Disability Discrimination and the Workplace

Related Titles from BNA Books

Age Discrimination in Employment Law

Employment Discrimination Law

Equal Employment Law Update

Mental and Emotional Injuries in Employment Litigation

Sexual Harassment in Employment Law

Disability Discrimination and the Workplace

Peter A. Susser

*Littler Mendelson, P.C.
Washington, D.C.*

The Bureau of National Affairs, Inc., Washington, D.C.

Copyright © 2005
The Bureau of National Affairs, Inc.
Washington, DC 20037

Library of Congress Cataloging-in-Publication Data

Susser, Peter.
  Disability discrimination and the workplace / by Peter A. Susser.
    p. cm.
  Includes index.
  ISBN-13: 978-1-57018-231-0
  ISBN-10: 1-57018-231-0
    1. People with disabilities–Employment–Law and legislation–United States–States. 2. Discrimination against people with disabilities–Law and legislation–United States–States. I. Title.

KF3469.Z95S87 2005
344.7301'59–dc22

2005045683

All rights reserved. Photocopying any portion of this publication is strictly prohibited unless express written authorization is first obtained from BNA Books, 1231 25th St., N.W., Washington, D.C. 20037, www.bnabooks.com. Authorization to photocopy items for internal or personal use, or the internal or personal use of specific clients, is granted by BNA Books for libraries and other users registered with the Copyright Clearance Center (CCC) Transactional Reporting Service, provided that $1.00 per page is paid directly to CCC, 222 Rosewood Dr., Danvers, MA 01923, www.copyright.com, Telephone: 978-750-8400, Fax: 978-646-8600.

Published by BNA Books
1231 25th St., NW, Washington, DC 20037
http://www.bnabooks.com

ISBN: 1-57018-2312-0; 978-1-57018-231-0
Printed in the United States of America

PREFACE

More than a dozen years after its employment provisions first took effect, the Americans with Disabilities Act (ADA) stands as a landmark piece of social and workplace legislation. It clearly has altered the design of public facilities and spaces, commercial activities and a vast array of workplaces. With respect to employment practices, the statute has had a substantial impact on job analysis and the designation of essential job functions, hiring practices, the accommodation of individuals with limiting conditions and capabilities, and many other facets of the employment relationship. In addition to the ADA (and the federal statute that preceded it, the Rehabilitation Act), a substantial volume of state and local measures—including both legislation and detailed regulations—also have been enacted and promulgated across the country.

Despite the sweeping reach of these statutes and the great impact they have had in many instances in opening the workplace (as well as public accommodations and commercial facilities) to the disabled, much controversy today surrounds this area of law. Many interested groups and individuals believe that the broad vision behind the 1990 enactment of the ADA has been severely constrained through the judicial process. By contrast, a number of employers have welcomed interpretations that some others view as narrowing in nature; and others believe that, notwithstanding the limiting construction applied in some circumstances, the statute remains both vague and burdensome as to its mandates on business and other employing organizations. To a great extent, this debate has focused on the interpretation and application of the ADA in the federal courts. Decisions of the U.S. Supreme Court, which obviously guide, if not directly determine, the outcome of many of those proceedings—and influence the views of comparable statutes by some (but not all) state courts, legislatures and agencies—have generated much of this criticism. Yet, the trends manifest in the larger number of ADA cases resolved in the federal court system have led to debate and—in some corners—frustration and dissent over the manner in which the measure's legal framework has been applied.

This treatise outlines the development of disability discrimination law in the U.S. workplace, with a major focus on the ADA. Also explored are the parameters of the Rehabilitation Act, with its development of key definitions, such as those that identify individuals with "handicaps"—in that statute's pre-ADA terminology—and the scope of the critical obligation to reasonably accommodate protected individuals. The proliferation of state disability discrimination protections, some of which that preceded the ADA and others of which that patterned their structure and scope in coordination with that measure (to extend the reach of disability discrimination protections, in some instances, beyond the federal law's coverage triggers), also are delineated. Many of the distinctive interpretations of some of these state measures—which, through court decision or legislative enactment, have extended beyond the judicial interpretations of the ADA to provide more expansive protections—also are noted.

The principle focus of this treatise, however, is on the development of the law under the 1990 federal disabilities statute. It includes a focus on the key definitions of conditions that are covered as protected disabilities under the ADA, a critical concept that accounted for much of the early litigation under the statute, and which remains a key issue in cases pending before the courts today. A second critical element of the statute is its requirement that employers not only refrain from discrimination against qualified individuals with protected disabilities, but that they also provide reasonable accommodations as to those limitations that still permit individuals to perform essential job functions unless they impose an undue hardship on the employer. These concepts are explored in some detail.

As many employment law practitioners can testify, the ADA has become an important component of almost every legal practice that focuses on workplace issues. While some plaintiffs and their counsel and representatives of the disability rights communities perceive that its influence has narrowed because of improperly constricted interpretations of its legal protections, it remains true that disability issues and potential accommodation obligations remain important and serious considerations in a vast number of workplace scenarios that play out every day in every sector of business and public-sector operation across the United States. The volume of cases in which such issues are raised is very substantial. In the 12 full federal fiscal years from the effective date of Title I of the ADA through 2004, the number of ADA charges filed with the EEOC ranged between 15,000 and 20,000, and amounted to 17.4% to just over 23% of the total volume of charges filed with the federal agency. While statistics on federal court filings referencing Title I of the ADA are not available, the experience of most employment attorneys reflects the perspective that a substantial percentage of workplace litigation incorporates such disability discrimination allegations (either as the principal focus of the dispute, or as an "add on" that sometimes assumes greater significance as the lawsuit proceeds). In addition, such federal charges and litigation describe only part of the picture, as plaintiffs increasingly seek to utilize state disability discrimination laws—such as those applicable in California and Massachusetts—that depart from interpretations of the U.S. Supreme Court on important aspects of the ADA, are more favorable to applicants and employees and more demanding of employers, and which may not have the same damages limitations that apply under the federal disabilities statute, as amended by the Civil Rights Act of 1991.

Apart from the employment requirements and obligations established by Title I of the ADA, many employers—and attorneys who work on employment matters—have faced additional substantial compliance questions that arise under other portions of the federal disabilities statute. Title III of the ADA deals with accessibility issues in a broad range of establishments and operations. As such, many employment lawyers regularly field requests for compliance advice in this area, and some become involved in litigation proceedings focused on accommodation issues involving access for customers and members of the public (as well as applicants and employees). Due to the substantial overlap between that portion of the statute—

which can have substantial impact on the design, construction, and operation of many establishments and operations—these access issues have drawn a greater focus from practitioners than some of the more intensely technical telecommunications and other requirements.

A challenge to all parties to employment relationships is the manner in which the ADA intersects with other federal and state statutes that impact on individuals who experience physical or mental impairments, such as may arise through on-the-job events (as are typically covered by workers' compensation statutes) or otherwise. The Family and Medical Leave Act of 1993 (FMLA) delineates certain minimum leave obligations of covered employers (with respect to eligible employees). The Employee Retirement Income Security Act regulates, in certain respects, employee benefits plans, including those that provide health benefits to employees and dependents that cover a range of accidents, illnesses, and disabilities. The National Labor Relations Act (NLRA) affords employees representation rights and allows for the role of labor organizations as exclusive representative of groups of employees for purposes of wages, hours, and other conditions of employment. The manner in which NLRA rights and obligations (e.g., the duty to represent all unit employees fairly and in good faith, or negotiated seniority systems) intersect with individual protections such as those provided by the FMLA have provided issues for all interested parties to contemplate.

This treatise is current through December 31, 2004. It is anticipated that future supplements and editions will update the developing law of disability discrimination in the workplace and preserve the utility of this lengthy analysis. Important developments in the courts continue to shape the evolution of the ADA, as do corresponding state law developments, and these holdings will steer the direction and content of future expansion and refinement of this volume.

PETER A. SUSSER
Washington, D.C.
August 2005

ACKNOWLEDGMENTS

As many readers will recognize, a project of this dimension requires the assistance of a number of very able professionals. In this case, the support of my law firm, Littler Mendelson, and the participation of a number of the Firm's attorneys at various phases of the publication's development have been invaluable. Littler Mendelson's Managing Directors during my years with the Firm—J. Richard Thesing (who subsequently served a term, through appointment by President Clinton, on the Architectural and Transportation Barriers Compliance Board), Wendy Tice-Wallner, and Marko Mrkonich —all have been devoted, both professionally and personally, to the principle and practice of inclusion and diversity, and have my appreciation for their support of this effort. Kevin Wright, Managing Shareholder in Littler's Washington, D.C. office, provided encouragement and support, which I very much appreciate, as this project advanced. In a changing legal profession, one means of measuring and enhancing attorneys' professional fulfillment—particularly in a large firm setting—is the ability they retain, among other practice imperatives, to pursue activities that they find meaningful and rewarding. Littler Mendelson's support of publications like this, and other initiatives pursued by its individual attorneys, contributes to the Firm's role as an attractive and rewarding environment for many employment law practitioners across the country.

A number of present and former attorneys at Littler provided assistance with the research, drafting, and editing of this volume. Most notably, Tessa Gelbman, a graduate of the Cornell University School of Industrial and Labor Relations and Harvard Law School, provided the largest quantity of assistance in this regard, involving substantial contributions on the ADA's legislative history as well as a number of other topics explored in this volume. In addition, several other attorneys in Littler's Washington, D.C. office—including Sue Marie King, a graduate of the William and Mary Law School, Gary Shapiro, a graduate of the Cornell ILR School and the Washington University School of Law, and Cristina Rodriquez, a graduate of the George Washington University Law School—made very helpful contributions as this volume moved towards publication. Margarita Santos Krncevic, currently working in-house at Fannie Mae in Washington, performed substantial research on state disability discrimination laws, with additional contributions by Tracy Arcaro and James McKinley. Attorneys in a number of Littler's other offices, from California to the East Coast, also provided valuable assistance. Krista Stevenson, a shareholder in the Firm's San Francisco office, assisted with one chapter, while Monica Hartman and Laura Shipley assisted with another. Judith Paulson, in Littler's Sacramento office, and David Neill prepared detailed material that contributed to one chapter. Bruce Young, Veronica Archederra Hall, and Wendy Medura Krincek in the Firm's Las Vegas office, assisted by Anthony Hall, contributed to another portion of the text. Jim Winkler, also of Littler's Las Vegas office, assisted with material on NLRA-related issues. Sven Collins (then residing in Littler's Denver office), assisted by Josh Kirkpatrick, developed a draft discussion of Rehabilitation Act issues. Steven Groode, Doug Adams, and Nora Sheehan were among others who also helped with research and drafting. All of these colleagues, and the others who provided assistance along the way, have my deepest appreciation for their invaluable assistance.

At BNA Books, Timothy J. Darby, Project Director, has worked with me throughout the long process from development through publication, and I appreciate his encouragement —and his patience—throughout this endeavor. Brian M. Malsberger was present at the outset of discussions that led to this book, and reconnected with the effort in the final months of the editorial process, and I thank him for his role in bringing this project to fruition.

My parents, Esther Susser and the late Myron Susser, provided much encouragement throughout my development and academic career, and were able to watch with satisfaction as my professional experiences advanced.

Finally, my wife, Jodi, and two terrific young men, our sons, Evan and Adam, always have provided love, motivation, patience and—sometimes, most importantly—humor, as this (and other) projects periodically diverted some of my attention. I greatly appreciate these contributions and all elements of the support they provide on a daily basis.

Peter Susser
Washington, D.C.
August, 2005

SUMMARY TABLE OF CONTENTS

PREFACE v

ACKNOWLEDGMENTS ix

DETAILED TABLE OF CONTENTS xv

CHAPTER 1. OVERVIEW OF FEDERAL DISABILITY DISCRIMINATION LAW 1

CHAPTER 2. THE REHABILITATION ACT OF 1973 41

CHAPTER 3. AMERICANS WITH DISABILITIES ACT: LEGISLATIVE HISTORY 119

CHAPTER 4. STATE DISABILITY DISCRIMINATION LAWS 259

CHAPTER 5. DISABILITIES PROTECTED BY THE AMERICANS WITH DISABILITIES ACT 481

CHAPTER 6. ACCESS AND ACCOMMODATION ISSUES: AMERICANS WITH DISABILITIES ACT'S TITLE III REQUIREMENTS ON PLACES OF PUBLIC ACCOMMODATIONS AND COMMERCIAL FACILITIES 609

CHAPTER 7. THE AMERICANS WITH DISABILITIES ACT AND THE HIRING PROCESS 699

CHAPTER 8. REASONABLE ACCOMMODATION 773

CHAPTER 9. INTERPLAY OF RELATED WORKPLACE STATUTES 835

CHAPTER 10. REMEDIES, LITIGATION STRATEGIES, AND ALTERNATIVE DISPUTE RESOLUTION 959

Appendix	List of Documents Included on CD-ROM	1053
Table of Cases		1059
Index		1099
About the Author		1133

DETAILED TABLE OF CONTENTS

PREFACE v

ACKNOWLEDGMENTS ix

SUMMARY TABLE OF CONTENTS xiii

CHAPTER 1. OVERVIEW OF FEDERAL DISABILITY
                  DISCRIMINATION LAW 1

I. Federal Disability Discrimination Legislation 2
  A. The Rehabilitation Act of 1973 3
     1. Section 501 4
     2. Section 503 5
     3. Section 504 6
     4. Section 508 7
  B. The Americans with Disabilities Act
     of 1990 7
     1. Progress in the Senate 9
     2. Progress in the House 10
     3. Food Industry Issue 11
     4. The Final Law 12
  C. Entities Covered by the ADA and the
     Rehabilitation Act 14
  D. What Is a Protected Disability? 15
     1. Impairment 17
     2. Limiting a Major Life Activity 18
     3. Previous or Misperceived Impairments 20
  E. The Reasonable Accommodation
     Obligation 21
  F. Defenses and Limitations to Employer
     Obligations 27
  G. Enforcement and Remedies 31

1. Administrative Relief	32
2. Private Right of Action	33
3. Available Remedies	33
II. Related Federal Statutes	35
A. Architectural Barriers Act	35
B. Individuals with Disabilities Education Act	36
C. Developmental Disabilities Assistance and Bill of Rights Act	37
D. Air Carrier Access Act	37
E. Telecommunications Act	38
F. Fair Housing Act	39
G. Social Security Act	40

CHAPTER 2. THE REHABILITATION ACT OF 1973 41

I. Overview	43
II. Enactment of and Subsequent Amendments to the Rehabilitation Act of 1973	45
A. Enactment	45
B. 1974 Rehabilitation Act Amendments	47
C. 1978 Rehabilitation Act Amendments	49
D. 1990 Rehabilitation Act Amendments	50
E. 1992 Rehabilitation Act Amendments	51
III. Scope of Key Employment Provisions	53
A. Overview	53
B. Application to Federal Agencies— Section 501	56
C. Application to Federal Contractors— Section 503	57
D. Application to Programs or Activities Receiving Federal Financial Assistance— Section 504	60
1. Meaning of "Program or Activity"	61
2. Meaning of "Receipt of Federal Financial Assistance"	63
3. Application to States	65
IV. Definition of "Protected Individual"	66
A. Evolution of the Definition	66

	B. Actual Disability		68
	1. Impairment		68
		a. General Definition	68
		b. Areas of Conflict	69
		i. Obesity	69
		ii. Drug and Alcohol Use	70
	2. Substantially Limits One or More Major Life Activities		72
		a. General Definition	72
		b. Area of Conflict	73
	C. Record of Having a Disability		74
	D. Being Regarded as Having a Disability		75
	E. Qualified Individual with a Disability		77
V.	Reasonable Accommodation Obligation		79
	A. Origin of the Obligation		79
	B. Definition of the Obligation		81
VI.	Rehabilitation Act Enforcement		85
	A. Overview		85
	B. Section 501		87
	1. Scope		87
	2. Enforcement Procedures		88
	3. Remedies		90
	4. Affirmative Action Plan Requirements		92
	C. Section 503		93
	1. Scope		93
	2. Enforcement Procedures		94
	3. Remedies		95
	4. Affirmative Action Plan Requirements		96
	5. Compliance Reviews		97
	D. Section 504		98
	1. Scope		98
	2. Enforcement Procedures		99
	3. Remedies		102
VII.	Defenses to Liability		105
	A. Type of Defenses		105
	1. Employer Is Not a Covered Entity		106
	2. Employee Is Not Covered by the Rehabilitation Act		107
		a. Employee Is Not Qualified	107

   b. Employee Is Not Disabled 108
  3. Reasonable Accommodation Is
   Not Possible 109
  4. Employer Lacks Knowledge of
   Employee's Disability 110
  5. Procedural Defenses 111
 B. Section 504 111
  1. Employer Is Not a Direct Recipient of
   Federal Aid 111
  2. Entire Employing Entity Is Not Covered 112
 C. Section 503 114
 D. Section 501 117

CHAPTER 3. AMERICANS WITH DISABILITIES ACT:
      LEGISLATIVE HISTORY 119

 I. Preliminary Analyses and Legislative Efforts 121
  A. The Disabilities Bill's First Draft 124
  B. The Disabilities Act Reaches Congress 128
 II. Senate Consideration of the ADA 131
  A. Tactical Revisions to Proposed Measure 133
  B. Other Changes 137
  C. Building Senate Support for S. 933 140
  D. Initial Senate Hearings and
    Legislative Progress 143
  E. Administration Deliberations 147
  F. Senate Obtains White House Approval 149
  G. Initial Senate Approval 152
 III. House Consideration of the ADA 156
  A. Committee on Education and Labor 159
   1. Committee on Education and
    Labor Hearings 159
   2. Committee on Education and Labor
    Report 172
  B. Committee on Energy and Commerce 184
   1. Committee on Energy and
    Commerce Hearings 184

		2. Committee on Energy and Commerce Report	186

    C. Committee Public Works and Transportation 191
        1. Committee on Public Works and Transportation Hearings 191
        2. Committee on Public Works and Transportation Report 192
    D. Committee on the Judiciary 198
        1. Committee on the Judiciary and Hearings 198
        2. Committee on the Judiciary Report 211
    E. Action on the House Floor: General Debate and Proposed Amendments 217
        1. Grace Period for Small Business 223
        2. Role of Written Job Descriptions in Assessing Essential Job Functions 226
        3. Effort to Quantify Undue Hardship 227
        4. Access to Wilderness Areas 230
        5. Food-Handling Jobs 231
        6. Additional Proposed Amendments 237
IV. House-Senate Conference and Final Passage 251

CHAPTER 4. STATE DISABILITY DISCRIMINATION LAWS 259

ALABAMA 278
  I. State Law 278

ALASKA 278
  I. State Law 278
    A. Overview 278
    B. Prohibited Discrimination 279
    C. Definitions 279
        1. Disability 279
    D. Covered Employers 280
    E. Reasonable Accommodation and Defenses 280

ARIZONA ... 281
I. State Law ... 281
- A. Overview ... 281
- B. Prohibited Discrimination ... 281
  1. Preemployment Inquiries ... 282
     a. Medical Examinations ... 282
- C. Definitions ... 282
  1. Disability ... 282
  2. Essential Job Functions ... 283
- D. Covered Employers ... 283
- E. Reasonable Accommodation and Defenses ... 284
  1. Reasonable Accommodation ... 284
  2. Defenses ... 284
     a. Direct Threat ... 284
     b. Undue Hardship ... 285

ARKANSAS ... 285
I. State Law ... 285
- A. Overview ... 285
- B. Prohibited Discrimination ... 285
  1. Genetic Testing ... 285
- C. Definitions ... 286
  1. Disability ... 286
- D. Covered Employers ... 286
- E. Reasonable Accommodation and Defenses ... 286

CALIFORNIA ... 287
I. State Law ... 287
- A. Overview ... 287
- B. Prohibited Discrimination ... 287
- C. Definitions ... 289
  1. Disability ... 289
  2. Essential Job Functions ... 291
  3. Major Life Activities ... 291
  4. Medical Conditions ... 292
- D. Covered Employers ... 292
- E. Reasonable Accommodation and Defenses ... 293
  1. Reasonable Accommodation ... 293

2. Defenses	295
a. Undue Hardship	295
II. Local Laws	296

COLORADO   296

I. State Law	296
A. Overview	296
B. Prohibited Discrimination	296
C. Definitions	297
1. Disability	297
D. Covered Employers	297
E. Reasonable Accommodation and Defenses	298
1. Defenses	298
a. Bona Fide Occupational Qualification	298
b. Business Necessity	299
c. Undue Hardship	299

CONNECTICUT   300

I. State Law	300
A. Overview	300
B. Prohibited Discrimination	301
1. Genetic Testing	301
C. Definitions	301
1. Disability	301
D. Covered Employers	303
E. Reasonable Accommodation and Defenses	304
1. Defenses	304
a. Bona Fide Occupational Qualification	304

DELAWARE   304

I. State Law	304
A. Overview	304
B. Prohibited Discrimination	305
1. Preemployment Inquiries	305
a. Medical Examinations	305
2. Genetic Testing	306
C. Definitions	306

	1. Disability	306
D.	Covered Employers	307
E.	Reasonable Accommodation and Defenses	307
	1. Reasonable Accommodation	307
	2. Defenses	308
	a. Undue Hardship	308

DISTRICT OF COLUMBIA 309
- I. State Law 309
  - A. Overview 309
  - B. Prohibited Discrimination 309
    1. Preemployment Inquiries 310
  - C. Definitions 310
    1. Disability 310
  - D. Covered Employers 311
  - E. Reasonable Accommodation and Defenses 311
    1. Reasonable Accommodation 311
    2. Defenses 312

FLORIDA 313
- I. State Law 313
  - A. Overview 313
  - B. Prohibited Discrimination 314
    1. Genetic Testing 314
    2. Harassment 314
    3. Medical Conditions 315
  - C. Definitions 315
    1. Disability 315
    2. Essential Job Functions 316
  - D. Covered Employers 316
  - E. Reasonable Accommodation and Defenses 316
    1. Reasonable Accommodation 316
    2. Defenses 317
       - a. Bona Fide Occupational Qualification ... 317
       - b. Direct Threat 318
       - c. Undue Hardship 318
- II. Local Laws 318

GEORGIA ... 319
I. State Law ... 319
- A. Overview ... 319
- B. Prohibited Discrimination ... 319
  1. Preemployment Inquiries ... 320
  2. Retaliation ... 320
- C. Definitions ... 320
  1. Disability ... 320
- D. Covered Employers ... 321
- E. Reasonable Accommodation and Defenses ... 321
  1. Reasonable Accommodation ... 321
  2. Defenses ... 322
     a. Infectious or Communicable Diseases ... 322

HAWAII ... 322
I. State Law ... 322
- A. Overview ... 322
- B. Prohibited Discrimination ... 323
  1. Genetic Testing ... 324
- C. Definitions ... 324
  1. Disability ... 324
  2. Employment ... 324
- D. Covered Employers ... 324
- E. Reasonable Accommodation and Defenses ... 325
  1. Reasonable Accommodation ... 325
  2. Defenses ... 325
     a. Bona Fide Occupational Qualification ... 325

IDAHO ... 325
I. State Law ... 325
- A. Overview ... 325
- B. Prohibited Discrimination ... 326
- C. Definitions ... 326
  1. Disability ... 326
- D. Covered Employers ... 326
- E. Reasonable Accommodation and Defenses ... 327
  1. Reasonable Accommodation ... 327
  2. Defenses ... 328
     a. Direct Threat ... 328

ILLINOIS	328
I. State Law	328
A. Overview	328
B. Prohibited Discrimination	328
1. Pregnancy-Related Disability	329
C. Definitions	329
1. Disability	329
D. Covered Employers	330
E. Reasonable Accommodation and Defenses	331
1. Reasonable Accommodation	331
2. Defenses	331
a. Bona Fide Occupational Qualification	332
b. Undue Hardship	332
II. Local Laws	333
INDIANA	333
I. State Law	333
A. Overview	333
B. Prohibited Discrimination	333
1. Preemployment Inquiries	335
a. Medical Examinations	335
C. Definitions	336
1. Disability	336
2. Employee	337
3. Person	337
D. Covered Employers	337
E. Reasonable Accommodation and Defenses	337
1. Reasonable Accommodation	337
2. Defenses	338
a. Infectious or Communicable Diseases	338
b. Qualification Standards	338
c. Undue Hardship	339
IOWA	339
I. State Law	339
A. Overview	339
B. Prohibited Discrimination	340
1. Preemployment Inquiries	341

		a. Medical Examinations	341
		2. Genetic Testing	341
		3. Pregnancy-Related Disability	342
	C.	Definitions	342
		1. Disability	342
		2. Major Life Activities	343
	D.	Covered Employers	343
	E.	Reasonable Accommodation and Defenses	344
		1. Reasonable Accommodation	344
		2. Defenses	344
		a. Affirmative Action	344
		b. Bona Fide Occupational Qualification	344
		c. Undue Hardship	345

KANSAS ... 345

I. State Law		345
A. Overview		345
B. Prohibited Discrimination		345
	1. Preemployment Inquiries	346
	a. Medical Exminations	346
	2. Genetic Testing	347
	3. Pregnancy-Related Disability	348
C. Definitions		348
	1. Disability	348
	2. Essential Job Function	349
	3. Major Life Activities	349
D. Covered Employers		349
E. Reasonable Accommodation and Defenses		350
	1. Reasonable Accommodation	350
	2. Defenses	350
	a. Affirmative Action	350
	b. Direct Threat	350
	c. Infectious or Communicable Diseases	351
	d. Undue Hardship	351

KENTUCKY ... 351

I. State Law	351
A. Overview	351

    B. Prohibited Discrimination 352
    C. Definitions 353
        1. Disability 353
    D. Covered Employers 353
    E. Reasonable Accommodation and Defenses 354
        1. Reasonable Accommodation 354
        2. Defenses 355
            a. Undue Hardship 355

LOUISIANA 355
  I. State Law 355
    A. Overview 355
    B. Prohibited Discrimination 355
        1. Genetic Testing 357
        2. Pregnancy-Related Disability 357
    C. Definitions 358
        1. Disability 358
        2. Major Life Activities 358
    D. Covered Employers 358
    E. Reasonable Accommodation and Defenses 359
        1. Reasonable Accommodation 359
        2. Defenses 359
            a. Affirmative Action 359
            b. Business Necessity 359
            c. Qualification Standards 360
            d. Undue Hardship 360

MAINE 360
  I. State Law 360
    A. Overview 360
    B. Prohibited Discrimination 361
        1. Preemployment Inquiries 361
            a. Medical Examinations 361
        2. Genetic Testing 362
    C. Definitions 362
        1. Disability 362
    D. Covered Employers 364
    E. Reasonable Accommodation and Defenses 364

        1. Reasonable Accommodation 364
        2. Defenses 365
           a. Undue Hardship 365

MARYLAND 365
   I. State Law 365
     A. Overview 365
     B. Prohibited Discrimination 366
        1. Genetic Testing 367
        2. Pregnancy-Related Disability 368
     C. Definitions 368
        1. Disability 368
        2. Major Life Activities 369
     D. Covered Employers 369
     E. Reasonable Accommodation and Defenses 369
        1. Reasonable Accommodation 369
        2. Defenses 370
           a. Bona Fide Occupational Qualification ... 370
           b. Future Hazard 371
           c. Preferential Treatment 371

MASSACHUSETTS 372
   I. State Law 372
     A. Overview 372
     B. Prohibited Discrimination 372
        1. Preemployment Inquiries 373
        2. Genetic Testing 374
        3. Retaliation 375
     C. Definitions 375
        1. Disability 375
        2. Major Life Activities 376
     D. Covered Employers 376
     E. Reasonable Accommodation and Defenses 377
        1. Reasonable Accommodation 377
        2. Defenses 377
           a. Bona Fide Occupational Qualification ... 377
           b. Undue Hardship 377

MICHIGAN 378
I. State Law 378
A. Overview 378
B. Prohibited Discrimination 378
1. Genetic Testing 379
C. Definitions 380
1. Disability 380
2. Major Life Activities 381
D. Covered Employers 381
E. Reasonable Accommodation and Defenses 382
1. Reasonable Accommodation 382
2. Defenses 382
a. Undue Hardship 382

MINNESOTA 383
I. State Law 383
A. Overview 383
B. Prohibited Discrimination 383
1. Preemployment Inquiries 384
a. Medical Examinations 384
2. Pregnancy-Related Disability 385
3. Genetic Testing 385
4. Retaliation 386
C. Definitions 387
1. Disability 387
D. Covered Employers 387
E. Reasonable Accommodation and Defenses 388
1. Reasonable Accommodation 388
2. Defenses 388
a. Direct Threat 388
b. Undue Hardship 388

MISSISSIPPI 389
I. State Law 389
A. Overview 389
B. Prohibited Discrimination 389
C. Definitions 389
1. Disability 389

  D. Covered Employees 390
  E. Reasonable Accommodation and Defenses 390

MISSOURI 390
 I. State Law 390
  A. Overview 390
  B. Prohibited Discrimination 391
   1. Preemployment Inquiries 391
    a. Medical Examinations 392
  C. Definitions 392
   1. Disability 392
   2. Major Life Activities 392
  D. Covered Employers 393
  E. Reasonable Accommodation and Defenses 393
   1. Reasonable Accommodation 394
   2. Defenses 394
    a. Affirmative Action 394
    b. Preferential Treatment 394

MONTANA 395
 I. State Law 395
  A. Overview 395
  B. Prohibited Discrimination 395
   1. Preemployment Inquiries 396
    a. Medical Examinations 396
  C. Definitions 397
   1. Disability 397
  D. Covered Employers 397
  E. Reasonable Accommodation and Defenses 397
   1. Reasonable Accommodation 397
   2. Defenses 398
    a. Bona Fide Occupational Qualification ... 398
    b. Undue Hardship 399

NEBRASKA 399
 I. State Law 399
  A. Overview 399
  B. Prohibited Discrimination 399

1. Preemployment Inquiries	400
a. Medical Examinations	400
2. Genetic Testing	401
C. Definitions	402
1. Disability	402
D. Covered Employers	403
E. Reasonable Accommodation and Defenses	403
1. Reasonable Accommodation	403
2. Defenses	404
a. Undue Hardship	404

NEVADA	404
I. State Law	404
A. Overview	404
B. Prohibited Discrimination	404
1. Genetic Testing	405
2. Pregnancy-Related Discrimination	405
C. Definitions	406
1. Disability	406
D. Covered Employers	406
E. Reasonable Accommodation and Defenses	407
1. Reasonable Accommodation	407
2. Defenses	407
a. Bona Fide Occupational Qualification	407
b. Preferential Treatment	407

NEW HAMPSHIRE	408
I. State Law	408
A. Overview	408
B. Prohibited Discrimination	408
1. Preemployment Issues	409
2. Genetic Testing	409
C. Definitions	410
1. Disability	410
D. Covered Employers	410
E. Reasonable Accommodation and Defenses	410

NEW JERSEY	410
I. State Law	410

A.	Overview	410
B.	Prohibited Discrimination	411
C.	Definitions	412
	1. Disability	412
D.	Covered Employers	413
E.	Reasonable Accommodation and Defenses	414
	1. Reasonable Accommodation	414
	2. Defenses	414
	a. Undue Hardship	415

NEW MEXICO 415
I. State Law 415
    A. Overview 415
    B. Prohibited Discrimination 416
    C. Definitions 416
        1. Disability 416
        2. Medical Conditions 417
    D. Covered Employers 418
    E. Reasonable Accommodation and Defenses 418
        1. Reasonable Accommodation 418

NEW YORK 418
I. State Law 418
    A. Overview 418
    B. Prohibited Discrimination 419
        1. Genetic Testing 419
    C. Definitions 420
        1. Disability 420
    D. Covered Employers 420
    E. Reasonable Accommodation and Defenses 421
        1. Reasonable Accommodation 421
II. Local Laws 421

NORTH CAROLINA 422
I. State Law 422
    A. Overview 422
    B. Prohibited Discrimination 422
        1. Genetic Testing 423
        2. Retaliation 423

	C. Definitions	424
	1. Disability	424
	D. Covered Employers	425
	E. Reasonable Accommodation and Defenses	425
	1. Reasonable Accommodation	425
	2. Defenses	426
	a. Undue Hardship	426

NORTH DAKOTA ... 427

- I. State Law ... 427
  - A. Overview ... 427
  - B. Prohibited Discrimination ... 427
  - C. Definitions ... 428
    1. Disability ... 428
  - D. Covered Employers ... 428
  - E. Reasonable Accommodation and Defenses ... 428
    1. Reasonable Accommodation ... 428
    2. Defenses ... 429
       a. Undue Hardship ... 429

OHIO ... 429

- I. State Law ... 429
  - A. Overview ... 429
  - B. Prohibited Discrimination ... 429
    1. Preemployment Inquiries ... 431
  - C. Definitions ... 431
    1. Disability ... 431
    2. Major Life Activities ... 433
  - D. Covered Employers ... 433
  - E. Reasonable Accommodation and Defenses ... 433
    1. Reasonable Accommodation ... 433
    2. Defenses ... 434
       a. Undue Hardship ... 434

OKLAHOMA ... 434

- I. State Law ... 434
  - A. Overview ... 434
  - B. Prohibited Discrimination ... 434
    1. Genetic Testing ... 435

C. Definitions	435
1. Disability	435
D. Covered Employers	436
E. Reasonable Accommodation and Defenses	437
1. Reasonable Accommodation	437
2. Defenses	438
a. Undue Hardship	438

OREGON 438
  I. State Law 438
    A. Overview 438
    B. Prohibited Discrimination 439
        1. Genetic Testing 439
    C. Definitions 440
        1. Disability 440
        2. Major Life Activities 441
    D. Covered Employers 442
    E. Reasonable Accommodation and Defenses 442
        1. Reasonable Accommodation 442
        2. Defenses 442
            a. Direct Threat 442

PENNSYLVANIA 443
  I. State Law 443
    A. Overview 443
    B. Prohibited Discrimination 443
        1. Medical Conditions 444
    C. Definitions 445
        1. Disability 445
        2. Major Life Activities 445
    D. Covered Employers 446
    E. Reasonable Accommodation and Defenses 446
        1. Reasonable Accommodations 446
        2. Defenses 446
            a. Undue Hardship 446

RHODE ISLAND 447
  I. State Law 447
    A. Overview 447

  B. Prohibited Discrimination 447
    1. Genetic Testing 448
  C. Definitions 448
    1. Disability 448
  D. Covered Employers 449
  E. Reasonable Accommodation and Defenses 449

SOUTH CAROLINA 450
 I. State Law 450
  A. Overview 450
  B. Prohibited Discrimination 450
    1. Preemployment Inquiries 451
     a. Medical Examinations 451
  C. Definitions 451
    1. Disability 451
  D. Covered Employers 452
  E. Reasonable Accommodation and Defenses 452
    1. Reasonable Accommodation 452

SOUTH DAKOTA 453
 I. State Law 453
  A. Overview 453
  B. Prohibited Discrimination 453
    1. Genetic Testing 454
  C. Definitions 454
    1. Disability 454
  D. Covered Employers 454
  E. Reasonable Accommodation and Defenses 455
    1. Reasonable Accommodation 455

TENNESSEE 455
 I. State Law 455
  A. Overview 455
  B. Prohibited Discrimination 455
    1. Retaliation 456
  C. Definitions 456
    1. Disability 456
  D. Covered Employers 456
  E. Reasonable Accommodation and Defenses 457

TEXAS 457
I. State Law 457
- A. Overview 457
- B. Prohibited Discrimination 458
  - 1. Genetic Testing 458
- C. Definitions 459
  - 1. Disability 459
- D. Covered Employers 459
- E. Reasonable Accommodation and Defenses 460
  - 1. Reasonable Accommodation 460
  - 2. Defenses 460
    - a. Business Necessity 460

UTAH 461
I. State Law 461
- A. Overview 461
- B. Prohibited Discrimination 461
  - 1. Preemployment Inquiries 461
  - 2. Genetic Testing 462
- C. Definitions 463
  - 1. Disability 463
  - 2. Major Life Activities 463
- D. Covered Employers 463
- E. Reasonable Accommodation and Defenses 464
  - 1. Reasonable Accommodation 464

VERMONT 465
I. State Law 465
- A. Overview 465
- B. Prohibited Discrimination 465
  - 1. Genetic Testing 466
- C. Definitions 466
  - 1. Disability 466
- D. Covered Employers 467
- E. Reasonable Accommodation and Defenses 467
  - 1. Reasonable Accommodation 467
  - 2. Defenses 467
    - a. Undue Hardship 467

VIRGINIA ... 468
I. State Law ... 468
A. Overview ... 468
B. Prohibited Discrimination ... 468
1. Genetic Testing ... 469
C. Definitions ... 469
1. Disability ... 469
D. Covered Employers ... 470
E. Reasonable Accommodation and Defenses ... 470
1. Reasonable Accommodation ... 470
2. Defenses ... 471
a. Direct Threat ... 471
b. Undue Hardship ... 471

WASHINGTON ... 471
I. State Law ... 471
A. Overview ... 471
B. Prohibited Discrimination ... 472
1. Preemployment Inquiries ... 472
a. Medical Examinations ... 472
C. Definitions ... 473
1. Disability ... 473
D. Covered Employers ... 473
E. Reasonable Accommodation and Defenses ... 474
1. Reasonable Accommodation ... 474

WEST VIRGINIA ... 474
I. State Law ... 474
A. Overview ... 474
B. Prohibited Discrimination ... 474
C. Definitions ... 475
1. Disability ... 475
D. Covered Employers ... 475
E. Reasonable Accommodation and Defenses ... 476
1. Reasonable Accommodation ... 476

WISCONSIN ... 476
I. State Law ... 476
A. Overview ... 476

B. Prohibited Discrimination		476
1. Genetic Testing		477
C. Definitions		477
1. Disability		477
D. Covered Employers		478
E. Reasonable Accommodation and Defenses		478
1. Defenses		478
a. Undue Hardship		478

WYOMING 478

I. State Law	478
A. Overview	478
B. Prohibited Discrimination	479
C. Definitions	479
1. Disability	479
D. Covered Employers	479
E. Reasonable Accommodation and Defenses	479
1. Defenses	479

CHAPTER 5. DISABILITIES PROTECTED BY THE AMERICANS WITH DISABILITIES ACT 481

I. The Rehabilitation Act Definition	483
II. Americans With Disabilities Act Statutory and Regulatory Framework	488
A. What Is an Impairment?	489
B. Major Life Activities	493
1. "Working" as a Major Life Activity	495
C. Substantial Limitation	496
1. Nature and Severity of the Impairment	496
2. Substantially Limited In Working	500
3. Temporary v. Permanent Impairment	504
4. The Effect of Mitigating Measures	506
D. Record of Impairment	510
E. Regarded as Disabled	512
1. Regarded as Substantially Limited in the Ability to Work	513
F. Drug and Alcohol Use	517

III. "Qualified" Individual With a Disability 520
   A. Otherwise Qualified 520
   B. What Is an Essential Job Function? 521
      1. Written Job Description 523
      2. Government Standards 524
      3. Percentage of Time Devoted to Job Function 526
      4. Consequences of Not Performing Job Function 526
      5. Other Factors 527
   C. Performance of Essential Functions With or Without a Reasonable Accommodation 527
IV. Interaction of Other Statutes' Provisions Regarding Disability With Those of the Americans With Disabilities Act 529
V. Common Illnesses and Conditions Examined Under the American With Disabilities Act 532
   A. Substance Abuse 534
      1. Current Drug Use 536
      2. Alcohol Use 539
      3. Being "Regarded as" or Having a Record of Substance Abuse–Related Disability 540
      4. Employer Rights With Respect to Employee Substance Abuse 543
         a. Last-Chance Agreements 544
         b. Off-Duty Conduct 544
         c. Discrimination/Pretext 545
      5. Medical Inquiries and Examinations Regarding Drug and Alcohol Use 546
         a. Drug Testing 547
      6. Employer Defenses 548
         a. Job-Related and Consistent With Business Necessity 548
         b. Direct Threat 550
      7. Compliance With Other Substance Abuse Laws and Regulations 551
      8. Reasonable Accommodation 552
   B. AIDS/HIV 554

    1. Qualified Individual With A Disability 559
     a. Not Qualified Because of Risk 561
     b. Ability to Make Inquiries or
      Mandate Tests 562
     c. Association 564
     d. Reasonable Accommodation 565
     e. Insurance 566
     f. Privacy 568
  C. Mental Disorders 570
    1. Substantially Limit Major Life Activity 571
    2. Mitigating or Corrective Measures 574
    3. Substantially Limited in the Ability
     to Work 575
    4. Qualified Individual 576
    5. Perceived as Being Disabled 578
    6. Benefits Distinguishing Between Physical
     and Mental Disabilities 580
    7. Reasonable Accommodation 581
  D. Diabetes 583
  E. Hypertension 590
  F. Heart Disease 592
  G. Cancer 593
  H. Epilepsy 595
VI. Conclusion 606

CHAPTER 6. ACCESS AND ACCOMMODATION ISSUES:
       AMERICANS WITH DISABILITIES ACT'S
       TITLE III REQUIREMENTS ON PLACES OF
       PUBLIC ACCOMMODATIONS AND
       COMMERCIAL FACILITIES 609

 I. Title III Compliance 614
 II. Who Is Covered Under Title III? 616
  A. What Is a Public Accommodation? 617
  B. Mixed-Use Facilities 621
  C. Physical Versus Nonphysical Places of
   Public Accommodation 623

		1. Lawsuits	625
		2. Viability of Claim	625
	D.	Other Intangible "Public Accommodations"	628
	E.	Private Companies	630
		1. When Web Sites Are Not Public Accommodations	631
		2. When Web Sites Are Public Accommodations	633
		3. Physical Location Versus Internet Only	634
		4. Current Law	635
	F.	Commercial Facilities	636
III.	Title III Exemptions		638
	A.	Religious Organizations	638
	B.	Private Clubs	639
	C.	Government Entities	641
IV.	Title III Requirements		642
	A.	Equal Participation	642
	B.	Direct Threat	644
	C.	Policy Modifications	646
	D.	Integrated Settings	648
	E.	Barrier Removal	649
		1. "Readily Achievable" Standard	651
		2. Assembly Seating	653
		3. Barrier Removal Priority	653
		4. Additional Measures	654
		a. Public Areas Only	654
		b. Historic Landmarks	655
	F.	Barrier Removal Guidelines	656
	G.	Alternatives to Barrier Removal	656
	H.	Provision of Auxiliary Aids	659
	I.	Alterations	661
	J.	Primary Function Area	663
	K.	Tax Credits	665
	L.	Franchise Liability	667
	M.	Landlord/Tenant Liability	668
	N.	New Construction	670
		1. Scoping Requirements	671
		2. Unclear Accessiblity Guidelines	673

O. Architect Liability 674
P. Transportation 675
   1. Fixed-Route System Requirements 677
   2. Demand-Responsive System Requirements 678
   3. Public Accommodations Primarily
      Engaged in the Business of
      Providing Transportation 679
   4. Over-the-Road Buses 680
Q. Examinations and Courses 684
V. Enforcement 687
   A. Remedies 688
   B. Role of Attorney General 689
   C. Exhaustion of Administrative Remedies 691
   D. Standing 693
   E. Attorneys' Fees 694
   F. Justice Department Enforcement Under
      Title III 696
VI. Conclusion 698

CHAPTER 7.   THE AMERICANS WITH DISABILITIES ACT
              AND THE HIRING PROCESS 699

I. Introduction 701
II. Prima Facie Case of Preemployment
    Discrimination Under the Americans with
    Disabilities Act 703
III. Proving Disability Discrimination in Hiring
     Procedures 705
IV. Accessibility of the Hiring Process 706
    A. Physical Access 707
    B. Interviewing 708
    C. Specific Disabilities 710
       1. Hearing-Impaired Applicants 710
       2. Visually Impaired Applicants 710
       3. Mobility-Impaired Applicants 711
       4. Speech-Impaired Applicants 711
V. Applications and Job Descriptions 711

	A. Applications	711
	1. The Application Form as Evidence	712
	2. Qualifications Comparison of Applicant With and Without Disability	713
	B. Job Descriptions	714
VI.	Preemployment Inquiries and Medical Examinations	718
	A. Disability-Related Inquiries	720
	1. The Prima Facie Case	720
	2. Purpose for Prohibiting Disability-Related Inquiries	721
	3. Permissible Inquiries in the Hiring Process	722
	a. Inquiries Regarding Nondisabling Impairments	723
	b. Inquiries Related to the Performance of Job-Related Functions	724
	c. Inquiries Related to Known Disabilities	725
	B. Medical Examinations	728
	1. Pre-Offer Medical Examinations	729
	2. Postoffer Medical Examinations	731
	3. What Is a Medical Examination?	733
	4. Disputes Over Conclusions of Medical Examinations	736
VII.	Preemployment Training Programs	738
VIII.	The Duty to Make Reasonable Accommodations for an Applicant	740
	A. Reasonable Accommodations Under the Rehabilitation Act of 1973	740
	B. Reasonable Accommodations Under the Americans With Disabilities Act	742
	1. Equal Employment Opportunity	743
	2. Employers' Duties	744
	3. Providing Information	746
	4. Employment Agencies	746
	5. Recruitment	747
	6. Applicants Request for or Advising About Need for Reasonable Accommodation	748

7. The Undue Hardship Analysis 750
   a. Undue Hardship Exception 752
8. The Essential Functions Analysis 753
   a. Determining Essential Job Function: EEOC Guidelines 754
   b. Rehabilitation Act/ADA Guidelines 755
   c. Private Employer Requirements 758
IX. Determining Whether a Requirement Is "Job-Related" and "Consistent With Business Necessity" 759
   A. Justified 759
   B. Not Justified 760
   C. Establishing Certain Job Requirements 761
X. Responding to a Claim of Disability Discrimination in Hiring 763
   A. No Reasonable Accommodation Existed 763
   B. Applicant Unable to Perform Essential Job Functions With a Reasonable Accommodation 764
   C. Disparate Treatment Based on Legitimate Nondiscriminatory Reason 765
      1. Applicant Posed Direct Threat 765
      2. Direct Threat Defense 766
      3. Function of Reasonable Accommodation ... 767
      4. Threat Assessment 768
      5. Employee Insubordination 770
   D. Nonstatutory Defenses 771

CHAPTER 8. REASONABLE ACCOMMODATION 773

I. Introduction 775
   A. Reasonable Accommodation Under the Rehabilitation Act of 1973 775
   B. Reasonable Accommodation Under the Americans With Disabilities Act 776
II. Reasonable Accommodation Defined/General Requirements 777
   A. Categories of Reasonable Accommodations ... 777

- B. Reasonable Accommodation Concepts 777
  - 1. Essential Functions of the Job 778
  - 2. Employers' Rights 781
- C. The Employer Must Provide Accommodations That Will Enable the Employee to Enjoy the Benefits and Privileges of Employment 782
- D. Establishing the Employer's Failure to Provide a Reasonable Accommodation 783

III. Requests for Accommodations 784
- A. "Interactive Process" Anticipated by the Regulations 784
  - 1. The Employee's Responsibility to Request a Reasonable Accommodation 785
    - a. Employer's Duty 787
  - 2. Form of the Request 789
  - 3. Employer's Responsibility to Engage in the Interactive Process to Formulate an Effective Accommodation 790
  - 4. The Responsibility of the Employee to Provide Requested Information 791
  - 5. Interactive Process Examples 793
- B. Documentation Requests by Employer 795
- C. Requirement of Additional Certification by Physician Selected by Employer 796
- D. Employer Policies 798
- E. Effect of a Collective Bargaining Agreement 801
- F. Confidentiality Issues 803

IV. What Type of Accommodation Is "Reasonable"? 804
- A. Making Existing Facilities Accessible to Disabled Employees 806
- B. Job Restructuring 807
- C. Job Reassignment 809
  - 1. Legitimate Policies Prohibiting a Transfer 811
  - 2. Vacant Positions 813
- D. Obligation to Provide a Leave of Absence as a Reasonable Accommodation 815

			1. Employer Policies Regarding Leaves of Absence and Attendance	817

        1. Employer Policies Regarding Leaves of Absence and Attendance 817
        2. Employee's Job Security While on Medical Leave 817
        3. Requiring Employee to Stay on the Job Rather Than Take a Leave as a Form of Reasonable Accommodation 818
        4. Providing a Modified or Part-Time Schedule 818
    E. Work at Home 820
    F. Issues Relating to Medication of a Disabled Employee 821
    G. Modification of the Employer's Work Site or Equipment 822
    H. Effect on Workplace Conduct Rules 822
  V. Undue Hardship Issues 823
    A. Undue Hardship Defined 823
    B. Undue Hardship Applied to Leave Cases 825
  VI. Direct-Threat Defense 826
  VII. Reasonable Accommodation and Job Applicants 828
    A. Duty to Provide Reasonable Accommodation to New Hires 828
    B. Preemployment Inquiries by an Employer as to the Need for a Reasonable Accommodation 829
        1. Preemployment Offer 829
        2. Post-Employment Offer 830
  VIII. Other Reasonable Accommodation Issues 830
    A. Interplay With Other Laws 830
    B. Providing Additional Accommodations 832
  IX. Public Accommodations 833

CHAPTER 9.   INTERPLAY OF RELATED WORKPLACE STATUTES 835

  I. The Family and Medical Leave Act 839

A.	Employer Coverage Under the ADA and the FMLA	841
B.	Employee Coverage Under the ADA and the FMLA	841
	1. Threshold Requirements as to Duration of Employment	841
	2. "Disability" Versus "Serious Health Condition"	842
	a. "Disability"	843
	b. "Serious Health Condition"	843
	c. Differing Requirements	845
C.	Terms and Conditions of Leave Under the ADA and the FMLA	847
	1. Limitations on the Availability of Leave Based on Hardship to the Employer Under the ADA and the FMLA	847
	2. Duration of Leave Under the ADA and the FMLA	850
	3. Availability of Reduced Schedule or Intermittent Leave	852
	4. Compensation While on Leave Under the ADA and the FMLA	854
	5. Continuation of Benefits While on Leave Under the ADA and the FMLA	855
	6. Treatment of Absenteeism under the ADA and the FMLA	856
D.	Availability of Light-Duty Work Under the ADA and the FMLA	857
E.	Medical Examinations and Inquiries Under the ADA and the FMLA	858
F.	Fitness-for-Duty Requirements Under the ADA and the FMLA	861
G.	Reinstatement Rights Under the ADA and the FMLA	862
H.	Antiretaliation Provisions Under the ADA and the FMLA	864
I.	Remedies Under the ADA and the FMLA	865
II. Workers' Compensation Laws		865

  A. The ADA and the Exclusive Remedy
    Provisions of Workers' Compensation Laws 867
  B. Pursuit of Discrimination Charges and
    Workers' Compensation Claims 869
    1. Judicial Estoppel 869
    2. EEOC Position 870
    3. Disability Benefits Versus ADA Claims 871
  C. Medical Inquiries and Confidentiality of
    Medical Information 873
    1. Medical Records 873
    2. Medical Examinations 873
    3. Fitness to Return-to-Work Policies 874
    4. Physical Agility Tests 875
    5. Medical Inquiries 875
  D. Accommodations, Light-Duty, and
    Leave Under the ADA and Workers'
    Compensation Laws 877
III. Social Security and Other Disability
  Benefits Programs 879
  A. "Disability" Under the Social
    Security Programs 881
    1. Duration of Social Security Benefits 883
  B. "Disability" Under the ADA 885
  C. Recognition of Conflict Between Social
    Security Disability and ADA Disability 887
    1. Administrative Recognition of Conflict 887
    2. Court Recognition of Conflict 887
  D. Receipt of Disability Benefits and
    ADA Recovery 890
    1. Social Security and ADA Disability
      Claims Conflict 890
    2. Genuine Conflicts 892
    3. "Sufficient Explanation" Burden 893
IV. Safety and Health Statutes and Regulations 895
  A. Balancing Individual Rights Against the Duty
    to Provide a Safe Workplace 897
    1. The Business Necessity Defense 898
    2. The Undue Hardship Defense 899

		3. The Direct-Threat Defense	900
		a. Opposing View	901
		4. The ADA's Conflict With Other Federal Laws as a Defense	904
	B.	Specific Occupational Safety and Health Act and ADA Tensions	907
		1. Employee Records	907
		2. Medical Examinations	909
		3. Abatement Requirements	910
	C.	State Medical and Safety Requirements	911
V.	The National Labor Relations Act		912
	A.	How the ADA and tje NLRA Interrelate	913
	B.	Conflicts Between the ADA and the NLRA	914
		1. The Implicit Duty to Meet Informally Versus the Prohibition Against Direct Dealing	914
		2. The Duty to Maintain Confidentiality Versus the Duty to Disclose	915
		3. The Duty to Reasonably Accommodate Versus the Duty to Bargain	917
		a. Collective Bargaining Agreement	917
	C.	Arbitration Issues Under the ADA	921
	D.	The Duty of Fair Representation	923
VI.	ERISA and the ADA's Application to Employee Benefits Plans		924
	A.	ADA Section 501(c)	927
		1. Historical Background/Legislative History	928
		a. Effect on ERISA's Preemption Provision	930
		b. Effect on Insurance Industry	930
		2. No Subterfuge	931
		3. Permitted Limitations	932
	B.	EEOC Guidance	934
		1. Level 1: Are Benefits "Unequal"?	937
		2. Level 2: Do the "Unequal" Benefits Arise from a "Disability-Based" Distinction?	937
		3. Level 3: Is the "Disability-Based" Distinction a "Subterfuge"?	939

			a. Circumstance 1	940

        a. Circumstance 1 940
        b. Circumstance 2 941
        c. Circumstance 3 942
        d. Circumstance 4 943
        e. Circumstance 5 944
        f. Summary 944
    C. Recurring Questions 944
        1. Standing to Sue Under the ADA 945
            a. No Longer Covered Under the ADA 946
            b. Judicial Estoppel 947
            c. EEOC's Position 947
            d. Disability-Based Risk Classifications 949
        2. Mental Versus Physical Health Care
           Coverage 952
    D. Violations and Permitted Distinctions 954

Chapter 10. Remedies, Litigation Strategies, and Alternative Dispute Resolution 959

I. Introduction 961
II. Administrative Procedures 962
    A. The Americans with Disabilities Act, Title I 962
        1. Filing a Discrimination Charge
           With the EEOC 962
        2. Exception to Time-Period Limitations:
           The *Edelman* Case 964
        3. EEOC Procedures: Probable Cause 965
        4. Civil Lawsuit 967
    B. The Americans with Disabilities Act,
        Title II 968
    C. The Americans with Disabilities Act,
        Title III 972
    D. The Rehabilitation Act of 1973 972
        1. Section 501 973
        2. Section 503 974
        3. Section 504 975
III. Sovereign Immunity 977
    A. The Americans With Disabilities Act 980

B. The Rehabilitation Act of 1973 984
IV. Remedies 986
　　A. Damages 986
　　　　1. The Americans with Disabilities Act 986
　　　　　　a. Title I 986
　　　　　　b. Title II 989
　　　　　　c. Title III 990
　　　　2. The Rehabilitation Act of 1973 992
　　B. Injunctions 994
V. Litigation Strategies 995
　　A. Plaintiff's Strategies 995
　　　　1. Filing the Charge of Discrimination at the
　　　　　　Administrative Level 996
　　　　2. Filing the Lawsuit in Court 997
　　　　3. Establishing a *Prima Facie* Case 999
　　　　　　a. Proving the Employee's Impairment
　　　　　　　　Is a Disability 999
　　　　　　　　i. Providing Proof 1000
　　　　　　b. Proving the Employee Is a Qualified
　　　　　　　　Individual With a Disability 1003
　　　　　　c. Reasonable Accommodation 1005
　　　　　　d. Making a Case for Punitive Damages 1009
　　B. Defendant's Strategies 1010
　　　　1. Disproving Plaintiff's Prima Facie Case 1011
　　　　　　a. Is the Employee Disabled? 1011
　　　　　　b. Affirmative Defenses 1014
　　　　　　　　i. Job-Related and Consistent With
　　　　　　　　　　Business Necessity 1016
　　　　　　　　ii. Leave Policies 1017
　　　　　　　　iii. Safety-Based Qualification
　　　　　　　　　　Standards 1017
　　　　　　　　iv. Direct Threat 1018
　　　　　　　　v. Undue Hardship 1021
　　　　　　　　vi. Seniority Systems and Collective
　　　　　　　　　　Bargaining Agreements 1024
　　　　　　　　vii. Conflict with Federal Law 1024
　　　　　　　　viii. Miscellaneous Defense 1025
VI. Arbitration 1026

    A. Americans With Disabilities Act 1026
        1. Unresolved Issues 1028
        2. Exceptions 1030
        3. Procedural Elements 1032
        4. Challenges to Arbitration Agreements 1033
        5. Unconscionable Arbitration Agreements ... 1035
        6. Collective Bargaining Agreements 1037
    B. The Rehabilitation Act of 1973 1039
VII. Attorneys' Fees, Costs, and Expenses 1041
    A. Americans With Disabilities Act 1041
        1. Legislative History 1042
        2. Obtaining an Award 1043
            a. Unsuccessful 1044
            b. Successful 1045
        3. Awards Against EEOC 1046
    B. The Rehabilitation Act of 1973 1047
    C. Claiming Attorneys' Fees Against
       State Governments 1047
    D. Recovery of Attorneys' Fees by the Prevailing
       Plaintiff for an Administrative Proceeding 1049

APPENDIX   LIST OF DOCUMENTS INCLUDED ON
                CD-ROM 1053

TABLE OF CASES 1059
INDEX 1099
ABOUT THE AUTHOR 1133

CHAPTER 1

OVERVIEW OF FEDERAL DISABILITY DISCRIMINATION LAW

I. Federal Disability Discrimination Legislation 2
   A. The Rehabilitation Act of 1973 3
      1. Section 501 4
      2. Section 503 5
      3. Section 504 6
      4. Section 508 7
   B. The Americans with Disabilities Act of 1990 7
      1. Progress in the Senate 9
      2. Progress in the House 10
      3. Food Industry Issue 11
      4. The Final Law 12
   C. Entities Covered by the ADA and the Rehabilitation Act 14
   D. What Is a Protected Disability? 15
      1. Impairment 17
      2. Limiting a Major Life Activity 18
      3. Previous or Misperceived Impairments 20
   E. The Reasonable Accommodation Obligation 21
   F. Defenses and Limitations to Employer Obligations 27
   G. Enforcement and Remedies 31
      1. Administrative Relief 32
      2. Private Right of Action 33
      3. Available Remedies 33
II. Related Federal Statutes 35
   A. Architectural Barriers Act 35
   B. Individuals with Disabilities Education Act 36
   C. Developmental Disabilities Assistance and Bill of Rights Act 37

D. Air Carrier Access Act 37
E. Telecommunications Act 38
F. Fair Housing Act 39
G. Social Security Act 40

I. FEDERAL DISABILITY DISCRIMINATION LEGISLATION

The federal statutes that grant formal protection to disabled individuals are among the most wide-ranging civil rights statutes that were passed in the 20th century. The disability laws not only prohibit discrimination in the workplace and beyond, they also establish obligations for employers, as well as people who own and maintain public facilities, to make necessary changes in operations as well as physical modifications so that disabled individuals are granted the same rights of access and enjoyment as others. This far-reaching obligation to provide reasonable accommodations is one characteristic that makes the disability statutes somewhat unique among federal discrimination laws. While Title VII of the Civil Rights Act of 1964,[1] with its obligation to refrain from discrimination based on religious practice, has been interpreted as imposing an obligation to reasonably accommodate religious belief and practice, the disability laws—and particularly, the Americans with Disabilities Act (ADA)[2]—create requirements that reach even farther in compelling organizations to deal with the conditions of individuals.

In the employment context, under disability discrimination laws, employers are required to engage both applicants and employees—in appropriate circumstances—in an interactive process through which they discuss the limitations imposed by the disability, the assistance that the individual requires, and what accommodations the employer is able and willing to provide. These accommodations range from changing the characteristics or requirements of a given job

---

[1] 42 U.S.C. §2000e et seq.
[2] 42 U.S.C. §12101 et seq.

assignment or offering to modify an employee's work shift to transferring an individual to a different position or providing specific equipment, devices, or assistance that would allow employees to perform the essential functions of their positions and responsibilities.

It was perhaps inevitable that this legislation would result in a great deal of litigation over whether an individual met the requirements for protection under the various laws,[3] but those consequences do not diminish the significance of this initiative.

The following discussion provides an overview of the principal elements of the federal disabilities statutes, as well as their application in the workplace and beyond.

A. The Rehabilitation Act of 1973

The legacy of the Rehabilitation Act of 1973[4] has been its initial role in dramatically altering the perceived limitations of disabled individuals as employees and helping to create a new environment in which they receive full access to the opportunities of the workplace. As the Supreme Court pointed out, the Rehabilitation Act was intended to remedy workplace discrimination against disabled individuals in all its forms, from malicious animus to stereotyping and thoughtless and indifferent benign neglect.[5] Chief among its provisions was Title V, which created unprecedented antidiscrimination and affirmative action requirements covering most federal workplaces and a number of private employers that are recipients of federal contracts or funding.

Congress passed the Rehabilitation Act in order to "promote and expand employment opportunities in the public and private sectors for handicapped individuals and to place such individuals in employment."[6] Its passage was designed to maintain and expand a federal vocational rehabilitation services

---

[3]This litigation is discussed in section I.D., "What Is a Protected Disability," below, and in subsequent chapters.
[4]Pub. L. No. 93-112, 87 Stat. 355 (1973) (codified as amended as 29 U.S.C. §701 et seq.).
[5]Alexander v. Choate, 469 U.S. 287, 295–96 (1985).
[6]Pub. L. No. 93-112, §2(8).

program for disabled individuals.[7] Title V, one of its key provisions, contains three substantive antidiscrimination provisions: section 501, which covers federal executive branch employees; section 503, which protects employees of contractors and subcontractors with federal contracts exceeding $10,000; and section 504, which prohibits discrimination in any program or activity that receives federal financial assistance or that is conducted by a federal executive agency or the U.S. Postal Service. President Richard Nixon signed the legislation into law in 1973 after vetoing two earlier versions of the measure, due to budgetary concerns that were unrelated to the provisions of Title V.

1. *Section 501*

As noted, above, section 501 protects qualified federal executive branch employees and applicants from discrimination on the basis of physical or mental disabilities.[8] This requirement was consistent with Congress's stated goal of making the federal government an exemplary equal opportunity employer of people with disabilities that protects against discrimination on the basis of a real or perceived disability.[9] In addition to its antidiscrimination provisions, section 501 also requires federal executive agencies to create affirmative action programs for hiring, placing, and advancing qualified disabled individuals. Finally, it obligates the agencies to provide reasonable accommodations to disabled federal employees or applicants to allow them to function effectively in positions for which they are qualified.

Today, each covered agency is independently responsible for the enforcement of section 501, in coordination with the

---

[7] 29 U.S.C. §§791–96.

[8] Section 501 provides, in relevant part, that coverage extends to "[e]ach department, agency or instrumentality (including the United States Postal Service and the Postal Rate Commission) in the executive branch and the Smithsonian Institute . . . ." 29 U.S.C. §791(b).

[9] 124 CONG. REC. 30,347 (1978) (comments of Sen. Alan Cranston (D-Cal.)); 29 C.F.R. §1614.203(b) (2003) ("The Federal Government shall become a model employer of individuals with disabilities.").

Equal Employment Opportunity Commission (EEOC), and must develop effective complaint and enforcement procedures. The EEOC regulations direct those agencies covered under section 501 to develop an annual written affirmative action plan that specifies goals for employment and for advancing employees with disabilities. Under this section, any aggrieved applicant or employee may file a complaint with the specific agency or the EEOC, or file a private action in federal court. In recent years, EEOC regulations have extended coverage to legislative competitive positions as well, but judicial branch competitive positions have been exempted from the scope of the Rehabilitation Act.[10]

2. Section 503

Section 503 creates similar obligations on federal government contractors and subcontractors with federal contracts greater than $10,000.[11] Under this provision, all such contractors and subcontractors are required to take affirmative action to employ and advance qualified individuals with disabilities. In addition, they must provide reasonable accommodations to all qualified individuals with disabilities, ensure nondiscriminatory hiring and employment practices, and engage in outreach to employ qualified individuals with physical or mental disabilities. These obligations continue for the duration of the contract, regardless of whether the value of the contract falls below $10,000 at any point. Contractors and subcontractors may petition for a waiver of section 503's requirements from either the President of the United States[12] or the Secretary of Labor.[13] In 1992, Congress passed an amendment stating that absent this waiver, *all* employees of federal contractors with contracts over $10,000 will be covered under the Rehabilitation Act. Unlike section 501, employees and applicants are not granted a private right of action against a contractor or subcontractor; the

---

[10] 29 C.F.R. §1614.103(b)(4) (2003) (as amended at 64 Fed. Reg. 37,655 (July 12, 1999)).
[11] 29 U.S.C. §793(a).
[12] *Id.* §793(c)(1).
[13] *Id.* §793(c)(2).

Department of Labor's Office of Federal Contract Compliance Programs (OFCCP) is responsible for enforcement.

3. Section 504

Section 504 incorporates the antidiscrimination principles of the two preceding sections and broadens their application, prohibiting discrimination against any "otherwise qualified individual with a disability" in any program or activity receiving federal financial assistance, or any program or activity conducted by a federal executive branch agency or the U.S. Postal Service.[14] This includes any entity, government or private, receiving assistance in almost any form, such as through the provision of money, personnel, services, or property. The measure of what constitutes "receiving federal financial assistance" has not been resolved definitively, but most agencies have adopted the broad mandate of the early Department of Health and Human Services regulations, which includes funding, service, or property as requisite financial assistance.[15] Unlike sections 501 and 503, however, section 504 does not have a distinct affirmative action mandate in addition to its antidiscrimination provisions. Each individual government agency is responsible for its implementation, in coordination with the Department of Justice (DOJ), and protected individuals are afforded both administrative remedies and a private right of action.[16]

---

[14] *Id.* §794(a).

[15] 45 C.F.R. §84.3(h) (2003) ("any grant, loan, contract (other than a procurement contract or a contract of insurance or guaranty), or any other arrangement by which the Department [of Health and Human Services] provides or otherwise makes available assistance in the form of: (1) Funds; (2) Services of Federal personnel; or (3) Real and personal property or any interest in or use of such property ....").

[16] In addition to the provisions of the Rehabilitation Act that are discussed above, section 508 of the statute, 29 U.S.C. §794d, has played a significant role in making electronic and information technology more accessible to individuals with disabilities (including both employees of a covered organization and members of the public). It sets forth requirements relating to such tools of technology when they are developed, maintained, procured, or used by the federal government. In this regard, it has emphasized principles of accessibility through the design of technology systems that do not rely solely on a single sense or ability of the individual user (such as visual or auditory formats). To guide federal agencies in this regard, the U.S. Access Board developed accessibility standards for electronic and information

4. Section 508

Section 508[17] deals with electronic and information technology that is developed, maintained, or procured by the federal government, and establishes standards requiring that such technology be accessible to individuals with disabilities. Accessibility for these purposes generally calls for systems that can be operated in more than one way and that are not dependent solely on a user's single sense or ability. These accessibility requirements apply regardless of the medium of technology and extend to both federal employees and members of the public. The requirement of accessibility is subject to a defense that compliance constitutes an undue hardship on the agency. The General Services Administration and the Architectural and Transportation Barriers Compliance Board provide technical assistance under section 508.

B. The Americans with Disabilities Act of 1990

In the decades following the passage of the Civil Rights Act of 1964[18] and its grant of employment and social protections to individuals on account of their race, color, religion, sex, and national origin, members of the disabled community had been seeking legislation far broader than the Rehabilitation Act that would guarantee them the same rights and benefits across all segments of society. Approximately a quarter-century after Congress enacted broad antidiscrimination protections in the Civil Rights Act of 1964, the House and Senate engaged in analysis and debate over the scope of civil rights protections that might be extended to disabled individuals. After the ADA was introduced in Congress, it passed both chambers with speed that was somewhat surprising, and it was immediately signed into law by President George H.W. Bush. Neither the relatively swift progress toward enactment nor the wide margins

---

technology, the General Services Administration issued related acquisition requirements, and the DOJ has provided compliance coordination assistance to the various agencies.

[17] 29 U.S.C. §794d.
[18] 42 U.S.C. §2000a et seq.

that voted for the measure on final passage, however, should imply that its path to the U.S. Code was simple or straightforward. Rather, the legislation survived multiple drafts and countless amendments before final passage, and survived the tensions between a Democratic Congress and a Republican White House, and their respective supporters.

While many factors contributed to the introduction and passage of the ADA, none was more important than the work of the National Council on Disability (NCD), a 15-member independent federal agency charged with reviewing and creating policies and laws affecting the disabled. The NCD issued a report entitled *Toward Independence,* which outlined many of the problems facing the disabled community and proposed a series of legislative reforms, many of which ultimately were incorporated into the enacted ADA. The report called for the expansion of the nation's broad antidiscrimination statutes to include the disabled community, guaranteeing them equal opportunities in employment and elsewhere, providing reasonable accommodations to ensure that equality, and creating appropriate enforcement mechanisms in order to guarantee compliance. Polling information also indicated that disabled individuals were facing persistent discrimination in the workplace and that only comprehensive legislative action could correct the problem.

In an attempt to expedite a legislative resolution, the NCD initially submitted a draft bill for Congress's consideration in 1988. The bill was designed to stand separately from the Rehabilitation Act and essentially would have extended the protections of Title VII of the Civil Rights Act to individuals with disabilities. The EEOC was to be charged with providing regulations for its enforcement, and those regulations would be similar to the existing provisions of Title VII, including administrative remedies, a private right of action in federal court, monetary damages, and injunctive relief.[19] Immediately, the bill generated intense interest among supporters and critics alike, and early controversy quickly surrounded the potential economic

---

[19] H.R. 4498, the "Americans with Disabilities Act of 1988," introduced on April 29, 1988 (200th Cong.), sponsored by Rep. Tony Coelho (D-CA), with 124

burden of compliance, the inclusion of Acquired Immune Deficiency Syndrome (AIDS) victims among the groups protected from discrimination, and what standard employers would be held to in providing reasonable accommodations.

1. Progress in the Senate

Originally introduced in the Senate as S. 2345, the bill was modified substantially before final passage in an effort to appeal to both advocates of the disabled and potential congressional opponents. The new bill, S. 933, focused on inequities in employment, public services such as mass transportation, public accommodations, and telecommunications. Legislators reduced the breadth and scope of the definition of "disability" to mirror the three-pronged definitional language of the Rehabilitation Act of 1973.[20] They also took steps to reduce the potential cost of compliance. For instance, rather than obligate employers to take all steps short of those that would bankrupt or change the essential nature of their business to ensure accessibility for the disabled, sponsors exempted them from any acts that would be considered an "undue hardship." Additionally, their responsibility to update public transportation vehicles and facilities was limited to a "good-faith effort," or where accessibility was "readily achievable." But the legislative process expanded the scope of the bill in other areas. For example, the list of "public accommodations" required to be handicapped-accessible was expanded to include virtually all privately owned facilities used by the general public and that affected commerce.

One final point of major contention remained: whether certain conditions such as homosexuality, voyeurism, kleptomania, and pyromania would be considered disabilities that received protection under the law. After an exhaustive debate

---

co-sponsors; S. 2345, "the Americans with Disabilities Act of 1988," introduced on April 28, 1988 (100th Cong.), sponsored by Sen. Lowell Weicker (R-CT), with 26 co-sponsors.

[20]S. Rep. No. 101-116 (1989). "The term 'disability' means, with respect to an individual—(1) a physical or mental impairment that substantially limits one or more of the major life activities of such individual; (2) a record of such impairment; or (3) being regarded as having such an impairment." *Id.* at 22.

concerning the moral overtones that might be implicit in the provision of federal protection to such individuals, the Senate decided to attach a list of conditions that would be expressly exempted from coverage under the ADA. Now approaching a consensus, the leaders of the bill in the Senate met with the White House to discuss any outstanding points of contention. In the course of those negotiations, senators agreed to restrict available remedies to those available under the Civil Rights Act, thereby quieting employer fears that they might face enormous punitive damage claims.[21] In turn, the administration agreed to support the broad definition of "public accommodations" under Title III, as outlined above. With that, the focus moved to the House of Representatives.

2. *Progress in the House*

The bill was introduced in the House for consideration on two separate occasions, and it was the second version, H.R. 2273, that ultimately passed. Four different committees reviewed and modified the bill before its submission to the full House for debate and a vote. During this process, a constant theme emerged—the bill became infused with the spirit of the civil rights movement, and its supporters declared it the next logical step in eliminating discrimination both in and out of the workplace. Nonetheless, substantial changes were made before its final passage.

- The House Committee on Education and Labor, the first to review the bill, modified it to allow state and local governments to develop their own standards for public accommodations, independent of Title III, so long as their versions met or exceeded the federal standard and received certification from the Attorney

---

[21]The subsequently enacted Civil Rights Act of 1991, Pub. L. No. 102-166, 105 Stat. 1071, extended the availability of punitive damages (capped on the basis of size of the employing entity) to actions under both Title VII and the ADA.

General. Like the Senate version, the House bill prohibited the recovery of punitive damages against employers under Title III and limited compensatory damages to out-of-pocket expenses and remuneration for pain and suffering.
- The Committee on Energy and Commerce added amendments that, among other things, created detailed accessibility guidelines for Amtrak trains and required closed-captioning for public service announcements.
- The Committee on Public Works and Transportation exempted historic vehicles from the requirement that remanufactured vehicles be made handicapped-accessible in the process.
- The final committee to review the bill, the Committee on the Judiciary, added a provision to encourage alternative dispute resolution, although not to the exclusion of those forms of relief made available pursuant to the ADA's enforcement provisions, and linked the remedies provided under the ADA to those set forth in Title VII of the Civil Rights Act. With the inclusion of these and other amendments, the bill moved to the full House for debate.

3. Food Industry Issue

Throughout the debate in the full House of Representatives, and in the House-Senate conference that followed House passage, one of the most contentious debates surrounded a proposed amendment that permitted the reassignment of food industry employees with AIDS or the human immunodeficiency virus to positions that did not involve food-handling. After several failed compromises, both sides ultimately agreed to authorize the Secretary of Health and Human Services to prepare and update an annual list of communicable and contagious diseases that can be transmitted via food-handling. A food industry employer would be permitted to transfer only those employees with those listed diseases from food-handling positions. With the resolution of that final matter, the bill was sent to President George H.W. Bush, who signed the Americans with Disabilities Act into law on July 26, 1990.[22]

4. *The Final Law*

The ADA was hailed as a combination of the Emancipation Proclamation and the Bill of Rights for people with disabilities. It noted that 43 million Americans were living with disabilities in 1990, and that the lack of effective antidiscrimination laws had impaired their ability to thrive both in and out of the workplace.[23] The legislation not only featured antidiscrimination language similar to that found in traditional civil rights statutes, it also required individualized reasonable accommodations and the redesign and construction of both new and existing buildings, facilities, and transportation that were accessible to the disabled. In all, the ADA covered four distinct spheres: employment, public services, public accommodations and services operated by private entities, and telecommunications relay services.

Title I, which governs employment, holds that "[n]o covered entity shall discriminate against a qualified individual with a disability because of the disability . . . in regard to job application procedures, the hiring, advancement, or discharge of employees, employee compensation, job training, and other terms, conditions, and privileges of employment."[24] It covers employers with more than 15 employees. Arguably its defining characteristic is the requirement that employers must "reasonably accommodate" qualified disabled individuals, and defining what constitutes a disability and what suffices as a "reasonable accommodation" became the most-litigated issues under the ADA in the first years after its enactment. Those issues are discussed in detail in the chapters that follow.

---

[22] S. 933 became Public Law No. 101-336.

[23] 42 U.S.C. §12101(a)(1). *See also* 42 U.S.C. §12101(a)(2) and (3) ("(2) historically, society has tended to isolate and segregate individuals with disabilities, and, despite some improvements, such forms of discrimination against individuals with disabilities continue to be a serious and pervasive social problem; (3) discrimination against individuals with disabilities persists in such critical areas as employment, housing, public accommodations, education, transportation, communication, recreation, institutionalization, health services, voting, and access to public services").

[24] 42 U.S.C. §12112(a).

Title II prohibits discrimination based on disability in all activities, programs, and services by any "public entity," which includes state and local governments and their instrumentalities. The scope of Title II is extremely broad and includes all three branches of state and local governments, as well as a wide variety of instrumentalities including public transit authorities, police departments, mayoral and planning commissions, and school boards.[25] This section also requires reasonable modifications to rules, policies, or practices in order to remove architectural, communication, or transportation barriers, and to ensure the provision of auxiliary aids and services.[26] Pursuant to section 505 of the Rehabilitation Act, those aggrieved are granted a private right of action against wrongdoers.

Title III prohibits discrimination in any place of public accommodation on the basis of disability. It identifies 12 categories of entities that are described as "public accommodations," the scope of which includes virtually every business or other establishment that has regular contact with the general public. It also covers commercial facilities and certain transportation services. The section requires that public accommodations make those reasonable modifications to policies, practices, or procedures necessary to allow disabled individuals to enjoy fully the services or goods provided, unless doing so would fundamentally alter the nature of the services or goods themselves. Other requirements include the provision of auxiliary aids and services and the removal of architectural and structural communications barriers, if removal is readily achievable. New facilities must be accessible to the disabled unless to do so is "structurally impracticable." Both the Attorney General and aggrieved individuals may seek relief under Title III.

Title IV covers telecommunications services—telephone transmissions and television public service announcements. This section obligates telephone companies that provide telephone service in a given area to also provide telephone relay services to those individuals who use telecommunications

---

[25]H.R. REP. No. 101-485, pt. 2, at 86 (1990), *reprinted in* 1990 U.S.C.C.A.N. 303, 369.
[26]42 U.S.C. §12131(2).

display devices or similar devices. It further requires that the content of all public service announcements be made available via closed captioning, in addition to verbal transmissions. The Federal Communications Commission is generally responsible for all necessary enforcement of Title IV.[27]

C. Entities Covered by the ADA and the Rehabilitation Act

Much of the ADA borrows the language of Title VII of the Civil Rights Act of 1964. Under Title I of the ADA, "covered entities" are prohibited from engaging in employment discrimination. Those covered entities include employers, employment agencies, labor organizations, and joint labor-management committees.[28] Employers are defined as those entities that employ 15 or more individuals over a 20-week period and also include those persons who are "agents" of an employer.[29] According to the EEOC, agents are those managers, supervisors, foremen, or others who act for or on behalf of the employer, such as agencies used to conduct background checks on candidates.[30] Like Title VII, the language of the ADA does not include the federal government and corporations wholly owned by the federal government—such organizations are covered under the Rehabilitation Act. However, unlike Title VII, the ADA does not exempt state-elected public officials or members of their personal staff from its coverage.[31]

Under Title II, the ADA prohibits discrimination on the part of public entities, including any state, city, or local government, or agency or department within the government.[32] This extends to those activities carried out by government contractors as well. Finally, Title V affords protections to applicants,

---

[27] Title V of the ADA, not addressed here, covers the General Accounting Office, the Government Printing Office, and the Library of Congress.
[28] 42 U.S.C. §§12111(2), 12112(a). *See also* 29 C.F.R. §1630.2(b) (2003).
[29] 42 U.S.C. §12111(5). *See also* 29 C.F.R. §1630.2(e)(1) (2003).
[30] EQUAL EMPLOYMENT OPPORTUNITY COMM'N, A TECHNICAL ASSISTANCE MANUAL ON THE EMPLOYMENT PROVISIONS (TITLE I) OF THE AMERICANS WITH DISABILITIES ACT at I-2 (1992).
[31] 42 U.S.C. §12111(5).
[32] 42 U.S.C. §§12132, 12131(1).

employees, and former employees of several government bodies, including the House of Representatives, the Senate, and the Congressional Budget Office.[33]

The Rehabilitation Act also covers a substantial number of employing entities within the U.S. government. Section 501 applies to every department, agency, and instrumentality in the Executive Branch.[34] Subsequent case law has further developed and defined the scope and extent of that coverage, and the resulting conclusions largely depend on whether the given agency or department truly resides in the Executive Branch or elsewhere, a conclusion that often is far from clear.

Under section 503, those private entities that hold government contracts and subcontracts in excess of $10,000 that furnish supplies and services and use real or personal property also are covered. At the same time, coverage of contracts that do not exceed that $10,000 threshold also may be waived under section 503 if "special circumstances in the national interest" apply.[35] With respect to separate agencies or facilities, the affirmative action requirement does not apply to any agency or subdivision of a state or local government that does not participate in the work of the contract or subcontract; separate facilities of a private contractor are not similarly exempted, however.[36]

Finally, section 504 borrows language from Title VI of the Civil Rights Act of 1964 and Title IX of the Education Amendments of 1972[37] in applying its prohibitions against discrimination to any "program or activity" that receives federal assistance or is under the direction of any Executive Branch agency or the U.S. Postal Service.[38] This applies in three separate areas: state and local government entities, educational systems, and private businesses. With respect to state and local

---

[33]Pub. L. No. 104-1, §101(3), 109 Stat. 4 (1995).
[34]29 U.S.C. §791(b).
[35]41 C.F.R. §60-741.3(a)(3) (1993); 29 U.S.C. §793; 29 U.S.C. §793(c)(1).
[36]41 C.F.R. §60-741.4.
[37]20 U.S.C. §1681 et seq.
[38]29 U.S.C. §794(a).

government entities, two general principles govern: if any department or agency of a state or local government receives federal funds, all operations of that particular department or agency are covered as a result; if a department or agency receives funds for the purpose of dispensing them, then both the distributor *and* the recipient must comply with the statute.[39] With respect to school systems, the provisions apply to a single school if it exists within an overall school system that receives aid, regardless of whether the aid is direct or indirect. Finally, private businesses are similarly included under this "umbrella" principle, depending on whether the aid is granted according to a company's geographic facilities, principal business focus, or on a companywide basis.[40]

D. What Is a Protected Disability?

Today, virtually all disability discrimination statutes—including those adopted at the state and local levels—have incorporated some version of the federal statutes' three-pronged concept of disability. Although the precise language varies slightly according to the context of the specific measure,[41] the multipart definition has gained wide acceptance. It defines a "disability" as: "(A) a physical or mental impairment that substantially limits one or more of the major life activities of [an] individual; (B) a record of such an impairment; or (C) being regarded as having such an impairment."[42] In practice, however, application of this definition does not always yield predictable or precise results. Determinations of "disability" status are made on a case-by-case basis, measuring the actual effect the impairment has on an individual's life and his or her ability to compensate for that impairment.[43] Therefore, it is incumbent on attorneys for employers and employees

---

[39] 29 U.S.C. §794(b)(1)(A)–(B).
[40] 29 U.S.C. §794(b)(3)(A)–(B).
[41] The Rehabilitation Act Amendments initially established this definition for a covered "handicapped individual," while the ADA adopted the three-pronged format to create a definition for a "disability" that may be protected by the statute.
[42] 42 U.S.C. §12102(2)(A)–(C).
[43] Toyota Motor Mfg., Inc. v. Williams, 534 U.S. 184, 12 AD Cases 993 (2002).

alike to recognize and understand the underlying definitional elements of a "disability," and how courts apply them in practice.

1. Impairment

As stated above, a disability is an "impairment that substantially limits one or more of the major life activities of [an] individual."[44] The first question that often is asked is, "What is an impairment?" Regulations promulgated under both the ADA and the Rehabilitation Act provide the relevant definitions: a "physical impairment" is defined as "any physiological disorder or condition, cosmetic disfigurement, or anatomical loss affecting one or more of the following body systems: neurological, musculoskeletal, special sense organs, respiratory (including speech organs), cardiovascular, reproductive, digestive, gentiro-urinary, hemic and lymphatic, skin, and endocrine."[45] A "mental impairment" is "any mental or psychological disorder, such as mental retardation, organic brain syndrome, emotional or mental illness, and specific learning disabilities."[46] Other types of impairments (e.g., environmental, cultural, and economic) generally are not considered handicapping conditions or disabilities.

Based on the sheer number of variations in human circumstance, any attempt to draft an exhaustive list covering all of the possible types of diseases and conditions that might constitute a protected physical or mental impairment certainly would be impossible. Therefore, neither Congress nor the courts have attempted to do so. The diversity of conditions also limits the viability of attempts to subdivide these conditions into useful categories or classifications. In fact, even a publication as comprehensive and authoritative as the American Psychiatric Association's *Diagnostic and Statistical Manual of Mental Disorders* does not include all of the conditions that might qualify as mental impairments, according to the March 1997 EEOC Guidelines. Therefore, litigating parties and the courts continue to work

---

[44] 42 U.S.C. §12102(2)(a).
[45] 29 C.F.R. §1630.2(h)(1) (2003); 45 C.F.R. §84.3(j)(2)(i)(A) (2003).
[46] 29 C.F.R. §1630.2(h)(2); 45 C.F.R. §84.3(j)(2)(i)(B).

2. Limiting a Major Life Activity

Obviously, not all physical or mental impairments qualify for legal protection as disabilities. In order to constitute a "disability," an impairment must also substantially limit one or more of the major life activities of the given individual. As defined in section 504 and elsewhere, "major life activities" include caring for one's self, performing manual tasks, walking, seeing, hearing, speaking, breathing, learning, and working.[47] In order to determine whether an impairment substantially limits one of those activities, one must consider: (1) the nature and severity of the impairment (*i.e.*, the extent of a limitation), (2) the permanent or long-term impact of the impairment (i.e., its impact), and (3) the duration or expected duration of the impairment (i.e., the duration of the impairment).[48] Generally, the standard used is a comparison to the "average person in the general population."[49] In that vein, temporary or nonchronic impairments that have little or no long-term impact, such as broken limbs, sprained joints, concussions, appendicitis, or influenza usually are not considered disabilities.[50] However, if an injury such as a broken leg was to heal improperly, and the person was left with a permanent limp, then that condition might qualify.[51] In addition, several courts have held that normal pregnancy is not a disability, so long as unusual complications do not result.[52] However, if abnormal

---

[47] As with impairments, this list of major life activities is not exhaustive. Although the previous list represents the broadest consensus of included activities, judicial decisions also have mentioned procreation, sexual conduct, normal social relationships, standing, and sitting. Oesterling v. Walters, 760 F.2d 859, 1 AD Cases 722 (8th Cir. 1985); Doe v. District of Columbia, 796 F. Supp. 559, 2 AD Cases 197 (D.D.C. 1992).

[48] 29 C.F.R. §1630.2(j)(2) (2003).

[49] *Id.*

[50] A person who suffers from transitory illnesses that have no permanent effect on the individual's health is not considered to be "disabled." Stevens v. Stubbs, 576 F. Supp. 1409, 1 AD Cases 546 (N.D. Ga. 1983).

[51] 29 C.F.R. pt. 1630, app. §1630.2(j) (2003).

[52] Gabriel v. City of Chicago, 9 F. Supp. 2d 974, 9 AD Cases 483 (N.D. Ill. 1998).

or unusual circumstances exist, and those conditions cause or result in an abnormal reproductive functioning (reproduction being a major life activity[53]), then the individual may satisfy the statutory definition of disability.[54]

This applies equally to mental impairments. If a psychological impairment lasts for a relatively short period of time and shows no sign of residual effects, then it does not qualify for disability status. However, if multiple impairments constitute a disability in the aggregate, that impact might qualify for protection.[55]

In some circumstances, a separate level of analysis applies depending on the specific major life activity involved. With respect to working, case law developing under the ADA suggests that it is not enough to show that the impairment limits an individual in the performance of only one particular job or a narrow range of specialized employment. Rather, an individual must show that he or she is significantly restricted in his or her ability to perform either a class of jobs or a broad range of jobs in various classes. For example, in 2002, the Supreme Court held that an assembly line worker suffering from carpal tunnel syndrome was not substantially limited from performing manual activities, because the interference with manual tasks was only minor and was limited to occupation-specific manual tasks.[56] Instead, the Court ruled, the plaintiff must demonstrate that the impairment "prevents or severely restricts" him or her from performing manual activities that are of "central importance" to most people's daily lives.[57]

Similarly, the U.S. Court of Appeals for the Ninth Circuit has held that even if a newspaper reporter was able to demonstrate injuries caused by a work-related repetitive stress disorder, the effect of those injuries was largely limited to her specific job, and being a reporter does not constitute a sufficiently

---

[53]Bragdon v. Abbott, 524 U.S. 624, 8 AD Cases 239 (1998).
[54]Gudenkauf v. Stauffer Communications, 922 F. Supp. 465, 5 AD Cases 1739, 77 FEP Cases 1723 (D. Kan. 1996), *aff'd*, 158 F.3d 1074, 77 FEP Cases 1742 (10th Cir. 1998).
[55]29 C.F.R. pt. 1630, app. §1630.2(j) (2003).
[56]Toyota Motor Mfg. v. Williams, 534 U.S. 184, 12 AD Cases 993 (2002).
[57]*Id.* at 190–91.

broad class of jobs under the ADA.[58] The employee was not able to demonstrate that she was substantially limited in the major life activity of performing manual tasks, because her ability to do a wide range of manual tasks outweighed her inability to type and write for extended periods of time.

Another consideration when making the determination of whether impairment substantially limits a major life activity is the mitigating or corrective measures that might be utilized or available to that individual. In 1999, the Supreme Court held that a disability exists only where an impairment actually limits a major life activity in a substantial manner, not in those situations where the impairment "would" or "could" be substantially limiting if mitigating measures were not taken.[59] Therefore, an individualized inquiry must be made that measures the individual's limitations in their "corrected" state and must consider any negative side effects of the corrective measures (e.g., side effects of medications).[60]

3. Previous or Misperceived Impairments

The federal statutes also provide protection to those individuals who have a history of, or have been misclassified as having, a mental or physical impairment that substantially limits one or more major life activities.[61] This aspect of the statutory provision was enacted, in part, to protect individuals who have recovered from a physical or mental impairment that previously limited them in a substantial manner in a major life activity, with the goal of preventing discrimination due to either prior conditions or misclassifications.

Discrimination also is prohibited against individuals who are treated as if they are disabled. This category includes individuals who have physical or mental impairments that substantially limit a major activity only as a result of the attitude of others toward that impairment, as well as those who have no

---

[58]Thornton v. McClatchy Newspapers, Inc., 261 F.3d 789, 12 AD Cases 211 (9th Cir. 2001).
[59]Sutton v. United Air Lines, 527 U.S. 471, 9 AD Cases 673 (1999).
[60]*Id.*
[61]29 U.S.C. §706(8)(b)(ii); 42 U.S.C. §12102(2)(A), (B), & (C).

physical or mental impairment, but are treated by an employer as if they did.[62] In *School Board of Nassau County v. Arline*,[63] a case under the Rehabilitation Act, the Supreme Court set the contemporary standard for addressing cases of this type. The individual in question had a prior record of impairment—an earlier case of tuberculosis. Stating that "society's accumulated myths and fears about disability and disease are as handicapping as are the physical limitations that flow from actual impairment,"[64] the Court held that the fact that the individual was contagious did not necessarily deprive her of the statutory protections. While some persons with contagious diseases may pose a serious health threat to others under certain circumstances, the Court concluded that fact did not justify excluding from the disability law's coverage all persons with actual or perceived contagious diseases. Trial courts were instructed to determine whether the individual was otherwise qualified to perform her job, which would require an individualized inquiry and findings of fact regarding the nature of the risk of transmission, its duration (how long the person will be contagious), the potential harm to third parties, and the probabilities that the disease will be transmitted and will cause varying degrees of harm.

E. The Reasonable Accommodation Obligation

The existence of a reasonable accommodation is one major factor distinguishing the federal disabilities statutes from other civil rights laws. Beyond the basic antidiscrimination provisions of most such statutes that require employers to treat all individuals equally, the Rehabilitation Act of 1973 and the ADA impose an affirmative duty on employers to provide special and unique treatment to disabled individuals. The principle underlying the obligation is that this special treatment will level the playing field on which employees compete, without affording disabled individuals an inherent or undue advantage.

---

[62] 45 C.F.R. §84.3(j)(2)(iv) (2003); 29 C.F.R. §1630.2(1).
[63] 480 U.S. 273, 1 AD Cases 1026 (1987).
[64] *Id.* at 284.

The nature of the obligation is as follows: employers are obligated to provide reasonable accommodations that allow otherwise qualified individuals to perform their essential job functions, so long as those accommodations do not impose an undue hardship on the employer.[65] That obligation extends to all aspects of employment, including recruiting, hiring, assignment of work, and advancement. The scope of these obligations represents some of the most litigated areas with respect to the disability statutes.

Because employers are only required to accommodate "qualified individuals with disabilities," the next stage in the inquiry concerning statutory application is defining those qualified individuals. Under the ADA, there are two relevant considerations: (1) whether the person possesses "the requisite skill, experience, education, and other job-related requirements" for the position; and (2) whether the individual is able to perform the essential functions of the position desired or held with or without a reasonable accommodation.[66]

The next component of an employer's reasonable accommodation obligation is to identify the essential functions of a given position. This assessment requires an examination of whether employees in a given position are actually required to perform those functions that are considered "essential," how much time an employee spends performing the given functions, the degree of expertise or skills required to perform the functions, and whether removal of those functions would fundamentally alter the position.[67] That inquiry is highly fact-specific, and the results vary widely according to the position, employer, and the industry involved. Under the federal statutes, employers retain the right to define a job and those functions that are required to perform it. This does not mean that the employer's judgment cannot be challenged; rather, that judgment is simply afforded a degree of weight under the

---

[65] 42 U.S.C. §12181.
[66] 29 C.F.R. §1630.2(m) (2003).
[67] 29 C.F.R. §1630.2(n) (2003).

statute.[68] If an employee challenges an assertion that a task is an "essential function" of a job, the employer bears the burden of demonstrating that the task at issue is, in fact, essential. Frequently, employers will develop or maintain formal job descriptions, and these may be offered as evidence that certain job components are essential job functions. Federal regulations under the ADA do not require employers to maintain such job descriptions. If employers do, however, they are well-advised to ensure that the job descriptions accurately describe the tasks and responsibilities of the employees occupying the position. If a job description declares that a given function is essential, but individuals performing that job fail to perform the function or perform it rarely, courts are likely to ignore the formalities of the job description in favor of the practical realities of the position.[69]

Under the ADA, an employer is only obligated to make accommodations to *known* limitations of an otherwise qualified individual with a disability.[70] Thus, the employee has the responsibility of notifying his or her employer of the need for an accommodation in the workplace. However, even if the employee has not made a specific request for an accommodation, the employer must explore possible accommodations as soon as the existence of a disability becomes known, regardless of the source.[71] There is no formulaic manner in which employees must request an accommodation; in fact, other people may make the request on their behalf.

According to the EEOC's regulations under the ADA, following that notification, the employer must initiate an interactive process with the individual needing the accommodation in order to identify the limitations resulting from the disability and what potential accommodations would be helpful.[72] The

---

[68]Pesterfield v. Tennessee Valley Auth., 941 F.2d 437, 1 AD Cases 1858 (6th Cir. 1991).
[69]29 C.F.R. pt. 1630, app. §1630.2(n) (2003); Durning v. Duffens Optical, Inc., 1996 U.S. Dist. LEXIS 1685, 1996 WL 67640 (E.D. La. 1996).
[70]Hedberg v. Indiana Bell Tel. Co., 47 F.3d 928, 4 AD Cases 65 (7th Cir. 1995).
[71]S. REP. NO. 101-116, at 34 (1989); H.R. REP. NO. 101-485, pt. 2, at 65 (1990).
[72]29 C.F.R. §1630.2(o)(3) (2003).

underlying theme is that the employer must provide those accommodations that will allow the employee to enjoy the benefits and privileges of employment. Generally speaking, the interactive process includes the following:

- exchanging information with the disabled individual about his or her disability and work restrictions,
- identifying the appropriate workplace accommodations, and
- reaching a mutually satisfactory decision about the reasonable accommodation to be provided.[73]

Throughout this process, the nature of the obligation is reciprocal; disabled individuals who request accommodations are obligated to cooperate in the accommodation process in a timely and responsive manner. For employees, this means providing requested information to the employer as part of the inquiry as to whether a reasonable accommodation can be made. However, the employer is only entitled to request information and documentation that would be necessary in determining whether the employee has a qualifying disability.

Beyond basic information, closer scrutiny may be triggered if the employer seeks medical certification to determine a reasonable accommodation. Because such an inquiry is more invasive, the permissibility of such an examination is limited to those occasions when the employer can demonstrate that it is "job-related and consistent with business necessity."[74] Those circumstances include: when an employee is having difficulty performing the job effectively; when an employee becomes disabled, either on or off the job; when an examination is necessary to determine a reasonable accommodation; or when examinations or medical monitoring are required by other laws.[75]

With respect to the general duty of cooperation, some appellate rulings held that reviewing courts should look for

---

[73] 29 C.F.R. pt. 1630, app. §1630.9 (2003).
[74] 42 U.S.C. §12112(d)(4)(A).
[75] EQUAL EMPLOYMENT OPPORTUNITY COMM'N, TECHNICAL ASSISTANCE MANUAL §6.6.

evidence demonstrating a lack of good faith between the parties, such as obstructing or delaying the interactive process, or failing to communicate, in evaluating this mutuality of commitment.[76] This duty of accommodation is ongoing and may require different accommodations at different times. Finally, while the interactive process should be conducted promptly, it does not necessarily have to take priority over all other legitimate business considerations.[77]

The duty to make reasonable accommodations applies to all aspects of employment, and those accommodations can assume a variety of forms. Some of most common categories of accommodations include:

- making existing facilities used by employees readily accessible to and usable by individuals with disabilities;
- job restructuring;
- part-time or modified work schedules;
- reassigning a disabled individual to a vacant position;
- acquiring or modifying equipment or devices;
- appropriately adjusting or modifying examinations, training materials, or policies; and
- providing qualified readers or interpreters.[78]

Often, more than one accommodation may be effective in resolving a situation; in those cases, the employer is free to choose among them, even if the decision is made with an eye toward issues such as cost or convenience, so long as the accommodation is effective.[79]

In the case of job restructuring, it may be possible to reassign certain duties or functions to another position within the company; however, the employer has the discretion to

---

[76] Beck v. University of Wis. Bd. of Regents, 75 F.3d 1130, 5 AD Cases 304 (7th Cir. 1996).
[77] Selenke v. Medical Imaging of Colo., 248 F.3d 1249, 11 AD Cases 1395 (10th Cir. 2001).
[78] 42 U.S.C. §12111(9)(A), (B).
[79] 29 U.S.C. §794a(a)(1).

determine the viability of such a transfer.[80] Similarly, an employer might offer to transfer or reassign the disabled individual to another position, or even to another geographic area within the company. However, there may be limitations on such transfers. For example, reassignments might only be considered in cases where the employee is qualified for the position in question.[81] Employers typically are not required to create new positions to accommodate disabled employees, nor must they displace another employee as a result. It also should be noted that the employer's responsibility may go beyond just the ability to perform certain work-related tasks; the accommodation also must protect the employee's ability to enjoy the benefits and privileges of employment, including company-sponsored training, services, and social functions.

With respect to making changes to training materials, the EEOC provides the following examples:

- providing accessible training sites;
- providing training materials in alternate formats, such as by making them available on tape, in large print, or on a computer diskette for an individual with a visual disability, or by providing a person with mental retardation with materials in a simplified form or with help in understanding the instructions; or
- modifying the way training is provided, such as by affording people with learning disabilities or mental impairments more time and extra assistance for training.[82]

The U.S. Court of Appeals for the Seventh Circuit held that an employee who could not perform the essential functions of his or her job was not entitled to promotion to a position for which another employee was better qualified.[83] Nor was the employer required to provide said employee with all of the

---

[80] 29 C.F.R. pt. 1630, app. §1630.2(o) (2003).
[81] Ozlowski v. Henderson, 237 F.3d 837, 11 AD Cases 671 (7th Cir. 2001).
[82] EQUAL EMPLOYMENT OPPORTUNITY COMM'N, TECHNICAL ASSISTANCE MANUAL §3.10, at III-30.
[83] Williams v. United Ins. Co. of Am., 253 F.2d 280, 11 AD Cases 1613 (7th Cir. 2001).

necessary training to qualify for the position. In reaching this conclusion, the court noted that the ADA does not require employers to provide special training to disabled employees that it does not provide to nondisabled individuals.[84] These illustrations represent several basic examples of reasonable ways in which employers can modify existing workplace behaviors to accommodate individuals with disabilities, as well as steps that employers are not expected to take in the normal course of business.

In many cases arising under the federal disabilities statutes, individuals assert that an employer has not satisfied its obligations with respect to reasonable accommodation. An individual can make this showing by demonstrating the following:

- the individual in question has a disability within the meaning of the statutes,
- the individual is "qualified" with respect to the position in question,
- the employer knew about the employee's disability,
- the employee requested accommodations or assistance for his or her disability,
- the employer did not make a good-faith effort to assist the employee in seeking accommodations, and
- the employee could have been reasonably accommodated but for the employer's lack of good faith.[85]

F. Defenses and Limitations to Employer Obligations

As an initial matter, parties to disability discrimination cases often contest the question of whether the individual is "disabled" within the meaning of the statute. A substantial number of cases pursued in the first decade of litigation under the ADA focused on this key question. To the dismay of some, and to the applause of others, the federal courts—led by the

---

[84] *Id.*
[85] 29 C.F.R. §1630.2(g), (n), (o).

Supreme Court's important decisions on this subject[86]—have construed that status in a narrow fashion.

Although the federal disabilities statutes were enacted to encourage employers to hire disabled individuals and provide them with the full benefits and privileges of full employment, employers generally retain the ability to establish appropriate job-related qualification standards. Typically, these standards cover employment characteristics such as education, skills, work experience, and physical and mental standards necessary for job performance, health, and safety. However, employers cannot incorporate or apply standards that screen out or tend to screen out individuals on the basis of a disability unless they are "job-related" and "consistent with business necessity."[87]

In order to be job-related, qualification standards, tests, or selection criteria must be a legitimate measure of qualification for a specific job or position at issue. Employers may evaluate and measure applicants on all functions of a job, including nonessential functions, and may continue to select and hire people who can perform all of these functions. However, to the extent that the specific qualification standards affect only marginal job functions, the federal disability statutes require the employer to evaluate an individual's qualifications based solely on his or her ability to perform the essential functions of the job, with or without an accommodation.[88]

A business necessity defense requires an employer to demonstrate that an individual is excluded from a position not because of the disability itself, but due to the relevant qualification standard, which must relate to the essential functions of the job.[89] For example, an employer may require applicants for a clerical job to possess a valid driver's license because it would be desirable to have a person who could occasionally

---

[86] *See, e.g.,* Toyota Motor Mfg. v. Williams, 534 U.S. 184, 12 AD Cases 993 (2002); Albertson's Inc. v. Kirkingburg, 527 U.S. 555, 9 AD Cases 694 (1999); Murphy v. United Parcel Serv., 527 U.S. 516, 9 AD Cases 691 (1999); Sutton v. United Airlines, 527 U.S. 471, 9 AD Cases 673 (1999).

[87] 29 C.F.R. §1630.10 (2003).

[88] S. REP. No. 101-116, at 36–37 (1989); H.R. REP. No. 101-485, pt. 2, at 71 (1990).

[89] 42 U.S.C. §12112(b)(6). *See also* 29 C.F.R. §1630.10 (2003).

run errands. However, in those circumstances, running errands appears to be an incidental job function rather than an essential one, so the employer could not claim that possessing a driver's license was a business necessity. As a result, the employer could not refuse to hire an applicant simply because the applicant's disability prevented him or her from obtaining a valid driver's license.

In *Morton v. United Parcel Service, Inc.*[90] a plaintiff had a serious hearing impairment that prevented her from obtaining Department of Transportation (DOT) certification. The company had a policy that DOT certification was required for advancement to a package car driver position; based on the aforementioned limitation, her request for promotion to a package car driver position was denied, even though some of those assignments did not require the use of DOT vehicles. The U.S. Court of Appeals for the Ninth Circuit reversed summary judgment in favor of the employer, holding that while the company was entitled to an undeniable interest in hiring safe drivers, there was insufficient evidence that an across-the-board exclusion was a matter of business necessity to prevent an unacceptable risk.[91]

The obligation to accommodate, however, is not unlimited. The federal disabilities statutes require employers only to *reasonably* accommodate an individual with a disability, and employers are not required to undergo *undue hardship* in the process. The ADA provides a list of factors to consider in the determination of what constitutes an undue hardship:

- the nature and cost of the accommodation needed;
- the overall financial resources of the facility or facilities involved;
- the number of persons employed at the facility;
- the effect on expenses and resources, and the impact on the operation of the facilities;
- the overall financial resources of the covered entity;
- the overall size of the business and number of its employees;

---

[90] 272 F.3d 1249, 12 AD Cases 897 (9th Cir. 2001).
[91] *Id.*

- the number, type, and location of its facilities;
- the type of operation or operations of the covered entity;
- the composition, structures, and functions of the workforce;
- the geographic separateness of the relevant facilities; and
- the administrative or fiscal relationship of the facility or facilities to the covered entity.[92]

Cost is only one form of undue hardship employers cite as a basis for failing to provide a reasonable accommodation. An accommodation that undermines the efficiency of job performance at a work site also might constitute an undue hardship. Employers may be expected to modify or slightly lower their own qualification standards, but not to the extent that the overall job performance is substantially impaired as a result.[93] Finally, to the extent that a proposed accommodation alters the nature of an employer's overall business or program, it well may constitute an undue hardship for the employer.

The ADA also provides employers with a "direct threat" defense, in which an employer may require as a qualification standard that an individual not pose a direct threat to health or safety, so long as that same standard is applied to all applicants for a particular job. A direct threat is a situation presenting a significant risk of substantial harm to the health or safety of the employee or others that cannot be eliminated or reduced by reasonable accommodation.[94] The assessment of whether the individual poses a significant risk of substantial harm to others must be based on objective, scientific evidence, not on subjective perceptions, irrational fears, or stereotypes. The risk must be present and concrete, and the employer must be prepared to show a high probability of substantial harm if the person were employed in the position at issue.[95] The employer also must show that it took into consideration the duration of

---

[92] 42 U.S.C. §12111(10)(B).
[93] Treadwell v. Alexander, 707 F.2d 473, 1 AD Cases 459 (11th Cir. 1983).
[94] 42 U.S.C. §12113(b); 29 C.F.R. §1630.2(r) (2003).
[95] 42 U.S.C. §12111(3).

the risk, the nature and severity of the potential harm, the likelihood that the potential harm would occur, and the imminence of potential harm.[96]

In *Chevron v. Echazabal*,[97] the Supreme Court upheld an EEOC regulation that allows employers to reject a disabled job applicant because the applicant's disability and the job would pose a direct threat to the applicant's own health. The Court reversed the U.S. Court of Appeals for the Ninth Circuit, holding that the threat-to-self regulation was within the EEOC's rulemaking discretion. According to the Court, the broad wording of the ADA indicates that the threat-to-others provision is an *example* of a legitimate qualification standard that is job-related and consistent with business necessity, not the only permissible standard. In addition, the Court found no deliberate congressional intent to exclude a threat-to-self defense from the ADA. The Court also noted that the EEOC regulation was entitled to deference because it was a reasonable interpretation of the ADA's direct threat provision. The employer had argued that the regulation was reasonable because of employer concerns regarding time lost to sickness, excessive turnover from medical complications, litigation under state tort law, and potential violations of the Occupational Safety and Health Act.[98] While the decision upheld an employer's right to deny employment because of a direct threat to the applicant's own health, the denial of a job under these circumstances must be based on reasonable medical judgment *and* an individualized assessment of the applicant's ability to perform the essential functions of the job safely.

G. Enforcement and Remedies

Assuming that the employees can establish that they are disabled individuals within the meaning of the employment

---

[96] Bekker v. Humana Health Plan, Inc., 229 F.3d 662, 10 AD Cases 1776 (7th Cir. 2000).
[97] 536 U.S. 73, 13 AD Cases 97 (2002).
[98] 29 U.S.C. §651 et seq.

discrimination statutes, and that they have suffered discrimination (in the form of adverse action, retaliation, harassment, or a failure to reasonably accommodate the condition in question), there are a variety of remedies available to plaintiffs under the various federal statutes.

- Under the Civil Rights Act of 1991, which amended Title VII and the ADA, individuals may seek awards for injunctive relief, back pay, reinstatement, promotion, and even affirmative relief, in certain cases.[99]
- The Civil Rights Act of 1991 formally allowed for awards of compensatory and punitive damages, in cases where an employer acted "with malice or with reckless indifference" to the rights protected under federal law.[100]
- As discussed earlier, an employer can avoid compensatory or punitive damages in cases where it can demonstrate a good-faith effort to accommodate an employee's disability.
- In addition, a prevailing party will be eligible for attorneys' fees or costs of the action.

Several avenues and procedural requirements may apply to claims of employment discrimination under the federal disability discrimination statutes.

1. Administrative Relief

Under sections 501, 503, and 504 of the Rehabilitation Act, employees can petition to agencies of the federal government to seek various forms of relief against offending parties. The EEOC, OFCCP, and the DOJ, respectively, are assigned said responsibility under those three sections. In addition to these external mechanisms, the agencies or employers are required to conduct investigations and self-audits, either as part of an internal investigative procedure or in response to formal demands from the external investigative authorities. Under the

---

[99]2 U.S.C. §§1201–1224; 29 U.S.C. §626(e); 42 U.S.C. §§1981a, 1988, 2000e, 2000e(f), 2000e-2, 2000e-4, 2000e4(h), 2000e5(e), 2000e-16, 12111, 12209.
[100]42 U.S.C. §1981a(b)(1).

ADA, the administrative procedure for handling complaints under Title I is the same as that used under Title VII of the Civil Rights Act. In fact, the ADA specifically incorporates those provisions, and the EEOC is charged with the investigatory and prosecutorial roles.[101] With respect to Title II, the range of potential parties covers all of the various state and local government departments, and this creates considerable overlap and confusion as to the appropriate investigatory authority.[102] Therefore, the DOJ serves a central processing role, identifying the appropriate federal agency to be responsible for an initial investigation and effort to bring about a nonadverserial solution to the given complaint.[103] If that initial attempt is unsuccessful, then the DOJ retains the authority and discretion to appoint an appropriate authority to prosecute the complaint.

2. *Private Right of Action*

In addition to the administrative procedure discussed above, federal disabilities statutes also typically provide complainants with the opportunity to raise their disputes privately in a courtroom setting. Under the Rehabilitation Act, employees are afforded the right to file their own lawsuit pursuant to sections 501 and 504. Section 503, however, does not afford a similar private right of action—plaintiffs are limited to filing with the OFCCP. By contrast, both Titles I and II of the ADA grant would-be plaintiffs a private right of action.

3. *Available Remedies*

Although the different sections of the disabilities statutes are relatively similar in the forums that they provide to individuals to file complaints and seek relief, the nature of the relief available varies widely from statute to statute and section to section.

---

[101] 42 U.S.C. §§12117(a), 12116.
[102] S. REP. No. 101-116, at 57–58 (1989); H.R. REP. No. 101-485, at 98 (1990); 28 C.F.R. pt. 35, app. A, at 553–54 (commentary on subpt. F, Compliance Procedures) (2003).
[103] S. REP. No. 101-116, at 44; H.R. REP. No. 101-485, at 98.

Section 501 of the Rehabilitation Act gives individuals the right to seek an injunction, as well as an award of back pay, placement or reinstatement, and other appropriate relief.[104] The subsequent cases demonstrate that plaintiffs can gain compensatory, but not punitive, damages. The specific amount of compensatory damages is limited, however, damage awards are apportioned according to the overall number of employees, and the total amount cannot exceed $300,000.[105] Damages are not available in disparate impact cases, or if an employer has made "good-faith efforts" to establish reasonable accommodation that provides "an equally effective [employment] opportunity [without causing an] undue hardship on the operation of the business."[106]

As stated above, section 503 limits relief to that which the OFCCP can gain on the employee's behalf. At the appropriate administrative proceeding, the agency can seek that payments due the employer be withheld, a contract or subcontract be canceled, and that the employer be denied future contracts.[107] The individual complainant can receive an award of back pay, placement or reinstatement, and other equitable relief.[108] Section 504 is similar to section 501, in that compensatory damages are not available in disparate impact cases, and injunctive relief is also available.

With respect to the ADA, Title I equitable remedies can include injunctive relief, front pay, job accommodation, or other relief.[109] Additionally, compensatory and punitive damages are now available.[110] Similarly, compensatory and punitive damages are available under Title II.[111] Under both sections,

---

[104] 2 U.S.C. §§1201-1224; 29 U.S.C. §626(e); 42 U.S.C. §§1981a, 1988, 2000e, 2000e(f), 2000e-2, 2000e-4, 2000e4(h), 2000e5(e), 2000e-16, 12111, 12209.

[105] 42 U.S.C. §1981a(b)(3)(D) (borrowing the language of Title VII of the Civil Rights Act of 1964).

[106] *Id.* §1981a(a)(3).

[107] 41 C.F.R. §60-741.66 (2003).

[108] E.E. Black, Ltd. v. Marshall, 497 F. Supp. 1088, 1 AD Cases 220 (D. Haw. 1980), *vacated on other grounds sub nom.* E.E. Black, Ltd. v. Donovan, 1981 WL 265, 1 AD Cases 266 (D. Haw. 1981).

[109] 42 U.S.C. §2000e-5.

[110] 42 U.S.C. §1981a.

[111] 42 U.S.C. §12133.

punitive damages are limited to cases in which the employer has violated the ADA and the plaintiff proves by clear and convincing evidence that the employer acted "with malice or with reckless indifference" to the rights protected by federal law.[112] In order to make this determination, courts evaluate the employer's state of mind, and whether it had knowledge that its conduct violated federal law.[113]

II. Related Federal Statutes

A. Architectural Barriers Act

The Architectural Barriers Act of 1968[114] requires that all buildings and facilities be accessible to, and usable by, individuals with physical disabilities, if they are designed, built, altered, or financed by the U.S. government or leased for occupancy by federal agencies. The statute's coverage is limited to new and altered buildings and newly leased facilities, and does not include coverage of the various activities for which those facilities are utilized. The Architectural and Transportation Barriers Compliance Board (Access Board) issued certain minimum design standards and guidelines under the statute,[115] and then four government agencies—the Department of Defense, the Department of Housing and Urban Development, the General Services Administration, and the U.S. Postal Service—developed formal accessibility standards pursuant to those guidelines. The four agencies then jointly issued a single set of accessibility standards—the Uniform Federal Accessibility Standards.[116] These standards dictate the necessity, quantity, and location of items such as walkways, ramps, elevators, entrances, rest rooms, and parking facilities. The Access Board,

---

[112]Kolstad v. American Dental Ass'n, 527 U.S. 526, 79 FEP Cases 1697 (1999).
[113]*Id.*
[114]42 U.S.C. §§4151–4157.
[115]The initial set of guidelines and requirements issued by the Access Board were published in 1982. 47 Fed. Reg. 33,864 (Aug. 4, 1982) (codified at 36 C.F.R. pt. 1190).
[116]49 Fed. Reg. 31,528 (Aug. 7, 1984).

which was established under section 502 of the Rehabilitation Act of 1973, also is responsible for enforcing the accessibility guidelines through complaints filed by aggrieved parties, administrative actions, and lawsuits.

B. Individuals with Disabilities Education Act

Originally known as the Education for All Handicapped Children Act of 1975,[117] the Individuals with Disabilities Education Act[118] (IDEA) uses the incentive of federal grant money to encourage states to improve the quality of their local educational programs for children with disabilities. If states were able to demonstrate the sufficiency of their respective programs, showing that all children with disabilities receive a free, appropriate public education, their educational agencies were to receive an infusion of federal funding (although such funding has been deficient, historically speaking). Under the IDEA, states must be able to identify and locate those children with disabilities and provide them with an Individualized Education Program (IEP) targeted to fit their specific needs. The IEP is to be developed by a knowledgeable team, generally including the child's teacher, parents, agency representatives, and others (such as special education personnel). Each of these individualized educational programs undergoes a formal review every year to determine its effectiveness. If parents do not agree with the IEP that is proposed, they can obtain a due process hearing and review by the applicable state education agency, and can pursue a private action in court. Through these mechanisms and other procedural requirements, the IDEA created safeguards for individuals—and obligations for education agencies—that produced many legal challenges regarding placement, program design, and funding under IEPs in its decades on the books.

This statutory commitment to individualized education is balanced with the mandate that children with disabilities must remain in the least restrictive environment, that is, that they be educated with nondisabled children to the maximum extent

---

[117] 20 U.S.C. §§1232, 1401, 1405–1420, 1453.
[118] The law was renamed in 1990. Pub. L. 101-476, 104 Stat. 1142 (1990).

possible. Finally, the state must submit for approval to the U.S. Secretary of Education an overall policy that outlines the goals, programs, and timetables in effect to guarantee each child a free, appropriate public education.

C. Developmental Disabilities Assistance and Bill of Rights Act

The Developmental Disabilities Assistance and Bill of Rights Act[119] offers federal assistance to "developmentally disabled" individuals—those with severe long-term disabilities that developed before age 22 and require extended care or treatment—along the same lines as the IDEA. Once again, states receive federal grant money in exchange for establishing a comprehensive system that provides care and treatment for a particular subset of disabled individuals. The Developmental Disabilities Assistance Act also features its own Bill of Rights, which declares that it is the right of each developmentally disabled person to have appropriate treatment, services, and habilitation in a way that creates the fewest restrictions on his or her personal freedoms.[120] At the least, covered state programs provide medical and dental services and a nutritional diet, and limit the use of physical and chemical restraints unless absolutely necessary. Although the language of the Bill of Rights is not strictly binding on states enrolling in the program, it provides a clear indication of the underlying legislative intent and the factors that the federal government will be considering when it reviews each state's practices and procedures.

D. Air Carrier Access Act

The Air Carrier Access Act[121] prohibits discrimination on the basis of disability in air travel and requires all air carriers to accommodate the needs of passengers with disabilities. Pursuant to the Air Carriers Access Act, the DOT has promulgated rules that further define the rights of passengers and obligations of air carriers. For example, air carriers may not refuse

---

[119] 42 U.S.C. §§6000–6081.
[120] Id. §6009.
[121] 49 U.S.C. §41705.

transportation or seat assignment on the basis of disability, except as Federal Aviation Administration rules require. With respect to the accessibility of certain facilities, certain aircraft models are required to provide movable armrests, accessible lavatories, wheelchair space, or even wheelchairs themselves. Beyond the aircraft itself, airlines are required to provide assistance with boarding, deplaning, and making flight connections, as well as making the necessary accommodations for individuals with mobility aids, hearing impairments, and service animals.[122] In the event that an airline fails to satisfy these and other standards, individuals may file a complaint with the DOT, or bring a lawsuit in federal court.

E. Telecommunications Act

The Communications Act of 1934, as amended by the Telecommunications Act of 1996,[123] requires both companies that manufacture telecommunications equipment and providers of telecommunications services to ensure that the equipment or the services are accessible to and usable by individuals with disabilities, if meeting that goal is readily achievable. The measure is designed to ensure that access to a wide range of products and services will be available to individuals with disabilities. Its provisions have been applied to telephones, mobile phones and pagers, and call-waiting devices, and to services such as those provided by operators.

The Access Board plays an important role under this statute as well, with responsibility for developing guidelines on accessible telecommunications products. In 1998, the Access Board published such guidelines, after receiving extensive input from the Telecommunications Access Advisory Committee, which consisted of product manufacturers, service providers, disability groups, and consulting experts. The guidelines, which are enforced by the Federal Communications Commission, specify those operating characteristics and product capabilities that are necessary to ensure access, which is focused on

---

[122] 14 C.F.R. §382.1–.65 (2003).
[123] 42 U.S.C. §§255, 251(a)(2).

individuals with limitations affecting hearing, vision, movement, manipulation, speech, and interpretation of information.

F. Fair Housing Act

Discrimination in housing is prohibited by the Fair Housing Amendments Act of 1988.[124] Amending Title VIII of the Civil Rights Act of 1968, it focuses on discrimination in the sale or rental of private property. It extends to the characteristics recognized in Title VII of the Civil Rights Act of 1964 (i.e., race, color, religion, sex, and national origin), and added to that list a new protected category: individuals with disabilities.

The measure describes actions that constitute disability-related discrimination and includes an obligation to make "reasonable accommodations" in order to provide such individuals with equal opportunities to use and reside in the housing facility. In addition to protections based on an individual's own condition, the statute bars discrimination because of his or her "association with" an individual with a disability, or because of a plan to have such a person live in the residence. In a structure that parallels federal requirements relating to the design and construction of covered businesses and commercial facilities, the housing statute establishes multiple accessibility requirements on the design and construction of new multifamily dwellings.[125]

G. Social Security Act

The Social Security Administration, implementing the Social Security Act,[126] administers two disability benefits programs to individuals who meet specified qualification criteria. The two programs—Supplemental Security Income (SSI) benefits and Social Security Disability Insurance (SSDI)—utilize similar definitions of disability as a threshold for coverage. Benefits are provided only to individuals who are totally disabled; no benefits are paid for partial or short-term disabilities. The

---

[124] 42 U.S.C. §3601 et seq. Regulations implementing the Fair Housing Act are found at 24 C.F.R. pt. 100 et seq. (2003).
[125] 42 U.S.C. §3604(f)(3)(C).
[126] 42 U.S.C. §301 et seq.

agency bases its disability determinations on an individual's inability to work, considering the work performed previously and the individual's ability to adjust to perform other work because of his or her medical condition. Its qualification criteria include an assessment of whether the applicant currently is working, whether his or her condition is severe, whether the condition is found on the agency's list of disabling conditions or is of equal severity to such listed conditions, whether the individual still can perform the work he or she did previously, and whether the applicant can perform any other type of work. Most people who qualify for benefits satisfy these criteria on their own records, however, there are special rules relating to individuals who are blind, widows or widowers who are disabled, and children who are disabled.

The SSI program—which can provide both cash payments and medical treatment benefits—is administered under Title XVI of the statute,[127] and applies need, income, and resources tests to determine eligibility for cash payments. Coverage through SSI also can provide eligibility to receive medical treatment. To qualify for benefits under the SSI program, an applicant must have had a physical or mental impairment that has prevented the performance of work for a period of at least 12 months. The SSDI program, administered under Title II of the Social Security Act,[128] requires satisfaction of the definition of disability and a background of performing a sufficient volume of work to have earned sufficient quarters of coverage and thus be judged fully insured.

In addition to these federal statutes, which cover a wide range of areas and activities impacting individuals with disabilities, a host of other employment laws[129] also affect workplace issues involving applicants and employees. Their intersection with the obligations imposed by the ADA and the Rehabilitation Act can raise additional questions that merit careful scrutiny.

---

[127] 42 U.S.C. §1381 et seq.
[128] 42 U.S.C. §401 et seq.
[129] Other employment laws are discussed in detail in Chapter 9, "Interplay of Related Workplace Statutes."

CHAPTER 2

THE REHABILITATION ACT OF 1973

I.	Overview	43
II.	Enactment of and Subsequent Amendments to the Rehabilitation Act of 1973	45
	A. Enactment	45
	B. 1974 Rehabilitation Act Amendments	47
	C. 1978 Rehabilitation Act Amendments	49
	D. 1990 Rehabilitation Act Amendments	50
	E. 1992 Rehabilitation Act Amendments	51
III.	Scope of Key Employment Provisions	53
	A. Overview	53
	B. Application to Federal Agencies—Section 501 ...	56
	C. Application to Federal Contractors— Section 503	57
	D. Application to Programs or Activities Receiving Federal Financial Assistance— Section 504	60
	1. Meaning of "Program or Activity"	61
	2. Meaning of "Receipt of Federal Financial Assistance"	63
	3. Application to States	65
IV.	Definition of "Protected Individual"	66
	A. Evolution of the Definition	66
	B. Actual Disability	68
	1. Impairment	68
	a. General Definition	68
	b. Areas of Conflict	69
	i. Obesity	69
	ii. Drug and Alcohol Use	70
	2. Substantially Limits One or More Major Life Activities	72

	a. General Definition	72
	b. Area of Conflict	73
C.	Record of Having a Disability	74
D.	Being Regarded as Having a Disability	75
E.	Qualified Individual with a Disability	77

V. Reasonable Accommodation Obligation 79
   A. Origin of the Obligation 79
   B. Definition of the Obligation 81
VI. Rehabilitation Act Enforcement 85
   A. Overview 85
   B. Section 501 87
      1. Scope 87
      2. Enforcement Procedures 88
      3. Remedies 90
      4. Affirmative Action Plan Requirements 92
   C. Section 503 93
      1. Scope 93
      2. Enforcement Procedures 94
      3. Remedies 95
      4. Affirmative Action Plan Requirements 96
      5. Compliance Reviews 97
   D. Section 504 98
      1. Scope 98
      2. Enforcement Procedures 99
      3. Remedies 102
VII. Defenses to Liability 105
   A. Type of Defenses 105
      1. Employer Is Not a Covered Entity 106
      2. Employee Is Not Covered by the
         Rehabilitation Act 107
         a. Employee Is Not Qualified 107
         b. Employee Is Not Disabled 108
      3. Reasonable Accommodation Is
         Not Possible 109
      4. Employer Lacks Knowledge of
         Employee's Disability 110
      5. Procedural Defenses 111
   B. Section 504 111

1. Employer Is Not a Direct Recipient of
    Federal Aid 111
 2. Entire Employing Entity Is Not Covered 112
C. Section 503 114
D. Section 501 117

I. Overview

The Rehabilitation Act of 1973[1] was the first major federal legislation aimed at providing equal rights for individuals with physical or mental disabilities. The centerpiece of the Rehabilitation Act is a broad, federally funded vocational rehabilitation program, which is beyond the scope of this treatise. The Rehabilitation Act also established unprecedented antidiscrimination and affirmative action obligations in employment reaching most federal and some private employers. These employment obligations will be the focus of this chapter.

The antidiscrimination and affirmative action mandates of the Rehabilitation Act are set forth in Title V. These mandates are found in three important statutory provisions: sections 501, 503, and 504. Section 501 requires federal executive agencies to establish affirmative action plans for employing and advancing qualified disabled individuals. Section 501 also commands federal executive agencies to make reasonable accommodations to qualified disabled applicants and employees. Section 503 imposes similar affirmative action and nondiscrimination requirements on federal contractors with contracts of at least $10,000. Finally, section 504 prohibits discrimination against qualified disabled individuals in any program or activity receiving federal financial assistance or any program or activity conducted by a federal executive agency or the U.S. Postal Service.

Title V of the Rehabilitation Act generally applies to federal executive agencies as well as to private employers that

---

[1]Pub. L. No. 93-112, 87 Stat. 355 (1973) (codified as amended at 29 U.S.C. §790–796).

either have federal contracts worth at least $10,000 or that receive "federal financial assistance."[2]

For almost two decades, the Rehabilitation Act was the sole federal law regulating the conduct of private employers with respect to the employment of disabled individuals. During this time, Congress, the courts, and federal agencies charged with implementing the Rehabilitation Act, in varying degrees, created and tested many of the key concepts of disability discrimination law. Many of these concepts have been incorporated into the statutory language and guiding case law principles developed under subsequent state and federal disability legislation.

In 1990, Congress vastly broadened the scope of federal prohibitions against disability discrimination with the enactment of the Americans with Disabilities Act (ADA).[3] The ADA's coverage overlaps substantially with that of the Rehabilitation Act, and the antidiscrimination provisions of the two acts are designed to be the same. Individuals alleging disability discrimination in employment often choose to bring claims under the ADA rather than under the Rehabilitation Act, even where both acts might apply. In this way, the ADA has rendered the Rehabilitation Act somewhat redundant.

Although its utility has been partially diminished by the ADA, the Rehabilitation Act remains a vital and important part of federal disability law for several reasons. First, it governs employers that either receive federal financial assistance or that have federal contracts over $10,000, irrespective of the number of employees an entity might have. In this manner, the Rehabilitation Act reaches some employers who do not have the 15 or more employees necessary to meet the jurisdictional limits of the ADA. The Rehabilitation Act also mandates that federal contractors take "affirmative action" to employ individuals with disabilities. The ADA, on the other hand, has

---

[2] See discussion in Chapter 1, section I.A., "The Rehabilitation Act of 1973," above. The criteria for determining whether a public or private entity is subject to Title V obligations is discussed in section IV., "Definition of 'Protected Individual,'" below.

[3] 42 U.S.C. §12101 et seq.

no affirmative action requirement. Most significantly, the ADA adopts almost verbatim the Rehabilitation Act's definition of disability and expressly incorporates judicial constructions of the Rehabilitation Act. Thus, the Rehabilitation Act and the almost two decades of decisions interpreting it have become the wellspring of many of the key concepts and issues arising in disability discrimination.

This chapter first discusses the factors leading to enactment of the Rehabilitation Act and its subsequent amendments. Next, it explains the scope of application of the three principal sections of the Rehabilitation Act regulating employment practices. Following this material are discussions and explanations of the concepts of "disabled individual" and "qualified individual with a disability." An employer's reasonable accommodation obligation is covered, as are issues relating to enforcement of various sections of the Rehabilitation Act with respect to both private and public entities. Finally, this chapter concludes with a discussion of defenses to liability available to entities charged with violations of the Rehabilitation Act.

II. Enactment of and Subsequent Amendments to the Rehabilitation Act of 1973

A. Enactment

Congress passed the Rehabilitation Act of 1973 in part to "promote and expand employment opportunities in the public and private sectors for handicapped individuals and to place such individuals in employment."[4] To achieve this goal, the Rehabilitation Act is devoted in large part to the continuation and expansion of a federally funded vocational rehabilitation services program for disabled individuals. The Rehabilitation Act also establishes certain nondiscrimination and affirmative action mandates with respect to the employment of disabled

---

[4]Pub. L. No. 93-112, §2(8), 87 Stat. 355 (1973).

individuals by some federal and private employers. These provisions regulating employment practices are set forth in Title V of the Rehabilitation Act, in sections 501, 503, and 504.

President Richard M. Nixon signed the Rehabilitation Act into law in 1973 after he had vetoed two prior versions of the legislation. President Nixon's stated objection to the previous bills principally concerned the cost of vocational rehabilitative services and programs, but did not focus on the novel provisions of Title V regulating employment practices.[5] As one federal circuit court has explained:

> The Rehabilitation Act of 1973 was adopted after presidential vetoes had stymied two earlier attempts to enhance federal aid to handicapped persons. Most of the controversy surrounding the bill and its predecessors focused on wide ranging programs, to be federally funded, designed to aid handicapped persons in assuming a full role in society, and on the appropriations that would be required if the measure were adopted. Consequently, Congress devoted little of its discussion to its intentions regarding section 503. *See* Sen. Rep. No. 93-318, 93d Cong., 1st Sess. pp. 12–16 (1973), U.S. Code Cong. & Admin. News, p. 2076. The statute's muteness, therefore is not given meaning by voices in the legislative background.[6]

Due to the lack of debate concerning Title V, there is scant legislative history illuminating its purposes.[7] From what little history there is, the Supreme Court has divined that Congress, in passing Title V, was concerned with remedying discrimination against disabled individuals that it perceived "to be most often the product, not of invidious animus, but rather of thoughtlessness and indifference—of benign neglect."[8]

Additionally, the Supreme Court has held that a portion of the legislative history of Title VI of the Civil Rights Act of 1964,[9] which prohibits discrimination in programs receiving

---

[5] S. Rep. No. 93-318, at 6 (1973), *reprinted in* 1973 U.S.C.C.A.N 2076, 2888, 2990.

[6] Rogers v. Frito Lay, Inc., 611 F.2d 1074, 1078, 1 AD Cases 131, 132 (5th Cir.), *cert. denied*, 449 U.S. 889 (1980).

[7] *See, e.g.*, Alexander v. Choate, 469 U.S. 287, 296 n.13 (1985); *Frito Lay, Inc.*, 611 F.2d at 1079 n.5.

[8] *Choate*, 469 U.S. at 292 n.7.

[9] 42 U.S.C. §2000d et seq.

federal assistance,[10] is informative as to the purposes of section 504 of the Rehabilitation Act. Section 504 mandates nondiscrimination under federal grants and programs.[11] Bills similar to section 504 were originally introduced as an amendment to Title VI of the Civil Rights Act of 1964. The intent of the Senate and House sponsors of these bills, respectively Senator Hubert H. Humphrey (D-Minn.) and Representative Charles A. Vanik (D-Ohio), is "a primary signpost on the road toward interpreting the legislative history of § 504."[12]

Since originally enacting the Rehabilitation Act in 1973, Congress has frequently amended it to both fine tune and broaden the Rehabilitation Act's provisions. The amendments making substantial revisions to the sections of the Rehabilitation Act governing employment practices are discussed below.

B. 1974 Rehabilitation Act Amendments

In 1974, Congress made an important change to the Rehabilitation Act's definition of "handicapped individual." The original Rehabilitation Act defined "handicapped individual" as

> any individual who (A) has a physical or mental disability which for such individual constitutes or results in a substantial handicap to employment and (B) can reasonably be expected to benefit in terms of employability from vocational rehabilitation services provided pursuant to [this Act].[13]

This definition was consistent with the Rehabilitation Act's primary purpose of providing vocational rehabilitation services to handicapped individuals. However, Congress recognized that the definition was "troublesome" when applied to the affirmative action and antidiscrimination provisions of sections

---

[10] *See* H.R. 14,033, 92d Cong., 2d Sess., 118 CONG. REC. 9712 (1972); H.R. 12,154, 92d Cong., 1st Sess., 117 CONG. REC. 45,945 (1971).

[11] Pub. L. No. 93-112, 87 Stat. 355 (1973) (codified as amended at 29 U.S.C. §790–794e).

[12] Alexander v. Choate, 469 U.S. 287, 296 n.13 (1985).

[13] Pub. L. No. 93-112, §7(6), 87 Stat. 361 (1973).

503 and 504, because it failed to reach key forms of disability-based discrimination.[14] In particular, in the context of employment, the definition did not protect individuals who "are discriminated against because they are classified or labeled, correctly or incorrectly, as handicapped" or those who "are discriminated against if they are regarded as handicapped, regardless of whether they are in fact handicapped."[15] Further, the original definition only prevented discrimination against individuals with disabilities who would reasonably expect to benefit in terms of employability from vocational rehabilitation services.[16] Congress had not intended the Rehabilitation Act to afford such limited protections when it was originally passed.[17]

To reach these other forms of disability discrimination, Congress added a new definition of "handicapped individual" for purposes of Titles IV and V of the Rehabilitation Act.[18] Under the revised definition, a "handicapped individual" is "any person who (A) has a physical or mental impairment which substantially limits one or more of such person's major life activities, (B) has a record of such an impairment, or (C) is regarded as having such an impairment."[19] The new definition has three distinct types of coverage. The first prong of the definition is designed to protect individuals with actual current disabilities. The second prong applies to individuals who have recovered—in whole or in part—from a disabling condition, such as a mental or neurological illness, a heart attack, or cancer, or who have been misclassified as having a disability. Finally, the third prong is intended to cover individuals who do not in fact have the condition they are perceived as having as well as those whose mental or physical condition is inaccurately perceived as substantially limiting.[20]

---

[14] S. Rep. No. 1297 (1974), *reprinted in* 1974 U.S.C.C.A.N. 6373, 6388.
[15] *Id.*, 1974 U.S.C.C.A.N. at 6389.
[16] *Id.* at 6388.
[17] *Id.* at 6389.
[18] *Id.*
[19] Pub. L. No. 93-516, §111(a)(6), 88 Stat. 1617 (1974) (originally codified at 29 U.S.C. §706(6); redesignated in 1998 as 29 U.S.C. §705(20) (Pub. L. No. 105-277, Div. A, §101(f), 112 Stat. 2681-412)).
[20] S. Rep. No. 1297 (1974), *reprinted in* 1974 U.S.C.C.A.N. 6373, 6389–6390.

The new comprehensive definition of handicapped individual, which has remained substantially unchanged for over a quarter century,[21] is the prototypical definition of disability in state and federal disability legislation, including the Americans with Disabilities Act.[22]

C. 1978 Rehabilitation Act Amendments

As originally enacted, the Rehabilitation Act contained no express provisions for enforcing violations of section 501 or 504.[23] Lacking express statutory language regarding remedies and enforcement procedures, the courts were forced to determine what implicit rights, remedies, and procedures were available under these two sections. With respect to section 501, most courts considering the issue held that no private right of action existed for federal employees or applicants alleging disability discrimination.[24] However, there was almost unanimous agreement among the federal circuit courts that section 504 did create a private right of action.[25]

In 1978, Congress amended the Rehabilitation Act by adding section 505, which expressly provides remedies and enforcement mechanisms for sections 501 and 504.[26] Congress made certain remedies, procedures, and rights set forth in the Civil Rights Act of 1964 available to aggrieved individuals

---

[21] In 1992, the Rehabilitation Act was amended to replace the term "handicapped individual" with "individual with a disability" and the definition section was changed accordingly. Pub. L. No. 102-569, §102(f) (codified at 29 U.S.C. §706(26); redesignated in 1998 as 29 U.S.C. §705(20) (Pub. L. No. 105-277, Div. A, §101(f), 112 Stat. 2681-412)).

[22] 42 U.S.C. §12102(2).

[23] See Pub. L. No. 93-112, §§501, 504, 87 Stat. 355 (1973); S. Rep. No. 1297 (1974), *reprinted in* 1974 U.S.C.C.A.N. 6373, 6390.

[24] See Prewitt v. U.S. Postal Serv., 662 F.2d 292, 303 n.12, 1 AD Cases 273 (5th Cir. 1981) (reciting cases holding that §501 does not provide a private right of action).

[25] See, e.g., Hart v. Alameda County Prob. Dep't, 485 F. Supp. 66, 69–70, 21 FEP Cases 233 (N.D. Cal. 1979) (reciting authority holding that §504 contains an implied private right of action).

[26] Comprehensive Rehabilitation Services Amendments of 1978, Pub. L. No. 95-602, §120(a), 92 Stat. 2955, 2982 (1978) (codified at 29 U.S.C. §794a(a)(1)).

seeking to enforce sections 501 and 504.[27] Those remedies, procedures, and rights generally include the right to file a complaint with the Equal Employment Opportunity Commission (EEOC), the right to file a private cause of action in court, and the availability of an award of attorneys' fees to prevailing parties.[28]

D. 1990 Rehabilitation Act Amendments

In the 1980s and 1990s, handling drug addiction moved from treating a disease to fighting a war. In response to the war on drugs and the perceived need to "get tough" with drug addicts, the 1990 amendments to the Rehabilitation Act, once again, altered the definition of "individual with handicaps" as it pertains to current drug abusers.[29] The amendment clarified that an individual with disabilities "does not include an individual who is currently engaging in the illegal use of drugs, when a covered entity acts on the basis of such use."[30] Additionally, as applied to sections 503 and 504, the definition was amended to exclude "an alcoholic whose current use of alcohol prevents such individual from performing the duties of the job in question or whose employment, by reason of such current alcohol abuse, would constitute a direct threat to property or the safety of others."[31]

These amendments allowed employers to take action against an alcoholic or drug addict currently engaging in drug use when "a covered entity acts on the basis of such use," while individuals without drug- or alcohol-related disabilities remain protected for actions done on the basis of their disability. This change ensured that while drug or alcohol addiction may, in limited circumstances, remain a covered disability under the Rehabilitation Act, individuals with current alcohol or drug

---

[27] Id.
[28] Id.
[29] Pub. L. No. 101-663, §512(a).
[30] 29 U.S.C. §705(20)(C).
[31] Id.

problems will not be provided the same, or any, protection as individuals with other types of disabilities.

E. 1992 Rehabilitation Act Amendments

In 1990, Congress passed the Americans with Disabilities Act, whose coverage overlaps substantially with the Rehabilitation Act. In part to harmonize implementation and enforcement of these acts, Congress amended the Rehabilitation Act in 1992. The 1992 amendments went a long way toward ensuring that these federal disability laws work in tandem and do not result in conflicting requirements and guidance. Most importantly, the 1992 amendments to the Rehabilitation Act mandated that the standards used to determine whether the Rehabilitation Act has been violated in a complaint alleging nonaffirmative action employment discrimination, under sections 501 or 503, or employment discrimination, under section 504

> shall be the standards applied under title I of the Americans with Disabilities Act of 1990 (42 U.S.C. 12111 et seq.) and the provisions of sections 501 through 504, and 510 of the Americans with Disabilities Act of 1990 (42 U.S.C. 12201-12204 and 12210), as such sections relate to employment.[32]

As the above-quoted passage indicates, the ADA standards were incorporated into all three relevant sections of the Rehabilitation Act, with the only distinction being the type of discrimination alleged. This distinction was Congress's first express recognition that the affirmative action mandates of sections 501 and 503 implicitly include a nondiscrimination requirement.

The 1992 amendments also made what may be considered more of a symbolic change to the Rehabilitation Act. The 1992 amendments replaced the term "handicap" with "disability" and the phrase "individuals with handicaps" with "individuals with disabilities" throughout the Act.[33] Consistent with this

---

[32] 29 U.S.C. §§791(g), 793(d), 794(d). The 1992 amendments were enacted in Pub. L. No. 102-569 (effective Oct. 26, 1992).
[33] Pub. L. No 102-569, §§102(p)(29)(A), 31(B), and (32), 106 Stat. 4360 (1992).

change, the Rehabilitation Act now contains a definition of the term "disability," rather than "handicap" as under the prior language of the Rehabilitation Act. With the 1992 amendments, "disability" is defined as "a physical or mental impairment that constitutes or results in a substantial impediment to employment; or (B) . . . a physical or mental impairment that substantially limits one or more major life activities."[34]

The 1992 amendments also added provisions specifically excluding certain conditions from coverage under the Rehabilitation Act. These conditions include: homosexuality or bisexuality,[35] transvestitism, transsexualism, pedophilia, exhibitionism, voyeurism, gender identity disorders not resulting from physical impairments, and other sexual behavior disorders.[36] The amendments further explicitly exclude the following impairments: compulsive gambling, kleptomania, or pyromania,[37] and psychoactive substance use disorders resulting from current illegal use of drugs.[38]

Additional, but less fundamental, changes made by the 1992 amendments included increasing the minimum threshold for federal contracts under section 503 from $2,500 to $10,000[39] and expanding section 503 coverage to include protection for all individuals working for contractors with federal contracts over $10,000.00.[40] Prior to 1992, only employees carrying out a federal contract of requisite value were protected by section 503. The 1992 amendments brought section 503 in line with the Vietnam Era Veterans Readjustment Assistance Act[41] and Executive Order 11,246 by mandating that all employees of contractors with federal contracts over $10,000 are

---

[34]Pub. L. No. 102-569, §102(n) (codified at 29 U.S.C. §705(9)).
[35]29 U.S.C. §705(20)(E) (as amended by Pub. L. No. 102-569, §102(f)(4)).
[36]*Id.* §705(20)(F)(i).
[37]*Id.* §705(20)(F)(ii).
[38]*Id.* §705(20)(F)(iii).
[39]Pub. L. No. 102-569, §505(a)(1).
[40]*Id.*, §505(a)(2).
[41]The Vietnam Era Veterans Readjustment Assistance Act of 1972, Pub. L. No. 92-540, requires all federal contractors with contracts over $10,000 to "take affirmative action to employ and advance in employment qualified special disabled veterans and veterans of the Vietnam era." 38 U.S.C. §2012(a), Pub. L. No. 92-540. The 1998 amendments to the Vietnam Era Veterans Readjustment Assistance Act increased the minimum threshold for federal contracts from $10,000 to $25,000,

CH. 2 III.A.   REHABILITATION ACT OF 1973   53

protected under the Rehabilitation Act and not simply those employed in carrying out the federal contract at issue.[42] All three statutes are enforced together by the Department of Labor's Office of Federal Contract Compliance Programs (OFCCP).

Finally, the 1992 amendments added new waiver provisions from coverage under section 503. The amendments authorize the Secretary of Labor to waive the affirmative action requirements required under section 503 for facilities that are "in all respects separate and distinct from activities of the prime contractor or subcontractor related to the performance or the contract or subcontract, if the Secretary of Labor also finds that such a waiver will not interfere with or impede the effectuation of [the Act]."[43] Previously, only the President of the United States was able to grant such waivers.[44]

III. SCOPE OF KEY EMPLOYMENT PROVISIONS

A. Overview

The Rehabilitation Act protects covered employees and applicants from discrimination on the basis of a disability. Each

---

and struck out "special disabled veterans and veterans of the Vietnam era" and inserted "special disabled veterans, veterans of the Vietnam era, and any other veterans who served on active duty during a war or in a campaign or expedition for which a campaign badge has been authorized." 38 U.S.C. §4212(a); Pub. L. No. 105-339. Each operation and facility of covered contractors is subject to the law's requirements without regard to whether they are involved with the covered contract. The Office of Federal Contract Compliance Programs (OFCCP) of the U.S. Department of Labor has promulgated and revised regulations requiring government contractors to invite voluntary self-identification by job applicants and employees as disabled veterans or veterans of the Vietnam era. *See* 41 C.F.R. pt. 60-250 (2003). Such voluntary identifications are to be kept confidential, and any relevant medical information provided to contractors must be maintained in distinct medical files. 41 C.F.R. §60-250.42(d), (e) (2003) (similar to requirements established by the ADA).

[42]Section 202 & Exec. Order No. 11,246 mandates that federal contractors with contracts over $10,000 "take affirmative action to ensure that applicants are employed, and that employees are treated during employment, without regard to their race, religion, sex, or national origin." 30 Fed. Reg. 12319, §202(2) (1965), as amended by Exec. Order 11375, 32 Fed. Reg. 14,303 (1967), and Exec. Order 12,086, 43 Fed. Reg. 46,501 (1978).

[43]29 U.S.C. §793(c)(2)(A) (as amended by Pub. L. No. 102-569, §505(b)).

[44]In addition to those provisions having a direct impact on employment issues, Section 508 of the Rehabilitation Act, as amended, 29 U.S.C. §794d, requires federal

of the sections of the Rehabilitation Act directly governing employment—sections 501, 503, and 504—protects a different class of employees, incorporates different requirements, such as affirmative action or antidiscrimination, and uses varied enforcement mechanisms. This section of the chapter begins with a brief overview discussing scope of coverage and protection under sections 501, 503, and 504. It then addresses in detail the scope of application of each of the three relevant sections of the Rehabilitation Act.

Section 501 of the Rehabilitation Act protects qualified federal executive branch employees and applicants against discrimination on the basis of physical or mental disabilities.[45] It mandates that covered federal employers shall not discriminate against a qualified individual with a physical or mental disability. Section 501's goals are to ensure that the federal government stands as a model employer and to provide protection to federal employees and applicants who feel they have been discriminated against on the basis of a real, or perceived, disability. To achieve these goals, section 501 obligates covered federal employers to use affirmative action in employing and advancing in employment qualified individuals with disabilities. Furthermore, it requires that covered federal employers provide reasonable accommodations to disabled federal employees or applicants to allow them to function effectively in positions for which they are qualified. Section 501 is enforced independently by covered federal agencies with coordination through the EEOC. Each covered federal agency or department is required to promulgate an affirmative action plan as well as enforcement and complaint procedures. Aggrieved federal applicants and employees have the right to file a complaint with the agency at issue, the EEOC, or to file a private action in federal court.

---

agencies to make electronic and information technology accessible to federal employees with disabilities and individuals with disabilities who are members of the public seeking information and services from such agencies.

[45]Section 501 provides, in relevant part, that coverage extends to "[e]ach department, agency, and instrumentality (including the United States Postal Service

Section 503 of the Rehabilitation Act protects employees of contractors and subcontractors with federal contracts greater than $10,000.[46] Pursuant to section 503, all contracts with the federal government over $10,000 must include a provision mandating that contractors take affirmative action to employ and advance in employment qualified individuals with disabilities. Federal contractors also must provide reasonable accommodations to all qualified individuals with disabilities, ensure nondiscriminatory hiring and employment practices, and engage in outreach to employ qualified individuals with physical or mental disabilities. Section 503 is enforced administratively through the Department of Labor's OFCCP, but does not provide aggrieved employees or applicants with a private right of action against either the contractor or the federal contracting entity.

Section 504 prohibits discrimination against any "otherwise qualified individual with a disability" in any program or activity receiving federal financial assistance, or any program or activity conducted by a federal executive agency or the U.S. Postal Service.[47] A program or activity receiving federal financial assistance is considered any entity, government or private, receiving assistance in almost any form, such as through the provision of money, personnel, services, or property.

The programs or activities conducted by an executive agency or by the U.S. Postal Service under section 504 are broadly construed to include virtually all agency actions. Section 504 has no affirmative action mandate but prohibits discrimination in the employment of qualified individuals with disabilities. Section 504 is implemented by each individual government agency with coordination through the Department of Justice. Section 504 provides protected individuals with both administrative remedies and a private right of action.

---

and the Postal Rate Commission) in the executive branch and the Smithsonian Institution." 29 U.S.C. §791(b).

[46] *Id.* §793(a).
[47] *Id.* §794(a).

B. Application to Federal Agencies—Section 501

Section 501 of the Rehabilitation Act of 1973 requires "[e]ach department, agency, and instrumentality (including the United States Postal Service and the Postal Rate Commission) in the executive branch and the Smithsonian Institution" to develop and implement "an affirmative action program plan for the hiring, placement, and advancement of individuals with disabilities."[48] The Rehabilitation Act continues:

> Such plan shall include a description of the extent to which and methods whereby the special needs of employees who are individuals with disabilities are being met. . . . Such plan shall . . . provide[] sufficient assurances, procedures and commitments to provide adequate hiring, placement, and advancement opportunities for individuals with disabilities.[49]

Section 501 is implemented and coordinated by the EEOC, which has issued regulations both prohibiting discrimination and mandating affirmative action in covered federal employment.[50]

The Rehabilitation Act covers every department, agency,[51] and instrumentality in the executive branch, and the U.S. Postal Service and Postal Rate Commission.[52] Executive departments include the departments of Agriculture, Commerce, Defense, Education, Energy, Health and Human Services, Housing and

---

[48] *Id.* §791(b).

[49] *Id.*

[50] "Employee" status, though crucial to claims under Section 501, is not defined by the statute, although courts have been able to distinguish (and dismiss) claims of contractors. *See, e.g.,* Lopez v. Johnson, 333 F.3d 459, 14 AD Cases 893 (9th Cir. 2003); Redd v. Summers, 232 F.3d 933, 11 AD Cases 410 (D.C. Cir. 2000).

[51] An executive agency is defined, in 5 U.S.C. §105, as "an executive department, a Government corporation, and an independent establishment." A government corporation, in turn, is defined as "a corporation owned or controlled by the Government of the United States." 5 U.S.C. §103(1). An independent establishment is defined as "(1) an establishment in the executive branch (other than the United States Postal Service and the Postal Rate Commission) which is not an Executive department, military department, Government corporation, or part thereof, or part of an independent establishment; and (2) the General Accounting Office." 5 U.S.C. §104.

[52] 29 U.S.C. §791(b).

Urban Development, Interior, Justice, Labor, State, Transportation, Treasury, and Veteran Affairs.[53] EEOC regulations extend section 501 coverage further to the Tennessee Valley Authority,[54] nonuniformed members of military departments,[55] the National Oceanic and Atmospheric Administration Commissioned Corps,[56] the Smithsonian Institution,[57] and the Government Printing Office.[58] Until 1992, the EEOC also attempted to extend coverage to most legislative and judicial branch competitive positions.[59] However, in 1992, amended EEOC regulations exempted legislative and judicial branch competitive positions from coverage under the Rehabilitation Act.[60] In 1999, the regulations were again amended to extend coverage for legislative competitive positions while maintaining the exclusion for judicial competitive positions under the Rehabilitation Act.[61] The Rehabilitation Act specifically excludes coverage for the General Accounting Office and the Library of Congress.[62]

As explained previously, the section 501 mandates encourage covered federal entities to act as model employers. As such, they are required to take affirmative action in employing and advancing qualified individuals with physical or mental disabilities. Covered federal employers also are required to provide all reasonable accommodations for qualified employers and applicants. They must submit plans annually to ensure compliance with the nondiscrimination and affirmative action mandates of section 501 and take all reasonable steps to ensure

---

[53] 5 U.S.C. §101.
[54] 29 C.F.R. §1614.103(b)(3) (2003).
[55] Id. §1614.103(b)(1), (d)(1) (2003).
[56] Id. §1614.103(b)(5) (2003).
[57] Id. §1614.103(b)(7) (2003).
[58] Id. §1614.103(b)(6) (2003).
[59] 29 C.F.R. §1613.701(b) (1991).
[60] 56 Fed. Reg. 12,646 (Apr. 10, 1992), as amended at 64 Fed. Reg. 37,655 (July 12, 1999).
[61] Id. §1614.103(b)(4) (2003) (as amended at 64 Fed. Reg. 37,655 (July 12, 1999)). The July 1999 amendments eliminated the phrase "legislative and" thereby removing legislative branch employees from protection under the Rehabilitation Act, Title VII, the Age Discrimination in Employment Act (ADEA), 29 U.S.C. §621 et seq., and the Equal Pay Act generally, 29 U.S.C. §206.
[62] 29 C.F.R. §1614.103(d)(2), (3) (2003).

covered federal employers provide model nondiscriminatory employment practices.

C. Application to Federal Contractors—Section 503

Section 503 of the Rehabilitation Act requires that

> [a]ny contract in excess of $10,000 entered into by any Federal department or agency for the procurement of personal property and nonpersonal services (including construction) for the United States shall contain a provision requiring that the party contracting with the United States shall take affirmative action to employ and advance in employment qualified individuals with disabilities.[63]

A government contract includes any government contract or subcontract consisting of an "agreement or modification . . . for the purchase, sale or use of personal property or nonpersonal property (including construction)," but excludes agreements in which the parties are acting as employer and employee, and of federally assisted contracts.[64] For contracts and subcontracts of indefinite quantities, such as "open end contracts, requirement-type contracts, Federal Supply Schedule contracts, 'call-type' contracts, and purchase notice agreements,"[65] the contractor or subcontractor is required to include the equal opportunity and affirmative action clauses "unless the contracting agency has reason to believe that the amount to be ordered in any year under such contract will not be in excess of $10,000."[66]

Once a contract is subject to the affirmative action provision of section 503, the contractor remains obligated for the duration of the contract, regardless of the amount spent under the contract.[67] Therefore, if the first year of a 5-year contract falls within section 503 requirements, the contractor will remain bound by section 503 throughout its entire term regardless of whether, during the remaining 4 years, the amount

---

[63] 29 U.S.C. §793(a).
[64] 41 C.F.R. §60-741.2 (2003).
[65] *Id.* §60-741.4(a)(3).
[66] *Id.*
[67] *Id.*

under the contract does not exceed $10,000. However, section 503 coverage exists only while there is a federal contract in place.[68] Therefore, if an alleged violation occurs during a lapse in a recurring federal contract, before a contract is initiated, or after a covered federal contract has been completed, the contractor cannot be sanctioned under section 503. The OFCCP may not charge a violation because it does not have jurisdiction in the absence of a federal contract. However, if a violation occurs while a contract is operative, it is not a defense that, at the time of enforcement, there was no longer a federal contract in place subjecting the contractor or subcontractor to section 503's requirements.[69]

Although generally all federal contracts and subcontracts in excess of $10,000 will subject a federal contractor or subcontractor to section 503 requirements, contractors and subcontractors may request a waiver from either the president of the United States[70] or the secretary of the Department of Labor.[71] A contractor may petition the president for a waiver where "the President determines that special circumstances in the national interest so require" a waiver, in whole or in part, of the particular contract or subcontract.[72] A contractor or subcontractor also may petition the Secretary of Labor to waive the section 503 affirmative action clause requirements "with respect to any of a prime contractor's or subcontractor's facilities that are found to be in all respects separate and distinct from activities of the prime contractor or subcontractor related to the performance of the contract or subcontract, if the Secretary of Labor also finds that such a waiver will not interfere with or impede the effectuation of [section 503]."[73]

---

[68]Burnett v. Brock, 806 F.2d 265, 267–68 (11th Cir. 1986) (no Section 503 jurisdiction over newspaper that contracted with federal government on three occasions for advertising; where advertisements were placed pursuant to separate contracts and no contract was in place at time of action alleged to have violated §503).
[69]41 C.F.R. §60-1.4(a)(6), (b)(6) (2003).
[70]*Id.* §793(c)(1).
[71]*Id.* §793(c)(2).
[72]*Id.* §793(c)(1).
[73]*Id.* §793(c)(2)(A).

Prior to amendments to section 503 in 1992, it was unclear whether such a waiver provision was necessary. The former version of section 503 provided that "*in employing persons to carry out such contracts,* the party contracting with the United States shall take affirmative action...."[74] This language raised the question whether affirmative action requirements, and thereby the nondiscrimination requirements, were only applicable to a contractor's employees who were carrying out the federal contract. The Department of Labor answered this question in the negative and interpreted this provision to encompass "all the contractor's employees... unless that contractor can come in and show that some are totally unconnected in any way ... [to the] government contracts."[75] However, in *Washington Metropolitan Area Transit Authority v. DeArment*,[76] the U.S. District Court for the District of Columbia found that this standard was inconsistent with the section 503's plain language.

In 1992, Congress amended section 503, and effectively reversed the *DeArment* ruling, by removing from section 503 the language "in employing persons to carry out such contract."[77] This amendment ensures that *all* employees of federal contractors with contracts over $10,000 will be covered under the Rehabilitation Act, unless the contractor receives a waiver.

D. Application to Programs or Activities Receiving Federal Financial Assistance—Section 504

Section 504 of the Rehabilitation Act provides that

> [n]o otherwise qualified individual with a disability ..., shall, solely by reason of her or his disability, be excluded from the participation in, be denied the benefits of, or be subjected to discrimination under any program or activity receiving Federal financial assistance or under any program or activity conducted by any Executive agency or by the United States Postal Service.[78]

---

[74] *Id.* §793(a) (emphasis added).
[75] Washington Metro. Area Transit Auth. v. DeArment, 1991 U.S. Dist. LEXIS 10391, at 3 (D.D.C. 1991).
[76] *Id.*
[77] Pub. L. No. 102-569, §505(a)(2), 106 Stat. 4427 (1992).
[78] 29 U.S.C. §794(a).

Each agency independently enforces section 504 for its aid recipients and programs, with coordination provided by the Department of Justice. However, each agency's section 504 regulations and compliance procedures must mirror the procedures in place for complying with Title VI of the Civil Rights Act of 1964.[79]

1. Meaning of "Program or Activity"

There are two questions subsumed in the analysis of the meaning of a program or activity receiving federal financial assistance: first, what constitutes a program or activity; and, second, what constitutes receipt of federal financial assistance. Early court decisions were in disagreement over whether Congress intended the phrase "program or activity" to encompass an institutionwide or program-specific approach. Under the program-specific approach, only the specific department or activity receiving aid was governed by section 504. Where aid was directed for a specific purpose, and not provided to the entity generally, the entity as a whole was not subject to section 504 requirements.[80] Some courts did, however, embrace the institutionwide approach, finding that once an entity received federal funds, the entire entity was subject to section 504 requirements, regardless of whether the aid was directed to a specific program or purpose.[81]

In 1982, the Supreme Court took an active role in the program or activity debate. In a series of cases, culminating in *Grove City College v. Bell*[82] and *Consolidated Rail Corp. v. Darrone*,[83]

---

[79] 28 C.F.R. §41.5(a)(1) (2003).

[80] Brown v. Sibley, 650 F.2d 760, 767–69, 1 AD Cases 254 (5th Cir. 1981); Simpson v. Reynolds Metals Co., 629 F.2d 1226, 1233 n.12, 1 AD Cases 206 (7th Cir. 1980).

[81] Garrity v. Gallen, 522 F. Supp. 171, 213 (D.N.H. 1981); Wright v. Columbia Univ., 520 F. Supp. 789, 792 (E.D. Pa. 1981). At least one appellate court has found that the reach of Section 504 is not limited by the ADA's coverage threshold of 15 employees. Schrader v. Fred A. Ray M.D., P.C., 296 F.3d 968, 13 AD Cases 481 (10th Cir. 2002).

[82] 465 U.S. 555 (1984).

[83] 465 U.S. 624, 1 AD Cases 567 (1984).

the Supreme Court held that the mandates of section 504 covered only the specific program receiving assistance.

Following *Darrone* and *Grove City College*, Congress enacted the Civil Rights Restoration Act of 1987,[84] to reinstate, generally, the institutionwide approach rejected by the Court. Although the Civil Rights Restoration Act did not mandate that the receipt of federal financial assistance would automatically subject an entire entity to section 504 coverage, it shifted the presumption to institutionwide coverage and placed the onus on the entity receiving aid to demonstrate that the entire entity should not be covered by section 504. The Civil Rights Restoration Act of 1987 provided, in relevant part, that, for private entities, aid provided generally would subject the entire operation to section 504.[85] However, it preserved the program-specific approach as it applied to separate facilities. Where aid is provided to a separate facility that is part of a larger entity and the aid is limited in scope to that separate facility, only that facility, and not the whole entity, will be subject to section 504 requirements.[86]

Additionally, the Senate Report accompanying the Civil Rights Restoration Act provided guidance on when the entity as a whole would be covered and when coverage may be limited.[87] Where federal funds are clearly designated for a specific purpose and that purpose is limited to a certain area or department, the aid will not subject the entity as a whole to section 504.[88] However, where the aid is not designated for a specific purpose but for a specific facility, the entire facility will be covered although the entity as a whole will remain exempt.[89] The Civil Rights Restoration Act thereby provides a compromise for section 504 coverage, mandating that, where the scope of the assistance is ambiguous, an entire entity is covered, but

---

[84] Pub. L. No. 100-259, 102 Stat. 28 (1988) (codified at 20 U.S.C. §§1681, 1687, 1688).
[85] 29 U.S.C. §794(b)(3)(A).
[86] 29 U.S.C. §794(b)(3)(B).
[87] S. Rep. No. 100-64, at 4–19 (1988), *reprinted in* 1988 U.S.C.C.A.N. at 3, 9–18.
[88] *Id.* at 17, 18.
[89] *Id.*

where funding is specific, coverage will remain limited to the specific facility, program, or purpose receiving funding.

2. Meaning of "Receipt of Federal Financial Assistance"

The next question presented by section 504, what constitutes "receiving federal financial assistance," has never been addressed by a legislative pronouncement. However, individual agency regulations and judicial interpretations have mapped out what qualifies as receipt of federal financial assistance for the purpose of section 504 coverage. Early Department of Health and Human Services regulations, for example, defined federal financial assistance as it applies to the Rehabilitation Act as

> any grant, loan, contract (other than a procurement contract or a contract of insurance or guaranty), or any other arrangement by which the Department [of Health and Human Services] provides or otherwise makes available assistance in the form of: (1) Funds; (2) Services of Federal personnel; or (3) Real and personal property or any interest in or use of such property....[90]

Other agency regulations have largely followed this broad definition. Early case law, however, took a very narrow view of what could constitute federal financial assistance, based on a tight construction of the 1978 amendments, which incorporated the "remedies, procedures, and rights set forth in title VI of the Civil Rights Act of 1964" into section 504 of the Rehabilitation Act.[91] Title VI was limited to federal financial assistance in providing employment. Courts reasoned that Congress intended this limitation of Title VI to apply to section 504 when it incorporated Title VI. However, the Supreme Court disagreed with this interpretation. In *Darrone*,[92] the Court found that the 1978 amendments and the incorporation of Title VI was intended to grant a private right to sue and not to limit drastically the applicability of section 504. The Court found

---

[90] 45 C.F.R. §84.3(h) (2003).
[91] 29 U.S.C. §794a(a)(2), Pub. L. No. 95-602, §120(a), 92 Stat. 2955, 2983 (1978).
[92] Consolidated Rail Corp. v. Darrone, 465 U.S. 624, 1 AD Cases 567 (1984).

that, where the legislative purpose was clearly to increase options for aggrieved parties, courts should not interpret the action to limit drastically those options, unless the statute is explicit in its limitation.[93]

Additional questions remain, however, as to how direct the receipt of federal financial assistance must be for section 504 coverage to apply. For example, if a federal agency provides aid to a corresponding state agency, which then provides aid to a designated private agency, which in turn distributes aid to numerous groups, it is unclear whether all of the entities coming into contact with this federal aid are subject to section 504 or whether the liability stops somewhere in the distribution chain. These issues have been clarified by statute and court action. First, Congress has expressly excluded ultimate beneficiaries of federal financial assistance from coverage under section 504.[94] This means that final individual aid beneficiaries, such as Social Security or Medicare recipients, need never fear that receipt of such aid will subject them to the requirements under the Rehabilitation Act. Second, the Supreme Court has held that a beneficiary does not have to receive the aid money directly from the federal government to be subject to section 504.[95] However, entities that merely benefit from federal assistance, but that do not receive the assistance, even indirectly, will not be covered by section 504.[96] The Supreme Court rationalizes the distinction on the basis that those who are not intended recipients of assistance, but who merely enjoy some benefits of assistance, have no opportunity to accept or reject the assistance and with it the concomitant obligations of section 504.[97]

---

[93] *Id.*

[94] 20 U.S.C. §1687.

[95] Grove City Coll. v. Bell, 465 U.S. 555, 571–75 (1984) (university "received" federal financial assistance for purposes of §504, where students of university used federal grants to pay for school tuition).

[96] Department of Transp. v. Paralyzed Veterans of Am., 477 U.S. 597, 605–07 (1986) (airlines, which benefited from federal funds provided to airport operators for construction projects, were not covered by Section 504 because airlines were not recipients of aid).

[97] *Id.* at 606.

In addition to excluding ultimate beneficiaries of aid, courts have found that indirect federal benefits, such as tax breaks or tax-exempt status, although they provide a concrete financial benefit, do not constitute federal financial assistance for the purpose of section 504.[98] Although tax breaks and incentives undeniably provide real financial benefits for the recipients, no court has found such credits and incentives sufficient to bring an entity within the Rehabilitation Act's coverage.

3. Application to States

The question of whether states are immune from lawsuits under the Rehabilitation Act remains in doubt despite the narrow view taken by the Supreme Court in key constitutional rulings in recent years. For example, in *Seminole Tribe v. Florida*,[99] the Court restated the test for Congress's lawful abrogation of states' immunity under the Eleventh Amendment, indicating that it must unequivocally express its intent to do so and act pursuant to a valid exercise of its power. In *University of Alabama v. Garrett*,[100] the Court held that despite Congress's clear intent to do so under Title I of the ADA, that statute's remedies were disproportionate to the perceived wrongs to which it was addressed and exceeded Congress's authority under the Fourteenth Amendment. In some respects, observers see the Rehabilitation Act as potentially more vulnerable to constitutional attack, because it failed to identify the infirmities at which its remedies were aimed. At the same time, the mechanism ultimately may find constitutional validation through the Spending Clause in Article I of the Constitution and the financial inducements provided the states under the funding program. To this point, the Supreme Court has let stand appellate court rulings that states waived their sovereign immunity to

---

[98]Bachman v. American Soc'y of Clinical Pathologists, 577 F. Supp. 1257, 1263–64 (D.N.J. 1983).
[99]517 U.S. 44 (1996).
[100]531 U.S. 356, 11 AD Cases 737 (2001).

Rehabilitation Act suits through the acceptance of federal funds.[101]

IV. Definition of "Protected Individual"

A. Evolution of the Definition

The Rehabilitation Act of 1973 originally provided protection to "any individual who (i) has a physical or mental impairment which for such individual constitutes or results in a substantial impediment to employment; and (ii) can benefit in terms of employment outcome from vocational rehabilitation services provided [under the Act]."[102] However, Congress soon realized that this narrow definition was insufficient to protect individuals intended to be covered by Titles IV and V of the Rehabilitation Act, including the central sections 501, 503, and 504. In 1974, Congress amended the Rehabilitation Act to include a second definition of "handicapped individual" better suited to the broad prohibition of discrimination in federal employment, contracts, and federal aid.[103] The revised definition of a "handicapped individual" (later amended as "disabled individual") provides protection under the Rehabilitation Act for "any person who (i) has a physical or mental impairment which substantially limits one or more of such person's major life activities; (ii) has a record of such an impairment; or (iii) is

---

[101] *See, e.g.*, Brookman v. Wyoming Dep't of Family Servs., 342 F.3d 1159, 14 AD Cases 1423 (10th Cir. 2003), *cert. denied,* 124 S. Ct. 1509 (2004); Koslow v. Pennsylvania, 302 F.3d 161, 13 AD Cases 769 (3d Cir. 2002), *cert. denied,* 537 U.S. 1232 (2003); Ohio Envtl. Prot. Agency v. Nihiser, 269 F.3d 626, 12 AD Cases 530 (6th Cir. 2001), *cert. denied,* 536 U.S. 922 (2002); Douglas v. California Dep't of Youth Auth., 271 F.3d 812, 12 AD Cases 826 (9th Cir. 2001), *cert. denied,* 536 U.S. 924 (2002). *See also* Savage v. Glendale Union High Sch. Dist. No. 205, 343 F.3d 1036, 14 AD Cases 1412 (9th Cir.), *cert. denied,* 124 S. Ct. 2067 (2004); Garrett v. Board of Trustees of Univ. of Ala., 344 F.3d 1288, 14 AD Cases 1386 (11th Cir. 2003).

[102] 87 Stat. 361 (1973) (codified at 29 U.S.C. §705(20)(A)).

[103] Pub. L. No. 93-516, §111(a)(6), 88 Stat. 1617 (1974) (originally codified at 29 U.S.C. §706(6); redesignated in 1998 as 29 U.S.C. §705(20) (Pub. L. No. 105-220, title IV, §403, 112 Stat. 1097)). The original definition was retained for the purpose of the vocational rehabilitation services portion of the Rehabilitation Act. *See* 29 U.S.C. §705(20)(A)(ii).

regarded as having such an impairment."[104] This three-pronged definition has been subsequently adopted by much of the federal and state legislation to protect disabled individuals, including the ADA.[105]

Prior to the enactment of the ADA, courts and regulators provided the primary elucidations of the definition of "handicapped individual." With the passage of the ADA in 1990, however, this term has been further illuminated by regulation and agency guidance. The ADA uses the term "disabled individual" rather than "handicapped individual."[106] The EEOC has provided guidance on the meaning of "disabled individual" through its regulations and guidance.[107] The EEOC's regulation and guidance with respect to this term has been made applicable to Rehabilitation Act as well with the 1992 amendments. The 1992 amendments mandate that the Rehabilitation Act apply the "substantive standards of Title I of the ADA" to sections 501, 503, and 504 of the Rehabilitation Act.[108] As a result, the ADA definition of disability and the accompanying EEOC guidance is applicable to the Rehabilitation Act. Therefore, most of the explication of terms used in the Rehabilitation Act now comes from ADA guidance and interpretations. In an effort to avoid redundancy with other chapters of this treatise, this section explains only the fundamental aspects of the Rehabilitation Act's "qualified individual with a disability" concept and identifies any differences between the ADA and the Rehabilitation Act with respect to this concept.

As discussed above, the Rehabilitation Act's definition of "disabled individual" covers three distinct types of individuals: those with actual disabilities, those with records of disabilities, and those who are regarded as having disabilities. Each of these three classifications is discussed below.

---

[104] 29 U.S.C. §705(20)(B).
[105] 42 U.S.C. §12102(2); 42 U.S.C. §12112(a) (Title I prohibition against employment discrimination "against a qualified individual with a disability because of the disability of such individual"); 42 U.S.C. §12132 (Title II prohibition against a "qualified individual with a disability" by a public entity).
[106] 42 U.S.C. §12102(2).
[107] *E.g.*, 29 C.F.R. pt. 1630 (2003).
[108] 29 U.S.C. §§791(g), 793(d), 794(d).

B. Actual Disability

The first classification of an "individual with a disability" under the Rehabilitation Act is any person with a physical or mental impairment that substantially limits one or more major life activities.[109] This category is meant to include any qualified person with an actual debilitating impairment. The analysis of actual disabilities turns on two issues: (1) The types of impairments are covered by the Rehabilitation Act? and (2) The definition of a substantial limitation on a major life activity.

1. Impairment

a. General Definition

The initial question the first prong of the definition of "disabled individual" presents is what types of impairments are sufficient to provide the basis for coverage under the Rehabilitation Act. Original guidance on this issue came in the section 504 regulations, which were subsequently adopted for use for other relevant provisions of the Rehabilitation Act, including sections 501 and 503, the ADA, and other state and federal disability discrimination statutes.[110] The Rehabilitation Act covers both physical and mental impairments. The section 504 regulations define a "physical impairment" as:

> any physiological disorder or condition, cosmetic disfigurement, or anatomical loss affecting one or more of the following body systems: neurological; musculoskeletal; special sense organs; respiratory, including speech organs; cardiovascular; reproductive, digestive, genito-urinary, hemic and lymphatic; skin; and endocrine ....[111]

A "mental impairment" is "any mental or psychological disorder, such as mental retardation, organic brain syndrome, emotional or mental illness, and specific learning disabilities."[112]

---

[109] 29 U.S.C. §705(20).
[110] *E.g.*, 29 C.F.R. §1630.2(h) (2003).
[111] 45 C.F.R. §84.3(j)(2)(i) (2003).
[112] *Id.* These definitions have been explicitly incorporated into the ADA at 29 C.F.R. §1630.2(h) (2003), and the appendix to pt. 1630 provides much of the interpretive guidance.

Although the above list of qualifying physical and mental impairments is fairly comprehensive, it has never been considered, nor was it ever intended to be, exclusive or exhaustive.[113] EEOC regulations implementing the ADA provide additional guidance on certain conditions that are to be included or excluded under this definition. The appendix to the regulations and EEOC guidance clarify that normal physical characteristics, such as "eye color, hair color, left-handedness, or height, weight or muscle tone that are in the normal range and are not the result of a physiological disorder," although they may result in disqualification for specific jobs, do not constitute impairments.[114] Additionally, the guidance provides that the definition of impairment does not include predisposition to illness, common personality traits, or environmental, cultural, or economic conditions, where the conditions do not result from a mental or psychological disorder.[115] Furthermore, the statute specifically provides that homosexuality, bisexuality,[116] transvestitism, transsexualism, and gender identity disorders do not constitute impairments under the Rehabilitation Act.[117]

b. Areas of Conflict

i. Obesity. Although many issues arising under the Rehabilitation Act's definition of impairment are adequately addressed by the statutory language and regulations, some confusing and contentious issues remain.[118] This section will highlight some of the fundamental confusion and detail areas where the ADA and the Rehabilitation Act differ or come into conflict on these issues. For example, there was early confusion over whether

---

[113] S. REP. NO. 101-116, at 21, 22 (1989); H.R. REP. NO. 101-485, pt. 2, at 50, 51 (1990), *reprinted in* 1990 U.S.C.C.A.N. 303, 332–34; H.R. REP. NO. 101-485, pt. 3, at 27 (1990), *reprinted in* 1990 U.S.C.C.A.N. 445, 450.

[114] 29 C.F.R. pt. 1630, app. §1630.2(h); EEOC COMPLIANCE MANUAL, *Definition of the Term "Disability,"* §902.2(c).

[115] *Id.*

[116] 29 U.S.C. §705(20)(E).

[117] *Id.* §705(20)(F)(i). This exclusion is consistent with the American Psychiatric Association's *Diagnostic and Statistical Manual of Mental Disorders* (4th ed. 1994).

[118] Many of these subtle issues are discussed in detail in Chapter 5, "Disabilities Protected by the ADA," and will not be addressed in this chapter.

obesity came within the definition of disability, as well over the applicability of the disability statutes to drug and alcohol use or addiction. Original regulatory guidance for the ADA generally excluded obesity from the definition of disabling impairment, "except in rare circumstances."[119] Federal courts, however, were not convinced by this guidance, and, in *Cook v. Rhode Island Dep't of Mental Health, Retardation, & Hospitals*,[120] the district court of Rhode Island found that where obesity is the result of systemic or metabolic dysfunction, it may be considered a physiological impairment qualifying as a disability. The district court continued that, if obesity were the result of voluntary overeating, it generally would not qualify as a disability under the ADA or the Rehabilitation Act. On appeal, however, the U.S. Court of Appeals for the First Circuit disagreed, finding that the voluntariness of a condition does not influence its qualification as a disability.[121] Subsequently, the EEOC softened its position, finding that obesity may be considered a disability under federal disability statutes.[122] Additionally, even if not qualifying under the first disability prong, obese individuals may be "regarded as" having an impairment and therefore may qualify under the definition's third prong.[123]

ii. Drug and Alcohol Use. Another area of initial confusion over the definition of impairment concerned the classification of drug and alcohol addiction as disabilities. Although drug and alcohol addiction are recognized disabilities and therefore

---

[119]EEOC *Interpretive Guidance on Title I of the Americans with Disabilities Act*, 56 Fed. Reg. 35,726, 35,741 (July 26, 1991) (codified at 29 C.F.R. pt. 1630 app. §1630.2(j) (1993)).

[120]783 F. Supp. 1569, 1573, 2 AD Cases 143 (D.R.I. 1992), *aff'd*, 10 F.3d 17, 2 AD Cases 1476 (1st Cir. 1993).

[121]Cook v. Rhode Island Dep't of Mental Health, Retardation, & Hosps., 10 F.3d 17, 2 AD Cases 1476 (1st Cir. 1993).

[122]Effective June 8, 2000, the *EEOC Interpretive Guidance on Title I of the Americans with Disabilities Act* (Interpretive Guidance) was amended to eliminate the presumption that obesity will not be considered a disability except in rare circumstances. 65 Fed. Reg. 36,327 (June 8, 2000). The *Interpretive Guidance* now provides that the "definition of the term 'impairment' does not include physical characteristics such as . . . weight or muscle tone that are within 'normal' range. . . ." 29 C.F.R. pt. 1630, app. §1630.2(h) (2003).

[123]See section III.C., "Being Regarded as Having a Disability," below, for a discussion of the "regarded as" prong.

are covered under the Rehabilitation Act, the precise protections afforded drug or alcohol users and addicts has undergone many changes over the years. From the beginning, drug or alcohol addiction was considered a disability. Consequently, the Rehabilitation Act protected those afflicted with these addictions, even if they might currently be using drugs or alcohol, so long as they could perform their job requirements and did not present a direct threat to health, safety, or property.[124] This protection was narrowed, however, by the ADA. With the passage of the ADA, and the Rehabilitation Act's subsequent incorporation of its standards, the Rehabilitation Act withdrew protection for individuals "currently engaging in the illegal use of drugs, when a covered entity acts on the basis of such use."[125] Interestingly, the statutory provision of the Rehabilitation Act covering the exemption of alcoholics "whose current use of alcohol prevents such individual from performing the duties of the job in question" only applies to sections 503 and 504, thereby implying that federal employees who currently use alcohol as a direct result of alcohol addiction would remain protected under section 501.[126] Therefore, an individual currently using illegal drugs, even if the use results from drug addiction, is not protected by either the ADA or the Rehabilitation Act. Employers may discipline or terminate such individuals without implicating either act, whereas alcoholic federal employees currently engaged in the use of alcohol may still be protected. In analyzing this seeming anomaly, courts have noted that the federal government has a duty to be a model employer and thus could be expected to provide greater protection to employees with disabilities or addictions.[127] However,

---

[124]Pub. L. No. 93-516, §111(a), 88 Stat. 1617 (1974) (codified as amended at 29 U.S.C. §705(20)(C)).

[125]29 U.S.C. §705(20)(C)(i).

[126]*Id.* 705(20)(C)(v). *See* Crewe v. Office of Pers. Mgmt., 834 F.2d 140, 1 AD Cases 1167 (8th Cir. 1987) (alcoholism exclusion does not operate under §501, relying on statutory language that restricts the exclusion to §§503 and 504 as well as the greater affirmative duty of federal employers); Whitlock v. Donovan, 598 F. Supp. 126, 1 AD Cases 630 (D.D.C. 1984), *aff'd sub nom.* Whitlock v. Brock, 790 F.2d 964, 2 AD Cases 624 (D.C. Cir. 1986).

[127]834 F.2d at 142.

this federal exception for alcoholics offers limited protection, because all individuals under the Rehabilitation Act must still prove they are "qualified," which is generally difficult to prove for many current abusers of alcohol.

2. Substantially Limits One or More Major Life Activities

a. General Definition

An impairment will not constitute a disability cognizable under the Rehabilitation Act unless it "substantially limits one or more . . . major life activities."[128] Although the Rehabilitation Act neither defines nor provides guidance for interpreting the term "substantially limits," the 1992 amendments expressly provide for reliance on the ADA for interpretive guidance.[129] The ADA defines "substantially limits" as a significant restriction "as to the condition manner or duration under which an individual can perform a particular major life activity . . . as compared to . . . the general population."[130] Further, courts have found the language "substantially limits" does not include impairments that are transitory or minor and only includes impairments that substantially limit an individual's ability to perform a major life activity.[131]

As discussed previously, an impairment must substantially limit a major life activity to meet the threshold for coverage under the Rehabilitation Act. "Major life activities" are defined in the section 504 regulations as "functions such as caring for one's self, performing manual tasks, walking, seeing, hearing, speaking, breathing, learning, and working."[132] This definition has been adopted for use in the ADA and has been incorporated into subsequent EEOC regulations for the ADA. Much of the definitional guidance comes from ADA interpretations. Early on, however, courts were faced with the task of interpreting this language without guidance from the ADA and EEOC.

---

[128] 29 U.S.C. §705(20)(B)(i).
[129] Id. §§791(g), 793(d), 794(d).
[130] 29 C.F.R. §1630.2(j)(1) (2003).
[131] EEOC COMPLIANCE MANUAL, *Definition of the Term Disability*.
[132] 45 C.F.R. §84.3(2)(ii) (2003).

Ch. 2 IV.B.2.b.   Rehabilitation Act of 1973   73

In *Oesterling v. Walters*,[133] the U.S. Court of Appeals for the Eighth Circuit found that the use of the phrase "such as" in the definition of major life activities clearly implies that the list of qualifying activities is not intended to be exhaustive. That court also held that the activities of sitting and standing qualify as major life activities.

b. Area of Conflict

One question that remains an area of confusion is whether work, or a specific work limitation, can constitute a substantial limitation on a major life activity. Regulations promulgated for implementation of section 503 provide:

> With respect to the major life activity of working (i) the term *substantially limits* means significantly restricted in the ability to perform either a class of jobs or a broad range of jobs in various classes as compared to the average person having comparable training, skills, and abilities. The inability to perform a single, particular job does not constitute a substantial limitation in the major life activity of working.[134]

The determination of whether an impairment "substantially limits one or more major life activities" must be made on a case-by-case basis, based on individual considerations and the limitations of each individual.[135] As under the ADA, employees often have faced difficulties in establishing that their conditions "substantially limits" them in a manner protected by the statute. Thus, a nurse who was unable to drive herself to and from work because of limitations imposed by taking medication for

---

[133] 760 F.2d 859, 1 AD Cases 722 (8th Cir. 1985).

[134] 41 C.F.R. §60-741.2(q)(3) (2003). The Supreme Court recently noted that "there may be some conceptual difficulty in defining 'major life activities' to include work, for it seems to argue in a circle to say that if one is excluded, for instance, by reason of an impairment, from working with others ... then that exclusion constitutes an impairment, when the question you're asking is, whether the exclusion itself is by reason of handicap." Sutton v. United Airlines, Inc., 527 U.S. 471, 492, 9 AD Cases 673 (1999) (internal quotation omitted). Nevertheless, the Supreme Court did not have to decide whether working would qualify as a major life activity in *Sutton* and assumed that it is. *Id.*

[135] This determination is discussed in further detail in Chapter 5, "Disabilities Protected by the ADA."

epilepsy was not disabled.[136] An agent of the Immigration and Naturalization Service who experienced chronic muscle pain was unable to show that her condition substantially limited her performance of any major life activity.[137] Similarly, an employee of the Tennessee Valley Authority who worked as a steamfitter and was laid-off after several years in a light-duty program due to a herniated disc was unable to establish that he was substantially limited in the performance of major life activities or that the employer regarded him as so limited.[138] A student with multiple personality disorder dismissed from a teacher certification program because it was believed she could not be left unsupervised with children had no viable claim because the defendant did not believe she was substantially limited from a broad range of jobs.[139] Finally, a surgical resident who experienced depression was not able to establish substantial limitations in one hospital when he subsequently moved to and successfully completed a residency at another hospital.[140]

C. Record of Having a Disability

The second classification of an "individual with a disability" under the Rehabilitation Act encompasses persons with "a record of" an impairment that substantially limits a major life activity.[141] Pursuant to section 504's implementing regulations, a person has "a record of" a disability if he or she either has "a history of, or has been misclassified as having, a mental or physical impairment that substantially limits one or more major life activities."[142] This definition also applies to the ADA.[143] As

---

[136] Chenoweth v. Hillsborough County, 250 F.3d 1328, 11 AD Cases 1421 (11th Cir. 2001), *cert. denied*, 534 U.S. 1131 (2002).

[137] Stein v. Ashcroft, 284 F.3d 721 (7th Cir. 2002).

[138] Mahon v. Crowell, 295 F.3d 585, 13 AD Cases 390 (6th Cir. 2002).

[139] Davis v. University of N.C. at Wilmington, 263 F.3d 95, 12 AD Cases 243 (4th Cir. 2001).

[140] Swanson v. University of Cincinnati, 268 F.3d 307, 12 AD Cases 417 (6th Cir. 2001).

[141] 29 U.S.C. §705(20)(B)(ii).

[142] 45 C.F.R. §84.3(j)(2)(iii) (2003) (Department of Health and Human Services regulations for implementing §504).

[143] 29 U.S.C. §12102(2)(B).

Congress has reported, this definition of disabled individual is intended to protect individuals "who have recovered—in whole or in part—from a handicapping condition, such as a mental or neurological illness, a heart attack, or cancer and to persons who were classified as handicapped (for example as mentally ill or retarded) but who may be discriminated against or otherwise in need of protection of sections 503 and 504."[144] Courts have found that the "record of" prong applies to individuals who, having recovered from a disability, still may be stigmatized from their past history or who have been incorrectly categorized as having a substantially limiting disability.[145]

D. Being Regarded as Having a Disability

The third prong of the definition of disabled individual protects individuals who are regarded as disabled. This is designed to protect those who do not have an actual disability, but who nevertheless are perceived as having an impairment that limits a major life activity. The section 504 implementing regulations explain that an individual "is regarded as having an impairment" where that person

> (A) has a physical or mental impairment that does not substantially limit major life activities but that is treated by a recipient as constituting such a limitation; (B) has a physical or mental impairment that substantially limits major life activities only as a result of the attitudes of others toward such an impairment; or (C) has none of the impairments defined in . . . this section but is treated by a recipient as having such an impairment."[146]

The Fifth Circuit explained, in *Carter v. Orleans Parish Public Schools*,[147] that the Rehabilitation Act protects "not only . . . persons who are excluded from . . . programs because they are handicapped but also . . . those who are excluded because

---

[144]S. Rep. No. 1297 (1974), *reprinted in* 1974 U.S.C.C.A.N. 6373, 6389–6390.
[145]School Bd. of Nassau County v. Arline, 480 U.S. 273, 284–86, 1 AD Cases 1026 (1987).
[146]45 C.F.R. §84.3(j)(2)(iv) (2003).
[147]725 F.2d 261 (5th Cir. 1984).

officials have incorrectly classified and treated them as being handicapped when they in fact are not."[148] Additionally, this prong of the disability definition protects those who, although they are disabled, are not disabled to such an extent so as to substantially limit a major life activity and those who, due to unfounded fears of or prejudice against disease or disfigurement, are incorrectly considered disabled.[149]

As the definition suggests, an individual is not regarded as disabled unless he or she is regarded as substantially limited in a major life activity. Thus, where an employer perceives that an individual is impaired in a manner that is not substantially limiting in a major life activity—for example, where the employer perceives the individual as unable to perform only one particular job—the individual will not meet the "regarded as" test.[150] On the other hand, where there is evidence that an employer perceived an employee as mentally ill, after publicly communicated suicide complaints, a claim based on an employer's perception of disability may be viable.[151]

The Supreme Court provided analysis of the Rehabilitation Act's "regarded as" definition of "disabled individual" in *School Board of Nassau County v. Arline*.[152] In that case, Gene Arline, a Nassau County schoolteacher was discharged because she had infectious tuberculosis. She brought a lawsuit under section 504 of the Rehabilitation Act and Nassau County defended by arguing she was not a "handicapped person" within the Rehabilitation Act's definition.[153] The Supreme Court ruled that Arline fit within the statutory definition of handicapped person under all three prongs of the definition. The Court held Arline's tuberculosis substantially limited her life activities as demonstrated by her hospitalization, and her hospitalization

---

[148] *Id.* at 262.
[149] Sutton v. United Air Lines, Inc., 527 U.S. 471, 489–90, 9 AD Cases 673 (1999); School Board of Nassau County v. Arline, 480 U.S. 273, 284, 1 AD Cases 1026 (1987).
[150] *Sutton*, 527 U.S. at 489–93.
[151] Peters v. Baldwin Union Free Sch. Dist., 320 F.3d 164, 13 AD Cases 1793 (2d Cir. 2003).
[152] 480 U.S. 273, 1 AD Cases 1026 (1987).
[153] *Id.* at 277.

demonstrated a record of impairment. More importantly, the Court ruled that the fact that the county dismissed Arline because the disease was infectious was not a defense and qualified Arline under the "regarded as" prong of the definition. The Court held that "Congress was as concerned about the effect of an impairment on others as it was about its effect on the individual."[154] The *Arline* case made clear that an individual may fall under the statutory definition of disabled individual solely as a result of prejudice, ignorance, or stigma and that the definition does not require a showing of actual disability.

E. Qualified Individual With a Disability

The Rehabilitation Act prohibits discrimination in employment against any "qualified individual with a disability" by any covered federal employer, contractor, or agency receiving federal funds. Although the statute does not define the term "qualified individual," regulations and court opinions clarify that the Rehabilitation Act does not require employers to hire disabled persons incapable of meeting the job criteria with or without reasonable accommodations, and "employers subject to the Rehabilitation Act need not hire handicapped individuals who cannot fully perform the required work, even with accommodation."[155] The Rehabilitation Act simply requires that covered employers treat qualified individuals with disabilities in a fair and evenhanded manner in work or employment and not discriminate against them solely because of a real or perceived disability. In addition, applying the Supreme Court's holding in *Cleveland v. Policy Mgmt. Sys. Corp.*,[156] the Sixth Circuit has held that an individual who received a disability pension was not barred from bringing a discrimination action under the Rehabilitation Act.[157]

---

[154]*Id.* at 282.
[155]Prewitt v. U.S. Postal Serv., 662 F.2d 292, 1 AD Cases 273, 283 (5th Cir. 1981).
[156]526 U.S. 795, 9 AD Cases 491 (1999).
[157]Justice v. Pike County Bd. of Educ., 348 F.3d 554, 14 AD Cases 1761 (6th Cir. 2003); Dotson v. Pike County Bd. of Educ., 2001 WL 1216998 (6th Cir. 2001).

Each section of the Rehabilitation Act covering employment has a slightly different test for determining which individuals with disabilities are protected. Section 501, which requires federal executive agencies to develop affirmative action plans for individuals with disabilities, does not expressly use limiting language regarding the qualification of disabled individuals.[158] However, the EEOC regulations implementing section 501 incorporate the "qualified" requirement. Those regulations define a "qualified individual with disabilities" as follows:

> [A]n individual with handicaps who, with or without reasonable accommodation, can perform the essential functions of the position in question without endangering the health and safety of the individual or others and who, depending upon the type of appointing authority being used:
> (i) Meets the experience or education requirements (which may include passing a written test) of the position in question; or
> (ii) Meets the criteria for appointment under one of the special appointing authorities for individuals with handicaps.[159]

The Department of Labor employs a different definition for purposes of section 503, which requires federal contractors to employ and advance qualified individuals with disabilities. Under the Department of Labor's regulations for section 503, a "qualified individual with a disability" is:

> [A]n individual with a disability who satisfies the requisite skill, experience, education and other job-related requirements of the employment position such individual holds or desires, and who, with or without reasonable accommodation, can perform the essential functions of such position.[160]

The Department of Labor regulations go on to define essential functions as "fundamental job duties of the employment position the individual with a disability holds or desires."[161]

Further variation is found in section 504, which protects otherwise qualified disabled individuals.[162] This resulted in

---

[158] 29 U.S.C. §791.
[159] 29 C.F.R. §1614.203(a)(6) (2001), text amended and changed to 29 C.F.R. §1630.2(m) (2003).
[160] 41 C.F.R. §60-741.2(t) (2003).
[161] Id. at §60-741.2(u).
[162] 29 U.S.C. §794.

some initial confusion as some courts were interpreting this language literally so as to protect all individuals who would be qualified absent a disability.[163] As the regulations implementing section 504 explained, the "otherwise qualified" language, if taken literally, would mean that a blind man would be otherwise qualified as a bus driver because the only qualification he lacked, sight, was a result of his disability.[164] The regulations rejected this absurd interpretation in favor of a reading of "otherwise qualified" to mean "qualified" as in sections 501 and 503, as section 504 was never intended to protect unqualified applicants and employees.[165] The Supreme Court followed this interpretation in *Southeastern Community College v. Davis*.[166]

The Supreme Court again addressed the issue of who is a qualified individual in *School Board of Nassau County v. Arline*.[167] In *Arline*, the Court held that for an individual to be qualified he or she must be able to perform all essential job functions, despite his or her disability, with or without the help of reasonable accommodation.[168] This holding of *Arline* raises the question of what constitutes an essential job function. The term "essential job function" has received most development in connection with the ADA, rather than under the Rehabilitation Act.[169]

V. REASONABLE ACCOMMODATION OBLIGATION

A. Origin of the Obligation

The Rehabilitation Act requires employers to provide reasonable accommodations in employment and application to qualified individuals with a disability. The term "reasonable

---

[163]Davis v. Southeastern Cmty. Coll., 574 F.2d 1158, 1160 (4th Cir. 1978), *rev'd*, 442 U.S. 397, 2 AD Cases 1 (1979).

[164]45 C.F.R. pt. 84, app. A, subpt. A, no. 5.

[165]*Id.*

[166]442 U.S. 397, 405–06, 2 AD Cases 1 (1979).

[167]480 U.S. 273, 1 AD Cases 1026 (1987).

[168]*Id.* at 287.

[169]"Essential job function" is explained in detail in Chapter 5, section III.B., "What Is an Essential Job Function?"

accommodation" first came about in connection with disability-related requirements found in OFCCP regulations for implementing section 503 of the Rehabilitation Act. The OFCCP required all covered federal contractors to "make a reasonable accommodation to the known physical and/or mental limitations of an otherwise qualified applicant or employee unless the contractor can demonstrate that such an accommodation would impose an undue hardship on the operation of its business."[170] Following the OFCCP's example, the Department of Health, Education and Welfare, the original implementing agency for section 504, included a reasonable accommodation requirement into its section 504 regulations in 1977.[171] The EEOC also included a reasonable accommodation mandate in its implementing regulations for section 501.[172]

Interestingly, the reasonable accommodation mandate in both the Rehabilitation Act and the ADA runs contrary to most other antidiscrimination laws. Laws concerning discrimination generally mandate that all people be treated equally without regard to the characteristic at issue, such as age, race, sex, or national origin.[173] However, with respect to disabilities, providing equal treatment, without accounting for disabilities, results in individuals being excluded from many aspects of life and employment for which they are qualified with some accommodations.[174] Therefore, legislators passing disability legislation recognized that a mandate of simple equality, without a requirement of reasonable accommodation, would do little to assist the disabled in their goal of achieving equality in the workplace. As the U.S. Commission on Civil Rights explained:

> Discrimination against handicapped people cannot be eliminated if programs, activities, and tasks are always structured in the ways people with "normal" physical and mental abilities customarily undertake them. Adjustments or modifications of opportunities to

---

[170] 41 C.F.R. §60-741.21(f)(1) (2002).
[171] 42 Fed. Reg. 22, 676–77 (1977) (codified at 45 C.F.R. §84.12 (2003)).
[172] 43 Fed. Reg. 12,295 (1978).
[173] Civil Rights Act of 1964, 42 U.S.C. §2000 et seq.
[174] *See, e.g.*, 42 U.S.C. §12101.

permit handicapped people to participate fully have been broadly termed "reasonable accommodation."[175]

In 1990, with the passage of the ADA, Congress codified the reasonable accommodation obligation with regard to individuals with disabilities.[176] Congress made the reasonable accommodation obligation set forth in the ADA applicable to the Rehabilitation Act with the 1992 amendments.[177] Pursuant to the 1992 amendments, all relevant guidance from regulations and court decisions concerning the interpretation of "reasonable accommodation" for the ADA also apply to the Rehabilitation Act.[178] This section discusses early guidance on the Rehabilitation Act's reasonable accommodation obligation and areas in which this obligation differs under the Rehabilitation Act and the ADA.

B. Definition of the Obligation

Although early Rehabilitation Act regulations imposed reasonable accommodation obligations, there was little early guidance as to what that obligation entailed. For example, the section 503 regulations, which first used the term reasonable accommodation, did not define that term.[179] Section 503 provided little guidance to employers beyond the inclusion of a sample notice to employees stating that employees covered under the Rehabilitation Act are entitled to reasonable accommodations that would "enable you to perform the job properly and safely, including special equipment, changes in the physical layout of the job, elimination of certain duties relating to the job, . . . or other accommodations."[180]

---

[175] U.S. COMMISSION ON CIVIL RIGHTS, ACCOMMODATING THE SPECTRUM OF INDIVIDUAL ABILITIES 153–54 (1983).

[176] 42 U.S.C. §12112(b)(5)(A).

[177] Pub. L. No. 102-569, 106 Stat. 4344 (codified at 29 U.S.C. §§791(g), 793(d), and 794(d)).

[178] *Id.* The reasonable accommodation obligation for the ADA is covered extensively in Chapter 8, "Reasonable Accommodation Requirements," and that analysis will not be duplicated here.

[179] 41 C.F.R. pt. 60-741 (effective Feb. 12, 1980).

[180] 41 C.F.R. pt. 60-741, app. B, no. 2 (2003).

The first definition of the reasonable accommodation obligation came in regulations implementing sections 501 and 504. This definition, however, was not an explication of the term but merely provided a nonexhaustive list of accommodations that reasonably could be required of employers. The regulations provided that

> [r]easonable accommodation may include, but shall not be limited to: (i) Making facilities readily accessible to and usable by individuals with handicaps; and (ii) job restructuring, part-time or modified work schedules, acquisition or modification of equipment or devices, . . . the provision of readers or interpreters, and other similar actions.[181]

The best explication of the term "reasonable accommodation" came in ADA regulations:

> The term reasonable accommodation means:
> (i) Modifications or adjustments to a job application process that enable a qualified applicant with a disability to be considered for the position such qualified applicant desires; or
> (ii) Modifications or adjustments to the work environment, or to the manner or circumstances under which the position held or desired is customarily performed, that enable a qualified individual with a disability to perform the essential functions of that position; or
> (iii) Modifications or adjustments that enable a covered entity's employee with a disability to enjoy equal benefits and privileges of employment as are enjoyed by its other similarly situated employees without disabilities[182]

This definition, and its application to the Rehabilitation Act through the 1992 amendments, clarifies that the reasonable accommodation obligation applies not only to current employees but also to qualified disabled applicants. Accommodations must be made in both the application process and during employment to ensure that reasonable accommodations are

---

[181] 29 C.F.R. §1614.203(c)(2) (2001), text amended and changed to 29 C.F.R. §1630.2(o) (2003); 42 U.S.C. §12111(9) (§501 regulations use the same list of examples, although they add appropriate adjustment or modification of examinations to the list).

[182] 29 C.F.R. §1630.2(o)(i)–(iii) (2003).

made to prevent qualified disabled individuals from being unnecessarily disadvantaged due to their disability.

Even with the ADA's more extensive definition of "reasonable accommodation," much confusion remained about the extent to which an employer needs to accommodate before doing so is no longer reasonable. Rehabilitation Act and ADA regulations clarify that employers are not required to implement any accommodation that would impose an "undue hardship" on the employer or its business operation.[183] The Rehabilitation Act does not provide a definition of "undue hardship," but its implementing regulations give factors to be considered in determining whether a given accommodation constitutes an undue hardship. For example, under section 501 or 504, relevant factors to be considered are (1) the size of the agency's program, (2) the type of agency operation and the structure of the workforce, and (3) the overall cost and nature of the accommodation.[184] Section 503 regulations contain a more comprehensive definition for "undue hardship":

> Undue hardship means, with respect to the provision of an accommodation, significant difficulty or expense incurred by the contractor, when considered in light of the [following] factors ....
> ...
> (i) The nature and net cost of the accommodation needed, taking into consideration the availability of tax credits and deductions, and/or outside funding;
> (ii) The overall financial resources of the facility or facilities involved in the provision of the reasonable accommodation, the number of persons employed at such facility, and the effect on expenses and resources;
> (iii) The overall financial resources of the contractor, the overall size of the business of the contractor with respect to the number of its employees, and the number, type and location of its facilities;
> (iv) The type of operation or operations of the contractor, including the composition, structure and functions of the work force of such contractor, and the geographic separateness and

---

[183] 29 C.F.R. §1614.102(a)(8) (2003); 29 C.F.R. §1630.2(p); 41 C.F.R. §60-741.2(v) (2002); 45 C.F.R. §84.12(a) (2003).

[184] 29 C.F.R. §1630.2(p)(2); 45 C.F.R. §84.12(c) (2003).

administrative or fiscal relationship of the facility or facilities in question to the contractor; and

(v) The impact of the accommodation upon the operation of the facility, including the impact on the ability of other employees to perform their duties and the impact on the facility's ability to conduct business.[185]

Additionally, the Rehabilitation Act was amended in 1978 to add section 505(a)(1), which requires that cost be taken into account in determining a reasonable accommodation under section 501:

> In fashioning an equitable or affirmative action remedy under [section 501], a court may take into account the reasonableness of the cost of any necessary work place accommodation, and the availability of alternatives therefor or other appropriate relief in order to achieve an equitable and appropriate remedy.[186]

As discussed previously, the Rehabilitation Act now incorporates the ADA's definitions and decisional guidance of the reasonable accommodation obligation.[187]

Consistent with the outcome of a number of ADA cases, employees have achieved some successes, but have faced difficult challenges under the Rehabilitation Act in establishing that the accommodations they seek are reasonable under the statute. In a case involving a request for an alternative work schedule desired as an accommodation for the individual's diagnosed obsessive-compulsive disorder, the D.C. Circuit decided that there were material issues of fact regarding the employing agency's response, and it allowed the claim to proceed.[188] However, other plaintiffs have had challenges to their employers' refusal to accommodate rejected by reviewing courts. Thus, in *Ozlowski v. Henderson*,[189] the Seventh Circuit found that the Postal Service did not discriminate against an employee with degenerative spinal disease when it failed to

---
[185]41 C.F.R. §60-741.2(w) (2002).
[186]29 U.S.C. §794a(a)(1).
[187]The duty to provide reasonable accommodation under the ADA is discussed in detail in Chapter 8, "Reasonable Accommodation Requirements."
[188]Breen v. Department of Transp., 282 F.3d 839, 12 AD Cases 1652 (D.C. Cir. 2002).
[189]237 F.3d 837, 11 AD Cases 671 (7th Cir. 2001).

commence an interactive accommodation process, since the employee had not identified any vacant position for which he was qualified. An employer's rejection of the request of an employee with spina bifida to work exclusively from home because his workplace presence was required to perform the job's essential functions was upheld by the First Circuit.[190] A machine operator with a shoulder problem who requested that he be accommodated by having another employee do the heaviest lifting components of his job did not seek a reasonable accommodation, because it would require another employee to perform an essential function of the job.[191] Where employees challenge a specific alternative accommodation provided by the employer, they also may face difficulties. For example, in *Webster v. Henderson*,[192] where postal employees on light-duty and limited-duty were assigned to a new facility that they considered to be less desirable (because of working conditions and work hours), the employees' challenge failed when the court accepted as legitimate and non-pretextual the business reasons advanced by the employer for the challenged actions.

VI. Rehabilitation Act Enforcement

A. Overview

When the Rehabilitation Act was originally passed in 1973, it mandated equal and nondiscriminatory treatment of handicapped persons in employment and application for employment by federal executive agencies, federal contractors, and organizations and programs receiving federal financial assistance.[193] However, as originally enacted, the Rehabilitation Act left many enforcement questions unanswered. For example, it did not contain any express mechanism for enforcing violations of either section 501 or section 504, and initially there was

---

[190] Kvorjak v. Maine, 259 F.3d 48, 12 AD Cases 160 (1st Cir. 2001).
[191] Peters v. City of Mauston, 311 F.3d 835 (7th Cir. 2002).
[192] 2002 U.S. App. LEXIS 2877 (4th Cir. 2002) (unpublished opinion).
[193] 29 U.S.C. §701 et seq.

much disagreement among the courts over the availability of a private right of action under those sections.[194] This was clarified, by amendment in 1978, with the addition of section 505, which sets forth remedies and enforcement mechanisms for sections 501 and 504. Additionally, although the Rehabilitation Act was originally promulgated in 1973, it was not until 1978 that regulations were first published and it became a viable law for the prevention of discrimination against individuals with disabilities.[195] With the regulations and the addition of section 505,[196] the Rehabilitation Act became an important tool for effecting the statute's original goal: "the tragically overdue goal of full integration of . . . handicapped [people] into normal community living, working and service patterns."[197]

Each of the provisions of the Rehabilitation Act governing employment has its own enforcement procedures and remediation schemes. In brief, section 501 enforcement is through individual federal agency employers with coordination through the EEOC.[198] It is enforced in accordance with the Title VII of the Civil Rights Act of 1964,[199] which includes administrative action and a private right of action. Section 503 is enforced through the OFCCP, Employment Standards Administration,[200] and is enforceable solely through administrative action with little judicial oversight or review.[201] Section 504 is enforced through the individual federal agencies providing aid or money to programs or entities and is enforceable both through administrative remediation and private right of action as a result of the incorporation of the rights, remedies, and procedures of Title VI of the Civil Rights Act of 1964. This discussion explains

---

[194] Briggs, *Note: Safeguarding Equality for the Handicapped: Compensatory Relief Under §504 of the Rehabilitation Act*, 1986 DUKE L.J. 197, 198.

[195] Tucker, *Section 504 of the Rehabilitation Act After Ten Years of Enforcement: The Past and the Future*, 1989 U. ILL. L. REV. 845, 845–46.

[196] Section 505 was added to the Rehabilitation Act of 1973 at 92 Stat. 2982, 29 U.S.C. §794(a) (1978).

[197] 118 CONG. REC. 3320 (1972) (statement of Sen. Williams (D-N.J.)).

[198] 29 U.S.C. §791(b).

[199] 29 U.S.C. §794a(a)(1).

[200] 29 U.S.C. §793(b); 41 C.F.R. §60-741.60 to §60-741.70 (2003).

[201] 29 U.S.C. §793(b); 41 C.F.R. §60-741.60 to §60-741.70 (2003).

the enforcement provisions of sections 501, 503, and 504 and evaluates both the administrative procedures for handling complaints under the Rehabilitation Act as well as the judiciary's role in enforcing the Rehabilitation Act.

B. Section 501

1. Scope

Section 501 covers federal executive agencies. Enforcement of section 501 is delegated to the EEOC through the enforcement procedures established in 29 C.F.R. part 1614.[202] The 1978 amendments, with the addition of section 505, provided a private right of action, which had previously been found lacking by most courts considering the issue.[203] Section 505 enables covered federal employees and applicants aggrieved by alleged section 501 violations to avail themselves of all the "rights, remedies and procedures" available under Title VII of the Civil Rights Act of 1964.[204]

Federal executive agency employees and applicants aggrieved by violations of section 501 have two possible remedial

---

[202] 29 C.F.R. pt. 1614 (2003). In 1992, the EEOC combined regulations for enforcing Section 501 of the Rehabilitation Act, as well as job discrimination on the basis of race, color, national origin, sex, age, and religion, in order to achieve a comprehensive and coordinated program to eradicate discrimination in federal employment under 29 C.F.R. pt. 1614 (2003).

[203] Pub. L. No. 95-602, 92 Stat. 2982 (effective Nov. 6, 1978). *See* Doe v. Garrett, 903 F.2d 1455, 1459, 1 AD Cases 1606 (11th Cir. 1990), *cert. denied*, 499 U.S. 904 (1991); Prewitt v. U.S. Postal Serv., 662 F.2d 292, 1 AD Cases 273 (5th Cir. 1981); Counts v. U.S. Postal Serv., 17 FEP Cases 1161 (N.D. Fla. 1978), *rev'd due to statutory changes*, 631 F.2d 46, 24 FEP Cases 677 (5th Cir. 1980); Coleman v. Darden, 15 FEP Cases 272 (D. Colo. 1977), *cert. denied*, 444 U.S. 927 (1979).

[204] Rehabilitation Act of 1978, 29 U.S.C. §794a(a)(1):

The remedies, procedures, and rights set forth in section 717 of the Civil Rights Act of 1964 (42 U.S.C. 2000e-16), including the application of sections 706(f) through 706(k) (42 U.S.C. 2000e-5(f) through (k)), shall be available, with respect to any complaint under section 791 of this title [501 of the Rehabilitation Act], to any employee or applicant for employment aggrieved by the final disposition of such complaint, or by the failure to take final action on such complaint. In fashioning an equitable or affirmative action remedy under such section, a court may take into account the reasonableness of the cost of any necessary work place accommodation, and the availability of alternatives therefor or other appropriate relief in order to achieve an equitable and appropriate remedy.

procedures available to them: administrative investigation and remediation, and a private right of action. However, in order to take advantage of the private right of action, the aggrieved party must exhaust all administrative remedies, unless a court determines such a course of action to be futile.[205]

2. Enforcement Procedures

The EEOC, in accordance with its mandate to enforce section 501, has promulgated regulations and procedures to guide federal employees and applicants in filing a complaint alleging section 501 violations. Federal employees or applicants who believe they have been discriminated against in violation of section 501 have 45 days from the date of the alleged discriminatory action to contact the agency's equal employment opportunity counselor and report the alleged violation.[206] The counselor is required to advise the complainant of his or her rights and responsibilities and begin an informal investigation, working with both the agency and the aggrieved party to attempt to resolve the dispute informally.[207] If the counselor is unable to resolve the dispute to the satisfaction of the claimant within 15 days, the counselor must file a written report with the agency and the grievant concerning the issues discussed

---

[205] Milbert v. Koop, 830 F.2d 354, 1 AD Cases 1148 (D.C. Cir. 1987) (Title VII and its exhaustion requirement were incorporated into remedy procedures of §501). Although Title VII regulations at 42 U.S.C. §2000e-16 require employees suing the federal government under the Rehabilitation Act to exhaust administrative remedies prior to filing suit, the U.S. Court of Appeals for the Second Circuit, in *Boos v. Runyon*, 201 F.3d 178, 10 AD Cases 198 (2d Cir. 2000), found that the exhaustion requirement was not jurisdictional and therefore may be waived and subject to equitable tolling. The futility exception applies where " 'following the administrative remedy would be futile because of certainty of an adverse decision.' " James v. U.S.. Dep't of Health & Human Servs., 824 F.2d 1132, 1138 (D.C. Cir. 1987) (quoting Randolph-Sheppard Vendors of Am. v. Weinberger, 795 F.2d 90, 105 (D.C. Cir. 1986) (quoting, in turn, 3 K. Davis, Administrative Law Treatise §20.07)); Randolph-Sheppard Vendors of Am. v. Weinberger, 795 F.2d 90, 105 (D.C. Cir. 1986) (quoting 3 K. Davis, Administrative Law Treatise §20.07).

[206] 29 C.F.R. §1614.105(a)(1) (2003). Failure to meet this deadline, or to establish the existence of a continuing violation will result in the rejection of an individual's discrimination. *See, e.g.*, Henrickson v. Potter, 327 F.3d 444 (5th Cir.), *cert. denied*, 124 S. Ct. 579 (2003); Cherosky v. Henderson, 330 F.3d 1243, 14 AD Cases, 673 (9th Cir. 2003).

[207] *Id.* §1614.105(b)(1).

and action taken.[208] If the complaint has not been resolved within 30 days of the original complaint, the counselor must complete the preliminary investigation and notify the grievant of his or her right to file a discrimination complaint with the agency in question.[209] The claimant then has 15 days from receipt of the notice of right to file complaint in which to file such a complaint with the alleged discriminatory agency.[210]

On receipt of a complaint, the agency has 180 days to conduct a complete and impartial investigation of the complaint and make findings.[211] The EEOC regulations describe the process by which an agency may attempt to investigate and address a complaint:

> Agencies may use exchange of letters or memoranda, interrogatories, investigations, fact-finding conferences or any other fact-finding methods that efficiently and thoroughly address the matters at issue. Agencies are encouraged to incorporate alternative dispute resolution techniques into their investigative efforts in order to promote early resolution of complaints.[212]

Within 180 days of receipt of the complaint, the agency must provide the complainant with a copy of the file and inform the complainant that he or she has 30 days to request a hearing and decision from an administrative law judge (ALJ) or request a final decision from the agency without a hearing.[213] On a timely request for a hearing, the EEOC must appoint an ALJ. The ALJ then has 180 days to conduct a hearing and issue findings.[214] On the decision of the ALJ, the agency may accept, reject, or modify the findings, conclusion, or relief ordered. If the agency takes no action within 40 days, the ALJ's decision becomes final.[215] The agency's final decision must include findings and remedies, where appropriate, and must inform the

---

[208] *Id.* §1614.105(c).
[209] *Id.* §1614.105(d).
[210] *Id.* §1614.106(b).
[211] *Id.* §1614.108(e).
[212] *Id.* §1614.108(b).
[213] *Id.* §1614.108(f).
[214] *Id.* §1614.109(h)(i).
[215] *Id.* §1614.110.

complainant of the right to file an appeal with the EEOC and the right to file a civil action in federal district court.[216]

If the claimant decides to pursue an EEOC appeal, he or she must begin by filing Form 573 Notice of Appeal/Petition with the EEOC, with a copy to the agency at issue.[217] Both the agency and the complainant may file supporting briefs or statements, and the agency is required to submit the complaint to the EEOC Office of Federal Operations (OFO), which is assigned to review all appeals to the EEOC filed under section 501.[218] The OFO may supplement the record as needed and request additional information from the parties.[219] The OFO does not hold hearings and will issue a decision and remedies, where appropriate, based solely on the record provided by the parties and additional information collected.[220] On an adverse decision, either party may petition the EEOC for reconsideration.[221] A party requesting reconsideration must establish that the decision was a "clearly erroneous interpretation of material fact or law" or that the "decision will have a substantial impact on the policies, practices or operation of the agency."[222] Absent a, or following an unsuccessful, demand for reconsideration, the final decision on appeal "is mandatory and binding on the agency."[223] If compliance is ordered but is not forthcoming, the EEOC may issue a "show cause notice"[224] or may notify the complainant of a right to file a civil action to obtain compliance.

3. *Remedies*

If a section 501 violation is found, an applicant or employee is entitled to a panoply of remedies under Title VII of

---

[216] *Id.*
[217] *Id.* §1614.403.
[218] *Id.*
[219] *Id.* §1614.404.
[220] *Id.* §§1614.404, 405.
[221] *Id.* §1614.405.
[222] *Id.* §1614.405(b).
[223] *Id.* §1614.502(a).
[224] A "show cause notice" provides the alleged violator with notice that the agency believes there to be a violation and provides the alleged violator with 30 days to resolve the violation or provide justification for failure to comply. *Id.* §§1614.503(e), 1614.504(b).

the Civil Rights Act of 1964.[225] Title VII explicitly mentions the award of back pay, instatement or reinstatement, or "any other equitable relief as the court deems appropriate."[226] Additionally, Title VII provides for the entry of injunctions, including preliminary injunctions,[227] to prevent continued violations as well as to compensate past harms.[228] The remedies are limited, however, by the inclusion of language into section 505(a)(1) that "[i]n fashioning an equitable or affirmative action remedy under such section [501], a court may take into account the reasonableness of the cost of any necessary work place accommodation, and the availability of alternatives therefor or other appropriate relief...."[229]

Although equitable relief has been made available under section 501, prior to 1991 federal employees and applicants suing for relief under section 501 could not receive legal relief in the form of monetary damage awards.[230] Courts found that, because Title VII did not expressly provide for the award of legal damages, damages were not available under Title VII and, therefore, were not available to section 501 plaintiffs.[231] With the passage of the 1991 Civil Rights Act, Congress statutorily reversed these decisions by providing that federal employers would be held liable for compensatory damage for *intentional* discrimination in violation of section 501.[232]

---

[225] As explained above, Title VII's rights, remedies, and procedures were made available to §501 plaintiffs through the 1978 Rehabilitation Act Amendments. 29 U.S.C. §794a. *See* Chapter 2, §II.C., "1978 Rehabilitation Act Amendments."

[226] 42 U.S.C. §2000e-5(g)(1).

[227] The appropriateness of a preliminary injunction is determined by the four-part test. A plaintiff must establish (1) they will likely prevail on the merits; (2) irreparable injury; (3) whether the injunction would harm other interested parties; and (4) whether the public interest would be served or harmed by issuing the injunction. *See* Holt v. Continental Group, Inc., 708 F.2d 87, 91, 31 FEP Cases 1468 (2d Cir. 1983), *cert. denied*, 465 U.S. 1030 (1984); EEOC v. Anchor Hocking Corp., 666 F.2d 1037, 27 FEP Cases 809 (6th Cir. 1981); Porter v. Adams, 639 F.2d 273, 25 FEP Cases 1107 (5th Cir. 1981).

[228] 42 U.S.C. §2000e-5(g).

[229] 29 U.S.C. §794a(a)(1).

[230] United States v. Burke, 504 U.S. 229, 238, 58 FEP Cases 1323 (1992); Walker v. Ford Motor Co., 684 F.2d 1355, 1363–64, 29 FEP Cases 1259 (11th Cir. 1982).

[231] *Id.*

[232] 42 U.S.C. §1981a(b).

Despite the availability of damage awards for federal employees and applicants discriminated against in violation of section 501, the extent of permissible damages remains severely limited. Compensatory damages against the federal government for section 501 violations are limited to cases involving intentional discrimination and are capped at $300,000. Punitive damages remain entirely barred.[233] Furthermore, damages are not available in disparate impact cases or where the government employer has made "good faith efforts" at providing reasonable accommodations.[234] The Rehabilitation Act provides that courts are required to assign costs to the federal government as they would to private individuals and allows for the award of prejudgment interest and attorneys' fees against the federal government.[235] The remedies available to aggrieved federal employees and applicants, although somewhat limited, provide some realistic possibility of recovery under section 501.

4. Affirmative Action Plan Requirements

In addition to its nondiscrimination requirements, section 501 mandates that every federal executive agency "submit to the [Equal Opportunity Employment] Commission and to the [Interagency] Committee [on Employees Who Are Individuals with Disabilities] an affirmative action program plan for the hiring, placement, and advancement of individuals with disabilities . . . ."[236]

> Such plan shall include a description of the extent to which and methods whereby the special needs of employees who are individuals with disabilities are being met. Such plan shall be updated annually, and shall be reviewed annually and approved by the Commission, if the Commission determines, after consultation with the Committee, that such plan provides sufficient assurances, procedures and commitments to provide adequate hiring,

---

[233]*Id.* §1981a(b)(3).
[234]*Id.* §1981 a(a)(2), and (3).
[235]Library of Congress v. Shaw, 478 U.S. 310, 41 FEP Cases 85 (1986).
[236]29 U.S.C. §791(b).

placement, and advancement opportunities for individuals with disabilities.[237]

In accordance with their affirmative action requirements, each federal agency is required to create a program that will ensure that the federal government acts as a model employer. Each agency is required to provide "sufficient resources to its equal opportunity program, . . . [and] [c]onduct a continuing campaign to eradicate every form of prejudice or discrimination from the agency's personnel policies, practices and working conditions."[238] Additionally, each agency is required to submit a plan that specifies goals for employing and advancing qualified individuals with disabilities and to set goals for the employment of such targeted individuals.[239] These affirmative action requirements may be enforced through all means available to enforce section 501 generally.

C. Section 503

1. Scope

Section 503 of the Rehabilitation Act of 1973 obligates federal contractors, falling under its requirements, both to maintain nondiscriminatory hiring practices and to take "affirmative action to ensure that applicants are employed and that employees are placed, trained, upgraded, promoted, and otherwise treated in accordance with [section 503 requirements]."[240] The U.S. Department of Labor's Employment Standards Administration, OFCCP, is charged with enforcing section 503.[241] Pursuant to this mandate, the OFCCP has promulgated regulations and procedures for processing grievances under section 503.[242]

---

[237] *Id.*
[238] 29 C.F.R. §1614.102(a)(1), (3) (2003).
[239] 29 U.S.C. §791(b); EEOC Management Directive 711 (1982).
[240] 41 C.F.R. §60-741.60(a) (2003).
[241] 29 U.S.C. §793(b).
[242] 41 C.F.R. §60-741.60 to §60.741.70 (2003).

2. Enforcement Procedures

Section 503 requires aggrieved employees or applicants to submit their complaints to the OFCCP within 300 days following the latest occurrence of alleged discrimination.[243] Once the OFCCP is notified of a complaint or alleged violation of section 503 against a federal contractor subject to the Rehabilitation Act, it must determine whether the contractor is also subject to the ADA. If a contractor is also subject to the ADA, the charge will fall within the overlapping jurisdiction of the EEOC and OFCCP. An overlapping charge filed with the OFCCP is considered simultaneously filed under the ADA.[244] This joint filing will ensure that the aggrieved individual's rights under the ADA are preserved and provides the aggrieved party a private right of action that is not available if the employer falls exclusively under section 503.[245] Next, the OFCCP examines the contractor's internal review procedures and, if such procedures are in place, submits the grievance to the contractor's internal processes to attempt an informal resolution.[246] If there is no satisfactory resolution through internal processes or the contractor lacks an internal process, the OFCCP will instigate an initial investigation of the claim and develop a "complete case record," including findings and recommendations for further action.[247]

If the OFCCP recommends against further action, either because of a no violation finding or a decision not to take further action, the complainant is informed of the decision and his or her right to seek review by the director of the

---

[243] Complaint of Discrimination in Employment Under Federal Government Contracts, Form CC-4, OMB No. 1215-0131.

[244] 41 C.F.R. §60-742.5 (2003). *See also* Employment Standards Administration, Office of Federal Contract Compliance Programs, *Memorandum of Understanding; Coordination of Functions—EEOC and DOL, Final Notice*, 6570-01, 4510-27 (Apr. 12, 1999). Allocation of responsibilities under charges filed under OFCCP and EEOC overlapping jurisdiction is governed by the memorandum of understanding and is beyond the scope of this chapter.

[245] 41 C.F.R. §60-742.5 (2003).

[246] 41 C.F.R. §60-741.44 (2003).

[247] *Id.*

OFCCP.[248] If the OFCCP finds a section 503 violation, the OFCCP will attempt to induce compliance through informal dialogue with the contractor. If noncompliance persists, the contractor is provided a hearing, conducted by an ALJ, in which the contractor is given the opportunity to explain or defend its lack of compliance. The ALJ's agreement that the contractor has violated section 503 triggers the OFCCP's authority to impose sanctions against the contractor.

3. Remedies

The OFCCP has the authority to impose sanctions of varying severity, ranging from terminating the contract at issue to barring the contractor from participating in any future federal contracts. Additionally, if the contractor is recalcitrant, the OFCCP is authorized to obtain an injunction to compel compliance. However, once the federal contract is terminated, the injunctive power is curtailed because the contractor no longer falls under the requirements of section 503 or the jurisdiction of the OFCCP.

Unlike sections 501 and 504, section 503 does not contain a private right of action. Therefore, contractor employers who do not simultaneously fall under the requirements of the ADA are protected from lawsuits and are subject only to OFCCP sanctions, which some believe to be ineffectual. Additionally, aggrieved employees or applicants whose claims are denied are left with no other recourse. Even if sanctions are imposed against a contractor, through loss of contracts or other penalties, the aggrieved party is rarely entitled to any direct compensation through section 503. Although the OFCCP is empowered, as one of its available remedies, to order the contractor to pay the aggrieved employee back pay, a 1978 study found that only 120 out of 2,700 complainants were awarded back pay.[249] Furthermore, most courts addressing the question have found

---

[248] *Id.*

[249] Comment, *Protecting the Handicapped From Employment Discrimination in Private Sector Employment: A Critical Analysis of §503 of the Rehabilitation Act of 1973*, 54 Tul. L. Rev. 717, 742 (1980).

that an OFCCP determination not to prosecute is a matter committed to agency discretion and, therefore, is not subject to judicial review.[250] Even when courts have found these decisions reviewable, the review is limited to verifying that the agency provided nonarbitrary reasons for its decision.[251]

4. *Affirmative Action Plan Requirements*

In addition to nondiscrimination obligations, federal government contractors are required, under section 503, to "take affirmative action to employ and advance in employment qualified individuals with disabilities."[252] Under this mandate, the OFCCP is empowered to conduct compliance reviews to determine whether federal contractors are complying with section 503 affirmative action mandates and "determine if the contractor maintains nondiscriminatory hiring and employment practices and ... that employees are placed, trained, upgraded, promoted, and otherwise treated in accordance with this part during employment."[253] Contractors are required to file periodic compliance reports. Detailed procedures for evaluating affirmative action programs and compliance reports are laid out in the *Federal Contract Compliance Manual.*[254] The OFCCP is empowered to engage in "comprehensive analysis and evaluation of all relevant hiring and employment practices"[255] and may impose sanctions where necessary to induce compliance,

---

[250]Andrews v. Consolidated Rail Corp., 831 F.2d 678, 1 AD Cases 1122 (7th Cir. 1987) (decisions not to prosecute are in discretion of OFCCP); Giacobbi v. Biermann, 780 F. Supp. 33, 2 AD Cases 104 (D.D.C. 1992); Kilmer v. U.S. Dep't of Labor, 1 AD Cases 1535 (S.D.N.Y. 1989).

[251]Moon v. Secretary, U.S. Dep't of Labor, 747 F.2d 599, 1 AD Cases 642 (11th Cir. 1984), *cert. denied*, 471 U.S. 1055 (1985) (only reviewable to determine if decision was arbitrary or capricious or otherwise not in accordance with law); Presinzano v. Hoffman-LaRoche, Inc., 726 F.2d 105, 112, 1 AD Cases 552 (3d Cir. 1984) (if nonenforcement decision is reviewable at all, record for review is sufficient if it contains statement of reasons).

[252]41 C.F.R. §60-741.1(a) (2003).

[253]41 C.F.R. §60-741.60 (2003).

[254]EMPLOYMENT STANDARDS ADMINISTRATION, OFFICE OF FEDERAL CONTRACT COMPLIANCE PROGRAMS, FEDERAL CONTRACT COMPLIANCE MANUAL, available at <www.dol.gov/esa/regs/compliance/ofccp/fccm/fccmanul.htm>.

[255]"Compliance Evaluation Procedures," OFCCP Directive: Transmittal No. 230: FCCM Notice CH2 (Dec. 22, 1998).

including, as explained above, withholding of payments, cancellation of contracts, and total debarment from participation in federal government contracts.[256]

5. Compliance Reviews

Generally, the OFCCP will conduct a review of a contractor on receipt of a discrimination complaint. However, reviews also may be initiated based on below average representation of disabled individuals or a preaward review. A compliance review has four phases: (1) the desk audit in which the contractor's affirmative action plan is reviewed, (2) an on-site review, (3) further off-site review of information, and (4) an exit conference with findings.[257] If an investigation determines that there has been a violation and the contractor is unable to provide an adequate defense, the OFCCP will propose a remedy and a conciliation agreement in which the contractor and the OFCCP agree to resolve the violation formally.[258] If this fails, or if the contractor refuses to participate in conciliation, the OFCCP may institute administrative enforcement procedures.[259] These conciliation agreements and administrative enforcement procedures can result in monetary penalties payable to either the government, the aggrieved parties, or both, and the OFCCP may enjoin violations or may institute sanctions as discussed above.[260] In addition, the OFCCP may refer the matter to the Department of Justice to enforce agreements where the threat of sanctions is ineffectual.

Although section 503 contains no private right of action, some courts have held that private citizens and groups may sue the OFCCP to enforce its affirmative action compliance obligations. For example, in *Legal Aid Society v. Brennan*,[261] the

---

[256]41 C.F.R. §60-741.66 (2003).
[257]"Compliance Check Procedure," OFCCP Directive: Transmittal No. 227: FCCM Notice CH2 (Sept. 10, 1998); "Compliance Evaluation Procedures," OFCCP Directive: Transmittal No. 230: FCCM Notice CH2 (Dec. 22, 1998).
[258]"Compliance Evaluation Procedures, Transmittal No. 230 (Dec. 22, 1998).
[259]41 C.F.R. §60-741.65 (2003).
[260]*Id.*
[261]608 F.2d 1319, 21 FEP Cases 605 (9th Cir. 1979), *cert. denied*, 447 U.S. 921 (1980).

U.S. Court of Appeals for the Ninth Circuit found that organizations and citizens may sue the OFCCP to force it to comply with its duty to accurately review affirmative action plans in compliance with OFCCP regulations.[262] However, other courts have found that a private right of action does not exist to challenge section 503 enforcement.[263] Additionally, the courts that have affirmed the existence of a right of action to challenge agency inaction have limited their review to nondiscretionary responsibilities.[264]

Section 503's mandates of affirmative action and nondiscrimination coupled with the OFCCP's compliance review procedures help to ensure that federal contractors comply with their antidiscrimination obligations. However, with the lack of private enforcement mechanisms for section 503 and the diminished likelihood that any individual will receive compensation to redress noncompliance, there is comparatively little incentive for individuals to report violations of section 503.

D. Section 504

1. Scope

Section 504 prohibits discrimination against any "otherwise qualified individual with a disability" in programs or activities that receive federal financial assistance.[265] It is enforced independently by each federal agency with coordination by the Department of Justice.[266] In the 1978 amendments, Congress expanded this protection to all federal executive agency programs or activities and the U.S. Post Office.[267] With this expansion, the scope of section 504 protection now reaches all executive agency programs in which the government conducts activities or provides financial assistance.

---

[262] *Id.* at 1321.
[263] *See e.g.,* Women's Equity Action League v. Cavazos, 906 F.2d 742, 750–51 (D.C. Cir. 1990).
[264] *Brennan,* 608 F.2d at 1331.
[265] 29 U.S.C. §794(a).
[266] Exec. Order No. 12,250; 45 Fed. Reg. 72,995 (Nov. 2, 1980).
[267] Pub. L. No. 95-602, 92 Stat. 2955, 2982 (1978) (codified at 29 U.S.C. §795(b), (c)).

The Department of Justice has issued regulations for federal agencies implementing section 504. These regulations require each agency to follow procedures for compliance with section 504 that the agency has adopted in complying with Title VI of the Civil Rights Act of 1964.[268] Furthermore, the Department of Justice requires all federal agencies to mandate that aid recipients notify their employees and beneficiaries of their rights under section 504 and conduct self-evaluations to ensure section 504 compliance.[269] Additionally, Title VI, the provision governing enforcement of section 504, mandates that federal agencies issue regulations to effectuate nondiscrimination in those programs or activities for which it provides aid.[270]

2. *Enforcement Procedures*

If an employee of a program receiving federal aid wishes to file a complaint of a violation of section 504, he or she must do so with the agency providing the program aid.[271] The agency providing the aid must investigate all complaints and determine whether they present meritorious claims.[272] If a violation is found, the agency must then attempt to induce voluntary compliance through informal means.[273] Where the agency determines that informal efforts at compliance are unsuccessful, the agency must inform the aid recipient of its failure to comply and may impose sanctions or initiate additional compliance efforts.[274]

Agencies are given alternative formal avenues for achieving compliance once informal methods have proved fruitless. The Department of Justice explains there are two main alternatives to secure compliance: court enforcement or administrative action.[275] Judicial enforcement mechanisms suggested by

---

[268] 28 C.F.R. §41.5 (2003).
[269] *Id.*
[270] *Id.* §50.3.
[271] *Id.* §42.107(b).
[272] *Id.* §42.107(c).
[273] *Id.* §42.107(d).
[274] *Id.* §42.108.
[275] *Id.* §50.3.I.b.

the Department of Justice guidelines include, among other things, suits to obtain specific performance of assurances of nondiscrimination contained in contracts with aid recipients.[276] The administrative action contemplated by the Department of Justice guidelines involves consulting with or seeking assistance from other agencies at the federal, state, or local level, or bypassing the violating entity and providing aid directly to a local agency or to the recipients or programs for which the aid is ultimately intended.[277]

If the efforts at obtaining enforcement remain ineffectual, the agency may "suspend or terminate, or refuse to grant or continue" aid to the recipient.[278] However, before any of these actions may be taken, the recipient must be provided a hearing with express findings on the record of both the recipient's failure to comply and the inability to induce voluntary compliance.[279] Additionally, the Attorney General must approve of the decision to cut off aid and the appropriate congressional committee must be notified of the agency's intention to cut off aid 30 days prior to any funding severance.[280]

Although originally not provided in the statute, courts have found that section 504, unlike section 503, does contain an implied private right of action for individuals discriminated against in violation of its provisions.[281] Prior to the 1978 amendments, the courts looked to the four-part test developed by the Supreme Court in *Cort v. Ash*,[282] to determine if a private right of action existed under section 504. Under the *Cort* test, the following factors are relevant in considering whether a private right of action exists:

> First, is the plaintiff "one of the class for whose especial benefit the statute was enacted"... that is, does that statute create a federal right in favor of the plaintiff? Second, is there any indication of

---

[276] *Id.* §50.3.I.b.1.
[277] *Id.* §50.3.I.b.2.
[278] *Id.* §42.108(a).
[279] *Id.* §28.108(c)(1).
[280] *Id.* §42.108(c)(3), (4).
[281] *E.g.*, Lloyd v. Regional Transp. Auth., 548 F.2d 1277 (7th Cir. 1977).
[282] 422 U.S. 66 (1975).

legislative intent, explicit or implicit, either to create such a remedy or to deny one? ... Third, is it consistent with the underlying purposes of the legislative scheme to imply such a remedy for the plaintiff? ... And finally, is the cause of action one traditionally relegated to state law, in an area basically the concern of the States, so that it would be inappropriate to infer a cause of action based solely on federal law?[283]

In 1977, in *Lloyd v. Regional Transportation Authority*,[284] the U.S. Court of Appeals for the Seventh Circuit found, under *Cort*, that a private cause of action must be implied under section 504. In 1978, Congress, through the 1978 amendments, explicitly affirmed this decision by incorporating, through the addition of section 505(a)(2) of the Rehabilitation Act, Title VI of the Civil Rights Act of 1964 and its "remedies, procedures, and rights."[285] The courts, and the later amendments, provided that a person, aggrieved by an aid recipient's actions or failure to act in violation of section 504, may look to the courts to have their grievances addressed. Unlike section 501, however, the incorporation of Title VI into section 504 does not require a person aggrieved by the actions of a private entity receiving aid to exhaust all administrative remedies prior to filing suit in federal court.[286] Covered federal employees, however, must exhaust administrative remedies to seek redress for violations of section 504, as they would under section 501.[287]

---

[283] *Id.* at 78 (citations omitted).
[284] 548 F.2d 1277 (7th Cir. 1977).
[285] Consolidated Rail Corp. v. Darrone, 465 U.S. 624, 1 AD Cases 567 (1984).
[286] Freed v. Consolidated Rail Corp., 201 F.3d 188, 10 AD Cases 169 (3d Cir. 2000) (private employees are not required to exhaust administrative remedies under §504); Brennan v. King, 139 F.3d 258 (1st Cir. 1998); Tuck v. HCA Health Servs. of Tenn., Inc., 7 F.3d 465, 470–71, 2 AD Cases 1349 (6th Cir. 1993); Smith v. Barton, 914 F.2d 1330, 1338, 1 AD Cases 1689 (9th Cir. 1990), *cert. denied*, 501 U.S. 1217 (1991); Miener v. Missouri, 673 F.2d 969, 978 (8th Cir.), *cert. denied*, 459 U.S. 909 (1982); Pushkin v. Regents of the Univ. of Colo., 658 F.2d 1372, 1382, 2 AD Cases 11 (10th Cir. 1981); *Lloyd*, 548 F.2d at 1287.
[287] Federal employees suing under §504 are still required to exhaust administrative remedies. *See, e.g.*, Spence v. Straw, 54 F.3d 196, 4 AD Cases 528 (3rd Cir. 1995); Doe v. Garrett, 903 F.2d 1455, 1 AD Cases 1606 (11th Cir. 1990), *cert. denied*, 499 U.S. 904 (1991); McGuinness v. U.S. Postal Serv., 744 F.2d 1318, 1332, 1 AD Cases 624 (7th Cir. 1984); Prewitt v. U.S. Postal Serv., 662 F.2d 292, 302–04, 1 AD Cases 273 (5th Cir. 1981).

3. Remedies

Although section 504 now explicitly provides a private right of action, the precise remedies available under this private right of action remain unsettled. The courts are in agreement that injunctive and equitable forms of relief are available under section 504. However, courts were originally split over the availability of compensatory damages for section 504 plaintiffs.[288] The Supreme Court weighed in on this debate for the first time in 1983, in *Guardians Ass'n v. City Civil Service Commission*,[289] a decision issued with five separate opinions. In *Guardians*, black and Hispanic members of the New York City police department brought suit to challenge the city's hiring policies under Title VI of the Civil Rights Act of 1964. A majority of the Court found that compensatory relief was available under Title VI for intentional discrimination.[290] With the Rehabilitation Act's incorporation of the remedies of Title VI for section 504 violations, the *Guardians* holding implicitly stands for the proposition that compensatory damages are available under section 504. However, the Court's split opinion left some confusion as to the availability of compensatory damages under section 504.

The Supreme Court resolved confusion about the availability of compensatory damages in two later decisions, *Consolidated Rail Corp. v. Darrone*[291] and *Franklin v. Gwinnett County Public Schools*.[292] In *Darrone*, the Supreme Court found that back pay was an available remedy for section 504 private plaintiffs. However, the Court, in *Darrone*, also found that back pay was an equitable remedy, thereby leaving the question of compensatory relief unsettled. The Supreme Court finally settled this question in *Gwinnett* when it said that it would "presume the availability of all appropriate remedies unless Congress has

---

[288] Miener v. Missouri, 673 F.2d 969 (8th Cir.), *cert. denied*, 459 U.S. 909 (1982).
[289] 463 U.S. 582, 32 FEP Cases 250 (1983).
[290] *Id.*
[291] 465 U.S. 624, 1 AD Cases 567 (1984).
[292] 503 U.S. 60, 59 FEP Cases 213 (1992).

expressly indicated otherwise."[293] The Court found that "where legal rights have been invaded, and a federal statute provides for a general right to sue for such invasion, federal courts may use any available remedy to make good the wrong done.'"[294] Although the *Gwinnett* case dealt specifically with Title IX, courts since *Gwinnett* have found that compensatory damages are available under section 504 as established under the principles elucidated in *Gwinnett*.[295] Additionally, some federal courts have found, relying on *Gwinnett*, that, in addition to compensatory damages, punitive damages may be allowed under section 504.[296]

Where courts have found compensatory or punitive damages are available under section 504, they have concomitantly found that plaintiffs have a right to a jury trial under the Seventh Amendment of the Constitution.[297] This private right of action and the availability of damage remedies are of importance to aggrieved individuals because the administrative remedies envisioned under section 504 do not provide for "equitable relief for the affected individual" but only allow for prospective relief such as funding termination.[298]

---

[293] *Id.* at 66.
[294] *Id.* (quoting Bell v. Hood, 327 U.S. 678, 684 (1946)).
[295] *See, e.g.*, Johnson v. City of Saline, 151 F.3d 564, 8 AD Cases 629 (6th Cir. 1998); W.B. v. Matula, 67 F.3d 484, 494 (3d Cir. 1995); Rodgers v. Magnet Cove Pub. Sch., 34 F.3d 642, 645, 3 AD Cases 971 (8th Cir. 1994); Waldrop v. Southern Co. Servs., 24 F.3d 152, 157 n.5, 3 AD Cases 595 (11th Cir. 1994); Pandazides v. Virginia Bd. of Educ., 13 F.3d 823, 830, 2 AD Cases 1711 (4th Cir. 1994).
[296] *See, e.g.*, Moreno v. Consolidated Rail Corp., 63 F.3d 1404, 4 AD Cases 1364 (6th Cir. 1995), *aff'd en banc*, 99 F.3d 782, 6 AD Cases 86 (6th Cir. 1996); Hernandez v. City of Hartford, 30 F. Supp. 2d 268 (D. Conn. 1998); Kilroy v. Husson Coll., 959 F. Supp. 22, 6 AD Cases 1033 (D. Me. 1997); DeLeo v. City of Stamford, 919 F. Supp. 70, 4 AD Cases 427 (D. Conn. 1995) (compensatory and punitive damages are available for intentional violations of §504); Kedra v. Nazareth Hosp., 868 F. Supp. 733, 3 AD Cases 1550 (E.D. Pa. 1994). *Cf.* Winfrey v. City of Chi., 957 F. Supp. 1014, 7 AD Cases 1525 (N.D. Ill. 1997); Cortes v. Board of Governors, 766 F. Supp. 623, 626, 3 AD Cases 271 (N.D. Ill. 1991) (Rehabilitation Act does not allow for punitive damages).
[297] *Waldrop*, 24 F.3d 1520; *Pandazides*, 13 F.3d 823; Smith v. Barton, 914 F.2d 1330, 1 AD Cases 1689 (9th Cir. 1990), *cert. denied*, 501 U.S. 1217 (1991).
[298] Pushkin v. Regents of the Univ. of Colo., 658 F.2d 1372, 2 AD Cases 11 (10th Cir. 1981).

In addition to a private right of action to remedy its violations, section 504, through Title VI and section 505, envisions the use of injunctions. The complication arises, however, that once an agency has terminated federal aid in response to a section 504 violation, the violating institute or program would no longer fall under the mandates of section 504 and, therefore, injunctive relief would be inappropriate. However, the use of preliminary injunctions remains available, and plaintiffs may turn to the court for preliminary relief while courts or relevant agencies are determining the existence of a section 504 violation.[299]

Section 504 and Title VI provide no guidance regarding the statute of limitations applicable to civil suits under section 504. The Supreme Court explained in *Wilson v. Garcia*[300] that where a federal statute lacks a limitations period, courts should look to the most analogous state statute of limitations. The Supreme Court further explained, in *Goodman v. Lukens Steel Co.*,[301] that discrimination suits most closely resemble actions for personal injury. Therefore, most state courts in analyzing the question have found that section 504 should be governed by the state's personal injury statute of limitations.[302]

The 1978 amendments expanded section 504 coverage to include federal executive agency and U.S. Postal Service programs and activities.[303] As a result, many federal executive employees are covered under both sections 501 and 504 of the Rehabilitation Act and may pursue administrative and judicial

---

[299] Chalk v. U.S. Dist. Court Cent. Dist. of Cal., 840 F.2d 701, 1 AD Cases 1210 (9th Cir. 1988).
[300] 471 U.S. 261, 266–67 (1985).
[301] 482 U.S. 656, 661, 44 FEP Cases 1 (1987).
[302] Ballard v. Rubin, 284 F.3d 957, 12 AD Cases 1646 (8th Cir. 2002); Everett v. Cobb County Sch. Dist., 138 F.3d 1407, 8 AD Cases 65 (11th Cir. 1998); Bates v. Long Island R.R., 997 F.2d 1028, 2 AD Cases 1038 (2d Cir.), *cert. denied*, 510 U.S. 992 (1993); Baker v. Board of Regents of State of Kan., 991 F.2d 628, 632 (10th Cir. 1993); Bush v. Commonwealth Edison Co., 990 F.2d 928, 2 AD Cases 679 (7th Cir. 1993); Hickey v. Irving Indep. Sch. Dist., 976 F.2d 980, 982–83 (5th Cir. 1992); Morse v. University of Vt., 973 F.2d 122, 127 (2d Cir. 1992); Hall v. Knott County Bd. of Educ., 941 F.2d 402 (6th Cir. 1991), *cert. denied*, 502 U.S. 1077 (1992); Henrickson v. Sammons, 263 Ga. 331, 434 S.E.2d 51, 2 AD Cases 1358 (1993).
[303] 29 U.S.C. §794.

remedies under either section or both sections.[304] Even though the language in section 504 appears to encompass federal employees and allow them to seek redress under both sections 501 and 504, some courts addressing the issue have held that federal employees and applicants are limited to proceeding under section 501.[305] These courts hold that section 501 provides the exclusive remedies to federal employees and applicants. Other courts do not find such a limitation and allow federal employee plaintiffs to proceed under both sections 501 and 504.[306] However, these courts have agreed that money damages may not be awarded against the United States because the United States has not abrogated its sovereign immunity against money damages under section 504.[307]

VII. Defenses to Liability

A. Type of Defenses

There are a number of possible defenses that will insulate employers from potential liability for alleged violations of the Rehabilitation Act. However, turning a blind eye to violations is never a defense for an employer. The Rehabilitation Act

---

[304]Milbert v. Koop, 830 F.2d 354, 1 AD Cases 1148 (D.C. Cir. 1987); Prewitt v. U.S. Postal Serv., 662 F.2d 292, 1 AD 273 (5th Cir. 1981).

[305]Barth v. Gelb, 2 F.3d 1180, 1183, 2 AD Cases 1180 (D.C. Cir. 1993), *cert. denied sub nom.* Barth v. Duffy, 511 U.S. 1030 (1994); Johnston v. Horne, 875 F.2d 1415, 1420–21, 49 FEP Cases 1806 (9th Cir. 1989); Johnson v. U.S. Postal Serv., 861 F.2d 1475, 1477–78, 48 FEP Cases 686 (10th Cir. 1988), *cert. denied*, 493 U.S. 811 (1989); Boyd v. U.S. Postal Serv., 752 F.2d 410, 413, 1 AD Cases 686 (9th Cir. 1985); McGuinness v. U.S. Postal Serv., 744 F.2d 1318, 1321, 35 FEP Cases 1762 (7th Cir. 1984); DiPompo v. West Point Military Acad., 708 F. Supp. 540, 1 AD Cases 1432 (S.D.N.Y. 1989), *aff'd*, 960 F.2d 326, 2 AD Cases 1514 (2d Cir. 1992). *Cf.* Cousins v. Secretary, Department of Transp., 880 F.2d 603, 1 AD Cases 1502 (1st Cir. 1989) (federal employees may sue under both §§501 and 504); Morgan v. U.S. Postal Serv., 798 F.2d 1162, 1164–65, 1 AD Cases 963 (8th Cir. 1986), *cert. denied*, 480 U.S. 948 (1987); De la Torres v. Bolger, 781 F.2d 1134, 1135–36, 1 AD Cases 852 (5th Cir. 1986); Smith v. U.S. Postal Serv., 742 F.2d 257, 259–60, 1 AD Cases 620 (6th Cir. 1984).

[306]Lane v. Pena, 518 U.S. 187, 5 AD Cases 973 (1996); Dorsey v. Department of Labor, 41 F.3d 1551, 3 AD Cases 1651 (D.C. Cir. 1994); Redd v. Rubin, 34 F. Supp. 2d 1, 8 AD Cases 1787 (D.D.C. 1998).

[307]*Lane*, 518 U.S. 187.

requires employers not only to examine possible accommodations, but, in many instances, to take affirmative steps to hire and employ qualified individuals with disabilities. This section will begin by examining defenses that employers may assert under any applicable section of the Rehabilitation Act and will then examine specific defenses unique to the individual sections of the Rehabilitation Act.

1. Employer Is Not a Covered Entity

The first defense an employer may be able to offer is that it is not, or was not at the time of the alleged violation, a covered entity under the Rehabilitation Act. This defense may be asserted in a number of circumstances. Most obviously, an employer that does not receive federal financial assistance or have a contract in excess of the jurisdictional minimum can successfully assert that it does not fall under the requirements of the Rehabilitation Act. Even if an employer is subject to the Rehabilitation Act at the time of suit, the employer may nevertheless escape liability if it did not fall under the Rehabilitation Act at the time of the alleged violation. This may be the case where contractors have a series of federal contracts or grants but, at the time of the violation, there was no contract or grant in place or there was a lapse in coverage. For example, in *Burnett v. Brock*,[308] the U.S. Court of Appeals for the Eleventh Circuit held that the defendant newspaper was not a contractor under section 503 even though the government had ordered more than $2,500 in advertising from it, because there was no purchase order in place at the time of the alleged violation.[309] The court held that an employer must be a covered entity at the time of the violation, and it was irrelevant that it was a covered entity both before and after the alleged violation.[310]

---

[308] 806 F.2d 265 (11th Cir. 1986).
[309] The jurisdictional threshold for contracts was increased from $2,500 to $10,000 in the 1992 Amendments. Pub. L. No. 102-569, §505(a)(1).
[310] 806 F.2d at 266.

2. Employee Is Not Covered by the Rehabilitation Act

a. Employee Is Not Qualified

Assuming an employer is covered by the Rehabilitation Act, the employer's next defense to examine is whether the individual employee or applicant is covered by the Rehabilitation Act. The Rehabilitation Act protects only "qualified individuals with disabilities," providing employers with a panoply of potential defenses. To begin with, an individual is not "qualified" unless he or she meets the educational and experience requirements of the job in question.[311] Additionally, an individual must be capable of performing the essential job functions with or without reasonable accommodations. Some disabilities preclude employment in certain fields or positions altogether. For example, a blind person would never be a "qualified individual with a disability" when applying for a job as a commercial driver.[312] Additionally, case law and EEOC guidance indicate that blind persons are not qualified for jobs that require reading as an essential job function, where the only possible accommodation is to have a second person perform the reading.[313] In such cases, the reader would be performing the essential function of the job and not simply assisting the disabled individual with job performance.[314] A person also is not a qualified individual with a disability if he or she is unable, despite reasonable accommodations, to perform essential job functions without endangering the health or safety of the individual or others.[315] Finally, an employer is never required to hire a disabled person over other, better qualified candidates.

Although an employer may defend a claim under the Rehabilitation Act by showing that the employee or applicant was not qualified for the job, with or without accommodations, this defense will not be available where the claimant would

---

[311] 41 C.F.R. §60-741.2 (2003).
[312] 42 Fed. Reg. 22,686 No. 5 (1977) (codified as reissued at 45 C.F.R. pt. 84, app. A (2003).
[313] 29 C.F.R. pt. 1630, app. §1630.2(o) (2003); Coleman v. Darden, 595 F.2d 533, 1 AD Cases 49 (10th Cir. 1979).
[314] *Coleman*, 595 F.2d at 540.
[315] 41 C.F.R. §60-741.2 (2003).

have been able to meet the job qualifications but for the lack of a reasonable accommodation. For example, an employer cannot claim a blind employee is not qualified based on the inability to take a written test, which necessarily precludes all blind applicants but which is not essential to the performance of the job. However, an employer may be able to defend such a test where reading or sight is an essential element of the job, for example, with a driving or proofreading job. In order to be allowed to eliminate a category of disabled employees or applicants, the employer must be able to establish that the condition precludes the employee/applicant from performing an essential job-related requirement with or without reasonable accommodations. In general, however, employers should require relevant qualifications (i.e., a driver's license) rather than attempting the dangerous prospect of presumptively excluding an entire category of disabled individuals.[316]

b. Employee Is Not Disabled

An employer also can defend an alleged Rehabilitation Act violation by arguing that the employee or applicant is not an "individual with a disability" as defined in the Rehabilitation Act. An "individual with a disability" is a person substantially limited in one or more major life activities, or has a record of, or is regarded as, having such an impairment.[317] The Rehabilitation Act specifically includes, and excludes, certain conditions and illnesses. The list of specifically excluded conditions is short and it is therefore unlikely that one of the listed conditions will be at issue in a given case. However, employers still may be successful in showing that an employee or applicant is not substantially limited in a major life activity. For example, the EEOC has clarified that temporary incapacities, such as

---

[316]This qualified individual with a disability concept is covered in more detail in section IV.E., "Qualified Individual with a Disability," above, with respect to the Rehabilitation Act, and Chapter 5, section III., "Qualified Individual with a Disability," with respect to the ADA.

[317]29 U.S.C. §705(2)(B).

broken bones, generally do not constitute a substantial impairment of a major life activity unless there are complications or the healing period is extremely protracted.[318]

Additionally, with respect to the major life activity of working, a condition that precludes an individual from a specific job generally is not sufficiently limiting to constitute a cognizable disability unless it also precludes the individual from an entire category or class of jobs.[319] Employers must remember, however, that if they do not employ an individual because of a belief that the individual is substantially limited in a major life activity, it will be no defense to liability later to assert and attempt to prove that the individual was not in fact so limited. The employer's belief at the time the employment decision was made is the critical inquiry, and the individual will likely be able to show that he or she was regarded as or had a record of a disability, either of which meets the definition of disability under the Rehabilitation Act.

3. Reasonable Accommodation Is Not Possible

Once it has been established that the employee or applicant is a qualified individual with a disability, the employer is required to provide all "reasonable accommodations." A reasonable accommodation allows the employee or applicant to perform the essential functions of the job while not imposing an undue burden on the employer or coworkers. Reasonable accommodations may involve alterations in equipment, modified work schedules, or any other accommodation that would allow the employee to adequately function in the position in question.[320] An employer may challenge a claimed Rehabilitation Act violation by establishing that there were no reasonable accommodations that could be provided or that the only accommodations available would impose an undue hardship on the employer.

---

[318] EQUAL EMPLOYMENT OPPORTUNITY COMM'N, TECHNICAL ASSISTANCE MANUAL ON THE EMPLOYMENT PROVISIONS (TITLE I) OF THE ADA §2.2(a)(iii) (1992).

[319] Murphy v. United Parcel Serv., Inc., 527 U.S. 516, 9 AD Cases 691 (1999); Sutton v. United Air Lines, 527 U.S. 471, 9 AD Cases 673 (1999).

[320] 29 C.F.R. §1630.2(o) (2003); 42 U.S.C. §12111(9).

The terms "reasonable accommodation" and "undue hardship" are so intertwined that a defense under one is likely to involve both terms. This is because what determines a reasonable accommodation depends, in large part, on whether it will impose an undue hardship on the individual employer. In determining the reasonableness of an accommodation under the Rehabilitation Act, courts and regulators are instructed to consider all relevant factors, including the cost of the accommodation, the size of the operation, and the disruption of business operations.[321] Of course, a defense of undue hardship is less likely to prevail where the cost of the accommodation is small in comparison to the overall cost of the operation. The larger the employer, the greater the barrier to an undue hardship defense. In addition to an undue hardship defense, an employer may defend the denial of an accommodation by arguing that, although it would not have been unduly burdensome, the accommodation was not reasonable. For example, an employer is not required to accommodate an employee or applicant by employing a second person to do the essential functions of the job for the disabled individual.[322]

4. Employer Lacks Knowledge of Employee's Disability

An employer's strongest defense may be that it was unaware that the employee or applicant was or is, in fact, disabled. An employer is not required to provide accommodations for a condition of which it is not aware.[323] Where a disabling condition is not obvious, an employer is under no affirmative obligation to determine whether individuals are disabled.[324] In fact, employers often are barred from making inquiries into disabilities.[325] Additionally, an employer that lacks knowledge of an employee's or applicant's disability also cannot regard that

---

[321] 29 C.F.R. §1630.2(p) (2003); 42 U.S.C. §12119(10)(B).
[322] 29 C.F.R. pt. 1630, app. §1630.2(o) (2003).
[323] *Id.* app. §1630.9 (2003).
[324] *Id.*; Woodman v. Runyon, 132 F.3d 1330, 1344, 7 AD Cases 1189 (10th Cir. 1997).
[325] 29 C.F.R. pt. 1630 app. §1630.13 (2003).

individual as disabled or substantially limited in one or more major life activities.

However, both employers and employees have obligations in addressing potential disabilities. If an employee with a known disability is having difficulty performing his job, an employer may inquire whether the employee is in need of a reasonable accommodation.[326] The employee, too, has an obligation to inform the employer about his or her disability, particularly if it is a nonobvious condition, the limitations it entails, and the need for accommodation. Failure to do so will be a defense to liability under the Rehabilitation Act.[327] This begins an interactive process in which the individual and the employer work together to establish reasonable accommodations that allow the individual to perform the essential functions of the job while not imposing an undue burden on the employer.[328]

5. Procedural Defenses

Finally, employers may have certain procedural defenses available to them when faced with a potential Rehabilitation Act violation. All sections of the Rehabilitation Act have timeliness requirements and applicable statutes of limitations for filing claims, either administrative or judicial. Additionally, section 504 requires an individual to exhaust administrative remedies before bringing a private right of action. These procedural defenses are discussed in more detail below with respect to the specific sections of the Rehabilitation Act.

B. Section 504

1. Employer Is Not a Direct Recipient of Federal Aid

An employer charged with a violation of section 504 may have defenses in addition to those discussed above. Section 504 covers recipients of federal financial aid and assistance. Direct recipients of aid are covered under section 504, whereas

---

[326] *Id.* app. §1630.9.
[327] *Id.*
[328] *Id.*

the ultimate beneficiaries of the aid are not.[329] However, an entity is not necessarily covered under the Rehabilitation Act simply because it is benefited in some indirect way by federal aid. Although indirect recipients of federal aid may be subject to section 504 requirements and liability for violations, it is unclear how indirect an aid recipient may be and still fall within section 504. For example, in *Grove City College v. Bell*,[330] the Supreme Court found that a college was subject to section 504 where its students used federal grants to pay tuition. The college was an actual recipient of the funding and thus was covered by the Rehabilitation Act.[331] However, in *Department of Transportation v. Paralyzed Veterans of America*,[332] the Supreme Court held that airlines, which benefited from federal funds provided to airport operators for construction projects, were not covered by section 504 because the airlines were not recipients of the aid. Although the airlines were clearly beneficiaries under the grant to the airports, they were not the intended recipients and, therefore, were not subject to the Rehabilitation Act.[333]

2. Entire Employing Entity Is Not Covered

Where federal financial aid is targeted for a specific purpose or sector, an entity receiving federal financial assistance may be able to argue that, although certain of its programs receive federal financial assistance and would be covered under section 504, it is not covered as a whole. Section 504 of the Rehabilitation Act of 1973 was amended by the Civil Rights Restoration Act of 1987[334] to include a definition of "program or activity" that, in general, encompassed a systemwide, instead of a program-specific, coverage approach.[335] The amendment places the onus on the entity to show that one of its programs

---

[329] 45 C.F.R. §84.3(f) (2003).
[330] 465 U.S. 555 (1984).
[331] *Id.* at 564–70.
[332] 477 U.S. 597 (1986).
[333] *Id.*
[334] 20 U.S.C. §1687.
[335] 41 C.F.R. §60-741.4(b)(3).

or subunits receiving aid is separate and distinct from the operation-as-a-whole.[336] Unless the distinction can be proved, it is presumed that the aid is given to the entity as a whole, thereby subjecting the entire operation to section 504 requirements and liabilities.[337]

For private business, section 504 defines a "program or activity" as

> all of the operations of—
> (A) an entire corporation, partnership, or other private organization, or an entire sole proprietorship—
> (i) if assistance is extended to such corporation, partnership, private organization, or sole proprietorship as a whole; or
> (ii) which is principally engaged in the business of providing education, health care, housing, social services, or parks and recreation; or
> (B) the entire plant or other comparable, geographically separate facility to which Federal financial assistance is extended, in the case of any other corporation, partnership, private organization, or sole proprietorship. . .
> any part of which is extended Federal financial assistance.[338]

This definition, and the accompanying Senate Report,[339] clarify that when an entity receives general aid or assistance, the entire entity will be covered under section 504, even where the aid is actually used in only one specific program. However, where federal aid has a limited purpose or designated use, such as job training for high-tech jobs, the coverage will extend only to the programs assisted.[340] This is true "even if it is used at several facilities and the corporation has the discretion to determine which of its facilities participate in the program."[341] Furthermore, if the aid is provided only to a specific facility within a larger entity, only that facility will fall under section 504

---

[336] *Id.*
[337] 29 U.S.C. §§794(b)(3)(A), (B).
[338] Pub. L. No. 100-259, 102 Stat. 28.
[339] S. Rep. No. 100-64, at 17 (1988), *reprinted in* 1988 U.S.C.C.A.N. 3, 19.
[340] *Id.* at 19–20.
[341] *Id.* at 19.

requirements.[342] However, part (A)(ii) of the definition clarifies that where an operation is principally engaged in education, health care, housing, social services, or parks and recreation, the entity as a whole will be subject to section 504 obligations if any part of the entity receives federal assistance.[343] It does not matter whether the entity has completely separate facilities or whether the operation is primarily a for-profit business, any receipt of federal aid will subject the entire operation to section 504.

Once it has been determined that a given entity is subject to section 504 requirements, the entity is left to defend the claim on the merits or on procedural grounds. As discussed above,[344] employers charged with violations may face administrative action to ensure compliance, such as conditioning present and future funding on compliance, and private suits from aggrieved parties in federal court. Plaintiffs suing nongovernmental entities are not required to exhaust administrative remedies prior to filing suit, and courts have ruled that the full panoply of Title VII remedies are available under section 504.[345] Therefore, employers covered under section 504 should take careful steps to avoid violations and subsequent liability under the Rehabilitation Act.

C. Section 503

Section 503 contractors face two types of potential section 503 action. First, an employee or applicant may file a section 503 complaint with the OFCCP. Second, federal contractors may be faced with an administrative action alleging noncompliance with section 503 affirmative action or nondiscrimination requirements as a result of an audit. Contractors faced with a potential Rehabilitation Act violation, discovered either through a complaint or an administrative audit or review, have

---

[342]*Id.*; 29 U.S.C. §794(b)(3)(B).
[343]29 U.S.C. §794(b)(3)(A)(ii).
[344]See section V.D., "Section 504," above.
[345]Franklin v. Gwinnett County Pub. Sch., 503 U.S. 60, 59 FEP Cases 213 (1992).

many chances to eliminate the violation once a complaint is made, due to the lack of a private right of action and a drawn-out administrative process. As explained above,[346] if a complaint or OFCCP action alleges a section 503 violation, the problem is first referred to the contractor's internal procedures to attempt to find a resolution satisfactory to all parties. This provides contractors with an opportunity to correct any problems and avoid any possible sanctions. If unsuccessful, the OFCCP will attempt reconciliation to correct the violation. The process will continue through hearings and appeals, providing ample opportunity for contractors to challenge the finding of a violation and remedy any existing violation. At any stage before an administrative hearing, the federal contractor may absolve itself of all liability by establishing a written "corrective action program,"[347] including the type of corrective action to be taken that is to be completed as soon as practicable.[348] Eventually, contractors can be faced with the loss of a contract and/or a ban on obtaining all future federal contracts.

In one interesting case, a federal contractor that previously defended a discrimination lawsuit initiated by the EEOC regarding the same policy and practice was able to block the enforcement efforts of the OFCCP challenging allegedly discriminatory acts. In *Exxon Corp. v. U.S. Department of Labor*,[349] the federal contracting agency attempted to challenge a policy adopted by Exxon in the aftermath of the Valdez oil spill that barred individuals with problems or a history of substance abuse from occupying designated safety-sensitive positions (which basically were those that had no on-site supervision). That proceeding was stayed for a period of years while the similar enforcement action initiated by the EEOC under the ADA advanced in the courts and was resolved, with the Fifth Circuit holding that defendants such as Exxon could attempt to defend their broad, safety-based standards as a "business

---

[346]See section V.C., "Section 503," above.
[347]41 C.F.R. §60-741.62(a).
[348]*Id.*
[349]2002 U.S. Dist. LEXIS 3540, 12 AD Cases 1665 (N.D. Texas 2002).

necessity" under the ADA.³⁵⁰ When the OFCCP attempted to move forward with its action under the Rehabilitation Act, the U.S. District Court for the Northern District of Texas held that the agency was collaterally estopped from litigating the complaint relating to the disability status and treatment of an Exxon employee who fell into the category of workers excluded from certain positions.

In addition to having ample opportunities to rectify section 503 violations, contractors may challenge a finding of section 503 coverage by arguing they are either a separate entity from the facility with the federal contract or that there was no government contract in place at the time of the alleged violation. The separate facilities exemption under section 503 is very similar to the separate facilities provisions under section 504, explained above.³⁵¹ Like the section 504 requirements, separate facilities of a private contractor are not automatically exempt from section 503 requirements. Contractors must request an exemption from the OFCCP and the facility must be "in all respects separate and distinct from activities of the [prime] contractor [or subcontractor] related to the performance of the contract or subcontract."³⁵² Additionally, the OFCCP may grant a waiver for facilities that are not completely separate, where such a waiver "will not interfere with or impede the effectuation of [§503]."³⁵³ Further, there must be a government contract in place at the time of the alleged violation. It is irrelevant that there may have been contracts in place for years prior or subsequent to the violation; the contract must have been in place at the time of the alleged violation for section 503 requirements to apply and confer OFCCP jurisdiction.³⁵⁴ OFCCP regulations also provide that federal contractors who perform all of the contract work exclusively outside of the United States are exempt from the affirmative action requirements of section

---

³⁵⁰EEOC v. Exxon Corp., 203 F.3d 871, 10 AD Cases 225 (5th Cir. 2000).
³⁵¹See section IV.B.2., "Entire Employing Entity Is Not Covered," above.
³⁵²41 C.F.R. §60-741.4(b)(3).
³⁵³*Id.*
³⁵⁴Burnett v. Brock, 806 F.2d 265 (11th Cir. 1986).

503, as long as the employees are not recruited within the United States.[355]

Although federal contractors have the more onerous responsibility of creating and following affirmative action plans,[356] they are concomitantly provided with more options and greater protection if they fall short. The absence of a private right of action, and the many procedural restrictions on administrative sanctions, allow federal contractors to correct noncompliance easily and avoid potential sanctions.

D. Section 501

Section 501 of the Rehabilitation Act requires every executive branch, agency, department, or instrumentality to develop and implement an "affirmative action program plan for the hiring, placement, and advancement of individuals with disabilities."[357] Although section 501 affords employees and applicants alleging violations of the Rehabilitation Act with a private right of action, federal executive agencies have many opportunities to redress any violations before any administrative action and before the filing of a private suit. Aggrieved employees and applicants are subject to strict deadlines throughout the complaint process and must exhaust administrative remedies prior to filing suit in federal court.[358] These strict procedural and timeliness requirements may allow federal agencies to defend a federal suit by arguing that the plaintiff did not jump through the proper procedural hoops before filing suit. Additionally, the exhaustion requirement gives agencies in violation substantial opportunities to redress the violations prior to the imposition of administrative sanctions or court action.

If a plaintiff does pursue the administrative remedies to exhaustion and then successfully files suit in federal court, a

---

[355] 41 C.F.R. §60-741.4(a)(4).
[356] 29 U.S.C. §793(a) (mandating that federal contracts "contain a provision requiring that the party contracting with the United States shall take affirmative action to employ and advance in employment qualified individuals with disabilities").
[357] *Id.* §791(b).
[358] 29 C.F.R. §§1614.101–.504 (2003).

federal court may order both legal and equitable remedies. However, there are substantial limitations on when these remedies are available, and to what extent. Back pay is limited to 2 years prior to the filing of a charge with the EEOC and is reduced by the amount of "[i]nterim earnings or amounts earnable with reasonable diligence by the person or persons discriminated against. . . ."[359] Additionally, compensatory damages are only available in cases of intentional discrimination and are limited in amount, based on the number of employees, to a maximum of $300,000.[360] Furthermore, compensatory damages are not available where the employer has made good-faith efforts to provide reasonable accommodations and "an equally effective opportunity and would not cause an undue hardship on the operation of the business."[361] Punitive damages are not available against the federal government under the Rehabilitation Act.[362] These limitations mean that damages often will be limited to actual damages, thus vastly reducing federal agency liability exposure.

---

[359] 42 U.S.C. §2000e-5(g).
[360] *Id.* §1981a(b)(3).
[361] *Id.* §1981a(a)(3).
[362] *Id.* §1981a(b)(1).

CHAPTER 3

AMERICANS WITH DISABILITIES ACT: LEGISLATIVE HISTORY

I. Preliminary Analyses and Legislative Efforts 121
   A. The Disabilities Bill's First Draft 124
   B. The Disabilities Act Reaches Congress 128
II. Senate Consideration of the ADA 131
   A. Tactical Revisions to Proposed Measure 133
   B. Other Changes 137
   C. Building Senate Support for S. 933 140
   D. Initial Senate Hearings and
      Legislative Progress 143
   E. Administration Deliberations 147
   F. Senate Obtains White House Approval 149
   G. Initial Senate Approval 152
III. House Consideration of the ADA 156
   A. Committee on Education and Labor 159
     1. Committee on Education and
       Labor Hearings 159
     2. Committee on Education and Labor Report .. 172
   B. Committee on Energy and Commerce 184
     1. Committee on Energy and
       Commerce Hearings 184
     2. Committee on Energy and
       Commerce Report 186
   C. Committee Public Works and Transportation ... 191
     1. Committee on Public Works and
       Transportation Hearings 191
     2. Committee on Public Works and
       Transportation Report 192
   D. Committee on the Judiciary 198
     1. Committee on the Judiciary and Hearings ... 198

  2. Committee on the Judiciary Report 211
E. Action on the House Floor: General Debate
 and Proposed Amendments 217
  1. Grace Period for Small Business 223
  2. Role of Written Job Descriptions in
   Assessing Essential Job Functions 226
  3. Effort to Quantify Undue Hardship 227
  4. Access to Wilderness Areas 230
  5. Food-Handling Jobs 231
  6. Additional Proposed Amendments 237
IV. House-Senate Conference and Final Passage 251

  While some observers felt that the Americans with Disabilities Act of 1990[1] (ADA) moved toward enactment with stunning speed, it resulted from years of analysis, lobbying, and debate. Nearly three decades after the Civil Rights Act of 1964[2] provided employment and social protections to individuals on account of their race, color, religion, sex, and national origin, the disabled community would finally see enacted a piece of legislation granting them similar rights.[3] The legislative route

---

  [1] 42 U.S.C. §12101 et seq.
  [2] 42 U.S.C. §2000 et seq.; Pub. L. No. 88-352, 78 Stat. 241.
  [3] The ADA guarantees equal opportunity for individuals with disabilities in employment, public accommodations, transportation, state and local government services, and telecommunications. Title I provides that:

> No covered entity shall discriminate against a qualified individual with a disability because of the disability of such individual in regard to job application procedures, the hiring, advancement, or discharge of employees, employee compensation, job training, and other terms, conditions, and privileges of employment.

42 U.S.C. §12112(a). Title II stipulates that:

> [n]o qualified individual with a disability shall, by reason of such disability, be excluded from participation in or be denied the benefits of the services, programs, or activities of a public entity, or be subjected to discrimination by any such entity.

42 U.S.C. §12132. Title III states:

> No individual shall be discriminated against on the basis of disability in the full and equal enjoyment of the goods, services, facilities, privileges, advantages, or accommodations of any place of public accommodation by any person who owns, leases (or leases to), or operates a place of public accommodation.

42 U.S.C. §12182(a).

to the final bill, however, was anything but direct. The following discussion explores some of the influential forces behind the ADA's introduction and tracks the most important legislative actions that impacted the infant bill as it took shape.

I. Preliminary Analyses and Legislative Efforts

The main congressional impetus for the ADA began with reports issued by the National Council on Disability (NCD),[4] an independent federal agency comprised of 15 members appointed by the President of the United States and confirmed by the Senate. Formed as a result of the 1984 amendments to the Rehabilitation Act of 1973,[5] the NCD is charged with, among other duties, reviewing and formulating policies and laws affecting the disabled.[6]

Additionally, the NCD receives mandates to develop reports on disability issues at Congress's behest. One report in particular, *Toward Independence* (NCD Report),[7] embodied many of the goals and aspirations that would become the ADA. This report was the result of a congressional mandate to evaluate current programs aimed at the disabled community, and

---

[4]Denominated the National Council on the Handicapped during its period of important work prior to the ADA's enactment, the NCD was established by the 95th Congress in Title IV of the Rehabilitation Act of 1973, 29 U.S.C. §780 (as amended by Public Law No. 95-602 in 1978). The NCD had been an advisory board within the Department of Education.

[5]29 U.S.C. §701 et seq.; Pub. L. No. 93-112, 87 Stat. 355 (1977).

[6]The NCD's original purpose was to review the programs of the Rehabilitation Services Administration, and evaluate and coordinate all federal programs affecting persons with disabilities.

[7]Toward Independence (National Council on Disability 1986) [hereinafter NCD Report]. This report was the result of a specific statutory mandate that the NCD

[a]ssess the extent to which [federal] programs provide incentives or disincentives to the establishment of community-based services for handicapped individuals, promote the full integration of such individuals in the community, in schools, and in the workplace, and contribute to the independence and dignity of such individuals ... [and] recommend to the President and the Congress legislative proposals for increasing incentives and eliminating disincentives in Federal programs based on the assessment made ...

Pub. L. No. 98-221, §401(a), §142(b).

make legislative proposals for increasing incentives and eliminating disincentives in federal programs.[8] One of the NCD Report's first recommendations was for Congress to enact "a comprehensive law requiring equal opportunity for individuals with disabilities, with broad coverage and setting clear, consistent, and enforceable standards prohibiting discrimination on the basis of handicap."[9] The NCD Report suggested that the statute be packaged as a single comprehensive bill entitled "The Americans with Disabilities Act of 1986."[10] Following this suggestion was a detailed list of entities to be covered by this proposed antidiscrimination law.[11] In essence, the provisions of the ADA would expand coverage of other antidiscrimination laws to reach individuals with disabilities. The NCD Report also suggested that the law provide a clear definition and standards for applying the law, and delineated specific enforcement standards, procedures, and timelines for the implementation of the bill's requirements.[12]

---

[8] Pub. L. No. 98-221, §401(a).
[9] NCD REPORT, available at <http:www.ncd/toward_ind.htm>.
[10] *Id.*
[11] The equal opportunity law for persons with disabilities should prohibit discrimination on the basis of handicap by:
- the federal government, all of its agencies and departments, and the U.S. Postal Service;
- all recipients of federal financial assistance, with coverage of all operations of the recipient and not just a particular program or activity;
- federal contractors and subcontractors and federal licensees;
- all employers engaged in an industry affecting commerce that have 15 or more employees, employment agencies, and labor unions;
- all sellers, landlords, and other providers of housing covered by Title VIII of the Civil Rights Act of 1968;
- all public accommodations covered by Title II of the Civil Rights Act of 1964;
- all persons, companies, and agencies that engage in the business of interstate transportation of persons, goods, documents, or data;
- all persons, companies, and agencies that make use of the mails or interstate communications and telecommunications services for the business of selling, arranging, or providing insurance; and
- states, counties, and local governments, pursuant to congressional authority to enact legislation abrogating the states' immunity under the Eleventh Amendment in order to enforce the Fourteenth Amendment guarantee of equal protection of the laws.

[12] NCD REPORT, *supra* note 7.

Some of the NCD Report's suggestions embodied the main controversies that would resurface during many of the disabilities bill's legislative debates. For example, the NCD stated that the law should have broad coverage, prohibiting "discrimination on the basis of handicap," without establishing any eligibility classification for the coverage of the statute.[13] The proposed law would ban discrimination in all situations in which a person would be subjected to unfair or unnecessary exclusion or disadvantage because of some mental or physical impairment, perceived impairment, or history of impairment. Additionally, the NCD Report recommended that discrimination based on disability should be defined to include: (1) intentional exclusion; (2) unintentional exclusion; (3) segregation; (4) unequal or inferior services, benefits, or activities; (5) less effective services, benefits, or activities; and (6) the use of screening criteria with a disparate impact on individuals with disabilities that do not correlate with actual ability.[14]

The NCD Report stipulated that the nondiscrimination requirements include a duty to make reasonable accommodations, defined as "providing or modifying devices, services, or facilities, or changing practices or procedures in order to allow a particular person to participate in a particular program, activity, or job."[15] This duty also entailed an obligation to remove architectural, transportation, and communication barriers.

Copies of the NCD Report were distributed to President Ronald W. Reagan, Vice President George H.W. Bush, and Speaker of the House James C. Wright (D-Tex.) on February 1, 1986. An additional 20,000 copies were distributed nationwide. The NCD Report's written and disseminated call for a national disability policy was a significant step forward in the ADA's history. Passage of such a comprehensive disability antidiscrimination policy was identified as the NCD's "top priority" in its 1986 report.

---

[13] *Id.*
[14] *Id.*
[15] *Id.*

Supporting the findings of the NCD Report were polls taken by Louis Harris and Associates: The ICD Survey of Disabled Americans: Bringing Disabled Americans into the Mainstream[16] and The ICD Survey II: Employing Disabled Americans.[17] These polls emphasized the need for a national disability law by focusing on personal accounts of individuals living with disabilities and the discrimination they faced. According to the poll, one-fourth of individuals with disabilities reported that they had experienced employment discrimination on the basis of their disabilities, and two-thirds of all Americans of working age with disabilities did not have jobs. The ICD polls keyed in on the barriers—both physical and psychological—that the disabled community faced in the workplace. The study also found that approximately 8.2 million people with disabilities who wanted to work were unable to find a job.[18] Additionally, the ICD poll found that a majority of top managers (72 percent), equal opportunity officers (76 percent), and department heads/line managers (80 percent) believed that the disabled faced job discrimination from employers and that the discrimination in the employment arena remained an inexcusable barrier to increased employment of the disabled.[19] By emphasizing the potential economic incentives to the proposed disabilities bill, the ICD polls and the NCD Report helped garner public support in favor of the bill.

A. The Disabilities Bill's First Draft

NCD Research Specialist Robert L. Burgdorf, Jr., completed a full draft of the proposed disabilities legislation by August 1987. Despite the positive political reception to the legislation, there was some initial concern that the new bill would undermine or weaken sections 503[20] and 504[21] of the Rehabilitation Act. Section 503 prohibits discrimination on

---

[16] The results of the poll were issued in March 1986.
[17] The results of this second poll were issued in 1987.
[18] *The ICD Survey of Disabled Americans: Bringing Disabled Americans into the Mainstream*, at 47–50.
[19] *The ICD Survey II: Employing Disabled Americans*, at 23.
[20] 29 U.S.C. §793.
[21] 29 U.S.C. §794.

the basis of disability in employment institutions that receive federal funding, including federal government contractors and subcontractors with contracts of more than $10,000.[22] Section 504 requires that qualified individuals with disabilities shall not be excluded from, denied access to, or be subjected to discrimination under any program or activity that either receives federal financial assistance or is conducted by any executive agency or by the U.S. Postal Service.[23]

Drafting and enforcing regulations for these sections of the Rehabilitation Act had been an uphill battle. Some disability groups argued that the proposed disabilities bill should merely fill in the gaps the Rehabilitation Act left open.[24] One particular concern was that any new disability rights legislation would undermine the Rehabilitation Act's definition of protected conditions.[25] Nonetheless, it was ultimately decided that

---

[22]Section 503 reads, in pertinent part:
Any contract in excess of $10,000 entered into by any Federal department or agency for the procurement of personal property and nonpersonal services (including construction) for the United States shall contain a provision requiring that the party contracting with the United States shall take affirmative action to employ and advance in employment qualified individuals with disabilities. The provisions of the section shall apply to any subcontract in excess of $10,000 entered into by a prime contractor in carrying out any contract for the procurement of personal property and nonpersonal services (including construction) for the United States. . . .
29 U.S.C. §793(a).

[23]29 U.S.C. §794(a).

[24]During the September 27, 1988, joint hearing of the Senate Labor and Human Resources Subcommittee on the Handicapped and the House Subcommittee on Select Education, Senator Tom Harkin (D-Iowa) stated that legislation is needed to fill in the gaps left by the Rehabilitation Act, which only prohibits discrimination against the disabled by the federal government and recipients of federal aid. "To this day, nothing prevents an employer or the owner of a hotel or restaurant from excluding a person because of disability . . . the courthouse door is still closed to Americans with disabilities." Americans With Disabilities Act of 1988: Joint Hearing before the Subcommittee on the Handicapped of the Committee on Labor and Human Resources, United States Senate, and the Subcommittee on Select Education of the Committee on Education and Labor, House of Representatives, 100th Cong., Second Session, on S. 2345, Sept. 27, S. Hrg. 100-926, p. 10.

[25]The provision now states:
The term "disability" means—
(A) except as otherwise provided in subparagraph (B), a physical or mental impairment that constitutes or results in a substantial impediment to employment; or

the disabilities bill would represent a new piece of legislation, and not simply fill in the gaps sections 503 and 504 left behind.

Meanwhile, the NCD faced another statutory mandate to update its findings in the NCD Report.[26] The result of this mandate, *On the Threshold of Independence*, not only updated the prior report, but included in the new report's equal opportunity law recommendation section a draft of the proposed disabilities bill. The first complete draft of the legislation was broad in scope and was divided up into 10 sections.[27] These sections both defined and prohibited discrimination against the disabled in a variety of circumstances and settings, including employment, housing, transportation, public accommodations, federal contracting, state and local government, and recipients of federal financial assistance.[28] The 1988 Draft Bill provided definitions of key terms in the ADA, including "on the basis of handicap," "physical or mental impairment," and "reasonable accommodation."[29] The first two phrases were lifted from section 504 of the Rehabilitation Act. "Reasonable accommodation" was taken from *Accommodating the Spectrum of Individual Abilities*, a report issued by the U.S. Commission on Civil Rights.[30]

(B) for purposes of sections 701, 713, and 712 of this chapter, and subchapters II [29 U.S.C.A. §790 et seq.], . . . and VII [29 U.S.C.A. §796 et seq.] of this chapter, a physical or mental impairment that substantially limits one or more major life activities.

29 U.S.C. §705(9).

[26]Pub. L. No. 99-506, §502(b), 100 Stat. 1807, mandated that the NCD, [n]ot later than January 30, 1988, and annually thereafter, the National Council on the Handicapped shall issue a report to the President and Congress on the progress that has been made in implementing the recommendations contained in the Council's January 30, 1986, report TOWARD INDEPENDENCE. The reports issued shall present, as appropriate, available data on health, housing employment, insurance, transportation, recreation, and education, and shall include appropriate information on the current status and trends in the status of individuals with disabilities.

[27](1) Short Title, (2) Findings and Purpose, (3) Definitions, (4) Scope of Discrimination Prohibited, (5) Forms of Discrimination Prohibited, (6) Discrimination in Housing, (7) Limitations on the Duties of Accommodation and Barrier Removal, (8) Regulations, (9) Enforcement, and (10) Effective Date.

[28]1988 ADA Draft Bill, §8, submitted by the NCD in *On the Threshold of Independence*.

[29]*Id.*, §3 summary.

[30]The United States Commission on Civil Rights is an independent, bipartisan, factfinding agency of the Executive Branch, first established under the Civil Rights

Although ambitious, the draft bill included some definitions that would later elicit concern. For instance, "physical or mental impairment" not only included a number of disorders or conditions affecting a number of body systems,[31] but also included "any mental or physiological disorder, such as mental retardation, organic brain syndrome, emotional or mental illness, and specific learning disabilities."[32] Including "mental impairments" would incite much debate later on in the process.[33]

Likewise a subject of debate was the definition of "reasonable accommodation," which was written to mean "providing or modifying devices, services, or facilities, or changing standards, criteria, practices or procedures for the purpose of responding to the specific functional abilities of a particular person with a physical or mental impairment in order to provide an equal opportunity to participate effectively in a particular program, activity, job, or other opportunity."[34] Failing to provide such accommodations—especially removing physical barriers[35]—was deemed discriminatory and unlawful under the draft bill.[36] Employers in particular were concerned about the expense

---

Act of 1957. On November 30, 1983, a new commission was established under the Civil Rights Act of 1983, Pub. L. No. 98-183.

[31] The term "physical or mental impairment" means:
(A) any physiological disorder or condition, cosmetic disfigurement, or anatomical loss affecting one or more of the following body systems: (i) neurological system; (ii) musculoskeletal system; (iii) the special sense organs, and respiratory organs, including speech organs; (iv) the cardiovascular system; (vi) the digestive and genitourinary systems; (vii) the hemic and lymphatic systems; (viii) the skin; and (ix) the endocrine system.
1988 ADA Draft Bill, §3(2)(B).

[32] *Id.*

[33] Many later debates focused on whether this definition provides protections for insanity, kleptomania, and homosexuality, among other conditions.

[34] 1988 ADA Draft Bill, §3(5).

[35] "Barriers.—It shall be discriminatory (A) to establish or impose; or (B) to fail or refuse to remove; any architectural, transportation, or communication barriers that prevent or limit the access or participation of persons on the basis of handicap." 1988 ADA Draft Bill, §5.

[36] "It shall be discriminatory to fail or refuse to make a reasonable accommodation to permit an individual with a physical or mental impairment, perceived impairment, or record of impairment to apply, have access to, or participate in a service, program, activity, benefit, job, or other opportunity." *Id.*

and possible liability that would result from the ADA's enforcement.[37]

B. The Disabilities Act Reaches Congress

Despite the broad scope of the ADA, Senator Lowell P. Weicker, Jr. (R-Conn.), introduced the proposed disabilities bill on the floor of the Senate on April 28, 1988.[38] Representative Tony Coelho (D-Cal.) introduced a companion bill the following day.[39] Senator Weicker would work with Senator Tom Harkin (D-Iowa), Chairman of the Subcommittee on the Handicapped in the Senate, to move the bill through committee.

The legislative proposal was designed to extend the protections afforded by Title VII of the Civil Rights Act of 1964 to individuals with disabilities, and would leave the Rehabilitation Act intact. The Equal Employment Opportunity Commission (EEOC) would be responsible for issuing, within one year, regulations for enforcing the bill. Such enforcement provisions would be analogous to those found in Title VII, and would include administrative remedies, a private right of action in federal court, monetary damages, and injunctive relief.[40]

---

[37]The U.S. Chamber of Commerce, the National Association of Machinists, and a number of business lobbyists voiced concern over the ADA's accommodation provisions.

[38]Senator Weicker introduced S. 2345—The Americans with Disabilities Act of 1988— on April 28, 1988. Twenty-six senators cosponsored the bill. This version of the ADA provides that no person shall be subjected to discrimination on the basis of handicap in: (1) employment practices and training covered by Title VII of the Civil Rights Act of 1964; (2) the sale or rental of housing covered by Title VIII of the Civil Rights Act of 1968 (Fair Housing Amendments Act, 42 U.S.C. §3601, et seq.); (3) any public accommodation covered by Title II of the Civil Rights Act of 1964 (42 U.S.C. §2000a); (4) transportation services; (5) the actions, practices, and operations of state and local governments; and (6) broadcasts, communications, or telecommunications services.

On May 9, 1989, during the next congressional session (101st Congress), Senator Harkin introduced S. 933—the revised version of the ADA that would eventually become law.

[39]Representative Coelho introduced H.R. 4498 on April 29, 1988, along with 124 cosponsors. During the 101st Congress, Representative Coelho introduced H.R. 2273, the House version of the ADA that better resembled the final version.

[40]H.R. 4498, 100th Cong. (1988); S. 2345, 100th Cong. (1988).

Many disability rights grass roots organizations began an intensive campaign to publicize and lobby for the bill.[41] Additionally, on May 2, 1988, less than a week after the ADA's introduction, Representative Major R. Owens (D-N.Y.) created the Task Force on the Rights and Empowerment of Americans with Disabilities. The purpose of the task force was to present to Congress evidence of discrimination and make policy recommendations. The task force ultimately held 63 forums to collect testimony regarding disability discrimination and collected over 5,000 documents in support of the ADA. The task force presented 11 interim reports and 37 statements from disability community leaders to Congress. Such active participation from the disabled community would continue through the legislation's passage.

The disabled community was not alone in its interest in the bill. Many members of the government also paid attention. Evan Kemp, then Commissioner of the EEOC, spoke of the ADA during a speech at the Employers Banquet of the President's Committee on Employment of the Handicapped on May 5, 1988.[42] Although the response was generally favorable, the potential economic burden of making reasonable accommodations gave many employers pause. Some suggestions to allay these fears included the possibility of government tax credits or subsidies for small businesses.[43]

Another controversial aspect of the bill was its inclusion of acquired immune deficiency syndrome (AIDS) victims in its prohibition of discrimination in employment, housing, and

---

[41] The Consortium for Citizens with Developmental Disabilities, the Association for Retarded Citizens, the Disability Rights Education and Defense Fund, the Epilepsy Foundation of America, and the National Association of Protection and Advocacy Systems are just some of the organizations instrumental in the ADA's ultimate passage.

[42] The President's Committee on Employment of the Handicapped was established pursuant to Exec. Order No. 10,994. The functions of the committee include facilitating "the development of maximum employment opportunities for the physically and mentally handicapped." *Id.* §2.

[43] "[W]e should take into consideration the burdens that are going to be placed upon small businesses. I think the tax credit approach is an appropriate remedy." 135 CONG. REC. S10,708, S10,715 (daily ed. Sept. 7, 1989) (statement of Sen. Orrin Hatch).

public accommodations. In June 1988, President Ronald W. Reagan's Commission on AIDS issued a draft report, which included a controversial call for a federal law banning discrimination against individuals suffering with AIDS and those who are human immunodeficiency virus (HIV) positive.[44] Admiral James Watkins, former chairman of the commission, testified at the September 27, 1988, joint hearing of the Senate Labor and Human Resources Subcommittee on the Handicapped and the House Subcommittee on Select Education that "without a strong federal anti-discrimination law, HIV-infected individuals would continue to face the same sort of discrimination that persons with disabilities always faced . . . it's time for federal action."[45] The controversy over the proposed bill's coverage of individuals with AIDS and those who are HIV positive would prove to be a major stumbling block in the road to the ADA's final passage.

In addition to employers, representatives of the Reagan administration also voiced concern. Acting Assistant Attorney General Thomas M. Boyd presented the position of the Reagan administration. Although in favor of disability rights legislation on the whole, the administration took issue with a number of the proposed disabilities bill's standards and broad scope. In particular, the legislation deviated from section 504 of the Rehabilitation Act in two important ways. First, it required barrier removal for both existing and new facilities.[46] Second, the draft bill stipulated that an employer could defend itself against discrimination charges for failing to make reasonable accommodations only if doing so "would fundamentally alter the essential nature, or threaten the existence of the program, activity, business, or facility in question."[47]

---

[44] The President's Commission on AIDS, Draft recommendations, Chapter 9: Legal and Ethical Issues, §1. Discrimination.

[45] S. Hrg. No. 100-926, 89 Congressional Information Service S. 54,117, at 39–58 (Testimony No. 2).

[46] 1988 ADA Draft Bill, §5.

[47] *Id.* §7(a)(1) (Limitations on the Duties of Accommodation and Barrier Removal).

The administration also took issue with the ADA's definitions of "handicap" and "reasonable accommodation," and questioned whether such accommodations were needed in settings other than employment. For example, the administration disagreed with the proposal for requiring all new transportation vehicles to be accessible[48] and all new homes to be of universal design.[49] Moreover, the administration called for a one-year delay in the ADA's enforcement. As written, the ADA would have become effective on the date of enactment.[50]

Despite these and other concerns, 26 senators and 117 representatives had endorsed the 1988 draft of the proposed disabilities bill by the close of the 100th Congress on October 22, 1988. Senate Labor and Human Resources Committee Chairman Edward M. Kennedy (D-Mass.) vowed that the ADA would be "the first order of business" when the 101st Congress convened the following year.[51]

II. Senate Consideration of the ADA

It took a little over a year for the draft disabilities bill—introduced in the Senate as S. 2345 by Senator Lowell P. Weicker, Jr. (R-Conn.), on April 28, 1988—to evolve into S. 933, the reformulated version of the bill introduced by Senator Tom Harkin (D-Iowa) on May 9, 1989. It would take even longer for S. 933 to become the Americans with Disabilities Act of 1990, the end product. Senate Bill 2345's transformation into S. 933 was a contentious process, presenting significant political, legal, and social hurdles.

The election of 1988 resulted in a setback to the progression of S. 2345 as Senator Weicker, a long-time supporter of individuals with disabilities and the Senate sponsor of the disabilities bill in 1988, lost his bid for reelection. The bill required

---

[48] *Id.* §7(c)(1).
[49] *Id.* §6(b)(3)(C).
[50] *Id.* §10 ("[t]his Act shall become effective on the date of enactment").
[51] S. Hrg. 100-926, 89 Congressional Information Service S. 54,117 (Sept. 27, 1988).

a new Senate leader, and Senator Harkin assumed the responsibility as chief sponsor of the bill. Harkin had been the chief Senate cosponsor of the original ADA bill, and had worked closely with Weicker, the NCD, and the disabled community in developing S. 2345.[52] Harkin also was the Chairman of the Labor and Human Resources' Subcommittee on the Handicapped and possessed firsthand experience with the needs of the disabled because his brother was hearing-impaired.[53]

Sponsorship of the proposed disabilities bill was a somewhat risky endeavor for the first-term Senator.[54] Harkin was advised that his leadership of the bill could jeopardize his political career.[55] However, Harkin was undaunted, and, with a vision for improving society through establishing civil rights protection for the disabled, he committed himself to move the legislation through the Senate.[56]

Senator Harkin established a strategic relationship with Senator Edward M. Kennedy (D-Mass.), who was the Chairman of the Committee on Labor and Human Resources. The bill needed to be successfully voted out of Kennedy's Committee on Labor and Human Resources as well as Harkin's Subcommittee on the Handicapped, and Kennedy's support of the bill would ease the transition from committee to the Senate floor. Moreover, Kennedy possessed decades of civil rights leadership, as well as personal experiences with disability through

---

[52] YOUNG, EQUALITY OF OPPORTUNITY: THE MAKING OF THE AMERICANS WITH DISABILITIES ACT 95 (National Council on Disability 1997).

[53] *Id.* at 96.

[54] *Id.*

[55] Senator Harkin was up for reelection in 1990, and no Democratic senator from Iowa had won a second term in the modern era. Additionally, as a relative newcomer to disability policy, Harkin would have to begin his relationship with the disability community by making compromises on provisions in the ADA in order to further the bill in the Senate. As the lead sponsor of the ADA, he would also become a target for those opposed to the bill. For more information on interview with Robert Silverstein dated Aug. 30, 1993, see *id.* at 96, 300 n.4.

[56] "I didn't get elected to get re-elected. My brother is deaf. I understand discrimination. I understand what it means and what this country can look like in thirty years. We are doing this legislation." Senator Harkin quote recounted by Silverstein in an interview dated Aug. 30, 1993. *See id.*

his son, who lost a leg to cancer, and his sister, who possessed a developmental disability.[57]

A. Tactical Revisions to Proposed Measure

With the goal of achieving the best possible civil rights coverage for individuals with disabilities, it was necessary to revise the bill in order to gain the bipartisan support necessary for the bill to become law. With this in mind, Carolyn Osolink from Kennedy's committee staff and Robert Silverstein, staff director and chief counsel for Harkin's Subcommittee on the Handicapped, reviewed S. 2345.[58] After their review, they solicited opinions of other groups such as the disability community, covered entities under the bill, both the Reagan and Bush administrations, and members of Congress and their staff, regarding their interests and reservations about the bill. From the insight provided by these groups, the bill was reshaped into an enforceable and significant bill that could withstand the gauntlet through Congress.[59]

The revised draft of the ADA bill contained substantial changes.[60] While the Findings and Purposes section included in the original bill, S. 2345, remained unchanged, S. 933 was more finely tuned and was comprised of titles that focused on the main areas of employment, public services such as mass transportation, public accommodations, and telecommunications.[61] The three main Titles—I, II, and III—covered the employment arena, public services, and public accommodations and services operated by private entities, respectively. The section covering entities that provided private housing was removed from the bill because the Fair Housing Amendments Act of 1988 already prohibited discrimination against people

---

[57] *Id.* at 97.
[58] *Id.* at 98.
[59] *Id.*
[60] S. 993, 1989 ADA Draft Bill.
[61] *Id.* S. 933 (May 9, 1989) also included Title V, which dealt with miscellaneous provisions.

with disabilities in residential housing.[62] There also was a noticeable change regarding the addition of language that built on existing legal precedent in civil rights law.[63] The structure and language of the bill was modified to build on the foundation of earlier legislation such as the Civil Rights Act of 1964, section 504 of the Rehabilitation Act, and the Fair Housing Amendments Act of 1988.[64] The text of S. 933 contained a stronger connectivity to established federal statutes compared with S. 2345, as numerous references to the Rehabilitation Act and the Civil Rights Act were inserted.[65] The final version also possessed a different tone from the original in that instead of emphasizing the discriminatory practices that would not be tolerated, the new version outlined positive, proactive steps that needed to be achieved to overcome discriminatory practices.[66]

---

[62]Discrimination in Housing section, S. 2345, 100th Cong., 2d sess. §6 (Apr. 28, 1988) (not included in S. 933).

[63]For example:

The Americans with Disabilities Act builds on earlier anti-discrimination statutes such as the Civil Rights Act of 1964, the Fair Housing Amendment [ ] Act of 1988, and most notably the Rehabilitation Act of 1973. To a large extent the Americans with Disabilities Act simply enhances the application of these earlier laws and in some cases extends to the private sector several of the safeguards against discrimination that already apply to the Federal Government.

135 CONG. REC. S4,998 (daily ed. May 9, 1989) (statement of Sen. James M. Jeffords (I-Vt.)).

[64]*Id.*

[65]"The ADA incorporates many of the standards of discrimination set out in regulations implementing section 504 of the Rehabilitation Act of 1973, including the obligation to provide reasonable accommodation unless it would result in an undue hardship on the operation of the business." S. REP. No. 101-116 pt. II, at 2 (to accompany S. 933, submitted by Senator Kennedy from the Committee on Labor and Human Resources on Aug. 2, 1989). "The ADA incorporates by reference the enforcement provisions under Title VII of the Civil Rights Act of 1964." *Id.*

[66]*Compare, e.g.,* S. 2345 §5(A) ("Forms of Discrimination Prohibited—It shall be discriminatory to . . ."); *id.* §5(D) ("A person, company, or agency may not, directly or through contractual or other arrangements, utilize criteria or methods of administration that . . ."); *id.* §5(D)(2) ("BARRIERS—It shall be discriminatory to . . ."); *id.* §6 ("DISCRIMINATION IN HOUSING (a) In General.— . . . , it shall be an act of discrimination to . . ."); *with* S. 933 §3(1) (May 9, 1989) ("The terms auxiliary aids and services shall include: (A) qualified interpreters or other effective methods of making aurally delivered materials available to individuals with disabilities."); *id.* §3(3) ("The term 'reasonable accommodations' shall include . . ."); Title III Public Services §301(2) ("such an individual or entity shall make demonstrated

In S. 2345, "disability" had been defined as "a physical or mental impairment, a perceived impairment, or a record of impairment."[67] This definition was more inclusive than the definition of "disability" found under section 504 of the Rehabilitation Act of 1973, in which "disability" is defined as a "physical or mental impairment which substantially limits one or more of a person's major life activities." Unlike the Rehabilitation Act, S. 2345's definition of a disability included anyone with a physiological disorder or condition, cosmetic disfigurement, anatomical loss, or any mental or psychological disorder.[68] Therefore, compared with the definition of a disability in section 504 of the Rehabilitation Act, coverage under S. 2345 was extremely broad.

The definition of a disability had been altered in S. 933 to strike a balance between being inclusive enough to cover diverse disabilities and limiting the universe of individuals that would be able to invoke the protection under the ADA. Thus, the definition of a disability under the ADA was revised to mirror the definition of a disability found in the Rehabilitation Act of 1973 and section 802(h) of the Fair Housing Act. One subtle change, however, was the use of the term "disability" instead of "handicap" and the term "individual with a disability" instead of "individual with handicaps." This change in terminology was an intentional shift away from language deemed "patronizing" and "overlaid with stereotypes."[69] The Senate therefore adopted the following three-prong definition of disability:

> The term "disability" means, with respect to an individual—
>
> (1) A physical or mental impairment that substantially limits one or more of the major life activities of such individual;
>
> (2) A record of such impairment; or
>
> (3) Being regarded as having such an impairment.[70]

---

good faith efforts to purchase or lease a used vehicle that is readily accessible to and usable by individuals with disabilities, including individuals who use wheelchairs").
[67] S. 2345, 1988 ADA Draft Bill, §3(1).
[68] Id. §3(2).
[69] S. REP. No. 101-116, at 21 (1989).
[70] Id. at 22.

The first prong was deemed to include (1) any physiological disorder or condition, cosmetic disfigurement, or anatomical loss affecting one or more of the following body systems: neurological; musculoskeletal; special sense organs; respiratory, including speech organs; cardiovascular, reproductive, digestive; genito-urinary; hemic and lymphatic; skin; and endocrine; or (2) any mental or psychological disorder, such as mental retardation, organic brain syndrome, emotional or mental illness, and specific learning disabilities.[71]

The second prong of the definition—having a record of such an impairment—was added in part to protect individuals who have recovered from a physical or mental impairment that previously substantially limited them in a major life activity. For example, it would be against the law to discriminate against an individual who has had a history of mental or emotional illnesses, heart disease, cancer, or who has been misclassified as having had such conditions.[72]

The third prong of the definition includes an individual who is regarded as having a covered impairment. The category includes an individual who has a physical or mental impairment that does not substantially limit major life activities, but is treated by a covered entity as having such a limitation. This prong also includes an individual who has a physical or mental impairment that substantially limits major activities only as a result of the attitudes of others toward such impairment, or who has no physical or mental impairment but is treated by a covered entity as having the impairment.[73]

The rationale for the third prong of this definition was articulated by the Supreme Court in a Rehabilitation Act case, *School Board of Nassau County v. Arline*.[74] In the *Arline* case, the Court emphasized that Congress included this third prong because it was as concerned about the effect of an impairment on others as it was about its effect on the individual. This aspect

---

[71] *Id.*
[72] *Id.* at 23.
[73] *Id.*
[74] 480 U.S. 273, 1 AD Cases 1026 (1987).

of the definition was designed to protect individuals who have impairments that do not in fact substantially limit their functioning. The Court explained that: "Such an impairment might not diminish a person's physical or mental capabilities, but could nevertheless substantially limit that person's ability to work as a result of the negative reactions of others to the impairment."[75]

This prong was designed to protect those with stigmatic conditions that are viewed as physical impairments, such as burn victims with disfiguring scars. Additionally, the third prong covers such situations involving an employer that refuses to hire an individual because of a fear of the "negative reactions" of others to the individual, or because the employer believes that the applicant had a disability that would prevent the individual from working.

This more inclusive definition of "disability" would fuel the fire of later debates in both the House and Senate.

B. Other Changes

The original draft of the ADA bill contained rigorous and rigid standards of accessibility that required immediate implementation.[76] In the revised language, timelines for compliance with the accessibility guidelines were extended and varied according to specific circumstances on a case-by-case basis.[77]

The cost and burden associated with accommodating a disability concerned entities that were covered under the ADA, and this was the most controversial issue in the redrafting

---

[75] *Id.* at 283. The Court went on to conclude that "[b]y amending the definition of 'handicapped individual' to include not only those who are actually physically impaired but also those who are regarded as impaired and who, as a result, are substantially limited in a major life activity, Congress acknowledged that society's accumulated myths and fears about disability and diseases are as handicapping as are the physical limitations that flow from actual impairment." *Id.* at 284.

[76] Discrimination in Housing section, S. 2345, 100th Cong. (1988).

[77] For example, key stations in intercity rail systems were required to make their stations accessible "as soon as practicable but in no event later than 3 years after the date of enactment of this Act, except that the time limit may be extended by the Secretary of Transportation up to 20 years for extraordinarily expensive

stage.[78] Defenses allowed under S. 2345 were limited to actions that "would fundamentally alter the essential nature or threaten the existence of, the program, activity, business or facility in question."[79] Although Robert Burgdorf wrote this provision to assure that compliance would not mean the closing of business, it became pejoratively known as the "bankruptcy provision" as it was interpreted to mean that a business would have to go to the brink of bankruptcy before it could defend discrimination charges.[80]

S. 933 revised this language so that it paralleled section 504 by using the "undue hardship" standard for determining whether employment accommodations were reasonable.[81] "Undue hardship" was defined as "an action that is unduly costly, extensive, substantive, disruptive, or that will fundamentally alter the nature of the program."[82] Whether an undue hardship existed would be determined on a case-by-case basis, and would vary depending on factors such as the size of the business, type of operations, and nature and cost of accommodation.[83]

Cost also shaped the new language requiring accessibility to public transportation in Title II of the ADA that deals with public services. S. 2345 required retrofitting of all public transportation vehicles and facilities to allow accessibility to individuals with disabilities.[84] S. 933, however, varied its demands according to whether vehicles and facilities were newly constructed or already in operation.[85] Operators of old vehicles

---

structural changes to, or replacement of, existing facilities necessary to achieve accessibility." Title III, §303(g)(3).

[78]YOUNG, *supra* note 52, at 100 n.11.
[79]1989 ADA Draft Bill, §7(a)(1).
[80]YOUNG, *supra* note 52, at 100 n.15.
[81]S. REP. No. 101-116, at 2 (1989).
[82]S. 2345, 1989 ADA Draft Bill, §202(b)(1).
[83]"The weight given to each factor in making the determination as to whether a reasonable accommodation nonetheless constitutes an 'undue hardship' will vary depending on the facts of a particular situation and turns on both the nature and cost of the accommodation in relation to the employer's resources and operations." 135 CONG. REC. S10,773 (daily ed. Sept. 7, 1989) (statement of Sen. Tom Harkin (D-Iowa)).
[84]S. 2345, §8(e)(3)(A).
[85]S. 933; 1989 ADA Draft Bill, §303(b)(1), (e).

were required to make a "good faith effort" to find accessible vehicles, and only some of the currently operating vehicles required immediate retrofitting.[86]

The potential costs involved in barrier removals shaped the Title III language regarding barrier removals in public accommodations. In what was referred to as the "flat earth" provision, the old bill required nearly every place of public accommodation to remove all barriers within five years.[87] S. 933's language omitted the concept of across-the-board retrofitting and required all new construction to be made accessible for use by disabled individuals. Changes to existing structures were to be made where accessibility was "readily achievable."[88] This section was interpreted to mean that, for existing structures, accessibility was easy to accomplish and able to be carried out without much difficulty or expense.[89] However, where structural changes were not "readily achievable," the covered entity was required to provide disabled individuals with "auxiliary aids and services" to enable the full and equal participation in the services and activities of public entities covered under Title II and of public accommodations covered under Title III.[90]

The new bill did, however, expand the scope of regulation in certain areas. Under the old bill only those public accommodations that were covered under the Civil Rights Act of 1964 regulations, such as places of lodging, eating, and entertainment, had to comply with the accessibility.[91] Under the new bill, S. 933, the definition of a public accommodation under Title III expanded coverage to include virtually every privately owned establishment that was used by the general public and that affected commerce.[92] Although this coverage deviated from the original plan to parallel the Civil Rights Act of 1964,

---

[86]*Id.*

[87]See YOUNG, *supra* note 52, at 100, for more information on the barrier removal language.

[88]1989 ADA Draft Bill §301(5)(A).

[89]*Id.*

[90]135 CONG. REC. S10,773 (daily ed. Sept. 7, 1989); 1989 ADA Draft Bill, §302(b)(2)(A)(iii).

[91]S. 2345, 100th Cong., §10773 (1988).

[92]S. 933, 1989 ADA Draft Bill, §401 (Title III, public accommodations).

the drafters considered the expanded coverage to be in line with the spirit of the ADA.[93]

The new bill also took steps to define the initial bill's prohibition of discrimination in broadcasts, communications, or telecommunications. In the revised draft, S. 933 specifically required that communication providers implement telecommunications relay services such as telecommunications display devices (TDD) for the deaf.[94]

The old version of the bill granted administrative agencies the authority to order all appropriate remedial relief and gave individuals the right to sue in district court for both injunctive relief and monetary damages, including punitive damages.[95] In S. 933, the remedies were modified so that they were tailored to each title. Only administrative remedies were available for the public accommodations and telecommunications provisions, private rights of actions were allowed for employment and public services, and punitive damages were made available for employment discrimination cases.[96]

C. Building Senate Support for S. 933

The disability community initially objected to the revised bill, because the modifications were perceived as weakening the statute.[97] However, political realists understood that the bill required the modifications if it were to survive passage. Realizing that the bill may be the best that could be achieved politically, the disability community gave their support to the revised draft.

---

[93] During the Senate hearings, witnesses testified about the need to define places of public accommodations "to include all places open to the public, not simply restaurants, hotels, and places of entertainment (which are the types of establishments covered by Title II of the Civil Rights Act of 1964) because discrimination against people with disabilities is not limited to specific categories of public accommodations." S. REP. No. 101-116 (1989).
[94] S. 933, 101st Cong., Title V, §502(a) (1989).
[95] S. 2345, 1988 ADA Draft Bill, §9(a)(2).
[96] S. 933 §§205, 305, 405.
[97] For more information, see YOUNG, *supra* note 52, at 103 n.21.

The next step was to engender support for the bill among members of Congress and procure the endorsement of newly-elected President George H.W. Bush. On the Senate side, ADA advocates desired the support of Senators Orrin G. Hatch (R-Utah) and Robert J. Dole (R-Kan.). Hatch played an influential role in policymaking because he was the ranking Republican on the Labor and Human Resources Committee. Hatch possessed a consistent and lengthy record of supporting disabled individuals, and like Senator Tom Harkin (D-Iowa) and Senator Edward M. Kennedy (D-Mass.), Hatch also knew about the difficulties of the disabled community through his personal experience with his brother, who had lost the use of his legs from polio.[98] Despite Hatch's record and personal experience, he had reservations about the bill. His areas of concern included proposing more limited remedies and the exemption of religious groups from the public accommodations provisions, and he also wanted to coordinate his position with the administration, so he declined to be the lead cosponsor of S. 933.[99]

Hatch directed his chief counsel, Mark Disler, to draft an alternative bill that would prohibit discrimination against disabled individuals. The bill Disler drafted was similar to the old bill, S. 2345, in that it was short and contained general broad principles of nondiscrimination that provided the executive agencies with the responsibility and authority to create nondiscrimination standards. This was a very different approach to eliminating discrimination compared to the specific responsibilities of covered entities contained in S. 933.

Senator Dole also possessed a consistent voting record in support of disability issues, and he was targeted by ADA supporters as a potential early cosponsor of the ADA. A vocal supporter of disability interests, on each anniversary of his World War II injury, which resulted in the paralysis of his arm, Dole spoke about disability on the Senate floor. Dole also possessed a solid voting record on disability issues and had

---

[98] *Id.* at 103.
[99] *Id.* at 104.

established the Dole Foundation in 1984, which is an organization that improves the employment prospects of individuals with disabilities. As the Senate minority leader, Dole had substantial influence over the progress of the ADA through the Senate committees and on the Senate floor. Dole, however, refrained from supporting S. 933 in its current form and considered introducing his own disability rights bill, even though he was 1 of the 14 original cosponsors of S. 2345.

Senator Harkin was prepared to introduce S. 933 in March, however, the White House was not yet ready to endorse the bill. The administration requested that Harkin delay its introduction, but, by April, the bill's supporters decided to move forward with or without President Bush.[100] Harkin scheduled the introduction of S. 933 for May 9, 1989, at which time Representative Tony Coelho (D-Cal.) would introduce the companion bill, H.R. 2273, in the House.[101] Even though the ADA lacked the endorsement of Hatch, Dole, and President George H.W. Bush, by May 9, 1989, the ADA had 33 Senate cosponsors and 84 House cosponsors.

The Senate was a strategic starting point for the ADA. In the Senate, a bill goes through only one committee with jurisdiction, and referrals to any additional committees are through requests. Kennedy was the chairman of the committee with jurisdiction, the Committee on Labor and Human Resources, and his committee had a Democratic majority. Additionally, Senator Harkin was the chairman of the subcommittee with jurisdiction. It also was advantageous that the ranking Republicans on the committee and subcommittee, Senators Hatch and David R. Durenberger (D-Minn.), respectively, were strong supporters of an enhanced federal disability discrimination policy in general. The Senate had a better working relationship with the White House than the House of Representatives, and because the administration's official support was still needed, beginning in the Senate seemed the logical choice.

---

[100] *Id.* at 105.
[101] *Id.* at 106.

S. 933 was scheduled for mark-up at the Committee on Labor and Human Resources' executive session on August 2, 1989, and for introduction on the Senate floor before the August recess. The bill then would be scheduled to go to the House with the version passed by the Senate.

D. Initial Senate Hearings and Legislative Progress

The Senate Labor and Human Resources Committee and the panel's Subcommittee on the Handicapped scheduled hearings for May 9, 10, and 16, 1989.[102] Individuals from the disability community testified and responded to questions of practical applicability, regarding how covered entities could respond to the ADA provisions. These Senate hearings would include very detailed, technical analysis of the ADA and would have testimony from those supporting as well as opposing the bill.

The Senate hearings on S. 933 began on May 9, 1989.[103] Senator Hatch in his opening statement declared his support for a civil rights bill for individuals with disabilities.[104] He also, however, stated specific concerns with the bill, namely, the extension of the public accommodations provisions of Title III of the ADA that went beyond the establishments covered under the Civil Rights Act of 1964. He also expressed his opposition to the provisions that remedied violations with monetary and punitive damages and stated that his reservations on these points of S. 933 might compel him to introduce his own bill or support a different bill, such as the one introduced by Senator Dole.

At this time, the Bush administration still had not developed a formal position on the bill and therefore did not participate in the tradition of providing the lead testimony at the hearings for a bill of this magnitude.[105] Instead, Representative

---

[102] *Id.* at 102.

[103] *Id.*

[104] *Hearings on S. 933, the Americans With Disabilities Act, Before the Sen. Subcomm. on the Handicapped*, 101st Cong. 1st Sess. (May 9, 1989) (statement of Sen. Hatch) [hereinafter S. Hrg. 101-156].

[105] YOUNG, *supra* note 52, at 108.

Coelho was selected to provide the lead statement at the Senate hearings on the measure. The selection was appropriate because Coelho was the sponsor of the ADA bill in the House and was an individual who had triumphed over disability discrimination. During his senior year in college, Coelho learned that he had epilepsy. Due to his disability, he was barred from the Catholic priesthood and his familial relationships were severely strained. Coelho persisted in pursuing his ministerial calling through public service and began a government career. He was elected to Congress in 1978, became the Chairman of the Democratic Congressional Campaign Committee in 1981, and five years later was elected by his party as the Majority Whip. As a national advocate for disability issues, Coelho also served as director of the Epilepsy Foundation of America. Emphasizing the testament his life example provided, Coelho stated at the hearing, "We can be productive, if you will give us that right, give us that opportunity. That is all we ask for, nothing more, but definitely nothing less."[106]

Coelho also addressed Senator Hatch's remarks and stressed the need for bipartisanship, urging Hatch not to introduce his own bill but to work on a common bill instead.[107] While Hatch replied that he would pledge his best efforts toward building consensus, he stated that in its present form he could not cosponsor the bill.[108] From the opening remarks it was clear that bipartisan support for the bill was not readily forthcoming and the prospect of a competing bill made matters more complicated. Bipartisan support would need to be established at the hearings if a unified front was to be presented before the bill went to the House.

Like the field hearings in 1988,[109] individuals with disabilities presented compelling testimony about their personal

---

[106]S. Hrg. 101-156, p. 7; *Hearings on S. 933, supra* note 104 (statement of Rep. Coelho).

[107]YOUNG, *supra* note 52, at n. 33; *Hearings on S. 933, supra* note 104 (statement of Rep. Coelho).

[108]S. Hrg. 101-156, at p. 6 (statement of Sen. Hatch).

[109]For a detailed list of individuals who testified at the September 27, 1988, joint hearing before the Senate Subcommittee on the Handicapped and the House Subcommittee on Select Education, regarding S. 2345, see 1 LEGISLATIVE HISTORY

experiences with disability from around the country.[110] The testimonials covered many aspects of day-to-day living such as finding a job, going to the movies, crossing the street without curb cuts, education, which became insurmountable due to discrimination, and lack of awareness of the needs of 43 million citizens.[111] Although testimony also came from those proposing changes to the bill, almost every witness pledged to support the overall concept of the ADA.[112]

The two dominant issues of concern that were raised were the cost burden and litigation potential under the ADA. Unlike other civil rights legislation, the ADA required businesses and employers to spend money on accommodations and modifications.[113] The fear of the litigation potential stemmed from terms such as "reasonable accommodation," "undue hardship," "readily achievable," "essential function," and "less effective."[114] Absent clear interpretation the courts would be the arbiter as to the meaning of these terms and the enforcement guidelines of the ADA.

Issues also were raised dealing with the public accommodations title of the ADA. The Association of Christian Schools

---

OF PUBLIC LAW 101-336, THE AMERICANS WITH DISABILITIES ACT, at 102 (Gov't Printing Office (1991)) [hereinafter LEGISLATIVE HISTORY].

[110] Justin Dart, Chair of the Task Force on the Rights and Empowerment of Americans with Disabilities, organized and collected the testimonials from across the United States.

[111] The statistic of 43 million disabled individuals in the United States was established in the ADA, §2, Findings and Purposes.

[112] YOUNG, *supra* note 52, at 111. For example, the Chamber of Commerce testified that the Chamber "shares the goal of the sponsors of this act," and pledged to "cooperate in trying to achieve a workable piece of legislation that we can fully support." *Id.* The National Federation of Independent Business endorsed, "the right of every American to have to opportunity to realize his or her full potential." *Id.*

[113] *See, e.g.*, S. 933, 101st Cong., §302(b)(2)(A)(iii) (1989) (regarding public accommodations); LEGISLATIVE HISTORY, *supra* note 109, at 160 (language specifies that discrimination includes a failure to make reasonable modifications in policies, practices, and procedures when such modifications may be necessary to afford such goods, services, facilities, privileges, advantages, and accommodations unless the entity can demonstrate that making such modifications would fundamentally alter the nature of such goods, services, facilities, privileges, advantages, and accommodations).

[114] YOUNG, *supra* note 52, at n.50; *Hearings on S. 933, supra* note 104 (statement of Lawrence Lorber).

International argued that religious organizations and religious schools should be exempt from the public accommodations provisions because the ADA would be too costly, might force the schools to hire drug and or alcohol abusers or homosexuals, and threatened the constitutional separation of church and state.[115] The small business community also argued for exempt status from the public accommodations provisions because of the associated costs and in keeping with past practice, as small business owners were exempt from other civil rights laws.[116] Defining the scope of a "public accommodation" was also at issue as ADA supporters advocated a definition that included all places open to the public and not simply restaurants, hotels, and places of entertainment, which are the types of establishments covered by Title II of the Civil Rights Act of 1964.[117] The American Bus Association also voiced in the deliberations its position against the controversial issue of mandatory lifts for intercity buses.[118]

Under pressure from the disability community, Senator Dole met with White House Counsel C. Boyden Gray, White

---

[115] *Id.* at n.51; *Hearings on S. 933, supra* note 104, at 73–74 (statement of William Ball).

[116] Senator Dole, for example, stated that Greyhound had estimated that the annual cost of ADA compliance would range from $40 to $100 million. 135 CONG. REC. S10,790 (daily ed. Sept. 7, 1989) (statement of Sen. Dole).

[117] For example,
"[I]t makes no sense to bar discrimination against people with disabilities in theaters, restaurants, or places of entertainment but not in regard to such important things as doctor's offices. It makes no sense for a law to say that people with disabilities cannot be discriminated against if they want to buy a pastrami sandwich at the local deli but that they can be discriminated against next door at the pharmacy where they need to fill a prescription. There is no sense to that distinction."
Hearings before the Committee on Labor and Human Resources and the Subcommittee on the Handicapped, supra note 104, at 100 (statement of Robert Burgdorf, Jr., National Easter Seal Society).

[118] Transportation is considered the linchpin that enables people with disabilities to be integrated into mainstream society, and accessibility and modification requirements for public transit buses were included in Title II of the ADA, which dealt with public services. The National Council on Disability declared that "accessible transportation is a critical component of a national policy that promotes the self-reliance and self-sufficiency of people with disabilities." NCD REPORT, *supra* note 7, at 33. Included in ADA §2, Senator Kennedy emphasized that the "removal of physical barriers AND access to reasonable accommodations are among the most

House Chief of Staff John Sununu, and the head of the Domestic Policy Council, Roger Porter, among others in the White House, to discuss achieving a bipartisan bill.[119] Dole also spoke with President Bush on May 9, prior to appearing before the Senate Committee on May 10 to make a statement. He asserted that he and the administration hoped to see before the year's end a "bipartisan piece of legislation passed by Congress, signed by the President, and embraced by hopefully, the business community and certainly by the disability community."[120] While Dole expressed the fear of potential litigation and promoted a gradual phase-in of small businesses under the statute, he nevertheless wanted to be a "positive force" and not an "obstructionist" to the bill, and he stated that the administration needed more time to formulate its position on the bill.

After consulting with the White House, Senator Hatch at the final hearing on May 16, 1989, said that it was "imperative that this committee hear testimony from the administration on this bill."[121] He requested that the Committee for Labor and Human Resources give the administration one more chance to support the bill, and suggested that the mark-up be delayed for five weeks and that it hold one more hearing for the week of June 19, where it could invite the administration to come forward with its support for the ADA. If at that time the administration did not come forward, Hatch pledged that he would not stand in the way of the bill. Senator Kennedy agreed to the proposal for more time, but stressed that if the administration did not come forward, the committee would move forward without its input.[122]

E. Administration Deliberations

President George H.W. Bush was committed to getting some form of disability nondiscrimination legislation passed,

---

essential elements of this measure. . . . If Rosa Parks had been disabled, she could not have boarded the bus at all." 135 CONG. REC. S4,993 (daily ed. May 9, 1989).
   [119]YOUNG, *supra* note 52, at 112.
   [120]*Id.*; *Hearings on S. 933, supra* note 104, at 87–89 (statement of Sen. Dole).
   [121]YOUNG, *supra* note 52, at 113; *Hearings on S. 933, supra* note 104, at 87, 89 (statement of Sen. Hatch).
   [122]YOUNG, *supra* note 52, at 113.

but officials within the administration had substantive reservations on several issues. At the forefront were the necessity for the individual to be qualified for any given job, that the original ADA definition of disability needed to be limited, and that there had to be a practical limit as to the covered entities' burden of providing reasonable accommodations for qualified individuals.[123]

Others, such as White House Counsel Gray and Attorney General Richard Thornburgh, advocated support for the ADA and Bush's desire to get such legislation passed. Attorney General Thornburgh represented the administration as the Department of Justice organized the various recommendations made by the executive agencies, and at the Senate Hearing on June 22, 1989, he presented the Bush administration's position on the ADA.[124] He explained that promoting and legally establishing civil rights for the disabled would help the American economy by supporting employment rather than dependence. Thornburgh also underscored the administration's support for linking the ADA to the Civil Rights Act of 1964 and the Rehabilitation Act of 1973. He did, however, express his concern that drug abusers should not be included in the definition of disability and that measures should be taken to lessen the burden on small businesses. While not directly opposed to the expansion of public accommodations that would be covered under Title III of the ADA, Thornburgh cautioned that the extension of public accommodations beyond the Civil Rights Act should be carefully analyzed.

Yet despite these perceived differences between the ADA drafters and the Bush administration, Thornburgh pledged to work toward obtaining bipartisan support for the ADA.[125] His testimony established that the Bush administration was working toward consensus on a bill that President Bush could endorse. Senators Harkin and Kennedy eagerly accepted the invitation

---

[123] *Id.* at 115 n.59.

[124] *Americans with Disabilities Act of 1989: Hearings Before the Comm. on Labor and Human Resources and the Subcomm. on the Handicapped*, 101st Cong., 1st Sess. 156 (1989) (statement of Attorney General Richard Thornburgh).

[125] *Id.*

to open negotiations with the Bush administration. Subsequently, Senators Dole and Hatch laid to rest possibilities of introducing competing bills.[126]

F. Senate Obtains White House Approval

Senator Edward M. Kennedy (D-Mass.), as the senior senator as well as the chair of the committee, led the negotiations with the White House even though he was not the ADA Senate sponsor.[127] At the first meeting, Dr. William Roper (who worked for Domestic Policy Council Chair Roger Porter) led the negotiations on behalf of the administration and worked closely with Robert Funk, who was a disability advocate from the Domestic Policy Council. Other representatives of the administration included John Wodatch from the Justice Department, who had a role in authoring section 504 of the Rehabilitation Act, and White House staff from the Department of Transportation and the Office of Management and Budget (OMB).[128]

Carolyn Osolink and Robert Silverstein were the lead staff negotiators for the Senate.[129] Other representatives of the Senate included staffers of Senators Robert J. Dole (R-Kan.), David F. Durenberger (D-Minn.), Tom Harkin (D-Iowa), Orrin G. Hatch (R-Utah), and Kennedy. Staffers from Senator John McCain's (R-Ariz.) office joined the discussions regarding Title IV of the ADA that dealt with provisions for telecommunications and were pivotal in shaping that portion of the bill. The Senate staff and the administration staff held 10 negotiation sessions between July 6 and July 18, 1989. The negotiations committees reached agreement on the majority of the issues; the outstanding key issues were left for the principals to resolve. These difficult issues included whether to include compensatory and punitive damages as remedies, whether the scope of public accommodations would go beyond the establishments covered by the Civil Rights Act, whether religious organizations

---

[126]YOUNG, *supra* note 52, at 116.
[127]Senator Harkin was the Senate sponsor.
[128]YOUNG, *supra* note 52, at 118.
[129]*Id.* at 117.

would be exempt from the public accommodations provisions, whether drug and alcohol users would be covered as disabled, and the definition of "disability."[130] Despite these major issues still left to be resolved, by July 18, 1989, 47 senators had cosponsored S. 933.[131]

On July 28, 1989, Senators Dole, Durenberger, Kennedy, Harkin, Hatch, Chief Counsel Gray, Chief of Staff Sununu, Secretary of Transportation Samuel K. Skinner, Attorney General Thornburgh, head of the Domestic Policy Council Porter, and others representing executive agencies covered by the ADA, met to continue the negotiations.[132] Not until three days after that session—when Senators Harkin and Kennedy and Attorney General Thornburgh met—were the remaining issues resolved, and the negotiations between the Senate and the White House concluded.

The breakthrough compromise that occurred at the final meeting was basically a swap concerning the scope of coverage in Title III, dealing with public accommodations, for the exclusion of compensatory and punitive damages as a remedy. The administration had argued that the ADA should only cover those establishments covered under the Civil Rights Act and that compensatory and punitive damages should be excluded. As a compromise, Harkin and Kennedy agreed to restrict remedies to those available under the Civil Rights Act in exchange for the administration's consent to apply the ADA to the broad spectrum of public accommodations.

Other major agreements were reached regarding provisions under Title I which dealt with employment, Title II regarding public transportation, and Title III regarding public accommodations. Negotiators incorporated a two-year delay in the effective date for operations with 25 or more employees with respect to the employment provisions under Title I. Additionally, stronger language was incorporated to ensure that

---

[130] *Id.* at 118.

[131] Smurr, Paralyzed Veterans of America, *ADA Update*, 43 PARAPLEGIA NEWS No. 9, at 16 (Sept. 1989).

[132] YOUNG, *supra* note 52, at 118.

employees who were currently abusing drugs and alcohol would not be a protected class.[133] It also was agreed that the Secretary of Transportation would have the authority to waive the requirement for bus lifts for fixed-route systems when lifts were unavailable.[134] For private intercity bus transportation, the agreement delayed implementation of lift requirements for at least five years and mandated a study to explore how best to make intercity buses accessible. Implementation of enforcement against public accommodations was delayed for 18 months, and religious organizations and private clubs were exempted from coverage. Also, elevators were only required in buildings with at least three stories or more than 3,000 square feet per floor.

Receiving the administration's endorsement was a major step. As Senator Kennedy stated, "with the administration support, we virtually clench [sic] the legislation this year."[135] Civil rights advocates hailed the bill being voted out of committee and marked it as a milestone of growing understanding that disability rights were civil rights.[136] The White House issued a statement, calling the Americans with Disabilities Act a "landmark legislation," and emphasized that President Bush was "committed to producing a bill that can be signed this year."[137]

---

[133] *Id.* The amendment does not require employers to make any reasonable accommodations for current illegal drug users including those addicted to illegal drugs—and does not require employers to offer such accommodations to any individual who violates any of the rules or requirements set out in the statute. This is because employers' obligations to make reasonable accommodations extend only to those who have a disability within the scope of the title. Since current illegal drug use—including addiction—does not constitute such a disability, no duty of reasonable accommodation exists with respect to any applicant or employee who currently uses illegal drugs. 135 CONG. REC. S10,777 (daily ed. Sept. 7, 1989) (statement of Sen. Harkin).

[134] YOUNG, *supra* note 52, at 119.

[135] Yost, *Accord Set on Disabled-Worker Bill; White House, Senators Endorse Anti-Discrimination Legislation*, WASH. POST, Aug. 3, 1989, at A6.

[136] "What a great day," said Pat Wright of the Disability Rights and Education Defense Fund. "This is a major victory for the disabled community." *Id.* Ralph Neas of the Leadership Conference on Civil Rights called the bill the most comprehensive civil rights measure in more than two decades. Neas also remarked that the endorsement reflected a growing understanding that disability rights are civil rights. *Id.*

[137] *Id.*

Others still remained skeptical as to the bill's practical application. Fred Krebs, manager of business and government policy for the U.S. Chamber of Commerce, stated that the term "reasonable accommodation" and the responsibilities for providing such accommodations created uncertainty for business owners across the country.[138] Susan Perry of the American Bus Association called the bill a "death sentence" for private bus systems because it would result in increased costs.

G. Initial Senate Approval

The Labor and Human Resources Committee mark-up session on August 2, 1989, was brief due to the prior detailed negotiations and the deference the committee members gave to Senators David F. Durenberger (D-Minn.), Tom Harkin (D-Iowa), Orrin G. Hatch (R-Utah), and Edward M. Kennedy (D-Mass.), who all supported the revised version of S. 933.[139] Before the end of the day the committee voted unanimously, 16 to 0, to report the ADA to the Senate floor for final consideration.[140]

Two days after the mark-up, the Senate closed for recess on August 4, 1989, but it scheduled the committee to convene again in the fall session, which opened on September 6, 1989. In order to make the ADA one of the first items of business when the Senate reconvened, the committee report needed to be filed by August 30 to give senators and their staffs sufficient time to review the issues prior to casting their votes.[141] During this break, Senators Harkin and Kennedy and their respective Republican and Democratic staff worked continuously with the administration, the disability community, and the business community to develop the committee report that provided an accurate historical record, reflecting the various negotiated agreements. A draft of the committee report was

---

[138] *Id.*
[139] *See* LEGISLATIVE HISTORY, *supra* note 109, at 119.
[140] *Id.*
[141] *Id.* at 120.

completed on August 22, and it was submitted along with the revised version of S. 933 on August 30.

By September 6, 1989, more than 60 senators had signed on as cosponsors of S. 933, and the ADA came up for a vote on September 7, just 1 day after the fall session had opened. The speed with which the Labor and Human Resources Committee had moved the ADA surprised and shocked many senators and staffers. Some senators were displeased at the momentum with which the bill was being moved and with the bill in general,[142] and the debate on the Senate floor lasted more than 14 hours prior to taking a vote.

One of the debated issues was a proposed amendment by Senator Hatch that provided a $5,000 tax credit to businesses for making accommodations and modifications as an alternative to complete exemption for small businesses from Title III's public accommodations provisions.[143] Hatch said that it was unfair to burden small businesses with the costs of implementation without placing any of the responsibility on the government. Senator Lloyd M. Bentsen (D-Tex.) argued that the Hatch amendment was a "killer amendment" because bills affecting revenue are constitutionally required to come from the House.[144] Hatch disagreed, as did the majority of the Senate, but because the Budget Act requires two-thirds majority for

---

[142]"Frankly, I am astounded that this bill has arrived on the floor in the shape we find it." 135 CONG. REC. S10,714 (daily ed. Sept. 7, 1989) (statement of Sen. Gordon J. Humphrey (R-N.H.)).

[143]Amendment No. 709's stated purpose was to "provide a refundable tax credit for the costs of small businesses complying with the public accommodations requirements." This amendment would revise Subpart C of part IV of subchapter A of chapter 1 of the Internal Revenue Code of 1986, 26 U.S.C. §35 (relating to refundable credits) to read:

Sec. 35. COSTS OF PROVIDING NONDISCRIMINATORY PUBLIC ACCOMMODATIONS TO DISABLED INDIVIDUALS.

(a) GENERAL RULE.—In the case of eligible small business, there shall be allowed as a credit against the tax imposed by this subtitle for the taxable year an amount equal to the lesser of—

(1) the eligible public accommodations access expenditure for the taxable year, or

(2) $5,000.

S. Amdt. 709 (Sept 7, 1989), Hatch Amendments Nos. 705 through 709, 101 Cong. Rec. S. 10663.

[144]135 CONG. REC. S10,714, 10,738 n.74 (statement of Sen. Bentsen).

such revenue amendments, the tax credit proposal failed because it did not get enough support in the Senate.[145]

Senator Charles E. Grassley (R-Iowa) introduced an amendment to the ADA that would make the provisions under the ADA applicable to the Senate and the House.[146] His rationale was that it was unfair for the Senate to impose a burden on the American people without sharing it. Senator Wendell H. Ford (D-Ky.) argued that giving the executive branch such administrative control over Congress would blur the balance of powers.[147] While Ford agreed with Senators Harkin and Kennedy that the ADA should apply to Congress, he thought the amendment warranted further careful consideration. Despite his objection, the Senate approved the amendment through a standing vote, with the supposition that the details of the intent would be worked out later in the House or in conference.[148]

A divisive debate centered on the definition of "disability," and Senator William J. Armstrong (R-Colo.) stated that the definition of "disability" in the ADA was too broad, because it included "mental disorders" and disorders with a "moral content" as warranting protection.[149] Armstrong questioned whether senators thought that homosexuality, bisexuality, exhibitionism, pedophilia, voyeurism, and kleptomania should be protected by the ADA.[150] Senator Jesse Helms (R-N.C.) agreed with Armstrong's views, especially with respect to homosexuality, asserting that 85 percent of individuals infected with the AIDS virus were homosexuals or drug users.[151] He feared that employers would no longer be allowed to maintain "moral standards" in their businesses with such a broad definition.[152]

---

[145] YOUNG at 121.
[146] *Id.*
[147] *Id.*
[148] *Id.*
[149] *Id.* at n.77; 135 CONG. REC. S10,714, S10,735 (Sept. 7, 1989) (statement of Sen. Armstrong).
[150] *Id.*
[151] Greene, *Bill Is Emancipation Proclamation for the Disabled*, ASSOCIATED PRESS, Sept. 8, 1989.
[152] YOUNG, *supra* note 52, at 121–22 n.78.

Senator Kennedy argued that the broad protection was necessary to prohibit discrimination against persons with HIV, as it would encourage people to reveal their illness, which is crucial to getting immediate medical care and controlling the epidemic.[153] Although Senators Harkin and Kennedy opposed further restriction of the definition of disability, it was clear that the bill would not proceed further in the Senate unless specific conditions were excluded from the bill. Under relentless pressure from conservatives, an amendment by Senator Armstrong prepared a long list of conditions that would not be considered a disability under the ADA.[154] The Armstrong amendment excluded homosexuals, bisexuals, transvestites, pedophiles, exhibitionists, voyeurs, compulsive gamblers, kleptomaniacs, transsexuals, pyromaniacs, those suffering from gender disorders, and drug users.[155] The Senate approved the amendment by a voice vote.

Once all these issues, as well as other smaller amendments, were considered and resolved, the Senate voted on the ADA, passing it by a vote of 76–8. When it passed the Senate, S. 933 was comprised of five titles: employment, public services, public accommodations and services operated by private entities, telecommunications relay services, and miscellaneous provisions. Of the senators who voted on the measure, all 44 of the Democratic senators voting supported the bill, while 32 of 40 Republican senators also voted in favor of the bill. Sixteen other senators did not vote. The bill achieved remarkably successful bipartisan support in the Senate, but a difficult time in the House of Representatives lay ahead.

---

[153]"As the chairman of the President's Commission on the HIV epidemic has pointed out, the linchpin of our ability to control the spread of this virus is protection against discrimination. If we fail to provide this protection, we will continue to drive this epidemic underground." 135 CONG. REC. S10,714, S10,768 (daily ed. Sept. 7, 1989) (statement of Sen. Kennedy).
[154]Gerstel, *Senate Passes Disability Bill*, UNITED PRESS INT'L, Sept. 8, 1989.
[155]MAYERSON, 1 AMERICANS WITH DISABILITIES ACT: LEGISLATIVE HISTORY, REGULATIONS & COMMENTARY, FINDINGS & PURPOSES §3(2), at 120 (2000).

III. House Consideration of the ADA

A substantial risk to the ADA's passage at this point was the fact that the deliberative process is more complicated on the House side. In the House of Representatives, a bill is submitted by placing a copy of it in the "hopper"—a wooden box located at the side of the dais in the House chamber.[156] The clerk then assigns the bill a number. Subsequently, the Speaker of the House, with the assistance of the Parliamentarian, directs the bill to the appropriate committee or committees. With every referral to a committee, there is a chance to kill or excessively amend a bill.

On April 29, 1988, Representative Tony Coelho (D-Cal.) introduced H.R. 4498, the first version of the Americans with Disabilities Act.[157] On that same day, the bill was referred to four committees: the Committee on Education and Labor, the Committee on Energy and Commerce, the Committee on the Judiciary, and the Committee on Public Works and Transportation. The bill already had 45 cosponsors and would eventually get 124 cosponsors. Despite this strong start, this initial legislative vehicle would be gone from the House, as would Representative Coelho, before the final enactment of the ADA.

The four committees to which the bill was referred each passed H.R. 4498 on to various subcommittees.[158] In all but one subcommittee, the bill simply was not acted upon and died. The only committee to actually hold hearings on the bill was the Subcommittee on Select Education of the Committee

---

[156] JOHNSON, HOW OUR LAWS ARE MADE, H.R. DOC. No. 108-93 (22d ed. 2000).

[157] *Bill Summary and Status for the 100th Congress,* H.R. 4498, *at* <http://www.thomas.loc.gov> (last visited May 3, 2004).

[158] *Id.* The Committee on Education and Labor referred it to the Subcommittee on Select Education and the Subcommittee on Employment Opportunities on May 25, 1988; the Committee on Energy and Commerce referred it to the Subcommittee on Telecommunications and Finance and the Subcommittee on Transportation, Tourism, and Hazardous Materials on May 9, 1988; the Committee on the Judiciary referred it to the Subcommittee on Civil and Constitutional Rights on May 5, 1988; the Committee on Public Works and Transportation referred it to the Subcommittee on Surface Transportation and the Subcommittee on Public Buildings and Grounds on May 12, 1988.

on Education and Labor.[159] The hearings consisted of various people reading statements and submitting written materials for Congress's consideration. The September 27 hearing was held jointly with the Subcommittee on the Handicapped of the Senate Committee on Labor and Human Resources.[160] Senator Lowell P. Weicker (R-Conn.) presided over the session and warned the members that

> the agenda of the Nation is going to be set in the next several weeks, not after the election is over. If both parties and their candidates can tiptoe off the stage without mentioning the Americans With Disabilities Act and its passage immediately in the next Congress, if they can do that, then there will be no Americans with Disabilities Act enacted by the next Congress.[161]

Most of the statements were simply declarations of support, as if the members knew that the bill would not be acted on until the next Congress. Indeed, Senator Tom Harkin (D-Iowa) stated flatly, "It is my expectation that this legislation will become the law of the land during the 101st Congress."[162] The September 27 and the October 24 hearings both served to gather statements and information for later discussions.

After negotiations between the Senate and the Bush administration and a complete revision of the bill, Representative Coelho reintroduced the ADA. In its new form—H.R. 2273—the bill was introduced on May 9, 1989, in the 101st session of Congress.[163] The bill was immediately referred to the same four committees, each of which set to work on a goal that seemed within reach.

---

[159] *Americans with Disabilities Act of 1988: Joint Hearing Before the Subcomm. on the Handicapped of the Committee on Labor and Human Resources and the Subcomm. on Select Education of the Comm. on Education and Labor*, 100th Cong. (1988) [hereinafter *ADA Joint Hearings 1988*]; *Oversight Hearing on H.R. 4498, Americans with Disabilities Act of 1988: Hearing Before the Subcomm. on Select Education of the Committee on Education and Labor*, 100th Cong. (1988).

[160] *ADA Joint Hearings 1988, supra* note 159.

[161] *Id.* at 2.

[162] *Id.* at 9.

[163] *Bill Summary and Status for the 101st Congress*, H.R. 2273, *at* <http://www.thomas.loc.gov> (last visited May 3, 2004).

Progress hit a snag, however, when, on July 15, 1989, Representative Coelho resigned from the House of Representatives.[164] Having been implicated in a financial scandal involving a junk bond investment and failure to disclose a $50,000 loan, he chose to resign rather than tarnish his party and his work with a protracted investigation and legal fight.[165] His departure left Representative Steny Hoyer (D-Md.) in charge of shepherding the bill through the procedural maze of House rules. Representative Hoyer was a very close friend of Representative Coelho and a savvy negotiator who would prove to be indispensable to the process of passing the ADA.[166] Despite Representative Coelho's departure, Hoyer would refer to the bill as the "Coelho bill," declaring that Representative Coelho remained the bill's principal sponsor.[167]

So, it was with a new bill and a new leader that the House of Representatives began to more fully consider the ADA. The process would take over a year[168] and involve 10 hearings, 6 subcommittees, and 4 full committees. In total, more than 160 representatives would witness and debate the bill before it ever even reached the floor.[169] The House committee process, arduous at times, produced needed changes and clarifications. The first to take up the bill was the Committee on Education and Labor. Allowing that particular body to set the conceptual terms of the ADA would prove to be a very wise move.

On May 9, 1989, the Speaker of the House referred H.R. 2273—the new House version of the ADA draft bill—to four committees: the Education and Labor Committee, the Energy

---

[164]"*It's Time for Me to Move On, for My Party to Move On*," WASH. POST, May 28, 1989, at A22.

[165]*Id.* In announcing his intention to resign, Rep. Coelho said, "I don't intend to put my party through more turmoil. I don't intend to put this institution through more turmoil." *Id.*

[166]Pianin, *House Shake-Up May Provide Opening for Hoyer to Advance*, WASH. POST, May 29, 1989, at B1.

[167]136 CONG. REC. H2423 (daily ed. May 17, 1990) (statement of Rep. Hoyer).

[168]The bill was introduced on May 9, 1989, and did not pass the House until May 22, 1990.

[169]136 CONG. REC. at H2424 (statement of Rep. Hoyer).

and Commerce Committee, the Public Works and Transportation Committee and the Committee on the Judiciary.[170] Because the bill was so important and so comprehensive, each of these committees was needed to fully examine the provisions of the ADA. However, the fact that there were four committees, which then referred the bill to six subcommittees, meant that the process in the House would take longer and subject the bill to more alterations. Each committee could potentially kill the bill or amend it beyond recognition. Thus, the process required a massive coordination effort and took nine months, as opposed to the Senate, which passed the bill in only four months.[171]

A. Committee on Education and Labor

1. *Committee on Education and Labor Hearings*

On June 9, 1989, the House Committee on Education and Labor referred the bill to two subcommittees: the Subcommittee on Select Education and the Subcommittee on Employment Opportunities.[172] The House Committee on Education and Labor heard more testimony than any other, and made numerous refinements and substantive changes in response to concerns articulated at the hearings.

The July 18, 1989, joint hearing of the Subcommittees on Select Education and Employment Opportunities heard testimony that would set the tone for the rest of the hearings before the Committee on Education and Labor.[173] Several

---

[170] *Bill Summary and Status for the 101st Congress,* H.R. 2273, at <http://www.thomas.loc.gov> (last visited May 3, 2004).
[171] *Id.*
[172] *Id.*
[173] *Joint Hearing on H.R. 2273, The Americans With Disabilities Act of 1989: Joint Hearing Before the Subcomm. on Select Education and Employment Opportunities of the Comm. on Education and Labor,* 101st Cong., 1st Session (July 18, 1989). The members of the Subcommittee on Employment Opportunities were Representatives Matthew G. Martinez (D-Cal.) (Chairman), Pat Williams (D-Mont.), Jamie B. Fuster (D-P.R.), Kweisi Mfume (D-Md.), Augustus F. Hawkins (D-Cal.) (ex officio), Steve Gunderson (R-Wis.), Paul B. Henry (R-Mich.), and Peter Smith (R-Vt.). The members of the Subcommittee on Select Education were Representatives Major R. Owens (D-N.Y.) (Chairman), Matthew G. Martinez (D-Cal.), Donald M. Payne (D-N.J.), Jim Jontz

members of Congress gave opening statements expressing their support for immediate passage of the bill. The members also heard testimony from civil rights leaders and other supporters of the disabled community. Several factors surfaced during this hearing and continued throughout the deliberative process in the House of Representatives. One theme to emerge was considering the ADA as the next logical step in the civil rights movement. Other recurrent themes included issues involving the measure's application to drug use and the use of technical assistance manuals to guide those responsible for compliance with the ADA.

Representative Ronald V. Dellums (D-Cal.), Chairman of the Congressional Black Caucus (CBC), issued a statement linking the disability movement to that of civil rights. Representative Dellums discussed the fact that, although the majority has power to act, partnerships among the oppressed could create numbers large enough to affect change.[174] He stated, "as African-Americans we have learned never to be intimidated because one is in the minority on an issue which you know to be right. This lesson we repeat for those who join us as advocates in seeking passage of these civil rights measures."[175]

When Jesse Jackson, President of the National Rainbow Coalition, spoke, he invoked images of the civil rights struggle and compared them to the struggles in the disability rights movement. During the questioning period, Representative Steve Bartlett (R-Tex.) posed a question that would be repeated throughout the committee hearings: Should an employer be forced to hire a drug or alcohol addict?[176] Jackson replied by

---

(D-Ind.), Augustus F. Hawkins (D-Cal.) (ex officio-chairman of full committee), Steve Bartlett (R-Tex.), Cass Ballenger (R-N.C.), Peter R. Smith (R-Vt.).

[174] *Id.* at 15 (statement of Rep. Dellums).

As beneficiaries of the 1964 CRA [Civil Rights Act], we understand the legacy that comes with an appreciation for the universality of the human condition and the sharing of a common destiny. While the will of the majority prevails, circumstances forge a special alliance among those who have suffered injustice.

Id.

[175] *Id.*

[176] *Id.* at 40 (statement of Rep. Bartlett). "[S]hould there be other exceptions, that is, should employers be able to deny employment to persons who are current

advising Representative Bartlett not to get caught up in extreme examples and to perhaps consider the possibility of employing addicts on a case-by-case basis.[177] He added, "some people who are really drug and alcohol abusers are not capable of working because they cannot stay awake long enough."[178] Connecting the rhetoric of the disability rights movement to the civil rights movement would later prove to be extremely important, not just in terms of public support, but also in helping disability proponents in their struggle for remedies that parallel the Civil Rights Act.

Last, the congressional panel heard from a panel of disability rights activists. Joseph Rauh from the Conference on Civil Rights spoke first. He emphasized that there should be a sense of urgency about the ADA since a unique situation was presented in which the administration and both parties in Congress all agreed on basic tenets of what should be done. He explained that "we have to go do this job this year while there is a chance," and, if that does not happen, "it is your fault and my fault too."[179] Calling for a provision that would eventually be added into the bill by the Committee, Sandra Parrino, Chairwoman of the National Council on Disability, spoke and asked that technical assistance manuals be provided.[180] For her, it was important "so that those responsible for complying with the legislation will be able to understand and receive guidance in how they are to fulfill their responsibility."[181] Having heard

---

abusers of alcohol or illegal drugs if, in fact, for other reasons, if the employer, for example, wants to maintain a drug free workplace?" *Id.*

[177] *Id.* (statement of Jesse Jackson). "Let's focus on all the possibilities out here and not get caught up, it seems to me, Mr. Bartlett, on the extremities. I think in some of those situations, it is almost case by case." *Id.*

[178] *Id.*

[179] *Id.* at 48 (statement of Joseph Rauh).

[180] *Id.* at 69 (statement of Sandra Parrino).

History shows us that technical assistance can be a powerful and effective tool for educating and enabling compliance. The technical assistance available in the mid 1970's, upon enactment of our current civil rights statute for persons with disabilities, §504 of the Rehabilitation Act, was considered especially valuable as it often provided recipients with practical solutions to difficult problems such as developing physical accessibility in older buildings and accommodating services for persons with sensory impairments.

Id.

[181] *Id.*

from members and advocates on general matters, the stage was set to begin investigating the real-world impact of the proposed legislation.

The next subcommittee meeting was held in Houston, Texas, at the Metropolitan Multiservice Center. Representative Bartlett had not fully come to support the ADA and the Democratic leadership needed his help to negotiate a workable bill. Thus, it was no coincidence that the area in which the field hearing was scheduled to take place was Representative Bartlett's district. He opened the hearing by outlining three principles that he would like to see guiding the discussion. First, he made it clear that the bill should not increase dependence of disabled people by giving more public benefits.[182] Second, he called for legislation that followed the existing laws. "We have a whole body of disability legislation on the book[s] and civil rights legislation such as the 1964 Civil Rights Act of 1964. . . . We should also, as much as possible, track Section 504 and Section 503 [of the Rehabilitation Act of 1973] that apply to recipients of Federal money."[183] Third, he asked for a bill with remedies that were straightforward and that did not encourage litigation, since the goal was to eliminate discrimination, not create financial windfalls or punishment.[184]

When Mayor Kathryn Whitmire of Houston spoke, she began by describing the Multiservice Center where the hearing was being held. She explained that it was a facility that housed 18 organizations that service the disabled, ranging from the Houston Council for the Blind to the Greater Houston Athletic Association for the Physically Disabled. She spoke about other strides Houston had made in its effort to accommodate the

---

[182] *Field Hearing on Americans With Disabilities Act: Hearing Before the Subcomm. on Select Education of the Comm. on Education and Labor*, 101st Cong. 3 (Aug. 28, 1989). "The first principle should be, it should be a principle of promoting independent living. This is not legislation, nor should it be, designed to increase public benefits." *Id.* (statement of Rep. Bartlett).

[183] *Id.* at 3–4.

[184] *Id.* "And third, the remedies for the legislation should be simple, should be easy to understand, and should be non-litigious. . . . The goal should be to end discrimination rather than to provide large amounts of lawsuits or punishment for wrongdoings." *Id.*

surrounding disabled community. For example, when the city passed an affirmative action program, disabled persons were included.[185] Additionally, in 1986, the city voted to make all new buildings accessible.[186] When asked by Representative Bartlett what other mayors thought of the ADA, she assured him that, "[I]n my role as President of the United States Conference of Mayors, I can report to you that our conference has adopted resolutions in support of civil rights legislation that would provide for opportunities for the disabled."[187]

When Nikki Van Hightower, Treasurer of Harris County, Texas, addressed the committee, she emphasized that, in her view, the bill was not just about disabled people, it was a symbol of society's collective morality.[188] She also made the point that continued discrimination against the disabled affects women much more drastically than men by citing a Census Bureau study that reported that the average disabled woman earns less than half of what the average disabled man makes. When Representative Bartlett asked her about what the law should do if there were a conflict between Section 504 and the ADA, she expressed her hope that whichever bill had the strongest provision relating to the particular situation would prevail. Representative Bartlett also asked her, "[W]ould you have us write out very specifically in the statute a definition for what reasonable accommodation is that's readily achievable, and undue hardship and the various other definitions that we have to have? Or would you rather leave that up to the administrative agencies for regulations, or for the courts to interpret?" As a

---

[185] *Id.* (statement of Kathryn Whitmire). "Within city government, when we passed the Affirmative Action Program for Equal Employment and Equal Opportunity, we included, of course, the disabled community in the provision of that ordinance." *Id.*

[186] *Id.* at 22. "We have given attention to the needs for independent living, the needs for a barrier-free environment, which I must [say] has not been an easy assignment. However, in 1986, our city did vote to amend our building codes so that newly constructed buildings in this city would be accessible to the disabled." *Id.*

[187] *Id.* at 23.

[188] *Id.* at 25 (statement of Nikki Van Hightower). "It says something about who are as a society. . . . Policies that allow for discrimination . . . endorse the idea that we will prey on others' misfortune in order to gain personal advantage or make ourselves feel superior." *Id.*

person who worked with government statutes regularly, she stated her preference for specificity.[189]

Melody Ellis, President of the Board of Education for the Houston Independent School District, spoke about the special treatment and facilities that Houston was making available to students in need. She expressed concern about the fact that the city was providing an education to disabled students who, when they graduated, found themselves unable to get jobs, find housing, or use transportation.[190] Representative Bartlett asked Ellis the same question as Van Hightower regarding the definitions of various terms in the statute. Ellis cited the city's record of compliance and challenged him to "be as specific, and if you like, you can make it as hard as you want. We are going to go an inch above whatever you say anyway."[191] He then challenged her with a hypothetical: If a person who was deaf or blind applied for a teaching job, would hiring and paying for an assistant be a reasonable accommodation? Ellis replied that it would definitely be reasonable because "we do have mandates now for the number of children that we have in classrooms to have aides for able-bodied persons. So I see no reason why we should not have aides for persons with disabilities."[192]

After the first panel, comprised of government officials who frequently worked with guidelines and mandates, the representatives then heard a panel who spoke about their perspectives as businesspeople and community leaders. First to testify was Judith Comfort, Division Manager of External Affairs for Southwestern Bell Telephone Company. She explained that at Southwestern Bell, there were many disabled employees and that it was the policy of the company to consult with each disabled person and jointly decide how to adapt the work environment. Some examples of accommodations that they

---

[189] *Id.* at 38.

[190] *Id.* (statement of Melody Ellis). "The graduate of our program faces enormous barriers to gaining full access to employment, housing, transportation, extrication, and opportunities that able-bodied person take for granted." *Id.*

[191] *Id.* at 39.

[192] *Id.* at 40.

had made were "flexible hours, adaptive devices for personal computers, Braille writers, adjustable furniture, wider doors, ramps, volume control headsets, TDDs and speaker phones."[193]

In what was one of the most informative witness statements of the day, Robert Lanier, Chairman of the Metropolitan Transit Authority of Harris County, spoke in favor of the bus-lift requirement. Noting that the city had voted for all new vehicles to be lift equipped, according to his own calculations, paratransit was cheaper. But after talking with some disabled people, he realized that they wanted to participate fully in society. "[T]hey (disabled people) resisted the notion that a group of our citizens could be separated from the rest of society and told, even if it was true, that these separated facilities are equal to what the rest of society has, and they wanted to participate."[194] When asked by Representative Bartlett if the bill should mandate lifts and paratransit service, Lanier responded in the affirmative, indicating that paratransit would still be necessary for some people with disabilities—like blind and severely mentally disabled people.[195] He answered the question of cost by saying that, "given the way the transit agencies spend their money, I do not think that this is below the cut line in terms of the priority of decisions."[196] He explained that the overall cost for paratransit would be $7 or $8 million dollars a year out of a $200 million dollar budget, so that item was unlikely to be cut.

After Lanier's testimony, Robert Mosbacher, Jr., Chairman of the Texas Department of Human Services Board, took the floor. He praised the leadership in Washington and spoke of the need for local governments to take up the effort. He pledged to make several changes to the local bureaucracy that would assist disabled persons.[197]

---

[193] *Id.* (statement of Judith Comfort).
[194] *Id.* (statement of Robert Lanier).
[195] *Id.* at 77.
[196] *Id.*
[197] *Id.* at 60–61 (statement of Robert Mosbacher).
As a next step in our commitment within the State of Texas to provide the necessary focus, inter-agency coordination, targeted services, and leverage of public and private resources in a more effective manner, I will recommend to the board of the Department of Human Services that we establish an Office

The chairman of the Board of Trustees of the Institute for Rehabilitation and Research, Howard Wolf, viewed the issue of discrimination from an economics and health angle.[198] He told the representatives that without support for independent living, many people end up in chronic hospital care and suffer from ailments that could have been prevented. Furthermore, because the person does not regain productivity, the financial losses to the government and to the person's family are unrecoverable. Later, Representative Bartlett asked questions about drug use and whether an employer should have to prove that the drug use was affecting the employee's performance in order to fire that person. When Wolf answered that a person using drugs should not be employed, Representative Major R. Owens (R-N.Y.) broke in with a hypothetical: "A young man graduated from law school, worked in the U.S. Attorney General's office in New York, and was found guilty of using cocaine. He has gone before a judge and was mandated to enter a treatment program. He is in the treatment program and it is publicly known that he is a drug user. Are you saying that this individual does not have a chance anymore in the work place?" At that point, Wolf admitted that someone one who has gone through rehabilitation should not be barred from employment.[199]

Having heard from people who were not only involved in business, but in the community as well, the subcommittee next heard from two state legislators. First, Representative Ashley Smith of the Texas state legislature asked that punitive damages be excluded from the remedy section of the bill.

---

of Disabilities within that department. Responsibilities of this office might include: planning, design, implementation, administration, coordination, and monitoring of services to persons with disabilities of all ages. In addition, I have called for the establishment of a Task Force on Disabilities to assist in the establishment of this new office and to help formulate its agenda. It is my intention that these initiatives create programmatic and financial assistance systems that address the goals of this legislation, which are independence and work force participation.

Id.

[198] Id. at 62 (statement of Howard Wolf).
[199] Id.

We would respectfully request that, in your deliberations over the ADA, that you would emphasize those aspects of the bill which would assist Texans in achieving full employment of its citizens while avoiding the burdens that might arise out of punitive damages and related expenses that small businesses in Texas cannot afford.[200]

Next, Senator Chet Brooks of the Texas legislature gave a statement that argued vehemently against exempting people with HIV.[201] Claiming that individual rights should be guaranteed regardless of how a person became disabled, he lamented the fact that the federal government recognized AIDS as a disability when making an eligibility determination for Social Security, and yet some in the federal government would deny them civil rights.[202]

At the Houston hearing, most of the witnesses were in favor of the ADA and presented compelling arguments for its success. At the next hearing, the Subcommittees on Employment Opportunities and Select Education would hear from more supporters and a few critics from the business community.

Evan Kemp, Commissioner of the EEOC and a person with a disability, testified first on September 13, 1989. He began by describing the difficulties he had experienced as a disabled person. When describing the frustration he felt at not being listened to, he pointed to the issue of paratransit. "If people would listen to what disabled people say, would look at the studies, it wouldn't be a controversy. Paratransit does not work for mainstreaming disabled people. It has never worked for getting people to a job. It is great for getting people to a doctor's appointment once a month, maybe to a shopping center, but it cannot work to mainstream people with disabilities."[203] He then recalled an incident at the White House when someone who was against the ADA said, "Who had the bright

---

[200] *Id.* at 79 (statement of Tex. Rep. Smith).
[201] *Id.* at 87 (statement of Tex. Sen. Brooks).
[202] *Id.* at 91.
[203] *Hearing on H.R. 2273, The Americans With Disabilities Act of 1989: Joint Hearing Before the Subcomms. on Employment Opportunities and Select Education of the Comm. on Education and Labor,* 101st Cong. 3 (Sept. 13, 1989) (statement of Evan Kemp).

idea of taking disabled people out of the charity pity model and put them in the civil rights model?" And that statement, according to Kemp, was precisely the reason why the ADA was necessary. Later, Representative Bartlett asked Kemp what the committee should do about the issue of preemption. Kemp claimed that he would like to see in place the Title VII approach, wherein the ADA preempts other laws unless state measures are more stringent.[204] Representative Bartlett pressed Kemp to explain why site-specific issues should not control the assessment of "undue hardship" in light of the fact that such laws as the federal "Plant Closing" statute[205] rely solely on site-specific factors. The commissioner replied that the Plant Closing statute deals with a particular site that is closing its doors, while the ADA seeks to mainstream people with disabilities. For example, if only one restaurant site out of a whole chain were made accessible, it would limit a disabled person who had earned a promotion but could not move to other locations of the company.

Kemp added two more important observations. First, he commended the fact that the answers to compliance were not specifically spelled out in the ADA, because it would make the employer see past a disabled person as a member of a group and start thinking about that person as an individual.[206] Second,

---

[204] *Id.* at 12.
  I think that the ADA is probably going to be the dominant bill in this area. I think that judges and lawyers, just like all of us, are lazy and are going to use the ADA as their model. I think in a few years that we can speak about 504 still being in existence, still being a way to go, but most people probably would be proceeding under the Americans with Disabilities Act. I think to clarify your first question, Steve, I don't think that—where it is inconsistent, why don't we follow the pattern that is done under Title VII of the Civil Rights Act? If it is inconsistent, Title VII is in control. If the states have a better system, we allow that to be the dominant law.
Id.

[205] Worker Adjustment and Retraining Notification Act (WARN), 29 U.S.C. §2101 et seq.

[206] *Hearing on H.R. 2273, supra* note 203, at 17.
  I think this is one of the revolutionary aspects of this bill. There are no really a, b, c, d, e answers that a corporation can do. I think what a corporation has to do is to start thinking of the individual and not the group, to really

he informed the representatives that "[m]ore than half of the disabled people don't need reasonable accommodations. There are people that ... had cancer 30 years ago and are discriminated because of that cancer. So we really are just talking about less than half the people."[207]

Later, Mark Donovan from the Marriott Corporation spoke about the efforts of his company to accommodate persons with disabilities.

> Marriott has assumed a leadership position in this area because it makes good business sense for Marriott.... I think in many cases, the accommodation issue is overblown and wrongly placed as a disability issue. Accommodation is not a disability issue. Accommodation is an employment issue, and, as such, should be seen as a cost of doing business, not as a cost of hiring people with disabilities.[208]

The representatives then heard from two members of the business community who had significant concerns about the bill. First to testify was Duane Rasmussen, Chief Executive Officer (CEO) of Sell Publishing Company, who spoke on behalf of the National Federation of Independent Business (NFIB).[209] He began with a complaint about Congress's general change in philosophy in which businesses were expected to pay for curing social problems.[210] He then asked a flurry of rhetorical questions:

---

   make the whole employment process meaningful to both himself and the individual that he is hiring.
Id. (statement of Evan Kemp).
   [207] *Id.* at 19.
   [208] *Id.* at 114–15 (statement of Mark Donovan).
   [209] *Id.* at 50 (statement of Duane Rasmussen).
   [210] *Id.*
   Before I get into the specifics, I would like to speak about the general change in philosophy of the U.S. House and Senate in recent years. Too many members of Congress have been introducing legislation to correct certain social problems which are to be paid for through specific costs to small businesses as opposed to being paid for by the general population through taxation methods already in place.
Id.

Now, if you will put yourselves in the place of a business person, you will quickly see how impossible H.R. 2273 is. How can a business owner make physical changes in the work place even before a specific disabled person begins work?[211]

... And even more importantly than all of the cost and compliance factors, why does the Act adopt a punitive approach in its philosophy which only encourages lawsuits, including those of a frivolous nature, instead of providing incentives to accomplish the retrofitting and hire the disabled?[212]

Later, Representative Bartlett criticized the NFIB and Rasmussen for their consistent complaints that the language of the bill is vague without ever giving an alternative idea or strategy.[213]

Paul Wharen, a project manager for a general contracting firm in Maryland was the next businessperson to speak at the hearing.[214] An official in the construction industry, his main concern was the safety of construction sites and the necessity for drug testing to maintain that safety.[215] Because so many work site accidents were caused by illegal drug and alcohol use, he cautioned the panel to "not tie employers' hands" with regard to drug testing. He articulated a desire to have a drug-free workplace, not a workplace that only tests people who pose a "direct threat."[216]

---

[211] *Id.* at 51. Later, Arlene Mayerson directing attorney, Disability Rights Education and Defense Fund, addressed this complaint with her statement: "Mr. Rasmussen asked, 'How can a business owner make physical changes to the work place even before a specific disabled person begins work?' In employment, the ADA like §504 requires the accommodation to the known physical or mental limitations of a qualified applicant or employee with a disability." *Id.* at 70 (statement of Arlene Mayerson).

[212] *Id.* at 52 (statement of Duane Rasmussen).

[213] *Id.* at 119 (statement of Rep. Bartlett).

[214] *Id.* at 61 (statement of Paul Wharen).

[215] *Id.* "Perhaps the second largest concern for construction employers is how the ADA bill will impact our ability to maintain safe work sites. As project manager, a large portion of my job focuses upon job site safety" *Id.*

[216] *Id.*
We must be certain that the ADA bill does not tie employers' hands who are taking steps to stop America's drug problem. The current language of H.R. 2273 merely states that "qualification standards" may include "requiring that the current use of alcohol or drugs by an alcoholic or drug abuser not pose a direct threat to property or the safety of others in the work place or program." ABC strongly supports the ability of employers to maintain a work place that

When Arlene Mayerson, directing attorney with the Disability Rights Education and Defense Fund, began her testimony, she immediately made her position clear when she said, "The business community has been more than reasonably accommodated. There is no more compromising to do and still maintain fundamental civil rights protection for persons with disabilities."[217]

Although only six people testified at the September 13, 1989, hearing, there was more interaction between the witnesses and the representatives. The issues they addressed—preemption, site-specific factors, drug testing, and vague terms—would all resurface in the other committees and on the House floor.

Representative James Jontz (D-Ind.) welcomed all the attendees to the field hearing of the Subcommittee on Select Education in Indianapolis, Indiana. He explained that he felt it was a good idea to gather some opinions from the Midwest before the bill reached its final stages.[218] Although 15 people testified, much of the commentary consisted of an outpouring of support and repetition of what the committee had heard before. There were, however, two new points that were brought to the forefront for consideration.

First, Chris Lee, an individual with cerebral palsy, called for not just remedies, but a serious focus on education for employers and operators of commercial facilities. To illustrate the need, he related the following:

> I was going to a meeting on home care. Mother was my chauffeur. When we got to the place there were handicap spaces as the law provides but they were all filled with what appeared to be all non-handicapped persons' cars. So we had to park in the street. [¶] There was a ramp entrance, again, according to law but the doorway was locked. Obviously the building's manager had complied

---

is drug-free, not simply monitored for those employees who pose a 'direct threat,' through illegal drug use.
Id.

[217] Id. at 70 (statement of Arlene Mayerson).

[218] Hearing on H.R. 2273, The Americans With Disabilities Act of 1989: Joint Hearing Before the Subcomms. on Employment Opportunities and Select Education of the Comm. on Education and Labor, 101st Cong. 1 (Oct. 6, 1989).

with the letter of the law, but had no understanding of the special needs of the disabled. This brings me to my recommendation. Use the time between the enactment of a law and the promulgation and the enforcement of the program to educate those affected by the laws. Use it for education in so that they become educated in the awareness and special needs of the disabled and not just comply to the letter of the law.[219]

Professor Jack Lewis, a disability rights activist, called for a narrower definition of the term "disabled."[220] He claimed that allowing so many people to fall under the umbrella of "disabled" might harm people with severe disabilities by allowing employers to believe that they are in compliance just because they hire someone with lower back pain or some other marginal problem. He worried that the ultimate result would be that marginally disabled people benefited greatly from the ADA, but that the severely disabled would still suffer from unemployment or underemployment.

After hearing such a large amount of testimony, dealing with everything from statistics to personal stories to legal theory, the committees met to consider amendments to the bill. As the committee report illustrates, the concerns, arguments, and stories were not lost on the representatives who listened and sometimes even took action based on witness testimony.

2. *Committee on Education and Labor Report*

The Committee on Education and Labor's markup session lasted for two days and resulted in the passage of only one amendment.[221] The first meeting was on November 9, 1989, and the second was on November 15, 1989. Representative

---

[219] *Id.* at 25 (statement by Chris Lee, read by his mother, Muriel Lee).
[220] *Id.* at 33 (statement of Jack Lewis).
And it says in effect that a person with a disability is a person that has a physical or mental impairment that substantially limits one or more of its major life activities, a person who has had such an impairment, a person who has been considered as having such an impairment. And the concern is, that just what does that mean?
Id.
[221] H.R. REP. No. 101-485, pt. II, at 50 (1990), *reprinted in* 1990 U.S.C.C.A.N. 303, 332.

Major R. Owens (D-N.Y.) offered the one amendment that was passed. Essentially, the members negotiated 11 main points of clarification and change to the Senate version of the bill.[222] Using S. 993 as a starting point, the agreed-upon committee changes were made. On November 9, 1989, Chairman Owens presented the new and improved document to the committee as a substitute for the original House version of the bill.[223] It was not passed until the November 15 meeting, however, because the committee considered 12 amendments to the new version. All 12 amendments were defeated, and the committee accepted the substitute bill presented by Representative Owens with a unanimous vote.[224]

Of the 12 amendments that were rejected, one would have eliminated the business necessity requirement for medical examinations and another would have provided a tax credit for small businesses for costs associated with the ADA. Still another would have limited the remedies in the public accommodation section to injunctive relief. A fourth amendment sought to postpone the effective date of the ADA's provisions regarding employment and public accommodations until after final regulations had been issued. A fifth proposal would have extended the law's coverage to Congress. An amendment was also offered that would have "limited the scope of the 'association' provision to relationships based on blood, marriage, or situations involving significant assistance." Although each of these amendments—in addition to six others—failed, several of the proposed changes would continue to be offered as improvements to H.R. 2273.

Although not technically offered as amendments, there were negotiated changes that the committee made to the bill that are noteworthy. Most of the changes were not substantive,

---

[222] *Id.* at 164–66.

[223] *Id.* at 50. "The markup was resumed on November 15, 1989, at which time Mr. Owens offered an amendment in the nature of a substitute to be considered as an original bill for the purpose of amendment." *Id.*

[224] *Id.* "Twelve amendments to this substitute were offered, all of which were defeated. The Committee voted to adopt and report H.R. 2273, as an amendment in the nature of a substitute, by a roll call vote of 35-0." *Id.*

but were meant to clarify existing provisions about which concerns had been expressed regarding ambiguities.

The committee added site-specific characteristics to the language of factors to consider when making an "undue hardship" or "readily achievable" determination. The Senate version provided that, when making a determination as to what constitutes an "undue hardship," the factors to be taken into account were: "(i) the overall size of the business of a covered entity with respect to the number of employees, number and type of facilities, and the size of the budget; (ii) the type of operation maintained by the covered entity, including the composition and structure of the workforce of such entity; and (iii) the nature and cost of the accommodation needed under this Act." The committee's new language would add "location" of the parent companies' various locations to (i).[225] Additionally, the "financial resources of its facility or facilities involved in the provision of the reasonable accommodation" would be considered under the change. Last, when looking specifically at the covered entity under (ii), the Committee added that "functions of the workforce, geographic separateness, and administrative relationship" also would be factors when making an "undue hardship" or "readily achievable" determination. Under the additional language, if one were assessing whether a type of accommodation posed an "undue hardship," one would examine the particulars and financial resources of that specific

---

[225] *Id.* at 4, §101(9)(B).

(B) Determination.—In determining whether an accommodation would impose an undue hardship on a covered entity, factors to be considered include—

(i) the overall size of the business of a covered entity with respect to the number of its employees; the number, type, and location of its facilities; the overall financial resources of the entity and the financial resources of its facility or facilities involved in the provision of the reasonable accommodation;

(ii) the type of operation or operations of the covered entity, including the composition and structure of the workforce, in terms of such factors as functions of the workforce, geographic separateness, and administrative relationship, to the extent that such factors contribute to a reasonable determination of undue hardship, and

(iii) the nature and cost of the accommodation needed under this Act.

See *id.* at 11 for similar "readily achievable" language at §301(5)(B)(i–iii).

store as well as the overall company.[226] This change came in response to members of the business community whose companies consisted of many distinct locations.[227] Since the financial resources of a location can vary considerably, the committee decided that taking local factors into account would be a fair way to make a determination of the factors constituting what is considered an "undue hardship" or what is "readily achievable."[228]

In the Senate version of the ADA, there were provisions that prohibited employers and operators of commercial facilities from entering into contracts that have a discriminatory effect. Essentially, the purpose of this provision was to make it clear that "any entity may not do through a contractual provision what it may not do directly."[229] However, there may be an occasion where the contract is nondiscriminatory but the contractor is discriminating against its own employees or customers. The language agreed to by the committee was inserted to clarify the extent of employer liability in that situation.[230] "[The contractual prohibition] does not apply to a

---

[226] *Id.* at 68.
The factors further reflect the Committee's intent that, in determining whether a reasonable accommodation would constitute an undue hardship, the financial resources of the larger covered entity, and any of those financial resources available to the local covered facility from the larger covered entity, should be looked at and may be weighed by the court as well.
Id.

[227] *Id.* "The specific factors added to section 101(9)(B) reflect concerns that were raised regarding covered entities that may operate separate, local facilities across the country." *Id.*

[228] *Id.*
The addition of these factors reflects the Committee's intent that, in determining whether a reasonable accommodation would constitute an undue hardship, courts should look at and may weigh the financial resources and operations of those local facilities that are being asked to provide an accommodation, because the financial resources of local facilities of a covered entity may vary significantly.
Id.

[229] *Id.* at 60.

[230] *Id.* at 59.
The phrase "the covered entity's" qualified applicants or employees was added to the Act in order to avoid any possible misunderstanding regarding this provision. This provision is intended to apply to a situation in which a covered entity enters into a contractual relationship with another entity, which has

situation in which a covered entity enters into a contractual relationship with another entity that is engaging in some form of discrimination against its own employees or applicants." Thus, the language was changed to state that discrimination consists of "participating in a contractual or other arrangement or relationship that has the effect of subjecting *a covered entity's qualified applicant or employee with a disability* to the discrimination prohibited by this title." Section 302(b)(1)(A)(iv) was added to make the same clarification in the public accommodation section.[231]

The committee also agreed to add two new provisions related to drug and alcohol abuse. Whereas the Senate bill already had a provision stating that users of illegal drugs were not covered by the ADA, the Committee on Education and Labor added another provision specifically exempting rehabilitated persons and allowing some safety-sensitive occupations to institute standards that would otherwise be discriminatory. First, section 104(b), following the drug user exemption in section 104(a), stated:

> Nothing in subsection (a) shall be considered to exclude as an individual with a disability an individual who (i) has successfully completed a supervised drug rehabilitation program and is no longer using illegal drugs, or has otherwise been rehabilitated successfully and is no longer using illegal drugs, or (ii) is participating in a supervised rehabilitation program and is no longer using illegal drugs, or (iii) is erroneously regarded as being an illegal drug user but is not using illegal drugs. Provided that it shall not be a violation of this Act for a covered entity to adopt or administer reasonable policies or procedures, including, but not limited to drug testing, designed to ensure that an individual defined in this paragraph is no longer using illegal drugs.[232]

---

the effect of subjecting the first entity's own employees or applicants to discrimination.
Id.

[231] *Id.* at 11. "For purposes of §302(b)(1)(A)(i)–(iii), the term 'individual or class of individuals' refers to the clients or customers of the covered public accommodation that enters into the contractual, licensing or other arrangement."

[232] *Id.* at 7.

The committee intended that this provision be made explicit because under the Rehabilitation Act and the ADA, persons were only protected because of a past or perceived disability if that problem was actually a disability. Since section 104(a) made it clear that drug use was not a disability for the purposes of the ADA, it was necessary, the committee agreed, to state that section 104(a) did not preclude a discrimination suit by a person who rehabilitated or regarded as having a drug problem.[233]

The second addition to section 104 was part (c)(5), which allowed for some employees in "sensitive positions" to be subjected to stricter regulations if the Department of Transportation, the Department of Defense, or the Nuclear Regulatory Commission had regulations that demanded more rigorous testing and selection of employees.[234] The committee reported that this provision allowed for potential employers to consider past drunk-driving convictions, off-duty drinking, and drug tests when regulations provided for such standards.[235]

Another change inserted new language into the section on alterations. The provision already mandated that, when renovating a structure for whatever reason, any changes that can be arranged to create an accessible building must be made. In the Senate version of the bill, accessibility alterations were required if the renovation was to be done "in a manner that affects or could affect the usability of the facility or part thereof." The language agreed to by the committee specifically required renovation if the "entity is undertaking an alteration that affects or could affect usability of or access to an area of the facility containing a primary function."[236] The committee defined the term "primary functions" to mean "those portions of a place of public accommodations where significant goods,

---

[233] *Id.*

[234] *Id.* at 7. "(A covered entity) may require employees in sensitive positions, as defined by the Department of Transportation regulations regarding alcohol and drug use, the Department of Defense drug-free workplace regulations, and the Nuclear Regulatory Commission regulations regarding alcohol and drug use, to comply with the standards established by such regulations." *Id.*

[235] *Id.* at 78.

[236] *Id.* at 12, §302(b)(2)(vi).

services, facilities, privileges, advantages, or accommodations are provided."[237] Thus, the committee version would set a higher standard in requiring that a primary area be affected, not just any area. Language also was added to the provision that required bathroom, telephone, and drinking fountain accessibility once it was established that a significantly major alteration was taking place. The qualifying phrase, "where such alterations to the path of travel to the bathrooms, telephones, and drinking fountains serving the altered area are not disproportionate to the overall alterations in terms of cost and scope," was added to the section.[238] The Architectural and Transportation Barriers Compliance Board would determine proportionality under the new provision and the committee agreed that the board could establish a numerical standard (*e.g.*, 30 percent of the costs of the renovation) to be used as a bright-line test of whether accessibility costs were disproportionately high.

Another clarifying amendment was the elimination of the term "potential places of employment" and the insertion of the term "commercial facilities" in section 301(2) and throughout Title III. The committee was concerned that there might be confusion between Title I and Title III.[239] For example, although new construction under the public accommodations title must be accessible, this did not include individual work stations. The committee emphasized that the two terms mean the same thing and that the definition of "commercial facilities" was to be consistent with the broad definition of "potential

---

[237] *Id.* at 112.
A mechanical room, boiler room, supply storage room, or janitorial closet is clearly not an area containing a primary function; the customer services lobby at a bank, the dining area of the cafeteria, the meeting rooms in a conference center, and the viewing galleries of a museum are areas containing a primary function.

Id.

[238] *Id.* at 12.

[239] *Id.* at 117. "The phrase 'commercial facilities' has been substituted for the phrase 'potential places of employment' of H.R. 2273 in order to eliminate any possible confusion between coverage of title III, concerning new construction, and coverage of title I, concerning employment practices." *Id.*

places of employment."[240] The committee report pointed out that, "To the extent that new facilities are built in a manner that makes them accessible to all individuals, including potential employees, there will be less of a need for individual employers to engage in reasonable accommodations for particular employees."

In the section concerning the enforcement of public accommodation accessibility, the committee added a qualifying phrase to the "about to be discriminated against" provision. The change inserted that a person must have "reasonable grounds" to believe that he or she is going to be subject to discrimination before a remedy is available under Title III.[241] The committee claimed that this language made the anticipatory discrimination section of Title III consistent with the Civil Rights Act.

In one of the few substantive changes to the bill, the committee added a provision that would allow state and local governments to have their local codes and ordinances certified by the attorney general. The certification would indicate that the statutes meet or exceed the public accommodations requirements under the ADA.[242] This certification would then

---

[240] *Id.*
The term "commercial facilities," retains the same definition as that given to "potential places of employment" in the Senate bill (S. 933). The new term therefore, is designed solely to eliminate any unnecessary confusion regarding coverage of employers; it is not intended to reduce the scope of the definition (i.e., any facility intended for non-residential use). Further, the term is not intended to be defined by dictionary or common industry definitions. Rather, "commercial facility," which is to be interpreted consistently with "potential places of employment," is defined as in S. 933, broadly to include any facility that is intended for nonresidential use and whose operations will affect commerce.
Id.

[241] *Id.* at 15, §308(a)(1). "The remedies and procedures set forth in section 204 of the Civil Rights Act of 1964 (42 U.S.C. sec. 2000a-3(a)) shall be available to any individual who is being or has reasonable grounds for believing that he or she is about to be subjected to discrimination on the basis of disability in violation of this title." *Id.*

[242] *Id.*
Upon the application of a state or local government, the Attorney General, in consultation with the Architectural and Transportation Barriers Compliance Board, may certify that a state law or building code, or similar ordinance

be used to create a rebuttable presumption of compliance if action is taken against an entity that followed the certified laws.[243] The new provision also provided that before a locale can become certified, a public hearing must be held in which disabled people and their advocates can voice their opinions on the subject of certification.[244] The committee stressed that

> this provision is intended simply to allow builders and architects to use codes and laws with which they are familiar, if those laws, in fact, meet or exceed the requirements of this Act. This provision is not intended in any way to allow entities to avoid the purposes and goals of this Act.

In another explanatory addition, section 308(b)(4) was added to the enforcement section of Title III. The new provision concerned the ability of the attorney general to ask for pecuniary damages on behalf of a victimized party.[245] Section 308(b)(2)(B) authorized that, when the attorney general takes up a pattern and practice case, the court may grant the "award [of] such other relief as the court considers appropriate, including monetary damages to persons aggrieved when requested by the Attorney General."[246] The new section added by the committee stated "for the purposes of subsection (b)(2)(B), the term 'monetary damages' and 'such other relief'

---

which establishes accessibility requirements, meets or exceeds the minimum requirements of this Act for the accessibility and usability of covered facilities under this title.
Id.

[243] *Id.*
At any enforcement proceeding under this section, any certification granted by the Attorney General shall be rebuttable evidence that such state law or ordinance does meet or exceed the minimum requirements of this Act. That is, the certification may be presented as evidence, but it can then be rebutted by the plaintiff.
Id.

[244] *Id.* "Such certification can occur only after public notice of such a request has been given and after a public hearing has been held in which individual with disabilities, and organizations representing such individuals, have been provided an opportunity to testify against such certification if they so wish." *Id.*

[245] *Id.* "Section 308(b)(4) clarifies that the term 'monetary damages' and 'other relief' in section 308(b)(2) does not include punitive damages." *Id.*

[246] *Id.* at 16, §308(b)(2)(B).

does not include punitive damages."[247] It was made clear that all other forms of compensatory damages would remain available, such as out-of-pocket expenses and remuneration for pain and suffering.

The Senate bill already contained a provision requiring the attorney general to consider "any good faith effort to attempt to comply with this Act by the entity." The Committee on Education and Labor agreed to add a sentence directing the court specifically to examine whether the need for the accommodation could have been foreseen. "In evaluating good faith, the court shall consider, among the other factors it deems relevant, whether the entity could have reasonably anticipated the need for an appropriate type of auxiliary aid needed to accommodate the unique needs of a particular individual with a disability."[248]

This amendment's purpose was to assuage the business community's fears that it would have to anticipate every kind of possible disability in making facilities accessible. But the committee also noted that if the disabled person asked for an accommodation, the operator could not then claim that such accommodations were not reasonably foreseeable and would not benefit from this provision.[249]

In another substantive addition, a special provision for historical buildings was inserted as section 504(c). This new language provided flexibility in the application of Titles II and III when making changes that would jeopardize the historical integrity of a building. Essentially, the amendment delineated that when the Architectural and Transportation Barriers Compliance Board issued guidelines for minimum requirements for accessibility for Titles II and III, the board would issue a special set of guidelines for historic buildings.[250] If the building

---

[247] *Id.* at 16, §308(b)(4).
[248] *Id.* at 16.
[249] *Id.* "Of course, once an individual has identified and requested a specific auxiliary aid, the public accommodation cannot subsequently claim that the aid could not have been reasonably anticipated. The public accommodation, of course, would still not have to provide the aid if it would impose an undue burden." *Id.*
[250] *Id.* at 19. Section 504(a) stated: "Not later than 6 months after the date of enactment of this Act, the Architectural and Transportation Barriers Compliance

qualified as "historic" under the National Historic Preservation Act of 1966,[251] the new guidelines were required by the amendment to be at least as stringent as the Uniform Federal Accessibility Standards.[252] If the structure were declared historic by another statute or by a state or local ordinance, the guidelines would have to establish, at a minimum, procedures and requirements that comply with the Uniform Federal Accessibility Standards.[253]

In an effort to encourage efficiency and consistency, the committee added language that would require agencies that have a duty to enforce the ADA to coordinate their policies and practices. In the enforcement section of this provision, a new paragraph was added that mandated coordinating efforts:

> The agencies with enforcement authority for action which allege employment discrimination under this title and under the Rehabilitation Act of 1973 shall develop procedures to ensure that administrative complaints filed under this title and under the Rehabilitation Act of 1973 are dealt with in a manner that avoids duplication of effort and prevents imposition of inconsistent or conflicting standards for the same requirements under this title and the Rehabilitation Act of 1973.[254]

Board shall issue minimum guidelines that shall supplement the existing Minimum Guidelines and Requirements for Accessible Design for purposes of titles II and III." Then §504(c)(i) provided: "The guidelines issued under subsection (a) shall include guidelines and requirements for alterations that will threaten to destroy the historic significance of qualified historic buildings and facilities as defined in the Uniform Federal Accessibility Standards 4.1.7(1)(a)." *Id.*

[251] 16 U.S.C. §470.

[252] H.R. REP. No. 101-485, pt. II, at 140 (1990), *reprinted in* 1990 U.S.C.C.A.N. 303, 423. "The provision further requires that, regarding alterations of buildings or facilities covered by the requirements of section 106 of the National Historic Preservation Act of 1966, the guidelines issued shall at a minimum maintain the procedures and standards established in the Uniform Federal Accessibility Standards 4.1.7(1) and (2)." *Id.*

[253] *Id.*

> [R]egarding alterations of qualified historic buildings designated as historic under a statute of the appropriate state or local government body, the guidelines shall establish procedures equivalent to those established by the Uniform Federal Accessibility Standards 4.1.7(1)(b) and (c) and shall require, at a minimum, compliance with the minimum requirements established in Uniform Federal Accessibility Standards 4.1.7(2).

Id.

[254] *Id.* at 7–8.

Furthermore, those responsible agencies would be required to issue technical assistance manuals within six months after the day the regulations were issued for any title. Moreover, although the manuals would be available to assist with compliance, "Failure to receive technical assistance in no event excuses entities from meeting the requirements of the Act."

Between the time of the markup session (Nov. 1989) and the final promulgation of the report (May 1990), the Civil Rights Act of 1990 was introduced.[255] The new civil rights bill would provide for punitive damages under Title VII, so that the linkage between the ADA and Title VII remedies would result in punitive damages under the ADA.[256] At the end of the committee report, the minority members angrily declared that, "Minority Members of this Committee supported this bill on the assumption that the agreement as struck in the Senate . . . with regard to remedies would be adhered to." They warned that, "This prospect (of punitive damages) threatens to undermine all support for this legislation and is the one issue which will result in complete opposition to the bill by the entire business community." Finally, the minority members articulated their support for an amendment on the floor of the House that would enshrine the existing remedies under Title VII.

After all the hearings and all the changes that were made, it was clear that the negotiations that allowed for such a productive and amicable process were responsible for the success of the bill in the Committee on Education and Labor proceedings. By listening to the concerns of those who wondered about the parameters of the provisions, and by not compromising in a way that would undermine the strength of the rights guaranteed therein, the bill that emerged from the Committee on Labor and Education seemed clear and fair. However, there were still three more committees and four more subcommittees yet to make their mark on the ADA.

---

[255] H.R. 4000, 101st Cong., 2d Sess. (Feb. 7, 1990).
[256] *Id.* at 167.

B. Committee on Energy and Commerce

1. *Committee on Energy and Commerce Hearings*

The Committee on Energy and Commerce referred H.R. 2273 to the Subcommittee on Telecommunications and Finance and the Subcommittee on Transportation and Hazardous Materials on May 22, 1989.[257] The two subcommittees represented the two areas over which the Committee on Energy and Commerce had jurisdiction: telecommunications and railroads.[258] The Subcommittee on Telecommunications and Finance dealt primarily with Title VI of the bill, entitled "Telecommunications." Railroads—specifically Amtrak—was the subject of the hearings conducted by the Subcommittee on Transportation and Hazardous Materials, which meant that its concerns were primarily Titles II and III. The process for the two subcommittees was eased by the fact that many questions had been answered in hearings for other committees. Additionally, the subjects of telephones and railroads were very technical and the representatives generally needed more factual information than opinion. Although debate was not extensive, concerns brought before the members often foreshadowed future amendments.

With respect to the telecommunications title of the bill, much of the testimony centered on how to pay for relay service. "In these systems, a relay operator, acting as an intermediary between the parties, translates typed TDD messages by voice and vice versa."[259] Because the system required a human translator, it was a costly endeavor for which advocates did not want the deaf community to be solely responsible. I. King Jordan, President of Gallaudet University, called for "a national system that provides full and equal accessibility and does not place a cost burden on the hearing-impaired users, and has no restrictions, such as

---

[257] *Bill Summary and Status for the 101st Congress*, H.R. 2273, *at* <http://www.thomas.loc.gov> (last visited May 3, 2004).

[258] H.R. REP. No. 101-485, pt. IV, at 80 (1990), *reprinted in* 1990 U.S.C.C.A.N. 512.

[259] *Id.* at 27.

length of call, or number of calls."²⁶⁰ Above and beyond the cost of the human translator, Representative Edward J. Markey (D-Mass.) pointed out that the length of the call must necessarily be longer because the parties are on the phone while the translation process continues. He asked Gail Garfield Schwartz, Deputy Chairman of the New York State Public Service Commission, what the billing rate was for relay calls. Although she did not have the actual numbers on hand, she did broach the idea of a congressional mandate for discounted interstate relay calls, calling it a "thorny issue." Representative Markey expressed the general sentiment of the day when he replied that "[W]e would not want to pass a law and then have the majority of the States then construct a system that discourages its use, and have to continue to revisit this issue."²⁶¹

When Jordan addressed the subcommittee, another issue that he brought up was closed-captioning for public service announcements. Claiming that many people cannot afford captioners for their home television sets, or are too proud to admit a hearing problem, Jordan pointed out that "public service announcements often provide emergency information that it is essential people see and understand."²⁶² This suggestion eventually would be added to the committee version of the bill. Later, it would be part of Public Law No. 101-336 as enacted.²⁶³

The hearings on railroads focused on crafting rules that would ensure access while accounting for the innumerable ways in which railroads were run. For example, where stations and trains may have any number of managerial configurations, the committee tried to determine who bore the responsibility and liability for compliance. Representative Alex McMillan (R-N.C.) asked Mark Lindsey, Chief Counsel for the Federal Railroad Administration, the following question: "Does the law

---

²⁶⁰ *Americans with Disabilities: Telecommunications Relay Services Hearing Before the Subcomm. on Telecommunications and Finance of the Comm. on Energy and Commerce*, 101st Cong. 56 (1989) (statement of I. King Jordan).
²⁶¹ *Id.* at 53–54 (statement of Rep. Markey).
²⁶² *Id.* at 56 (statement of I. King Jordan).
²⁶³ 42 U.S.C. §611 (1990).

impose the cost entirely upon Amtrak, or does it recognize that many stations are maintained at the request of the local community, and in some cases are owned by the local community or some other transportation authority, and that that cost perhaps should be borne by them rather than Amtrak."[264] Because the statute read "intercity transit stations" shall ensure compliance, Lindsey interpreted it to mean that the owners and operators, whether public or private, all had a duty to comply.[265]

Finally, although the exchanges between witnesses and representatives were congenial in most instances, because the president had proposed cutting money for the nearly defunct Amtrak, Representative Thomas A. Luken (D-Ohio) took a very personal interest in the testimony of Philip Calkins from the President's Committee on Employment of People with Disabilities.[266]

In all, the subcommittees held tightly-run hearings that did not include information outside their specific jurisdictions. Hearing testimony from a variety of people with a variety of different situations, at the very least showed the members that whatever bill was passed would have to be expansive and flexible.

2. Committee on Energy and Commerce Report

While the committee reviewed and passed numerous changes to the text of the Senate bill, there were several amendments of significance. First, the committee eliminated the "undue burden" exception for nationwide telephone relay service. Second, an amendment that would mandate closed captioning for public service announcements was added. Third, the committee included a long and very detailed provision guiding accessibility for Amtrak trains. Fourth, a section that would clarify the responsible party in case of a lawsuit was inserted.

Not all of the proposed amendments passed the scrutiny of the committee, however. An amendment by Representative

---

[264] *Americans with Disabilities Act Hearing Before the Subcomm. on Transportation and Hazardous Materials of the Comm. on Energy and Commerce*, 101st Cong. 121 (1989).
[265] H.R. 2273, 101st Cong., at 66 (1990).
[266] *Americans with Disabilities Act Hearing Before the Subcomm. on Transportation and Hazardous Materials of the Comm. on Energy and Commerce*, 101st Cong. 148 (1989).

William E. Dannenmeyer (R-Cal.) that would have excluded "behavioral disorders" and "contagious diseases and sexually transmittable diseases or infections," in addition to an amendment that would have eliminated coverage for people who are perceived as having a disability, failed.[267]

In the Senate version of the bill, section 401 required telecommunications services, particularly relay services, to be accessible to all individuals.[268] That section also included the following provision: "(5) UNDUE BURDEN.—If the Commission finds that full compliance with the requirements of this section would unduly burden one or more common carriers, the Commission may extend the date for full compliance by such carrier for a period not to exceed 1 additional year."[269]

The committee did not include that section in their final draft of the bill because of the immediate need for disabled persons to have access to telephones in society. The committee report comment cited the reality that "[t]he telephone is . . . no longer a luxury item but an essential component of our daily lives."[270]

Although the committee report does not discuss the impetus behind this amendment, it appears to have come at the suggestion of I. King Jordan, President of Gallaudet University, who testified in the hearing by the Subcommittee on Telecommunications and Finance.[271] Ultimately, the following was inserted into the ADA:

SEC. 711. CLOSED-CAPTIONING OF PUBLIC SERVICE ANNOUNCEMENTS.

Any television public service announcement that is produced or funded in whole or in part by any agency or instrumentality of Federal government shall include closed captioning of the verbal

---

[267] H.R. REP. No. 101-485, pt. IV, at 80–82 (1990), *reprinted in* 1990 U.S.C.C.A.N. 512.

[268] S. 933, 101st Cong., at 19 §202 (1989).

[269] *Id.* §202(c)(2).

[270] H.R. REP. No. 101-485, pt. IV, at 27 (1990), *reprinted in* 1990 U.S.C.C.A.N. 512.

[271] *Americans with Disabilities: Telecommunications Relay Services Hearing Before the Subcomm. on Telecommunications and Finance of the Comm. on Energy and Commerce*, 101st Cong. 56 (1989) (statement of I. King Jordan).

content of such announcement. A television broadcast station licensee—

(1) shall not be required to supply closed captioning for any such announcement that fails to include it; and

(2) shall not be liable for broadcasting any such announcement without transmitting a closed caption unless the licensee intentionally fails to transmit the closed caption that was included with the announcement.[272]

When identifying the needs of new railroad legislation, the committee specifically referred to the lack of specificity in Amtrak regulations.[273] The then-existing regulations dictated that an accessible car consisted of a place to store and park more than one wheelchair and a wheelchair accessible bathroom.[274] There was concern among the representatives because, depending on whether the car was single-level or bi-level, accessibility issues were very different.[275] "Legislation should require refinement of the section 504 regulations to address the need to treat these differing cars and trains appropriately."[276] Essentially, the new requirements clarified three things: guidelines for current single-level cars and dining facilities, the number of wheelchair spaces per single-level cars, and provisions in new dining cars for single-level cars.

First, the new provision stated that, in order for single-level cars to be accessible, people in wheelchairs must be able to (1) enter the car, (2) park their wheelchair (in case they wish to remain in the wheelchair), (3) sit in a seat if they choose, and (4) use the restroom facilities.[277] Second, the amendment

---

[272]H.R. 2273, 101st Cong., at 330 (1990).

[273]H.R. REP. No. 101-485, pt. IV, at 26 (1990), *reprinted in* 1990 U.S.C.C.A.N. 512. "[T]he section 504 regulations applicable to Amtrak demonstrate little regard for the different types of equipment used in various Amtrak trains." *Id.*

[274]*Id.* (citing 49 C.F.R. §27.73(b)(2) (1990)). "Instead, they simply provide that to be considered accessible a rail passenger car must have (1) space to park and secure one or more wheelchairs, (2) space to store and fold one or more wheelchairs, and (3) a restroom large enough to accommodate a wheelchair." *Id.*

[275]*Id.* "Accessibility issues, however, differ from car type to car type and from train to train, depending on the function a car is intended to serve and on whether the train is composed of single-level or bi-level cars." *Id.*

[276]*Id.*

[277]H.R. 2273, 101st Cong., at 285 §222(a)(2)(B)(i)–(iii) (1990).

linked the number of spaces for handicapped people to either sit in their chair or move to a seat, to the number of cars in the train altogether. For the first five years after the bill's enactment, the number of available spaces had to be at least one-half the number of cars in the train (*e.g.*, in a six-car train, three spaces would have to be available).[278] After five years, the number of spaces would have to be equal to the number of cars in the trains (using the previous example, six spaces would then have to be available).[279] However, regardless of the number of spaces that would have to be made available, no more than two of those spaces could be located on one car (preventing the "cattle car" effect).[280] Third, if a dining car was bought after the date of enactment, it would have to provide table service to persons in wheelchairs as long as the car adjacent to the dining car was accessible, the train would not have to be moved if the person had to get out of one car and go up a ramp into the dining car and there was space available.[281] Although the provision only explicitly refers to people in wheelchairs, the committee stated that, "The section specifically refers to 'individuals who use wheelchairs' among the individuals with disabilities who must be provided access in order to emphasize clearly that the section's requirements apply even to those individuals whose particular disability requires the most extensive modifications in order to assure access."[282]

According to former 49 C.F.R. §27.73(a)(2), statutory and pecuniary obligations could be imposed on a private party that owned a rail station, a proposition rejected by the committee.[283] As an example, the committee cited the fact that most of Amtrak's stations were owned by freight railroads with no real

---

[278] *Id.* at 286–87 §222(a)(3)(i).
[279] *Id.* at 287–88 §222(a)(3)(ii).
[280] *Id.* at 288 §222(a)(3)(c).
[281] *Id.* at 289–90 §222(a)(4).
[282] H.R. REP. No. 101-485, pt. IV, at 45 (1990), *reprinted in* 1990 U.S.C.C.A.N. 512.
[283] *Id.* at 42. "The inclusion in the ADA of the term 'responsible person' is designed to improve upon current law, which arguably subjects private parties owning passenger rail stations to the legal and financial obligations imposed under 49 C.F.R. 27.73(a)(2)." *Id.*

interest in the passenger use of the stations.[284] "The Committee believes that the legal an[d] financial responsibilities . . . should be . . . upon those parties that actually operate the rail service being provided to passengers at each location or, where applicable, upon those public entities that own all or a share of such stations."[285] The final definition of "responsible person" read:

> (6) the term "responsible person" means—
>
> (A) in the case of a station more than 50 percent of which is owned by a public entity, such public entity;
>
> (B) in the case of a station more than 50 percent of which is owned by a private party, the persons providing intercity or commuter rail transportation to such station, as allocated on an equitable basis by regulation by the Secretary of Transportation; and
>
> (C) in a case where no party owns more than 50 percent of a station, the persons providing intercity or commuter rail transportation to such station and the owners of the station, other than private party owners, as allocated on an equitable basis by regulation by the Secretary of Transportation.[286]

The fact that telecommunication access was a unanimously accepted proposition combined with the Amtrak provisions that only the Committee on Energy and Commerce had the expertise to draft, made for smooth hearings and several helpful amendments. Indeed, the most controversial issue to come out of the committee was a provision that was left untouched—the provision requiring that all new cars and remanufactured cars be accessible. The Committee on Public Works and Transportation tried to amend the section and the Rules Committee eventually had to decide which committee had proper jurisdiction. The Rules Committee ultimately decided that the Committee on Energy and Commerce had jurisdiction, leaving the section intact—nonetheless, this provision did not stay in the bill without a fight on the floor of the House from proponents of the alternative provision.

---

[284] *Id.* at 42–43. "The vast majority of Amtrak's 499 stations, for example, are owned by freight railroads who have little or no business interest in the continuation of rail passenger service at these stations." *Id.*

[285] *Id.* at 43.

[286] H.R. 2273, 101st Cong., at 282–83 §221(6) (1990).

C. Committee Public Works and Transportation

1. *Committee on Public Works and Transportation Hearings*

In accordance with House Rule X(1)(q)(20), the Committee on Public Works and Transportation had jurisdiction over all transportation issues except for automobile safety. Thus, when the full committee referred H.R. 2273 to the Subcommittee on Surface Transportation on May 22, 1989, the main focus of that subcommittee would be Title II, "Public Services." Although the subcommittee met twice and heard from many witnesses, many of those testifying simply read a statement and were excused without questioning. Additionally, much of what is on the record from the hearings is written statements from advocates, business people, and other interested parties. Thus, the Subcommittee on Surface Transportation did not hear as much debate as did some of the other hearings. When debate did take place, it was almost always concerned with either the paratransit or the bus accessibility provisions.

Representative Thomas E. Petri (R-Wis.) began his opening statement with a reminder that the subject of universal bus access and paratransit were not new topics. He reminded members that the subject of requiring all buses to be lift equipped or leaving transportation options to localities was also a point of contention when section 504 of the Rehabilitation Act was debated.[287] However, criticizing previous attempts was Committee Chairman Norman Y. Mineta (D-Cal.), who stated that the logic behind making all buses accessible and providing paratransit so that disabled persons could choose was "lacking in our earlier attempts to address this issue. That is why we've had such a long and tangled legal history of

---

[287] *Hearings Before the Subcomm. on Surface Transportation of the Comm. on Public Works and Transportation*, House of Representatives, 101st Cong., 1st Sess., 7 (Sept. 20 & 26, 1989).

Back in 1980 and 1981, in the 96th and 97th Congresses, the same subject was addressed as part of the implementation process for §504 of the Rehabilitation Act. The principal issue then as now was requiring that buses be equipped with lifts, regardless of local needs and conditions, or alternative means of transportation tailored by localities for themselves.

Id. (statement of Rep. Petri).

court decisions dealing with accessibility regulations in this country today."[288]

As the debate over paratransit service took place, with disagreement over how much should be provided and how effective it was in bringing the disabled into the mainstream, some wondered if it would not be better to take money from paratransit and use it to make all buses accessible. Representative Bud Shuster (R-Pa.), however, told the members that "having lifts on every bus does not do a thing for those thousands of disabled people who need door-to-door transportation. I think we have got to be very careful that we don't limit our focus in this area."[289] He then emphasized the need for a bill that would take into account the diversity among the disabled—geographically and medically. Indeed, when arguing against mandatory bus accessibility, he pointed to cities with cold climates and contended that the unique challenges posed by cold and snow required flexibility in choosing to what extent paratransit was necessary as opposed to buses.[290]

Many people who spoke gave estimates on how much the bill would cost, how much lifts cost, and how much paratransit costs—but rarely were the reported figures remotely similar. Those in favor of the ADA provisions gave small, manageable numbers while those in opposition quoted astronomical figures. The difficulty in calculating an actual cost highlighted the fact that the statute as passed by the Senate was vaguely worded. Thus, when making amendments to the bill in markup, the Committee on Public Works and Transportation made several changes for the sake of clarification.

2. *Committee on Public Works and Transportation Report*

The committee met for its markup session on April 3, 1990, making it the third committee to finish deliberations on the ADA.[291] The expertise of the committee led to some smaller,

---

[288] *Id.* at 1 (statement of Rep. Mineta).
[289] *Id.* at 4 (statement of Rep. Shuster).
[290] *Id.* at 4.
[291] *Bill Summary and Status for the 101st Congress,* H.R. 2273, *at* <http://www.thomas.loc.gov> (last visited May 3, 2004). The Committee on Education and Labor

very technical changes and a number of major additions to the bill. One major amendment provided an exception from accessible remanufacturing for historic vehicles. Another clarified and added to the paratransit requirements. A new section also defined discrimination for accessible vehicles. A fourth amendment allowed for an exception to the accessibility requirements for rail transportation as long as one car was accessible. Finally, a specific process for the issuance of guidelines for over-the-road buses was added to the ADA.

In the provision that required that remanufactured vehicles be made accessible,[292] the committee added an amendment that would protect historic vehicles by exempting them from accessibility if they serviced a location that was in the National Register of Historic Places.[293] The members explained, "Vehicles used solely on such segments need only be made accessible

---

held their markup session on November 9, 1989, and the Committee on Energy and Commerce held their markup session on March 13, 1990.

[292]H.R. 2977, 101st Cong., at 24 §203(c)(1) (1990):

(c) REMANUFACTURED VEHICLES.—

(1) GENERAL RULE.—Except as provided in paragraph (2), it shall be considered discrimination for purposes of this Act and section 504 of the Rehabilitation Act of 1973 (29 U.S.C. 794) for a public entity which operates a fixed route system—

(A) to remanufacture a vehicle for use on such system so as to extend its usable life for 5 years or more, which remanufacture begins (or for which the solicitation is made) after the 30th day following the effective date of this subsection; or

(B) to purchase or lease for use on such system a remanufactured vehicle which has been remanufactured so as to extend its usable life for 5 years or more, which purchase or lease occurs after such 30th day and during the period in which the usable life is extended; unless, after remanufacture, the vehicle is, to the maximum extent feasible, readily accessible to and usable by individuals with disabilities, including individuals who use wheelchairs.

[293]The exemption amendment states:

(2) EXCEPTION FOR HISTORIC VEHICLES.—

(A) GENERAL RULE.—If a public entity operates a fixed route system any segment of which is included on the National Register of Historic Places and if making a vehicle of historic character to be used solely on such segment readily accessible to and usable by individuals with disabilities would significantly alter the historic character of such vehicle, the public entity only has to make (or to purchase or lease a remanufactured vehicle with) those modifications which are necessary to meet the requirements of paragraph (1) and which do not significantly alter the historic character of such vehicle.

to the extent that the modifications needed to provide accessibility to the vehicle do not significantly alter the historic character of such vehicles."[294]

The amended paratransit provision was a reflection of negotiations that took place during the hearings. For example, although section 204 retained the "undue financial burden" limitation on the extent to which paratransit must be made available,[295] it also added a provision allowing the Secretary of Transportation to override the limitation.[296] Among the other new provisions was subsection 204(c)(B), which allowed for one person to accompany the disabled person as long as they both were going to the same place and there were available seats.[297] In order to keep the number of persons entitled to

---

(B) VEHICLES OF HISTORIC CHARACTER DEFINED BY REGULATIONS.—For purposes of this paragraph and section 209(b), a vehicle of historic character shall be defined by the regulations issued by the Secretary to carry out this subsection.

Id. §203(c)(2).

[294] H.R. Rep. No. 101-485, pt. I, at 28 (1990), reprinted in 1990 U.S.C.C.A.N. 267.

[295] H.R. 2273, 101st Cong., at 28 §204(c)(B)(4) (1990):
UNDUE FINANCIAL BURDEN LIMITATION.—The regulations issued under this section shall provide that, if the public entity is able to demonstrate to the satisfaction of the Secretary that the provision of paratransit and other special transportation services otherwise required under this section would impose an undue financial burden on the public entity, the public entity, notwithstanding any other provision of this section (other than paragraph (5)), shall only be required to provide such services to the extent that providing such services would not impose such a burden.

[296] H.R. Rep. No. 101-485, pt. I, at 31, *reprinted in* 1990 U.S.C.C.A.N. 267, 275. Section (c)(5) specifies that the Secretary of Transportation may require a public entity to provide service beyond the undue financial burden limit. Among others, this provision addresses a potential situation in which a fixed route operator cannot provide even the most basic level of paratransit service without triggering the undue financial burden limitation. In that case, the Committee expects the regulations issued by the Secretary under this section to require a basic level of paratransit service to be provided by the fixed route operator.

Id.

[297] Id.
Subsection (c) also specifies that paratransit service must be provided to one associate of each individual with a disability. The Committee anticipates occasions on which seats may be available on paratransit vehicles which could be used by additional associates—that is, in addition to the one associate accompanying the individual with a disability—wishing to accompany an

paratransit low, the same section provided that, unless one is so disabled that they could not "board, ride, or disembark" from a readily accessible vehicle, the inability to travel to, or get home from the vehicle did not entitle one to paratransit.[298] Amended section 204 did mandate that each public entity must have a hearing in which disabled people could comment and consult with the leadership about what sort of plan for paratransit should be promulgated.[299] Once a locality decided on a way to provide the necessary paratransit service, this plan would have to be written and submitted to the Secretary of Transportation.[300] The "plan" mandated by the amendment would be subject to the disapproval of the secretary, who could demand that it be redone.[301] Finally, the new section encouraged localities to go above and beyond what was required by the provision.

The committee reported that, with this amendment, paratransit did not have to be provided by a public entity if another entity could provide the service.[302] However, if the public entity indicated in its plan that the other service provider will be providing paratransit assistance, then the public entity had a duty to make sure that the service actually was being provided. If, however, the paratransit provider was not listed on the plan submitted to the secretary, then there would be no responsibility for the public entity to ensure that service was being provided. "[S]ince the public entity is ultimately responsible for

---

individual with a disability. The Committee anticipates that these additional persons may be allowed to ride in the same paratransit vehicle as the individual with a disability and his or her associate, as long as the additional persons are going to the same destination, as the individual with a disability and do not use seats which would have otherwise been used by individuals with disabilities.
[298] H.R. 2273, 101st Cong., at 27 §204(c)(B) (1990).
[299] *Id.* at 28–20 §204(c)(B)(6).
[300] *Id.* at 29 §204(c)(B)(7).
[301] *Id.* at 30 §204(d).
[302] H.R. REP. No. 101-485, pt. I, at 31, *reprinted in* 1990 U.S.C.C.A.N. 267, 275: Subsection (8) states that a public entity is not required to provide paratransit service provided by another public entity or person in a given service area. A public entity may identify in its paratransit service plan other entities or persons which are providing a sufficient level of paratransit service so that the public entity can state that, because of the existence of that service, it has met its obligation to provide paratransit service under the Act.

the provision of the paratransit service required of it under the Act, the public entity must only monitor and ensure adequate service from those entities or persons which it has identified in its paratransit plan as surrogates to meet its responsibilities under the Act."[303]

The new and improved section 209 provided that, when facilities are accessible, it would be discriminatory to fail to operate the vehicles in a nondiscriminatory way.[304] One way to avoid a discrimination charge, according to the amendment, would be to have one car per train that is accessible to disabled people.[305] The section even provided for a "historic train" exception so that trains with historical significance would only be required to do as much as possible without significantly altering the train.

In what would prove to be the most controversial amendment from the Committee on Public Works and Transportation, a new section 213 was added to the statute.[306] This provision, over which there was very little debate in the

---

[303] *Id.* at 32, 1990 U.S.C.C.A.N. at 276.
[304] H.R. 2273, 101st Cong., at 37–38 §209(a) (1990).
[305] *Id.* at 38 §209(b)(1).
[306] The new amendment stated:
SEC. 213. APPLICABILITY TO CERTAIN COMMUTER RAIL SYSTEMS.
(a) GENERAL RULE.—Subject to subsection (b), a public entity which operates a fixed route system providing commuter rail service does not have to purchase or lease readily accessible and usable commuter rail vehicles to meet the requirements of this title and does not have to remanufacture commuter rail vehicles to meet the requirements of this title—
(1) if such entity is meeting the requirement of this title relating to 1 car per train being accessible to individuals with disabilities;
(2) if such entity provides clear, concise, and adequate notice, in its stations, of which cars are so accessible and the location of such cars on its trains; and
(3) if, in any case in which additional services are offered in a nonaccessible car of a train, such entity makes reasonable provision to ensure that such services are available to individuals with disabilities in the accessible car or cars of such train.
(b) ADDITIONAL ACCESSIBLE CARS TO MEET DEMAND.—In order for a public entity to be exempt under subsection (a), in any case in which actual continuing demand for accessible service cannot be met by the public entity with 1 accessible car per train, the public entity must use such additional accessible cars per train as may be necessary to meet such demand.
Id. at 38, §213.

subcommittee hearings, permitted an exemption from the requirement that all new vehicles be lift-equipped and remanufactured vehicles had to be accessible.[307] As long as one car per train was accessible and the entrance to the accessible car was visible and all amenities provided to the other cars was provided to the accessible car, an entity did not have to purchase lift-equipped vehicles or remanufacture vehicles in a such a way as to make them accessible.[308]

This amendment led to a jurisdictional challenge by the Committee on Energy and Commerce. That committee left in the provision stipulating that all new and remanufactured vehicles be accessible. The conflict eventually was settled by the Rules Committee in favor of the Committee on Energy and Commerce.[309] However, the Rules Committee allowed the provision to be debated on the floor as an amendment, where it also failed.

The final major change to the ADA dealt with accessibility requirements for over-the-road buses. It first mandated that, within one year of the enactment of the bill, the Secretary of Transportation would issue accessibility guidelines to be followed until the issuance of final guidelines.[310] The interim guidelines would not require structural changes, but would require minor changes.[311] The committee explained that "the regulations in effect during this period may require additions to an over-the-road bus to aid accessibility which do not require structural changes or boarding assistance devices, such as the installation of non-skid strips on stairs."[312] The amendment

---

[307] *Id.* at 41 §213(a)(1).
[308] H.R. REP. No. 101-485, pt. I, at 35 (1990), *reprinted in* 1990 U.S.C.C.A.N. 267: Subsection (a) of this section provides a partial exemption to the accessible commuter rail vehicle purchase and remanufacturing requirements under section 203 as long as (1) the one car per train requirements under section 209 is met, (2) clear, concise, and adequate notice is provided identifying accessible vehicles and their location on a train, and (3) reasonable provision is made to ensure that additional services provided on nonaccessible vehicles are provided to individuals with disabilities traveling on accessible vehicles.
[309] H.R. REP. No. 101-485 (1990).
[310] H.R. 2273 at 62 §306(a)(1).
[311] *Id.* at 62–63 §306(a)(2)(A)(i).
[312] H.R. REP. No. 101-485, pt. I, at 43, *reprinted in* 1990 U.S.C.C.A.N. 267.

also provided that once the study mandated by section 305 was complete,[313] the Secretary would issue the final guidelines, which would have to be implemented within seven years for small bus service providers and six years for all others.[314] The amendment also specified that the Secretary would not require that restrooms be made accessible as part of the compliance requirements.

In all, there were over 13 changes made to the Senate version of the bill, not all as technical and extensive as the aforementioned amendments. The Committee on Public Works and Transportation felt that extensive explanations and processes were necessary additions, perhaps because the ADA only went through one committee in the Senate, the Committee on Labor and Human Resources, or perhaps it was because the Committee on Public Works and Transportation had more time to examine the provisions and their effects. One thing is certain—the result of the committee negotiations was a substantially longer and more detailed bill for the whole House of Representatives to consider.

D. Committee on the Judiciary

1. *Committee on the Judiciary and Hearings*

Charged with jurisdiction over that which restrains trade and commerce, the Judiciary Committee had the difficult task of dealing with provisions that not only were vague, but that had the potential to be monumentally expensive. Although the committee received its fair share of written amendments and basic witness statements, most of the action occurred during the Judiciary Committee hearings. Issues of drug use, HIV

---

[313] *Id.* at 40.
Section 305(a) directs the Office of Technology Assessment (OTA) to conduct a study to determine (1) the access needs of individuals with disabilities to over-the-road buses and to over-the-road bus service; and (2) the most-cost effective methods for providing access to over-the-road buses and over-the-road bus service to individuals with disabilities through all forms of boarding options.
Id.

[314] H.R. 2273, 101st Cong., at 64 §306(a)(2)(B)(iii) (1990).

coverage, and imprecise statutory language were the subjects of much of the questioning as the committee looked for a way to make the bill work for all Americans.

The Subcommittee on Civil and Constitutional Rights of the Judiciary Committee held its first hearing to address H.R. 2273 on August 3, 1989.[315] The Senate Committee on Labor and Human Resources had marked up S. 933 only the day before. The six-member subcommittee was primarily concerned with Title III, which dealt with public accommodations. The subcommittee heard three witnesses, all of whom were disability rights advocates: James Brady of the National Organization on Disability; Peter Addesso of the Paralyzed Veterans of America; and Chai Feldblum, counsel for the American Civil Liberties Union (ACLU).

Feldblum made general remarks and expressed her organization's strong support for the ADA. She then was sharply questioned by Representative William E. Dannemeyer (R-Cal.), who immediately began interrogating her about ADA coverage of communicable diseases. After she explained that the ACLU would not support a bill without the coverage of people with communicable diseases, he moved to another topic. As he had done with other witnesses, Dannemeyer brought up drug addicts and those with HIV, but Feldblum reminded him that those with HIV are covered under section 504 of the Rehabilitation Act.[316] He went on to ask about the "rationale and necessity" of protecting those who are associated with a disabled person and covering persons who are about to be discriminated

---

[315] *Americans with Disabilities Act: Hearings on H.R. 2273 Before the Subcomm. on Civil and Constitutional Rights of the House Comm. on the Judiciary*, 101st Cong. 1 (1989) [hereinafter *ADA Judiciary Comm. Hearings*].

[316] *Id.* at 72 n.308. "Section 504 has been used in many cases by people who have AIDS or HIV who have been unjustifiably discriminated from their jobs, unjustifiably tossed out of places where they don't pose a threat to others." *Id.* (statement of Chai Feldblum). *See* 24 C.F.R. §100.201(a)(2) (2003) (interpreting section 504). "The term *physical or mental impairment* includes, but is not limited to, such diseases and conditions as orthopedic, visual, speech and hearing impairments, cerebral palsy, autism, epilepsy, muscular dystrophy, multiple sclerosis, cancer, heart disease, diabetes, Human Immunodeficiency Virus infection, mental retardation, emotional illness, drug addiction (other than addiction caused by current, illegal use of a controlled substance) and alcoholism." *Id.* (emphasis in original).

against.[317] As to both points, Feldblum answered that these provisions were already in the Fair Housing Amendments Act.[318] Furthermore, where one is about to be discriminated against,

> You have to prove that discrimination is going to occur.... [This provision is useful] [i]f you find out that there are blueprints for a building that's going to be built, that is going to be built nonaccessible, instead of waiting until that building is built and then bring the lawsuit, which will be incredibly expensive.[319]

Representative Craig T. James (R-Fla.) spoke to Feldblum next, asking her more questions related to drug and alcohol addicts. Specifically, he wanted to know what antidrug and alcohol policies an employer could implement that would not run afoul of the law.[320] He gave a hypothetical situation in which an employer required at least two days of sobriety before hiring someone, and insisted that former alcoholics go to Alcoholics Anonymous.[321] Feldblum pointed out that the employer

---

[317] *ADA Judiciary Comm. Hearings, supra* note 315, at 74–75 (statement of Rep. Dannenmeyer).

[318] *Id.* at 74. *See* 45 U.S.C. §3604(f)(1)(C) and (f)(2)(C) (Statement of unlawful practices):

(f) (1) To discriminate in the sale or rental, or to otherwise make unavailable or deny, a dwelling to any buyer or renter because of a handicap of—

(A) that buyer or renter;

(B) a person residing in or intending to reside in that dwelling after it is so sold, rented, or made available; or

(C) any person associated with that buyer or renter.

(2) To discriminate against any person in the terms, conditions, or privileges of sale or rental of a dwelling, or in the provision of services or facilities in connection with such dwelling, because of a handicap of—

(A) that person; or

(B) a person residing in or intending to reside in that dwelling after it is so sold, rented, or made available; or

(C) any person associated with that person.

See also 45 U.S.C. §3602(i) (Definitions):

(i) "Aggrieved person" includes any person who—

(1) claims to have been injured by a discriminatory housing practice; or

(2) believes that such person will be injured by a discriminatory housing practice that is about to occur.

[319] *ADA Judiciary Comm. Hearings, supra* note 315, at 74–75 (statement of Chai Feldblum).

[320] *Id.* at 75 (statement of Rep. James).

[321] *Id.* at 76.

maintains all rights under the Drug-Free Workplace Act of 1988.[322] After some further questioning by James, Feldblum concluded by stating that "Section 504, which has been on the books since 1973, applies to many, many employers. We have not had troubles with either the coverage of alcoholism or drug addiction under that law."[323]

After Feldblum was excused, the hearing was over and the subcommittee would not resume its deliberations until almost three months later, after the Senate had already passed its version.[324]

The October 11 hearing of the Subcommittee on Civil and Constitutional Rights saw three representatives from the business community who opposed the bill, a disabled lawyer, and a Baptist preacher who worked for a charitable AIDS organization.[325] With the Senate bill already passed, the imminence of the passage of the ADA was becoming clear. The three business representatives who testified also submitted lengthy written statements to the subcommittee, detailing the concerns of their respective organizations.

First, John Motley of the NFIB spoke to the subcommittee on behalf of small businesses. He first explained that the costs of compliance are high, citing, among other examples, the fact that it costs $1,000 to $10,000 for a concrete ramp, $300 to $3,000 to modify a restroom, and $23 an hour for a certified signer.[326] He then complained that the statute lacks definition because it does not list the disabilities covered, but requires the business owner to "know which conditions are legitimate and therefore must be accommodated." He then added that "readily achievable," "reasonable accommodation," and "undue hardship" are vague terms. In Title I of the ADA, employers who employ fewer than 15 people are exempt, but in Title III

---

[322] 41 U.S.C. §701 et seq.

[323] *ADA Judiciary Comm. Hearings, supra* note 315, at 77 (statement of Chai Feldblum).

[324] S. 933, 101st Cong. (1990) (passed on Sept. 7, 1989).

[325] *ADA Judiciary Comm. Hearings, supra* note 315, at 79–187.

[326] *Id.* at 82 (statement of John Motley, Director of Federal Government Relations for the NFIB).

there was no such exemption. Motley argued that the Title I exemption should be extended to Title II as well, "Since the burdens we believe are relatively the same for those businesses under both sections of the bill."[327] Second to testify was Christopher J. Hoey on behalf of the International Mass Retail Association (IMRA).[328] He expressed the desire to extend the readily achievable standard to the employment provisions, which functioned under the "undue burden" standard. He also argued that, when determining whether something is readily achievable, only site-specific factors should be taken into consideration, not the overall company resources.

The third business representative was James DiLuigi from the American Hotel and Motel Association (AH&MA).[329] In his statement to the committee, he echoed the previous two witnesses' testimonies by objecting to the vagueness of the terms of the bill, namely, "readily achievable" and "maximum extent possible." The approach he advocated was one of incentives and flexibility, not legislated rules. He suggested a "10-year tax credit for implementing certain standards with a diminishing return," so that the longer it takes to implement changes, the smaller the tax credit. He then cited the efforts of the AH&MA to work with the Paralyzed Veterans of America to implement changes in hotels and motels. He later stated that "[t]he legislation would be best suited to allow . . . for the kind of exchange to occur between businesses, between the design community and the disabled, to come up with good solutions."[330]

The next witness to make a statement was Laura Cooper, a disabled attorney.[331] Despite having been diagnosed with multiple sclerosis in 1979, she went to law school, where she was close to the top of her class, on law review, and a recognized moot court competitor. She had also interned with a federal

---

[327] *Id.*

[328] *Id.* at 99 (Christopher J. Hoey, Assistant Treasurer and Assistant General Counsel, Woolworth Corp., on behalf of IMRA).

[329] *Id.* at 125 (James A. DiLuigi, AIA, Director, Technical Information, Marriott Corp., on behalf of AH&MA).

[330] *Id.*

[331] *Id.* at 151 (Laura Cooper, Attorney, Pettit & Martin, San Francisco, Cal.).

appellate court and worked at a renowned law firm. Despite all this, she testified to having been rejected over 400 times by legal employers. She described numerous accounts of discrimination as a result of inadequate access to public facilities. She emphasized the fact that, when a firm finally did hire her, she "became a productive, taxpaying citizen and consumer," and no longer collected social security, medicare, or vocational rehabilitation funding. During questioning of the witnesses, Representative Don Edwards (D-Cal.) inquired as to what Cooper thought "readily achievable" meant. She pointed out that "'readily achievable' is a lower standard than 'undue burden,' which is in the employment section." And furthermore, "It is my understanding that that the standard was incorporated specifically in order to address the concerns of business." Cooper was then asked by Colleen Kiko, minority counsel, whether the exclusion of homosexuals from protection in the Senate bill was nullified by the coverage of people with HIV, since homosexuals could sue for being "regarded as" having HIV.[332] "[I]f somebody's operating on the assumption that all homosexuals are HIV positive, that's a pretty irrational fear and it seems like that's exactly what the 'regarded as' category is designed to address—irrational fears that employers have," was her response.[333]

Next to testify was Reverend Scott Allen from the National Commission on AIDS.[334] As the head advisor to Congress on implementing the recommendation of the President's Commission on the HIV Epidemic, he stated the need for comprehensive federal legislation against HIV discrimination.[335] Essentially, his message was that "[a]ll persons with symptomatic or asymptomatic HIV infections should be clearly included as persons with disabilities who are covered by the antidiscrimination protections of this legislation."[336] In addition to describing the need for the ADA because of the "dual tragedy" of

---

[332] *Id.* at 185 (statement of Colleen Kiko, present as counsel for the minority).
[333] *Id.* at 186 (statement of Laura Cooper).
[334] *Id.* at 170 (Reverend Scott Allen, member of the National Commission on AIDS).
[335] *Id.* (statement of Rev. Allen).
[336] *Id.*

HIV and discrimination, he warned the subcommittee that if HIV status is left unprotected, it will serve as a disincentive for people to get tested and receive treatment. When questioned by Representative F. James Sensenbrenner, Jr. (R-Wis.), about how to "deal with" the protection of people with HIV but exclusion of homosexuals, he emphasized that, "We're dealing with someone who is disabled. So one's sexuality should not be an issue in this decision process of an employer."[337] Later, when addressing the point of Colleen Kiko on the "regarded as" aspect of homosexuals and HIV status, he cited a case where a woman who volunteered for an AIDS organization was forced to quit volunteering by her employer because of a perception that she would inevitably catch the virus. The fact that there is no protection for people "regarded as" having HIV, he warned, will have a chilling effect on the number of volunteers willing to help people who are HIV positive.[338]

The October 12, 1989, session of the full Committee on the Judiciary saw only one witness—Attorney General Richard Thornburgh.[339] With Chairman Jack B. Brooks (D-Tex.) presiding and Representative Steny Hoyer (D-Md.) present, Thornburgh gave his statement to the committee. He began by reminding the committee that he testified at the June 22, 1989, hearing of the Senate Committee on Labor and Human Resources, where he pledged the administration's support for S. 933 as comprehensive legislation on disability rights. While testifying at that hearing, he did raise some issues that the administration wanted to address, but "during this past summer, representatives of the administration engaged in prolonged negotiations with the Senate on this bill."[340] Since the administration's concerns had been addressed in the Senate, he felt it was appropriate to fully extend the administration's support of the ADA. Thornburgh's assessment of the bill began

---

[337] *Id.*

[338] *Id.* at 186 (statement of Rev. Allen). "[I]f its found out that you're helping someone and you lose your job, then that's going to diminish the potentiality of getting individuals to care." *Id.*

[339] *Id.* 189–232.

[340] *Id.* at 191.

with his praise for the similarities between the language of the employment section of the ADA with Title VII and the Rehabilitation Act.

> The Americans with Disabilities Act wisely parallels in the disability area title VII of the Civil Rights Act of 1964, the landmark statute that prohibits discrimination in employment on the basis of race, color, national origin, sex, or religion.[341]

> Furthermore, the administration is pleased that the employment provisions of the Americans with Disabilities Act closely follow the standards provided by section 504 of the Rehabilitation Act of 1973.[342]

He then performed essentially a section-by-section analysis and approval of the ADA, reiterating the merits of each provision. Among the merits, he emphasized that the earlier version of the Senate bill provided for punitive damages, while this negotiated bill limits remedies to those compensatory damages available under Title VII of the Civil Rights Act. He closed by saying, "On behalf of the Administration, I pledge to this committee and to Congress our support to produce a bill that can be signed this year."[343]

Representative Edwards questioned the lack of precision regarding the definitions of such terms as "readily achievable" and "undue burden." Attorney General Thornburgh responded by emphasizing that many of these definitions were extracted from existing legislation—namely, the Rehabilitation Act.[344]

---

[341] *Id.* at 192 (statement of Attorney General Thornburgh).

[342] *Id.* at 193. Thornburgh added:
The fact that many of the employment provisions of the Americans with Disabilities Act are drawn directly and, in many instances, even taken verbatim from the Federal regulations, implementing section 504 represents a particularly wise choice. The section 504 standards are familiar to large segments of the private sector already covered by the Rehabilitation Act. Experience has shown that these standards do not result in undue costs or excessive litigation.
Id.

[343] *Id.*

[344] The question and response were as follows:
EDWARDS: Would you suggest that additional attention be given to providing more precise statutory definitions of such terms as "readily achievable" and "undue burden" in the law [*sic*].

Representative Hamilton Fish, Jr. (R-N.Y.), inquired as to whether the requirement that all new buildings be accessible means that every part of a new building must be accessible.[345] Thornburgh assured him that a standard of "reasonableness" would be applied to accessibility situations under section 303.[346] Representative Bill McCollum (R-Fla.) then asked Thornburgh if any consideration had been given to a small business exception for Title III. Thornburgh explained that, if the same small business exception in Title I were extended to Title III, it would exempt over 90 percent of the public accommodations.[347] He emphasized the fact that the "readily achievable" standard is very low, requiring only those changes that can be done without much difficulty or expense.[348] The issue of a tax credit was the next item Thornburgh dealt with, in a question posed by Representative Michael DeWine (R-Ohio), who inquired as to the administration's view of such an incentive.[349] After stating clearly that "the administration does not support any such provision" due to "fiscal restrictions and restraints," he reminded the committee that, under section 190 of the Code of

---

> THORNBURGH: I think it is important to note that most of the terms used in the Americans with Disabilities Act that prompt such inquiries, terms such as "reasonable accommodation" derive from already existing legislation, section 405 of the Rehabilitation Act of 1972 [*sic*]. The term "readily achievable" is fairly narrowly defined in this legislation. ... With regard to the others, what one might call "terms of art," they have acquired it the 15 or 16 years that they have been part of the accepted meaning in the courts and through regulatory practices that ought to reduce any confusion or litigation to an absolute bare minimum. ... Obviously, applying these terms to new factual situations is going to create new questions. But the notion that the whole flood of undefined terms is being loosed on an unsuspecting public, I believe it much exaggerated.

Id. at 213.

[345] *ADA Judiciary Comm. Hearings, supra* note 315, at 215 (statement of Rep. Fish).

[346] *Id.* at 216 (statement of Attorney General Thornburgh). "I think the only answer to that is to look at it from the point of view of the standard of reasonableness which excludes the notion that every portion of every building, every service included within that building, must be accessible, under the standard of reasonableness." *Id.*

[347] *Id.* at 221. By contrast, it was estimated that the Title I exemption would only exempt about 20 percent of employers. *Id.* at 220–21.

[348] *Id.*

[349] *Id.* at 223 (statement of Rep. DeWine).

the Internal Revenue Service (IRS), if one wishes to make qualified architectural or transportation changes, a $35,000 deduction is available.[350] Representative Dannemeyer then asked Thornburgh about coverage for people who have acquired their disability through "intentional conduct" when "they knew the consequences."[351] "The President has made a pledge to support legislation against AIDS discrimination based on the findings of the Watkins Commission," was the Attorney General's response.[352] The last issue that was discussed and resolved was the issue of intentional versus unintentional discrimination. Representative McCollum asked, "Shouldn't there be more punishment for the guy who says, 'I know what the rule is, but I am going to refuse to remove the barrier?'"[353] Thornburgh reassured him that, although the law "allows [the Attorney General] to act unreasonably," the attorney general's office would assign the larger fines to the "intentional egregious violator."[354]

The October 12, 1989, hearing of the Subcommittee on Civil and Constitutional Rights was held a few minutes after the entire Committee on the Judiciary had its hearing.[355] Four witnesses testified, but few questions were asked of them. In general, the first two witnesses wanted to see changes made to the bill, while the second two simply expressed their support for H.R. 2273.

Paul Roth was the first to address the subcommittee. As a representative of an association of theater owners, he testified to structural specifics of making theaters accessible. He cited

---

[350] *Id.* (statement of Attorney General Thornburgh).

[351] *Id.* at 225 (statement of Rep. Dannemeyer). Specifically, he asked about drug addicts, alcoholics, and persons with communicable diseases. He characterized the attitude of these people as, "not unlike a young man who kills both parents and then throws himself in the mercy of the court because he is an orphan." *Id.* at 226.

[352] *Id.* at 226 (statement of Attorney General Thornburgh).

[353] *Id.* at 231 (statement of Rep. McCollum).

[354] *Id.* (statement of Attorney General Thornburgh). McCollum then expressed ambivalence because the law would see many other administrations and attorneys general—and this law gives lots of discretion (statement of Rep. McCollum).

[355] *Id.* at 232–33. The Committee on the Judiciary adjourned at 12:20 p.m. and the subcommittee met at 12:30 p.m.

section 302(1)(b), which "requires that seating for patrons in wheelchairs be integrated within an auditorium. Depending on how far you go with the definition of integration, that becomes impractical and potentially unsafe."[356] Furthermore, he explained that older theaters tend to be without the resources to make accommodations, since they are in low-income neighborhoods and charge bargain prices. He also spoke about the difficulty in changing the various movie theater jobs that require heavy lifting or the ability to reach over the counter to deliver merchandise. His main complaint was the same as many other people who represented businesses, that "the law is not clear."[357]

Next to testify was Robert Lynch of the American Institute of Architects (AIA).[358] He proposed four changes to H.R. 2273. First, he suggested that, as was done in Pennsylvania, "renovation value to building value ratio" be adopted to distinguish between major and minor alterations, so that minor alterations, do not set off the need to make costly compliance changes. Second, he suggested that a historical building exception be applied to "all qualified properties including those listed on, or eligible for the National Register of Historic Places, or designated historic by a state statute or local ordinance." Lynch expressed anxiety over a provision that would apply the "new facility" standard of accessibility to any facility that is open for the first time 30 months after the enactment of the ADA. To remedy the costly renovations on projects already underway, he suggested that the law apply only to projects that receive a design contract after the enactment date of the statute.[359] Fourth, he suggested that the Department of Justice certify some state and local officials to certify buildings as compliant so that certification can be used as a defense against a charge of violating Title III. Last, Lynch noted extreme dearth of "barrier free design"/"universality" education available to architects and architecture students and asked that resources be

---

[356] *Id.* at 292 (statement of Paul Roth).
[357] *Id.* at 294.
[358] *Id.* at 307.
[359] *Id.* (statement of Robert Lynch).

directed to that area. He closed by saying "we architects, the designers and builders of the environment of man, must broaden our spectrum of design parameters to help improve the quality of life for those who cannot walk or talk or see or hear."[360]

The last person to testify was Professor Robert Burgdorf, Jr., of the University of the District of Columbia David Clark School of Law.[361] After talking about the Louis Harris poll, which illustrated the isolation felt by disabled people, he went on to address some of the points brought up by the previous witnesses.[362] First, he addressed Roth and other advocates for the small business community, stating that, "At every juncture in the bill, there is deference paid to the size and to the difficulties faced by smaller businesses."[363] He further asserted that the ADA considers and gives deference to the needs of businesses, particularly small businesses, "more than any other civil rights bill that has ever been before Congress."[364] Second, he addressed Lynch's concerns about minor alterations triggering the need for major construction. Burgdorf pointed out that the bill addresses only those alterations that affect the usability of a facility, not minor alterations. The alteration must also be a structural alteration that changes the physical components of the facility. Finally, the alteration must be major, so "a change in the broom closet is not a major structural change, no matter how extensive it is, and a change in a bank lobby would be a change in a major area of a bank."[365] During questioning, Representative Edwards asked Burgdorf to comment on the "renovation value to building value ratio" that Lynch suggested as a way to determine what are major and what

---

[360] *Id.*

[361] *Id.* at 327 (statement of Robert Burgdorf, Jr.).

[362] *Id.* Burgdorf cited the Louis Harris poll that reported that, for example, 75% of disabled persons did not see a movie or live music performance in 1985, as opposed to only 40% of the general population.

[363] *Id.* at 328.

[364] *Id.*

[365] *Id. See* S. REP. No. 101-116, at 329. The term "major structural alteration" is used to identify what type of alteration would trigger the need for accessibility.

are minor alterations. Burgdorf explained that, if a building was constructed for $50,000 years ago, and is worth $1 million dollars today, the alteration would have to be valued at $500,000 to trigger the need for accessibility. The person making alterations then has an incentive to keep the cost just under that amount, for example, $499,000. The fact that the building, post-alteration would be worth $1,499,000.00 means that, the next year, the cost of the alteration would have to be over $700,000 to trigger the requirement. "We don't think that is what they are intending or what the bill is intending," he observed.[366] Finally, Representative Edwards asked him about the term "readily achievable," to which he responded, "I don't see how anybody could object to doing what is easy to do."[367]

On May 1, 1990, the Committee on the Judiciary met again for a markup session. There, it considered amendments, armed not only with the information ascertained from the hearing testimony, but also the written statements submitted by interested parties. They included legal analysis, statements from business-oriented groups,[368] and submissions from disability rights advocates.[369] The interests of the submitting parties spanned a broad spectrum of viewpoints and were illustrative of the diverse interests of the American public. For example, Kathy Hogancamp, who was a quadriplegic, wrote, "Yes, it can be frustrating as a disabled consumer not to be able to go to a movie or restaurant because of a lack of accessibility. But what about the rights of the private sector, of the private, small business owners? The private sector does not owe me—or any other disabled person—a frustration free life."[370] With these

---

[366] *ADA Judiciary Comm. Hearings, supra* note 315, at 381 (statement of Robert Burgdorf).

[367] *Id.* at 382.

[368] *Id.* (Nancy Fulco, U.S. Chamber of Commerce, prepared statement, *id.* at 424; Roy Bredder, director, Washington office, American Dental Association, letter to Hon. Jack B. Brooks, Oct. 24, 1989, *id.* at 434; James P. Cramer, executive vice president and CEO of AIA, letter to Hon. Don Edwards, Oct. 26, 1989, *id.* at 444).

[369] *Id.* at 416 (James Ellis, president, American Association on Mental Retardation, prepared statement).

[370] *Id.* at 439 (Kathy Hogancamp, testimony submitted to the Committee on the Judiciary, Oct. 27, 1989).

numerous conflicting interests in mind, the committee met to make amendments and submit a final version of the bill as the Committee on the Judiciary would like it to be.

2. Committee on the Judiciary Report

The Committee on the Judiciary considered five potential amendments to the legislation.[371] The first added a section 513 to the bill to encourage alternative dispute resolution.[372] The new section read:

> Where appropriate and to the extent authorized by law, the use of alternative means of dispute resolution, including settlement negotiations, conciliation, facilitation, mediation, factfinding, minitrials, and arbitration, is encouraged to resolve disputes arising under this Act.[373]

The committee made it clear that this encouragement did not preclude the aggrieved party from seeking relief under the enforcement provisions of the ADA. "This view is consistent with the Supreme Court's interpretation of Title VII of the Civil Rights Act of 1964, whose remedial provisions are incorporated by reference in title I."[374]

The second amendment passed by the committee was one that articulated additional factors to be considered in making a determination as to what is "undue hardship" under Title I and what is "readily achievable" under Title III.[375] The same set of new factors would apply to both definitions. For "undue

---

[371] H.R. REP. No. 101-485, pt. 3, at 23 (1990), *reprinted in* 1990 U.S.C.C.A.N. 445. In total, there were five amendments.

[372] *Id.* This amendment was proposed by Representative Dan Glickman (D-Kan.) to "serve as a reminder that rights and litigation are not one in the same." 136 CONG. REC. H2431 (daily ed. May 17, 1990) (statement of Rep. Glickman).

[373] H.R. REP. No. 101-485, pt. 3 at 22.

[374] *Id.* at 77. "The Committee believes that the approach articulated by the Supreme Court in *Alexander v. Gardner-Denver Co.* [415 U.S. 36, 49, 7 FEP Cases 81 (1974)] applies equally to the ADA." *Id.* Where an African-American man submitted a race discrimination claim to arbitration pursuant to a collective bargaining agreement and then, receiving an unfavorable judgment, brought suit in federal court, "Title VII's purpose and procedures strongly suggest that an individual does not forfeit his private cause of action if he first pursues his grievance to final arbitration under the nondiscrimination clause of a collective-bargaining agreement." *Id.*

[375] *Id.* at 23.

hardship," the new set of factors would be used to determine whether the accommodation would require "significant difficulty or expense."[376] For "readily achievable," the factors would be used to determine whether the accommodation would be "easily accomplishable and able to be carried out without much difficulty or expense."

In particular, three new provisions were added. First, section 101(10)(B)(ii) added the consideration of site-specific factors. Specifically, "the overall financial resources of the facility or facilities involved in the provision of the reasonable accommodation; the number of persons employed at the facility; the effect on expenses, resources, or the impact otherwise of such accommodation upon the operation of the facility."[377] Second, the amendment included consideration of parent company factors in section 101(10)(B)(iii) by stating that "the overall financial resources of the covered entity; the overall size of the business of a covered entity with respect to the number of its employees, the number, type and location of its facilities," should all be considered. Third, the committee added section 101(10)(B)(iv), a provision that included consideration of the fiscal and administrative relationship between the covered entity and facility involved.[378] Namely, "the type of operation or operations of the covered entity, including the compensation and structure of the workforce of such entity; the geographic separateness, administrative, and fiscal relationship to the facility or facilities in question to the covered entity."[379]

---

[376] *Id.* at 4 (Bill proposed by the Committee on the Judiciary, §101(10)(A)).

[377] *Id.* (Bill proposed by the Committee on the Judiciary, §101(10)(B)(ii)). This is the same as §301(5)(B), but instead of "facilities involved in the reasonable accommodation," it says "facilities involved in the action" because reasonable accommodation is not required under Title III. *Id.* at 11.

[378] *Id.* §101(10)(B)(iv). The committee added:

The Committee does not intend for the requirements of the Act to result in the closure of neighborhood stores or in loss of jobs. The Committee intends for courts to consider in determining "undue hardship" whether the local store is threatened with closing by the parent company or is faced with job loss as a result of the requirements of this Act.

Id. at 41.

[379] *Id.*

The Committee also amended section 101(A) by adding the phrase "when considered in light of the factors set forth in subparagraph (B)," because accommodating actions may be significant in the abstract, but, given all the factors, they may still be required. Then the committee cited to *Nelson v. Thornburgh*,[380] a section 504 case in which blind workers needed accommodations that would cost a "substantial" amount of money. The court held that, since the cost would be a small fraction of the company's personnel budget, it did not qualify as "significant expense."[381]

The committee report further noted that an amendment was rejected that would "set a fixed limit of over 10 percent of the disabled employee's salary as a *per se* undue hardship."[382]

The third amendment that passed was one that clarified the fact that the remedies provided in Titles I, II, III, are tied to the remedies set forth the Title VII of the Civil Rights Act.[383] Thus, "If those remedies are amended in the future, such remedies will also apply to the ADA."[384] The amendment struck out the provision "shall be available" and substituted "available, with respect" to "the powers, remedies and procedures this

---

[380] 567 F. Supp. 369, 1 AD Cases 463 (E.D. Pa. 1983).

[381] H.R. REP. No. 101-485, pt. III, at 41 (1990), *reprinted in* 1990 U.S.C.C.A.N. 445 (citing *Thornburgh*, 567 F. Supp. at 380–82). "[I]n view of (plaintiff's) $300,000 administrative budget, the modest cost of providing half-time readers, and the ease of adopting that accommodation without any disruption of (plaintiff's) services, it is apparent that (plaintiff) has not met its burden of showing undue hardship." *Thornburgh*, 567 F. Supp. at 380.

[382] H.R. REP. No. 101-485, pt. III, at 41.

[383] *Id.* at 7. The bill proposed by the Committee on the Judiciary, §107(a) stated:
The powers, remedies, and procedures set forth in §§705, 706, 707, 709, and 710 of the Civil Rights Act of 1964 (42 U.S.C. §§2000e-4, 2000e-5, 2000e-6, 2000e-8, and 2000e-9) shall be the powers, remedies, and procedures this title provides to the Commission, to the Attorney General, or to any person alleging discrimination on the basis of disability in violation of any provisions of this Act, or regulation promulgated under section 106, concerning employment.
Id. (provisions conveying similar authority were included in §205 as to transportation and in §308 relating to public accommodation).

[384] *Id.* at 48.
The Committee intends that persons with disabilities have remedies and procedures parallel to those available under comparable civil rights laws. Thus, if the remedies and procedures change in title II of the 1964 Act, for persons discriminated against in public accommodations on account of race,

title provides." The committee was worried that this provision could be construed to mean that the specific remedies are available, but aggrieved parties do not have to abide by them. The amendment did not affect remedies available under state laws or other federal laws and clearly tied remedies to Title VII and throughout ADA.

The report noted that an amendment was proposed that would strike out the language that tied ADA remedies to Civil Rights Act remedies and specifically articulate that the only relief available would be equitable relief—injunctions and back pay. However, "[t]his amendment was rejected as antithetical to the purpose of the ADA—to provide civil rights protections for persons with disabilities that are parallel to those available to minorities and women."[385]

A fourth amendment consisted of an attempt to clarify the phrases "direct threat," "essential functions" (of a job), and "anticipatory discrimination." This amendment also delineated what entities are covered under the "general rule" provision of Title III, stated that commercial facilities are covered by the alterations provision, and added a section that mandated that exams and classes relating to application, licensing, certifications, or credentialing must be held in an accessible place and manner.

With regard to the term "direct threat," the amendment added the definition: "a significant risk to the health or safety of others that cannot be eliminated by reasonable accommodation."[386] This amendment[387] served to codify *School Board of Nassau County v. Arline*.[388] Thus, where a direct threat to the

---

color, religion, or national origin, they will change identically in this title for persons with disabilities.
Id.

[385] *Id.*

[386] *Id.*; Bill proposed by the Judiciary Committee, section 101(8) (for employment settings), at 4; and 302(b)(3) (for public accommodation settings), at 13.

[387] *Id.* at 34.

[388] 480 U.S. 273, 1 AD Cases 1026 (1987). Where a school teacher was susceptible to tuberculosis relapses, the Supreme Court held that while "avoiding exposing others to significant health and safety risks," one must "evaluate, in light of [the] medical findings, whether the employer could reasonable accommodate the employee under the established standards for that inquiry." *Id.* at 289.

health and safety of others exists, the bill would not require entities to allow such a person to benefit from the available goods and services.[389]

The section on essential functions adopted language to state explicitly that "consideration shall be given to employer's judgement as to what functions are essential."[390] Additionally, the report pointed out that the committee rejected an amendment that would have created a presumption in favor of the employer's determination of essential functions.

With regard to the "general rule" provision,[391] the committee adopted an amendment in which the prohibition preventing discrimination "in the full and equal enjoyment of the goods, services, facilities, privileges, advantages, and accommodations of any place of public accommodation," applies to "any person who owns, leases (or leases to), or operates a place of public accommodation."[392] With this change, both the owner and the operator of a building would be obligated to make the facility accessible and both could be held liable.[393] Additionally, the amendment clarifies one aspect of the "anticipatory discrimination provision."[394] If, "[f]or example, . . . the corporate headquarters of a chain of restaurants designs all new restaurants to contain barriers to access," the corporation could be enjoined from all inaccessible new construction.

---

[389] H.R. REP. No. 101-485, pt. III, at 13 (1990), *reprinted in* 1990 U.S.C.C.A.N. 445. The bill proposed by the Committee on the Judiciary, §302(b)(3) states:
Nothing in this title shall require an entity to permit an individual to participate in or benefit from the goods, services, facilities, privileges, advantages and accommodations of such entity where such individual poses a direct threat to the health or safety of others. The term "direct threat" means a significant risk to the health or safety of others that cannot be eliminated by a modification of policies, practices, or procedures or by the provision of auxiliary aids or services.

[390] *Id.* at 4; Bill proposed by the Committee on the Judiciary, §101(7).

[391] *ADA Judiciary Comm. Hearings, supra* note 315, at 26; Bill as introduced in the House of Representatives, §402(a).

[392] H.R. REP. No. 101-485, pt. III, at 11 (1990), *reprinted in* 1990 U.S.C.C.A.N. 445; Bill proposed by the Committee on the Judiciary §302(a).

[393] H.R. REP. No. 101-485, pt. III, at 55. "For example, if an office building contains a doctor's office, both the owner of the building and the doctor's office are required to make readily achievable alterations." *Id.*

[394] *Id.* at 56; Bill proposed by the Committee on the Judiciary §308(a)(1).

The amendment also moved the section that mandated alterations for existing structures from section 302(b)(2)(vi), where it only applied to public accommodations, and put it in section 303 so that it would apply to both public accommodations and commercial facilities.[395]

Finally, the amendment added a new section that addressed the problem of inaccessibility to testing facilities. Section 309 states that "an entity cannot offer its program in an inaccessible site without providing persons with disabilities an alternative accessible arrangement which provides comparable conditions provided to others."[396]

The purpose of the fifth and final proposed amendment was to make technical changes to interim accessibility standards under Title III, which mandated that the new facility accessibility requirements applied to any building that will first be occupied within 30 months after the date of enactment of the ADA. Specifically, the amendment linked interim accessibility standards to the date the builder gets a permit to build that building within the time specified in the permit. In other words, the amendment gives builders a specific timeframe.[397]

It was clear from the successful amendments that the House members had listened to the witnesses and considered their hesitations about the ADA. Passing two amendments

---

[395] H.R. Rep. No. 101-485, pt. III, at 63. "This provision does not require alterations. Rather it simply provides that, when alterations are being made, they must be done in a manner such that, to the maximum extent feasible, the altered area is readily accessible to and usable by individuals with disabilities." *Id.* at 55.

[396] *Id.* at 69. *See id.* at 16; Bill proposed by the Committee on the Judiciary, §309. "Any person that offers examination or course related to application, licensing, certification, or credentialing for secondary or postsecondary education, professional, or trade purposes shall offer such examinations or courses in place and manner accessible to persons with disabilities or offer alternative accessible arrangements for such individuals." H.R. Rep. No. 101-485, pt. III, at 16.

[397] H.R. Rep. No. 101-485, pt. III, at 15; Bill proposed by the Committee on the Judiciary, §306(d). "For new construction or alterations for which a valid and appropriate [s]tate or local building permit is obtained prior to the issuance of final regulations under this section, and for which the construction or alteration authorized by such permit begins within [1] year of the receipt of such permit and is completed under the terms of such permit, compliance with the Uniform Federal Accessibility Standards in effect at the time the building permit is issued shall suffice

clarifying the language of the bill, expanding the scope of the "Public Accommodations" title, and refusing to back down on remedies, the members demonstrated a capacity for compromise and a willingness to address the concerns brought before them. As the last committee to consider the bill, the Committee on the Judiciary markup session was the final chance to openly submit amendments. That which was not passed in the markup session would have to make it past the Rules Committee in order to be debated on the floor.

E. Action on the House Floor: General Debate and Proposed Amendments

According to the procedures adopted by the House of Representatives, after deliberations and action on legislation by committees with substantive jurisdiction, the Rules Committee submits a "rule," in the form of a "House Resolution," that delineates the method by which the bill can be considered in the full House.[398] The rule can either be accepted or rejected, but once accepted, it is the authority on how the debate will proceed. In the case of the ADA, the Rules Committee presented House Resolution (H.R. Res.) 394.[399] This resolution provided that the House would dissolve into the Committee on the Whole for consideration of H.R. 2273. The Committee on the Whole is a way to expedite debate, because it requires that only 100 representatives be present to conduct business, instead of the usual number required for a quorum. After the Committee on the Whole debates and considers amendments, the entire House votes to accept or amend the actions of the committee. Resolution 394 from the Rules Committee also specified which and for how long the amendments would be considered. It provided for two hours of general debate—30

---

to satisfy the requirement that facilities be readily accessible to and [usable] by persons as required under §§302(b)(2)(A)(vi) and 303. . . ." *Id.*
[398] JOHNSON, HOW OUR LAWS ARE MADE, H.R. DOC. NO. 108-93 (22d ed. 2000).
[399] 136 CONG. REC. H2410 (daily ed. May 17, 1990).

minutes for each committee to be divided between the chair and the ranking minority member. Because the members of the House can vote whether to abide by the rule, the first order of ADA business on May 17, 1990, was to debate and vote on acceptance of H.R. Res. 394.

Although 45 amendments were submitted to the Rules Committee for consideration, under the rule only eight were to be considered. Thus, the provision that limited the number of amendments on the floor was by far the most contentious. Many representatives rose to defend the validity of their neglected amendments and the amendments of colleagues. For example, Representative Lynn M. Martin (R-Ill.) and Representative Newt Gingrich (R-Ga.) decried the fact that Representative Tom DeLay (R-Tex.) had offered 11 amendments, none of which made it to the floor. Among the amendments that were left out was an amendment by Representative Bill McCollum (R-Fla.) that would define the term "association" for the purposes of determining whether one could bring suit for having been "associated" with a disabled person. Another amendment by Representative H. Martin Lancaster (R-N.C.) would have provided that the same negotiations that are required between employer and disabled employee for determining reasonable accommodation be extended to the public accommodation title. Additionally, Representative Chuck Douglas (R-N.H.) had proposed that police not be required to hire "psychopaths." Representative William E. Dannemeyer's (R-Cal.) amendment would have exempted persons with communicable diseases from ADA coverage and Representative Dan Burton (R-Ind.) would have proposed stringent food-handling prohibitions for people with communicable diseases.

Such paring down of amendments was considered "totalitarian rule," an "abomination," and "a very bad rule" by the bill's critics. However, proponents of the rule claimed that, after 11 hearings, 7 subcommittee and committee markups, 6 subcommittees, and 4 full committee considerations, H.R. 2273 should not be subjected to more debate and wasting of time. Representative Steny Hoyer (D-Md.) spoke last and pointed out that, with all the committee considerations, a third of the members had already considered the bill and heard amendments, so there had certainly been full consideration of many of the amendments. In the end, the House voted to accept the rule by a vote of 251 for, 162 against, and 19 abstentions.[400]

Once the parameters of H.R. Res. 394 were accepted, the House Committee on the Whole moved into general debate. The chairman and ranking minority member on each of the four committees that considered H.R. 2273 were each given 15 minutes. The way general debate proceeds is that, when a member is allotted time, he then yields it out in small parts to other members who wish to speak in agreement with his stance. Thus, the fact that only the chairman and the ranking minority member were allotted time does not mean they were the only ones to speak. For example, Representative Major R. Owens (D-N.Y.), Chairman of the Education and Labor Committee, was allotted 15 minutes and immediately yielded time to Representative Hoyer to kick off the debate.

Representative Hoyer began his remarks by acknowledging the effort of the thousands of people who worked to make the ADA a reality. He then launched into a wrenching description of what it was like to be disabled in America.[401]

Decrying the loss of productivity and manpower, he informed his colleagues that $170 billion a year was spent on maintaining the dependency of disabled people. He went on to discuss the fact that the "next great world competition" would be economic, and not militaristic, so it would be of the

---

[400] *Id.* at H2424.
[401] *Id.* at H2426 (statement of Rep. Hoyer):
Imagine living in a world where every curb is a barrier; where nearly every telephone is useless and where most stores and businesses are unavailable to you. Where you and your family's tax dollars go to fund buses you cannot use, trains you cannot ride on, Government programs you cannot get to and jobs you cannot have. A world where you want to be included just like all your friends and relatives. Where you are frustrated at receiving a check from the Government every month, a check that effectively serves as compensation for all this discrimination. And where you want desperately to challenge your mind and your body in the day-to-day world or work and in the world at large that everyone else takes for granted. That is the world of most Americans with disabilities.
Id.

utmost importance that all our human resources be tapped for their potential. Having talked about the justification for the legislation, he spoke about the process of making a workable bill and how so many changes and compromises were made in the name of fairness.[402] He also noted that, in the interest of mutual understanding and legal certainty, wherever feasible the drafters of the bill used existing language from the Civil Rights Act and the Rehabilitation Act.

Representative William F. Goodling (R-Pa.) extolled the cooperation between the Republicans and Democrats and cited the bipartisan nature of the process as the reason the bill was dealt with quickly and sincerely. When Representative Owens rose before the House, he pointed out that the reason there was so much bipartisan support for the bill was because the bill merited such cooperation and respect. Thereafter, Representative Steve Bartlett (R-Tex.) and Representative Hoyer engaged in a colloquy that clarified the meaning of "qualification standards" as it appears in section 103(b) of the bill.[403]

---

[402] *Id.*
When the Americans with Disabilities Act came over from the other body last fall, we heard from many corners of the business community about concerns they had over this bill. We have worked closely with them, and adopted numerous amendments, to ensure that American business can work with the ADA.

Id.

[403] The exchange between Reps. Bartlett and Hoyer follows:
BARTLETT: Mr. Chairman, I would like to ask the gentleman from Maryland [Rep. Hoyer] for some clarification concerning the meaning of the term qualification standards as it appears in section 103(b) of the bill. That standard, as modified by the Judiciary Committee, permits a requirement that an individual with a disability not pose a direct threat to the health or safety of other individuals in the workplace if reasonable accommodation will not eliminate the direct threat. Direct threat is defined in section 101 of the bill to mean significant risk. As I understand it, this qualification standard is intended to spell out clearly the right of an employer to take action to protect the right of its employees and other individuals in the workplace, including not assigning an individual to a job if such assignment would pose a direct threat to those individuals. Is my understanding correct?
HOYER: Mr. Chairman, if the gentleman will yield, the gentleman's understanding is correct, assuming the employer cannot eliminate the direct threat by making reasonable accommodation.
BARTLETT: If I may further inquire of the gentleman, it is also my understanding that in determining what constitutes a significant risk, the employer

Representative Bartlett went on to discuss another reason why the ADA was so important—people are living longer and there is technology to assuage illnesses like never before. Then, again using his alloted time for clarification purposes, he gave examples as to what would constitute "undue hardship" and "readily achievable." By way of illustration, he noted that a $6 an hour reader for a $5 an hour employee would be an undue hardship, but a $6 an hour reader for one hour a year would not be an undue hardship.[404] Finally, he acknowledged that the best source for information about what a business should do are the disabled themselves: "[T]hey know what they need and what they don't need to level the playing field—simply ask them."[405]

When the time came to hear from the Committee on Energy and Commerce, Representative Thomas A. Luken (D-Ohio) articulated an unexpected benefit from the committee hearings: the dialogue that was begun between the disabled community and the commuter rail community.[406] The connection that was made and awareness that resulted were probably,

---

> may take into consideration factors such as the magnitude, severity, or likelihood of the risk to other individuals in the workplace, again assuming that such factors could not be eliminated by reasonable accommodation. I yield to the gentleman.
>
> HOYER: The gentleman's understanding is correct. Of course, the burden will be on the employer to show the relevance of such factors in relying on the qualification standard.
>
> BARTLETT: I thank the gentleman.
>
> *Id.* at H2428.

[404]Some of Rep. Bartlett's comments regarding the scope of accommodation and accessibility obligations foreshadowed debates that later unfolded regarding the scope of the obligations of commercial establishments. He opined that a store would not have to change its whole floor plan to accommodate patrons in wheelchairs. Rather, he suggested that simply having a sales representative who could assist a customer with reaching items and putting popular items near the front would be making a "readily achievable" accommodation. *Id.*

[405] *Id.* at H2428.

[406] *Id.* at H2433.

> Testimony at our subcommittee's hearing last fall indicated that Amtrak and many commuter railroads already do a fairly good job of serving disabled persons. This is not to say that there are not some problems. But the discussions and negotiations on this bill, at a minimum, have raised the level of

according to him, as important as the changes that the committee made to the bill.

Later in the debate, Representative Jolene Unsoeld (D-Wash.) spoke about the experience of her home state of Washington. She claimed that, despite having a law similar to the ADA on the books for over 10 years, not one business had ever been forced to shut down by having to make accommodations or employ the disabled.[407]

Representative Bud Shuster (R-Pa.) dominated debate by the Committee on Public Works and Transportation, setting the stage for an amendment he would later advance during the floor debate. His main criticism was with the potential cost of the bill.

> I must reluctantly state that I have serious problems with certain provisions of this legislation. First and foremost, there is not one penny in this bill to implement the tremendous costs of the various mandates and provisions which we are laying on the American people, on public transit systems, for example, across America.[408]

He denied that the ADA was a civil rights bill at all, claiming that it was merely a feel-good bill that was being passed without providing funding to make change happen.

Representative Norman Y. Mineta (D-Cal.) also addressed the issue of costs by warning that leaving such a large segment of society out in the cold will cost America much more, as the country can no longer afford to maintain a separate but equal situation.[409]

---

awareness for the legitimate concerns that exist on all sides of the fence, and have improved communication between the parties.

Id. (statement of Rep. Luken).

[407] *Id.* at H2434.

A number of those who have spoken in opposition to this legislation have expressed the concern that enactment of the ADA is going to create an unreasonable burden on small business, drive up the cost of operation, and ultimately threaten the very survivability of some businesses. My own State of Washington has proven the fallacy of this fear. For over 10 years Washington State has had similar statutes on the books, yet I have found no evidence of even one business being forced out of operation by having to accommodate or hire the handicapped.

Id. (statement of Rep. Unsoeld).

[408] *Id.* at H2436 (statement of Rep. Shuster).

[409] *Id.* at H2438.

Declaring the ADA a just and appropriate balance between business concerns and the concerns of disabled people, Representative Fish reminded the members that the job of Congress was to find the right balance—not the perfect bill for one side or the other.[410]

Much of the general debate was spent by members thanking fellow members for cooperation and support, in particular, many members expressed gratitude for the work of Representatives Bartlett and Hoyer and former Representative Tony Coelho (D-Cal.). Several members read general statements that expressed their happiness with the bill and summarized its provisions. Still others used their time to advocate amendments that the House would soon be discussing, for this was their very last chance to make changes. Indeed, over two days, the legislators would spend more than twice as much time discussing amendments as they did in general debate.[411]

1. *Grace Period for Small Business*

The House then turned to consideration of specific amendments to the legislation. The first to be taken up was an amendment introduced by Representative John J. LaFalce (D-N.Y.) and Representative Tom Campbell (R-Cal.), which read:

> Sure, there are costs associated with this bill, but these costs are manageable. But the cost of not allowing disabled Americans to be full participants in our society will be much greater. "Separate but equal" is not civil rights. So we must turn back those amendments that may provide that kind of "separate but equal" treatment.

Id. (statement of Rep. Mineta).

[410] *Id.* at H2440.

> This bill aims at opening up opportunities for all persons with disabilities. At the same time the bill does not put an undue burden on employers, businesses or the community at large. It strikes a balance. I understand that there are concerns from the business community that the bill goes too far and from the disabled community that the bill does not go far enough. The responsibility of the Congress is to ensure the protection of the rights of disabled people and to ensure that the community at large is not unduly financially burdened. This bill does just that. Not all will be happy but I know that we have reached a balance for justice.

Id. (statement of Rep. Fish).

[411] *Id.* at H2410. H.R. Res. provided that 4 hours and 20 minutes be spent in official debate.

> In section 310 (relating to effective dates), redesignate subsection (b) as subsection (c) and insert after subsection (a) the following new subsection:
>
> (b) **Civil Actions:** Except for any civil action brought for a violation of section 303, no civil action shall be brought—
>
> (1) during the first 6 months after the effective date, against businesses that employ 25 or fewer employees and have gross receipts of $1,000,000 or less; and
>
> (2) during the first year after the effective date, against businesses that employ 10 or fewer employees and have gross receipts of $500,000 or less.
>
> In subsection (a) of section 310, strike 'subsection (b)' and insert 'subsections (b) and (c)'.[412]

After being allotted 10 minutes to speak on the amendment, Representative LaFalce explained that the amendment was the result of concerns voiced in the Committee on Small Business, which he chaired. While he acknowledged the need for the ADA, he reported that, "On the other hand, no one wants a small business to fail because complying with or defending oneself under the ADA requires costly and time-consuming lawsuits or because regulations have not been issued informing businesses about the ADA's requirements."[413] Postponing the date at which a civil action can be brought against a public or commercial facility, he reasoned, would give smaller businesses time to figure out a way to come into compliance without jeopardizing their (often meager) resources.[414]

Representative LaFalce then yielded to Representative Campbell, co-author of the amendment, who clarified the fact that the "grace period" being extended to small businesses meant that the covered entities could not later be sued

---

[412] *Id.* at H2464.
[413] *Id.*
[414] *Id.*
> In light of this, our amendment provides a period of protection from civil action for the smallest businesses after the title goes into effect. Small businesses deserve a period of protection—a period without fear of penalty—as they seek to come into compliance with the ADA's requirements—an entirely new aspect of doing business for many of them.
>
> *Id.* (statement of Rep. LaFalce).

under the ADA for violations that occurred in that six-month period.[415] Representative Steny Hoyer (D-Md.) spoke in favor of the amendment and emphasized the provisions already in place to assist small businesses in the transition from inaccessible to accessible. He mentioned the 18-month "phase-in period," the guidelines from the Architectural Transportation Barriers Compliance Board to be issued nine months before the effective date of the ADA, and the technical assistance guides mandated for development by the Attorney General and the EEOC. The purpose was to create an effort "to educate the small business community and give them time."[416]

When Representative William F. Goodling (R-Pa.) spoke on the amendment, however, he summarized the sentiment of the House very concisely:

> While the concepts underpinning the ADA have parallels in existing law under the Rehabilitation Act, the reach of that act had been limited to Federal contractors and those entities receiving Federal financial assistance. Thus, the requirements of the ADA were completely novel to many aspects of the private sector, most particularly small businesses. Further, let's be honest, the ADA will impose costs, sometimes substantial. In this light, the perceived need for an exemption was hardly irrational.
>
> On the other hand, the disability community was rightfully concerned that a small business exemption would simply result in the continued denial of retail, entertainment, and other services—many of which are provided by small businesses—which led to the development of this legislation in the first place.
>
> Mr. Chairman, I believe the amendment before us, developed on a bipartisan basis, is a reasonable and sound compromise between these two competing concerns.[417]

After Representative Steve Bartlett (R-Tex.) gave a brief speech in favor of the amendment, the House voted unanimously to approve it.[418]

---

[415] *Id.* "I think the question should be made very clear that for actions or failures to take action during that period a lawsuit could not be brought once the 6 months is over." *Id.* (statement of Rep. Campbell).
[416] *Id.* (statement of Rep. Hoyer).
[417] *Id.* at H2466 (statement of Rep. Goodling).
[418] *Id.* at H2467, Roll No. 116 (401-0-31).

2. Role of Written Job Descriptions in Assessing Essential Job Functions

The next amendment that was considered by the Committee of the Whole House was one presented by Representative Bill McCollum (R-Fla.). It read: "and if an employer has prepared a written description before advertising or interviewing applicants for the job, this description shall be considered evidence of the essential functions of the job."[419]

Representative McCollum explained that the impetus for the bill was the uncertainty surrounding who would decide what are the "essential functions" of a particular job. This concern, he explained, is what prompted the Committee on the Judiciary to adopt an initial amendment that added the phrase "For the purposes of this title, consideration shall be given to the employer's judgment as to what functions of a job are essential," to the definition of "qualified individual with a disability." Representative McCollum's amendment would add to that provision by stating clearly that a written description by the employer is to be used as evidence. He pointed out that the protected person would still have freedom to present whatever relevant evidence is available, but that clarity in this provision would be essential to the success of the employment title. Representative Don Edwards (D-Cal.) then spoke and made it abundantly apparent that he and others were supporting the amendment because they felt that this amendment only clarified what the bill already said about employer consideration and did not add substance to the ADA. He went on to state that, "The weight that evidence of a job description will be given will depend directly on how closely it is tailored to the essential duties of the

---

[419] *Id.* at H2469. Although the record does not indicate where the wording was intended to go, the discussion suggests that it would go in section 101(8), immediately after the text

> Qualified individual with a disability: The term "qualified individual with a disability" means an individual with a disability who, with or without reasonable accommodation, can perform the essential functions of the employment position that such individual holds or desires. For the purposes of this title, consideration shall be given to the employer's judgment as to what functions of a job are essential [amendment].

Id. at H2451.

actual job. Writing down discriminatory criteria certainly does not shield them," and even that "[i]n fact, a job description can also be used as evidence of discrimination."[420]

No representative spoke out against the bill, and it passed by unanimous voice vote.

3. Effort to Quantify Undue Hardship

The next amendment was submitted by Representative James R. Olin (R-Va.):

> In section 101, at the end of paragraph (10) (relating to undue hardship), insert the following: "(C) **Excessive cost hardship:** For the purpose of this title, it is presumed an undue hardship if an employer incurs costs in making an accommodation which exceeds 10 percent of the [annual] salary or the annualized hourly wage of the job in question."[421]

This amendment caused the first actual amendment debate between members of the House. First, Representative Olin spoke about the context in which this change seemed necessary and the purpose of the amendment. He described the obligation of employers under the bill to provide a reasonable accommodation that is not an undue hardship, which, in turn, means without significant difficulty or expense. He then complained that the line between what is and is not an undue hardship will be "any person's guess."[422] Finally, Representative Olin claimed that his amendment would help remedy that vagueness by setting a cap at 10 percent of an employee's salary, beyond which there would be a presumption of an undue hardship.[423]

---

[420] Id. (statement of Rep. Edwards).

[421] Id. at H2470.

[422] Id. "The bill makes an attempt to define what the obligation of the employer is, but really when we come right down to it, it is going to be any person's guess what really is the dividing line between a sufficient response by the employer and an insufficient response." Id. (statement of Rep. Olin).

[423] Id.

> My amendment says that it is presumed to be undue hardship if an employer incurs costs making accommodation of more than 10 percent of the annual salary or the annualized hourly rate of the job in question. This is a limit that is easier to administer. It is fair. It is more likely not to cause problems.

Id. at H2471.

Representative Bill McCollum (R-Fla.) spoke in favor of the amendment, noting that he had sponsored a very similar one in the Committee on the Judiciary, but that it had failed. Undaunted, he stated that "it is my judgment that of all the amendments we are going to be considering on the floor today, this one may be the most significant one from the standpoint of mitigating the cost to small business."[424] He went on to state that this amendment would cut down on litigation because protected persons will not ask for, or expect, more than 10 percent of their salaries to be expended for the purpose of accommodation.[425]

A House Republican, Representative Steve Bartlett (R-Tex.) spoke out against the amendment. He claimed that the amendment would, in fact, cause harm to employers as well as disabled people. Individuals with disabilities would be harmed, he argued, because the concept of reason that permeated the bill would be replaced by a fixed sum of money. For businesses, he claimed that, in cases where there is an inexpensive way to accommodate a disabled person, this amendment would artificially set a floor of 10 percent and require more money than is necessary. He cited the following as an example of how the amendment will operate as a floor and not a ceiling, as Representative Olin claimed:

> Let us consider the reality. With an employee who is hired with a speech impediment, the employer makes a reasonable accommodation of no cost, of simply not requiring that employee to take his turns on the telephone in the reception area during the noon area [*sic*] and dividing that time among the other employees. There would be no cost to the employer, and it would be a modest, reasonable accommodation by the employees. The employee with the speech impediment gets the position and then goes to the employer and says, "Wait a minute, I earned $20,000 a year with

---

[424] *Id.* He went on to cite the support of the amendment by the NFIB.

[425] *Id.* at H2474 "[This amendment] does reduce the litigation opportunities because everybody looking at this is going to know from day one that they certainly are not going to get the employer to spend more than that 10 percent." *Id.* (statement of Rep. McCollum).

this company. Where is my 10 percent, my $2,000 for speech therapy?"[426]

The representative also made the point that the term "undue hardship" had been adjudicated in every court in the country, so there should be no question about what that term entails.[427]

Directly thereafter, Representative H. Martin Lancaster (R-N.C.) spoke about his state's experience with a 5 percent rule and assured the members of the House that it had imparted some certainty for the business community, and had not been a floor or a ceiling.

When Representative Major R. Owens (D-N.Y.) spoke out against the amendment, he questioned the origin of the 10 percent figure. Arguing that the number was arbitrary, he warned that its adoption would lead to unjust results. He asked about accommodations that are used concurrently by several employees, and facilities that will be used by numerous disabled people over time, such as ramps. After pointing out the difficulties in the amendment, he concluded, "The language is quite clear and quite simple already. This amendment only complicates matters a great deal despite its seeming simplicity, and I would urge a no vote on the amendment."[428]

Representative Tom DeLay (R-Tex.) next spoke on behalf of those who favored the amendment. He responded to Representative Bartlett's assertion that the amendment would hurt businesses by pointing out that the NFIB supported the change. He claimed that employers would rather pay higher costs for making accommodations than to let the courts decide the fate of their businesses.[429]

Representative Pat Schroeder (D-Colo.) responded by stating that this amendment would provide lesser accommodations

---

[426] *Id.*

[427] *Id.* "[The] same definition that has been in public law since 1973, and the country knows exactly what it means because it has been well defined; it has been tested in every court in the land, and in fact it is very clear what 'undue hardship' means." *Id.* (statement of Rep. Bartlett).

[428] *Id.* (statement of Rep. Owens).

[429] *Id.*

for the hardest hit—poor, disabled people. Particularly hard hit, according to Schroeder, would be female and minority workers and those who work in temporary and transitional jobs.[430]

The final congressman to speak against the amendment was Representative Steny Hoyer (D-Md.), who suggested that, for some small businesses, even 10 percent would be unworkable. He admonished the members to "[t]hink, if you will, if a small business only has three employees and the employee is making $20,000 so that the 10 percent would be $2,000, but the gross income of that company may be very small. In fact, significant difficulty or expense may be $400, it may be $300, depending on the resources of the company."[431] He argued that big business may not want this amendment either, citing a letter from the disability director at Dupont who stated that the 10 percent rule is not reasonable from the standpoint of a large company.[432] Last, he noted that the language used in the ADA was the same as section 503 of the Rehabilitation Act, which had never caused a business owner to declare that it could not meet the "reasonable accommodation" requirements of the bill.

Representative Olin spoke on the amendment last and made a final plea that, "We should not be passing laws that affect almost all the businessmen in this country where the proprietor of that business does not know what he needs to do to abide by the law."[433] Despite his efforts and the efforts of his colleagues, the amendment failed by a vote of 187 in favor, 213 against and 32 not voting.[434]

4. Access to Wilderness Areas

The fourth amendment to be considered had been proposed by Representative James V. Hansen (R-Utah). As one of

---

[430] *Id.*

[431] *Id.*

[432] *Id.* "[Allow me to refer you to the] remarks made just yesterday by Dick Drach, the manager of the disability program at E.I. Dupont, who said that 10 percent of salary as a definition of undue hardship does not make any sense from the perspective of a large corporation." *Id.* (statement of Rep. Hoyer).

[433] *Id.* at H2475 (statement of Rep. Olin).

[434] *Id.*

the original authors of the Wilderness Act of 1964,[435] he wanted to make sure that people in wheelchairs could have access to wilderness areas. On the House floor, however, a modification to the pending bill was proposed by Representative Bruce F. Vento (D-Minn.) stating:

> (c) **Specific Wilderness Access:** Congress reaffirms that nothing in the Wilderness Act is to be construed as prohibiting use of a wheelchair in a wilderness area by an individual whose disability requires use of a wheelchair, but no agency is required to provide any form of special treatment or accommodation, or to construct any facilities or modify any conditions of lands within a wilderness area in order to facilitate such use.[436]

Representative Hansen explained that the Wilderness Act was silent as to whether wheelchairs are allowed. Because of this silence, the Wilderness Act had been construed to mean that wheelchairs were prohibited because it was a form of mechanized transportation, which is specifically banned in the Wilderness Act. His amendment would make it clear that wheelchairs are not to be interpreted as banned transportation, but would not require wilderness areas to make special accommodations.

Representative Ron Marlenee (R-Mont.) asked the members to consider the fact that, "One of the groups supporting this amendment is the Disabled Veterans of America. Let us think about that. These are disabled veterans who fought to protect every acre of America, and they are forcibly prohibited from enjoying our wilderness areas."[437] Soon thereafter the amendment passed by a voice vote.

5. Food-Handling Jobs

The amendment offered by Representative Jim Chapman (D-Tex.), less than 70 words in total, generated the most charged debate of the day on May 17. It stated:

> (d) **Food Handling Job:** It shall not be a violation of this Act for an employer to refuse to assign or continue to assign any employee

---

[435]Pub. L. No. 88-577, 78 Stat. 890 (codified at 16 U.S.C. §§1131–1136).
[436]136 CONG. REC. H2471, H2476 (daily ed. May 17, 1990).
[437]*Id.* at H2477–78 (statement of Rep. Marlence).

with an infectious or communicable disease of public health significance to a job involving food handling, provided that the employer shall make reasonable accommodation that would offer an alternative employment opportunity for which the employee is qualified and for which the employee would sustain no economic damage . . .[438]

The debate over the measure began with Representative Chapman offering an explanation of the problem he perceived and how the proposed amendment would solve that difficulty. He observed that "the bill as currently drafted will not provide an employer the flexibility to move an employee out of [a] food-handling position if that employee were diagnosed as having an infectious or contagious disease such as AIDS."[439] The inability to transfer an employee to a non-food-handling job might result in small businesses having to shut down entirely if customers are too afraid to patronize the establishment.[440] He acknowledged early on that there was no evidence that AIDS could be spread by food-handling, but he did warn that, according to the Centers for Disease Control (CDC), there were 4,428 cases where the cause of AIDS was not ascertainable.[441] He admonished the members to look at the problem faced by small business owners realistically, and see that it was a distinct possibility that an establishment could go out of business if forced to retain food-handlers who are HIV-

---

[438] *Id.* at H2478 (statement of Rep. Chapman).

[439] *Id.*

[440] *Id.* "Damage to the business can be severe and not only cause the owner the loss of his business but could cause the loss of all the jobs of the employees that work there and result in the loss of . . . their livelihood." *Id.* at H2478.

[441] *Id.*
Let me hasten to add that I am not here to say that there is any evidence that AIDS can be transferred in the process of handling food. To the contrary, the Centers for Disease Control seems to say or does say that there is not a case that they can determine and document found in over 130,000 cases through April 1990 of the disease of AIDS being transmitted in this way. At the same time, however, the Centers for Disease Control said as of yesterday that there are 4,428 cases of AIDS where the cause is undetermined or unknown.

Id.

positive.[442] Finally, Representative Chapman pointed out that the hospitality industry, which includes food service, is the largest employer of disabled people, and so Congress should protect those who have taken the lead in disability integration.

Representative J. Roy Rowland (D-Ga.), a doctor himself, spoke against the amendment on the grounds that Congress simply did not have the medical knowledge to pass such sweeping legislation. He made it clear that he would feel better if the CDC were to issue the guidelines on what ailments constituted a "communicable disease of public health significance."[443] He even went so far as to ask, "How many of you know whether schistosomiasis, leishmaniasis, fascitis, trigonitis, and meningococcus are infectious or contagious diseases? Can any of you tell me that? Of course, Mr. Chairman, my colleagues cannot because they do not know, and they are not expected to know."[444] He concluded by stating that these matters need to be left up to health officials, not politicians.

Representative Charlie Rose (D-N.C.) then spoke about his personal view and about sound public policy. First, he declared his sentiments by stating: "Now do not ask me to risk my health, and the health of my children and the health of my family to prove how liberal and unprejudiced I am about communicable diseases."[445] He then spoke about how the government mandates that pilots retire at age 60 even though

---

[442] *Id.*
> We are dealing in the real world with real people who have real businesses that create real jobs, and I think it is a very reasonable accommodation to those people that we provide that they can make a reassignment to a different job of those who have a disease that the owner and all of us in this Chamber know can bankrupt that business and cause this loss of those jobs.

Id.

[443] *Id.*
> Who makes the determination about what is an infectious or communicable disease of public health significance? Mr. Chairman, if he had put after that, "as specified by CDC," then I think the amendment would be much more acceptable, but we have no standard. We have no base there. Health officials are expected to know whether those diseases are communicable and whether or not they are infectious, and we should leave that decision to health professionals.

Id. (statement of Rep. Rowland).

[444] *Id.* at H2479.

[445] *Id.* (statement of Rep. Rose).

they may still be able to fly, simply because it is good public policy and Congress decided that "they ought to be doing something else, like fishing."[446]

Arguing that the major authorities on restaurants and disease were in opposition to this amendment, Representative Frank McCloskey (D-Ind.) spoke to the House. He stated that, although restaurateurs want this amendment, the National Restaurant Association declared in a recent report that persons with AIDS should not be kept from duties or facilities because there is no evidence linking the transmission of the disease and food-handling. Furthermore, he pointed out that the National Council of Churches and the American Medical Association both opposed the amendment as well.[447] Representative Henry A. Waxman (D-Cal.) reminded the House that, at other times in history, persons have been treated unfairly, based not on medical evidence but because of social prejudices. For example, people used to believe that cancer was contagious and that blood transfusions from another race would not "settle" effectively. For Representative Waxman, the Chapman amendment was the result of similar, bigoted thinking.

Then Representative Steve Bartlett (R-Tex.) addressed the House in favor of the amendment. He began by asking the members to read the amendment again and see that it was not in conflict with the letter or spirit of the ADA. Specifically, the amendment

> does not allow an employer to fire anyone because of a public health disease in this case, nor to refuse to hire someone unless there is a direct threat, nor does it change the prohibition against discrimination against someone who has a disability, nor does it redefine disability from current law which does include those with contagious diseases.[448]

He went on to explain that the change would mean that, if someone had a disease covered by the amendment, moving

---

[446] *Id.*
[447] *Id.* (statement of Rep. McCloskey).
[448] *Id.* (statement of Rep. Bartlett).

them to a different job at the same pay would *be* the reasonable accommodation, along with any other adaptations.[449]

Another doctor, Representative Jim McDermott (D-Wash.), spoke next about the harm of the amendment from a medical standpoint. He first made it clear that, having taken an oath to protect public health, he would be forced to vote for anything that might be beneficial for the public's health and safety. But when acknowledging that the amendment was not about public safety, he stated, "Let us be honest: It is about the fear of AIDS."[450] He called the amendment the product of policy based on myth, fear, and ignorance and declared that making policy without knowing all the facts is one thing, but making policy directly in opposition to what is known is unacceptable.[451] Representative McDermott concluded with the following: "The amendment is bad medicine, bad science, bad public policy. It is indigestible. I urge my colleagues to send it back to the kitchen."[452]

Representative Beverly B. Byron (D-Md.) then addressed the House about the "direct threat" provision, stating that there are people with diseases that should not be handling food, but the instances with actual merit fall under the direct threat provision of the bill, which dictates that they can be fired.[453]

---

[449] *Id.*
What this amendment does is a very reasonable and careful balancing of the equities in which the amendment would say that, if there is an infectious or communicable disease that has a public health significance, then the employer may, first, make a reasonable accommodation that would, first, offer an alternative employment opportunity for the employee, and, second, for which the employee would suffer no economic damage.

Id.

[450] *Id.* at H2480 (statement of Rep. McDermott).
[451] *Id.*
This is what happens when you make public policy on the basis of myth, on the basis of fear and ignorance. It is one thing to make policy without knowing all the facts. This amendment asks us to make policy in spite of the facts we know, in deliberate deference to the fears and prejudices of others.

Id.

[452] *Id.*
[453] *Id.*
I agree that there are diseases that should disqualify food handlers from the working place. I could not agree more. People with illnesses that can be transmitted on the job, like infectious tuberculosis, hepatitis, should be

Thus, the amendment was unnecessary. Then Representative Chuck Douglas (R-N.H.) addressed the members on the subject of perception versus reality, stating that "perception is reality. Every one in this room knows that. We run election campaigns on perception. It is reality for our voters." He made it clear that the restaurant owners know the medical facts, but their patrons may not, and instead of creating a situation in which the business has to close, this amendment balances everyone's interests by providing for a lateral job change.[454] Later, Representative Paul B. Henry (D-Mich.) would urge, "if you want to vote perception, then support the amendment. But if you want to vote reality, and if you want to vote truthfulness as we understand it in science and the medical profession, you will oppose this amendment."[455]

Representative John Lewis (D-Ga.) issued an appeal based on civil rights ideals. He called the arguments used to defend this amendment "tired," as they had been used for so long to rationalize segregation.[456] He then urged the other representative to listen to the "health experts, not the hate experts." Finally, he reminded the members that "separate is never equal." Representative Tom DeLay (R-Tex.) later spoke and called the continued reference to race "incredible." He explained that problem at issue with the Chapman amendment was simply about changing employment areas, and nothing

---

disqualified from the workplace. They can be dismissed from their jobs because they pose a direct threat to public health and safety, and this bill guarantees that.

Id. (statement of Rep. Byron).

[454] *Id.*

It recognizes that unfortunately today there is a perception and there are cases unknown as to the cause of AIDS or some other disease that could be transmitted by blood, could be done by the chef in the kitchen, and it is just a realistic way of saying we are not going to shut down our restaurants because of that perception. We are going to be fair to them, as well as fair to the folks who have the disease.

Id. (statement of Rep. Douglas).

[455] *Id.* at H2482 (statement of Rep. Henry).

[456] *Id.* at H2481 (statement of Rep. Lewis). "Twenty-five years after the passage of the major civil rights legislation of the 1960's, we are still hearing the same tired arguments that were used to justify segregated restaurants. They have been dusted off and used again to defend discrimination." *Id.*

else—not racism or sexism.[457] Representative John R. Miller (R-Wash.) responded that, "this is as if businesses 40 years ago had pointed to the public perception of blacks and said our customers will not understand our hiring blacks, so allow us to discriminate against blacks."[458]

The final plea came from Representative Hamilton Fish, Jr. (R-N.Y.), who declared "Mr. Chairman, the Congress must not enshrine ignorance and prejudice in the law."[459] Regardless, the amendment passed by a narrow count of 199 for, 187 against, and with 46 abstentions.[460]

6. Additional Proposed Amendments

The House met again on May 22, 1990, to continue considering amendments on H.R. 2273. Representative William O. Lipinski (D-Ill.) had sponsored the first amendment that was considered.[461] Essentially, Representative Lipinski was reintroducing the same amendment that he had proposed and passed

---

[457] *Id.* (statement of Rep. DeLay). "This is not a racist issue. This is not sexist issue. This is a simple health issue that says that if you have an infectious or communicable disease, you can be moved to another part of your employment area. That is all it is. This is a health issue." *Id.*

[458] *Id.* (statement of Rep. Miller).

[459] *Id.* at H2483 (statement of Rep. Fish).

[460] *Id.*

[461] Amendment offered by Rep. Lipinski:

In section 242(b), strike paragraph (2) and insert the following:

(2) New commuter rail cars:

(A) General rule: Subject to subparagraph (B), a public entity which operates a fixed route system providing commuter rail service does not have to purchase or lease readily accessible and usable commuter rail vehicles to meet the requirements of this title—

(i) if such entity is meeting the requirements of subsection (b)(1) of this section relating to one car per train being accessible to individuals with disabilities within five years of the enactment of this Act;

(ii) if such entity provides clear, concise, and adequate notice, in its stations, of which cars are so accessible and the location of such cars on its trains;

(iii) if, in any case in which additional services are offered in a nonaccessible car of a train, such entity makes reasonable provision to ensure that such services are available to individuals with disabilities in the accessible car or cars of such train.

(B) Additional accessible cars to meet demand: In order for a public entity to be exempt under subparagraph (A), in any case in which actual continuing

in the Committee on Public Works and Transportation.[462] The amendment would allow commuter trains to make only one car accessible and negate the requirement that all newly purchased cars be accessible. The Rules Committee had accepted the jurisdiction of the Committee on Energy and Commerce, and their provision had been the one incorporated into H.R. 2273 as presented to the House for consideration.

Representative Lipinski acknowledged that, although all buses in a system should be accessible in order for that resource to be available, when it came to commuter rail, he proposed that the train be looked at as a whole and not several parts strung together. The amendment provided that, within 5 years, all commuter trains must have at least one accessible car, and to require that car to stop in the same, identifiable place every time.[463] In addition, whatever amenities were offered on other cars had to be offered on the accessible car and, if there was

---

demand for accessible service cannot be met by the public entity with one accessible car per train, the public entity must use additional accessible cars per train as may be necessary to meet such demand.

Id. at H2600.

[462] Id.

As you know, the Committee on Public Works and Transportation took a long look at the ADA, with the goal of providing complete accessibility while maintaining the highest level of public transit service possible. In the process of marking up the bill, the Committee on Public Works adopted an amendment of mine pertaining to commuter rail and accessibility. As we all know, in the final version of H.R. 2273 the issue of commuter rail will be addressed by the provisions of the Committee on Energy and Commerce. My amendment would essentially reinstitute the Public Works and Transportation version.

Id. (statement of Rep. Lipinski).

[463] Id.

First, the amendment maintains the one car per train rule, mandating that at least one car must be accessible as soon as practicable but no later than within 5 years. Additionally, it demands that the position of the accessible car on the platform be clearly indicated at all rail stations. This is designed to decrease train boarding confusion, allowing the disabled rider to expect the accessible car in the same place everyday. Furthermore, if any amenities are provided anywhere else on the train, such as bathrooms, diner or bar cars, they must be provided in the accessible car or cars. If these conditions are met in providing one accessible car per train, then commuter rail operators do not have to buy all new cars accessible.

Id.

a demonstrated need, additional cars had to be made accessible. He assured the members that "the existing commuter rail provisions do not guarantee even these simple solutions."[464]

Representative Lipinski emphasized his stringent equal accommodation requirement.

> You will notice my amendment requires that any services available anywhere on the commuter train, such as a bathroom, diner car or bar car, must be provided to the accessible car as well. The existing bill says no bathroom is required, even if every non-accessible car on the train includes a bathroom.[465]

Further, he pointed out that the Committee on Energy and Commerce provision did not ensure that all train stations had to be accessible, even if all the cars were. He declared that the ability to get on a train but inability to get off at one's desired stop did not constitute accessibility. However, with his proposed amendment, all stations would be required to be accessible.[466] Because his amendment called for the expansion of accessibility if there was "continuing demand," he also clarified that the term was to be construed broadly, and included special events and nonsequential busy days.[467] Representative Cardiss Collins (D-Ill.) would later counter that, "If you used a wheelchair, would you show up for a ride on a train that experience tells you can't accommodate your needs? Of course not. Demand for services by the disabled can only manifest itself when the supply already exists."[468]

---

[464] *Id.*

[465] *Id.*

[466] *Id.* "In sharp contrast, the Public Works version along with my report language makes clear each station must be accessible, and even outline requirements for special events and other situations which will arise." *Id.*

[467] *Id.*

> By no means does a given train need to operate over capacity five or seven days a week to be considered as "continuing demand." Rather, the demand, whether once a week or five times, must be regular or predictable. For instance, a person may have a part-time job and only ride a train three times a week. A student may ride to attend classes twice a week, or a person may travel to the hospital once a week. In all cases, if the demand is continuing and consistent to a train sometimes filled to capacity, the additional space must be provided.

Id.

[468] *Id.* (statement of Rep. Collins).

After making his initial case, Representative Lipinski yielded to Representative J. Dennis Hastert (R-Ill.), who advocated the amendment by pointing out the exceptions in the provision that the amendment sought to replace: "For example: only 'key' stations in a system must be accessible. In New York City, only 38 of 465 stations, eight percent, are classified as key stations. In Philadelphia, fewer than 20 percent. San Francisco cable cars and New Orleans street cars are entirely exempt from accessibility requirements."[469]

Representative Thomas A. Luken (D-Ohio) was the first to speak against the amendment, basing his objections on three grounds. First, he claimed that the amendment would be a step backward in disability legislation, because the Rehabilitation Act mandated that entities receiving federal assistance buy accessible new cars as well as have one accessible car per train. Second, he pointed out that the current provision was the result of negotiations with disability advocates and the administration—neither of which supported the Lipinski amendment. Third, many commuter systems had made efforts to improve their accessibility and the amendment would lower the expectations for those systems. Additionally, he maintained that "[t]he amendment also encourages segregation instead of integration."[470]

Next, Representative Collins decried the amendment, and, as she recalled a time when she had to sit in the back of the bus, she insisted that disabled people be extended full civil rights.[471] She went on to state:

> To be segregated is to be misunderstood, even feared. . . . Imagine, if you will, that you are an employer deciding whether to hire someone with a mobility impairment; you may have concerns about

---

[469] *Id.* at H2602 (statement of Rep. Hastert).

[470] *Id.* (statement of Rep. Luken).

[471] *Id.* at H2603.

There was a time in this country when I was required to ride in the back of the bus. I could not accept that kind of discrimination then, and I will not accept it now for any American. Allowing a few disabled passengers to ride a train is not enough. What disabled Americans seek with this legislation is the dignity which can only come with the full recognition of their civil rights.

Id. (statement of Rep. Collins).

whether that person can get to work every day on time. However, if you sit next to someone in a wheelchair every day on the train, I doubt that the question would enter your mind.[472]

Representative Nita M. Lowey (D-N.Y.) brought up another aspect of concern—the fact that the rail cars in her district were not amenable to having the same car stop in the same place every time.[473] The rotation system of the cars in her district and in many other districts prevented the sort of consistency required by the Lipinski amendment. Representative Norman Y. Mineta (D-Cal.) reminded the members that the purpose of making sure all new cars are accessible is because, over time, that practice will ensure that all trains are accessible.

Representative Steny Hoyer (D-Md.) rose to speak out against the provision and attempted to point out that the Bush administration and the mayor of Chicago (about whose rail system Representative Lipinski continually referred) did not support the amendment.[474] Representative Hoyer indicated that the Chicago system was facing legal problems because of its inaccessibility under state laws and was about to purchase new cars—a project that the city had postponed because of the requirement that they buy accessible cars. Time for debate ran out shortly thereafter, and the Lipinski amendment failed by a vote of 110 in favor, 290 against, and 32 not voting.[475]

The "Shuster amendment" offered after the Lipinski amendment had, like other proposed modifications, been offered in committee before. By far the lengthiest amendment,

---

[472] *Id.*
[473] *Id.* (statement of Rep. Lowey).
The commuter railroad in my district, Metro-North, is adamantly opposed to this amendment because of the severe difficulties it would pose to the management of their system. The cars on Metro-North trains are reordered frequently during each day in order to meet ridership demands. If Metro-North is forced to keep one accessible car in a specific place on each train, it will increase costs and interfere with their schedules. In fact, they consider this requirement to be more burdensome than the requirements that are already in the bill.
Id.
[474] *Id.*
[475] *Id.*

it provided "a very restricted annual waiver on mandating 100 percent life-equipped buses for those small communities an rural areas, small areas of 200,000 or less as defined by the Urban Mass Transit Administration, or rural areas."[476] The waiver, Representative Bud Shuster (R-Pa.) clarified, would be conditioned on the meeting of several standards. First, the applying locality would be required to submit a written plan for meeting the particular needs of the disabled in its district. Then the applicant would be required to prove that the needs of the disabled community will be met at least as well at they would have been met with 100 percent lift-equipped buses. Third, an advisory committee of disabled people would have to be established and the disabled community in general would be required to approve of the new plan to meet their needs. With regard to the latter requirement, Representative Shuster emphasized that its addition was "a fundamental difference between this amendment and the previous amendment which was offered. In this amendment, the local disabled community has a veto over such a waiver. In effect, this shifts the power and the authority and responsibility away from the Washington disabled lobby to the local disabled community."[477]

The bill as it was presented to the House, Representative Shuster argued, presented a "loophole" ("undue financial burden") that would allow localities to opt out of paratransit services where the financial burden was too high. He reasoned that if Congress gave a costly mandate for bus accessibility, the financial burden would almost always be too high—causing paratransit services to suffer.[478] Referring to the station exceptions for commuter rail in big cities, he claimed that "[t]he big cities have been taken care of with their exceptions, but

---

[476] *Id.* at H2606.
[477] *Id.* (statement of Rep. Shuster).
[478] *Id.*
Think about it for a minute. If we must, without exception, put lifts on every bus, if we do not get one cent more money to do this, and if we have a loophole that says we do not have to use paratransit if is an undue financial burden, then obviously it is the paratransit that is going to suffer.
Id.

small community America, rural America, has been given absolutely no latitude at all."[479]

In response, Representative Glenn M. Anderson (D-Cal.) pointed out that since public transit is paid for with 80 percent federal funding, the federal government ought to have a say in how the facilities are handled.[480] He then accused supporters of the amendment of believing that people in smaller, rural communities have fewer rights than people who live in big cities.[481] Pointing out the diversity of support for bus accessibility requirements, he asked, "[H]ow can we pass an amendment which takes away a civil right which the Senate, the White House, and even the Department of Transportation in its recent notice of proposed rulemaking are willing to extend to individuals with disabilities. The answer is—we cannot."[482] He further reminded delegates that "separate but equal is inherently unequal."[483]

Representative Donald J. Pease (D-Ohio) expressed anxiety over the fact that purchasing the more expensive, lift-equipped buses would result in fewer buses overall, which would limit transportation for everyone.[484] Addressing the issues of prior negotiation and local control, Representative

---

[479] *Id.*

[480] *Id.* (statement of Rep. Anderson). "I strongly believe that every public transit bus, most of which are paid for with 80 percent Federal funds, should have a wheelchair lift so the disabled can ride these buses just like their friends, fellow employees, and families." *Id.*

[481] *Id.* "More importantly, how can anyone believe that the disabled have less of a right to transportation if they live in a city of 200,000 or fewer than those who live in larger cities." *Id.*

[482] *Id.*

[483] *Id.*

[484] *Id.* at H2608 (statement of Rep. Pease). "Fixed resources and more expensive buses mean few buses. Yet transit systems need more, not fewer, buses." *Id.* Later, Representative Thomas E. Petri (R-Wis.) painted this picture:
> In my home town of Fond du Lac, population 35,000, the public transit authority currently operates an extensive paratransit service well beyond the operating hours for its main-line bus service. To ensure that its needs would be adequately met, the local disabled community was actively involved in structuring this successful plan. If Fond du Lac and hundreds of other small cities are forced to incur the additional expense of equipping and maintaining lifts on all of their buses, resources will necessarily be diverted from alternatives which in some cases are preferred by local disabled residents. In Fond du

Mineta spoke against the amendment. He asked the members how they were supposed to tell the disability community about this measure if it passed—about going back on their previously negotiated promise of full access to public transportation.[485] He questioned reliance on the decisions of local communities given the fact that they had not fixed the problem of disability access to date. "[I]f [the] local option works," he asked, "then why are we still debating the issue of accessibility for the disabled today?"[486] The answer, according to Representative Mineta, was that "local option simply does not work as a national policy."[487] Representative Thomas Petri (R-Wis.) rose to clarify that the local exemption option could only happen if the local disabled community approved the alternative system.

In defense of paratransit, Representative Bob McEwen (R-Ohio) expressed his incredulity at the idea that buses are better than paratransit:

> Let me repeat what we just heard on the floor. It [was] said that, if we gave door-to-door service to the disabled communities in small towns, that somehow or another we were doing them a disservice because we were not mainstreaming them. If we did not force them to sit in the wheelchair in the snow on the corner there and wait for the bus, then, if we went to the house and picked them up, that that somehow was unfair. Mr. Chairman, I would submit that the Rockefellers, and the Carnegies and the Vanderbilts did not feel it was unfair to have door-to-door service, personalized service.[488]

Lac, that means that paratransit will be cut back to only that which is required by the new ADA law: that is, service comparable to the existing main line bus service. In other words, for Fond du Lac and other cities the new ADA law without the Shuster amendment will result in a reduction rather than an increase in service for the disabled.
Id. at H2609 (statement of Rep. Petri).

[485] *Id.* at H2608 (statement of Rep. Mineta). "How can we tell a disabled individual gladdened by the recent notice of proposed rulemaking issued by DOT [Department of Transportation], which will allow that individual to use a public transit bus for the first time, that this Congress is withdrawing that promise of access?" *Id.*

[486] *Id.*

[487] *Id.*

[488] *Id.* at H2609 (statement of Rep. McEwen).

Concluding the proponent side of the debate, Representative Shuster made a final plea to members not to place further demands on struggling localities that had already suffered funding cuts from the federal government.[489] The final speaker for the opponents of the amendment was Representative Hoyer, who got into a heated debate with Representative McEwen.

When Representative Hoyer spoke, he again invoked civil rights rhetoric and proclaimed that localities should not be given the option as to whether they want to maintain segregated facilities. Following this lead, the amendment failed by a vote of 148 for, 266 against, and 18 not voting.[490]

With the possibility of the passage of H.R. 4000—the Civil Rights Act of 1990—looming, Representative F. James Sensenbrenner, Jr. (R-Wis.), with the backing of the Bush administration, proposed an amendment that would spell out the remedies available under the ADA instead of having them connected to the remedies available under Title VII of the Civil Rights Act.

While debates on this amendment proved to be some of the most lengthy and lively of the session, it began with a simple explanation by Representative Sensenbrenner, who stated that the amendment's purpose was to clarify that equitable relief is the remedy for discrimination under the ADA. The amendment would not take away a right or give any new right, only "de-link" the remedies for employment discrimination from Title VII remedies.[491] He reminded the members that the Civil

---

[489] *Id.* at H2610.

Mr. Chairman, in conclusion I would emphasize that the facts of the matter are that our public transit service systems across America in this decade have suffered a 50 percent reduction in real money, real funding from the Federal Government—a 50 percent reduction, my colleagues, and this bill does not provide one penny, not 1 cent, to provide for the increased costs that the bill mandates. . . . Let us support our localities, rather than letting Big Brother here in Washington make all these decisions.

Id. (statement of Rep. Shuster).

[490] *Id.* at H2611.

[491] *Id.*

The amendment will neither expand nor contract the employment remedies currently available under the ADA which are the same as those afforded to women and racial minorities. This amendment will simply delink the remedies

Rights Act of 1990 might pass, which would provide for punitive damages and jury trials under Title VII. First, he insisted that punitive damages in the ADA would be an affront to the deal that was made between proponents of the ADA and the Bush administration and other Republicans who insisted that the first draft (which included punitive damages because it was connected to section 1981) be rewritten to provide only compensatory damages.[492] Second, he worried that the business community would be particularly hard hit, because many of them did not have experience with this sort of compliance and potentially could be sued for intentional and unintentional conduct. He clarified his position by stating that, "I believe it is sound policy is to have the money that businesses spend to comply with the ADA used to make facilities accessible and provide additional employment opportunities for the disabled rather than to provide a windfall to ambulance chasing attorneys."[493]

Leading the opposition to the amendment was Representative Don Edwards (D-Cal.), who called the parity in remedies between Title VII and the ADA the "heart" of the bill and called the amendment premature, advance discrimination.

---

for employment discrimination in the Americans With Disabilities Act from the remedies contained in Title VII of the Civil Rights Act of 1964.
Id. (statement of Rep. Sensenbrenner).

[492] *Id.*
As originally introduced, the Americans With Disabilities Act would have provided greater remedies for the disabled than provided under current title VII law. H.R. 2273 originally contained a provision calling for the "remedies and procedures available under section 1981" of the Civil Rights Act of 1866. Section 1981 has been interpreted by the courts to allow for recovery of punitive and compensatory damages and jury trials in certain cases of employment discrimination. Inclusion of this language in the original version of the ADA would have allowed the recovery of expanded damages and jury trials for employment discrimination against the disabled under the ADA. After intense negotiations between the other body and the Bush administration, an agreement was reached in August 1989 to, among other items, delete the reference to section 1981 procedures from the employment remedies provision in exchange for broadening the coverage under the public accommodations title. Thus, the ADA's employment remedies were limited to current title VII remedies.
Id.

[493] *Id.*

Representative Pat Schroeder (D-Col.), concurred by stating that "there are no rights without remedies. But you have lesser rights if you have lesser remedies."[494]

Representative Steve Bartlett (R-Tex.) then rose to give the most compelling legal defense of the amendment. He noted that compensatory damages were the norm in almost every other similar law—the National Labor Relations Act,[495] the Rehabilitation Act,[496] the Davis-Bacon Act,[497] the Equal Pay Act,[498] the Fair Labor Standards Act,[499] the Age Discrimination in Employment Act,[500] and the Worker Adjustment and Retraining Notification Act.[501] Even the Civil Rights Act had used compensatory damages for 25 years. He also argued that compensatory damages deter unwanted, discriminatory behavior and result in disputes being settled rather quickly—allowing the victim to return to work quickly.[502] He cited case law under the Age Discrimination in Employment Act in which courts ruled against allowing punitive damages because they were deterrents to the conciliation process, provided no incentive to settle in mediation, and impeded good will between the parties.[503]

---

[494] *Id.* (statement of Rep. Schroeder).
[495] 29 U.S.C. §151 et seq.
[496] 29 U.S.C. §790–796.
[497] 40 U.S.C. §276a to 276a-7.
[498] 29 U.S.C. §206.
[499] 29 U.S.C. §201 et seq.
[500] 29 U.S.C. §621 et seq.
[501] 29 U.S.C. §2101 et seq.
[502] 136 CONG. REC. H2410, H2611 (daily ed. May 17, 1990). "Remedies allowing for injunctive relief and backpay, and excluding punitive and compensatory damages, both deter discrimination and promote the prompt resolution of disputes, a resolution which puts the employee back to work in this or her rightful position as soon as possible." *Id.* (statement of Rep. Bartlett).
[503] *Id.* at H2616–17.
This [danger that will come from punitive damages] is not some prediction made up yesterday; it is a well-recognized result arising from these kinds of damages, as reflected by the analysis in numerous courts which considered, and ultimately rejected, compensatory and punitive damages under the Age Discrimination in Employment Act [ADEA]. For example, the Third Circuit in *Rogers v. Exxon Research & Engineering Co.*, 550 F.2d 834, 841 ([3d Cir.] 1977) reasoned that compensatory damages would: Introduce an element of uncertainty which would impair the conciliation process. Haggling over an appropriate sum could become a three-sided conflict among the employer,

Other proponents of the bill included Representative Charles W. Stenholm (D-Tex.) and Representative Peter Smith (R-Vt.). Representative Stenholm brought up the point that identical remedies might not be appropriate in this situation.

> Identical remedies on paper do not necessarily translate into identical results in the real world. For example, under current Title VII remedies, injunctive relief for a race, religion, or sex-based violation could include simple placement in the job the plaintiff sought. Under the ADA, current Title VII injunctive relief could require expensive alterations for accessibility in order to accomplish that job placement. Maybe we do want ADA remedies to be exactly the same as whatever remedies are available under Title VII. Or, maybe we would want, after careful consideration of how the two laws could interact, to fine tune some differences, for purposes of equity and more consistent results.... [W]e shouldn't put the legislative process on autopilot by dismissing the request for considered debate. We shouldn't avoid reasonable questions with a superficial one-size-will-fit-all attitude.[504]

In an attempt to predict what might happen if the Civil Rights Act and the ADA were both given punitive damages and jury trial remedies, Representative Smith cited the statistic

---

the [EEOC], and the claimant. . . . [T]he possibility of recovering a large verdict for pain and suffering will make a claimant less than enthusiastic about accepting a settlement for only out-of-pocket loss in the administrative phase of the case. The net result can only be to substantially increase the volume of litigation in the trials.

The Fifth Circuit echoed that compensatory damages would: Introduc[e] a volatile ingredient into the tripartite negotiations involving [EEOC], employee, and employer which might well be calculated to frustrate rather than to "effectuate the purposes" of the Act. *Dean v. American Security Insurance Co.*, 559 F.2d 1036, 1039 ([5th Cir.] 1977), *cert. denied*, 434 U.S. 1066 (1978).

The Second Circuit has stated: If an individual alleging discrimination knew he could recover compensatory damages if he refused to settle during the administrative process and commenced a civil suit, he would have little incentive to resolve the dispute during the conciliation process. *Johnson v. Al Tech Specialties Steel Corp.*, 34 FEP Cases 861, 864 (1984).

One trial court observed: "If large tort recoveries are allowable under the ADEA, it is doubtful that alleged age discriminatees will enter into good faith conference and conciliation when around the corner lies the possibility of large dollar pain and suffering recoveries." *Sant v. Mack Trucks, Inc.*, 424 F. Supp. 621 (N.D. Cal. 1976).

Id. (statement of Rep. Bartlett).

[504] *Id.* at H2619 (statement of Rep. Stenholm).

that, although under a compensatory remedy scheme only 6 percent of Title VII cases go to trial, of those that do, the attorneys' fees alone average over $96,000 per case.[505]

The arguments against the amendment were just as impassioned. Representative Craig A. Washington (D-Tex.) stated simply that, "If we have apples and oranges, and you choose one remedy for the apples and a different remedy for the oranges, if that is not discrimination, I do not know what is,"[506] while Representative Morrison argued that the amendment would not be necessary if there were not some desire to distinguish between the remedies in the future.[507] In his final appeal, Representative Hoyer alluded to the testimony of Attorney General Richard Thornburgh and to the Declaration of Independence:

> All persons discriminated against ought to have the same remedies. As a matter of fact, Attorney General Thornburgh said exactly that. He said, "The ADA wisely parallels in the disability area Title VII of the Civil Rights Act of 1964." What did that mean? It meant, ladies and gentlemen, that we hold these truths to be self-evident, that all men are created equal and are endowed by their creator with certain unalienable rights, and among these are life, liberty, and the pursuit of happiness. Because they are all created equal, in the eyes of our law we will treat them equal.[508]

---

[505] *Id.* at H2620 (statement of Rep. Smith).
What happens if employment discrimination damages get expanded under ADA and title VII? Under title VII with its current remedies, only 6 percent of the charges filed with the EEOC end up as lawsuits. The rest are disposed of through title VII's mediation and conciliation procedures. Of those cases that go to trial—an average of over 1,500 cases litigated each year—the attorneys fees average more than $96,000 per case.

Id.

[506] *Id.* (statement of Rep. Washington).
[507] *Id.* (statement of Rep. Morrison).
This amendment is about discriminating against the disabled, or it is about nothing at all. This amendment would not be needed in any way, shape or form unless there is a desire down the road to have different remedies, different protections for the disabled from the protections we give in our other civil rights legislation under title VII.

Id.

[508] *Id.* at H2622 (statement of Rep. Hoyer).

The vote on the controversial amendment followed, and it failed by a margin of 192 for, 227 against, and with 13 not voting.

After consideration of the amendments to the legislation, Representative Tom DeLay (R-Tex.) offered a "motion to recommit" the bill, which would have sent H.R. 2273 back to the Rules Committee.[509] Specifically, he wanted the Rules Committee to reconsider adding a provision that would allow an employer to consider a history of drug and alcohol abuse. Additionally, the new provision would extend coverage of the ADA to the executive and judicial branches of the government. Representative DeLay explained that, "What this amendment does is give employers a little more discretion in looking at the record of those drug addicts and alcoholics that may have been rehabilitated, and take a period of time as far as proving whether they have been rehabilitated or not, especially in safety-sensitive areas."[510] Arguing against the motion, Representative Hoyer expressed concern because there was no limit on how long the employer could wait to allow the employee to "prove" his or her rehabilitation. Allowing for a one-year or five-year "proving" period would be discrimination, according to Representative Hoyer. As for ADA coverage of the executive and judicial branches, Representative DeLay pointed out that the only remedy for disability discrimination against these two branches was under the Rehabilitation Act. Because, under the Rehabilitation Act, the only remedy is the restriction of federal funds, there was essentially no remedy, as the federal government would not cut off its own financial lifeline. Representative Hoyer assured him that "the executive is going to carry out the act and is in fact carrying it out."[511] In the end, the motion to recommit failed by a margin of 143 voting yes, 280 voting no, and 9 not voting.[512]

H.R. 2273 was finally voted on by the entire House and passed by an overwhelming 403 in favor, 20 against, and

---

[509] 136 CONG. REC. H2636 (daily ed. May 22, 1990).
[510] *Id.* (statement of Rep. DeLay).
[511] *Id.* (statement of Rep. Hoyer).
[512] *Id.*

9 members not voting. Aside from the one-car-per-train controversy between the Committee on Energy and Commerce and the Committee on Public Works and Transportation, the House bill incorporated all of the major amendments passed by the committees. Having aired their concerns about illegal drug use, contagious diseases, vague terminology, and preemption, the House managed to create and pass a bill that 93 percent of the House could agree on. The endless negotiations led to more specific definitions and procedures while maintaining and sometimes even expanding the rights enjoyed by disabled individuals under the law. In the end, rehabilitated drug users, alcoholics, and individuals with asymptomatic HIV were covered by the ADA. Additionally, Title VII remedies and preemption provisions were in place. Nonetheless, a few issues still remained to be ironed out in the joint conference committee.

IV. House-Senate Conference and Final Passage

Despite the overwhelming support for the ADA's passage, a few sticking points impeded total congressional approval of the bill. On May 24, 1990, two days after the House passed the ADA, the House and Senate met to resolve some of the outstanding issues. Conferees from each of the committees participated in the discussions that followed.

First, on June 6, 1990, the Senate met to consider the House's substitute bill. The Chapman amendment, introduced by Representative Jim Chapman (D-Tex.), triggered a great amount of debate and controversy. Senator Jesse Helms (R-N.C.) introduced a motion to instruct the Senate conferees to support the controversial amendment, which would permit restaurant owners and other employers in the food industry to reassign employees with AIDS or the HIV virus to positions that do not involve food-handling.[513] Helms said that the Chapman amendment was intended to protect food-industry

---

[513]The Senate adopted the motion on June 6, 1990, by voice vote after a tabling motion was defeated by a vote of 40 to 53.

employers from the "public's perception" of AIDS as a communicable disease. Many business interests strongly supported the amendment. For instance, the National Restaurant Association and the National Federation of Indepedent Business expressed their support of the motion. The National Restaurant Association, in a May 23, 1990, letter to the members of the Senate, stated that the Chapman amendment "strikes a balance for food service operators who must respond to current public health concerns while allowing those with infectious and communicable diseases the opportunity to continue their employment and maintain their standards of living."[514]

Others vehemently opposed the measure.[515] Secretary of Health and Human Services Louis Sullivan wrote a letter to House Speaker Thomas S. Foley (D-Wash.) describing the misconceptions surrounding the disease. Sullivan emphasized that "there is no medical reason for singling out individuals with AIDS or HIV infection for differential treatment under the Act."[516] William Roper, the Director of the Centers for Disease Control, also opposed the measure. In a June 15, 1990, letter to Senator Edward M. Kennedy (D-Mass.), Roper stated that the "scientific data clearly show lack of threat to food safety by HIV infection or HIV-infected persons," and that "food-service workers known to be infected with HIV need not be restricted from work unless they have evidence of other infections or illnesses for which a non HIV-infected food-service worker should also be restricted." Senate Majority Leader

---

[514] *AIDS Amendment to Disability Act Seen Facing Challenge in Conference*, 114 Daily Lab. Rep. (BNA), at A-20 (June 13, 1990).

[515] In addition to the members of Congress opposed to the measure, a consortium of 78 groups representing individuals with disabilities also opposed the amendment. Other organizations opposed to the amendment included the American Medical Association, the American Public Health Association, the American Nurses Association, the Centers for Disease Control, the American Bar Association, and the National Commission on AIDS.

[516] Additionally, Sullivan stated that he felt that the measure was "not needed or justified in terms of the protection of the public health" and that "the Administration is strongly committed to ensuring that all Americans with disabilities, including HIV infection, are protected from discrimination, and believes that the Americans with Disabilities Act should furnish that protection." (Letter from Sullivan to Foley, 1990).

George J. Mitchell (D-Me.) tried to block Helms's motion by instituting his own motion to table the issue. However, only 40 senators supported Mitchell's effort, and the Senate agreed, by voice vote, to Helms's motion.

In the meantime, the House and Senate were able to resolve 79 of the 81 issues left open-ended. The two main sticking points remained the Chapman amendment and congressional coverage by the ADA. Congress initially agreed to congressional coverage by a compromise under which Senate employees can sue in federal court to enforce their rights under the ADA, while House employees and those employed by "instrumentalities"[517] of Congress can seek redress through internal grievance procedures only. However, providing Senate employees with private rights of action in federal court was an issue that ultimately would be shot down. Nonetheless, Congress had reached a tentative compromise regarding this issue.

Consensus over the Chapman amendment would be a more contentious battle. On June 25, a House-Senate conference committee approved the ADA after the House conferees voted 12 to 10 to delete the Chapman amendment.[518] On June 6, the Senate had voted 53 to 40 to instruct its conferees to accept the amendment, but, according to conference chairman Senator Kennedy, the motion was "purely advisory" and thus was not binding on the conferees. The House conferees ultimately agreed to remove the amendment and approved the conference report.

On June 28, although the Senate had not yet voted on the report, Senator Kennedy attempted to send the conference report to the House for a vote. However, a few stumbling blocks kept the ADA from final vote. First, Senate Minority Leader

---

[517]For example, the Library of Congress, the General Accounting Office, and the Government Printing Office. 42 U.S.C. §12209.

[518]Representative Steny Hoyer (D-Md.) proposed the motion to agree to the Senate conferees' demand to remove the Chapman amendment. House Energy and Commerce Committee Chairman John D. Dingell (D-Mich.) and House Judiciary Committee Chairman Jack B. Brooks (D-Tex.) joined Chapman as the three Democrats opposing the Hoyer motion while Representative Hamilton Fish, Jr. (R-N.Y.) was the only Republican conferee to vote for the option to delete the Chapman amendment.

Robert J. Dole (R-Kan.) thwarted Senator Kennedy's attempt to send the report to the House through a parliamentary objection on behalf of other Republican senators over the jurisdictional dispute regarding the means of handling ADA claims against the Senate. The conference report had subjected the Senate to federal court action over potential ADA claims, but allowed House members to resolve such disputes through internal dispute resolution channels. This split method raised some constitutional separation of powers concerns. Both houses agreed that Congress should be subject to the ADA, but disagreed on how such a ban on disability discrimination should be enforced. The House bill enabled both House employees and those of Congress' "instrumentalities", to pursue their claims internally. Complaints would be handled pursuant to H.R. Res. 15, a House rule authorization for that chamber's Office of Fair Employment Practices.[519] The Senate bill, however, merely made the provisions of the ADA applicable to the Senate and its instrumentalities. Although some favored the notion that proponents of the bill should in turn be subject to its provisions, others expressed concern over the constitutional limitations of such a measure. Some believed that allowing individuals to sue in federal court violated the separation of powers principle by allowing members of the executive branch to administer the law. Senate Minority Ethics Committee leader Warren B. Rudman (R-N.H.) emphasized how congressional members are legally distinct from private entities and should not be susceptible to some of the ADA's enforcement measures. Senator J. Bennett Johnston (D-La.) commented that such enforcement measures "could result in a judge ordering a senator to hire someone as a 'confidential political adviser who was neither sympathetic with his politics or perhaps not even of the same party.' "[520] Thus, the issue of congressional coverage was far from settled.

---

[519] Rovner, *Law/Judiciary: Last-Minute Snag Means Delay for Disabled Rights Measure*, CG WKLY. REP., June 30, 1990.

[520] Rovner, *Congress Clears Sweeping Bill to Guard Rights of Disabled*, CQ WKLY. REP., July 14, 1990.

Debates over the Civil Rights Act of 1990[521] wound up determining the scope of congressional coverage for the ADA. On July 11, 1990, the Senate approved an amendment to the Civil Rights Act of 1990 offered by Senate Rules Committee Chairman Wendell H. Ford (D-Ky.) to codify an existing Senate rule providing civil rights protections for Senate employees. The ADA sponsors, favoring Senator Ford's language, agreed to permit the Senate to send the bill back to conference to incorporate the congressional enforcement provisions of the Civil Rights Act into the ADA.

In the version adopted by the conferees, the ADA prohibited members, officers, and employees of Congress and its agencies from refusing to hire, discharge, or otherwise discriminate in employment against individuals with disabilities. Complainants are limited to administrative relief and may not file civil suits against either the Senate or the House. Moreover, each legislative agency is responsible for developing remedies and procedures to enforce the ADA internally.[522]

After the congressional coverage question was resolved, the remaining issue to stall the ADA's passage was the decision to delete the Chapman amendment. Senator Helms threatened to sponsor a motion to send the ADA back to committee. Thus, the vote would have to wait until after the July 4th recess.

By July 11, 1990, Senators Helms and Orrin G. Hatch (R-Utah) took the debate over the Chapman amendment to a new level. Senator Helms had planned to introduce an amendment that would ultimately force the conferees to put the Chapman amendment back into the report. Senator Hatch, meanwhile, had come up with a plan to let the Secretary of Health and Human Services play a role. Hatch proposed that the Secretary of Health and Human Services prepare a list of communicable and contagious diseases that would be transmitted via food handling.[523] An employer in the food industry

---

[521] S. 2104.
[522] 42 U.S.C. §12209(2).
[523] Amendment SP 2118, introduced July 11, 1990. The amendment summary stated that it was intended "to permit the reassignment of food handlers with

could transfer employees with those listed diseases away from food-handling positions. The Secretary of Health and Human Services would update this list annually. Moreover, this amendment would not preempt state and local ordinances. The idea of allowing science to decide the issue spurred Helms to come up with a competing amendment. Helms put similar language into his amendment, except that instead of a list of diseases that would be transmitted through food-handling, Helms wanted the Secretary of Health and Human Services to compose a list of diseases that *may* be transmitted via food-handling.[524] The difference was that Helms's amendment did not require proof or evidence of transmittal. Ultimately, this more stringent amendment was rejected by a vote of 61 to 39. As to the Hatch amendment, Representative Steve Bartlett (R-Tex.) proposed to modify the measure so that food-industry employers would be placed under no greater burden than other employers in refusing to hire or transfer individuals whose disabilities pose a "direct threat" to the health or safety of others in the workplace.[525] However, Representative Steny Hoyer (D-Md.) argued that the Hatch amendment does not impose a greater burden on food-industry employers, and that they could avail themselves of the "direct threat" exemption. The House conferees rejected the Bartlett amendment by a vote of 14 to 6. Hatch's amendment, however, was approved by an overwhelming 99 to 1.

The National Restaurant Association, the organization that spurred the Chapman amendment in the first place, was disappointed by this turn of events. Mark Gorman, the

---

infectious and communicable diseases and to grant State and local food handling laws preeminence over Federal laws in this area."

[524] Amendment SP 2119, introduced July 11, 1990. The amendment's summary states that its purpose is "[t]o include the human immunodeficiency virus (HIV) on the list of infectious diseases that may be transmitted through food supply, and to grant employers the right to reassign food handlers with HIV or AIDS."

[525] Representative Bartlett's proposed clarification of the Hatch amendment would provide that food-industry employers need only accommodate individuals with communicable diseases "to the extent required" by section 103 of the ADA. Section 103 absolves an employer from having to hire or provide reasonable accommodations to an individual whose disability poses a "direct threat" to the health and safety of others.

association's senior director of government affairs, believed that restaurant owners would have to compare the Health and Human Services list with local health regulations to determine their ADA compliance, and therefore the ADA placed additional burdens on food-industry employers.[526]

Additional attempts to revive the Chapman amendment also failed. Representative William E. Dannemeyer's (R-Cal.) motion to recommit the conference report back to conference with mandates that the House conferees accept the Chapman amendment failed by a vote falling along party lines—77 percent of Democrats opposed the amendment, while 75 percent of Republicans voted in favor. In the end, the House narrowly elected to reject the language of the Chapman amendment.[527] On July 12, 1990, the House approved the ADA by a vote of 377 to 28.

Thus, despite the long and protracted battle over the Chapman amendment, the House passed the ADA by an overwhelming margin. Over 90 percent of House members voted in favor of the bill's passage. On July 13, 1990, the Senate voted in a similar fashion—91 Senators voted in favor the bill, while 6 opposed the measure, and 3 members did not vote.[528] The final bill was the result of more than 20 House and Senate committee hearings and markup sessions, in addition to two House-Senate conference committee sessions. Senator Tom Harkin (D-Iowa), who first delivered his remarks in sign language, emphasized that the ADA was an "emancipation proclamation" for individuals with disabilities:

> Today, we say no to second-class citizenship for people with disabilities, no to segregation, isolation, and exclusion, and no to

---

[526] *House Passes Disabilities Act After Conference Approves Report*, 135 Daily Lab. Rep. (BNA), A-15 (July 13, 1990).

[527] The final vote was 224 to 180 against Representative Dannemeyer's motion. Fifty-five percent of the House voted to reject adding the language of the Chapman amendment.

[528] The following Senate Republicans voted against the ADA's passage: E.J. (Jake) Garn (Utah), Malcolm Wallop (Wyo.), Gordon J. Humphrey (N.H.), Christopher S. Bond (Mo.), Steve Symms (Idaho), and Jesse Helms (N.C.). The following senators did not vote: James A. McClure (R-Idaho), Alan K. Simpson (R-Wyo.), and John D. (Jay) Rockefeller IV (D-W. Va.). 42 U.S.C. §12209(2).

patronizing attitudes. Today, we say yes to treating people with disabilities with dignity and respect, yes to empowerment, and yes to judging people on the basis of their abilities, not on the basis of fear, ignorance, and prejudice.[529]

President George H.W. Bush signed the ADA into law on July 26, 1990.[530]

---

[529] 136 Cong. Rec. S9698 (daily ed. July 13, 1990) (statement of Sen. Harkin).
[530] S. 933 became Pub. L. No. 101-336.

CHAPTER 4

STATE DISABILITY DISCRIMINATION LAWS

ALABAMA	278
I. State Law	278
ALASKA	278
I. State Law	278
A. Overview	278
B. Prohibited Discrimination	279
C. Definitions	279
1. Disability	279
D. Covered Employers	280
E. Reasonable Accommodation and Defenses	280
ARIZONA	281
I. State Law	281
A. Overview	281
B. Prohibited Discrimination	281
1. Preemployment Inquiries	282
a. Medical Examinations	282
C. Definitions	282
1. Disability	282
2. Essential Job Functions	283
D. Covered Employers	283
E. Reasonable Accommodation and Defenses	284
1. Reasonable Accommodation	284
2. Defenses	284
a. Direct Threat	284
b. Undue Hardship	285

ARKANSAS ... 285
I. State Law ... 285
   A. Overview ... 285
   B. Prohibited Discrimination ... 285
      1. Genetic Testing ... 285
   C. Definitions ... 286
      1. Disability ... 286
   D. Covered Employers ... 286
   E. Reasonable Accommodation and Defenses ... 286

CALIFORNIA ... 287
I. State Law ... 287
   A. Overview ... 287
   B. Prohibited Discrimination ... 287
   C. Definitions ... 289
      1. Disability ... 289
      2. Essential Job Functions ... 291
      3. Major Life Activities ... 291
      4. Medical Conditions ... 292
   D. Covered Employers ... 292
   E. Reasonable Accommodation and Defenses ... 293
      1. Reasonable Accommodation ... 293
      2. Defenses ... 295
         a. Undue Hardship ... 295
II. Local Laws ... 296

COLORADO ... 296
I. State Law ... 296
   A. Overview ... 296
   B. Prohibited Discrimination ... 296
   C. Definitions ... 297
      1. Disability ... 297
   D. Covered Employers ... 297
   E. Reasonable Accommodation and Defenses ... 298
      1. Defenses ... 298
         a. Bona Fide Occupational Qualification ... 298
         b. Business Necessity ... 299
         c. Undue Hardship ... 299

CONNECTICUT	300
I. State Law	300
A. Overview	300
B. Prohibited Discrimination	301
1. Genetic Testing	301
C. Definitions	301
1. Disability	301
D. Covered Employers	303
E. Reasonable Accommodation and Defenses	304
1. Defenses	304
a. Bona Fide Occupational Qualification	304
DELAWARE	304
I. State Law	304
A. Overview	304
B. Prohibited Discrimination	305
1. Preemployment Inquiries	305
a. Medical Examinations	305
2. Genetic Testing	306
C. Definitions	306
1. Disability	306
D. Covered Employers	307
E. Reasonable Accommodation and Defenses	307
1. Reasonable Accommodation	307
2. Defenses	308
a. Undue Hardship	308
DISTRICT OF COLUMBIA	309
I. State Law	309
A. Overview	309
B. Prohibited Discrimination	309
1. Preemployment Inquiries	310
C. Definitions	310
1. Disability	310
D. Covered Employers	311
E. Reasonable Accommodation and Defenses	311
1. Reasonable Accommodation	311
2. Defenses	312

FLORIDA	313
I. State Law	313
A. Overview	313
B. Prohibited Discrimination	314
1. Genetic Testing	314
2. Harassment	314
3. Medical Conditions	315
C. Definitions	315
1. Disability	315
2. Essential Job Functions	316
D. Covered Employers	316
E. Reasonable Accommodation and Defenses	316
1. Reasonable Accommodation	316
2. Defenses	317
a. Bona Fide Occupational Qualification	317
b. Direct Threat	318
c. Undue Hardship	318
II. Local Laws	318
GEORGIA	319
I. State Law	319
A. Overview	319
B. Prohibited Discrimination	319
1. Preemployment Inquiries	320
2. Retaliation	320
C. Definitions	320
1. Disability	320
D. Covered Employers	321
E. Reasonable Accommodation and Defenses	321
1. Reasonable Accommodation	321
2. Defenses	322
a. Infectious or Communicable Diseases	322
HAWAII	322
I. State Law	322
A. Overview	322
B. Prohibited Discrimination	323
1. Genetic Testing	324

C. Definitions 324
   1. Disability 324
   2. Employment 324
D. Covered Employers 324
E. Reasonable Accommodation and Defenses 325
   1. Reasonable Accommodation 325
   2. Defenses 325
      a. Bona Fide Occupational Qualification 325

IDAHO 325
I. State Law 325
   A. Overview 325
   B. Prohibited Discrimination 326
   C. Definitions 326
      1. Disability 326
   D. Covered Employers 326
   E. Reasonable Accommodation and Defenses 327
      1. Reasonable Accommodation 327
      2. Defenses 328
         a. Direct Threat 328

ILLINOIS 328
I. State Law 328
   A. Overview 328
   B. Prohibited Discrimination 328
      1. Pregnancy-Related Disability 329
   C. Definitions 329
      1. Disability 329
   D. Covered Employers 330
   E. Reasonable Accommodation and Defenses 331
      1. Reasonable Accommodation 331
      2. Defenses 331
         a. Bona Fide Occupational Qualification 332
         b. Undue Hardship 332
II. Local Laws 333

INDIANA 333
I. State Law 333

A. Overview	333
B. Prohibited Discrimination	333
1. Preemployment Inquiries	335
a. Medical Examinations	335
C. Definitions	336
1. Disability	336
2. Employee	337
3. Person	337
D. Covered Employers	337
E. Reasonable Accommodation and Defenses	337
1. Reasonable Accommodation	337
2. Defenses	338
a. Infectious or Communicable Diseases	338
b. Qualification Standards	338
c. Undue Hardship	339
IOWA	339
I. State Law	339
A. Overview	339
B. Prohibited Discrimination	340
1. Preemployment Inquiries	341
a. Medical Examinations	341
2. Genetic Testing	341
3. Pregnancy-Related Disability	342
C. Definitions	342
1. Disability	342
2. Major Life Activities	343
D. Covered Employers	343
E. Reasonable Accommodation and Defenses	344
1. Reasonable Accommodation	344
2. Defenses	344
a. Affirmative Action	344
b. Bona Fide Occupational Qualification	344
c. Undue Hardship	345
KANSAS	345
I. State Law	345
A. Overview	345

B.	Prohibited Discrimination	345
	1. Preemployment Inquiries	346
	a. Medical Exminations	346
	2. Genetic Testing	347
	3. Pregnancy-Related Disability	348
C.	Definitions	348
	1. Disability	348
	2. Essential Job Function	349
	3. Major Life Activities	349
D.	Covered Employers	349
E.	Reasonable Accommodation and Defenses	350
	1. Reasonable Accommodation	350
	2. Defenses	350
	a. Affirmative Action	350
	b. Direct Threat	350
	c. Infectious or Communicable Diseases	351
	d. Undue Hardship	351

KENTUCKY 351
I. State Law 351
  A. Overview 351
  B. Prohibited Discrimination 352
  C. Definitions 353
    1. Disability 353
  D. Covered Employers 353
  E. Reasonable Accommodation and Defenses 354
    1. Reasonable Accommodation 354
    2. Defenses 355
      a. Undue Hardship 355

LOUISIANA 355
I. State Law 355
  A. Overview 355
  B. Prohibited Discrimination 355
    1. Genetic Testing 357
    2. Pregnancy-Related Disability 357
  C. Definitions 358
    1. Disability 358

   2. Major Life Activities 358
 D. Covered Employers 358
 E. Reasonable Accommodation and Defenses 359
   1. Reasonable Accommodation 359
   2. Defenses 359
    a. Affirmative Action 359
    b. Business Necessity 359
    c. Qualification Standards 360
    d. Undue Hardship 360

MAINE 360
I. State Law 360
 A. Overview 360
 B. Prohibited Discrimination 361
   1. Preemployment Inquiries 361
    a. Medical Examinations 361
   2. Genetic Testing 362
 C. Definitions 362
   1. Disability 362
 D. Covered Employers 364
 E. Reasonable Accommodation and Defenses 364
   1. Reasonable Accommodation 364
   2. Defenses 365
    a. Undue Hardship 365

MARYLAND 365
I. State Law 365
 A. Overview 365
 B. Prohibited Discrimination 366
   1. Genetic Testing 367
   2. Pregnancy-Related Disability 368
 C. Definitions 368
   1. Disability 368
   2. Major Life Activities 369
 D. Covered Employers 369
 E. Reasonable Accommodation and Defenses 369
   1. Reasonable Accommodation 369
   2. Defenses 370

   a. Bona Fide Occupational Qualification 370
   b. Future Hazard 371
   c. Preferential Treatment 371

MASSACHUSETTS 372
I. State Law 372
 A. Overview 372
 B. Prohibited Discrimination 372
  1. Preemployment Inquiries 373
  2. Genetic Testing 374
  3. Retaliation 375
 C. Definitions 375
  1. Disability 375
  2. Major Life Activities 376
 D. Covered Employers 376
 E. Reasonable Accommodation and Defenses 377
  1. Reasonable Accommodation 377
  2. Defenses 377
   a. Bona Fide Occupational Qualification 377
   b. Undue Hardship 377

MICHIGAN 378
I. State Law 378
 A. Overview 378
 B. Prohibited Discrimination 378
  1. Genetic Testing 379
 C. Definitions 380
  1. Disability 380
  2. Major Life Activities 381
 D. Covered Employers 381
 E. Reasonable Accommodation and Defenses 382
  1. Reasonable Accommodation 382
  2. Defenses 382
   a. Undue Hardship 382

MINNESOTA 383
I. State Law 383
 A. Overview 383

    B. Prohibited Discrimination 383
        1. Preemployment Inquiries 384
            a. Medical Examinations 384
        2. Pregnancy-Related Disability 385
        3. Genetic Testing 385
        4. Retaliation 386
    C. Definitions 387
        1. Disability 387
    D. Covered Employers 387
    E. Reasonable Accommodation and Defenses 388
        1. Reasonable Accommodation 388
        2. Defenses 388
            a. Direct Threat 388
            b. Undue Hardship 388

MISSISSIPPI 389
I. State Law 389
    A. Overview 389
    B. Prohibited Discrimination 389
    C. Definitions 389
        1. Disability 389
    D. Covered Employees 390
    E. Reasonable Accommodation and Defenses 390

MISSOURI 390
I. State Law 390
    A. Overview 390
    B. Prohibited Discrimination 391
        1. Preemployment Inquiries 391
            a. Medical Examinations 392
    C. Definitions 392
         1. Disability 392
         2. Major Life Activities 392
    D. Covered Employers 393
    E. Reasonable Accommodation and Defenses 393
        1. Reasonable Accommodation 394
        2. Defenses 394

a. Affirmative Action	394
b. Preferential Treatment	394

MONTANA 395
I. State Law 395
   A. Overview 395
   B. Prohibited Discrimination 395
      1. Preemployment Inquiries 396
         a. Medical Examinations 396
   C. Definitions 397
      1. Disability 397
   D. Covered Employers 397
   E. Reasonable Accommodation and Defenses 397
      1. Reasonable Accommodation 397
      2. Defenses 398
         a. Bona Fide Occupational Qualification 398
         b. Undue Hardship 399

NEBRASKA 399
I. State Law 399
   A. Overview 399
   B. Prohibited Discrimination 399
      1. Preemployment Inquiries 400
         a. Medical Examinations 400
      2. Genetic Testing 401
   C. Definitions 402
      1. Disability 402
   D. Covered Employers 403
   E. Reasonable Accommodation and Defenses 403
      1. Reasonable Accommodation 403
      2. Defenses 404
         a. Undue Hardship 404

NEVADA 404
I. State Law 404
   A. Overview 404
   B. Prohibited Discrimination 404
      1. Genetic Testing 405

  2. Pregnancy-Related Discrimination 405
 C. Definitions 406
  1. Disability 406
 D. Covered Employers 406
 E. Reasonable Accommodation and Defenses 407
  1. Reasonable Accommodation 407
  2. Defenses 407
   a. Bona Fide Occupational Qualification 407
   b. Preferential Treatment 407

NEW HAMPSHIRE 408
I. State Law 408
 A. Overview 408
 B. Prohibited Discrimination 408
  1. Preemployment Issues 409
  2. Genetic Testing 409
 C. Definitions 410
  1. Disability 410
 D. Covered Employers 410
 E. Reasonable Accommodation and Defenses 410

NEW JERSEY 410
I. State Law 410
 A. Overview 410
 B. Prohibited Discrimination 411
 C. Definitions 412
  1. Disability 412
 D. Covered Employers 413
 E. Reasonable Accommodation and Defenses 414
  1. Reasonable Accommodation 414
  2. Defenses 414
   a. Undue Hardship 415

NEW MEXICO 415
I. State Law 415
 A. Overview 415
 B. Prohibited Discrimination 416
 C. Definitions 416

	1. Disability	416
	2. Medical Conditions	417
D.	Covered Employers	418
E.	Reasonable Accommodation and Defenses	418
	1. Reasonable Accommodation	418

NEW YORK 418
I. State Law 418
   A. Overview 418
   B. Prohibited Discrimination 419
      1. Genetic Testing 419
   C. Definitions 420
      1. Disability 420
   D. Covered Employers 420
   E. Reasonable Accommodation and Defenses 421
      1. Reasonable Accommodation 421
II. Local Laws 421

NORTH CAROLINA 422
I. State Law 422
   A. Overview 422
   B. Prohibited Discrimination 422
      1. Genetic Testing 423
      2. Retaliation 423
   C. Definitions 424
      1. Disability 424
   D. Covered Employers 425
   E. Reasonable Accommodation and Defenses 425
      1. Reasonable Accommodation 425
      2. Defenses 426
         a. Undue Hardship 426

NORTH DAKOTA 427
I. State Law 427
   A. Overview 427
   B. Prohibited Discrimination 427
   C. Definitions 428
      1. Disability 428

D. Covered Employers	428
E. Reasonable Accommodation and Defenses	428
1. Reasonable Accommodation	428
2. Defenses	429
a. Undue Hardship	429

OHIO 429
I. State Law	429
A. Overview	429
B. Prohibited Discrimination	429
1. Preemployment Inquiries	431
C. Definitions	431
1. Disability	431
2. Major Life Activities	433
D. Covered Employers	433
E. Reasonable Accommodation and Defenses	433
1. Reasonable Accommodation	433
2. Defenses	434
a. Undue Hardship	434

OKLAHOMA 434
I. State Law	434
A. Overview	434
B. Prohibited Discrimination	434
1. Genetic Testing	435
C. Definitions	435
1. Disability	435
D. Covered Employers	436
E. Reasonable Accommodation and Defenses	437
1. Reasonable Accommodation	437
2. Defenses	438
a. Undue Hardship	438

OREGON 438
I. State Law	438
A. Overview	438
B. Prohibited Discrimination	439
1. Genetic Testing	439

C. Definitions	440
1. Disability	440
2. Major Life Activities	441
D. Covered Employers	442
E. Reasonable Accommodation and Defenses	442
1. Reasonable Accommodation	442
2. Defenses	442
a. Direct Threat	442

PENSYLVANIA 443
I. State Law 443
  A. Overview 443
  B. Prohibited Discrimination 443
     1. Medical Conditions 444
  C. Definitions 445
     1. Disability 445
     2. Major Life Activities 445
  D. Covered Employers 446
  E. Reasonable Accommodation and Defenses 446
     1. Reasonable Accommodations 446
     2. Defenses 446
        a. Undue Hardship 446

RHODE ISLAND 447
I. State Law 447
  A. Overview 447
  B. Prohibited Discrimination 447
     1. Genetic Testing 448
  C. Definitions 448
     1. Disability 448
  D. Covered Employers 449
  E. Reasonable Accommodation and Defenses 449

SOUTH CAROLINA 450
I. State Law 450
  A. Overview 450
  B. Prohibited Discrimination 450
     1. Preemployment Inquiries 451

   a. Medical Examinations 451
  C. Definitions 451
   1. Disability 451
  D. Covered Employers 452
  E. Reasonable Accommodation and Defenses 452
   1. Reasonable Accommodation 452

SOUTH DAKOTA 453
I. State Law 453
  A. Overview 453
  B. Prohibited Discrimination 453
   1. Genetic Testing 454
  C. Definitions 454
   1. Disability 454
  D. Covered Employers 454
  E. Reasonable Accommodation and Defenses 455
   1. Reasonable Accommodation 455

TENNESSEE 455
I. State Law 455
  A. Overview 455
  B. Prohibited Discrimination 455
   1. Retaliation 456
  C. Definitions 456
   1. Disability 456
  D. Covered Employers 456
  E. Reasonable Accommodation and Defenses 457

TEXAS 457
I. State Law 457
  A. Overview 457
  B. Prohibited Discrimination 458
   1. Genetic Testing 458
  C. Definitions 459
   1. Disability 459
  D. Covered Employers 459
  E. Reasonable Accommodation and Defenses 460
   1. Reasonable Accommodation 460

| 2. Defenses .... | 460 |
| a. Business Necessity .... | 460 |

UTAH 461
I. State Law 461
   A. Overview 461
   B. Prohibited Discrimination 461
      1. Preemployment Inquiries 461
      2. Genetic Testing 462
   C. Definitions 463
      1. Disability 463
      2. Major Life Activities 463
   D. Covered Employers 463
   E. Reasonable Accommodation and Defenses 464
      1. Reasonable Accommodation 464

VERMONT 465
I. State Law 465
   A. Overview 465
   B. Prohibited Discrimination 465
      1. Genetic Testing 466
   C. Definitions 466
      1. Disability 466
   D. Covered Employers 467
   E. Reasonable Accommodation and Defenses 467
      1. Reasonable Accommodation 467
      2. Defenses 467
         a. Undue Hardship 467

VIRGINIA 468
I. State Law 468
   A. Overview 468
   B. Prohibited Discrimination 468
      1. Genetic Testing 469
   C. Definitions 469
      1. Disability 469
   D. Covered Employers 470
   E. Reasonable Accommodation and Defenses 470

1. Reasonable Accommodation	470
2. Defenses	471
a. Direct Threat	471
b. Undue Hardship	471

WASHINGTON 471
I. State Law 471
    A. Overview 471
    B. Prohibited Discrimination 472
        1. Preemployment Inquiries 472
            a. Medical Examinations 472
    C. Definitions 473
        1. Disability 473
    D. Covered Employers 473
    E. Reasonable Accommodation and Defenses 474
        1. Reasonable Accommodation 474

WEST VIRGINIA 474
I. State Law 474
    A. Overview 474
    B. Prohibited Discrimination 474
    C. Definitions 475
        1. Disability 475
    D. Covered Employers 475
    E. Reasonable Accommodation and Defenses 476
        1. Reasonable Accommodation 476

WISCONSIN 476
I. State Law 476
    A. Overview 476
    B. Prohibited Discrimination 476
        1. Genetic Testing 477
    C. Definitions 477
        1. Disability 477
    D. Covered Employers 478
    E. Reasonable Accommodation and Defenses 478
        1. Defenses 478
            a. Undue Hardship 478

WYOMING	....	478
I. State Law	....	478
A. Overview	....	478
B. Prohibited Discrimination	....	479
C. Definitions	....	479
1. Disability	....	479
D. Covered Employers	....	479
E. Reasonable Accommodation and Defenses	....	479
1. Defenses	....	479

The enactment of federal disability discrimination statutes—initially, the Rehabilitation Act,[1] followed by the Americans with Disabilities Act (ADA)[2]—served as the model for many states to enact stand-alone disability discrimination measures or to amend their general employment discrimination statutes to extend protections to individuals with handicaps or disabilities. These measures remain critically important today, even after the enactment of sweeping federal legislation that extends to most employers and workplaces. In a number of jurisdictions, employers must abide by and plaintiffs can utilize differing—often, more expansive—requirements and interpretations that go beyond the rights or causes of action recognized under the federal statutes. Thus, despite the fact that the ADA in particular has had important effects throughout society, it is not unusual for individuals bringing discrimination actions to pursue claims that rely exclusively or alternatively on state law theories or protections.

This has been particularly true following important rulings under the ADA in recent years, including those of the Supreme Court, which appeared to embrace a narrow view or construction of that legislation. In the aftermath of those decisions, some states reinforced the broader protections offered by their

---

[1] 29 U.S.C. §701 et seq.
[2] 42 U.S.C. §12101 et seq.

statutes—through legislative enactments, agency interpretations, or significant state court rulings—and their continuing importance was evident to employers, interest groups, and affected individuals alike. The following summary briefly describes the disability discrimination measures in effect in the states and highlights treatment of certain key issues, such as coverage, protections, remedies, and defenses.

ALABAMA

I. STATE LAW

Alabama has no general employment statute of broad application, nor does it have a specifically focused disability discrimination law that applies to most of the state's private-sector employers. One portion of the state's statutes contains an expression of Alabama's policy that the blind, visually handicapped, and those who are otherwise physically disabled shall be employed in the state service, as well as in the service of the state's political subdivisions, including its public schools. This provision further states that unless a particular disability prevents a person from performing a job, people with visual and other physical disabilities are to be employed on the same basis as people without physical handicaps in employment supported by public funds.[3]

ALASKA

I. STATE LAW

A. Overview

Alaska's Human Rights Law protects employees and applicants with disabilities from employment discrimination. The statute enunciates the policy of the state to encourage and

---

[3]ALA. CODE §21-7-8.

enable physically and mentally disabled persons to participate fully in the social and economic life of the state and to engage in remunerative employment.[4]

B. Prohibited Discrimination

Under the Alaska Human Rights Law, employers cannot discriminate against workers on the basis of mental or physical disabilities in hiring (including in the use of recruiting materials[5] and application forms[6] that express a limitation based on disability, unless the limitation is based on a bona fide occupational qualification), compensation, or other terms, conditions, or privileges of employment.[7] Unless a limitation is based on a bona fide occupational qualification, employers are prohibited from making preemployment inquiries that communicate or inquire into a limitation based on physical or mental disability.[8]

C. Definitions

1. Disability

Alaska's Human Rights Law defines "physical or mental disability" in a manner similar to that contained in federal law. It means a physical or mental impairment that: "(A) substantially limits one or more major life activities; (B) a history of, or a misclassification as having, a mental or physical impairment that substantially limits one or more major life activities; [or] (C) having a physical or mental impairment that does not substantially limit a person's major life activities but that is treated by the person as constituting such a limitation," or such an impairment that limits the individual's "major life activities only as the result of the attitudes of others toward the impairment;" or without such an impairment but is "treated

---

[4]ALASKA STAT. §18.80.200(b).
[5]*Id.* §§18.80.220(a)(3), (6), 18.80.225(2).
[6]*Id.* §18.80.220(a)(3).
[7]*Id.* §§18.80.220(a)(1), 18.80.220(a)(3).
[8]*Id.* §§18.80.220(3), (6).

by others as having such an impairment."[9] The definition of physical and mental disabilities in the Alaska statute also specifically includes conditions that may require the use of a prosthesis, special equipment for mobility, or a service animal.

The statute also defines "physical or mental impairment" as including a "physiological disorder or condition, cosmetic disfigurement, or anatomical loss affecting one or more of the following body systems: neurological, musculoskeletal, special sense organs, respiratory including speech organs, cardiovascular, reproductive, digestive, genito-urinary, hemic and lymphatic, skin, and endocrine[, as well as] mental or psychological disorder[s], including mental retardation, organic brain syndrome, emotional or mental illness and specific learning disabilities."[10]

D. Covered Employers

Employers covered by Alaska's Human Rights Law include states, political subdivisions of states, and other entities employing one or more employees in the state. Excluded are social clubs, and entities that are "fraternal, charitable, educational, or religious [in nature that are] not organized for private profit."[11]

E. Reasonable Accommodation and Defenses

According to the Alaska Supreme Court's decision in *Moody-Herrara v. State*,[12] the Alaska Human Rights Act, which prohibits discrimination against disabled employees, establishes an implied duty to reasonably accommodate disabled employees. In reaching this conclusion, the court looked for guidance to the rulings of federal courts under the ADA, and concluded that, unless there is a duty to reasonably accommodate disabled employees, the statute's purpose could not be fully realized.

---

[9] *Id.* §18.80.300(12).
[10] *Id.* §18.80.300(13).
[11] *Id.* §18.80.300(4).
[12] 967 P.2d 79 (Alaska 1998).

ARIZONA

I. State Law

A. Overview

The Arizona Civil Rights Act[13] contains broad prohibitions on discrimination in employment on the basis of disability by both public and private employers. The statute's restrictions extend to all facets of the hiring process and selection criteria and require reasonable accommodations of otherwise qualified individuals with disabilities.

B. Prohibited Discrimination

The Arizona Civil Rights Act prohibits employers from engaging in any of a number of prohibited acts, including: (1) participating in "contractual or other arrangement[s that have] the effect of subjecting a qualified individual with a disability who applies" for a job with or is employed by a "covered entity to unlawful employment discrimination"; (2) using "standards, criteria or methods of administration that have the effect of discriminating on the basis of disability, or that perpetuate the discrimination of others who are subject to common administrative control"; (3) excluding or otherwise denying "equal jobs or benefits to a qualified individual because of" his or her relationship or association with an individual with a known disability; (4) not making "reasonable accommodations to the known physical or mental limitations of an otherwise qualified individual with a disability who is an applicant or employee unless the" employer can establish an "undue hardship;" (5) denying employment opportunities based on the employer's need to make reasonable accommodation; (6) using "qualification standards, employment tests or other selection criteria that screen out or tend to screen out individuals" with disabilities, unless such "criteria, as used . . . is shown to be job related . . . and consistent with business necessity";

---

[13]Ariz. Rev. Stat. Ann. §41-1401 et seq.

and (7) failing "to select and administer tests . . . in the most effective manner to ensure that [the tool accurately reflects] the skills, aptitudes or other relevant factors of the tested individual, rather than reflect their "impaired sensory, manual or speaking skills" (except if they are the factors the test purports to measure).[14]

1. Preemployment Inquiries

a. Medical Examinations

Arizona law provides that the prohibition against discrimination on the basis of a disability extends to medical examinations and inquiries. Such scrutiny properly may include preemployment inquiries into the ability of an applicant to perform job-related functions, and medical examinations conducted in accordance with the statute's requirements, if it uses such results in accordance with the law's parameters and is shown to be job-related and consistent with business necessity. Medical exams can be required "after an offer of employment has been made to a job applicant and before" employment has commenced (and employment can be conditioned on the results) if "[a]ll entering employees are subjected to the examination regardless of disability [and] information obtained regarding the medical condition or history of the applicant is . . . maintained separately as a confidential medical record." The statute limits circulation of information derived from such exams, and excludes tests to determine the illegal use of drugs from the definition of medical examinations for these purposes.[15]

C. Definitions

1. Disability

The Arizona Civil Rights Act defines "disability" as "[a] physical or mental impairment that substantially limits one or

---

[14] *Id.* §41-1463(F).
[15] *Id.* §41-1466.

more of an individual's major life activities ... [a] record of such a physical or mental impairment[; or] [b]eing regarded as having such a physical or mental impairment."[16] "[I]mpairment caused by current use of illegal drugs" is specifically excluded from this definition.[17]

Under Arizona's Civil Rights Act an individual is a "qualified individual with a disability" if he or she "is capable of performing the essential functions of the employment position the individual holds or desires," with or without reasonable accommodation.[18]

The Arizona statute uses the familiar definition of "disability," stating that it "means, with respect to an individual . . . : (a) A physical or mental impairment that substantially limits one or more of the major life activities of the individual[;] (b) A record of such a physical or mental impairment[; or] (c) Being regarded as having such a physical or mental impairment."[19]

2. *Essential Job Functions*

The statue provides that "in determining what functions of a particular job are essential, consideration [is to] be given to the employer's judgment as to what functions of the job are essential, and if the employer has prepared a written description of the job before advertising [for the position] or interviewing applicants," that document may serve as evidence of the job's essential functions.[20]

D. Covered Employers

The Arizona Civil Rights Act covers employers of 15 "or more employees for each working day in each of [20] or more calendar weeks in the current or preceding calendar year" and their agents. These include employers, employment agencies,

---

[16] *Id.* §41-1461.2.
[17] *Id.*
[18] *Id.* §41-1461.8.
[19] *Id.* §41-1461.2.
[20] *Id.* §41-1467.

labor organizations, and joint labor-management committees. However, the Civil Rights Act excludes agencies of the federal government, bona fide private membership clubs, Indian tribes, religious organizations, and employers "of aliens outside any state."[21] The statute exempts employment outside the state, or employment by "a religious corporation, association, educational institution or society with respect to the employment of individuals of a particular religion to perform work connected with the carrying on . . . of its activities."[22]

E. Reasonable Accommodation and Defenses

1. *Reasonable Accommodation*

Under Arizona's Civil Rights Act, required reasonable accommodations are defined as follows:

> (a) Making existing facilities used by employees readily accessible to and usable by individuals with disabilities.
> (b) Job restructuring, part-time or modified work schedules, reassignment to a vacant position, acquisition or modification of equipment or devices, appropriate adjustment or modification of examinations, training materials or policies, the provision of qualified readers or interpreters and other similar accommodations for individuals with disabilities.[23]

2. *Defenses*

a. *Direct Threat*

An employer lawfully "may require that an individual with a disability shall not pose a direct threat to the health or safety of other individuals in the workplace." In this regard, the term " 'direct threat' means a significant risk to the health or safety of others than cannot be eliminated [through] reasonable accommodation."[24]

---

[21] *Id.* §§41-1461(4), 41-1462.
[22] *Id.* §41-1462.
[23] *Id.* §41-1461.9.
[24] *Id.* §41-1463(M).

b. Undue Hardship

"Undue hardship," an important factor in the accommodations process, is defined as "an action requiring significant difficulty or expense when" considering such factors as the nature and cost of an accommodation, the overall financial resources of the facility involved in the matter, and the overall financial resources of the employer.[25]

ARKANSAS

I. STATE LAW

A. Overview

Under the Arkansas Civil Rights Act, an otherwise qualified person has a right to hold employment without discrimination because of sensory, mental, or physical disability,[26] and freedom from disability discrimination is a civil right.[27] Moreover, under the Public Health and Welfare laws, the state, political subdivisions, public schools, and all other employment supported by public funds must employ people with sensory, mental, and physical disabilities on the same terms and conditions as persons who are not disabled, unless the person's disability "prevents the performance of the work involved."[28] It is a misdemeanor to interfere with an individual's rights under the Public Health and Welfare laws.[29]

B. Prohibited Discrimination

1. Genetic Testing

Apart from general prohibitions of discrimination on the basis of disability status, state law includes limitations on the

---
[25] *Id.* §41-1461.11.
[26] ARK. CODE ANN. §16-123-105(a).
[27] *Id.* §§16-123-101–16-123-108.
[28] *Id.* §20-14-301(b).
[29] *Id.* §20-14-302.

use of genetic information in the workplace statute.[30] That measure bars employers from utilizing genetic tests or information regarding applicants or employees for the purpose of discriminating against that individual or restricting any right or benefit of employment.[31]

C. Definitions

1. Disability

The Arkansas Civil Rights Act defines "disability" as "a physical or mental impairment that substantially limits a major life function, [but does] not include: (A) [c]ompulsive gambling, kleptomania, or pyromania; (B) [c]urrent use of illegal drugs or psychoactive substance use disorders resulting from illegal use of drugs; or (C) [a]lcoholism."[32]

D. Covered Employers

The Arkansas statute covers employers of nine or more employees "in each of twenty (20) or more calendar weeks in the current or preceding calendar year," and their agents.[33] Persons employed outside Arkansas or by (1) religious organizations;[34] (2) their parent, spouse, or child; or (3) a special license in "a nonprofit sheltered workshop or rehabilitation facility" are not covered by Arkansas Civil Rights Act.[35]

E. Reasonable Accommodation and Defenses

The Arkansas statute places damage caps on awards for compensatory and punitive damages for intentional employment discrimination: (1) $15,000 for employers of fewer than 15 workers; (2) $50,000 for employers of more than 14 and

---

[30] *Id.* §11-5-403.
[31] *Id.* §20-14-302.
[32] *Id.* §16-123-102(3).
[33] *Id.* §16-123-102(5).
[34] *Id.* §16-123-103(a).
[35] *Id.* §16-123-102(4).

fewer than 101 workers; (3) $100,000 for employers who employ more than 100 and fewer than 201 workers; (4) $200,000 for employers who employ more than 200 but fewer than 501 workers; and (5) $300,000 for employers who employ more than 500 employees.[36]

CALIFORNIA

I. STATE LAW

A. Overview

California has a variety of equal employment statutes that address disability discrimination in the workplace. For the most part, these laws, which cover most California employers, are found in the California Fair Employment and Housing Act (FEHA)[37] and the California Labor Code.

For public-sector employers, the California Civil Service Act provides the applicable prohibitions against disability discrimination. The Civil Service Act prohibits discrimination on the basis of physical or mental disability, and state agencies must establish and implement effective affirmative action programs to ensure access to state civil service employment for individuals with disabilities capable of remunerative employment.[38] In addition, other statutes prohibit disability discrimination by contractors performing public works contracts,[39] and in public schools.[40]

B. Prohibited Discrimination

The FEHA is one of the broadest employment discrimination statutes in the nation, and it has been expanded in recent years in the area of disability discrimination to deal with—and

---

[36]*Id.* §16-123-107(c)(1)(B).
[37]CAL. GOV'T CODE §12900 et seq.
[38]*Id.* §19230 et seq.
[39]CAL. LAB. CODE §1735 (Deering).
[40]CAL. EDUC. CODE §§44337, 44338 (Deering).

take a different approach from—the interpretations of the ADA at the federal level (chiefly those of the Supreme Court).

The terms of the statute spell out the state's distinctive approach, as compared with the federal statute. The California Legislature declared its intention to provide "protections independent from those in the" ADA, noting that even prior to enactment of the federal statute, California law "afforded additional protections."[41]

It made clear its desire "that the definitions of physical disability and mental disability be construed so that applicants and employees are protected from discrimination due to an actual or perceived physical or mental impairment that is disabling, potentially disabling, or perceived as disabling or potentially disabling."[42] It declared that "[p]hysical and mental disabilities include, but are not limited to, chronic or episodic conditions such as HIV/AIDS [human immunodeficiency virus/acquired immunodeficiency syndrome], hepatitis, epilepsy, seizure disorder, diabetes, clinical depression, bipolar disorder, multiple sclerosis, and heart disease."[43] In addition, it stated its determination that protected physical and mental disabilities "require a 'limitation' upon a major life activity, but do not require, as does the [ADA], a 'substantial limitation,'" which specifically was "intended to result in broader coverage under the law of this state than under that federal act."[44]

Moreover, under California law, "whether a condition limits a major life activity shall be determined without respect to any mitigating measures, unless the mitigating measure itself limits a major life activity, regardless of federal law under the [ADA].... 'Working' is a major life activity [under the FEHA], regardless of whether the actual or perceived working limitation implicates a particular employment or a class or broad

---

[41]CAL. GOV'T CODE §12926.1(a).
[42]*Id.* §12926.1(b).
[43]*Id.* §12926.1(c).
[44]*Id.* §12926.1(k)(B)(i). *See* Bryan v. United Parcel Serv. Inc., 2004 US Dist. LEXIS 3382 (N.D. Cal. Mar. 2, 2004) (district court held that because "working" qualifies as a major life activity, an individual may qualify as "disabled" under the

range of employments" (again, contrary to Supreme Court's interpretation of the ADA).[45] Thus, the FEHA requires only "a 'limitation,' rather than a 'substantial limitation' of a major life activity," and provides "protection when an individual is erroneously or mistakenly believed to have any physical or mental condition that limits a major life activity."[46]

C. Definitions

1. Disability

Under the FEHA, covered "physical disabilities" include, but are not limited to all of the following:

> (1) Having any physiological disease, disorder, condition, cosmetic disfigurement, or anatomical loss that does both of the following:
> (A) Affects one or more of the following body systems: neurological, immunological, musculoskeletal, special sense organs, respiratory, including speech organs, cardiovascular, reproductive, digestive, genitourinary, hemic and lymphatic, skin, and endocrine.
> (B) Limits a major life activity. For purposes of this section:
> (i) "Limits" shall be determined without regard to mitigating measures such as medications, assistive devices, prosthetics, or reasonable accommodations, unless the mitigating measure itself limits a major life activity.
> (ii) A physiological disease, disorder, condition, cosmetic disfigurement, or anatomical loss limits a major life activity if it makes the achievement of the major life activity difficult.
> (iii) "Major life activities" shall be broadly construed and includes physical, mental, and social activities and working.
> (2) Any other health impairment not described in paragraph (1) that requires special education or related services.
> (3) Having a record or history of a disease, disorder, condition, cosmetic disfigurement, anatomical loss, or health impairment described in paragraph (1) or (2), which is known to the employer or other entity covered by this part.

FEHA if he or she is "unable (due to an impairment) to perform a single job for a single employer.")
  [45] CAL. GOV'T CODE §12926.1(c).
  [46] *Id.* §12926.1(d).

(4) Being regarded or treated by the employer or other entity covered by this part as having, or having had, any physical condition that makes achievement of a major life activity difficult.

(5) Being regarded or treated by the employer or other entity covered by this part as having, or having had, a disease, disorder, condition, cosmetic disfigurement, anatomical loss, or health impairment that has no present disabling effect but may become a physical disability as described in paragraph (1) or (2).

(6) "Physical disability" does not include sexual behavior disorders, compulsive gambling, kleptomania, pyromania, or psychoactive substance use disorders resulting from the current unlawful use of controlled substances or other drugs.

(*l*) Notwithstanding subdivisions (i) and (k), if the definition of "disability" used in the Americans with Disabilities Act of 1990 (Public Law 101-336) would result in broader protection of the civil rights of individuals with a mental disability or physical disability, as defined in subdivision (i) or (k), or would include any medical condition not included within those definitions, then that broader protection or coverage shall be deemed incorporated by reference into, and shall prevail over conflicting provisions of, the definitions in subdivisions (i) and (k) [of mental and physical disabilities].[47]

A covered "mental disability" extends to individuals having any mental or psychological disorder or condition, such as mental retardation, organic brain syndrome, emotional or mental illness, or specific learning disabilities, which limits a major life activity, having a record of such a disability, or being regarded as having (or having had) such a disability, which "makes achievement of the major life activity difficult."[48] Also covered are circumstances in which an individual is "[b]eing regarded or treated by the employer . . . entity . . . as having, or having had, a mental or psychological disorder or condition that has no present disabling effect, but that may become a mental disability. . . ."[49] For purposes of the FEHA, the term " 'mental disability' does not include sexual behavior disorders, compulsive gambling, kleptomania, pyromania, or psychoactive substance use disorders resulting from the current unlawful use of controlled substances or other drugs."[50]

---

[47] *Id.* §12926(k), (*l*).
[48] *Id.* §12926(i)(B).
[49] *Id.* §12926(i)(C)(4).
[50] *Id.* §12926(i).

2. Essential Job Functions

The statute incorporates a very detailed definition of the term "essential functions." It states:

> "Essential functions" means the fundamental job duties of the employment position the individual with a disability holds or desires. "Essential functions" does not include the marginal functions of the position.
>
> (1) A job function may be considered essential for any of several reasons, including, but not limited to, any one or more of the following:
>
> (A) The function may be essential because the reason the position exists is to perform that function.
>
> (B) The function may be essential because of the limited number of employees available among whom the performance of that job function can be distributed.
>
> (C) The function may be highly specialized, so that the incumbent in the position is hired for his or her expertise or ability to perform the particular function.
>
> (2) Evidence of whether a particular function is essential includes, but is not limited to, the following:
>
> (A) The employer's judgment as to which functions are essential.
>
> (B) Written job descriptions prepared before advertising or interviewing applicants for the job.
>
> (C) The amount of time spent on the job performing the function.
>
> (D) The consequences of not requiring the incumbent to perform the function.
>
> (E) The terms of a collective bargaining agreement.
>
> (F) The work experiences of past incumbents in the job.
>
> (G) The current work experience of incumbents in similar jobs.[51]

3. Major Life Activities

With respect to limitations on major life activities, the statute provides that the term "'limits' shall be determined without regard to mitigating measures such as medications, assistive devices, prosthetics, or reasonable accommodations,

---

[51] *Id.* §12926(f).

unless the mitigating measure itself limits a major life activity."[52] A mental or psychological disorder or condition limits a major life activity if it makes the achievement of the major life activity difficult. "Major life activities" are to be "broadly construed[, according to the statute,] and shall include physical, mental, and social activities and working."[53]

4. Medical Conditions

Another important term defined in the FEHA is "medical condition." It includes health impairments "related to or associated with a diagnosis of cancer, or a record or history of cancer," as well as genetic characteristics.[54] Genetic characteristics include

> [a]ny scientifically or medically identifiable gene or chromosome, or combination or alteration thereof, that is known to be a cause of a disease or disorder in a person or his or her offspring, or that is determined to be associated with a statistically increased risk of development of a disease or disorder, and that is presently not associated with any symptoms of any disease or disorder[, and any] [i]nherited characteristics that may derive from the individual or family member

similarly linked to potential disease or disorder.[55]

D. Covered Employers

Employers of five or more full-time or part-time employees are subject to the FEHA's prohibitions against disability discrimination. Moreover, employers of at least one employee are prohibited from unlawful harassment based on disability.[56] In addition, an employer's agents, cities, the state, and any political or civil subdivision are covered by the FEHA.[57] However,

---

[52] *Id.* §12926(k)(1)(B)(i).
[53] *Id.* §12926(i)(1)(B).
[54] *Id.* §12926(h)(1).
[55] *Id.* §12926(h)(1)–(2)(A)–(B).
[56] *See* Robinson v. Fair Employment & Hous. Comm'n, 2 Cal. 4th 226, 825 P.2d 781, 58 FEP Cases 887 (1992).
[57] CAL. GOV'T CODE §12926(d) (Deering).

the FEHA does not apply to an out-of-state employer that hires California residents when that employer does not employ at least five employees within the state.[58] Similarly, non-California residents who work outside the state, but whose employer is a California-based company, are outside the protection of the FEHA.[59] Nonprofit religious organizations are also excluded from FEHA's reach.[60]

E. Reasonable Accommodation and Defenses

1. *Reasonable Accommodation*

Another key concept, "reasonable accommodation," is defined in the statute. The FEHA notes that it may include either "[m]aking existing facilities . . . readily accessible to, and usable by, individuals with disabilities," or involve a range of job modification measures. These may include "[j]ob restructuring, part-time or modified work schedules, reassignment to a vacant position, acquisition or modification of equipment or devices, adjustment or modifications of examinations, training materials or policies, the provision of qualified readers or interpreters, and other similar accommodations . . . ."[61]

In 2001, the California Supreme Court considered the extent of an employer's liability for an alleged failure to provide accommodations in an appropriate manner for an employee with multiple sclerosis. In *Richards v. CH2M Hill, Inc.*,[62] the court reviewed an employer's appeal of a jury award in excess of $1.4 million in damages relating to an alleged failure to provide accommodation and harassment over a 5-year period. At issue in the appeal was the statute's 1-year statute of limitations, which the employer argued rendered the former employee's evidence of conduct 5 years earlier untimely. The California Supreme Court ruled that, in that context, the conduct

---

[58] *See* Clopton v. Global Computer Assocs., 4 AD Cases 360 (C.D. Cal. 1995).
[59] *See* Campbell v. Arco Marine, Inc., 42 Cal. App. 4th 1850, 50 Cal. Rptr. 2d 626, 70 FEP Cases 262 (1996).
[60] CAL. GOV'T CODE §§12926 (d)(1), 12940(h)(3)(B) (Deering).
[61] *Id.* §12926(n).
[62] 26 Cal. 4th 798, 12 AD Cases 129 (2001).

over the 5-year period of time could be construed to be a single course of conduct, and the evidence potentially admissible in some circumstances.

In another accommodation case, an individual who experienced degenerative disc disease was allowed to proceed with a claim that her employer failed to meet its statutory obligations when it failed to reassign her to a vacant position that was less physically demanding, despite multiple transfer requests made to four managers over an extended period of time.[63] The company attempted to defend by noting that it had provided leave time, permitted rest breaks, and allowed the use of a chair on its sales floor, yet the court ruled that this was insufficient and did not satisfy an undue hardship standard.

The reasonable accommodation obligation is only triggered, however, if the individual in question is "otherwise qualified" for the position. Where an applicant failed a medical examination due to a hearing impairment but was hired because of a clerical error, his subsequent termination when the mistake was discovered was rejected, because the employer had established appropriate and legitimate criteria for the position that the individual failed to satisfy.[64]

Furthermore, employers cannot reject, terminate, or determine the insurability or suitability for employment of individuals whose blood test reflects that they have been exposed to the HIV virus or who suffer from AIDS based on those medical characteristics.[65] Moreover, because persons diagnosed with AIDS often experience certain cancers, including Kaposi's sarcoma, employees with such conditions could bring both disability discrimination and medical condition discrimination actions under the FEHA.

Among modifications found to be reasonable accommodations: (1) installation of a ramp to enable wheelchair access, (2) permitting an employee to telecommute 1 day per week,[66]

---

[63]Spitzer v. Good Guys, Inc., 80 Cal. App. 4th 1376, 96 Cal. Rptr. 2d 236, 10 AD Cases 1638 (2000).
[64]Quinn v. City of Los Angeles, 84 Cal. App. 4th 472, 11 AD Cases 207 (2000).
[65]CAL. HEALTH & SAFETY CODE §120980(f).
[66]See Bell v. Wells Fargo Bank, N.A., 62 Cal. App. 4th 1382, 73 Cal. Rptr. 2d 354, 8 AD Cases 95 (1998).

(3) investigating the possibility of other job positions or alternative work,[67] (4) holding an employee's job open for a few months,[68] providing training material or policies,[69] and providing qualified readers or interpreters.[70]

2. Defenses

a. Undue Hardship

An employer is not required to undergo "undue hardship" in providing a reasonable accommodation. The FEHA defines the term as an action requiring significant difficulty or expense, when considered in light of several specific factors. Among these are:

> (1) the nature and cost of the accommodation needed.
> (2) The overall financial resources of the facilities involved in the provision of the reasonable accommodations, the number of persons employed at the facility, and the effect on expenses and resources or the impact otherwise of these accommodations upon the operation of the facility.
> (3) The overall financial resources of the covered entity, the overall size of the business of a covered entity with respect to the number of employees, and the number, type, and location of its facilities.
> (4) The type of operations, including the composition, structure, and functions of the workforce of the entity.
> (5) The geographic separateness, administrative, or fiscal relationship of the facility or facilities.[71]

Among accommodations that would pose an undue burden on employers: (1) holding an employee's job open for 1 year,[72] (2) having an employee telecommute 5 days per week, and (3) employing a worker who is too ill to perform any alternative work.[73]

---

[67] *See* Prillman v. United Air Lines, Inc., 53 Cal. App. 4th 935 (1997).
[68] *See* LeBourgeois v. Fireplace Mfrs., Inc., 68 Cal. App. 4th 1049 (1998).
[69] CAL. GOV'T CODE §12926(n),(2).
[70] *Id.*
[71] *Id.* §12926(s).
[72] *See* LeBourgeois, 68 Cal. App. 4th 1049.
[73] *See* Prillman, 53 Cal. App. 4th 935 (1997).

II. Local Laws

A Santa Cruz ordinance prohibits discrimination on the basis of height or weight (or perceptions of a person's height or weight), as well as a person's physical characteristics, including a person's mannerisms, bodily conditions, and characteristics.[74]

COLORADO

I. State Law

A. Overview

Colorado law broadly protects individuals from employment discrimination on the basis of disability with respect to virtually all aspects of the employment relationship, including hiring, promotions, demotions, compensation, and terminations. Employer actions in these areas are insulated if they can establish that there is no reasonable accommodation that the employer can make in regard to the disability at issue, the disability actually disqualifies the individual from the job, or the disability has a significant impact on the job.[75]

B. Prohibited Discrimination

Colorado's statutes bar employment discrimination on the basis of disability in both the public and private sectors. Section 24-34-402 of the Colorado Revised Statutes encompasses a broad range of discriminatory employment practices relating to hiring, termination, promotion or demotion, harassment, retaliation, and discrimination in compensation, and extends to employers, employment agencies, and labor organizations. The state's courts have indicated that disabled or handicapped persons are "otherwise qualified" if they are capable of performing the reasonable, legitimate, and necessary functions of the job with reasonable accommodations. *See e.g., AT&T Techs. Inc. v. Royston*, 772 P.2d 1182 (Colo. Ct. App. 1989).

---

[74]Santa Cruz, Cal., Mun. Code ch. 9.83.
[75]Colo. Rev. Stat. §24-34-402 et seq.

C. Definitions

1. Disability

Under Colorado law, a disability is defined as a (1) "physical impairment which substantially limits one or more of a person's major life activities," (2) "a record of such impairment," or (3) "being regarded as having such an impairment."[76] Mental impairments such as "any mental or psychological disorder, such as developmental disability, organic brain syndrome, mental illness, or specific learning disabilities," are also protected disabilities under Colorado law.[77] Employers are not required to accommodate an employee if a "reasonable accommodation" cannot be made and the disability actually disqualifies the person from the job and poses a significant impact on the job.[78]

In addition to statutory provisions, the Colorado Civil Rights Commission has promulgated rules relating to discrimination on the basis of physical or mental disability.[79] These guidelines, which closely follow rules and interpretations promulgated at the federal level with respect to the ADA, indicate the manner that agency will consider in determining whether or not there has been a violation of state law.

Individuals seeking accommodation under the Colorado statute must establish that they are "otherwise qualified," meaning that they can perform the reasonable, legitimate, and necessary functions of the job if they are provided with an appropriate and reasonable accommodation.[80]

D. Covered Employers

Employers covered by Colorado's statutory disability discrimination rights and obligations include the state of Colorado and all political subdivisions, commissions, departments,

---

[76] *Id.* §24-34-301(2.5)(a).
[77] *Id.* §24-34-301(2.5)(b)(III).
[78] *See* Gamble v. Levitz Furniture Co. of Midwest, 759 P.2d 761, 2 AD Cases 1539 (Colo. Ct. App. 1988).
[79] 3 COLO. CODE REGS. §708-1, Rules 60.1 & 60.2.
[80] AT&T Techs. v. Royston, 772 P.2d 1182, 2 AD Cases 1564 (Colo. Ct. App. 1989).

institutions, or school districts, and every other person employing persons within the state. Excluded are "religious organizations or associations, except [for those] organizations or associations supported in whole or in part by money raised by taxation or public borrowing."[81]

E. Reasonable Accommodation and Defenses

1. Defenses

The burden of proving a defense of reasonable accommodation falls on the employer.[82] Once the employee makes a prima facie case of disability discrimination,[83] the employer must establish that there is no reasonable accommodation that it can make regarding the individual's limitations. As the Colorado court of appeals has noted, however, a reasonable accommodation must strike a balance between protecting those with disabilities and the legitimate concerns of the employer, which may have safety or business considerations motivating its posture on the question of accommodation.[84]

a. Bona Fide Occupational Qualification

The Colorado statute essentially requires a case-by-case determination of whether a disabled individual actually can perform the job in a safe and efficient manner, and a bona fide occupational qualification defense will not apply.[85] What is required is an examination of the number and types of jobs from which the individual is disqualified, the geographical

---

[81] COLO. REV. STAT. §24-34-401(3).
[82] *See, e.g.,* Healion v. Great-West Life Assurance Co., 830 F. Supp. 1372 (D. Colo. 1993).
[83] *Id.*
[84] Coski v. City & County of Denver, 795 P.2d 1364, 2 AD Cases 1525 (Colo. App. 1990).
[85] COLO. REV. STAT. §24-34-402 (1)(a); *see* Colorado Civil Rights Comm'n v. ConAgra Flour Milling Co., 736 P.2d 842, 2 AD Cases 1554 (Colo. Ct. App. 1987) (discrimination defense must relate to treatment of individuals, rather than classes of individuals).

area to which the individual had access, and the individual's expectations and training.[86]

b. Business Necessity

In the specific context of preemployment tests that have the alleged effect of inappropriately disqualifying disabled applicants, the Colorado supreme court has applied a process to consider claims of business necessity. It requires the employer to specify the particular characteristic or trait the selection device is being used to measure or identify, then determine whether that factor is an important element of the work activity, and then must demonstrate by professionally acceptable methods that the selection device is predictive or significantly correlated with that element of work activity.[87]

c. Undue Hardship

Differing from requirements imposed by federal law, the Colorado statute provides that no employer is "required to alter, modify, or purchase any building, structure, or equipment, or incur any additional expense which would not otherwise be incurred in order to comply with" the provisions of the discrimination law.[88] Also, other accommodations are not required if they are shown to impose an "undue hardship" on the operations of the employer, considering a number of different factors. These include: (1) the overall size of the employer's business; (2) number of employees, (3) number and type of facilities; (4) size of budget; (5) type of employer's operation; (6) composition and structure of employer's work force; (7) the nature, cost, and funding for the accommodation needed"; (8) whether funding is available for auxiliary aids or accommodations through public or private sources; and (9) the employee's willingness and ability to potentially absorb some or all of the cost of accommodation.[89]

---

[86] Colorado Civil Rights Comm'n v. North Wash. Fire Prot. Dist., 772 P.2d 70, 2 AD Cases 1545 (Colo. 1989).
[87] *Id.*
[88] COLO. REV. STAT. §24-34-305(2). *See also* 3 COLO. CODE REGS. §708-1, Rule 60.1(E).
[89] 3 COLO. CODE REGS. §708-1, Rule 60.2(c)(3).

CONNECTICUT

I. State Law

A. Overview

The Connecticut Fair Employment Practices Act (CFEPA) prohibits employers, except in the case of a bona fide occupational qualification or need, from refusing to hire, discharging, or otherwise discriminating against individuals in terms, conditions, or privileges of employment because of the employee's present or past history of mental disorder, mental retardation, physical disability, learning disability, or genetic information.[90] In addition, an individual who is perceived as being disabled is also protected against discrimination.[91]

These prohibitions also apply to an employer's agents, employment agencies, labor organizations,[92] licensing agencies,[93] or educational or vocational training programs run or participated in by state agencies.[94] In addition, the CFEPA and the government contracts statute prohibit government contractors and subcontractors from discriminating on the basis of mental disorder, past or present history of mental disorder, mental retardation, learning disability or physical disability, including but not limited to, blindness.[95] The Connecticut Commission on Human Rights and Opportunities is the administrative agency that has jurisdiction over complaints filed under the CFEPA. Under the Human Rights and Opportunities Law, it also is unlawful for an employer to refuse to grant an employee a reasonable leave of absence for disability resulting from her pregnancy.[96]

---

[90] Conn. Gen. Stat. §46a-60 et seq.
[91] *See* Connecticut Comm'n on Human Rights & Oppportunities ex rel. Tucker v. General Dynamics Corp., No. 517054, 1991 Conn. Super. LEXIS 2704 (Conn. Super. Ct. Nov. 22, 1991) (unpublished).
[92] Conn. Gen. Stat. §46a-60(a).
[93] *Id.* §46a-73(a).
[94] *Id.* §46a-75(a).
[95] *Id.* §4(a)-60(a), 4(a)-60(e).
[96] *Id.* §46a-60(7).

B. Prohibited Discrimination

Covered Connecticut employers are barred from discriminating against an individual due to a physical disability, present or past history of mental disorder, mental retardation, or learning disability.

1. Genetic Testing

State law prohibits an employer from requesting or requiring genetic information from an employee or applicant and bars discharge or discrimination on the basis of such information.[97]

C. Definitions

1. Disability

The Connecticut statute defines "physically disabled" as "any individual who has any chronic physical handicap, infirmity or impairment, whether congenital or resulting from bodily injury, organic processes or changes or from illness, including, but not limited to, epilepsy, deafness or hearing impairment or reliance on a wheelchair or other medical appliance or device."[98] The CFEPA further defines a "chronic impairment" as a condition that requires "reliance on a wheelchair or other medical appliance or device."[99]

In addition, the statute defines mental retardation and blindness. "Mental retardation" is defined as a significantly subaverage general intellectual functioning existing concurrently with deficits in adaptive behavior and manifested during the developmental period.[100] The state law defines "mental disability" as having "one or more mental disorders, as defined in the

---

[97] *Id.* §46a-60 (11). Genetic information is defined in the statute as "information about genes, gene products or inherited characteristics that may derive from an individual or a family member." *Id.*

[98] *Id.* §46(a)-51(15). Transsexuality is excluded from this definition. *See* Conway v. City of Hartford, Civ. 950553003, 1997 Conn. Super. LEXIS 282 (Conn. Super. Ct. Feb. 4, 1997).

[99] CONN. GEN. STAT. §46(a)-51(15).

[100] *Id.* §1-1g.

most recent edition of the American Psychiatric Association's 'Diagnostic and Statistical Manual of Mental Disorders' [DSM-IV-TR]."[101] With respect to other mental or psychological limitations, the statute defines "protected learning disabled individuals as those who exhibit severe discrepancies "between educational performance and measured intellectual ability and who [exhibit disorders in any] of the basic psychological processes involved in understanding or [using written or spoken language], which may manifest itself in a diminished ability to listen, speak, read, write, spell, or to do mathematical calculations."[102] The state law also defines a blind individual as one "whose central visual acuity does not exceed 20/200 in the better eye with correcting lenses, or whose visual acuity is greater than 20/200 but is accompanied by a limitation in the fields of vision such that the widest diameter of the visual field subtends an angle no greater than [20] degrees."[103]

The Connecticut statute also provides that in order to qualify as a disability, the condition cannot be temporary in nature. Accordingly, Connecticut courts have declined to qualify temporary symptoms of carpal tunnel syndrome[104] and temporary eye conditions[105] as disabilities. In addition, Connecticut law—in line with the treatment provided by the ADA, excludes coverage of transsexualism from the statute's category of protected disabilities.[106]

---

[101] *Id.* §46a-51(20). For example, the DSM-IV-TR includes depression as a mental disorder within the larger subtopic of mood disorders. AMERICAN PSYCHIATRIC ASSOCIATION, DIAGNOSTIC AND STATISTICAL MANUAL OF MENTAL DISORDERS 349–56, 369–81 (4th ed., text rev., 2000).

[102] CONN. GEN. STAT. §46(a)-51(19).

[103] *Id.* §46(a)-51(1).

[104] *See* Gilman Bros. Co. v. Connecticut Comm'n on Human Rights and Opportunities, No. CV 950536075, 1997 Conn. Super. LEXIS 1311 (Conn. Super. Ct. May 14, 1997).

[105] *See* Charbonneau v. United Grinding, Inc., 1995 Conn. Super. LEXIS 3305 (Super. Ct. Nov. 20, 1995).

[106] *See* Conway v. City of Hartford, Civ. 950553003, 1997 Conn. Super. LEXIS 282 (Conn. Super. Ct. Feb. 4, 1997).

The U.S. Court of Appeals for the Second Circuit has construed the scope of Connecticut's disability discrimination protections, finding that the state law's concept of protected "physical disabilities" is more expansive than the ADA, as the latter statute has been interpreted.[107] The Connecticut Commission on Human Rights and Opportunities also has recognized the difference between Connecticut and federal law regarding the definition of disability.[108] Nonetheless, the Second Circuit held that Connecticut state law does not provide a cause of action for cases of "perceived" physical disability discrimination.[109]

D. Covered Employers

Employers of three or more workers are subject to the Connecticut Fair Employment Practices Act's prohibitions against disability discrimination, a category that includes the state and all of its political subdivisions.[110]

---

[107] Beason v. United Techs. Corp., 337 F.3d 271, 14 AD Cases 1121 (2d Cir. 2003). In this regard, the appeals court noted a lower court holding in *Shaw v. Greenwich Anesthesiology Assocs., P.C.*, 137 F. Supp. 2d 48, 11 AD Cases 1354 (D. Conn. 2001), in which the district court dismissed a plaintiff's ADA claim on summary judgment, finding that her arthritis did not substantially limit a major life activity, but refused to grant summary judgment with respect to the plaintiff's CFEPA claim, ruling that " '[t]o be "disabled" under Connecticut law is different from being "disabled" under the ADA'." *Beason*, 337 F.3d at 278, 14 AD Cases 1125 (quoting *Shaw*, 137 F. Supp. 2d at 65, 11 AD Cases at 1364). *See also* Tordonato v. Colt's Mfg. Co., No. CV 970481610S, 2000 Conn. Super. LEXIS 3615 (Conn. Super. Ct. Dec. 26, 2000); Venclauskas v. State, No. CV 960471879, 1997 Conn. Super. LEXIS 1643 (Conn. Super. Ct. May 14, 1997) (rejecting defendant's assertion that CFEPA plaintiff, "by analogy to federal anti-discrimination statutes," could not be considered disabled within the meaning of the CFEPA); Gilman Bros., No. CV 950536075, 1997 Conn. Super. LEXIS 1311 (Conn. Super. Ct. May 13, 1997).

[108] *See, e.g.*, Connecticut Comm'n on Human Rights & Opportunities ex rel. Kowalczyk v. City of New Britain, CHRO No. 9810482. at *25–*26 (Mar. 15, 2002) ("The definitions of 'disability' in the ADA and [C]FEPA—and the interpretive case law—differ significantly.... [C]FEPA, unlike the ADA, does not require the complainant to prove that she is substantially limited in a major life activity."); Connecticut Comm'n on Human Rights & Opportunities ex rel. Saksena v. State, CHRO No. 9940089, at *10 (Aug. 9, 2001) (same); Connecticut Comm'n on Human Rights & Opportunities ex rel. Secondo v. Housing Auth., CHRO No. 9710713, at *24 (June 9, 2000) ("Although the complainant is not disabled under the ADA ... the broader definition of disability under state law yields a different result than the federal definition.").

[109] *Beason*, 337 F.3d 271.

[110] CONN. GEN. STAT. §46a-51(10).

E. Reasonable Accommodation and Defenses

1. Defenses

a. Bona Fide Occupational Qualification

While the state statute prohibits discrimination based on disability, an employer is permitted to discharge an employee who is disabled if the employer can establish a bona fide occupational qualification or need.[111] The employer has the burden of establishing that a certain job requires a bona fide occupational qualification possessed only by people outside of the protected disabled category.[112] Thus, employers can establish bona fide qualifications for certain jobs, such as vision for drivers.

Accordingly, employers are not required to retain employees who cannot perform their jobs even if the inability to perform is due to the disabling condition. Thus, Connecticut courts have upheld terminations of a cleaner who was unable to perform the essential job functions of regular movement, bending, shifting, and working with his hands,[113] and of a hearing-impaired worker who was required to operate a forklift throughout a shipyard.[114]

DELAWARE

I. STATE LAW

A. Overview

Delaware's Handicapped Persons Employment Protection Act prohibits discrimination against qualified handicapped individuals on the basis of the handicap.[115] However, the statute

---

[111] *Id.* §46a-60(1).
[112] *Id.* §46a-51.
[113] *See* McBrearity v. Connecticut Comm'n on Human Rights & Opportunities, 1995 Conn. Super. LEXIS 2669 (Conn. Super. Ct. Sept. 19, 1995).
[114] *See* Connecticut Comm'n on Human Rights & Opportunities v. General Dynamics Corp., 1995 Conn. Super. LEXIS 1318 (Conn. Super. Ct. May 1, 1995).
[115] DEL. CODE tit. 19, §720 et seq.

allows employers latitude in determining whether or not a handicapped individual is qualified to perform certain jobs.

B. Prohibited Discrimination

Delaware's Handicapped Persons Employment Protection Act broadly bars covered entities from taking various prohibited actions relating to the employment relationship on the basis of handicap. Such constraints apply to recruiting, hiring and promotion, discharge or other adverse actions, and other limitations on individuals that deprive them of employment opportunities, due to protected conditions.[116]

1. Preemployment Inquiries

The statute does not prohibit preemployment and prepromotion inquiries about handicaps that directly relate to an applicant's ability to perform essential job functions; or the termination or change of employment status when the employee, even after a reasonable accommodation has been provided, cannot adequately perform essential job functions.[117]

While employers may not require applicants to identify themselves as disabled prior to a conditional offer of employment, they can make inquiries into the ability of candidates to perform essential job functions. Employers can also require preemployment tests that accurately measure job-related abilities and are required for all applicants for the same positions.[118]

a. Medical Examinations

Some medical examinations and preemployment tests are permitted. Employers can require medical examinations to determine an individual's ability to safely and satisfactorily perform a job, or for identifying potential reasonable accommodations. They can also require a standard preemployment test

---

[116]DEL. CODE tit. 19, §724(a).
[117]*Id.* §724(f).
[118]DEL. CODE tit. 19, §724(f)(5).

that measures all applicants' job-related abilities, or a test designed to identify possible accommodations or handicaps that interfere with safe job performance.[119]

2. Genetic Testing

The state's general Fair Employment Practices Act effectively bars the use of genetic information in the employment context. For these purposes, the discrimination statute adopts a definition of the term "genetic test" as otherwise utilized in state law, which extends to "test[s] for determining the presence or absence of an inherited genetic characteristic in an individual, including tests of nucleic acids such as DNA, RNA and mitochondrial DNA, chromosomes or proteins in order to identify a predisposing genetic characteristic associated with disease, disorder or syndrome."[120]

C. Definitions

1. Disability

Delaware's Handicapped Persons Employment Protection Act defines a "handicapped person" as: one who "[h]as a physical or mental impairment which substantially limits 1 or more major life activities[; or] [h]as a record of such an impairment; or [i]s regarded as having such an impairment."[121] Key terms, such as "major life activities," "record of such an impairment," "regarded as having an impairment," and "substantially limits" are defined in the state law, through terminology that bears substantial relation to the definitions of such terms under the ADA.[122] Excluded are alcoholics or drug abusers whose current use of those substances prevents performance of particular job duties, "or whose employment . . . would constitute a direct threat to the property or the safety of others" from this definition.[123]

---

[119] *Id.* §724(f)(4)–(5).
[120] *Id.* §710(5); *see also* DEL. CODE tit. 18, §2317(a)(3).
[121] DEL. CODE tit. 19, §722(4).
[122] *Id.* §722(4)(c)(1)–(4).
[123] *Id.* §722(4)(c)(5).

In addition, the Delaware Handicapped Persons Employment Protection Act defines a "qualified handicapped" individual as: one who can "satisfactorily perform the essential functions of the job in question," under the same performance standards applied to other employees, without creating "an unreasonable and demonstrable risk to the" health and safety of that individual or others.[124] The Delaware statute further notes the duties imposed by state law may entail consideration of "higher or more comprehensive obligations" established by other federal, state, or local laws.[125]

D. Covered Employers

The Delaware handicap discrimination statute covers employers, employment agencies, labor organizations, and joint labor-management apprenticeship committees from discriminating against qualified handicapped individuals.[126] Employers covered by the statute include the State of Delaware and "any political subdivision or board, department, commission or school district . . . and any person employing . . . 15 or more employees for each working day in each of 20 or more calendar weeks in the current or preceding calendar year."[127]

E. Reasonable Accommodation and Defenses

1. *Reasonable Accommodation*

The Delaware statute requires covered employers to make reasonable accommodations for qualified handicapped individuals. Reasonable accommodations are described as reasonable changes to the workplace to enable the disabled person to perform the job's essential functions.[128]

The following are some examples of reasonable changes in the workplace that would satisfy the statute's reasonable

---

[124]*Id.* §722(5).
[125]*Id.* §721(b).
[126]DEL. CODE tit. 19, §724.
[127]*Id.* §722(2).
[128]*Id.* §722(6).

accommodation requirement: (1) making facilities accessible, (2) modifying equipment, (3) providing mechanical aids, or (4) making reasonable changes in schedules or duties so that a qualified handicapped person may satisfactorily perform essential duties.[129]

In contrast, reasonable accommodations would not include: (1) providing "eyeglasses, hearing aids or prostheses," unless these devices are generally provided to employees; (2) reassigning job duties to other employees without a corresponding reassignment of other duties to the qualified handicapped worker; (3) reassignments of duties to significantly "increase the skill, effort or responsibility required" from the employee to whom the duties are assigned; (4) accommodations for new employees that cost more than 5 percent of the annual salary or wage of the jobs at issue, or accommodations for existing employees that bring the total cost of changes since initial hire to more than 5 percent of the employee's current annual salary or wage; and (5) accommodations that would impose an undue hardship on the employer.[130] The statute provides that a qualified individual with a disability is not required to accept a particular accommodation. At the same time, if the individual cannot satisfactorily perform the essential functions of the job despite a reasonable accommodation, the employer would have an effective affirmative defense, as the individual will not be judged to be a qualified individual with a disability.[131]

2. Defenses

a. Undue Hardship

Employers who can show that an accommodation would pose an undue hardship also would have a successful affirmative defense.[132] They would need to analyze their operations and the impact of the accommodation on the facility's operation,

---

[129] *Id.*
[130] *Id.*
[131] *Id.* §725(1).
[132] *Id.* §725(3).

including the question of cost (less than 5 percent of the individual's annual wage or salary will not be presumed undue hardship)[133] as well as its impact on the ability of other employees to perform their duties and the impact on the facility's ability to conduct business.

Employers are also justified in discriminating against individuals on the basis of handicaps if their employment would pose an unreasonable and demonstrable risk to the safety or health of the handicapped person, other employees, the employer's customers, or the public.[134]

DISTRICT OF COLUMBIA

I. STATE LAW

A. Overview

The District of Columbia's Human Rights law,[135] one of the broadest employment discrimination statutes in the nation, prohibits discrimination on the basis of disability and covers any employer of one or more employees.[136] The District of Columbia Office of Human Rights and the District of Columbia Commission on Human Rights enforces the Human Rights Act's provisions.[137]

B. Prohibited Discrimination

The Human Rights Act prohibits discrimination in hiring, promotion, discharge, compensation, and conditions or privileges of employment.[138] Under the statute, employers are prohibited from discriminating against employees or job applicants because of disability, a record of a disability, or who are perceived as having a disability.[139]

---

[133] *Id.* §722(6)(d)-(e).
[134] *Id.* §725(2).
[135] D.C. CODE ANN. §2-1401.01, et seq.
[136] *Id.* §2-1401.02.
[137] *Id.* §2-1411.03(2).
[138] *Id.* §2-1402.11.
[139] *Id.* §2-1401.02(5A).

Employers also are prohibited from discriminating against applicants and employees on the basis of blindness or physical disability, unless employers can demonstrate that the blindness or particular disability prevents blind workers from performing job duties.[140]

Employers are prohibited from failing or refusing to hire, or to discharge, or otherwise to discriminate against any individual with respect to compensation or terms and conditions of employment, including promotion. Moreover, they may not "limit, segregate, or classify employees in any way which would deprive or tend to deprive any individual of employment opportunities, or otherwise adversely affect his status as an employee."[141]

1. Preemployment Inquiries

Employers can make preemployment inquiries about the physical condition or past medical history of applicants if the inquiry is based on a business necessity or required to comply with the District of Columbia's and/or the federal government's affirmative action provisions.[142] For example, employers may only consider if an individual's physical impairment is likely to prevent the applicant from performing safely and effectively.[143] However, employers are not required to hire workers who are unable to fulfill the duties listed in a job description.[144] Employers can give applicants and employees only tests that are job related.[145]

C. Definitions

1. Disability

The Human Rights Act defines a "disability" as "a physical or mental impairment that substantially limits one or more of

---
[140] *Id.* §7-1005.
[141] *Id.* §2-1402.11(1).
[142] D.C. Department of Human Rights, "Employment Guidelines for Human Rights Law," §513.4.
[143] *Id.*
[144] *Id.* §502.5.
[145] *Id.* §513.11.

the major life activities of an individual, having a record of such an impairment and being regarded as having such an impairment."[146] Construing the District of Columbia statute in accord with the federal ADA, the U.S. Court of the Appeals for the District of Columbia has declared that mitigating factors must be taken into account in determining if an individual's condition substantially limits a major life activity.[147]

D. Covered Employers

The District of Columbia Human Rights Act applies to employers through a very broad definition of regulated entities. Under the statute, the term "employer" means any person who employs an individual for compensation, which covers virtually all individuals or entities who hire others to perform work (with very limited exceptions provided for members of an employer's family and domestic household help).[148] This category also extends to any persons acting in the interest of such an employer, either directly or indirectly. Thus, individual supervisors may be liable for violations of the District of Columbia's Human Rights Act.[149]

E. Reasonable Accommodation and Defenses

1. Reasonable Accommodation

Employers are required to provide reasonable accommodations to otherwise qualified disabled individuals. For example, employers can satisfy this requirement through job restructuring or renovation when an employee's disability prevents satisfactory performance in the current conditions. Factors to consider in such a change are: (1) the nature and cost of the change; (2) the number of people who will benefit from the

---

[146]D.C. CODE ANN., §2-1401.02(5A).
[147]Grant v. May Dep't Store Co., 786 A.2d 580, 12 AD Cases 1308 (D.C. 2001). *See also* Woodland v. State, County & Mun. Employees Dist. Council 20, 777 A.2d 795, 7 WH Cases 2d 312 (D.C. 2001).
[148]D.C. Code Ann. §2-1401.02(10).
[149]Wallace v. Skadden, Arps, Slate, Meagher & Flom, 715 A.2d 873, 14 IER Cases 851 (D.C. 1998).

change, including the number of disabled people who could be employed after the modification; (3) the detriments and benefits resulting from the change; and (4) whether an employer engaged in commercial construction, remodeling, or major redesign must provide increased accessibility.[150] If employees become disabled on the job, employers must continue to employ those workers as long as a reasonable accommodation can be made.[151] Employers cannot escape the duty of providing reasonable accommodations to their disabled workers based on customer, client, tenant, patron, or other preferences that exclude disabled workers.[152]

The burden of proving disability discrimination lies with employees, who have to demonstrate that the employer could have made a reasonable accommodation that would have allowed the employee to perform essential job functions.[153] Employees who apply for and receive Social Security benefits are not barred from also filing lawsuits against employers on the basis of disability discrimination and failure to provide reasonable accommodations.[154]

2. *Defenses*

The guidelines issued by the Office of Human Rights states that employees may be terminated for excessive absenteeism, even if injury or illness causes the absenteeism, if the absenteeism interferes with, or causes an undue hardship on, the employee's job performance.[155]

Challenged employment practices may be defended with proof that they were not adopted with an intent to contravene

---

[150] D.C. Department of Human Rights, "Employment Guidelines for Human Rights Law," §513.11.
[151] *Id.* §513.13.
[152] *Id.* §513.12.
[153] *See* Miller v. American Coalition of Citizens with Disabilities, Inc., 485 A.2d 186, 1 AD Cases 649 (D.C. 1984).
[154] *See* Whitbeck v. Vital Signs, Inc., 116 F.3d 588, 6 AD Cases 1540 (D.C. Cir. 1997).
[155] D.C. Department of Human Rights, "Employment Guidelines for Human Rights Law," §513.6-8.

the Human Rights Act's constraints, and are justified by business necessity. Such a business necessity defense can be applicable only in an individual case in which it can be shown that without such an exception, business cannot be conducted. A "business necessity" exception may not be justified on the basis "of increased cost to business, business efficiency," customer preference, or stereotyped characterizations "of one group as opposed to another."[156]

FLORIDA

I. State Law

A. Overview

The Florida Civil Rights Act of 1992 prohibits employment discrimination on the basis of handicap.[157] Public employers, such as counties and municipalities, are also prohibited from discrimination in employment on this basis.[158]

The Florida Commission on Human Relations (Commission) is the enforcement authority for the Florida Civil Rights Act.[159] The Commission has the authority to adopt rules implementing its statutory authority to investigate and hold hearings on complaints alleging discriminatory employment practices.[160] Aggrieved persons can bring an administrative action and must exhaust their administrative remedies before filing a private a discrimination action in court.[161]

---

[156] D.C. Code Ann., Chapter 14, §2-1401.03
[157] Fla. Stat. §760.10(1)(a).
[158] Id. §112.042 et seq.
[159] Id. §760.06.
[160] Publix Supermarkets v. Commission on Human Relations, 470 So. 2d 754 (Fla. Dist. Ct. App. 1985).
[161] Fla. Stat. §760.07; see also Armstrong v. Lockheed Martin Beryllium Co., 990 F. Supp. 1395, 1399 (M.D. Fla. 1997).

B. Prohibited Discrimination

Employers are expressly prohibited from discriminating against a qualified individual with a handicap.[162] In addition, employers are prohibited from depriving or denying employment opportunities to a qualified individual with a handicap.[163]

Employers are prohibited from: (1) segregating or classifying employees or applicants because of their disabilities[164]; (2) retaliating against applicants or employees who oppose unlawful discrimination or make a charge or complaint of discrimination[165]; and (3) discriminating in "job training programs," licensing, or required association membership.[166]

Employers, including labor organizations and employment agencies are also prohibited from discriminating in employment advertising. These employers cannot publish any notice or advertising relating to employment that indicates "preference, limitation, specification, or discrimination based on . . . absence of a handicap."[167]

1. Genetic Testing

The Florida Civil Rights Act allows for genetic testing in the form of DNA analysis "only with the informed consent of the person to be tested." In addition, the results of such testing "are confidential [and] the exclusive property of the person tested, and may not be disclosed without the consent of the person tested."[168] Notice that the analysis was performed or that the information was received must be provided to the person tested if the results are used to deny employment.[169]

2. Harassment

Under Florida law, an employer can be held liable for a hostile work-environment harassment claim based on disability.

---

[162]FLA. STAT. §760.10(1)(a).
[163]Id. §760.10(1)(b).
[164]Id.
[165]Id. §760.10(7).
[166]Id. §760.10(4)–(6).
[167]Id. §760.10(6).
[168]Id. §760.40(2)(a).
[169]Id. §760.40(3).

Therefore, continuously subjecting a disabled employee to jokes, threats, ridicule, and other harassing behavior because of the employee's disability, is prohibited.[170]

3. Medical Conditions

In Florida, it is unlawful for employers to deny or refuse employment to individuals based on their sickle-cell trait.[171]

Under the Florida Civil Rights Act, protections for disabled workers also applies to persons with acquired immunodeficiency syndrome (AIDS) or human immunodeficiency virus (HIV), or who are perceived as having AIDS or HIV.[172] Employers cannot refuse to hire, discharge, segregate, or otherwise discriminate against any individual with respect to compensation, terms, conditions, or privileges of employment on the basis of (1) knowledge or belief that the individual has taken an HIV test, or (2) the results or perceived results of such a test.[173] In addition, employers cannot require an individual to take an HIV test, unless the absence of HIV "is a bona fide occupational qualification for the job. . . ."[174]

The Florida Civil Rights Act, although not expressly defining morbid obesity as a "handicap," protects employment discrimination based on obesity, because obesity is a perceived disability based on the definition of handicap, which is a physical impairment that substantially limits a major life activity if so regarded by the employer.[175]

C. Definitions

1. Disability

The Florida Fair Housing Act defines a handicapped individual as a "person [who] has a physical or mental impairment which substantially limits one or more major life activities, or

---

[170] *Id.* at 648.
[171] FLA. STAT. §448.075.
[172] *Id.* §760.50(2).
[173] *Id.* §760.50(3)(b).
[174] *Id.* §760.50(3)(a).
[175] Greene v. Seminole Elec. Coop., 701 So. 2d 646 (Fla. Dist Ct. App. 1997).

[who] has a record of having, or is regarded as having, such physical or mental impairment"[176]

Florida has adopted the ADA's definition of a "qualified individual." Consequently, in Florida a qualified individual is an "individual with a disability who, with or without reasonable accommodation, can perform the essential functions of the employment position that such individual holds or desires."[177]

2. *Essential Job Functions*

Florida courts consider the following factors in determining whether a job function is "essential": (1) the terms of a collective bargaining agreement, (2) the work experience of past and present employees performing similar jobs, (3) the consequences of not requiring the employee to perform the function, and (4) the amount of time spent performing the task.[178]

D. Covered Employers

The Florida Civil Rights Act applies to employers with 15 or more workers, labor organizations, employment agencies, and joint labor-management committees.[179] Religious organizations and institutions that limit employment opportunities to applicants and employees who subscribe to the religious tenets of the organization's teachings and beliefs, however, are exempt from the Florida Civil Rights Act's prohibitions.[180]

E. Reasonable Accommodation and Defenses

1. *Reasonable Accommodation*

The Florida Civil Rights Act requires employers to reasonably accommodate a qualified handicapped individual's known

---

[176] FLA. STAT. §760.22.
[177] 42 U.S.C. §12111(8).
[178] *See* Vincent v. Wells Fargo Guard Servs., Inc. of Fla., 3 F. Supp. 2d 1405, 1416 (S.D. Fla. 1998) (cited 29 C.F.R. §1630.2(n)(3)(iii)–(vii)).
[179] FLA. STAT. §760.02(6)–(9).
[180] *Id.* §760.10(9).

disability.[181] However, an employee is responsible for notifying the employer or making the employer aware of the employee's disability and for requesting a reasonable accommodation.[182]

Examples of reasonable accommodations in Florida include: (1) a modified work schedule, including a part-time work schedule; (2) reassignment to a vacant position; (3) modifications or adjustments to the work environment; and (4) modifications or adjustments to manner in which the job is usually performed.[183]

2. *Defenses*

An employer is not, however, required to accommodate an employee when an accommodation would not enable the individual to perform the essential functions and fundamental duties of the job, as differentiated from marginal functions.[184]

a. Bona Fide Occupational Qualification

Employers can defend against claims of unlawful discrimination by raising the affirmative defense that the discriminatory criteria the employer used was a bona fide occupational qualification that was reasonably related to the performance of a particular job.[185] Employers can raise this defense against an employment practice that discriminates on its face.[186] However, employers have had varying degrees of success using this defense because courts place a high burden of proof on employers and carefully scrutinize the bona fide occupational qualification defense.[187]

---

[181] *See* Hernandez v. Prudential Ins. Co., 977 F. Supp. 1160, 1165 (M.D. Fla. 1997).

[182] *See* Morisky v. Broward County, 80 F.3d 445, 448, 5 AD Cases 737 (11th Cir. 1996).

[183] *See* Salmon v. Dade County Sch. Bd., 4 F. Supp. 2d 1157, 1161 (S.D. Fla. 1998).

[184] *See* LaChance v. Duffy's Draft House, Inc., 146 F.3d 832, 835, 8 AD Cases 652 (11th Cir. 1998).

[185] FLA. STAT. §760.10(8)(a).

[186] *See* Davidson v. Iona-McGregor Fire Prot. & Rescue Dist., 674 So. 2d 858, 860–61 (Fla. Dist. Ct. App. 1996).

[187] *See* O'Loughlin v. Pinchback, 579 So. 2d 788, 792–93 (Fla. Dist. Ct. App. 1991) (employee's pregnancy status was not a bona fide occupational qualification, because the employee could still perform her position successfully).

In Florida, an employer can require an individual to undergo HIV testing if the employer can demonstrate that the absence of HIV is a bona fide occupational qualification.[188] However, the employer must also demonstrate that a reasonable accommodation does not exist.[189]

b. Direct Threat

Employers are not required to accommodate an individual who represents a direct threat of harm to the individual or to the safety of others, regardless of an accommodation.[190]

c. Undue Hardship

Employers are not required to accommodate a person's disability if it imposes an undue hardship on the employer.[191] Under Florida law, an accommodation poses an undue hardship if (1) it would require significant difficulty or expense on the part of the employer, (2) it would impose an undue financial and administrative burden, or (3) it would require a fundamental alteration in the nature of the program.[192]

II. Local Laws

Some municipalities in Florida have enacted local ordinances that are broader than the Florida Civil Rights Act. Below are examples of some of the more expansive ordinances.[193]

1. Miami Beach's ordinance prohibits employment discrimination by employers of five or more workers for a minimum of 4 calendar weeks.[194]

---

[188] FLA. STAT. §760.50(3)(c).

[189] Id. §760.50(3)(c)(2).

[190] See LaChance v. Duffy's Draft House, Inc., 146 F.3d 832, 835–36, 8 AD Cases 652 (11th Cir. 1998).

[191] See Salmon v. Dade County Sch. Bd., 4 F. Supp. 2d 1157, 1160–62 (S.D. Fla. 1998).

[192] Id.

[193] The cities of Clearwater, St. Petersburg, Tampa, Jacksonville, and Orlando, and the counties of Hillsborough, Lee, and Pinellas, have also enacted some form of local antidiscrimination laws.

[194] MIAMI BEEACH, FLA., CODE §62-31.

2. Similarly, Dade County's local ordinance applies to employers with five or more workers.[195]
3. Key West's Human Rights Ordinance goes beyond employers and prohibits discrimination by any person, implying that individual workers and supervisors may be liable for employment discrimination.[196]

GEORGIA

I. State Law

A. Overview

The Georgia Equal Employment for Persons with Disabilities Code provides protection for persons with disabilities.[197]

B. Prohibited Discrimination

The Georgia Equal Employment for Persons with Disabilities Code prohibits covered employers from discriminating against disabled individuals with respect to hours, wages, rates of pay, or other terms and conditions of employment, unless the disability limits the person's ability to do a particular job or occupation.[198]

In addition, employers may not "limit, segregate, or classify" an individual with a disability in a way that deprives that person of employment opportunities.[199] Employers cannot advertise a preference, limitation, specification, or discrimination based on disability, unless the criteria are job related.[200] An employer also may not discriminate against an individual because of his or her disability in admission to an apprenticeship or training program.[201]

---

[195] Miami-Dade County, Fla., Code §11A-25(2).
[196] Key West, Fla., Code §72.26(f).
[197] Ga. Code Ann. §34-6A-1 et seq.
[198] Id. §34-6A-4(a).
[199] Id.
[200] Id. §34-6A-4(e).
[201] Id. §34-6A-4(d).

1. Preemployment Inquiries

Georgia employers are permitted to make preemployment inquiries of job applicants about whether they have a disability.[202] Employers can also make employment decisions, including the rejection of a prospective employee, based on a good-faith reliance on the opinion a licensed health-care professional, such as a "licensed physician, rehabilitation specialist, psychologist, physical therapist, or dentist," about the disabled person's condition.[203]

Employees and applicants can obtain a health-care professional's assessment of his or her disability independently. A conflict may arise when the employer, and employee or applicant, obtain different assessments of the employee or applicant's disability. In some cases, courts have permitted the employer to use its own doctor's opinion, even if it is less favorable than the one the employee obtained.[204]

2. Retaliation

Employers cannot retaliate against an employee with a disability by discharging, expelling, refusing to hire, or otherwise discriminating against the employee for opposing any unfair employment practice as defined in the Georgia Equal Employment for Persons with Disabilities Code.[205]

C. Definitions

1. Disability

The Georgia Equal Employment for Persons with Disabilities Code defines persons with disabilities as "any person who has a physical or mental impairment which substantially limits one or more of such person's major life activities and who has a record of such impairment."[206] However, employers may

---

[202] *Id.* §34-6A-3(a).
[203] *Id.* §34-6A-3(c).
[204] *See* Daugherty v. Metropolitan Atlanta Rapid Transit Auth., 187 Ga. App. 864, 371 S.E.2d 677, 4 AD Cases 1315 (1988); Spicer v. Martin-Brower Co., 177 Ga. App. 197, 338 S.E.2d 773, 58 FEP Cases 1372 (1985).
[205] Ga. Code Ann. §34-6A-5.
[206] *Id.* §34-6A-2(3).

reject applicants because of a disability if the disability "interferes with a person's ability to perform" job duties adequately.[207]

Persons addicted to the use of any drug, "illegal or federally controlled substance," or alcohol are not considered disabled under Georgia law,[208] and neither are persons afflicted with claustrophobia or depression.[209] Indeed, most emotional disorders probably do not qualify as disabilities under the Georgia Equal Employment for Persons with Disabilities Code.[210] However, any psychological disorder or condition affecting one or more of the following systems is an impairment: "neurological, musculoskeletal, special sense organs, respiratory [speech], cardiovascular, reproductive, digestive, genitourinary, hemic and lymphatic, skin, or endocrine" systems.[211] In addition, "[m]ental retardation and specific learning disabilities" are protected from discrimination.[212]

D. Covered Employers

The Georgia Equal Employment for Persons with Disabilities Code covers employers and governmental units or officers that employ 15 or more individuals, or agents of the employer.[213] The Code also applies to employment agencies, placement services, training schools or centers, and labor organizations.[214]

E. Reasonable Accommodation and Defenses

1. *Reasonable Accommodation*

Because the Georgia Equal Employment for Persons with Disabilities Code does not prohibit employers from discriminating against individuals whose disability limits the person's

---

[207] *Id.* §34-6A-3(b)(1).
[208] *Id.* §34-6A-2(1), (3).
[209] *Id.*; *see also* Bowers v. Estep, 204 Ga. App. 615, 420 S.E. 2d 336 (1992).
[210] GA. CODE ANN. §34-6A-2.
[211] *Id.* §34-6A-2(7)(A).
[212] *Id.* §34-6A-2(7)(B).
[213] *Id.* §34-6A-2(2).
[214] *Id.* §34-6A-4(b).

ability to do a particular job or occupation,[215] employers are not required to provide any reasonable accommodation for an employee's disability.[216]

Similarly, employers are not required to modify their workplace facilities or grounds to accommodate disabled workers.[217] Indeed, employers do not have to "exercise a higher degree of caution for a handicapped individual than for any person who is not a handicapped individual."[218]

2. Defenses

a. Infectious or Communicable Diseases

Employers are not required to hire or accommodate persons who are carriers of, or are afflicted with, communicable or infectious diseases.[219] Employers also are not prevented from making a job-related inquiry about the extent to which a "disability has been overcome by treatment, medication, or other rehabilitation."[220]

HAWAII

I. STATE LAW

A. Overview

In Hawaii, it is against public policy to discriminate against an applicant or employee on the basis of disability.[221] Hawaii's

---

[215] *Id.* §34-6A-4(a).
[216] *Id.* §34-6A-4.
[217] *Id.* §34-6A-4(a). *See* Davis v. Sea Island Co., 43 FEP Cases 997 (Ga. Super. Ct. 1987) (employer could deny employment to deaf mute, because his disability would interfere with his ability to perform duty of kitchen utility worker).
[218] GA. CODE ANN. §34-6A-4(a). *See* Dugger v. Delta Airlines, 325 S.E.2d 394 (Ga. Ct. App. 1984) (in upholding termination of receptionist who had problems working because of back pain, court noted employers not required to accommodate disabled employee or even to take any more precautions for disabled worker, but are merely required to refrain from discriminating if disability does not limit employee's ability to perform job).
[219] GA. CODE ANN. §34-6A-3(b)(2).
[220] *Id.* §34-6A-3(a).
[221] HAW. REV. STAT. ANN. §368-1.

Civil Rights Commission is the mechanism by which a uniform procedure for the enforcement of the state's discrimination laws is made.[222] In addition, Hawaii has a Fair Employment Practices Law that also prohibits employment discrimination based on disability.[223]

B. Prohibited Discrimination

In Hawaii, it is unlawful for any employer to refuse to employ or hire, "to bar or discharge from employment, or otherwise discriminate against any individual in compensation or in the terms, conditions, or privileges of employment" based on disability.[224] In addition, employers and employment agencies must not use any advertisement or make any preemployment inquiry that "expresses, [either] directly or indirectly, any limitation, specification, or discrimination."[225]

It is also unlawful for any employer to retaliate against an individual who "has filed a complaint, testified, or assisted in any proceeding" regarding discriminatory practices, by discharging, expelling, or otherwise discriminating against the individual.[226]

Additionally, any employer, employment agency, or labor organization is prohibited from excluding or otherwise denying "equal jobs or benefits to a qualified individual" based on his or her association or relationship with an individual who has a known disability.[227] However, employers are not required to accommodate "the needs of a nondisabled person associated with or related to a person with a disability in any way not required by the" ADA.[228]

---

[222] *Id.* §368-2.
[223] *Id.* §378-1 et seq.
[224] *Id.* §378-2(1)(A). Employees can also bring claims of intentional infliction of emotional distress against their employers for violations of §378-2. *See also* Lesane v. Hawaiian Airlines, 75 F. Supp. 2d 1113 (D. Haw. 1999).
[225] HAW. REV. STAT. ANN. §378-2(1)(C).
[226] *Id.* §378-2(2).
[227] *Id.* §378-2(6).
[228] *Id.* §378-3(11).

Employers, employees, and others also are prohibited from aiding, abetting, inciting, coercing, or compelling a discriminatory practice, and from attempting to do so.[229]

However, employers are not prohibited "from refusing to hire, refer, or discharge any [person] for reasons relating to [that person's] ability to perform" a job.[230]

1. Genetic Testing

Employment discrimination on the basis of an individual's genetic information is prohibited, as well as genetic testing or use of genetic information as a prerequisite for certain types of insurance.[231]

C. Definitions

1. Disability

In Hawaii, a "disability" is a physical or mental impairment that substantially limits one or more major life activities, having a record of such impairment, or being regarded as having such an impairment.[232]

2. Employment

A person is employed if he or she performs any services for another person under any contract of hire, whether express or implied, oral or written, regardless of whether the contract was lawfully entered into.[233] However, employment does not include domestic services by an individual in the home of another person.[234]

D. Covered Employers

Hawaii's Fair Employment Practices Law covers employers of one or more workers, including the state and its political

---

[229] *Id.* §378-2(3).
[230] *Id.* §378-3(3).
[231] *See id.* §§432:1-607, 432D-26, 431:10A-118.
[232] *Id.*
[233] *Id.*
[234] *Id.*

subdivisions.[235] The Fair Employer Practices Law also covers discriminatory acts by employment agencies and labor organizations.[236]

E. Reasonable Accommodation and Defenses

1. Reasonable Accommodation

Hawaiian employers are not required "to execute unreasonable structural changes or expensive equipment alterations to accommodate the employment of" persons with disabilities.[237]

In addition, employers are not required to accommodate the needs of a nondisabled person associated with or related to a person with a disability in any way that is not mandated by the ADA.[238]

2. Defenses

a. Bona Fide Occupational Qualification

In Hawaii, employers are permitted to establish bona fide occupational qualifications that are reasonably necessary for the normal operations "of a particular business or enterprise and that have a substantial relationship to the functions and responsibilities of prospective or continued employment."[239]

IDAHO

I. State Law

A. Overview

The Idaho Human Rights Act protects individuals from employment discrimination based on disability.[240] In fact, it is

---

[235] *Id.* §378-1. Hawaii's legislature intended the Fair Employment Practice Law's discrimination prohibitions to apply to all employers, regardless of size. *See* Sam Teague, Ltd. v. Hawaii Civil Rights Comm'n, 89 Haw. 269, 971 P.2d 1104 (1999).
[236] *Id.* §378-2.
[237] *Id.* §378-3(7).
[238] *Id.* §378(11).
[239] *Id.* §378-3(2).
[240] IDAHO CODE §67-5901.

the public policy of Idaho to encourage and otherwise "enable the blind, the visually handicapped, the hearing impaired, and [persons] otherwise physically disabled . . . to engage in remunerative employment."[241]

B. Prohibited Discrimination

In Idaho, it is unlawful for covered employers "to fail or refuse to hire, to discharge, or to otherwise discriminate against an individual with respect to compensation or the terms, conditions or privileges of employment or to reduce the wage of any employee," on the basis of disability, unless the disability, even with a reasonable accommodation, prevents the individual from performing the required work.[242]

Employers also are prohibited from publishing a notice or advertisement that indicates "a preference, limitation, specification, or discrimination," unless the preference, limitation, specification, or discrimination is a bona fide occupational qualification for employment.[243]

C. Definitions

1. Disability

In Idaho, a disability is a physical or mental condition, whether congenital or acquired, that constitutes a substantial limitation to that person and is demonstrable by medically accepted clinical or laboratory diagnostic techniques.[244]

A disabled person is one who either has a disability, or a record of such a disability, or is regarded as having a disability.[245]

D. Covered Employers

Employers in Idaho who hire "five (5) or more employees for each working day in each of twenty (20) or more calendar

---

[241] *Id.* §56-701.
[242] *Id.* §67-5909(1).
[243] *Id.* §67-5909(4).
[244] *Id.* §67-5902(15).
[245] *Id.*

weeks in the current or preceding calendar year [and] whose services are to be partially or wholly performed in" Idaho are covered by the Idaho Human Rights Act's prohibitions against discrimination.[246] The term "employer" also includes any contractor or subcontractor furnishing material or performing work for the state, any governmental entity within the state, and any agent of such employer.[247] Labor organizations and employment agencies are also covered employers.[248]

Although the Idaho Human Rights Act's provisions protect employees, they do not apply to independent contractors.[249] Moreover, individual supervisors, agents, and employees cannot be held individually liable for violations of the Idaho Human Rights Act.[250] In addition, persons employing domestic servants to work in and about their households are not employers.[251]

E. Reasonable Accommodation and Defenses

1. Reasonable Accommodation

Employers are required to provide adjustments that do not "(a) unduly disrupt or interfere with the employer's normal operations; (b) threaten the health or safety" of the disabled person or others; "(c) contradict [the employer's] business necessity[;] or (d) impose [an] undue hardship" based on the employer's size, type of business, financial resources, and extent of the adjustment.[252]

---

[246] *Id.* §67-5902(6).

[247] *Id.* §67-5902(6)(a)–(c).

[248] *Id.* §§67-5909(2), (3).

[249] *See* Ostrander v. Farm Bureau Mut. Ins. Co., 123 Idaho 650, 851 P.2d 946, 8 IER Cases 1063 (1993).

[250] *See* Foster v. Shore Club Lodge, Inc., 127 Idaho 921, 908 P.2d 1228 (1995) (agents or employees are not employers for the purposes of establishing liability under the Idaho Human Rights Act); *see also* Paterson v. State, 128 Idaho 494, 915 P.2d 724 (1996) (there is no individual liability under the Idaho Human Rights Act).

[251] IDAHO CODE §67-5902(6).

[252] *Id.* §67-5902(16).

2. Defenses

a. Direct Threat

Employers are not required to hire or employ disabled individuals when employment of the disabled person "poses a serious threat to the health or safety of the" disabled person or to others.[253] The burden on proving this defense is on the employer.

ILLINOIS

I. STATE LAW

A. Overview

In Illinois, workers have both a constitutional and statutory right to be free from handicap discrimination in employment.[254]

B. Prohibited Discrimination

In Illinois, workers with a physical or mental handicap have a constitutional right to be "free from discrimination unrelated to ability" in an employer's hiring and promotion practices.[255]

In addition, the Illinois Human Rights Act prohibits employment discrimination on the basis of handicap.[256] Under the Illinois Human Rights Act, employers are prohibited from refusing to hire, segregating, or otherwise discriminating against a person on the basis of a physical or mental handicap unrelated to ability.[257]

---

[253] *Id.* §67-5910(2)(d).
[254] ILL. CONST. art. I, §19; 775 ILL. COMP. STAT. 5/1-101 et seq.
[255] ILL. CONST. art. I, §19.
[256] 775 ILL. COMP. STAT. 5/1-103(Q).
[257] *Id.* 5/2-101 et seq.

To proceed with a disability discrimination claim, employees must first exhaust the administrative remedies provided in the Illinois Human Rights Act.[258]

1. Pregnancy-Related Disability

In Illinois, pregnancy-related disability leave "may not be more restrictive," or more generous, than other disability leaves.[259] Thus, employers must give these employees the same rights and treatment as it would for any other temporarily disabled worker in terms of the rules for reinstatement, leave, seniority, benefits, insurance, and any similar leave terms and conditions.[260]

C. Definitions

1. Disability

Under the Illinois Human Rights Act, a handicap is

> [A] determinable physical or mental characteristic of a person, including, but not limited to, a determinable physical characteristic which necessitates the person's use of a guide, hearing or support dog, the history of such characteristic, or the perception of such characteristic by the person complained against, which may result from disease, injury, congenital condition of birth or functional disorder and which characteristic . . . is unrelated to the person's ability to perform the duties of a particular job or position . . . .[261]

While the definition of "handicap" may seem broad, it does not cover conditions that are temporary or "not significantly debilitating or disfiguring," but is limited to "physical and mental conditions" that are extreme or serious.[262] In addition, the

---

[258] *Id.; see also* Yount v. Hesston Corp., 124 Ill. App. 3d 943, 464 N.E.2d 1214, 45 FEP Cases 371 (Ill. Ct. App. 1984).
[259] ILL. ADMIN. CODE tit. 56, §5210.110.
[260] *Id.*
[261] 775 ILL. COMP. STAT. 5/1-103(I)(1).
[262] ILL. ADMIN. CODE tit. 56, §2500.20(b).

"condition must be 'determinable' [and capable of being recognized by] clinical or laboratory diagnostic techniques"[263] and the employee has the burden of proving that the condition is the result of injury, disease, or a "congenital condition of birth or [a] functional disorder.[264]

The statute provides that an individual is protected against discrimination if he or she is "currently afflicted" with a condition that constitutes a handicap."[265] An individual can show a history of a handicap if the person "is restored or recovered from a prior" condition or if the person's "symptoms are in remission[, such as] those who have" suffered heart attacks, cancer, or who are mentally restored or have "orthopedic findings."[266]

A person can be perceived as handicapped if the individual "has been misdiagnosed, misclassified," mistakenly viewed as having a handicap, and for having a current nondisabling condition that the employer views as creating the potential for future disability, such as hypertension.[267]

D. Covered Employers

For handicap discrimination, the Human Rights Act applies to employers of one or more workers, employment agencies, and labor organizations.[268] The state and any political subdivision, municipal corporation, other governmental agency, any party to a public contract, a joint apprenticeship, or training committee is a covered employer without regard to the number of employees.[269] Religious associations, however, may limit employment to persons of a particular religion to perform work connected with carrying on the organization's activities.[270]

---

[263] *Id.* §2500.20(6)(2).
[264] *Id.* §2500.20(c).
[265] 775 ILCS 5/1-103(1); 56 ILL. ADMIN. CODE §2500.30(a)(1).
[266] 56 ILL. ADMIN. CODE §2500.30(b).
[267] *Id.*
[268] 775 ILL. COMP. STAT. 5/2-101(B)(1), (C), (D); *see also* Dana Tank Container, Inc. v. Human Rights Comm'n, 687 N.E.2d 102 (Ill. Ct. App. 1997).
[269] 775 ILL. COMP. STAT. 5/2-101(B)(e).
[270] *Id.* 5/2-101(B)(2).

E. Reasonable Accommodation and Defenses

1. Reasonable Accommodation

Illinois requires employers to provide a reasonable accommodation for known physical limitations of otherwise qualified handicapped individuals.[271] The employee bears the burden of (1) asserting the duty to accommodate, (2) showing that an accommodation was requested, and (3) demonstrating that the accommodation was necessary for adequate job performance.[272] An employer cannot refuse to employ or accommodate a handicapped person based on factors such as (1) the preferences of clients, customers, or coworkers; (2) "potential workers compensation liability;" or (3) "the expense of providing fringe benefits," like insurance.[273]

In addition, an employer must provide reasonable accommodations to a person whose handicap is unrelated to his or her ability to perform a job or occupation, such as when the handicap only limits the individual's ability to perform incidental or peripheral job functions.[274]

2. Defenses

An employer does not have to hire or employ a worker whose handicap is related to his or her ability to perform a job and would pose a demonstrably hazardous risk to the person's health or safety, the health or safety of others, or the handicap results in behavior that "fails to meet acceptable standards," such as chronic absenteeism.[275]

---

[271] *See* Department of Corr. v. Illinois Human Rights Comm'n, 699 N.E.2d 143 (Ill. Ct. App. 1998); ILL. ADMIN. CODE tit. 56, §2500.40.
[272] ILL. ADMIN. CODE tit. 56, §2500.40(c).
[273] *Id.* §§2500.20(d)(1), 5210.90.
[274] *Id.* §2500.20(d)(1).
[275] *Id.* §2500.20(d)(2).

a. Bona Fide Occupational Qualification

Employers are not liable for handicap discrimination that results in handicapped individuals being denied employment on the basis of a bona fide occupational qualification.[276] An employer has the burden of establishing that the exclusion of an entire group of individuals is necessary for the safe and efficient operation of a particular job.[277] For instance, sight could be a bona fide occupational qualification for a school bus driver just as speech could be a bona fide occupational qualification for a radio disc jockey.

b. Undue Hardship

Similarly, an employer can refuse to provide a reasonable accommodation if it poses an undue hardship that is prohibitively expensive or would unduly disrupt the ordinary conduct of the employer's business.[278] In deciding whether an accommodation poses an undue burden, employers must weigh the costs and inconvenience of the accommodation versus the immediate benefit of facilitating a handicapped person's employment, and the potential benefits of facilitating access for other disabled employees, applicants, clients, and customers.[279]

Job restructuring, such as part-time work, or alterations of the work facility to make it more accessible for handicapped persons are examples of reasonable accommodations.[280] Providing employees with accommodations of a personal nature, such as eyeglasses, transportation to work, or eliminating a job, however, is not required.[281]

---

[276] 775 ILL. COMP. STAT. 5/2-104(A)(1).
[277] Id.
[278] See Department of Corr. v. Illinois Human Rights Comm'n, 298 Ill. App. 3d 536, 699 N.E.2d 143 (3d Dist. 1998); ILL. ADMIN. CODE tit. 56, §2500.40(a).
[279] ILL. ADMIN. CODE tit. 56, §2500.40(a).
[280] Id.
[281] Id.

II. Local Laws

Chicago and Cook County employers with one or more employees are also subject to local human rights ordinances.[282]

INDIANA

I. State Law

A. Overview

It is the policy of Indiana "to encourage and enable the blind, the visually disabled, and the otherwise physically disabled [persons] to engage in remunerative employment."[283] Indeed, the state's public policy is "to eliminate segregation or separation based solely on" disability and to provide equal employment opportunities to all of its citizens.[284] However, it is also Indiana's public policy "to protect employers [against] unfounded charges of discrimination."[285]

B. Prohibited Discrimination

Employers are prohibited from discriminating against an otherwise qualified disabled person with regard to job application procedures, hiring, advancement, discharge, compensation, training, and other "terms, conditions, and privileges of employment."[286] It is also unlawful to exclude "or otherwise deny equal [job opportunities] or benefits to a qualified individual because" of his or her association or relationship with a known disabled person.[287]

Employers are also prohibited from denying employment opportunities to an otherwise qualified disabled job applicant

---

[282]Chicago Mun. Code Ordinance No. 93-0-13 (Human Rights), Cook County, Illinois.
[283]Ind. Code Ann. §16-32-3-1.
[284]*Id.* §22-9-1-2(a).
[285]*Id.* §22-9-1-2(c).
[286]*Id.* §22-9-5-19.
[287]*Id.* §22-9-5-7(4).

or employee based on the employer's need "to make a reasonable accommodation to the physical or mental impairments of" the applicant or employee.[288] However, there is no intention on the part of the legislature to require an employer to employ a person who simply for whatever reason, handicapped or otherwise, cannot reasonably perform the job offered.[289]

It is discrimination to exclude "a person from equal opportunities because of ... disability," or to maintain a "system that excludes persons from equal opportunities because of ... disability."[290] "Limiting, segregating, or classifying a job applicant or an employee in a way that adversely affects the opportunities or status of the" person on the basis of disability is discrimination.[291]

Additionally, employers are prohibited from using "standards, criteria," or administrative methods that have the effect of discriminating based on disability.[292] Employers cannot use "qualification standards, employment tests, or other selection criteria that screen out or tend to screen out" persons with disabilities, unless the criteria are job related and are "consistent with business necessity."[293] Moreover, when an employer administers tests to employees and applicants, the tests must be done "in the most effective manner to ensure" that persons with disabilities that impair their "sensory, manual, or speaking skills" are not adversely affected, except where those skills are the factors that the test is aimed to measure.[294]

Participating in a contract or other arrangement with employment or referral agencies, labor unions, and other organizations when the relationship "has the effect of subjecting [the employer's] qualified applicant[s] or employee[s] with a disability to" discrimination is also prohibited.[295]

---

[288] *Id.* §22-9-5-7(6).
[289] Indiana Civil Rights Comm'n v. Southern Ind. Gas & Elec. Co., 553 N.E. 2d 840 (Ind. 1990).
[290] IND. CODE ANN. §22-9-1-3(*l*)(1)–(2).
[291] *Id.* §22-9-5-7(1).
[292] *Id.* §22-9-5-7(3)(A)–(B).
[293] *Id.* §22-9-5-7(7).
[294] *Id.* §22-9-5-7(8).
[295] *Id.* §22-9-5-7(2).

1. Preemployment Inquiries

a. Medical Examinations

Generally, employers cannot require medical examinations and inquire about an employee or applicant's disability status "unless the examination or inquiry is . . . job related and consistent with business necessity."[296]

Employers are prohibited from making preemployment inquiries about a job applicant's disability status and about the severity of the disability, if one exists.[297] However, preemployment inquiries about an applicant's ability to perform job-related functions is permissible.[298]

Employers are not permitted to require preemployment medical examinations of its applicants; however, employers can require post-offer medical examination prior to actual commencement of employment and can condition an offer on the results of a medical examination if the employer complies with the following requirements: (1) "[a]ll entering employees," regardless of disability status, must be tested; and (2) the information regarding the medical condition or applicant history must be "collected and maintained on separate forms and in separate medical files . . . ."[299] The information collected also must be treated as confidential medical information, except that the employer may disclose the information to supervisors, managers, first aid and safety personnel, and certain government officials where necessary and permitted by statute.[300]

Employers are not prohibited from conducting "voluntary medical examinations, including [obtaining] voluntary medical histories, as part of an employee health [plan that is] available to employees at" the work facility.[301] In addition, employers

---

[296] *Id.* §22-9-5-20(d).
[297] *Id.* §22-9-5-20(a).
[298] *Id.* §22-9-5-20(b).
[299] *Id.* §22-9-5-20(c)(1)–(2).
[300] *Id.* §22-9-5-20(c)(2).
[301] *Id.* §22-9-5-20(e).

may inquire "into the ability of an employee to perform job related functions."[302]

C. Definitions

1. Disability

A disability is a physical impairment "that substantially limits at least one" major life activity, "a record of such an impairment," or [b]eing regarded as having an impairment . . . ."[303] In the employment context, a disability is also a "physical or mental condition . . . that constitutes a substantial disability . . . unrelated to the person's ability to engage in a particular occupation."[304]

"Homosexuality, bisexuality, transvestism, transsexualism, pedophilia, exhibitionism, voyeurism, gender identity disorders not resulting from physical impairments, . . . other sexual behavior disorders, compulsive gambling, kleptomania, [and] pyromania" are not considered disabilities in Indiana.[305]

In Indiana, a person using illegal drugs or alcohol is not disabled unless the person has "successfully completed[, or is participating in,] a supervised drug rehabilitation program . . . or has otherwise been rehabilitated[,]and is no longer engaging in the illegal use of drugs . . . or [i]s erroneously regarded" as using illegal drugs.[306] Similarly, psychoactive substance abuse "disorders resulting from current illegal use of drugs" is not a disability.[307]

Disabled individuals who can perform the essential job functions, "with or without reasonable accommodation[s]," are qualified individuals.[308] An employer's written job description, prepared "before advertising or interviewing applicants," and the employer's judgment are evidence of what is "essential."[309]

---

[302] *Id.*
[303] *Id.* §22-9-5-6(a)(1)–(3).
[304] *Id.* §22-9-1-3(r).
[305] *Id.* §22-9-5-6(d)(1)–(4).
[306] *Id.* §22-9-5-6(b)(1)–(3).
[307] *Id.* §22-9-5-6(d)(5).
[308] *Id.* §22-9-5-16.
[309] *Id.*

2. Employee

An employee is a "person employed by another for wages or salary," but not employed by a "parent, spouse, or child[, nor i]n the domestic service of any person."[310]

3. Person

For the purposes of determining liability under Indiana's Civil Rights Act, a "person" includes one "or more individuals, partnerships, associations, organizations, limited liability companies, corporations, labor organizations, . . . and other organized groups of persons."[311]

D. Covered Employers

Any person who employs six "or more persons within" Indiana is covered by Indiana's prohibitions against discrimination.[312] Covered employers include employers, employment agencies, labor organization, and joint labor-management committees.[313]

This definition does not include nonprofit corporations "organized exclusively for fraternal or religious purposes . . . any religious institution owned or . . . affiliated with a church or religious institution," or any social club "not organized for profit."[314]

E. Reasonable Accommodation and Defenses

1. Reasonable Accommodation

Employers must make "reasonable accommodations to the known physical or mental [disabilities] of an otherwise qualified" applicant or employee, unless the employer can show "that the accommodation would impose an undue hardship"

---

[310] *Id.* §22-9-1-3(i).
[311] *Id.* §22-9-1-3(a).
[312] *Id.* §22-9-1-3(h).
[313] *Id.* §22-9-5-4.
[314] *Id.* §22-9-1-3(h).

on its operation.[315] Under the Indiana Civil Rights Act, a reasonable accommodation includes "[m]aking existing facilities . . . readily accessible to individuals with disabilities." It also includes "[j]ob restructuring, [including] part-time or modified work schedules, reassignment to [vacant positions,] acquisition [of] or modification [to] equipment or devices, appropriate adjustment or modification of examinations, [including] training materials or policies," and "providing qualified readers or interpreters [or] similar accommodations . . . ."[316]

2. Defenses

Employers are not required "to modify any physical accommodations or administrative procedures" in order to accommodate a disabled person.[317] Moreover, once a disabled worker is hired, employers are not required "to promote or transfer [the worker] to another job or occupation, unless, prior to such transfer," the disabled worker, through "training or experience is qualified for [the] job or occupation."[318]

a. Infectious or Communicable Diseases

An employer "may refuse to assign" or discontinue assignment to a food-handling job for persons who have infectious or communicable diseases that are "transmitted to others through the handling of food," and constitute "a significant risk to the health or safety of others that cannot be eliminated by reasonable accommodation."[319]

b. Qualification Standards

Selection criteria, standards, tests, and other qualification standards "that screen out or tend to screen out . . . or otherwise deny a job or benefit" to a disabled person may be defended by an employer if the criteria are "shown to be job related . . . consistent with business necessity, and performance cannot

---

[315] *Id.* §22-9-5-7(5).
[316] *Id.* §22-9-5-17(1)–(2).
[317] *Id.* §22-9-1-13(c).
[318] *Id.* §22-9-1-13(b).
[319] *Id.* §22-9-5-23.

be accomplished by reasonable accommodation . . . ."[320] For example, a corporation did not engage in unlawful discriminatory practices when it rejected an application of employment from a man with cerebral palsy and presented a legitimate business reason for not hiring him.[321]

Qualification standards may also include a requirement that the disabled person not pose a direct threat to the health or safety of other individuals in the workplace.[322]

Employers are not required "to employ or retain" a disabled person who, because of the disability, "is physically or otherwise unable to efficiently and safely perform" the job duties consistent with standards set by the employer.[323]

c. Undue Hardship

An undue hardship defense requires "significant difficulty or expense when" factoring in the "nature and cost of the accommodation," the overall financial resources and size of the employer and facility at issue, including the facility's structure, workforce, geographic separateness, and the effect on expense and resources, or the impact of the accommodation on the employer's operations.[324]

IOWA

I. STATE LAW

A. Overview

The Iowa Civil Rights Act of 1965 established the Iowa Civil Rights Commission, which promotes the elimination and

---

[320] *Id.* §22-9-5-21.
[321] Robinson v. Dana Corp., 656 N.E.2d 540 (Ind. Ct. App. 1995).
[322] *Id.*
[323] IND. CODE ANN. §22-9-1-13(a). *See also* Indiana Civil Rights Comm'n v. Southern Ind. Gas & Elec. Co., 553 N.E.2d 840 (Ind. 1990) (employers not required to hire person who cannot reasonably perform job regardless of whether person is handicapped; thus, employer not required to hire 5'1", 124-pound woman with congenital back condition for job requiring heavy lifting); *Robinson*, 656 N.E.2d 540 (corporation rightfully rejected applicant who had cerebral palsy because company presented legitimate business reason for not hiring applicant).
[324] *Id.* §22-9-5-18.

minimization of disability discrimination in employment.[325] In addition, the Iowa Department of Human Rights' Commission of Persons with Disabilities promotes "the employment of persons with disabilities."[326]

B. Prohibited Discrimination

It is unlawful discrimination for employers "to hire, accept, register, [discharge,] classify, or refer for employment, ... or to otherwise discriminate in employment against any applicant ... or any employee because of ... disability," unless the discrimination is "based upon the nature of the occupation."[327] However, if a disabled person is qualified by training or experience "to perform a particular" job, the nature of the occupation cannot serve as the basis for exception to discrimination.[328]

Employers and their employees or agents are prohibited from advertising or publicizing in any manner that disabled individuals "are unwelcome, objectionable, not acceptable, or not solicited for employment," unless the discriminatory advertising or publication is "based on the nature of the occupation."[329] However, if a disabled person is qualified by training or experience to perform a particular job, the nature of the occupation cannot serve as the basis for exception to advertisement or publication.[330]

Employers "may offer employment ... to only persons with disabilities when other applicants have" employment available "compatible with their ability which would not be available to persons with disabilities . . . ."[331]

The Iowa Civil Rights Commission, the enforcement arm for the state's civil rights laws, has published additional antidiscrimination policies and regulations. For example, employers are prohibited from discriminating between disabled persons

---

[325] IOWA CODE ANN. §216.5 et seq.
[326] Id. §216A.77.
[327] Id. §216.6(1)(a).
[328] Id.
[329] Id. §216.6(1)(c).
[330] Id.
[331] Id.

and persons who are not disabled, with regard to fringe benefits, unless there are bona fide underwriting criteria.[332]

1. Preemployment Inquiries

a. Medical Examinations

Employers may not solicit or require as a condition of employment of any applicant or employee a test for the presence of human immunodeficiency virus (HIV) "or affect the terms, conditions, or privileges of employment or terminate the employment of any employee solely as a result of the employee obtaining a test for the presence of an antibody" to this virus.[333] In addition, agreements between employers and employees regarding "employment, pay, or benefits to an employee" or applicant in exchange "for taking a test for the presence of the antibody to the ... virus, is prohibited."[334]

2. Genetic Testing

Employers may not (1) "[s]olicit, require, or administer a genetic test to a person as a condition of employment, preemployment application, labor organization membership, or licensure;" or (2) "[a]ffect the terms, conditions, or privileges of employment, preemployment application, labor organization membership, or licensure, or terminate the employment, labor organization membership, or licensure of any person who obtains a genetic test."[335] However, genetic testing of an employee is permitted if the employee "requests a genetic test and ... provides written" consent in these situations: (1) the investigation of "a workers' compensation claim"; or (2) the determination of "the employee's susceptibility or level of exposure to potentially toxic" substances, if the employer does not take adverse action against the employee that "affects any term,

---

[332] IOWA ADMIN. CODE §161-8.29.
[333] IOWA CODE ANN. §216.6(d).
[334] Id.
[335] Id. §729.6(2).

condition, or privilege of the ... employment as a result of the genetic test."[336]

3. Pregnancy-Related Disability

In Iowa, "[d]isabilities caused or contributed to by the employee's pregnancy, miscarriage, childbirth, ... legal abortion and recovery therefrom are, for all job-related purposes, temporary disabilities ...."[337] Consequently, these temporary conditions must be treated as disabilities under any "temporary disability insurance or sick leave plan available in connection with employment [and must be applied on] the same terms and conditions as they are applied to other temporary disabilities."[338]

Moreover, employers cannot terminate the employment of a person disabled by pregnancy.[339] In addition, employers must provide leave to employees who are disabled by pregnancy, childbirth, or related medical conditions, with "timely notice" by the employee, when the employer's current leave or insurance policy provides insufficient leave.[340]

C. Definitions

1. Disability

A disability is the "physical or mental condition of a person which constitutes a substantial disability, and the condition of a person with a positive [HIV] test result, a diagnosis of acquired immune deficiency syndrome [(AIDS)]-related complex, or any other condition related to [AIDS]."[341]

---

[336] *Id.* §729.6(7).
[337] *Id.* §216.6(2)(b)–(c). Employers are permitted "to exclude health insurance coverage for abortion from a plan ... except when the life of the mother [is endangered] if the fetus is carried to [full] term or where medical complications have arisen from an abortion." *Id.* §216.6(2)(c).
[338] *Id.*
[339] *Id.* §216.6(2)(d).
[340] *Id.* §216.6(2)(e).
[341] *Id.* §216.2(5).

The Iowa Civil Rights Commission has published additional definitions for disability discrimination that track federal law.[342]

Any person who has a physical or mental impairment that "substantially limits one or more major life activities, has a record or such an impairment, or is regarded as having such impairment," is a substantially handicapped person.[343]

"Any physiological disorder or condition, cosmetic disfigurement, or anatomical loss affecting one or more of the ... neurological; musculoskeletal; special sense organs; respiratory, including speech organs; cardiovascular; reproductive; digestive; genito-urinary; hemic and lymphatic; skin; and endocrine" body systems is a physical or mental impairment.[344] In addition, "mental retardation, organic brain syndrome, emotional or mental illness, [certain] learning disabilities," and any mental or psychological disorder are also physical or mental impairments.[345]

2. Major Life Activities

"Functions such as caring for one's self, performing manual tasks, walking, seeing, hearing, speaking, breathing, learning, and working" are examples of major life activities.[346]

D. Covered Employers

Iowa's discrimination provisions apply to employers who regularly employ four or more workers, not including family members, to labor organizations, and to employment agencies.[347] However, persons who employ domestic workers in their homes and religious institutions that base employment on a bona fide religious purpose are not covered employers.[348]

---

[342] IOWA ADMIN. CODE §161-8.26(216).
[343] Id. §161-8.26(1).
[344] Id. §161-8.26(2).
[345] Id.
[346] Id. §161-8.26(3).
[347] IOWA CODE ANN. §216.6(6).
[348] Id.

E. Reasonable Accommodation and Defenses

1. Reasonable Accommodation

Under Iowa's regulations, employers are required to "make reasonable accommodation[s] to the known physical or mental limitations of an otherwise qualified handicapped applicant or employee unless the employer can demonstrate that the accommodation would impose an undue hardship" on its operations.[349] The following are examples of reasonable accommodations: (1) job restructuring, such as a modified or part-time work schedule; (2) acquiring or modifying equipment or devices; (3) making facilities "readily accessible to and usable by handicapped persons"; and (4) providing "readers or interpreters."[350]

2. Defenses

a. Affirmative Action

Employers "may offer employment or advertise for employment" exclusively to disabled individuals, "when other applicants have ... other employment compatible with their ability" available to them, "which would not be available to persons with disabilities ...."[351] Any such employment or offer shall not be made by discriminating among disabled persons "on the basis of race, color, creed, sex, or national origin."[352]

b. Bona Fide Occupational Qualification

Employers have the ability to use bona fide occupational qualifications as a defense to a claim of discrimination if the qualification is "reasonably necessary to the normal operation of the particular business."[353] However, employers must be aware that the "qualification is narrow in scope and [does]

---

[349] IOWA ADMIN. CODE §161-8.27(6).
[350] Id.
[351] IOWA CODE ANN. §216.6(1)(c).
[352] Id.
[353] IOWA ADMIN. CODE §161-8.32(1).

not ... include the mere preference or convenience of the employer."[354]

c. *Undue Hardship*

Employers should consider the following factors when deciding whether a reasonable accommodation poses an undue hardship: (1) the size and type of the employer's facility and budget; (2) the nature and cost of the accommodation; and (3) the type of operation, including the structure of the workforce.[355] Employers are prohibited from denying an employment "opportunity to a qualified handicapped" applicant or employee because of the need to accommodate the person's disability.[356]

KANSAS

I. STATE LAW

A. Overview

Under the Kansas Act Against Discrimination, every citizen has a civil right to have the opportunity to secure and hold employment, regardless of disability.[357] It is the policy of the state to assure equal employment opportunities to citizens regardless of disability.[358]

B. Prohibited Discrimination

The Kansas Act Against Discrimination makes it unlawful for an employer "to refuse to hire or employ[,] ... bar or discharge, ... limit, segregate, separate, classify," or otherwise discriminate against any individual on the basis of disability

---

[354] *Id.* §161-8.32(2).
[355] Id. §161-8.27(6).
[356] *Id.*
[357] KAN. STAT. ANN. §44-1001 et seq.
[358] *Id.*

with respect to compensation, or in other "conditions or privileges of employment" (including transfers, assignments, layoffs, training, and promotions), or to follow any employment procedure or practice "that results in discrimination, segregation or separation without a valid business necessity."[359]

Employers are also prohibited from printing or circulating any statement, advertising, or publication that "expresses . . . any limitation, specification or discrimination" against disabled persons, unless it is "based on a bona fide occupational qualification."[360] In addition, employers are prohibited from retaliating against any person because they have opposed any discriminatory practice.[361]

The Kansas Act Against Discrimination has additional prohibitions against discrimination on the basis of disability, including utilizing discriminatory standards or criteria and discriminating against a person who is associated or has a relationship with someone with a known disability.[362] Employers are also prohibited from using "qualification standards, employment tests or other selection criteria that screen out or tend to screen out [individuals with disabilities] unless the [method used is] job-related [and] consistent with business necessity";[363] the tests or methods used must also be accurate and nondiscriminatory.[364] Finally, it is unlawful for any person, to aid, abet, incite, compel or coerce, or attempt discrimination.[365]

1. Preemployment Inquiries

a. Medical Exminations

Employers are prohibited from requiring medical examinations and inquiring whether an employee is disabled, or "the nature or severity of the disability," if any, unless the

---

[359] *Id.* §44-1009(a)(1), (6).
[360] *Id.* §44-1009(a)(3).
[361] *Id.* §44-1009(a)(4).
[362] *Id.* §44-1009(a)(8).
[363] *Id.* §44-1009(a)(8)(G).
[364] *Id.* §44-1009(a)(8)(H).
[365] *Id.* §44-1009(c)(2).

examination or inquiry is "job-related and consistent with business necessity," or related to an applicant's ability to perform job-related functions.[366]

Generally, employers are not permitted to "conduct a medical examination or make inquiries of a job applicant as to whether the applicant is an individual with a disability or as to the nature or severity of the applicant's disability . . . ."[367] Employers are, however, permitted to make preemployment inquiries and require medical examinations after a job offer has been made, but before employment has commenced, "and may condition an offer . . . on the results of the examination or inquiry, or both" as long as: (1) "all entering employees in the same job category are subjected" to the examination or inquiry; and (2) the "information obtained" through the examination or inquiry is maintained and collected on separate forms, "in separate medical files, and is treated as a confidential medical record . . . ."[368] Under certain circumstances, supervisors, managers, first aid, safety personnel, and government officials may be informed of the results of the examination or inquiry.[369]

In addition, employers are permitted to make inquiries about "the ability of an employee to perform job-related functions."[370] Employers may also "conduct voluntary medical examinations, including . . . medical histories, [as] part of an employee health program.[371]

2. *Genetic Testing*

It is unlawful for employers to "[s]eek to obtain, or obtain or to use genetic screening or testing information of an employee or prospective employee [in order to] discriminate against or restrict any right or benefit otherwise due or available

---

[366] KAN. ADMIN. REGS. §§21-34-5, 21-34-3(b).
[367] *Id.* §21-34-3(a).
[368] *Id.* §21-34-4(a), (b).
[369] *Id.* §21-34-4(b)(1), (2).
[370] *Id.* §21-34-6(a).
[371] *Id.*

to an employee or a prospective employee."[372] In addition, employers may not "subject, directly or indirectly, any employee or prospective employee to any genetic screening or test."[373]

3. Pregnancy-Related Disability

Kansas employers are permitted to provide leaves of absence to employees suffering pregnancy-related disabilities.[374]

C. Definitions

1. Disability

A disability is a physical or mental impairment that substantially limits one or more major life activities, a record of such impairment, or being regarded as having such impairment.[375] While current use of illegal drugs is not a disability,[376] persons who have completed or are currently enrolled in a "supervised drug rehabilitation program," are no longer using illegal drugs, or are "erroneously regarded as engaging in the illegal use of drugs" can be considered qualified individuals with disabilities.[377]

"[A]ny physiological disorder or condition, cosmetic disfigurement, or anatomical loss affecting one or more of [the] neurological, musculoskeletal, special sense organs, respiratory [and] speech organs, cardiovascular, reproductive, digestive, genitourinary, hemic and lymphatic, skin, and endocrine" body systems, and any mental or psychological disorder, such as mental retardation, organic brain syndrome, emotional or

---

[372] *See* Kansas Gas & Elec. Co. v. Kansas Comm'n on Civil Rights, 750 P.2d 1055 (Kan. 1988).
[373] KAN. STAT. ANN. §44-1009(a)(9)(A).
[374] *Id.* §44-1009(a)(9)(B).
[375] *Id.* §44-1002(j)(1)–(3). *See* Padilla v. City of Topeka, 238 Kan. 218, 708 P.2d 543, 2 AD Cases 1605 (1985) (myopia corrected to 20/20 vision not substantial disability).
[376] KAN. STAT. ANN. §44-1002(j).
[377] KAN. ADMIN. REGS. §21-34-11(b).

mental illness, and specific learning disabilities are examples of physical or mental impairments.[378]

A person is "substantially limited" if he or she is "unable to perform a major life activity that the average person in the general population can perform; or [is] significantly restricted [in] the condition, manner, or duration under which" the person can do so.[379]

2. *Essential Job Function*

A job function may be essential when: "(1) the job exists to perform that function, (2) the function is highly specialized" and requires expertise or ability, and "(3) a limited number of employees" are available to perform that function.[380] "[T]he employer's judgment as to which functions are essential; written job descriptions prepared before advertising [for] or interviewing applicants for the job; . . . the terms of a collective bargaining agreement; the work experience of past [or present] incumbents in the job [or similar jobs,] and "the amount of time spent" performing the function are evidence of whether the function is essential.[381]

3. *Major Life Activities*

"[C]aring for oneself, performing manual tasks, walking, seeing, hearing, speaking, breathing, learning, and working" are examples of major life activities.[382]

D. Covered Employers

The Kansas Act Against Discrimination covers any person in Kansas "employing four or more persons and any [other] person acting directly or indirectly for the employer," including employment agencies and labor organizations.[383]

---

[378] *Id.* §21-34-1(h).
[379] *Id.* §21-34-1(k).
[380] *Id.* §21-34-14(a).
[381] *Id.* §21-34-14(b).
[382] *Id.* §21-34-1(g).
[383] KAN. STAT. ANN. §44-1002(b).

E. Reasonable Accommodation and Defenses

1. Reasonable Accommodation

Employers are required to "make reasonable accommodations to the known physical or mental limitations of an otherwise qualified" applicant or employee with a disability, unless the employer can prove "that the accommodation would pose an undue hardship on the operation . . . ."[384] It is also unlawful to "deny employment opportunities to" applicants and employees because of the need to accommodate their disabilities.[385]

The following are examples of reasonable accommodations: (1) making existing facilities readily accessible to disabled individuals; (2) job restructuring, including a part-time or modified work schedule, or reassignment to a vacant position; (3) acquiring or modifying equipment or devices, examinations, training materials, or policies; (4) providing qualified readers or interpreters; and (5) other similar accommodations.[386]

2. Defenses

a. Affirmative Action

It is not unlawful for an employer "to fill vacancies in such a way as to eliminate or reduce imbalance [in the workforce] with respect to . . . disability . . . ."[387]

b. Direct Threat

Employers may use direct threat as a qualification standard, including "a requirement that an individual shall not pose a direct threat to the health or safety of that individual or others in the workplace."[388] "The determination that an individual with a disability poses a 'direct threat' [must] be based on an individualized assessment of the individual's present ability to safely perform the essential functions of the job."[389]

---

[384] Id. §44-1009(a)(8)(E).
[385] Id. §44-1009(a)(8)(F).
[386] Id. §44-1009(k)(1)–(2).
[387] Id.
[388] KAN. ADMIN. REGS. §21-34-15.
[389] Id. §21-34-13(a).

The assessment should be based on the following factors: "(1) the duration of the risk; (2) the nature and severity of the potential harm; (3) the likelihood that the potential harm will occur; and (4) the imminence of the potential harm."[390]

c. Infectious or Communicable Diseases

An employer is not required "to assign or continue to assign" a disabled individual with an infectious or communicable disease if the risk of transmitting the disease in food-handling jobs cannot be eliminated by reasonable accommodation.[391] An employer must, however, attempt to accommodate a disabled worker by reassigning the worker to a vacant non-food-handling job.[392]

d. Undue Hardship

An undue hardship requires "significant difficulty or expense."[393] In determining whether an accommodation would pose an undue hardship, an employer should consider the following factors: (1) "nature and net cost of the accommodation," including tax credits, deductions, and funding; (2) the overall financial resources of, number of workers at, and size of the facility involved; (3) the type of operation; and (4) "the geographic separateness, administrative, or fiscal relationship of the facility or facilities" requiring the accommodation.[394]

KENTUCKY

I. State Law

A. Overview

Kentucky's Civil Rights Act prohibits discrimination in employment against qualified persons with disabilities.[395] Kentucky has executed within the state the policies embodied in the ADA.[396]

---

[390] Id. §21-34-13(b).
[391] Id. §21-34-16(a).
[392] Id.
[393] Id. §21-34-19(a).
[394] Id. §21-34-19(b).
[395] Ky. Rev. Stat. Ann. §344.040.
[396] Id. §344.020(1)(a).

Kentucky also has an Equal Opportunities Act[397] that prohibits discrimination, including retaliation, against disabled individuals, and defines disability as a "physical condition, . . . congenital or acquired, which constitutes a substantial disability . . . and is demonstrable by medically accepted clinical or laboratory diagnostic techniques."[398] The Equal Opportunities Act also protects persons with acquired immune deficiency syndrome-related complex, or human immunodeficiency virus (HIV) from discrimination in employment.[399]

Specifically, the Equal Opportunities Act prohibits an employer from failing or refusing to "hire, discharge, or discriminate against any individual with a disability" in terms of wage, pay rates, "hours, or other terms and conditions of employment," unless the disability (including HIV status) limits the individual's ability to perform the job functions or because of a bona fide occupational qualification.[400] The Equal Opportunites Act covers employers that employ eight or more individuals and the employer's agent.[401]

B. Prohibited Discrimination

It is unlawful for employers to discriminate against a qualified individual with a disability in hiring, in discharging, or "with respect to compensation, terms, conditions, or privileges of employment, . . . or to limit, segregate, or classify [these] employees in any way that would deprive or tend to deprive an individual of employment opportunities or otherwise adversely affect the individual's status as an employee . . . ."[402]

Employers are prohibited from printing or publishing any advertising or notice related to employment that expresses a

---

[397] *Id.* §207.130 et seq.
[398] *Id.* §207.130(2).
[399] *Id.* §207.135.
[400] *Id.* §207.150.
[401] *Id.* §207.130 (3). *See* Whitlow v. Kentucky Mfg. Co., 762 S.W.2d 808 (Ky. Ct. App. 1988) (person who had problems with coordination, vision, and varicose veins was not physically handicapped).
[402] *Id.* §344.040(1)–(2).

"preference, limitation, specification, or discrimination" because of disability, unless it is for a bona fide occupational qualification.[403] In addition, employment agencies,[404] labor organizations,[405] or joint labor-management committees[406] are prohibited from discriminating against persons with disabilities in employment matters, including admission to or employment in apprenticeship or training programs.[407]

C. Definitions

1. Disability

A disability is a physical or mental impairment that substantially limits one (1) or more ... major life activities ..., [a] record of such impairment; or being regarding as having such impairment."[408] "Persons with current or past controlled substance abuse or alcohol abuse problems" are excluded from this definition.[409]

A qualified individual with a disability is a person who, "with or without reasonable accommodation, can perform" essential job functions, unless the employer "is unable to reasonably accommodate" the applicant or employee "without undue hardship" on the employer's business.[410]

D. Covered Employers

The Kentucky Civil Rights Act applies to an employer "engaged in an industry affecting commerce [that] has fifteen (15) or more employees for each working day in each of twenty

---

[403] *Id.* §344.080.
[404] *Id.* §344.050.
[405] *Id.* §344.060.
[406] *Id.* §344.070.
[407] *Id.*
[408] *Id.* §344.010(4).
[409] *Id. See* Howard Baer Inc. v. Schave, 127 S.W.3d 589 (Ky. 2003) (holding that an employee was not disabled due to his alleged inability to perform the major life function of working because he was unable to perform a single, task-specific job.)
[410] *Id.* §344.030(1). *See* Brohm v. JH Properties, Inc., 947 F. Supp. 299, 6 AD Cases 1489 (W.D. Ky. 1996) (hospital's termination of doctor with sleep apnea who fell asleep during surgery was not discriminatory).

(20) or more calendar weeks in the current or preceding calendar year, and any agent of" the employer.[411] In addition, employment agencies,[412] labor organizations,[413] or joint labor-management committees[414] are prohibited from discriminating against persons with disabilities in employment matters, including "admission to or employment in" apprenticeship or training programs.[415]

Individual supervisors cannot be held liable for discrimination in Kentucky.[416] Similarly, an individual supervisory employee is not an employer within the meaning of the statute.[417] "A bona fide private membership club" is also excluded from coverage.[418]

E. Reasonable Accommodation and Defenses

1. *Reasonable Accommodation*

In Kentucky, employers are required to provide reasonable accommodations to qualified disabled applicants or employees by (1) making existing facilities readily accessible for use by disabled individuals; (2) job restructuring, including a part-time or modified work schedule, or "reassignment to a vacant position"; (3) acquiring, adjusting, or modifying examinations, devices, training materials, and policies; or (4) providing "qualified readers or interpreters, and other similar accommodations," without undue hardship.[419]

---

[411] *Id.* §344.030(2).
[412] *Id.* §344.050.
[413] *Id.* §344.060.
[414] *Id.* §344.070.
[415] *Id.*
[416] *See* Effinger v. Philip Morris, Inc., 984 F. Supp. 1043 (W.D. Ky. 1997) (under Kentucky Civil Rights Act, employers are ultimately responsible for discriminatory acts of their employees and, thus, supervisor could not be held liable for discrimination).
[417] Boone v. Kent Feeds, Inc., 2001 U.S. Dist. LEXIS 9616, 2001 WL 1775375 (W.D. Ky. July 10, 2001).
[418] KY. REV. STAT. ANN. §344.030(2)(b).
[419] *Id.* §344.030(6).

2. Defenses

It is not illegal discrimination in Kentucky if discrimination in wages or conditions of employment is made for a reason other than that the person is a qualified individual with a disability.[420] An employer may apply different standards, as long as the "differences are not the result of an intention to discriminate," if the compensation or terms, conditions, or privileges of employment are pursuant to (1) "a bona fide seniority or merit system," (2) "a system which measures earnings by quantity or quality of production," or (3) different work locations of employees.[421]

a. Undue Hardship

An action that requires "significant difficulty or expense" poses an undue hardship on the employer when factoring (1) the nature and cost of the accommodation; (2) the overall financial resources, size, and number workers of the facility involved; and (3) the type of operation.[422]

LOUISIANA

I. STATE LAW

A. Overview

Under the Louisiana Employment Discrimination Law, an otherwise qualified disabled person has the right to be free from employment discrimination.[423]

B. Prohibited Discrimination

Employers cannot "[f]ail or refuse to hire, promote, or reasonably accommodate an otherwise qualified disabled person on the basis of a disability, when [the disability] is unrelated

---

[420] *Id.*
[421] *Id.* §344.100.
[422] *Id.* §344.030(9).
[423] La. Rev. Stat. Ann. §§23:301, 23:323(A).

to the [person's] ability, with reasonable accommodation, to perform the duties of a particular job or position."[424] Employers are also prohibited from discharging or otherwise discriminating "against an otherwise qualified disabled person with respect to compensation or the terms, conditions, or privileges of employment on the basis of a disability when it is unrelated to the individual's ability to perform" job duties.[425] Nor can employers "[l]imit, segregate, or classify an otherwise qualified disabled [individual] in a way [that] deprives the [person] of employment opportunities or otherwise adversely affects the status of the individual on the basis of a disability when it is unrelated to the [person's] ability to perform" job duties, or "[f]ail or refuse to hire or promote an otherwise qualified disabled person, . . . [d]ischarge or take other discriminatory action . . . on the basis of physical or mental examinations or preemployment interviews that are not directly related to the requirements of the specific job, or are not required of all employees or applicants."[426] In addition, employers are prohibited from failing or refusing to hire or to promote, discharging, or taking any "other discriminatory action against an otherwise qualified disabled person when adaptive devices or aids may need to be utilized to enable that individual, at [his or her] own expense, to perform specific" job requirements.[427]

Making or using "a written or oral inquiry or form of application" or advertisement that seeks or attempts to seek information about a prospective employee's disability, or "that expresses a preference, limitation, or specification based on" disability for discriminatory purposes is prohibited.[428] Finally, making or keeping "a record of information," or disclosing information about "the disability of a prospective employee for discriminatory purposes" is prohibited.[429]

---

[424] *Id.* §23:323(B)(1).
[425] *Id.* §23:323(B)(2).
[426] *Id.* §23:323(B)(3)–(5).
[427] *Id.* §23:323(B)(6), (7).
[428] *Id.* §§23:323(B)(8), (10); §23:323(D)(2).
[429] *Id.* §23:323(B)(9).

1. Genetic Testing

Employment discrimination by employers, labor organization, employment agencies, and joint labor-management training committees on the basis of genetic testing and information is barred under the Louisiana Employment Discrimination Law.[430] In addition, labor organizations may not discriminate in membership practices or job referrals on the basis of genetic information.[431] Genetic information about an employee may not be disclosed except to the employee, occupational or other health researcher, certain government officials, and federal and state courts if subpoenaed.[432]

Genetic information may be requested or required of an employee or applicant under certain conditions: (1) if the information is used "to assess whether further medical evaluation is needed to diagnose a current [condition that] could prevent the [employee/applicant] from performing" essential job functions; (2) for "therapeutic purposes," if the employee uses employer-provided health care services and has provided written authorization; and (3) for "monitoring [the] biological effects of toxic substances in the workplace," if the employee has provided written authorization and is told how to obtain the results of the monitoring, and the employer receives results in a form that does not disclose individual identities.[433] Employers must display a state labor department poster on the law.[434]

2. Pregnancy-Related Disability

Employers are required to give the same benefits or privileges to female employees affected by "pregnancy, childbirth, or related medical condition" that they do to other similarly situated employees, including providing disability leave "or any other accrued leave [that] is made available . . . to temporarily

---

[430] *Id.* §23:368(B).
[431] *Id.* §23:368(C)(1).
[432] *Id.* §23:368(B)(4).
[433] *Id.* §23:368(E).
[434] *Id.* §23:369.

disabled employees."[435] In addition, employers who have "a policy, practice, or collective bargaining agreement requiring or authorizing the transfer of temporarily disabled employees to less strenuous or hazardous positions for the duration of the disability" must provide the same benefit to a pregnant female employee who requests it.[436]

C. Definitions

1. Disability

"[A]ny person who has a physical or mental impairment [that] substantially limits one or more" major life activity, "or has a record of such an impairment, or is regarded as having such an impairment" is disabled.[437]

An impairment is any current or prior physical or mental disorder, condition, including retardation, but, at the employer's discretion, "may not include chronic alcoholism or any other form of active drug addiction, any cosmetic disfigurement, or an anatomical loss of body systems."[438]

A disabled applicant or employee who, with or without reasonable accommodation, "can perform the essential functions" of a job is otherwise qualified for that position.[439]

2. Major Life Activities

"[C]aring for one's self, performing manual tasks, walking, seeing, hearing, speaking, breathing, learning, and working" are major life activities.[440]

D. Covered Employers

The Louisiana Employment Discrimination Law defines an "employer" as "a person, association, legal or commercial

---

[435] *Id.* §23:342(2)(a).
[436] *Id.* §23:342(3).
[437] *Id.* §23:322(3).
[438] *Id.* §23:322(6).
[439] *Id.* §23:322(8).
[440] *Id.* §23:322(7).

entity, the state, or any state agency, board, commission, or political subdivision of the state . . . who employs twenty or more employees . . . for each working day in each of twenty or more calendar weeks in the . . . calendar year."[441] However, employers are not those who employ "a parent, spouse, child," or the domestic service of another.[442]

E. Reasonable Accommodation and Defenses

1. *Reasonable Accommodation*

A reasonable accommodation is "an adjustment or modification to a known physical limitation of an otherwise qualified disabled person which would not impose an undue hardship on the employer."[443] Employers are not, however, required "to spend more for architectural modifications than" the amount currently "allowed as a federal tax deduction."[444] However, the duty to reasonably accommodate does not impose on an employer a duty to incur "any additional costs" to hire or promote a disabled person.[445]

2. *Defenses*

a. *Affirmative Action*

It is permissible for employers to adopt and carry out a plan to fill vacancies or hire new employees so as to eliminate or reduce imbalance in the workplace with respect to disability, if the plan is filed with the Louisiana Commission on Human Rights and the Commission has not disapproved of the plan.[446]

b. *Business Necessity*

In Louisiana, an employer may defend against a charge "that an alleged application of a qualification" standard, test, or selection criteria that screens out or tends to screen out or

---

[441] *Id.* §23:302(2).
[442] *Id.* §23:302(2)(a).
[443] *Id.* §23:322(9).
[444] *Id.*
[445] *Id.*
[446] *See* LA. ADMIN. CODE tit. 40 §XVII.2501 et seq.

otherwise denies a job or benefit to a disabled person by showing it to be job related and consistent with business necessity.[447]

c. Qualification Standards

Qualification standards may include requirements that applicants or employees "not pose a direct threat to the health or safety of" the disabled person or others in the workplace.[448]

d. Undue Hardship

In Louisiana, whether a reasonable accommodation imposes an "[u]ndue hardship is determined on a case-by-case basis" considering all of the following factors: (1) the employee or applicant who is to be accommodated, (2) the employee or applicant's specific disability, (3) "the essential job duties of the position," and (4) the work environment.[449]

MAINE

I. State Law

A. Overview

Maine has extensive laws that specifically prohibit disability discrimination in employment. Indeed, Maine's public policy seeks to prevent discrimination in employment because of physical or mental disability,[450] and persons with physical or mental disabilities have a civil right to be free from employment discrimination.[451] It is the policy of the Maine Human Rights Act "to keep continually in review all practices infringing on the basic human right to a life with dignity."[452]

---

[447] *Id.* §23:324(A).
[448] *Id.* §23:324(B).
[449] *Id.* §23:322(9).
[450] 5 Me. Rev. Stat. Ann. §4552.
[451] *Id.* §4571.
[452] *Id.* §4552.

It is also Maine's policy in the state's Model White Cane Law "to encourage and enable the blind, the visually handicapped and the otherwise physically disabled" persons to engage in remunerative employment.[453]

B. Prohibited Discrimination

The Maine Human Rights Act prohibits discrimination in employment, "except when based on a bona fide occupational qualification."[454] Employers are prohibited from discriminatory practices in failing to hire, retaliating, discharging, promoting, transferring, compensating, or otherwise discriminating against an applicant or employee in the "terms, conditions, or privileges of employment," including job-training and application procedures, on the basis of physical or mental disability.[455] Employers also are forbidden from using an employment agency in recruiting individuals if the employer knows or has reason to know that the agency discriminates on the basis of physical or mental disability.[456]

It is unlawful discrimination for employers to "[e]licit or attempt to [e]licit information," including application forms that pertain to physical or mental disability, or to make or keep a record of physical or mental disability, unless the "employer requires a physical or mental examination prior to employment."[457] Employers are similarly prohibited from publishing, advertising, or announcing any policy of denying employment to disabled persons, or expressing a preference, limitation, or specification based on physical or mental disability.[458]

1. Preemployment Inquiries

a. Medical Examinations

Employers are prohibited from conducting "a medical examination" or making inquiries of job applicants regarding

---

[453] 17 Me. Rev. Stat. Ann. §1311.
[454] 5 Me. Rev. Stat. Ann. §4572(1).
[455] Id. §4572(1)(A).
[456] Id. §4572(1)(D).
[457] Id. §4572(1)(D)(1)–(3).
[458] Id. §4572(1)(D)(4).

the existence and extent of a disability, "unless the examination or inquiry [is] job-related and consistent with business necessity."[459]

However, employers are permitted to require post-offer medical examinations, "prior to the commencement" of employment, and can condition a job offer on the results of the medical examination if (1) "[a]ll entering employees are subjected to the same examination;" and (2) any "[i]nformation obtained about an applicant's medical condition or history is kept in separate medical files and is treated as" confidential, except that certain disclosures may be made to supervisors, managers, first aid and safety personnel, and government officials.[460] Other voluntary medical examinations for health programs are permissible.[461]

2. Genetic Testing

Employers "may not fail or refuse to hire, discharge or otherwise discriminate against [an individual] on the basis of genetic information concerning that individual or because of the individual's refusal to submit to a genetic test or make available the results of a genetic test or on the basis that the individual received a genetic test or genetic counseling, except when based on a bona fide occupational qualification."[462]

C. Definitions

1. Disability

A "disabled person" is one who "[h]as a physical or mental disability," a record of such a disability, or is regarded as having a disability.[463]

Discrimination against individuals with physical or mental disabilities includes the following: (1) "limiting, segregating,

---

[459] Id. §4572(2)(B), (D).
[460] Id. §4572(2)(C).
[461] Id. §4572(2)(E).
[462] Id. §19302.
[463] Id. §4553(7-B).

or classifying a job applicant or employee in a way that adversely affects the opportunities or status of the applicant or employee because of the disability"; (2) "[p]articipating in a contractual or other arrangement or relationship that has the effect of subjecting a covered entity's qualified [disabled] applicant or employee with a disability to" discrimination; or (3) "[u]tilizing standards, criteria or methods of administration that have the effect of" discriminating or perpetuating discrimination "on the basis of disability."[464]

It is also discriminatory to exclude or otherwise deny "equal jobs or benefits to a qualified" person because of his or her association or relationship with a known disabled person.[465] Failure to make a reasonable accommodation "to the known physical or mental limitations of an otherwise qualified" disabled applicant or employee is also discriminatory, unless the employer "can demonstrate that the accommodation would impose an undue hardship on the" employer's operation.[466] In addition, employers are prohibited from denying employment opportunities to an otherwise qualified disabled job applicant or employee based on the employer's need to reasonably accommodate the applicant or employee.[467]

Employers cannot discriminate against otherwise qualified disabled employees or applicants by (1) "[u]sing qualification standards, employment tests or other selection criteria that screen out or tend to screen out" individuals with disabilities unless it "is shown to be job-related . . . and is consistent with business necessity";[468] or (2) "[f]ailing to select and administer tests concerning employment in the most effective manner to ensure that . . . the test results accurately reflect the skills, aptitude or any other factor of the applicant or employee . . . rather than reflecting [his or her] impaired sensory, manual or speaking skills."[469]

---

[464] *Id.* §4553(2)(A–C).
[465] *Id.* §4553(2)(D).
[466] *Id.* §4553(2)(E).
[467] *Id.* §4553(2)(F).
[468] *Id.* §4553(2)(G).
[469] *Id.* §4553(2)(H).

Any "infirmity, malformation, disfigurement, congenital defect or mental condition caused by bodily injury, accident, disease, birth defect, environmental conditions or illness, [including] the physical or mental condition of a person that constitutes a substantial disability as determined by a physician or, ... a psychiatrist or psychologist, as well as any other health or sensory impairment that requires special education, vocational rehabilitation or related services," is a physical or mental disability.[470]

"[A]n individual with a physical or mental disability who, with or without reasonable accommodation, can perform" essential job functions is a qualified person with a disability.[471]

D. Covered Employers

The Maine Human Rights Act covers an employer (or agent) with "any number of employees [in the state], whatever the place of employment of the employees, and any person outside [Maine] employing any number of employees whose usual place of employment is in" Maine.[472] Covered employers also include employment agencies and labor organizations.[473]

E. Reasonable Accommodation and Defenses

1. Reasonable Accommodation

The following are examples of acts that an employer can take to reasonably accommodate a disabled employee or applicant: (1) making facilities "readily accessible to ... individuals with disabilities"; (2) job restructuring, including a part-time or modified work schedule or "reassignment to a vacant position"; (3) "adjustment or modifications of examinations, training materials or policies"; and (4) providing "qualified readers or interpreters."[474]

---

[470] *Id.* §4553 (7-A).
[471] *Id.* §4553 (8-D).
[472] *Id.* §4553(4).
[473] *Id.* §4572.
[474] *Id.* §4553 (9-A).

2. Defenses

Employers are not prohibited "from discharging or refusing to hire" disabled persons who are "unable to perform" job duties in a way that does not endanger their health or safety or that of others, and from discharging or refusing to hire disabled persons who are "unable to be at, remain at or go to or from" the employment site.[475]

a. Undue Hardship

An undue hardship or burden is an action that requires excessive "financial or administrative hardship." In determining whether providing an accommodation would pose and undue burden or hardship, employers should consider the following factors: (1) "[t]he nature and cost of the accommodation . . ."; (2) the overall financial resources of the affected facilities, including the number of employees at the facility; (3) the employer's overall financial resources and size of the business; (4) the geographic separateness, administrative or fiscal relationship of the facility and overall operations; (5) the resources available to meet the accommodation; (6) "[d]ocumented good faith efforts to explore less restrictive or less expensive alternatives"; (7) "availability of equipment and technology for the accommodation"; and (8) "whether an accommodation would result in a fundamental change in the nature of the public accommodation."[476]

MARYLAND

I. State Law

A. Overview

It is Maryland's policy "to assure all persons equal opportunity in . . . employment" regardless of "disability unrelated in

---

[475] *Id.* §4573-A(1-B).
[476] *Id.* §4553 (9-B)(A)–(J).

nature and extent so as to reasonably preclude the performance of the employment, and to . . . prohibit discrimination in employment by any" employer.[477]

B. Prohibited Discrimination

Maryland prohibits covered employers from failing or refusing "to hire or discharge any individual, or otherwise to discriminate . . . with respect to the individual's compensation, terms, conditions, or privileges of employment, because of [the person's] disability unrelated in nature and extent so as to reasonably preclude the performance of the employment . . . ."[478] It is also prohibited for an employer to

> limit, segregate, or classify its employees or applicants for employment in any way which would deprive or tend to deprive any individual of employment opportunities or otherwise adversely affect the individual's status as an employee, because of the individual's . . . disability unrelated in nature and extent so as to reasonably preclude the performance of the employment . . . .[479]

Employment agencies may not "fail or refuse to refer for employment . . . any individual because of the [person's] disability unrelated in nature and extent so as to reasonably preclude the performance of the employment, or to classify" any individual on the basis of disability.[480] Labor unions may not

> classify or fail or refuse to refer for employment any individual, in any way which would deprive or tend to deprive any individual of employment opportunities, . . . because of such individual's . . . disability unrelated in nature and extent so as to reasonably preclude the performance of the employment, or . . . to cause or attempt to cause an employer to discriminate against an individual . . . ."[481]

In addition, no employer may "discriminate against any individual because of the individual's . . . disability . . . in admission

---
[477] MD. ANN. CODE art. 49B, §14.
[478] Id. §16(a)(1).
[479] Id. §16(a)(2).
[480] Id. §16(b).
[481] Id. §16(c).

to, or employment in, any program established to provide apprenticeship or other training."[482]

It is an unlawful employment practice for a covered employer to print or publish any "advertisement relating to employment . . . indicating any preference, limitation, specification, or discrimination," on the basis of a disability.[483] However, an advertisement "may indicate a preference, limitation, specification, or discrimination based [on disability] when religion, sex, age, national origin or disability is a bona fide occupational qualification for employment."[484]

It also is unlawful "for an employer to discriminate against any of its employees or applicants for employment, . . . because the individual has opposed" any unlawful employment practice "or because the individual has made a charge, testified, assisted, or participated in any manner in an investigation, proceeding, or hearing" regarding an unlawful employment practice.[485]

1. Genetic Testing

Employers may not

(1) fail or refuse to hire or to discharge any individual, or otherwise to discriminate against any individual with respect to the individual's . . . genetic information, . . . or because of the individual's refusal to submit to a genetic test or make available the results of a genetic test;
(2) . . . limit, segregate, or classify . . . employees or applicants [in a way that] adversely affect[s] the individual's status as an employee, because of the individual's . . . genetic information . . . or because of the individual's refusal to submit to a genetic test or make available the results of a genetic test; or
(3) . . . request or require genetic tests or genetic information as a condition for hiring or determining benefits.[486]

---

[482] *Id.* §16(d).
[483] *Id.* §16(e).
[484] *Id.*
[485] *Id.* §16(f).
[486] *Id.* §16(a).

2. Pregnancy-Related Disability

Any "disabilities caused or contributed to by pregnancy or childbirth, are temporary disabilities for all job-related purposes, and [are] treated as such under any health or temporary disability insurance or sick leave plan available in connection with employment."[487]

C. Definitions

1. Disability

A "disability"

> means any physical disability, infirmity, malformation or disfigurement which is caused by bodily injury, birth defect or illness including epilepsy, and which shall include, but not be limited to, any degree of paralysis, amputation, lack of physical coordination, blindness or visual impairment, deafness or hearing impairment, muteness or speech impediment or physical reliance on a seeing eye dog, wheelchair, or other remedial appliance or device; and any mental impairment or deficiency as, but not limited to, retardation or such other which may have necessitated remedial or special education and related services.[488]

A disability is

> (b) A physical or mental impairment . . . that is caused by bodily injury, birth defect, or illness, which substantially limits one or more of an individual's major life activities;
> (c) A record of a physical or mental impairment . . . including having a history of, or being misclassified as having, such an impairment;
> (d) Being regarded as having a physical or mental impairment . . . including one that:
>   (i) does not substantially limit major life activities; . . . or
>   (ii) Substantially limits major life activities as a result of the attitude of the covered entity or of others towards the impairment; or

---

[487] *Id.* §17.
[488] *Id.* §15(g).

(e) being treated by a covered entity as having an impairment, even if there is no physical or mental impairment.[489]

A "'[q]ualified individual with a disability' means an individual with a disability who: (a) With or without reasonable accommodation can perform the essential functions of the job in question; or (b) Is otherwise qualified for the benefit, term, condition, or privilege of employment at issue."[490]

2. *Major Life Activities*

"Major life activities" include, but are not "limited to, functions such as caring for oneself, performing manual tasks, walking, seeing, hearing, speaking, breathing, learning, working, driving a vehicle, socializing, and engaging in procreation and recreation."[491]

D. Covered Employers

Maryland's discrimination provisions cover employers who have "fifteen or more employees for each working day in each of twenty or more calendar weeks . . . ."[492] Also included in this definition is the state of Maryland, employment agencies, and labor organizations.[493]

E. Reasonable Accommodation and Defenses

1. *Reasonable Accommodation*

A covered entity (1) must

make a reasonable accommodation to the known physical or mental limitations of a qualified individual with a disability;
(2) Is not required to provide an accommodation, if it demonstrates that the accommodation would impose undue hardship on the operation of its business or program; and

---

[489] MD. REGS. CODE tit. 14, §14.03.02.02(6)(b)-(e).
[490] *Id.* §14.03.02.02(10).
[491] *Id.* §14.03.02.02(7).
[492] MD. ANN. CODE art. 49B, §15(b).
[493] *Id.* §15(b)-(d).

3) May not deny an employment opportunity to a qualified individual with a disability, if the basis for the denial is the need to accommodate the individual's physical or mental limitations, and this accommodation, if attempted, would be reasonable.[494]

Some examples

of a reasonable accommodation include, but are not limited to:

(1) Making existing facilities used by employees readily accessible to, and usable by, individuals with disabilities;

(2) Providing or modifying equipment or devices;

(3) Job restructuring;

(4) Part-time or modified work schedules;

(5) Reassigning or transferring an employee to a vacant position, light duty job, different work location, or other alternative employment opportunity which is available under the employer's existing policies or practices;

(6) Teleworking;

(7) Permitting an employee to use paid or unpaid sick leave, disability leave, medical leave, or other leave which is available under the employer's existing policies or practices;

(8) Adjusting or modifying examinations, training materials, or policies;

(9) Waiving a no-pet requirement to allow use of a service animal;

(10) Providing applicants or employees with a disability with an opportunity to demonstrate their pertinent knowledge, skills, and abilities by testing methods adapted to their special circumstances if employment tests are used;

(11) Making reasonable modifications in the covered entity's rules, policies, and practices if the modification may enable an applicant or employee with a disability to perform the essential functions of the job; and

(12) Reanalyzing, with full consideration to the needs of the applicant or employee with a disability, job specifications, qualifications, or criteria to determine if they may be waived or modified.[495]

2. Defenses

a. Bona Fide Occupational Qualification

An employer "may take discriminatory actions otherwise prohibited under this chapter if mental or physical ability is

---

[494] Md. Regs. Code tit. 14, §14.03.02.05(A).
[495] Id. §14.03.02.05(B).

a bona fide occupational qualification (BFOQ), reasonably necessary to the normal operation of the business or program."[496]

Further, an employer

has the burden of establishing the existence of a BFOQ. In determining whether the BFOQ defense, narrowly construed, has been met, a covered entity shall show that the particular standard or regulation is reasonably necessary to the normal operation of that business, and that:
(a) All or substantially all individuals with the particular disability would be unable, even with reasonable accommodation, to perform the duties of the job in question; or
(b) It is impossible or highly impractical to determine, on an individual basis, whether an individual with the particular disability would be able to perform the duties of the job in question.[497]

b. Future Hazard

An employer "may take discriminatory actions otherwise prohibited by this chapter, if the applicant's or employee's disability would create a future hazard to health or safety.[498]

In order to

establish a future hazard defense, a covered entity must show that:
(a) it conducted an individualized assessment of the individual's ability to perform the essential functions of the job in question; and
(b) to a reasonable probability, the individual's disability, even with reasonable accommodation, would render the individual unable to perform the duties of the position in question without endangering the health or safety of the individual with a disability or others.[499]

c. Preferential Treatment

Employers are not required

to grant preferential treatment to any individual . . . because of the . . . disability of the individual . . . which may exist with respect to the total number or percentage of persons . . . with disabilities

---

[496] *Id.* §14.03.02.08(A)(1).
[497] *Id.* §14.03.02.08(A)(2).
[498] *Id.* §14.03.02.08(B)(1).
[499] *Id.* §14.03.02.08(B)(2).

employed by any employer, . . . in comparison with the total number or percentage of . . . persons with disabilities in any community, State, section, or other area, or in the available work force in any community, State, section, or other area."[500]

MASSACHUSETTS

I. State Law

A. Overview

Massachusetts law broadly prohibits discrimination in employment on the basis of a handicap.[501] In addition to the statutory prohibition, the state's antidiscrimination agency—the Massachusetts Commission Against Discrimination (MCAD)—has published extensive guidelines that discuss the provisions of state law, which note the manner in which state law differs from the requirements and interpretations of the federal ADA.[502]

B. Prohibited Discrimination

In Massachusetts, employers and their agents are prohibited from discriminating against an otherwise "qualified handicapped person, capable of performing the essential functions of [a job with] reasonable accommodation, unless the employer can demonstrate that the accommodation . . . would impose an undue burden [on] the employer's business."[503] Specifically, employers are prohibited from dismissing from employment or refusing to hire, rehire, promote, or otherwise discriminate against a disabled person because of his or her handicap.[504]

---

[500] Md. Code Ann. art. 49B, §16(h).
[501] Mass. Gen. Laws Ann. ch. 151B, §§2, 4:16.
[502] Massachusetts Commission Against Discrimination, "Guidelines: Employment Discrimination on the Basis of Handicap—Chapter 151B," *available at www.mass.gov/mcad/disability1a.html.*
[503] Mass. Gen. Laws Ann. ch. 151B, §4:16.
[504] *Id.; see also* Mass. Regs. Code tit. 804, §3.01(4)(a)(2), (3), (5)(d).

It is also unlawful for any employer to advertise or publish any statement, application, or notice, "or to make any inquiry or record . . . in connection with employment, which expresses any . . . limitation, specification or discrimination" regarding a person's handicap.[505]

Employers and their agents are also prohibited from refusing, "unless based on a bona fide occupational qualification, to hire or employ or to bar or discharge from employment any person [due to his or her] failure to furnish information regarding . . . admission . . . to any public or private facility for the care of mentally ill persons, provided that such person has been discharged from" the mental health facility and can establish mental competence.[506] In addition, employers are prohibited from giving applicants forms or applications that contain "any questions or requests for information regarding" their previous admission to any public or private mental health facility.[507]

Employers are prohibited from terminating or causing an employee to be terminated or otherwise disciplining or in any manner discriminating or threatening any employee, client, or other person for participating in protected activity, including testifying or filing a complaint of discrimination.[508]

1. Preemployment Inquiries

In Massachusetts, employers are prohibited from making preemployment inquiries about an applicant's handicap status or "the nature and severity of the handicap, except that an employer may condition an offer of employment on the results of a medical examination conducted [exclusively for] determining whether the employee, with reasonable accommodation, is capable of performing the essential functions of the job."[509] Employers are not, however, prohibited from inviting job "applicants to voluntarily disclose their handicap [status]

---
[505] Mass. Gen. Laws Ann. ch. 151B, §4:3; Mass. Regs. Code §3.01(4)(a)(1).
[506] Id. §4:9(A).
[507] Id.
[508] Id. Mass. Gen. Laws Ann. ch. 151B, §4:4.
[509] Id. §4:16.

for purposes of assisting the employer in its affirmative action efforts."[510]

2. Genetic Testing

A genetic test is any test of "human DNA, RNA, mitochondrial DNA, chromosomes or proteins for the purpose of identifying genes or genetic abnormalities, or the presence or absence of inherited or acquired characteristics in genetic material [but is not a test] given for the exclusive purpose of determining the abuse of drugs or alcohol."[511]

Genetic information is

> any written, recorded individually identifiable result of a genetic test ... or explanation of such a result or family history pertaining to the presence, absence, variation, alteration, or modification of a human gene or genes, ... but is not information pertaining to the abuse of drugs or alcohol which is derived from tests given for the exclusive purpose of determining the abuse of drugs or alcohol.[512]

Employers may not

(1) refuse to hire or employ ... on the basis of [a] person's genetic information;
(2) collect, solicit or require disclosure of genetic information from any person as a condition of employment ... ;
(3) ... administer ... ; [or]
(4) offer ... an inducement to undergo a genetic test to any person as a condition of employment ... ;
(5) question a person about ... genetic information ... ;
(6) use the results of a genetic test to ... affect the terms, conditions, compensation or privileges of a person's employment ... ;
(7) terminate or refuse to renew a person's employment ... ; or
(8) otherwise seek, receive, or maintain genetic information for non-medical purposes.[513]

---

[510] *Id.*
[511] *Id.* §1:23.
[512] *Id.* §1:22.
[513] *Id.* §4:19(a).

3. Retaliation

Employers are also prohibited from retaliating or otherwise discriminating against any person who has opposed discriminatory practices or who has filed a complaint, testified, or assisted in any discrimination proceedings.[514] In addition, any person is forbidden from aiding, abetting, inciting, compelling, or coercing the doing of any discriminatory act against a person with a handicap.[515]

C. Definitions

1. Disability

In Massachusetts, a handicap is "a physical or mental impairment [that] substantially limits one or more major life activities . . . a record of . . . such impairment, or . . . being regarded as having such impairment. . . ."[516] However, "current, illegal use of a controlled substance" is not a handicap.[517]

In contrast to the holdings of the Supreme Court under the ADA, employees in Massachusetts with disabilities that can be corrected through the use of devices or medications remain protected under state law.[518] In this regard, the Massachusetts Supreme Judicial Court referenced the interpretations of the MCAD, which previously opined that the existence of an impairment should be determined without regard to whether its effects can be mitigated by measures such as auxiliary aids, medication, or prosthetic devices.

A "qualified handicapped person" is an individual "who is capable of performing the essential functions of a particular job" with or without reasonable accommodation.[519] In *Sullivan*

---

[514]*Id.* ch. 19C, §11; MASS. REGS. CODE §3.01(4)(d)(3).
[515]MASS. GEN. LAWS ANN. ch. 151B, §4:5; MASS. REGS. CODE §3.01(4)(d)(1).
[516]MASS. GEN. LAWS ANN. ch. 151B, §1:17.
[517]*Id.*
[518]Dahill v. Police Dep't of Boston, 434 Mass. 233, 748 N.E. 3d 956, 11 AD Cases 1377 (2001).
[519]MASS. GEN. LAWS ANN. ch. 151B, §1:16. *See* Gauthier v. Natick, 20 MDLR 41 (M.C.A.D. 1998) (applicant who weighed approximately 250 lbs. failed to establish she was handicapped and was properly denied employment, where she did not allege she was "morbidly obese" or she was limited in any major life activity); Beele

v. Raytheon Co.,[520] the U.S. Court of Appeals for the First Circuit—applying Massachusetts law—found that an individual was unable to demonstrate that he was a "qualified handicapped person" who could be accommodated in the job at the same time that he was pursuing long-term disability benefits on the basis that workplace injuries left him totally disabled. At the same time, the Supreme Judicial Court has adopted and applied the U.S. Supreme Court's holding in *Cleveland v. Policy Management System Corp.*,[521] which declared that an individual seeking disability insurance benefits as "totally disabled" still may bring a disability discrimination complaint (however, such individuals generally must provide a sufficient explanation for the apparent contradiction).[522]

2. Major Life Activities

Functions such as "caring for one's self, performing manual tasks, walking, seeing, hearing, speaking, breathing, learning and working" are examples of major life activities.[523]

D. Covered Employers

Massachusetts' disability discrimination laws cover employers of six or more persons,[524] labor organizations,[525] and employment agencies.[526]

---

v. Donohue & Donohue, P.C., 20 MDLR 5 (1998) (legal secretary with multiple sclerosis had physical impairment that limits one or more major life activities and was handicapped person under Massachusetts law); Lakota v. Sonoco Prod. Co., 2002 U.S. Dist. LEXIS 6422 (D. Mass. 2002) (deep vein thrombosis is not "handicap" under Massachusetts law).

[520] 262 F.3d 41, 12 AD Cases 634 (1st Cir. 2001), *cert. denied*, 534 U.S. 1118 (2002).

[521] 526 U.S. 795, 9 AD Cases 491 (1999).

[522] *See* Russell v. Cooley Dickinson Hosp., Inc., 437 Mass. 433, 772 N.E.2d 1054, 13 AD Cases 709 (2002).

[523] Mass. Gen. Laws Ann. ch. 151B, §1:20.

[524] *Id.* §1:5; Mass. Regs. Code §3.01(1).

[525] Mass. Gen. Laws Ann. ch. 151B, §4:2.

[526] *Id.* §4:3.

An individual is not considered an employee if employed by a parent, spouse, child, "or in the domestic service of any person."[527]

E. Reasonable Accommodation and Defenses

1. Reasonable Accommodation

"An accommodation is 'reasonable' if it does not impose [an] undue hardship on the employer."[528]

2. Defenses

a. Bona Fide Occupational Qualification

It is not unlawful for employers to "observe the terms of a bona fide seniority system or any bona fide employee benefit plan such as a retirement, pension, or insurance plan."[529] Although the MCAD does not define bona fide occupational qualification, it "takes the position that it provides only the narrowest of exceptions" and decides the "issues on a case by case basis . . . ."[530] If an employer wishes to use a "physical or mental job requirement with respect to hiring, promotion, demotion or dismissal from employment," the employer must ensure that the requirement is "functionally related to the specific job . . . and . . . consistent with the safe and lawful performance of the job."[531]

b. Undue Hardship

Employers should look at the following factors in determining whether an accommodation "would impose an undue hardship on the conduct of the employer's business": (1) the size of an "employer's business[,] number of employees, number and type of facilities, and size of budget or available assets; (2) the type of . . . operation, including the composition and

---

[527] *Id.* §1:6.
[528] MASS. REGS. CODE §3.01(5)(c).
[529] MASS. GEN. LAWS ANN. ch. 151B, §4:17(a).
[530] 804 MASS. REGS. CODE §3.01(3)(a), (b).
[531] *Id.* §3.01(5)(f).

structure of the ... workforce; and (3) the nature and cost of the accommodation ... ."[532]

MICHIGAN

I. STATE LAW

A. Overview

In Michigan, the Michigan Persons with Disabilities Civil Rights Act protects disabled person against discrimination in employment.[533] "The opportunity to obtain employment ... without discrimination because of disability is ... a civil right in Michigan.[534]

B. Prohibited Discrimination

Employers are prohibited from failing or refusing to hire, recruit, discharge, promote, limit, segregate, classify or otherwise discriminate against an "individual with respect to compensation or the terms, conditions, or privileges of employment, because of a disability ... that is unrelated to the individual's ability to perform the duties of a particular job or position."[535] In addition, employers are prohibited from failing or refusing to hire, recruit, discharge, promote, or other discriminatory action against "an individual on the basis of physical or mental examinations that are not directly related to the requirements of the specific job."[536]

Employers may not discharge, "fail or refuse to hire, recruit, or promote ... , or take other discriminatory action

---

[532] MASS. GEN. LAWS ANN. ch. 151B, §4:16; MASS. REGS. CODE §3.01(5)(e); see Beele v. Donohue & Donohue, 20 MDLR 5 (1998) (law firm provided reasonable accommodations for legal secretary with flair ups of multiple sclerosis, where she was permitted to wear sneakers in office, revise her work schedule, change her work station, and receive assistance in walking).
[533] MICH. COMP. LAWS §37.1101.
[534] Id. §37.1102(1).
[535] Id. §37.1202(1)(a)–(c).
[536] Id. §37.1202(1)(d).

against an individual when adaptive devices or aids may be utilized" to enable the "individual to perform the specific" job requirements.[537] Employers are also prohibited from discharging or taking "other discriminatory action against [a person] on the basis of physical or mental examinations that are not directly related to the requirements of the specific job."[538] In addition, employers are not permitted to discriminate against a disabled individual in admission to, employment in, or continuation in a training or apprenticeship program.[539]

Employers are prohibited from making or using "a written or oral inquiry or form of application that elicits or attempts to elicit information" regarding a prospective employee's disability.[540] In addition, employers are prohibited from expressing "a preference, limitation, or specification based on the" prospective employee's disability.[541]

1. Genetic Testing

"Genetic information" is "information about a gene, gene product, or inherited characteristic of an individual derived from the individual's family history or [a] genetic test."[542] A "genetic test" is "the analysis of human DNA, RNA, chromosomes, and those proteins and metabolites used to detect heritable or somatic disease-related genotypes or karyotypes for clinical purposes."[543] However, a genetic test "does not include a routine physical examination or a routine analysis including, but not limited to, a chemical analysis of body fluids unless conducted specifically to determine the presence, absence, or mutation of a gene or chromosome."[544]

Employers may not

---

[537] *Id.* §§37.1202(1)(f), (g).
[538] *Id.* §37.1202(1)(e).
[539] *Id.* §37.1205.
[540] *Id.* §37.1206(2)(a).
[541] *Id.* §37.1206(2)(c).
[542] *Id.* §37.1201(d).
[543] *Id.* §37.1201(e).
[544] *Id.*

(a) Fail or refuse to hire, recruit, or promote an individual because of... genetic information that is unrelated to the individual's ability to perform the duties of a particular job....

(b) Discharge or otherwise discriminate against an individual with respect to compensation or the terms, conditions, or privileges of employment, because of... genetic information that is unrelated to the individual's ability to perform the duties of a particular job....

(c) Limit, segregate, or classify an employee or applicant... in a way which deprives or tends to deprive... employment opportunities or... the status of an employee because of... genetic information that is unrelated to the individual's ability to perform the duties of a particular job....

...

(d) Require an individual to submit to a genetic test or to provide genetic information as a condition of employment or promotion."[545]

Employers may not directly or indirectly "acquire or have access to... genetic information concerning an [individual,] or a member of the [individual's] family."[546] However, individuals are not prohibited "from voluntarily providing to an employer genetic information that is related to the employee's health or safety," nor are employers prohibited "from using genetic information... to protect an employee's health or safety."[547]

C. Definitions

1. *Disability*

A "disability" is a "determinable physical or mental characteristic [that] may result from disease, injury, congenital condition of birth, or functional disorder, if the characteristic... substantially limits 1 or more of [a person's] major life activities ... and is unrelated to the individual's ability to perform the duties of a particular job... or is unrelated to the individual's qualifications for employment or promotion."[548] However, a

---

[545] *Id.* §§37.1202(1)(a),(b),(c),(h).
[546] *Id.* §37.1202(4).
[547] *Id.* §37.1202(2).
[548] *Id.* §37.1103(d).

disability does not include a "determinable physical or mental characteristic caused by the current, illegal use of a controlled substance" or alcoholic liquor.[549]

A person with a disability or disabilities is "an individual who has 1 or more disabilities."[550]

If a person's disability does not prevent that individual from performing the duties of a particular position, with or without accommodation, then that person's disability is unrelated to his or her ability.[551]

2. Major Life Activities

The Michigan statute generally protects individuals from discrimination based on physical or mental disabilities that substantially limit one or more major life activities of the individual, but that do not prevent the applicant or employee from performing the essential functions of the job in question (as measured with or without reasonable accommodation). That assessment is made based on the condition as it actually exists, with the benefit of mitigating measures such as medication.[552]

D. Covered Employers

An "employer" is a "person who has 1 or more employees or a person who as a contractor or subcontractor is furnishing material or performing work for the state or a governmental

---

[549] *Id.* §37.1103(f); *see* Means v. Jowa Sec. Servs., 440 N.W.2d 23 (Mich. Ct. App. 1989) (pseudofolliculitis barbae, skin condition particularly aggravated by shaving, is handicap); Doman v. City of Grosse Pointe Farms, 170 Mich. App. 536, 428 N.W.2d 708, 50 FEP Cases 982 (1988) (handicap includes determinable mental characteristic or history, which is significantly subaverage general intellectual functioning, and to a mentally ill restored condition, which is mental health that is either normal or stabilized with medication); Wilson v. Acacia Park Cemetery Ass'n, 162 Mich. App. 638, 413 N.W.2d 79, 47 FEP Cases 1309 (1987) (disability related to person's ability to perform duties of particular job now a handicap under Michigan Persons with Disabilities Civil Rights Act).

[550] MICH. COMP. LAWS §37.1103(h).

[551] *Id.* §37.1103(*l*).

[552] Peden v. City of Detroit, Detroit Police Dep't, 470 Mich. 195, 680 N.W. 2d 857 (2004); Chmielewski v. Xermac, Inc., 457 Mich. 593, 606–07, 580 N.W. 2d 817 (1998) (interpreting the predecessor version to the Persons with Disabilities Civil Rights Act, the Handicappers' Civil Rights Act).

entity . . . [including] an agent of such" persons.[553] The Michigan Persons with Disabilities Civil Rights Act also covers discriminatory employment practices by labor organizations and employment agencies.[554]

E. Reasonable Accommodation and Defenses

1. Reasonable Accommodation

Employers are required to accommodate persons with disabilities, unless the employer can demonstrate that the accommodation would impose an undue hardship.[555]

2. Defenses

a. Undue Hardship

Michigan law limits the amount of money that employers are required to spend in purchasing "any equipment or device to accommodate [a] person with a disability," depending on the number of employees that the affected employer has in the state.[556] However, the cost limitations do not include "the cost of reasonable routine maintenance or repair of equipment or devices needed to accommodate a [disabled] person . . . ."[557] In addition, a "person who employs fewer than 15 [workers] is not required to restructure a job or alter the schedule of employees as an accommodation . . . ."[558]

---

[553] *Id.* §37.1201(b).
[554] *Id.* §§37.1203, .1204.
[555] *Id.* §37.1102(2) *See* Rouke v. Oakwood Hosp. Corp., 580 N.W.2d 397 (Mich. App. 1998) (employer's duty to accommodate handicapped employee does not include duty to transfer that employee to different job); Bowerman v. Malloy Lithographing, Inc., 171 Mich. App. 110, 430 N.W.2d 742, 48 FEP Cases 635 (1988) (in Michigan, duty of employer to accommodate handicapped employees is limited to alteration of physical structures to allow access to place of employment and modification of peripheral duties to allow job performance).
[556] MICH. COMP. LAWS §37.1210.
[557] *Id.* §37.1210(7).
[558] *Id.* §37.1210(14); *see* Hall v. Hackley Hosp., 210 Mich. App. 48, 532 N.W.2d 893, 4 AD Cases 961 (1995) (Michigan Persons with Disabilities Civil Rights Act places burden of proof on handicapped person to demonstrate that employer failed to accommodate handicap).

MINNESOTA

I. STATE LAW

A. Overview

The Minnesota Human Rights Act prohibits employment discrimination because of disability.[559] It is the public policy of Minnesota "to secure for persons in [Minnesota] freedom from discrimination in employment[, because such] discrimination threatens the rights and privileges of the inhabitants of [Minnesota] and menaces the institutions and foundations of democracy."[560] "It is also the public policy of [Minnesota] to protect all persons from wholly unfounded charges of discrimination."[561] Nothing in the Minnesota Human Rights Act restricts "the implementation of positive action programs to combat discrimination."[562] In addition, the "opportunity to obtain employment" without discrimination is a civil right in Minnesota.[563] Minnesota construes the provisions of the Minnesota Human Rights Act liberally.[564]

B. Prohibited Discrimination

Employers cannot discriminate against a person based on disability in "hiring, [discharging,] tenure, compensation, terms, upgrading, conditions, facilities, or privileges," or by maintaining "a system of employment which unreasonably excludes" a disabled applicant, except "when based on a bona fide occupational qualification."[565] In addition, employers are prohibited from printing, publishing, or advertising a notice that "discloses a preference, limitation, specification, or discrimination based on . . . disability . . . ."[566] Except when based

---

[559] MINN. STAT. §§363A.01 et seq., .02, subd. 1(a)(1).
[560] Id. §363A.02, subd. 1(a), (b).
[561] Id. §363A.02, subd. 1(b).
[562] Id.
[563] Id. §363A.02, subd. 2.
[564] Id. §363A.04.
[565] Id. §363A.08, subd. 2.
[566] Id. §363A.08, subd. 4(3).

on a bona fide occupational qualification, employers may not "seek and obtain . . . information from any source that pertains to the person's . . . disability" for the purpose of making an employment decision.[567]

1. Preemployment Inquiries

a. Medical Examinations

Employers are precluded from requesting preemployment information about disabilities, or requesting or requiring a physical examination.[568]

However, employers can require or request that an applicant or employee undergo a physical examination to determine his or her capability of performing a job if: (1) "an offer of employment has been made on [the] condition that the person meets the physical or mental requirements of the job; . . . [(2)] the examination tests only for essential job-related" functions and "is required of all persons conditionally offered employment for [that job] regardless of disability; and [(3)] the information obtained regarding the medical condition or history . . . is collected and maintained on separate forms and in separate medical files and is treated as a confidential medical record, except that" essential persons, including supervisors and safety personnel may be informed where appropriate.[569]

It is not unlawful for employers to administer preemployment tests if they (1) "measure only essential job-related abilities; [(2)] are required of all applicants for the same position regardless of disability . . . ; and [(3)] accurately measure the applicant's aptitude, achievement level, or . . . other factors . . . rather than reflecting the applicant's impaired sensory, manual, or speaking skills[, unless] those skills are the factors" the test is measuring.[570]

If any health or medical records or information adversely affects an employee or applicant, "the employer must notify

---

[567] *Id.* §363A.08, subd. 4(2).
[568] *Id.* §363A.08, subd. 4(1).
[569] *Id.* §363A.20, subd. 8(a)(1).
[570] *Id.* §363A.20, subd. 8(a)(3).

the affected [individual] within 10 days" of making the final employment decision.[571]

2. Pregnancy-Related Disability

Employers must treat women "with disabilities related to pregnancy or childbirth, the same as other" similarly situated disabled persons, including providing a reasonable accommodation.[572] In addition, employers are permitted "to provide special safety considerations for pregnant women involved in tasks which are potentially hazardous to the health of the unborn child, as determined by medical criteria."[573]

3. Genetic Testing

Protected genetic information is "(1) information about a person's genetic test; or (2) information about a genetic test of a blood relative of a person."[574] A genetic test is "the analysis of human DNA, RNA, chromosomes, proteins, or certain metabolites in order to detect disease-related genotypes or mutations."[575]

"No employer . . . shall directly or indirectly: (1) administer a genetic test or request, require, or collect protected genetic information . . . as a condition of employment; or (2) affect the terms or conditions of employment or terminate [a person's] employment . . . based on protected genetic information."[576] In addition, "[n]o person shall provide or interpret for any employer . . . genetic information on a current or prospective employee."[577]

"Any person aggrieved by a violation of" protected genetic information "may bring a civil action, in which the court may award: (1) up to three times the actual damages suffered due to the violation; (2) punitive damages; (3) reasonable costs

---

[571] *Id.* §363A.20, subd. 8(c).
[572] *Id.* §363A.08, subd. 5.
[573] *Id.* §363A.20, subd. 8(a)(5).
[574] *Id.* §181.974, subd. 1(d).
[575] *Id.* §181.974, subd. 1(a).
[576] *Id.* §181.974, subd. 2(a).
[577] *Id.* §181.974, subd. 2(b).

and attorney fees; and (4) injunctive or other equitable relief as the court may deem appropriate."[578]

4. Retaliation

Employers are also prohibited from retaliating against a person who engaged in protected conduct under Minnesota law.[579] It is a reprisal for any employer to engage in any of these activities against a person who either has opposed an illegal practice by the employer or has associated with a disabled person: (1) to "refuse to hire" the person, (2) to "depart from . . . customary employment practice, (3) to "transfer [the person] to a lesser position," or (4) to inform another employer "of the person's engagement in protected activities."[580] However, the fact that an employer's disability benefit plan provides less coverage for individuals with mental disabilities in comparison to those with physical disabilities does not violate the Minnesota Human Rights Act.[581] In interpreting the Minnesota statute's prohibition against reprisal discrimination, the federal courts have narrowed the scope of the term "adverse employment action" by noting:

> Although actions short of termination may constitute an adverse employment action within the meaning of the statute, not everything that makes an employee unhappy is an actionable adverse action. Otherwise, minor and even trivial employment actions that an irritable, chip-on-the-shoulder employee did not like would form the basis of a discrimination suit. Rather, for an action to be considered adverse, it must have had a materially adverse impact on the plaintiff's employment terms and conditions.[582]

---

[578] *Id.* §181.974, subd. 3.
[579] *Id.* §363A.15.
[580] *Id.*
[581] Kolton v. Anoka County, 645 N.W.2d 403, 13 AD Cases 337 (Minn. 2002).
[582] Grozdanich v. Leisure Hills Health Ctr., Inc., 25 F. Supp. 2d 953, 975 n.6 (D. Minn. 1998) (quoting Greser v. Department of Corr., 145 F.3d 979, 984 (8th Cir. 1998)).

C. Definitions

1. Disability

A disability is "any condition or characteristic that renders a person disabled,"[583] but "excludes any condition resulting from alcohol or drug abuse which prevents a person from performing" essential job functions "or constitutes a direct threat to property or the safety of others."[584] The definition has been construed in a broad fashion, including a holding by the Minnesota Supreme Court that authorized an individual who suffered from fibromyalgia to proceed with disability and retaliatory discharge claims.[585]

"[A]ny person who (1) has a physical, sensory, or mental impairment which materially limits one or more major life activities; (2) has a record of such an impairment; or (3) is regarded as having such an impairment" is a disabled person.[586]

"[A] disabled person who . . . can perform the essential job functions required of all applicants for the job" with reasonable accommodation is a qualified disabled person.[587]

D. Covered Employers

Minnesota's discrimination provisions cover employers who have "one or more employees,"[588] except with regard to providing reasonable accommodations.[589] In addition, the discrimination provisions cover discriminatory actions by labor organizations and employment agencies.[590]

---

[583] *Id.* §363A.03, subd. 12.
[584] *Id.* §363A.03, subd. 36; *see* Liljedahl v. Ryder Student Transp. Serv., Inc., 341 F.3d 836, 14 AD Cases 1390 (8th Cir. 2003) (lung cancer not disability under Minnesota Human Rights Act, and knowledge by employer of cancer surgery did not put company on notice of employee's emphysema or breathing problems).
[585] Hoover v. Norwest Private Mortgage Banking, 632 N.W.2d 534, 12 AD Cases 360 (Minn. 2001).
[586] MINN. STAT. §363A.03, subd. 12.
[587] *Id.* §363A.03, subd. 36.
[588] *Id.* §363A.03, subd. 16.
[589] *Id.* §363A.08, subd. 6.
[590] *Id.* §363A.08, subd. 4.

E. Reasonable Accommodation and Defenses

1. *Reasonable Accommodation*

Employers with 15 or more full- or part-time "employees for each working day in each of 20 or more calendar weeks in the current or preceding calendar year" are required to make a "reasonable accommodation to the known disability of a qualified disabled [employee or] applicant, unless the employer ... can demonstrate that the accommodation would impose an undue hardship" on its business.[591] A reasonable accommodation is comprised of "steps which must be taken to accommodate the known physical or mental limitations of a qualified disabled person."[592]

Examples of reasonable accommodation under Minnesota law may include: (1) "making facilities readily accessible [for use] by disabled persons; [(2)] job restructuring[, including] modified work schedules [or] reassignment to a vacant position"; (3) acquiring or modifying "equipment or devices"; and (4) "providing aides on a temporary or periodic basis."[593] However, a prospective employer is not required to pay for an applicant's accommodation "if it is available from an alternative source without cost" to either party.[594]

2. *Defenses*

a. *Direct Threat*

Employers can defend against a charge of employment discrimination by demonstrating that the disabled person, even with reasonable accommodation, poses a threat to his or her safety or health or that of others.[595]

b. *Undue Hardship*

Employers should consider the following factors in deciding whether an accommodation would impose an undue hardship on its business: (1) the size of the business, including the

---

[591] *Id.* §363A.08, subd. 6.
[592] *Id.*
[593] *Id.*
[594] *Id.*
[595] *Id.* §363A.25.

number of employees; (2) the "composition and structure of the work force and the number of employees at the [affected] location; [(3)] the nature and cost of the ... accommodation; [(4)] the reasonable ability to finance the accommodation; and [(5)] the documented good-faith efforts [by the employer] to explore less restrictive or less expensive alternatives, including [consulting] with the disabled person or ... organizations."[596]

MISSISSIPPI

I. STATE LAW

A. Overview

Mississippi does not have extensive laws dealing with discrimination in the employment setting.

B. Prohibited Discrimination

Mississippi prohibits handicap discrimination in employment by the state, political subdivisions, public schools, and any other employment that is "supported in whole or in part by public funds...."[597]

C. Definitions

1. Disability

Handicapped persons include persons who are "blind, visually handicapped, deaf, or otherwise physically handicapped, unless [the] disability materially" affects the job performance.[598]

The terms "blind, totally blind, visually handicapped, partially blind," "mean having central visual acuity not to exceed 20/200 in the better eye, with corrected lenses as measured by the Snellen test, or having visual acuity greater than 20/

---

[596] *Id.* §363A.08, subd. 6(a)–(e).
[597] MISS. CODE ANN. §43-6-15.
[598] *Id.*

200, but with a limitation in the field of vision such that the widest diameter of the visual field subtends an angle not greater than twenty (20) degrees."[599]

A person "who cannot readily understand spoken language through hearing alone with or without a hearing aid, and who may also have a speech defect which renders [the] speech unintelligible to most people with normal hearing" is deaf.[600]

D. Covered Employees

The Mississippi statutes provide, at MISS. CODE ANN. §25-9-149, that individuals seeking employment by the state will not be discriminated against on the basis of handicap. *See also* MISS. CODE ANN. §43-6-15. These provisions are not applicable to private-sector employers in the state.

E. Reasonable Accommodation and Defenses

The terms of the Mississippi statutes that deal with discrimination against the handicapped in state employment are very limited. Beyond definitional terms, they do not describe obligations to engage in reasonable accommodation, other than language which limits non-discrimination obligations in situations in which the individual's disability affects the performance of the work required by the job in question. MISS. CODE ANN. §43-6-15.

MISSOURI

I. STATE LAW

A. Overview

The Missouri Commission on Human Rights seeks to eliminate and prevent employment discrimination against persons with disabilities.[601]

---
[599] *Id.* §43-6-1.
[600] *Id.*
[601] MO. ANN. STAT. §213.020.2.

B. Prohibited Discrimination

Employers are prohibited from failing or refusing to hire or discharge, limiting, segregating, or classifying, adversely affecting the employee's status, or otherwise discriminating "against any individual with respect to compensation, terms, conditions, or privileges of employment" because of disability.[602] Employers are also prohibited from printing, circulating, or causing "any statement, advertisement or publication [that] expresses ... any limitation, specification, or discrimination" based on disability, unless the limitation is "based upon a bona fide occupational qualification . . . ."[603]

However, employers are permitted "to apply different standards of compensation or ... terms, conditions or privileges of employment pursuant to a bona fide seniority or merit system, or [to have] a system which measures earnings by quantity or quality of production, or to [have different standards for] employees who work in different locations, provided that such" a practice does not discriminate on the basis of disability.[604]

It is unlawful for anyone to "aid, abet, incite, compel, coerce ... retaliate or discriminate in any manner against [a] person [who] has opposed any" discriminatory practice, such as complaining, testifying, assisting, or participating in any protective activity.[605] In addition, it is unlawful to "discriminate in any manner against [another] person because of [his or her] association" with a disabled person.[606]

1. Preemployment Inquiries

Employers are prohibited from making any preemployment inquiries of applicants "as to whether the applicant has a physical or mental impairment or [about] the nature or

---

[602] *Id.* §213.055(1)(1).
[603] *Id.* §213.055(1)(3); Mo. CODE REGS. ANN., tit. 8, §60-3.020(2).
[604] Mo. ANN. STAT. §213.055(3)2.
[605] *Id.* §213.070(1)–(2).
[606] *Id.* §213.070(4).

severity of [the] impairment."[607] However, employers may inquire "into an applicant's ability to perform specific job-related functions."[608]

a. Medical Examinations

Employers "may conduct pre-employment medical examinations relating to minimum physical standards for employment if: "1. All applicants . . . are subjected to examination regardless of physical or mental impairment. 2. The minimum physical standards for employment related to the [applicant's] ability to perform essential" job functions. [and] 3. [The results of the medical examinations] are given the same consideration in employment decisions for all applicants regardless of physical or mental impairment."[609] An employer must not use "any employment test or any other selection criteria which screens out, or [attempts] to screen out . . . any class of [disabled] persons, unless . . . the . . . criterion is shown to be job related . . . ."[610]

C. Definitions

1. Disability

A person who has "a physical or mental impairment which substantially limits one (1) or more . . . major life activities; or who has a record of such impairment; or is regarded as having such an impairment," is disabled under Missouri law.[611] However, "[m]inor temporary illnesses [such as] broken bones, sprains or colds" are not considered disabilities.[612]

A person is regarded as having an impairment if the person "[h]as a physical or mental impairment that does not substantially limit a major life activities, but is treated by an employer

---

[607] Mo. Code Regs. Ann., tit. 8, §60-3.060(2)(A).
[608] Id.
[609] Id. §60-3.060(2)(B).
[610] Id. §60-3.060(3)(A)(1).
[611] Id. §60-3.060(1)(B); Mo. Ann. Stat. §213.010(4).
[612] Mo. Code Regs. Ann., tit. 8, §60-3.060(1)(B)1.

or by others as" having a disability, or does not have any impairment "but is treated by an employer or by others as having [a disability] which substantially limits a major life activity."[613] The "current, illegal use of or addiction to a controlled substance" is not a disability unless the person has "successfully completed a supervised rehabilitation program," is no longer illegally using a controlled substance, "and is not currently addicted to . . . a controlled substance or has otherwise been "successfully rehabilitated, or [i]s erroneously regarded as currently illegally using, or being addicted to, a controlled substance."[614]

A disability "is not job related if, with reasonable accommodation, [the disability] does not prevent" the employee or applicant from performing essential job functions.[615] A disability is not job related merely because the job may pose a threat of harm, unless the threat is one of demonstrable serious harm to the safety of others.[616]

2. Major Life Activities

Activities that affect "communication, ambulation, self-care, socialization, education, vocational training, employment and transportation," are examples of major life activities.[617]

D. Covered Employers

Employers who employ six or more persons within Missouri, and, their agents, are covered by Missouri's employment discrimination prohibitions.[618] Labor organizations and employment agencies are also prohibited from engaging in employment discrimination against persons with disabilities.[619]

---

[613] *Id.* §60-3.060(1)(E).
[614] Mo. Ann. Stat. §213.101(4).
[615] Mo. Code Regs. Ann., tit. 8, §60-3.060(1)(f)4.
[616] *Id.* §60-3.060(1)(F)3.
[617] *Id.* §60-3.060(1)(C).
[618] Mo. Ann. Stat. §213.010(7).
[619] *Id.* §213.055(2), (3).

E. Reasonable Accommodation and Defenses

1. *Reasonable Accommodation*

Reasonable accommodations include (1) making facilities readily accessible to handicapped persons; (2) proper job structuring, including part-time or modified work schedules; (3) acquisition or modification of equipment or devices systems; and (4) the provision of readers or interpreters.[620] An employer should consider the following factors in determining whether an accommodation is reasonable: (1) the nature and cost of the accommodation; (2) the size and nature of the employer's business, including the number and type of facilities, structures, and compensation of the workforce; and (3) the employer's previous good-faith efforts to accommodate disabilities.[621]

2. *Defenses*

a. *Affirmative Action*

The Missouri Commission on Human Rights has published extensive regulations dealing with voluntary affirmative action, which is appropriate under certain circumstances, including analyses that reveal employment practices causing potential adverse impact and historic restrictions by employers.[622]

b. *Preferential Treatment*

The Missouri Commission on Human Rights does not require that employers grant preferential treatment to any person because of the person's disability.[623]

---

[620] Mo. Code Regs. Ann., tit. 8, §60-3.060(1)(g)(2).
[621] *Id.* §60-3.060(1)(g)(3).
[622] *Id.* §60-3.080(2).
[623] Mo. Ann. Stat. §213.055.3.

MONTANA

I. State Law

A. Overview

In Montana, the "right to be free from discrimination" in employment based on physical or mental disability is a civil right.[624]

B. Prohibited Discrimination

Employers are prohibited from refusing to employ, barring from employment, or discriminating "against a person in compensation," terms, conditions, or privileges of employment based on "physical or mental disability."[625] However, there "is no discrimination when the nature or extent of the disability reasonably precludes the performance of the particular employment or when the particular employment may subject the person with a disability or that person's fellow employees to physical harm."[626] Employers are also prohibited from printing or circulating "a statement, advertisement, [application,] or publication . . . that expresses . . . a limitation, specification, or discrimination [on the basis of] physical or mental disability, . . . unless [the limitation is] based upon a bona fide occupational qualification.[627]

It is unlawful for an employer "to discharge, expel, blacklist, or otherwise discriminate against an individual" who has opposed discriminatory practices, or who "has filed a complaint, testified, assisted, or" engaged in any protective activity.[628] It is also "unlawful for a person . . . to aid, abet, incite, compel, coerce [discrimination,] or to attempt to do so."[629]

---

[624] Mont. Code Ann. §49-1-102(1).
[625] *Id.* §49-2-303(1)(a).
[626] *Id.* §49-4-101.
[627] *Id.* §49-2-303(1)(c).
[628] *Id.* §49-2-301.
[629] *Id.* §49-2-302.

In Montana, discriminating against disabled person in employment is a misdemeanor and also subjects the employer to liability for civil damages and attorneys' fees, including punitive damages for an intentional reckless violation.[630]

1. *Preemployment Inquiries*

Employees are prohibited from making preemployment inquiries "in connection with" a prospective employee's "physical or mental disability, [unless] the inquiry is required for implementation of a bona fide lawful affirmative action plan" or a bona fide occupational qualification.[631]

a. Medical Examinations

Employers are prohibited from requiring "medical examinations . . . for the purposes of determining whether [a prospective] employee has a physical or mental disability or to determine the nature [and extent] of [the] disability unless the examination . . . is . . . job-related and consistent with business necessity."[632]

However, employers "may make pre-employment inquiries into the [applicant's] ability . . . to perform job-related functions."[633] In addition, employers "may require a medical examination . . . after an offer of employment has been made and prior to the commencement of . . . employment duties and may condition the offer of employment on the results of the [medical] examination."[634] However, the medical examination must (1) be required of "all entering employees . . . in the same job category . . . regardless of disability"; (2) maintain "information obtained regarding the medical condition or history . . . as a confidential medical record"; and (3) maintain the information collected "in accordance with the requirements of the" ADA.[635]

---

[630] *Id.* §49-4-102; *see* Owens v. Parker Drilling Co., 207 Mont. 446, 676 P.2d 162, 2 AD Cases 312 (1984).
[631] Mont. Admin. R. 24.9.1406(1).
[632] *Id.* at 24.9.607(1).
[633] *Id.* at 24.9.607(3).
[634] *Id.* at 24.9.607(4).
[635] *Id.*

C. Definitions

1. Disability

A physical or mental disability is (1) "a physical or mental impairment that substantially limits one or more of a person's major life activities; [(2)] a record of such an impairment; or [(3)] a condition regarded as such an impairment."[636]

"A person with a physical or mental disability is qualified to hold an [appointed] position if the person can perform the essential [job functions] with or without a reasonable accommodation...."[637]

D. Covered Employers

Covered employers are employers "of one or more persons or an agent of the employer, [not including] fraternal, charitable, or religious association[s] ... if the association ... is not organized either for private profit or to provide accommodations or services that are available on a nonmembership basis."[638]

E. Reasonable Accommodation and Defenses

1. Reasonable Accommodation

It is unlawful for employers, or their agents, to "fail to make reasonable accommodations to the known physical or mental limitations of an otherwise qualified employee [or applicant], unless [the employer] can demonstrate that the accommodation would impose an undue hardship on the operation of [its] business...."[639] Similarly, it is unlawful for an employer to "deny equal employment opportunities to a person with a physical or mental disability because of the need to make a reasonable accommodation to the person's disability...."[640]

---

[636] *Id.* at 24.9.606(2).
[637] MONT. CODE ANN. §49-2-101(19)(a).
[638] *Id.* §49-2-101(11).
[639] MONT. ADMIN. R. 24.9.606(1)(a).
[640] *Id.* at 24.9.606(1)(b).

Reasonable accommodations may include (1) "making existing facilities . . . readily accessible to" disabled individuals; (2) "job restructuring, [including] part-time or modified work schedules, reassignment to vacant positions [that] the employee is qualified to hold"; (3) acquiring or modifying "equipment or devices, . . . examinations or training materials or policies"; and (4) providing qualified interpreters or readers.[641]

"Discrimination based on, because of, on the basis of, or on the grounds of physical or mental disability includes the failure to make reasonable accommodations that are required by an otherwise qualified person who has a physical or mental disability."[642]

2. Defenses

"An accommodation that would require an undue hardship or that would endanger the health or safety of any person is not a reasonable accommodation."[643]

Employers are not required to accommodate a person with a physical or mental disability if enabling that "person to perform the essential functions of an employment position . . . would endanger the health or safety of any person."[644] However, "any grounds urged as a 'reasonable basis' for an exemption . . . shall be strictly construed."[645]

a. Bona Fide Occupational Qualification

Employers are permitted to make distinctions based on "physical or mental disability . . . when the reasonable demands of the [job] or program require the distinction."[646] However, this exception is construed strictly "against allowing the exception."[647]

---

[641] *Id.* at 29.9.606(3).
[642] MONT. CODE ANN. §49-2-101(19)(b).
[643] *Id.*
[644] MONT. ADMIN. R. 24.9.606(6).
[645] MONT. CODE ANN. §49-2-402.
[646] *Id.* at 24.9.605(1).
[647] *Id.* at 4.9.605(2).

b. Undue Hardship

"An accommodation to a person with a physical or mental disability [to enable] the person to perform the essential functions of [a] position is reasonable unless it would impose an undue hardship upon the employer."[648] An act that requires undue hardship presents "significant difficulty or extraordinary costs when considered in light of" the following factors: (1) "the nature and expense of the accommodation needed; [(2)] the overall financial resources of the [business or] facility . . . and the number of persons employed at the facility" or by the employer; and (3) "the type of operation . . . including [the] compensation, structure, and functions of the work force, and the geographic separateness and administrative or fiscal relationship of the facility . . . in question . . . ."[649]

NEBRASKA

I. STATE LAW

A. Overview

It is Nebraska's "policy to encourage and enable blind, visually handicapped, hearing-impaired, or physically disabled persons to" engage in remunerative employment.[650] However, under the Nebraska Fair Employment Practice Act employers are not required to give "preferential treatment to any [person] or to any group because of . . . disability . . . ."[651]

B. Prohibited Discrimination

In Nebraska, it is unlawful for employers to discriminate against disabled applicants or employees in hiring, termination, "compensation, terms, conditions, or privileges of employment," and to adversely "limit, advertise, solicit, [retaliate,]

---

[648] MONT. ADMIN. R. 24.9.606(4).
[649] *Id.* at 24.9.606(5).
[650] NEB. REV. STAT. ANN. §20-126.
[651] *Id.* §48-1113.

segregate, or classify" disabled persons.[652] It also is unlawful for employers to hire and employ workers on the basis of disability, unless its based on a bona fide occupational qualification that is reasonably necessary to the employer's normal business operations.[653]

Employers are, however, permitted "to apply different standards of compensation, or different terms, conditions, or privileges of employment" in accordance with "a bona fide seniority or merit system or a system which measures earnings by quantity or quality of production or to employees who work in different locations" that are not a result of intentional discrimination based on disability.[654]

Employers also are permitted "to give and to act upon the results of any professionally developed ability test [when] its administration ... is not designed, intended, or used to discriminate" against disabled persons.[655] In addition, employers may deny employment to a disabled person when the "selection criteria used is job-related and consistent with business necessity and ... performance cannot be accomplished by reasonable accommodation," or when the disabled person poses "a direct threat, involving a significant risk to the health or safety of other individuals" or the disabled person.[656]

1. Preemployment Inquiries

Employers may inquire about a job applicant's ability to perform job-related functions.[657]

a. Medical Examinations

Employers can also "require a medical examination after [the employer has made] an offer of employment ... to the applicant and prior to the commencement of ... employment ... and may condition an offer on the results of the examination if:

---

[652] *Id.* §48-1104.
[653] *Id.* §48-1108(1).
[654] *Id.* §48-1111.
[655] *Id.* §48-1111(1).
[656] *Id.*
[657] *Id.* §48-1107.02(9).

... all entering employees are subjected to [the same] examination regardless of disability," and any information obtained as a result of the examination is treated as a medical record and is kept confidential, only disclosing necessary information to essential personnel, for safety and health reasons, or to the government.[658]

2. *Genetic Testing*

Genetic information is "information about a gene, gene product, or inherited characteristic derived from a genetic test."[659] A genetic test is "the analysis of human DNA, RNA, and chromosomes and those proteins and metabolites used to detect heritable or somatic disease-related genotypes or karyotypes for clinical purposes."[660] However, a "[g]enetic test does not include a routine physical examination or a routine analysis, including a chemical analysis, of body fluids unless conducted specifically to determine the presence, absence, or mutation of a gene or chromosome."[661]

Employers may not

> (a) Fail or refuse to hire, recruit, or promote an [individual] because of genetic information that is unrelated to the ability to perform the duties of a particular job or position;
>
> (b) Discharge or otherwise discriminate against an [individual] with respect to compensation or the terms, conditions, or privileges of employment because of genetic information that is unrelated to the ability to perform the duties of a particular job or position;
>
> (c) Limit, segregate, or classify an [individual] for employment in a way which deprives or tends to deprive a [person] of employment opportunities or otherwise adversely affects the status of an employee ... because of genetic information that is unrelated to the ability to perform the duties of a particular job or position; or
>
> (d) Require an [individual] to submit to a genetic test or to provide genetic information as a condition of employment or promotion.[662]

---

[658] *Id.*
[659] *Id.* §48-236(1)(c).
[660] *Id.* §48-236(1)(d).
[661] *Id.*
[662] *Id.* §48-236(2).

However, an employee may voluntarily provide "genetic information that is related to the employee's health or safety in the workspace," and an employer may use "genetic information received from an employee . . . to protect the employee's health or safety."[663]

C. Definitions

1. Disability

A disability is "a physical or mental impairment that substantially limits one or more of [an individual's] major life activities . . . , a record of such an impairment, or . . . being regarded as having such an impairment."[664] However, "homosexuality, bisexuality, transvestism, transsexualism, pedophilia, exhibitionism, voyeurism, gender-identity disorders not resulting in physical impairments, [compulsive] gambling, kleptomania, pyromania, or psychoactive substance [abuse] disorders resulting from" illegal drug use, are not disabilities.[665]

An employer can hold alcoholics and illegal drug users "to the same qualification standards for employment . . . , job performance and behavior" that apply to other employees.[666]

A person who "can perform the essential functions" of a job, with or without reasonable accommodation, is a qualified individual with a disability.[667] Persons who are currently engaging in illegal drug use are not qualified individuals with disabilities.[668]

---

[663] *Id.* §48-236(3).

[664] *Id.* §48-1102(9).

[665] *Id. See* Father Flannagan's Boy's Home v. Goerke, 401 N.W.2d 461 (Neb. 1987) (epilepsy is disability if related to person's ability to engage in particular occupation); Bradley v. Pizzaco of Neb., Inc., 939 F.2d 610 (8th Cir. 1991) (pseudofolliculitis barbae is not disability).

[666] NEB. REV. STAT. ANN. §48-1108.1(4).

[667] *Id.* §48-1102(10)(a). *See* Woodyard v. Hoover Group, Inc., 985 F.2d 421, 2 AD Cases 467 (8th Cir. 1993) (employee who admitted she required another employee's assistance in order to perform job duties essentially conceded her disability was related to and adversely affected her ability to perform job duties and was not within protected class of qualified persons with disabilities).

[668] NEB. REV. STAT. ANN. §48-1102(10)(b).

"[T]erms and conditions . . . , opportunities for advancement . . . , and plant conveniences" are examples of employment privileges.[669]

D. Covered Employers

Nebraska's antidiscrimination laws apply to employers and their agents "who have fifteen or more employees for each working day in each of twenty or more calendar weeks in the current or preceding calendar year . . . ."[670] Labor organization and employment agencies are also considered covered entities under the laws.[671]

E. Reasonable Accommodation and Defenses

1. Reasonable Accommodation

Employers are required to make "reasonable accommodations to the known physical or mental limitations of an otherwise qualified individual with a disability . . . , unless [the employer] can demonstrate that the accommodation would impose an undue hardship on the operation of the [employer's] business."[672] In addition, it is unlawful for employers to deny employment opportunities to an otherwise qualified job applicant or employee based on the need to make a reasonable accommodation for the individual's physical or mental impairments.[673]

An employer can reasonably accommodate applicants and employees through (1) job restructuring, including a part-time or modified work schedule, or reassignment to a vacant position; (2) acquiring or modifying equipment or devices, examinations, training manuals, or policies; and (3) providing qualified readers or interpreters.[674]

---

[669] *Id.* §48-1102(6).
[670] *Id.* §48-1102(2).
[671] *Id.* §48-1102(5).
[672] *Id.* §48-1107.02(5).
[673] *Id.* §48-1107.02(6).
[674] *Id.* §48-1107.02(11).

2. Defenses

a. Undue Hardship

In determining whether an accommodation would pose an undue hardship, employers should consider the following: (1) the nature and cost of the accommodation; (2) the overall financial resources of the affected facility and the number of employees at the facility; (3) the employer's overall resources; (4) and composition of the workforce.[675]

NEVADA

I. State Law

A. Overview

In Nevada, it is unlawful for employers to discriminate or segregate on the basis of disability.[676]

B. Prohibited Discrimination

Employers are prohibited from failing or refusing to hire, discharge, limit, segregate, classify, or otherwise discriminate against a disabled person in compensation, or other terms and conditions of employment, except on the basis of a bona fide, and relevant, occupational qualification that is necessary to the normal operation of the employer's business.[677] In addition, employers must permit employees "with a visual or aural disability" to use a guide dog, hearing dog, helping dog, or other "service animal" at work.[678]

It also is unlawful for employers to discriminate against a disabled person in training or apprenticeship programs.[679] Employers are similarly prohibited from discriminating in

---

[675] Id. §48-1102(11).
[676] Nev. Rev. Stat. Ann. §613.330.
[677] Id. §§613.330(1), 613.350.
[678] Id. §613.330(6).
[679] Id. §613.330(4).

advertising employment opportunities and soliciting applicants.[680]

In addition, it is unlawful "for an employer to discriminate against any of his employees or applicants for employment," because he or she has opposed any unlawful employment practice, or because he or she "has made a charge, testified, assisted, or participated in any manner in an investigation, proceeding or hearing" regarding an unlawful employment practice.[681]

1. *Genetic Testing*

Genetic information is "information that is obtained from a genetic test."[682] A genetic test is one

> that uses deoxyribonucleic acid extracted from the cells of a person, or a diagnostic test that uses another substance extracted or otherwise obtained from the body of a person, which determines the presence of an abnormality or deficiency that:
> (1) Is linked to a physical or mental disorder or impairment; or (2) Indicates a susceptibility to an illness, a disease, an impairment or another physical or mental disorder.[683]

A genetic test is not "a test that determines the presence of alcohol or a controlled substance in the system of the person tested."[684]

2. *Pregnancy-Related Discrimination*

Pregnant females are accorded the same benefits as other employees:

> If an employer grants leave with pay, leave without pay, or leave without loss of seniority to his employees for sickness or disability because of a medical condition, it is an unlawful employment practice to fail or refuse to extend the same benefits to any female employee who is pregnant. The female employee who is pregnant must be allowed to use the leave before and after childbirth,

---
[680] *Id.* §613.340(2).
[681] *Id.* §613.340(1).
[682] *Id.* §613.345(2)(a).
[683] *Id.* §613.345(2)(b).
[684] *Id.*

miscarriage or other natural resolution of her pregnancy, if the leave is granted, accrued or allowed to accumulate as a part of her employment benefits.[685]

"It is an unlawful employment practice for an employer, a labor organization or an employment agency" to engage in any of the following practices:

> (a) To ask or encourage a prospective or current employee or member of the labor organization to submit to a genetic test.
> (b) To require or administer a genetic test to a person as a condition of employment or membership in the labor organization.
> (c) To deny employment or membership in the labor organization based on genetic information.
> (d) To alter the terms, conditions or privileges of employment or membership in the labor organization based on genetic information.
> (e) To terminate employment or membership in the labor organization based on genetic information.[686]

C. Definitions

1. Disability

" 'Disability' means, with respect to a person: (a) A physical or mental impairment that substantially limits one or more of the major life activities of the person; (b) A record of such an impairment; or (c) Being regarded as having such an impairment."[687]

D. Covered Employers

A covered employer is "any person who has 15 or more employees for each working day in each of 20 or more calendar weeks in the current or preceding calendar year . . . ."[688] An employer is also a labor organization or employment agency.[689]

---

[685] *Id.* §613.335.
[686] *Id.* §613.345(1).
[687] *Id.* §613.310(1).
[688] *Id.* §613.310(2).
[689] *Id.* §613.310(3), (4).

E. Reasonable Accommodation and Defenses

1. *Reasonable Accommodation*

An employer does not have an obligation to accommodate a disability, or even to enter into discussions with an employee concerning appropriate accommodations, until the employee requests a reasonable accommodation.[690] However, the U.S. Court of Appeals for the Ninth Circuit has expanded an employer's obligation to engage in the interactive process and discuss with the employee appropriate accommodations.[691] Now, an employer's obligation to engage in the interactive process arises when the employee requests an accommodation or when the employer recognizes the employee's need for an accommodation.[692]

2. *Defenses*

a. *Bona Fide Occupational Qualification*

"It is not an unlawful employment practice for an employer to hire and employ employees . . . on the basis of his . . . disability . . . in those instances where [a] physical, mental, or visual condition . . . is a bona fide occupational qualification reasonably necessary to the normal operation of that particular business or enterprise,"[693] and if it is shown that the particular disability would prevent proper performance of the work for which the disabled person would otherwise have been hired . . . ."[694]

b. *Preferential Treatment*

Nothing "requires any employer . . . to grant preferential treatment to any person" with a disability because "of an imbalance which exists with respect to the total number or percentage of persons of any . . . disability . . . employed by any employer, . . . in comparison with the total number or percentage

---

[690] Maes v. Henderson, 33 F. Supp. 2d 1281 (D. Nev. 1999).
[691] Barnett v. U.S. Air, 228 F.3d 1105, 10 AD Cases 1761 (9th Cir. 2000).
[692] *Id.*
[693] Nev. Rev. Stat. Ann. §613.350(1).
[694] *Id.* §613.350(2).

of persons of that ... disability ... in any community, section or other area, or in the available workforce in any community, section or other area."[695]

NEW HAMPSHIRE

I. STATE LAW

A. Overview

New Hampshire's Law Against Discrimination prohibits employment discrimination on the basis of physical or mental disability.[696] In New Hampshire, citizens have a civil right to be free from employment discrimination based on physical or mental disability.[697] However, citizens do not have a private right of action based on unlawful discriminatory practices, but are limited to seeking relief through New Hampshire's administrative process and may seek judicial review of the results of that process.[698]

B. Prohibited Discrimination

It is unlawful for employers to discriminate against persons with physical or mental disabilities in hiring, termination, compensation, or other terms and conditions of employment, except on the basis of a "bona fide occupational qualification."[699]

However, New Hampshire's protections against disability discrimination do not apply when the disability interferes "with the individual's ability to perform" job functions, or when the person presents "a significant risk [or] direct threat, to the health or safety of himself or others when performing the

---

[695] *Id.* §613.400.
[696] N.H. REV. STAT. ANN. §354-A:1.
[697] *Id.* §354-A:6.
[698] *See* Carparts Distribution Ctr. of New England v. Automotive Wholesaler's Ass'n, Inc., 987 F. Supp. 77, 7 AD Cases 759 (D.N.H. 1997); Nedder v. Rivier Coll., 944 F. Supp. 111, 5 AD Cases 1691 (D.N.H. 1996); Tsetseranos v. Tech Prototype, Inc., 893 F. Supp. 109, 4 AD Cases 1635 (D.N.H. 1995).
[699] N.H. REV. STAT. ANN. §354-A:7.I.

job...."[700] Employers cannot base "an employment decision ... on [speculation of a] future risk to health or safety," or on assumptions and stereotypes.[701]

Employers also are barred from printing, circulating, advertising, or publishing any application or notice that expresses "any limitation, specification or discrimination" based on physical or mental disability, unless it is based on "a bona fide occupational qualification."[702]

1. Preemployment Issues

Employers are also prohibited from making any inquiries or records "in connection with employment" based on physical or mental disability, unless it is based on "a bona fide occupational qualification."[703] However, employers are permitted to make inquiries and keep records "of any existing ... physical or mental conditions" after the employer makes a job offer to an applicant.[704]

2. Genetic Testing

Employers may not "(a) Solicit, require or administer genetic testing relating to any individual as a condition of employment; [or] (b) Affect the terms, conditions, or privileges of employment ... based on genetic testing."[705] However, employers may administer genetic testing to

> an employee who requests to undergo genetic testing and who provides written and informed consent to genetic testing for any of the following purposes:
> (a) [the investigation of] a worker's compensation claim ... ; [or]
> (b) [the determination of] the employee's susceptibility or level of exposure to potentially ... toxic substances ... , if the employer

---

[700] N.H. CODE ADMIN. R. ANN. Hum. 406.02(a).
[701] *Id.* 406.02(b).
[702] N.H. REV. STAT. ANN. §354-A:7.III.
[703] *Id.*
[704] *Id.*
[705] *Id.* §141-H:3.I.

does not [take any] action that adversely affects any term, condition, or privilege of the employee's employment, as a result of genetic testing."[706]

In addition, employers may use "genetic testing for evidence of insurability with respect to . . . disability income [ ] or long-term care insurance under the terms of an employee benefit plan."[707]

C. Definitions

1. Disability

A disability "is [a] physical or mental impairment . . . , [a] record of having such an impairment, or [b]eing regarded as having such an impairment."[708] In addition, transsexualism is considered a disability in New Hampshire.[709]

D. Covered Employers

In New Hampshire, an employer is "any person acting in the interest of an employer directly or indirectly."[710]

E. Reasonable Accommodation and Defenses

The New Hampshire Law Against Discrimination does not require that employers "make accommodations for the limitations of applicants or employees with disabilities."[711]

NEW JERSEY

I. STATE LAW

A. Overview

The New Jersey Law Against Discrimination (NJLAD) prohibits discrimination in any employment-related action against

---

[706] *Id.* §141-H:3.IV.
[707] *Id.* §141-H:3.V.
[708] *Id.* §354-A:2.IV.
[709] Jane Doe v. Electro-Craft Corp., No. 87-E-132 (Rockingham Super. Ct. 1988).
[710] N.H. REV. STAT. ANN. §275:36.
[711] N.H. CODE ADMIN. R. ANN. Hum. 406.01.

handicapped individuals, unless the employer determines that "the nature and extent of the disability reasonably precludes the" safe performance of the particular job.[712] The NJLAD applies to all persons presently or previously handicapped.[713]

The prohibitions of the NJLAD are quite expansive: in addition to mental and physical disabilities, acquired immune deficiency syndrome (AIDS) and human immunodeficiency virus (HIV) infection are specified under the NJLAD's definition of disability";[714] genetic information and an applicant's or worker's refusal to submit to a genetic test are protected;[715] persons with "atypical hereditary cellular or blood" traits, such as sickle cell disorders, are protected;[716] and the NJLAD also protects handicapped, blind, and deaf persons from job bias based on their use of service animals.[717]

B. Prohibited Discrimination

New Jersey employers must give persons with disabilities equal consideration with nondisabled persons in "hiring, promotion, tenure, training, assignment, transfers," fringe benefits, wages, leaves, and all other aspects of employment.[718] Employers are prohibited from knowingly using an "employment agency or recruitment source which does not refer [persons] with disabilities" for employment.[719] Employers are also prohibited from using any employment tests or other selection criteria "that screens out or has the effect of screening out people with disabilities unless" the tests or criteria are job-related and alternative methods are not available.[720] In addition, it is unlawful for employers to advertise employment in a manner that discourages disabled persons from applying, by using words

---

[712] N.J. STAT. ANN. §10:5-4.1.
[713] Id.
[714] Id. §10:5-5(q).
[715] Id. §10:5-12(a).
[716] Id.
[717] Id. §10:5-29.1
[718] N.J. ADMIN. CODE tit. 13, §13:13-2.5(a).
[719] Id. §13:13-2.2(a).
[720] Id. §13:13-2.3(a).

like "'ablebodied persons wanted' or their equivalent."[721] Employers are, however, permitted to "include a statement of the particular physical or mental abilities reasonably necessary" to perform the job.[722]

It is unlawful for an employer to elicit any information about "the existence of a disability or health condition," or to ask any question that tends to divulge that information, unless required by law.[723] However, employers may inquire about "whether an applicant is precluded from satisfactorily performing the job duties . . . ."[724] Furthermore, employers may condition job offers "on the results of a medical examination" conducted after the offer, but before employment commences, as long as all "entering employees are subjected to the same examination; and [t]he results of [the] examination . . . are not used to disqualify an applicant [unless] any disability discovered would, even with reasonable accommodation, preclude the safe or adequate performance of the job . . . ."[725]

C. Definitions

1. Disability

The NJLAD explicitly defines "Disability" as meaning:

> physical disability, infirmity, malformation or disfigurement which is caused by bodily injury, birth defect or illness including epilepsy . . . and which shall include, but not be limited to, any degree of paralysis, amputation, lack of physical coordination, blindness or visual impediment, deafness or hearing impediment, muteness or speech impediment or physical reliance on a service or guide dog, wheelchair, or other remedial appliance or device, or [from] any mental, psychological or developmental disability resulting from anatomical, psychological or developmental disability resulting from anatomical, psychological, physiological or neurological conditions which prevents the normal exercise of any bodily or mental

---

[721] *Id.* §13:13-2.1(a).
[722] *Id.*
[723] *Id.* §13:13-2.4(a).
[724] *Id.*
[725] *Id.* §13:13-2.4(e)(2).

functions or is demonstrable, medically or psychologically, by accepted clinical or laboratory diagnostic techniques. Disability shall also mean AIDS or HIV infection.[726]

In addition, blindness is defined as a "central visual acuity [that] does not exceed 20/200 in the better eye with correcting lens or visual acuity is better than 20/200 if accompanied by a limit to the field of vision in the better eye to such a degree that its widest diameter subtends an angle of no greater than 20 degrees."[727] Deafness is defined as hearing that is so "impaired that the person is unable to hear and understand normal conversational speech through the unaided ear alone, and who must depend primarily on a supportive device or visual communication such as writing, lip reading, sign language, and gestures."[728]

"Atypical hereditary cellular or blood trait[s]" are defined under the statute as "sickle cell trait, hemoglobin C trait, thalassemia trait, Tay-Sachs trait, or cystic fibrosis trait."[729]

The NJLAD's definition of disabled contrasts with the ADA's definition, which incorporates the additional requirement that the condition result in a substantial limitation on a major life activity.[730] The NJLAD's definition imposes a lesser standard of proof than the ADA's definition; New Jersey courts have recognized that this results in coverage of a wider array of conditions.[731]

D. Covered Employers

The NJLAD applies to all private and public employers, including the state and its political subdivisions, state and municipal contractors, and all public officers, agencies, and

---

[726] N.J. STAT. ANN. §10:5-5(q).
[727] *Id.* §10:5-5(r).
[728] *Id.* §10:5-5(w).
[729] *Id.* §10:5-5(x).
[730] 42 U.S.C. §12103(2)(A).
[731] Failla v. City of Passaic, 146 F.3d 149, 8 AD Cases 275 (3d Cir. 1998).

boards.[732] The law also applies to employment agencies and labor organizations[733]

E. Reasonable Accommodation and Defenses

1. Reasonable Accommodation

In New Jersey, employers are required to reasonably accommodate the limitations of a disabled employee "unless the employer can demonstrate that the accommodation would impose an undue hardship on the operation of its business."[734] In order for a decision to be reasonable, the employer must determine that the employee's disability precludes performance of essential duties and does not merely hinder the execution of some tasks. Furthermore, before deciding that a person's disability precludes the safe performance of a particular job, the employer must first consider the possibility of making reasonable accommodations that may enable the person to perform the essential functions of the position. The following are examples of reasonable accommodations: (1) making facilities readily accessible for persons with disabilities; (2) job restructuring, including reassignment, and "part-time or modified work schedules"; and (3) [a]cquisition or modification of equipment or devices...."[735] Employers are required to consider whether a reasonable accommodation is possible "before firing, demoting or refusing to hire or promote a" disabled person on the basis that the "disability precludes job performance."[736]

2. Defenses

Employers are permitted to refuse employment to disabled individuals when employing the disabled person in a particular position is "hazardous to the safety or health of [the] individual, other employees, clients or customers."[737]

---

[732] N.J. STAT. ANN. §10:5-5(e).
[733] Id. §10:5-12(b)–(c).
[734] N.J. ADMIN. CODE tit. 13, §13:13-2.5(b).
[735] Id. §13:13-2.5(b)1.
[736] Id. §13:13-2.5(b)2.
[737] Id. §13:13-2.8(a)2.

Employers are not required to hire or retain an individual who is not otherwise qualified to perform a job; indeed, where "the nature and extent of the disability reasonably precludes" or impedes the adequate and safe performance of the essential functions of the job, an employer does not violate the NJLAD by taking an adverse action with respect to the individual's employment.[738] The essential inquiry in assessing whether an employee must be retained and accommodated is whether the handicapped employee, with reasonable accommodation, is performing or can perform at an acceptable level in comparison to other employees.[739]

a. Undue Hardship

Employers should consider the following factors in deciding whether providing an accommodation would pose an undue burden: (1) size of the employer's business, including personnel, budget, and number of facilities; (2) the nature and cost of the accommodation; and (3) the extent to which an accommodation is a waiver of an essential job requirement or a nonbusiness necessity.[740]

NEW MEXICO

I. STATE LAW

A. Overview

New Mexico's Human Rights Act[741] and White Cane Law[742] protect persons with disabilities from discrimination in employment. Indeed, it is New Mexico's policy to encourage the blind, visually handicapped, and otherwise physically disabled to engage in remunerative employment.[743]

---

[738] N.J. STAT. ANN. §10:5-4.1
[739] DCR Response to Public Comments on N.J.A.C. 13:13-1.1 et seq., N.J. STAT. ANN. §10:5-2.1.
[740] N.J. ADMIN. CODE tit. 13, §13:13-2.5(b)3.
[741] N.M. STAT. ANN. §28-1-1.
[742] Id. §28-7-1.
[743] Id. §22-14-24.

B. Prohibited Discrimination

Employers are prohibited from discriminating against persons with physical or mental handicaps or serious medical conditions in hiring, discharging, promoting, demoting, compensating, or other terms, "conditions, or privileges of employment" unless based on a bona fide occupational qualification.[744] Employers are not permitted to advertise or use any form of employment application that expresses "any limitation, specification or discrimination as to . . . physical or mental handicap or serious medical condition, . . . unless based on a bona fide occupational qualification."[745] New Mexico's AIDS Testing Law prohibits testing for human immunodeficiency virus (HIV) status unless a negative HIV status "is a bona fide occupational qualification [for] the job in question."[746]

C. Definitions

1. Disability

A person who has "a physical or mental impairment that substantially limits one or more . . . major life activities," has a record of such impairment, or is regarded as having such impairment, is considered to be handicapped or disabled under New Mexico's Human Rights Act.[747] Examples of major life activities for purposes of the statute include caring for "one's self, performing manual tasks, walking, seeing, hearing, speaking, breathing, learning, and working."[748] Physical and mental impairments are

---

[744] *Id.* §28-1-7.A. *See* Stock v. Grantham, 125 N.M. 564, 964 P.2d 125, (1998) (termination of ill nanny not unlawful because ability to attend to work regularly is bona fide occupational qualification).

[745] N.M. STAT. ANN. §28-1-7(D). *See* Kitchell v. Public Serv. Co., 126 N.M. 525, 972 P.2d 344 (1998) (employee who admitted in his workers' compensation claims that he was totally disabled also admitted thereby that he was not otherwise qualified disabled individual).

[746] N.M. STAT. ANN. §28-10A-1.

[747] *Id.* §28-1-2.M.

[748] *Id.* §28-1-2.N.

defined to include, but [are] not limited to, any physiological disorder or condition, cosmetic disfigurement or anatomical loss affecting one or more of the following body systems: neurological; musculoskeletal; special sense organs; respiratory, including speech organs; cardiovascular; reproductive; digestive; genitourinary; hemic and lymphatic; skin; endocrine; or any mental or psychological disorder, such as mental retardation, organic brain syndrome, emotional or mental illness and specific learning disabilities.[749]

A qualified handicapped person is one "who, with reasonable accommodation, can perform the essential functions of the job."[750] A record is "a history or recorded classification of having a mental or physical impairment or [serious medical condition] that substantially limits one or more major life activities."[751] A person is regarded as having a handicap if the person: (1) has "a physical or mental impairment that does not substantially limit major life activities, but [is] treated as ... having such a limitation; (2) has "a physical or mental impairment that substantially limits major life activities only as a result of the attitudes of others ... ; or (3) does not have a physical or mental impairment, "but [is] treated as having such an impairment."[752]

2. Medical Conditions

"The term 'serious medical condition' [applies] to serious health-related impairment that requires protection against discrimination due to the severity and/or duration ...."[753] A serious health impairment is one that "substantially limits one or more ... major life activities, [and] is verifiable by medical diagnosis."[754] A person "is also considered to have a serious medical condition, if he or she (a) has a record of a serious

---

[749] N.M. ADMIN. CODE tit. 9, §1.1.7.W.
[750] Id. §1.1.7.AA.
[751] Id. §§1.1.7.22.2.V(2), 1.1.7.33.GG.
[752] Id. §1.1.7.22.3.V(3).
[753] Id. §1.1.7.33.GG.
[754] Id. §1.1.7.GG.

health-related impairment; or (b) is regarded as having a serious health-related impairment."[755] A person is regarded as having a serious health-related impairment if the person: (1) has "a serious medical condition that does not substantially limit major life activities, but is treated . . . as having such a limitation; (2) has "a serious medical condition that substantially limits major life activities only as a result of the attitudes of others . . . "; or (3) does not have a serious medical condition, but is treated "as having such an impairment."[756]

D. Covered Employers

All private employers of four or more employees, employment agencies, and labor organizations are subject to the Human Rights Act's prohibitions.[757]

E. Reasonable Accommodation and Defenses

1. Reasonable Accommodation

Employers must accommodate an individual's "physical or mental handicap or serious medical condition, unless [the] accommodation is unreasonable or [imposes] an undue hardship" on the employer.[758] Reasonable accommodations are necessary "modifications or adaptations of the work environment or job responsibilities [that enable] a handicapped person . . . to perform the essential [job functions] and do not impose an undue hardship on the employer."[759]

NEW YORK

I. State Law

A. Overview

The New York State Human Rights Law generally prohibits discrimination in employment against disabled individuals who

---

[755] *Id.* §1.1.7.33.GG(1).
[756] *Id.* §1.1.7.33.GG(3).
[757] N.M. Stat. Ann. §28-1-2B.
[758] *Id.* §28-1-7J.
[759] N.M. Admin. Code tit. 9, §1.1.7.DD.

are reasonably able to do what the position requires on the provision of a reasonable accommodation by the employer.[760] Under the Equal Opportunities for Disabled Persons Law, employers who hire individuals with disabilities are allowed a state tax credit of up to $2,100.[761]

B. Prohibited Discrimination

Employers in New York are prohibited from discriminating against disabled persons in hiring, employment, discharge, compensation, and "terms, conditions or privileges of employment."[762] It is also unlawful for employers "to print or circulate" any advertisement, publication, or application, or make any inquiries that express "any limitation, specification or discrimination" on the basis of disability.[763] Employers cannot deny employment opportunities to disabled individuals merely because they are "accompanied by a guide dog, hearing dog or service dog . . . ."[764] Retaliation against persons who have engaged in protected activity is also prohibited.[765]

1. Genetic Testing

Under the Nondiscrimination Against Genetic Disorders Law, it is unlawful in New York for an employer to discriminate on the basis of, or to inquire into, genetic predisposition or carrier status.[766] The New York statute specifically prohibits testing for sickle-cell trait, Tay-Sachs syndrome, and Cooley's anemia; furthermore, individuals with a history of cancer are protected against discrimination.[767] However, the law permits genetic testing if the testing is based on a bona fide occupational qualification (BFOQ).[768]

---

[760] N.Y. Exec. Law §§292(21), 296(1).
[761] N.Y. Tax Law §187-a.
[762] N.Y. Exec. Law §296(1)(a).
[763] Id. §296(1)(d).
[764] N.Y. Civ. Rights. Law §47-a.
[765] Id.
[766] N.Y Lab. Law §292(21-b), (21-c).
[767] Id. §296(1)(a).
[768] Id. §296(1)(d).

C. Definitions

1. Disability

A disability is "a physical, mental or medical impairment resulting from anatomical, physiological, genetic or neurological conditions which prevents the exercise of a normal bodily function or is demonstrable by medically accepted clinical or laboratory diagnostic techniques ... a record of such an impairment or ... a condition regarded by others as such an impairment...."[769] However, disabilities are limited to those that, with reasonable accommodation, "do not prevent the [person] from performing" job activities in a reasonable manner.[770]

The New York Division of Human Rights has issued a policy statement declaring that acquired immune deficiency syndrome (AIDS) is a disability under the New York State Human Rights Law and that it will process AIDS discrimination complaints.

D. Covered Employers

Employers with four or more employees, employment agencies, labor organizations, licensing agencies, and apprenticeship training programs are subject to New York's antidiscrimination laws.[771]

---

[769] N.Y. EXEC. LAW §292(21). *See* Delta Air Lines v. New York State Div. of Human Rights, 91 N.Y.2d 65, 666 N.Y.S.2d 1004, 689 N.E.2d 898 (1997) (employer did not discriminate against flight attendants who failed to meet weight standards and failed to prove they were medically incapable of meeting weight requirements, because weight, without more, is not disability); State Div. of Human Rights v. Xerox Corp., 102 A.D. 2d 543, 478 N.Y.S.2d 982, 35 FEP Cases 819 (1984) (employer unlawfully refused to hire applicant with active gross obesity, which without more, is mental and physical impairment).

[770] N.Y. EXEC. LAW §292(21).

[771] §§292(5), 296(1)(a)–(c), (1-a).

E. Reasonable Accommodation and Defenses

1. *Reasonable Accommodation*

Providing "an accessible worksite, acquisition or modification of equipment, support services for persons with impaired hearing or vision, and job restructuring [including] modified work schedules," are examples of reasonable accommodations, provided that they "do not impose an undue hardship" on the employer.[772] An employer must provide employees with pregnancy-related disabilities the same leave terms that they provide employees with other disabilities.[773]

II. Local Laws

The disability discrimination provisions in the New York City Human Rights Law differ significantly from the New York State Human Rights Law and the ADA in their definitions of disability. Under the New York City Human Rights Law, "disability" is defined to mean "any physical, medical, mental, or psychological impairment, or a history or record of such impairment."[774] Physical and medical impairments are further defined to mean "an impairment of any system of the body."[775] At least one court has found that under the New York City law, a condition that impairs any system of an individual's body qualifies as a disability, so that to be covered by the New York City law, an individual's impairment need not "substantially limit a major life activity" or be "demonstrable by medically accepted techniques" as required under the New York State law.[776] Thus, protection under the New York City law appears to be far broader than its state or federal counterparts.

---

[772] §292(21-e).
[773] *See* Brooklyn Union Gas Co. v. New York State Human Rights Appeal Bd., 41 N.Y.2d 84, 390 N.Y.S.2d 884, 359 N.E.2d 393, 14 FEP Cases 42 (1976).
[774] N.Y.C. Admin. Code §8-102(16)(a).
[775] *Id.* §8-102(16)(b)(1).
[776] Hazeldine v. Beverage Media, 954 F. Supp. 697, 706, 6 AD Cases 1821 (S.D.N.Y. 1997).

NORTH CAROLINA

I. STATE LAW

A. Overview

North Carolina public policy[777] and the North Carolina Persons With Disabilities Protection Act[778] prohibit discrimination in employment on the basis of handicap or disability. However, North Carolina's standards are narrower than those of the ADA.[779]

B. Prohibited Discrimination

Employers are prohibited from discriminating against a qualified person with a disability in hiring, compensation, discharge, promotion, or "other terms, conditions, or privileges of employment. . . ."[780] Moreover, it is discriminatory for employers to require an applicant to disclose whether he or she is disabled "prior to a conditional offer of employment. . . ."[781] However, employers can invite applicants to identify themselves as disabled "in order to act affirmatively on his behalf."[782]

Employers are permitted to ask whether an applicant "has the ability to perform" job duties.[783] Similarly, an employer may require or request that an applicant undergo a post-offer "medical examination, which may include a medical history, [to determine] the person's ability or capacity to safely and satisfactorily perform [job duties], or to aid in determining

---

[777] N.C. GEN. STAT. §143-422.2.
[778] Id. §168A-1.
[779] See Williams v. Channel Master Satellite Sys., 101 F.3d 346, 6 AD Case 131 (4th Cir. 1996); see also Burgess v. Your House of Raleigh, Inc., 326 N.C. 205, 388 S.E.2d 134, 2 AD Cases 672 (1990) (a person who has human immunodeficiency virus, but is asymptomatic is not protected by the North Carolina Persons With Disabilities Protection Act).
[780] N.C. GEN. STAT. §168A-5(a)(1).
[781] Id. §168A-5(a)(4).
[782] Id.
[783] Id. §168A-5(b)(5).

possible accommodations for an" impairment, where the employer has conditioned the offer on the person's ability to meet the job's mental and physical requirements "with or without reasonable accommodation."[784] Furthermore, employers are permitted "[t]o obtain medical information or to require . . . a medical examination . . . for the purpose of establishing an employee health record."[785] Employers can also "administer pre-employment tests . . . that the tests (i) measure only job-related abilities, (ii) are required of all applicants for the same [job], and (iii) accurately measure the applicant's [ability] rather than reflecting . . . a disability . . . ."[786]

1. Genetic Testing

Employers are prohibited from discriminating against persons with sickle cell or "hemoglobin C trait . . . ,"[787] and acquired immune deficiency syndrome or human immunodeficiency virus.[788] Furthermore, the Genetic Testing Law prohibits discrimination by public and private employers against an individual who has "requested genetic testing . . . or on the basis of genetic information . . . ."[789]

2. Retaliation

The Retaliatory Employment Discrimination law, which applies to all employers, including the state and its subdivisions, prohibits retaliatory actions because of filing, providing information in, or the investigation of an employment bias complaint.[790]

---

[784] *Id.* §168A-5(b)(6).
[785] *Id.* §168A-5(b)(7).
[786] *Id.* §168A-5(b)(8).
[787] *Id.* §95-28.1.
[788] *Id.* §130A-148(i).
[789] *Id.* §95-28.1A.
[790] *Id.* §95-241.

C. Definitions

1. Disability

Handicaps or disabilities include "physical, mental and visual" impairments.[791] "[A]ny condition or characteristic that" causes a person to be disabled is a disabling condition.[792]

"[A]ny person who (i) has a physical or mental impairment which substantially limits one or more major life activities, (ii) has a record of such an impairment, or (iii) is regarded as having such impairment" is a person with a disability.[793] A person who "has a history of, or has been misclassified as having, a mental or physical impairment that substantially limits [one or more] major life activities" has a record of such impairment.[794] A person is regarded as having an impairment if he or she "(i) has a physical or mental impairment that does not substantially limit major life activities but" is treated as having such limitations; (ii) has a physical or mental impairment that substantially limits major life activities because of the attitudes of others; or (iii)" does not have any impairment "but is treated" as being impaired.[795] Examples of major life activities include "caring for one's self, performing manual tasks, walking, seeing, hearing, speaking, breathing, learning, and working."[796]

Physical or mental impairments are defined as:

> (i) any physiological disorder or abnormal condition, cosmetic disfigurement, or anatomical loss, caused by bodily injury, birth defect or illness, affecting one or more of the following body

---

[791] *Id.* §168-1. *See* Pressman v. UNC-Charlotte, 78 N.C. App. 296, 337 S.E.2d 644 (1985) (person suffering from occasional episodes of stress, depression, and mental exhaustion not a handicapped person); Burgess v. Joseph Schlitz Brewing Co., 298 N.C. 520, 259 S.E.2d 248, 1 AD Cases 121 (1979) (person with eye disease but whose vision functioned normally with glasses not visually disabled); GASP v. Mecklenburg County, 42 N.C. App. 225, 256 S.E.2d 477 (1979) (persons with minor pulmonary problems and who are harmed or irritated by tobacco smoke not included within definition of handicapped persons).

[792] N.C. Gen. Stat. §168A-3(1).

[793] *Id.* §168A-3(7a).

[794] *Id.* §168A-3(7a)(c).

[795] *Id.* §168A-3(7a)(d).

[796] *Id.* §168A-3(7a)(b). *See* Gravitte v. Mitsubishi Semiconductor Am., Inc., 109 N.C. App. 466, 428 S.E.2d 254, 2 AD Cases 669 (1993) (plaintiff who experienced

systems: neurological; musculoskeletal; special sense organs; respiratory, including speech organs; cardiovascular; reproductive; digestive; genitourinary; hemic and lymphatic; skin; and endocrine [body systems]; or (ii) any mental disorder, such as mental retardation, organic brain syndrome, mental illness, specific learning disabilities, and other developmental disabilities, but (iii) [excluding] (A) sexual preferences; (B) active alcoholism or drug addiction or abuse; and (C) any disorder, condition or disfigurement which is temporary in nature leaving no residual impairment."[797]

A disabled person "who can satisfactorily perform [job duties] with or without reasonable accommodation" is a qualified person with a disability, as long as the disabled person is "held to the same standards as other similarly situated employees, and "that the disabling condition does not [pose] an unreasonable risk to the safety or health [of the disabled person], other employees, the employer's customers, or the public."[798]

D. Covered Employers

North Carolina's employment discrimination provisions apply to employers who "regularly employ 15 or more employees."[799]

E. Reasonable Accommodation and Defenses

1. *Reasonable Accommodation*

Reasonable accommodations include "making physical changes in the workplace, [such as] making facilities accessible, modifying equipment and providing mechanical aids to assist in operating equipment, or making reasonable changes in" job duties that would enable the employee or applicant to satisfactorily perform job duties.[800]

---

lower back pain on repetitive twisting, turning, reaching, stooping, and bending did not have impairment that limited major life activity).
[797] N.C. GEN. STAT. §168A-3(7a)(a).
[798] *Id.* §168A-3(9)(a).
[799] *Id.* §143-422.2.
[800] *Id.* §168A-3(10)(a).

2. Defenses

However, employers are not required to do any of the following: (1) "hire one or more employees, other than the" disabled person, to enable the disabled person's employment; (2) reassign job duties at issue "to other employees without assigning the [disabled employee] duties that would compensate for those reassigned"; (3) reassign job duties to "one or more employees [that] would increase the skill, effort or responsibility" than that previously required; or (4) "provide accommodations of a personal nature [such as] eyeglasses, hearing aids, and prostheses...."[801]

a. Undue Hardship

The North Carolina Persons with Disabilities Protection Act outlines the circumstances in which an employer may be able to present an "undue hardship" defense to a claim of discrimination or failure to reasonably accommodate an individual with a disability. The term "undue hardship" is defined by the state law to mean "a significant difficulty or expense."[802] The state law outlines a number of factors that will be considered in determining whether an accommodation would impose an undue hardship, including the nature and cost of the accommodations required, the overall financial resources of the particular facility or facilities involved (including the number of persons employed at the facility, the effect on expenses and resources at the facility, and any other impact on the operation of the facility), the overall effect on the financial resources of the covered entity, and the type of operations of the covered entity. This latter factor would include analysis of the composition, structure, and functions of the workforce of the entity, the geographic separateness of the particular facility to the covered entity, and the administrative or fiscal relationship of the particular facility to the covered entity.[803]

---

[801] *Id.*
[802] *Id.* §168A-3 (11).
[803] *Id.*

NORTH DAKOTA

I. State Law

A. Overview

The North Dakota Human Rights Act prohibits discrimination on the basis of the presence of any mental or physical disability.[804] Under the North Dakota statute, it is a discriminatory practice for an employer not to make reasonable accommodations for an otherwise qualified person with a physical or mental disability.[805]

B. Prohibited Discrimination

Employers are prohibited from discriminating against a person with physical or mental disabilities in hiring, application procedures, discharge, training, apprenticeship, tenure, promotion, upgrading, compensation, layoff, or in terms, conditions, or privileges of employment.[806] It is also unlawful discrimination for employers to fail or refuse to make reasonable accommodations for otherwise qualified persons with physical or mental disabilities.[807] Employers are also prohibited from retaliating against applicants or employees who engage in protected activity, and from aiding, abetting, compelling, coercing, inciting, or inducing discrimination.[808] Similarly, employers are prohibited from advertising or using an application, or making a record or inquiry, or any device to facilitate discrimination.[809]

However, it is not discriminatory for employers to fail or refuse to hire, or discharge, a disabled employee based on a bona fide occupational qualification that is reasonably necessary to the normal operations of the employer's business.[810]

---

[804] N.D. Cent. Code §14-02.4-01.
[805] Id. §14-02.4-03.
[806] Id.
[807] Id.
[808] Id. §14-02.4-18.
[809] Id.
[810] Id. §14-02.4-08. See Soentgen v. Quain & Ramstad Clinic, 467 N.W.2d 73 (N.D. 1991) (even assuming alcoholism and drug addiction are handicaps in North

C. Definitions

1. Disability

A "disability" is a physical or mental impairment that substantially limits one or more major life activities; furthermore, a record of such impairment, or being regarded as having such impairment, is included in the state's definition of disability.[811]

Segregating, separating, treating inequitably, or denying, preventing, limiting, or otherwise adversely affecting a disabled person's enjoyment of employment is a discriminatory practice.[812]

D. Covered Employers

North Dakota's Human Rights Act applies to employers within the state that employ one or more employees for more than one-quarter of the year and to employers wherever situated that employ one or more employees whose services are performed within the state.[813] The law also applies to employment agencies[814] and labor organizations.[815]

E. Reasonable Accommodation and Defenses

1. Reasonable Accommodation

Accommodations that do not unduly disrupt or interfere with an employer's normal operations, or threaten the health or safety of the disabled person or others, or contradict a

---

Dakota, employer did not discriminate against physician by requiring him to take leave and secure treatment for his addictions, because employer's actions were based on bona fide occupational qualification reasonably necessary for physician).

[811] N.D. CENT. CODE §14-02.4-02(3). *See* Krein v. Martin Manor Nursing Home, 415 N.W.2d 793 (N.D. 1987) (plaintiff who weighed over 300 pounds not handicapped, where she failed to demonstrate that she was disabled; mere assertion that person is overweight or obese alone not enough to put that person in protected class of being disabled).

[812] N.D. CENT. CODE §14-02.4-02(4).
[813] *Id.* §14-02.4-02(6).
[814] *Id.* §14-02.4-04.
[815] *Id.* §14-02.4-05.

business necessity of the employer, or impose an undue hardship on the employer are reasonable accommodations.[816]

2. Defenses

a. Undue Hardship

Employers are not required to provide accommodations that pose an undue hardship based on the size of the employer's business, the type of business, the employer's financial resources, and estimated cost and extent of the accommodation.[817]

OHIO

I. STATE LAW

A. Overview

The Ohio Fair Employment Practice Law prohibits discrimination in employment based on disability.[818]

B. Prohibited Discrimination

It is unlawful for employers "to discharge without just cause, to refuse to hire, or otherwise to discriminate against [a] person with respect to" hiring, recruitment, promotions, demotions, transfers, layoffs, compensation, assignments, leaves, fringe benefits, employer-sponsored social or recreational activities, "tenure, terms, conditions, or privileges of employment, or any matter directly or indirectly related to employment" on the basis of disability.[819] Employers are also prohibited from discriminating on the basis of disability "in admission to, or employment in, any program established to provide apprenticeship training."[820] It is unlawful to retaliate

---

[816] *Id.* §14-02.4-02(16).
[817] *Id.*
[818] OHIO REV. CODE ANN. §4112.02(A); OHIO. ADMIN. CODE §4112-5-08(A).
[819] *Id.*
[820] OHIO REV. CODE ANN. §4112.02(D).

against an employee who has engaged in protected activity[821] and "to aid, abet, incite, compel, or coerce, unlawful discrimination, or to obstruct," or prevent nondiscriminatory practices.[822] In addition, employers are prohibited from doing any of the following, unless based "on a bona fide occupational qualification [that has been] certified in advance by the" Ohio Human Rights Commission: (1) using any employment application or form that seeks or attempts to elicit information about a disability;[823] (2) printing or publishing any advertisement that expresses any preferences, limitations, specifications, "or discrimination based on . . . disability . . . ";[824] (3) making or keeping a record of the disability of an applicant;[825] or (4) use any employment agency or recruiter "known to discriminate against persons" with disabilities.[826] Bona fide occupational qualifications are narrowly construed in Ohio. Permissible bona fide occupational qualifications include specific requirements established in state, local, or federal statutes and regulations.[827] In contrast, the "[p]references or objections of co-workers, the employer, clients, or customers" are not bona fide occupational qualifications.[828]

Ohio does not require employers to employ or train disabled persons if it "would significantly increase the occupational hazards affecting either the [disabled] person . . . , other employees, or the general public . . . ."[829] In addition, employers are not required to employ or train a disabled person in a job that requires the person to perform routinely tasks that

---

[821] *Id.* §4112.02(I).
[822] *Id.* §4112.02(J).
[823] *Id.* §4112.02(E)(1).
[824] *Id.* §4112.02(E)(4).
[825] *Id.* §4112.02(E)(2).
[826] *Id.* §4112.02(E)(6).
[827] OHIO ADMIN. CODE §4112-5-08(D)(2).
[828] *Id.*
[829] OHIO REV. CODE ANN. §4112.02(L); *see also* OHIO ADMIN. CODE §4112-5-08(D)(3); City of Columbus v. Liebhart, 86 Ohio App. 3d 469, 621 N.E.2d 554, 2 AD Cases 1508 (1993) (firefighter candidate with stutter did not pose occupational hazard on basis of his speech impediment).

are "substantially and inherently impaired by the person's disability."[830]

1. Preemployment Inquiries

An employer is permitted to require a preemployment examination "after a conditional offer of employment has been extended to" an applicant, but only for legitimate purposes, such as determining whether the applicant poses a safety hazard.[831] Employers are permitted to make preemployment inquiries about an applicant's disability if the following conditions are met: (1) the employer precedes any inquiry with "a statement that discrimination on the basis of" disability is prohibited by law; (2) the inquiry is designed to determine if an applicant can perform the job without significantly increasing occupational hazards to the applicant, others, the general public, or workplace, or to determine if the applicant can perform essential job functions with or without reasonable accommodation; and (3) the employer treats the applicant's information as a confidential medical record.[832]

The Ohio Civil Rights Commission has issued a policy statement that prohibits job bias based on acquired immune deficiency syndrome or human immunodeficiency virus (HIV) status.

C. Definitions

1. Disability

A "disability" is "a physical or mental impairment that substantially limits one or more major life activities," a record of such impairment, "or being regarded as having [such] impairment."[833] Any person who has a disability, "is treated ...

---

[830] OHIO REV. CODE ANN. §4112.02(L); *see also* OHIO ADMIN. CODE §4112-5-08(D)(4).
[831] OHIO ADMIN. CODE §4112-5-08(C).
[832] *Id.* §4112-5-08(B).
[833] OHIO REV. CODE ANN. §4112.01(A)(13).

as having such a disability, ... or is regarded" as having a disability is a disabled person.[834]

The following are examples of mental and physical impairments in Ohio:

> (a))(i) Any physiological disorder or condition, cosmetic disfigurement, anatomical loss affecting [a major body system, including] neurological; musculoskeletal; special sense organs; respiratory, including speech organs; cardiovascular; reproductive; digestive; genito-urinary; hemic and lymphatic; and endocrine;
> (ii) Any mental or psychological disorder, including ... mental retardation, organic brain syndrome, emotional or mental illness, and specific learning disabilities;
> (iii) Diseases and conditions, including ... orthopedic, visual, speech and hearing impairments, cerebral palsy, autism, epilepsy, muscular dystrophy, multiple sclerosis, cancer, heart disease, diabetes, [HIV] infection, mental retardation, emotional illness, drug addiction, and alcoholism.[835]

However,

> (b) "Physical or mental impairment does not include ...
> (i) Homosexuality and bisexuality;
> (ii) Transvestism, transsexualism, pedophilia, exhibitionism, voyeurism, gender identity disorders not resulting from physical impairments, or other sexual behavior disorders;
> (iii) Compulsive gambling, kleptomania, or pyromania;
> (iv) Psychoactive substance use disorders resulting from current illegal use of a controlled substance.[836]

An accommodation is "a reasonable adjustment to a job and/or the work environment that enables a qualified" person

---

[834] OHIO ADMIN. CODE §4112-5-02(H).

[835] OHIO REV. CODE ANN. §4112.01(A)(16)(a). *See* Hayes v. Cleveland Pneumatic Co., 92 Ohio App. 3d 36, 634 N.E.2d 228, 3 AD Cases 646 (1993) (even though chemical dependency is handicap, employees can still be terminated when chemical dependency adversely affects job performance through chronic unexcused absences); Stevanovic v. Modern Tool & Die Co., No. 67225, 1995 Ohio App. LEXIS 1628 (8th App. Dist. Apr. 20, 1995) (chronic tinnitus does not limit one or more major life activities and, consequently, is not disability); Kent State Univ. v. Ohio Civil Rights Comm'n, 64 Ohio App. 3d 427, 581 N.E.2d 1135, 2 AD Cases 1496 (1989) (employee's laryngeal stidor with laryngaspasm was medically diagnosable handicap that significantly increased hardship in employee's daily life).

[836] OHIO REV. CODE ANN. §4112.01(A)(16)(b).

with a disability to perform job duties safely and substantially.[837] Bona fide occupational qualifications are "special job situations where an employer may hire employees or take other" action based on disability, "justified by business necessity."[838]

2. Major Life Activities

Major life activities include "caring for one's self, performing manual tasks, walking, seeing, hearing, speaking, breathing, learning, and working . . . ."[839] A disabled person who can safely and substantially perform essential job functions, with or without reasonable accommodation, is a qualified disabled person.

D. Covered Employers

The Fair Employment Practice Law applies to state and local government agencies, private employers that employ "four or more [employees] within the state," employment agencies, personnel placement services, and labor organizations.[840] In addition, individual supervisors may be personally liable for acts of discrimination.[841] However, the statute does not cover domestic servants.[842]

E. Reasonable Accommodation and Defenses

1. Reasonable Accommodation

"An employer must make reasonable accommodation" for a disabled employee, unless making the accommodation imposes "an undue hardship on the conduct of the employer's business."[843] Examples of reasonable accommodations include

---

[837] Ohio Admin. Code §4112-5-02(A).
[838] *Id.* §4112-5-02(D).
[839] Ohio Rev. Code Ann. §4112.01(A)(13).
[840] *Id.* §4112.01(A)(2), (4), (5).
[841] *See* Garraway v. Diversified Material Handling, Inc., 975 F. Supp. 1026, 74 FEP Cases 1593 (N.D. Ohio 1997).
[842] Ohio Rev. Code Ann. §4112.01(3).
[843] Ohio Admin. Code §4112-5-08(E)(1).

job restructuring, acquiring or modifying equipment or devices, and modifying a work schedule.[844]

2. Defenses

a. Undue Hardship

An employer can consider the following factors in determining if a particular accommodation imposes an undue hardship on the employer's business: (1) "business necessity"; (2) unreasonably high financial costs and expenses "in view of the size of the employer's business [and] the value of the disabled employee's work"; and (3) "[o]ther appropriate considerations...."[845]

OKLAHOMA

I. State Law

A. Overview

Oklahoma's Anti-Discrimination Act prohibits employment discrimination based on handicap.[846]

B. Prohibited Discrimination

In Oklahoma, employers are prohibited from failing or refusing to hire, discharging, limiting, segregating, classifying,

---

[844] *Id.* §4112-5-08(E)(2). *See also* Martinez v. Ohio Dep't of Admin. Servs., 118 Ohio App. 3d 687, 693 N.E.2d 1152 (1997) (when employee's handicap was result of sick building syndrome, reassignment of employee to different location was reasonable accommodation even if this caused employee to have longer commute); Wooten v. City of Columbus, 91 Ohio App. 3d 326, 632 N.E.2d 605, 3 AD Cases 631 (1993) (reasonable accommodation of employee's handicap may include reassignment to vacant position for which employee is qualified); Greater Cleveland Reg'l Transit Auth. v. Ohio Civil Rights Comm'n, 58 Ohio App. 3d 20, 567 N.E.2d 1325, 55 FEP Cases 826 (1989) (employers have obligation to avoid any occupational hazards involved in retaining alcoholic employee through reasonable accommodation and employer did not fulfill this obligation by refusing to permit employee to second chance at rehabilitation through alcohol addiction recovery program).
[845] Ohio Admin. Code §4112-5-08(E)(3).
[846] Okla. Stat. tit. 25, §1302(A).

or otherwise discriminating against an individual in compensation, training programs, or other terms, conditions, "privileges, or responsibilities of employment," or otherwise adversely affect the status of an employee on the basis of handicap, "unless such action is related to a bona fide occupational qualification reasonably necessary to the normal operation of the employer's business or enterprise."[847] Employers also are prohibited from printing, or publishing "a notice or advertisement" that indicates "a preference, limitation, specification, or discrimination based on" handicap.[848] However, employers in Oklahoma can hire, employ, or admit a person to a training, retraining, or apprenticeship program on the basis of "a handicap if such action is related to a bona fide occupational qualification [that is] reasonably necessary to the normal operation of the business or enterprise . . . ."[849]

1. Genetic Testing

Oklahoma's Genetic Nondiscrimination in Employment Act prohibits employers from discriminating against employees and prospective employees on the basis of genetic test results or genetic information.[850] Violation of the genetic nondiscrimination statute is a misdemeanor punishable by a fine of up to $25,000, imprisonment for up to 1 year, or both.[851]

C. Definitions

1. Disability

The Oklahoma Anti-Discrimination Act defines a handicapped person as one "who has a physical or mental impairment which substantially limits one or more . . . major life activities, has a record of such an impairment or is regarded

---

[847] *Id.*
[848] *Id.* §1306.
[849] *Id.* §1308.
[850] OKLA. STAT. tit. 36, §3614.2.C.
[851] *Id.* §3614.2.D.

as having such an impairment . . . ."[852] The Oklahoma Administrative Code explicitly adopts the "same terms used in the Federal Rehabilitation Act of 1973, as amended."[853] Thus,

> (A) "Life-Activities" may be considered to include communication, ambulation, selfcare, socialization, education, vocational training, employment, transportation, adapting to housing, etc. . . . [P]rimary attention is given to those life activities that affect employability.
> (B) The phrase "substantially limits" means the degree that the impairment affects employability. A handicapped individual who is likely to experience difficulty in securing, retaining, or advancing in employment would be considered substantially limited.
> (C) "Has a record of such an impairment" means that an individual may be completely recovered from a previous physical or mental impairment. . . . [T]his part of the definition [includes] individuals who may have been erroneously classified and may experience discrimination based on this misclassification [and] persons such as those who have been misclassified as mentally retarded or mentally restored.
> (D) "Is regarded as having such an impairment" refers to those individuals who are perceived as having a handicap, whether an impairment exists or as handicapped by employers or supervisors who have an effect on the individual securing, retaining, or advancing in employment.[854]

The Oklahoma Human Rights Commission also adopted "the Rehabilitation Act's definition of 'qualified' handicapped person to mean a person with a handicap who with reasonable accommodation can perform the essential functions of the job in question."[855]

D. Covered Employers

The Oklahoma Anti-Discrimination Act applies to private employers of 15 or more employees within the state, to state contractors, and to the state and its political subdivisions.[856]

---

[852] OKLA. STAT. tit. 25, §1301(4).
[853] OKLA. ADMIN. CODE §335:15-9-1(a).
[854] Id. §335:15-9-1(b)(1).
[855] Id. §335:15-9-1(b)(2).
[856] OKLA. STAT. tit. 25, §1301(1).

The law also applies to employment agencies[857] and labor organizations.[858] Labor-management committees controlling apprenticeship and other on-the-job training programs are also prohibited from discriminating under the Oklahoma Anti-Discrimination Act.[859]

The Oklahoma Anti-Discrimination Act does not apply to individuals employed by their "parents, spouse, or child," to domestic servants,[860] or to religious organizations that employ "individuals of a particular religion" to carry out their activities.[861]

E. Reasonable Accommodation and Defenses

1. *Reasonable Accommodation*

An employer must make reasonable accommodations

to the known limitations of an otherwise qualified handicapped applicant or employee unless the employer can demonstrate that the accommodation would impose an undue hardship.
(2) Reasonable accommodation by an employer may include:
(A) Modification of work sites and commonly used areas, such as parking lots, lunch rooms, restrooms, desks and work benches.
(B) Job restructuring, modified work or attendance schedules, modification of equipment, purchase of assistive devices and other similar actions.[862]
To determine whether an accommodation would impose an undue hardship on an employer[']s normal operations, [an employer should consider] the essential functions of the job; that is, what basic qualifications are necessary to perform all the essential functions, or, what bona fide occupational qualifications are reasonably necessary to the normal operation of the employer[']s business.[863]

---

[857] *Id.* §1303.
[858] *Id.* §1304.
[859] *Id.* §1305.
[860] *Id.* §1302.
[861] *Id.* §1307.
[862] OKLA. ADMIN. CODE §335:15-9-2(1)–(2).
[863] *Id.* §335:15-9-2(3)(A).

Furthermore, an employer should consider whether there are "reasonable accommodations available that would enable the qualified handicapped person to perform the essential job functions."[864] Other factors

> to consider in determining whether an employer can reasonably accommodate the qualified handicapped person include:
> (A) The overall size of the employer's operations, number of employees, number and type of facilities, location of facilities, and ease of alterations of the employer's facilities.
> (B) The type of the employer's operation, including the composition and structure of the employer's work force.
> (C) The nature, cost, and funding for the accommodation needed.[865]

2. Defenses

a. Undue Hardship

In determining whether a handicap accommodation would constitute an undue hardship on the employer, the following factors should be considered:

> (1) The extent to which the employer demonstrates that compliance with the law would require alteration, modification, or purchase of any building structure, or equipment, or would require additional expenses which would not otherwise be incurred, and
> (2) The extent to which the employer demonstrates the unavailability of alternatives not requiring additional expenses.[866]

OREGON

I. STATE LAW

A. Overview

The Oregon Fair Employment Practice Act prohibits discrimination on the basis of physical or mental disability.[867]

---

[864] Id. §335:15-9-2(3)(B).
[865] Id. §335:15-9-2(4).
[866] Id. §335:15-9-3.
[867] OR. REV. STAT. §659A.112.

Furthermore, Oregon's public policy guarantees persons with disabilities full "participation in the social and economic life of the state," including employment and the right to be free from employment without discrimination due to disability.[868]

B. Prohibited Discrimination

It is unlawful for employers "to refuse to hire, employ or promote, to bar or discharge from employment," limit, segregate, classify, or "discriminate in compensation or [other] terms, conditions or privileges of employment because an otherwise qualified person is" disabled.[869] Employers are not permitted to consider the attitudes or preferences of "co-workers, [supervisors,] customers, clients or the general public toward" disabled persons in making employment decisions.[870] Employers are also prohibited from discriminating against a worker who has opposed an unlawful employment practice or who has assisted in a complaint proceeding,[871] and in the use of employment tests or other selection criteria.[872] Employers are prohibited from asking job applicants if they are disabled, but can inquire into an applicant's ability to perform job-related functions, consistent with business necessity.[873] However, employers can require post-offer medical examinations and "condition the employment on the results of the examination," if employers adhere to certain regulations such as requiring medical examinations of all applicants and keeping the results confidential.[874]

1. Genetic Testing

The Nondiscrimination Against Genetic Disorders Law, a portion of the Fair Employment Practice Act, prohibits employers from obtaining genetic information from employees, persons who are prospective employees, or blood relatives of an

---

[868] *Id.* §659A.103; OR. ADMIN. R. §839-006-0200.
[869] OR. REV. STAT. §659A.112(1)–(2)(a).
[870] OR. ADMIN. R. §839-006-0250.
[871] OR. REV. STAT. §659A.030(f).
[872] *Id.* §659A.112(g).
[873] *Id.* §659A.136.
[874] *Id.* §659A.133(3)(a)–(b); OR. ADMIN. R. §839-006-0242(2).

employee or prospective employee for the purposes of hiring for employment.[875] The law also prohibits discrimination in any benefits related to employment and provides remedies for employees or prospective employees.[876]

C. Definitions

1. *Disability*

A person "who has a physical or mental impairment that substantially limits one or more major life activities, has a record of such an impairment or is regarded as having such an impairment" is disabled.[877] "[A] disabled person is otherwise qualified for a position if the person ... can perform the essential functions of the position," with or without reasonable accommodation.[878] A person who is substantially limited in his or her ability to work "must be significantly restricted in the ability to perform a class" or a broad range of jobs in various areas when compared with other average workers with comparable skills, "experience, education or other job-related requirements . . . ."[879]

Physical or mental impairments include "physiological disorder[s], condition[s], cosmetic disfigurement[s] or anatomical loss affecting" major body systems such as the neurological, musculoskeletal, special sense organs, respiratory (including speech organs), cardiovascular, reproductive, digestive, genitourinary, hemic and lymphatic, skin, and endocrine systems, and mental or psychological disorders, such as mental retardation, organic brain syndrome, emotional or mental illness, and specific learning disabilities.[880] However, homosexuality, bisexuality, "[t]ransvestitism, pedophilia, exhibitionism, voyeurism . . . ,

---

[875] OR. REV. STAT. §659A.303(1).
[876] *Id.* §659A.303(2).
[877] *Id.* §659A.100(1)(a).
[878] *Id.* §659A.115.
[879] *Id.* §839-006-0205(6)(b).
[880] *Id.* §839-006-0205(10).

[c]ompulsive gambling, kleptomania[,] or pyromania," temporary nonchronic impairments of short duration, "and [p]sychoactive substance use disorders resulting from current illegal use of drugs" are not impairments that render someone disabled.[881]

If a person "has a history of, or has been misclassified as having, a mental or physical impairment that substantially limits one or more major life activities," then that person has a record of impairment.[882] A person is regarded as impaired when an employer or supervisor treats the person as having an impairment that substantially limits a major life activity when the impairment does not limit such activity, the person does not have an impairment, or when the person's impairment limits a major life activity only as a result of other persons views toward such impairment.[883] An impairment substantially limits a person's major life activities if it keeps a person from performing activities that an "average person in the general population" is able to perform.[884] In addition, employers should consider the following factors, on a case-by-case basis, in deciding whether an impairment substantially limits a major life activity: (1) the nature and severity of the impairment; (2) the duration of the impairment; and (3) its permanent or long-term impact.[885]

2. *Major Life Activities*

Major life activities include self-care, ambulation, communication, transportation, education, socialization, employment, and the ability to acquire, rent or maintain property,"[886] "walking, sitting, standing lifting, reaching, speaking, interacting with others, seeing, hearing, breathing, learning, sleeping, performing manual tasks, reproduction and working.[887]

---

[881] OR. REV. STAT. §659A.130(A)–(C); OR. ADMIN. R. §839-006-0240(1).
[882] OR. REV. STAT. §659A.100(d)(2)(b).
[883] *Id.* §659A.100(2)(c).
[884] *Id.* §659A.100(2)(d).
[885] OR. ADMIN. R. §839-006-0212(1).
[886] *Id.* §659A.100(d)(2)(a).
[887] OR. ADMIN. R. §839-006-0205(6)(a).

D. Covered Employers

The Oregon Fair Employment Practices Act applies to employers who employ six or more employees, including the state and its political subdivisions, employment agencies, and labor organizations.[888]

E. Reasonable Accommodation and Defenses

1. *Reasonable Accommodation*

Oregon employers are required to make a reasonable accommodation to the known physical or mental limitations of an otherwise qualified disabled job applicant or employee, unless the employer demonstrates that the accommodation would impose an undue hardship on its operation.[889] Reasonable accommodations for otherwise qualified disabled individuals include modifications, acquisitions, or adjustments to the job application process, work environment, position, examination, schedule, equipment, or facilities that enable disabled employee to enjoy equal benefits and privileges in the same manner that they are enjoyed by other similarly situated employees without disabilities.[890] Employers are also prohibited from denying job opportunities to an applicant or employees when based on an applicant or employee's need for a reasonable accommodation.[891]

2. *Defenses*

a. *Direct Threat*

Employers can deny employment to a disabled person who poses a direct threat to the health and safety of the disabled person or others.[892] The direct threat must pose a "significant

---

[888] Or. Rev. Stat. §659A.106.
[889] *Id.* §§659A.118, .121.
[890] Or. Admin. R. §839-006-0205(11), Or. Rev. Stat. §659A.118.
[891] Or. Rev. Stat. §659A.112(2)(f).
[892] Or. Admin. R. §839-006-0244.

risk of substantial harm that cannot be eliminated or reduced" by reasonable accommodation.[893]

PENNSYLVANIA

I. State Law

A. Overview

The Pennsylvania Human Relations Act prohibits discrimination in jobs and benefits against individuals with disabilities.[894]

B. Prohibited Discrimination

In Pennsylvania, employers are prohibited from discriminating against handicapped or disabled persons with non-job-related handicaps or disabilities (or against persons who "use a guide or support animal because of . . . blindness, deafness or physical handicap") in hiring, recruiting, termination, compensation, tenure, or otherwise discriminating against such persons in "conditions or privilege of employment," unless based on a bona fide occupational qualification.[895] In addition, an employer cannot limit, segregate, or classify handicapped or disabled persons in a manner "that adversely affects their [employment] opportunities."[896]

Employers are also prohibited from discriminating against disabled or handicapped persons in recordkeeping, advertising employment positions, recruiting, job applications, or based on "a prior handicap or disability," or retaliating against persons who engage in protected activity.[897]

Employers also must refrain from eliciting or disseminating information about an employee's handicap or disability

---

[893]*Id.*
[894]Pa. Stat. Ann. tit. 43, §§951 et seq.
[895]*Id.* §955(a).
[896]16 Pa. Code §44.5(a).
[897]Pa. Stat. Ann. tit. 43, §955(b)(1), (2), (4)–(5).

and must keep information about employee medical records, histories, or conditions confidential and can only disclose such information to certain essential supervisors, safety personnel, and the government."[898]

In addition, employers must not discriminate against an applicant or employee "because of present handicap or disability which is not job-related, but which may [deteriorate] and become job-related or because of a past job-related handicap or disability" that could potentially recur, unless it imposes "an undue hardship on the employer."[899] Employers are not permitted to make preemployment inquiries about an applicant's disability status, but they can inquire about a person's ability to perform job duties.[900]

1. *Medical Conditions*

The State Employees' AIDS Policy establishes an acquired immune deficiency syndrome (AIDS) policy in the workplace that prevents state employers from discriminating against state employees with AIDS or human immunodeficiency virus (HIV) infection or requiring individuals to be tested for AIDS or HIV as a condition of employment.[901] Moreover, because of the episodic nature of the secondary illnesses that afflict persons with AIDS or HIV, affected state employees may request reasonable accommodations that will allow them to continue to work with their handicap.[902] Otherwise, Pennsylvania has no statute that specifically prohibits private employers from requiring employees or applicants to submit to HIV/AIDS tests; however, the Pennsylvania Human Relations Act, as stated above, prohibits employers from inquiring into whether an individual has a disability or handicap prior to an offer of employment. The

---

[898] 16 PA. CODE §44.12.

[899] *Id.* §44.15. *See* Pennsylvania State Police v. Pennsylvania Human Relations Comm'n, 72 Pa. Commw. 520, 457 A.2d 584, 36 FEP Cases 602 (1983) (determination that applicant's disability was not job-related was consistent with Pennsylvania law, where employer failed to show that applicant posed demonstrable or serious threat of harm to applicant or that employer would suffer undue hardship if applicant were employed).

[900] PA. STAT. ANN. tit. 43, §955(b)(1); *see also* 16 PA. CODE §44.11(d).

[901] 4 PA. CODE §7.432(b).

[902] *Id.* §7.432(c).

Pennsylvania Human Relations Act specifies that an employer may inquire as to an individual's ability to perform the essential functions of the position. Thus, unless an employer can establish that an HIV/AIDS test is related directly to an employee's ability to perform the essential functions of the position, an employer should refrain from requiring such tests.[903]

C. Definitions

1. Disability

A person is handicapped or disabled if he or she has "1. a physical or mental impairment which substantially limits one or more . . . major life activities; 2. a record of . . . such an impairment; or 3. [is] regarded as having such an impairment . . . ."[904] An impairment can be actual or perceived by others.[905] A " 'non-job related handicap or disability' means any handicap or disability which does not substantially interfere with the ability [of an applicant or employee] to perform essential" job functions.[906] "Uninsurability or increased cost of insurance under a group . . . plan does not render a handicap or disability job related."[907]

"[C]urrent, illegal use of or addiction to a controlled substance" is not included as a disability.[908]

2. Major Life Activities

"[C]aring for one's self, performing manual tasks, walking, seeing, hearing, speaking, breathing, learning and working" are examples of major life activities.[909]

---

[903] PA. STAT. ANN. tit. 43, §955.
[904] Id. §954(p.1).
[905] Id. §954(p.1).
[906] Id. §954(p). See Murphy v. Cartex Corp., 377 Pa. Super. 181, 546 A.2d 1217, 1220, 52 FEP Cases 1267 (1988) (epilepsy considered job-related handicap or disability because it posed demonstrable threat to health and safety of others); Philadelphia Elec. Co. v. Pennsylvania Human Relations Comm'n, 68 Pa. Commw. 212, 448 A.2d 701, 36 FEP Cases 593 (1982) (morbid obesity alone is not handicap or disability).
[907] PA. STAT. ANN. tit. 43, §954(p).
[908] Id.
[909] 16 PA. CODE §44.4(ii)(B).

D. Covered Employers

The Pennsylvania Human Relations Act applies to employers having four or more employees, and to "the Commonwealth [of Pennsylvania and] any political subdivision or board, department, commission or school district . . . within the Commonwealth."[910] "Religious, fraternal, charitable or sectarian corporations" that receive government appropriations and employ "four or more [employees] within the Commonwealth" are subject to the Pennsylvania Human Relations Act.[911]

E. Reasonable Accommodation and Defenses

1. *Reasonable Accommodations*

Employers are required to make reasonable accommodations for handicapped or disabled persons by making existing facilities accessible by eliminating "architectural and other barriers or omissions that interfere with [the] use . . . enjoyment . . . , ingress to, egress from" the building, and mobility within the building, unless the modification would pose an undue hardship on the employer or if the employer is otherwise exempt.[912] Employers also must make reasonable accommodations by modifying a job's requirements and equipment provided that the accommodations do not pose an undue hardship on the employer.[913]

2. *Defenses*

a. *Undue Hardship*

Employers should consider the following factors in determining whether an accommodation imposes an undue hardship: "(i) The overall size and nature of [the employer's] business, . . . including [the] number of employees, structure and composition of [the] workforce, and [the] number and type of facilities . . . ."[914] (ii) [Prior g]ood faith efforts . . . made to

---

[910] PA. STAT. ANN. tit 43, §954(b).
[911] *Id.*
[912] 16 PA. CODE §44.6(d).
[913] *Id.* §44.13–.14.
[914] *Id.* §44.4(Undue Hardship).

accommodate similar handicaps or disabilities. (iii) The extent, nature and cost of the . . . accommodation . . . ." However, the "financial ability to make reasonable accommodations [can] only be a factor when [it is] raised as part of an undue hardship defense."[915]

RHODE ISLAND

I. STATE LAW

A. Overview

Under Rhode Island's Fair Employment Practices Act, an employer is prohibited from discriminating against a worker with a disability.[916] The Rhode Island Handicapped Discrimination Law further prohibits bias against disabled people in hiring, compensation, promotion, leave, fringe benefits, or "[a]ny other term, condition, or privilege of employment."[917] State agencies are prohibited from discriminating against qualified individuals with disabilities under the State Employees' Handicapped Bias Rules.[918]

B. Prohibited Discrimination

In Rhode Island, it is unlawful for an employer to refuse to hire, discharge, or otherwise discriminate against an individual in hiring, "tenure, compensation, terms, conditions, or privileges of employment or any other matter directly or indirectly related to employment."[919] Rhode Island's civil rights statute gives workers additional protections against discrimination.[920]

---

[915] *Id.* §44.4(Undue Hardship)(i).
[916] R.I. GEN. LAWS §28-5-5.
[917] *Id.* §42-87-3(2)(i), (ii), (v), (vi), (x).
[918] R.I. ADMIN. CODE 3.092.
[919] R.I. GEN. LAWS §28-5-7(1)(i)–(ii).
[920] *Id.* §42-112-1. *See* Wyss v. General Dynamics Corp., 24 F. Supp. 2d 202 (D.R.I. 1998) (civil rights statute protects workers against any discrimination that interferes with benefits, terms, and conditions of employment relationship).

Employers also are prohibited from using any type of employment or placement agency in recruiting or hiring that discriminates against people with disabilities.[921] Employers are prohibited from discriminating against people who have tested positive for the human immunodeficiency virus (HIV), and employers cannot require an applicant or employee to take an HIV test "as a condition of employment."[922] Rhode Island also prohibits anyone from aiding, abetting, inciting, compelling, or coercing another to commit unlawful discrimination.[923]

1. Genetic Testing

Genetic testing by employers for abnormalities or deficiencies that are linked to physical or mental disorders or impairments is prohibited.[924] A court may award punitive damages, actual damages, and reasonable attorneys' fees to an applicant or employee in a civil action alleging a violation of this law.[925] Rhode Island in 2002 added to its genetic nondiscrimination statute a provision barring discrimination against persons who refuse to submit to genetic testing, reveal genetic information, submit a family history, or reveal whether they have submitted to genetic testing. The legislation also outlaws the revelation of "genetic information about employees, licensees, or applicants," as well as the use of such information to otherwise adversely affect the employment, licensure, or application for employment or licensure of any individual.[926]

C. Definitions

1. Disability

A "disability" is any "physical or mental impairment that substantially limits one or more major life activities," a record of such impairment, or being "regarded as having such an

---

[921] R.I. GEN. LAWS §28-5-7(iii).
[922] Id. §23-6-22.
[923] Id. §28-5-7(6).
[924] Id. §28-6.7-1.
[925] Id. §28-6.7-3.
[926] Id.

impairment."[927] Physiological disorders or conditions, "cosmetic disfigurements, or anatomical loss affecting one or more of the following body systems: neurological; musculoskeletal; special sense organs; respiratory, including speech organs; cardiovascular; reproductive; digestive; genito-urinary; hemic and lymphatic; skin; and endocrine; or any mental or psychological disorder such as mental retardation, emotional or mental illness, and specific learning disabilities" are examples of physical or mental impairments.[928] "Caring for one's self, performing manual tasks, walking, seeing, hearing, speaking, breathing, learning, and working" are examples of major life activities.[929] An individual who "can perform the essential functions of the job," with or without reasonable accommodation, is an otherwise qualified disabled person.[930]

D. Covered Employers

Rhode Island's antidiscrimination in employment laws apply to "the state and all political subdivisions of the state" and to all labor organizations, employment agencies, and any person who employs four or more persons, and any person acting for the employer.[931]

E. Reasonable Accommodation and Defenses

Employers are required to provide a reasonable accommodation to employees or applicants, unless the accommodation imposes an undue "hardship on the employer's program, enterprise, or business."[932]

---

[927] *Id.* §42-87-1(7).
[928] *Id.* §42-87-1(8). *See* Tadie v. Rehabilitation Hosp., 6 F. Supp. 2d 125, (D.R.I. 1998) (employee's heart condition that prevented her from performing essential functions of job not qualifying disability for bringing claim under civil rights law).
[929] R.I. GEN. LAWS §42-87-1(5).
[930] *Id.* §42-87-1(6).
[931] *Id.* §28-5-6(7), (8), (11).
[932] *Id.* §28-5-7(1)(iv). *See* Moran v. State Comm'n for Human Rights, 121 R.I. 978, 404 A.2d 857 (1979) (employer justified in terminating employee from job that required heavy lifting because employee's physical examination showed preexisting back injuries and job posed serious risk of aggravating injury).

SOUTH CAROLINA

I. State Law

A. Overview

South Carolina's public policy promotes the employment of "the blind, visually handicapped, and the otherwise physically disabled" persons in employment "supported in whole or in part by public funds . . . ."[933] In addition, the South Carolina Human Affairs Law prohibits bias against disabled persons based on a qualified individual's physical or mental disability.[934] The South Carolina Human Affairs Law specifically excludes from coverage anyone whose disability poses a direct threat "to the health or safety of" other workers when the disability "cannot be eliminated by reasonable accommodation"[935] and anyone who engages in illegal drug use.[936]

B. Prohibited Discrimination

Employers are prohibited from failing or refusing to hire, bar, discharge from employment, or otherwise discriminating against an individual in "compensation or terms, [training,] tests, conditions, or privileges of employment, [or] to limit, segregate, [adversely] classify, . . . or otherwise adversely affect" an individual's employment status based on disability.[937] Employers must not "exclude or otherwise deny equal job [opportunities] or benefits to a qualified individual because" of his or her association or relationship with someone who is known to be disabled.[938] Employers are also prohibited from denying

---

[933] S.C. Code Ann. §43-33-60.
[934] Id. §1-13-30(S).
[935] Id. §1-13-30(P).
[936] Id. §1-13-30(Q).
[937] Id. §1-13-80(A).
[938] Id. §1-13-80(D)(1).

employment opportunities to an otherwise qualified job applicant or employee based on the employer's need to reasonably accommodate their "known physical or mental limitations...."[939]

1. Preemployment Inquiries

Employers are prohibited from conducting medical examinations or making "inquiries of a job applicant [about] whether the applicant is" disabled or about the "nature or severity" of any disability.[940]

a. Medical Examinations

Employers can, however, make preemployment inquiries about an applicant's ability "to perform job-related functions."[941] Employers may also "require a medical examination after an offer of employment has been made to an applicant," but prior to "the commencement of the employment... and may condition an offer of employment on the results of the examination, if" the employer's reasons are nondiscriminatory and comply with statutory requirements.[942] Finally, any medical examination or inquiries must "be job related and consistent with business necessity."[943]

C. Definitions

1. Disability

A person's disability is only a direct threat "to the health or safety of the" disabled employee, or others, if it poses a significant risk "that cannot be eliminated by reasonable accommodation."[944] A "disability" is "a physical or mental impairment that substantially limits one or more of the major life activities, ... a record of [such] an impairment, or ... being

---
[939] *Id.* §1-13-80(D)(2).
[940] *Id.* §1-13-85(B).
[941] *Id.*
[942] *Id.* §1-13-85(C).
[943] *Id.* §1-13-85(E).
[944] *Id.* §1-13-30(P).

regarded as having [such] an impairment."[945] A person who "can perform the essential functions of" a job, with or without reasonable accommodation, is a "[q]ualified individual with a disability."[946] An "employer's judgment [regarding] what [job functions] are essential," and written job descriptions prepared before advertising or interviewing job applicants, are evidence of essential job functions.[947]

D. Covered Employers

The South Carolina Human Affairs Law applies to state agencies, departments, and local subdivisions; private employers "of fifteen or more [workers] for each working day in each of twenty or more calendar weeks in the current or preceding" year, and their agents; and all public officers, agencies, and boards and are subject to South Carolina's employment discrimination prohibitions.[948] The law also applies to employment agencies, labor organizations, or joint labor-management committees.[949]

E. Reasonable Accommodation and Defenses

1. Reasonable Accommodation

In South Carolina, employers are required to "make reasonable accommodations to the known physical or mental limitations of an otherwise qualified disabled ... applicant or employee, unless the [employer] can demonstrate that the accommodation would impose an undue hardship" on its business operations,[950] and employers are prohibited from using unrelated job qualification "standards, employment tests, or

---

[945] Id. §1-13-30(N).
[946] Id. §1-13-30(S).
[947] Id.
[948] Id. §1-13-30(d)–(f), (h).
[949] Id. §1-13-30(M).
[950] Id. §1-13-80(D).

other selection criteria that [may] screen out" qualified disabled individuals.[951] Employers can provide reasonable accommodations by "(1) making existing facilities . . . accessible" to persons with disabilities; "(2) job restructuring, . . . reassignment to a vacant position," "part-time or modified work schedule," "acquisition or modification of equipment or devices, . . . examinations, training materials or policies"; and (4) providing "qualified readers or interpreters . . . ."[952]

SOUTH DAKOTA

I. STATE LAW

A. Overview

The South Dakota Human Relations Act prohibits employment discrimination on the basis of disability.[953] The Genetic Information Bias in Employment Law prohibits employers from seeking, obtaining, or using any "genetic information" . . . to discriminate against employees or prospective employees . . . ."[954] and the Discrimination in Public Employment Law prohibits bias against state employees based on physical disability, unless the physical requirements of the job constitute a bona fide occupational qualification.[955]

B. Prohibited Discrimination

Employers are prohibited from failing or refusing to hire, discharge, give adverse or unequal treatment in hiring, applying for a position, "training, apprenticeship, tenure, promotion, upgrading, compensating, layoff, or any term or condition of employment" because a person has a disability.[956] Employers

---
[951] *Id.* §1-13-80(D)(3).
[952] *Id.* §1-13-30(T).
[953] S.D. CODIFIED LAWS §20-13-10.
[954] *Id.* §60-2-20.
[955] *Id.* §3-6A-15.
[956] *Id.* §20-13-10.

are also prohibited from discriminating against disabled persons by directly or indirectly advertising, indicating, or publicizing that disabled individuals" are unwelcome, objectionable, not acceptable, or not solicited for employment . . . ."⁹⁵⁷

1. Genetic Testing

The state law that prohibits employers from obtaining the genetic information of employees and applicants or using it to discriminate against them provides exceptions for criminal investigations conducted by law enforcement agencies, in which case an employer may use the test results to take "disciplinary action against" an employee.⁹⁵⁸

C. Definitions

1. Disability

A "disability" is defined as "a physical or mental impairment . . . resulting from disease, injury, congenital condition . . . , or functional disorder which substantially limits one or more . . . major life functions [and] is unrelated to an individual's ability to perform the major duties of a . . . job or position or is unrelated to the [person's] qualifications for employment or promotion."⁹⁵⁹ A record of having such an impairment or being regarded as having such an impairment is also included in the definition of disability.⁹⁶⁰

D. Covered Employers

South Dakota's prohibitions against discrimination in employment apply to "any person within the State," including the state and all its political subdivisions and agencies, employment agencies, and labor organizations, who hire or employ any worker, and any person (wherever situated) "who hires or

---

⁹⁵⁷ *Id.* §20-13-13.
⁹⁵⁸ *Id.* §60-2-20.
⁹⁵⁹ *Id.* §20-13-1(4)(a).
⁹⁶⁰ *Id.*

employs any [workers] whose services are to be partially or wholly performed in . . . South Dakota."[961]

E. Reasonable Accommodation and Defenses

1. Reasonable Accommodation

Employers in South Dakota can administer, and act "upon the results of any professionally developed ability test [if the administration of the test or action thereafter] is not designed, intended or used to discriminate" on the basis of disability.[962]

"[E]mployment practices and policies, except for insurance, [must] be applied to pregnancy and childbirth on the same terms and conditions as . . . temporary disabilities."[963]

TENNESSEE

I. STATE LAW

A. Overview

The Tennessee Handicap Discrimination Law prohibits bias based on a person's physical, mental, or visual disability.[964] The law also provides that the state of Tennessee will encourage and support the employment of disabled persons in public service.[965]

B. Prohibited Discrimination

Employers cannot discriminate against any applicant based solely on any physical, mental, or visual handicap, "unless [the] handicap, to some degree, prevents the applicant from performing required" job duties or impairs performance.[966] In addition, an employer cannot discriminate against a blind person based on the person's use of a guide dog.[967]

---

[961] *Id.* §20-13-1(7).
[962] §20-13-15.
[963] S.D. ADMIN. R. 20:03:09:12.
[964] TENN. CODE ANN. §8-50-103(a).
[965] *Id.* §8-50-104.
[966] *Id.* §8-50-103(a).
[967] *Id.*

"[C]urrent, illegal use of, or addiction to, a controlled substance" is specifically excepted from the definition of handicap under Tennessee law.[968] Moreover, employees or job applicants who refuse "to submit to a drug or alcohol test" may be terminated or disciplined.[969]

1. Retaliation

It is a prohibited discriminatory practice for any person or legal entity to retaliate against persons who file complaints, to "[a]id, abet, incite, compel or command" others to engage in discriminatory acts, or to willfully obstruct the law's enforcement.[970]

C. Definitions

1. Disability

A "handicap" is "(i) [a] physical or mental impairment which substantially limits one (1) or more . . . major life activities; (ii) [a] record of having such an impairment; or (iii) [b]eing regarded as having such an impairment."[971]

D. Covered Employers

In Tennessee, private employers of "eight (8) or more persons within the state, or any person acting as an [employer's] agent," and the state and its political subdivisions are subject to its antidiscrimination laws.[972] The law also applies to employment agencies[973] and labor organizations.[974] Labor-management committees that control apprenticeship and

---

[968] Id. §4-21-102(9)(B).
[969] Id. §50-9-108(f).
[970] Id. §4-21-301.
[971] Id. §4-21-102(9)(A); See Forbes v. Wilson County Emergency, 966 S.W.2d 421 (Tenn. 1998) (cancer qualifies as handicap).
[972] Tenn. Code Ann. §4-21-102(4). See Burnett v. Tyco Corp., 932 F. Supp. 1039 (W.D. Tenn. 1996) (employee or supervisor is not agent of employer and thus is not individually liable for violations of Tennessee's Human Rights Act); see also Carr v. United Parcel Serv., 955 S.W.2d 832, 83 FEP Cases 341 (Tenn. 1997).
[973] Tenn. Code Ann. §4-21-403.
[974] Id. §4-21-402.

other on-the-job training programs are also subject to the state's antidiscrimination laws.[975]

E. Reasonable Accommodation and Defenses

The Tennessee statutes do not specify a requirement of reasonable accommodation with respect to individuals who are handicapped within the meaning of state law. While the Tennessee Code bars discrimination in hiring by public and private employers in the state, and provides means of redress through complaints filed with the state's human rights commission, it does not define the notion of reasonable accommodation with specificity. (The statute does specify that no blind person shall be discriminated against in employment because that individual uses a guide dog.)[976] At the same time, the statute limits employment decisions based solely upon an applicant's handicaps, unless that condition "to some degree" prevents the individual from performing the job duties or "impairs the performance of the work involved."[977]

TEXAS

I. STATE LAW

A. Overview

Texas's Employment Discrimination Law prohibits job bias based on disability.[978] Discrimination on the basis of physical or mental disability by private and public employers is also prohibited under the Texas Disability Discrimination Law.[979] The Texas Disability Discrimination Law provides that violations are misdemeanors punishable by a $30–$1,000 fine and

---

[975] *Id.* §4-21-404.
[976] *Id.* §8-50-103.
[977] *Id.*
[978] TEX. LAB. CODE ANN. §21.002(4), (6).
[979] 40 TEX. ADMIN. CODE §121.001.

that a person whose civil rights are violated may bring an action for damages of at least $100.[980]

B. Prohibited Discrimination

An employer is prohibited from failing or refusing to hire, discharge, limit, segregate, adversely classify or affect, or otherwise discriminate against a person in "compensation on the terms, conditions or privileges of employment" based on disability.[981] However, disability discrimination must be based on a physical or mental condition that does not impair a person's ability to reasonably perform a job.[982] Employers cannot publish a notice or advertise any preferences, limitations, specifications, or discrimination based on disability,[983] unless based on a bona fide occupational qualification.[984]

The Texas Communicable Disease Law prohibits, with some exceptions, testing for the human immunodeficiency virus (HIV) in connection with employment, unless testing negative for HIV is a bona fide occupational qualification.[985] However, the Texas Employment Discrimination Law specifically excludes from the definition of "disability" a person with a communicable disease, including acquired immune deficiency syndrome (AIDS) or HIV, "that constitutes a direct threat to the health or safety of [that person or other persons] or that makes the affected person unable to perform" his or her job duties.[986]

1. Genetic Testing

Employers are prohibited from discriminating on the basis of genetic or family health information or on an individual's refusal to submit to genetic testing.[987]

---

[980] *Id.* §121.004.
[981] Tex. Lab. Code Ann. §21.051.
[982] *Id.* §21.105.
[983] *Id.* §21.059(a).
[984] *Id.* §21.059(b).
[985] Tex. Health & Safety Code Ann. §§81.101, .102.
[986] Tex. Lab. Code Ann. §21.002(6)(B).
[987] *Id.* §21.401.

C. Definitions

1. Disability

A "disability" or "handicap" is "a mental or physical impairment that substantially limits at least one major life activity . . . , a record of such [an] impairment, or being regarded as having such an impairment."[988] Current addiction to alcohol, or illegal or federally controlled drugs or substances are not disabilities.[989] As noted above, communicable diseases or infections, including HIV or AIDS are not disabilities if they pose "a direct threat to the health or safety of others," or prevent an employee from performing job duties.[990]

The following are examples of impairments recognized in Texas: (1) physiological disorders or conditions, cosmetic disfigurement, or anatomical loss affecting major body systems; (2) mental or physical disorders, such as mental retardation, organic brain syndrome, emotional or mental illness and specific learning disabilities; and (3) certain diseases or conditions, including, but not limited to hearing impairments, heart disease, diabetes, autism, cerebral palsy, cancer, and HIV (as long as it does not pose a direct threat to the health and safety of others and does not impair the individual's ability to perform the job).[991]

D. Covered Employers

The Texas Employment Discrimination Law applies to employers with 15 or more employees, to any agent of that employer, to state agencies (including educational institutions), and to people "elected to public office in [the] state or a political subdivision of [the] state."[992] The law also applies

---

[988] 40 TEX. ADMIN. CODE §321.1(14).
[989] Id. §321.1(14)(A).
[990] Id. §321.1(14)(B).
[991] Id. §7819.151(18).
[992] Id. §21.002(8).

to employment agencies,[993] labor organizations,[994] and labor-management committees that control apprenticeship training programs.[995]

E. Reasonable Accommodation and Defenses

1. Reasonable Accommodation

It is unlawful for employers "to fail or refuse to make a reasonable workplace accommodation to a known physical or mental limitation of an otherwise qualified [employee] or applicant . . . , unless the . . . accommodation would impose an undue hardship on the" employer's business operation.[996] The "reasonableness of the cost of any necessary workplace accommodation and the availability of alternatives" should be considered.[997]

A qualification "that is reasonably related to the satisfactory performance of" job duties and that there "is a factual basis for believing that no persons of the excluded group would be able to perform satisfactorily" job duties, safely, and efficiently, is a bona fide occupational qualification.[998]

2. Defenses

a. Business Necessity

Employers may engage in a practice that has discriminatory effects if the practice "is not intentionally devised or operated to contravene" the discrimination prohibitions "and is justified by business necessity."[999] However, employers may not use this defense "against a complaint of intentional discrimination."[1000]

---

[993] Id. §21.002(9).
[994] Id. §§21.002(10), .053.
[995] Id. §21.054.
[996] Id. §21.128(a).
[997] Id. §21.128(b).
[998] 40 TEX. ADMIN. CODE §321.1(4).
[999] TEX. LAB. CODE ANN. §21.115.
[1000] Id. §21.123.

UTAH

I. State Law

A. Overview

Utah's Antidiscrimination Act prohibits discrimination in employment on the basis of disability.[1001] A new law, the Genetic Testing Privacy Act, prohibits employers from using private genetic information for hiring and promotion purposes, and places restrictions on health insurers' use of genetic information, with limited exceptions.[1002]

B. Prohibited Discrimination

Employers are prohibited from refusing "to hire, promote, discharge, demote, or terminate any person, or to retaliate against, harass, or discriminate in matters of compensation or in terms, privileges, and conditions of employment against any" otherwise qualified person because of disability.[1003]

Utah's policy promotes employment of the "blind, visually impaired, and otherwise physically disabled [individuals in] employment supported in whole or in part by public funds on the same terms and conditions as able-bodied persons, unless . . . the particular disability prevents performance of the work involved."[1004] Employers are prohibited from printing or circulating any statement, or advertising, or using any application, or making any inquiry that expresses "any limitation, specification, or discrimination on the basis of" disability, unless it is based on a bona fide occupational qualification.[1005]

1. Preemployment Inquiries

Employers may ask applicants about their "ability to perform job-related functions as long as the questions are not

---

[1001] UTAH CODE ANN. §34A-5-101.
[1002] Id. §§26-45-103–104.
[1003] Id. §34A-5-106(1)(a)(i)(H).
[1004] Id. §26-30-3.
[1005] Id. §34A-5-106(1)(d)(i)(H).

phrased in terms of a disability."[1006] Employers can also ask job applicants "to describe or demonstrate, with or without reasonable accommodation, [their] ability to perform job-related functions."[1007] Employers are not, however, permitted to ask "whether an applicant is disabled or about the nature or severity of a disability."[1008] Employers similarly are not permitted to require that "an applicant take a medical examination prior to [making] an offer of employment."[1009]

2. Genetic Testing

The state of Utah in 2002 addressed the issue of genetic discrimination with comprehensive legislation that includes prohibitions with respect to employers making hiring, "promotion, retention, or related decisions."[1010] Employers may not access or consider private genetic information, request or require consent to the release of such information, "request or require an individual or his [or her] blood relative to submit to a genetic test," or inquire into or consider "the fact that an individual or his [or her] blood relative has taken or [has] refused to take" such a test.[1011] An employer may, however, seek an "order compelling the disclosure of private genetic information [if] the employer has a reasonable basis to believe that the individual's health condition poses a real and unjustifiable safety risk requiring the change or denial of an assignment."[1012] A private right of action is available for violations after June 2003.[1013] Insurers and employers may be liable in an amount equal to "actual damages sustained as a result of the violation; [an additional] $100,000 if the violation is" intentional and willful, and for "punitive damages if the violation is the result of a malicious act," as well as "reasonable attorneys'

[1006] UTAH ADMIN. CODE §R606-2-2(F)1.a.
[1007] *Id.* §606-2-2(F)1.b.
[1008] *Id.* §606-2-2(F)2.a.
[1009] *Id.* §606-2-2(F)2.b.
[1010] UTAH CODE ANN. §26-45-103(1).
[1011] *Id.*
[1012] *Id.* §26-45-103(2)(a)(ii).
[1013] *Id.* §26-45-105.

fees."[1014] The state attorney general also may bring civil actions that carry fines of up to $25,000 per violation.[1015]

C. Definitions

1. Disability

A "disability" is a physical or mental impairment that substantially limits one or more major life activities.[1016] A "bona fide occupational qualification" is a characteristic that is necessary to an employer's operation or "is the essence of the" business.[1017] An otherwise qualified applicant must possess the "education; training; ability with or without reasonable accommodation; moral character; integrity; disposition to work; adherence to reasonable rules and regulations; and other job related" criteria required by an employer for a "particular job, job classification, or position."[1018]

The following conditions are not disabilities in Utah: transvestitism, transsexualism, pedophilia, exhibitionism, voyeurism, gender identity disorders not resulting from physical impairments, compulsive gambling, kleptomania, pyromania, and psychoactive substance abuse disorders resulting from current illegal use of drugs.[1019]

2. Major Life Activities

"[C]aring for one's self, performing manual tasks, walking, seeing, hearing, speaking, breathing, learning, and" working are examples of major life activities.[1020]

D. Covered Employers

The Utah Antidiscrimination Act applies to employers of 15 or more employees, including the state and its political

---

[1014] *Id.* §26-45-105(2).
[1015] *Id.* §26-45-106.
[1016] *Id.* §34A-5-102(5).
[1017] *Id.* §34A-5-102(2).
[1018] *Id.* §34A-5-106(1)(a)(ii).
[1019] UTAH ADMIN. CODE §R280-201-1(D).
[1020] *Id.* R277-606-E.3.

subdivisions, but does not include religious organizations or associations.[1021] The law also applies to labor organizations, employment agencies, and joint apprenticeship committees, and vocational schools that control apprenticeship programs.[1022]

E. Reasonable Accommodation and Defenses

1. *Reasonable Accommodation*

The Utah Administrative Code provides that an employer must make reasonable accommodations for known physical or mental limitations of otherwise qualified disabled applicants or employees unless the employer can demonstrate that the accommodation would impose an undue hardship.[1023] What accommodations would qualify as reasonable depends upon the circumstances of the individual's disability.[1024] Examples of reasonable accommodations may include making the work facility accessible to and useable by disabled individuals as well as restructuring jobs, modifying work schedules, and acquiring or modifying work equipment or devices.[1025]

To determine whether an accommodation would qualify as an undue hardship, relevant factors include "the overall size of the employer's program with respect to number of employees, number and type of facilities, and size of budget; the type of the employer's operation, including the composition and structure of the employer's work force; and the nature and cost of the accommodation needed."[1026] However, an employer may not deny employment or advancement within the company to a qualified individual with a disability if the basis for the denial is the need to make reasonable accommodation to the physical or mental limitations of the individual.[1027]

[1021] UTAH CODE ANN. §34A-5-102(8)(a)(i)–(ii), (iv), (8)(h).
[1022] *Id.* §34A-5-106(9)–(11).
[1023] UTAH ADMIN. CODE R606-1-2(I)(1).
[1024] *See id.* R606-1-2(I)(5).
[1025] *See id.* R606-1-2(I)(1).
[1026] *See id.* R606-1-2(I)(3).
[1027] *See id.* R606-1-2(I)(4).

VERMONT

I. State Law

A. Overview

The Vermont Fair Employment Practices Act prohibits discrimination in employment against a "qualified individual with a disability."[1028] Vermont's Genetic Testing in Employment law prohibits employers from discriminating against employees who have undergone genetic testing, from requiring genetic testing, and from using genetic test results or genetic information as a condition of employment, or to affect the terms of employment.[1029]

B. Prohibited Discrimination

Employers are prohibited from discriminating against a qualified individual with a disability "except where a bona fide occupational qualification requires persons of a particular ... physical or mental condition."[1030]

Employers are also prohibited from printing, publishing or circulating "any notice or advertisement relating to employment [that indicates a] preference, limitation, specification or discrimination based" on disability.[1031] In addition, employers cannot discharge or discriminate, in any manner, against an employee who has engaged in protected activity, such as filing a complaint of discrimination.[1032]

Employers may not discriminate against persons who have tested positive for the human immunodeficiency virus (HIV), or require applicants to have an HIV test as a condition of employment.[1033]

[1028] Vt. Stat. Ann. tit. 21, §495(a)(1).
[1029] Vt. Stat. Ann. tit. 18, §9333.
[1030] Vt. Stat. Ann. tit. 21, §495(a)(1).
[1031] *Id.* §495(a)(2).
[1032] *Id.* §495(a)(5).
[1033] *Id.* §495(a)(6)–(7).

1. Genetic Testing

Employers are prohibited from requiring genetic testing or using genetic test results, and are also prohibited from disclosing any genetic test results or genetic information.[1034]

C. Definitions

1. Disability

A "disability" is "(A) a physical or mental impairment which limits one or more major life activities, (B) a history or record of such an impairment, or (C) being regarded as having such an impairment."[1035] Physical and mental impairments include

> (A) any physiological disorder or condition, cosmetic disfigurement, anatomical loss affecting one or more ... major body systems: neurological; musculoskeletal; special sense organs; respiratory, including speech organs; cardiovascular; reproductive; digestive; genito-urinary; hemic and lymphatic; skin; or endocrine;
> (B) any mental disorders, such as mental retardation, organic brain syndrome, emotional or mental illness, and specific learning disabilities; [and]
> (C) ... such diseases and conditions as orthopedic, visual, speech and hearing impairments, cerebral palsy, epilepsy, muscular dystrophy, multiple sclerosis, cancer, heart disease, diabetes, mental retardation, and drug addiction and alcoholism.[1036]

A person "who is an alcoholic or drug abuser[, however, is not a handicapped individual] who, by reason of current alcohol

---

[1034] VT. STAT. ANN. tit. 18, §9333.

[1035] VT. STAT. ANN. tit. 9, §4501(2). *See* Lowell v. International Bus. Machs. Corp., 955 F. Supp. 300, 6 AD Cases 1269 (D. Vt. 1997) (generally, plaintiff's condition must foreclose type of employment at issue for employee to show that his or her ability to work is substantially limited).

[1036] VT. STAT. ANN. tit. 9, §4501(3). *See* Potvin v. Champlain Cable Corp., 165 Vt. 504, 687 A.2d 95, 6 AD Cases 1493 (1996) (ulcerative colitis that lasted at least 5 months and was result of long-term illness that required three separate surgeries was impairment); Hodgdon v. Mt. Mansfield Co., 160 Vt. 150, 624 A.2d 1122, 2 AD Cases 499 (1992) (lack of upper teeth is physical impairment, because it is cosmetic disfigurement and anatomical loss affecting musculoskeletal and digestive systems).

or drug use, [poses] a direct threat to the property or safety of others."[1037]

A person who can perform the essential functions of a job with reasonable accommodation to the disability, is a qualified individual with a disability.[1038] However, persons who are alcoholics or drug abusers whose current use of drugs or alcohol prevents them from performing job duties, or whose employment poses a direct threat to the property or safety of others is not a qualified person with a disability.[1039]

D. Covered Employers

Any employer who has one or more persons performing services for it within the state, any agent of that employer, employment agencies, and labor organizations are subject to Vermont's antidiscrimination laws.[1040]

E. Reasonable Accommodation and Defenses

1. *Reasonable Accommodation*

Reasonable accommodations are the changes and modifications that can be made in the structure of a job, or in the manner a job is performed, unless it imposes an undue hardship on the employer.[1041]

2. *Defenses*

a. Undue Burden

An "undue burden" is a "significant difficulty or expense [when considering] (A) The nature and cost of the action

---

[1037] VT. STAT. ANN. tit. 9, §4501(3).

[1038] VT. STAT. ANN. tit. 21, §495d(6)(A).

[1039] *Id.* §495d(6)(B). *See* Decker v. Vermont Educ. Television, 13 F. Supp. 2d 569 (D. Vt. 1998) (relevant time for assessing whether employee is capable of performing essential job functions is when employee requests accommodation).

[1040] VT. STAT. ANN. tit. 21, §495d(1). *See* Fernot v. Crafts Inn, Inc., 895 F. Supp. 668 (D. Vt. 1995) (definition of employer does not contain requirement that to be employer person must have power to terminate employees).

[1041] VT. STAT. ANN. tit. 21, §495d(12). *See* Brace v. International Bus. Machs. Corp., 953 F. Supp. 561 (D. Vt. 1997) (reasonable accommodations for employee

needed. (B) The overall financial resources of the ... sites involved ... ; the number of persons employed at the site; ... legitimate safety requirements necessary for safe operation.... (C) The geographic separateness and the administrative or fiscal relationship of the site ... to any parent corporation or entity."[1042]

VIRGINIA

I. STATE LAW

A. Overview

It is the policy of the Commonwealth of Virginia to safeguard all persons in Virginia from unlawful employment discrimination on the basis of disability under the Virginia Human Rights Act[1043] and to encourage and enable persons with disabilities to engage in remunerative employment through the Virginians With Disabilities Act.[1044] The Genetic Testing and Genetic Characteristics Bias in Employment Law prohibits employers from using genetic information to affect an employee's job.[1045]

B. Prohibited Discrimination

All employers are prohibited from discriminating "in employment or promotion practices against an otherwise qualified" disabled person solely on the basis of disability.[1046] Moreover, employers are required to "make reasonable accommodation to the known physical and mental impairments of an otherwise qualified person with a disability, if necessary to assist" the person perform a particular job, unless

---

disabilities do not include obligation to transfer employee solely to allow him or her to work for another supervisor).
[1042] VT. STAT. ANN. tit. 9, §4501(10)(A)-(C).
[1043] VA. CODE ANN. §2.2-3900.
[1044] *Id.* §51.5-1.
[1045] *Id.* §40.1-28.7:1.A.
[1046] *Id.* §51.5-41(A).

the accommodation imposes a demonstrated "undue burden on the employer."[1047]

Employers are not, however, prohibited "from refusing to hire or promote, from disciplining, transferring, or discharging or taking any other personnel action pertaining to an applicant or employee who, because of [a] disability, is unable to adequately perform [job] duties, or cannot perform such duties in a manner which would not endanger" health and safety.[1048]

The Virginia Human Rights Act makes any violation of a federal statute or regulation governing discrimination on the basis of disability a violation of Virginia law as well.[1049]

1. Genetic Testing

Under the Genetic Testing and Genetic Characteristics Bias in Employment Law, no employer can "[r]equest, require, solicit or administer a genetic test . . . to any person as a condition of employment" or use any genetic testing results obtained by any means to adversely affect an employee's terms or conditions of employment.[1050]

C. Definitions

1. Disability

"[A]ny person who has a physical or mental impairment that substantially limits one or more . . . major life activities or has a record of such impairment and that [is] unrelated to the [person's] ability to perform [particular job duties], or is unrelated to the individual's qualifications for employment or promotion," is a person with a disability.[1051] An "otherwise qualified person with a disability" is "a person with a disability

---

[1047] *Id.* §51.5-41(C). *See* Yates v. Volunteer Health Care Sys., 783 F. Supp. 1002 (W.D. Va. 1992).

[1048] Va. Code Ann. §51.5-41(D).

[1049] *Id.* §2.2-3901. *See* Grimes v. Canadian Am. Transp. Inc., 72 F. Supp. 2d 629, 81 FEP Cases 428 (W.D. Va. 1999).

[1050] Va. Code Ann. §40.1-28.7:1.A.

[1051] *Id.* §51.5-3.

who . . . is qualified to perform the duties of a particular job or position."[1052]

A "mental impairment" is

> (i) a disability attributable to mental retardation, autism, or any other neurologically handicapping condition closely related to mental retardation and requiring treatment similar to that required by mentally retarded individuals; or
>
> (ii) an organic or mental impairment that has substantial adverse effects on an individual's cognitive or volitional functions, including central nervous system disorders or significant discrepancies among mental functions of an individual.[1053]

Active alcoholism or current drug addiction are not, however, mental impairments.[1054]

"[A]ny physical condition, anatomic loss, or cosmetic disfigurement that is caused by bodily injury, birth defect, or illness" is a physical impairment.[1055]

D. Covered Employers

The Virginia Human Rights Act prohibits bias in employment without specifying any minimum number of employees.[1056] However, special provisions are given for state court actions by employees discriminatorily discharged by employers with more than 5 but fewer than 15 employees.[1057]

E. Reasonable Accommodation and Defenses

1. Reasonable Accommodation

Employers are required to make "reasonable accommodation to the known physical and mental impairments of an

---

[1052] *Id.*
[1053] *Id.*
[1054] *Id.*
[1055] *Id.*
[1056] *Id.* §2.1-715.
[1057] *Id.* §2.1-725.

otherwise qualified person with a disability, . . . unless the employer can demonstrate that the accommodation would impose an undue burden . . . ."[1058]

2. Defenses

a. Direct Threat

An employer is not required to hire a person with a disability who is a threat to the health or safety of that person or others.[1059]

b. Undue Hardship

Employers should consider the

> a. [h]ardship on the conduct of the employer's business, considering the nature of the employer's operation, including composition and structure of the . . . work force; b. [s]ize of the facility . . . ; c. . . . nature and cost of the" accommodation, possibility that other employees can use the accommodation, and other health and safety considerations when making this determination.[1060]

In Virginia, any accommodation that exceeds $500 in cost is "rebuttably presumed to impose an undue burden upon any employer with fewer than [50] employees."[1061] In addition, employers have "the right to choose among equally effective accommodations."[1062]

WASHINGTON

I. State Law

A. Overview

Washington's Law Against Discrimination in Employment protects persons with "any sensory, mental, or physical disability

---

[1058] *Id.* §51.5-41(C).
[1059] *Id.* §51.5-46(B).
[1060] *Id.* §51.5-41(C)(1).
[1061] *Id.* §51.5-41(C)(2).
[1062] *Id.* §51.5-41(C)(3).

or the use of a trained dog guide or service animal by a disabled person," from discrimination in employment.[1063] In addition, certain unlawful employment practices with respect to the human immunodeficiency virus (HIV) infection are specifically prohibited.[1064]

B. Prohibited Discrimination

Employers are prohibited from refusing "to hire any person because of . . . the presence of any sensory, mental, or physical disability or the use of trained dog guide or service animal by a disabled person, unless based upon a bona fide occupational qualification."[1065] The prohibition against discrimination because of disability does not apply, however, if the particular disability prevents the worker from properly performing the job.[1066]

It is also unlawful for employers to discriminate against disabled persons in discharge, compensation, or other terms or conditions of employment, or to print or circulate any statement or publication, or to make an inquiry prior to employment, that "expresses any limitation, specification, or discrimination" based on disability (unless based on a bona fide occupational qualification).[1067]

1. Preemployment Inquiries

a. Medical Examinations

Employers may not "require an individual to take an HIV test . . . or hepatitis C test, as a condition of hiring, promotion, or continued employment unless the absence of HIV or hepatitis C infection is a bona fide occupational qualification," which exists when performing a job presents a significant risk of transmitting HIV, and there is no means of eliminating the risk through job restructuring.[1068] In addition, employers may

---

[1063] WASH. REV. CODE. §49.60.010.
[1064] Id. §49.60.172.
[1065] Id. §49.60.180(1).
[1066] Id.
[1067] Id. §49.60.180(2), (3), (4).
[1068] Id. §49.60.172(1), (3).

not "discharge or fail or refuse to hire, . . . segregate, or classify . . . or otherwise discriminate against any individual [in] compensation, terms, conditions, or privileges of employment on the basis of the results of an HIV test or hepatitis C test," unless based on a bona fide occupational qualification.[1069]

C. Definitions

1. Disability

Washington's antidiscrimination statute does not define handicap or disability.[1070] A dog guide "is trained for the purpose of guiding blind persons or . . . assisting hearing impaired persons."[1071] A service animal is trained to assist or accommodate "a disabled person's sensory, mental, or physical disability."[1072]

D. Covered Employers

Washington's Law Against Discrimination in Employment applies to employers of eight or more employees, including the state and its political subdivisions, cities, counties, public schools, public colleges, public universities, and other governmental instrumentalities.[1073] The law also applies to labor unions[1074] and employment agencies.[1075]

[1069] *Id.* §49.60.172(2). "Employers are immune from civil action for damages arising out of transmission of HIV or hepatitis C to employees or to members of the public unless [the] transmission occurs as a result of" gross negligence by the employer. *Id.* §49.60.172(5).

[1070] *See* Kimbro v. Atlantic Richfield Co., 889 F.2d 869, 1 AD Cases 1537 (9th Cir. 1989) (cluster migraine headache condition is handicap); Hume v. American Disposal Co., 124 Wash.2d 656, 880 P.2d 988, 3 AD Cases 1208 (1994); Doe v. Boeing Co., 121 Wash.2d 8, 846 P.2d 531, 2 AD Cases 548 (1993) (gender dysphoria is not handicap); Reese v. Sears, Roebuck & Co., 107 Wash.2d 563, 731 P.2d 497, 1 AD Cases 1012 (1987) (chronic bronchitis is handicap).

[1071] WASH. REV. CODE. §49.60.040(22).

[1072] *Id.* §49.60.040(23).

[1073] *Id.* §49.60.040(1), (3). *See* Brown v. Scott Paper Worldwide Co., 98 Wash. App. 349, 989 P.2d 1187, 81 FEP Cases 1267 (1999) (eight-employee threshold does not provide protection from lawsuits to managers and other individual employees who act in interest of employer, either directly or indirectly); Thompson v. Berta Enters., Inc., 72 Wash. App. 531, 864 P.2d 983, 68 FEP Cases 1643 (1994) (supervisor who had apparent authority to make employment decisions, including determining hours and schedules of employees, was employer).

[1074] *Id.* §49.60.190.

[1075] *Id.* §49.60.200.

E. Reasonable Accommodation and Defenses

1. Reasonable Accommodation

Employers may have a duty to provide reasonable accommodations to disabled workers if the employer is made aware of an employee's disability and need for an accommodation.[1076]

WEST VIRGINIA

I. State Law

A. Overview

The West Virginia Human Rights Act prohibits job bias against blind or otherwise disabled individuals.[1077]

B. Prohibited Discrimination

Employers are prohibited, except where based on a bona fide occupational qualification, from discriminating against a person in compensation, hiring, hiring, "tenure, terms, conditions or privileges of employment if the [person] is able and competent to perform the" required services.[1078]

Employers may not "print or publish ... any notice or advertisement relating to employment ... indicating any preference, limitations, specifications" that discriminate based on disability or blindness.[1079]

[1076] *See* Maxwell v. State, 91 Wash. App. 171, 956 P.2d 1110 (1998). *See also* Staub v. Boeing Co., 919 F. Supp. 366, 8 AD Cases 323 (W.D. Wash. 1996) (Washington antidiscrimination law does not require employers to fire other employees in order to promote disabled workers to jobs for which they are not qualified, or to create new jobs); Snyder v. Medical Serv. Corp., 98 Wash. App. 315, 988 P.2d 1023, 16 IER Cases 1337 (1999) (employer not required to accommodate employee's request for new supervisor even though employee's supervisor was rude and overbearing and employee sustained emotional injuries as result); Curtis v. Security Bank of Wash., 69 Wash. App. 12, 847 P.2d 507, 2 AD Cases 573 (1993) (bank discriminated against employee handicapped by arthritic hip condition when her position was being eliminated by offering her teller position that she could not perform, rather than train her for position she could perform).

[1077] W. Va. Code §5-11-9(1).

[1078] *Id.* §5-11-9(1).

[1079] *Id.* §5-11-9(2)(B).

C. Definitions

1. Disability

"A mental or physical impairment which substantially limits one or more . . . major life activities . . .; [a] record of such impairment; or [b]eing regarded as having such an impairment," is a disability.[1080] "[C]urrent use of or addiction to alcohol or drugs [that] prevents [an individual] from performing job duties or who poses a "threat to [the] property or safety of others," however, is not a disability.[1081] "[C]aring for one's self, performing manual tasks, walking, seeing, hearing, speaking, breathing, learning and working" are major life activities.[1082]

A person who is able and competent, with reasonable accommodation, to perform essential job functions is a qualified handicapped person.[1083]

D. Covered Employers

The state, any political subdivisions of the state, and employers of 12 or more workers within West Virginia "for [20] or more calendar weeks in the calendar year in which the [alleged] act of discrimination [occurred], or the preceding calendar year" in which an alleged act of discrimination occurred, are covered by West Virginia's antidiscrimination laws.[1084]

[1080] *Id.* §5-11-3(m).

[1081] *Id. See also* Anderson v. Live Plants, Inc., 187 W. Va. 365, 419 S.E. 2d 305, 6 AD Cases 1045 (1992) (impairment of severely deformed hand and arm are handicaps); Benajmin R. v. Orkin Exterminating Co., 182 W.Va. 615, 390 S.E. 2d 814, 2 AD Cases 389 (1990) (person at any state of human immunodeficiency virus HIV infection is a person with a handicap).

[1082] W. VA. CODE §5-11-3(m)(1).

[1083] *Id.* §5-11-1 et seq.

[1084] *Id.* §5-11-3(d). Under the West Virginia Human Rights Act, an individual person (including supervisors) and other employees can be held liable for discrimination. *See* St. Peter v. AMPAK-Div. of Gatewood Prods., Inc., 199 W. Va. 365, 484 S.E.2d 481, 7 AD Cases 1709 (1997); Holstein v. Norandex, Inc., 194 W. Va. 727, 461 S.E. 2d 473 (1995).

E. Reasonable Accommodation and Defenses

1. Reasonable Accommodation

Employers must provide reasonable accommodations for qualified handicapped persons such as job modifications including reassignment, transfer, or a part-time work schedule.[1085]

WISCONSIN

I. STATE LAW

A. Overview

Wisconsin's Fair Employment Act prohibits job discrimination against properly qualified disabled individuals.[1086]

B. Prohibited Discrimination

"[N]o employer . . . may engage in any act of employment discrimination . . . against any individual on the basis of . . . disability . . . ."[1087] These acts include refusing "to hire, employ, admit or license, to bar or terminate . . . , or to discriminate . . . in promotion, compensation or [other] terms, conditions or privileges of employment . . . ."[1088]

"Employment discrimination . . . includes . . . [c]ontributing a lesser amount to [an employee's] fringe benefits, including life or disability insurance coverage . . . because of [an] employee's disability."[1089] Employers are also prohibited from discharging or otherwise discriminating against any individual who engages in protected activity.[1090]

[1085] *See* Hurst v. St. Mary's Hosp., 867 F. Supp. 435 (S.D. W. Va. 1994); Skaggs v. Elk Run Coal Co., 198 W. Va. 51, 479 S.E. 2d 561, 6 AD Cases 965 (1996).
[1086] WIS. STAT. §111.31.
[1087] *Id.* §111.321.
[1088] *Id.* §111.322(1).
[1089] *Id.* §111.34(1), (1)(a).
[1090] *Id.* §111.322(2m), (3).

It is not unlawful, "because of disability to refuse to hire, employ, admit or license . . . , to bar or terminate . . . , or to discriminate . . . in promotion, compensation or in terms, conditions or privileges of employment if the disability is reasonably related to the individual's ability to adequately undertake the job-related responsibilities of that [person's] employment . . . ."[1091]

1. Genetic Testing

Wisconsin's Fair Employment Act also prohibits employers, labor organizations, employment agencies, and licensing agencies from soliciting, requiring, or administering "a genetic test . . . as a condition of employment."[1092] An employee, however, can give consent to taking a genetic test for the purpose of determining exposure to potentially toxic substances in the workplace.[1093]

C. Definitions

1. Disability

A person who "[h]as a physical or mental impairment which makes achievement unusually difficult or limits the capacity to work; . . . [h]as a record of such an impairment; or . . . [i]s perceived as having such impairment" is an "individual with a disability."[1094] Determining if a disabled individual "can adequately undertake . . . job-related responsibilities" must be made on a case-by-case basis.[1095] In making this determination, employers should evaluate "the present and future safety of the [disabled] individual, of the individual's coworkers, and [even] the general public," if applicable.[1096]

[1091] *Id.* §111.34(2)(a).
[1092] *Id.* §111.372(1), (1)(a).
[1093] *Id.* §111.372(4), (4)(b).
[1094] *Id.* §111.32(8).
[1095] *Id.* §111.34(2)(b).
[1096] *Id.*

D. Covered Employers

Any person employing at least one worker is considered an "employer" and is subject to the Wisconsin Fair Employment Act's antidiscrimination provisions.[1097] The Wisconsin Fair Employment Act applies to employers, employment agencies, labor unions, and licensing agencies.[1098] Organizations that hold contracts with the state of Wisconsin are covered by provisions of the Discrimination by State Contractors Law.[1099]

E. Reasonable Accommodation and Defenses

1. Defenses

a. Undue Hardship

Employers cannot refuse "to reasonably accommodate an employee's or prospective employee's disability unless the employer can demonstrate that the accommodation [poses] a hardship on the employer's program, enterprise or business."[1100]

WYOMING

I. State Law

A. Overview

The Wyoming Fair Employment Practices Act of 1965 prohibits discrimination against employees or prospective employees with disabilities as long as they are able to perform their job duties with a reasonable accommodation by the employer.[1101]

[1097] *Id.* §111.32(6)(a).
[1098] *Id.* §111.32(6), (7), (9), (11).
[1099] *Id.* §111.32(6)(a).
[1100] *Id.* §111.34(1)(b).
[1101] Wyo. Stat. Ann. §§27-9-101, -105.

B. Prohibited Discrimination

Employers are prohibited from refusing "to hire, to discharge, to promote or demote, or to discriminate in . . . compensation on the terms, conditions or privileges of employment against" an otherwise qualified handicapped person.[1102]

C. Definitions

1. Disability

A handicapped person is "a disabled person who is capable of performing a particular job, or who would be capable of performing a particular job with reasonable accommodation" to the handicap.[1103]

D. Covered Employers

Any person employing two or more workers within the state of Wyoming, and all of its political subdivisions, boards, commissions, departments, institutions, and school districts are subject to Wyoming's Fair Employment Practices Act.[1104] The law does not apply to "religious organizations or associations."[1105]

E. Reasonable Accommodation and Defenses

1. Defenses

In order to avoid liability under the Wyoming Fair Employment Practices provisions against bias based on liability, employers must be able to demonstrate that a reasonable accommodation to the known physical or mental limitations of otherwise qualified employees would impose an undue hardship on the operation of their business.[1106]

[1102] *Id.* §27-9-105(a)(i).
[1103] *Id.* §27-9-105(d).
[1104] *Id.* §27-9-102(b).
[1105] *Id.*
[1106] WYOMING RULES OF PRACTICE, DISABILITY DISCRIMINATION RULES, Ch. V, §§1–3, Wyoming Department of Employment, Labor Standards Office, effective Nov. 30, 2001.

Chapter 5

DISABILITIES PROTECTED BY THE AMERICANS WITH DISABILITIES ACT

I. The Rehabilitation Act Definition 483
II. Americans With Disabilities Act Statutory and Regulatory Framework 488
   A. What Is an Impairment? 489
   B. Major Life Activities 493
      1. "Working" as a Major Life Activity 495
   C. Substantial Limitation 496
      1. Nature and Severity of the Impairment 496
      2. Substantially Limited In Working 500
      3. Temporary v. Permanent Impairment 504
      4. The Effect of Mitigating Measures 506
   D. Record of Impairment 510
   E. Regarded as Disabled 512
      1. Regarded as Substantially Limited in the Ability to Work 513
   F. Drug and Alcohol Use 517
III. "Qualified" Individual With a Disability 520
   A. Otherwise Qualified 520
   B. What Is an Essential Job Function? 521
      1. Written Job Description 523
      2. Government Standards 524
      3. Percentage of Time Devoted to Job Function 526
      4. Consequences of Not Performing Job Function 526
      5. Other Factors 527
   C. Performance of Essential Functions With or Without a Reasonable Accommodation 527

IV. Interaction of Other Statutes' Provisions Regarding Disability With Those of the Americans With Disabilities Act	529
V. Common Illnesses and Conditions Examined Under the American With Disabilities Act	532
A. Substance Abuse	534
1. Current Drug Use	536
2. Alcohol Use	539
3. Being "Regarded as" or Having a Record of Substance Abuse–Related Disability	540
4. Employer Rights With Respect to Employee Substance Abuse	543
a. Last-Chance Agreements	544
b. Off-Duty Conduct	544
c. Discrimination/Pretext	545
5. Medical Inquiries and Examinations Regarding Drug and Alcohol Use	546
a. Drug Testing	547
6. Employer Defenses	548
a. Job-Related and Consistent With Business Necessity	548
b. Direct Threat	550
7. Compliance With Other Substance Abuse Laws and Regulations	551
8. Reasonable Accommodation	552
B. AIDS/HIV	554
1. Qualified Individual With A Disability	559
a. Not Qualified Because of Risk	561
b. Ability to Make Inquiries or Mandate Tests	562
c. Association	564
d. Reasonable Accommodation	565
e. Insurance	566
f. Privacy	568
C. Mental Disorders	570
1. Substantially Limit Major Life Activity	571
2. Mitigating or Corrective Measures	574
3. Substantially Limited in the Ability to Work	575

    4. Qualified Individual 576
    5. Perceived as Being Disabled 578
    6. Benefits Distinguishing Between Physical
       and Mental Disabilities 580
    7. Reasonable Accommodation 581
  D. Diabetes 583
  E. Hypertension 590
  F. Heart Disease 592
  G. Cancer 593
  H. Epilepsy 595
VI. Conclusion 606

Under the Americans with Disabilities Act of 1990 (ADA),[1] the definition of protected "disabilities" has been a subject critical to coverage and statutory protection. Indeed, following the ADA's enactment, questions regarding the scope of the statute's definition of protected "disabilities" and "qualified individuals with disabilities" were among the most frequently litigated aspects of this legislation. Although regulations, policy guidance, and a number of key court cases have helped refine what it is to be both disabled and a qualified individual with a disability under the ADA, the parameters of these definitions are far from clear. In order to understand the current state of the law and how it has evolved, a look at the definition of "disability" under the ADA's precursor, the Rehabilitation Act of 1973,[2] is warranted.

I. The Rehabilitation Act Definition

The definition of the term "disability" in the ADA is drawn almost verbatim from the definition of "handicap" that evolved under the Rehabilitation Act[3] as well as the Fair Housing Act

---

[1] 42 U.S.C. §12101 et seq.
[2] 29 U.S.C. §701 et seq.
[3] Three major sections of the Rehabilitation Act define its scope: (1) section 501, 29 U.S.C. §791, applies to all agencies and departments of the federal government; (2) section 503, 29 U.S.C. §793, extends to government contractors, including those who have contracts that exceed $2,500 with federal departments or agencies;

Amendments of 1988.[4] The Rehabilitation Act, first passed in 1973, provided vocational rehabilitation to certain individuals whose handicaps adversely affected their employment prospects. When certain terms of the statute were amended in 1974, the protected class encompassed those who fell within the statutory phrase "person with a handicap." This phrase was defined in Title V of the Rehabilitation Act as including any person who: "(i) has a physical or mental impairment which substantially limits one or more major life activities; (ii) has a record of such an impairment, or (iii) is regarded as having such an impairment."[5] This definition originated with Congress' desire to address discrimination stemming from simple prejudice as well as from "the fact that the American people are simply unfamiliar with and insensitive to the difficulties confront[ing] individuals with handicaps."[6] The revised definition was developed to deal with erroneous but prevalent perceptions about the handicapped, and to prevent discrimination against individuals who have a record of, or are regarded as, having an impairment, but do not currently suffer from an actual incapacity.[7]

Under the Rehabilitation Act, the Department of Health, Education and Welfare (HEW) was responsible for coordinating the implementation and enforcement of section 504 of the Rehabilitation Act,[8] which prohibits federal agencies and entities receiving federal assistance from discriminating against

---

and (3) section 504, 29 U.S.C. §794, covers other recipients of federal funds, in addition to all federal agencies. Each provision requires covered entities to refrain from discrimination in employment on the basis of handicap (now disability), and further imposes affirmative action obligations on federal agencies and contractors.

[4] 42 U.S.C. §3602(h)(1).

[5] 29 U.S.C. §706 (7)(B). This formulation replaced an earlier definition that focused solely on employability, and the potential for such handicapped persons to benefit from vocational rehabilitation programs.

[6] S. Rep. No. 93-1297, at 50 (1974).

[7] Southeastern Cmty. Coll. v. Davis, 442 U.S. 397, 405–06 n.6, 2 AD Cases 1 (1979).

[8] *See* Exec. Order No. 11,194, 3 C.F.R. 117 (1976–1980 Comp.) (subsequently revoked by Exec. Order 12250, 45 Fed. Reg. 72995 (1980); *see also* Consolidated Rail Corp. v. Darrone, 465 U.S. 624, 1 AD Cases 567 (1984).

qualified individuals with disabilities.[9] HEW also drafted the first regulations interpreting the Rehabilitation Act. The Supreme Court has noted that because these regulations were drafted with the oversight and approval of Congress, they provide important guidance in interpreting the Rehabilitation Act's definitions.[10] That agency defined covered "physical or mental impairments" as meaning:

> (A) any physiological disorder or condition, cosmetic disfigurement, or anatomical loss affecting one or more of the following body systems: neurological; musculoskeletal; special sense organs; respiratory, including speech organs; cardiovascular; reproductive, digestive, genito-urinary; hemic and lymphatic; skin; and endocrine; or
> (B) any mental or psychological disorder, such as mental retardation, organic brain syndrome, emotional or mental illness, and specific learning disabilities.[11]

Concerned that any attempt to delineate covered physical or mental disorders that constitute physical or mental impairments would not be comprehensive, HEW did not include such a description in the regulations. It did, however, publish accompanying commentary that contained a representative list of disorders and conditions, including "such diseases and conditions as orthopedic, visual, speech, and hearing impairments, cerebral palsy, epilepsy, muscular dystrophy, multiple sclerosis, cancer, heart disease, diabetes, mental retardation, emotional illness, and . . . drug addiction and alcoholism.[12] Thus, rather than providing a definitive enumeration of those conditions and limitations that would trigger the statute's definition of disability, the regulations developed a representative list, which was illustrative and not exhaustive.[13] The agency also made clear that "a physical or mental impairment does not constitute a handicap for purposes of Section 504 unless its severity is

---

[9] 29 U.S.C. §794d.
[10] Alexander v. Choate, 469 U.S. 287, 304 n.24 (1985); *Darrone*, 465 U.S. at 634–35 & nn.14–16.
[11] *See* 42 Fed. Reg. 22,685 (1977) (codified at 45 C.F.R. §84.3(j)(2)(i) (2003)).
[12] 45 C.F.R. pt. 84, app. A 3 (2003) (commentary).
[13] *See* Bragdon v. Abbott, 524 U.S. 624, 8 AD Cases 239 (1998).

such that it results in a substantial limitation of one or more major life activities."[14]

With respect to individuals covered because they have a record of impairment, the regulations promulgated by HEW describe such persons as those who have a history of a physiological or mental disorder that substantially limited him or her at one time, but no longer, and individuals who are misclassified as having that type of impairment.[15] Concerning the "regarded as" prong of the Rehabilitation Act's definition, the HEW regulations described coverage applying to: (1) individuals who have a physical or mental impairment that does *not* substantially limit a major life activity, but are treated by a covered entity as experiencing such a limitation; (2) individuals who have a substantially limiting physical or mental impairment solely because of the attitudes of others toward that impairment; and (3) individuals with no such impairment who are treated as having a substantially limiting physical or mental impairment.[16] The Rehabilitation Act's legislative history uses a visibly physically impaired individual to illustrate that although an individual is not substantially limited in function, he or she may be substantially limited in working because others react negatively to the impairment.[17] As the Supreme Court observed, "Congress was as concerned about the effect of an impairment on others as it was about its effect on the individual."[18]

On November 2, 1980, President Jimmy Carter transferred HEW's responsibilities under the Rehabilitation Act to the attorney general.[19] The implementing regulations promulgated by the Department of Justice adopted without change certain of the key definitions initially developed by HEW, including the critical definition of covered "physical impairment," as well as

---

[14] 45 C.F.R. pt. 84, app. A 3 (2003) (commentary).
[15] 45 C.F.R. §84.3(j)(2)(iii) (2003).
[16] S. REP. No. 93-1297, at 64 (1974).
[17] 45 C.F.R. §84.3(j)(2)(iv) (2003).
[18] School Bd. of Nassau County v. Arline, 480 U.S. 273, 282, 1 AD Cases 1026, 1030 (1987).
[19] *See* Exec. Order No. 12,250, 3 C.F.R. 298 (1980).

the representative list of covered conditions developed by that agency.[20]

During the 1980s, several Rehabilitation Act cases focused on whether specific conditions qualified as impairments. Among conditions found to be "physical or mental impairments" were chronic tuberculosis,[21] legal blindness,[22] blindness in one eye,[23] manic depressive syndrome,[24] ankylosing spondylitis (which caused stiffens the joints, and limits the plaintiff's movement of his or her spine, knees, elbows, and wrists),[25] heart condition,[26] nervous and heart conditions,[27] multiple sclerosis,[28] permanent osteoporosis of the knee joints,[29] cerebral palsy, nocturnal epilepsy and dyslexia,[30] right leg amputated below the knee cap,[31] and hypersensitivity to tobacco smoke,[32] among other impairments.

While this representative list of impairments ranges in severity, courts sought to limit the statute's reach to avoid providing a vehicle to those individuals with minor or temporary impairments. As the U.S. Court of Appeals for the Fourth Circuit has stated:

> The Rehabilitation Act assures that truly disabled, but genuinely capable, individuals will not face discrimination in employment because of stereotypes about the insurmountability of their handicaps. It would debase this high purpose if the statutory protections

---

[20] *See* 28 C.F.R. §41.31(b)(1) (2003).

[21] *Arline*, 480 U.S. 273.

[22] Norcross v. Sneed, 755 F.2d 113, 1 AD Cases 689 (8th Cir. 1985).

[23] Holly v. City of Naperville, Ill., 603 F. Supp. 220, 37 FEP Cases 1615 (N.D. Ill. 1985), *aff'd*, 861 F.2d 723, 48 FEP Cases 235 (7th Cir. 1988).

[24] Gardner v. Morris, 752 F.2d 1271, 1 AD Cases 673 (8th Cir. 1985).

[25] Sisson v. Helms, 751 F.2d 991, 1 AD Cases 670 (9th Cir.), *cert. denied*, 474 U.S. 846, 1 AD Cases 830 (1985).

[26] Bento v. I.T.O. Corp. of R.I., 599 F. Supp. 731, 1 AD Cases 653 (D.R.I.1984).

[27] Treadwell v. Alexander, 707 F.2d 473, 1 AD Cases 459 (11th Cir. 1983).

[28] Pushkin v. Regents of the Univ. of Colo., 658 F.2d 1372, 2 AD Cases 11 (10th Cir. 1981).

[29] Guinn v. Bolger, 598 F. Supp. 196, 36 FEP Cases 506 (D.D.C. 1984).

[30] Fitzgerald v. Green Area Educ. Agency, 589 F. Supp. 1130, 1 AD Cases 601 (S.D. Iowa 1984).

[31] Longoria v. Harris, 554 F. Supp. 102, 38 FEP Cases 738 (S.D. Tex. 1982).

[32] Vickers v. Veterans Admin., 549 F. Supp. 85, 1 AD Cases 366 (W.D. Wash. 1982).

available to those truly handicapped could be claimed by anyone whose disability was minor and whose relative severity of impairment was widely shared.[33]

Litigation under the Rehabilitation Act did not definitively determine which impairments and under what circumstances those impairments constitute protected disabilities under the law. Instead, this debate would gain even greater momentum following the enactment of the ADA.

II. AMERICANS WITH DISABILITIES ACT STATUTORY AND REGULATORY FRAMEWORK

At the time of the ADA's enactment, Congress was aware of the various judicial interpretations of early regulatory definitions of such terms as "impairment" and "disability." In drafting the ADA, Congress relied on the rule of statutory construction that a repetition of well-established terms meant their later use should be interpreted in accordance with prior holdings. To emphasize that terms used in the ADA should mirror those established in the Rehabilitation Act, Congress adopted an explicit statutory provision that states that: "[e]xcept as otherwise provided . . . nothing in this chapter shall be construed to apply a lesser standard than the standards applied under title V of the Rehabilitation Act . . . or the regulations issued by Federal agencies pursuant to such title."[34]

The ADA's statutory language reflected the same terminology used in the Rehabilitation Act with respect to covered individual conditions. The ADA states that the term "disability" means:

(A) a physical or mental impairment that substantially limits one or more of the major life activities of such individual;
(B) a record of such an impairment; or
(C) being regarded as having an impairment.[35]

---

[33]Forrisi v. Bowen, 794 F.2d 931, 934, 1 AD Cases 921 (4th Cir. 1986).
[34]42 U.S.C. §12201(a).
[35]42 U.S.C. §12102(2).

The heavy reliance on the Rehabilitation Act's definition and application is also evident in the ADA's legislative history, which makes numerous references to the same descriptions of covered physical or mental impairments as those that appear in the HEW regulations.[36]

Following the ADA's enactment, the Equal Employment Opportunity Commission (EEOC), which was charged with drafting the ADA's Title I regulations, issued regulations interpreting key terms embodied in this statutory definition of disability. Among the terms and phrases the EEOC addressed in regulations published exactly 1 year after the statute's enactment were: "physical or mental impairment," "major life activities," "substantially limits," "has a record of such impairment," and "regarded as having such an impairment."[37] Accompanying the regulatory text were two section-by-section discussions that expanded on the agency's views, its "analysis of comments and revisions" in the Preamble to the regulations,[38] and "Interpretive Guidance," published as an appendix to the agency's regulations.[39] In addition, prior to the initial effective date of Title I of the ADA, the EEOC published its *Technical Assistance Manual for the Americans with Disabilities Act*, which provided the public with further insight into its views on the ADA's proper application and interpretation.

A. What Is an Impairment?

The EEOC adopted the definition of "physical and mental impairments" from the regulations implementing Section 504 of the Rehabilitation Act.[40] In essence, the definition describes an impairment as a physiological disorder or condition that affects one or more body systems.[41] Certain

---

[36] *See, e.g.*, H.R. REP. No. 101-485, pt. II, at 51 (1990), *reprinted in* 1990 U.S.C.C.A.N. 267; S. REP. No. 101-16, at 22 (1989).
[37] 56 Fed. Reg. 35,726 (July 26, 1991).
[38] *Id.* at 35,727.
[39] *Id.* at 35,739.
[40] *See* 34 C.F.R. pt. 104 (2003).
[41] The regulations define the term as:
(1) Any physiological disorder, or condition, cosmetic disfigurement, or ana-

mental or psychological disorders also qualify as impairments.[42] Thus, blindness is a physiological condition that affects the body's ability to see, emphysema is a physiological condition that impact's the ability to breathe, and schizophrenia is a psychological disorder that manifests itself as a mental illness. Therefore, all three of these conditions would be considered impairments under the ADA.

Not all impairments, however, are as easy to identify as the examples above. The relatively open-ended nature of the definition of impairment has been clarified, to some extent, by ruling out conditions that *do not* constitute impairments. For example, Title I regulations distinguish between impairments and physical, psychological, environmental, cultural, and economic characteristics that are not impairments. The EEOC noted, for instance, that physical characteristics such as eye color, hair color, left-handedness, or height, weight, and muscle tone within "normal" range and are not the result of a physiological disorder do not qualify as impairments. Also outside the definition of covered disabilities are predispositions to illness or disease, common personality traits (such as quick temper) that are not symptoms of a mental or psychological disorder, and environmental, cultural, or economic disadvantages.

For example, the EEOC's *Technical Assistance Manual* explains that an individual who cannot read because of dyslexia, a learning disability, is an individual with a disability, because learning disabilities are impairments. A person who cannot read because he or she dropped out of school, however, is not disabled, because laziness or lack of education is not an

---

tomical loss affecting one or more of the following body systems: neurological, musculoskeletal, special sense organs, respiratory (including speech organs), cardiovascular, reproductive, digestive, genito-urinary, hemic and lymphatic, skins, and endocrine; . . . .

56 Fed. Reg. 35,735 (July 26, 1991) (codified at 29 C.F.R. §1630.2(h)(1) (2003)).

[42] (2) Any mental or psychological disorder, such as mental retardation, organic brain syndrome, emotional or mental illness and specific learning disabilities.

Id. 29 C.F.R. §1630.2(h)(2) (2003).

impairment.[43] Similarly, while an inability to work due to general stress encountered on the job is inadequate to establish a statutory disability,[44] a diagnosed stress disorder *is* an impairment that could constitute a disability.

Certain personality traits, unless triggered by an underlying disorder, are not disabilities under the ADA. Temperament, irritability,[45] grief,[46] and poor judgment[47] have all been adjudicated as not rising to the level of "impairment." For example, a police officer who alleged that coworkers viewed him as "disgruntled," "threatening," and "difficult to work with" failed to establish the existence of a mental impairment.[48] The court held that evidence of the officer's conduct and behavior that created personality conflicts with fellow officers did not rise to the level of a mental impairment.

Old age, in and of itself, is not an impairment, although various medical conditions commonly associated with old age (e.g., hearing loss, osteoporosis, and arthritis) may constitute impairments within the meaning of Title I. Nicotine addiction is not a disability, as it does not substantially limit any major life activity.[49] Pregnancy, a temporary condition, is also unprotected under the ADA.[50]

Having autoimmune deficiency syndrome (AIDS) or testing positive for the human immunodeficiency virus (HIV) *does*,

---

[43]A Technical Assistance Manual on the Employment Provisions (Title I) of the Americans With Disabilities Act [hereinafter Title I Technical Assistance Manual] §2.1(a)(i).

[44]Kolpas v. G.D. Searle & Co. 959 F. Supp. 525, 8 AD Cases 1285 (N.D. Ill. 1997). *See also* Mundo v. Sanus Health Plan of Greater N.Y., 966 F. Supp. 171, 8 AD Cases 937 (E.D.N.Y. 1997).

[45]Duda v. Board of Educ. of Franklin Park Pub. Sch. Dist. No. 84, 133 F.3d 1054, 8 AD Cases 99 (7th Cir. 1998).

[46]Johnson v. Boardman Petroleum, Inc., 923 F. Supp. 1563, 5 AD Cases 983 (S.D. Ga. 1996).

[47]Greenberg v. New York State Dep't of Corr. Servs., 919 F. Supp. 637, 5 AD Cases 1851 (E.D.N.Y. 1996).

[48]Watson v. City of Miami Beach, 177 F.3d 932, 9 AD Cases 760 (11th Cir. 1999).

[49]Stevens v. Inland Waters, Inc., 220 Mich. App. 212, 559 N.W.2d 61, 6 AD Cases 490 (1996) (addiction to nicotine was not a disability because it did not substantially limit any major life activity).

[50]29 C.F.R. pt. 1630, app. §1630.2(h) (2003).

however, rise to the level of impairment. In *Bragdon v. Abbott*,[51] the Supreme Court first considered the question of whether HIV infection constituted an impairment under the ADA. Tracing the progress of the disease in infected individuals, the Court concluded that "HIV infection must be regarded as a physiological disorder with a constant and detrimental effect on the infected person's hemic and lymphatic systems from the moment of infection," and thus "satisfies the statutory and regulatory definition of a physical impairment during every stage of the disease."[52]

The Department of Justice's early interpretation of the statute's definition of disability was echoed in the Court's ruling, which noted that the agency added "HIV infection (symptomatic and asymptomatic)" to the disorders constituting a "physical impairment" under the statute.[53] This view was incorporated into the technical assistance published by the department's Civil Rights Division,[54] and the Supreme Court noted that these views were endorsed in the interpretations developed by federal agencies authorized to administer other aspects of the ADA, including the EEOC.[55]

Once it has been established that an individual has an impairment, the next step is to determine what impact, if any, that impairment has on the individual's major life activities.

---

[51] 524 U.S. 624, 8 AD Cases 239 (1998).

[52] *Id.* at 637, 8 AD Cases at 244. The Court noted that its conclusion regarding the coverage of asymptomatic HIV was confirmed by the consistent course of agency interpretations both before and after the enactment of the ADA. The Court took particular note of a 1988 opinion issued by the Office of Legal Counsel of the Department of Justice, which concluded that the Rehabilitation Act " 'protects symptomatic and asymptomatic HIV-infected individuals against discrimination in any covered program.' Application of Section 504 of the Rehabilitation Act to HIV-Infected Individuals", 12 Op. Off. Legal Counsel 264, 264–65 (Sept. 27, 1988) (citing a letter from then Surgeon General C. Everett Koop stating that "from a purely scientific perspective, persons with HIV are clearly impaired . . . ," *id.* at 642, 8 AD Cases 246).

[53] 28 C.F.R. §35.104 (1)(iii) (1997).

[54] THE AMERICANS WITH DISABILITIES ACT TITLE III TECHNICAL ASSISTANCE MANUAL 9.

[55] *See* TITLE I, TECHNICAL ASSISTANCE MANUAL, *supra* note 43, §2.3; 29 C.F.R. pt. 1630, app. §1630.1(a) (2003); AMERICANS WITH DISABILITIES ACT TITLE II

B. Major Life Activities

The EEOC's regulations define the term "major life activities" as functions such as "caring for oneself, performing manual tasks, walking, seeing, hearing, speaking, breathing, learning, and working."[56] The EEOC adopted the definition of "major life activities" from that found in the Rehabilitation Act regulations, which identify major life activities as "those basic activities that the average person in the general population can perform with little or no difficulty."[57] This list is not intended to be exhaustive, and potentially includes other activities, such as "sitting, standing, lifting, reaching."[58] Indeed, at least one appellate court has held that "interacting with others" can qualify as a major life activity under the statute.[59]

Despite the potentially open-ended nature of this list, courts have tended to construe the definition of major life function narrowly. Further, a major life function for one individual will not necessarily be placed on the same footing for another. For example, while reproduction can be considered a major life activity,[60] an individual may need to show that he or she intended to have children, and could have done so, but for the impairment.[61] Thus, an individual who has undergone a

---

Technical Assistance Manual §4; 28 C.F.R. §35.104(1)(iii) (1997); 49 C.F.R. §§37.3 (1997).

[56] 29 C.F.R. §1630.2(h)(i) (2003).

[57] 29 C.F.R. pt. 1630 app. §1630.2(i) (2003).

[58] *Id. See also* Fraser v. Goodale, 342 F.3d 1032, 10 AD Cases 1377 (9th Cir. 2003), *cert. denied*, 541 U.S. 937, 15 AD Cases 608 (2004) (eating recognized as a major life activity), echoing conclusions reached by three other appellate courts. Lawson v. CSX Transp., Inc., 245 F.3d 916, 11 AD Cases 1025 (7th Cir. 2001) (diabetes); Forest City Daly Hous., Inc. v. Town of N. Hempstead, 175 F.3d 144 (2d Cir. 1999) (dicta in case involving assisted living facility); Land v. Baptist Med. Ctr., 164 F.3d 423 (8th Cir. 1999). At the same time, courts often have viewed the term "major life activities" narrowly. In *Popko v. Pennsylvania State University*, 994 F. Supp. 293, 299, 9 AD Cases 131 (M.D. Pa. 1998), *aff'd*, 254 F. 3d 1078 (3d Cir. 2001), the court noted that leisure activities (e.g., playing piano, swimming, playing sports involving arm dexterity) are not major life activities.

[59] Jacques v. DiMarzio, Inc., 386 F.3d 192, 16 AD Cases 1 (2d Cir. 2004).

[60] *See, e.g.*, Bragdon v. Abbott, 524 U.S. 624, 8 AD Cases 239 (1998) (individual who is HIV-positive is substantially limited in the major life activity of reproduction).

[61] *See, e.g.*, Blanks v. Southwestern Bell Communications, Inc., 310 F.3d 398, 13 AD Cases 1253 (5th Cir. 2002) (HIV-positive individual was not substantially

sterilization procedure cannot claim that his or her impairment substantially limits the ability to reproduce. Certain other bodily functions, such as normal kidney function that allows the body to cleanse blood and eliminate waste, also have been judged to be major life activities.[62] On the other hand, chronic pancreatitis may not necessarily establish that an individual is substantially limited in the major life activity of eating.[63]

Additionally, sleeping[64] is a major life activity, but some secondary effects from lack of sleeping—such as poor concentration[65] and stamina[66]—are not. Similarly, awareness, in and of itself, is not considered a major life activity, despite its potential connection to the major life activities of seeing, hearing, and speaking.[67]

Many other common activities do not rise to the level of "major." Driving, for example, is not a major life activity, as many members of the general public do not drive and the activity itself requires a revocable license.[68] Other household activities other than basic chores, such as going shopping in a mall, shoveling snow, mowing the lawn, painting, plastering, and performing mechanical work on cars, and recreational activities such as playing tennis, fishing, skiing, and golfing, also are not considered major life activities.[69]

---

limited in major life activity of reproduction, because he had decided not to have any more children, and his wife had undergone a sterilization procedure).

[62] Fiscus v. Wal-Mart Stores Inc., 385 F.3d 378, 16 AD Cases 10 (3d Cir. 2004).

[63] Waldrip v. General Elec. Co., 325 F.3d 652, 14 AD Cases 301 (5th Cir. 2003).

[64] *See* Boerst v. General Mills Operations, Inc., 25 Fed. Appx. 403, 2002 WL 59637, 2002 U.S. App. LEXIS 813 (6th Cir.), *cert. denied*, 535 U.S. 1097 (2002); Pack v. Kmart Corp., 166 F.3d 1300, 8 AD Cases 1880 (10th Cir.), *cert. denied*, 528 U.S. 811 (1999).

[65] *Id.*

[66] *Boerst*, 2002 WL 59637.

[67] Deas v. River W., L.P., 152 F.3d 471, 8 AD Cases 989 (5th Cir. 1998), *cert. denied*, 527 U.S. 1035, 1044 (1999).

[68] Chenoweth v. Hillsborough County, 250 F.3d 1328, 1329–30, 11 AD Cases 1421, 1422 (11th Cir. 2001) ("We are an automobile society and an automobile economy, so that it is not entirely farfetched to promote driving to a major life activity; but millions of Americans do not drive, millions are passengers to work, and deprivation of being self-driven to work cannot be sensibly compared to inability to see or to learn."), *cert. denied*, 534 U.S. 1131 (2002).

[69] *See* Weber v. Strippit, Inc., 186 F.3d 907, 9 AD Cases 961 (8th Cir. 1999), *cert. denied*, 528 U.S. 1078 (2000); Colwell v. Suffolk County Police Dep't, 158 F.3d 635, 8 AD Cases 1232 (2d Cir. 1998), *cert. denied*, 526 U.S. 1018 (1999).

Additionally, the inability to perform certain functions related to one's job does not render a person disabled under the ADA. For example, lifting in and of itself is not likely a major life activity.[70] Similarly, typing and handwriting are not central to people's lives, and therefore not major life activities.[71]

1. "Working" as a Major Life Activity

The EEOC also declared that the term "major life activities," through which individual impairments and restrictions might be judged, includes "working."[72] The agency stated that the question of limitations in the major life activity of "working" should be considered only if the individual is not limited with respect to any other major life activities. For example, if a blind individual is substantially limited in the major life activity of seeing, then it is the EEOC's position that there is no reason to consider if he or she is also substantially limited in the major life activity of working. In *Sutton v. United Air Lines, Inc.*,[73] the Supreme Court questioned sharply, but did not resolve, whether the EEOC's regulatory definition of "major life activities" correctly included the activity of "working."[74] Nonetheless, a number of federal courts have accepted the EEOC's view that "working" is, indeed, a major life activity under the ADA.

---

[70]Huckans v. U.S. Postal Serv., 1999 U.S. App. LEXIS 30755, *10 (10th Cir. 1999) ("thirty-five pound lifting restriction is not an impairment substantially limiting the major life activity of lifting"); Ray v. Glidden Co., 85 F.3d 227, 5 AD Cases 991 (5th Cir. 1996) (inability to lift or reach may qualify as a disability, but inability to perform discrete task of "heavy lifting" does not render one substantially limited in a major life activity).

[71]Thornton v. McClatchy Newspapers, Inc., 292 F.3d 1045, 13 AD Cases 203 (9th Cir. 2002) (a reporter's inability to type or write for an extended period of time not a disability).

[72]29 C.F.R. §1630.2(h)(2)(i) (2003).

[73]527 U.S. 471, 9 AD Cases 673 (1999).

[74]Justice O'Connor, writing for the majority in *Sutton*, stated:
Because the parties accept that the term "major life activities" includes working, we do not determine the validity of the cited regulations. We note, however, that there may be some conceptual difficulty in defining "major life activities" to include work, for it seems "to argue in a circle to say that if one is excluded, for instance, by reason of [an impairment, from working with others] . . . then that exclusion constitutes an impairment, when the

If an impairment is found to limit a major life activity, the final inquiry under the first prong of the definition of disability is to determine whether that impairment *substantially limits* that major life activity.

C. Substantial Limitation

To be considered disabled for purposes of Title I coverage, the impairment must be "substantially limiting." The EEOC explains in its regulations that this phrase refers to an inability to perform a major life activity that an average person in the general population can perform.[75] Alternatively, a person can be substantially limited for purposes of Title I coverage if he or she is "[s]ignificantly restricted as to the condition, manner or duration under which [he or she] can perform a particular major life activity as compared to the condition, manner, or duration under which the average person in the general population can perform that same major life activity."[76] In addition, the impairment or impact of the impairment must be severe and either permanent or long-term.[77]

1. *Nature and Severity of the Impairment*

The determination of substantial limitation must be made on a case-by-case basis under the ADA. Part of this determination involves comparing the effects of the individual's impairment to those limitations endured by the average person in the general population. By way of illustration, an individual who once could walk at an extraordinary speed but whose impairment limits his or her ability such that he or she now

---

question you're asking is, whether the exclusion itself is by reason of handicap."
Id. at 527 U.S. 471, 492, 119 S. Ct. 2139, 2151 (quoting Tr. of oral argument in *School Bd. of Nassau County v. Arline*, O.T. 1986, No. 85-1277, at 15 (argument of solicitor general)).
[75]29 C.F.R. §1630.2(j)(1)(ii) (2003).
[76]*Id.*
[77]Toyota Motor Mfg., Ky. Inc. v. Williams, 534 U.S. 184, 12 AD Cases 993 (2002).

can only walk at an average speed would not be impaired.[78] Individuals with monocular vision are not likely to be substantially limited in the ability to see, as using only one eye to see does not prevent or severely restrict the ability to see as compared with the way that the average person uses eyesight in daily life.[79] For the same reason, an individual with hearing loss in one ear is not substantially limited in his or her ability to hear.[80] Moreover, although sleep is a major life function, the degree of sleep deprivation caused by an impairment must be considerably greater than that suffered by the general population to be considered substantially limiting.[81]

In essence, an impairment is viewed as substantially limiting only if it imposes a significant restriction on the duration, manner, and condition under which a major life activity is performed. Stated differently, how an impairment affects an individual's activities will determine whether that impairment substantially limits a major life activity. The same condition may have very different impacts on various individuals, and therefore be considered substantially limiting impairments in some people, but not others. For example, one person's obsessive compulsive disorder may cause him or her to take considerably more time in performing such basic tasks as bathing and dressing than it would take the average person, thus substantially limiting his or her ability to care for himself or herself.[82] This same disorder in another individual, however, may not rise

---

[78] 29 C.F.R. pt. 1630, app. §1630.2(j) (2003).

[79] Dyke v. O'Neal Steel, Inc., 14 AD Cases 481, 2003 WL 21000819 (7th Cir. 2003) (individual with one eye is not substantially limited in his ability to see, where his only limitations were the inability to drive at night, hold his head straight when looking to either side, and engage in some recreational activities); EEOC v. United Parcel Serv., Inc., 306 F.3d 794, 13 AD Cases 961 (9th Cir. 2002) (monocular vision did not keep plaintiffs from using eyesight as most people do in their daily lives).

[80] See Clemente v. Executive Airlines, Inc., 213 F.3d 25, 10 AD Cases 996 (1st Cir. 2000) (flight attendant with hearing loss in only one ear was not impaired under the ADA).

[81] See EEOC v. Sara Lee Corp., 237 F.3d 349, 11 AD Cases 595 (4th Cir. 2001) (seizure disorder reduced quality of sleep, but not beyond that suffered by general public).

[82] Humphrey v. Memorial Hosps. Ass'n, 239 F.3d 1128, 11 AD Cases 765 (9th Cir. 2001), cert. denied, 535 U.S. 1011 (2002).

to the level of substantial impairment, if the disorder manifests itself in ways that do not affect the ability to care for oneself.[83] Similarly, in some instances, asthma may substantially limit the major life activity of breathing, while in other individuals, this condition may be completely controlled by medication, and thus not rise to the level of a substantially limiting impairment.[84]

The effects of multiple impairments taken together that act to substantially limit one or more major life activities also constitute an impairment, according to the EEOC.[85] For example, asthma, obesity, and emphysema are conditions that may act in concert to substantially limit an individual's ability to breathe.

To be substantially limited in the ability to perform manual tasks, an individual must have an impairment that prevents or severely restricts the individual from doing activities that are of central importance to most people's daily lives.[86] For example, in *Toyota Motor Manufacturing, Kentucky Inc. v. Williams*,[87] the Supreme Court held that an employee who developed carpal tunnel syndrome needed to prove that she was substantially limited in performing a range of manual tasks, not just those discrete tasks associated with her job. According to the Court, "household chores, bathing, and brushing one's teeth are among the types of manual tasks of central importance to people's daily lives, and should have been part of the assessment of whether respondent was substantially limited in performing manual tasks."[88] Although the employee presented evidence that she could not sweep or dance, and had to drive

---

[83] *See, e.g.*, Steele v. Thiokol Corp., 241 F.3d 1248, 11 AD Cases 859 (10th Cir. 2001) (plaintiff's obsessive compulsive disorder, which interrupted his sleeping, causing him to be fatigued during day, did not adversely impact his overall health in severe or permanent way).

[84] Russell v. Clark County Sch. Dist., 2000 U.S. App. LEXIS 17460 at *3 (9th Cir. 2000) (proof of asthma, in and of itself, is not sufficient to establish disability without proving the "severity or frequency of her asthma attacks or the effect her asthma had generally on her life activities").

[85] 29 C.F.R. pt. 1630, app. §1630.2(j), 2000 U.S. App. LEXIS 174603 (2003).

[86] Toyota Motor Mfg. Ky. Inc. v. Williams, 534 U.S. 184, 198, 12 AD Cases 993 (2002).

[87] 534 U.S. 184, 12 AD Cases 993 (2002).

[88] *Id.* at 201, 12 AD Cases at 1000.

and play with her children in moderation, the Court held that these changes did not amount to severe restrictions in important life tasks that establish a manual-task disability as a matter of law. In the aftermath of the *Toyota* decision, most of the federal appellate courts have applied to other classes of major life activities the standard enunciated by the Supreme Court in that opinion relating to manual tasks.[89]

As in other areas, mental impairments may be sufficiently disabling to trigger statutory coverage. Thus, in *Taylor v. Phoenixville School District*,[90] the Third Circuit—after the Supreme Court's decision in *Sutton* and *Murphy*—remanded a case for trial on the question of whether an employee suffering from bipolar disorder, who was confined to a hospital because she was delusional, increasingly agitated, and psychotic, was substantially limited in major life activities even while medicated with lithium.[91] An employee's claimed post-traumatic stress disorder, however, did not substantially limit his major life activities, despite contentions that he had a history of episodes of fatigue, thoughts of suicide, and overeating to the point of nausea, where he no longer suffered from these impairments.[92]

---

[89] Fenney v. Dakota, Minnesota & R.R. Co., 327 F.3d 707, 14 AD Cases 385 (8th Cir.), *reh'g denied*, 2003 U.S. App. LEXIS 10769 (8th Cir. 2003); Waldrip v. General Elec., 325 F.3d 652, 14 AD Cases 301 (5th Cir. 2003); Mack v. Great Dane Trailers, 308 F.3d 776, 13 AD Cases 1153 (7th Cir. 2002); EEOC v. United Parcel Serv., Inc., 306 F.3d 794, 13 AD Cases 961 (9th Cir. 2002); Mulholland v. Pharmacia & Upjohn, Inc., 2002 U.S. App. LEXIS 24200, 13 AD Cases 1632 (6th Cir. 2002). *But see* Rakity v. Dillon Cos., 302 F.3d 1152, 13 AD Cases 896 (10th Cir. 2002) (assuming that the *Toyota* holding was limited to the major life activity of performing manual tasks).

[90] 184 F.3d 296, 9 AD Cases 1187 (3d Cir. 1999).

[91] *But see* Hoeller v. Eaton Corp., 149 F.3d 621, 8 AD Cases 537 (7th Cir. 1998) (former employee with bipolar disorder failed to establish statutory disability through substantially limiting impairment, where claim made in only cursory fashion). *See also* McGuiness v. University of N.M. Sch. of Med., 170 F.3d 974, 9 AD Cases 297 (10th Cir. 1998), *cert. denied*, 526 U.S. 1051 (1999) (anxiety disorder manifesting itself in certain areas does not establish substantial limitation on working).

[92] Hamilton v. Southwestern Bell Tel. Co., 136 F.3d 1047, 8 AD Cases 1219 (5th Cir. 1998). *See also* Carroll v. Xerox Corp., 294 F.3d 231, 13 AD Cases 396 (1st Cir. 2002) (former sales manager did not show statutory violation because he failed to show that job-related stress qualified as a disability, because evidence was insufficient to establish that condition substantially limited the asserted major life activity of working).

In many instances, however, it will remain a factual dispute if an individual with a claimed history of impairment remains an individual with a disability as of the date of a scheduled critical employment decision.[93]

2. Substantially Limited In Working

A person may be able to work in some capacity and still be deemed substantially limited in the life activity of working.[94] The individual must, however, be "significantly restricted in the ability to perform either a class of jobs or a broad range of jobs in various classes as compared to the average person having comparable training, skills and abilities."[95] "The inability to perform a single, particular job" does not render a person substantially limited in the ability to work.[96]

The following factors should be taken into consideration when determining whether an individual is substantially limited in the ability to work:

- the geographical area in which the person may reasonably expect to find a job;
- the type of "job from which the individual has been disqualified because of" the impairment;
- "the number and types of jobs" using similar training, knowledge, skills, or abilities from which the individual is disqualified within the geographical area; and/or
- "the number and types of other jobs" in the area that do not involve similar training, knowledge, skills, or abilities from which the individual also is disqualified because of the impairment.[97]

For example, an individual with a heart condition may be precluded from jobs that require heavy lifting. However, that

---

[93] *See, e.g.,* Mustafa v. Clark County Sch. Dist., 157 F.3d 1169, 8 AD Cases 1119 (9th Cir. 1998).
[94] TITLE I TECHNICAL ASSISTANCE MANUAL, *supra* note 43, §2.2(a)(iii).
[95] 29 C.F.R. §1630(j)(3)(i) (2003).
[96] *Id.*
[97] 29 C.F.R. §1630(j)(3)(ii) (2003); *see also* TITLE I TECHNICAL ASSISTANCE MANUAL, *supra* note 43, §2.2(a)(iii).

same individual may be perfectly able to perform other types of manual labor that do not involve heavy lifting, or be qualified to perform a number of nonmanual tasks. Thus, that person is not substantially limited in working, as he or she would be limited only in performing a small range of jobs.[98] The inability to lift heavy objects, however, *could* qualify as an impairment that substantially limits an individual's ability to work, if the person is precluded from working in a broad range of physically demanding jobs, the geographic area predominantly consists of manual labor positions, and the individual's education and skill level do not allow him or her to work in nonlabor intensive positions.[99]

An employee who can no longer perform his or her job because of an impairment but continues to work in another occupation is not substantially limited in working, as he or she is capable of performing other jobs.[100] Also, the inability to

---

[98] *See, e.g.*, Brunko v. Mercy Hosp., 260 F.3d 939, 12 AD Cases 256 (8th Cir. 2001) (nurse whose back injury prevented her from meeting the hospital's lifting requirement was limited from working in only a narrow range of nursing jobs, as evidenced by her ability to obtain other nursing positions at other hospitals).

[99] *See, e.g.*, Webner v. Titan Distribution, Inc., 267 F.3d 828, 12 AD Cases 513 (8th Cir. 2001) (assembly line worker's back injury could substantially limit his ability to work, where evidence indicated that he could not work in heavy and very heavy industrial positions); Burns v. Coca-Cola Enters., Inc., 222 F.3d 247, 10 AD Cases 1409 (6th Cir. 2000) (inability to lift heavy objects is impairment that substantially limits employee's ability to work, as restriction precludes him or her from performing 50% of the jobs he or she is qualified to perform in light of limited education and work experience); Wellington v. Lyon County Sch. Dist., 187 F.3d 1150, 9 AD Cases 1177 (9th Cir. 1999) (factual issue whether maintenance worker with limited education and trade school certification was substantially limited by carpal tunnel syndrome).

[100] *See* Sheehan v. City of Gloucester, 321 F.3d 21, 14 AD Cases 1 (1st Cir. 2003) (police lieutenant who worked as part-time security guard following involuntary retirement because of hypertension is capable of performing a range of jobs, and is therefore not substantially limited in working); Gonzalez v. El Dia, Inc., 304 F.3d 63, 13 AD Cases 889 (1st Cir. 2002) (employee unable to perform job because of diabetes and obesity could not prove that she was precluded from performing a broad range of jobs given that she found alternative employment); *Brunko*, 260 F.3d 939 (nurse whose back injury prevented her from meeting hospital's lifting requirement was limited from working in only a narrow range of nursing jobs, as evidenced by her ability to obtain other nursing positions at other hospitals); Berg v. Norand Corp., 169 F.3d 1140, 9 AD Cases 207 (8th Cir), *cert. denied*, 528 U.S. 872 (1999) (department manager whose diabetes limited her working time to no more than 40–50 hours per week is not substantially limited in her ability to work

perform one of many job tasks is not indicative of a substantially limiting impairment,[101] nor is the inability to perform the tasks required by one employer. For example, the EEOC's Interpretive Guidance under the ADA explains that "an individual who cannot be a commercial airline pilot because of a minor vision impairment, but who can be a commercial airline co-pilot or a pilot for a courier service, would not be substantially limited in the major life activity of working."[102]

Moreover, impairments that limit employees' working hours do not substantially limit their ability to work if they could perform other jobs within the limited time frame. For example, an employee whose impairment limits him or her to working no more than 40 hours per week is not likely to be substantially limited in the ability to work, as many jobs can be completed in 40 or fewer hours per week.[103]

An employee who is unable to perform a particular job in one location only cannot establish that he or she is substantially limited in the ability to work. For example, an employee claiming that his or her depression is instigated by a poor working relationship with certain coworkers is not substantially limited in the ability to work, as the stressful conditions are present in one location only.[104] Similarly, personality conflicts are not substantially limiting if the employee is able to work under different supervision or with different coworkers.[105]

Proving that an individual's impairment prevents him or her from working in a class or broad range of jobs is not an onerous burden, but does require more than unsupported

---

in part because she was able to find alternative employment in her field following her discharge).

[101] Marinelli v. City of Erie, Pa., 216 F.3d 354, 10 AD Cases 1157 (3d Cir. 2000) (street crew worker unable to drive snow plows due to arm pain is not substantially limited in his ability to work).

[102] 29 C.F.R. pt. 1630, app. §1630.2(j) (2003).

[103] See Boerst v. General Mills Operations, Inc., 25 Fed. Appx. 403, 2002 WL 59637, 2002 U.S. App. LEXIS 813 (6th Cir.), cert. denied, 535 U.S. 1097 (2002) (limited to no more than 8 hours per day); Kellogg v. Union Pac. R.R., 233 F.3d 1083, 11 AD Cases 385 (8th Cir. 2000) (limited to 40 hours per week); Berg, 169 F.3d 1140 (limited to 40–50 hours per week).

[104] Aldrup v. Caldera, 274 F.3d 282, 12 AD Cases 1044 (5th Cir. 2001).

[105] See Schneiker v. Fortis Ins. Co., 200 F.3d 1055, 10 AD Cases 75 (7th Cir. 2000).

assertions. At the very least, an individual must present evidence of the local job market, including the jobs he or she can no longer perform because of an impairment.[106] Vocational expert testimony is instructive, but not necessary.[107]

Additionally, presenting generic evidence of work restrictions without indicating how these restrictions limit one's ability to work in a particular location in light of one's skills, training, education, and employment experience, will not suffice as proof that the impairment substantially limits the ability to work.[108] If an employee qualifies for a substantial number of jobs he or she was qualified for prior to suffering the impairment, then the impairment does not substantially limit the employee's ability to work.[109] Receiving compensation for a partial disability is also insufficient to prove that an individual is precluded from working in a class or broad range of jobs.[110]

Finally, a workplace accommodation cannot be taken into consideration when determining whether an individual is substantially limited in working.[111] For example, that one employer allows an employee with a back injury to work on a reduced

---

[106] *See, e.g.*, Duncan v. Washington Metro. Area Transit Auth., 240 F.3d 1110, 11 AD Cases 833 (D.C. Cir.) (en banc), *cert. denied*, 534 U.S. 818 (2001) (employee with degenerative disc disease resulting in lifting restriction failed to present evidence of number and types of jobs available in local labor market, and thus could not establish that he could not perform a class or broad range of jobs).

[107] *Id. See also* Mullins v. Crowell, 228 F.3d 1305, 11 AD Cases 38 (11th Cir. 2000) (vocational expert testimony may be persuasive, but not necessary to satisfy evidentiary burden).

[108] *See* Gelabert-Ladenheim v. American Airlines, Inc., 252 F.3d 54, 11 AD Cases 1581 (1st Cir. 2001) (multilevel analysis of whether an impairment substantially limits working requires individual to present evidence of how impairment restricts one's ability to work in job market).

[109] Mahon v. Crowell, 295 F.3d 585, 13 AD Cases 390 (6th Cir. 2002) (injured steamfitter who presented evidence that he suffered 47% loss of access to job market was not substantially limited in his ability to work, as he was still qualified to perform over half of the jobs he was qualified for prior to being injured).

[110] Lebron-Torres v. Whitehall Robins Labs., 251 F.3d 236, 11 AD Cases 1491 (1st Cir. 2001) (evidence that employee received compensation for a 20% disability insufficient to prove she had impairment that prevented her from working in a class or broad range of jobs).

[111] Black v. Roadway Express, Inc., 297 F.3d 445, 13 AD Cases 581 (6th Cir. 2002) (determination of whether truck driver's knee injury precluded him from a class or broad range of jobs should not consider how other trucking company accommodated this injury).

schedule does not necessarily indicate that the employee is disabled.

3. Temporary versus Permanent Impairment

Other factors to consider when assessing whether an impairment substantially limits a major life function are the duration and impact of the impairment.[112] The duration of an impairment is the length of time the condition or disorder persists, while the impact of the impairment refers to the condition's residual effects. As an illustration, a broken leg, which heals in 8 weeks, is a condition of fairly short duration. Thus, while the broken leg may affect the individual's ability to walk, this limitation will last for a relatively short period of time, and would not be deemed a substantial limitation under the ADA. If, however, the break fails to heal properly, the "impact" of the impairment might be a permanent resulting limp, an impairment that could substantially limiting a person's ability to walk on a permanent or long-term basis.[113]

As a general rule, temporary, nonchronic impairments of short duration—such as "broken limbs, sprained joints, concussions, appendicitis, and influenza"—usually are not considered disabilities.[114] Even serious conditions may not qualify an individual for statutory protection if their effects are temporary. For example, a severe back injury that prevents an individual from working for months is not considered a disability if the individual is expected to make a full recovery.[115] Similarly, in *Colwell v. Suffolk County Police Dep't*,[116] an individual hospitalized for 30 days following a cerebral hemorrhage did not establish a record of impairment that showed a substantial limitation in major life activities. Although serious, the effects of the

---

[112] 29 C.F.R. §1630.2(j)(2)(iii) (2003).

[113] 29 C.F.R. pt. 1630, app. §1630.2(j) (2003).

[114] *Id.*

[115] *See* Pollard v. High's of Balt., Inc., 281 F.3d 462, 12 AD Cases 1409 (4th Cir.), *cert. denied*, 517 U.S. 827 (2002).

[116] 158 F.3d 635, 8 AD Cases 1232 (2d Cir. 1998), *cert. denied*, 526 U.S. 1018 (1999).

hemorrhage were not shown to be permanent.[117] Likewise, in *Pryor v. Trane Co.*,[118] a cervical vertebrae injury, subsequent surgery, hospitalization, inability to work for 2 years, and work restrictions did not establish that an assembly line worker was disabled or that her impairment limited her major life activities. In *Korzeniowski v. ABF Freight Systems, Inc.*,[119] a former line haul supervisor for a freight line who was diagnosed with arteriosclerotic heart disease was not disabled, despite recurring impotence, because testimony indicated that his condition was a temporary problem experienced while taking previous medication.

In at least one instance, an individual's carpal tunnel syndrome was not judged to be a "temporary" impairment, even though physicians described it as an "irritation" of the median nerve that produced a recurrent and permanent condition.[120] Thus, so long as the effects of a condition are permanent and severe, a seemingly minor ailment may qualify as a disability.

However, not all impairments need to be permanent to rise to the level of a disability. Some conditions may be long-term, or potentially long-term, in that their duration is indefinite and unknowable or is expected to last at least several months. Such conditions, if severe, are substantially limiting and thus may constitute disabilities.[121]

Even conditions perceived to be benign, such as psoriasis, can represent a physical impairment within the meaning of

---

[117]*See also* Ogburn v. United Food & Commercial Workers Local No. 881, 305 F.3d 763, 13 AD Cases 1071 (7th Cir.), *reh'g denied*, 2002 U.S. App. LEXIS 7394 (7th Cir. 2002) (union business agent fired while on medical leave for depression did not violate ADA because condition did not limit him in major life activity except during 8-week period during which he sought treatment).

[118]138 F.3d 1024, 8 AD Cases 271 (5th Cir. 1998). *See also* McKiver v. General Elec. Co., 11 F. Supp. 2d 755, 9 AD Cases 30 (M.D.N.C. 1997) (cervical and lumbar sprains producing 15-pound lifting restriction did not limit ability to work substantially, due to limited duration and severity); Green v. Rosemont Indus., 5 F. Supp. 2d 568, 9 AD Cases 121 (S.D. Ohio 1998) (hernia limitation of insufficient duration).

[119]38 F. Supp. 2d 688, 9 AD Cases 393 (N.D. Ill. 1999).

[120]Quint v. A.E. Staley Mfg. Co., 172 F.3d 1, 9 AD Cases 242 (1st Cir.), *cert. denied*, 535 U.S. 1023 (1999).

[121]EEOC, INTERPRETIVE MANUAL (1995), *reprinted in* 2 EEOC COMPLIANCE MANUAL §902.4(d), at 902–30 (BNA 1997); *see also* Aldrich v. Boeing Co., 146 F.3d 1265, 8 AD Cases 424 (10th Cir. 1998), *cert. denied*, 526 U.S. 1144 (1999).

the ADA, when its occasional flareups are combined with its psychological impact, even in its dormant stage.[122] Similarly, permanent conditions that are episodic in nature, such as epilepsy, can be considered disabilities.[123]

4. The Effect of Mitigating Measures

When determining the existence of a disability, measures that mitigate an individual's impairment, such as corrective lenses and medication, must be taken into consideration.[124] For example, in *Sutton v. United Air Lines, Inc.*,[125] prospective commercial airline pilots with severe myopia accused the airline of discrimination under the ADA for rejecting their employment applications because of their vision. Although the plaintiffs wore corrective lenses that allowed them to function identically to individuals without similar impairments, they could not meet the minimum uncorrected vision standards the airlines maintained.

The airline argued, and the Supreme Court agreed, that the plaintiffs could not bring a claim under the ADA, as they did not have a disability. An impairment does not substantially limit a major life activity if it is corrected. According to the plain language of the ADA, that an impairment "substantially limits one or more major life activities" means that substantial limitations actually and presently exist. By disregarding such mitigating measures, the airline argued, the Court would ignore the statute's command that impairments be measured in

---

[122]Cehrs v. Northeast Ohio Alzheimer's Research Ctr., 155 F.3d 775, 8 AD Cases 825 (6th Cir. 1998).

[123]Otting v. J.C. Penney Co., 223 F.3d 704, 10 AD Cases 1549 (8th Cir. 2000) (severe epilepsy is a disability, where seizures substantially limit major life activities of speaking, walking, seeing, working, and controlling one's body). *See also* EEOC v. Sara Lee Corp., 237 F.3d 349, 11 AD Cases 595 (4th Cir. 2001) (intermittent manifestations of illness should not be used to determine whether person is substantially limited in major life activity); Taylor v. Phoenixville Sch. Dist., 184 F.3d 296, 9 AD Cases 1187 (3d Cir. 1999) (individual with bipolar disorder may be substantially limited in ability to think, where illness caused episodic—as opposed to continuous—bouts of paranoia and mood irregularities).

[124]Murphy v. United Parcel Serv., Inc., 527 U.S. 516, 9 AD Cases 691 (1999); Sutton v. United Air Lines, Inc., 527 U.S. 471, 9 AD Cases 673 (1999).

[125]527 U.S. 471, 9 AD Cases 673 (1999).

their effect on the major life activities of each individual. The Supreme Court concurred, concluding that the effects—both positive and negative—of mitigating measures used in relation to a physical or mental impairment, must be considered in determining if an individual is "substantially limited" in a major life activity and "disabled" within the meaning of the statute.

Similarly, in *Murphy v. United Parcel Service, Inc.*,[126] the Supreme Court held that a mechanic suffering from hypertension was not disabled under the ADA, as his condition was controlled by medication. Therefore, his termination for failing to meet health requirements[127] established by the Federal Highway Administration of the U.S. Department of Transportation (DOT) was not in violation of the ADA.

The Supreme Court rulings in *Sutton* and *Murphy* engendered harsh criticism from representatives of the disability rights community, many of whom suggested that the decisions radically revised and limited the obligations of employers as well as the rights of applicants and employees under the statute. Prior to these decisions, the EEOC,[128] the Department of Justice,[129] and several federal circuit courts of appeal[130] favored

---

[126] 527 U.S. 516, 9 AD Cases 691 (1999).

[127] *See* 49 C.F.R. pt. 391 (2003). Among these regulations is a requirement that commercial motor vehicle operators have "no current clinical diagnosis of high blood pressure likely to interfere with his/her ability to operate a commercial motor vehicle safely." *Id.* §391.41(b)(6).

[128] The EEOC stated in its interpretive guidance that "[t]he determination of whether an individual is substantially limited in a major life activity must be made on a case by case basis, without regard to mitigating measures such as medicines, or assistive or prosthetic devices." 29 C.F.R. pt. 1630, app. §1630.2(j) (1999).

[129] The Department of Justice guidelines for Title II of the ADA described a similar viewpoint, noting, "The question of whether a person has a disability should be assessed without regard to the availability of mitigating measures, such as reasonable modification or auxiliary aids and services." 28 C.F.R. pt. 35, app. A §35.104; pt. 36, app. B §36.104.

[130] *See* Bartlett v. New York State Bd. of Law Exam'rs, 156 F.3d 321, 8 AD Cases 1004 (2d Cir. 1998), *vacated*, 527 U.S. 1031, 9 AD Cases 768 (1999); Washington v. HCA Health Servs. of Tex., Inc., 152 F.3d 464, 8 AD Cases 1044 (5th Cir. 1998), *vacated*, 527 U.S. 1032, 9 AD Cases 768 (1999); Baert v. Euclid Beverage, Ltd., 149 F.3d 626, 8 AD Cases 973 (7th Cir. 1998); Matczak v. Frankford Candy & Chocolate Co., 136 F.3d 933, 7 AD Cases 1050 (3d Cir. 1997); Arnold v. United Parcel Serv., 136 F.3d 854, 7 AD Cases 1489 (1st Cir. 1998); Doane v. City of Omaha, 115 F.3d 624, 6 AD Cases 1553 (8th Cir. 1997); Harris v. H&W Contracting Co., 102 F.3d

the opposite view that mitigating measures *should not* be taken into consideration when assessing whether an individual has a disability.

Following these Supreme Court decisions, a number of courts applied the holdings in *Sutton* and *Murphy* to a variety of circumstances. Because an individual's condition must be assessed on a case-by-case basis, any one impairment may or may not be considered a disability, depending on how the individual is able to cope with that impairment. For example, if an individual with diabetes is able to sufficiently control his or her blood sugar with insulin injections and diet without incident, then that person's diabetes does not constitute a disability under the ADA.[131] A factfinder, however, could determine that an individual's diabetes does constitute a disability, where, for instance, diet and medication do not completely control an individual's blood sugar levels, subjecting the diabetic to hypoglycemic episodes and frequent blood sugar monitoring,[132] or if the medication itself poses life-threatening consequences.[133]

Similarly, clinical depression, if controlled by medication and/or counseling, is not a disability.[134] Moreover, failure to

---

516, 6 AD Cases 460 (11th Cir. 1996); Holihan v. Lucky Stores, Inc., 87 F.3d 362, 5 AD Cases 1068 (9th Cir. 1996), *cert. denied*, 520 U.S. 1162 (1997).

[131]*See, e.g.,* Orr v. Wal-Mart Stores, Inc., 297 F.3d 720, 13 AD Cases 577 (8th Cir. 2002) (employee failed to show how his diabetes, which was controlled through diet and medication, substantially affected his major life activities).

[132]*See, e.g.,* Nawrot v. CPC Int'l, 277 F.3d 896, 12 AD Cases 1138 (7th Cir. 2002) (employee with Type I diabetes is substantially limited in the major life activities of thinking and caring for himself, where treatment for illness includes injecting insulin 3 times per day and monitoring his blood sugar 10 times per day).

[133]*See, e.g.,* Lawson v. CSX Transp., Inc., 245 F.3d 916, 11 AD Cases 1025 (7th Cir. 2001) (reasonable jury could find that Type I diabetic who had difficulty metabolizing food even after taking insulin was substantially limited in life function of eating). *See also* Kapche v. San Antonio, 304 F.3d 493, 13 AD Cases 907 (5th Cir. 2002) (an insulin-dependent diabetic applying to police department should be evaluated individually to consider whether that condition limited his ability to perform essential job functions).

[134]*See, e.g.,* Swanson v. University of Cincinnati, 268 F.3d 307, 12 AD Cases 417 (6th Cir. 2001) (surgical resident was not substantially limited in sleeping and communicating, and was therefore not disabled, where his depression was controlled by medication); Spades v. City of Walnut Ridge, Ark., 186 F.3d 897, 9 AD Cases

take medication that would enable an individual to function normally does not render that person disabled.[135]

Nonetheless, individuals may be considered disabled even if assistive devices enable them to function with their impairments. For example, a person who uses a cane may still be substantially limited in the ability to walk where the device does not adequately mitigate the underlying impairment, but rather enables the individual to walk greater distances without falling.[136] By the same token, an amputee who wears a prosthetic device is still likely deemed disabled, as the device does not sufficiently compensate for the loss of limb function enjoyed by the nondisabled public.[137] Thus, to determine whether mitigating measures adequately counteract the effects of an individual's impairment, a factfinder must examine whether those measures enable the individual to function at a level on a par with that of the general public. As in the case of a prosthesis, such a device may mitigate, but can never sufficiently compensate for, the impairment. This assessment must necessarily be conducted on a case-by-case basis.

Corrective measures include the steps taken by one's own body to compensate for an impairment. For example, in *Albertsons, Inc. v. Kirkingburg*,[138] an individual with monocular vision had subconsciously learned to cope with his visual impairment, allowing him to effectively compensate for his visual limitation. The Supreme Court stated that there is "no principled basis for distinguishing between measures undertaken with artificial

---

1015 (8th Cir. 1999) (police officer with depression treated by medication and therapy was able to function without limitations, and thus not disabled).

[135] Hein v. All Am. Plywood Co., 232 F.3d 482, 11 AD Cases 308 (6th Cir. 2000) (individual with hypertension is not substantially limited in any major life function, where medication allows individual to function normally).

[136] EEOC v. Sears, Roebuck & Co., 233 F.3d 432, 11 AD Cases 193 (7th Cir. 2000) (individual with neuropathy is substantially limited in her ability to walk even though she uses cane for support).

[137] *See, e.g.,* Sutton v. United Air Lines, 527 U.S. 471, 488, 9 AD Cases 673 (1999) ("The use or nonuse of a corrective device does not determine whether an individual is disabled; that determination depends on whether the limitations an individual with an impairment *actually* faces are in fact substantially limiting" (emphasis in original)).

[138] 527 U.S. 555, 9 AD Cases 694 (1999).

aids, like medications and devices, and measures undertaken, whether consciously or not, with the body's own systems."[139] Because the individual's coping mechanisms provided him with a degree of vision enjoyed by the general public, he was not disabled under the ADA.

The mitigating effect of corrective measures, therefore, must be taken into consideration when assessing whether an impairment is, indeed, substantially limiting for purposes of ADA coverage.

D. Record of Impairment

While a person is considered disabled under the ADA if he or she has a mental or physical impairment that substantially limits one or more major life activities, there are other ways in which an individual may receive statutory protection under the ADA. For example, an individual who has a record of an impairment is considered disabled under the ADA.[140] The EEOC regulations define the term "has a record of such an impairment" as meaning that the individual "has a history of, or has been misclassified as having, a mental or physical impairment that substantially limits one or more major life activities."[141] As the language suggests, this portion of the definition of disability is intended to ensure that employers do not make adverse employment decisions based on the individual's history of having a disability. This part of the ADA protects a person who has a history of cancer, heart disease, or other illness that is now cured, in remission, or otherwise under control.[142] Moreover, people who have been misclassified or misdiagnosed as having a disability are also protected under this section.[143]

According to the EEOC, the record relied on by an employer in making a challenged employment decision must indicate that the individual has or has had a bona fide disability.[144]

---

[139] *Id.* at 565.
[140] 29 C.F.R. §1630.2(g)(2) (2003).
[141] 29 C.F.R. §1630.2(k) (2003).
[142] TITLE I TECHNICAL ASSISTANCE MANUAL, *supra* note 43, §2.2(b).
[143] *Id.*
[144] 29 C.F.R. pt. 1630, app. §1630.2(k) (2003).

The EEOC makes clear that "[t]he impairment indicated in the record must be an impairment that would substantially limit one or more of the individual's major life activities."[145] Thus, a record of minor or short-term limitations, such as temporary lifting restrictions, does not constitute a record of having a disability.[146] Similarly, a record of absences and hospital stays without more is insufficient to qualify as a record of an impairment.[147]

A record of an employee's past drug addiction would, however, constitute a valid record of an impairment, as addiction is a disability under the ADA.[148] Casual or current drug use, however, is not statutorily protected.[149] Thus, information regarding an individual's stay at a rehabilitation center would likely constitute a record of an impairment, while similar information about a person's recreational drug use would not.

Finally, a record of being a disabled veteran, receipt of disability retirement, or a classification as being disabled for other purposes does *not* necessarily ensure that the individual will satisfy this prong of the definition of disability. For example, the receipt of social security disability insurance may be used as relevant evidence to establish that the individual has or had an impairment, but is not dispositive of that issue.[150]

---

[145] *Id.*

[146] *See* Rakity v. Dillon Cos., 302 F.3d 1152, 13 AD Cases 896 (10th Cir. 2002).

[147] *See* Sorensen v. University of Utah Hosp., 194 F.3d 1084, 9 AD Cases 1490 (10th Cir. 1999) (employee with multiple sclerosis did not have record of impairment, as employee's hospital stays and limitations were temporary in nature); *see also* Hilburn v. Murata Elecs. N. Am., Inc., 181 F.3d 1220, 9 AD Cases 908 (11th Cir. 1999) (38-day absence stemming from employee's coronary heart disease insufficient to establish record of impairment); *cf.* EEOC v. R.J. Gallagher Co., 181 F.3d 645, 9 AD Cases 917 (5th Cir. 1999) (employee's visual limitations associated with blood cancer in addition to 30-day hospital stay and accompanying chemotherapy treatments may constitute record of substantial limitation in major life activity of working, among others).

[148] *See, e.g.,* Hernandez v. Hughes Missile Sys. Co., 292 F.3d 1038, *as amended,* 298 F.3d 1030, 13 AD Cases 198 (9th Cir. 2002), *vacated sub nom.* Raytheon Co. v. Hernandez, 540 U.S. 44, 14 AD Cases 1825 (2003).

[149] TITLE I TECHNICAL ASSISTANCE MANUAL, *supra* note 43, §2.2(b).

[150] *See, e.g.,* Lawson v. CSX Transp., Inc., 245 F.3d 916, 11 AD Cases 1025 (7th Cir. 2001) (receipt of social security disability insurance for almost 12 years may be used as evidence that employee had record of being disabled).

E. Regarded as Disabled

The final prong of the regulatory definition of disability promulgated by the EEOC involves individuals who are "regarded as having such an impairment." Congress added this section to the definition of disability in order to protect people from a range of discriminatory conduct based on "myths, fears and stereotypes" about disabilities, which are "as handicapping as are the physical limitations that flow from actual impairments."[151]

Employees may be "regarded as" disabled in one of three circumstances. First, if they have physical or mental impairments that do not substantially limit major life activities but are *treated* by a covered entity as having such limitations, the employees are regarded as having a disability. For example, an individual with high blood pressure would not be substantially limited in any major life activity if he or she is able to keep this condition under control. If this individual were reassigned to carry out less strenuous work because of an unsubstantiated concern that the employee would suffer a heart attack performing a more arduous task, "the employer would be regarding the individual as disabled."[152]

Second, if individuals have physical or mental impairments that substantially limit major life activities only as a result of the *attitudes of others* toward such impairment(s), the individuals would be disabled. Thus, an employee with a prominent facial disfigurement that does not limit the individual's major life activities is *regarded as* having a disability by an employer who refuses to hire him or her because of anticipated negative customer reactions. Similarly, an employer that refuses to allow an individual to apply for a job on the grounds that the applicant looks as if he or she would fail a required physical exam is regarding that individual as disabled.[153]

---

[151] TITLE I TECHNICAL ASSISTANCE MANUAL, *supra* note 43, §2.2(c).
[152] 29 C.F.R. pt. 1630, app. §1630.2(*l*) (2003).
[153] *See, e.g.*, Dyke v. O'Neal Steel, Inc., 2003 WL 21000819, 14 AD Cases 481 (7th Cir. 2003) (employer that refused to give individual vision test for position

Finally, individuals are regarded as being disabled if they have no impairments that presently limit major life activities, but are treated as if they do. For example, an employer that discharges an employee because of a false rumor that he or she is HIV positive would be regarding that individual as disabled, as the termination is premised on the *perception* that the employee is disabled.[154]

1. Regarded as Substantially Limited in the Ability to Work

Proving that an employer regards an individual as substantially limited in the ability to work is a difficult burden. The individual must show that the employer regards him or her as unable to perform a broad range or class of jobs, not merely unable to carry out a discrete number of tasks specific to a particular position.[155] For example, an employee who was fired

---

that requires minimum level of vision on grounds that he "looked odd" and that he might have "some problem" regarded him as disabled).

[154] 29 C.F.R. pt. 1630, app. §1630.2(*l*) (2003).

[155] *See, e.g.*, Murphy v. United Parcel Serv., Inc., 527 U.S. 516, 9 AD Cases 691 (1999) (mechanic with hypertension was regarded as being unable to perform only small subset of mechanics jobs, not mechanic positions generally); Sutton v. United Air Lines, Inc., 527 U.S. 471, 9 AD Cases 673 (1999) (pilot with substandard vision was precluded from only a narrow range of jobs, so was not regarded as disabled); EEOC v. J.B. Hunt Transp., Inc., 321 F.3d 69, 13 AD Cases 1697 (2d Cir. 2003) (over-the-road truck driver applicants who were rejected because of their use of prescription medications were not regarded as substantially limited in their ability to work, as they did not prove that employer thought that they were unqualified to be drivers at all); Sheehan v. City of Gloucester, 321 F.3d 21, 14 AD Cases 1 (1st Cir. 2003) (police officer who was involuntarily retired from service because of his hypertension could not prove that employer regarded him as unable to perform a broad range of jobs); Blanks v. Southwestern Bell Communications, Inc., 310 F.3d 398, 13 AD Cases 1253 (5th Cir. 2002) (HIV-positive employee could not prove that employer believed he was unable to perform a broad range of jobs); Mack v. Great Dane Trailers, 308 F.3d 776, 13 AD Cases 1153 (7th Cir. 2002) (limitations on lifting and squatting were occupation-specific, and did not prevent employee from working entirely); EEOC v. Woodbridge Corp., 263 F.3d 812, 12 AD Cases 254 (8th Cir. 2001) (inability to perform single job does not constitute a disability); EEOC v. Rockwell Int'l Corp., 243 F.3d 1012 (7th Cir. 2001) (plaintiff must provide some demographic information from relevant labor market as evidence that employer regarded employee as precluded from broad range of jobs, and not merely discrete set of jobs requiring particular skill); Cash v. Smith, 231 F.3d 1301, 11 AD Cases 203 (11th Cir. 2000) (firefighter must show that he was regarded as being unable to perform broad class of jobs); Shipley v. City of University City, Mo., 195 F.3d 1020, 9 AD Cases 1775 (8th Cir. 1999) (same), *reh'g denied* (2000).

because he was deemed unfit to work as a city police officer following heart surgery was not regarded as disabled, because he was, at most, regarded as unable to work in positions requiring substantial risk of physical confrontation only.[156] Similarly, a surgical resident suffering from major depression who was terminated from his medical residency program was not regarded as disabled in his ability to work where his supervisors believed he could work in a different medical field and encouraged him to switch specialties.[157] Likewise, an employer that was aware of a therapist's attention deficit disorder (ADD) did not regard her as disabled despite its conclusion that her condition prevented her from fulfilling certain responsibilities in *its* therapist positions, as the employer did not perceive her as unfit to be a psychotherapist in other settings.[158]

In essence, that an employer believes an employee incapable of performing some job-related tasks does not automatically indicate that it regards the employee as disabled. If, for example, the employer actively seeks to find alternative positions for that employee, it does not regard the employee as substantially limited in the ability to work.[159] Similarly, temporarily switching an employee to light duty does not equate to regarding that employee as substantially limited in the ability to work.[160] Thus, only where an employee can prove that the employer thought he or she was unable to perform a broad range of jobs can the employee establish that he or she was regarded as unable to work.

---

[156] Giordano v. City of New York, 274 F.3d 740, 12 AD Cases 1053 (2d Cir. 2001).

[157] Swanson v. University of Cincinnati, 268 F.3d 307, 12 AD Cases 417 (6th Cir. 2001); *see also* Rhoads v. Federal Deposit Ins. Corp., 257 F.3d 373 (4th Cir. 2001), *cert. denied*, 535 U.S. 933 (2002) (employer who thought employee with smoke-induced asthma could function in a smoke-free environment did not regard employee as disabled).

[158] Davidson v. Midelfort Clinic Ltd., 133 F.3d 499, 8 AD Cases 77 (7th Cir. 1998).

[159] Talk v. Delta Airlines, Inc., 165 F.3d 1021, 9 AD Cases 5 (5th Cir. 1999).

[160] Richards v. City of Topeka, 173 F.3d 1247, 9 AD Cases 333 (10th Cir. 1999) (city did not regard pregnant firefighter as disabled when it assigned her to light duty and did not permit her to return to full duty during her pregnancy, which plaintiff conceded was not substantially limiting impairment).

Determining whether an employer deems an employee unable to work is necessarily a fact-specific inquiry. Written or spoken comments expressing concern about an individual's ability to perform his or her job can serve as evidence that the employer regards that employee as substantially limited in this capacity.[161] However, simple awareness that an employee is sick does not prove that the employer regarded the employee as unable to work.[162]

Even an innocent mistake on the part of the employer is sufficient to subject the employer to liability under the ADA. For example, an employer that discharges an employee after relying on information in an employee's file to falsely conclude that he or she is incapable of working impermissibly regards that employee as substantially limited in the ability to work. The employee does not need to prove that the employer acted

---

[161] *See, e.g.*, Adams v. Master Carvers of Jamestown Ltd., 2004 U.S. App. LEXIS 3381 (2d Cir. 2004) (unpublished opinion) (officer's comments expressing doubts about whether plaintiff was healthy enough or could physically do the job raised a triable issue as to whether he was "regarded" as disabled); Buskirk v. Apollo Metals, 307 F.3d 160 (3d Cir. 2002) (letter from human resources to employee's union representative expressing doubts about employee's ability to fill vacant positions because of a back injury served as evidence that employer regarded him as disabled); Ross v. Campbell Soup Co., 237 F.3d 701, 11 AD Cases 577 (6th Cir. 2001) (supervisor's memo describing employee with back injury as a "problem person" with a "back case" indicates that employee was regarded as substantially limited in his ability to work); Heyman v. Queens Vill. Comm. for Mental Health for Jamaica Cmty. Adolescent Program, Inc., 198 F.3d 68, 10 AD Cases 27 (2d Cir. 1999) (factfinder could determine that employee with asymptomatic lymphoma was regarded as having impairment that substantially limited his ability to work, where employer drafted report expressing concern about his ability to work, and where another employee with same condition was unable to work). At the same time, the Seventh Circuit has held that a manager's use of terms such as "crippled," "handicapped," or "disabled" do not—by themselves—connote a belief that an individual has an ADA-protected disability. Tockes v. Air-Land Transp. Serv., Inc., 343 F.3d 895, 14 AD Cases 1389 (7th Cir. 2003), *cert. denied*, 124 S. Ct. 1414, 15 AD Cases 416 (2004).

[162] *See* Rinehimer v. Cemcolift, Inc., 292 F.3d 375, 13 AD Cases 110 (3d Cir. 2002) (managers' comments that employee was sick and had difficulty breathing was insufficient to establish that employee was regarded as disabled); Genthe v. Quebecor World Lincoln, 383 F.3d 713, 15 AD Cases 1697 (8th Cir.), *reh'g denied*, 2004 U.S. App. LEXIS 21634 (2004), *cert. denied*, 2005 U.S. LEXIS 2805 (2005) (factory worker with vision and heart problems produced insufficient evidence for inference that employer denied promotions because it perceived him to be disabled).

negligently or with malice, although the employer's state of mind is clearly relevant to the appropriate remedies.[163]

An employer does not, however, violate the ADA by basing decisions on objective evidence rather than opinion or conjecture. For example, an employer who relies on a doctor's written evaluation of an employee's condition in determining the employee's lifting restriction does not mistakenly regard the employee as disabled.[164] In this instance, the employer does not substitute its own judgment for that of the medical records, nor does it base its impression on speculation, stereotypes, or myth. However, if the employer misinterprets a doctor's medical report or otherwise makes an erroneous conclusion about the employee's condition based on that report, the employee may be regarded as having an impairment.[165]

Requesting that an employee submit to a medical examination prior to returning to work following an injury does not necessarily prove that an employer regards the employee as disabled.[166] In fact, if the employee is *not* limited in the ability to work or perform any other major life activities and refuses an employer's lawful request for medical information, the employee may be precluded from alleging that the employer regarded him or her as being disabled.[167] The medical inquiry, however, should be limited to the injury, and not be used as a fishing expedition into the mental or physical condition of

---

[163] *Id.* (citing Deane v. Pocono Med. Ctr., 142 F.3d 138, 143 n.4, 7 AD Cases 1809 (3d Cir. 1998)).

[164] Rakity v. Dillon Cos., 302 F.3d 1152, 13 AD Cases 896 (10th Cir. 2002).

[165] *See, e.g.*, Taylor v. Pathmark Stores, 177 F.3d 180, 9 AD Cases 497 (3d Cir. 1999) (employer regarded employee as substantially limited in ability to work after misinterpreting medical report of employee's condition).

[166] *See, e.g.*, Tice v. Centre Area Transp. Auth., 247 F.3d 506, 11 AD Cases (3d Cir. 2001) (employer's request for medical examination of bus driver following extended medical leave, without more, does not prove that employer regarded employee as disabled); Sanchez v. Henderson, 188 F.3d 740, 9 AD Cases 1006 (7th Cir. 1999), *cert. denied*, 528 U.S. 1173 (2000) (fitness-for-duty examination does not constitute evidence that employer regarded postal carrier as disabled, especially where examination was requested only after employee refused to return to work for medical reasons, and employer believed employee was qualified to perform nonstrenuous job tasks).

[167] *See, e.g.*, Haulbrook v. Michelin N. Am., Inc., 252 F.3d 696, 11 AD Cases 1407 (4th Cir. 2001) (chemical engineer cannot allege that inquiries regarding his

the employee. Merely expressing concern for an employee's illness through an offer for medical leave or a get well card, however, does not rise to an actionable level.[168]

The "regarded as" prong of the definition requires an employer to form an opinion about an employee's condition. Therefore, it follows that if the employee never informs the employer about past or existing impairments, the employer cannot be guilty of regarding him or her as disabled.[169]

F. Drug and Alcohol Use

Although addiction is an impairment under the ADA, *current* abuse of drugs or alcohol is not protected by the ADA.[170] Drug or alcohol abuse is considered "current" if the employee's activity is periodic or ongoing, and has not yet permanently ended, even if the employee is participating in a drug or alcohol rehabilitation program or is otherwise drug or alcohol free at the time of the discharge or other disciplinary action.[171] Thus, only past drug or alcohol addition is protected under Title I of the ADA.

Given the ADA's intent to protect reformed addicts in most circumstances, an employer may not impose a blanket policy against rehiring employees who had been discharged for any reason, because this policy precludes the rehire of any individual

---

breathing difficulties on return from sick leave prove that his employer regarded him as being disabled, where employee refused to respond).

[168] *See, e.g.,* Taylor v. Nimock's Oil Co., 214 F.3d 957, 10 AD Cases 1069 (8th Cir. 2000) (receipt of get well card does not constitute evidence that employee with heart disease was regarded as disabled).

[169] *See, e.g.,* Amadio v. Ford Motor Co., 238 F.3d 919, 11 AD Cases 641 (7th Cir. 2001) (auto assembly worker with number of medical conditions was not regarded as disabled, as he never informed employer of these conditions).

[170] 29 C.F.R. §1630.3(a) (2003); *see also* Bekker v. Humana Health Plan, Inc., 229 F.3d 662, 10 AD Cases 1776 (7th Cir. 2000) (terminating doctor who treated patients while under influence of alcohol did not violate Title I of the ADA).

[171] Shafer v. Preston Mem'l Hosp. Corp., 107 F.3d 274, 6 AD Cases 682 (4th Cir. 1997); *see also* Collings v. Longview Fibre Co., 63 F.3d 828, 4 AD Cases 1278 (9th Cir. 1995) (employees terminated for drug use while on job were considered current users, even though they had entered rehabilitation program and were not using drugs at time of discharge).

fired solely for drug or alcohol addiction, but who has been completely rehabilitated.[172] This rule does not, however, prevent an employer from enforcing a drug-testing policy in the workplace.[173] Random tests do not amount to proof that an employer regards an individual as being an illegal drug user.[174]

In addition, it is within the employer's right to institute a policy that permanently removes employees who have undergone treatment for substance abuse from safety-sensitive positions, even if this policy excludes individuals with past substance abuse problems. As long as the policy's rationale is job-related and consistent with business necessity,[175] the employer does not need to prove that the excluded employee would pose a direct threat.[176] For example, a school district's refusal to hire a past employee as a school bus driver was legitimate, where the employee had been disciplined in the past for drinking on the job.[177] Fear that the employee could repeat his behavior was a sufficient rationale for this employment decision.[178] However, a conference center's ban on prescription drug use without prior company approval *did* violate an account manager's rights under the ADA, as the employer could not prove that the policy was job-related or consistent with business necessity.[179]

An employer need not excuse poor behavior or performance because of an employee's substance abuse. For example,

---

[172] Hernandez v. Hughes Missile Sys. Co., 292 F.3d 1038, *as amended*, 298 F.3d 1030 (9th Cir. 2002), *vacated sub nom.* Raytheon Co. v. Hernandez, 540 U.S. 44, 14 AD Cases 1825 (2003).

[173] 29 C.F.R. §1630.3(c) (2003).

[174] Parry v. Mohawk Motors of Mich., Inc., 236 F.3d 299, 11 AD Cases 538 (6th Cir. 2000), *cert. denied*, 533 U.S. 951 (2001).

[175] In deciding whether a policy is consistent with business necessity, an employer must take into account the magnitude of possible harm as well as the probability of that harm occurring. EEOC v. Exxon Corp., 203 F.3d 871, 10 AD Cases 225 (5th Cir. 2000).

[176] *Exxon*, 203 F.3d 871.

[177] Martin v. Barnesville Exempted Vill. Sch. Dist. Bd. of Educ., 209 F.3d 931, 10 AD Cases 787 (6th Cir. 2000).

[178] *Id.*

[179] Roe v. Cheyenne Mountain Conference Resort, 124 F.3d 1221, 7 AD Cases 779 (10th Cir. 1997). The company's prescription drug disclosure provisions violated §102 of the ADA, 42 U.S.C. §12112(d)(4), which prohibits a medical examination or inquiries as to whether an employee is an individual with a disability, unless shown to be job-related and consistent with business necessity).

an employee who threatens his or her employer while intoxicated is not immune from disciplinary action.[180] Similarly, the ADA does not protect egregious off-duty conduct. An employer may terminate an employee who engages in off-duty criminal or threatening behavior, even if this behavior is spurred on by alcohol or drug abuse.[181]

Moreover, simply being an alcoholic or having a record of drug use does not automatically render an individual a "qualified individual with a disability" under the ADA. The individual must show that the alcoholism or past drug use substantially limits major life activities, or that the employee has a record of these substantial limitations, or that he or she is regarded as being disabled.[182] For instance, an individual whose off-duty drinking caused him to perform his job with a hangover, and eventually forced him to check himself into a rehabilitation center, could not prove that his alcoholism substantially limited any major life activity, including working, and was therefore not protected under Title I from any adverse employment action.[183]

An individual may be protected under the ADA for being *regarded* as an alcoholic or illicit drug user. For example, in *Miners v. Cargill Communications, Inc.*,[184] after an employee was observed drinking with clients, the employer gave her an ultimatum of either alcohol rehabilitation treatment or termination. When she refused treatment, the employee was fired. The employee later successfully sued on the grounds that her

---

[180] *See, e.g.*, Williams v. Widnall, 79 F.3d 1003, 5 AD Cases 663 (10th Cir. 1996) (employer did not violate ADA for firing alcoholic employee who threatened supervisor and coworkers).

[181] *See, e.g.*, Johnson v. New York Hosp., 96 F.3d 33, 5 AD Cases 1537 (2d Cir. 1996) (nurse who became intoxicated, returned to work while off-duty and engaged security guards in fight was validly terminated for posing safety risk to patients); Maddox v. University of Tenn., 62 F.3d 843, 4 AD Cases 1253 (6th Cir. 1995) (university lawfully terminated assistant coach for drunk driving arrest).

[182] *See, e.g.*, Bailey v. Georgia-Pacific Corp., 306 F.3d 1162, 13 AD Cases 1066 (1st Cir. 2002) (employee failed to show that his alcoholism prevented him from working in broad range of jobs, could not show that his alcohol-related incarceration prevented him from working for long period of time, and presented no evidence of any past limitations or that employer regarded him as being disabled).

[183] Burch v. Coca-Cola Co., 119 F.3d 305, 7 AD Cases 241 (5th Cir. 1997).

[184] 113 F.3d 820, 6 AD Cases 1229 (8th Cir. 1997).

employer regarded her as an alcoholic. Providing her with the option to enter rehabilitation was not a reasonable accommodation, because the company never determined that the employee was, indeed, an alcoholic.

III. "Qualified" Individual With a Disability

To be protected against employment discrimination under Title I of the ADA, an individual must not only be disabled, but must be considered a *qualified* individual with a disability. Thus, individuals with disabilities who are protected under other sections of the ADA are not necessarily shielded from adverse employment actions under Title I.

A "qualified" individual with a disability possess the requisite "skill, experience, education and other job-related requirements of the employment position such individual holds or desires," and is able to perform the essential functions of that position "with or without reasonable accommodation."[185] Determining whether a disabled individual is qualified for purposes of Title I entails two key steps. First, it must be determined whether the individual meets the necessary prerequisites for the job, that is, is "otherwise qualified" to perform the job despite his or her disability. Factors involved in making this assessment include the individual's education, work experience, training, skills, licenses, certificates, and other job-related requirements.[186] Thus, an individual with a disability is not otherwise qualified to be a doctor, for example, if he or she does not have a medical degree or license to practice medicine.

A. Otherwise Qualified

If, however, an individual meets all the necessary job requirements *except* those that he or she cannot meet because of the disability, and therefore alleges discrimination because he or she is otherwise qualified, it would be incumbent on the

---

[185] 29 C.F.R. §1630.2(m) (2003).
[186] Title I Technical Assistance Manual, *supra* note 43, §2.3.

employer to show that these job requirements are "job related and consistent with business necessity."[187] For example, if a hearing-impaired individual meets all of an employer's stated job requirements except the ability to answer phones, the burden is on the employer to show that phone work is a necessary part of the job.[188]

Once it is determined that the individual satisfies the job requirements, an employer must assess whether the individual can perform the *essential* functions of the job, with our without a reasonable accommodation.[189] This step involves isolating the job tasks/skills that are deemed essential to the performance of the job from those that are considered marginal or incidental.

B. What Is an Essential Job Function?

Identifying the essential job functions of a business is not always a clear-cut task, and has led to a considerable amount of litigation. First and foremost, if a function is essential, employees must be required to perform that function.[190] Therefore, although a written job description may require employees to be able to type 75 words per minute, if employees are not held to that standard, then it is not an essential job function. Similarly, an ability to rotate through a variety of tasks is not an essential function if the employer does not enforce a full job rotation policy.[191]

Second, if removing that function would fundamentally change the nature of the job, then it qualifies as an essential job function. The regulations to Title I of the ADA provide some guidance in making this assessment. A job function in question might be essential if, for example, "the reason the

---

[187] *Id.*

[188] *See, e.g.*, Ward v. Massachusetts Health Research Inst., Inc., 209 F.3d 29, 10 AD Cases 776 (1st Cir. 2000) (burden is on employer to show that set schedule is essential job function where flexible policy was in place).

[189] *Id.*

[190] TITLE I TECHNICAL ASSISTANCE MANUAL, *supra* note 43, §2.3(a).

[191] *See* Kiphart v. Saturn Corp., 251 F.3d 573, 11 AD Cases 1473 (6th Cir. 2001); *see also* Hamlin v. Charter Township of Flint, 165 F.3d 426, 8 AD Cases 1688 (6th Cir. 1999) (firefighting duties were not essential to assistant fire chief with heart condition who performed mainly administrative tasks).

position exists is to perform that function."[192] The ability to work nights, for instance, is an essential job function for a third-shift position. By its very nature, a third-shift position necessitates late night work. It follows that a time-shift change would fundamentally change the nature of the position, and therefore could not be requested as a reasonable accommodation for an individual with a sleep disorder.

Additionally, a function is essential if there are a limited number of employees capable of performing the particular job task, or among whom the function can be distributed.[193] For example, the ability to lift a certain amount of weight has been found to be an essential job function for nurses where staff shortages or emergencies could require them to assist patients on their own.[194] Moreover, if only a few employees are trained to do a particular job, regular attendance itself can become an essential job function.[195]

In certain instances, *all* of an employer's job functions may become essential. The *EEOC's Technical Assistance Manual* explains that during peak performance times, a limited number of employees curbs the employer's flexibility to reassign any particular job, thereby making each job task essential to the business operation.[196]

If an employee is hired for his or her ability to perform a highly specialized task, then that task would be considered an essential job function.[197] The ability to speak a particular language is an essential job function of an interpreter hired to speak that language. Moreover, direct interaction with patients

---

[192] 29 C.F.R. §1630.2(n)(2)(i) (2003).
[193] 29 C.F.R. §1630.2(n)(2)(ii) (2003).
[194] Lenker v. Methodist Hosp., 210 F.3d 792, 10 AD Cases 782 (7th Cir. 2000).
[195] *See* Maziarka v. Mills Fleet Farm, Inc., 245 F.3d 675, 11 AD Cases 1140 (8th Cir. 2001) (denial of receiving clerk's request for leave to accommodate illness not deemed discriminatory because of limited number of employees trained to perform essential functions of job); *see also* EEOC v. Yellow Freight Sys. Inc., 253 F.3d 943, 11 AD Cases 1569 (7th Cir. 2001) (en banc) (attendance an essential function for dockworker); Earl v. Mervyns, Inc., 207 F.3d 1361, 10 AD Cases 673 (11th Cir. 2000) (same); Buckles v. First Data Res., Inc., 176 F.3d 1098, 9 AD Cases 765 (8th Cir. 1999) (same).
[196] TITLE I TECHNICAL ASSISTANCE MANUAL, *supra* note 43, §2.3(a)(2).
[197] 29 C.F.R. §1630.2(n)(2)(iii) (2003).

would be an essential job function for a psychologist hired to perform individual counseling.[198] Thus, a psychologist unable to interact with potentially violent and/or infectious patients because he was suffering from asthma and a weakened immune system would not be considered a "qualified" individual with a disability.[199]

A number of factors may be used as evidence that a function is essential. A great deal of deference is placed on the employer's judgment.[200] Courts are reluctant to second guess an employer's production standards, methods, and output. For example, it is an employer's prerogative to mandate that all of its employees be able to perform a range of duties, all of which would therefore be deemed essential job functions.[201] Similarly, an employer may require its employees to work from 8:30 a.m. to 4:30 p.m., even if the employees could perform the same work on 9-to-5 schedule.

1. Written Job Description

The importance an employer places on a particular job function may be evident by its mention in the employee's job description, handbook, or collective bargaining agreement, and by any disciplinary policy in place for failure to perform the job function.[202] The job description, while neither essential nor dispositive as to what constitutes a position's essential job functions, does provide some evidence—along with other factors—that certain tasks are considered essential to the position.[203] The job description, however, must have been prepared

---

[198] Webb v. Clyde L. Choate Mental Heath Ctr., 230 F.3d 991, 11 AD Cases 97 (7th Cir. 2000).

[199] Id.

[200] 29 C.F.R. §1630.2(n)(3)(i) (2003).

[201] See, e.g., Peters v. City of Mauston, 311 F.3d 835, 13 AD Cases 1351 (7th Cir. 2002) (heavy lifting is essential job function, where employer requires all employees to be able to perform variety of operational and construction tasks).

[202] See, e.g., Earl v. Mervyns, Inc., 207 F.3d 1361, 10 AD Cases 673 (11th Cir. 2000) (employer's priority on punctuality was evident by its mention in employee handbook, and by comprehensive system of warnings and reprimands in place for tardiness).

[203] 29 C.F.R. §1630(n)(3)(ii) (2003).

before the employer began advertising or interviewing applicants for the job in question, and be up-to-date, to be considered legitimate.[204] Additionally, the description must emphasize which functions are essential to the performance of the job. It may not suffice to simply label any one task or skill as merely a job "requirement" without stipulating that the task or skill is essential.[205]

In establishing a job description, an employer must be able to distinguish between the essential function itself and the various means of performing that essential job function. If more than one means can achieve the same end, any one method of achieving that end cannot be deemed essential.[206] For example, typing may not be an essential function for a computer programmer, if other assistive devices, such as voice recognition software, could enable an employee with a disability to perform the job without manually inputting text.[207]

In essence, it is the employer's right to define the jobs within its business, and delineate the functions and standards required to perform those jobs, so long as those functions and standards are legitimate and not in place merely to screen out potential employees with disabilities.[208] An employer may also change a position's job functions for legitimate reasons. For example, an employer may restructure or combine positions, thereby adding essential functions to an established job.

2. Government Standards

Federal safety standards may serve as the basis for a job's essential functions, even if that federal standard may be waived

---

[204] TITLE I TECHNICAL ASSISTANCE MANUAL, *supra* note 43, §2.3(a)(3)(b).

[205] *See, e.g.*, Skerski v. Time Warner Cable Co., 257 F.3d 273, 11 AD Cases 1665 (3d Cir. 2001) ("climbing" is not essential function for cable installer even though this skill was listed as job requirement in position description, where climbing was not explicitly labeled "essential function" of job, but was just one method of performing essential function of job).

[206] *Id.*

[207] *See* TITLE I TECHNICAL ASSISTANCE MANUAL, *supra* note 43, §2.3(a)(3)(b).

[208] Anderson v. Coors Brewing Co., 181 F.3d 1171, 9 AD Cases 835 (10th Cir. 1999).

under certain conditions.[209] Even qualification standards "that screen out or tend to screen out or otherwise deny a job or benefit to an individual with a disability" may be considered essential job functions, so long as the standards are "job-related and consistent with business necessity, and . . . performance cannot be accomplished by reasonable accommodation . . . ."[210] The business necessity standard requires an employer to demonstrate that the screening criteria at issue substantially promotes the employer's business needs.[211] In addition, to justify the use of a safety standard that tends to exclude individuals with disabilities, the employer must "demonstrat[e] the correlation between the qualification standard and the safe job performance and . . . prov[e] the difficulty of using less restrictive alternatives."[212] In other words, an employer must show that the safety standard screens out all individuals who pose an unacceptable risk of danger, or that it is "highly impractical" to weed out the individuals who pose the risk in question.[213]

An employer cannot, however, invoke a federal safety standard to exclude a class of disabled job applicants if that safety standard does not apply to the position at issue. For example, an employer cannot rely on Department of Transportation hearing standards in refusing to hire hearing-impaired individuals to drive trucks if those vehicles are not covered by the DOT regulations in the first place.[214]

---

[209] *See, e.g.,* Albertsons, Inc. v. Kirkingburg, 527 U.S. 555, 9 AD Cases 694 (1999) (employer could enforce DOT visual acuity standard as essential job function, even if agency permitted standard waiver in certain instances); *see also* Tate v. Farmland Indus., Inc., 268 F.3d 989, 12 AD Cases 519 (10th Cir. 2001) (employer may use DOT's advisory Medical Advisory Criteria as essential job functions for its truck drivers, where criteria are job-related and consistent with business necessity).

[210] 42 U.S.C. §12113(a).

[211] *See, e.g.,* Cripe v. City of San Jose, 261 F.3d 877, 12 AD Cases 225 (9th Cir. 2001) (requirement that police officers serve as patrol officers prior to receiving specialized assignments, which screens out officers whose injuries preclude them from serving as patrol officers, must be examined under business necessity standard, not undue hardship defense).

[212] Morton v. United Parcel Serv., Inc., 272 F.3d 1249, 1262, 12 AD Cases 897, 906 (9th Cir. 2001), *cert. denied,* 535 U.S. 1054 (2002).

[213] *Id.* at 1260, 12 AD Cases at 905.

[214] *Id.* at 1263, 12 AD Cases at 907.

3. Percentage of Time Devoted to Job Function

The amount of time an employee devotes to performing a particular task is not necessarily indicative of whether or not that task is essential. Even if an employee has never performed a particular task in the course of his or her employment, that task still may be considered essential if it is included in the job description, other employees perform the task, and failure to perform this function would fundamentally impact the operation of the business.[215] If an employee may be required to perform a particular job function—even if these instances are few and far between—then that function is essential.[216] A job function can be essential even if an employee is informally excused from performing the task.[217]

4. Consequences of Not Performing Job Function

The consequences of not performing the job function in question may shed light on whether that function is essential under the ADA.[218] For example, the ability to make forcible arrests is an essential function of a police officer, even though this action is not routine, because failure to make a forcible arrest could pose a threat to both the officer and the public at large.[219] Similarly, the ability of a customer service representative to

---

[215] *See, e.g.*, Dropinski v. Douglas County, 298 F.3d 704, 13 AD Cases 676 (8th Cir. 2002) (contention that equipment operator had not performed general labor functions in past 5 years did not negate fact that these functions were essential).

[216] *See, e.g.*, Winfrey v. City of Chi., 259 F.3d 610, 12 AD Cases 21 (7th Cir. 2001) (removing job functions from clerk position to accommodate employee's blindness does not render these functions nonessential, because other employees may be required to perform these functions at any time); *see also* Anderson v. Coors Brewing Co., 181 F.3d 1171, 9 AD Cases 835 (10th Cir. 1999) (if employer requires employee to be able to perform multiple tasks, all of those tasks are deemed essential, not just those employee performs the majority of time).

[217] *See, e.g.*, Phelps v. Optima Health, Inc., 251 F.3d 21, 11 AD Cases 1487 (1st Cir. 2001) (ability to lift 50 pounds still essential job function even after one nurse was informally excused from this requirement after injuring her back, because exemption was never formalized or made known to human resources).

[218] 29 C.F.R. §1630.2(n)(3)(iv) (2003).

[219] *See* Cripe v. City of San Jose, 261 F.3d 877, 12 AD Cases 225 (9th Cir. 2001).

handle emergency phone calls is an essential function, even if such calls comprise a small percentage of the job.[220]

5. Other Factors

Examining the work experiences of other employees who hold or have held the same or similar positions to the one at issue is another means of determining which job functions are essential.[221] Additionally, the employer's operations and organization structure also factor into what functions are essential. For example, if an employer maintains a flexible arrival/departure schedule, then punctuality is not an essential job function.[222]

An employer is not required to perform a formal job analysis to identify its essential functions.[223] However, it is recommended that the employer informally analyze its organization and job categories in order to separate essential from marginal job skills/tasks.

C. Performance of Essential Functions With or Without a Reasonable Accommodation[224]

While many individuals with disabilities are able to perform the essential functions of their jobs without any assistive devices or job modifications, an individual is still considered a qualified individual with a disability if he or she can perform those functions only once reasonable accommodations to an employer's policies, practices, or operations are made. The regulations to Title I define "reasonable accommodations" as:

---

[220] *See* Emerson v. Northern States Power Co., 256 F.3d 506, 11 AD Cases 1683 (7th Cir. 2001) (responding to safety-sensitive calls, such as reports of gas leaks, is essential function of customer-service consultant for power company).
[221] 29 C.F.R. §1630.2(n)(3)(vi)–(vii) (2003).
[222] *See, e.g.*, Ward v. Massachusetts Health Research Inst., Inc., 209 F.3d 29, 10 AD Cases 776 (1st Cir. 2000) (ability to arrive at job by 9:00 a.m. is not essential function, where employer permits employees to arrive within 2-hour window so long as they complete full day of work).
[223] TITLE I TECHNICAL ASSISTANCE MANUAL, *supra* note 43, §2.3(b).
[224] For a more detailed discussion of reasonable accommodations, see Chapter 8, "Reasonable Accommodation Requirements."

(i) Modifications or adjustments to a job application process that enable a qualified applicant with a disability to be considered for the position such qualified applicant desires; or
(ii) Modifications or adjustments to the work environment, or to the manner or circumstances under which the position held or desired is customarily performed, that enable a qualified individual with a disability to perform the essential functions of that position; or
(iii) Modifications or adjustments that enable a covered entity's employee with a disability to enjoy equal benefits and privileges of employment as are enjoyed by its other similarly situated employees without disabilities.[225]

Reasonable accommodations include, but are not limited to:

(i) Making existing facilities used by employees readily accessible to and usable by individuals with disabilities; and
(ii) Job restructuring; part-time or modified work schedules; reassignment to a vacant position; acquisition or modifications of equipment or devices; appropriate adjustment or modifications of examinations, training materials, or policies; the provision of qualified readers or interpreters; and other similar accommodations for individuals with disabilities.[226]

Identifying and implementing an appropriate reasonable accommodation is intended to be a collaborative process between the employer and employee.[227] An employer may, but is not required to, reassign a marginal job function to another employee instead of providing a reasonable accommodation to a qualified employee with a disability.[228]

Determining what types of work accommodations are considered "reasonable" under Title I is a fact-specific process, and has been subject to a considerable amount of litigation. Generally, an employer is not required to alter its operations

---

[225] 29 C.F.R. §1630.2(o)(1)(i)–(iii) (2003).
[226] *Id.* §1630.2(o)(2)(i)–(ii) (2003).
[227] 29 C.F.R. pt. 1630, app. (2003) (commentary).
[228] *See* Hoffman v. Caterpillar, Inc., 256 F.3d 568, 11 AD Cases 1674 (7th Cir. 2001).

fundamentally to accommodate an individual with a disability, nor is it required to incur an unreasonable expense.[229]

IV. Interaction of Other Statutes' Provisions Regarding Disability With Those of the Americans With Disabilities Act

Another hotly contested issue since the enactment of the ADA has been the ability of individuals to simultaneously assert claims under the ADA and apparently contradictory claims under other statutes. For example, an individual may claim to be a qualified individual with a disability under the ADA—that is, able to perform the essential job functions with or without a reasonable accommodation—while at the same time claim to be completely disabled for purposes of receiving social security disability benefits or workers compensation payments. In this instance, the principle of judicial estoppel—sometimes referred to as the doctrine of preclusion of inconsistent positions—may apply. Judicial estoppel precludes a party from gaining an advantage by taking one position, and then seeking a second advantage by taking an incompatible position.[230]

The federal circuits that have addressed this issue are split as to whether a claimant may be estopped judicially from bringing an ADA claim after asserting that he or she is completely disabled in another proceeding.[231]

---

[229]The complexities of this topic are discussed in greater detail in Chapter 8, "Reasonable Accommodation Requirements."

[230]18B ALAN WRIGHT, ARTHUR R. MILLER & EDWARD H. COOPER, FEDERAL PRACTICE AND PROCEDURE *Federal Jurisdiction* §4477 (2002).

[231]*Compare, e.g.,* Rascon v. U.S. W. Communications, Inc., 143 F.3d 1324, 8 AD Cases 541 (10th Cir. 1998), Griffith v. Wal-Mart Stores, Inc., 135 F.3d 376, 7 AD Cases 1233 (6th Cir. 1998), *and* Swanks v. Washington Metro. Transit Auth., 116 F.3d 582, 6 AD Cases 1544 (D.C. Cir. 1997) (application for and receipt of Social Security Disability Insurance (SSDI) benefits is relevant to, but does not bar plaintiff from, bringing ADA claim), *with* McNemar v. Disney Store, Inc., 91 F.3d 610, 5 AD Cases 1227 (3d Cir. 1996) (judicial estoppel barred plaintiff who filed disability benefits application from bringing ADA suit), Rissetto v. Plumbers & Steamfitters Local 343, 94 F.3d 597, 71 FEP Cases 1057 (9th Cir. 1996) (same), *and* Kennedy v. Applause, Inc., 90 F.3d 1477, 5 AD Cases 1249 (9th Cir.1996) (refusing to apply judicial estoppel but holding that claimant failed to raise genuine issue

The EEOC, however, has taken the position that post-termination representations made in connection with an application for disability benefits should not be an automatic bar to an ADA claim.[232] According to the agency, statements about the extent of one's impairments made after being discharged are irrelevant as to whether an indiviudal was unfairly treated because of his or her disability. One rationale is that judicial estoppel applies to judicial proceedings only. Therefore, according to this reasoning, statements made regarding the status of one's disability in an administrative proceeding or on an application for benefits do not bar claims made under the ADA. However, a number of courts *have* applied the doctrine of judicial estoppel to statements made in administrative proceedings.[233]

Another rationale is that statements made in different proceedings are not necessarily mutually exclusive. The Supreme Court weighed in on this debate in the context of Social Security Disability Insurance (SSDI) benefits, concluding that the application for and receipt of such benefits do not operate to bar individuals from pursuing an ADA claim automatically.[234] The Court noted, however, that a person pursuing both types of recovery must explain why the disability contentions advanced in the SSDI context are consistent with the assertion

---

of material fact concerning her status as qualified individual with a disability where she declared total disability in benefits application).

[232] EEOC Notice No. 915.002, Feb. 12, 1997.

[233] *See* Chaveriat v. Williams Pipe Line Co., 11 F.3d 1420, 1427 (7th Cir. 1993) ("Though called judicial estoppel, the doctrine has been applied, rightly in our view, to proceedings in which a party to an administrative proceeding obtains a favorable order that he seeks to repudiate in a subsequent judicial proceeding."); Smith v. Montgomery Ward & Co., 388 F.2d 291, 292 (6th Cir. 1968) (position taken in workers' compensation proceeding estopped party in subsequent personal injury action); Simo v. Home Health & Hospice Care, 906 F. Supp. 714, 718, 5 AD Cases 1461 (D.N.H. 1995) (Social Security Administration disability proceeding); UNUM Corp. v. United States, 886 F. Supp. 150, 158 (D. Me. 1995) (Maine Bureau of Insurance approval proceeding); Zapata Gulf Marine Corp. v. Puerto Rico Mar. Shipping Auth., 731 F. Supp. 747, 750 (E.D. La. 1990) (Interstate Commerce Commission proceeding); Muellner v. Mars, Inc., 714 F. Supp. 351, 357–58 (N.D. Ill. 1989) (Social Security Administration proceeding, applying Illinois law).

[234] Cleveland v. Policy Mgmt. Sys. Corp., 526 U.S. 795, 9 AD Cases 491 (1999).

that he or she can perform the essential functions of the job, at least with a reasonable accommodation.

The Court reviewed the purposes of the SSDI program, and its definition of the term "disability," which applies to an

> inability to engage in any substantial gainful activity by reason of any . . . physical or mental impairment which can be expected to result in death or which has lasted or can be expected to last for a continuous period of not less than 12 months; . . .[235]

To qualify for SSDI benefits, an applicant's impairment must be so severe that he or she is not only unable to perform his or her previous work, but cannot engage in any other kind of substantial gainful work that exists in the national economy (bearing in mind the individual's age, education, and work experience). The Court noted that disability representations made by applicants in this context must essentially be viewed as implying a context-related legal conclusion (that is, "I am disabled for purposes of the Social Security Act") rather than a purely factual statement of physical disability.[236]

The Supreme Court rejected the conclusion that a special "rebuttable presumption" was appropriate for ADA claims in the context of a concurrent SSDI filing, finding instead that "there are too many situations in which an SSDI claim and ADA claim can comfortably exist side by side."[237] The Court noted the abbreviated analysis employed by the federal agency in making SSDI eligibility determinations (due to the very substantial volume of required claim adjudication), and the fact that these benefits examination do *not* take into account considerations of possible reasonable accommodations. This approach to the question of "disability" determination differs significantly from the analysis applied to discrimination and accommodation questions under the ADA, and does not justify the application of a legal presumption of judicial estoppel.[238]

---

[235] *Id.* at 801, 9 AD Cases at 494 (quoting 42 U.S.C. §423(d)(1)(A)).
[236] *Id.* at 802, 9 AD Cases at 494.
[237] *Id.* at 802–03, 9 AD Cases at 495.
[238] *Id.*

Nonetheless, the Supreme Court acknowledged that in some cases, a prior claim for SSDI benefits may genuinely conflict with an ADA claim.[239] Indeed, a plaintiff's sworn assertion that he or she is "unable to work" for purposes of the SSDI application appears to negate a necessary element of an ADA claim (that is, that he or she is a qualified individual with a disability capable of performing a job's essential functions with or without reasonable accommodation).[240] Justice Breyer, writing for the court, held that these apparent contradictions must be remedied by sufficient explanations.

> When faced with a plaintiff's previous sworn statement asserting "total disability" or the like, the court should require an explanation of any apparent inconsistency with the necessary elements of an ADA claim. To defeat summary judgment, that explanation must be sufficient to warrant a reasonable juror's concluding that, assuming the truth of, or the plaintiff's good faith belief in, the earlier statement, the plaintiff could nonetheless "perform the essential functions" of her job, with or without "reasonable accommodation".[241]

Thus, an individual may still be considered a qualified individual with a disability, even though he or she receives benefits for being completely disabled.

A substantial amount of litigation under the ADA has focused on the appropriate interpretations of the key statutory terms—"disability" and "qualified individual with a disability"—which are fundamental starting points in assessing the ADA's protections and an employer's obligations. Despite the EEOC's regulations, interpretive guidance, and a number of Supreme Court rulings, it is clear that these definitions and their applications will remain fluid for years to come.

V. Common Illnesses and Conditions Examined Under the Americans With Disabilities Act

The ADA has forced employers to reexamine their treatment of job applicants and current employees suffering from

---

[239] *Id.* at 805, 9 AD Cases at 496.
[240] *Id.* at 806, 9 AD Cases at 496.
[241] *Id.* at 807, 9 AD Cases at 496.

a variety of common illnesses and conditions. Similarly, many individuals—both applicants and employees—have sought to assert their statutory rights and protections in a broad range of circumstances. Although few conditions or illnesses are considered per se disabilities under the ADA, many can be deemed to be disabilities if they substantially limit one or major life activities. Similarly, many individuals suffering from serious ailments are not classified as disabled, as the criteria for being considered disabled under the ADA—as interpreted by the federal courts—are quite stringent. Thus, it is important for parties to the employment relationship and their legal counsel to be aware of the ADA's nuances with respect to various medical conditions.

The general paradigm for the analysis of medical conditions under the ADA has proven to follow a common approach, as similar issues have been litigated in circumstances involving many specific illnesses and conditions. Among these have been the question of whether a limitation alleged to be a protected disability under the ADA actually falls into that category if its effects have been or can be mitigated through medications, assistive devices, or other means. In addition, many cases have turned on whether a condition that limits an employee or applicant actually disqualifies that person from performance of a range of jobs (in either the employer's operations or across the economy). The impact of other laws and regulations, apart from the ADA, in limiting an individual's ability to lawfully or appropriately perform specific jobs also has figured into cases assessing potential status of applicants and employees as qualified individuals with disabilities. These and other issues are explored below in the context of some of the most common conditions, illnesses, and circumstances considered by the courts in applying the ADA.

In contrast to the discussion in other chapters of this publication, this analysis may seem somewhat focused on the employer perspective of actions that are required and those that are prohibited under the ADA in the context of specific conditions. However, because of the nature of the statute's requirements, and the interactions that involve employees and employers—and, often, their legal counsel—such an analysis should be helpful in identifying the impact of a given condition, accommodation processes, and requirements. An understanding on both sides of the hiring and employment perspective may be beneficial in considering appropriate standards and modifications, as that may maximize the prospects for a successful outcome from the interactive process that often characterizes compliance with the reasonable accommodation obligation.

A. Substance Abuse

Alcoholics and past or recovering drug addicts may qualify as individuals with disabilities under the ADA under certain circumstances.[242] Covered individuals enjoy some degree of protection against discrimination, termination, demotion, and other adverse employment actions. This does not mean, however, that employers have no recourse against employees or job applicants with substance abuse problems. Moreover, for purposes of ADA coverage, abuse of drugs is treated differently from abuse of alcohol. This section will address both types of substance abuse and explain an employer's obligation to individuals with these problems under the ADA.

Former drug addicts who participate in a supervised rehabilitation program, have successfully completed such a program, or who are otherwise rehabilitated and are no longer taking drugs are considered individuals with disabilities under the ADA.[243] Rehabilitation programs "include in-patient, outpatient, or employee assistance programs, or recognized self-help programs such as Narcotics Anonymous."[244] Individuals who are falsely regarded as being a drug addict are also protected by the ADA.[245]

In order to be substantially limited by drug use, and thus protected under the ADA, an individual must be addicted to

---

[242]TITLE I TECHNICAL ASSISTANCE MANUAL, *supra* note 43, §8.5.
[243]42 U.S.C. §12114(b)(1)–(2).
[244]TITLE I TECHNICAL ASSISTANCE MANUAL, *supra* note 43, §8.5.
[245]42 U.S.C. §12114(b)(3).

that drug.[246] Thus, casual or social drug users do not receive the same shielding under the law.[247]

Employers, however, need not make allowances for present drug users. The ADA specifically *excludes* from coverage employees or job applicants who *currently* use illegal drugs.[248] Drug use considered illegal includes the use, possession, or distribution of drugs banned by the Controlled Substances Act.[249] Using drugs under the supervision by a licensed healthcare professional or authorized by the Controlled Substances Act or other federal law is not considered illegal.[250] Thus, abuse of, or addiction to, lawfully obtained prescription drugs, is not subject to the ADA's coverage exclusion. For example, a dependence on opiates prescribed by a psychiatrist is not considered an illegal use of drugs, even though these pain killers are controlled substances, because the drugs were procured through and monitored by a licensed healthcare professional.[251] Similarly, the use of methadone as part of a drug maintenance treatment program, or morphine prescribed by a physician to alleviate pain, is not deemed unlawful, even though morphine and amphetamines are controlled substances.[252]

An individual addicted to drugs that are not considered controlled substances is not precluded from coverage under the ADA, even if such drugs are used illegally. Abusing noncontrolled, prescription pills obtained without a prescription, for instance, would not exclude an individual from ADA coverage.[253]

---

[246] TITLE I TECHNICAL ASSISTANCE MANUAL, *supra* note 43, §8.5.

[247] *See, e.g.*, Montegue v. City of New Orleans, No. Civ. A. 95-2420, 1997 WL 327113 (E.D. La. 1997) (firefighter who occasionally used cocaine and marijuana could not prove he was drug addict, and was thus not individual with disability).

[248] The ADA states: "the term 'qualified individual with a disability' shall not include any employee or applicant who is currently engaging in the illegal use of drugs, when the covered entity acts on the basis of such use." 42 U.S.C. §12114(a).

[249] 21 U.S.C. §812.

[250] 42 U.S.C. §12111(6)(A).

[251] *See* Toscano v. National Broadcast. Co., 12 AD Cases 768 (S.D.N.Y. 2000) (employee's addition to prescription pain pills taken under supervision of licensed healthcare profession not illegal drug use under ADA).

[252] *See* TITLE I TECHNICAL ASSISTANCE MANUAL, *supra* note 43, §8.3.

[253] *See, e.g.*, Adams v. Rite Aid of Me., Inc., 6 WH Cases 2d 1481 (D. Me. 2001) (pharmacist's excessive use of pain-killer Ultram without prescription was not considered illegal drug use under, as Ultram is not controlled substance).

However, the current *illegal* use of prescription drugs that *are* considered controlled substances *is* considered an unlawful action under the Controlled Substances Act, and therefore excludes a user from ADA's protections. For example, the use of amphetamines—a controlled substance that may be legally prescribed—without a prescription is deemed illegal drug use.[254]

It bears noting that controlled substances do not "include distilled spirits, wine, malt beverages, or tobacco."[255] Thus, the abuse of alcohol receives different treatment under the ADA.

1. Current Drug Use

How temporal an employee's drug use must be in relation to the adverse employment action has been a subject of much litigation. According to the EEOC's *Technical Assistance Manual*, current drug use is "the illegal use of drugs [that has] occurred recently enough to justify a[n] employer's reasonable belief that" the employee's drug use is ongoing.[256] "Current" is not limited to the day of use, or recent weeks or days in relation to the adverse employment action. The determination of whether an individual's drug use is current does not follow a specific formula, but rather must be made on a case-by-case basis.

Current drug use is often indicated by a positive result of a properly administered drug test. Once an employee or applicant tests positive for illegal drug use, and is therefore deemed a current drug user, he or she cannot use the participation in a rehabilitation program as a shield against any adverse employment action. An individual who tests positive for current drug use then immediately enters into a rehabilitation program does not enjoy the same protection afforded to former or

---

[254]TITLE I TECHNICAL ASSISTANCE MANUAL, *supra* note 43, §8.3.
[255]21 U.S.C. §802(6).
[256]TITLE I TECHNICAL ASSISTANCE MANUAL, *supra* note 43, §8.3; *see also* Salley v. Circuit City Stores, Inc., 7 AD Cases 852 (E.D. Pa. 1997), *aff'd on other grounds*, 160 F.3d 977, 8 AD Cases 1407 (3d Cir. 1998) ("currently engaging" is term that can be applied to illegal drug use that is close enough in time to challenged employment action to indicate that illegal drug use is ongoing problem).

current participants in rehabilitation programs who no longer use drugs.

Exactly how long an individual must remain drug-free in order to be considered a "former" drug user is unclear. In the majority of jurisdictions that have addressed this issue, so long as it can be shown that an employee was an illegal drug user in the weeks or months prior to the challenged employment action, he or she may be deemed a current user even if clean and sober at the time the disciplinary action is carried out. For example, in *Shafer v. Preston Memorial Hospital Corp.*,[257] a hospital nurse addicted to narcotics was placed on medical leave and enrolled in a rehabilitation program. The hospital fired the nurse the day she completed the inpatient portion of the rehabilitation program. The nurse sued her employer, alleging that she had been discriminated against because of her drug addiction. Because she was drug-free when the hospital fired her, the nurse contended that she was no longer a current illegal drug user. The court disagreed, finding that "currently" means a periodic or ongoing activity that has not yet permanently ended, and emphasized that "an employee illegally using drugs in a periodic fashion during the weeks or months prior to discharge is 'currently engaging in the illegal use of drugs,'" notwithstanding the fact that she is participating in a drug rehabilitation program and is no longer using drugs on the date of termination.[258]

Similarly, in *Collings v. Longview Fibre Co.*,[259] employees fired while undergoing rehabilitation were deemed current illegal drug users, and thus not protected by the ADA. According to the U.S. Court of Appeals for the Ninth Circuit in this case, current drug use is not measured in days or weeks, but rather by whether the use is "recently enough" to give employers a reason to believe that the drug use is continuing. Other courts

---

[257] 107 F.3d 274, 6 AD Cases 682 (4th Cir. 1997).
[258] *Id.* at 278, 6 AD Cases at 685.
[259] 63 F.3d 828, 4 AD Cases 1278 (9th Cir. 1995), *cert. denied*, 516 U.S. 1048 (1996).

have found that time periods of 1 month[260] and 6 weeks[261] of abstinence from illegal drug still qualify an individual as a current user of illegal drugs.

In general, the date the decision is made to fire or otherwise discipline an employee for illegal drug use is more important than the date the action is actually carried out. If the employee is a current illegal drug user at the time of the decision, it does not matter if the employee is clean and sober when the disciplinary measure actually takes effect. In *Zenor v. El Paso Healthcare System*,[262] a hospital recommended a detoxification and rehabilitation program to a pharmacist employee addicted to cocaine. The hospital then informed the employee that he would be discharged as soon as his medical leave expired. The U.S. Court of Appeals for the Fifth Circuit affirmed the legality of his discharge, finding that at the time the employee was informed of the decision to terminate his employment, he was a current user of illegal drugs.

The U.S. Court of Appeals for the Second Circuit, however, maintains a different view of the "current user" exception to ADA coverage. In *Teahan v. Metro-North Commuter Railroad Co.*,[263] this court determined in a Rehabilitation Act[264] case that the relevant inquiry is not when the adverse employment decision is made or communicated to the employee, but rather when the date of termination becomes effective. In *Teahan*, an employee was terminated for absenteeism, which was allegedly caused by substance abuse. Although the court ultimately determined that the employee was not "otherwise qualified" to perform the job due to his severe substance abuse and history

---

[260] Quigley v. Austeel Lemont Co., 79 F. Supp. 2d 941, 10 AD Cases 351 (N.D. Ill. 2000) (10-day treatment program and 1-month abstinence from drug use constitutes current drug use); Scott v. Beverly Enter.-Kansas, Inc., 968 F. Supp. 1430 (D. Kan. 1997) (staying clean for 30-day period when employee was hired and fired is not long enough to render employee former drug user).

[261] McDaniel v. Mississippi Baptist Med. Ctr., 877 F. Supp. 321, 4 AD Cases 241 (S.D. Miss.), *aff'd*, 74 F.3d 1238, 6 AD Cases 800 (5th Cir. 1995) (6 weeks of abstinence insufficient to be regarded as former drug addict).

[262] 176 F.3d 847, 9 AD Cases 609 (5th Cir. 1999).

[263] 80 F.3d 50, 5 AD Cases 603 (2d Cir. 1996).

[264] The relevant provisions of the Rehabilitation Act are virtually identical to those of the ADA.

of relapse, the court ruled that employers must consider the employee's drug use at the time of discharge. This case represents the minority opinion on this matter.

Thus, for the most part, the ADA permits employers to take adverse actions against employees or job applicants who are deemed current users of drugs, even if the individuals are drug-free and/or are participating in a rehabilitation program at the time those employment decisions are carried out. The same exception, however, does not necessarily apply to individuals who abuse alcohol.

2. Alcohol Use

Alcoholics are treated differently from illegal drug addicts under the ADA, in that current alcohol use does not automatically exclude an alcoholic from ADA protection. Because the ADA specifically excludes current illegal drug users from its definition of a "qualified individual with a disability," and the term "illegal use of drugs" does not include the consumption of alcohol, alcoholics are given more leeway under the statute than are illegal drug addicts.[265]

Under the ADA, current alcoholics, recovering alcoholics, and those erroneously perceived as being alcoholics may be deemed disabled.[266] This does not mean that an employee is immune from termination or other action if he or she engages in discipline-worthy behavior as a result of alcoholism. According to the EEOC's *Technical Assistance Manual*, an employer may "discipline, discharge or deny employment to an alcoholic whose use of alcohol adversely affects job performance or conduct to the extent that s/he is not qualified [to perform the job]."[267]

---

[265] *See, e.g.*, Mararri v. WCI Steel Inc., 130 F.3d 1180, 7 AD Cases 978 (6th Cir. 1997) (plain language of ADA does not exclude alcoholics from coverage, because alcohol is not "drug" within meaning of statute); Flynn v. Raytheon Co., 868 F. Supp. 383, 386 n6, 3 AD Cases 1495 (D. Mass. 1994) ("Congress did not exclude alcoholics from ADA protection as it did current illegal drug users.").

[266] *See* TITLE I TECHNICAL ASSISTANCE MANUAL, *supra* note 43, §8.4.

[267] *Id.*

Whether alcoholism is a per se disability under the ADA, or whether an individual must first prove that his or her alcoholism substantially limits the ability to perform a major life activity to be considered a disability is an unsettled issue. Representing the minority view, the U.S. Court of Appeals for the Seventh Circuit has found that alcoholism *is* a per se disability.[268] In contrast, the U.S. Court of Appeals for the First,[269] Fifth,[270] and Tenth[271] Circuits, in addition to the Federal District Court in the District of Columbia,[272] have all determined that an employee's alcoholism must limit the performance of a major life activity substantially to constitute a disability. Thus, while current use of alcohol does not automatically render an alcoholic employee ineligible to receive ADA protection, in most jurisdictions the individual must be prepared to show how alcoholism adversely affects his or her ability to perform at least one major life activity.

3. Being "Regarded as" or Having a Record of Substance Abuse–Related Disability

An employee or job applicant who is mistakenly believed to be an alcoholic or drug addict is also deemed disabled under the ADA. For example, an employer that erroneously perceives

---

[268] *See* Duda v. Board of Educ. of Franklin Park Pub. Sch. Dist. No. 84, 133 F.3d 1054, 8 AD Cases 99 (7th Cir. 1998) (alcoholism is per se disability); Huels v. Exxon Coal USA, Inc., 121 F.3d 1047, 1049, 7 AD Cases 10 (7th Cir. 1997) (acknowledging without discussion that alcoholism is disability); Bryant v. Madigan, 84 F.3d 246, 248, 5 AD Cases 833 (7th Cir. 1996) (same); DeSpears v. Milwaukee County, 63 F.3d 635, 635, 4 AD Cases 1313 (7th Cir. 1995) (noting parties' acknowledgement that alcoholism is disability under ADA).

[269] Bailey v. Georgia-Pacific Corp., 306 F.3d 1162, 13 AD Cases 1066 (1st Cir. 2002) (employee failed to show that his alcoholism substantially limited his ability to work).

[270] Burch v. Coca-Cola Co., 119 F.3d 305, 7 AD Cases 241 (5th Cir. 1997), *cert. denied*, 522 U.S. 1084 (1998) (EEOC has not attempted to classify alcoholism as per se disability).

[271] Nelson v. Williams Field Serv. Co., Nos. 99-8041, 98-CV-242-D, 2000 WL 743684 (10th Cir. 2000) (employee's alcoholism was not disability because it did not interfere with his ability to perform his job duties).

[272] Wilson v. Teamsters, 47 F. Supp. 2d 8 (D.D.C. 1999) (employee could not demonstrate that his union regarded him as substantially limited in one or more major life activities).

an employee who slurs his or her speech and walks with an uneasy gait as an alcoholic could be liable for discrimination under the ADA if the employer bases an adverse employment decision on that misperception. An individual who is mistakenly viewed as merely a *casual* drug or alcohol user, however, is not protected under the ADA.[273]

In some instances, an employee's refusal to seek treatment for drug or alcohol abuse has led employers to mistakenly perceive such actions as admissions of addiction. In *Miners v. Cargill Communications, Inc.*,[274] for example, an employee seen drinking at a bar with clients was mistakenly assumed to be an alcoholic and was given an ultimatum of either entering into an alcohol treatment program or termination. After refusing to participate in the treatment program on the grounds that she was not an alcoholic, the employee was fired. The employee sued under the ADA, alleging that her employer regarded her as an alcoholic, and terminated her employment on that basis. The U.S. Court of Appeals for the Eighth Circuit agreed, reversing a grant of summary judgment in the employer's favor. Similarly, in *Jones v. Corrections Corp. of America*,[275] a corrections employee who tested positive for marijuana use was offered drug rehabilitation. The employee refused, maintaining he was not a current illegal drug user and that the drug test results were faulty. The employee sued, alleging that because the employee regarded him as a drug user, he was a protected individual under the ADA. The district court denied the employer's motion to dismiss this claim.

A drug test indicating that an employee takes prescription drugs may lead an employer to erroneously conclude that the employee is an illegal drug user. An individual who is believed to be unfit to perform a safety-sensitive job because of prescription drug use may similarly be "regarded as" disabled.[276]

---

[273]TITLE I TECHNICAL ASSISTANCE MANUAL, *supra* note 43, §8.6.
[274]113 F.3d 820, 6 AD Cases 1229 (8th Cir.), *cert. denied*, 522 U.S. 981 (1997).
[275]993 F. Supp. 1384, 8 AD Cases 1561 (D. Kan. 1998).
[276]*See* Shiplett v. National R.R. Passenger Corp., 182 F.3d 918 (6th Cir. 1999), *cert. denied*, 528 U.S. 1078 (2000). However, an employer that adheres to other federal

Individuals who claim to be regarded as being disabled must show that their employer considers them to have an impairment that substantially limits their ability to perform major life activities. Thus, simply participating in a drug or alcohol rehabilitation program does not necessarily mean the employer regards an employee as disabled, unless that employer believes the substance abuse treatment renders the individual unable to perform major life activities.[277]

Even if the employer regards the employee as being a drug addict, the employee still must show that the employer viewed this drug addiction as substantially limiting.[278] Moreover, merely being asked to take a drug test does not indicate that the employer regards an employee as an illegal drug user.[279]

If an employee claims that he or she has a record of substance abuse, he or she must demonstrate that the employer was aware of this past substance abuse.[280] Simply showing that an employee or applicant was hospitalized for substance abuse, without more, has been shown to be insufficient to prove that one has a record of being disabled.[281]

---

laws or regulations that preclude employees in certain safety-sensitive positions from taking particular prescription drugs does not violate the ADA.

[277] See, e.g., Martin v. Barnesville Exempted Vill. Sch. Dist. Bd. of Educ., 209 F.3d 931, 10 AD Cases 787 (6th Cir.), cert. denied, 531 U.S. 992 (2000) (employee who participated in alcohol rehabilitation program and denied safety-sensitive position could not prove that employer regarded her as disabled). For a discussion of what does and does not constitute a major life activity, see section II.B., "Major Life Activities," above.

[278] See Zenor v. El Paso Healthcare Sys., Ltd., 176 F.3d 847, 860, 9 AD Cases 609 (5th Cir. 1999) (perceived as being drug addict is not same as perceived as being disabled; "[E]ven a plaintiff who suffers from a condition such as alcoholism or drug addiction—or is perceived as suffering from such a condition—must demonstrate that the condition substantially limits, or is perceived by his employer as substantially limiting, his ability to perform a major life function."); see also Burch v. Coca-Cola Co., 119 F.3d 305, 7 AD Cases 241 (5th Cir. 1997).

[279] Parry v. Mohawk Motors of Mich., Inc., 236 F.3d 299, 11 AD Cases 538 (6th Cir. 2000), cert. denied, 533 U.S. 951 (2001) (random drug test insufficient to prove that employer regarded employee as having substantially limiting impairment).

[280] See Pace v. Paris Maint. Co., 107 F. Supp. 2d 251, 11 AD Cases 990 (S.D.N.Y. 2000), aff'd, 14 AD Cases 672 (2d Cir. 2001).

[281] See also Burch, 119 F.3d at 316 (having undergone hospitalization for alcoholism does not necessarily give rise to disability).

4. Employer Rights With Respect to Employee Substance Abuse

The ADA permits an employer to prohibit the illegal use of drugs and the use of alcohol at the workplace, and to discipline employees for being under the influence of illegal drugs or alcohol while working.[282] Therefore, an employee who shows up to work intoxicated or under the influence of illegal drugs cannot invoke the protections of the ADA by claiming to be an alcoholic or recovering drug addict. Similarly, it is permissible to terminate or otherwise discipline an employee for drug possession at the workplace without running afoul of the ADA.[283] Moreover, firing an employee for testing positive for illegal drug use does not equate to an unlawful action against an individual based on his or her addiction-related disability.[284]

In addition, the ADA does not require an employer to provide alcoholics or recovering drug addicts with extra leeway when it comes to performance or qualification standards, even if lapses in performance are the direct result of alcoholism or illegal drug use.[285] In other words, an employer's adverse actions against an employee for misconduct or subpar performance do not necessarily amount to discrimination based on that employee's status as an alcoholic or illegal drug user.[286] For example, if an employee is repeatedly absent because of excessive alcohol and/or illegal drug use, that employee may be terminated or disciplined for failing to meet an employer's legitimate work expectations, as attendance is usually deemed an essential job function.

By the same token, the ADA does not shield an alcoholic or drug-addicted employee from the same behavioral standards

---

[282] 42 U.S.C. §12114(c)(1), (2).

[283] *See, e.g.,* Pernice v. City of Chi., 237 F.3d 783, 11 AD Cases 608 (7th Cir. 2001); Collings v. Longview Fibre Co., 63 F.3d 828, 4 AD Cases 1278 (9th Cir. 1995), *cert. denied*, 516 U.S. 1048 (1996); Fitzgerald v. Caldera, 216 F.3d 1087 (10th Cir. 2000); Figueroa v. Fajardo, 1 F. Supp. 2d 117 (D.P.R. 1998).

[284] *See, e.g.,* Salisbury v. Art Van Furniture, 938 F. Supp. 435 (W.D. Mich. 1996); Toussaint v. Sheriff of Cook County, No. 97 C 7866, 2000 WL 656642 (N.D. Ill. 2000).

[285] 42 U.S.C. §12114(c)(4).

[286] *See* Martin v. Barnesville Exempted Vill. Sch. Dist. Bd. of Educ., 209 F.3d 931, 10 AD Cases 787 (6th Cir. 2000) (school bus driver who had been disciplined

imposed on all other employees.[287] This principle applies even if the employee's alcoholism or drug addiction was the only reason the employer's standards of conduct were violated.[288]

a. Last-Chance Agreements

Often, employers enter into last-chance agreements (LCAs) with employees, through which employers refrain from terminating the employment of an individual who has violated an employer's substance abuse policy, in exchange for assurances from the employee that he or she will abstain from drugs and/or alcohol, and agree to drug and/or alcohol testing, among other conditions. Violating the LCA has been held to be a legitimate grounds for termination, despite the employee's substance abuse–related disability.[289]

b. Off-Duty Conduct

Even off-duty drug and alcohol abuse may constitute legitimate grounds for disciplinary action. For example, in *Johnson v. New York Hospital*,[290] a nurse who had arrived at his workplace drunk and engaged in a violent altercation with security guards was validly terminated, according to the U.S. Court of Appeals for the Second Circuit, even though the alcohol use was the result of his alcoholism, and the incident occurred off-duty.

---

for alcohol abuse while on duty in past was legitimately denied safety-sensitive position, as decision was based on prior misconduct, not on status as alcoholic).

[287] *See, e.g.*, Brown v. Lucky Stores Inc., 246 F.3d 1182, 11 AD Cases 1195 (9th Cir. 2001) (ADA clearly states that employer may hold alcoholics and drug addicts to same performance and behavioral standards to which it holds other employees); Renaud v. Wyoming Dep't of Family Servs., 203 F.3d 723, 5 WH Cases 2d 1505 (10th Cir. 2000) (ADA does not protect alcoholic from consequences of misconduct caused by drinking).

[288] *See, e.g.*, Williams v. Widnall, 79 F.3d 1003, 5 AD Cases 663 (10th Cir. 1996) (discharge of alcoholic employee who made threats against coworkers while drunk not unlawful, as employer may hold alcoholic employee to same behavioral standards as those applicable to all employees).

[289] *See, e.g.*, Mararri v. WCI, Steel Inc., 130 F.3d 1180, 7 AD Cases 978 (6th Cir. 1997); Wobser v. PPG Indus., Inc., 208 F.3d 224 (9th Cir. 2000); Nelson v. Williams Field Servs. Co., Nos. 99-8041, 98-CV-242-D, 2000 WL 743684 (10th Cir. 2000).

[290] 96 F.3d 33, 5 AD Cases 1537 (2d Cir. 1996).

The court reasoned that the nurse's off-duty conduct was "relevant to whether his employment may pose a threat to the safety of others."[291]

An employee's criminal conduct often serves as grounds for termination, even if that conduct stems from alcohol or drug abuse. In *DeSpears v. Milwaukee County*,[292] an employee was demoted to a position that did not require driving after his fourth drunk-driving conviction and loss of license. Although the employee claimed the employer violated the ADA, as he alleged his convictions were the result of alcoholism, the U.S. Court of Appeals for the Seventh Circuit affirmed the employer's decision, finding that the decision to demote the employee was due to his off-duty criminal conduct, not his alcohol use.[293] Similarly, in *Newland v. Dalton*,[294] a federal employee who attempted to fire an assault rifle at people in a bar was found to have been justifiably discharged, given that the employee's behavior was the kind of "egregious and criminal conduct that employees are responsible for regardless of any disability."[295]

c. Discrimination/Pretext

Although an employer has the right to maintain a drug- and alcohol-free workplace, and may discipline employees for drug- or alcohol-related misconduct, it cannot treat the transgressions of alcoholics or former illegal drug users more harshly than those committed by other employees. For example, if an employer discharges an alcoholic employee who arrives at work under the influence of alcohol, it cannot impose a lesser punishment on nonalcoholic employees who are inebriated at the workplace.[296] Similarly, an employer cannot fire an alcoholic employee for missing work because of his or her drinking if

---

[291] *Id.* at 34, 5 AD Cases at 1538.
[292] 63 F.3d 635, 4 AD Cases 1313 (7th Cir. 1995).
[293] *See also* Maddox v. University of Tenn., 62 F.3d 843, 4 AD Cases 1253 (6th Cir. 1995) (assistant coach's termination was due to his arrest for drunk driving, not for his status as alcoholic, even if event was triggered by his condition).
[294] 81 F.3d 904, 5 AD Cases 735 (9th Cir. 1996).
[295] *Id.*
[296] *See* Flynn v. Raytheon Co., 868 F.Supp. 383, 3 AD Cases 1495 (D. Mass. 1994).

the employer does not enforce such a stringent penalty for absenteeism by other employees. In these instances, the reason provided for the employee's termination is pretextual, and thus unlawful under the ADA.

5. Medical Inquiries and Examinations Regarding Drug and Alcohol Use

While employers may inquire as to a job applicant's current use of illegal drugs or alcohol, they may not ask whether the individual is an alcoholic or a drug addict, or whether he or she has ever participated in a substance abuse rehabilitation program.[297] Once a conditional offer of employment has been made, however, an employer is permitted to inquire about the individual's past or present use of drugs or alcohol, but may not discriminate against the individual based on this information—such as precluding the employee from a safety-sensitive position—unless doing so is job-related and consistent with business necessity. Moreover, an employer must be prepared to show that there is no reasonable accommodation that would allow the alcoholic or recovering drug addict to work in spite of the disability.[298]

Additionally, employers are limited in their ability to perform medical examinations of prospective employees. An employer may, however, order a medical examination and/or make medical inquiries regarding a job applicant's condition after making a job offer and before he or she begins employment, making the final job offer contingent on the results of the medical examination and/or inquiry, so long as all prospective employees are treated in this manner.[299]

For example, in *EEOC v. J.B. Hunt Transp., Inc.*,[300] an employer, as part of medical screening, asked employees who had been given a conditional offer of employment about their drug use, including prescription drugs. The names of the drugs the

---

[297] TITLE I TECHNICAL ASSISTANCE MANUAL, *supra* note 43, §8.8.
[298] *Id.*
[299] 29 C.F.R. §1630.14(b) (2003).
[300] 128 F. Supp. 2d 117, 12 AD Cases 1805 (N.D.N.Y. 2001), *aff'd*, 321 F.3d 69, 13 AD Cases 1697 (2d Cir. 2003).

employees admitted taking were placed on a "Drug Review List." The employer, which was subject to DOT regulations for commercial drivers that prohibited the use of certain medications while on the job, then required the employees either to get medical authorization to work or be disqualified from employment. The New York federal district court that presided over this case ruled that this safety-related policy did not violate the ADA, because taking prescription drugs in and of itself is not a disability.

Once employed, individuals may lawfully be subject to medical examinations or inquiries by the employer, so long as doing so is job-related and consistent with business necessity.[301] The ADA, however, specifically exempts drug testing from its definition of "medical examination."[302] Thus, an employer need not make a conditional offer of employment to a job applicant before administering a drug test. Because tests to detect the use of alcohol, however, *are* still considered "medical examinations" under the ADA, the ADA's restrictions regarding medical tests apply for alcohol testing. Nonetheless, it is permissible to administer a follow-up test for alcohol to an employee who has returned from leave due to alcohol abuse so long as the employer has a reasonable belief that the employee poses a direct threat in the workplace in the absence of such testing.

a. Drug Testing

As discussed above, the ADA does not prohibit (or authorize) the use of drug testing for the alleged use of drugs by applicants or employees, nor does it bar employers from making employment decisions based on the results of such tests.[303] A positive test result cannot, however, be used to screen out individuals with other disabilities unless doing so is job-related and consistent with business necessity.

---

[301] 29 C.F.R. §1630.14(c) (2003).
[302] 42 U.S.C. §12114(d).
[303] 42 U.S.C. §12114(d)(2).

6. Employer Defenses

The ADA recognizes that employers may have legitimate justifications for refusing to hire an alcoholic or recovering drug addict (as discussed above, current drug users are not covered under the ADA). If the reason for excluding these individuals from employment is job-related and consistent with business necessity, and/or the applicant would pose a direct threat to himself or herself and others in the workplace, then an employer may lawfully behave in an otherwise discriminatory manner.

a. Job-Related and Consistent With Business Necessity

An employer may implement a policy that precludes individuals with a history of substance abuse so long as that policy is deemed "job-related and consistent with business necessity."[304] The EEOC's *Technical Assistance Manual* provides the example of a policy denying an individual with a history of illegal drug use an opportunity to become a police officer on the grounds that the applicant's illegal conduct would undermine the credibility of an officer serving as a witness for the prosecution in a criminal case.[305] The example then explains, however, that if the individual were able to prove that he or she had successfully performed the job as a police officer following the period of drug use, then the policy's necessity may not be so justified.[306]

If an employer implements a uniformly applied safety-based qualification standard that tends to screen out individuals with substance abuse–related disabilities, then the assessment of whether that standard is job-related and consistent with business necessity takes into consideration both the magnitude and probability of possible harm that such an individual could cause if employed.[307] In *EEOC v. Exxon*

---

[304] TITLE I TECHNICAL ASSISTANCE MANUAL, *supra* note 43, §8.7.
[305] *Id.*
[306] *Id.*
[307] *See, e.g.*, Morton v. United Parcel Serv., Inc., 272 F.3d 1249, 12 AD Cases 897 (9th Cir. 2001), *cert. denied*, 535 U.S. 1054, 13 AD Cases 96 (2002); EEOC v. Exxon Corp., 203 F.3d 871, 10 AD Cases 225 (5th Cir. 2000). The courts in these cases rejected the EEOC's position, as stated in 29 C.F.R. pt. 1630, app. §1630.15(b)

Corp.,[308] the standard for evaluating whether an employer's policy that permanently removed any employee who had undergone substance abuse treatment from safety-sensitive positions was discriminatory was brought into question. The U.S. Court of Appeals for the Fifth Circuit remanded the case, holding that so long as the employer could prove that the rate of recidivism among recovering substance abusers constituted a safety risk sufficient to prove business necessity, then the policy did not violate the ADA.[309]

It may be more difficult for an employer in the U.S. Court of Appeals for the Ninth Circuit, however, to invoke the business necessity defense to justify a policy that discriminates against former drug addicts. In *Hernandez v. Hughes Missile Systems Co.*,[310] the court held that an employer's policy against rehiring employees who had been terminated for misconduct or who had resigned in lieu of termination discriminated against an employee who had quit because of his drug addiction. The employee at issue was a recovering substance abuser who reapplied to his employer 2 years after resigning. The Ninth Circuit held that the employer's blanket policy as applied to employees who were terminated for substance abuse problems violated the ADA.

The Supreme Court, however, vacated this decision on the grounds that the Ninth Circuit applied the wrong standard to what amounted to a disparate treatment case, as opposed to a broader disparate impact claim.[311] Because the issue in

---

& (c) (2003), that in order to show that safety requirements that screen out or tend to screen out an individual with a disability or a class of individuals with disabilities are job-related and consistent with business necessity, an employer must demonstrate that the requirements, as applied to the individual, satisfy the "direct threat" standard in 29 C.F.R. §1630.2(r) (2003). This position, which was not articulated in the regulations, has not been given much deference.

[308] 203 F.3d 871, 10 AD Cases 225 (5th Cir. 2000).

[309] *Id.*

[310] 292 F.3d 1030 (9th Cir. 2002), *vacated sub nom.* Raytheon Co. v. Hernandez, 540 U.S. 44, 14 AD Cases 1825 (2003).

[311] Raytheon v. Hernandez, 540 U.S. 44, 14 AD Cases 1825 (2003). Because a disparate impact claim was not timely pleaded or raised, the legality of the employer's policy was not subject to a disparate impact analysis.

Hernandez was whether the employer's uniformly applied, facially neutral rehire policy was a legitimate, nondiscriminatory reason for failing to rehire one particular employee, *not* whether such a policy has a discriminatory impact on former drug abusers in general, the Supreme Court held that the Ninth Circuit erred in its analysis, and remanded the case for further review. Despite the Supreme Court's ruling, the Ninth Circuit's decision in *Hernandez* indicates that this jurisdiction would likely view such a blanket rehiring policy as having a disparate impact on recovering or former drug addicts, and therefore it would be an ADA violation.

A ban on prescription drug use without prior company approval was found to be unlawful under the ADA in the U.S. Court of Appeals for the Tenth Circuit, as the employer could not demonstrate how such a ban was job-related and consistent with business necessity.[312] Thus, if an employer seeks to defend a policy that adversely affects individuals with histories of substance abuse, it must establish how that policy is truly necessary, and not merely convenient or desirable.

b. Direct Threat

If an individual with a substance abuse–related disability poses a direct threat to himself or herself or others in the workplace, then an employer is allowed to fire or refuse to hire that individual without running afoul of the ADA. The ADA defines "direct threat" as "a significant risk to the health or safety of others that cannot be eliminated by reasonable accommodation."[313] An employer may also invoke the direct threat defense when refusing to reinstate a former employee to the same position he or she held prior to going on leave for substance abuse.[314]

In order to prove that an alcoholic of former illegal drug user poses a direct threat, an employer must show that there is a high probability that the individual will likely abuse drugs

---

[312] Roe v. Cheyenne Mountain Conference Resort, 124 F.3d 1221, 7 AD Cases 779 (10th Cir. 1997).

[313] 42 U.S.C. §12111(3).

[314] *See* Altman v. New York City Health & Hosps. Corp., 100 F.3d 1054, 6 AD Cases 73 (2d Cir. 1996).

or alcohol in the future, that there is a risk of substantial harm as a result of this probable substance abuse, and that this risk cannot be reduced or eliminated via a reasonable accommodation.[315] To establish that there is a high probability that the employee or applicant would start using drugs or alcohol again, an employer must make an individual assessment of the person's likelihood to do so, as opposed to merely citing general reports or statistics of recovering substance abuser recidivism rates.[316] Moreover, an assessment of any significant risk of substantial harm must be made by examining the individual's particular history of substance abuse, and the type of job at issue. For example, an alcoholic employee with a history of recidivism may be barred from a safety-sensitive position, such as ship's captain.[317]

Several courts have dealt with the direct threat defense as it applies to substance abuse. In *Bekker v. Humana Health Plan, Inc.*,[318] a doctor with a longstanding history of alcohol abuse was found to have been justifiably terminated, because her condition posed imminent harm to patients, and she declined a reasonable accommodation of alcohol treatment. Similarly, in *Griel v. Franklin Medical Center*,[319] a nurse who was a recovering illegal drug addict was found to pose a direct threat to patient safety when she failed to follow proper procedures for dispensing narcotics to patients. An employee who makes threats to supervisors and coworkers while drunk has also been adjudged to pose a direct threat to the safety of others, and thus lawfully terminated.[320]

7. Compliance With Other Substance Abuse Laws and Regulations

The ADA permits employers to require that their employees adhere to other laws and regulations regarding drug and

---

[315] TITLE I TECHNICAL ASSISTANCE MANUAL, *supra* note 43, §8.7.
[316] *Id.*
[317] *Id.*
[318] 229 F.3d 662, 10 AD Cases 1776 (7th Cir. 2000), *cert. denied*, 532 U.S. 972 (2001).
[319] 234 F.3d 731, 11 AD Cases 469 (1st Cir. 2000).
[320] Williams v. Widnall, 79 F.3d 1003, 5 AD Cases 663 (10th Cir. 1996).

alcohol use, such as the Drug-Free Workplace Act of 1988,[321] DOT regulations for airline employees, interstate motor carrier drivers, and railroad engineers, and regulations promulgated by the Department of Defense (DOD) and the Nuclear Regulatory Commission (NRC) for certain safety-sensitive positions.[322] The NRC regulations, for example, require that nuclear power plant operators ensure that their employees do not work under the influence of any substances that would impair their ability to perform their jobs.[323] These fitness-for-duty requirements preclude individuals under the influence of certain prescription drugs from working in safety-sensitive positions.[324] Therefore, an employer following these requirements will not run afoul of the ADA if it prevents an individual who uses prescription drugs from obtaining a safety-sensitive position because of this legal drug use. Meeting the NRC's fitness-for-duty requirements can be deemed an essential function of the job.[325]

In essence, an employer covered under other such laws and regulations may rely on such stringent rules and regulations regarding drug and alcohol use when making hiring, placement, and termination decisions.

8. *Reasonable Accommodation*

Rehabilitated drug addicts who no longer use illegal drugs and alcoholics who remain qualified to perform the essential

---

[321] 41 U.S.C. §701.

[322] 42 U.S.C. §12114(5); TITLE I TECHNICAL ASSISTANCE MANUAL, *supra* note 43, §8.10.

[323] 10 C.F.R. §26.10(a) (2004).

[324] *Id.* §26.10: General performance objectives.

Fitness-for-duty programs must: (a) Provide reasonable assurance that nuclear power plant personnel, transporter personnel, and personnel of licensees authorized to possess or use formula quantities of SSNM [strategic special nuclear material], will perform their tasks in a reliable and trustworthy manner and are not under the influence of any substance, legal or illegal, or mentally or physically impaired from any cause, which in any way adversely affects their ability to safely and competently perform their duties.

[325] *See* Mathieson v. American Elec. Power, 2002 U.S. Dist. LEXIS 6560 (W.D. Mich. 2002) (following NRC regulations, employee who took prescription medications was lawfully precluded from working in position that permitted unescorted access to nuclear power plant).

functions of their jobs, are entitled to reasonable accommodations of their disabilities.[326] Courts that have addressed the issue of reasonable accommodations for individuals with substance abuse problems have often held that the provision of drug or alcohol treatment services is an appropriate reasonable accommodation.[327] Providing employees with a more flexible schedule so that they may attend Alcoholics Anonymous meetings or other self-help programs also qualifies as a reasonable accommodation.[328]

However, if the employee is not a qualified individual with a disability, the employer is not required to provide a reasonable accommodation. For example, in *Wood v. Indianapolis Power & Light Co.*,[329] the U.S. Court of Appeals for the Seventh Circuit held that an employer's failure to offer an employee who was a current illegal drug user a reasonable accommodation did not violate the ADA, because current drug users are not qualified individuals with disabilities under the ADA.

In *Morgan v. N.W. Permanente, P.C.*,[330] a federal district court in Oregon held that a medical facility was under no obligation to provide a reasonable accommodation to a doctor who had lost his license due to alcohol abuse, because the individual was not qualified to serve as a doctor without a valid medical license.

Finally, at least one court has held that an employer need not provide a reasonable accommodation to an employee who divulges his or her substance abuse–related disability only after the adverse employment decision has been made. In *Peyton v. Otis Elevator Co.*,[331] an employee who was terminated for

---

[326]TITLE I TECHNICAL ASSISTANCE MANUAL, *supra* note 43, §8.7.
[327]*See* Bekker v. Humana Health Plan, Inc., 229 F.3d 662, 10 AD Cases 1776 (7th Cir. 2000), *cert. denied*, 532 U.S. 972 (2001) (offer of alcohol treatment program reasonable accommodation); Redding v. Chicago Transit Auth., 11 AD Cases 157 (N.D. Ill. 2000) (provision of drug treatment services reasonable, good-faith effort to accommodate employee's drug addiction).
[328]TITLE I TECHNICAL ASSISTANCE MANUAL, *supra* note 43, §8.7.
[329]210 F.3d 377 (7th Cir. 2000).
[330]989 F. Supp. 1330 (D. Or. 1997).
[331]72 F. Supp. 2d 915, 10 AD Cases 1148 (N.D. Ill. 1999).

absenteeism informed his employer that alcoholism was the reason for the excessive absenteeism, and requested a reasonable accommodation. In the litigation that followed the employer's refusal, the court found that an employer is not required to accommodate a disability about which it has no knowledge until after the employee has already been discharged. Doing so would provide alcoholic employees with an unfair advantage unavailable to other employees, the court indicated.

In sum, while the ADA protects alcoholics and former or recovering drug addicts from adverse employment actions based on their addiction, the ADA does not require employers to absolve employees who currently abuse illegal drugs from discipline, or to tolerate misconduct or poor performance because of drug or alcohol use.

B. AIDS/HIV

Acquired immunodeficiency syndrome (AIDS) and human immunodeficiency virus[332] (HIV) infection, while not per se disabilities, may be considered protected disabilities under the ADA.

The Supreme Court first considered whether an individual who is HIV-positive, but exhibits no symptoms of HIV infection or AIDS, can be categorized as "disabled" under the ADA in *Bragdon v. Abbott*.[333] Prior to the Court's consideration of the issue in *Bragdon*, a number of federal agencies had concluded that that asymptomatic HIV infection constitutes a handicap for purposes of the Rehabilitation Act,[334] and subsequently, under the ADA.[335] Moreover, every court that had addressed

---

[332] HIV is the virus that causes AIDS.

[333] 524 U.S. 624, 8 AD Cases 239 (1998).

[334] *See, e.g. Application of Section 504 of the Rehabilitation Act to HIV-Infected Individuals*, 12 OP. OFF. LEGAL COUNSEL 264, 264–65 (Sept. 27, 1988) (Office of Legal Counsel, Department of Justice); *In re* David Ritter, No. 03890089, 1989 WL 609697 (EEOC, Dec. 8, 1989); REPORT OF THE PRESIDENTIAL COMMISSION ON THE HUMAN IMMUNODEFICIENCY VIRUS EPIDEMIC 113–14, 122–23 (June 1988).

[335] *See, e.g.*, 5 C.F.R. §1636.103 (2003); 7 C.F.R. §15e.103 (2004); 22 C.F.R. §1701.103 (2001); 24 C.F.R. §9.103 (2004); 34 C.F.R. §1200.103 (2004); 45 C.F.R. §§2301.103, 2490.103 (2004); *In re* David T. Martin, No. 01954089, 1997 WL 151524

the issue under the Rehabilitation Act concluded that HIV-positive status was within its coverage.[336] Additional courts found HIV infection to be a protected handicap without distinguishing between symptomatic and asymptomatic states of the disease.[337]

These decisions set the stage for the Supreme Court in *Bragdon*. In this case, Abbott, who was HIV-positive but exhibited no symptoms of the infection's advanced stages, disclosed her HIV status on a patient registration form at her dentist's office. After finding a cavity, the dentist refused to fill it at his office because of the patient's HIV status. Instead, he offered to provide the service at a local hospital at no extra charge for his services, although the patient would be forced to incur larger costs because the procedure would utilize the hospital's facilities. Abbott filed suit under the ADA, alleging that the dentist had breached his obligation under Title III of the ADA,[338] which deals with the obligations of a "public accommodation"[339] under the ADA.

(EEOC, Mar. 27, 1997); *In re* Rosebud Sioux Tribe, No. 93-504-1, 1994 WL 603015 (Department of Health & Human Servs., Departmental Appeals Bd., Sept. 25, 1992).

[336]*See* Doe v. Garrett, 903 F.2d 1455, 1 AD Cases 1606 (11th Cir. 1990), *cert. denied*, 499 U.S. 904 (1991); Ray v. School Dist. of DeSoto County, 666 F. Supp. 1524 (M.D. Fla. 1987); Thomas v. Atascadero Unified Sch. Dist., 662 F. Supp. 376 (C.D. Cal. 1987); District 27 Cmty. Sch. Bd. v. Board of Educ. of New York, 130 Misc. 2d 398, 502 N.Y.S.2d 325 (Sup. Ct. Queens County 1986); *cf.* Baxter v. City of Belleville, 720 F. Supp. 720 (S.D. Ill. 1989).

[337]*See* Martinez ex. rel. Martinez v. School Bd. of Hillsborough County, 861 F.2d 1502 (11th Cir. 1988); Chalk v. United States Dist. Court Central Dist. of Cal., 840 F.2d 701, 1 AD Cases 1210 (9th Cir. 1988); Doe v. Dolton Elementary Sch. Dist. No. 148, 694 F. Supp. 440 (N.D. Ill. 1988); Robertson v. Granite City Cmty. Unit Sch. Dist. No. 9, 684 F. Supp. 1002 (S.D. Ill. 1988); Local 1812, Government Employees (AFGE) v. U.S. Dep't of State, 662 F. Supp. 50, 1 AD Cases 1060 (D.D.C. 1987); *cf.* Association of Relatives & Friends of AIDS Patients v. Regulations & Permits Admin., 740 F. Supp. 95 (D.P.R. 1990).

[338]42 U.S.C. §§12181–12189.

[339]Title III of the ADA defines the following private entities as "public accommodations":
    (A)   an inn, hotel, motel, or other place of lodging, except for an establishment located within a building that contains not more than five rooms for rent or hire and that is actually occupied by the proprietor of such establishment as the residence of such proprietor;
    (B)   a restaurant, bar, or other establishment serving food or drink;

Both the United States and the state of Maine intervened as plaintiffs in the case, and the trial court ruled in the plaintiff's favor, holding that Abbott's asymptomatic HIV infection satisfied the ADA's definition of protected disabilities.[340] The U.S. Court of Appeals for the First Circuit affirmed, agreeing that Bragdon treating Abbott in his dental office would not have posed a "direct threat" (within the meaning of the ADA) to the health and safety of others.[341]

In its decision, the Supreme Court first considered the question of whether Abbott's HIV infection constituted a disability under the ADA. Tracing the progress of the disease in infected individuals, the Court concluded that "HIV infection must be regarded as a physiological disorder with a constant and detrimental effect on the infected person's hemic and lymphatic systems from the moment of infection," and thus

---

(C) a motion picture house, theater, concert hall, stadium, or other place of exhibition or entertainment;
(D) an auditorium, convention center, lecture hall, or other place of public gathering;
(E) a bakery, grocery store, clothing store, hardware store, shopping center, or other sales or rental establishment;
(F) a laundromat, dry-cleaner, bank, barber shop, travel service, shoe repair service, funeral parlor, gas station, office of an accountant or lawyer, pharmacy, insurance office, professional office of a health care provider, hospital or other service establishment;
(G) a terminal, depot, or other station used for specified public transportation;
(H) a museum, library, gallery, or other place of public display or collection;
(I) a park, zoo, amusement park, or other place of recreation;
(J) a nursery, elementary, secondary, undergraduate, or postgraduate private school, or other place of education;
(K) a day care center, senior citizen center, homeless shelter, food bank, adoption agency, or other social service center establishment; and
(L) a gymnasium, health spa, bowling alley, golf course, or other place of exercise or recreation.

42. U.S.C. §12181(7).

[340]Abbott v. Bragdon, 912 F. Supp. 580, 585–87, 5 AD Cases 1673 (D. Me. 1995), *aff'd*, 107 F.3d 934, 6 AD Cases 780 (1st Cir. 1997), *vacated*, 524 U.S. 624, 8 AD Cases 239 (1998).

[341]Abbott v. Bragdon, 107 F. 3d 934, 939–43, 6 AD Cases 780 (1st Cir. 1997). The appellate court's holding on the "direct threat" issue was based on the Dentistry Guidelines issued in 1993 by the Centers for Disease Controls, U.S. Department of Health and Human Services, and by the Policy on AIDS, HIV Infection and the Practice of Dentistry, promulgated by the American Dental Association in 1991.

satisfies the statutory and regulatory definition of a physical impairment during every stage of the disease.[342] Abbott then argued that her infection substantially limited her in the major life activity of reproduction, asserting that she had decided not to have children after learning of her HIV disease. The Court agreed, noting that reproduction and the sexual dynamics surrounding it are central to the life process itself. The Court also noted that "[g]iven the pervasive, and invariably fatal, course of the disease, its effect on major life activities of many sorts might have been relevant" to the inquiry.[343] The Court determined that the risks of transmitting the virus to partners through sexual intercourse and to children through gestation and childbirth constituted a "substantial limitation" on the major life activity of reproduction.[344] Indeed, the Court stated, "[w]hen significant limitations result from the impairment, the definition is met even if the difficulties are not insurmountable."[345] In coming to this conclusion, the Court rejected Bragdon's contention that only "major life activities" that have a public or economic character warrant protection under the ADA.

Buttressing its own conclusions, the Court majority cited the relevant agency interpretation issued under the ADA, and in particular, the views of the Department of Justice, the agency

---

[342] Bragdon v. Abbott, 524 U.S. 624, 8 AD Cases 239, 244 (1998). The Court noted that its conclusion regarding the coverage of asymptomatic HIV was confirmed by the consistent course of agency interpretations both before and after the enactment of the ADA. It took particular note of a 1988 opinion issued by the Office of Legal Counsel of the Department of Justice, which concluded that the Rehabilitation Act "protects symptomatic and asymptomatic HIV-infected individuals against discrimination in any covered program." *Application of Section 504 of the Rehabilitation Act to HIV-Infected Individuals*, 12 Op. Off. Legal Counsel 264, 264–65 (Sept. 27, 1988) (citing a letter from then–Surgeon General C. Everett Koop stating that "from a purely scientific perspective, persons with HIV are clearly impaired").

[343] *Bragdon*, 524 U.S. at 637, 8 AD Cases at 244.

[344] *Id.* at 639–41, 8 AD Cases at 246. While Bragdon argued that with drug therapy, the risk of transmitting HIV to an unborn fetus might be reduced to as low as 8%, the Court observed that "It cannot be said as a matter of law that an 8% risk of transmitting a dread and fatal disease to one's child does not represent a substantial limitation on reproduction." *Id.* at 641, 8 AD Cases at 246.

[345] *Id.*, at 641, 8 AD Cases at 246.

charged by Congress with development of implementing regulations under Title III. In interpreting the ADA's definition of disability, the Department of Justice added "HIV infection (symptomatic and asymptomatic)" to the disorders constituting a "physical impairment" under the statute.[346] This view was incorporated into the technical assistance published by the department's Civil Rights Division,[347] and echoed in the interpretations developed by federal agencies authorized to administer other aspects of the ADA, including the EEOC.[348]

The Court nonetheless declined to consider whether HIV infection is a per se protected disability under the ADA, and instead declared that the "determination of whether an individual has a disability is not necessarily based on the name or diagnosis of the impairment the person has, but rather on the effect of that impairment on the life of the individual."[349]

Thus, while it is significant that an individual who exhibits no symptoms of either AIDS or HIV infection may be protected under the ADA, such protection is not automatic. The Supreme Court has emphasized in a number of cases that the ADA requires an individualized assessment of whether a job applicant or employee's illness substantially limits any major life activity.[350] Thus, it is incumbent on the individual who is HIV-positive to demonstrate how the virus substantially limits his or her ability to perform a major life activity.

---

[346] 28 C.F.R. §36.104 (2002).

[347] AMERICANS WITH DISABILITIES ACT TITLE III TECHNICAL ASSISTANCE MANUAL §III.2.2000 (1993).

[348] See TITLE I TECHNICAL ASSISTANCE MANUAL §2.2(a)(i); 29 C.F.R. pt. 1630, app. §1630.2(j) (2003); AMERICANS WITH DISABILITIES ACT TITLE II TECHNICAL ASSISTANCE MANUAL §II.2.2000 (1993); 28 C.F.R. §35.104 (2003); 49 C.F.R. §37.3 (2003).

[349] Bragdon v. Abbott, 524 U.S. 624, 8 AD Cases 239 (1998).

[350] See Albertson, Inc. v. Kirkinburg, 527 U.S. 555, 9 AD Cases 694 (1999) (ADA imposes statutory obligation to determine existence of disabilities on case-by-case basis, based on actual effect of impairment on life of individual in question); Murphy v. United Parcel Serv., Inc., 527 U.S. 516, 9 AD Cases 691 (1999) (truck driver with hypertension did not suffer "disability" under ADA, where medication he took enabled him to perform major life activities without substantial limitation); Sutton v. United Air Lines, Inc., 527 U.S. 471, 483, 9 AD Cases 673, 678 (1999) (mitigating or corrective measures must be taken into account in judging whether

In *Blanks v. Southwestern Bell Communications, Inc.*,[351] for example, a plaintiff who was HIV-positive could not show that he was substantially limited in the area of reproduction, where he and his wife decided not to have any more children, and where his wife had undergone a surgical procedure to physically prevent conception. Unlike the situation in *Bragdon*, factors *other* than the HIV virus substantially limited the plaintiff in *Blanks* from bearing children, a major life activity. Similarly, the plaintiff in *Gutwaks v. American Airlines, Inc.*[352] could not show that his HIV status substantially limited any major life activity, because he declared he did not want to have children, and failed to demonstrate how any other major life activity would be impacted by his infection. Thus, it is crucial for a plaintiff to be able to show how an HIV infection substantially limits a major life activity to merit ADA protection.

1. Qualified Individual With A Disability

In addition to proving that AIDS or HIV infection substantially limits a major life activity, an individual seeking protection under the ADA must demonstrate that he or she is qualified to perform the essential functions of the job despite his or her illness. If an employee can no longer perform the job, then he or she is not considered a qualified individual with a disability, and thus cannot take advantage of ADA coverage. For instance, in *DiSanto v. McGraw-Hill, Inc./Platt's Division*,[353] an individual who was HIV-positive sued his former employer, arguing, among other things, that he was discriminatorily terminated because of his disability in violation of the ADA. The employer countered this allegation by claiming that because the former employee could not perform the essential functions of his job as a salesman, he was not a "qualified individual with a disability" under the ADA. In support of this defense, the employer pointed to the fact that on his application for Social

---

individual possesses disability, because doing otherwise would "run[] directly counter to the individualized inquiry mandated by the ADA").

[351] 310 F.3d 398, 13 AD Cases 1253 (5th Cir. 2002).
[352] No. 3:98-CV-2120-BF, 1999 WL 1611328 (N.D. Tex. Sept. 2, 1999).
[353] 220 F.3d 61, 10 AD Cases 1364 (2d Cir. 2000).

Security benefits, the former employee represented that he had been completely unable to work because of his condition. Thus, an employee unable to perform the job is not a qualified individual with a disability, and therefore receives no protection under the ADA. The U.S. Court of Appeals for the Second Circuit agreed, affirming a lower court's ruling in the employer's favor.

Although statements claiming that one is completely unable to work for the purposes of securing Social Security benefits do not necessarily bar a disabled individual from maintaining that he or she is able to perform the essential functions of the job in order to set forth a viable claim under the ADA,[354] the individual must offer some explanation for the inconsistency.[355] The reconciliation between these inconsistent positions must be "sufficient to warrant a reasonable juror's concluding that, assuming the truth of, or the plaintiff's good-faith belief in [the statement to the Social Security Administration], the plaintiff could nonetheless 'perform the essential functions' of her job, with or without 'reasonable accommodation.'"[356] In *DiSanto*, the former employee offered no viable explanation for the inconsistent statements.

A similar fact pattern prevented an individual suffering from AIDS from asserting that he was a qualified individual with a disability under the ADA, after he certified under penalty of perjury that he had been totally and permanently disabled and unable to work in order to receive stated disability and Social Security benefits. The U.S. Court of Appeals for the Third Circuit ruled in *McNemar v. Disney Store, Inc.*[357] that the district court was within its discretion in holding that the former employee was estopped from arguing that he was "qualified" under the ADA, because the two positions he took on his ability to work could not be reconciled.

---

[354] *See* Cleveland v. Policy Mgmt. Sys. Corp., 526 U.S. 795, 9 AD Cases 491 (1999).
[355] *Id.*
[356] *Id.* at 807, 9 AD Cases at 496.
[357] 91 F.3d 610, 5 AD Cases 1227 (3d Cir. 1996), *cert. denied*, 519 U.S. 1115 (1997).

a. Not Qualified Because of Risk

An employer need not hire or retain an employee who has AIDS or is HIV-positive if that person poses a direct threat to himself or herself or others in the workplace.[358] A "direct threat" is defined as a "significant risk to the health or safety of others that cannot be eliminated by reasonable accommodation."[359]

In determining whether an individual poses a direct threat, an employer must make an individualized assessment of the employee's ability to perform the job safely. This determination must be based on a reasonable medical judgment that relies on the most current medical knowledge and/or the best objective evidence. Additionally, four factors—"the duration of the risk; [t]he nature and severity of the potential harm; [t]he likelihood that the potential harm will occur; and [t]he imminence of the potential harm"—must be considered in assessing the direct threat.[360]

For example, a worker in a safety-sensitive position whose medication for AIDS causes him or her to suffer from dizzy spells would likely pose a direct threat in the workplace. If no reasonable accommodation existed, such as offering to transfer the employee to a non–safety-sensitive position, then the employer would not run afoul of the ADA if it terminated the employee.

A number of courts have addressed situations in which individuals whose AIDS or HIV status has rendered them a direct threat to others. Several of these cases involve the medical profession. In *Doe v. University of Maryland Medical System Corp.*,[361] for instance, a neurosurgical resident who was HIV-positive was deemed a direct threat to patients, as determined by a panel of experts on blood-borne pathogens. An HIV-positive medical technician in *Estate of William C. Mauro v.*

---

[358] 42 U.S.C. §12113(b); 29 C.F.R. §1630.15(b)(2) (2003).
[359] 42 U.S.C. §12111(3); *see also* 29 C.F.R. §1630.2(r) (2003).
[360] 29 C.F.R. §1630.2(r) (2003).
[361] 50 F.3d 1261, 4 AD Cases 379 (4th Cir. 1995).

Borgess Medical Center[362] was characterized as a direct threat to others, because his work often involved placing his hands in patients' body cavities along with sharp medical instruments, thereby posing an increased risk of blood-to-blood transmission.

Dental hygienists with HIV infection also have been shown to pose substantial risk to patients. In *Waddell v. Valley Forge Dental Associates, Inc.*,[363] an HIV-positive dental hygienist was found to cause a direct threat to patients, even though the risk of transmission was small, given that the consequence of infection is severe. The lower court found that the hygienist's job entailed "exposure-prone" procedures, as defined by the Centers for Disease Control and Prevention,[364] and that the necessity of performing the procedures made the hygienist a direct threat. In essence, although all four factors (duration of the risk, nature and severity of the potential harm, likelihood that the potential harm will occur, and the imminence of the potential harm) should be considered when making a direct threat assessment, a strong showing in one of these factors may outweigh a weaker showing in another. Because HIV infection is lethal, an employer need not prove that the risk of infection is particularly likely or imminent, so long as the risk is real.

b. Ability to Make Inquiries or Mandate Tests

An employee who is HIV-positive or who has the AIDS virus may also be deemed a direct threat in nonmedical settings. In *EEOC v. Prevo's Family Market, Inc.*,[365] an employer was permitted to require a produce clerk[366] who was HIV-positive to undergo a medical examination to determine whether he posed

---

[362] 137 F.3d 398, 7 AD Cases 1571 (6th Cir.), *cert. denied*, 525 U.S. 815 (1998).

[363] 276 F.3d 1275, 12 AD Cases 1029 (11th Cir. 2001), *cert. denied*, 535 U.S. 1096, 13 AD Cases 192 (2002).

[364] Centers for Disease Control and Prevention, *Recommendation for Preventing Transmission of Human Immunodeficiency Virus and Hepatitis B Virus to Patients During Exposure-Prone Invasive Procedures*, at 4 (Apr. 12, 2004).

[365] 135 F.3d 1089, 8 AD Cases 401 (6th Cir. 1998).

[366] Although individuals with infectious or communicable diseases may lawfully be precluded from food-handling positions so long as a reasonable accommodation cannot eliminate the risk of spreading disease through the handling of food, AIDS and HIV are specifically not included on the Centers for Disease Control and

a direct threat to customers and fellow employees. Because the employee at issue handled knives and was in fact prone to cuts and scrapes on a regular basis, the employer was justified in requiring the clerk to take a medial exam as part of the individualized assessment to determine his threat level. The U.S. Court of Appeals for the Sixth Circuit held that the employer's mandate that the employee undergo such an examination was jobrelated and consistent with business necessity, and therefore not in violation of the ADA.

An employer generally is not permitted to conduct a medical examination or make inquires to determine the presence or extent of an individual's disability before making an offer of employment.[367] Once hired, however, an employer may inquire about the nature and extent of an individual's disability so long as doing so is job-related and consistent with business necessity.[368] In *Prevo's*, the court found that the employer's desire for a medical examination had the legitimate business purpose of protecting the health and safety of its employees and the general public from HIV infection.

General inquiries or examinations not directly related to the individual's ability to perform his or her job safely are not permissible under the ADA. For example, in *Doe v. An Oregon Resort*,[369] an Oregon federal court ruled that a ski resort violated the ADA when it demanded that a ski patroller provide a negative HIV test result or face termination. In discussing an insurance coverage matter with his supervisor, the employee disclosed that his wife was HIV-positive. The employee was then given the ultimatum of either taking a test to prove his HIV status, or lose his position. Although the employer argued that a ski patroller faced the possibility of blood exposure to skiers in an emergency, the court rejected this rationale, finding that the ADA requires more than a remote possibility of risk before

---

Prevention list of such diseases that can be transmitted in this manner. *See* "Diseases Trasmitted Through the Food Supply," Department of Health and Human Services, Centers for Disease Control and Prevention, 68 Fed. Reg. 62809 (2003).

[367] 42 U.S.C. §12112(d)(2)(a).
[368] 42 U.S.C. §12112(d)(4)(A).
[369] 11 AD Cases 1824 (D. Or. 2001).

a medical examination could be deemed job-related and consistent with business necessity. At the same time, an employee who disclosed that he had AIDS was unable to show that he suffered unlawful discrimination as his job was in jeopardy due to absenteeism and the assault of a co-worker prior to the disclosure.[370]

c. Association

The ADA's "association provision" protects qualified individuals from employment discrimination based on the "known disability of an individual with whom the qualified individual is known to have a relationship or association."[371] The purpose of this provision is to protect qualified individuals from adverse employment actions based on "unfounded stereotypes and assumptions" arising from the employees' relationships with particular disabled people.[372] Thus, for example, it is illegal under the ADA to discriminate against a job applicant or employee because he or she associates with or is related to an individual who has AIDS or HIV infection.[373] It would also be unlawful under the ADA to discriminate against an employee because that employee does volunteer work with people who have AIDS, and the employer fears that the employee may contract the disease.[374] At least one court, however, has held that the ADA does not cover individuals who advocate on behalf of individuals with AIDS or on behalf of those who are HIV-positive, on the grounds that this type of association falls short of the kind meriting protection under the ADA.[375] In addition, another court rejected the attempt of a terminated employee to tie his relation and association with his premature twin daughters—

---

[370] Buie v. Quad/Graphics Inc., 366 F.3d 496, 15 AD Cases 790 (7th Cir. 2004).
[371] 42 U.S.C. §12112(b)(4).
[372] See Den Hartog v. Wasatch Acad., 129 F.3d 1076, 1081–85, 7 AD Cases 764 (10th Cir. 1997) (discussing provision's legislative history and stating that prima facie case includes showing that plaintiff was known by his employer to have "a relative or associate with a disability," id. at 1085, 7 AD Cases at 772).
[373] See 29 C.F.R. §1630.8 (2003).
[374] 29 C.F.R. pt. 1630, app. §1630.8 (2003).
[375] See Oliveras-Sifre v. Puerto Rico Dep't of Health, 214 F.3d 23, 10 AD Cases 1083 (1st Cir. 2000).

whose medical care triggered nearly $20,000 in medical expenses—to his subsequent termination.[376]

Likewise, an employer is under no obligation to provide a reasonable accommodation to nondisabled employees so that they may care for relatives or associates who have AIDS or are HIV-positive, although the Family and Medical Leave Act (FMLA)[377] or comparable state laws may provide leave rights to eligible employees with respect to family or household members covered by the terms of those statutes.[378]

d. Reasonable Accommodation

If an individual with AIDS or HIV is disabled legitimately for purposes of the ADA, then the employer is required to provide him or her with a reasonable accommodation, if necessary, so long as doing so does not pose an undue hardship.[379] An undue hardship is an action that requires "significant difficulty or expense" when considered in light of, among other factors, the nature of the employer's business, its size, and resources.[380] Potential loss of customers or other employees because of their attitude toward individuals with HIV or AIDS does not constitute an undue hardship.

Examples of reasonable accommodations for an employee with HIV or AIDS include providing breaks so that the employee can take necessary medication, so long as the employee completes his or her work; allowing the employee to take time off for doctor visits, provided that the employee can make up the lost time; and installing a ramp so that an individual whose illness requires him or her to use a scooter or wheelchair may work on-site. An employer is not required to alter the nature

---

[376]Larimer v. International Bus. Machs. Corp., 370 F.3d 698, 15 AD Cases 1070 (7th Cir.), *cert. denied*, 125 S. Ct. 477, 33 EB Cases 3015 (2004).

[377]29 U.S.C. §2601 et seq.

[378]29 C.F.R. pt. 1630, app. §1630.8 (citing S. Rep. No. 101-116, at 30 (1989)); H.R. Rep. No. 101-485, pt. 2, at 61–62 (1990), *reprinted in* 1990 U.S.C.C.A.N. 303, 343–44; H.R. Rep. No. 101-485, pt. 3, at 38–39 (1990), *reprinted in* 1990 U.S.C.C.A.N. 445, 461–62).

[379]42 U.S.C. §12112(b)(5); 29 C.F.R. §1630.15(d) (2003).

[380]42 U.S.C. §12111(10); 29 C.F.R. §1630.2(p)(1)–(2) (2003).

of its business fundamentally in order to accommodate an individual with AIDS/HIV.[381]

e. Insurance

An issue that has arisen with some frequency involves an employer's obligation to provide insurance benefits to individuals suffering from AIDS or HIV infection. While the ADA requires an employer to provide the same level of benefits to all employees regardless of disability, problems arise when the benefits themselves discriminate on the basis of a particular illness, including AIDS or HIV infection.[382] For example, an insurance policy may place a lower benefits cap on AIDS-related conditions than for cancer or diabetes, or exclude AIDS coverage altogether. Which disparities in insurance coverage constitute discrimination in violation of the ADA is not always a clear determination.

In some jurisdictions, courts have decided that the contents of an insurance policy do not fall within the purview of the ADA. In other words, an employee would not be able to invoke the ADA when challenging a policy that, for instance, does not cover AIDS-related medications. The rationale for limiting the ADA's scope in this capacity is that while insurance *offices* must not discriminate against individuals with disabilities, insurance polices are not subject to ADA regulation, according to some jurisdictions.[383] Nonetheless, other courts have determined that the contents of insurance policies *are* subject to

---

[381] *See, e.g.*, Montalvo v. Radcliffe, 167 F.3d 873, 9 AD Cases 15 (4th Cir.), *cert. denied*, 528 U.S. 813 (1999) (in Title III action, martial arts business was not required to soften its program to accommodate student with AIDS, as doing so would fundamentally alter nature of business).

[382] For a more extensive discussion of the ADA's impact on employee benefits programs maintained by employers, including health insurance, see Chapter 9, "Interplay of Related Workplace Statutes."

[383] The U.S. Courts of Appeal for the Third, Sixth, and Ninth Circuits have held that a physical place is required for ADA coverage, and that the contents of insurance policies are not subject to ADA's nondiscrimination provisions. *See* Kolling v. Blue Cross Blue Shield of Mich., 318 F.3d 715, 14 AD Cases 384, 29 EB Cases 2597 (6th Cir. 2003) (Title III does not govern the contents of an employer-sponsored health plan, as they are not goods offered by place of public accommodation); Chabner v. United of Omaha Life Ins. Co., 225 F.3d 1042, 10 AD Cases 1705 (9th Cir. 2000) (insurance company administering employer-provided disability

the ADA's nondiscrimination provisions,[384] and therefore subject to scrutiny.[385]

Even in the jurisdictions where the terms of an insurance policy may be viewed in light of the ADA's nondiscrimination requirements, offering lesser benefits for AIDS/HIV-related conditions is not necessarily unlawful. The ADA does not prevent an insurer from underwriting or classifying risks that are based on, or are not inconsistent with, state law.[386] Thus, if the reason for a disparity in benefits coverage is due to legitimate actuarial, financial, or other considerations, as opposed to serving as subterfuge for discrimination, then the policy does not violate the ADA.

For example, in *Doe v. Mutual of Omaha Insurance Co.*,[387] the U.S. Court of Appeals for the Seventh Circuit held that a lifetime cap on AIDS-related coverage that was substantially

---

plan was not place of public accommodation under Title III because employees received their benefits through employment, not place of public accommodation); Weyer v. Twentieth Century Fox Film Corp., 198 F.3d 1104, 1114–16, 10 AD Cases 65 (9th Cir. 2000); McNeil v. Times Ins. Co., 2000 U.S. App. LEXIS 2710 (5th Cir. 2000) (Title III does not prohibit group health plan's limitation on AIDS treatment); Ford v. Schering-Plough Corp., 145 F.3d 601, 8 AD Cases 190 (3d Cir. 1998), *cert. denied*, 525 U.S. 1093 (1999) (because plaintiff received her disability benefits through employment, she had no nexus to MetLife's insurance office, and thus was not discriminated against in connection with public accommodation); Parker v. Metropolitan Life Ins. Co., 121 F.3d 1006, 1015, 6 AD Cases 1865 (6th Cir. 1997), *cert. denied*, 522 U.S. 1084 (1998) (Title III does not apply to insurance policy obtained from employer).

[384]Section 302(a) of the ADA provides that, "No individual shall be discriminated against on the basis of disability in the full and equal enjoyment of the goods, services, facilities, privileges, advantages, or accommodations of any place of public accommodation by any person who owns, leases (or leases to), or operates a place of public accommodation." 42 U.S.C. §12182(a).

[385]*See* Tompkins v. United Healthcare of New England, Inc., 203 F.3d 90, 23 EB Cases 2967 (1st Cir. 2000) (public accommodations are more than physical spaces); Doe v. Mutual of Omaha Ins. Co., 179 F.3d 557, 9 AD Cases 657 (7th Cir. 1999), *cert. denied*, 528 U.S. 1106 (2000) (same); Carparts Distribution Ctr., Inc. v. Automotive Wholesaler's Ass'n of New England, Inc., 37 F.3d 12, 3 AD Cases 1237 (1st Cir. 1994) (Title III is not limited to actual physical structures). *See also* Wai v. Allstate Ins. Co., 75 F. Supp. 2d 1, 9 AD Cases 1588 (D.D.C. 1999) (protections of Title III extend beyond physical access to insurance offices and include denial of insurance policies that are equal or comparable to those offered to nondisabled).

[386]42 U.S.C. §12201(c).

[387]179 F.3d 557, 9 AD Cases 657 (7th Cir. 1999), *cert. denied*, 528 U.S. 1106 (2000).

less than that provided for other medical conditions did not violate the ADA, because the ADA does not require that insurers make their products equally valuable to the disabled and to the nondisabled. According to the court, the plaintiffs were not denied insurance policies because they had AIDS, but—along with individuals who did not have AIDS—they were denied coverage for certain AIDS-related treatments.

Thus, while individuals with this disease may have a cause of action under the ADA if the employer refuses to offer them insurance, provides different policies to them because of their disability, or fires or refuses to hire them because of a fear that the company's insurance premiums will rise, such individuals likely have little or no recourse if the insurance policies themselves are less advantageous for AIDS-related illnesses.

f. Privacy

The ADA requires that the results of any lawful medical examination or inquiry be kept confidential.[388] There are only a limited set of circumstances under which an employer is permitted to disclose information about an individual's disability. An employer may discuss an employee's work restrictions and/or need for a reasonable accommodation to the employee's manager or supervisor.[389] The ADA also allows an employer to provide information about the employee's disability to emergency personnel in the event of a medical crisis, and requires that employers disclose relevant information to government officials investigating charges of discrimination.[390] The purpose of these confidentiality provisions is to permit employers to inquire into employees' medical conditions in order to provide reasonable accommodations, while helping employees avoid the "blatant and subtle sigma" that attaches to "being identified as disabled."[391]

---

[388] 42 U.S.C. §12112(d).
[389] 42 U.S.C. §12112(d)(3)(B)(i).
[390] 42 U.S.C. §12112(d)(3)(B)(ii)–(iii).
[391] H.R. REP. NO. 101-485, pt. II, at 75 (1990), *reprinted in* 1990 U.S.C.C.A.N. 303, 357–58.

These confidentiality protections do not apply if an individual voluntarily discloses his or her HIV status.[392] For example, if an employee, through his or her own volition mentions to a coworker that he or she has AIDS, the employer need not adhere to the ADA's confidentially provisions. Information about an employee's HIV status is not considered to have been voluntarily given, however, if the employer requests medical information through some other channel. For example, in *Doe v. U.S. Postal Service*,[393] the U.S. Court of Appeals for the District of Columbia Circuit held in a Rehabilitation Act case that an employee's disclosure of his HIV-positive status on a FMLA form *was* subject to confidentiality requirements, even though requesting FMLA leave is a voluntary act. To rule otherwise, the court said,

> would force employees to choose between waiving their right to avoid being publicly identified as having a disability and exercising their statutory rights—including the rights to FMLA leave and to "reasonable accommodations" for their disabilities . . . that may depend on disclosure of their medical conditions.[394]

Employers, therefore, should refrain from disclosing an employee's HIV status unless doing so is medically necessary, unless requested by a government agency, or unless integral to the provision of a reasonable accommodation.

Keeping an employee's illness confidential is especially important in light of the fact that courts are finding that hostile work environment claims are cognizable under the ADA.[395] In *Flowers v. Southern Regional Physician Services, Inc.*,[396] for example, an employee who was HIV-positive claimed that when word of her illness spread in the office, employees refused to shake her

---

[392] *See, e.g.*, Ballard v. Healthsouth Corp., 147 F. Supp. 2d 529, 11 AD Cases 1717 (N.D. Tex. 2001) (disclosure of HIV status not given through job-related medical examination or inquiry does not merit ADA's confidentiality protections).

[393] 317 F.3d 339, 13 AD Cases 1801 (D.C. Cir. 2003).

[394] *Id.* at 344, 13 AD Cases at 1805.

[395] *See, e.g.*, Fox v. v. General Motors Corp., 247 F.3d 169, 11 AD Cases 1121 (4th Cir. 2001); Flowers v. Southern Reg'l Physician Servs., Inc., 247 F.3d 229, 11 AD Cases 1129 (5th Cir. 2001).

[396] 247 F.3d 229, 11 AD Cases 1129 (5th Cir. 2001).

hand, stopped socializing with her, intercepted her telephone calls, and eavesdropped on her conversations. The plaintiff also claimed that she was required to take four random drug tests in a 1-week period, was lured into adversarial meetings on false pretenses, received negative performance appraisals, and was ultimately terminated because of her disability. Relying on the purpose, language, and remedial structure of Title VII of the Civil Rights Act of 1964,[397] the U.S. Court of Appeals for the Fifth Circuit held that the plaintiff could assert a cause of action under the ADA based on hostile work environment. Thus, employers should be mindful of an employee's medical privacy rights or be prepared to defend against a hostile work environment claim, among others.

Because AIDS and HIV infection still carry a strong social stigma, workplace discrimination against infected individuals will likely persist. Employers, therefore, must be particularly aware of their responsibilities under the ADA with respect to this disease.

C. Mental Disorders

The term "disability" under the ADA specifically includes mental impairments.[398] These impairments include "[a]ny mental or psychological disorder, such as mental retardation, organic brain syndrome, emotional or mental illness, and specific learning disabilities."[399] Thus, it is clear that mental illnesses and psychological disorders may benefit from ADA protection.

Nonetheless, merely having a mental illness or disorder does not necessarily render an individual disabled. A person

---

[397] 42 U.S.C. §2000e et seq.
[398] The ADA definition is as follows:
The term "disability" means, with respect to an individual—
   (A) a physical or mental impairment that substantially limits one or more of the major life activities of such individual;
   (B) a record of such an impairment; or
   (C) being regarded as having such an impairment.
42 U.S.C. §12102(2).
[399] 29 C.F.R. §1630.2(h)(2) (2003).

with a mental condition must prove that this condition is an impairment that substantially limits a major life activity. Once this burden is satisfied, the individual must still demonstrate how he or she is a *qualified* individual with a disability, that is, that he or she can perform the essential functions of the job with or without a reasonable accommodation.

1. Substantially Limit Major Life Activity

A variety of mental disorders can rise to the level of "disability" under the ADA so long as they substantially limit at least one major life activity. Any one mental condition, however, will necessarily affect different people in different ways. Depression, for instance, can range from mild to debilitating. Often, this mental disorder causes sleep difficulties, loss of appetite, and anxiety, among other symptoms. However, in order to qualify as a disability under the ADA, these symptoms must render the individual unable to perform a major life activity that an average person in the general population can perform.[400] For example, if a case of severe depression renders an individual utterly incapable of caring for himself or herself, then that person may be disabled, because "caring for oneself" is a major life activity.[401] Alternatively, the individual must show that the effects of the mental disorder significantly restrict "the condition, manner or duration under which an individual can perform a particular major life activity as compared to the condition, manner, or duration under which the average person in the general population can perform that same major life activity."[402] Thus, although a person's depression may cause lack of sleep, he or she must show that this sleep loss is significantly greater than the sleep deprivation suffered by the general public.[403]

---

[400] 29 C.F.R. §1630.2(j)(1)(ii) (2003).
[401] *Id.* §1630.2(i) (2003).
[402] *Id.* §1630.2(j)(1)(ii) (2003).
[403] *See* EEOC v. Sara Lee Corp., 237 F.3d 349, 11 AD Cases 595 (4th Cir. 2001) (seizure disorder reduced quality of sleep, but not beyond that suffered by general public).

It has proven difficult for an employee with depression to prove that this condition rises to the level of "disability." In *Leisen v. City of Shelbyville*,[404] a firefighter with depression could not show that she was substantially limited in any major life activity, even though she claimed that she suffered from sleep and memory problems, crying, anxiety, and suicidal thoughts. Similarly, an elementary school guidance counselor in *Olson v. Dubuque Community School District*[405] could not demonstrate that she was disabled because of her depression, because she reported to work regularly and believed that she was able to perform her job satisfactorily despite her episodes of depression. An actress whose post-traumatic stress disorder, producing flashback episodes to sexual abuse and incest in childhood that interfered, with her performance in a traveling theater company did not demonstrate that she was substantially limited in the major life activity of interacting with others.[406] Demonstrating that depression causes one to feel anxious in elevators, while driving, and traveling through high-crime areas is also insufficient to prove a substantial impairment under the ADA.[407] Thus, a diagnosis of a mental condition alone does not necessarily render a person disabled for purposes of ADA coverage.

Mental disorders affect individuals in a variety of ways, some triggering rights and protections under the ADA.[408] Not all conditions, however, impact major life activities. Although the EEOC's regulations define the term "major life activities" as functions such as "caring for oneself, performing manual tasks, walking, seeing, hearing, speaking, breathing, learning,

---

[404] 135 F.3d 805, 8 AD Cases 892 (7th Cir. 1998).

[405] 137 F.3d 609, 7 AD Cases 1598 (8th Cir. 1998).

[406] Rohan v. Networks Presentations LLC, 375 F.3d 266, 15 AD Cases 1313 (4th Cir. 2004).

[407] *See* Cody v. CIGNA Healthcare of St. Louis, 139 F.3d 595, 7 AD Cases 1716 (8th Cir. 1998) (at most, fears and anxiety cause difficulties in life, but do not constitute substantially limiting impairments).

[408] *See, e.g.*, "Questions and Answers About Persons with Intellectual Disabilities in the Workplace and the Americans with Disabilities Act" (EEOC, 2004), accessible at http://www.eeoc.gov/facts/intellectual_disabilities.html.

and walking,"[409] this list is not exhaustive. In *Amir v. St. Louis University*,[410] an individual was able to demonstrate that his obsessive-compulsive disorder affected his ability to eat, drink, and learn. In *Pack v. Kmart Corp.*,[411] however, a former employee who claimed that her depression compromised her ability to concentrate was unable to prove that she was disabled, because concentration, in and of itself, was held not to be a major life activity.

Employees who are harassed, intimidated, and fired because of a mental disability—such as bipolar disorder—may bring actions alleging discrimination and/or retaliation under the ADA.[412] At the same time, courts often look narrowly at claims of discrimination linked to conditions such as attention deficit disorder (ADD),[413] attention deficit hyperactivity disorder (ADHD)[414] and learning disabilities,[415] and reject many such claims.

"Every day mobility," such as traveling over bridges and tunnels, boarding trains unaccompanied, and driving along commonly congested roadways, was questioned as a major life activity in *Reeves v. Johnson Controls World Services*.[416] The U.S. Court of Appeals for the Second Circuit, in *Reeves*, found that the plaintiff, who suffered from a panic disorder and agoraphobia, was able to travel to and from work on a regular basis despite her limitations, and was therefore not substantially limited in her mobility. Even if the plaintiff were substantially limited in this regard, the court doubted whether "every day mobility" is, indeed, a major life activity. Thus, unless a mental disorder substantially impacts a major life activity, it is not a

---

[409] 29 C.F.R. §1630(i) (2003).

[410] 184 F.3d 1017, 9 AD Cases 999 (8th Cir. 1999).

[411] 166 F.3d 1300, 8 AD Cases 1880 (10th Cir.), *cert. denied*, 528 U.S. 811 (1999).

[412] *See, e.g.*, Doebele v. Sprint/United Mgmt. Co., 342 F.3d 1117, 14 AD Cases 1281 (10th Cir. 2003).

[413] Ristrom v. Asbestos Workers Local 34 Joint Apprentice Comm., 370 F.3d 763, 15 AD Cases 1057 (8th Cir.), *reh'g denied*, 2004 U.S. App. LEXIS 15037 (2004).

[414] Calef v. Gillette Co., 322 F.3d 75, 14 AD Cases 110 (1st Cir. 2003).

[415] Palotai v. University of Md. at Coll. Park, 2002 U.S. App. LEXIS 12757 (4th Cir. 2002), *cert. denied*, 537 U.S. 1107 (2003).

[416] 140 F.3d 144, 7 AD Cases 1675 (2d Cir. 1998).

disability, even if the condition adversely affects the individual's life in other ways.

2. Mitigating or Corrective Measures

The Supreme Court has made it clear that the determination of whether an individual's impairment substantially limits a major life activity must take mitigating or corrective measures into consideration.[417] It follows that if therapy and/or medication control an individual's mental disorder or illness sufficiently, that person cannot be considered disabled under the ADA. Many individuals with depression, for example, are able to function at a satisfactory level with counseling and antidepressants.[418] Often, plaintiffs admit that while taking their medications, they are able to fully perform their job functions, and are not substantially limited in any major life activity.[419]

In many instances, however, medications will not completely alleviate the effects of a mental impairment. Additionally, if the medication itself substantially limits major life activities, then the individual may be considered disabled. In

---

[417] *See* Albertson, Inc. v. Kirkinburg, 527 U.S. 555, 9 AD Cases 694 (1999) (ADA mandates individualized inquiry into whether person is disabled based on actual effect of impairment on life of person in question); Murphy v. United Parcel Serv., Inc., 527 U.S. 516, 9 AD Cases 691 (1999) (truck driver with hypertension was not disabled, as his condition was controlled by medication); Sutton v. United Air Lines, Inc., 527 U.S. 471, 483, 9 AD Cases 673, 678 (1999) (mitigating or corrective measures must be considered in assessing whether individual is disabled, because to do otherwise would "run[] directly counter to the individualized inquiry mandated by the ADA").

[418] *See, e.g.*, Swanson v. University of Cincinnati, 268 F.3d 307, 12 AD Cases 417 (6th Cir. 2001) (surgical resident suffering from depression was not substantially limited in his ability to sleep and communicate while on medication); Spades v. City of Walnut Ridge, Ark., 186 F.3d 897, 9 AD Cases 1015 (8th Cir. 1999) (police officer with depression was able to function normally with medication and therapy); Robb v. Horizon Credit Union, 66 F. Supp. 2d 913, 9 AD Cases 1365 (C.D. Ill. 1999) (employee taking antidepression medication admitted she was capable of working and not substantially limited in any major life activity so long as she remained on medication).

[419] *See* McConnell v. Pioneer Hi-Bred Int'l, 10 AD Cases 578 (D.S.D. 2000) (employee with bipolar disorder was not disabled, as he conceded that he felt fine while taking Lithium to treat his condition); *Robb*, 66 F. Supp. 2d 913 (use of antidepressants enabled individual to function normally); Sherer v. GE Capital Corp., 59 F. Supp. 2d 1132, 9 AD Cases 1820 (D. Kan. 1999) (employee with bipolar disorder and obsessive compulsive disorder acknowledged that he could generally control his symptoms while on medication).

McAlindin v. County of San Diego,[420] for example, an employee suffering from anxiety, panic, and somatoform disorders argued that the medications he took for these disorders disrupted his sleep and rendered him impotent. Because reproduction and sleep have been considered major life activities,[421] the court held that the plaintiff presented a triable issue of fact as to whether his medications caused him to be disabled. In *Taylor v. Phoenixville School District*,[422] the U.S. Court of Appeals for the Third Circuit held that a jury may decide whether an employee's bipolar disorder and the side effects of Lithium, which the employee used to treat the condition, substantially limited her ability to think, care for herself, and interact with others, among other activities.

3. Substantially Limited in the Ability to Work

If an individual alleges that he or she is substantially limited in the ability to work, the disability in question must prevent him or her from working in a class or broad range of jobs.[423] This is a tough hurdle to clear if the disability is a mental or psychological condition. A number of court decisions have shown that it is very difficult for employees with mental impairments to prove that such conditions preclude them from working not simply in their old position but in a broad range of positions.

Conditions such as depression and bipolar disorder, for example, may make working at a particular job stressful and difficult. Nonetheless, an inability to work in stressful jobs or situations does not prove that the individual is unable to work

---

[420] 201 F.3d 1211, 10 AD Cases 252 (9th Cir. 1999), *cert. denied*, 530 U.S. 1243 (2000).

[421] *See* Bragdon v. Abbott, 524 U.S. 624, 8 AD Cases 239 (1998) (reproduction may be considered major life activity); Pack v. Kmart Corp., 166 F.3d 1300, 8 AD Cases 1880 (10th Cir.), *cert. denied*, 528 U.S. 811 (1999) (sleep is major life activity).

[422] 174 F.3d 142, 9 AD Cases 311 (3d Cir. 1999).

[423] *See, e.g.*, Murphy v. United Parcel Serv., Inc., 527 U.S. 516, 9 AD Cases 691 (1999) (mechanic with hypertension was regarded as being unable to perform only small subset of mechanics' jobs, not mechanic positions generally); Sutton v. United Air Lines, Inc., 527 U.S. 471, 9 AD Cases 673 (1999) (pilot with substandard vision was precluded from only narrow range of jobs, so was not regarded as disabled).

in a class of jobs.[424] Moreover, the inability to work in one particular job because of a mental disability does not necessarily preclude that individual from working in other jobs.[425]

Other restrictions, such as not being able to work more than 40 hours per week because of major depression and anxiety does not constitute a substantially limiting factor, because a number of jobs can be performed within that time frame.[426] Temporary incapacity to work also does not render an individual disabled.[427]

Successful employment following termination can counter an employee's contention that his or her mental condition substantially limits the ability to work.[428] In essence, an employee must do more than show that a mental condition prevents him or her from working at one particular position. The condition must be so debilitating as to preclude the individual from working almost entirely.

4. Qualified Individual

Even if the employee or applicant has a legitimate mental disability, he or she must be qualified to perform the job with

---

[424] *See* Aldrup v. Caldera, 274 F.3d 282, 12 AD Cases 1044 (5th Cir. 2001) (inability to work with certain coworkers because of depression not substantially limiting, as employee could not show that he was unable to work at different location with different colleagues); Schneiker v. Fortis Ins. Co., 200 F.3d 1055, 10 AD Cases 75 (7th Cir. 2000) (personality conflict with supervisor and ensuing stressful work situation does not prevent employee from working in different job and/or under different supervisor); Gaul v. AT&T, Inc., 955 F. Supp. 346, 6 AD Cases 705 (D.N.J. 1997), *aff'd sub nom.* Gaul v. Lucent Techs., Inc., 134 F.3d 576, 7 AD Cases 1223 (3d Cir. 1998) (because "unduly stressful" jobs is not recognized occupational classification).

[425] *See, e.g.*, Leisen v. City of Shelbyville, 135 F.3d 805, 8 AD Cases 892 (7th Cir. 1998) (firefighter able to show, at most, that she was limited in ability to perform one particular job due to her depression, and therefore was not disabled under ADA); Lusk v. Christ Hosp., 10 AD Cases 534 (N.D. Ill. 2000) (inability to work as nurse does not prove that individual is prevented from working generally).

[426] *See* Kellogg v. Union Pac. R.R., 233 F.3d 1083, 11 AD Cases 385 (8th Cir. 2000).

[427] Ogborn v. Food & Commercial Workers Local 881, 305 F.3d 763, 13 AD Cases 1071 (7th Cir.) (inability to work for 8 weeks because of depression did not prove that employee was substantially limited in ability to work), *reh'g denied*, 2002 U.S. App. LEXIS 7394 (7th Cir. 2002).

[428] Bowers v. Multimedia Cablevision, Inc., 10 AD Cases 671 (D. Kan. 1999) (employee who got job as computer programmer after being terminated not substantially limited in ability to work because of his psychological condition).

or without a reasonable accommodation in order to receive the ADA's protections. If an employee's mental illness or condition prevents him or her from performing the essential functions of the position, then he or she is not qualified, and therefore is not covered under the ADA.

For example, an employee who is chronically absent from the workplace is not a qualified individual, even if those absences are caused by depression, as regular attendance is considered an essential function of most jobs.[429] By the same token, if the qualifications of a position require a license, degree, or other form of certification, then an individual without such credentials is not a qualified individual under the ADA, even if the inability to meet these requirements is caused by a mental disability.[430]

An employee who is fired or otherwise reprimanded for misconduct or criminal behavior stemming from a mental disorder cannot benefit from ADA protection. For example, employees who are verbally or physically abusive because of mental illness may be treated as other employees without a mental disability would be treated.[431] Thus, an employer is not required to provide more leeway to the mentally disabled when it comes to meeting work requirements or adhering to conduct standards. Moreover, an employer legitimately may require that an individual pose no direct threat either to himself or herself

---

[429] *See, e.g.*, Greer v. Emerson Elec. Co., 185 F.3d 917, 9 AD 1100 (8th Cir. 1999) (employee with depression was legitimately discharged for absenteeism, as regular and reliable attendance essential job function).

[430] *See, e.g.*, Leisen v. City of Shelbyville, 153 F.3d 805, 8 AD Cases 892 (7th Cir. 1998) (firefighter unable to obtain required paramedic certification was not qualified individual with disability, even though she claimed that her depression substantially limited her ability to learn).

[431] *See, e.g.*, Hamilton v. Southwestern Bell Tel. Co., 136 F.3d 1047, 8 AD Cases 1219 (5th Cir. 1998) (employee fired for verbally abusing and striking coworker not protected under ADA, even if conduct was caused by post-traumatic stress disorder); Barbera v. Di Martino, 305 N.J. Super. 617, 702 A.2d 1370, 7 AD Cases 1178 (1997), *cert. denied*, 708 A.2d 64 (1998) (employee suffering from psychiatric disability justifiably terminated for assaulting his supervisor, as court "[saw] no reason why . . . employers subject to law protecting the handicapped and disabled nonetheless should not be able to take appropriate action on account of egregious or criminal conduct of an employee, regardless of whether the employee's disability contributed to the conduct").

or others in the workplace.[432] Accordingly, the ADA offers no protection for an employee whose mental disability causes threatening or violent behavior, or places himself or herself or coworkers at risk of danger.[433]

5. Perceived as Being Disabled

An individual who is regarded as being disabled is protected under the ADA. Therefore, an employer who treats an applicant or employee as having a mental impairment that substantially limits one or more major life functions can be liable for discrimination under the ADA if it makes adverse employment decisions based on that faulty perception. For example, in *Peters v. Baldwin Union Free School District*,[434] an employer regarded an employee as substantially limited in the ability to care for herself because it thought the employee's mental illness rendered her suicidal. Thus, the employer's actions in terminating the employee because of these perceptions violated the ADA.

In *Mattice v. Memorial Hospital of South Bend, Inc.*,[435] an anesthesiologist with a history of depression and panic disorder was able to state a claim under the ADA that his employer regarded him as substantially limited in his cognitive thinking abilities. After returning to work from leave due to depression, the employee alleged that his employer hospital subjected him to rigorous and critical monitoring, and eventually terminated his employment because of his perceived inability to think critically. The U.S. Court of Appeals for the Seventh Circuit

---

[432] 42 U.S.C. §12113(b). In order to prove that an individual poses a direct threat, an employer must demonstrate that the person poses "a significant risk of substantial" and imminent harm that cannot be diminished through use of a reasonable accommodation. 29 C.F.R. §1630.2(r) (2003).

[433] *See, e.g.*, Palesch v. Missouri Comm'n on Human Rights, 233 F.3d 560, 85 FEP Cases 75 (8th Cir. 2000) (employee with depression who told coworker that she could have shot someone legitimately deemed direct threat to others); Collins v. Blue Cross/Blue Shield of Mich., 228 Mich. App. 560, 579 N.W.2d 435 (1998) (employee who expressed having homicidal thoughts about killing her supervisor not discriminated against after being terminated because of this threatening behavior).

[434] 320 F.3d 164, 13 AD Cases 1793 (2d Cir. 2003).

[435] 249 F.3d 682, 11 AD Cases 1339 (7th Cir. 2001).

denied the employer's motion to dismiss on the grounds that the employee provided sufficient information to state a viable claim that he was regarded as being disabled under the ADA.

Merely being ordered to undergo a fitness-for-duty medical or psychological evaluation, however, does not indicate that the employer regards an employee as disabled. So long as the medical exam is job-related and consistent with business necessity, an employer is within its right to require such an exam without running afoul of the ADA.[436]

An employee who alleges that he or she is regarded as substantially limited in the ability to work must show that the employer believes that the individual is unable to perform a class or broad range of jobs, not just the position at hand. For example, in *Witter v. Delta Air Lines, Inc.*,[437] an airline pilot who suffered from bipolar disorder and narcissistic personality disorder was unable to show that he was regarded as substantially limited in the ability to work, because he was precluded from working only in an airline pilot position. Likewise, an employee who is permitted to continue working despite an adverse employment action allegedly taken because of a perceived mental illness cannot be regarded as substantially limited in the ability to work.[438]

---

[436] *See, e.g.*, Sullivan v. River Valley Sch. Dist., 197 F.3d 804, 9 AD Cases 1711 (6th Cir. 1999), *cert. denied*, 530 U.S. 1262 (2000) (school district permitted to require mental and physical fitness-for-duty examinations for teacher who allegedly exhibited odd behavior); Krocka v. City of Chi., 203 F.3d 507, 10 AD Cases 289 (7th Cir. 2000) (requiring police officer in Rehabilitation Act case with depression to undergo medical evaluation not evidence that employer perceived him as disabled); Cody v. CIGNA Healthcare of St. Louis, 139 F.3d 595, 599, 7 AD Cases 1716, 1719 (8th Cir. 1998) (offering employee suffering from depression and anxiety paid medical leave and ordering her to see psychologist prior to returning to work "is not equivalent to treatment of the employee as though she were substantially impaired"); Miller v. City of Springfield, 146 F.3d 612, 8 AD Cases 321 (8th Cir. 1998) (police department allowed to require officer applicants to take and achieve particular score on psychological test designed, in part, to measure depression); Watson v. City of Miami Beach, 177 F.3d 932, 9 AD Cases 760 (11th Cir. 1999) (in Rehabilitation Act case, fitness-for-duty exam for officer who had displayed antagonistic behavior not indicative that employer regarded officer as paranoid).

[437] 138 F.3d 1366, 8 AD Cases 747 (11th Cir. 1998).

[438] *See Krocka*, 203 F.3d 507 (police officer suffering from depression not regarded as being unable to work after being placed in program for poor performers, because he was allowed to continue to perform duties of his position).

6. Benefits Distinguishing Between Physical and Mental Disabilities

It is not uncommon for an employee benefit package to distinguish between mental and physical conditions. For example, an employer-provided health plan may cover doctor visits for physical ailments or preventive care, but not psychological counseling. Or, a benefit plan may place a lower coverage cap on mental conditions than that provided for physical conditions.

By and large, courts have found that employers offering this type of benefits distinction do not violate Title I of the ADA.[439] Title I prohibits discrimination in the terms and conditions of employment, and requires, in relevant part, that

> [n]o covered entity shall discriminate against a qualified individual with a disability because of the disability of such individual in regard to job application procedures, the hiring, advancement, or discharge of employees, employee compensation, job training, and other terms, conditions, and privileges of employment.[440]

The term "discriminate" includes:

> participating in a contractual or other arrangement or relationship that has the effect of subjecting a covered entity's qualified applicant or employee with a disability to the discrimination prohibited by this subchapter (such relationship includes a relationship with ... an organization providing fringe benefits to an employee of the covered entity...).[441]

Although the provision of health insurance constitutes a fringe benefit, and offering lesser benefits for mental as opposed

---

[439] *See, e.g., Ford v. Schering-Plough Corp.*, 145 F.3d 601, 8 AD Cases 190 (3d Cir. 1998), *cert. denied*, 525 U.S. 1093 (1999) (employer-provided insurance plan that provided coverage for mental impairments for 2 years but provided coverage for physical impairments for employees up until age 65 did not violate ADA); Lenox v. Healthwise of Ky., 149 F.3d 453, 8 AD Cases 521 (6th Cir. 1998) (ADA does not prohibit insurance company from differentiating between different disabilities); Weyer v. Twentieth Century Fox Film Corp., 198 F.3d 1104, 10 AD Cases 65 (9th Cir. 2000) (ADA does not prevent employer from offering insurance policy that capped benefits for mental conditions, but provided coverage for physical conditions for people up to age 65).
[440] 42 U.S.C. §12112(a).
[441] 42 U.S.C. §12112(b)(2).

to physical conditions would seemingly discriminate against a mentally disabled employee in the terms, conditions, and privileges of employment, doing so does not likely violate the ADA. So long as mentally or psychologically disabled employees are offered the same set of benefits offered to nondisabled employees and on equal terms (i.e., offered the same mental health benefits, however limited, that other employees are offered), then there is no violation.

In support of this position, many courts have relied on the legislative history of the ADA. In 1996, the Senate defeated an amendment to the Health Insurance Portability and Accountability Act of 1996 (HIPAA),[442] which would have required equal insurance coverage for mental and physical illnesses. Had the ADA as originally passed already required such parity, courts have reasoned, then there would have been no need for such an amendment.[443]

Thus, an employer is not required to ensure that its benefits plans provide equal benefits for mental and physical impairments, but must not offer a lesser benefits package to those employees with mental disabilities.

7. *Reasonable Accommodation*

An employer is required to reasonably accommodate an employee's mental disability so long as doing so does not pose an undue hardship. An employer first must be made aware, however, that the employee suffers from a mental disability and is in need of a reasonable accommodation.[444] Additionally,

---

[442] Pub. L. No. 104-191, 110 Stat. 1936 (1996) (codified primarily in Titles 18, 26, and 42 of the U.S. Code).

[443] *See* 142 CONG. REC. S9477-02 (daily ed. Aug. 2, 1996) (statement of Sen. Heflin (D-Ala.)); *see also* EEOC v. CNA Ins. Co., 96 F.3d 1039, 1044, 5 AD Cases 1769 (7th Cir, 1996). It bears noting, however, that the final version of the HIPAA statute prohibits insurance companies from placing a cap on mental health benefits if no such cap exists for medical benefits in general. *See* Pub. L. No. 104-204, tit. VII, 110 Stat. 2944 (1996) (codified at 29 U.S.C. §1185a and 42 U.S.C. §300gg-5).

[444] *See* Reed v. LePage Bakeries, Inc., 244 F.3d 254, 11 AD Cases 1150 (1st Cir. 2001) (employer not required to provide reasonable accommodation for employee who never informed employer of her bipolar disorder); Corr v. MTA Long Island Bus, 27 F. Supp. 2d 359, 369 (E.D.N.Y. 1998) (" 'An employer is not obligated to observe employees for any behavior that may be symptomatic of a disability, and

it is the employee's burden to show that a particular accommodation would enable him or her to perform the essential functions of that job.[445] An employee, however, is not entitled to his or her choice of reasonable accommodations.[446] Nor is an employee with a mental disability entitled to a "stress free" working environment.[447]

In certain instances, providing an employee with leave is an acceptable means of accommodating the employee's mental disability. The determination of whether this option is reasonable is necessarily made on a case-by-case basis. In *Criado v. IBM Corp.*,[448] the U.S. Court of Appeals for the First Circuit sanctioned a 1-month leave of absence as a reasonable accommodation for an employee suffering from depression, taking into consideration the fact that the employer provided all employees with 52 weeks of paid disability leave, and that such an extended leave would not financially burden the company.

When leave would pose an undue burden on the operation of the business, or the period of requested leave is open-ended, the employer is under no obligation to provide it. For example, the employer in *Walton v. Mental Health Association of Southeastern Pennsylvania*[449] was not required to extend an employee's leave taken because of depression. After the employee's period

---

then divine that the employee actually suffers from a disability;'" (quoting Hedberg v. Indiana Bell Tel. Co., 47 F.3d 928, 934 (7th Cir. 1995)).

[445] *See, e.g.*, Cannice v. Norwest Bank Iowa, N.A., 189 F.3d 723, 9 AD Cases 1103 (8th Cir. 1999), *cert. denied*, 529 U.S. 1019 (2000) (employer did not fail to reasonably accommodate employee suffering from depression, where employee could not show that accommodation would enable him to keep his job); Seaman v. CSPH, Inc., 179 F.3d 297, 301, 5 WH Cases 2d 673, 675 (5th Cir. 1999) (employee cannot "expect his employer to bear the burden of identifying the need for and suggesting appropriate accommodation").

[446] *See, e.g.*, Keever v. City of Middletown, 145 F.3d 809, 8 AD Cases 388 (6th Cir.), *cert. denied*, 525 U.S. 963 (1998) (police officer suffering from stress and subsequently assigned to desk position as accommodation not entitled to his choice as night-shift detective instead).

[447] *See* Kennedy v. Dresser Rand Co., 193 F.3d 120, 9 AD Cases 1335 (2d Cir. 1999) (presumption exists that request by employee suffering from depression to replace his supervisor is unreasonable); Gaul v. Lucent Techs. Inc., 134 F.3d 576, 7 AD Cases 1223 (3d Cir. 1998) (providing stress-free working environment would impose unreasonable and "wholly impracticable obligation" on employer).

[448] 145 F.3d 437, 8 AD Cases 336 (1st Cir. 1998).

[449] 168 F.3d 661, 9 AD Cases 34 (3d Cir. 1999).

of leave ended, she failed to return to work, and was therefore terminated. The employee argued that the employer should have extended her period of leave as a reasonable accommodation. The U.S. Court of Appeals for the Third Circuit disagreed, finding such a request unreasonable.

In sum, when determining the reasonableness of an accommodation for an individual with a mental disability, counsel must consider the impact that leave would have on the operation of the business.

While mental disorders can rise to the level of "disability" under the ADA, proving that a mental impairment substantially limits a major life activity is a difficult burden. Nonetheless, because mental conditions may be covered, an employer must be cognizant of an employee's rights under the ADA.

D. Diabetes

Diabetes, a disease in which the body does not produce or properly manufacture insulin, is not a per se disability. Rather, diabetes qualifies as a disability when this condition substantially limits one or more major life activities.[450] Thus, it is important to evaluate how diabetes affects a particular individual when determining whether that person is disabled for purposes of ADA coverage.

Diabetes most commonly interferes with an individual's ability to eat and care for oneself. Individuals with this disease need to monitor their blood sugar carefully and continually, and regulate their medication and food intake accordingly. The severity of this condition varies; thus, proper nutrition and exercise can keep some forms of diabetes under control, while more critical cases of this disease require constant monitoring and medical intervention. The steps an individual must take to control this disease factor into whether or not his or her diabetes is a disability.

Additionally, any mitigating measures, such as insulin and proper nutrition, must be considered when evaluating whether

---

[450] *See* Sutton v. United Air Lines, Inc., 527 U.S. 471, 483, 9 AD Cases 673 (1999).

diabetes constitutes a disability.[451] For example, in *Orr v. Wal-Mart Stores, Inc.*,[452] the U.S. Court of Appeals for the Eighth Circuit found that an employee with diabetes was not disabled under the ADA, where he was able to control his disease thorough insulin injections and diet. An employee, therefore, who is able to keep his or her diabetes effectively in check through medication, diet, exercise, or other means, is not disabled for ADA purposes.

If, however, despite these mitigating measures an employee is still substantially limited in the ability to perform major life activities, then he or she properly may be classified as disabled. For instance, if an individual who takes insulin continues to have difficulty regulating his or her blood sugar and metabolizing food, and therefore must constantly monitor this condition and food intake, then that person can be considered substantially limited in the ability to eat.[453] Similarly, if treating one's diabetes involves a significant amount of time and energy, such as testing one's blood sugar and taking insulin numerous times a day, then that individual may be substantially limited in the ability to care for himself or herself.[454] Additionally, the possible effects of the disease, such as kidney and nerve damage, circulatory impairments, depression, mood swings, and hypoglycemic episodes, can also substantially limit major life activities such as walking and thinking.[455] Thus, it is essential to assess the nature and severity of an individual's diabetes and its impact on his or her major life activities in determining whether the disease amounts to a bona fide disability under the ADA.

---

[451] *See, e.g, id.*, at 482–83, 9 AD Cases at 678 ("[a] person whose physical or mental impairment is corrected by medication or other measures does not have an impairment that presently 'substantially limits' a major life activity.").

[452] 297 F.3d 720, 13 AD Cases 577 (8th Cir. 2002), *cert. denied*, 541 U.S. 1070, 15 AD Cases 960 (2004).

[453] *See* Lawson v. CSX Transp., Inc., 245 F.3d 916, 11 AD Cases 1025 (7th Cir. 2001) (severity of diabetic's limitations on ability to eat rendered him disabled); Branham v. Snow, 392 F.3d 896, 16 AD Cases 454 (7th Cir. 2004) (applying same conclusion to Rehabilitation Act claim).

[454] *See* Nawrot v. CPC Int'l, 277 F.3d 896, 12 AD Cases 1138 (7th Cir. 2002).

[455] *See id.*

If an employee alleges that diabetes substantially limits his or her ability to work, it must be shown that the employee is precluded from working in a class or broad range of jobs, not just the position at issue.[456] It is incumbent on the employee to demonstrate this limitation using demographic, local labor market, or other data.[457] This is a relatively difficult showing. Merely demonstrating that diabetes limits one's ability to work no more than 40–50 hours per week, for example, does not suffice to prove that the disease substantially limits one's ability to work in general, as many jobs can be performed in that time frame.[458] By the same token, an incapacity to perform one particular job does not render an individual substantially limited in the ability to work in general.[459]

Finally, if an employer perceives the diabetic employee to be substantially limited in any major life activity, or if the employee has a record of having such limitations because of diabetes, then the employee may be protected under the ADA even if the disease is *not* substantially limiting for that individual. For example, if an employer falsely assumes that a person with diabetes is not qualified to work, then that employer regards that employee as being disabled. Similarly, an employee who experienced diabetic episodes in the past but who currently has the disease under control may have a record of being impaired. If an employer bases an adverse employment decision on this record, the diabetic employee may have standing to sue under the ADA.

---

[456] 29 C.F.R. §1630.2(j)(3) (2003).

[457] *See* Gonzalez v. El Dia, Inc., 304 F.3d 63, 13 AD Cases 889 (1st Cir. 2002) (employee suffering from diabetes and obesity provided no labor market data or other evidence that her impairments rendered her unable to perform broad range of jobs).

[458] *See* Berg v. Norand Corp., 169 F.3d 1140, 9 AD Cases 207 (8th Cir.), *cert. denied*, 528 U.S. 872 (1999) (monitoring blood sugar at least 10 times and taking insulin at least 3 times per day were found to limit an individual's ability to care for oneself substantially).

[459] *See Gonzalez*, 304 F.3d at 63; Mohr v. Hoover Co., 2004 U.S. App. LEXIS 9689 (unpublished opinion) (6th Cir. 2004) (diabetic forklift driver transferred from her position because of recommended limitations on operating dangerous machinery not significantly restricted in broad class of jobs).

If an employee's diabetes is found to constitute a disability, that individual must still be able to perform the essential functions of the job with or without a reasonable accommodation in order to be protected under the ADA. If, for example, a job requires an employee to have good concentration, and an employee's diabetes impairs the ability to concentrate, then that employee is not qualified for the position under the ADA.[460]

Additionally, a diabetic employee is not a qualified individual with a disability if he or she poses a direct threat to himself or herself or others in the workplace. A "direct threat" is "a significant risk to the health or safety of others that cannot be eliminated by reasonable accommodation."[461] According to the EEOC's implementing regulations, the determination of whether an employee "poses a 'direct threat' shall be based on an individualized assessment of the [person's] present ability to safely perform the essential functions of the job."[462] Thus, a general policy banning insulin-dependent diabetics from a safety-sensitive position on the grounds that they would pose a direct threat in the workplace would likely violate the ADA, since the ADA requires that individualized assessments be made with respect to the direct-threat analysis.[463]

In *Hutton v. Elf Atochem North America, Inc.*,[464] however, a chlorine-finishing operator with Type I diabetes was held to pose a direct threat to himself and others, because his mental and physical lapses stemming from diabetic episodes could potentially cause "catastrophic" repercussions in the event of a chlorine spill. Similarly, a chemical process operator was

---

[460] *See* Turco v. Hoechst Celanese Chem. Group, Inc., 101 F.3d 1090, 6 AD Cases 278 (5th Cir. 1996) (chemical process operator with diabetes was not qualified individual with disability under ADA, as disease affected his ability to concentrate, an essential job function); Brenneman v. MedCentral Health Sys., 366 F.3d 412, 15 AD Cases 769 (diabetic technician's inability to satisfy employer's basic attendance requirements barred ADA claim), *reh'g denied*, 2004 U.S. App. LEXIS 16569 (2004), *cert. denied*, 125 S. Ct. 1300 (2005).

[461] 42 U.S.C. §12111(3).

[462] 29 C.F.R. §1630.2(r) (2003).

[463] *See, e.g.*, Kapche v. City of San Antonio, 304 F.3d 493, 13 AD Cases 907 (5th Cir. 2002) (policy precluding insulin-dependent diabetics from becoming police officers unlawful without individualized assessment of risk).

[464] 273 F.3d 884, 12 AD Cases 909 (9th Cir. 2001).

deemed unqualified in *Turco v. Hoechst Celanese Chemical Group*,[465] because his diabetes caused a loss of concentration while operating machinery and handling chemicals, an occurrence that could result in substantial harm.

An employer does not violate the ADA if it adheres to federal laws or regulations that limit the hiring of insulin-dependent individuals. For example, some federal agencies have implemented regulations applicable to work in particular safety-sensitive positions prohibiting the employment of individuals who take certain medications. The Nuclear Regulatory Commission's fitness-for-duty requirements, for instance, require that nuclear power plant operators ensure that their employees do not work under the influence of any substances that would impair their ability to perform their jobs and prohibit employees under the influence of certain prescription drugs from working in safety-sensitive positions.[466] Thus, if a diabetic employee's medication impairs his or her ability to work, a nuclear power plan operator may fire or refuse to hire that employee without violating the ADA. Compliance with these regulations, however, must be shown to be mandatory if the employer is to rely on them as an affirmative defense to a charge of disability discrimination.[467]

Generally, an employer may not conduct a medical examination or make inquiries regarding an employee's diabetes before making an offer of employment.[468] This prohibition includes asking an applicant whether he or she has diabetes and/or takes medication such as insulin. Once an employee has been hired, however, an employer may inquire about the nature and degree of the employee's disease if doing so is job-related and consistent with business necessity.[469] Any information gathered as a result of such inquiries or medical exams

---

[465] 101 F.3d 1090, 6 AD Cases 278 (5th Cir. 1996) (per curiam).

[466] 10 C.F.R. §26.10 (2004).

[467] *See EEOC Fact Sheet: Questions and Answers About Diabetes in the Workplace and the Americans with Disabilities Act (ADA)*, (Oct. 29, 2003), *published at* http://www.eeoc.gov/facts/diabetes.html [hereinafter *EEOC Fact Sheet*].

[468] 42 U.S.C. §12112(d)(1).

[469] 42 U.S.C. §12112(d)(4)(A). An employer may not withdraw an offer of employment once finding out that an individual has diabetes, so long as he or

must be kept confidential.[470] However, if information about an individual's diabetes is given voluntarily, no such confidentiality requirements apply.[471]

There are a number of instances in which an employer may legitimately disclose that an employee has diabetes. For instance, managers and supervisors often must be informed of the disease in order to reasonably accommodate the employee's condition and be made aware of his or her work restrictions. Additionally, an employer may reveal the employee's diabetes to medical personnel in the event of an emergency, to government personnel during an investigation into possible ADA and/or state/local law violations, and to the appropriate authorities involved in workers' compensation or insurance matters.[472]

An employer is permitted to ask an employee about his or her diabetes if the employer suspects that it may be causing performance problems.[473] For example, if an employee's job performance begins to decline while displaying symptoms of diabetes, an employer may ask the employee whether he or she has diabetes or request a medical examination based on the belief that the performance problems may be related to the disease. However, an employer does not have the authority to request a medical exam whenever an employee known to have diabetes exhibits poor performance. The employer must have objective evidence that diabetes may be the cause of the performance issues.

Additionally, an employer may inquire about an employee's diabetic status and/or require a medical examination if it suspects the employee poses a direct threat to himself or herself or others.[474] This suspicion must have some basis in

---

she can perform the essential functions of the job with or without a reasonable accommodation, and without posing a direct threat in the workplace.

[470] *See* 29 C.F.R. §1630.14(c)(1) (2003).

[471] *See, e.g.,* Cash v. Smith, 231 F.3d 1301, 11 AD Cases 203 (11th Cir. 2000) (employer did not violate confidentiality provisions of ADA when manager told diabetic employee's colleagues about employee's disease, as this information had been voluntarily disclosed).

[472] *See EEOC Fact Sheet, supra* note 453.

[473] *Id.*

[474] *Id.*

objective fact, and cannot be rooted in myths or stereotypes attributed to people with diabetes.

There are other instances in which asking an employee about his or her disability is permissible under the ADA. If a diabetic employee requests a reasonable accommodation for the disease, and/or is participating in a voluntary wellness program focusing on early detection, screening, and management of diseases such as diabetes, then it is appropriate for an employer to make inquiries about the employee's condition.[475] Moreover, employees can be required to provide a doctor's note verifying that sick leave was related to a legitimate medical condition such as diabetes, so long as this practice is required of all employees.

An employer may require a medical exam and/or a return-to-work notice from an employee's doctor on the employee's completion of diabetes-related medical leave. The employer must have a reasonable belief, however, that the employee may be unable to perform the essential functions of the job, or poses a direct threat in the workplace. Thus, an employer may not require such an exam of or documentation from a diabetic employee who happens to take leave for nonmedical reasons.

There are a number of ways in which an employer can reasonably accommodate an individual with diabetes. Some of the more common methods of accommodation include allowing diabetic employees breaks so that they can test their blood sugar, eat, rest, or take medication; providing private areas in which employees can test their blood sugar; allowing employees to take leave in order to seek medical treatment or information on managing their disease, or simply to recover from diabetic episodes; providing diabetic employees with modified or flexible work schedules; and allowing employees with circulatory or nerve problems resulting from the disease to sit while working. An employer is not responsible for ensuring that a diabetic employee takes his or her medication or monitors his or her blood sugar level.

---

[475] *Id.*

In sum, diabetes can constitute a disability under the ADA if this disease or its treatments substantially limit one or more major life activities. However, the employee must still be able to perform the essential functions of the job with or without a reasonable accommodation in order to receive ADA protection.

E. Hypertension

Hypertension (high blood pressure), like many other medical conditions, is considered a disability only if the ailment substantially limits one or more major life activities. Assessing whether a limitation is substantial must take into consideration any medications or other mitigating factors, such as diet and exercise, used by the individual.[476] As is often the case, medication taken for high blood pressure usually allows an individual to function normally. Thus, only in extreme cases, such as where hypertension is uncontrollable, or the medication taken to regulate blood pressure itself causes severe side effects, will hypertension rise to the level of "disability" for ADA purposes.

The Supreme Court examined hypertension in an ADA context in *Murphy v. United Parcel Serv., Inc.*[477] In this case, a United Parcel Service (UPS) mechanic was fired because his blood pressure exceeded DOT requirements. Under the DOT health certification requirements, a driver of a commercial vehicle must have "no current clinical diagnosis of high blood pressure likely to interfere with his/her ability to operate a commercial vehicle safely."[478] The mechanic was mistakenly granted certification to work, then terminated when the error was discovered. The employee sued UPS on the grounds that the company regarded him as disabled, a violation of the ADA. The Supreme Court affirmed the lower court's ruling that UPS did not fire the mechanic because of a perceived disability,

---

[476] *See* Murphy v. United Parcel Serv., Inc., 527 U.S. 516, 9 AD Cases 691 (1999).
[477] 527 U.S. 516, 9 AD Cases 691 (1999).
[478] 49 C.F.R. §391.41(b)(6) (2003).

but rather because he did not meet the DOT requirements.[479] Thus, an employer is permitted to adhere to more stringent federal requirements when making employment decisions, even if doing so discriminates against an individual with high blood pressure.

Further, the Court in *Murphy* affirmed the determination that the mechanic's hypertension did not constitute a disability, because his own doctor testified that when medicated, the employee functioned normally and was able to carry out everyday activities performed by the general public. High blood pressure, therefore, is not a disability if it is kept in check.

It is the individual's responsibility to ensure that he or she takes measures to counter the effects of hypertension. In *Hein v. All America Plywood Co.*,[480] a truck driver was fired after refusing to make an out-of-town delivery that was assigned to him almost a week in advance. The driver sued his employer under the ADA, alleging, among other things, that he could not make the delivery because he would have run out of blood pressure medication. The U.S. Court of Appeals for the Sixth Circuit affirmed the lower court's grant of summary judgment in the company's favor, finding that the driver was not disabled under the ADA, because his condition was controlled by his medication. The potential inaccessibility to medication was caused by the driver's own lack of foresight, according to the court, not the employer's action.

Finally, employees who claim that hypertension substantially limits their ability to work must demonstrate that they are precluded from a class or broad range of jobs. Merely being unable to work at one particular job because of hypertension

---

[479] EEOC v. J.B. Hunt Transp., Inc., 321 F.3d 69, 13 AD Cases 1697 (2d Cir. 2003) (employer that chose not to employ over-the-road truck drivers whose medications could impair ability to drive safely did not violate ADA by regarding drivers as disabled, but rather was following DOT mandate to restrict drivers from operating vehicles "while the driver's ability to alertness is so impaired, or so likely to become impaired, through fatigue, illness, or any other cause, as to make it unsafe for him/her to begin or continue to operate the commercial motor vehicle." 49 C.F.R. §392.3) (2003).

[480] 232 F.3d 482, 11 AD Cases 308 (6th Cir. 2000).

does not automatically render a person disabled under the ADA.[481]

In sum, the determination of whether an individual with hypertension has a cognizable disability depends on the effects this condition has on the person's ability to perform major life activities. In most instances, medication and proper diet prevent hypertension from rising to the level of "disability" under the ADA.

F. Heart Disease

Like hypertension, heart disease is not a per se disability.[482] Rather, an individual with heart disease who seeks ADA protection must establish that this condition substantially limits one or more major life activities.[483]

Proving that heart disease rises to the level of "disability" is a difficult burden. Often, individuals with heart disease are restricted in such strenuous activities as shoveling snow, mowing the lawn, lifting heavy objects, and engaging in vigorous exercise. However, these activities are not likely to be considered major life activities.[484] Even if an individual is restricted in certain activities such as lifting, walking long distances, performing manual tasks, and climbing stairs, moderate limitations do not equate to substantial limitations for purposes of ADA coverage. Moreover, an individual must show more than conclusory statements that he or she is substantially limited in performing any one major life activity.[485]

---

[481] *See, e.g.*, Sheehan v. City of Gloucester, 321 F.3d 21, 14 AD Cases 1 (1st Cir. 2003) (police lieutenant forced to retire because of hypertension could not show that he was precluded from working in other jobs, especially because he was able to work 24–32 hours per week as security guard following his retirement).

[482] *See, e.g.*, Weber v. Strippit, Inc., 186 F.3d 907, 9 AD Cases 961 (8th Cir. 1999), *cert. denied*, 528 U.S. 1078 (2000).

[483] 42 U.S.C. §12102(2)(A).

[484] *See, e.g.*, Weber, 186 F.3d 907 (engaging in yard work, playing tennis, and fishing not major life activities).

[485] *See* Hilburn v. Murata Elec. N. Am., Inc., 181 F.3d 1220, 9 AD Cases 908 (11th Cir. 1999) (conclusory allegations without specific supporting facts have no probative value).

An individual who claims that heart disease substantially limits his or her ability to work must demonstrate that health-related restrictions preclude a wide variety of employment. A lifting restriction that prevents an employee from working in only one position, for example, does not render that person disabled.[486]

In certain instances, federal rules and regulations prevent individuals with heart disease from working in specific occupations. The DOT, for example, requires drivers of large commercial vehicles to obtain medical certification attesting to their fitness to operate such vehicles safely. According to the DOT's regulations, the driver's examining physician must certify "[i]n the interest of public safety" that "the driver does not have any physical, mental, or organic condition that might affect the driver's ability to operate a commercial motor vehicle safely."[487] These regulations specifically note that cardiovascular disease, accompanied by known congestive cardiac failure, disqualifies a driver from obtaining such certification.[488] Thus, an employer that follows this directive will not run afoul of the ADA.

In sum, unless individuals with heart disease are severely restricted from performing major life activities, they are not deemed disabled under the ADA. Moreover, adhering to federal regulations that preclude individuals with heart disease from obtaining certain safety-sensitive positions will not violate the ADA.

G. Cancer

Although classified as an impairment under the ADA,[489] cancer is not always considered a disability. If cancer or its treatment substantially limits an individual's ability to perform major life activities, then this disease constitutes a disability.

---

[486] *See id.* (employee with 10-pound lifting restriction was not prevented from performing class or broad range of jobs, and therefore not disabled under ADA); *see also* Taylor v. Nimock's Oil Co., 214 F.3d 957, 10 AD Cases 1069 (8th Cir. 2000) (same).
[487] 49 C.F.R. §391.43 (2003).
[488] 49 C.F.R. §391.41(4) (2003).
[489] *See* 28 C.F.R. §35.104(1)(ii) (2003).

Whether an individual's cancer rises to the level of a disability must be determined on a case-by-case basis.

In *EEOC v. R.J. Gallagher Co.*,[490] a company president who was demoted after receiving cancer treatment was found not to be substantially limited in his ability to work, even though his treatments impaired his ability to perform some of his job functions. In this instance, the U.S. Court of Appeals for the Fifth Circuit noted that the employee's cancer had been in remission, and that his doctor had cleared him for an unqualified return to work. The court remanded to the lower court, however, the issue of whether the employee had a record of or was regarded as having a disability. To prove that he was regarded as disabled, the employee would need to establish that his employer believed that he was substantially limited in performing one or more major life activities, the appellate court stated. Similarly, the Fifth Circuit specified, in order to prove that he had a record of being disabled, the employee would be required to demonstrate that he had a record of an impairment that substantially limited one or more major life activities, not merely that he had a record of a cancer diagnosis. In so holding, the Fifth Circuit rejected the EEOC's statement in its *Interpretive Guidance* that the ADA "protects former cancer patients from discrimination based on their prior medical history."[491]

With respect to being regarded as unable to work, it is unlawful for an employer to assume that an employee with cancer can no longer perform the essential functions of his or her job. Such a faulty perception can result in large damages awards. In *EEOC v. AIC Security Investigations, Ltd.*,[492] for example, the EEOC won a jury verdict finding that the defendant company had terminated its executive director on the belief that he could no longer perform his job because of his diagnosis of terminal brain cancer. The jury concluded that the employer

---

[490] 181 F.3d 645, 9 AD Cases 917 (5th Cir. 1999).
[491] 29 C.F.R. pt. 1630, app. §1630.2(k) (2003).
[492] 820 F. Supp. 1060, 2 AD Cases 561 (N.D. Ill. 1993).

unlawfully regarded the employee as disabled under the ADA, and awarded the plaintiff $222,000 in damages.

Although not a per se disability, cancer can be considered a disability under the ADA if it substantially limits one or more major life activities. In litigation under the ADA regarding cancer, it has been more common, however, for employers to be found to have falsely regarded an employee with cancer as being disabled, even if this condition was not substantially limiting, than for the condition itself to be found to be substantially limiting.

H. Epilepsy

It is widely acknowledged that epilepsy, a neurological condition that makes people susceptible to seizures, can be a disabling condition.[493] In fact, epilepsy was one of the conditions Congress specifically considered when it enacted the ADA.[494] However, not all individuals suffering from epilepsy are deemed disabled for purposes of ADA coverage. Because epilepsy is not a per se disability, determining whether one is disabled under the ADA must be conducted on a case-by-case basis.

To receive protection under the ADA, an individual must have "a physical or mental impairment that substantially limits one or more" major life activities.[495] Although epilepsy qualifies as an impairment, the manifestations of this condition range from mild to severe. In some people with this disease, seizures are infrequent, short in duration, and cause minor disruptions to the individual's ability to perform everyday tasks.[496] More

---

[493] *See, e.g.*, 29 C.F.R. §1615.103(1)(ii) (2003) (definition of "physical or mental impairment" includes epilepsy); Sutton v. United Air Lines, Inc., 527 U.S. 471, 488, 9 AD Cases 673 (1999) (using epilepsy as example of a condition included in the definition of disability); LaChance v. Duffy's Draft House, Inc., 146 F.3d 832, 8 AD Cases 652 (11th Cir. 1998) (epilepsy qualifies as disability under ADA); Martinson v. Kinney Shoe Corp., 104 F.3d 683, 6 AD Cases 434 (4th Cir. 1997) (same).

[494] *See, e.g.*, H.R. Rep. No. 101-485, pt. II, at 52, *reprinted in* 1990 U.S.C.C.A.N. 303, 334 (epilepsy can be an impairment that substantially limits major life activity).

[495] 42 U.S.C. §12102(2)(A).

[496] *See, e.g.*, Matczak v. Frankford Candy & Chocolate Co., 136 F.3d 933, 938, 7 AD Cases 1050, 1053 (3d Cir. 1997) ("Some individuals suffer from relatively

acute cases of epilepsy can significantly impair an individual's life activities, and require surgery and/or hospitalization. Whether and to what extent an individual's epilepsy impacts a major life activity will therefore determine whether he or she is disabled under the ADA.

The most common life activities deemed "major" under the ADA include "caring for oneself, performing manual tasks, walking, seeing, hearing, speaking, breathing, learning, and working."[497] While this list is not exhaustive, not all functions an individual participates in on a daily basis are considered "major" life activities under the ADA. Driving, for example, has *not* been recognized as a major life activity for ADA purposes.[498] This is significant for people suffering from epilepsy, as many are medically and legally precluded from driving, depending on the severity and frequency of their seizures caused by this condition. Thus, individuals with epilepsy cannot use the fact that they are substantially limited in the ability to drive to support their contention that they are disabled under the ADA. Such may be the case even in rural areas, or where access to reliable public transportation is minimal or non-existent.[499]

Even if epilepsy does impact an individual's ability to breathe, care for oneself, sleep, or perform any other major life function, this impact must be regarded as substantial in order to constitute a disability under the ADA. A limitation is considered substantial if the individual cannot perform—or is significantly limited in the ability to perform—an activity that an average person in the general population can carry out.[500] This assessment must take into consideration any mitigating

---

mild forms of epilepsy which cause nothing more than 'minor isolated muscle jerks'—so we cannot and do not conclude that all epileptics are substantially limited by the impairment.").

[497] 29 C.F.R. §1630.2(i) (2003).

[498] Chenoweth v. Hillsborough County, 250 F.3d 1328, 11 AD Cases 1421 (11th Cir. 2001).

[499] *Id. See also* Lovejoy-Wilson v. NOCO Motor Fuel, Inc., 263 F.3d 208, 12 AD Cases 340 (2d Cir. 2001).

[500] *See* EEOC TITLE I TECHNICAL ASSISTANCE MANUAL, *supra* note 43, §2.2(a)(iii); 29 C.F.R. §1630.2(j) (2003).

measures, such as medication or behavioral modification to control epilepsy.[501] Therefore, if medication or other mitigating measures effectively controls an individual's seizures and enables that person to function at a level comparable to that of the general public, then epilepsy is not a disabling condition.[502]

Nonetheless, medication does not always completely negate the effects of epilepsy. Individuals with epilepsy who continue to suffer from seizures despite medication can still be considered disabled under the ADA if those seizures substantially limit major life activities.

Additionally, the medication taken to ease the symptoms of epilepsy can cause adverse side effects in some people. For example, certain medications cause drowsiness, irritability, difficulty concentrating, memory lapses, among other symptoms, which may impair an individuals' ability to work, care for oneself, or perform other life functions substantially. Thus, even if medication does control the effects of epilepsy, the side effects from the medications themselves may be substantially limiting.

---

[501] *See* Albertsons, Inc. v. Kirkinburg, 527 U.S. 555, 9 AD Cases 694 (1999) (ADA mandates individualized inquiry into whether person is disabled based on actual effect of impairment on life of person in question); Murphy v. United Parcel Serv., Inc., 527 U.S. 516, 9 AD Cases 691 (1999) (truck driver with hypertension not disabled, as his condition was controlled by medication); Sutton v. United Air Lines, Inc., 527 U.S. 471, 483, 9 AD Cases 673, 678 (1999) (mitigating or corrective measures must be considered in assessing whether individual is disabled, because to do otherwise would "run[] directly counter to the individualized inquiry mandated by the ADA").

[502] *See, e.g.*, Arnold v. City of Appleton, Wis., 97 F. Supp. 2d 937, 10 AD Cases 1474 (D. Wis. 2000) (ADA claimant whose epilepsy had been under control through medication for 19 years not disabled in light of *Sutton*); Popko v. Pennsylvania State Univ., 84 F. Supp. 2d 589, 10 AD Cases 1404 (M.D. Pa. 2000), *aff'd*, 254 F. 3d 1078 (3d Cir. 2001) (claimant whose epilepsy is completely controlled by appropriate amount of sleep not disabled); Treglia v. Town of Manlius, 68 F. Supp. 2d 153, 10 AD Cases 1486 (N.D.N.Y. 1999), *vacated in part*, 313 F.3d 713, 13 AD Cases 1537 (2d Cir. 2002) (claimant who admitted epilepsy was under control through medication and did not allege that epilepsy substantially limited any major life activities not disabled under ADA); Todd v. Academy Corp., 57 F. Supp. 2d 448, 9 AD Cases 1306 (S.D. Tex. 1999) (claimant who suffered eight "light" seizures, lasting approximately 15 seconds each, over a 5-month period not disabled under ADA). *But see* Rowles v. Automated Prod. Sys., Inc., 92 F. Supp. 2d 424, 10 AD Cases 1542 (M.D. Pa. 2000) (claimant with epilepsy could be considered disabled even though seizures

Therefore, although mitigating measures can prevent epilepsy from becoming a full-fledged disability under the ADA, the effects of those mitigating measures must also be evaluated when determining an individual's disability status.

In *EEOC v. Sara Lee Corp.*,[503] the U.S. Court of Appeals for the Fourth Circuit held that an individual with epilepsy was not substantially limited in the ability to sleep, think, or care for herself, and was therefore not disabled under the ADA. Although the plaintiff in this case alleged that she had difficulty sleeping at night because of her seizures, she could not prove that her sleep deprivation was any worse than that suffered by the general public, as she often slept through the night without any seizures, and on several occasions did not even remember having them. Ordinary sleep disturbances do not rise to the level of substantial, as many people without epilepsy do not receive a full night's sleep.[504]

By the same token, the appellate court noted that having forgetful episodes a few times a week does not amount to a substantial limitation in the ability to think, as "many other adults in the general population suffer from a few incidents of forgetfulness a week, and indeed must write things down in order to remember them."[505]

Finally, requiring assistance during and occasionally after suffering from seizures does not automatically render a person substantially limited in the ability to care for oneself, according to the Fourth Circuit. Because the individual at issue could still perform a variety of everyday tasks, such as drive, work, and care for her child, she was not substantially limited in the ability to care for herself, and was thus not disabled. The court

---

were controlled by medication, because precautions he took to prevent seizures could be viewed as substantially limiting).

[503] 237 F.3d 349, 11 AD Cases 595 (4th Cir. 2001).

[504] *See* Pack v. Kmart Corp., 166 F.3d 1300, 1306, 8 AD Cases 1880 (10th Cir. 1999) (ADA plaintiff could not demonstrate that her sleep was significantly worse than that of average person in general population, and therefore was not disabled); Colwell v. Suffolk County Police Dep't, 158 F.3d 635, 644, 8 AD Cases 1232 (2d Cir. 1998), *cert. denied*, 526 U.S. 1018 (1999) (same).

[505] *Sara Lee*, 237 F.3d at 354, 11 AD Cases at 597.

in *Sara Lee* emphasized that the individual suffered from a mild form of epilepsy that did not involve grand mal seizures.

Generally, epilepsy that results in infrequent and minor seizures usually does not render an individual disabled.[506] Similarly, being unable to see, hear, or speak for a period of several seconds is not necessarily a substantial limitation.[507] In *Deas v. River West, L.P.*,[508] for example, the U.S. Court of Appeals for the Fifth Circuit found that such momentary losses of sensory function, when compared with the degree of sensory function enjoyed by the general population, did not amount to a "significant restriction."

In contrast, the U.S. Court of Appeals for the Eighth Circuit, in *Otting v. J.C. Penney Co.*,[509] found that seizures rendering an individual unable to bathe herself and drive, and causing her to be lethargic, shaky, and have difficulty concentrating for up to 36 hours following each episode, rose to the level of disability under the ADA. In evaluating whether the claimant's limitations were substantial, the court emphasized that the individual's epilepsy was severe, resistant to control, and most likely permanent.

In sum, because no bright-line test exists to determine whether an individual's epilepsy is sufficiently severe to constitute a disabling condition, each situation must be assessed on a case-by-case basis. Some factors to take into consideration include the frequency, duration, and intensity of the seizures, whether medications sufficiently control these episodes, and whether medications or other mitigating measures cause side effects that substantially limit one or more major life activities.

---

[506] *See, e.g.*, Moreno v. American Ingredients Co., 10 AD Cases 1483 2000 WL 527808 (D. Kan. Apr. 7, 2000) (suffering from seizure approximately once every 1–2 months does not render individual substantially limited in ability to work under ADA); *cf. Rowles*, 92 F. Supp. 2d 424 (claimant who suffered from seizures approximately once a year met definition of disabled, as precautions he took to prevent seizures could be viewed as substantially limiting).

[507] *See, e.g.*, Deas v. River W., L.P., 152 F.3d 471, 478, 8 AD Cases 989 (5th Cir. 1998), *cert. denied*, 527 U.S. 1035, 1044 (1999).

[508] 152 F.3d 471, 478, 8 AD Cases 989 (5th Cir. 1998).

[509] 223 F.3d 704, 10 AD Cases 1549 (8th Cir. 2000).

Once it has been established that an individual's epilepsy is a disabling condition, the claimant still must demonstrate that he or she is qualified to perform the essential functions of the position with or without a reasonable accommodation. If epilepsy prevents an employee from adequately performing his or her job, then that individual is not a qualified individual with a disability, and therefore not protected under the ADA.

For example, In *Jacques v. Clean-Up Group, Inc.*,[510] the U.S. Court of Appeals for the First Circuit held that an epileptic employee precluded from driving was not a qualified individual with a disability, as he was unable to report to work by the designated start time. Because arriving to work on time is often deemed an essential job function, terminating an employee for failing to meet that legitimate job expectation does not run afoul of the ADA.

In *Martinson v. Kinney Shoe Corp.*,[511] the U.S. Court of Appeals for the Fourth Circuit held that a shoe store justifiably terminated a salesman suffering from epilepsy, as his seizures jeopardized his ability to safeguard the store. The court agreed with the employer that one of the essential functions of the salesman's job was to provide security, and that the employee would be unable to do so in the event of a seizure. Thus, the employee was not a qualified individual with a disability. The court further noted that hiring an additional employee to perform the security function would not be a reasonable accommodation, as the ADA does not require an employer to hire additional personnel to perform essential job functions.[512]

An employee who is not medically cleared to work for a certain time period because of epilepsy is similarly not a qualified individual with a disability. In *Mathews v. Denver Post*,[513] an employee alleged that his employer laid him off for a 2-year

---

[510] 96 F.3d 506, 5 AD Cases 1594 (1st Cir. 1996).
[511] 104 F.3d 683, 6 AD Cases 434 (4th Cir. 1997).
[512] *See* 29 C.F.R. pt. 1630, app. §1630.2(o) (2003) ("An employer or other covered entity is not required to reallocate essential functions.").
[513] 263 F.3d 1164, 12 AD Cases 250 (10th Cir. 2001).

period in violation of the ADA. The employee's doctor, however, had ordered him not to drive or operate heavy machinery during this period. Because the employee's job as a journey-level mailer necessitated work with such machinery, the employer contended, and the court agreed, that the employee was not qualified to perform his job while medically restricted, and was therefore legitimately terminated from his position. The court in *Mathews* paid particular attention to the job description at issue, which described the need to work with heavy machinery.

In sum, if an individual's epilepsy renders him or her unable to perform the essential functions of the job, and no reasonable accommodation exists to help that person perform these job tasks, then the employee is not a qualified individual with a disability.

An employer may require that an employee not pose a direct threat to himself or herself or others in the workplace.[514] The ADA defines "direct threat" as "a significant risk to the health or safety of others that cannot be eliminated by reasonable accommodation."[515] In assessing an individual's threat potential, the regulations provide the following criteria to be taken into consideration: "(1) The duration of the risk [posed by the employee]; (2) The nature and severity of the potential harm; (3) The likelihood that the potential harm will occur; and (4) The imminence of the potential harm."[516] While no strict formula exists, a strong showing in one or more of these categories will bolster the argument that an epileptic employee poses a direct threat.

Epileptics in safety-sensitive positions or who work with potentially dangerous equipment are most susceptible to the argument that their condition poses a direct threat in the workplace. For example, positions that require work on elevated platforms, or with fast-moving conveyor belts, exposed

---

[514] *See* 29 C.F.R. §1630.15(b)(2) (2003) ("The term 'qualification standard' may include a requirement that an individual shall not pose a direct threat to the health or safety of the individual or others in the workplace.").

[515] 42 U.S.C. §12111(3).

[516] 29 C.F.R. §1630.2(r) (2003).

running machinery, or hot or sharp equipment could prove dangerous for individuals with seizure disorders.[517]

The potential injury an epileptic employee could sustain on the job must be significant if that person is to be deemed a direct threat. Sustaining only a minor injury does not suffice as proof that an epileptic employee poses a direct threat to himself or herself or others.[518]

In sum, determining whether an individual with epilepsy poses a direct threat to himself or herself or others in the workplace must be made on a case-by-case basis. Further, efforts must be made to assess whether a reasonable accommodation can eliminate this threat. Such an accommodation, however, must not pose an undue hardship on the employer.[519]

The antidiscrimination provisions of the ADA do not affect federal regulations or laws in place that restrict epileptics from certain types of employment. For example, the DOT has regulations that prevent individuals with epilepsy from driving trucks in interstate commerce.[520] Under these regulations, commercial vehicle employers are permitted to disqualify anyone with an established medical history or diagnosis of epilepsy permanently, regardless of present ability to control seizures.[521]

---

[517] *See, e.g.*, LaChance v. Duffy's Draft House Inc., 146 F.3d 832, 8 AD Cases 652 (11th Cir. 1998) (line cook suffering from seizures posed direct threat to himself and others, as his job required him to cook on flat top grill, use fryer filled with hot grease, and use slicing machines); Moses v. American Nonwovens, Inc., 97 F.3d 446, 5 AD Cases 1651 (11th Cir. 1996) (epileptic employee whose medication did not sufficiently control his seizures posed direct threat, as his assigned tasks all involved work with heavy and dangerous machinery, such as conveyor belts and elevated platforms), *cert. denied*, 519 U.S. 1118 (1997).

[518] *See, e.g.*, Lovejoy-Wilson v. NOCO Motor Fuel, Inc., 263 F.3d 208, 12 AD Cases 340 (2d Cir. 2001) (employee who sustained minor injury to her elbow as result of seizure did not pose direct threat to herself or others).

[519] 42 U.S.C. §12112(b)(5)(A). Accommodation efforts are considered undue hardships if they require "significant difficulty or expense when considered in light of the" cost of the accommodation, the overall financial resources of the employer, and the type of operation of the employer, among other criteria. 42 U.S.C. §12111(10)(A), (B).

[520] 49 C.F.R. §391.41.

[521] 49 C.F.R. §391.41(b)(8) ("A person is physically qualified to drive a commercial motor vehicle if that person . . . [h]as no established medical history or clinical diagnosis of epilepsy or any other condition which is likely to cause loss of consciousness or any loss of ability to control a commercial motor vehicle.").

Similarly, epileptics are not permitted to pilot commercial airplanes.[522] Thus, adhering to federal regulations regarding the employment of epileptics does not violate the ADA. However, an employer cannot rely on these regulations to justify denying an epileptic a job for which the regulations do not apply. For instance, a transportation employer cannot use the DOT regulations to exclude an individual with epilepsy from working in a position that does not require driving a DOT-regulated vehicle automatically.[523]

While an employer may not ask a job applicant whether he or she has epilepsy, an employer can condition an offer of employment on a bona fide medical examination, if such an examination is required of all applicants regardless of disability.[524] If such a medical examination acts to exclude individuals with epilepsy, this exclusionary criteria must be job-related and consistent with business necessity.[525] For example, an employer can withdraw an offer of employment after finding out the individual's medical condition if it can demonstrate that epilepsy would preclude him or her from performing the essential functions of the job with or without a reasonable accommodation, and/or if the person would pose a significant risk of causing substantial harm to himself or herself or others, and such a threat could not be abated via a reasonable accommodation.

Once hired, an employee may be subject to medical inquiries or examinations if job-related and consistent with business necessity.[526] For example, if an individual suffers seizures while on the job, an employer may require the employee to submit to a medical examination to determine whether he or she is medically able to perform the essential functions of the job,

---

[522] 14 C.F.R. §67.109(a)(1) (2004).

[523] *See, e.g.,* Morton v. United Parcel Serv. Inc., 272 F.3d 1249, 12 AD Cases 897 (9th Cir. 2001) (relying on DOT regulation to deny employment to hearing impaired individual not proper, where employer had not examined business necessity of applying such regulations to non-DOT vehicles), *cert. denied,* 535 U.S. 1054 (2002).

[524] 29 C.F.R. §1630.14(b) (2003).

[525] *Id.* §1630.14(b)(3) (2003).

[526] 29 C.F.R. §1630.14(c) (2003).

and/or to determine the appropriate types of reasonable accommodations that would enable the employee to perform such functions. Any information garnered through such medical inquiries or exams are subject to the ADA's confidentially provisions.[527]

Even if an individual with epilepsy is not substantially limited in any major life activity, he or she may be protected by the ADA if an employer believes that he or she is disabled. In order to succeed on the "regarded as" theory, the individual must show that the employer "mistakenly believes that [he or she] has a physical impairment that substantially limits one or more major life activities," or, alternately, that it "mistakenly believes that an actual, nonlimiting impairment substantially limits one or more major life activities."[528]

If an individual with epilepsy believes that an employer falsely regards him or her as substantially limited in the ability to work, the individual must demonstrate that the employer believes that he or she is precluded from a class or broad range of jobs, not just the position at hand.[529] In *Schuler v. SuperValu, Inc.*,[530] for example, an epileptic individual medically restricted from driving a forklift and working at dangerous heights who was denied employment as a warehouse worker was not regarded as disabled, as he could not prove that the employer

---

[527] *Id.* §1630.14(d)(1) (2003):
Information obtained . . . regarding the medical condition or history of any employee shall be collected and maintained on separate forms and in separate medical files and be treated as a confidential medical record, except that:
   (i) Supervisors and managers may be informed regarding necessary restrictions on the work or duties of the employee and necessary accommodations;
   (ii) First aid and safety personnel may be informed, when appropriate, if the disability might require emergency treatment; and
   (iii) Government officials investigating compliance with this part shall be provided relevant information on request.

[528] Sutton v. United Air Lines, Inc., 527 U.S. 471, 489, 9 AD Cases 673, 680 (1999).

[529] *See* 29 C.F.R. §1630.2(j)(3)(i) (2003) (a person is substantially limited in major life activity of working if that person is "significantly restricted in the ability to perform either a class of jobs or a broad range of jobs in various classes as compared to the average person having comparable training, skills and abilities").

[530] 36 F.3d 702, 14 AD Cases 1115 (8th Cir. 2003).

viewed him as substantially limited in the ability to work in other positions.

It is discriminatory under the ADA for an employer to fail to make reasonable accommodations to the known limitations of an otherwise qualified individual with a disability. The ADA defines a qualified individual with a disability as a person "who, with or without reasonable accommodation, can perform the essential functions of the employment position that such individual holds or desires."[531]

In determining whether a reasonable accommodation is appropriate, one must assess whether a particular job function is essential, or whether it is just one of many means of accomplishing an essential task. For example, while depositing store receipts in a safe and timely manner may be an essential job function for a store manager, driving to the bank may be just one way of performing this task.[532] Thus, while an employee with epilepsy may not be able to drive to the bank due to medical restrictions, he or she may be able to complete this errand with a reasonable accommodation. Such feasible alternatives could include riding with another store manager or hiring a car service at either the employer or the employee's expense.[533]

An employer is not required to provide a reasonable accommodation that would pose an undue hardship. An accommodation effort constitutes an undue hardship if it would require "significant difficulty or expense, when considered in light of," among other factors, the cost of the accommodation, the overall financial resources of the employer, and the type of operation of the employer.[534] For example, it would be unlikely to pose an undue hardship for an employer to provide an employee whose seizures are triggered by blinking or flashing lights with a glare guard for his or her computer. Similarly, if an epileptic employee of a large department store is restricted

---

[531] 42 U.S.C. §12111(8).
[532] *See, e.g.*, Lovejoy-Wilson v. NOCO Motor Fuel, Inc., 263 F.3d 208, 12 AD Cases 340 (2d Cir. 2001).
[533] *Id.*
[534] 42 U.S.C. §12111(10)(A), (B).

from working at dangerous heights, an employer could, as a reasonable accommodation, have another employee retrieve or restock items that require the use of a ladder. This example assumes, of course, that the ability to retrieve or restock items from high places is not an essential job function.

The assessment of whether any accommodation would pose an undue hardship must necessarily be made on an individualized basis. Certain accommodations, for example, may be more disruptive for small employers. Rearranging schedules or providing frequent leaves of absence to an employee with epilepsy may pose undue burdens for employers with few qualified employees. Additionally, an employer is not required to violate the terms of a collective bargaining agreement or bona fide seniority system to accommodate an individual with epilepsy.[535] Nor must an employer bypass a more qualified applicant when awarding a job to an individual with a disability as a reasonable accommodation.[536]

In sum, depending on its severity, epilepsy may constitute a disability under the ADA. Thus, if an individual with epilepsy is a qualified individual with a disability, an employer has a duty, if requested, to reasonably accommodate the employee's condition, unless doing so would create an undue hardship, or the employee poses a direct threat to himself or herself or others in the workplace.

VI. Conclusion

Although few conditions or illnesses are considered per se disabilities under the ADA, many can be deemed disabilities

---

[535] *See, e.g.*, U.S. Airways, Inc. v. Barnett, 535 U.S. 391, 12 AD Cases 1729 (2002) (employer is not required to give disabled employee "super seniority" to enable him to retain his job in violation of established seniority system); EEOC v. Sara Lee Corp., 237 F.3d 349, 11 AD Cases 595 (4th Cir. 2001) (employer not required to circumvent seniority system and give job-bidding preference to employee with epilepsy so that she may request nonrotating shift as reasonable accommodation).

[536] Mays v. Principi, 301 F.3d 866, 13 AD Cases 985 (7th Cir. 2002) (employer did not violate its duty of reasonable accommodation by giving job to better-qualified applicants).

so long as they substantially limit one or major life activities. By the same token, many individuals suffering from serious ailments are not classified as disabled, as the criteria for being considered disabled under the ADA are quite stringent. Thus, it is important for interested parties and their legal counsel to be aware of the ADA's nuances with respect to various medical conditions.

CHAPTER 6

ACCESS AND ACCOMMODATION ISSUES: AMERICANS WITH DISABILITIES ACT'S TITLE III REQUIREMENTS ON PLACES OF PUBLIC ACCOMMODATIONS AND COMMERCIAL FACILITIES

I. Title III Compliance 614
II. Who Is Covered Under Title III? 616
    A. What Is a Public Accommodation? 617
    B. Mixed-Use Facilities 621
    C. Physical Versus Nonphysical Places of Public Accommodation 623
        1. Lawsuits 625
        2. Viability of Claim 625
    D. Other Intangible "Public Accommodations" 628
    E. Private Companies 630
        1. When Web Sites Are Not Public Accommodations 631
        2. When Web Sites Are Public Accommodations 633
        3. Physical Location Versus Internet Only 634
        4. Current Law 635
    F. Commercial Facilities 636
III. Title III Exemptions 638
    A. Religious Organizations 638
    B. Private Clubs 639
    C. Government Entities 641
IV. Title III Requirements 642
    A. Equal Participation 642
    B. Direct Threat 644
    C. Policy Modifications 646

D.	Integrated Settings	648
E.	Barrier Removal	649
	1. "Readily Achievable" Standard	651
	2. Assembly Seating	653
	3. Barrier Removal Priority	653
	4. Additional Measures	654
	a. Public Areas Only	654
	b. Historic Landmarks	655
F.	Barrier Removal Guidelines	656
G.	Alternatives to Barrier Removal	656
H.	Provision of Auxiliary Aids	659
I.	Alterations	661
J.	Primary Function Area	663
K.	Tax Credits	665
L.	Franchise Liability	667
M.	Landlord/Tenant Liability	668
N.	New Construction	670
	1. Scoping Requirements	671
	2. Unclear Accessiblity Guidelines	673
O.	Architect Liability	674
P.	Transportation	675
	1. Fixed-Route System Requirements	677
	2. Demand-Responsive System Requirements	678
	3. Public Accommodations Primarily Engaged in the Business of Providing Transportation	679
	4. Over-the-Road Buses	680
Q.	Examinations and Courses	684
V.	Enforcement	687
A.	Remedies	688
B.	Role of Attorney General	689
C.	Exhaustion of Administrative Remedies	691
D.	Standing	693
E.	Attorneys' Fees	694
F.	Justice Department Enforcement Under Title III	696
VI.	Conclusion	698

The implementation of Title III of the Americans with Disabilities Act (ADA)[1] had a dramatic impact of the way private entities conducted business. Title III makes it illegal for certain private establishments that provide products or services to the public to discriminate against individuals with disabilities. In addition, Title III sets standards for new construction of most private structures and imposes affirmative duties on businesses to make their facilities and services accessible to the disabled.

While the ADA focus of most employment lawyers is on Title I of the statute—with its prohibition of employment discrimination on the basis of disability, and its obligation that covered employers engage in reasonable accommodation—such counsel often confront issues arising under Title III. These issues can overlap with questions of accommodation involving applicants and employees, and are relevant to employment practitioners to a degree that some other ADA requirements, such as the technical telecommunications rules, are not. Accordingly, the following analysis examines Title III's requirements and its impact on many facets of the operations of covered entities.

Much of what Title III accomplished already is taken for granted today. Prior to the ADA's enactment, now-customary features such as ramps, automatic doors, wheelchair-accessible restrooms, and Braille lettering on elevator buttons were relatively uncommon. Designing facilities to be accessible to those with disabilities was not a common practice, let alone a broadly applicable legal requirement at the federal level. Individuals with hearing, visual, speaking, mobility, mental, and other impairments constituted a small and insular minority with limited opportunity to enjoy the goods and services offered to the general public and little legal recourse in the event of discrimination. Title III attempts to remedy this oversight by closing gaps left open by prior disability-based antidiscrimination legislation. While litigation in the wake of the statute's implementation continues to clarify the scope of regulated entities' obligations, and many issues remain the subject of strong contention,

---

[1] 42 U.S.C. §§12181–12189.

there can be no doubt that Title III of the ADA has had a substantial impact on American society. In fact, it is no exaggeration to observe that most Americans now encounter accessibility features made common by the statute on multiple occasions throughout each day.[2]

The first laws targeting discrimination against the disabled applied to members of the federal government and recipients of federal assistance. For example, section 504 of the Rehabilitation Act of 1973[3] prohibits federal agencies and recipients of federal funding from discriminating against individuals with disabilities. The purpose of Title III of the ADA, therefore, is to "extend these general prohibitions against discrimination to privately operated public accommodations and to bring individuals with disabilities into the economic and social mainstream of American life."[4] Ambitious in scope, Title III strives to accomplish this goal in two ways: first, by proscribing discriminatory behavior and, second, by mandating that covered entities take proactive measures to promote accessibility and equal opportunity.

---

[2] In addition to the accessibility requirements found in Title III of the ADA, a number of states have enacted companion measures that may cover additional facilities, require further accommodation measures and/or authorize different forms of damages and recoveries. For example, under California's Unruh Act, aggrieved parties may seek injunctive relief, attorney's fees, general and compensatory damages, and treble damages pursuant to Cal. Civil Code §54.3 for each day access to the public accommodation was allegedly denied. The California statute created a right for disabled persons to full and equal access, as other members of the public, to accommodations, advantages, facilities, and privileges of all places of public accommodation. CAL. CIV. CODE §54. The Unruh Act requires that public accommodations constructed and/or altered after 1970, comply with access standards contained in the California Building Code. The Unruh Act further states that any violation of the ADA is a violation of the Unruh Act. CAL. CIV. CODE §51.5. Unlike the ADA, the Unruh Act permits private parties to not only seek injunctive relief and attorney's fees, but also monetary damages, i.e., potential liability for each offense for actual damages, up to a maximum of three times of the amount, but in no case less than $4,000. CAL. CIV. CODE §52. Actual damages mean compensatory damages, which include both special damages and out-of-pocket losses and general damages for emotional distress. CAL. CIV. CODE §51; Boemio v. Loves Rest., 954 F. Supp. 204, 208–09 (S.D. Cal. 1997).

[3] 29 U.S.C. §794(a).

[4] S. REP. NO. 101-116, at 58 (1989); H.R. REP. NO. 101-485 pt. 2 (1990), *reprinted in* 1990 U.S.C.C.A.N. 303, 382.

In the first respect, Title III resembles other discrimination statutes by laying out what acts/omissions are unlawful. Specifically, Title III prohibits discrimination against any individual "on the basis of disability in the full and equal enjoyment of the goods, services, facilities, privileges, advantages, or accommodations of any place of public accommodation by any person who owns, leases (or leases to), or operates a place of public accommodation."[5] In support of this general principle, Title III enumerates a number of specific prohibitions deemed unlawful under the ADA.[6]

Unlike other civil rights statutes, Title III does not just identify and prohibit acts of discrimination. In addition to requiring that covered private entities refrain from discriminating against individuals with disabilities, Title III mandates that they take a number of affirmative steps as well. This subsection of the ADA requires that business owners, operators, landlords, and tenants make their facilities accessible by eliminating physical and communication barriers that ordinarily prevent individuals with disabilities from benefiting from the "goods, services, facilities, privileges, advantages, or accommodations of [that] entity."[7] Moreover, any new construction or alteration of a covered facility must comply with specific accessibility guidelines.[8]

Private entities offering educational or professional "examinations or courses related to applications, licensing, certification," or credentialing must offer them in an accessible manner

---

[5] 42 U.S.C. §12182(a).

[6] For a more detailed discussion of Title III's antidiscrimination provisions, see section IV below.

[7] 42 U.S.C. §12182(b)(A)(i). At the same time, Title III does not require covered entities to permit an individual to participate in or benefit from the goods, services, facilities, privileges, advantages, and accommodations of such entity where that individual poses a direct threat to the health or safety of others. 42 U.S.C. §12182(b)(3). See Bragdon v. Abbott, 524 U.S. 624, 8 AD Cases 239 (1998) (when considering whether a patient's HIV status poses a direct threat, courts must determine whether a significant risk exists from the standpoint of the health care professional who refuses treatment or accommodation; risk assessments must be based on medical or other objective, scientific evidence available to the provider and the profession, not simply on the individual's good-faith belief that a significant risk existed).

[8] Id. §12183.

or offer alternative arrangements.[9] Finally, Title III prohibits discrimination in public transportation services provided by private entities, and requires that private providers of transportation adhere to accessibility standards as well.[10]

I. TITLE III COMPLIANCE

In drafting the ADA, Congress directed the Architectural and Transportation Barriers Compliance Board (Access Board)[11] to devise detailed design and construction guidelines for covered entities in accordance with Title III principles.[12] These guidelines were to supplement the existing Minimum Guidelines and Requirements for Accessible Design that the Access Board had devised previously under the Architectural Barriers Act (ABA).[13] Congress imbued the Department of

---

[9] 28 C.F.R. §36.309(a) (2003).

[10] 42 U.S.C. §12184(a): "No individual shall be discriminated against on the basis of disability in the full and equal enjoyment of specified public transportation services provided by a private entity that is primarily engaged in the business of transporting people and whose operations affect commerce."

[11] The Access Board, established by §502 of the Rehabilitation Act of 1973 (codified as amended at 29 U.S.C. §792), is an independent federal agency created in 1985 to devise standards for and enforce the Architectural Barriers Act (ABA), 42 U.S.C. §§4151–4157. The ABA requires that federally owned, leased, or financed facilities that are open to the public, employ or house individuals with disabilities, and those facilities "constructed under authority of the National Capital Transportation Act of 1960, [1965], or title III of the Washington Metropolitan Area Transit Regulation Compact," make such facilities accessible in accordance with the limited scope of the ABA. 42 U.S.C. §4151. The Access Board, comprised of 25 members, 13 of whom are appointed by the president from the general public and 12 from various federal agencies, is responsible for, among other things, issuing and maintaining guideline requirements for accessible design for newly constructed buildings, additions to existing buildings, alterations to existing buildings, and leased buildings covered by the ABA and Titles II and III of the ADA. 29 U.S.C. §792(b)(3); 42 U.S.C. §12204(a).

[12] 42 U.S.C. §12204. The Department of Justice was given responsibility to issue regulations to enforce Title III's mandate that "no individual shall be discriminated against on the basis of disability in the full and equal enjoyment of the goods, services, facilities, privileges, advantages, or accommodations of any place of public accommodation by any person who owns . . . or operates a place of public accommodation." 42 U.S.C. §12182(a).

[13] 42 U.S.C. §4151 et seq. The set of standards created pursuant to the ABA is known as the Uniform Federal Accessibility Standards (UFAS), which established uniform standards for the design, construction, and alteration of buildings to enable

Justice (DOJ) with the power to develop and enforce regulations consistent with the Access Board's minimum guidelines.[14] Likewise, the Department of Transportation (DOT) was charged with drafting and enforcing regulations for the Title III provisions that apply to private entities providing transportation services.[15]

Following this mandate, in July 1991, the Access Board created, and the DOJ subsequently adopted as enforceable standards, a set of technical requirements known as the Americans with Disabilities Act Accessibility Guidelines (ADAAG, or Accessibility Guidelines).[16] The Accessibility Guidelines provide detailed construction and design specifications aimed at creating greater accessibility for individuals with disabilities. Additionally, the DOT promulgated two sets of regulations, one of which adopts the Accessibility Guidelines,[17] explains

---

physically disabled individuals to have access to those facilities. A 1978 amendment to §502 of the Rehabilitation Act ordered the Access Board to devise minimum guidelines and requirements for the UFAS. The Access Board drafted these guidelines to be consistent with the existing standards published by the American National Standards Institute (ANSI) for general use. The ANSI is a nongovernmental national organization that publishes a wide variety of recommended standards. The ANSI's standards for barrier-free design, called ANSI A117.1, "Specifications for Making Buildings and Facilities Accessible to, and Usable by, Physically Handicapped People," were adopted in 1961. These standards laid the technical groundwork for the UFAS, and subsequently the ADAAG.

[14] 42 U.S.C. §12163.

[15] *Id.* §12186(a)(1).

[16] In 2004, the Access Board published a final rule containing its revisions and updates to the accessibility guidelines for buildings and facilities covered by the ADA and the ABA. 69 Fed. Reg. 44084 (July 23, 2004). The final rules were published at the conclusion of an extensive rulemaking process that included advisory committee recommendations, a published proposed rule, public comments, and public hearings. Shortly after the Access Board finalized its revised guidelines, the Department of Justice published an Advance Notice of Proposed Rulemaking, seeking public comment on various issues relating to the potential application of the revised standards, and to obtain background information for the regulatory assessment it needs to perform before adopting them as regulations. 69 Fed. Reg. 58768 (Sept. 30, 2004). The DOJ rulemaking extended into 2005, and likely will go beyond that date before being formalized as any form of final action. Following the Justice Department notice, a degree of opposition to the revised rules began to surface in the business community, focusing on questions of cost and the guidelines' intrusion on employee work areas, among other questions.

[17] The vehicle guidelines address buses, vans, a variety of rail vehicles, trams, and other modes of public transportation.

which transportation entities are covered by Title III, and sets forth general nondiscrimination requirements.[18] The second set of regulations provides specific accessibility requirements for covered transportation entities.[19]

To further aid covered entities with compliance, the DOJ published a *Title III Technical Assistance Manual* that offers guidance for public accommodations, commercial facilities, and private entities offering certain examinations and courses.[20] Divided into nine sections, the *Technical Assistance Manual* describes in detail the obligations under Title III to adhere to nondiscriminatory policies and procedures, remove architectural and communication barriers in facilities where readily achievable, and provide effective communication to individuals with disabilities. Taken together, the *Technical Assistance Manual*, Accessibility Guidelines, and DOJ and DOT regulations offer a great deal of guidance to comply with Title III of the ADA.[21]

II. Who Is Covered Under Title III?

There are four broad categories of entities that Title III addresses: public accommodations,[22] commercial facilities,[23]

---

[18] 49 C.F.R. pt. 37 (2003).

[19] *Id.* pt. 38 (2003).

[20] AMERICANS WITH DISABILITIES ACT TITLE III TECHNICAL ASSISTANCE MANUAL (1993), Introduction.

[21] In addition to these federal sources of authority, there are vast numbers of code jurisdictions across the country that enforce various combinations of state and local building codes (which may, or may not, incorporate accessibility requirements). For building owners and developers, compliance with local codes does not constitute compliance with ADA Title III requirements unless the Department of Justice certifies that those ordinances meet or exceed applicable ADA standards for alterations and new construction to public accommodations and commercial facilities. 42 U.S.C. §12188(b)(1)(A)(ii) of the ADA; 28 C.F.R. §36.604. The benefit to affected parties of that certification is that builders, developers, architects, and other members of the public are able to work with and rely on the building inspection and plan approval processes at the state and local level. In addition, DOJ certification serves as rebuttable evidence in an enforcement action under the statute that a building that has been constructed or altered in accordance with the requirements of a certified code in compliance with the ADA.

[22] 42 U.S.C. §12182.

[23] *Id.* §12183.

privately owned transportation operations,[24] and private entities that offer certain examinations and courses for educational and occupational certification.[25] These categories are not clear-cut and have invited debate over what does and does not constitute a covered entity under the ADA.

The "public accommodation" and "commercial facilities" categories are especially fluid. Much litigation has centered on the correct labeling for various business facilities or services.[26] The main distinction between the two terms for compliance purposes is that commercial facilities are subject only to the new construction and alterations standards; commercial facilities *are not* required to adhere to the other Title III provisions, including those mandating nondiscrimination, barrier removal, and the provision of auxiliary aids.[27]

A. What Is a Public Accommodation?

Under the general rule of Title III,

> [n]o individual shall be discriminated against on the basis of disability in the full and equal enjoyment of the goods, services, facilities, privileges, advantages, or accommodations of any *place of public accommodation* by any person who owns, leases (or lease to), or operates a *place of public accommodation*.[28]

---

[24]*Id.* §12184.

[25]*Id.* §12189. Apart from the requirements of Title III (which are applicable to private entities), Title II of the ADA prohibits discrimination against qualified individuals with disabilities in all programs, activities, and services of public entities. It applies to all state and local governments, their departments and agencies, and any other instrumentalities or special purpose districts of state or local governments. In *Tennessee v. Lane,* 541 U.S. 509, 15 AD Cases 865 (2004), the Supreme Court upheld the constitutionality of Title II as applied to the courthouses of state and local governments, ruling that such entities are not immune from suit under those provisions of the statute. In contrast to its 2001 decision in *Board of Trustees of the University of Alabama v. Garrett,* 531 U.S. 356, 11 AD Cases 737 (2001), in which it held that suits to recover money damages from state governments are barred by the Eleventh Amendment to the Constitution, the Court—in a 5-4 ruling—limited its holding to access to the courts (based on the legislative history demonstrating pervasive unequal treatment in the administration of services and program by states).

[26]For a more detailed discussion of what constitutes a public accommodation versus a commercial facility, see sections II.A. & II.F., below.

[27]TITLE III TECHNICAL ASSISTANCE MANUAL, *supra* note 20, at §1.1000.

[28]42 U.S.C. §12182(a) (emphasis added).

Thus, the first question facing any business entity is whether or not the facility in question qualifies as a "public accommodation." This is no easy determination and has generated a significant amount of controversy.

A "public accommodation" is defined as "a private entity that owns, leases (or leases to), or operates a place of public accommodation."[29] This somewhat circular definition is not alleviated by a clear explanation of what constitutes a "place of public accommodation." Rather, the ADA provides 12 categories of public accommodations, each of which contains a series of related entities.[30] To be considered a *place* of public accommodation for purposes of Title III, the entity must be a facility[31] operated by a private entity, its operations must affect commerce,[32] and it must fall into 1 of these 12 categories:

> (A) an inn, hotel, motel, or other place of lodging, except for an establishment located within a building that contains not more than five rooms for rent or hire and that is actually occupied by the proprietor of such establishment as the residence of such proprietor;
>
> (B) a restaurant, bar, or other establishment serving food or drink;
>
> (C) a motion picture house, theater, concert hall, stadium, or other place of exhibition or entertainment;
>
> (D) an auditorium, convention center, lecture hall, or other place of public gathering;

---

[29] 28 C.F.R. §36.104 (2002).

[30] 42 U.S.C. §12181(7).

[31] "Facility means all or any portion of buildings, structures, sites, complexes, equipment, rolling stock or other conveyances, roads, walks, passageways, parking lots, or other real or personal property, including the site where the building, property, structure, or equipment is located." 28 C.F.R. §36.104 (2002).

[32] The term "commerce" as used in this title means "travel, trade, traffic, commerce, transportation, or communication—(A) among the several States; (B) between any foreign country or any territory or possession and any State; or (C) between points in the same State but through another State or foreign country." 42 U.S.C. §12181(1). To determine whether an entity affects commerce, some factors to consider are whether the facility is open to out-of-state visitors, whether the products it exhibits or sells originated out of state, or have traveled through other states; and whether operations of this kind, in the aggregate, would affect interstate commerce. H.R. Rep. No. 101-485, pt. 3, at 53, 54 (1990), *reprinted in* 1990 U.S.C.C.A.N 445, 476, 477.

(E) a bakery, grocery store, clothing store, hardware store, shopping center, or other sales or rental establishment;
(F) a laundromat, dry-cleaner, bank, barber shop, beauty shop, travel service, shoe repair service, funeral parlor, gas station, office of an accountant or lawyer, pharmacy, insurance office, professional office of a health care provider, hospital, or other service establishment;
(G) a terminal, depot, or other station used for specified public transportation;
(H) a museum, library, gallery, or other place of public display or collection;
(I) a park, zoo, amusement park, or other place of recreation;
(J) a nursery, elementary, secondary, undergraduate, or postgraduate private school, or other place of education;
(K) a day care center, senior citizen center, homeless shelter, food bank, adoption agency, or other social service center establishment; and
(L) a gymnasium, health spa, bowling alley, golf course, or other place of exercise or recreation.[33]

Although the above list is exhaustive, the examples within each category are meant to be illustrative.[34] The categories are to be interpreted broadly in order to place a wide range of entities within at least 1 of the 12 categories.[35] An individual alleging discrimination need not prove that an entity in question is similar to the examples listed in a particular category. Instead, the person must show only that the facility fits within one of the overall categories.[36] For example, as the *Technical Assistance Manual* explains, the category "sales or rental establishments" includes entities other than those listed, including video stores, carpet showrooms, and athletic equipment stores.[37]

The common thread among the 12 categories is that the facilities, products, or services of the listed entities are open or

---

[33] 42 U.S.C. §12181(7)(A)–(L).
[34] *See* TITLE III TECHNICAL ASSISTANCE MANUAL, *supra* note 20, at §1.2000.
[35] S. REP. No. 101-116, at 58, 59 (1989) *reprinted in* 1989 U.S.C.C.A.N.; H.R. REP. No. 101-485, pt. 2, at 99, 100 (1990), *reprinted in* 1990 U.S.C.C.A.N. 303, 382, 383. *See* PGA Tour, Inc. v. Martin, 532 U.S. 661, 676–77, 11 AD Cases 1281 (2001).
[36] H.R. REP. No. 101-485, pt. 3, at 53, 54 (1990), *reprinted in* 1990 U.S.C.C.A.N. 445, 476, 477.
[37] *Id.* at 54, 1990 U.S.C.C.A.N. at 486.

otherwise made available to the community. Thus, the determination of whether a facility is a "public accommodation" for purposes of ADA coverage often turns on whether the facility is open indiscriminately to other members of the general public.[38]

For instance, a wholesale sales establishment that sells its merchandise only to other businesses would not be considered a public accommodation, even though it is a "sales or rental establishment," because it is not generally open to the public.[39] Similarly, a private movie studio not open to the general population except for limited private tours is not a public accommodation.[40] Moreover, any area within a public accommodation that is off-limits to both disabled and nondisabled individuals—such as an employee-only restroom—is not a place of public accommodation and therefore need not comply with the public accommodation requirements of Title III.[41]

Title III provisions with respect to public accommodations—such as those dealing with barrier removal and nondiscrimination obligations—apply only to those aspects of a business that constitute *places* of public accommodation. For example, a department store would be responsible for complying with these Title III obligations only in areas where the public is invited, such as the sales floor and the parking garage. The store's administrative office that is not open to the public would not be considered a place of public accommodation.[42] Thus, while the store on the whole would be considered a public accommodation, it would be subject to the more stringent Title III requirements only over areas open to the public.[43]

---

[38] *See, e.g.,* Jankey v. Twentieth Century Fox Film Corp., 14 F. Supp. 2d 1174, 1178 (C.D. Cal. 1998), *aff'd,* 212 F.3d 1159, 10 AD Cases 1002 (9th Cir. 2000) (movie studio lot not public accommodation as it was not available indiscriminately to nondisabled members of public).

[39] 28 C.F.R. pt. 36, app B §36.104 (2003).

[40] *Jankey,* 14 F. Supp. 2d at 1174.

[41] Louie v. Ideal Cleaners, 1999 WL 1269191 (N.D. Cal. 1999) (employee-only restroom in dry cleaner was not public accommodation, even though dry cleaner itself was place of public accommodation, because both disabled and nondisabled customers were denied access).

[42] Although a business in this scenario need not comply with Title III of the ADA, it would have to make its administrative office accessible to any employee with disabilities under Title I of the ADA, 42 U.S.C. §12112 et seq.

[43] *See, e.g.,* TITLE III TECHNICAL ASSISTANCE MANUAL, *supra* note 20, at §1.2000.

The remaining areas of the facility would, however, be subject to the Title III provisions pertaining to commercial facilities.[44]

In one of the first Title III cases to reach the Supreme Court, the PGA attempted to draw a distinction between the operation of its golf course facilities during tournaments as a "place of exhibition or entertainment" for observers or patrons, and the role of a professional golfer as a provider of entertainment (similar to an actor in a theater production) not entitled to accommodation under this portion of the statute. Rather, it argued that the claim of discrimination he brought was "job related" and might only be brought under Title I, but was barred because he was an independent contractor rather than an "employee." In *PGA Tour, Inc. v. Martin*,[45] the Supreme Court rejected the suggestion that there was a distinction between this set of customers—players in tournaments (who pay entry fees and succeed in qualifying rounds)—and another class of clients or customers (spectators at tournaments), and embraced the broader concept of coverage under Title III.

B. Mixed-Use Facilities

Some facilities ordinarily exempt from Title III may be subject to Title III requirements for what would be considered "mixed-use" areas within that facility. For example, residential housing facilities (other than inns, hotels, and similar establishments) are not considered places of public accommodation under the ADA.[46] However, a residential facility may contain places of public accommodation, such as a home office in a private residence that is open to clients. In this instance, that portion of the private residence used as the office is covered under Title III.[47] Additionally, areas of the private residence made available to clients or customers or otherwise used by

---

[44] Commercial facilities are subject to Title III's requirements for new construction and alterations only.
 [45] 532 U.S. 661, 11 AD Cases 1281 (2001).
 [46] *See* 28 C.F.R. §36.104 (listing covered categories under term "place of accommodation"). Residential facilities are, however, subject to the nondiscrimination provisions of the Fair Housing Act, 42 U.S.C. §3601 et seq. The Fair Housing Act prohibits discrimination on the basis of disability in the sale or rental of dwellings.
 [47] 28 C.F.R. §36.207(a) (2003).

these individuals to access that place of public accommodation are subject to Title III's provisions. For instance, the home's sidewalk, door or entryway, and hallway(s) leading to the private office must be made accessible under Title III. A restroom made available for the client or customer's use must also comply with Title III.[48]

An apartment complex, which is considered a residential facility, is immune from Title III obligations, with the exception of the facility's sales rental office, community room, or other facility available to members of the general public. Because an individual with a disability must be able to access this rental office or community room, parking spaces, entryways and walkways, and public restrooms must comply with Title III's provisions for public accommodations as well.[49] In a similar vein, a hotel, which is covered under Title III,[50] may contain a separate residential apartment wing, which is not covered under the ADA.[51] In essence, Title III requirements are apportioned only to those areas considered places of public accommodation.

Sometimes the line between residential and nonresidential areas is not as clear-cut, and must be evaluated on a case-by-case basis. For example, a homeless shelter that provides social services and anticipates short-term stays by members of the public would likely be deemed a "social service center" covered under Title III.[52] However, if that shelter provides long-term residential facilities for the homeless and does not provide other types of social services, the facility is more residential in nature, and likely covered only by the Fair Housing Act,[53] which prohibits discrimination in the sale or renting of certain housing. Regardless of whether any particular facility is covered

---

[48] *Id.* §36.207(b) (2003).

[49] *See, e.g.,* Sapp v. MHI P'ship, 199 F. Supp. 2d 578 (N.D. Tex. 2002) (model home containing administrative sales office is place of public accommodation under 42 U.S.C. §12181(7)(E), and therefore must be made accessible).

[50] 42 U.S.C. §12181(7)(A).

[51] The residential area would, however, be subject to nondiscrimination provisions under the Fair Housing Act, 42 U.S.C. §3604; *see also* 28 C.F.R. pt. 36, app. B §36.104 (2003).

[52] 42 U.S.C. §12181(7)(K); 28 C.F.R. pt. 36, app. B §36.104 (2003).

[53] *Id.* §3601 et seq.

by the Fair Housing Act or other law, the ADA requires an independent analysis to determine applicability.[54]

Entities may be subject to more than one set of access and nondiscrimination requirements. A residential facility that contains a place of public accommodation must comply with both the ADA and the Fair Housing Act. Similarly, a private entity that receives federal assistance would be obligated to comply with section 504 of the Rehabilitation Act of 1973[55] in addition to Title III. A privately owned, operated, or leased place of public accommodation housed in a federally owned facility would also be covered by the ABA. Thus, the nondiscrimination and access requirements of these various laws are not mutually exclusive.

C. Physical Versus Nonphysical Places of Public Accommodation

Determining what is and is not a public accommodation under the ADA has become increasingly more difficult. Many companies, for instance, conduct business over the phone, facsimile, or via the Internet. These companies offer their products or services to the public without requiring a visit to the entity's physical location. Indeed, many businesses are entirely virtual—that is, they exist only in cyberspace without operating from a physical location. Thus, whether these companies constitute public accommodations under the ADA is a controversial—and unresolved—question.

Several courts have examined whether a public accommodation must be a physical location in the context of an employer-provided insurance plan.[56] In general, the ADA does not preclude insurance companies and employers from underwriting, classifying, or administering risks in insurance policies, as long as doing so is not a subterfuge for discriminating against

---

[54] 28 C.F.R. pt. 36, app. B §36.104 (2003).
[55] 29 U.S.C. §794.
[56] For a greater discussion of employee benefits and the ADA, see Chapter 9.

individuals with disabilities.[57] This section of the ADA enables employers and/or insurance providers to cap benefits coverage for certain ailments or refuse to cover certain conditions entirely as long as the decision to do so is based on economic as opposed to discriminatory reasons.[58] Nonetheless, a number of individuals with disabilities who have been adversely affected by a perceived discriminatory insurance policy or denied coverage altogether have sued under Titles I[59] and III of the ADA.

---

[57]Section 501(c) of the ADA, commonly known as the "safe harbor" provision, excludes from coverage of the ADA a bona fide benefit plan that (i) is consistent with or not regulated by state law, and (ii) does not use §501 as a "subterfuge" to evade the purposes of the ADA. 42 U.S.C. §12201(c). Such benefits include employer-provided insurance plans. Title III regulations explain that:
    (a) This part shall not be construed to prohibit or restrict—
    (1) An insurer, hospital or medical service company, health maintenance organization, or any agent, or entity that administers benefit plans, or similar organizations from underwriting risks, classifying risks, or administering such risks that are based on or not inconsistent with State law; or
    (2) A person or organization covered by this part from establishing, sponsoring, observing or administering the terms of a bona fide benefit plan that are based on underwriting risks, classifying risks, or administering such risks that are based on or not inconsistent with State law; or
    (3) A person or organization covered by this part from establishing, sponsoring, observing or administering the terms of a bona fide benefit plan that is not subject to State laws that regulate insurance.
    (b) Paragraphs (a) (1), (2), and (3) of this section shall not be used as a subterfuge to evade the purposes of the Act [ADA] or this part.
    (c) A public accommodation shall not refuse to serve an individual with a disability because its insurance company conditions coverage or rates on the absence of individuals with disabilities.
28 C.F.R. §36.212 (2003).

[58]The legislative history on this point explains that
while a plan which limits certain kinds of coverage based on classification of risk would be allowed under this section [codified at 42 U.S.C. §12201(c)], the plan may not refuse to insure, or refuse to continue to insure, or limit the amount, extent, or kind of coverage available to an individual, or charge a different rate for the same coverage solely because of a physical or mental impairment, except where the refusal, limitation, or rate differential is based on sound actuarial principles or is related to actual or reasonably anticipated experience.
    For example, a blind person may not be denied coverage based on blindness independent of actuarial risk classification.
H.R. REP. No. 101-485, pt. 2, at 136–37 (1990), *reprinted in* 1990 U.S.C.C.A.N. 267, 303, 419–20.

[59]Claims of discrimination under Title I, which governs discrimination against the disabled in employment, will not be addressed in this chapter but, instead, in chapters 5, 7, and 8.

1. Lawsuits

Lawsuits under Title III invoke the "general rule" of this subsection, which provides that "[n]o individual shall be discriminated against on the basis of disability in the full and equal enjoyment of the goods, services, facilities, privileges, advantages, or accommodations of any place of public accommodation...."[60] Among the more detailed prohibitions under this subsection, Title III deems it discriminatory to "afford an individual... on the basis of a disability... with the opportunity to participate in or benefit from a good... that is not equal to that afforded to other individuals."[61] Further, under Title III it is discriminatory

> to provide an individual... on the basis of a disability... with a good... that is different or separate from that provided to other individuals, unless such action is necessary to provide the individual or class of individuals with a good, service, facility, privilege, advantage, or accommodation, or other opportunity that is as effective as that provided to others.[62]

Taken together, these provisions support the argument that a denial of insurance coverage or benefits equates to a denial of services, privileges, or advantages under Title III. Moreover, under Title III, an "insurance office" is among the categories listed as a place of public accommodation.[63] Therefore, individuals alleging discrimination based on an insurance policy argue that the plain language of these Title III provisions covers "insurance products," because insurance products are goods or services provided by a person (employer or insurance provider) who owns a public accommodation (insurance office).

2. Viability of Claim

The viability of this claim, however, depends on whether Title III guarantees access to and mandates nondiscrimination

---

[60] 42 U.S.C. §12182(a).
[61] 42 U.S.C. §12182(b)(1)(A)(ii).
[62] *Id.* §12182(b)(1)(A)(iii).
[63] *Id.* §12181(7)(F).

for the physical insurance office only, or whether such protections extend to the contents of those insurance policies. Under the former, more limited interpretation, only claims regarding the physical structure could survive. Interpreted more broadly, Title III permits individuals with disabilities to challenge the substance of insurance policies. The courts are currently split on this issue.

The U.S. Courts of Appeal for the Third, Fifth, Sixth, and Ninth Circuits have weighed in on this debate, and have ruled that Title III requires a physical place.[64] These courts have determined that because a benefit plan offered by an employer is not a "good" offered by a place of public accommodation, Title III does not regulate the contents of such a plan.[65] Moreover, under the definitions section of Title III, "insurance office" is grouped with other *physical* structures.[66] Strictly construed, this definition implies that the physical office of an insurance provider, not the policy itself, is considered a public accommodation. Because an insurance policy is not a public accommodation, according to this line of reasoning, an individual cannot challenge the substantive provisions of that policy.

---

[64]McNeil v. Times Ins. Co., 2000 U.S. App. LEXIS 2710 (5th Cir. 2000) (Title III does not prohibit group health plan's limitation on acquired immune deficiency syndrome treatment); Kolling v. Blue Cross Blue Shield of Mich., 318 F.3d 715, 14 AD Cases 384 (6th Cir. 2003) (Title III does not govern contents of employer-sponsored health plan, as they are not goods offered by place of public accommodation); Chabner v. United of Omaha Life Ins. Co., 225 F.3d 1042, 10 AD Cases 1705 (9th Cir. 2000) (insurance company administering employer-provided disability plan was not place of public accommodation under Title III, because employees received benefits through employment, not place of public accommodation); Weyer v. Twentieth Century Fox Film Corp., 198 F.3d 1104, 1114–16, 10 AD Cases 65 (9th Cir. 2000); Ford v. Schering-Plough Corp., 145 F.3d 601, 8 AD Cases 190 (3d Cir. 1998), *cert. denied*, 525 U.S. 1093 (1999) (because plaintiff received her disability benefits through employment, she had no nexus to MetLife's insurance office, and thus was not discriminated against in connection with public accommodation); Parker v. Metropolitan Life Ins. Co., 121 F.3d 1006, 1015, 6 AD Cases 1865 (6th Cir. 1997), *cert. denied*, 522 U.S. 1084 (1998) (Title III does not apply to insurance policy obtained from employer).

[65]*See, e.g., Parker*, 121 F.3d at 1015.

[66]42 U.S.C. §12181(7)(F). The entities in this category include "a laundromat, dry-cleaner, bank, barber shop, beauty shop, travel service, shoe repair service, funeral parlor, gas station, office of an accountant or layer, pharmacy, *insurance office*, professional office of a health care provider, hospital, or other service establishment[;]" (emphasis added).

The U.S. Courts of Appeal for the First and Seventh Circuits, however, have found that Title III *does not* require a physical place.[67] These courts have determined that because of the perceived ambiguity of Title III's definition section, the ADA's regulations and public policy concerns favor a looser interpretation of the ADA that does not limit public accommodations to physical structures.[68] For example, "insurance office" is grouped with "travel service."[69] According to the U.S. Court of Appeal for the First Circuit, in *Carparts Distribution Center, Inc. v. Automotive Wholesaler's Ass'n of New England, Inc.*,[70]

> [b]y including "travel service" among the list of services considered "public accommodations," Congress clearly contemplated that "service establishments" include providers of services which do not require a person to physically enter an actual physical structure. Many travel services conduct business by telephone or correspondence without requiring their customers to enter an office in order to obtain their services. Likewise, one can easily imagine the existence of other service establishments conducting business by mail and phone without providing facilities for their customers to enter in order to utilize their services. It would be irrational to conclude that persons who enter an office to purchase services are protected by the ADA, but persons who purchase the same services over the telephone or by mail are not. Congress could not have intended such an absurd result.[71]

In essence, the court determined that because certain businesses grouped with "insurance office" often provide services to individuals who are not physically present in the office or building, a "public accommodation" can be a product as

---

[67] *See* Tompkins v. United Healthcare of New England, Inc., 203 F.3d 90 (1st Cir. 2000) (public accommodations are more than physical spaces); Doe v. Mutual of Omaha Ins. Co., 179 F.3d 557, 9 AD Cases 657 (7th Cir. 1999), *cert. denied*, 528 U.S. 1106 (2000) (same); Carparts Distribution Ctr., Inc. v. Automotive Wholesaler's Ass'n of New England, Inc., 37 F.3d 12, 3 AD Cases 1237 (1st Cir. 1994) (Title III not limited to actual physical structures). *See also* Wai v. Allstate Ins. Co., 75 F. Supp. 2d 1, 9 AD Cases 1588 (D.D.C. 1999) (Title III protections extend beyond physical access to insurance offices and include denial of insurance policies equal or comparable to those offered to nondisabled).

[68] *See, e.g., Carparts,* 37 F.3d at 19.
[69] 42 U.S.C. §12181(7)(F).
[70] 37 F.3d 12, 3 AD Cases 1237 (1st Cir. 1994).
[71] *Id.* at 19, 3 AD Cases at 1242–43.

well as a structural entity. Because the circuits are split on this issue, where an insurance policy or employer-provided benefit is challenged could dictate the viability of a claim under Title III.

D. Other Intangible "Public Accommodations"

Courts have likewise grappled with the issue of whether a membership organization qualifies as a "public accommodation." At least two federal district courts have held that sports associations are to be treated as public accommodations under the ADA.[72] According to the courts' rationale, athletic associations control access to sports facilities, which are public accommodations under Title III.[73] Because athletic membership organizations exert such control over the physical sports facility, they are covered under Title III.

This view is not universal, however. A number of courts have found insufficient connections between the membership organization and the physical structure. For example, an organization organizing bicycle races had no connection to a concrete place, and was therefore not a public accommodation subject to Title III.[74] Similarly, the U.S. Court of Appeals for the Sixth Circuit has held that the National Football League is not a "place," and therefore is not a public accommodation.[75] This reasoning does not apply just to sports membership organizations. A professional organization's creation of a study group and workshop sessions was deemed not to fall within

---

[72] *See* Matthews v. National Collegiate Athletic Ass'n, 179 F. Supp. 2d 1209 (E.D. Wash. 2001) (National Collegiate Athletic Association is a public accommodation, as it is a private entity, its operations of stadiums affect commerce, and it regulates terms and conditions of participation in sanctioned athletic activities); Bowers v. National Collegiate Athletic Ass'n, 118 F. Supp. 2d 494, 11 AD Cases 415 (D.N.J. 2000) (athletic association is public accommodation).

[73] 42 U.S.C. §12181(7)(L).

[74] *Brown v. 1995 Tenet ParaAmerica Bicycle Challenge*, 959 F. Supp. 496, 498–99, 6 AD Cases 1137 (N.D. Ill. 1997).

[75] Stoutenborough v. National Football League, 59 F.3d 580, 583, 4 AD Cases 1035 (6th Cir.) *cert. denied*, 516 U.S. 1028 (1995) (only stadium is place of public accommodation; live broadcasts of events at that stadium were not services of that public accommodation, and thus not covered under Title III). *See also* Elitt v. USA Hockey, 922 F. Supp. 217, 223, 5 AD Cases 648 (E.D. Mo. 1996) (hockey organization not subject to Title III as it is not sufficiently linked to "place").

Title III's purview, as the organization was found to have no connection to any particular place of public accommodation.[76]

Although the question of whether a public accommodation must be a physical structure remains open, the greater the nexus between the entity and a physical place, the more likely courts will be to deem the entity a public accommodation.

The advent of electronic communication and commerce has further complicated an already muddled legal area. Title III requires public accommodations, among other things, to "furnish appropriate auxiliary aids and services where necessary to ensure effective communication with individuals with disabilities."[77] Whether this requirement applies to a private company's web site is uncertain. The rise in electronic and digital technology has brought a number of new questions to the forefront of ADA analysis. Specifically, is a company's web site a public accommodation under Title III? Would it matter if these sites enabled individuals to make business transactions over the Internet, or whether the sites provided information only? What if the entire company was Internet-based, such as on-line auction entities? Would the same analysis apply to a company's telephone or facsimile line? The answers to these questions are still evolving.

While these topics pose new challenges for the private sector, federal agencies have already confronted electronic accessibility issues. Federal agencies and entities receiving federal assistance or under contract with the federal government[78] are required to make their web sites accessible to people with vision impairments, hearing problems, limited dexterity, and other disabilities.[79] Section 508, an amendment to the Rehabilitation Act of 1973, "requires that when Federal agencies develop, procure, maintain, or use electronic and information technology, [they must ensure that] Federal employees with

---

[76] Schaaf v. Association of Educ. Therapists, 1995 WL 381979 (N.D.Cal. 1995).
[77] 28 C.F.R. §36.303(c) (2003).
[78] Only the portion of a private entity's web site pertaining to the federal contract or receiving federal funds must comply with the accessibility requirements under §508 of the Rehabilitation Act.
[79] Section 508 of the Rehabilitation Act, "Electronic Equipment Accessibility," Pub. L. No. 93-112, Title V, §508, as added Pub. L. No. 99-506, Title VI, §603(a), Oct. 21, 1986, 100 Stat. 1830.

disabilities" are able to obtain such information in a manner comparable to that enjoyed by nondisabled employees, unless doing so would create a substantial burden on the agency.[80] Section 508 also requires that members of the public with disabilities have access to web sites made available to the general public.[81] These accessibility requirements took effect on June 21, 2001.

The Access Board was charged with publishing standards defining electronic and information technology, and creating technical and functional performance criteria necessary for accessing such technology.[82] These standards provide technical specifications for various types of technologies, including software applications and operating systems, web-based information and applications, telecommunications products, video and multimedia products, self-contained, closed products (e.g., information kiosks, calculators, and fax machines), and desktop and portable computers.[83]

Although section 508 applies only to federal agencies and those private entities under contract with or receiving assistance from the federal government, questions remain as to whether other private companies must make their web sites or other electronic components of their operations accessible. The DOJ has taken the position that Internet web sites are public accommodations, and therefore must be make accessible.[84]

E. Private Companies

Company web sites are becoming increasingly more common. Some businesses create sites for advertising purposes only, while others provide interactive services, such as offering

---

[80] 36 C.F.R. pt. 1194 (2003).
[81] *Id.*
[82] *Id.*
[83] 36 C.F.R. pt. 1194.21–26. *See also* http://www.section508.gov/.
[84] Policy Ruling, Sept. 9, 1996: "ADA Accessibility Requirements Apply to Internet Web Pages," 10 NDLR 240 (also available at http://www.usdoj.gov/crt/foia/tal712.txt). ("Covered entities under the ADA are required to provide effective communication, regardless of whether they generally communicate through print media, audio media, or computerized media such as the Internet. Covered entities that use the Internet for communications regarding their programs, goods, or

merchandise for sale on-line. Some sites are clearly linked to a physical entity, such as a bank's web site enabling customers to manage their accounts on-line, while others exist apart from any concrete structure, such as Internet search engines. Whether any of these sites constitute public accommodations is an unsettled issue.

The idea that a private entity would be required to make its web-based technology accessible drew attention in 1999, when the National Federation of the Blind (NFB) sued internet service provider (ISP) America Online (AOL) for an alleged violation of Title III.[85] The lawsuit claimed that AOL's proprietary software was not compatible with screen access programs that would have enabled AOL's content to be accessible to the blind. Because this lawsuit was settled,[86] the court did not resolve whether Title III of the ADA applies to ISPs.

1. When Web Sites Are Not Public Accommodations

Cases that have addressed whether web sites are public accommodations have examined the nexus between the site and the physical public accommodation. For instance, in *Access Now, Inc. v. Southwest Airlines Co.*,[87] a federal district court in Florida held that Southwest Airline's web site, www.southwest.com, through which the public could purchase airline tickets and obtain information about flights and fares, was not a place of public accommodation under Title III. The company, therefore, had no obligation to make its site accessible to the visually impaired. According to the court, "a public accommodation must be a physical, concrete structure. To expand the ADA to cover 'virtual' spaces would be to create new rights without well-defined standards."[88]

---

services must be prepared to offer those communications through accessible means as well.").

[85] National Fed'n of the Blind (NFB) v. America Online, Inc., 99CV12303EFH (D. Mass 1999).

[86] As part of the settlement, AOL agreed to make its version 6.0 software accessible. The settlement agreement in this case can be found at http://www.nfb.org/Tech/accessibility.htm.

[87] 227 F. Supp. 2d 1312, 13 AD Cases 1186 (S.D. Fla. 2002).

[88] *Id.* at 1318, 13 AD Cases at 1190.

The plaintiff in this case attempted to fit the web site into a few Title III categories considered public accommodations.[89] According to the plaintiff, a web site was analogous to a place of "exhibition," "public display," and a "sales establishment."[90] However, none of these places is 1 of the 12 categories of public accommodations under Title III, but rather a grouping culled from three separate categories of public accommodations: "a motion picture house, theater, concert hall, stadium, or other place of *exhibition* or entertainment";[91] "a museum, library, gallery, or other place of public *display* or collection";[92] and "a bakery, grocery store, clothing store, hardware store, shopping center, or other *sales* or rental establishment."[93] "Under the rule of *ejusdem generis*, 'where general words follow a specific enumeration of persons or things, the general words should be limited to persons or things similar to those specifically enumerated.' "[94] Therefore, the terms "exhibition," "display," and "sales establishment," are limited to their specific category groupings, all of which are physical, concrete structures.[95] Therefore, according to the court in this case, a web site is *not* a public accommodation.

Further, there was an insufficient nexus between the web site and a physical, concrete place of public accommodation. "[B]ecause the Internet website, southwest.com, does not exist in any particular geographical location, Plaintiffs are unable to demonstrate that Southwest's website impedes their access to a specific, physical, concrete space such as a particular airline ticket counter or travel agency."[96] Because of this lack of connection to a physical place of public accommodation, the claim under Title III fails.

---

[89] *See* 42 U.S.C. §12181(7).
[90] *Id.* §12181(7)(C), (H), and (E).
[91] *Id.* §12181(7)(C) (emphasis added).
[92] *Id.* §12181(7)(H) (emphasis added).
[93] *Id.* §12181(7)(E) (emphasis added).
[94] Access Now v. Southwest Airlines, 227 F. Supp. 2d 1312, 1318, 13 AD Cases 1186, 1191 (S.D. Fla. 2002) (quoting Allen v. A.G. Thomas, 161 F.3d 667, 671 (11th Cir. 1998) (in turn quoting United States v. Turkette, 425 U.S. 576, 581–82 (1981))).
[95] *Id.* at 1319, 13 AD Cases at 1191.
[96] *Id.* at 1321, 13 AD Cases at 1193.

Similarly, a federal district court in California dismissed a Title III claim against a cable service provider on the grounds that "nether the digital cable system nor its on-screen channel menu can be considered a place of public accommodation within the meaning of the ADA."[97] In this instance, a cable service provider was sued for failure to make its on-screen channel menu accessible to the visually impaired.

2. When Web Sites Are Public Accommodations

However, this "nexus" test was used to achieve the opposite conclusion in *Rendon v. Valleycrest Productions*.[98] The plaintiff in *Rendon*, who had hearing and upper-body mobility impairments, sought to be a contestant on the game show "Who Wants to Be a Millionaire?" The game show used a telephonic application process whereby prospective contestants participated in a dial-in, "fast-finger" quiz response screening test. The plaintiff sued on the grounds that this selection process was inaccessible to people with disabilities, thereby precluding the disabled from participating in the game show. The U.S. Court of Appeals for the Eleventh Circuit agreed, holding that the dial-in system was a barrier to access to participation in the game show, which took place in a television studio, a place of public accommodation. Because the plaintiff could demonstrate "a nexus between the challenged service and the premises of the pubic accommodation," the telephone hotline application process was covered under Title III.[99] The court explained that

> the definition of discrimination provided in Title III covers both tangible barriers . . . and intangible barriers, such as eligibility requirements and screening rules or discriminatory policies and procedures that restrict a disabled person's ability to enjoy the defendant entity's goods, services and privileges. . . . There is

---
[97]Torres v. AT&T Broadband, LLC, 158 F. Supp. 2d 1035, 1038 (N.D. Cal. 2001). *See also* Access Now, Inc. v. Claire's Stores, Inc., No. 00-14017-CIV-MOORE, 2002 WL 1162422, at *5 (S.D. Fla. May 7, 2002) ("No court has held that internet websites made available to the public by retail entities must be accessible.").

[98]294 F.3d 1279, 13 AD Cases 404 (11th Cir. 2002).

[99]*Id.* at 1284 n.8., 13 AD Cases at 408 n.8.

nothing in the text of the statute to suggest that discrimination via an imposition of screening or eligibility requirements must occur on site to offend the ADA.[100]

Therefore, like the U.S. Courts of Appeals for the First and Seventh Circuits, the Eleventh Circuit does not require a public accommodation to be a physical place.

In fact, in *Doe v. Mutual of Omaha Insurance Co.*,[101] which addressed Title III's application to the substance of insurance policies, the U.S. Court of Appeals for the Seventh Circuit noted in dicta that

> [t]he core meaning of [Title III's general nondiscrimination provision], plainly enough, is that the owner or operator of a store, hotel, restaurant, dentist's office, travel agency, theater, *Web site*, or other facility (whether in physical space or electronic space . . .) that is open to the public cannot exclude disabled persons from entering the facility and, once in, from using the facility in the same way that the nondisabled do.[102]

While not precedent-setting, the inclusion of "web site" in a list of physical structures indicates that this Circuit deems web sites to be public accommodations.

3. *Physical Location Versus Internet Only*

Whether a company providing services exclusively over the Internet constitutes a place of public accommodation was at issue in *Hooks v. Okbridge*.[103] In this case, an individual with bipolar disorder sued a commercial web site on which customers played bridge for a fee, alleging that his membership was terminated because of his illness. The plaintiff appealed after

---

[100] *Id.* at 1283–84, 13 AD Cases at 407 (footnote omitted).

[101] 179 F.3d 557, 559, 9 AD Cases 657 (7th Cir. 1999), *cert. denied*, 528 U.S. 1106 (2000).

[102] *Id.* at 559, 9 AD Cases at 658 (emphasis added; citation omitted). Title III's general nondiscrimination provision follows:
> 42 U.S.C. §12182(a): General Rule. No individual shall be discriminated against on the basis of disability in the full and equal enjoyment of the goods, services, facilities, privileges, advantages, or accommodations of any place of public accommodation by any person who owns, leases (or leases to), or operates a place of public accommodation.

[103] 232 F.3d 208 (5th Cir. 2000) (decision without published opinion).

a federal court in Texas ruled that such a web-based company was not a public accommodation, and that the company was otherwise exempt for being a private club.[104] On appeal, the U.S. Court of Appeals for the Fifth Circuit did not address these unresolved issues under the ADA. Instead, the court held that because the company was not aware of the plaintiff's medical status when it terminated his membership, he could not make out a claim under the ADA.[105]

What makes this case unique is that the DOJ submitted an amicus brief in support of the plaintiff's assertion that public accommodations under Title III are not limited to companies providing services to customers at a physical location and that the entertainment or recreation services provided by the web-based company made it a place of public accommodation.[106] According to the DOJ, the computerized bridge tournaments offered by the company "[are], under any ordinary understanding of the terms, a 'service establishment,' or an entity offering 'entertainment' or 'recreation.'"[107] Therefore, the Internet-based services are covered under Title III of the ADA.

Moreover, according to the DOJ, the ADA is not restricted to services provided at or in a place of public accommodation. "If Congress had intended to limit Title III to services provided at a business's physical premises, it presumably would have used the words 'at' or 'in' rather than 'of.'"[108]

4. Current Law

While it is clear that the DOJ considers Internet-based services and web sites to be public accommodations, the current state of the law is less certain. Furthermore, it is unclear how

---

[104] Private clubs are exempt from Title III requirements. 42 U.S.C. §12187. A more detailed discussion of this exemption can be found in section III.B., below.
[105] *Hooks*, 232 F.3d 208.
[106] *See* Brief of the United States as Amicus Curiae in Support of Appellant, published at http://www.usdoj.gov/crt/briefs/hooks.htm.
[107] *Id.*
[108] *Id.* The brief also averred that the gaming web site was not a private club—and thus not exempt under Title III—because it was a profit-making business with more than 18,000 fee-paying members in over 90 countries, and was essentially open to all members of the public willing to pay for its services.

the ADA would apply to other web-based enterprises, such as Internet auction sites that provide their services entirely in cyberspace, and subscriber-only web sites. It is also unclear what steps a business must take to make their web-based operations accessible. While the standards governing section 508 compliance are instructive, other organizations have considered the issue as well.

For example, the World Wide Web Consortium (W3C) is an international association of businesses that develops specifications, guidelines, software, and tools to promote Internet commerce and communication. The W3C spearheaded the Web Accessibility Initiative, which created a set of web content accessibility guidelines for developers and users of the Internet.[109] These guidelines address the visual layout, color cues, text size, audio/video features, and site navigability of web sites, and provide suggestions on how to make these sites more accessible. By way of example, the W3C promotes the use of web site assistive technology, including screen reader technology, which enables the visually impaired to navigate the Internet by converting text to speech or refreshable Braille display. Moreover, voice recognition and closed-captioning programs are also available for individuals with disabilities.

Although creating accessible web sites is not currently mandatory for private entities under the ADA, the law is far from settled in this area. At least in certain jurisdictions, the trend appears to favor a broad definition of "public accommodation," which includes Internet-based operations. Additionally, even if an entity does not fall under the category of "public accommodation," it may still need to comply with some provisions of Title III. Many businesses not directly providing services to the public may nonetheless be considered "commercial facilities" under the ADA, and thus subject to Title III's new construction and alterations requirements.

F. Commercial Facilities

Under the ADA, a "commercial facility" is an entity that is "intended for nonresidential use; and whose operations . . .

---

[109] *See* http://www.w3.org.

affect commerce."[110] Aircraft, railroad locomotives and cars, in addition to facilities covered or expressly exempted from coverage under the Fair Housing Act are specifically excluded from this definition.[111]

This definition of "commercial facility" is quite broad. That the nonresidential entity must "affect commerce" is not very limiting. The phrase "'commerce' means travel, trade, traffic, commerce, transportation, or communication (A) among the several States; (B) between any foreign country or any territory or possession and any State; or (C) between points in the same State but through another State or foreign country."[112] The DOJ in its interpretive guidance explains that "[t]he use of the phrase 'operations affect commerce' applies the full scope of coverage of the Commerce Clause of the Constitution in enforcing the ADA," and that it will have "extremely broad application."[113] Thus, qualifying as a commercial facility is not a difficult hurdle to clear.

For example, office buildings, factories, or warehouses that are not considered public accommodations because they are not ordinarily open to the general public would be considered commercial facilities.[114] Being open to vendors, salespersons, or job applicants does not render such facilities places of public accommodation.[115] Thus, while all public accommodations are commercial facilities, not all commercial facilities are public accommodations. Moreover, a business may contain both commercial facilities and places of public accommodation. For example, the *Technical Assistance Manual* explains that a manufacturing company with a customer service unit that takes customer complaints and provides related services is such a dual enterprise. The customer service operation is a "service establishment" under Title III, and is thus a place of public accommodation. The manufacturing operation, however,

---

[110] 42 U.S.C. §12181(2).
[111] 28 C.F.R. §36.104 (2002).
[112] 42 U.S.C. §12181(1).
[113] 28 C.F.R. pt. 36, app. B §36.104 (2003).
[114] *See, e.g.*, H.R. REP. No. 101-485, pt. 3, at 53 (1990), *reprinted in* 1990 U.S.C.C.A.N. 445, 476.
[115] TITLE III TECHNICAL ASSISTANCE MANUAL, *supra* note 20, §1.3100.

which does not directly serve the public, is a commercial facility.[116]

Distinguishing between an entity's places of public accommodation and commercial facilities becomes significant when determining which requirements of Title III must be met.

III. TITLE III EXEMPTIONS

While the range of business operations falling under the ADA's purview is quite expansive, private clubs and religious organizations, including the vehicles used by such entities, are exempt from Title III requirements.[117]

A. Religious Organizations

The religious organization exemption includes both "religious organizations [and] entities controlled by religious organizations, including places of worship."[118] This very broad exemption enables a variety of religious organizations and facilities to escape coverage and the requirements of Title III.

Even if a religious organization provides services to the general public, the exemption applies. The test is whether the organization or place of worship operates the facility or provides the public service, not who receives this service or who has access to the facility in question.[119] For example, even if a church operates a day-care facility or a school open to nonchurch members, the organization is still exempt from Title III requirements so long as it is controlled by a religious entity. Moreover, the use of lay boards or other secular or corporate means of operating the organization's social services does not necessarily abrogate the exemption. The applicability of the exemption hinges on whether the religious organization controls the operations of the day care, school, or other service

---

[116] *Id.*
[117] 42 U.S.C. §12187; 28 C.F.R. §36.102(e) (2003). *See also* 49 C.F.R. §37.37(e) (2003).
[118] 42 U.S.C. §12187.
[119] 28 C.F.R. pt. 26, app. B §36.104 (2003).

or whether the service itself is considered a religious organization.[120] If the answer is "yes," then the exemption applies.

However, any service or facility connected to a place of worship or other religious entity is not necessarily immune from Title III requirements. A religious-based place of public accommodation is subject to Title III if, for example, the organization rents space on its property to the public for nonreligious purposes and relinquishes control over such activities. Title III requirements would then apply to the activities of the secular organization over which the religious organization has no control. In order for Title III to apply, a lease or other rental agreement must exist, and consideration must be paid.[121] Therefore, if a church or synagogue operated a school open to the public on its premises, the organization would be exempt from Title III requirements because the religious organization controlled that public accommodation. If the church or synagogue rented out the same space to a nonreligious organization, however, Title III would apply to the operation of any services provided by that nonreligious organization.

B. Private Clubs

Private clubs are similarly exempt from Title III's requirements to the extent they do not make their facilities available to members of the general public. The term "private club" is defined as those establishments exempt from coverage under Title II of the Civil Rights Act of 1964.[122] Exempt establishments under Title II of the Civil Rights Act include any "private club or other establishment not in fact open to the public, except to the extent that the facilities of such establishment are made available to the customers or patrons of [a place of public accommodation as defined in title II]."[123] Therefore, if a private club rents space to any other private entity for the operation of a place of public accommodation, Title III applies. In its

---

[120] *Id.*
[121] 28 C.F.R. pt. 26, app. B §36.104 (2003).
[122] 42 U.S.C. §2000a et seq.
[123] 42 U.S.C. §2000a(e).

Technical Assistance Manual, the DOJ provides the example of a private country club leasing space for a day-care center open to children of nonmembers. The country club would be obligated to comply with Title III with respect to the operation of the day-care facility, but not to the operation of the rest of the private country club.[124]

It should be noted, however, that occasional use of a private club's facilities by the general public does not automatically render that facility a public accommodation subject to Title III's requirements. For example, a private club with a limited guest policy in which guests are not permitted "unfettered use" of the club's facilities is not converted into a public accommodation.[125]

Determining what constitutes a private club is a fact-specific inquiry. A number of factors have been taken into consideration by various courts, including the following:

- whether the club is highly selective in choosing members;
- whether the club membership exercises a high degree of control over the establishment's operation;
- whether historically the organization has been intended to be a private club;
- the degree to which the establishment is opened up to nonmembers;
- the purpose of the club's existence;
- the breadth of the club's advertising for members;
- whether the club is nonprofit;
- the degree to which the club observes formalities;
- whether substantial membership fees are charged;
- the degree to which the club receives public funding; and

---

[124] TITLE III TECHNICAL ASSISTANCE MANUAL, *supra* note 19, at §1.6000.
[125] Kelsey v. University Club of Orlando, 845 F. Supp. 1526, 1529, 3 AD Cases 459 (M.D. Fla. 1994) (private club with limited guest policy is not public accommodation, despite evidence of "isolated incidents" in which policy was not followed).

- whether the club was created or is being used to avoid compliance with a civil rights act.[126]

While there are no hard and fast rules, the more exclusive, formal, and financially self-sufficient the organization, the more likely the entity will be viewed as a private club, and thus exempt from Title III's requirements.

C. Government Entities

Title III applies only to *private* entities. State and local governments are covered under Title II of the ADA.[127] Therefore, while a privately owned store would have to adhere to the accessibility mandates under Title III of the ADA, the local government-controlled sidewalk in front of the store would have to be accessible pursuant to Title II of the ADA.

The federal government is not covered under either Titles II or III of the ADA. Rather, the executive branch of the federal government is covered by section 504 of the Rehabilitation Act of 1973, as amended,[128] and the Architectural Barriers Act of 1968.[129] The activities of the legislative branch, including Congress, are covered under title V of the ADA.[130]

---

[126] *See, e.g.,* Tillman v. Wheaton-Haven Recreation Ass'n, 410 U.S. 431 (1973); Daniel v. Paul, 395 U.S. 298 (1969); Olzman v. Lake Hills Swim Club, Inc., 495 F.2d 1333 (2d Cir. 1974); Anderson v. Pass Christian Isles Golf Club, Inc., 488 F.2d 855 (5th Cir. 1974); Smith v. Young Men's Christian Ass'n of Montgomery, 462 F.2d 634 (5th Cir. 1972); Stout v. Young Men's Christian Ass'n of Bessemer, Ala., 404 F.2d 687 (5th Cir. 1968); United States v. Richberg, 398 F.2d 523 (5th Cir. 1968); Nesmith v. YMCA, 397 F.2d 96 (4th Cir. 1968); United States v. Lansdowne Swim Club, 713 F. Supp. 785 (E.D. Pa. 1989); Durham v. Red Lake Fishing & Hunting Club, Inc., 666 F. Supp. 954 (W.D. Tex. 1987); New York v. Ocean Club, Inc., 602 F. Supp. 489 (E.D.N.Y. 1984); Brown v. Loudoun Golf & Country Club, Inc., 573 F. Supp. 399 (E.D. Va. 1983); United States v. Trustees of Fraternal Order of Eagles, Milwaukee, 472 F. Supp. 1174 (E.D. Wis. 1979); Cornelius v. Benevolent Protective Order of Elks, 382 F. Supp. 1182 (D. Conn. 1974).

[127] 42 U.S.C. §§12131–12134. Title II applies to *all state* and local government entities, regardless of whether they receive federal funding.

[128] 29 U.S.C. §794. Section 504 of the Rehabilitation Act requires program accessibility in all services provided with federal dollars.

[129] The ABA requires physical access to federal buildings and facilities, and those financed by the federal government.

[130] 42 U.S.C. §12209.

IV. Title III Requirements

The ADA first and foremost is a nondiscrimination statute. Therefore, a large portion of Title III is devoted to prohibiting various activities and polices that constitute discrimination against individuals with disabilities. The antidiscrimination provisions of Title III apply only to public accommodations, not to the parts of an entity's operations that are considered commercial facilities.[131]

A. Equal Participation

In addition to the general rule regarding discrimination against the disabled,[132] Title III specifically outlaws a public accommodation's activities that prevent individuals with disabilities from participating in or benefiting from the "goods, services, facilities, privileges, advantage, or accommodations of an entity."[133] Moreover, it is unlawful to provide unequal or separate benefits to an individual with disabilities than those provided to the general public.[134]

---

[131] 28 C.F.R. §36.102(b)(2) (2003).

[132] 42 U.S.C. §12182(a):
No individual shall be discriminated against on the basis of disability in the full and equal enjoyment of the goods, services, facilities, privileges, advantages, or accommodations of any place of public accommodation by any person who owns, leases (or leases to), or operates a place of public accommodation.

[133] 42 U.S.C. §12182(b)(A)(i):
Denial of participation
It shall be discriminatory to subject an individual or class of individuals on the basis of a disability or disabilities of such individual or class, directly, or through contractual, licensing, or other arrangements, to a denial of the opportunity of the individual or class to participate in or benefit from the goods, services, facilities, privileges, advantages, or accommodations of an entity.

[134] 42 U.S.C. §12182(b)(A)(ii):
Participation in unequal benefit
It shall be discriminatory to afford an individual or class of individuals, on the basis of a disability or disabilities of such individual or class, directly, or through contractual, licensing, or other arrangements with the opportunity to participate in or benefit from a good, service, facility, privilege, advantage, or accommodation that is not equal to that afforded to other individuals.

42 U.S.C. §12182(b)(A)(iii):
Separate benefit

Public accommodations can achieve these goals by eliminating application or eligibility criteria that screen out or otherwise negatively impact individuals with disabilities,[135] modifying policies, practices, or procedures when necessary to confer benefits to or accommodate individuals with disabilities,[136] providing auxiliary aids to assist individuals with disabilities,[137] and removing architectural and communication barriers.[138]

For example, in providing goods and services, a public accommodation cannot impose eligibility requirements that exclude or segregate individuals with disabilities, unless these

---

It shall be discriminatory to provide an individual or class of individuals, on the basis of a disability or disabilities of such individual or class, directly, or through contractual, licensing, or other arrangements with a good, service, facility, privilege, advantage, or accommodation that is different or separate from that provided to other individuals, unless such action is necessary to provide the individual or class of individuals with a good, service, facility, privilege, advantage, or accommodation, or other opportunity that is as effective as that provided to others.

[135] 42 U.S.C. §12182(b)(2)(A)(i): discrimination includes
the imposition or application of eligibility criteria that screen out or tend to screen out an individual with a disability or any class of individuals with disabilities from fully and equally enjoying any goods, services, facilities, privileges, advantages, or accommodations, unless such criteria can be shown to be necessary for the provision of the goods, services, facilities, privileges, advantages, or accommodations being offered[.]"

[136] 42 U.S.C. §12182(b)(2)(A)(ii): discrimination includes
a failure to make reasonable modifications in policies, practices, or procedures, when such modifications are necessary to afford such goods, services, facilities, privileges, advantages, or accommodations to individuals with disabilities, unless the entity can demonstrate that making such modifications would fundamentally alter the nature of such goods, services, facilities, privileges, advantages, or accommodations[.]"

[137] 42 U.S.C. §12182(b)(2)(A)(iii): discrimination includes
a failure to take such steps as may be necessary to ensure that no individual with a disability is excluded, denied services, segregated or otherwise treated differently than other individuals because of the absence of auxiliary aids and services, unless the entity can demonstrate that taking such steps would fundamentally alter the nature of the good, service, facility, privilege, advantage, or accommodation being offered or would result in an undue burden[.]"

[138] 42 U.S.C. §12182(b)(2)(A)(iv): discrimination includes
a failure to remove architectural barriers, and communication barriers that are structural in nature, in existing facilities, and transportation barriers in existing vehicles and rail passenger cars used by an establishment for transporting individuals (not including barriers that can only be removed through the retrofitting of vehicles or rail passenger cars by the installation of a hydraulic or other lift), where such removal is readily achievable[.]"

requirements are necessary for the operation of the public accommodation.[139] Examples include: (1) requiring a customer to produce a driver's license to receive a benefit or service, which discriminates against individuals who are medically or physically unable to obtain such a license; (2) refusing to allow vans into a privately run parking lot, even if there is sufficient clearance, which discriminates against vehicles designed to accommodate wheelchairs;[140] and (3) a doctor or dentist requiring that a patient prove that he or she is not infected with the human immunodeficiency virus (HIV), unless that knowledge is necessary to provide services to that patient.[141]

Public accommodations also cannot impose additional burdens on individuals with disabilities than those imposed on the general public.[142] For instance, a business cannot require that a patron with mental retardation be accompanied by an attendant.[143]

However, if certain neutral eligibility requirements are necessary for the safe operation of the public accommodation's business, they are not unlawful. "For example, a height limit" on amusement park rides that tends to screen out adults with short stature may be "a legitimate safety criterion."[144] Such safety requirements must be based on actual risk and not on "mere speculation, stereotypes, or generalizations about individuals with disabilities."[145]

B. Direct Threat

Nevertheless, the ADA does not require a public accommodation to engage in any activity that would pose a "direct threat" to the health or safety or others.[146] A direct threat means "a

---

[139] 42 U.S.C. §12182(b)(2)(A)(i).
[140] TITLE III TECHNICAL ASSISTANCE MANUAL, *supra* note 19, at §4.1100.
[141] 136 CONG. REC. S9697 (daily ed. July 13, 1990) (statement of Sen. Kennedy—D. Mass.).
[142] 28 C.F.R. pt. 36, app. B §36.301 (2003).
[143] Preamble to Regulations, 28 C.F.R. 36.301.
[144] H.R. REP. No. 101-485, at 105 (1990), *reprinted in* 1990 U.S.C.C.A.N. 303, 388.
[145] 28 C.F.R. §36.301(b) (2003).
[146] 42 U.S.C. §12182(b)(3); 28 C.F.R. §36.208(a) (2003).

significant risk to the health or safety of others that cannot be eliminated by a modification of policies, practices, or procedures, or by the provision of auxiliary aids or services."[147] Direct threats must be assessed on a case-by-case basis, using reasonable judgment that relies on current medical evidence or on the best available objective evidence to determine:

1. The nature, duration, and severity of the risk;
2. The probability that the potential injury will actually occur; and
3. Whether reasonable modifications of policies, practices, or procedures will mitigate or eliminate the risk.[148]

Because there is no bright-line test for determining what constitutes a direct threat, each case is necessarily fact-specific. For example, the refusal to admit an individual who is HIV-positive into a restaurant or health club is unlawful under Title III, as the virus cannot be transmitted through casual contact.[149] Refusing to move wheelchair-accessible seating from the back of a theater to the front on the grounds that wheelchairs in the front could pose a safety hazard is not justified unless such as assessment can be proven and that no other accommodations could be made to eliminate any perceived danger.[150] Moreover, a doctor or dentist cannot refuse to treat patients who are HIV-positive.[151] Although the existence of a significant risk is determined from the standpoint of the treating health care professional, such risk cannot rely simply on a good-faith

---

[147] 42 U.S.C. §12182(b)(3); 28 C.F.R. §36.208 (2003). This section of the ADA codifies the standard first applied in School Board of Nassau County v. Arline, 480 U.S. 273, 1 AD Cases 1026 (1987), in which the Supreme Court recognized that an individual with a contagious disease could be considered "disabled" under §504 of the Rehabilitation Act. In balancing the interests between the rights of the individual with the disease and the rights of the public to remain free from harm, the Court explained that if modifications could not eliminate the risk posed by the individual, he or she could be excluded from the activities/areas in question.

[148] TITLE III TECHNICAL ASSISTANCE MANUAL, *supra* note 19, at §3.8000; 28 C.F.R. 36.208(c) (2003).

[149] TITLE III TECHNICAL ASSISTANCE MANUAL, *supra* note 19, at §3.8000.

[150] *Fiedler v. American Multi-Cinema, Inc.*, 871 F. Supp. 35, 3 AD Cases 1610 (D.D.C. 1994).

[151] *Bragdon v. Abbott*, 524 U.S. 624, 8 AD Cases 239, 250 (1998).

belief that a significant risk exists. All risk assessments must be based on scientific, medical, or other objective evidence.[152]

Public accommodations are required to make reasonable modifications in order to eliminate a direct threat. For example, instead of banning an autistic child with aggressive tendencies from a day-care facility, instructors can attempt behavior modifications to curb those tendencies.[153]

Facilities are not, however, required to implement modifications that would change the nature of the service provided. Softening the teaching style of a martial arts course in order to accommodate a minor who is HIV-positive, for example, does not constitute a reasonable modification, as it would fundamentally change the nature of the program.[154]

C. Policy Modifications

Similarly, a public accommodation is required to make reasonable modifications to its policies, practices, and procedures that adversely affect individuals with disabilities, unless doing so would fundamentally alter the nature of the goods and services provided by that public accommodation.[155] "A fundamental alteration is a modification that is so significant that it alters the essential nature of the goods, services, facilities, privileges, advantages, or accommodations offered."[156] For example, a department store may need to modify its policy of permitting only one person to enter a dressing room at a time if an individual in a wheelchair or a customer with mental

---

[152]*Id.*; *see also* 28 C.F.R. §36.208(c) (2003).

[153]Burriola v. Greater Toledo YMCA, 133 F. Supp. 2d 1034, 12 AD Cases 1710 (N.D. Ohio 2001) (autistic child with aggressive tendencies not direct threat to others, where behavior modifications had not yet been implemented and evidence indicated that other children had also engaged in aggressive behavior).

[154]Montalvo v. Radcliffe, 167 F.3d 873, 9 AD Cases 15 (4th Cir.), *cert. denied*, 528 U.S. 813 (1999) (minor who was HIV-positive posed direct threat to others in intensive martial arts course, as potential for transmission of disease was high due to frequent cuts and scrapes endured in program).

[155]42 U.S.C. §12182(b)(2)(A)(ii); 28 C.F.R. §36.302(a) (2003).

[156]TITLE III TECHNICAL ASSISTANCE MANUAL, *supra* note 19, at §4.3600; *See also* PGA Tour, Inc. v. Martin, 532 U.S. 661, 11 AD Cases 1281 (2001) (allowing participant in professional golf tournament to use golf cart would not fundamentally alter nature of game).

retardation requires assistance. A store must also ensure that a sufficient number of wheelchair-accessible checkout aisles are in operation during business hours. Therefore, if the only accessible aisle is primarily used as an "express" checkout, the store must suspend this rule for an individual in a wheelchair.[157] By the same token, a "no pets" policy would not apply to service animals,[158] and a "no eating or drinking" policy might be challenged if a diabetic needs food in order to regulate his or her blood sugar level, since eligibility criteria that tend to screen out individuals with disabilities must yield, unless they are shown to be necessary for the provision of goods, services, and accommodations in question.[159]

Once again, however, nothing in the legislation requires a public accommodation to fundamentally alter its goods or services. While a doctor may not refuse to treat a patient who is HIV-positive, he or she could refuse to provide medical services that are outside his or her area of expertise to that individual.[160] Additionally, a museum would not need to permit individuals with visual impairments to touch priceless works of art.[161] Also, although a store must sell items to individuals with disabilities, it need not alter its inventory.[162] For example, a book store does not need to stock books written in Braille.[163]

In addition, a public accommodation is *not* required to provide personal or individually prescribed devices or services

---

[157] 28 C.F.R. §36.302(d) (2003).
[158] The DOT regulations define "service animal" as
any guide dog, signal dog, or other animal individually trained to do work or perform tasks for the benefit of an individual with a disability, including, but not limited to, guiding individuals with impaired vision, alerting individuals with impaired hearing to intruders or sounds, providing minimal protection or rescue work, pulling a wheelchair, or fetching dropped items.
28 C.F.R. §36.104 (2002). However, the ADA does not specifically require that entities suspend their "no pets" policy for people who *train* service animals. DOJ Opinion Letter, July 3, 1997.
[159] TITLE III TECHNICAL ASSISTANCE MANUAL, *supra* note 19, at §4.1100.
[160] 28 C.F.R. §36.302(b)(2) (2003).
[161] 28 C.F.R. pt. 36, app. B §36.302 (2003).
[162] 28 C.F.R. §36.307 (2003).
[163] 28 C.F.R. pt 36, app. B §36.302 (2003).

to individuals with disabilities. Such devices include wheelchairs, prescription eyeglasses, and hearing aids. Personal services include "assistance in eating, toileting, or dressing."[164] Thus, while a store may be required to bend its rule regarding the number of people allowed in a dressing room in order to accommodate a disabled individual's nurse or companion, the store does not need to personally assist the customer with trying on clothes. When a plaintiff shows that a modification was requested, and the modification was reasonable, some courts have held that defendants must make the reasonable accommodation unless it establishes that the requested accommodation would fundamentally alter the nature of the program.[165]

D. Integrated Settings

One of the main goals of the ADA is to promote the equal participation of individuals with disabilities in the mainstream of society. Therefore, Title III requires a public accommodation to take steps to ensure that individuals with disabilities are able to take advantage of the goods and services provided in the most integrated setting possible.[166] Thus, a restaurant cannot require that patrons with disabilities be seated in any one particular area of the premises.[167]

A public accommodation may create a separate program for the disabled where necessary to ensure equal opportunity. However, individuals with disabilities cannot be excluded from

---

[164] *See, e.g.*, TITLE III TECHNICAL ASSISTANCE MANUAL, *supra* note 19, at §4.2600.

[165] Colorado Cross Disability Coalition v. Hermanson Family Ltd. P'ship I, 264 F.3d 999, 12 AD Cases 351 (10th Cir. 2001); Johnson v. Gambrinus Co./Spoetzl Brewery, 116 F.3d 1052, 7 AD Cases 837 (5th Cir. 1997).

[166] 42 U.S.C. §12182(b)(1)(B): Integrated settings
 Goods, services, facilities, privileges, advantages, and accommodations shall be afforded to an individual with a disability in the most integrated setting appropriate to the needs of the individual.
42 U.S.C. §12182(b)(1)(C): Opportunity to participate
 Notwithstanding the existence of separate or different programs or activities provided in accordance with this section, an individual with a disability shall not be denied the opportunity to participate in such programs or activities that are not separate or different.

[167] TITLE III, TECHNICAL ASSISTANCE MANUAL, *supra* note 19, at §4.1100.

a regular program, or otherwise be required to participate in the special program or accept specially created services or benefits.[168] For example, a movie theater that installs accessible seating cannot require that individuals with disabilities take advantage of such seating.[169] Additionally, a public accommodation cannot impose extra charges on the disabled in order to cover the cost of the measures taken to ensure nondiscriminatory treatment. Thus, if a business incurs costs in creating wheelchair-accessible seating, it may not charge extra for use of those seats.[170]

Title III also protects those associated or believed to be associated with an individual with a disability.[171] It would thus be unlawful for a doctor to refuse to treat the mother of a child who is HIV-positive.[172] This provision covers any type of association, not just familial relationships. Thus, a building owner could not refuse to lease space to a medical facility that specializes in treating patients who are HIV-positive.[173]

E. Barrier Removal

Title III requires a public accommodation to actively remove architectural and communication barriers that are structural in nature from its premises if doing so is "readily achievable."[174] Architectural barriers are those physical portions of a

---

[168] 28 C.F.R. §36.203(c) (2003); *see also* TITLE III TECHNICAL ASSISTANCE MANUAL, *supra* note 19, at §3.4000.

[169] See 28 C.F.R. §36.203 ("Nothing in this part shall be construed to require an individual with a disability to accept an accommodation . . . that such an individual refuses to accept."

[170] However, a modest, refundable security deposit on certain items, such as a cassette recorder used by the visually impaired on a museum tour, would be acceptable. Preamble to the Regulations, 28 C.F.R. §36.301 (July 26, 1991).

[171] 42 U.S.C. §12182(b)(1)(E): Association
It shall be discriminatory to exclude or otherwise deny equal goods, services, facilities, privileges, advantages, accommodations, or other opportunities to an individual or entity because of the known disability of an individual with whom the individual or entity is known to have a relationship or association.

[172] TITLE III TECHNICAL ASSISTANCE MANUAL, §3-5000.

[173] TITLE III TECHNICAL ASSISTANCE MANUAL, *supra* note 19, at §3.5000.

[174] 42 U.S.C. §12182(b)(2)(A)(iv): discrimination includes
a failure to remove architectural barriers, and communication barriers that are structural in nature, in existing facilities, and transportation barriers

facility that impede access for people with disabilities.[175] Some physical barriers are obvious impediments, such as curbs, steps, deep pile carpeting, and bathroom stalls, which present challenges for people who use wheelchairs, walkers, or other assitive devices. Other physical barriers are less obvious, such as conventional doorknobs and operating controls, which are barriers to individuals with manual dexterity problems. Temporary impediments, such as furniture and movable display racks, are also considered architectural barriers subject to Title III.[176]

Communication barriers that are structural in nature are those that are integral to the structure of the public accommodation. Examples include signs in a facility, which are inaccessible to individuals with visual impairments, and audible fire alarms, which are inaccessible to individuals with hearing impairments.[177]

Types of barrier removal include:

(1) Installing ramps;
(2) Making curb cuts in sidewalks and entrances;
(3) Repositioning shelves;
(4) Rearranging tables, chairs, vending machines, display racks, and other furniture;
(5) Repositioning telephones;
(6) Adding raised markings on elevator control buttons;
(7) Installing flashing alarm lights;
(8) Widening doors;
(9) Installing offset hinges to widen doorways;
(10) Eliminating a turnstile or providing an alternative accessible path;
(11) Installing accessible door hardware;
(12) Installing grab bars in toilet stalls;

---

in existing vehicles and fail passengers cars used by an establishment for transporting individuals (not including barriers that can only be removed through the retrofitting of vehicles or rail passenger cars by the installation of a hydraulic or other lift), where such removal is readily achievable[.]"
[175] TITLE III TECHNICAL ASSISTANCE MANUAL, *supra* note 19, at §4.4100.
[176] *Id.*
[177] *Id.*

(13) Rearranging toilet partitions to increase maneuvering space;
(14) Insulating lavatory pipes under sinks to prevent burns;
(15) Installing a raised toilet seat;
(16) Installing a full-length bathroom mirror;
(17) Repositioning the paper towel dispenser in a bathroom;
(18) Creating designated accessible parking spaces;
(19) Installing an accessible paper cup dispenser at an existing inaccessible water fountain;
(20) Removing high pile, low density carpeting; or
(21) Installing vehicle hand controls.[178]

1. "Readily Achievable" Standard

Public accommodations are required to remove these barriers to existing entities if "readily achievable";[179] they are not required to retrofit their facilities.[180] "Readily achievable" is a lenient standard that depends on the business in question, what type of barrier removal is required, and the degree or ease of difficulty imposed in removing the barrier(s).[181] Under the ADA, "readily achievable" is defined as "easily accomplishable and able to be carried out without much difficulty or expense."[182] The prohibitive degree of cost or difficulty is measured on a case-by-case basis, taking the following factors into consideration:

- The nature and cost of the barrier removal;
- The overall financial resources of the public accommodation, including the effect on expenses and resources

---

[178] 28 C.F.R. §36.304 (2003).

[179] "Readily achievable" is a more lenient standard than "undue hardship," as defined in Title I of the ADA.

[180] The ADA imposes more stringent standards regarding alterations and new construction of a facility, as the cost of making the facility accessible can be taken into consideration at the planning stage.

[181] See S. Rep. No. 101-116, at 65, 66 (1989).

[182] 28 C.F.R. §36.104 (2002).

and the overall impact on the public accommodation's operations;
- the number of employees at the site;
- "legitimate safety requirements that are necessary for safe operation [of the business,] including crime prevention measures";
- "The geographic separateness, and the administrative or fiscal relationship of the site or sites [of the public accommodation] in question to any parent corporation or entity";
- The overall financial resources [of any parent corporation or entity], including the overall size of the parent corporation or entity with respect to the number of its employees; [and] the number, type, and location of its facilities"; and
- The type of operation or operations of any parent corporation or entity, including the composition, structure, and functions of the workforce of the parent corporation or entity.[183]

This relatively flexible standard balances the need to provide access to individuals with disabilities against the economic realities faced by many businesses. If removing a barrier is beyond an entity's financial or operational means, and/or entails extensive restructuring, then removing the barrier is not required.[184] Thus, a small, independently owned and operated restaurant has different obligations to removal barriers under the ADA than does a large, national restaurant chain.

A public accommodation with a flight of steps would not be required to provide physical access if significant ramping or the installation of an elevator would be the only means of providing access. Similarly, if lowering store shelves or rearranging display racks would significantly decrease the amount of selling space, this measure is not required.[185] However, in

---

[183] 42 U.S.C. §12181(9); 28 C.F.R. §36.104 (2002).
[184] See S. Rep. No. 101-116, at 65, 66 (1989).
[185] 28 C.F.R. §36.304(f) (2003).

most instances, selectively widening aisles and repositioning merchandise displays are readily achievable methods of barrier removal, and should be undertaken to maximize accessibility for individuals in wheelchairs.[186]

The ADA does not require that a public accommodation undertake measures of barrier removal that would fundamentally alter the nature of the goods or services provided. For example, a casino need not change the height of its gambling tables, as doing so would fundamentally alter the nature of the game.[187]

2. Assembly Seating

Title III regulations specifically address barrier removal requirements for public accommodations that provide assembly seating.[188] Generally, a public accommodation is required to provide a reasonable number of wheelchair-accessible seating spaces and seats with removable aisle-side armrests, disperse these seats throughout the seating area, provide an accessible emergency route to these seats, and permit friends and family members to sit with individuals using this accessible seating.[189] If removing seats is not readily achievable, then the public accommodation is required to provide a portable chair for friends or family members so that they can sit near the customer using the wheelchair.

3. Barrier Removal Priority

Given a public accommodation's limited resources, the ADA encourages entities to prioritize which barriers to remove.[190] First, a public accommodation should remove barriers

---

[186] *See, e.g.,* Lieber v. Macy's W., Inc., 80 F. Supp. 2d 1065 (N.D. Cal. 1999) (Macy's department store violated ADA by failing to provide adequate level of access, including clearance between display units).

[187] *See, e.g.,* Access Now v. Holland Am. Line-Westours, Inc., 147 F. Supp. 2d 1311 (S.D. Fla. 2001).

[188] 28 C.F.R. §36.308 (2003).

[189] *Id.*

[190] *See id.* §36.304(c) (2003).

that impede access to the facility from public sidewalks, parking, or public transportation. Such barrier removal efforts include installing entrance ramps, widening entrances, and providing accessible parking spaces.

Second, the public accommodation should remove barriers to enable individuals with disabilities to access areas where goods and services are made available to the public. These barrier removal efforts include "adjusting the layout of display racks, rearranging tables, providing Brailled and raised character signage, widening doors, providing visual alarms, and installing ramps."[191]

Third, access should be provided to restroom facilities. Access can be provided by, among other measures, removing furniture or other obstructions, widening doors, installing ramps, providing accessible signage, widening toilet stalls, and installing grab bars.[192]

4. Additional Measures

Once these barrier removal priorities are met, a public accommodation is encouraged to take any additional measures necessary to ensure that individuals with disabilities have access to all the goods and services provided by that place of public accommodation.

a. Public Areas Only

A public accommodation is required to remove barriers in areas open to the public only.[193] Moreover, a public accommodation need only remove barriers within its control. For example, the issue of whether movie theaters are required to provide close-captioning for customers with hearing impairments was raised during the legislative debates on the ADA. Congress heard testimony from several members of the motion

---

[191] *Id.* §36.304(c)(2) (2003).
[192] *Id.* §36.304(c)(3) (2003).
[193] Employee-only areas are, however, subject to reasonable accommodation requirements under Title I of the ADA.

picture industry and from owners and operators of movie theaters. Because theater owners exert little control over the films they show, legislators determined that the obligation to eliminate the communication barrier should not fall on the theater itself. Theater owners *are* required, however, to take other steps within their control, such as rotating film schedules that provides reasonable access for individuals in wheelchairs, and providing notice of the theater's accessible movie showings.[194]

b. *Historic Landmarks*

Title III also requires that barriers to historic buildings or facilities[195] be removed if readily achievable. However, if removing barriers would threaten or destroy the significant historic features of the public accommodation, alterations to provide accessibility are not required. The ADA Accessibility Guidelines contain special provisions regarding historic building barrier removal.[196] These guidelines take into consideration the need to protect the authenticity of historic resources while promoting the accessibility goals under the ADA. For example, if installing a ramp or lift in a historic building preserved because of its unique architecture would threaten or destroy the architecturally significant elements of the building, then doing so is not readily achievable.[197]

If removing barriers in the historic facility is not readily achievable, the ADA requires that the entity provide the goods or services of the historic facility via alternative means, if readily achievable.[198] For example, if the second floor of a historic house museum cannot be made accessible to individuals in

---

[194] 28 C.F.R. §36.305(c) (2003); *see also* TITLE III TECHNICAL ASSISTANCE MANUAL, *supra* note 19, at §4.5200.

[195] A historic building or facility is a building or facility that is: (i) Listed in or eligible for listing in the National Register of Historic Places; or (ii) Designated as historic under an appropriate State or local law. TITLE III TECHNICAL ASSISTANCE MANUAL, at III-4.4200.

[196] ADAAG §4.1.7.

[197] *See, e.g.,* TITLE III TECHNICAL ASSISTANCE MANUAL, *supra* note 19, at §4.4200.

[198] *Id.*

wheelchairs, providing pictures or a video of the items on this level could be readily achievable alternatives.[199]

F. Barrier Removal Guidelines

Barrier removal must comply, when readily achievable, with the alteration requirements outlined in the ADA Accessibility Guidelines. If following the Accessibility Guidelines is not readily achievable, then alternative measures that are readily achievable should be taken.

An individual may bring a claim against a public accommodation for failing to remove barriers that are readily achievable. The aggrieved individual must show that (1) he or she is disabled; (2) the place in question is a public accommodation; (3) the individual was denied full and equal treatment because of the disability; and (4) the existing facility presented an architectural barrier that is prohibited under the ADA, the removal of which is readily achievable.[200] Once the plaintiff makes this initial showing, the public accommodation has the opportunity to rebut this claim by demonstrating that removal of the disputed barrier could not be accomplished without much difficulty and/or expense.[201]

G. Alternatives to Barrier Removal

If removal of existing architectural or communication barriers is not readily achievable, the ADA requires that the public accommodation take alternative measures to make its goods or services accessible to individuals with disabilities.[202] Examples of alternative measures include "(1) [p]roviding curb service or

---

[199] *Id.*

[200] *See, e.g.,* Colorado Cross Disability Coalition v. Hermanson Family Ltd. P'ship, 264 F.3d 999, 12 AD Cases 351 (10th Cir. 2001); Johnson v. Gambrinus Co./Spoetzl Brewery, 116 F.3d 1052 (5th Cir. 1997).

[201] *Id.*

[202] 42 U.S.C. §12182(b)(2)(A)(v): "[W]here an entity can demonstrate that the removal of a barrier . . . is not readily achievable, [discrimination would include] a failure to make such goods, services, facilities, privileges, advantages, or accommodations available through alternative methods if such methods are readily achievable."

home delivery; (2) [r]etrieving merchandise from inaccessible shelves or racks; [and] (3) [r]elocating activities to accessible locations."[203] If an alternative method of barrier removal is not readily achievable, then the public accommodation has no further barrier removal obligations under Title III.[204]

A public accommodation may not charge an individual with a disability with the cost of providing alternatives to barrier removal.[205] For example, a restaurant may not charge a customer using a wheelchair extra for home delivery when it is provided as an alternative to barrier removal.[206] However, the ADA does not require that disabled individuals be afforded a greater opportunity to receive a benefit than nondisabled individuals, such

---

[203] 28 C.F.R. §36.305(b) (2003).

[204] The following exchange explaining a public accommodation's obligations to provide an alternative means of barrier removal took place on the Senate floor between Senators Dale Bumpers (D-Ark.) and Tom Harkin (D-Iowa)
 Mr. HARKIN: . . . access may be readily achievable or may not. The providing of services again may be readily achievable or it may not. . . . For example, let us say there are 3 or 4 or 5 steps going up to a dry cleaning establishment, the mom and pop operation on the corner. To put a ramp up and remove the steps might come as an undue amount. But if a handicapped person came to the door and said, I want to leave my dry cleaning and go to the door, fine.
 Mr. BUMPERS: That is all well and good. That is an easy example. The one I gave you is not so easy. I am not talking about where somebody who can drive up to the drive-in window and come up to the first step and hand in their dry cleaning. I am talking about a case where the cost of providing the access may very well cost as much as that businessman is going to take in the next 30 days.
 Mr. HARKIN: Well then, if that is not readily achievable he would not have to do it.
 Mr. BUMPERS: But you are telling me if that is not readily achievable then he must provide similar services if it is readily achievable.
 Mr. HARKIN: If the service is readily achievable.
 Mr. BUMPERS: Let us go further. Let us assume there is no alternative that is readily achievable. Then what happens?
 Mr. HARKIN: He has no obligation.
 Mr. BUMPERS: He is free.
 Mr. HARKIN: Yes.
 Mr. BUMPERS: So the disabled just do not have access to his place of business, is that correct?
 Mr. HARKIN: That is correct.
135 CONG. REC. S10760, S10761 (daily ed. Sept. 7, 1989) (statements of Sens. Bumpers and Harkin).

[205] Preamble to the Regulations, 28 C.F.R. §36.305.
[206] Id.

as providing free parking in a paying zone.[207] For instance, an events facility is not required to give disabled customers a special right to purchase tickets for performances if comparable tickets are not available for nondisabled patrons.[208] Similarly, a random ticket disbursement lottery for sporting events does not violate Title III, even if such a system could prevent disabled customers from obtaining accessible seating.[209]

Additionally, if the public accommodation customarily charges for a particular service, such as home delivery, it need not provide that option for free for an individual with a disability, so long as at least one other barrier removal alternative is provided.[210]

A covered entity is not required to provide individuals with assistive devices as an alternative to barrier removal.[211] Such devices include wheelchairs, prescription eyeglasses, and hearing aids. In addition, while an entity may be required to assist a customer or client with a disability, such as retrieving an item from an inaccessible shelf or reading items from a menu, the ADA does not require the provision of services of a personal nature, such as dressing or toileting.[212] Nor does the ADA require a public accommodation to alter its inventory to include accessible or special goods that are designed for, or facilitate use by, individuals with disabilities.[213] However, if it is a common practice for the business to make special orders for customers, then the entity cannot refuse to do so for an individual with a disability, so long as the specialized goods can be obtained from the entity's usual supplier.[214] For instance, if a book store honors customer requests for out-of-stock editions,

---

[207] *See, e.g.,* DOJ Technical Assistance Letter No. 839, Sept. 14, 2001.

[208] *See, e.g.,* Access Now, Inc. v. South Fla. Stadium Corp., 161 F. Supp. 2d 1357, 12 AD Cases 1384 (S.D. Fla. 2001); Independent Living Res. v. Oregon Arena Corp., 1 F. Supp. 2d 1159 (D. Or. 1998).

[209] Louie v. National Football League, 185 F. Supp. 2d 1306, 12 AD Cases 1394 (S.D. Fla. 2002).

[210] Preamble to the Regulations, 28 C.F.R. §36.305; *see also* Preamble to the Regulations, 28 C.F.R. §36.301.

[211] 28 C.F.R. §36.306 (2003).

[212] *Id.*

[213] Preamble to the Regulations, 28 C.F.R. §36.307.

[214] *Id.*

it must also be willing to special order books written in Braille on request for customers with visual impairments.[215]

Finally, a public accommodation is not required to risk the health or safety of its employees in providing barrier removal alternatives.[216] For example, a sole cashier of a convenience store is not required to leave his or her post to assist a customer with a disability, as doing so increases the risk of theft.[217]

H. Provision of Auxiliary Aids

While the ADA does not require a public accommodation to provide personal aids or services of a personal nature to individuals with disabilities, it must furnish appropriate auxiliary aids and services where necessary to afford effective communication for persons with vision, hearing, speech, and language disabilities, so long as doing so would not be a fundamental alteration or undue burden.[218] Examples of "auxiliary aids and services" for the hearing-impaired include "interpreters, notetakers, computer-aided transcription services, written materials, telephone handset amplifiers, assistive listening devices, assistive listening systems, telephones compatible with hearing aids, closed caption decoders, open and closed captioning, telecommunications devices for deaf persons (TDD's), [and] videotext displays...."[219] Auxiliary aids for individuals with vision impairments include "[q]ualified readers, taped texts, audio recordings, Brailled [and] large print materials...."[220]

A public accommodation is required to provide the use of a TDD only if the entity "offers its customer, client, patient, or participant the opportunity to make outgoing telephone calls on more than an incidental convenience basis...."[221] For example, hotels and hospitals must provide TDDs on request to their guests and patients where in-room phone service is

---

[215] *Id.*
[216] Preamble to the Regulations, 28 C.F.R. §36.305.
[217] Preamble to the Regulations, 28 C.F.R. §36.307.
[218] 28 C.F.R. §36.303(a) (2003).
[219] *Id.* §36.303(b)(1) (2003).
[220] *Id.* §36.303(b)(2) (2003).
[221] *Id.* §36.303(d) (2003).

typically provided. In addition, hotels or other places of lodging that offer "televisions in five or more guest rooms and hospitals that provide televisions" in patient rooms must offer closed-captioning services on request.[222]

According to Title III's regulations, a public accommodation must absorb the costs associated with providing the auxiliary aids or services, unless doing so would be an "undue burden."[223] An "undue burden" is defined as a "significant difficulty or expense."[224] Determining what measures would result in an undue burden must be made on a case-by-case basis, taking into consideration the factors used to assess whether a method of barrier removal is readily achievable. These factors include the cost of the auxiliary aid or service, the overall financial resources of the pubic accommodation, the degree of burden on the entity, the availability of alternative measures, and, if applicable, the overall financial resources of any parent company.[225]

For example, whether a doctor's office must provide an interpreter for a hearing-impaired patient will depend on a number of issues, including the size and financial resources of the practice. If hiring an interpreter would pose an undue burden, then the doctor's office must provide an alternative means of communicating with the patient, such as writing out instructions.[226] Generally, a large company is usually in a better position than a sole proprietor or small business owner to afford the costs of an interpreter or other assistive devices or services, and would therefore be required to provide them.[227]

---

[222] 28 C.F.R. §36.303(e) (2003).
[223] 28 C.F.R. §§36.301(c), 36.303(f) (2003).
[224] 28 C.F.R. §36.303(f) (2003).
[225] *See* 28 C.F.R. §36.104 (2002).
[226] 28 C.F.R. §36.303(f).
[227] For example, publishing company Harcourt Brace agreed in a consent decree to provide qualified sign language interpreters, assitive listening devices, and Brailled materials to students with disabilities who participate in the company's legal bar examination course, Bar/Bri. In addition, Harcourt Brace agreed to pay $28,000 in compensatory damages, and pay $25,000 in civil penalties to the United States, and to adopt a policy ensuring that auxiliary aids and services are provided, educate staff about the needs of students with disabilities, and promote the availability of auxiliary aids and services in its advertising. *See, e.g.,* United States v. Harcourt

A public accommodation may, however, charge a reasonable, refundable deposit for providing auxiliary aids. For instance, a museum may ask for a deposit on audiotape players and cassettes of audio tours lent to patrons with visual impairments.

A public accommodation is not required to provide any one auxiliary aid or service over another simply because a customer or client chooses it. Nor is a public accommodation required to provide an auxiliary aid or service that would fundamentally alter the nature of the goods or services provided.[229]

In general, the Title III directives regarding nondiscrimination, barrier removal, and the provision of auxiliary aids for individuals with disabilities are relatively lenient inasmuch as the entity's financial and operational circumstances are taken into consideration. Additionally, these requirements are applicable only to public accommodations. When an entity—be it a public accommodation or a commercial facility—renovates or otherwise alters its facility, however, a more stringent set of requirements comes into play.

I. Alterations

Alterations to places of public accommodation and commercial facilities *must* be accessible "to the maximum extent feasible" to individuals with disabilities.[230] This provision applies to all alterations commenced after January 26, 1992.[231] Title III regulations define "alteration" as "a change to a place of public accommodation or a commercial facility that affects or could affect the usability of the building or facility or any

---

Brace Legal & Prof'l Publ'ns, Inc. settlement agreement, http://www.usdoj.gov/crt/ada/archive/pubs/reg10rpt.htm.

[228] [*Reserved.*]

[229] 28 C.F.R. §36.303(f) (2003).

[230] 42 U.S.C. §12183(a)(2):

[W]ith respect to a facility or part thereof that is altered by, on behalf of, or for the use of an establishment in a manner that affects or could affect the usability of the facility or part thereof, a failure to make alterations in such manner that, to the maximum extent feasible, the altered portions of the facility are readily accessible to and usable by individuals with disabilities, including individuals who use wheelchairs. . . .

[231] 28 C.F.R. §36.402(a) (2003).

part thereof."[232] Such changes "include, but are not limited to, remodeling, renovation, rehabilitation, reconstruction, historic restoration, changes or rearrangement in structural parts or elements, and changes or rearrangement in the plan configuration of walls and full-height partitions."[233] For example, if during a renovation a restaurant remodels its restrooms, it must ensure that the new toilet stalls, sinks, and other fixtures conform to the ADA Accessibility Guidelines. Similarly, if a hotel remodels the floor of its lobby, the floor must comply with the requirements for nonslip surfaces or carpeting.[234]

Only significant structural alterations trigger the compliance requirements. Alterations do not include "[n]ormal maintenance, reroofing, painting or wallpapering, asbestos removal, or changes to mechanical and electrical systems . . . unless [such changes] affect the usability of the building or facility."[235] For instance, if electrical wiring inside a wall is being changed, it need not comply with the ADA Accessibility Guidelines. However, if an electrical outlet—which may be used by individuals with disabilities—is being altered, then the Guidelines must be adhered to.

Anytime a facility alters its premises, the ADA Accessibility Guidelines must be followed to the "maximum extent feasible." This qualification applies to the rare situations where the very nature of the facility makes it impossible to fully comply with the Guidelines.[236] For example, it is virtually impossible to alter a gangway of a ship so that its slope, which changes with the tide, conforms to the ADA Accessibility Guidelines.[237]

Unlike the determination of whether a method of barrier removal is "readily achievable," cost is *not* a consideration in determining whether an accessible alteration is feasible.[238] A public accommodation or commercial facility must evaluate

---

[232] *Id.* §36.402(b) (2003).
[233] *Id.* §36.402(b)(1) (2003).
[234] Preamble to Regulations, 28 C.F.R. §36.402.
[235] *Id.*
[236] *Id.* §36.402(c) (2003).
[237] *See* Association for Disabled Ams. v. Concorde Gaming Corp., 158 F. Supp. 2d 1353, 12 AD Cases 453 (S.D. Fla. 2001).
[238] TITLE III TECHNICAL ASSISTANCE MANUAL, *supra* note 19, at §6.1000.

whether adhering to the Guidelines would be *technically* feasible. A store undergoing a major renovation would not have to widen its front entrance if doing so would impact the overall building structure, thereby requiring a new frame. In this instance, widening the door is not technically feasible. However, if an increased cost is the only factor preventing the installation of a wider entrance, then the entity must comply with the Guidelines.[239] If adhering to the guidelines is impracticable, the facility must do what it can to make the facility as accessible as possible.

J. Primary Function Area

When alterations are made to a "primary function" area, a public accommodation or commercial facility must ensure that the path of travel to the altered location, in addition to the bathrooms, telephones, and drinking fountains serving that area, are accessible as well, so long as the cost of doing so is not disproportionate to the cost of the entire renovation.[240] A "primary function" is a "major activity for which the facility is intended."[241] Typical primary function areas include lobbies, dining areas, meeting rooms, and work areas. Attics, basements, boiler rooms, utility closets, and corridors are not likely to be considered "primary function" areas.

> A "path of travel" includes a continuous, unobstructed way of pedestrian passage by means of which the altered area may be approached, entered, and exited, and which connects the altered area with an exterior approach (including sidewalks, streets, and

---

[239] *Id.*
[240] 42 U.S.C. §12183(a)(2):
Where the entity is undertaking an alteration that affects or could affect usability of or access to an area of the facility containing a primary function, the entity shall also make the alterations in such a manner that, to the maximum extent feasible, the path of travel to the altered area and the bathrooms, telephones, and drinking fountains servicing the altered area, are readily accessible to and usable by individuals with disabilities where such alterations to the path of travel or the bathrooms, telephones, and drinking fountains serving the altered area are not disproportionate to the overall alterations in terms of cost and scope . . . .
[241] 28 C.F.R. §36.403(b) (2003).

parking areas), an entrance to the facility, and other parts of the facility.[242]

These areas include sidewalks, interior and exterior ramps, clear floor paths, parking access aisles, elevators, restrooms, drinking fountains, and telephones. Alterations to windows, hardware, controls, electrical outlets, and signage in primary function areas do not trigger the path of travel requirement.[243]

The cost of making a path of travel accessible is deemed disproportionate to the overall renovation if it exceeds 20 percent of the cost of the alteration to the primary function area.[244] Stated differently, an entity is expected to allocate up to 20 percent of its renovation budget to making its paths of travel to the altered primary function areas accessible. Costs that may be factored into this 20 percent figure include those "associated with providing an accessible entrance and an accessible route to the altered area," "making restrooms accessible," "providing accessible telephones," and "relocating inaccessible drinking fountain[s]."[245] If costs exceed 20 percent, an entity should apply its renovation funds, up to the 20 percent requirement, to projects that provide the greatest degree of access for individuals with disabilities. An entity's first priority is providing "an accessible entrance," followed by "[a]n accessible route to the altered area." Next, the entity should provide "[a]t least one accessible restroom for each sex or a single unisex restroom." If funds remain, telephones and drinking fountains should be made accessible, followed by any additional "elements, such as parking, storage, and alarms."[246]

An entity cannot evade the path of travel requirement by renovating its primary function area in a piecemeal fashion, if all of the alterations could have been completed at one time. The total costs of alterations made within a 3-year period are to be used in calculating whether the added accessibility costs are disproportionate to the renovations as a whole.[247]

---

[242] *Id.* §36.403(e)(1) (2003).
[243] Technical Assistance Manual §6.200.
[244] *Id.*
[245] 28 C.F.R. §36.403(f)(2) (2003).
[246] *Id.* §36.403(g)(2)(i)–(vi) (2003).
[247] 28 C.F.R. §403(h)(2) (2003).

Public accommodations or commercial facilities are not required to install elevators in facilities under three stories or with fewer than 3,000 square feet per floor, "unless the building is a shopping center or shopping mall,"[248] professional office of a health care provider, or station used for public transportation.[249]

Because alterations are usually voluntary,[250] they are held to a higher accessibility standard than that for barrier removal under Title III. As noted in the report of the House Committee on the Judiciary:

> The ADA is geared to the future—the goal being that, over time, access will be the rule rather than the exception. Thus, the [ADA] only requires modest expenditures to provide access in existing facilities, while requiring all new construction to be accessible. The provision governing alterations is akin to new construction because it is only applicable to situations where the commercial facility itself has chosen to alter the premises.[251]

K. Tax Credits

In order to ease the financial burden of the alterations requirement for small businesses, Congress enacted a new section of the Internal Revenue Code known as the "access

---

[248] Shopping centers and shopping malls are described as follows:
(2) For the purposes of this section, shopping center or shopping mall means—
(i) A building housing five or more sales or rental establishments; or
(ii) A series of buildings on a common site, connected by a common pedestrian access route above or below the ground floor, that is either under common ownership or common control or developed either as one project or as a series of related projects, housing five or more sales or rental establishments. ... The facility housing a shopping center or shopping mall only includes floor levels housing at least one sales or rental establishment, or any floor level designed or intended for use by at least one sales or rental establishment.
28 C.F.R. §36.404(a)(2)(i)–(ii) (2003).

[249] TITLE III TECHNICAL ASSISTANCE MANUAL, *supra* note 19, at §5.40000.

[250] Major reconstruction after a natural disaster such as flood or fire is considered an "alteration" subject to Title III requirements. However, if the restoration is mainly cosmetic, i.e., limited to cleaning, repainting or rewallpapering, such acts are not deemed "alterations" under the ADA.

[251] H.R. REP. No. 101-485, pt. 3, at 63 (1990), *reprinted in* 1990 U.S.C.C.A.N. 445, 486.

credit."[252] This new section provides certain eligible small businesses with a nonrefundable tax credit of up to 50 percent of the business' "eligible access expenditures" that exceed $250 but not more than $10,250 for the taxable year.[253]

To qualify as an "eligible small business," the entity must have gross receipts for the preceding tax year that do not exceed $1 million or, if gross receipts were greater, the business must have employed not more than 30 full-time employees during the preceding tax year.[254] The business must elect this credit by filing Form 8826 with its tax return.

A business seeking to use the access credit must have incurred expenses by removing architectural, communication, or transportation barriers, providing auxiliary aids, acquiring or modifying its equipment or devices for individuals with disabilities, altering its facilities to comply with the ADA Accessibility Guidelines, or providing other similar services, modifications, materials, or equipment.[255] These expenditures must be reasonable, necessary, and used to bring an existing building into compliance with the ADA.[256] In addition, to be deductible, removal of barriers must conform to the DOJ's standards for new construction and alterations. A business must claim the deductions in the year that the alterations are made and cannot be claimed for new construction or complete renovation.[257]

If a business avails itself of the disabled access credit, then it cannot take any other deductions or credits for the amount of the access credit under any other provision of Chapter 1 of the Internal Revenue Code (IRC).[258] Moreover, using the access credit will not allow the business to increase the adjusted basis of the property in the amount of the credit taken.[259]

---

[252] IRC §44. IRC §44 was created as part of the Omnibus Budget Reconciliation Act of 1990, Pub. L. No. 101-508.
[253] IRC §44. *See* IRS Publication 334 & Form 8826.
[254] IRC §44(b)(1).
[255] *Id.*
[256] *Id.* §44(c)(3).
[257] 26 U.S.C. §44(c).
[258] IRC §44(d)(7)(A).
[259] *Id.* 44(d)(7)(B).

Alternatively, a business tax credit of up to $15,000 per year is available to offset expenses incurred in removing architectural or transportation barriers. Section 190 of the IRC enables businesses that own or lease a facility or public transportation vehicle to deduct the costs of making that facility or vehicle more accessible to and usable by individuals with disabilities.[260] A business entity availing itself of this credit cannot deduct costs already paid or incurred to completely renovate a building, facility, or public transportation vehicle or to replace depreciable property in the normal course of business.[261]

L. Franchise Liability

Title III requires that anyone "who owns, leases (or leases to), or operates a place of public accommodation" abide by its nondiscrimination principles.[262] In essence, whoever exercises any control over the condition of the facility is responsible for Title III compliance. Whether a franchiser can be held liable for a Title III violation in one of its branch operations therefore depends on the degree of control it exerts over that facility. Courts have looked to the franchise agreement in place for guidance in deciding this issue. For example, if in a franchise agreement the franchiser does not reserve the right to control entry to the facility in question, then the franchiser cannot be liable to a customer using that facility.[263]

Similarly, a franchiser who has no control over a facility's structural modifications does not "operate" the public accommodation in question, and therefore is not liable under Title III.[264] That the franchiser may veto any proposed modifications

---

[260] 26 U.S.C. §190.
[261] See 26 C.F.R. §1.190-2.
[262] 42 U.S.C. §12182(a)(1).
[263] See, e.g., Pona v. Whittaker's, Inc., 155 F.3d 1034, 8 AD Cases 968 (8th Cir. 1998), cert. denied, 526 U.S. 1131 (1999) (restaurant franchiser is not liable to customer for Title III violations, as franchiser did not own, lease, or operate restaurant, and franchiser agreement did not reserve right for franchiser to control entry into restaurant).
[264] See Neff v. American Dairy Queen Corp., 58 F.3d 1063, 1066, 4 AD Cases 1170 (5th Cir. 1995), cert. denied, 516 U.S. 1045 (1996) (in determining whether franchiser operates franchise for purposes of Title III coverage, relevant inquiry is

to the building or equipment does not confer on him or her the status of "operator" for Title III purposes. Such a limited form of control that is negative in character is supervisory and thus insufficient to render the franchiser liable for Title III violations.[265]

M. Landlord/Tenant Liability

According to Title III's regulations, "[b]oth the landlord who owns the building that houses a place of public accommodation and the tenant who owns or operates the place of public accommodation are public accommodations subject to the requirements of [Title III]."[266] A landlord and tenant are nevertheless permitted to allocate ADA compliance responsibility via lease or contract.[267] For instance, a building proprietor may stipulate in a lease with a tenant store owner that it is the responsibility of the tenant to ensure that the premises are accessible to individuals with disabilities. This arrangement, however, is effective only "[a]s between the parties,"[268] and does not absolve either party of liability in the event of a Title III violation.[269] Under the ADA, each party has an independent obligation to comply with Title III.[270] Title III explains that

> [i]t shall be discriminatory to subject an individual or class of individuals on the basis of a disability or disabilities of such individual or class, directly, *or through contractual, licensing, or other arrangements,* to a denial of the opportunity of the individual or class

---

whether franchiser is responsible for modifying facility to improve accessibility; franchise agreement in question gave franchiser right to set standards for building and equipment maintenance and to veto proposed structural modifications); *see also* Independent Living Resources v. Oregon Arena Corp., 982 F. Supp. 698, 767 (D. Or. 1997), *supplemental*, 1 F. Supp. 2d 1159 (D. Or. 1998) (landlord responsible for Title III compliance in common areas).

[265] *Neff*, 58 F.3d at 1068–69.
[266] 28 C.F.R. §36.201(b) (2003).
[267] *Id.*
[268] *Id.* pt. 36, app. B §36.201 (2003).
[269] *See, e.g.*, Botosan v. Paul McNally Realty, 216 F.3d 827, 10 AD Cases 1185 (9th Cir. 2000) (individual allegedly denied access to realty office for lack of accessible parking sued property owners and real estate company lessee; despite lease agreement that transferred responsibility for ADA compliance to lessee, nonetheless landlord still responsible to third party for ADA violation).
[270] *Id.*

to participate in or benefit from the goods, services, facilities, privileges, advantages, or accommodations of an entity.[271]

Therefore, while a landlord may require the tenant (or vice versa) to indemnify him or her against any losses caused by the tenant's failure to comply with Title III, such an arrangement has no effect on either party's compliance obligations to third parties.

The legislative history clarifies that

> the reference to contractual arrangements is to make clear that an entity may not do indirectly through contractual arrangements what it is prohibited from doing directly under this Act. . . . [O]f course, a covered entity may not use a contractual provision to reduce any of its obligations under this Act. In sum, a public accommodation's obligations are not extended or changed in any manner by virtue of its lease with the other entity.[272]

Thus, Title III obligations cannot be contractually eliminated. The rationale behind making both landlords and tenants independently liable under Title III is to prevent landlords from leasing only to small entities with limited financial resources. Barrier removal measures would be less likely to be readily achievable for a tenant with a limited cash flow. Therefore, by renting only to operations that could not afford barrier removal, a landlord could circumvent the requirements under Title III.

A tenant is required to abide by Title III's mandates even if the landlord is not subject to the ADA. For example, a business owner operating a place of public accommodation in a federal building, which the ADA does not cover, still must comply with Title III.[273] A tenant is not, however, required to remove barriers to areas over which it has no control.[274] A lobby area in an office building is the landlord's responsibility, even if shared by all the tenants. Generally, if either party has

---

[271] 42 U.S.C. §12182(b)(1)(A)(i) (emphasis added).
[272] H.R. REP. No. 101-485, pt. 2, at 104, *reprinted in* 1990 U.S.C.C.A.N. 303, 387.
[273] TITLE III TECHNICAL ASSISTANCE MANUAL, *supra* note 19, at §1.2000.
[274] *See, e.g.*, Independent Living Res. v. Oregon Arena Corp., 982 F. Supp. 698, 767 (D. Or. 1997), *supplemented*, 1 F. Supp. 2d 1159 (D. Or. 1998) (landlord responsible for Title III compliance in common areas).

the power to remove access barriers, then both parties are liable for Title III violations; if a party has no authority to make the requisite modifications, then it has no compliance responsibility.

N. New Construction

In addition to ensuring that all alterations made to public accommodations and commercial facilities be made accessible, Title III stipulates that all new construction be readily accessible and usable by individuals with disabilities unless its is "structurally impracticable" to do so.[275] A facility is considered to be "readily accessible and usable" by an individual with a disability if built in strict compliance with the ADA Accessibility Guidelines.[276] The purpose of this high standard is to ensure that persons with disabilities are able to get to, enter, and use a facility.[277] This provision applies to all public accommodations and commercial facilities designed and constructed for first occupancy after January 26, 1993.[278]

Compliance with this section will be considered structurally impracticable only when the unique characteristics of the

---

[275] 42 U.S.C. §12183(a)(1):
[D]iscrimination . . . includes (1) a failure to design and construct facilities for first occupancy later than 30 months after July 26, 1990, that are readily accessible to and usable by individuals with disabilities, except where an entity can demonstrate that it is structurally impracticable to meet the requirements of such subsection in accordance with standards set forth or incorporated by reference in regulations issued under this subchapter[.]

[276] TITLE III TECHNICAL ASSISTANCE MANUAL, *supra* note 19, at §5.1000.

[277] H.R. REP. No. 101-485, pt. 3, at 59–63 (1990), *reprinted in* 1990 U.S.C.C.A.N. 445, 482–86.

[278] The provision states:
For purposes of this section, a facility is designed and constructed for first occupancy after January 26, 1993, only—
 (i) If the last application for a building permit or permit extension for the facility is certified to be complete, by a State, County, or local government after January 26, 1992 (or, in those jurisdictions where the government does not certify completion of applications, if the last application for a building permit or permit extension for the facility is received by the State, County, or local government after January 26, 1992); and
 (ii) If the first certificate of occupancy for the facility is issued after January 26, 1993.
28 C.F.R. §28.401(a)(2)(i)–(ii) (2003).

area make it impossible to construct the facility according to the ADA Accessibility Guidelines.[279] This exception is extremely limited, and does not absolve an entity from making accessible those portions of the facility that *can* be made accessible. For example, if one end of a planned building will be constructed in marshland, then it may be structurally impractical to design an entryway accessible to individuals using wheelchairs. However, the remainder of the building must be built according to the ADA Accessibility Guidelines.[280]

1. Scoping Requirements

The Guidelines contain general technical design standards for buildings and related structures, such as parking lots, stairs, restrooms, and ATM machines.[281] In addition, the Guidelines contain scoping requirements, that is, how many and under what circumstances must features be accessible in a given location. For example, at least 50 percent of public entrances to a covered facility must be accessible;[282] every public and common use restroom must be accessible, and generally one stall in that restroom must be accessible;[283] both audio and visual alarms are required when emergency warning systems are provided;[284] and where dressing rooms are provided at a facility, 5 percent or at last one dressing room must be assessable.[285] The Guidelines' scoping requirements provide specific mandates for a number of additional building elements, including telephones, automated teller machines, signage, and parking.

The Guidelines also set forth specific technical standards for restaurants, medical care facilities, mercantile facilities, libraries, and transient lodging facilities, such as hotels and

---

[279] 28 C.F.R. §36.401(c) (2003).
[280] *See* TITLE III TECHNICAL ASSISTANCE MANUAL, *supra* note 19, at §5.1000.
[281] 28 C.F.R. pt. 36 (2003); *see also* ADAAG 4.1.3 (as amended through Sept. 2002); TITLE III TECHNICAL ASSISTANCE MANUAL, *supra* note 19, at §7.5000 et seq.
[282] ADAAG 4.1.3(8) (as amended through Sept. 2002).
[283] *Id.* 4.1.3(11).
[284] *Id.* 4.1.3(14).
[285] *Id.* 4.1.3(21).

homeless shelters. For instance, at least one of each type of sales or service counter containing a cash register must be accessible.[286] All dining areas and 5 percent of fixed tables (but not less than 1) must be accessible in any restaurant and cafeteria.[287] Also, 5 percent of fixed tables or study carrels (or at last 1) in a library must be accessible.[288]

If no standards exist for a particular building structure, then the public accommodation or commercial facility must adhere to the guidelines as closely as possible for all surrounding structures. For example, there is no Accessibility Guidelines standard for exercise equipment. Therefore, a health club is not required to special order accessible gym equipment for its facility. However, the health club must adhere to the other accessibility requirements, such as providing accessible drinking fountains, restrooms, locker rooms, and entryways.

Moreover, where there are no appropriate scoping requirements for the building element in question, an entity must provide a reasonable number (but not less than one) of those elements. For example, while there are no scoping requirements for bowling alleys, making at least one lane accessible is a reasonable measure to comply with the ADA.[289]

While a public accommodation or commercial facility does not need to make individual work spaces accessible,[290] the DOJ's standards for accessible design require that these entities allow individuals with disabilities to approach, enter, and exit work areas.[291] A "work area" is limited to those spaces used exclusively by employees as work areas.

Moreover, access is not required in nonoccupiable spaces accessed only by ladders, catwalks, crawl spaces, very narrow passageways, or freight elevators and frequented only by service

---

[286] *Id.* 7.
[287] *Id.* 5.
[288] *Id.* 8.
[289] *See* TITLE III TECHNICAL ASSISTANCE MANUAL, *supra* note 19, at §5.3000.
[290] Under Title I of the ADA, however, facilities may be required to make reasonable accommodations for employees with disabilities.
[291] ADAAG 4.1.1(3) (as amended Sept. 2002).

personnel for repair purposes. These spaces include elevator pits, elevator penthouses, piping, or equipment catwalks.[292]

2. Unclear Accessiblity Guidelines

The ADA Accessibility Guidelines are not always clear. For example, standard 4.33.3, which addresses the placement of wheelchair locations, has sparked substantial litigation against public accommodations with arena-type seating. Standard 4.33.3 stipulates that:

> Wheelchair areas shall be an integral part of any fixed seating plan and shall be provided so as to provide people with physical disabilities a choice of admission prices and lines of sight comparable to those for members of the general public.[293]

The DOJ regulations reiterate this standard by requiring, among other things, that covered facilities "[p]rovide a reasonable number of wheelchair seating spaces and seats with removable aisle-side arm rests," locate these spaces "so that they are dispersed throughout the seating area[, and] [p]rovide lines of sight and choice of admission prices comparable to those for members of the general public."[294]

It is clear that under these dispersal and line-of-sight requirements, a covered entity must provide accessible seating options for patrons using wheelchairs in order to provide them with lines of sight comparable to those available to the general public. What is less clear is whether these lines of sight must take standing spectators into consideration.

It is the DOJ's position that in assembly areas hosting events where spectators commonly stand, such as ballgames and concerts, facilities must provide seating that affords individuals in wheelchairs angles of sight similar to those of other spectators.[295] However, courts are split as to whether the DOJ's

---
[292] Id. 4.1.1(5)(b)(ii).
[293] Id. 4.33.3.
[294] 28 C.F.R. §36.308(a)(1) (2003).
[295] According to the DOJ interpretation of Standard 4.33.3:
   In addition to requiring companion seating and dispersion of wheelchair locations, ADAAG requires that wheelchair locations provide people with disabilities lines of sight comparable to those for members of the general

position is entitled to the force of law. Some courts have argued that the DOJ's position as stated in the supplement to its *Technical Assistance Manual* is an impermissible attempt to promulgate a new regulation.[296] Therefore, a comparable line of sight would not include lines of sight over standing spectators. If, however, the DOJ's position is merely an interpretation of a regulation already in effect, then the more stringent line-of-sight requirement is acceptable.[297] Other courts have held that standard 4.33.3 does not even address lines of sight over standing spectators.[298] Thus, it is unclear whether public accommodations must construct wheelchair-accessible seating that would provide the viewer with various viewing angles above standing patrons.

O. Architect Liability

Section 303 of the ADA makes it unlawful for public accommodations and commercial facilities to design and construct new facilities that are not readily accessible to and usable by individuals with disabilities.[299] Under this section, parties who

---

public. Thus, in assembly areas where spectators can be expected to stand during the event or show being viewed, the wheelchair locations must provide lines of sight over spectators who stand. This can be accomplished in many ways, including placing wheelchair locations at the front of a seating section, or by providing sufficient additional elevation for wheelchair locations placed at the rear of seating sections to allow those spectators to see over the spectators who stand in front of them.

1994 Title III TECHNICAL ASSISTANCE MANUAL SUPPLEMENT, at 13.

[296] *See, e.g.,* Lara v. Cinemark USA, Inc., 207 F.3d 783, 789, 10 AD Cases 683, 687 (5th Cir.), *cert. denied,* 531 U.S. 944 (2000) (reversing lower court finding that "comparable" line of sight includes lines of sight over standing spectators: "[W]e cannot conclude that the phrase 'lines of sight comparable' requires anything more than that theaters provide wheelchair-bound patrons with unobstructed views of the screen").

[297] *See, e.g.,* Oregon Paralyzed Veterans of Am. v. Regal Cinemas, Inc., 339 F.3d 1126, 14 AD Cases 1779 (9th Cir. 2003); Paralyzed Veterans of Am. v. D.C. Arena L.P., 117 F.3d 579, 6 AD Cases 1614 (D.C. Cir. 1997), *cert. denied sub nom.* Pollin v. Paralyzed Veterans of Am., 523 U.S. 1003 (1998) (athletic arenas required to maintain wheelchair-accessible seating that provides lines of sight over standing spectators).

[298] *See, e.g.,* Caruso v. Blockbuster-Sony Music Entm't Ctr. at the Waterfront, 193 F.3d 730, 9 AD Cases 1601 (3d Cir. 1999).

[299] 42 U.S.C. §12183.

engage in this unlawful activity, including architects, contractors, and owners of the facility, may be found jointly liable for violating Title III. In essence, whoever has a hand in designing, building, and approving the construction of the facility has a shared responsibility to ensure that it complies with the statute. However, at least two courts have found that architects are not covered by Title III, and therefore could not be held liable for potential violations.[300]

States, cities, and localities often devise their own building and construction codes. To avoid potential conflict between the ADA standards for alterations and new construction and local building codes, the ADA authorizes the DOJ, upon request of state or local officials, to certify that the state or local building codes meet or exceed the ADA standards. A facility built in accordance with the certified code can rely on it as rebuttable evidence of compliance with the ADA. Although not a guarantee of compliance, certification enables building owners, architects, and design professionals to rely on their local codes instead of having to resolve any tensions among state, local, and federal codes.[301]

P. Transportation

Private providers of transportation services also are required to adhere to the ADA's nondiscrimination principles, as well as make their vehicles accessible to individuals with disabilities if readily achievable. Title III requirements apply to public accommodations that are in the business of providing transportation services, and to those entities whose provision of transportation services is incidental to their primary business. For example, a private charter bus company and a taxi service are in the business of providing transportation services.[303]

---

[300] *See* Paralyzed Veterans of Am. v. Ellerbe Becket Architects & Eng'rs, P.C., 945 F. Supp. 1, 5 AD Cases 1494 (D.D.C. 1996), *aff'd sub nom.* Paralyzed Veterans of Am. v. D.C. Arena L.P., 117 F.3d 579, 6 AD Cases 1614 (D.C. Cir. 1997), *cert. denied sub nom.* Pollin v. Paralyzed Veterans of Am., 423 U.S. 1003 (1998).
[301] 28 C.F.R. §36.602 (2003).
[302] [*Reserved.*]
[303] 49 C.F.R. §37.29.

These entities are subject to regulations promulgated by the DOT.[304] Other entities provide transportation as an auxiliary service to their main business. Examples include "airport shuttle services operated by hotels" and bus, van, or other transportation service operated by shopping centers, colleges and universities, and places of recreation.[305] These public accommodations must also comply with applicable regulations drafted by the DOJ.[306]

Entities that provide transportation services as an auxiliary service to their main business must "remove transportation barriers in existing vehicles and rail passenger cars" where doing so "is readily achievable."[307] A business is not required to retrofit its vehicles, or otherwise install hydraulic wheelchair lifts.[308] For example, announcing passenger stops and transfer points and providing ramps at train depots or service stations are some measures that improve communication and mobility for individuals with disabilities.[309] As with existing buildings or other structures, the requirements for existing transportation vehicles is not too stringent.[310]

If a public accommodation not primarily engaged in the business of providing transportation services purchases or leases a new vehicle, the requirements for that new vehicle vary depending on whether the entity offers a fixed-route or a demand-responsive transportation service. A "'fixed route

---

[304] The DOT has issued two sets of regulations. One set (49 C.F.R. pt. 37 (2003)) provides general nondiscrimination rules, specifies who is covered by these rules, and requires that new and altered transportation facilities and vehicles be accessible. This set of regulations adopts the ADA Accessibility Guidelines' section on transportation facilities as the standards that new and altered facilities must meet to be accessible under the ADA. The second set of regulations (49 C.F.R. pt. 38 (2003)) provides accessibility specifications for vehicles covered under Title III.

[305] *See, e.g.,* TITLE III TECHNICAL ASSISTANCE MANUAL, *supra* note 19, at §4.4700.

[306] 28 C.F.R. §36.310 (2002); 49 C.F.R. §37.21(a)(3) (2003).

[307] 28 C.F.R. §36.310(b) (2002).

[308] TITLE III TECHNICAL ASSISTANCE MANUAL, *supra* note 19, at §4.4700.

[309] 49 C.F.R. §37.167.

[310] *See, e.g.,* Access Board's Technical Assistance document to Transportation Accessibility Guidelines, accessible at www.access-board.gov/transit/manuals/Transit%20Manual%20#-#%20Intro.htm.

system' means a system of providing transportation of individuals (other than by aircraft) on which a vehicle is operated along a prescribed route according to a fixed schedule."[311] For example, an amusement park tram shuttle that transports customers to and from the entrance and fixed areas in a parking lot constitutes a fixed-route system.[312] Similarly, a hotel shuttle that brings guests to and from the airport runs on a fixed-route schedule. A "'demand responsive system' means any system of providing transportation of individuals by a vehicle, other than a system which is a fixed route system."[313] For instance, a business that provides an executive limousine service for its clients operates on a demand-responsive system.[314]

1. Fixed-Route System Requirements

An entity providing a fixed-route system that plans to purchase or lease a vehicle with a capacity of more than 16 individuals, including the driver, must ensure that such a "vehicle is readily accessible to and usable by individuals with disabilities, including individuals" using wheelchairs.[315] A vehicle is "readily accessible to and usable" if it is able to be entered into and exited from and safely and effectively used by individuals with disabilities, including individuals who use wheelchairs,[316] and if it meets the standards and requirements set forth in the DOT regulations.[317]

This criterion applies as well to newly purchased or leased vehicles with a seating capacity of 16 or fewer, unless the business operation, when viewed as a whole, offers an equivalent level of service to individuals with disabilities that it offers to

---

[311] 42 U.S.C. §12181(4).
[312] 49 C.F.R. §37.37.
[313] 42 U.S.C. §12181(3).
[314] Please note, however, that if the car service transports employees *only*, Title III regulations would not apply. Instead, such a service would be subject to the regulations issued by the Equal Employment Opportunity Commission under Title I of the ADA.
[315] 42 U.S.C. §12182(b)(2)(B)(i); 49 C.F.R. §37.101(b) (2003).
[316] *See* S. REP. No. 101-116, at 73–75 (1989); H.R. REP. No. 101-485, pt. 2, at 122 (1990), *reprinted in* 1990 U.S.C.C.A.N. 303, 405, 407.
[317] *See* 49 C.F.R. pts. 37 (2003) & 38 (2003).

those without disabilities.[318] The services that must be equivalent include:

> (a)(1) Schedules/headways (if the system is fixed route);
> (2) Response time (if the system is demand responsive);
> (b) Fares;
> (c) Geographic area of service;
> (d) Hours and days of service;
> (e) Availability of information;
> (f) Reservations capability (if the system is demand responsive);
> (g) Any constraints on capacity or service availability;
> (h) Restrictions priorities based on trip purpose (if the system is demand responsive).[319]

For example, a hotel shuttle service could make alternative arrangements for a guest who uses a wheelchair, such as using a portable lift or by making special arrangements with another company that has an accessible vehicle.[320] Because this level of service is equivalent to that offered to nondisabled guests, and assuming the shuttle seats 16 or fewer passengers, the hotel is not required to purchase or lease an accessible vehicle.[321]

2. Demand-Responsive System Requirements

Entities operating a demand-responsive system must meet the "readily achievable and usable" standard for vehicles seating more than 16 individuals, unless the system as a whole meets the "equivalent service" standard.[322] This is a less stringent requirement than that for fixed-route systems. No specific requirements other than the "equivalent service" standard apply to demand-responsive vehicles seating 16 or fewer individuals for entities not in the business of providing transportation services. Thus, an employer would not need to provide a car service to its clients that is wheelchair accessible so long as

---

[318] *Id.* 37.105 (2003).
[319] *Id.* 37.105(a)–(h) (2003).
[320] *See* 49 C.F.R. §37.101.
[321] *Id.*
[322] 42 U.S.C. §12182(b)(2)(C).

alternative arrangements are made in the event a such a vehicle is warranted.[323]

3. Public Accommodations Primarily Engaged in the Business of Providing Transportation

Companies that *are* in the business of providing transportation services face more stringent barrier removal and new purchase requirements. In addition to making reasonable modifications to its business practices, providing auxiliary aids and services, and removing structural barriers for individuals with disabilities,[324] companies in the business of providing transportation must ensure greater accessibility for newly leased or purchased vehicles.[325] A transportation entity operating a fixed-route system must ensure that its newly purchased or leased vehicles are readily accessible to and usable by individuals with disabilities, including individuals with wheelchairs, unless the vehicle is a car, "a van with a seating capacity of [fewer] than eight [individuals] (including the driver), or an over-the-road bus."[326] Entities operating a demand-responsive system must purchase or lease vehicles (excluding automobiles and over-the-road buses) that are readily accessible and usable by individuals with disabilities, unless the system as a whole provides equivalent service.[327] "Vans with a [seating] capacity of fewer than" eight people used in either fixed-route or demand-responsive systems must meet the same requirement.[328]

Any new rail passenger car used to provide public transportation also must be "readily accessible to, and usable by, individuals with disabilities, including individuals who use wheelchairs."[329] Rail passenger cars remanufactured to extend their useful lives another 10 years or more must be "readily accessible to and usable by individuals with disabilities" "to the maximum

---

[323] *Id.*
[324] *Id.* §12184(b)(2)(A)–(C).
[325] *See* 49 C.F.R. §37.103 (2003).
[326] *Id.* §37.103(b) (2003).
[327] *Id.* §37.103(c) (2003).
[328] *Id.* §37.103(d) (2003).
[329] 42 U.S.C. §12184(b)(6); 49 C.F.R. §37.107(a) (2003).

extent feasible."³³⁰ Making a remanufactured rail car accessible to individuals with disabilities is feasible "unless an engineering analysis demonstrates that doing so would have a significant adverse effect on the structural integrity of the car."³³¹

Historic and antique rail cars are exempt from this section if compliance would alter the historic or antiquated character of the rail car, or would violate "any rule, regulation, standard, or order" related to the Railroad Safety Act of 1970.³³²

In addition to these vehicle structural specifications, all providers of public transportation, including those in the business of providing transportation and those not primarily in the business of providing transportation, must not discriminate in the provision of transportation services, such as refusing to allow individuals with disabilities to use the service if they are capable of doing so, requiring an individual with a disability to use a designated priority seat, charging extra to accommodate the passenger with a disability, and requiring that the individual be accompanied by an attendant.³³³ These entities must also ensure that certain service standards are maintained for individuals with disabilities. For example, transit providers must announce stops and transfer points, allow service animals, respirators or portable oxygen supplies on board, provide sufficient time for an individual with a disability to board and disembark the vehicle, and provide "adequate information concerning transportation services."³³⁴

In addition, each transportation provider must train its appropriate personnel to "safely and properly assist and treat individuals with disabilities . . . in a respectful and courteous" manner.³³⁵

4. *Over-the-Road Buses*

When the DOT issued its regulations in 1991, the agency specifically excluded design requirements for over-the-road

---

[330] 42 U.S.C. §12184(b)(7); 49 C.F.R. §37.107(b) (2003).
[331] 49 C.F.R. §37.107(b) (2003).
[332] 49 U.S.C. §§20101–21311; *see also* 42 U.S.C. §12184(c); 49 C.F.R. §37.107(c) (2003).
[333] 49 C.F.R. §37.5 (2003).
[334] *Id.* §37.167 (2003).
[335] *Id.* §37.173 (2003).

buses. Over-the-road buses are defined as buses "characterized by an elevated passenger deck located over a baggage compartment."[336] Over-the-road buses include various local and national bus lines, such as Greyhound, in addition to charter and tour bus operators. Public busing services, such as municipal transit lines, are not included.

When the ADA was being drafted, the busing industry expressed concern over the potential cost and viability of making intercity buses wheelchair accessible. Conflicting reports of how expensive the installation of wheelchair ramps and lifts would be, in addition to alarm over the predicted loss of passenger seating and baggage space and rise in ticket prices, led Congress to delay complete implementation of Title III requirements for over-the-road buses.[337] Instead, Congress included a section in Title III that commissioned the Office of Technology Assessment to examine "the access needs of individuals with disabilities [with respect] to over-the-road buses and over-the-road bus service[s]," and to determine "the most cost-effective" means of achieving those needs.[338] The DOT was directed to draft design requirement regulations for over-the-road buses and services in light of this study, which was completed in 1993.[339]

Prior to the issuance of these final regulations, over-the-road bus operators were not completely immune from Title III mandates. The DOT issued interim requirements for over-the-road buses in 1991 that did not require any structural

---

[336] 42 U.S.C. §12181(5).

[337] *See, e.g.*, 135 CONG. REC. S10756-S10758 (daily ed. Sept. 7, 1989) (statements of Sens. Hollings (D-S.C.), Kennedy (D-Mass.), Chafee (R-R.I.), Wirth (D-Colo.), and Harkin (D-Iowa)); S10762, S10763 (daily ed. Sept. 7, 1989) (statements of Sens. Bumpers (D-Ark.) and Harkin (D-Iowa)); S9687 (daily ed. July 13, 1990) (statement of Sen. Harkin (D-Iowa)).

[338] 42 U.S.C. §12185(a).

[339] The study found that it was economically and technologically feasible to build new over-the-road buses accessible to individuals with disabilities. Viable features include having extra-wide doors, movable armrests, and wheelchair lifts. The study determined, however, that providing wheelchair-accessible restrooms on board that would not displace passenger seating would present a greater challenge. According to this study, this problem could be alleviated by scheduling a suitable number of stops where accessible restrooms are available. Section 306 of the ADA stipulates that installing "accessible restrooms in over-the-road buses" is not required if doing so "would result in a loss of seating capacity." 42 U.S.C. §12186(a)(2)(C).

changes to them.[340] The interim requirements adopted the Access Board's accessibility guidelines for over-the-road buses that provide technical requirements for nonstructural design features such as floor surfaces, lighting, and handrails.[341] In addition, the DOT established interim requirements for accommodating wheelchairs and other mobility aids, as well as providing general boarding and disembarking assistance.[342]

The DOT issued its final regulations regarding design standards and purchase requirements for over-the-road buses in 1998. These regulations went into effect for large operators[343] of over-the-road buses on October 30, 2000, and on October 29, 2001 for small operators.[344]

The final regulations for over-the-road buses were hotly debated. The regulations call for large carriers operating fixed-route systems to ensure that at least half of the buses in their fleet be readily accessibly and usable by individuals with disabilities by October 30, 2006, with the ultimate goal of having their entire fleet accessible by October 29, 2012.[345] Despite this strict requirement, an over-the-road bus carrier may request an extension for compliance. The deadline for compliance may be extended if the company has not been able to purchase or lease a sufficient number of accessible vehicles to meet the 50 and 100 percent quotas. A carrier cannot, however, circumvent the deadline by purchasing a large number of inaccessible vehicles.[346] No deadlines exist for small carriers to make their

---

[340] 49 C.F.R. §37.169 (2003).

[341] 36 C.F.R. §§1192.151, 153, 155, 157 (2003).

[342] 49 C.F.R. §37.169 (2003).

[343] Large over-the-road bus operators are those with operating revenues of $5 million or more; all other carriers are considered small operators. 63 Fed. Reg. 14,566 (Mar. 25, 1998).

[344] Under the ADA, the accessibility requirements for over-the-road buses were originally to have taken effect by the end of July 1996 and July 1997 for large and small operators, respectively. However, the National Highway System Designation Act of 1995, Pub. L. No. 104-59, 49 U.S.C. §3113, note, amended the ADA by eliminating specific compliance dates and instead requiring large and small operators to comply with the regulations within 2 and 3 years, respectively, from the date of the regulations' issuance.

[345] 49 C.F.R. §37.185(a)–(b) (2003).

[346] Id. §37.185(c)(1)–(2) (2003).

fleet accessible, although these entities face new purchase and lease requirements, as discussed below.

Large over-the-road bus carriers operating fixed-route systems must ensure that any newly purchased or leased vehicle is accessible.[347] Small operators must either make sure that its new vehicles are accessible, or that it satisfies the equivalent service standard.[348] The requirements that apply to small operators also apply to over-the-road bus operators who are not primarily in the business of providing transportation services.[349]

All over-the-road bus carriers—including those not primarily in the business of providing transportation services—operating demand-responsive systems are *not* required to purchase or lease accessible vehicles.[350] They must, however, ensure that any passenger with a disability who requests service from an accessible vehicle receives such service. This provision also applies to mixed-service operators—those operators providing both demand-responsive and fixed-route services—so long as no more than 25 percent of their buses provide fixed-route services.[351]

Any large or small over-the-road bus carriers providing demand-responsive services may require up to 48 hours' advance notice to make an accessible vehicle available to the requester.[352] "If the individual with a disability does not provide [such] advance notice," then the operator must nonetheless make a reasonable effort to obtain an accessible vehicle, but "is not required to fundamentally alter its normal reservation policies or displace" a passenger with a reservation.[353]

The DOT plans to review the practical and financial impact of the above requirements in 2006 and determine whether they need to be modified.[354]

---

[347] *Id.* §37.183(a) (2003).
[348] *Id.* §37.183(b)(1)–(2) (2003).
[349] *Id.* §37.195(a) (2003).
[350] *Id.* §§37.189(a), 37.195(b) (2003).
[351] *Id.* §37.191 (2003).
[352] *Id.* §37.189(b)–(c) (2003).
[353] *Id.* §37.189(d)–(e) (2003).
[354] *Id.* §37.215 (2003).

Q. Examinations and Courses

Title III requires private entities that offer examinations or courses related to "applications, licensing, certification, or credentialing" for higher education, "professional or trade purposes" to do so "in a place and manner accessible to [individuals] with disabilities."[355] In the alternative, such entities may offer substitute arrangements that are accessible.

The purpose of this provision is to ensure that individuals with disabilities are not precluded from attending schools or entering professions that require licensing or credentialing exams simply because the exams are located in an inaccessible location or administered in an inaccessible manner. Because licensing certification and other testing authorities are not covered by section 504 of the Rehabilitation Act or Title II of the ADA, this provision fills a significant gap for individuals with disabilities.[356]

Examinations must be selected and administered in a manner that accurately reflects an individual's aptitude or achievement level rather than his or her disability, such as visual, hearing, sensory, speaking, or manual impairments.[357] This duty does not apply if the test at issue is intended to measure a skill directly affected by the individual's disability. For example, a blind test-taker is not entitled to an accessible means of taking a test that purports to measure an individual's vision.

In order to make a test accessible to individuals with disabilities, an entity may be required to make reasonable modifications to its testing practices and procedures. Such modifications include changing the length of time permitted for completion of the exam and modifying the manner in which the test is given.[358] An entity administering the exam must also provide appropriate auxiliary aids when needed, such as

---

[355] 42 U.S.C. §12189.
[356] *See* H.R. REP. NO. 101-485, pt. 3, at 68, 69 (1990), *reprinted in* 1990 U.S.C.C.A.N. 445, 491, 492.
[357] 28 C.F.R. §36.309(b)(1)(i) (2003).
[358] *Id.* §36.309(b)(2) (2003).

offering a version of the exam in Braille, large print, or audiotape, or providing a test-taker with an interpreter, transcriber, or reader.[359] Providing auxiliary aids is not required if doing so "would fundamentally alter the measurement of the skills or knowledge the examination is intended to test, or [if it] would result in an undue burden."[360] The testing examiner may require an individual to provide documentary proof of a disability in order to receive modifications and/or auxiliary aids. While it is the test-taker's responsibility to pay for and obtain the documentary evidence of the disability, the examiner cannot require the individual to pay for those modifications or auxiliary aids.[361]

An exam specially tailored for disabled test-takers must be administered at equally convenient locations and as often as those ordinarily provided to the general public.[362] For instance, in 1994 the Educational Testing Service, the administrator of the high school Scholastic Aptitude Test (SAT), and the College Entrance Examination Board agreed to schedule additional dates during which individuals with disabilities could take the new version of the SAT in light of Title III requirements. Only one date had been scheduled for individuals wishing to take an accessible version of the exam, while nondisabled students had been offered a variety of dates.

In addition, the location of the examination must be accessible to individuals with disabilities.[363] If an accessible location is not available, the exam may be given in the individual's home accompanied by a proctor.[364] Whatever alternative arrangement is made, the conditions under which the test is taken must be similar to those faced by nondisabled test-takers. A test given in a well-lit, temperature-controlled but inaccessible room can be administered to a disabled test-taker in a

---

[359] *Id.* §36.309(b)(3) (2003).
[360] *Id.*
[361] TITLE III TECHNICAL ASSISTANCE MANUAL, *supra* note 19, at §4.6100.
[362] 28 C.F.R. §36.309(b)(1)(ii) (2003).
[363] *Id.* §36.309(b)(1)(iii) (2003).
[364] *Id.* §36.309(b)(4) (2003).

separate, accessible room, so long as the alternative location is also well-lit and temperature controlled.

An entity is required to offer accessible examinations and testing environments to individuals with disabilities even if the test-takers would be unable to satisfy other requirements of the profession or license for which the test is being given.[365] For example, an individual with vision impairments is entitled to take a medical school entrance exam, even if the testing examiner harbors doubts about the individual's ability to become a doctor.

Private entities offering courses related to applications, licensing, certification, or credentialing for professions or higher education must also provide its instruction in an accessible manner. Course modifications and auxiliary aids for individuals with seeing, hearing, sensory, manual, or speaking impairments are essentially the same as those required for examinations under Title III.[366] A private course must ensure that its instruction is conducted and materials distributed in a place and manner accessible to individuals with disabilities. Modifications to the coursework include providing more time for an individual to complete the course, substituting specific requirements, or changing the manner in which the material is presented.[367]

Auxiliary aids such as "taped texts, interpreters, Brailled or large print texts, [and] qualified readers" are required for individuals who need them unless providing these aids "would fundamentally alter" the nature of the course or otherwise cause an undue burden on the course provider.[368]

The larger the company administering the course of study, the less likely that providing an auxiliary aid would constitute an undue burden. It is not an undue burden, for example, for a national law school bar examination preparatory course to provide qualified sign language interpreters, assistive listening

---

[365] TITLE III TECHNICAL ASSISTANCE MANUAL, *supra* note 19, at §4.5100.
[366] 28 C.F.R. §36.309(c) (2003).
[367] *Id.* §36.309(c)(2) (2003).
[368] *Id.* §36.309(c)(3) (2003).

devices, and Brailled materials to students with disabilities.[369] Alternatively, the course materials may be provided in an alternative format, such as via "videotape, [audio] cassettes, or prepared notes."[370]

However, if the course uses materials published by a third party, then it is not within the course provider's control to modify the materials. In this instance, a course provider is under no obligation to make the course materials accessible, but should inform potential students in advance what the materials will be so that they can attempt to obtain the materials in an accessible format.[371] In addition, the course must be offered in an accessible location.[372]

V. Enforcement

When Congress was drafting Title III, some lawmakers expressed concern over an anticipated spate of litigation against business entities for failing to sufficiently remove access barriers.[373] The enforcement provisions of Title III quelled this fear, to some degree, by offering a compromise: individuals would have a private right of action under Title III, but for injunctive relief only.[374] Aggrieved individuals filing civil suits may not seek monetary damages, although they may be entitled to an award of reasonable attorneys' fees, including associated costs, if they are the prevailing party in their lawsuit.[375] At least one appellate court has held that individuals named as defendants in a Title III action involving a college's accessibility would not be subject to personal liability.[376]

---

[369] *See, e.g.*, United States v. Harcourt Brace Legal & Prof'l Publ'ns, Inc. settlement agreement, http://www.usdoj.gov/crt/ada/archive/pubs/reg10rpt.htm.
[370] 28 C.F.R. §36.309(c)(5) (2003).
[371] *See* TITLE III TECHNICAL ASSISTANCE MANUAL, *supra* note 19, at §4.6200.
[372] 28 C.F.R. §36.309(c)(4) (2003).
[373] *See, e.g.*, 135 CONG. REC. S10755, S10756 (daily ed. Sept. 7, 1989) (statement of Sens. Boschwitz (R-Minn.) and Harkin (D-Iowa)).
[374] 42 U.S.C. §12188(a)(2); *see also* Disabled Rights Action Comm. v. Santa Fe Gaming Corp., 2002 U.S. App. LEXIS 4803 (9th Cir. 2002); Wander v. Kaus, 304 F.3d 856, 13 AD Cases 1619 (9th Cir. 2002).
[375] See discussion of attorneys' fees, section V.E., below.
[376] Emerson v. Thiel Coll., 296 F.3d 184, 13 AD Cases 493 (3d Cir. 2002).

A. Remedies

Remedies for the individual include temporary or injunctive relief, a restraining order, or other order mandating compliance with Title III.[377] Such orders could require the entity to provide an auxiliary aid, modify a service, or provide alternative measures, as appropriate. For example, if a hotel lacks a teletype machine, an individual with hearing impairments is entitled to seek a court order requiring the hotel to obtain this auxiliary device.[378]

In addition to providing individuals with a private right of action in the event of discrimination, Title III allows a plaintiff to instigate a lawsuit on reasonable belief that he or she is *about* to become a victim of discrimination.[379] For example, if the blueprints for a restaurant undergoing renovations indicate that the restrooms do not comply with the ADA Accessibility Guidelines, a potential plaintiff need not wait until the renovations are complete to commence a lawsuit. This statutory grant of standing is justified by practical concerns. Obtaining an injunction against the planned renovations at the outset is a more sensible measure than waiting until the construction is completed and then filing suit. Title III specifically notes that an individual with a disability is not required to "engage in a futile gesture" if he or she has knowledge that the public accommodation or commercial facility does not intend to comply with the ADA.[380] A plaintiff need only allege that he or she

---

[377] 42 U.S.C. §12188(a)(2).
[378] *Id.*
[379] 42 U.S.C. §12188(a)(1):
Availability of remedies and procedures
The remedies and procedures set forth in section 2000a-3(a) of this title are the remedies and procedures this subchapter provides to any person who is being subjected to discrimination on the basis of disability in violation of this subchapter or who has reasonable grounds for believing that such person is about to be subjected to discrimination in violation of section 12183 of this title. Nothing in this section shall require a person with a disability to engage in a futile gesture if such person has actual notice that a person or organization covered by this subchapter does not intend to comply with its provisions.
[380] *Id. See* Pickern v. Holiday Quality Foods Inc., 293 F.3d 1133, 13 AD Cases 409 (9th Cir. 2002).

is likely to be served by the defendant in the future and that the defendant is likely discriminative against the plaintiff.

B. Role of Attorney General

Individuals may also file complaints of Title III violations with the attorney general, who in turn is authorized to bring lawsuits in cases of general public importance or in "pattern or practice" cases of discrimination.[381] In addition to seeking equitable remedies such as an injunction against a discriminatory practice and order to provide an auxiliary aid or service, Title III imbues the attorney general with the power to impose a fine against the offending entity and collect compensatory damages on behalf of the aggrieved individual(s).[382] The attorney general may assess a penalty of up to $50,000 for the first violation of Title III, and up to $100,000 for any subsequent violations.[383] The purpose of this penalty is to "vindicate the public interest."[384] Permitting only the attorney general to bring lawsuits that could generate monetary penalties alleviated additional concern that private lawyers would view Title III litigation as a potential windfall.[385]

In determining a penalty, the court will take into consideration the entity's good-faith attempt to comply with Title III, including whether the entity could have reasonably anticipated

---

[381] 42 U.S.C. §12188(b)(1)(B).

[382] *Id.* §12188(b)(2).

[383] *Id.* §12188(b)(2)(C). More than one discriminatory act will be collectively considered a "first" violation if covered under a single settlement or judgment. A second violation would not accrue to the entity until a second lawsuit is brought. 42 U.S.C. §12188(b)(3); 28 C.F.R. §36.504(b) (2003).

[384] 28 C.F.R. §36.504(a)(3) (2003); *see also* H.R. REP. No. 101-485, pt. 2, at 64 (1990), *reprinted in* 1990 U.S.C.C.A.N. 512, 553. *See also* TITLE III TECHNICAL ASSISTANCE MANUAL, *supra* note 19, at III-8.4000.

[385] *See* 135 CONG. REC. S10790 (daily ed. Sept. 7, 1989) (statement of Sen. Dole (R-Kan.)):

> [T]he only person who can bring suit for civil penalties and monetary damages under the bill's public accommodation's section is the Attorney General. So—as you can see—lawyers will not be able to build careers out of law suits against public accommodations brought on a contingency fee basis. . . . So those who would suggest that the ADA will unleash a mountain of litigation . . . are simply missing the point.

the need for an appropriate auxiliary aid or modification to its policy or practice.[386] This "good-faith" standard is not equivalent to a "willful" or "intentional" standard.[387] In other words, a public accommodation cannot be absolved of a Title III violation simply by demonstrating that it did not willfully, intentionally, or recklessly violate the law. Proof that the entity did not act willfully, however, may be used as a factor in assessing whether it acted in good faith.[388] For example, if a public accommodation "reasonably and honestly could not have anticipated" the need for a particular policy modification, the fact that the entity did not modify its policy for an individual with a disability would not likely result in a monetary penalty. However, if an individual with a disability identified the need for the policy modification, yet the entity still failed to act, the good-faith defense loses credibility.[389]

An important difference between the attorney general's and a private party's remedial authority under Title III is the former's ability to obtain monetary damages on behalf of the individual. Although an award of punitive damages is not allowed under Title III,[390] compensatory damages are permitted if the suit is brought by the attorney general.

In addition to investigating charges of Title III violations and initiating civil suits, the attorney general is also responsible for conducting periodic compliance reviews of public accommodations and commercial facilities, and certifying, in consultation with the Access Board, that state and local building codes meet or exceed Title III requirements.[391]

Through the initiation and pursuit of lawsuits—as well as the settlement of investigations and complaints through both formal and informal settlement agreements—the Department of Justice has engaged in a substantial volume of enforcement cases under Title III. By way of illustration, there has been

---

[386] 42 U.S.C. §12188(b)(5).
[387] *See, e.g.,* H.R. REP. No. 101-485, pt. 2, at 128 (1990), *reprinted in* 1990 U.S.C.C.A.N. 303, 411.
[388] *Id.*
[389] *Id.*
[390] 42 U.S.C. §12188(b)(4).
[391] *Id.* §12188(b)(1)(A).

substantial litigation in the federal courts over the question of "line of sight" for accessible seating in theaters and arenas, through cases initiated by the federal government (as well as private parties).[392]

C. Exhaustion of Administrative Remedies

Whether an individual needs to exhaust his or her administrative remedies—that is, file a complaint of discrimination with a state or local antidiscrimination agency prior to filing a private lawsuit under Title III—is an unsettled issue. The ADA explicitly adopts the enforcement provisions laid out in Title VII of the Civil Rights Act of 1964:[393]

> The remedies and procedures set forth in section 2000a-3(a) [of the Civil Rights Act] are the remedies and procedures [Title III] provides to any person who is being subjected to discrimination on the basis of disability in violation of [Title III] or who has reasonable grounds for believing that such person is about to be subjected to discrimination . . . .[394]

Section 2000a-3(a), however, is qualified by section 2000a-3(c) of the Civil Right Act. Section 2000a-3(c) requires an individual to exhaust his or her administrative remedies prior to filing a suit in federal court. This step entails filing a claim with the appropriate state or local agency if state or local law prohibits the same type of conduct precluded by federal law. Therefore, the question becomes whether an individual with a disability who believes he or she was discriminated against in violation of Title III must first file that discrimination claim with the appropriate state or local agency before filing a federal suit, assuming that the state or locality enforces a law analogous to Title III.

---

[392] *See e.g.,* U.S. v. Hoyts Cinemas Corp., 380 F.3d 558, 15 AD Cases 1774 (1st Cir. 2004); Lara v. Cinemark USA, Inc., 207 F.3d 783 (5th Cir. 2000), *cert. denied,* 531 U.S. 944, (2000); United States v. Cinemark USA Inc., 348 F.3d 569, 14 AD Cases 1788 (6th Cir. 2003), *cert. denied,* 124 S. Ct. 2905, 15 AD Cases 1216 (2004); Oregon Paralyzed Veterans of Am. v. Regal Cinemas, Inc., 339 F.3d 1126, 14 AD Cases 1779 (9th Cir. 2003), *cert. denied,* 124 S. Ct. 2903 (2004).
[393] *Id.* §2000 et seq.
[394] *Id.* §12188(a)(1).

Some courts have held that because Title III explicitly adopts section 2000a-3(a) *only*, the administrative exhaustion requirement under section 2000a-3(c) is inapplicable.[395] Therefore, an aggrieved individual can bypass state or local authorities and proceed directly in federal court.

Title III's legislative history supports this interpretation to some degree. The following exchange took place between Senators Dale Bumpers (D-Ark.) and Tom Harkin (D-Iowa) during the drafting of Title III:

> Mr. BUMPERS: Is it correct to say that one who is aggrieved by failure of anybody to comply with this act must exhaust ... his or her administrative remedies before they proceed to file suit.
>
> Mr. HARKIN: That is affirmative.
>
> Mr. BUMPERS: In that connection, Senator, if somebody who is disabled goes into a place of business ... and they say, "You do not have a ramp out here and I am in a wheelchair and I just went to the restroom here and it is not suitable for wheelchair occupants," are they permitted at that point to bring an action administratively against the owner of that business, or do they have to give the owner some notice prior to pursuing a legal remedy?
>
> Mr. HARKIN: First of all, Senator, there would be no administrative remedy in that kind of a situation. The administrative remedies only apply in the employment situation. In the situation you are talking about—
>
> Mr. BUMPERS: That is true. So one does not have to pursue or exhaust his administrative remedies in title III if it is title II that is the public accommodations.[396]

Despite the clear intent by one of the ADA's prime drafters, other courts have reached the opposite conclusion, finding that Title III of the ADA *does* require a claimant to exhaust his or her administrative remedies prior to filing an action in federal court. Federal courts in New Hampshire and Colorado

---

[395] *See* Burkhart v. Widener Univ., Inc., 2003 U.S. App. LEXIS 9004 (3d Cir. 2003); Botosan v. Paul McNally Realty, 216 F.3d 827, 10 AD Cases 1185 (9th Cir. 2000); Bercovitch v. Baldwin Sch., 964 F. Supp. 597, 7 AD Cases 1378 (D.P.R. 1997), *rev'd on other grounds*, 133 F.3d 141, 8 AD Cases 259 (1st Cir. 1998).

[396] 135 CONG. REC. S10759, S10760 (daily ed. Sept. 7, 1989) (statements of Sens. Bumpers (D-Ark.), Harkin (D-Iowa), and Hatch (R-Utah)).

have concluded as much without explanation.[397] Other courts have relied on different interpretations of the ADA's legislative history, concluding that "Congress wished . . . [to give] people discriminated against on the basis of disability the same means of redress possessed by people discriminated against on the basis of distinctions that the law already prohibited . . ."[398] Therefore, because Title VII of the Civil Rights Act provided for administrative exhaustion, so too does Title III of the ADA.

In addition, the DOJ interpreted Title III to incorporate the attorneys' fees statutory section of Title VII,[399] even though Title III does not expressly adopt this section. Thus, the argument has been made that because the DOJ believes the ADA intended to include a section of the Civil Rights Act other than section 2000a-3(a), the administrative exhaustion requirement is impliedly incorporated into Title III.[400]

D. Standing

In order to bring a claim of discrimination under Title III a claimant must show, among other things, that he or she was denied the opportunity to participate in or benefit from services or accommodations on the basis of his or her disability.[401] In essence, to have standing to sue, an individual must have been harmed by the public accommodation or commercial entity's failure to adhere to the tenets of Title III. Once harmed, however, the individual is not required to have been impacted by each and every Title III violation present in the facility in order to seek redress from those violations.[402] Such a rule would be inefficient and impractical, as it would result

---

[397] *See* Daigle v. Friendly Ice Cream Corp., 957 F. Supp. 8, 9, 6 AD Cases 554 (D.N.H. 1997); Howard v. Cherry Hills Cutters, Inc., 935 F. Supp. 1148, 1150, 5 AD Cases 1579 (D. Colo. 1996).

[398] Snyder v. San Diego Flowers, 21 F. Supp. 2d 1207, 1210, 8 AD Cases 1050 (S.D. Cal. 1998) (citing the Joint Explanatory Statement of the Committee of Conference); Mayes v. Allison, 983 F. Supp. 923, 925, 7 AD Cases 1063 (D. Nev. 1997).

[399] 42 U.S.C. §2000a-3(b).

[400] *See Mayes*, 983 F. Supp. at 925.

[401] *See, e.g.*, PGA Tour, Inc. v. Martin, 532 U.S. 661, 11 AD Cases 1281 (2001).

[402] *See, e.g.*, Steger v. Franco, Inc., 228 F.3d 889, 11 AD Cases 51 (8th Cir. 2000) (blind man with mobility impairments has standing to sue building over

in "piecemeal compliance."[403] Thus, an individual using a wheelchair can sue a facility for failing to eliminate physical access barriers on every floor, even if the individual was personally impacted by those barriers on the first floor only. Moreover, a plaintiff's ability to institute an action may not depend on how many attempts he or she has made to overcome a discriminatory barrier, but rather, on whether the barrier remains in place.[404]

The key for standing purposes is that the individual already has or would likely be affected by those access barriers. For example, in *Association for Disabled Americans Inc. v. 7-Eleven, Inc.*,[405] a disability rights organization, along with two individuals on their own behalf and on behalf of similarly situated individuals, sued a convenience store for failure to comply with Title III's mandate to remove physical and communication barriers. The court denied the class certification on the grounds that the plaintiffs could not prove that they had the same interests or injuries as all purported members of the class. In order to have standing under Title III, the plaintiffs in this case had to demonstrate that each of its members could have raised claims against the facility on their own behalf. The claim that the association membership consisted of individuals with visual, hearing, mobility, and other mental and physical impairments was deemed too broad to demonstrate that each of its members would be impacted by the outcome of the case.[406] Thus, to have standing in a Title III case, the plaintiff must be able to show how he or she was or could be impacted by the alleged violations.

E. Attorneys' Fees

Although not expressly stated in the statute itself, the DOJ's regulations provide that in any action or administrative

---

failure to make facility accessible, even though he personally was not impacted by each and every access barrier).

[403] *Id.* at 894, 11 AD Cases at 53.
[404] Dudley v. Hannaford Bros. Co., 333 F.3d 299, 14 AD Cases 901 (1st Cir. 2003).
[405] No. 3:01-CV-0230-H (N.D. Tex. 2002).
[406] *Id.*

proceeding under Title III, a successful plaintiff (other than the U.S. government) is entitled to an award of reasonable attorneys' fees and related costs and expenses incurred in the litigation.[407] A successful *defendant*, however, is entitled to fees and expenses only if the plaintiffs acted in bad faith in bringing the lawsuit. This is a difficult standard, especially since the attorney general lacks the authority to investigate or prosecute plaintiffs or attorneys who file frivolous or harassing claims under Title III. Responsibility for investigating the private attorneys who file frivolous enforcement actions lies with the state bar or with the judiciary system in which the lawsuit was filed.[408]

Although a prevailing party may seek attorneys' fees under Title III, this entitlement is not without qualifications. In *Buckhannon Board & Care Home, Inc. v. West Virginia Department of Health & Human Resources*,[409] the Supreme Court held that in order to qualify as a "prevailing party," the claimant must secure either a judgment on the merits or a court-ordered consent decree. The Court rejected the so-called "catalyst theory," which posits that a plaintiff qualifies as a "prevailing party" if the initiation of the lawsuit causes the defendant to voluntarily alter its actions, thereby achieving the desired result. According to the Court:

> A defendant's voluntary change in conduct, although perhaps accomplishing what the plaintiff sought to achieve by the lawsuit, lacks the necessary judicial *imprimatur* on the change. Our precedents thus counsel against holding that the term "prevailing party" authorizes an award of attorney's fees *without* a corresponding alteration in the legal relationship of the parties.[410]

Judicially sanctioned settlements also qualify as outcomes sufficient to trigger an award of attorneys' fees. In *Barrios v.*

---

[407] 28 C.F.R. §36.505 (2003). The following, 42 U.S.C. §12205 of the ADA, which is found under Title IV, "Miscellaneous Provisions," stipulates that:
In any action or administrative proceeding commenced pursuant to this chapter, the court or agency, in its discretion, may allow the prevailing party, other than the United States, a reasonable attorney's fee, including litigation expenses, and costs, and the United States shall be liable for the foregoing the same as a private individual.
[408] DOJ Opinion Letter, No. 820, Apr. 13, 2000.
[409] 532 U.S. 598 (2001).
[410] *Id.* at 605 (emphasis in original).

California Interscholastic Federation,[411] an individual using a wheelchair sued an athletic association for discrimination for allegedly preventing him from becoming a high school basketball coach. The parties eventually agreed to settle the case, but stipulated in the settlement agreement that the issue of attorneys' fees would be determined by the judge. The district court entered a judgment according to the terms of the settlement, but denied the motion for attorneys' fees. On appeal, the U.S. Court of Appeals for the Ninth Circuit reversed the denial of fees, holding that the plaintiff could enforce the judicially sanctioned settlement against the defendant, and therefore qualified as a "prevailing party" under the ADA.

Similarly, in *American Disability Ass'n Inc. v. Chmielarz*,[412] the parties, a disability rights advocacy association and a gas station owner who allegedly did not comply with Title III's barrier removal requirements, entered into a settlement agreement that placed the decision regarding attorneys' fees up to the court. Although the agreement itself was judicially enforced, the court declined to award the plaintiff attorneys' fees on the grounds that it was not a "prevailing party." The U.S. Court of Appeals for the Eleventh Circuit disagreed, finding that the court's authority to enforce the settlement agreement rendered the agreement the functional equivalent of a consent decree.

Therefore, so long as plaintiffs can judicially enforce their victory, be it a judgment, consent decree, or settlement, they are entitled to an award of attorneys' fees and litigation costs.

F. Justice Department Enforcement Under Title III

The Department of Justice, with enforcement responsibilities under Title III of the ADA, has sought to assure access rights for individuals with disabilities in a substantial number of cases. The agency initially seeks to resolve such disputes through negotiations with affected parties prior to initiating

---

[411] 277 F.3d 1128, 12 AD Cases 1145 (9th Cir.), *cert. denied*, 537 U.S. 820 (2002).
[412] No. 01-15366 (11th Cir. 2002).

litigation. Many cases are concluded through informal settlements that result from the Department's investigations. Mediation procedures also have been utilized to resolve Title III disputes, primarily through a DOJ contract with the Key Bridge Foundation, which utilizes professional mediators who have been trained in the requirements of the ADA. The agency reports that more than 400 professional mediators have been active nationally in resolving these cases, and that mediation has proved to be successful in more than 75 percent of disputes.[413]

When cases advance to litigation, many proceedings are resolved through formal agreements, as well as consent decrees. Illustrative settlements and consent decrees have been achieved with hotels,[414] rental car systems,[415] entertainment venues,[416] educational operations,[417] correctional institutions,[418] as well as other public agencies and a wide variety of other businesses and facilities.[419] In addition, the Department participates in a number of cases initiated by private parties through amicus filings, in attempts to guide courts in interpreting Title III of the statute.

---

[413] *See e.g.*, "Enforcing the ADA: A Status Report from the Department of Justice" (2004, Issue 3), accessible at http://www.usdoj.gov/crt/ada/julsep04.htm.

[414] *See e.g.*, agreements with Westin Convention Center Hotel, Pittsburgh, PA, accessible at http://www.usdoj.gov/crt/ada/westcctr.htm; Super 8 Motel and Comfort Inn Motel, Annapolis, MD, accessible at http://www.usdoj.gov/crt/ada/super8.htm.

[415] *See e.g.*, agreement with ANC Rental Corporation, Alamo Rent-A-Car, LLC and National Car Rental System, Inc., accessible at http://www.usdoj.gov/crt/ada/alamonat.htm.

[416] *See e.g.*, Consent Order and Final Judgment, United States v. SFX Entertainment, Inc., Civil Action No. 02-CV-1929 (E.D Pa. 2003), accessible at http://www.usdoj.gov/crt/ada/sfxinc.htm.

[417] *See e.g.*, agreement with Portable Practical Educational Preparation, Inc., accessible at http://www.usdoj.gov/crt/ada/ppedprep.htm.

[418] *See e.g.*, agreement with the New York City Department of Corrections, accessible at http://www.usdoj.gov/crt/ada/nycdocrikers.htm.

[419] *See* "ADA Settlements and Consent Agreements," accessible at http://www.usdoj.gov/crt/ada/settlemt.htm.

VI. Conclusion

Title III of the ADA has been instrumental in providing individuals with disabilities access to previously unattainable goods and services. Although not without controversy, Title III proved to be an ambitious piece of legislation that has altered many business designs, practices, and procedures. Since Title III is both broad in scope and application, its requirements impact on virtually all employers, and they—and their counsel—need to be familiar with this key portion of the ADA.

CHAPTER 7

THE AMERICANS WITH DISABILITIES ACT AND THE HIRING PROCESS

I.	Introduction	701
II.	Prima Facie Case of Preemployment Discrimination Under the Americans with Disabilities Act	703
III.	Proving Disability Discrimination in Hiring Procedures	705
IV.	Accessibility of the Hiring Process	706
	A. Physical Access	707
	B. Interviewing	708
	C. Specific Disabilities	710
	1. Hearing-Impaired Applicants	710
	2. Visually Impaired Applicants	710
	3. Mobility-Impaired Applicants	711
	4. Speech-Impaired Applicants	711
V.	Applications and Job Descriptions	711
	A. Applications	711
	1. The Application Form as Evidence	712
	2. Qualifications Comparison of Applicant With and Without Disability	713
	B. Job Descriptions	714
VI.	Preemployment Inquiries and Medical Examinations	718
	A. Disability-Related Inquiries	720
	1. The Prima Facie Case	720
	2. Purpose for Prohibiting Disability-Related Inquiries	721
	3. Permissible Inquiries in the Hiring Process	722

		a. Inquiries Regarding Nondisabling Impairments	723
		b. Inquiries Related to the Performance of Job-Related Functions	724
		c. Inquiries Related to Known Disabilities	725
	B.	Medical Examinations	728
		1. Pre-Offer Medical Examinations	729
		2. Postoffer Medical Examinations	731
		3. What Is a Medical Examination?	733
		4. Disputes Over Conclusions of Medical Examinations	736
VII.	Preemployment Training Programs		738
VIII.	The Duty to Make Reasonable Accommodations for an Applicant		740
	A.	Reasonable Accommodations Under the Rehabilitation Act of 1973	740
	B.	Reasonable Accommodations Under the Americans With Disabilities Act	742
		1. Equal Employment Opportunity	743
		2. Employers' Duties	744
		3. Providing Information	746
		4. Employment Agencies	746
		5. Recruitment	747
		6. Applicants Request for or Advising About Need for Reasonable Accommodation	748
		7. The Undue Hardship Analysis	750
		a. Undue Hardship Exception	752
		8. The Essential Functions Analysis	753
		a. Determining Essential Job Function: EEOC Guidelines	754
		b. Rehabilitation Act/ADA Guidelines	755
		c. Private Employer Requirements	758
IX.	Determining Whether a Requirement Is "Job-Related" and "Consistent With Business Necessity"		759
	A. Justified		759
	B. Not Justified		760
	C. Establishing Certain Job Requirements		761

X. Responding to a Claim of Disability
Discrimination in Hiring 763
  A. No Reasonable Accommodation Existed 763
  B. Applicant Unable to Perform Essential
     Job Functions With a Reasonable
     Accommodation 764
  C. Disparate Treatment Based on Legitimate
     Nondiscriminatory Reason 765
     1. Applicant Posed Direct Threat 765
     2. Direct Threat Defense 766
     3. Function of Reasonable Accommodation ... 767
     4. Threat Assessment 768
     5. Employee Insubordination 770
  D. Nonstatutory Defenses 771

I. INTRODUCTION

The Americans with Disabilities Act (ADA)[1] is one of the most important and pervasive pieces of modern civil rights legislation.[2] Confronting the obstacles facing disabled individuals, Congress enacted comprehensive legislation designed to eliminate unjust discrimination against the disabled in employment, public accommodation, and transportation. In a speech marking the signing of the ADA, President George H.W. Bush stated, "as the Declaration of Independence has been a beacon for people all over the world seeking freedom, it is my hope that the Americans with Disabilities Act will likewise come to be a model for the choices and opportunities of future generations around the world."[3]

---

[1] 42 U.S.C. §12101 et seq. (1995).
[2] *See White House Briefing*, FED. NEWS SERV., Nov. 22, 1991. President Bush's press secretary, Marlin Fitzwater, stated that the ADA is "one of the most important civil rights acts of this century . . . . It is a dramatic piece of legislation that brings millions of Americans under the protection of the civil rights laws." *Id.*
[3] Statement by President George H.W. Bush Upon Signing S. 933, 1990 U.S.C.C.A.N. 267, 602.

Title I of the ADA not only prohibits discriminatory employment practices against incumbent employees, it also provides protections for job applicants.[4] Under the ADA, an employer may not discriminate against a qualified individual with a disability in regard to job application procedures, hiring, or job training.[5] To further this objective in the context of hiring, the ADA permits the employer's use of "qualification standards, employment tests, or other selection criteria that screen out or tend to screen out an individual with a disability" *only* if such criteria are job-related and consistent with business necessity.[6]

A primary objective of the ADA's protections for job applicants is dismantling unfounded fears and bias against applicants with disabilities.[7] Recognizing that employment discrimination may occur at any stage of employment, including the hiring process, Congress incorporated numerous provisions into the ADA that were designed to apply to the preemployment[8] stage of the relationship between a potential employer and an applicant.[9] To assist in eradicating prejudice in the

---

[4] *See* Holiday v. City of Chattanooga, 206 F.3d 637, 642, 10 AD Cases 501 (6th Cir. 2000) ("ADA protects employees and job applicants from discrimination based on their disabilities.").

[5] *See* 42 U.S.C. §12112(a) (1995).

[6] 42 U.S.C. §12112(b)(6) (1995).

[7] *See* 42 U.S.C. §12101(a)(2) (1995) ("Historically, society has tended to isolate and segregate individuals with disabilities, and, despite some improvements, such forms of discrimination against individuals with disabilities continue to be a serious and pervasive social problem"); *see also* Smith v. Chrysler Corp., 155 F.3d 799, 805, 8 AD Cases 1084 (6th Cir. 1988) (quoting Sen. Tom Harkin's (D-Iowa) statement in 136 CONG. REC. §7422-03, 7347 (daily ed. June 6, 1990), "The thesis of the [ADA] is simply this: That people with disabilities ought to be judged on the basis of their abilities; they should not be judged nor discriminated against based on unfounded fear, prejudice, ignorance, or mythologies; people ought to be judged upon the relevant medical evidence and the abilities they have.").

[8] For the purposes of this chapter, the term "preemployment," refers to all employment decisions and relations between the employer and the applicant before the final hiring decision.

[9] *See* 42 U.S.C. §§12111(8) (1995) (a person covered under the ADA includes "an individual with a disability who, with or without reasonable accommodation, can perform the essential functions of the employment position that such individual holds or desires"); *id.* 12112(a) ("[n]o covered entity shall discriminate . . . in regard to job application procedures [and] hiring . . . ."); *id.* 12112(b)(5)(A) and (B) (discrimination includes "(A) not making reasonable accommodations to the known physical or mental limitations of an otherwise qualified individual with a disability

hiring process, Congress designated the Equal Employment Opportunity Commission (EEOC) as the enforcement agency for Title I of the ADA.[10] Through an analysis of the language of the ADA preemployment provisions, recent case law, legislative history of the ADA, and enforcement guidelines of the EEOC, this chapter examines the ADA's impact on the hiring process.

The ADA does not prevent employers from adopting job-related qualifications, such as education level, skills, work experience, and physical and mental abilities necessary for work performance, health, and safety. At their discretion, employers may establish relevant job standards, ensuring that workers will be competent, and that workers will be minimally qualified. The ADA constraints simply require that disabled individuals are not arbitrarily disqualified from jobs that they can perform because of their disability.

II. Prima Facie Case of Preemployment Discrimination Under the Americans with Disabilities Act

In analyzing claims under the ADA, the allocation of the evidentiary burdens remains the same, whether the claim involves hiring, firing, or other aspects of the employment relationship.[11] This burden scheme is derived from the burden-shifting analysis enunciated in *McDonnell Douglas Corp. v.*

---

who is an applicant or employee . . .; (B) denying employment opportunities to a job applicant . . . ;"); *id.* 12112(b)(6) (discrimination includes "using qualification standards, employment tests or other selection criteria that screen out or tend to screen out an individual with a disability . . ."); *id.* 12112(b)(7) (discrimination includes "failing to select and administer tests . . . in the most effective manner . . . to a job applicant . . ."); *id.* 12113(a) (providing a defense of job-relatedness and business necessity for employer selection criteria); *id.* 12114(a) (ADA coverage shall not "include . . . applicant who is currently engaging in the illegal use of drugs").

[10] *See* 42 U.S.C. §12117 (1995); Francis v. City of Meriden, 129 F.3d 281, 284 n.1, 7 AD Cases 955, 957 n.1 (2d Cir. 1997) (recognizing that courts should give "great deference to the EEOC's interpretation of the ADA, since it is charged with administering the statute").

[11] Cole v. Staff Temps, 554 N.W.2d 699, 703 (Iowa 1996).

Green.[12] To prevail on a claim of unlawful employment discrimination under the ADA, the applicant must make preliminary showings that collectively constitute the prima facie case.[13]

The elements of the prima facie case in the hiring context include: (1) the applicant is an individual with a disability;[14] (2) the applicant is otherwise qualified to perform the job requirements, with or without reasonable accommodation; and (3) the applicant suffered an adverse employment action because of the applicant's disability.[15] The prima facie case represents a burden of production, which the applicant must satisfy in order to proceed with a claim of discrimination.[16]

If the applicant can set forth the prima facie case, the burden of production then shifts to the employer.[17] The employer has the burden of production insofar as it may assert a legitimate nondiscriminatory reason for not hiring the applicant.[18] A legitimate nondiscriminatory reason can be any reason, lawful or unlawful, that is not based on the applicant's

---

[12] 411 U.S. 792, 5 FEP Cases 965 (1973). *See also* Martin v. Allegheny Airlines, Inc., 126 F. Supp. 2d 809, 815 n.3 (E.D. Pa. 2000) "Although the burden-shifting framework for analyzing discrimination claims was originally developed in the Title VII context, . . . courts have routinely applied this framework to discrimination claims under the ADA as well." (citing Matczak v. Frankford Candy & Chocolate Co., 136 F.3d 933, 938, 7 AD Cases 1050 (3d Cir. 1997), citation omitted), *aff'd*, 261 F.3d 492 (3d Cir. 2001).

[13] *See* St. Mary's Honor Ctr. v. Hicks, 509 U.S. 502, 506–07, 62 FEP Cases 96 (1993). At least one appellate court has held that a plaintiff's standing under Title I of the ADA requires proof that there is an actual employment relationship with an employer defendant. Brennan v. Mercedes Benz USA, 388 F.3d 133, 16 AD Cases 15 (5th Cir. 2004) (individual with dyslexia and attention deficit disorder enrolled in training program supported by employers, including putative defendant, could not bring a failure-to-accommodate claim regarding advanced training program).

[14] Murray v. John D. Archbold Mem'l Hosp., Inc., 50 F. Supp. 2d 1368, 1375 (M.D. Ga. 1999) ("A plaintiff-applicant must prove that she has a disability as an element of her prima facie case for discrimination in violation of the ADA.").

[15] Holiday v. City of Chattanooga, 206 F.3d 637, 642, 10 AD Cases 501 (6th Cir. 2000); Sanders v. Arneson Prods., 91 F.3d 1351, 1353, 5 AD Cases 1292, 1294 (9th Cir. 1996), *cert. denied*, 520 U.S. 1116 (1997) ("To state a prima facie case under the ADA, a plaintiff must prove that he is a qualified individual with a disability who suffered an adverse employment action because of his disability.").

[16] *St. Mary's Honor Ctr.*, 509 U.S. at 506–07.

[17] *Id.*

[18] *See id.*

disability.[19] Thus, if the employer presents evidence that it made its decision not to hire the applicant because of reasons not involving any consideration of the applicant's disability, no violation of the ADA exists.[20]

Following the employer's showing of a legitimate nondiscriminatory reason for its challenged action, the applicant must prove that the employer's proffered reason is "pretextual."[21] The proffered reason may be characterized as pretextual if the applicant can show that the actual reason for the employer's refusal to hire the applicant is because of the applicant's disability. This final burden, which rests with the applicant, is a burden of persuasion. Ultimately, after establishing the prima facie case, the applicant bears the burden of proving the actual existence of a discriminatory motive.[22]

III. Proving Disability Discrimination in Hiring Procedures

A plaintiff alleging that disability discrimination occurred during the employer's hiring process, must first sufficiently assert the prima facie case detailed above.[23] Commonly heard issues related to discrimination in hiring involve: accessibility to the interview sites and testing facilities, disability-related questions before an offer of employment is made, written job descriptions and job applications, and prehire disability-related inquiries and medical examinations. While disputes in these

---

[19] *See* Fuentes v. Perskie, 32 F.3d 759, 763, 63 FEP Cases 890 (3d Cir. 1994).

[20] *See* Morisky v. Broward County, 80 F.3d 445, 448, 5 AD Cases 737, 739 (11th Cir. 1996) (quoting Hedberg v. Indiana Bell Tel. Co., 47 F.3d 928, 932, 4 AD Cases 65 (7th Cir. 1995), " '[A]n employer cannot be liable under the ADA for firing an employee when it indisputably had no knowledge of the disability . . . . At the most basic level, it is intuitively clear when viewing the ADA's language in a straightforward manner that an employer cannot fire an employee *"because of"* a disability unless it knows of the disability. If it does not know of the disability, the employer is firing the employee *"because of"* some other reason.' (emphasis added).").

[21] St. Mary's Honor Ctr. v. Hicks, 509 U.S. 502, 507, 62 FEP Cases 96 (1993).

[22] *Id.*

[23] See section VI.A.1. "The Prima Facie Case," below. Some courts have ruled that an applicant need not prove disability status when challenging preemployment disability-related inquiries and medical examinations.

areas frequently form the basis for a preemployment discrimination claim, they are by no means exhaustive of the possible conflicts that can emerge. By its terms, the ADA broadly acknowledges that disability discrimination in the hiring process, through any preemployment selection criterion,[24] may be challenged as a discriminatory procedure.[25]

Qualification standards that eliminate, or tend to eliminate, disabled persons on the basis of a disability must be job-related and consistent with business necessity. If the job requirement, or a selection criterion, is job-related and consistent with business necessity, and it eliminates an applicant on the basis of his or her disability, the employer must consider whether the applicant could perform the job function, or satisfy the selection criterion, if given a reasonable accommodation. While an employer does have a duty under the ADA to provide reasonable accommodations, an employer is not required to lower its production standards applicable to the quality or quantity of work for a given job when considering qualifications of an individual with a disability. If an applicant with a disability cannot perform the essential functions of the job because of a disability, an employer may reject that applicant if no reasonable accommodation exists that would allow the applicant to perform the essential job functions.

IV. Accessibility of the Hiring Process

The ADA requires that an employer reasonably accommodate applicants with disabilities. Given this duty to accommodate, an employer must consider ways to make an interview

---

[24] ADA requirements govern all selection criteria and procedures, including, but not confined to: education and work experience requirements, physical and mental requirements, safety requirements, paper-and-pencil tests, physical or psychological tests, interview questions, and rating systems. However, an ADA plaintiff must establish standing. *See* Breman v. Mercedez Benz USA, 383 F.3d 133, 16 AD Cases 15 (5th Cir. 2004); Green v. Joy Cone Co., 2004 U.S. App. LEXIS 16612 (3d Cir. 2004) (unpublished opinion) (nondisabled applicant, who challenged employer's requirement mandating signed medical release during application process, lacked standing to sue).

[25] 42 U.S.C. §12112(a) (1995).

site accessible.[26] In securing an accessible interview site, the employer must take several preinterview measures.[27]

A. Physical Access

To begin making the interview site accessible, employers should make sure that the parking area is physically accessible. Providing easily identifiable spaces reserved for disabled individuals promotes accessibility. As another practical suggestion, the entrance to the interview site should have a drop-off zone for persons with disabilities who depend on transportation services. Moreover, a smooth pathway should extend from the parking area to the building entrance. Similarly, the entrance to the interview site should comply with standards that promote wheelchair accessibility. The doors at the entrance should open with ease, that is, they should be light and easy to grasp. Lastly, employers should avoid designating a service entrance as the only physically accessible building entrance unless no other entrance exists.

Once inside the building, the route to the personnel office must be equally accessible. For instance, a personnel office situated on the entrance level should permit applicants to enter without steps, sharp corners, or other obstructions. If the personnel office is located on a higher level, the call button for the elevator should be low to the ground. Also, the elevator door should open wide enough to enable an applicant in a wheelchair to enter. Additionally, the elevator control buttons should not be too high, making the buttons unreachable for persons seated in a wheelchair. Finally, applicants using walking devices and wheelchairs may require a hard floor surface.

Some of the changes needed to make the interview site accessible require minimal effort on the employer's part. For example, moving interview rooms to the first floor could easily make the site accessible for an applicant with a disability. Of

---

[26] *See* 42 U.S.C. §12111(9)(A)–(B) (Supp. III 1991).
[27] *See* A TECHNICAL ASSISTANCE MANUAL ON THE EMPLOYMENT PROVISIONS (TITLE I) OF THE AMERICANS WITH DISABILITIES ACT ("TECHNICAL ASSISTANCE MANUAL") (1992), at 76–81.

course, some modifications may involve more complicated structural changes. While considering such modifications, companies should meet with expert consultants in order to reduce costs and maximize the effectiveness of structural changes.

B. Interviewing

Another form of accessibility pertains to social rather than physical barriers. Employers, through training, should advise interviewers of the goals and requirements of the ADA, particularly in the preemployment context. Interviewers must be cognizant that bias and unfounded fears projected toward persons with disabilities should not interfere with the hiring process. For instance, interviewers who feel uneasy with disabled applicants may avoid asking questions integral to the hiring decision. In addition, uncomfortable or biased interviewers may be tempted to shorten interview sessions with disabled applicants. Interviewers should not avoid particular questions because they assume that applicants are easily offended. Most significantly, interviewers who unjustifiably assume that disabled applicants do not meet the job requirements violate the ADA.

Employers should not presume that disabled individuals need help, but should be prepared to offer help if it appears reasonably necessary. However, employers should encourage interviewers to facilitate a comfortable environment when interviewing disabled applicants. Employers should instruct interviewers to maintain eye contact with all applicants when speaking to them. When reasonably necessary, the interviewer may engage the applicant in a discussion regarding the easiest way to communicate with him or her. If someone escorts the applicant, the interviewer should speak directly to the applicant and not the escort.

Even when interviewers feel at ease with disabled applicants, they may be ignorant about the limitations created by various disabilities. It is incumbent on employers to educate themselves about disabilities as they are presented in the preemployment context.[28] Although employers cannot expect to

---

[28] *See* Hoffman v. Fidelity Brokerage Servs., 959 F. Supp. 452, 460, 6 AD Cases 651 (S.D. Ohio 1997).

understand the indicators and effects of all disabling conditions, there are some procedures that may provide disabled applicants with the necessary assistance while promoting fairness in the hiring process.

In general, employers interviewing disabled applicants should focus on job-related issues and not the disability.[29] They should fully understand the qualifications of the job for which the applicant is applying. This will assist interviewers in organizing interviews and tying all inquiries to job-related functions. Under the ADA, interviewers may not presume that an applicant will not be able to perform an essential job duty because of the interviewer's prior experience with similarly disabled individuals.[30] Rather, they must conduct the interview in terms of the applicant's ability, not disability. In some instances, the interviewer must allow the applicant to either demonstrate or explain how he or she will perform the essential job functions despite his or her disability.

While an interviewer may not ask the applicant about accommodations to perform the job, the interviewer may inquire as to any accommodations the applicant will need for the hiring process.[31] The interviewer cannot presume that the employer will not be able to accommodate the applicant. Rather, interviewers must engage the applicant in an interactive process aimed at discovering possible accommodations.[32] To further the dialogue regarding potential accommodations, the employer may take the applicant on a tour of the work site.

---

[29] *See* 42 U.S.C. §12112(b)(1) (Supp. III 1991) (discrimination includes "limiting, segregating, or classifying a job applicant or employee in a way that adversely affects the opportunities or status of such applicant or employee because of the disability of such applicant or employee"). This section was modeled on the language in Section 504's regulations in the Rehabilitation Act of 1973, 29 U.S.C. §701 et seq., e.g., 29 U.S.C. §794. *See* 42 Fed. Reg. 22,680, 45 C.F.R. §84.11(a)(3) (2003) (original Department of Health, Education and Welfare (HEW) regulations) ("A recipient... may not limit, segregate, or classify applicants or employees in any way that adversely affects their opportunities or status because of handicap.") (codified as reissued at 45 C.F.R. §84.11(a)(3) (2003) (Department of Health and Human Services (HHS) regulations).

[30] *See* 42 U.S.C. §12112(b).

[31] *See* Hall v. U.S. Postal Serv., 857 F.2d 1073, 1079–80, 1 AD Cases 1368 (6th Cir. 1988); *see also* 29 C.F.R. pt. 1630, app. (2003).

[32] *Id.*

As noted in the "fact sheet" on the application process and the ADA published by the EEOC, there are a number of questions that employers may not ask in a job application or during a job interview.[33] These include questions about specific conditions—e.g., "Do you have a heart condition?" "Do you have asthma or other difficulties breathing?"—as well as more general inquiries (such as the number of days an employee was sick in the prior year). Questions relating to an applicant's history ("Have you ever been treated for mental health problems?"), prior compensable workplace injuries or illnesses ("Have you ever filed for worker's compensation?"), or current treatment or presciption medications also are off-limits, according to the agency's summary.

C. Specific Disabilities

1. Hearing-Impaired Applicants

As a practical point, when communicating with hearing-impaired applicants who read lips, interviewers should face them directly, speaking slowly and clearly. They should avoid making nonverbal hand or body motions that applicants may not perceive or that may draw attention from the interviewer's lips. In addition, interviewers may want to shave or trim facial hair that inhibits a hearing-impaired applicant's ability to read lips. If needed, a sign language interpreter should be provided. The interpreter should sit next to the interviewer so that the hearing-impaired applicant can quickly move his gaze from the interpreter to the interviewer. Lastly, employers should not hesitate to flag the applicants' attention by tapping them on the shoulder.

2. Visually Impaired Applicants

When interviewing blind or visually impaired applicants, interviewers need not increase their voice level. While a blind

---

[33] See "Fact Sheet: Job Applicants and the Americans With Disabilities Act," Equal Employment Opportunity Commission, accessible at http://www.eeoc.gov/facts/jobapplicant.html, applying criteria contained in the agency's proper guid-

applicant may use voices to gauge direction, the increased level of the voice adds nothing instructive for the applicant with a visual impairment. Additionally, interviewers should introduce each person in the room so that the applicant is aware of all people present.

3. Mobility-Impaired Applicants

When interviewing mobility-impaired applicants, interviewers should offer assistance when reasonably necessary. Interviewers should know the location of wheelchair ramps. Lastly, they should not be afraid that wheelchair users will be offended by terms such as "walk" or "run."

4. Speech-Impaired Applicants

In interacting with applicants who have speech impairments or cognitive disabilities, interviewers should first provide detailed, specific information on the position. They then should listen carefully to the applicant, asking the applicant to repeat statements that the interviewer failed to comprehend.

V. APPLICATIONS AND JOB DESCRIPTIONS

A. Applications

An employer may not ask questions on a written application form concerning "whether an applicant will need [a] reasonable accommodation for a job."[34] Moreover, an employer may not list physical defects on an application form requiring that applicants indicate which ailments they have.[35] Because

---

ance document "Pre-employment Disability-Related Questions and Medical Examinations," EEOC Notice No. 915.002 (Oct. 10, 1995).

[34] EQUAL EMPLOYMENT OPPORTUNITY COMMISSION: ADA ENFORCEMENT GUIDANCE: PREEMPLOYMENT DISABILITY-RELATED QUESTIONS AND MEDICAL EXAMINATIONS, No. 915.002, Oct. 10, 1995 [hereinafter ADA ENFORCEMENT GUIDANCE].

[35] Downs v. Massachusetts Bay Trans. Auth., 13 F. Supp. 2d 130, 138, 8 AD Cases 447, 455 (D. Mass. 1998) ("[T]he EEOC explains that 'inquiries into the ability of an applicant to perform job-related functions . . . must be narrowly tailored,' and, more to the point, that '[a]n employer may not use an application form that lists

such questions tend to elicit whether the applicant has a disability, they are prohibited under the ADA. However, some courts, in examining the employer's application form, found that the ADA permits such questioning in certain situations.[36]

One such circumstance involved the employer's inclusion of a list of physical defects on an application form followed by a question requiring that the applicant indicate whether he or she suffered from any of the listed defects.[37] While such a question immediately arouses suspicion about the employer's preemployment practices, the court found that the employer stayed within the bounds of the law.[38] However, in its holding, the court did not broadly approve of questions regarding an applicant's physical defects on an application form. Rather, the court contained its reasoning within the facts of the case. It concluded that, because the list of physical defects on the application precisely mirrored the list of defects provided under the federal regulations governing the qualifications for the type of job the applicant sought, the employer correctly framed its preemployment inquiry as job-related and consistent with the employer's business necessity. Such an inquiry, on an application form, or in any other preemployment context, is permissible under the ADA.[39]

1. *The Application Form as Evidence*

The application form may serve as evidence of the preemployment inquiry contested in a claim alleging discriminatory

---

a number of potentially disabling impairments and ask the applicant to check any of the impairments he or she may have'," quoting 29 C.F.R. pt. 1630, app. §1630.14(a)).

[36] *See* EEOC v. Texas Bus Lines, 923 F. Supp. 965, 981, 5 AD Cases 878 (S.D. Tex. 1996).

[37] *Id.* at 981–82 (applicant claimed employer violated ADA by making disability-related inquiry on application form, which required applicant to list any physical defects, such as eyesight, hearing, limb impairment, diabetes, back or heart trouble, high blood pressure, fits, convulsions, fainting).

[38] *Id.* (employer successfully defended discrimination claim by arguing that application form merely requests applicant list defects expressly addressed by federal regulations and, therefore, are job-related and consistent with employer's business purpose).

[39] 42 U.S.C. §12112 (b)(6) (1995); *see also* 42 U.S.C. §12113(a) (1995) ("It may be a defense to a charge of discrimination . . . that an alleged application of

hiring practices.[40] The plaintiff, often an applicant rejected for a position, can rely on the application form to prove that the employer posed a question relating to the applicant's disability. By contrast, an employer can use the application form to show that it treated all applicants similarly during the hiring process. Additionally, an employer can use the application to show that the question posed on the application form would not likely elicit a response related to an applicant's disability. Also, the employer can offer the application to prove that the language of the question was directly relevant to job-relatedness and business necessity.

2. Qualifications Comparison of Applicant With and Without Disability

Another evidentiary use of an application form arises in the context of comparing the qualifications of an applicant with a disability with the qualifications of the applicant whom the employer hired.[41] For example, if a qualified applicant with a disability applies for a position but is rejected, and the applicant selected for the job appears less qualified than the rejected applicant, the rejected applicant with a disability may assert a claim alleging that the employer engaged in discriminatory hiring practices.

To bolster the discriminatory hiring claim, the disabled applicant might raise the argument that he or she was more qualified than the applicant whom the employer hired.[42] In response to such an argument, a court can examine and compare the application completed by the disabled applicant with the application of the applicant who received an offer of employment. If the court concludes that a reasonable employer would have found the applicant with the disability *significantly*

---

qualification standards, tests, or selection criteria that ... deny a job ... to an individual with a disability has been shown to be job-related and consistent with business necessity ...").

[40] *See id.*

[41] *See* Aka v. Washington Hosp. Ctr., 156 F.3d 1284, 8 AD Cases 1093 (D.C. Cir. 1998).

[42] *See id.* at 1294.

better qualified for the job, the court can then infer that the employer consciously selected a less-qualified candidate. Because employers typically do not overlook significantly better qualified candidates, the court can conclude further that some other strong consideration, such as disability discrimination, interfered with the hiring process.[43]

At the same time, it is not accurate to suggest that any employer selecting a candidate who, on his or her application, appears less qualified than another applicant with a disability, risks the inference of disability discrimination. On the contrary, courts recognize that an employer may, for subjective reasons, such as personality traits exhibited in an interview, favor a less-qualified candidate. However, if the disabled applicant has outstanding qualifications for the position that far outweigh the qualifications of the hired applicant, the employer may be forced to confront a strong inference of discrimination with only the slight protection of a subjective reason defending its preference for the less-qualified applicant. Thus, an employer, primarily defending itself based on subjective reasons, may find it difficult to overcome the inference created by its refusal to hire a significantly more qualified candidate with a disability.[44]

B. Job Descriptions

Like job application forms, written job descriptions serve many purposes in claims of discriminatory hiring practices. For one, an unsuccessful applicant with a disability may rely on the employer's job description to show that he or she was a more qualified applicant.[45] By listing the job responsibilities

---

[43] *Id.* at 1295, 1299–1300 (finding sufficient evidence creating inference of discrimination).

[44] *Id.* at 1298, 8 AD Cases at 1105 (citing Perfetti v. First Nat'l Bank of Chi., 950 F.2d 449, 457, 57 FEP Cases 720 (7th Cir. 1991), *cert. denied*, 505 U.S. 1205 (1992); cautioning that, "courts traditionally treat explanations that rely heavily on subjective considerations with caution. Particularly in cases where a jury could reasonably find that the plaintiff was otherwise significantly better qualified that the successful applicant, an employer's asserted strong reliance on subjective feelings about the candidates may mask discrimination").

[45] *Id.* at 1295–96.

in a job description, the employer provides key points of comparison for a court analyzing whether the applicant with a disability is significantly better qualified than the person hired for the position.[46] After a comparison of each candidate's qualifications within the scope of the job description, an inference of discriminatory animus may emerge.[47] Accordingly, for all practical purposes, the employer then must rebut the inference with a legitimate nondiscriminatory reason for rejecting the applicant.

Just as the applicant may use the job description in illustrating that he is the significantly better qualified candidate for the position, conversely, the employer may rely on the job description to refute the caliber of the disabled applicant's qualifications. The employer may rely on the job description to demonstrate that the successful applicant was in fact more qualified. More strongly, the employer can rely on the job description to show that the unsuccessful applicant was, in fact, unqualified. If an employer relies on the job description as evidence of a legitimate nondiscriminatory reason for not selecting an applicant with a disability, the job description, to be credible, must meet certain statutory requirements.

Generally, job descriptions are used to prove the employer's conceptualization of the essential functions of the job. According to the precepts of the ADA, an individual with a disability who brings a claim that he or she is better qualified than the person hired by the employer, must, at the very least, show that he or she could perform the essential functions of the position, with or without a reasonable accommodation.[48]

---

[46] *Id.* (closely examining job responsibilities and qualifications delineated in job description to decide whether inference of discrimination against disabled applicant could be raised).

[47] *Id.* (comparing qualifications of rejected applicant against those of successful applicant, court examined employer's job description, which listed as qualification for position, "previous hospital experience in pharmacy services," finding support for inference of disability discrimination in fact that applicant with disability had 19 years' experience in pharmacy services while person hired for position merely had 2 months' experience).

[48] 42 U.S.C. §12111(8) (1995) (defining who is covered individual under ADA, states that "an individual with a disability who, with or without reasonable

If the individual cannot make this showing, an employer may reject the applicant. No obligation exists under the ADA requiring an employer to hire an applicant who cannot perform the essential functions of the job. Therefore, deciding what functions are "essential functions" can be crucial to a disability discrimination case.

The ADA instructs courts to recognize the employer's job description when determining which job functions are essential.[49] The federal regulations implementing the ADA also require that the employer's job description serve as evidence of the essential functions of the job.[50] In accordance, many courts have explained the evidentiary role of the job description in the context of claims raising challenges to employers' preemployment practices.[51] When examining an employer's hiring decisions, courts allow the employer ample room to exercise its business judgment.[52] However, courts will limit an employer's business judgment by requiring that decisions be made without impermissible considerations of disability. In sum, the statutorily prescribed deference to the employer's business judgment

---

accommodation, can perform the essential functions of the employment position that such individual holds *or desires*. [emphasis added]).

[49] 42 U.S.C. §12111(8) (1995) ("For the purposes of this subchapter, consideration shall be given to the employer's judgment as to what functions of a job are essential, and if an employer has prepared a written description before advertising or interviewing applicants for the job, this description shall be considered evidence of the essential functions of the job.").

[50] 29 C.F.R. pt. 1630, app. §1630.2 (n) (2003).

[51] *See, e.g.*, Hoffman v. Fidelity Brokerage Servs., 959 F. Supp. 452, 460, 6 AD Cases 651 (S.D. Ohio 1997); Leverett v. City of Indianapolis, 51 F. Supp. 2d 949, 951 n.7, 9 AD Cases 1812, 1815 n.7 (S.D. Ind. 1999) ("The parties agree[d] that the essential [job] functions for a firefighter include[d] at least those duties listed in the [employer's] official job description."); Stinson v. West Suburban Hosp. Med. Ctr., 1998 WL 188938 *1, *7 (N.D. Ill. 1998) ("Ultimately, it is [the employer's] prerogative to establish reasonable qualifications for . . . [a] position" and that, as long as qualification is job related and consistent with business necessity, an employer is "free to use reasonable qualifications to screen out potential employees").

[52] *Hoffman*, 959 F. Supp. at 461, 6 AD Cases at 658, 659 ("[i]t is not the role of the . . . trier-of-fact to second-guess [an employer's] business judgment" when employer chose not to hire trainee with disability after trainee failed to perform at level of accuracy and speed required by employer for persons in position and that "[i]t is not necessary . . . that an employer's performance standards be quantifiable. Rather, an employer is permitted to exercise its business judgment in establishing performance standards and in determining whether an individual can meet its

remains constant, unless the rejected applicant can cast doubt on whether the employer exercised its business judgment in good faith.[53] For instance, if the employer uses the job description as evidence of the essential functions of the job, the duties listed as "essential" must, in fact, constitute essential job functions. If the job functions can be better characterized as inessential duties, the persuasiveness of the employer's job description as evidence of the essential job functions greatly diminishes.[54]

The ADA expressly provides another limitation on the court's willingness to defer to an employer's delineation of the essential job functions in the job description.[55] This limitation focuses on the time at which the employer makes the job description available to applicants. Under the ADA, an employer may only use a job description as evidence of the essential functions of the job if it was created before the employer advertises or interviews applicants for the job.[56]

The purpose underlying this provision is best understood through a hypothetical. Assume that an individual with a disability brings a claim arguing that the employer refused to hire her because of her disability. As explained previously, the applicant must set forth a prima facie case.[57] To establish a prima facie case, the applicant must show that he or she is a qualified individual entitled to the ADA's protections.[58] To be a qualified individual, the applicant must allege that he or she can perform the essential functions of the position, with or

---

standards, 'whether qualitative or quantitative,'" *id.* at 460, 6 AD Cases at 658 (quoting 29 C.F.R. pt. 1630, app. §1630.2(n))).

[53] *See Hoffman*, 959 F. Supp. at 461.

[54] *See* Doe v. New York Univ., 666 F.2d 761, 776 (2d Cir. 1981) (interpreting evidentiary effect of job description under Rehabilitation Act); Simon v. St. Louis County, 656 F.2d 316, 320, 1 AD Cases 268 (8th Cir. 1981) (same).

[55] 42 U.S.C. §12111(8) (1995).

[56] *Id.*; *see also* Deane v. Pocono Med. Ctr., 142 F.3d 138, 146, 7 AD Cases 1809 (3d Cir. 1998).

[57] See section II., "Prima Facie Case for Preemployment Discrimination Under the Americans With Disabilities Act," above.

[58] *See* Matczak v. Frankford Candy & Chocolate Co., 136 F.3d 933, 937, 7 AD Cases 1050, 1054 (3d Cir. 1997) (clarifying that, to present a prima facie case, "plaintiff need only show she or he was qualified member of protected class...," citing Waldron v. SL Indus., 56 F.3d 491, 67 FEP Cases 1577 (3d Cir. 1995)).

without a reasonable accommodation.[59] Therefore, an available defense for an employer may be that the applicant is not a qualified individual because he or she could not perform the essential functions of the job, with or without a reasonable accommodation. However, if the employer failed to describe the essential functions of the job when the applicant applied, the candidate effectively never received the opportunity to describe or demonstrate how he or she could perform the essential functions.

In one case, the U.S. Court of Appeals for the Tenth Circuit addressed an employer's policy of hiring only internal candidates for customer care positions that did not involve voicephone services.[60] It held that the lower court had erred in finding that a deaf applicant was not a "qualified applicant" under the ADA because the only departmental positions available under the employer's policy were voicephone positions. The applicant could not perform the essential functions of those jobs because of his hearing impairment, and the district court limited its analysis of his qualifications to those positions. However, the appellate court held that the non-voicephone positions—which certain incumbent employees who were hearing-impaired occupied successfully—should have been considered in the analysis of whether the candidate was a "qualified individual." It also held that the employer's policy of limiting the non-voicephone positions to current company employees raised questions that should have gone to the jury.

VI. Preemployment Inquiries and Medical Examinations

Prohibited discrimination under the ADA includes preemployment medical examinations and disability-related inquiries.[61] An employer may not conduct a medical examination

---

[59] 42 U.S.C. §12111(8) (1995).
[60] Davidson v. America Online, Inc., 337 F.3d 1179, 14 AD Cases 1185 (10th Cir. 2003).
[61] 42 U.S.C. §12112(d)(2) (1995).

of an applicant.[62] Additionally, an employer may not ask if a job applicant has a disability or inquire as to the nature and severity of such a disability.[63] As a general principle, an employer may only ask disability-related questions[64] and require medical examinations of an applicant *after* the applicant receives a conditional job offer.[65]

The ADA provides separate rules for medical examinations and disability-related inquiries.[66] These rules are further classified by their application to particular stages in the employment process.[67] For example, one provision applies to medical examinations and disability-related inquiries of applicants at the pre-offer stage of employment.[68] At a later point in the hiring process, the postoffer stage, another provision applies.[69] Under this provision, employers can condition an offer of employment

---

[62] *Id.* §12112(d)(2)(A) (1995).

[63] *Id.*

[64] According to the EEOC, a "disability-question" is a question that is likely to elicit information about a disability. *See* ADA ENFORCEMENT GUIDANCE, *supra* note 34 (explaining 42 U.S.C. §12112(d)(2)); *see also* Grenier v. Cyanamid Plastics, 70 F.3d 667, 671–72, 673, 5 AD Cases 75, 80 (1st Cir. 1995) ("The Guidance was designed 'for interim use by EEOC investigators, pending coordination with other federal agencies.' . . . It is not binding law, but as a detailed analysis of the relevant ADA provisions, it aids our interpretation of the statute," quoting ADA ENFORCEMENT GUIDANCE, *supra* note 34).

[65] Cole v. Staff Temps., 554 N.W.2d 699, 706 (Iowa 1996); *see also* ADA ENFORCEMENT GUIDANCE, *supra* note 34) (explaining 42 U.S.C. §12112(d)(2)).

[66] *See* Grenier, 70 F.3d at 671–72 (citing 42 U.S.C. §12112(d)(1)).

[67] *See* Harris v. Harris & Hart, Inc., 206 F.3d 838, 841, 10 AD Cases 481, 483 (9th Cir. 2000) ("With regard to an employer's request for medical examinations and inquiries, the ADA sets up separate rules for pre-offer job applications . . . ."); 42 U.S.C. §§12112(d)(2)(A), (d)(3), (d)(4)(A). (Note, however, that §12112(d)(4), providing that "a covered entity shall not require a medical examination and shall not make *inquiries of an employee*," is not relevant to the hiring process, which is the focus of this chapter, and will not be discussed. (emphasis added)).

[68] 42 U.S.C. §12112(d)(2)(A) (1995) ("a covered entity shall not conduct a medical examination or make inquiries of a *job applicant* as to whether such applicant is an individual with a disability or as to the nature or severity of such disability" (emphasis added)).

[69] 42 U.S.C. §12112(d)(3) (1995) ("A covered entity may require a medical examination *after an offer of employment has been made* to a job applicant and prior to the commencement of the employment duties of such applicant, and may condition an offer of employment on the results of such examination, if—(A) all entering employees are subjected to such an examination regardless of disability; (B) information obtained regarding the medical condition or history of applicant is collected and maintained on separate forms and in separate medical files and is treated as

on the results of a medical examination.[70] However, such a postoffer medical examination may not be administered in a discriminatory manner.[71] Furthermore, to protect the applicant's privacy, the ADA requires that an employer store the results of an applicant's postoffer medical examination in a file separate from the applicant's employee file.[72]

A. Disability-Related Inquiries

1. The Prima Facie Case

The ADA explicitly prohibits an employer from making disability-related inquiries of employees, unless the inquiry is job-related or consistent with business necessity.[73] This prohibition also applies to inquiries directed at job applicants.[74] The prima facie case for claims asserting that an employer asked a disability-related question differs from the prima facie case that an applicant must set forth in other ADA claims. When alleging that an employer violated the ADA by making disability-related inquiries, an applicant need not show that he is an individual with an actual disability. Therefore, unlike other claims under the ADA, an applicant need not necessarily be disabled to bring a section 12112(d)(2)(A) claim or a section 12112(d)(4)(A) claim.

Some jurisdictions hold that requiring an applicant to prove that he has a disability while such applicant attempts to preserve his right not to be arbitrarily asked about a disability,

---

a confidential medical record . . .; (C) the results of such examination are used only in accordance with [the ADA]" (emphasis added)).

[70] 42 U.S.C. §12112(d)(3) (1995).
[71] *Id.* §12112(d)(3)(A) (1995).
[72] *Id.* §12112(d)(3)(B) (1995).
[73] *See* Roe v. Cheyenne Mountain Conference Resort, Inc., 124 F.3d 1221, 1229, 7 AD Cases 779 (10th Cir. 1997) (citing 42 U.S.C. §12112(d)(4)(A), which prohibits employers from subjecting current employees to disability-related inquiries).
[74] *But see* Griffin v. Steeltek, Inc., 261 F.3d 1026, 12 AD Cases 248 (10th Cir. 2001) (employer's questions regarding an applicant's medical history and condition technically violated ADA's prohibitions, but did not necessarily constitute a compensable injury, unless plaintiff shows employer engaged in unlawful intentional discrimination).

defies the logic of the ADA's prohibition of disability-related questioning.[75] As a result, an applicant may, under narrow circumstances, seek protection under the ADA despite the fact that the applicant is not disabled. The likely scenario from which such a claim could arise exists when an employer asks an applicant a disability-related question, the applicant responds to the impermissible inquiry, and then the employer rejects the applicant on the basis of the applicant's response to the disability-related question. In this context, the applicant, although not disabled, may make a prima facie case for disability discrimination. However, if the applicant does not provide information or provides false information[76] in response to the employer's disability-related question, he may not later bring a claim under the provision of the ADA that prohibits employers from asking disability-related inquiries.[77]

2. Purpose for Prohibiting Disability-Related Inquiries

The purpose underlying the prohibition of disability-related inquiries at the preoffer stage of employment is to provide applicants with an immediate safeguard against disability discrimination.[78] The EEOC, interpreting the ADA's pre-employment protections, recognized that employers subject

---

[75] *Griffin*, 160 F.3d at 593–94. *But see* Brennan v. Mercedes Benz USA, 388 F.3d 133, 16 AD Cases 15 (5th Cir. 2004); Green v. Joy Cone Co., 2004 U.S. App. LEXIS 16612 (3d Cir. 2004) (unpublished opinion).

[76] *See* Downs v. Massachusetts Bay Transp. Auth., 13 F. Supp. 2d 130, 133, 8 AD Cases 447 (D. Mass. 1998) (On a medical history form asking whether the applicant had received workers' compensation, the applicant answered "no" despite the fact that he had received workers' compensation on several prior occasions. While finding that the application question constituted an impermissible disability-related inquiry, the court decided that the employer was not liable when, after hiring the applicant, the employer fired the applicant for falsifying information on the medical history form. The reasoning for the holding centered on the conclusion that the employee was not a qualified individual with a disability under the ADA because the employee was not actually disabled and the employee could not show that the employer regarded the employee as being disabled.).

[77] *See* Armstrong v. Turner Indus., 141 F.3d 554, 558, 8 AD Cases 118 (5th Cir. 1998) (§12112(d)(2)(A) does not present cognizable harm for nondisabled applicant).

[78] Harris v. Harris & Hart, 206 F.3d 838, 842, 10 AD Cases 481 (9th Cir. 2000) (citing 135 CONG. REC. S10,768 (daily ed. Sept. 7, 1989) (statement of Sen. Tom Harkin (D-Iowa)), explaining purpose of preoffer prohibition of disability-related

applicants to many types of preemployment reviews.[79] Simultaneously, employers may evaluate applicants through interviews, written tests, reference checks, and applications.[80] Under such systems of review, if an applicant with a disability received a rejection for the position, he or she could not know whether the rejection occurred because of a negative job reference or because the employer asked the applicant to indicate whether he or she had a disability. Confronting the intermingling mechanics of the hiring decision, Congress devised preemployment protections under the ADA.

3. Permissible Inquiries in the Hiring Process

Exceptions exist to the ADA's prohibition of preoffer disability inquiries.[81] One exception permits the use of preoffer inquiries when the inquiry relates "to the ability of an applicant to perform job-related functions."[82] Another exception applies when an employer can reasonably believe that an applicant's known disability will interfere with the performance of job-related functions.[83] Finally, an exception exists when the applicant requests a reasonable accommodation for the application process or for the employment position.[84] Along with various exceptions, there is an exclusion to the rule prohibiting disability-related inquiries. While an employer cannot make disability-related inquiries, an employer can pose questions regarding a physical impairment that is not considered a disability.[85]

---

inquiries as follows, "[t]he rationale behind the prohibition is that 'individuals with disabilities must be allowed a fair opportunity to be judged on their qualifications, 'to get past that initial barrier' where an employment judgment might be unfairly made . . . .").

[79] See ADA ENFORCEMENT GUIDANCE, supra note 34.
[80] See id.
[81] See Harris, 206 F.3d at 843.
[82] Id. (citing 42 U.S.C. §12112(d)(2)(B) (1995)).
[83] Id. (citing 29 C.F.R. §1630.14(a) (1991)).
[84] Id. at 842 n.3, 10 AD Cases at 484 n.3 (citing ADA ENFORCEMENT GUIDANCE, supra note 34, §IV.B.6.b.).
[85] See Murray v. John D. Archbold Mem'l Hosp., 50 F. Supp. 2d 1368, 1379 (M.D. Ga. 1999) (employer's preemployment inquiry regarding weight-to-height ratio of applicant did not violate §12112(d)(2) because "weight policy inquired into an applicant's weight, and not into an applicant's would-be 'disability,' as that term is defined by the ADA").

a. Inquiries Regarding Nondisabling Impairments

While the ADA prohibits disability-related inquiries, it does not restrain inquiries that pertain to nondisabling conditions.[86] Generally, an employer may ask a question regarding an applicant's physical impairment if the question will not likely elicit information about whether the applicant has a disability.[87] More precisely, an employer may ask an applicant with a broken leg how he or she broke his or her leg, because such impairments typically do not rise to the same level as a disability. Alternatively, an employer may not ask an applicant with a broken leg whether his or her bones are fragile, because this sort of question will likely elicit an underlying permanently disabling condition.[88]

Along the same line of reasoning, an employer may ask an applicant if he or she currently uses illegal drugs, because the ADA does not cover such persons. However, in most circumstances, an employer may not ask an applicant about the lawful use of prescription drugs, because such an inquiry may lead to information related to an underlying disability. At the same time, courts have on some occasions upheld an employer's exclusion of job applications taking certain prescription drugs. In *EEOC v. J.B. Hunt Transport, Inc.*,[89] the U.S. Court of Appeals for the Second Circuit rejected the agency's challenge to the employer's practice of rejecting certain truck driver applicants who took certain medications that could impair their ability to drive, because their exclusion from those specific jobs did not establish that the employer perceived them to be substantially limited in a broad range of jobs.

Additionally, an employer may not inquire about an applicant's past illegal drug use because such a question may lead to information about past drug addiction, which is protected under the ADA as a disabling condition. As a general guideline, employers should avoid asking questions related to major life

---

[86] *Id.*
[87] *See* ADA ENFORCEMENT GUIDANCE, *supra* note 34.
[88] *Id.*
[89] 321 F.3d 69, 13 AD Cases 1697 (2d Cir. 2003).

activities such as walking, breathing, standing, or reproduction. Almost always, questions about major life activities seem related to a disability, unless they are specifically connected to performing job functions.[90]

b. Inquiries Related to the Performance of Job-Related Functions

Federal regulations, promulgated for the purpose of enforcing the ADA, specifically authorize employers to make certain preemployment inquiries with regard to disabled applicants.[91] To supplement the federal regulations permitting disability-related inquiries under particular circumstances, the EEOC created an appendix to its ADA regulations.[92] Some jurisdictions rely on the appendix when interpreting the ADA preemployment provisions.[93] However, the same jurisdictions remain mindful of the principle that, while the EEOC's administrative interpretations of the ADA may serve as guidance, the interpretations are not controlling on the courts.[94]

Under the federal regulations, an employer may ask an applicant to describe or demonstrate how the applicant will perform job-related functions with or without a reasonable accommodation.[95] However, in making such a request, the

---

[90] *Id.*

[91] *See* 29 C.F.R. §1630.14(a) (2003); Downs v. Massachusetts Bay Transp. Auth., 13 F. Supp. 2d 130, 138, 8 AD Cases 447, 455 (D. Mass. 1998) ("The ADA Enforcement Guidance includes examples which are useful in discerning the line between improper disability-related questions and acceptable questions about job performance.").

[92] *See* 29 C.F.R. pt. 1630, app. (2003).

[93] *See* Grenier v. Cyanamid Plastics, 70 F.3d 667, 672, 5 AD Cases 75 (1st Cir. 1995) (citing Carparts Distribution Ctr., Inc. v. Automobile Wholesaler's Ass'n, 37 F.3d 12, 16, 3 AD Cases 1237 (1st Cir. 1994)); *Downs*, 13 F. Supp. 2d at 138, 8 AD Cases at 455 ("Further guidance can be found in the appendix to the implementing regulations.").

[94] *Grenier*, 70 F.3d at 672 (citing Meritor Sav. Bank v. Vinson, 477 U.S. 57, 40 FEP Cases 1822 (1986)).

[95] *See, e.g., id.* at 672 (citing 29 C.F.R. §1630.14(a)); Hoffman v. Fidelity Brokerage Servs., 959 F. Supp. 452, 458, 6 AD Cases 651, 657 (S.D. Ohio 1997) ("A covered entity may make pre-employment inquiries into the ability of an applicant to perform job-related functions, and/or may ask an applicant to describe or to demonstrate how, with or without reasonable accommodation, the applicant will be able to perform job-related functions."); Barnes v. Cochran, 944 F. Supp. 897, 905, 5 AD

employer's inquiry must be narrowly tailored, merely asking about the applicant's *ability* to perform the job, rather than framing the inquiry in terms of the applicant's disability.[96] For example, an employer may state the physical requirements of a job and then ask if the applicant can meet the stated requirements.[97]

c. Inquiries Related to Known Disabilities

Following this reasoning, courts allow employers to extend the breadth of a disability-related inquiry when an employer is *aware* of an applicant's disability.[98] The federal regulations provide authority for expanding the scope of the employer's inquiry in this context.[99] Under the federal regulations, an

---

Cases 1685, 1690 (S.D. Fla. 1996) (The ADA "does not completely preclude [employers] from making pre-employment inquiries into the abilities of its applicants to perform the jobs they seek, but instead 'permits an "interactive process" beneficial to both the employer and applicant;'" quoting *Grenier*, 70 F.3d at 675).

[96] *See e.g.*, Harris v. Harris & Hart, 206 F.3d 838, 842 n.5, 10 AD Cases 481, 484 n.5 (9th Cir. 2000); *Grenier*, 70 F.3d at 673 ("An employer also may ask an applicant to describe or demonstrate, at the pre-offer stage, how [he or she] would perform job-related functions, with or without reasonable accommodation, because these inquiries elicit information about an applicant's ability, not information about an applicant's disability," quoting ADA ENFORCEMENT GUIDANCE, *supra* note 34, §IV.B.6.a.); Cole v. Staff Temps, 554 N.W.2d 699, 706–07 (Iowa 1996) ("an inquiry into a job-related function must be narrowly tailored, and it should not be phrased in terms of disability").

[97] *See Cole*, 554 N.W.2d at 707 (recognizing that "an employer may state its attendance requirements and ask whether an applicant can meet them, but it may not, at the pre-offer stage, ask how many days an applicant was sick . . . [or inquire about] job-related injuries or workers' compensation history" (citation omitted)).

[98] *Barnes*, 944 F. Supp. at 905, 5 AD Cases at 1690 (citing *Grenier*, 70 F.3d at 675 n.4) (employer does not have to "ignore any disabilities of which it is aware," but rather, "the permissible range of an employer's inquiry may be extended when it is aware of an applicant's disability"). *Harris*, 206 F.3d at 842; Grenier v. Cyanamid Plastics, 70 F.3d 667, 673, 5 AD Cases 75, 80 (1st Cir. 1995) (quoting ADA ENFORCEMENT GUIDANCE, *supra* note 34, *reprinted in* EEOC Compl. Man. (CCH) ¶ 6093, at 5371), providing that "allowing an employer to ask an applicant with a known disability to describe or demonstrate how he would perform a job-related function 'is in the interest of both applicants and employers.'" §IV.B.5.b. n.23. "Employers are entitled to know whether an applicant with an apparently interfering disability can perform job-related functions, with or without reasonable accommodation. It is in the interest of an applicant with such a disability to describe or demonstrate performance in order to dispel notions that [he or she] is unable to perform the job because of the disability," *id.* §IV.B.5.b.

[99] *See Hoffman*, 959 F. Supp. at 460, 6 AD Cases at 658 (employer did not violate ADA's preemployment provisions by making prehire inquiries into whether

employer may make requests of an applicant whose known disability may interfere with, or prevent, the performance of a job-related function, whether or not the employer routinely makes such a request of all applicants vying for the job.[100] The employer may be deemed "aware" if the applicant voluntarily discloses that she has a disability or if the disability is obvious to the employer.[101] An example of an obvious disability may be the applicant's use of a wheelchair during an interview, apparently indicating that the applicant cannot walk. In this context, if an essential functions of the job is driving, an employer may ask an applicant to describe or demonstrate how she will drive if the employer reasonably believes that the applicant will not be able to drive because of the disability.[102]

If an employer asks an applicant with a known disability to demonstrate how the applicant will perform the job functions, the employer must provide the applicant with a reasonable accommodation for the purpose of demonstrating the job function.[103] If an accommodation for the demonstration cannot be provided at the time of the interview, the employer must permit the applicant to explain how she could perform the job function if a reasonable accommodation were later provided.[104] This describes the employer's affirmative duty to accommodate

---

applicant's known disability (applicant voluntarily disclosed to employer during interview that she was legally blind) would prevent her from performing certain job functions, because such inquiry was expressly permitted under federal regulations at 29 C.F.R. §1630.14(a)).

[100] *Id.* at 458, 6 AD Cases at 657 (citing 29 C.F.R. pt. 1630, app. §1630.14(a)).

[101] *See* ADA ENFORCEMENT GUIDANCE, *supra* note 34; *Grenier,* 70 F.3d at 673; Hoffman v. Fidelity Brokerage Servs., 959 F. Supp. 452, 460, 6 AD Cases 651 (S.D. Ohio 1997).

[102] *See* ADA ENFORCEMENT GUIDANCE, *supra* note 34; *Grenier,* 70 F.3d at 672–73, 5 AD Cases at 79–80 ("For example, an employer may ask an individual with one leg who applies for a position as a home washing machine repairman to demonstrate or to explain how, with or without accommodation, he would be able to transport himself and his tools down the basement stairs. However, the employer may not inquire as to the nature or severity of the disability. Therefore, for example, the employer cannot ask how the individual lost the leg or whether the loss of the leg is indicative of an underlying impairment.").

[103] *Hoffman,* 959 F. Supp. at 458, 6 AD Cases at 657 (citing 29 C.F.R. pt. 1630, app. §1630.14(a)).

[104] *Id.*

a job applicant with a known disability. The duty to provide reasonable accommodations for the hiring process is triggered when the employer knows of an applicant's disability, inquires about the ability of the applicant to perform the job tasks, and then requires the applicant to explain or demonstrate how the applicant will perform the essential job functions.[105]

The employer may not exclude the applicant from consideration for the job if the task that the applicant cannot perform is not an essential function of the job.[106] Thus, if an employer requires the applicant with a known disability to demonstrate her ability to perform a job function, the job function must be essential to the position that the applicant seeks. If the job function is not essential, the applicant may require that the employer reasonably accommodate her by either transferring the function to another employee or exchanging the function for a function that the applicant can perform.[107]

Before providing any reasonable accommodations, the employer may ask an applicant for documentation of her disability.[108] Under such circumstances, the employer may also ask a third party whether the applicant has a disability.[109] A request for documentation of the applicant's disability underscores the employer's willingness to participate in the process of determining whether reasonable accommodations exist.[110]

---

[105] Note, however, that while an employer may ask applicants whether they need a reasonable accommodation for the hiring process, the employer may not ask if an applicant needs a reasonable accommodation to perform the job functions unless the applicant's disability is obvious or known to the employer by virtue of the applicant's voluntary disclosure. EEOC, Enforcement Guidance: Pre-employment Disability Related Questions and Medical Examinations, No. 915.002 (Oct. 10, 1995); Grenier v. Cyanamid Plastics, 70 F.3d 667, 673–74 (1st Cir. 1995).

[106] *Hoffman*, 959 F. Supp. at 458–59, 6 AD Cases at 657 (citing 29 C.F.R. pt. 1630, app. §1630.14(a)).

[107] *Id.* at 459, 6 AD Cases at 657 (citing 29 C.F.R. pt. 1630, app. §1630.14(a)).

[108] Grenier v. Cyanamid Plastics, 70 F.3d 667, 674, 5 AD Cases 75, 81 (1st Cir. 1995) ("EEOC reasoned that such requests are not prohibited pre-offer inquiries because: [r]equesting such documentation is consistent with the ADA's legislative history. For example, Congress specifically anticipated that when an applicant requests reasonable accommodation for the application process..., the employer should engage in an interactive process with the individual to determine an effective reasonable accommodation.").

[109] *Id.* at 676.

[110] *Id.* at 674.

Thus, an employer's request for documentation of the applicant's disability supports the ADA's objectives.

In some cases, even if an employer's inquiries at the pre-employment stage regarding an applicant's medical history or condition violate the ADA, courts may find that the plaintiff has failed to establish any compensable injury.[111]

B. Medical Examinations

Like disability-related inquiries, the ADA imposes specific conditions on the employer's use of medical examinations.[112] For instance, the ADA distinguishes pre- and postoffer medical examinations.[113] Separate ADA provisions exist for the two categories of medical examinations.[114] This pre-/postoffer medical examination distinction may seem arbitrary. However, the distinction provides several important purposes.[115]

For one, the distinction allows an applicant to demonstrate that he or she has the necessary job qualifications without regard to a disability.[116] Reserving the use of a medical examination until the employer makes a conditional offer of employment reduces the risk that qualified applicants with disabilities will be summarily excluded at the initial stage of the hiring process. For example, suppose an applicant meets the minimal qualifications for the position, except for satisfying the medical examination. By making an offer of employment conditioned on favorable results of the medical examination, an employer admits, to some extent, that the applicant is minimally qualified. Reciprocally, the applicant accepts the possibility of rejection for the job if the applicant receives poor medical examination results. Given these two acknowledgments, the employer

---

[111] *See, e.g.,* Griffin v. Steeltek, Inc., 261 F.3d 1026, 12 AD Cases 248 (10th Cir. 2001).

[112] 42 U.S.C. §12112(d)(1) (1995).

[113] 42 U.S.C. §12112(d)(2)(A) (1995) (referring to the general prohibition of pre-offer medical examinations) and 42 U.S.C. §12112(d)(3) (1995) (describing the proper use of postoffer medical examinations).

[114] *See id.*

[115] Barnes v. Cochran, 944 F. Supp. 897, 905 n.3, 5 AD Cases 1685, 1690 n.3 (S.D. Fla. 1996) (citing Bagley, *Enough is Enough! Congress and the Courts React to Employers' Medical Screening and Surveillance Procedure,* 99 Dick. L. Rev. 723, 730–31 (1995)).

[116] *Id.*

and the applicant are more informed about the reasons supporting the applicant's rejection. With this shared information, it is more likely that an employer and the applicant will engage in discussions that explore reasonable accommodations allowing the applicant to perform the required functions of the job despite the applicant's disabling condition. In effect, the pre-/postoffer distinction permits an applicant and an employer the opportunity to discuss reasonable accommodations.

Another important function served by the distinction is that, with pre-employment medical examinations administered before a conditional offer of employment, an employer must show that its purpose for testing the applicant is job-related or consistent with a business necessity.[117] However, if the employer recognizes that the applicant is minimally qualified for the position and makes an offer of employment conditioned on the results of a preemployment medical examination, the employer need not show that the examination is job-related or consistent with a business necessity.[118] In this manner, the ADA makes an employer's rejection of an applicant based on the results of a preoffer medical examination much more difficult to justify. This is particularly true when the employer interprets medical examination test results in an overly broad manner, such as circumstances in which one excludes applicants based on a physician's opinion that the individual "may have difficulty" in the work environment.[119]

1. Pre-Offer Medical Examinations

Generally, the ADA prohibits an employer from requiring an applicant to submit to a medical examination before the employer extends a conditional offer of employment.[120] This prohibition applies to pre-offer medical examinations, unless

---

[117] *Id.*
[118] EEOC v. Blue Cross Blue Shield of Conn., 30 F. Supp. 2d 296, 303 (D. Conn. 1998) (citing 29 C.F.R. pt. 1630, app. §1630.14(b), and Norman-Bloodsaw v. Lawrence Berkeley Lab., 135 F.3d 1260, 1273, 7 AD Cases 1395 (9th Cir. 1998). Medical examinations required of individuals to whom a job offer has been extended need not be job-related nor justified by business necessity.
[119] Ollie v. Titan Tire Corp., 336 F.3d 680, 14 AD Cases 993 (8th Cir. 2003).
[120] 42 U.S.C. §12112(d)(2)(A) (1995).

the employer can show that the medical examination was job-related or consistent with the employer's business necessity.[121] An employer's reliance on a preoffer medical examination to determine whether an applicant has the requisite minimal qualifications satisfies the "job-relatedness" or "business necessity" requirement.[122] Therefore, if the preoffer medical examination reveals whether an applicant is minimally qualified for the job, the examination is permissible under the ADA. However, if the employer unjustifiably relies on results from a preoffer medical examination administered in a discriminatory manner, or if the employer improperly characterizes the minimal qualifications, the employer may be held liable under the ADA.[123]

Like disability-related inquiries, an applicant need not prove that he or she is a qualified individual with a disability to challenge preoffer medical examinations under the ADA.[124] In the definitional section of the ADA, the statute's coverage is restricted to "qualified individual[s] with a disability."[125] However, this language, "qualified individual[s] with a disability,"

---

[121] 42 U.S.C. §12113(a) (1995); *see also* 29 C.F.R. §1630.14(a) (2003); Prado v. Continental Air Transp. Co., 982 F. Supp. 1304, 1306–07 (N.D. Ill. 1997) (applicant with atrophied leg who applied for driver position was required to submit to physical examination before receiving conditional offer of employment; court found that even though medical examination was administered before conditional offer of employment, such requirement was not in violation of ADA, because minimum safety standards required all drivers to pass physical exam and therefore, in failing exam, applicant was not qualified individual subject to protections of ADA.); *but see* EEOC v. Texas Bus Lines, 923 F. Supp. 965, 973, 5 AD Cases 878 (S.D. Tex. 1996) (Employer interviewed applicant for a bus driver position and then, without extending a conditional offer of employment, asked applicant to undergo a physical examination as mandated by department of transportation regulations. The examining doctor erroneously refused to certify the applicant and the employer rejected the applicant based on the medical report. The employer was held liable under the ADA, because the court found that the employer knew, or should have known, that the regulations did not mandate that applicants be disqualified due to excessive weight. Thus, the employer could not escape liability by shielding itself under the mandate of the regulations, because the employer's belief that the applicant did not meet the minimal requirements of the position was "wholly unreasonable.").

[122] *See Prado*, 982 F. Supp. at 1306–07.

[123] *See Texas Bus Lines*, 923 F. Supp. at 973, 979.

[124] Fredenburg v. Contra Costa County Dep't of Health Servs., 172 F.3d 1176, 1179, 9 AD Cases 385 (9th Cir. 1999) (agreeing with *Roe v. Cheyenne Mountain Conference Resort, Inc.*, 124 F.3d 1221, 1229, 7 AD Cases 779 (10th Cir. 1997)).

[125] 42 U.S.C. §12112(a) (1995).

is not reproduced in the preemployment provisions pertaining to the discriminatory use of disability-related inquiries[126] and medical examinations. Because of the ADA's omission of the "qualified individual" language in the preemployment provisions, courts have interpreted the medical examination provisions to not only protect qualified individuals with disabilities, but also protect those employees and applicants without disabilities.[127] For example, courts reason that an employer violates the ADA when it requires applicants to take a human immunodeficiency virus (HIV) test that is not job-related even when the applicant does not have a disabling condition.[128] According to these decisions, requiring the applicants who challenge the HIV testing to establish that they actually have HIV defeats the purpose of the prohibition, which is to prevent employers from using medical examinations arbitrarily to discover whether a disabling condition exists.[129] In other settings, however, employers have turned back challenges to applicant testing.[130]

2. *Postoffer Medical Examinations*

The language of the ADA does not require that an employer's preemployment medical examination be job-related or consistent with a business necessity if the examination occurs after an applicant receives an offer of employment.[131] By releasing an

---

[126] 42 U.S.C. §12112(d)(2), (d)(3) & (d)(4) (1995) (these sections only refer to "employee" and "applicant," not a "qualified individual with a disability").

[127] *Fredenburg*, 172 F.3d at 1182, 9 AD Cases at 390 ("protecting only qualified individuals would defeat much of the usefulness of those sections.")

[128] *Id.*

[129] *Id.*

[130] The EEOC failed in two challenges to employers who denied employment based on the results of tests intended to identify susceptibility to carpal tunnel syndrome, because view of applicants as limited in performing a specific job did not constitute perception as to broad category of jobs, and therefore, did not violate the ADA. *See* EEOC v. Woodbridge Corp., 263 F.3d 812, 12 AD Cases 254 (8th Cir. 2001); EEOC v. Rockwell Int'l Corp., 243 F.3d 1012, 11 AD Cases 929 (7th Cir. 2001).

[131] *See* 42 U.S.C. §12112(d)(3) (1995); *see also* ADA ENFORCEMENT GUIDANCE, *supra* note 34; *see also* EEOC v. Blue Cross Blue Shield of Conn., 30 F. Supp. 2d 296, 303 (D. Conn. 1998). Thus, even where an employer used blood and urine samples obtained in a post-offer exam to test prospective employees for sickle cell trait, pregnancy, and syphilis, that did not rise to the level of a cognizable ADA claim (although Constitutinal limitations on search and seizure by that employer were violated). Norman-Bloodsaw v. Lawrence Berkeley Labs, 135 F.3d 1260 (9th Cir. 1998).

employer from the prerequisite showings of job-relatedness and business necessity, the ADA indirectly encourages the use of employment offers conditioned on preemployment medical examinations.[132] Unlike preoffer medical examinations, which require job-relatedness and business necessity, the ADA specifies three alternative procedural safeguards for postoffer medical examinations.[133] First, the employer must administer the medical examinations in a nondiscriminatory manner.[134] Additionally, the employer must adhere to confidentiality requirements under the ADA by storing medical examination results in a file separate from the employee file.[135] Finally, more broadly, the ADA dictates that an employer shall not use the results of the postoffer medical examination to defy the antidiscriminatory purpose of the ADA.[136] As a whole, these postoffer restrictions are more easily satisfied by employers than the burdensome preoffer "job-relatedness and business necessity" counterparts. By way of example, an employer was able to defeat an applicant's discrimination allegations when it failed to hire him following a physical examination conducted after a conditional offer of employment was made. When the medical exam indicated that the applicant was restricted in performing

---

[132] 42 U.S.C. §12112(d)(3) (1995).

[133] 42 U.S.C. §12112(d)(3)(A), (B), & (C) (1995); Blue Cross Blue Shield of Conn., 30 F. Supp. at 303.

[134] 42 U.S.C. §12112(d)(3)(A) (1995); Stinson v. West Suburban Hosp. Med. Ctr., 1998 WL 188938 (N.D. Ill. 1998) (employer entitled to make employment offer conditioned on results of postoffer medical examination as long as examination is administered in nondiscriminatory manner).

[135] 42 U.S.C. §12112(d)(3)(B) (1995).

[136] 42 U.S.C. §12112(d)(3)(C) (1995); see EEOC v. Dolphin Cruise Line, Inc., 945 F. Supp. 1550, 6 AD Cases 187 (S.D. Fla. 1996) (ADA violation when employer, after applicant tested positive for HIV, rescinded employment offer conditioned on medical examination that included HIV test); Holiday v. City of Chattanooga, 206 F.3d 637, 641–45, 10 AD Cases 501 (6th Cir. 2000) (employer unlawfully rescinded conditional offer of employment to applicant for police officer position, because at physical examination applicant revealed he was HIV-positive and employer withdrew offer based on unsupported belief that applicant, although asymptomatic, could not perform police work); Doe v. District of Columbia, 796 F. Supp. 559, 2 AD Cases 197 (D.D.C. 1992) (employer violated Rehabilitation Act when it withdrew its offer of employment based on applicant's HIV status although employer lacked any objective medical evidence supporting its belief that applicant's physical condition rendered him unable to perform essential functions of job as firefighter).

the job at issue (order-selector in a warehouse), the employer was not informed of the specific condition causing the limitation, assisting its subsequent argument that it did not view him as unable to perform other manual labor positions, or other positions in warehouses.[137] Similarly, a medical exam required for a police officer was an appropriate postoffer examination, because all relevant non-medical information has been evaluated by the employer prior to making the offer and the requirement was applied to all candidates at that stage of the hiring process.[138]

In contrast, the U.S. Court of Appeals for the Tenth Circuit upheld a jury's conclusion that an employer had improperly utilized a postoffer medical exam when it withdrew a conditional job offer for reasons that were neither job-related nor consistent with business necessity.[139] Rather, the jury's conclusion that the employer improperly focused on injuries by the plaintiff in a short period of time to predict that he posed a high risk of future injury, due to a perceived disability.

3. What Is a Medical Examination?

Because the ADA subjects the employer's use of medical examinations to specific limitations, determining what constitutes a "medical examination" for the purposes of the ADA becomes extremely important. Neither the ADA nor the federal regulations define the term "medical examination."[140] The EEOC, however, defines a medical examination as "a procedure or test that seeks information about an individual's physical or mental impairment or health."[141] Frequently, courts must

---

[137] Schuler v. SuperValu Inc., 336 F.3d 702, 14 AD Cases 1115 (8th Cir. 2003).
[138] O'Neal v. City of New Albany, 293 F.3d 998, 13 AD Cases 289 (7th Cir. 2002).
[139] Garrison v. Baker Hughes Oilfield Operations, Inc., 287 F.3d 955 (10th Cir. 2002).
[140] Thompson v. Borg-Warner Protective Servs. Corp., 1996 U.S. Dist. LEXIS 4781, *11–12 (N.D. Cal. 1996) (relying on EEOC's guidelines as the "most comprehensive statement on pre-employment medical examinations to date").
[141] See ADA ENFORCEMENT GUIDANCE, supra note 34.

decide what constitutes a medical examination under the ADA.[142]

The courts identify many factors that can be used when determining whether an examination constitutes a medical examination under the ADA.[143] If the examination tends to disclose specific physical or mental disabilities, the examination may be characterized as a medical examination.[144] Also, if the examination is conducted by a medical professional, the court is more likely to describe the test as a medical examination for the purposes of the ADA.[145] Moreover, whether the examiner reviews the applicant's past medical records could prove the existence of a medical examination under the ADA.[146]

Like the courts, the EEOC lists several factors that are helpful in determining whether the employer's preemployment test can be considered a medical examination under the ADA.[147] If the examination is administered by a health care professional, or someone trained by a health professional, the test could be a medical examination. Another factor that suggests a test is actually a medical examination focuses on whether the examination is designed to reveal an impairment in physical or mental health. Also, if the test involves invasive procedures such as drawing blood samples from applicants, it likely may be considered a medical examination. If the test measures the applicant's physiological response to performing a job task

---

[142] Grenier v. Cyanamid Plastics, 70 F.3d 667, 676, 5 AD Cases 75, 82 (1st Cir. 1995) ("Medical examinations are procedures or tests that seek information about the existence, nature, or severity of an individual's physical or mental impairment, or that seek information regarding an individual's physical or psychological health."); Barnes v. Cochran, 944 F. Supp. 897, 904, 5 AD Cases 1685 (S.D. Fla. 1996) (under ADA, preoffer medical examinations include psychological examinations).

[143] Barnes, 944 F. Supp. at 905 (after examining "nature and extent" of medical examination, preemployment medical examination violated 42 U.S.C. §12112(d)(2)(A)).

[144] Id. (persuasive factor in determining whether preemployment psychological test constituted medical examination was that psychologist's questions probed areas "tending to disclose specific psychological disabilities, such as Post Traumatic Stress Disorder").

[145] Id. (while finding preemployment medical examination violated ADA, court considered fact that test was performed by licensed psychologist).

[146] Id.

[147] See ADA ENFORCEMENT GUIDANCE, supra note 34.

rather than the applicant's ability to perform the task, the test may be construed as a medical examination. The fact that the test involves the use of medical equipment or is performed in a medical setting can support the conclusion that the test is a medical examination.[148]

The EEOC lists several tests that are not considered to be medical examinations under the ADA's preemployment provisions. For example, physical fitness tests that do not measure the applicant's physiological responses are not considered medical examinations. Psychological exams, if used to measure qualities such as honesty or personal tastes, are not deemed medical examinations. Similarly, vision tests that do not require an ophthalmologist or eye charts, but which are given to determine whether an applicant can read labels or differentiate objects are not medical examinations under the ADA. Because the drafters of the ADA refrained from definitively delineating medical examinations from nonmedical preemployment tests, the courts may consider whether a test constitutes a medical examination through an analysis of the facts of each case.

An employer must keep any medical information on applicants or employees confidential, with the following limited exceptions: (1) supervisors and managers may be told about necessary restrictions on the work or duties of the employee and about necessary accommodations; (2) first aid and safety personnel may be told if the disability might require emergency treatment; (3) government officials investigating compliance with the ADA must be given relevant information on request; (4) employers may use the information for insurance purposes;[149] (5) employers may share the information with their employees who are making hiring decisions so the decisionmakers may comply with the ADA.[150] Absent these exceptions, "an employer must keep medical information confidential even if someone is no longer an applicant (for example, [he or she] was'nt hired) or is no longer an employee."[151]

---
[148] *Id.*
[149] *See* 29 U.S.C. §501(c); 42 U.S.C. §12201 (Supp. III 1991).
[150] *See* ADA ENFORCEMENT GUIDANCE, *supra* note 34.
[151] *Id.*

The U.S. Court of Appeals for the Fifth Circuit has held that a veteran pipefitter could not proceed with a discriminatory hiring claim because he had failed to create a triable issue through his allegation that the weightlifting test used by his prospective employer was unrelated to the functions of the job at issue. In *Fuzy v. S&B Engineers & Constructors, Ltd.*,[152] the applicant was unable to lift 100 pounds without assistance, a standard that the company drew from the *Dictionary of Occupational Titles* published by the U.S. Department of Labor. He was unable to rebut the company's evidence that the lifting requirement was job-related, and the appellate court affirmed the dismissal of his claim.

4. Disputes Over Conclusions of Medical Examinations

The ADA permits employers to use preemployment medical examinations of applicants after extending a bona fide conditional offer of employment.[153] However, the employer's reliance on the results of postoffer medical examinations may be disputed. When an employer rejects an applicant for a position because of examination results reached by a doctor who did not use objective medical knowledge, the employer's reliance on the doctor's conclusions appears irrational. If the court finds that the employer's reliance on the results was indeed irrational, the employer can be held liable under the ADA.[154] Therefore, the employer cannot shield itself from liability by relying on an examining doctor's opinion, if such reliance can be deemed unreasonable[155] or they may be misinterpreted or misapplied by the employer.[156]

---

[152] 332 F.3d 301, 14 AD Cases 676 (5th Cir. 2003), *cert. denied*, 540 U.S. 1108, 15 AD Cases 128 (2004).

[153] 42 U.S.C. §12112(d)(3) (1995).

[154] EEOC v. Texas Bus Lines, 923 F. Supp. 965, 5 AD Cases 878 (S.D. Tex. 1996).

[155] *See id.* at 973 (employer could determine from doctor's examination report that doctor's opinion was not supported by any objective medical evidence and, because employer knew or should have known that doctor's conclusion was unfounded, employer's reliance on the doctor's opinion was unreasonable).

[156] *See* Ollie v. Titan Tire Corp., 336 F.3d 680, 14 AD Cases 993 (8th Cir. 2003), *reh'g denied*, 2003 U.S. App. LEXIS 17250 (2003) (employer relying on doctor's

Thus, employers often must exercise caution if they contemplate rejecting applicants for employment because of the results of a post-offering preemployment medical examination.[157] Because examining physicians typically do not know the essential functions of the job or the requirements of the ADA, the opinions in the examination reports may contain inappropriate conclusions. If an employer suspects that the examination results are unsupported by objective medical evidence, courts suggest that the employer seek a second opinion.[158] If, however, the doctor discovers the presence of a disability that would legitimately interfere with the applicant's ability to perform the essential functions of the position, the employer can lawfully exclude the applicant from further consideration for the job.

When an individual with epilepsy alleged that a grocery chain withdrew a job offer following a post-offer medical exam, the U.S. Court of Appeals for the Eighth Circuit held that this complaint should be dismissed because he failed to show that the employer had knowledge of his specific condition, or that it regarded him as substantially limited in the major life activity of working. In *Schuler v. Supervalu, Inc.*,[159] the company utilized an independent medical examiner, which was advised of the applicant's epilepsy but which did not directly advise the employer of that fact. Instead, it reported the applicant as medically recommended for employment, but with limitations on performance of certain functions and on operation of certain machinery. When the employer withdrew its offer of employment, the applicant asserted that the independent medical examiner's knowledge should be imputed to the company, a position that was rejected by the appellate court.

At the same time, when an individual's medical exam indicated that he was an insulin-dependent diabetic, the U.S. Court of Appeals for the Fifth Circuit (the views of which had

---

evaluation that applicant "may have difficulty" working near dust and fumes inappropriately refused to hire asthmatic job candidate.

[157] *Id.*
[158] *Id.* at 978.
[159] 336 F.3d 702, 14 AD Cases 1115 (8th Cir. 2003).

evolved over the course of the litigation) concluded that the applicant for a law enforcement position should be evaluated individually to determine potential ADA protection. It reversed its prior approach to cases involving insulin-dependent diabetics seeking positions requiring driving. They previously had been viewed as per se presenting a substantial risk that prevented the performance of essential job requirements.[160]

In a 2002 ruling, the Supreme Court held that employers could refuse to hire individuals who pose a "direct threat" to their health or safety, if based on reasonable medical judgment derived from current medical knowledge and/or the best available medical evidence.[161] Such conclusions must be based on individualized assessment of the individual's current ability to perform the job's essential functions.[162]

VII. Preemployment Training Programs

Employers may place applicants who fail to meet the minimal qualifications for the job in training programs.[163] For example, an applicant for a position as a police officer may lack prior policing experience and because of his or her inexperience may be sent to a regional police academy to attain the minimal requirements for the position of a police officer.[164] The possibility of future employment can then be conditioned on successful completion of the training program.[165] Thus, if

---

[160]Kapche v. San Antonio, 304 F.3d 493, 13 AD Cases 907 (5th Cir. 2002).

[161]Chevron U.S.A. Inc. Echazabal, 536 U.S. 73, 13 AD Cases 97 (2002).

[162]Id. On remand, the U.S. Court of Appeals for the Ninth Circuit held that the employer failed to prove that its decision was based on the best available medical evidence. Echazabal v. Chevron U.S.A., Inc., 336 F.3d 1023, 14 AD Cases 1089 (9th Cir. 2003).

[163]Hoffman v. Fidelity Brokerage Servs., 959 F. Supp. 452, 454, 6 AD Cases 651 (S.D. Ohio 1997) (employer required applicants for customer service position to complete computer training for customer service position).

[164]Ethridge v. State, 860 F. Supp. 808, 3 AD Cases 1013 (M.D. Ala. 1994).

[165]Id. at 814 (employer lawfully excluded disabled applicant from consideration for position as police officer when applicant could not successfully complete police academy training requirements).

an applicant with a disability cannot complete the training program, with or without reasonable accommodation, the employer may remove the applicant from the pool of employees considered for the position.[166]

During training, applicants with disabilities are entitled to reasonable accommodations to complete the training program.[167] Preemployment training typically requires that the applicant meet specific standards in order to be considered for employment. By failing to meet such standards, an applicant may be rejected for the position. However, if an applicant has a disability, the employer has a duty to provide reasonable accommodations allowing the applicant the opportunity to fulfill the requirements of the training program.[168] By initiating an informal and interactive process aimed at identifying the applicant's disability-related limitations, the employer satisfies its obligation under the ADA.[169] If the applicant declines a reasonable accommodation offered by the employer, the employer has no further obligations to the applicant under the ADA.[170]

In at least one case, an appeals court held that an individual dropped from a joint labor-management apprenticeship

---

[166] *Id.* (because applicant was unable to safely fire handgun, even with reasonable accommodations, applicant was not qualified individual with disability subject to protections under ADA).

[167] *Hoffman*, 959 F. Supp. at 460 (employer satisfied any obligation it had to reasonably accommodate legally blind applicant when employer discussed assistive technology with applicant, investigated availability and compatibility of such technology, and offered applicant position at another office that had computer system that could operate with assistive technology); *Ethridge*, 860 F. Supp. at 814 (disabled applicant, otherwise qualified to gain entrance into training course, must be reasonably accommodated during that course even if applicant is ultimately deemed not otherwise qualified for position sought).

[168] *Hoffman*, 959 F. Supp. at 460 (employer lawfully rejected legally blind applicant who could not pass computer accuracy tests during training course); *Ethridge*, 860 F. Supp. at 814 (employer met its duty to reasonably accommodate police academy trainee when it allowed trainee to shoot handgun from different stance, permitted retest in handgun course, provided additional instruction during training, and placed trainee on side of shooting range that most benefited his shooting style).

[169] *Hoffman*, 959 F. Supp. at 460, 6 AD Cases at 657 (citing 29 C.F.R. §1630.2(o)(3)).

[170] *Id.* at 460.

program failed to establish that his separation was caused by his attention deficit disorder and depression.[171] The court ruled that the fact that he was unable to succeed in the academic aspects of the training program did not establish that he was unable to learn and had an ADA-protected disability. The fact that he could not pass a few highly specialized courses did not establish a limited ability to learn, particularly in light of the individual's history of academic and job success.

VIII. The Duty to Make Reasonable Accommodations for an Applicant

Reasonable accommodation is a unique and important concept under the ADA. Other federal antidiscrimination statutes, such as Title VII of the Civil Rights Act of 1964,[172] the Age Discrimination in Employment Act of 1967,[173] or the Pregnancy Discrimination Act of 1978[174] typically do not require reasonable accommodations for members of protected categories. Rather, other federal antidiscrimination statutes focus on equal treatment for similarly situated employees and applicants. In contrast, the ADA places an affirmative duty to reasonably accommodate qualified individuals with disabilities within the meaning of the statute.[175]

A. Reasonable Accommodations Under the Rehabilitation Act of 1973

The concept of reasonable accommodations first appeared in section 504 of the Rehabilitation Act.[176] Since the enactment of the Rehabiliation Act, numerous courts have

---

[171] Ristrom v. Asbestos Workers Local 34 Joint Apprentice Comm., 370 F.3d 763, 15 AD Cases 1057 (8th Cir. 2004), *cert. denied,* 2004 U.S. App. LEXIS 15037 (2004).

[172] *See* 42 U.S.C. §2000 et seq.

[173] *See* 29 U.S.C. §626(e).

[174] *See* 42 U.S.C. §2000e(k); 29 C.F.R. §1604.10 (2003).

[175] *See* 29 C.F.R. pt. 1630, app. §1630.2(o) (2003).

[176] *See* 29 U.S.C. §794a(a)(1) (1988) for the requirement of reasonable accommodations under the Rehabilitation Act.

addressed employers' obligation to reasonably accommodate. Because the ADA specifically adopts section 504 case law, the significant cases under the Rehabilitation Act are relevant to an understanding of the development of modern law governing reasonable accommodations.

The Rehabilitation Act requires employers to make reasonable accommodations to work sites that permit otherwise qualified applicants to perform essential job functions.[177] The objectives underlying this provision are to create equal opportunity for disabled persons and to remove obstacles facing applicants.

Regulations formulated under the Rehabilitation Act give examples of the kind of reasonable accommodations intended by the drafters of the ADA.[178] The regulations mention changes to physical structures and job requirements that create increased opportunities for disabled applicants.[179] The list of suggested modifications is not comprehensive, however, and Congress expected employers to adapt to the unanticipated, reasonable needs of disabled applicants as well.[180] An employer does not have to make an accommodation that will place an undue hardship on it.[181] This process requires a fact-specific analysis of each case.[182]

As a general matter, employers must only assess applicants' ability to perform the essential functions of the position for which they are applying.[183] If an applicant is incapable of performing the essential functions of a position, an employer must consider whether it is capable of providing a reasonable accommodation that would enable the applicant to perform the essential functions. A reasonable accommodation is one

---

[177] *Id.*

[178] *See* 29 C.F.R. §1613.704 (1993).

[179] *See* 29 C.F.R. §1613.704(b) (1993). Changing job requirements may include the following: "job restructuring, part-time or modified work schedules, acquisition or modification of equipment or devices, appropriate adjustment or modification of examinations, the provision of readers and interpreters, and other similar actions." *Id.*

[180] *See* 29 C.F.R. §1613.704 (1993).

[181] *See* 29 U.S.C. §794a(a)(1) (1988).

[182] *See* Hall v. U.S. Postal Serv., 857 F.2d 1073, 1079–80, 1 AD Cases 1368 (6th Cir. 1988); *see also* 29 C.F.R. pt. 1630, app. (2003).

[183] *See* 29 C.F.R. §1630.2(m) & (n) (2003).

that would not place an undue hardship on the employer. Thus, employers do not have to change the essential character of a position in order to accommodate a disabled applicant.[184] However, in some circumstances, courts may question an employer's self-imposed limitation on the types of jobs it would consider for external candidates.[185]

Employers may hire a nondisabled applicant instead of a disabled applicant for legitimate reasons unconnected to the disability of the applicant.[186] For instance, if two applicants for an administrative position have different levels of proficiency with certain word processing programs, the employer may legitimately choose to hire the applicant who is most skilled, as long as the ability to use the programs is an essential function of the position.[187] An employer may not, however, favor a nondisabled applicant when a disabled applicant could also meet the requirements if the employer simply provided a reasonable accommodation.[188] The reasonable accommodations provision is an integral component in attaining the objectives of the Rehabilitation Act, and now the ADA, by removing obstacles to employment confronting otherwise qualified disabled applicants.

B. Reasonable Accommodations Under the Americans With Disabilities Act

The reasonable accommodations requirements introduced in the Rehabilitation Act were incorporated into the

---

[184] *See* Strathie v. Department of Transp., 716 F.2d 227, 230, 1 AD Cases 486 (3d Cir. 1983) (accommodation is unreasonable if employer must change essential function of position or if accommodation places excessive financial burden on employer).

[185] *See* Davidson v. America Online, Inc., 337 F.3d 1179, 14 AD Cases 1185 (10th Cir. 2003) (questioned employer's limitation of "qualified individual" analysis to exclude jobs for which it hired only internal candidates).

[186] *See* 29 C.F.R. §1630, app. (2003).

[187] *Id.*

[188] *See* Southeastern Cmty. Coll. v. Davis, 442 U.S. 397, 2 AD Cases 1 (1979) (employer did not have to provide accommodations for hearing-impaired applicant for nursing program, where such accommodations would require wide-ranging changes and impose unreasonable expenses); *see also* 29 C.F.R. §1630.9 (2003).

ADA.[189] The ADA likewise requires employers to determine whether a reasonable accommodation would allow an otherwise qualified disabled applicant to meet job requirements.[190] An employer who fails to make this analysis or who refuses to make reasonable accommodations is liable for illegal discrimination under the ADA.[191] The ADA allows two exceptions to the reasonable accommodations requirement. The first exception is that employers do not have to consider reasonable accommodations unless an applicant qualifies as a disabled individual under the ADA.[192] The second exception, also found in the Rehabilitation Act, is that an employer does not have to make accommodations that would create an undue hardship.[193]

Reasonable accommodation is a crucial provision of the ADA because many disabled applicants are turned down for jobs that they would be able to perform were it not for easily remedied hindrances at work sites. Workplace obstacles may discriminate against disabled applicants as much as personal prejudices. The ADA thus incorporates reasonable accommodation as a means of eliminating needless obstacles that limit job opportunities and promoting equal employment opportunity for otherwise qualified disabled applicants.

1. *Equal Employment Opportunity*

An equal employment opportunity means an opportunity to attain an equal job ranking or to enjoy a salary and benefits comparable to those received by standard, nondisabled applicants. Reasonable accommodations must be made available in

---

[189] *See infra* notes 191–199 and accompanying text. The legislative history of the ADA affirms that it was modeled on the Rehabilitation Act. *See* H.R. REP. NO. 101-485, pt. 2, at 23 (1990), *reprinted in* 1990 U.S.C.C.A.N. 303, 304.

[190] *See* 29 C.F.R. pt. 1630, app. (2003). The House Committee on Education and Labor stated that the requirement of reasonable accommodations is a "key requirement of the Rehabilitation Act and of this Act." H.R. REP. NO. 101-485, pts. 1 & 2, at 33, *reprinted in* 1990 U.S.C.C.A.N. 267, 315.

[191] *See* 42 U.S.C. §12112(b)(5)(A)–(B).

[192] *See* 42 U.S.C. §12112(b)(5)(B). The ADA defines qualified individual with a disability as "an individual with a disability who, with or without reasonable accommodation, can perform the essential functions of the employment position that such individual holds or desires." *Id.* §12111(8).

[193] 42 U.S.C. §12112(b)(5)(A).

all areas of the hiring process to create a level playing field on which qualified disabled applicants can compete for jobs. The ADA calls for reasonable accommodation for three reasons: (1) to promote equal opportunity in the hiring process, (2) to make it possible for disabled individuals to perform the necessary functions of a job, and (3) to make it possible for disabled individuals to enjoy equal benefits and privileges of employment.[194]

Making a reasonable accommodation may involve an alteration to the nature of a position, the work environment, the way in which job duties are performed, or providing devices that would enable the applicant to perform the essential functions of the job.[195] Some examples of reasonable accommodation include: (1) making current premises accessible to, and usable by, disabled individuals; (2) job restructuring; (3) obtaining or altering equipment or policies; (4) adapting or changing tests, training equipment, or procedures; and (5) supplying competent readers or interpreters. Where a particular function is not essential to the job, an employer must provide either an accommodation that will assist the applicant in performing the job, transfer the function to another position, or exchange the function with one that the applicant can perform.[196]

2. Employers' Duties

Several sections of the ADA govern employers' duties to make facilities accessible. Private employers' duties regarding

---

[194] *See* Bureau of National Affairs, Americans With Disabilities Act Manual §90:0518.

[195] *See* 42 U.S.C. §12111(9)(A)–(B). The ADA states that:

"reasonable accommodations" may include—(A) making existing facilities used by employees readily accessible to and usable by individuals with disabilities; and (B) job restructuring, part-time or modified work schedules, reassignment to a vacant position, acquisition or modification of equipment or devices, appropriate adjustment or modifications of examinations, training materials or policies, the provision of qualified readers or interpreters, and other similar accommodations for individuals with disabilities.

Id.

[196] *See* Hoffman v. Fidelity Brokerage Servs., Inc., 959 F. Supp. 452, 6 AD Cases 651 (S.D. Ohio 1997).

accessibility are governed by Title I of the ADA,[197] while public employers' duties to its customers and clients and the duties of owners of newly built or renovated public accommodations and commercial buildings are governed by Title III.[198] The responsibilities of state and local governments to provide access for applicants and employees under Title I varies from their responsibility to provide accessibility under Title II.[199] Under Title I, employers must provide access for an *individual* applicant to take part in the hiring process unless it would cause an undue hardship. Employers are not required to make their buildings and facilities accessible until a particular applicant needs an accommodation, and then the alterations should meet that applicant's work requirements. Employers do not have to modify facilities to provide access to activities or benefits that are not employment-related.

In contrast, Title III forces public facilities (including banks, retail stores, theaters, hotels, and restaurants) to make their goods and services accessible generally to all disabled individuals. Under Title III, current public accommodation sites must be made accessible by eliminating architectural obstacles or structural communications impediments if this is "readily achievable." If this is not readily achievable, some type of alternative services must be provided to disabled individuals.

State and local governments' duty to create "program accessibility" in current facilities under Title II also varies from their duty as employers under Title I to make facilities accessible. Title II establishes that state and local governments must manage each service, course, or activity in current facilities so that, when viewed as a whole, it is readily accessible to and usable by disabled individuals, unless this would produce a "fundamental alteration" in the nature of the program or service, or would create "undue financial and administrative burdens." Moreover, private employers that use commercial buildings or run public facilities and state and local governments

---

[197] 42 U.S.C. §12112.
[198] *Id.* §12181.
[199] *Id.* §12131.

must abide by more stringent accessibility requirements under Title II and Title III when modifying existing buildings or starting new construction projects.

3. Providing Information

Even before making reasonable accommodations to work sites, employers must ensure that information about available positions is accessible to people with various disabilities. The ADA does not require employers to supply written information in assorted formats before an applicant requests it, but employers must be prepared to supply job information in an accessible format once a request has been made. For instance, information should be available in a location that is accessible to people with mobility impairments. If a job announcement provides only a telephone number to call for information, a telecommunication display device (TDD) for the deaf number should be provided, unless a telephone relay service has been set up.[200] Written information in large type should be placed in employment offices or posted on bulletin boards for individuals with visual difficulties. Employers can make audio tapes of job advertisements or provide someone to read to applicants with more acute vision impairments.

4. Employment Agencies

Employment agencies are "covered entities" under the ADA, and must abide by all relevant ADA guidelines. The ADA classifies "employment agencies" in the same way as does Title VII of the Civil Rights Act. It incorporates private and public employment agencies and other businesses, such as college placement organizations, that regularly provide employees to companies. Thus, when companies use an employment agency to recruit, interview, or hire potential employees, both the

---

[200]Title IV, 42 U.S.C. of the ADA required all telephone companies to have established relay services by July 1993 that would allow people who use TDDs to speak directly to another person by using relay operators. Both before and after enactment of the ADA, many states had instituted and continue to operate relay services, as described at the website of the Federal Communications Commission, at www.fcc.gov/cgb/dro/state.html.

employer and the employment agency may be liable if the agency does not abide by ADA guidelines.

For instance, an employer uses an employment agency to recruit applicants and the agency places an advertisement with a telephone number that all job applicants must call because the advertisement does not provide a street address. However, there is no TDD number provided in the advertisement. If there is no telephone relay service, and a deaf person does not have access to information about a position he or she could perform and makes a discrimination charge, both the employer and the agency may be legally responsible.

Because of this potential liability, employers should instruct all employment agencies that they are also under an obligation to comply with ADA guidelines. Employment agencies should be particularly knowledgeable regarding the guidelines on qualification standards, preemployment inquiries, and reasonable accommodations. If an employer hires an employment agency, the employer may wish to incorporate into its contract a requirement that the agency will recruit, screen, and hire applicants in accordance with all nondiscrimination laws, including the ADA.

5. Recruitment

The ADA does not force employers to take extraordinary actions to recruit disabled individuals. However, it does require employers to increase their efforts to find qualified disabled employees. Recruitment activities that eliminate potential disabled applicants may contravene the ADA. For instance, if an employer conducts recruitment events at any site that is not accessible to people with physical, visual, auditory or other impairments, it may be subject to a successful discrimination claim.

There are many methods of finding qualified disabled persons. Indeed, the disabled population is a resource waiting to be developed. For instance, many colleges have employees hired to organize services for disabled students who can provide valuable information on recruitment and accessibility. Local

6. Applicants Request for or Advising About Need for Reasonable Accommodation

The burden of requesting a reasonable accommodation from an employer rests with the disabled individual.[201] Employers do not have to make an accommodation if they do not realize the need. However, employers must advise job applicants of the employer duty to accommodate qualified disabled individuals. The ADA requires employers to put up signs, supplied by the EEOC, regarding their duties under the ADA, including the duty to provide reasonable accommodations, in prominent areas at work sites. Employers should make sure to hang signs in employment offices and other locations where applicants are likely to notice them. Information about employers' duties also can be incorporated into applications, job advertisements, company handbooks, and informational lectures.

Job applicants do not have to ask explicitly for a "reasonable accommodation," but must only advise an employer that they need some type of modification in order to perform their job because of their disability. If an applicant has a disability that is not apparent, it is the applicant's responsibility to advise the employer of his or her need for a modification. If an applicant has an obvious disability, which an employer clearly can see would restrict or prohibit the applicant from meeting job requirements, the interviewer(s) may request that he or she explain or show how he or she would perform the duties with or without a reasonable accommodation.

If an applicant asks for an accommodation and the need for the accommodation is not apparent, or if the employer does not believe the accommodation is required, the employer

---

[201] *See* Spitzer v. Good Guys, Inc., 80 Cal. App. 4th 1376, 1384, 10 AD Cases 1638 (1st Dist. 2000) (if employee with known disability is having difficulty performing his or her job, employer may inquire whether employee is in need of reasonable accommodation; in general, however, it is responsibility of individual with a disability to inform employer that accommodation is needed.).

may ask the applicant for proof of his or her impairment. For instance, an employer may request records from a physician, psychiatrist, rehabilitation adviser, physical therapist, independent living assistant, or other person who has witnessed the applicant's impairment(s). There are three exceptions to the ADA's general rule barring preoffer medical inquiries: (1) inquiries relating to the applicant's ability to perform job-related functions;[202] (2) when an employer reasonably believes that the applicant's known disability will interfere with the performance of a job-related function; and (3) when an applicant requests a reasonable accommodation for the job, or the application process itself.[203]

Moreover, employers may require applicants to request accommodations for taking an examination a reasonable time before the administration of the examination. A qualified disabled applicant may decline an accommodation, but if he or she cannot meet job requirements without the accommodation, he or she may not be competent for the position. An employer is not expected to lower quality or quantity standards to accommodate an applicant or to provide objects such as glasses or hearing aids. However, the ADA may require an employer to reassign a disabled employee to a different position as a reasonable accommodation if an already funded, vacant position at the same level exists and the employee can no longer perform the essential functions of his or her current position.[204]

In the absence of the reasonable accommodations provision, many disabled applicants would be denied access to the hiring process for jobs in which they are interested. Frequently,

---

[202] *See* 42 U.S.C. §12112(d)(2)(B) (1995).

[203] *See* Harris v. Harris & Hart, Inc., 206 F.3d 838, 841–42, 845, 10 AD Cases 481 (9th Cir. 2000) (employer's request for medical release prior to rehiring former employee with known disability did not violate ADA); Grenier v. Cyanamid Plastics, 70 F.3d 667, 5 AD Cases 75 (1st Cir. 1995) (employer's request that former employee provide certification from his doctor that (1) identified necessary reasonable accommodations, and (2) provided that employee could work without restrictions, did not violate ADA); *cf.* Barnes v. Cochran, 944 F. Supp. 897, 5 AD Cases 1685 (S.D. Fla. 1996) (employer's preemployment psychological exam violated ADA).

[204] *See Spitzer*, 80 Cal. App. 4th at 1389.

a suitable accommodation will be apparent and can be prepared with little trouble or expense. Disabled applicants can often propose an easy and less expensive modification based on their experiences in managing their disability. Thus, employers should always seek advice from applicants before making an accommodation.

7. *The Undue Hardship Analysis*

An employer does not have to make an accommodation if doing so will impose an undue hardship on the company. The legislative history of the ADA defines undue hardship as "an action that is unduly costly, extensive, substantial, disruptive, or that will fundamentally alter the nature of the program."[205] In analyzing whether a particular accommodation will create an undue hardship, employers may consider congressional intent, EEOC regulations, and the Rehabilitation Act.[206] The ADA and EEOC regulations list five factors that employers should consider when deciding whether an accommodation will create an undue hardship:[207]

1. The nature and expense of the accommodation. The expense to be factored in is the net expense to the company after accounting for federal tax credits, deductions, and any other sources of funding.
2. The financial assets of the site(s) providing the accommodation, the number of employees at the particular site(s), and the effect on the financial solvency of the site(s).
3. The overall financial assets, size, number of employees, type, and location of businesses of the company governed by the ADA (if the businesses involved in the accommodation are part of a larger company).
4. The organization and duties of employees, the geographic layout of the company, and the administrative or monetary interactions between the business making

---

[205] *See* H.R. REP. No. 101-485, pt. 2, at 67, *reprinted in* 1990 U.S.C.C.A.N. 303, 349.
[206] *See id.*; *see also* 29 C.F.R. §1630.2(p) (2003) (defining undue hardship).
[207] *See* 29 C.F.R. §1630.2(p)(2) (2003).

the accommodation and its holding company. Also, whether the company involves any unique kind of operation that would make it unusually difficult to make the accommodation.[208]

Factor 4 will be weighed, in conjunction with factors 2 and 3, when a company runs more than one site, in order to determine the financial resources of the site making the accommodation, and in consideration of the relationship between the site and the larger company. At times, such an analysis may not be appropriate because the site making the accommodation may not receive funding from the larger company.

For instance, "an independently owned fast food franchise" of a national company may claim that "it would be an undue hardship to provide an interpreter to enable" a deaf applicant to take part in staff meetings if it is solely reliant on its own money and is connected only by name to a larger organization. If the financial interactions between the national company and the local company are restricted to the payment "of an annual franchise fee, only the" resources of the local franchise would be factored into a determination of whether the accommodation would create an undue hardship. If, however, the local company was part of a national company with financial and administrative management over all of its sites, the funds of the larger company would be taken into account.[209]

5. The effect of the accommodation on the functioning of the local work site.

These factors center on each employer's ability to shoulder the financial burden of providing the accommodation. Thus, companies cannot assert undue hardship simply because accommodating an individual will harm company morale or create disturbances because of employees' various fears or biases. Under the ADA's individualized analysis, an accommodation that is reasonable for one employer may impose an undue

---
[208] *Id.*
[209] 29 C.F.R. pt. 1630, app. §1630.2(p) (2003).

hardship on another.[210] As a rule, larger companies are expected to have more resources and manpower to spend making accommodations than are smaller companies.

a. Undue Hardship Exception

An employer may be able to demonstrate that making a certain accommodation would seriously impact its workforce or operations as a whole. For instance, an individual with a visual disability who needs bright light to see well applies for a wait staff job at a nightclub. The club keeps the premises dimly lit to generate an intimate mood, and reduces the lighting more during the shows. If the applicant requested bright lighting as an accommodation so that she could see to take customers' orders, the employer could validly claim that this would create an undue hardship because it would change the type of establishment and thus drastically affect operations.[211]

If the expense of an accommodation would inflict an undue hardship on the employer, the employer should give the applicant the alternative of supplying the accommodation or reimbursing the employer for that share of the expense that would represent an undue hardship. Hence, an accommodation that imposes an undue hardship on one employer at a certain time may not impose an undue hardship on a different employer, or even on the same employer at a different time.[212]

To overcome the duty to provide accommodations under the undue hardship exception, the employer must show that the costs of accommodations would threaten the company's ability to maintain current production levels.[213] Thus, increased budgetary concerns alone are not a sufficient argument to

---

[210] *See* H.R. REP. No. 101-485, pt. 2, at 70 (1990), *reprinted in* 1990 U.S.C.C.A.N. 303, 352. For instance, a neighborhood store would have an easier time demonstrating that providing an accommodation creates an undue hardship than would a national chain. *Id.* pt. 3, at 40–41, *reprinted in* 1990 U.S.C.C.A.N. 445, 463.

[211] 29 C.F.R. pt. 1630, app. §1630.2(p) (2003).

[212] H.R. REP. No. 101-485, pt. 2, at 70.

[213] *See* Nelson v. Thornburgh, 567 F. Supp. 369, 380, 1 AD Cases 463 (E.D. Pa. 1983), aff'd, 732 F.2d 146, 1 AD Cases 573 (3d Cir. 1984), *cert. denied*, 469 U.S. 118 (1985) (determining, under Rehabilitation Act, that it would not create undue hardship for Pennsylvania's Department of Public Welfare to supply readers as accommodation to blind applicants).

overcome the duty.[214] Individually determining the cost and difficulty of each potential accommodation is one of the more difficult challenges of employers trying to comply with the ADA. Employers should analyze the above-mentioned factors for each disabled applicant carefully and rely as much as possible on legislative guidelines and existing case law under the Rehabilitation Act and the ADA.

8. *The Essential Functions Analysis*

If the disabled applicant can meet the job requirements, the employer must then decide whether he or she can carry out the essential functions of the job for which he or she is applying, with or without reasonable accommodations.[215] As part of this determination, the employer must decide what functions are essential to various jobs. Essential functions are those "job tasks that are fundamental and not marginal."[216] The essential function requirement is consistent with the legislative purpose of providing equal opportunity to the disabled. Employers must determine whether an applicant can perform the essential functions at the time he or she applies for the position. Employers may not, however, discriminate on the basis of potential future disabilities.[217]

The ADA gives employers the discretion to determine each position's essential functions and the qualifications necessary for applicants.[218] Thus, employers will not usually violate the ADA by their determinations of what constitutes the "essential functions" of a particular job, but will violate the ADA if they

---

[214] *See* 29 C.F.R. §1630, app. §1630.2(p) (2003).

[215] *See* 42 U.S.C. §12111(8) (1995).

[216] *See* H.R. REP. No. 101-485, pt. 2, at 55, *reprinted in* 1990 U.S.C.C.A.N. 303, 337. Congress adopted this definition to "ensure that employers can continue to require that all applicants and employees, including those with disabilities, are able to perform the essential, i.e., the non-marginal functions of the job in question." *Id.* For instance, a policy that requires employees to hold driver's licenses, if driving is not part of the job, is a marginal requirement, and employers cannot exclude a disabled worker who could otherwise perform the essential functions. *Id.*

[217] *See id.* at 55, 1990 U.S.C.C.A.N. at 357.

[218] *See* Webster v. Methodist Occupational Health Ctrs., Inc., 141 F.3d 1236, 8 AD Cases 33 (7th Cir. 1998); Dalton v. Subaru-Isuzu Auto., Inc., 141 F.3d 667, 7 AD Cases 1872 (7th Cir. 1998).

do not expect all employees in that job to perform what they have determined to be the essential functions.[219] However, the EEOC does provide employers with guidelines on how to determine if a job function is "essential" and distinguish between essential and nonessential job functions. In general, when trying to decide whether a job function is essential, employers should consider "whether removing the function would fundamentally alter at position."[220]

a. Determining Essential Job Function: EEOC Guidelines

Where a position was created in order to complete a particular function, that function is clearly "essential."[221] For instance, in the case of a person who checks identification cards, the ability to read the cards is an essential function of the job. The only reason the job exists is to have identification cards checked.[222] Likewise, in an example given by the EEOC, the ability to proofread written materials would be an essential function of a proofreader's job, because the job was created for this sole purpose.[223] The second factor in deciding whether a function is essential, under the EEOC's guidelines, is "the number of other employees available to perform the job function or among whom the performance of that job function can be distributed."[224] This factor is particularly significant when the total number of employees is low or when there are variable demands for the business operation. If there are a small number of employees for the amount of work to be performed, each employee may be needed to perform a number of different functions. In such circumstances, an employee's ability to perform each function becomes significant and,

---

[219] See DePaoli v. Abbott Labs., 140 F.3d 668, 7 AD Cases 1828 (7th Cir. 1998); Mason v. South Bend Cmty. Sch. Corp., 9 AD Cases 979 (N.D. Ind. 1998).

[220] 29 C.F.R. pt. 1630, app. §1630.2(n) (2003).

[221] See id.

[222] See Bureau of National Affairs, AMERICANS WITH DISABILITIES ACT MANUAL §90:0525.

[223] See 29 C.F.R. pt. 1630, app. §1630.2(n) (2003).

[224] See id. By referring to the "number of available employees," rather than simply the "number of employees," the EEOC has stated that its purpose is not to require "an assessment of whether a job function could be distributed among all employees in any job at any level." 56 Fed. Reg. 35,726, 35,729 (July 26, 1991).

as a result, the employer may not have the ability to delegate job duties easily among other employees.[225]

A comparable situation may face employers handling larger workforces where periods of heavy demand for work are often followed by low demand periods. While job duties could be transferred among employees during the low demand periods, during the heavy demand periods performance of each duty becomes more crucial and might restrict the employer's ability to easily reorganize operations.[226]

The third and final factor supplied by the EEOC to determine what job functions are essential relates to the level of expertise or skill necessary to perform the particular job function. The EEOC regulations recognize that in specialized jobs, employees are often hired for their expertise or special knowledge of particular job functions. In such cases, the ADA regulations provide that the performance of that specialized duty would represent an "essential function."[227]

In considering various job duties based on these factors, the decision of whether a particular function is "essential" must be made on a case-by-case basis and only after a careful analysis. The EEOC has stated: "[i]n determining whether or not a particular function is essential, all relevant evidence should be considered."[228]

b. Rehabilitation Act/ADA Guidelines

Cases decided under the Rehabilitation Act and regulations provide additional instruction on the manner in which one can determine whether a function is essential.[229] In performing a case-specific analysis, the EEOC's regulations list the

---

Instead, an assessment should be limited to those employees within the same group or job classification.

[225] See 29 C.F.R. pt. 1630, app. §1630.2(n) (2003).
[226] Id.
[227] See id.
[228] Id. See Benson v. Northwest Airlines, Inc., 62 F.3d 1108, 4 AD Cases 1234 (8th Cir. 1995) (reversing district court's grant of summary judgment in favor of employer, because employer made insufficient factual showing as to what comprised essential functions of position).
[229] See, e.g., 29 C.F.R. §1630.2(n)(3) (2003); Southeastern Cmty. Coll. v. Davis, 442 U.S. 397, 2 AD Cases 1 (1979); Hall v. U.S. Postal Serv., 857 F.2d 1073, 1 AD

following as some indications of whether a particular function is "essential":[230]

- The employer's determination of what functions are essential;
- The employer's written job description, created before advertising or interviewing applicants for the job;
- The length of time spent by employees performing the particular job duty;
- The work experience of past employees in the position;
- The current work experience of those working in similar positions; and
- The provisions of a collective bargaining agreement.[231]

This list is not comprehensive, and other factors may be considered as part of an "essential functions" analysis.[232] However, the list reflects examples of the type of analysis required

---

Cases 1368 (6th Cir. 1988); Nelson v. Thornburgh, 567 F. Supp. 369, 1 AD Cases 463 (E.D. Pa. 1983).

[230] *See* 29 C.F.R. §1630.2(n) (2003), (1991). *See also* Kalekiristos v. CTF Hotel Mgmt. Corp., 958 F. Supp. 641, 660, 6 AD Cases 1725 (D.D.C. 1997), *aff'd*, 132 F.3d 1481 (D.C. Cir. 1997) ("courts defer to the employer's judgment as to what functions of the job are essential"); 42 U.S.C. §12111(8) ("consideration shall be given to the employer's judgment as to what functions of a job are essential . . .").

[231] 29 C.F.R. §1630.2(n)(3) (2003). Evidence regarding the provisions of a collective bargaining agreement was not included by the EEOC in its proposed Title I regulations. *See* 56 Fed. Reg. 8,578, 8,588 (Feb. 28, 1991). In response to complaints by employers and unions, the EEOC added collective bargaining agreements to that section of the final regulations providing factors for determining the essential functions of a job. *See* 56 Fed. Reg. 35,726, 35,729 (July 26, 1991). In making this addition, the EEOC stated that this provision was consistent with the legislative history of the ADA. *Id.* (citing S. Rep. No. 101-116, at 32 (1989), H.R. Rep. No. 101-485, pt. 2, at 63 (1990), *reprinted in* 1990 U.S.C.C.A.N. 303.

[232] *See* 56 Fed. Reg. 35,726, 35,729 (July 26, 1991). Other relevant evidence in ascertaining the essential functions of a position include the nature of the work operation and the employer's organizational structure. *See* A Technical Assistance Manual on the Employment Provisions (Title I) of the Americans with Disabilities Act (1992) ("EEOC Technical Assistance Manual") at II–18. For example, an employer's production operations are performed by a team of workers; each worker may perform a distinct function, but every worker is required, on a rotating basis, to perform each different function. In this situation, the EEOC recognizes that all of the functions may be deemed essential for the job, rather than restricting essential functions to the function that one worker performs at a particular period in the process. *Id.*

under the ADA.²³³ However, the EEOC has advised that "[g]reater weight will not be granted to the types of evidence included on the list than to the types of evidence not listed."²³⁴

The legislative history of the ADA provides another example of the type of factual analysis that is necessary to determine the essential functions of a job:

> In one case, a person with epilepsy applied for the job group counselor at a juvenile hall. After receiving a job offer, the offer was withdrawn when the employer learned that the applicant did not have a driver's license. Driving was required for emergencies, such as taking a juvenile to the hospital, for example, and to transport the juveniles to court appearances. While it was necessary that *some* of the group counselors be able to drive, it was not essential that *all* group counselors be available to drive. On any given shift, another group counselor could perform the driving duty.²³⁵

In light of these facts, the Judiciary Committee concluded that having a driver's license would not be an essential qualification for the particular position of a group counselor because not all counselors necessarily would be called upon to drive. Therefore, the fact that a person had epilepsy and could not drive would not be a legitimate disqualification for the particular position.²³⁶

However, the ability to drive would be an essential function of at least some counseling jobs; otherwise, no counselor would be available to drive in emergency situations.²³⁷ Thus, in determining the essential functions of a job, employers must consider the job responsibilities in the context of the real work environment. At the same time, courts sometimes question an employer's conclusions about whether particular functions truly are essential, even in circumstances that appear,

---

[233] *See* 29 C.F.R. §1630.2(n)(3) (2003).

[234] *See* 29 C.F.R. pt. 1630, app. §1630.2(n) (2003). This creates another difficulty with the ADA. Because of the indefinite requirements provided by Congress and the EEOC, the uncertainty may be expensive for employers and pose risks of litigation.

[235] *See* H.R. REP. No. 101-485, pt. 3, at 33 (1990), *reprinted in* 1990 U.S.C.C.A.N. 445, 456.

[236] *Id.*

[237] *Id.*

superficially, to present a strong position in favor such a classification.[238]

The ADA guidelines instruct employers initially to determine whether employees actually perform the essential function.[239] An employee will not be able to justify a function as "essential" based on an illusory or paper-only written description of the function.[240] For instance, an employer may state that typing is an essential function of the position. However, if the employer has never required any employee in that position to type, that will be evidence that typing is not actually an essential function.[241] Under the Rehabilitation Act, the duty to provide job opportunities for the handicapped does not create a duty to change the essential nature of the business.[242] In comparison, the ADA requires a much more individualized and case-specific analysis.[243] Thus, the ADA arguably may require more modifications to job functions than were required under the Rehabilitation Act.

c. Private Employer Requirements

Although employers have a statutory duty to reasonably accommodate disabled individuals, private employers do not have a duty to implement affirmative action hiring policies for the disabled under the ADA. In fact, the ADA legislative history warns against private employers going beyond reasonable accommodation to give "preferences" to disabled applicants.[244]

---

[238] *See, e.g.,* Gillen v. Fallon Ambulance Serv., Inc., 283 F.3d 11, 12 AD Cases 1633 (1st Cir. 2002) (whether substantial lifting capability was essential function for position of emergency medical technician questionable). By contrast, certain other courts have little difficulty in finding attacks on lifting requirements insufficient to survive resolution through summary judgment. Fuzy v. S&B Engrs. & Constructors, 332 F.3d 301, 14 AD Cases 676 (5th Cir. 2003).

[239] *See* 29 C.F.R. pt. 1630, app. 1630.2(n) (2003).

[240] *Id.*

[241] *Id.*

[242] *See* Southeastern Cmty. Coll. v. Davis, 442 U.S. 397, 410, 2 AD Cases 1 (1979) (modification of nursing training program not required, because it would fundamentally alter nature of program).

[243] *See, e.g.,* School Bd. of Nassau County v. Arline, 480 U.S. 273, 287–89, 1 AD Cases 1026 (1987) (remanding case for more detailed inquiry into defendant's contagious disease).

[244] *See* Johnson v. Brown, 26 F. Supp. 2d 147, 150 n.4 (D.D.C. 1998).

An individual has no right under the ADA to a particular job.[245] "The Rehabilitation Act requires employers to actively recruit individuals with disabilities, but it does not require them to automatically hire an individual who [has] shown that he/she is a 'qualified individual with a disability.'"[246]

IX. Determining Whether a Requirement Is "Job-Related" and "Consistent With Business Necessity"

A. Justified

If a job requirement or test tends to eliminate disabled applicants on the basis of their disabilities it must be a justifiable standard or qualification for the position it is being used for and cannot apply generally to a class of jobs. For example, a requirement that a secretary have the ability to take shorthand dictation is not job-related if the current secretary in fact transcribes taped dictation.

Under the ADA, as under the Rehabilitation Act, if a test or other selection criterion excludes an individual with a disability because of the disability and does not relate to the essential functions of a job it is not consistent with business necessity.[247] This standard is similar to the legal standard under Title VII of the Civil Rights Act, which states that a job qualification that excludes a disproportionate number of people of a certain race, sex, or national origin "class" must be justifiable as a "business necessity."[248] However, under the ADA, the standard may be applied to an applicant who is excluded by a job qualification because of a disability *and* to a class of applicants. Thus,

---

[245] *See* Gutridge v. Clure, 153 F.3d 898, 8 AD Cases 705 (8th Cir. 1998), *cert. denied sub nom.* Gutridge v. Midland Computer, 526 U.S. 1113 (1999); Swain v. Hillsborough County Sch. Bd., 146 F.3d 855, 8 AD Cases 488 (11th Cir. 1998); Thompson v. Holy Family Hosp., 121 F.3d 537, 7 AD Cases 308 (9th Cir. 1997); McKay v. Toyota Motor Mfg. U.S.A., Inc., 110 F.3d 369, 6 AD Cases 933 (6th Cir. 1997); Dutcher v. Ingalls Shipbuilding, 53 F.3d 723, 4 AD Cases 802 (5th Cir. 1995); Daley v. Koch, 892 F.2d 212, 1 AD Cases 1549 (2d Cir. 1989).

[246] Duren v. Johnson, Dkt. No. 01934068, 1995 WL 114286, *2 (EEOC).

[247] 42 U.S.C. §12112(b)(6) (1995).

[248] *See* 42 U.S.C. §2000 et seq.

the ADA does not require statistical comparisons between classes of applicants with disabilities and classes of applicants who are not disabled to show that an applicant with a disability is excluded by a job qualification. Due to this distinction between the ADA and the Civil Rights Act, the federal Uniform Guidelines on Employee Selection Procedures[249] that govern selection criteria on the basis of race, sex, and national origin under Title VII of the Civil Rights Act[250] and other federal authorities do not govern selection criteria under the ADA.

There are so many different types of disabilities that it is nearly impossible to make generalizations about the effect of particular standards and procedures on disabled applicants. Often there is a dearth of statistical data regarding the impact of a procedure on any "class" of applicants with a particular disability compared with applicants without disabilities. Thus, the exclusionary effect of job qualifications usually must be looked at in relation to a particular applicant who has particular restrictions caused by a disability.

B. Not Justified

A requirement may be job-related but not justified by business necessity because it does not pertain to an essential function of a position. For instance, an interviewer may ask applicants for an administrative position if they have a driver's license, because it would be helpful to have an employee who could sporadically run errands. This qualification is "job-related," but it relates to a minor, not an essential, job duty. The employer, hence, would not be able to reject an applicant based on this criterion and justify his or her decision as a "business necessity."

Moreover, the ADA requires that even if a condition of employment is job-related and consistent with business necessity, it may not be used to reject a disabled applicant if the applicant could satisfy the condition with a reasonable accommodation. For instance, it may be job-related and necessary

---

[249] 29 U.S.C. §1607; 41 C.F.R. pt. 60.3 (2003).
[250] 42 U.S.C. §2000 et seq.

for a company to require that a secretary type documents. But a company could not exclude an applicant whose disability prevented manual typing, but who could "type" using a computer-assistive device, if supplying this device would not create an undue hardship.

C. Establishing Certain Job Requirements

The ADA recognizes that employers may establish certain job requirements based on such criteria as:

- educational level;
- work experience;
- particular expertise; and
- licenses.[251]

For instance, a disabled individual who applies to work as a lawyer for a firm must first be able to show that he or she has passed the bar examination of the state in which he or she is seeking to practice. If the applicant does not have the necessary license, then the interview need not continue, as there is no need to ascertain whether the applicant can perform the essential functions of the job.[252] The EEOC has also stated that job qualifications may include such subjective criteria as

---

[251] As originally written, the EEOC's definition of a "qualified individual with a disability" pertained only to "skill, experience and education" job qualifications. *See* 56 Fed. Reg. 8,578, 8,588 (Feb. 28, 1991). Many employers complained that this definition was too narrow because it "did not permit employers to consider other job-related qualifications." *See* 56 Fed. Reg. 35,726, 35,728 (July 26, 1991). In response to these complaints, the EEOC recognized that employers may establish more than the three types of qualification standards provided in EEOC regulations. Hence, in the final regulations, the definition of "qualified individual" was modified to make clear that the reference to "skill, experience, and education" is not an "exhaustive list of permissible qualification requirements." *Id.* The EEOC made this clarification in the final regulations by including the phrase "and other job-related requirements" following the mention of "skill, experience, and education." As the EEOC stated, "[t]his revision recognizes that other types of job-related requirements may be relevant to determining whether an individual is qualified for a position." *Id.*

[252] Under the Rehabilitation Act, courts recognized that an employer lawfully could reject applicants who were not qualified for a position as long as their failure to meet job standards was not due to any physical or mental restrictions caused by the disability.

good judgment and ability to interact and communicate with coworkers.[253]

Cases construing the Rehabilitation Act have consistently held that regular, predictable attendance and the ability to keep a regular work schedule may be minimum requirements of any job and that refusing to hire an applicant, or discharging an employee, who cannot satisfy these requirements is not unlawful discrimination. This is true even if the employee's inability to satisfy the requirements is due to a disability.[254] The case law under the ADA has followed these Rehabilitation Act cases by similarly defining a "qualified individual with a disability" to mean not only that the applicant has the skills to perform

---

[253] A TECHNICAL ASSISTANCE MANUAL ON THE EMPLOYMENT PROVISIONS (TITLE I) OF THE AMERICANS WITH DISABILITIES ACT ("EEOC TECHNICAL ASSISTANCE MANUAL") at II-12. *See also* Grenier v. Cyanamid Plastics, Inc., 70 F.3d 667, 674, 5 AD Cases 75, 81, 82 (1st Cir. 1995) (recognizing that "[t]echnical skills and experience are not the only essential requirements of a job," *id.* at 674, 5 AD Cases at 81, and that the "ability to function effectively in the workplace and to get along," *id.* at 675, 5 AD Cases at 82, with coworkers and supervisors also may be essential functions); Voytek v. University of Cal., 5 AD Cases 1255, 1266–67 (N.D. Cal. 1994) (employee legally denied reemployment after period of disability, where he "could not continue to perform all of the tasks assigned to him" due in part to ongoing conflict with his supervisor). For more elaboration on how employers can defend a decision not to hire a disabled applicant who poses a "direct threat" in the work environment with such subjective criteria, see section J(d), below.

[254] *See, e.g.*, D'Antonio v. Runyon, 3 AD Cases 1658, 1662 (E.D. Pa. 1994) ("Attendance is almost by definition an essential function of any job."); Carr v. Reno, 23 F.3d 525, 3 AD Cases 434 (D.C. Cir. 1994); Leatherwood v. Houston Post Co., 59 F.3d 533, 4 AD Cases 1091 (5th Cir. 1995) (employee's disability-based absence from his job for 33–44% of his last 9 months of employment indicated his disability rendered him unqualified for his job as matter of law); Cromer v. Greenwood Comm'n of Pub. Works, 2 AD Cases 683 (S.C. Ct. Com. Pl. 1993) (no violation of State Bill of Rights for Handicapped Persons, where employee discharged because of prolonged absences occasioned by Crohn's disease; employee missed almost half the total number of scheduled work days and did not have regular and predictable attendance); Jackson v. Veterans Admin., 22 F.3d 277, 279, 3 AD Cases 483, 484 (11th Cir.), *cert. denied* sub. nom. Jackson v. Department of Veterans Affairs, 513 U.S. 1052 (1994) (regular, predictable attendance was essential function of plaintiff's job as janitor because "[u]nlike other jobs that can be performed off site or deferred until a later day, the tasks of a housekeeping aide by their very nature must be performed daily at a specific location"); *cf.* Dutton v. Johnson County Bd. of County Comm'rs, 859 F. Supp. 498 (D. Kan. 1994) (fact that employee's disability may cause employee to have unpredictable absences does not necessarily render employee unqualified to perform essential functions of job, and issue must be determined on case-by-case basis).

the job, but also that the applicant is able to perform the skills by attending work regularly.[255]

X. Responding to a Claim of Disability Discrimination in Hiring

A. No Reasonable Accommodation Existed

When an applicant claims that an employer failed to provide reasonable accommodation, the employer may assert that no reasonable accommodation existed. Under the ADA, an employer is not required to hire an applicant or trainee who cannot perform the essential functions of the position with or without an accommodation. For instance, an applicant was lawfully rejected because he could not pass a handgun qualification test during training at a police academy.[256] In another case, an applicant was lawfully rejected for a firefighter position when he failed a required hearing examination.[257] When permitted to take the hearing test with a hearing device, the applicant still failed. The court concluded that the applicant was not a qualified individual under the ADA because he could not perform the essential function of localizing sound with or without a reasonable accommodation.[258] As another example, a trainee was lawfully rejected when an employer called the

---

[255] *See, e.g., Carr*, 23 F.3d 525 (essential function of job at issue was "coming to work regularly"); Howard v. North Miss. Med. Ctr., 939 F. Supp. 505, 509, 5 AD Cases 1723, 1727 (N.D. Miss. 1996) ("[a]ttendance at work is an essential function of all jobs" and plaintiff, whose migraine headaches resulted in her being confined to bed, was therefore unqualified for employment); Kennedy v. Applause, Inc., 3 AD Cases 1734, 1736–37 (C.D. Cal. 1994) ("Numerous federal courts have held that disabled employees cannot establish that they can sufficiently perform the essential functions of a job without showing they can maintain a regular and reliable level of attendance at that job.").

[256] *See* Ethridge v. State, 860 F. Supp. 808, 816, 3 AD Cases 1013 (M.D. Ala. 1994).

[257] *See* Leverett v. City of Indianapolis, 51 F. Supp. 2d 949, 955, 9 AD Cases 1812 (S.D. Ind. 1999); *see also* Karbusicky v. City of Park Ridge, 950 F. Supp. 878, 6 AD Cases 661 (N.D. Ill. 1997) (same hearing aid did not improve police officer's ability to localize sound).

[258] *Leverett*, 51 F. Supp. at 955.

manufacturer of an assistive device and was informed that no plans existed to develop technology that would permit the applicant to perform the essential functions of the position sought.[259]

The burden rests on the employer to show that there are no existing reasonable accommodations and that the job requirement is job-related and consistent with business necessity.[260] Once the employer has shown this, the burden shifts to the applicant to rebut the employer's evidence by showing that a reasonable accommodation is feasible.[261]

B. Applicant Unable to Perform Essential Job Functions With a Reasonable Accommodation

When an applicant claims that an employer failed to provide reasonable accommodation, the employer may propose that the applicant is not a qualified individual under the ADA because the applicant could not perform the essential functions of the job with a reasonable accommodation.[262] "It is not the role of the . . . trier-of-fact to second-guess [an employer's] business judgment" when the employer chooses not to hire a trainee with a disability after the trainee failed to perform at a level of accuracy and speed required by the employer for persons in the position.[263] "It is not necessary . . . that an employer's performance standards be quantifiable. Rather, an employer is permitted to exercise its business judgment in establishing performance standards and in determining whether an individual can meet its standards, 'whether qualitative or quantitative.' "[264]

---

[259] *See* Hoffman v. Fidelity Brokerage Servs., 959 F. Supp. 452, 458, 6 AD Cases 651 (S.D. Ohio 1997).

[260] *See* Treadwell v. Alexander, 707 F.2d 473, 475, 1 AD Cases 459 (11th Cir. 1983); *Ethridge*, 860 F. Supp. at 816 n.19.

[261] *See* Chiari v. City of League City, 920 F.2d 311, 318, 1 AD Cases 1721 (5th Cir. 1991).

[262] *See Hoffman*, 959 F. Supp. at 460.

[263] *Id.* at 461, 6 AD Cases at 659.

[264] *Id.* at 460, 6 AD Cases at 658 (quoting 29 C.F.R. pt. 1630, app. §1630.2(n)).

Yet, it is clear that an employer's assumption about job requirements and potential accommodations are not always persuasive. Thus, when a female applicant with only one completely functioning arm sued an ambulance service for its refusal to hire her as an emergency medical technician, the U.S. Court of Appeals for the First Circuit vacated summary judgment awarded to the employer by the trial court.[265] The lower court had found that the applicant was not disabled because she was not substantially limited in her ability to lift (she could lift 40 to 50 pounds); the appellate court rejected that conclusion, based, in part, on the candidate's "upbeat" opinion of her condition. The First Circuit also was dubious about the employer's assertion that the lifting requirement was essential to the job, because no other employees had been tested to see if they could satisfy the lifting standard. It also found that the employer's reliance on its physician's opinion did not automatically absolve the employer of liability; rather, remanding the case for further proceedings, it held that employers must assess the objective reasonableness of those conclusions.

C. Disparate Treatment Based on Legitimate Nondiscriminatory Reason

When an applicant claims that an employer discriminated in the hiring process (disparate treatment claim), the employer may assert that such treatment was based on a legitimate nondiscriminatory reason.[266] For instance, a legitimate, nondiscriminatory reason is that an applicant would pose a direct threat to the safety of other employees or to the public.[267]

1. Applicant Posed Direct Threat

Employers may refuse to hire applicants who present a "direct threat" to the health or safety of others or to themselves

---

[265] Gillen v. Fallon Ambulance Serv. Inc., 283 F.3d 11, 12 AD Cases 1633 (1st Cir. 2002).

[266] See 29 C.F.R. §1630.15(a) (2003); Ethridge v. State, 860 F. Supp. 808, 817, 3 AD Cases 1013 (M.D. Ala. 1994).

[267] See Ethridge, 860 F. Supp. at 817–18.

under the theory of legitimate business necessity.[268] A health or safety threat is a valid defense only if it is "a significant risk of substantial harm."[269] Thus, an "'elevated risk of injury',"[270] which is not based on "actual proof of a significant risk," is insufficient to satisfy the direct threat test. A consideration of whether an applicant creates a risk must be founded only on legitimate medical diagnoses and/or other objective facts, and not on conjecture.[271] This requirement reflects Congress' purpose of discouraging employers from making decisions that an applicant is a danger to others that are not based on "objective evidence about the individual involved."[272] At the same time the standard also protects employers, who otherwise would be exposed to the constant threat of tort litigation because of dangerous employees.

2. Direct Threat Defense

In the regulations promulgated by the EEOC under the ADA, the agency extended the language employed by Congress in the statute's "direct threat" defense to cover circumstances in which the threat posed by the individual does not run to third parties, but rather, to the applicant or employee. In *Chevron U.S.A., Inc. v. Echazabal*,[273] the Supreme Court approved the agency's regulation, in the context of a challenge brought by a job applicant who sought employment in a refinery position that posed exposure hazards that would have exacerbated his diagnosed medical condition.

---

[268] *See* 42 U.S.C. §12113(b); *see also* H.R. REP. NO. 101-485, pt. 3, at 45, *reprinted in* 1990 U.S.C.C.A.N. 445, 468.

[269] 42 U.S.C. §12111(3) (Supp. III 1991).

[270] *See* H.R. REP. NO. 101-485, pt. 3, at 46; *reprinted in* 1990 U.S.C.C.A.N. 445, 469.

[271] *See id.* at 45–46, 1990 U.S.C.C.A.N. at 468–69. For instance, an employer must consider the risk of a direct threat based on "the behavior of the particular disabled person, not merely on generalizations about the disability." H.R. Rep. No. 101-485, pt. 2 at 57, *reprinted in* 1990 U.S.C.C.A.N. 303, 339.

[272] H.R. REP. NO. 101-485 (II), at 56, *reprinted in* 1990 U.S.C.C.A.N. 338–339; H.R. REP. NO. 101-485 (III), at 45–46, *reprinted in* 1990 U.S.C.C.A.N. 468–469.

[273] 536 U.S. 73, 13 AD Cases 97 (2002).

The direct threat affirmative defense is triggered only after an ADA plaintiff makes out a prima facie case.[274] The defendant then has the burden to demonstrate that a qualification standard is job-related and consistent with business necessity.[275] However, "[t]he lack of a precise or universally perfect fit between a job requirement and actual effective performance is not fatal to a claim [by an employer] of business necessity, particularly when the public health and safety are at stake."[276]

3. Function of Reasonable Accommodation

Before rejecting an applicant who poses a direct threat, the employer must first attempt to eliminate or reduce the risk to an acceptable level with a reasonable accommodation.[277] Only if a reasonable accommodation cannot be made may the employer reject the applicant.[278] If the cost of accommodating an applicant with a disability creates an undue hardship, the employer must give the applicant the opportunity to provide the accommodation or pay for that portion of the accommodation that constitutes an undue hardship.[279] In determining whether employment of an applicant in a particular job would create a direct threat, the factors to be weighed include the following: "(1) The duration of the risk; (2) The nature and severity of the potential harm; (3) The likelihood that the potential harm will occur; and (4) The imminence of the potential harm."[280]

---

[274] *See* Koshinski v. Decatur Foundry, Inc., 177 F.3d 599, 602, 9 AD Cases 353 (7th Cir. 1999); *see also* Andrews v. Ohio, 104 F.3d 803, 808, 6 AD Cases 322 (6th Cir. 1997).

[275] *See* Andrews, 104 F.3d at 807–08.

[276] Smith v. City of Des Moines, Iowa, 99 F.3d 1466, 1473, 6 AD Cases 14, 19 (8th Cir. 1996).

[277] *See* 42 U.S.C. §12112(b)(5)(A)–(B) (Supp. III 1991).

[278] *Id.*

[279] *See* H.R. REP. No. 101-485, pt. 2, at 67–68, *reprinted in* 1990 U.S.C.C.A.N. 303, 350; 29 C.F.R. pt. 1630, app. §1630.2(p) (2003).

[280] *See* 29 C.F.R. pt. 1630, app. §1630.2(r) (2003). *See also* Rizzo v. Children's World Learning Ctrs., 84 F.3d 758, 763, 5 AD Cases 1155 (5th Cir. 1996), *cert. denied*, 531 U.S. 958 (2000); EEOC v. Dolphin Cruise Line, Inc., 945 F. Supp. 1550, 1554–55, 6 AD Cases 187 (S.D. Fla. 1996) (rejecting employer's argument that cruise ship entertainer applicant who tested HIV-positive would pose direct threat after considering above-listed factors and current medical knowledge that teaches

4. Threat Assessment

Although EEOC regulations require an individualized assessment of a job applicant's "present ability to safely perform the essential functions of the job,"[281] there is nothing in the express language of the ADA that requires an individualized assessment.[282] Some courts have not used an individualized assessment, but rather, found, as a matter of law, that some conditions fall under the direct threat defense. For instance, an insulin-dependent diabetic applicant for a police officer position was removed from a list of eligible candidates after a medical examination revealed the applicant's diabetic condition.[283] This precedent created an exception to the individualized assessment of the direct threat, holding that drivers with insulin-dependent diabetes pose a direct threat *as a matter of law*.[284] The court stated that, without en banc review for guidance, it would "operate under the assumption that an exception to the EEOC regulation requiring individualized assessment is permissible."[285]

EEOC regulations provide that an employer may legitimately deem a disabled applicant to be a direct threat if the

---

that significant risk of harm defense is without merit in position sought by applicant and based on "speculation and stereotyping").

[281] 29 C.F.R. §1630.2(r) (2003). Disability groups argued that the EEOC standard perpetuated stereotypical attitudes explicitly rejected in the legislative history of the ADA. *See* 56 Fed. Reg. 35,726, 35,730 (July 26, 1991).

[282] *See* Kapche v. City of San Antonio, 176 F.3d 840, 844, 9 AD Cases 623 (5th Cir. 1999).

[283] *See id.* at 840. The *Kapche* court relied on precedent, Daugherty v. City of El Paso, 56 F.3d 695, 4 AD Cases 993 (5th Cir. 1995), *cert. denied*, 516 U.S. 1172 (1996); Chandler v. City of Dallas, 2 F.3d 1385, 2 AD Cases 1326 (5th Cir. 1993), *cert. denied*, 511 U.S. 1011 (1994) (as matter of law, applicant was not qualified to be police officer because of his diabetic condition, which presented genuine substantial risk that he could injure himself or others; the essential job function at issue was "defensive and high performance driving," *Kapche*, 176 F.3d at 843).

[284] *Kapche*, 176 F.3d 840 at 843.

[285] *Id.* at 845–86. However, the court went on to examine whether the exception, as it applies to drivers who are insulin-dependent diabetics, should be modified in light of recent studies and advances in medical technology. Because Department of Transportation regulations abolished prohibitions of diabetic drivers and the American Diabetes Association offered cogent support through several recent studies, the court found a genuine issue of material fact in dispute regarding the safety risk posed and vacated the lower decisions. *See id.* at 846–47.

applicant lacks good judgment or the ability to interact and communicate effectively with coworkers or supervisors.[286] The EEOC's acknowledgment follows case law interpreting the Rehabilitation Act.[287] For instance, one court held that an employee who claimed to have a mental disability was not otherwise qualified under the Rehabilitation Act in light of "repeated disruptive and abusive behavior," which demonstrated "his inability to accept criticism or to deal with his co-workers in a civil manner."[288] The court found that the employer would not be required to employ plaintiff inasmuch as it would expose the other employees with whom plaintiff would work to a "hostile and potentially threatening work environment."[289] According to the court, "[t]hese fundamental requirements that an

---

[286] A TECHNICAL ASSISTANCE MANUAL ON THE EMPLOYMENT PROVISIONS (TITLE I) OF THE AMERICANS WITH DISABILITIES ACT, at II-12. *See also* Grenier v. Cyanamid Plastics, Inc., 70 F.3d 667, 5 AD Cases 75, 81 (1st Cir. 1995) (recognizing that "[t]echnical skills and experience are not the only essential requirements of a job" and that "ability to function effectively in the workplace and to get along" with coworkers and supervisors also may be essential functions); Voytek v. University of Cal., 5 AD Cases 1255, 1266–67 (N.D. Cal. 1994) (employee legally denied reemployment after period of disability, where he "could not continue to perform all of the tasks assigned to him" due in part to ongoing conflict with supervisor).

[287] *See* Pesterfield v. Tennessee Valley Auth., 941 F.2d 437, 1 AD Cases 1858 (6th Cir. 1991) (employee's psychological condition, which caused inability to tolerate any criticism and to withstand ordinary workplace pressures, rendered him unqualified to perform essential functions of tool room attendant job (decided under Rehabilitation Act of 1973)); Mancini v. General Elec. Co., 820 F. Supp. 141, 2 AD Cases 764 (D. Vt. 1993) (employee, who had emotional condition characterized by feelings of inferiority and unacceptability and was insubordinate on several occasions, was not qualified individual with disability, because he was incapable of performing essential functions of job even with reasonable accommodation) (decided under Vermont Fair Employment Practices Act, 21 U.S.A. §495 et seq.); Russell v. Frank, 2 AD Cases 243, 247 (D. Mass. 1991), *aff'd*, 971 F.2d 744, 2 AD Cases 1872 (1st Cir. 1992), *cert. denied*, 507 U.S. 925 (1993) ("ability to tell the truth" has been recognized to be "an essential part of every job") (decided under §504 of the Rehabilitation Act of 1973).

[288] Gordon v. Runyon, 1994 U.S. Dist. LEXIS 4959 at *13, 3 AD Cases 784 (E.D. Pa. 1994).

[289] *Id. See also* Mazzarella v. U.S. Postal Serv., 849 F. Supp. 89, 94, 3 AD Cases 232, 236 (D. Mass. 1994) ("the essential functions of any job include avoidance of violent behavior that threatens the safety of other employees.... [t]o qualify for employment of any nature, the employee must have the ability to refrain from willfully destroying his employer's property"). The EEOC has also recognized that the ADA does not protect an employee from the consequences of his or her misconduct, even though such conduct may be caused by an employee's disability.

employee not engage in violent or destructive behavior are a matter of common sense."[290] Thus, an employee who has aggressive outbursts, even if caused by a mental impairment, is unqualified to perform the essential functions of a job. [291]

5. Employee Insubordination

Courts interpreting the Rehabilitation Act and similar state antidiscrimination laws likewise have held that the ability to follow the orders of superiors is an essential function of any position. In other words, employees who are insubordinate are not otherwise qualified for a position.[292] As the District Court for the Southern District of New York recognized, "an employer may . . . require that employees, whether handicapped or not, not cause, or contribute to, undue interruptions and hostility in the workplace."[293]

Some state health or safety laws may allow or require an employer to reject a disabled applicant in situations where the ADA would not because the applicant would pose a direct threat. Because the ADA supersedes such state laws, employers may not defend their rejection of applicants based on these laws.

See Letter from Clare Gonzales, Director of Communications and Legislative Affairs, EEOC, to Honorable John B. Breaux, United States Senate, January 4, 1995.

[290] *Mazzarella,* 849 F. Supp. at 94.

[291] *See also* Magruder v. Runyon, 844 F. Supp. 696, 705, 3 AD Cases 120 (D. Kan. 1994), *aff'd,* 54 F.3d 787, 6 AD Cases 1440 (10th Cir. 1995) (employee disabled by alcoholism, who was discharged for forging the signature of a supervisor, was not "otherwise qualified" for his job and, therefore, employer did not violate Rehabilitation Act in discharging employee for misconduct).

[292] *See* Thomas v. General Servs. Admin., 49 FEP Cases 1602 (D.D.C. 1989) (employee who was insubordinate not otherwise qualified); Mancini v. General Elec. Co., 820 F. Supp. 141, 147, 2 AD Cases 764 (D. Vt. 1993); Dowden v. Tisch, 729 F. Supp. 1137, 1138–39, 52 FEP Cases 93 (E.D. Tex. 1989), *aff'd,* 902 F.2d 957, 53 FEP Cases 912 (5th Cir. 1990).

[293] Misek-Falkoff v. International Bus. Machs. Corp., 854 F. Supp. 215, 227, 3 AD Cases 449, 457 (S.D.N.Y. 1994), *aff'd,* 60 F.3d 811, 6 AD Cases 576 (2d Cir.), *cert. denied,* 516 U.S. 991 (1995) ("it is certainly a 'job-related requirement' that an employee, handicapped or not, be able to get along with co-workers and supervisors"); *cf.* Hindman v. GTE Data Servs., 3 AD Cases 641 (M.D. Fla. 1994) (individual with poor judgment and irresponsible behavior, which were symptoms of a mental disorder, is not necessarily unqualified to perform essential functions of job).

Employers must consider the actual threat to third parties and avoid stereotypes and misconceptions about an applicant's disability.[294] An employer cannot deny an otherwise qualified applicant a position based on speculation that he or she will not be able to perform the job in the future, or because by hiring him or her the employer's workers' compensation or health insurance costs may increase.[295] In addition, an employer cannot reject an applicant merely because he or she sustained a work injury in the past. While prior occupational injuries may be relevant to a direct threat analysis, they do not establish the existence of a direct threat.[296]

D. Nonstatutory Defenses

Federal regulations drafted to implement the ADA similarly recognize that "[i]t may be a defense to a charge of discrimination . . . that a challenged action is required or necessitated by another Federal law or regulation. . . ."[297] For instance, a legitimate nondiscriminatory reason may be that a state law requires licenses or qualification standards to be met.[298]

---

[294] *See* H.R. REP. NO. 101-485, pt. 3, at 45, *reprinted in* 1990 U.S.C.C.A.N. 445, 468.

[295] *See id.*

[296] *See, e.g.*, EEOC Guidance on Workers' Compensation and the ADA, No. 915.002 (Sept. 1996).

[297] 29 C.F.R. §1630.15(e) (2003).

[298] *See* Ethridge v. State, 860 F. Supp. 808, 820, 3 AD Cases 1013 (M.D. Ala. 1994) (pertaining to handgun course required by state Peace Officers' Standards and Training Commission, commission created by state law); *see also* Fitzpatrick v. City of Atlanta, 2 F.3d 1112, 1115, 2 AD Cases 1270 (11th Cir. 1993) (pertaining to Occupational Safety and Health Administration regulations requiring no beards for firefighters).

CHAPTER 8

REASONABLE ACCOMMODATION

I. Introduction 775
   A. Reasonable Accommodation Under the
      Rehabilitation Act of 1973 775
   B. Reasonable Accommodation Under the
      Americans With Disabilities Act 776
II. Reasonable Accommodation Defined/General
    Requirements 777
   A. Categories of Reasonable Accommodations 777
   B. Reasonable Accommodation Concepts 777
      1. Essential Functions of the Job 778
      2. Employers' Rights 781
   C. The Employer Must Provide Accommodations
      That Will Enable the Employee to Enjoy the
      Benefits and Privileges of Employment 782
   D. Establishing the Employer's Failure to
      Provide a Reasonable Accommodation 783
III. Requests for Accommodations 784
   A. "Interactive Process" Anticipated by
      the Regulations 784
      1. The Employee's Responsibility to Request
         a Reasonable Accommodation 785
         a. Employer's Duty 787
      2. Form of the Request 789
      3. Employer's Responsibility to Engage in the
         Interactive Process to Formulate an
         Effective Accommodation 790
      4. The Responsibility of the Employee to
         Provide Requested Information 791
      5. Interactive Process Examples 793
   B. Documentation Requests by Employer 795

	C. Requirement of Additional Certification by Physician Selected by Employer	796
	D. Employer Policies	798
	E. Effect of a Collective Bargaining Agreement ..	801
	F. Confidentiality Issues	803
IV.	What Type of Accommodation Is "Reasonable"? ..	804
	A. Making Existing Facilities Accessible to Disabled Employees	806
	B. Job Restructuring	807
	C. Job Reassignment	809
	1. Legitimate Policies Prohibiting a Transfer	811
	2. Vacant Positions	813
	D. Obligation to Provide a Leave of Absence as a Reasonable Accommodation	815
	1. Employer Policies Regarding Leaves of Absence and Attendance	817
	2. Employee's Job Security While on Medical Leave	817
	3. Requiring Employee to Stay on the Job Rather Than Take a Leave as a Form of Reasonable Accommodation	818
	4. Providing a Modified or Part-Time Schedule	818
	E. Work at Home	820
	F. Issues Relating to Medication of a Disabled Employee	821
	G. Modification of the Employer's Work Site or Equipment	822
	H. Effect on Workplace Conduct Rules	822
V.	Undue Hardship Issues	823
	A. Undue Hardship Defined	823
	B. Undue Hardship Applied to Leave Cases	825
VI.	Direct-Threat Defense	826
VII.	Reasonable Accommodation and Job Applicants	828
	A. Duty to Provide Reasonable Accommodation to New Hires	828

B. Preemployment Inquiries by an
Employer as to the Need for a
Reasonable Accommodation 829
1. Preemployment Offer 829
2. Post-Employment Offer 830
VIII. Other Reasonable Accommodation Issues 830
A. Interplay With Other Laws 830
B. Providing Additional Accommodations 832
IX. Public Accommodations 833

I. Introduction

Reasonable accommodation is a unique and important concept under the Americans with Disabilities Act (ADA).[1] While other federal antidiscrimination statutes focus on equal treatment for similarly situated employees and applicants, the ADA provides for special treatment of persons with disabilities by placing on the employer an affirmative duty to identify and provide a reasonable accommodation to any qualified employee or applicant with a disability.[2]

A. Reasonable Accommodation Under the Rehabilitation Act of 1973

The concept of reasonable accommodation was first developed under the Rehabilitation Act of 1973 (Rehabilitation Act),[3] a federal precursor to the ADA that applies to federal government employees. The Rehabilitation Act requires employers to make reasonable accommodations to work sites that permit otherwise qualified applicants to perform essential job

---

[1] 42 U.S.C. §12101 et seq.
[2] 42 U.S.C. §12112(b)(5)(A) (under the ADA, failure to accommodate a qualified individual with a disability is unlawful discrimination); see 29 C.F.R. pt. 1630, app. (2003) ("Background") (the "ADA requires employers to consider whether [a] reasonable accommodation could remove the barrier [created by an individual's disability]").
[3] 29 U.S.C. §701 et seq.

functions.[4] The Rehabilitation Act regulations suggest changes to physical structures and job requirements that create increased opportunities for disabled applicants.[5] Under the Rehabilitation Act, however, an employer is not required to make an accommodation that will place an undue hardship on the employer.[6]

The ADA, by its terms, evidences an intent to follow Rehabilitation Act principles.[7] Additionally, Congress used the same definition of the term "disabled" in the ADA as was used in the definition of "individual with handicaps" in the Rehabilitation Act of 1973.[8] These factors reflect the intent of Congress to make the relevant case law developed under the Rehabilitation Act applicable to the interpretation of relevant ADA concepts. Additionally, Congress has subsequently amended the Rehabilitation Act to provide that the standards for employment discrimination under that act will be construed in concert with the ADA and other federal employment statutes.[9] Thus, the courts will look to Rehabilitation Act cases for interpretation of how employers should accommodate employees with disabilities under the ADA.

B. Reasonable Accommodation Under the Americans With Disabilities Act

The concepts behind the regulations promulgated under the Rehabilitation Act that pertain to reasonable accommodation were incorporated into the ADA.[10] Under the ADA, an employer must reasonably accommodate individuals with disabilities.[11] The duty to provide a reasonable accommodation

---

[4] *See* 29 U.S.C. §794a(a)(1) for the requirement of reasonable accommodations under the Rehabilitation Act.
[5] *Id.* §794b(a).
[6] *See* 29 U.S.C. §794(a)(1) (1988).
[7] 42 U.S.C. §12201(a).
[8] *See* 29 C.F.R. pt. 1630, app. §1630.2(g) (2003).
[9] 29 U.S.C. §§791(g), 793(d), and 794(d).
[10] *See* H.R. REP. No. 101-485, pt. 2, at 23, *reprinted in* 1990 U.S.C.C.A.N. 303, 304.
[11] 42 U.S.C. §12112(b)(5)(A), (B).

applies to all aspects of employment including recruiting, hiring, and assignment of work.[12] An employer may not deny a reasonable accommodation to an individual unless the accommodation would pose an undue hardship to the employer.[13] However, an employer may screen out individuals who pose a direct threat to the health or safety of other individuals in the workplace, or to the individual himself or herself.[14]

II. Reasonable Accommodation Defined/General Requirements

A. Categories of Reasonable Accommodations

There are three categories of accommodations contemplated by the regulations interpreting the ADA:

> (1) accommodations that are required to ensure equal opportunity in the application process; (2) accommodations that enable the employer's employees with disabilities to perform the essential functions of the position held or desired; and (3) accommodations that enable the employer's employees with disabilities to enjoy equal benefits and privileges of employment as are enjoyed by employees without disabilities.[15]

B. Reasonable Accommodation Concepts

Employers are required to accommodate only "qualified" individuals with disabilities.[16] Two inquiries determine whether

---

[12] *Id.* §12112(a).

[13] *Id.* §12112(b)(5)(A).

[14] *Id.* §§12112(b)(6), 12113(a), (b). The regulations promulgated by the Equal Employment Opportunity Commission (EEOC) under the ADA provide that an employer can screen out a potential worker with a disability—and defend against a claim of discrimination—not only for risks that he or she would pose to others in the workplace but for risks on the job to his or her own health or safety as well: "The term 'qualification standard' may include a requirement that an individual shall not pose a direct threat to the health or safety of the individual or others in the workplace." 29 C.F.R. §1630.15 (b)(2) (2003).

[15] 29 C.F.R. pt. 1630, app. §1630.2 (o) (2003).

[16] 42 U.S.C. §§12111(8); 12112(a); *see* Criado v. IBM Corp., 145 F.3d 437, 443, 8 AD Cases 336 (1st Cir. 1998).

a person is a qualified individual under the ADA: (1) whether the person possesses "the requisite skill, experience, education and other job-related requirements" for the position; and (2) whether the individual is able to perform the essential functions of the position desired or held with or without a reasonable accommodation.[17] In considering the categories of individuals who may be entitled to a reasonable accommodation under the ADA, a dispute has developed in the federal courts as to whether such an accommodation must be provided to individuals whose claim to status as disabled individuals under the statute rests on their being "regarded as" individuals with a disability, with most courts holding that such an entitlement does not exist.[18] In addition, where the disabling limitation of an individual's capabilities involve a major life activity unconnected to work functions, an accommodation may not be required.[19]

1. *Essential Functions of the Job*

The essential functions of a job or, the "fundamental job duties of the employment position" must first be identified to determine whether a disabled individual is qualified for the position and how best to accommodate the individual.[20] The analysis of whether a function is essential requires consideration of: (1) "whether the employer actually requires employees in the

---

[17] *Criado*, 145 F.3d at 443, 8 AD Cases at 340 (quoting 29 C.F.R. §1630.2(m)).

[18] *Compare* Kaplan v. City of N. Las Vegas, 323 F.3d 1226, 14 AD Cases 295 (9th Cir.), *cert. denied* 14 AD Cases 1920 (2003); Weber v. Strippit, Inc., 186 F.3d 907, 9 AD Cases 961 (8th Cir. 1999); Workman v. Frito-Lay, Inc., 165 F.3d 460, 8 AD Cases 1761 (6th Cir. 1999); Newberry v. East Tex. State Univ., 161 F.3d 276, 8 AD Cases 1595 (5th Cir. 1998); Deane v. Pocono Med. Ctr., 142 F.3d 138, 7 AD Cases 1809 (3d Cir. 1998), all holding no entitlement to reasonable accommodation for individuals regarded as disabled, *with* Katz v. City Metal Co., 87 F.3d 26, 5 AD Cases 1120 (1st Cir. 1996); Jacques v. DiMarzio, Inc., 200 F. Supp. 2d 151, 13 AD Cases 1014 (E.D.N.Y. 2002).

[19] Wood v. Crown Redi-Mix, 339 F.3d 682, 14 AD Cases 1204 (8th Cir. 2003) (individual whose major life activity of procreation was substantially limited could not establish prima facie case of disability discrimination due to rejection of his requested accommodation in his position as non-ready-mix trucker). *See also* Felix v. New York City Transit Auth., 324 F.3d 102, 14 AD Cases 193 (2d Cir. 2003) (request for reassignment to above-ground position by subway clerk with posttraumatic stress disorder not reasonable, because it did not flow from her disability).

[20] 42 U.S.C. §12111(8).

position to perform the functions that the employer asserts are essential;" and (2) "whether removing the function would fundamentally alter that position."[21] A job function is essential if the job exists to perform the function.[22] It may also be essential if there are a "limited number of employees available" to perform the function, or among whom the "function can be distributed."[23] Thus, although answering the telephone may not be an essential function for a file clerk in many offices, it may be an essential function for a file clerk to answer the telephone at a small, busy office where each employee must perform many different tasks, including answering the telephone.[24] Additionally, a job function is essential if it is highly specialized so that the incumbent is hired for his or her ability to perform that function.[25]

Other factors that are considered to determine if a particular job function is "essential" are:

1. "the degree of expertise or skill required to perform the function;"
2. "written job descriptions;"
3. "the employer's judgment as to what functions are essential;"
4. "terms of a collective bargaining agreement;"
5. "[t]he work experience of past employees in the [same] job or [of] current employees in similar jobs;"
6. "the time spent performing the particular [job];" and
7. "the consequences of failing to require the employee to perform the function."[26]

Thus, an employee's inability to perform the essential functions of his or her job disqualifies the employee from ADA protection, because the employee is not a "qualified individual

---

[21] 29 C.F.R. pt. 1630, app. §1630.2 (n) (2003).
[22] 29 C.F.R. §1630.2(n)(2)(i) (2003).
[23] *Id.* §1630.2(n)(2)(ii) (2003).
[24] 29 C.F.R. pt. 1630, app. §1630.2(n) (2003) (citing Treadwell v. Alexander, 707 F.2d 473, 1 AD Cases 459 (11th Cir. 1983)).
[25] 29 C.F.R. §1630.2(n)(2)(iii) (2003).
[26] 29 C.F.R. pt. 1630, app. §1630.2(n) (2003).

with a disability."[27] Thus, in *Dropinski v. Douglas County*,[28] the accommodation sought by a truck driver who was unable to fulfill his job's essential functions of performing its sporadic manual labor requirements—that is, occasional coworker assistance—was not viewed as appropriate.

Courts have determined that an employee who is unable to come to work on a regular basis is unable to satisfy the essential functions of the job.[29] Additionally, the U.S. Court of Appeals for the Eleventh Circuit has held that arriving at work on time can be an essential function of an employee's position of retail store area coordinator.[30] The court noted that the employer's policies placed a high value on punctuality, the importance that the area coordinator be at her shift on time to prepare the store or to relieve another area coordinator, and that there were few employees in the area coordinator position and few area coordinators on duty at any given time.[31] The court found that the employee failed to prove that any accommodation would enable her to arrive at work on time, and thus, the employee did not qualify for protection under the ADA.[32] Similarly, in *Durning v. Duffers Optical, Inc.*,[33] a court dismissed the claims of an outside salesperson whose disability rendered him unable to communicate effectively, make in-person sales calls to distant locations, or to make presentations to customers.

---

[27] *Id.*

[28] 298 F.3d 704, 13 AD Cases 676 (8th Cir. 2002).

[29] Nesser v. Trans World Airlines, Inc., 160 F.3d 442, 8 AD Cases 1348 (8th Cir. 1998) (employee suffering from Crohn's disease could not perform essential functions of his job without accommodation, because he was unable to attend work on regular basis); Halperin v. Abacus Tech. Corp., 128 F.3d 191, 198, 7 AD Cases 406, 409 (4th Cir. 1997) ("Because Halperin was unable to come to work on a regular basis, he was unable to satisfy any of the functions of the job in question, much less the essential ones.").

[30] Earl v. Mervyns, 207 F.3d 1361, 10 AD Cases 673 (11th Cir. 2000) (a woman suffering from obsessive compulsive disorder was not qualified individual with disability, because her disability prevented her from coming to work on time); *see also* Jackson v. Veterans Admin., Dep't of Veterans Affairs, 22 F.3d 277, 279, 3 AD Cases 483 (11th Cir.), punctuality an essential function of housekeeping aide position), *cert. dismissed*, 513 U.S. 1052 (1994).

[31] *Earl*, 207 F.3d 1361.

[32] *Id.*

[33] 1996 U.S. Dist. LEXIS 1685 (E.D. La. 1996) (because employee could not perform essential functions of his position, he was not qualified for ADA protection).

2. Employers' Rights

As a general matter, the courts and the Equal Employment Opportunity Commission (EEOC) will not use the analysis of the essential functions of the job as a vehicle to second-guess the employer or require a company to lower its standards.[34] The employer has the right to define the job and the functions required to perform it. Preexisting written job descriptions will provide evidence of what functions are "essential" to a position.[35] However, if an employer's actions are challenged in a court or administrative action, neither the employer's judgment nor a job description will be dispositive in defining the "essential functions" of a particular job or whether an applicant or employee is a qualified individual with a disability.[36] For example, where an employee and the employer presented conflicting evidence regarding an HIV-infected police officer's ability to perform the essential functions of his job safely, the court found that it could not conclude as a matter of law that the officer was unable to perform the essential functions of his position.[37] However, in another case, the U.S. Court of Appeals for the Sixth Circuit agreed with the employer that an employee was unable to perform the essential functions of his sales representative position where he was unable to bend, lift, twist, or walk for extended periods of time, and where the doctor's report stated that he was "fit only for the most sedentary type of employment."[38] Whether a function is essential is a highly fact-specific inquiry that may vary depending on the employer and the type of position at issue.[39]

---

[34] 29 C.F.R. pt. 1630, app. §1630.2(n) (2003); *see Durning*, 1996 U.S. Dist. LEXIS 1685.

[35] *Id.*

[36] *See* Holiday v. City of Chattanooga, 206 F.3d 637, 643, 10 AD Cases 501 (6th Cir. 2000) (employer cannot use doctor's report as dispositive evidence of employee's inability to perform essential functions of job).

[37] *Id.* at 643.

[38] Smith v. Ameritech, 129 F.3d 857, 861, 7 AD Cases 917, 919 (6th Cir. 1997).

[39] *See, e.g.,* Laurin v. Providence Hosp. & Mass. Nurses Ass'n, 150 F.3d 52, 8 AD Cases 768 (1st Cir. 1998) (requirement to work rotating schedule was essential function for maternity nurse position where night shift undesirable and all employees required to take turn); Martinson v. Kinney Shoe Corp., 104 F.3d 683, 687, 6

C. The Employer Must Provide Accommodations That Will Enable the Employee to Enjoy the Benefits and Privileges of Employment

The EEOC published a guidance document intended to assist employers in correctly applying the requirements of the ADA and its implementing regulations.[40] Although the Enforcement Guidance is not strictly binding on courts, it is a statement of how the EEOC believes the ADA should be construed.[41] The Enforcement Guidance provides that aside from accommodating the employee's ability to work, the employer must also accommodate the employee's ability to enjoy the "benefits and privileges of employment."[42] Benefits and privileges include, among other things:

1. employer-sponsored training, including optional training, whether it occurs on the employer's premises or elsewhere;
2. employer-sponsored services (e.g., employee assistance programs, credit unions, cafeterias, lounges, gymnasiums, auditoriums, and transportation);

AD Cases 434, 437 (4th Cir. 1997) (provision of store security is of such nature that it "cannot reasonably be abandoned for even 'a brief period' "); Jasany v. U.S. Postal Serv., 755 F.2d 1244, 1251, 1 AD Cases 706 (6th Cir. 1985) (defining scheduling flexibility as essential function under analogous Rehabilitation Act); Salmon v. Dade County Sch. Bd., 4 F. Supp. 2d 1157, 1161 (S.D. Fla. 1998) ("Unlike other jobs that can be . . . deferred until a later day, a guidance counselor must counsel students at the school during the hours in which the children are in attendance."); Mackie v. Runyon, 804 F. Supp. 1508, 1511, 2 AD Cases 260 (M.D. Fla. 1992) (scheduling flexibility essential function).

[40] EQUAL EMPLOYMENT OPPORTUNITY COMM'N, REVISED ENFORCEMENT GUIDANCE: REASONABLE ACCOMMODATION AND UNDUE HARDSHIP UNDER THE AMERICANS WITH DISABILITIES ACT, <http://www.eeoc.gov/docs/accommodation.html> [hereinafter EEOC ENFORCEMENT GUIDE]. The guidance document was published initially on March 1, 1999, and was superseded by an updated document published on October 17, 2002.

[41] *See* Sutton v. United Airlines, 527 U.S. 471, 481–84, 9 AD Cases 673 (1999) (declining to follow "unreasonable" interpretation of ADA contained in regulations and interpretive guidelines); Grenier v. Cyanamid Plastics, Inc., 70 F.3d 667, 672, 5 AD Cases 75 (1st Cir. 1995) (EEOC regulations interpreting ADA, while not controlling, constitute " 'a body of experience and informed judgment to which courts . . . may properly resort for guidance;' " quoting Meritar Sav. Bank v. Vinson, 477 U.S. 57, 65, 40 FEP Cases 1822 (1986)).

[42] EEOC ENFORCEMENT GUIDE, *supra* note 40, at 11–12.

3. employer-sponsored parties or other social functions (e.g., parties to celebrate retirements and birthdays, and company outings);
4. equal access to any information communicated in the workplace, regardless of whether the information is necessary to perform the job.[43]

The Enforcement Guidance provides the following example of an effective reasonable accommodation of the benefits and privileges of employment: An employer regularly communicates information about meetings and upcoming events to employees via the public intercom system. To accommodate a hearing-impaired employee's inability to hear these office announcements, the EEOC suggests that the employer send an electronic mail message to the deaf employee in advance of the broadcast conveying the information that will be communicated. Thus, even where the communications may not be essential to the employee's positions, the employee is entitled to the same benefits and privileges of the employees who are able to hear.

D. Establishing the Employer's Failure to Provide a Reasonable Accommodation

The failure of an employer to provide a reasonable accommodation where it would be possible to do so is a violation of the ADA. A plaintiff establishes that an employer has failed to accommodate a disability of the employee by demonstrating the following: "'1) the employer knew about the employee's disability; 2) the employee requested accommodations or assistance for his or her disability; 3) the employer did not make a good faith effort to assist the employee in seeking accommodations; and 4) the employee could have been reasonably accommodated but for the employer's lack of good faith.'"[44]

---

[43]*Id.*

[44]Jones v. United Parcel Serv., 214 F.3d 402, 408, 10 AD Cases 1064 (3d Cir. 2000) (quoting Taylor v. Phoenixville Sch. Dist., 184 F.3d 296, 319–20, 9 AD Cases 1187 (3d Cir. 1999)); *see also* Mantolete v. Bolger, 767 F.2d 1416, 1423–24, 1 AD Cases 811 (9th Cir. 1985); Treadwell v. Alexander, 707 F.2d 473, 478, 1 AD Cases

In cases involving a request for reassignment as a reasonable accommodation, the plaintiff bears the burden of demonstrating: (1) that there was a vacant position, (2) that the position was at or below the level of the plaintiff's former job, and (3) that the plaintiff was qualified to perform the essential duties of this job with or without reasonable accommodation.[45] If the employee meets his or her burden, the employer has the burden to show that transferring the employee would cause unreasonable hardship.[46] Thus, where an employee with performance problems challenged the refusal of her supervisor to recommend her for a transfer after her work deteriorated despite earlier accommodations, her ADA complaint was rejected.[47]

III. Requests for Accommodations

A. "Interactive Process" Anticipated by the Regulations

When resolving issues relating to accommodating individuals with disabilities, the regulations require that the employer

> initiate an informal, interactive process with the qualified individual with a disability in need of the accommodation. This process should identify the precise limitations resulting from the disability and potential reasonable accommodations that could overcome those limitations.[48]

The EEOC and courts will consider the following elements to determine whether an employer has failed to engage in the interactive process required by the regulations:

---

459 (11th Cir. 1983); Prewitt v. U.S. Postal Serv., 662 F.2d 292, 310, 1 AD Cases 273 (5th Cir. 1981).

[45]Donahue v. Consolidated Rail Corp., 224 F.3d 226, 230, 10 AD Cases 1505 (3d Cir. 2000) (Rehabilitation Act case); Burns v. Coca-Cola Enters., Inc., 222 F.3d 247, 258, 10 AD Cases 1409 (6th Cir. 2000) (outlining burden in ADA case).

[46]*Burns*, 222 F.3d at 258.

[47]Burchett v. Target Corp., 340 F.3d 510, 14 AD Cases 1296 (8th Cir. 2003).

[48]29 C.F.R. §1630.2(o)(3) (2003); *see also* Cravens v. Blue Cross & Blue Shield of Kansas City, 214 F.3d 1011, 1021, 10 AD Cases 1057 (8th Cir. 2000) (once employee requests assistance in accommodating disability, employer has duty to initiate interactive process in effort to come up with appropriate accommodation).

1. Whether the employer knew of the disability;
2. Whether the employee requested assistance or accommodation;
3. Lack of good faith effort by the employer to "assist the employee"; and
4. Whether "the employee could have been reasonably accommodated but for the employer's lack of good faith."[49]

The interactive process between the employer and the employee generally begins with notification to the employer of the employee's disability and limitations and the employee's desire for a particular reasonable accommodation or reassignment. Thereafter, both parties have an obligation to proceed in a reasonably interactive manner. However, " '[t]he exact shape of this interactive [process] will necessarily vary from situation to situation and no rules of universal application can be articulated.' "[50]

1. The Employee's Responsibility to Request a Reasonable Accommodation

The employee has the obligation to notify the employer in some form of the employee's need for an accommodation. Therefore, "an employer would not be expected to accommodate disabilities of which it is unaware."[51] Thus, in *Ballard v.*

---

[49] *See* Cravens, 214 F.3d at 1021, 10 AD Cases at 1063.

[50] Hines v. Chrysler Corp., 2000 U.S. App. LEXIS 11338, *6 (10th Cir. May 19, 2000) (unpublished opinion) (quoting Smith v. Midland Brake, 180 F.3d 1154, 1173, 9 AD Cases 738, 750 (10th Cir. 1999)).

[51] 29 C.F.R. pt. 1630, app. §1630.9 (2003). *See* Reed v. LePage Bakeries, Inc., 244 F.3d 254, 11 AD Cases 1150 (1st Cir. 2001) (employer never informed of employee's bipolar disorder has no obligation to provide reasonable accommodation to deal with conflicts in workplace); Jovanovic v. In-Sink-Erator Div., Emerson Elec. Co., 201 F.3d 894, 10 AD Cases 193 (7th Cir. 2000) (general rule is that employee with disability must request reasonable accommodation before employer can be found liable for failure to provide one); Mole v. Buckhorn Rubber Prods., Inc., 185 F.3d 1212, 8 AD Cases 1873 (8th Cir.), *cert. denied*, 528 U.S. 821 (1999) (employer that previously made accommodations relating to employee's multiple sclerosis cannot be found liable under ADA for failure to provide additional accommodation if employee fails to request one); Hill v. Kansas City Area Transp. Auth., 181 F.3d 891, 9 AD Cases 833 (8th Cir. 1999) (request for reasonable accommoda-

Rubin,[52] an employee's memo containing contradictory statements regarding the individual's desire for an accommodation could not be construed to be a request for that type of adjustment or modification. In *Morisky v. Broward County*,[53] a job applicant informed the administrators of a qualifying examination for county employment that she was illiterate. After being refused the opportunity to take the test with a reader, the individual sued the county, alleging that it should have known that she suffered from a learning disability based on the information she had provided—that she could not read and that she had taken special education courses. The court found that an employee's vague, conclusory statements to the test administrators did not put the employer on notice of her need for an accommodation.[54] Similarly, in *Kennedy v. Chemical Waste*

---

tion comes too late when it is made after employee has committed infraction warranting termination); Gaston v. Bellingrath Gardens & Home, Inc., 167 F.3d 1361, 8 AD Cases 1862 (11th Cir. 1999) (employer is not required to provide disabled employee with reasonable accommodation until and unless employee asks for it); Hammon v. DHL Airways, Inc., 165 F.3d 441, 450, 8 AD Cases 1707 (6th Cir. 1999) (quoting Gantt v. Wilson Sporting Goods Co., 143 F.3d 1042, 1046, 8 AD Cases 308 (6th Cir. 1998) (employer " 'is not required to speculate as to the extent of the employee's disability or the employee's need or desire for an accommodation' ")); Hunt-Golliday v. Metropolitan Water Reclamation Dist. of Greater Ohio, 104 F.3d 1004, 6 AD Cases 725 (7th Cir. 1997) (same); Office of Senate Sergeant-at-Arms v. Office of Senate Fair Employment Practices, 95 F.3d 1102, 6 AD Cases 1237 (Fed. Cir. 1996) (duty to accommodate arises when employer first learned of employee's need for accommodation); Miller v. National Cas. Co., 61 F.3d 627, 4 AD Cases 1089 (8th Cir. 1995) (employer did not know of employee's disability because employee's symptoms were not so severe as to put employer on notice of such disability); Hedberg v. Indiana Bell Tel. Co., 47 F.3d 928, 4 AD Cases 65 (7th Cir. 1995) (ADA does not require employers to retain unproductive employees on chance they may suffer from disability); Whillock v. Delta Air Lines, 926 F. Supp. 1555, 5 AD Cases 1027 (N.D. Ga. 1995), *aff'd*, 86 F.3d 1171,7 AD Cases 1267 (11th Cir. 1996) (recognizing that employer's duty to provide its employee with reasonable accommodation sets in once employer is made aware of employee's disability); McAlpin v. National Semiconductor Corp., 921 F. Supp. 1518, 1525, 5 AD Cases 1047, 1052 (N.D. Tex. 1996) ("[A]n employer does not have the responsibility to go in search of information, such as medical advice, that is uniquely in the hands of the employee, particularly when the employee appears not to have been responsive to requests for further information."); Mears v. Gulfstream Aerospace Corp., 905 F. Supp. 1075, 1080, 5 AD Cases 1295 (S.D. Ga. 1995), *aff'd*, 87 F.3d 1331, 6 AD Cases 1152 (11th Cir. 1996) (employee must inform employer of need for reasonable accommodation).

[52]284 F.3d 957, 12 AD Cases 1646 (8th Cir. 2002).
[53]80 F.3d 445, 448, 5 AD Cases 737 (11th Cir. 1996).
[54]*Id.*

Management, Inc.,[55] the court held that an employer had no obligation to restore seniority to a rehired employee who had quit because of his disability without informing his employer of a need for an accommodation.[56]

a. Employer's Duty

In most circumstances the employee, his or her doctor, family member, or other representative must inform the employer of the need for an accommodation because of a disability. However, according to the EEOC, the employer has a duty to explore accommodations any time the disability is known, even if the employee has not specifically requested an accommodation.[57] The agency's *Enforcement Guidance* states that the employer should initiate the interactive process if the employer knows of an employee's disability, knows or has reason to know that the employee is experiencing difficulty in the workplace because of the disability, and knows or has reason to know that the disability prevents the employee from requesting an accommodation.[58] For example, in *Cravens v. Blue Cross & Blue Shield of Kansas City*,[59] the court found that the employer knew about the employee's bilateral carpal tunnel syndrome after receiving several notes from her doctor and after the employee had asked to be reassigned to another job because of her disability. Thus, the court found that because the employer had been put on notice of the qualifying disability, the employer had the duty to initiate the interactive process to reasonably accommodate her condition, even though she had not specifically requested an accommodation.[60]

---

[55] 79 F.3d 49, 5 AD Cases 565 (7th Cir. 1996).

[56] *Id.*; *see also* Jones v. United Parcel Serv., 214 F.3d 402, 10 AD Cases 1064 (3d Cir. 2000) ("constructive notice" of employee's disability insufficient to prompt employer's duties to accommodate under ADA).

[57] 29 C.F.R. pt. 1630, app. §1630.9 (2003).

[58] EEOC ENFORCEMENT GUIDE, *supra* note 40, at 23.

[59] Cravens v. Blue Cross & Blue Shield of Kansas City, 214 F.3d 1011, 10 AD Cases 1057 (8th Cir. 2000).

[60] *Id.*; *see also* Schmidt v. Safeway, Inc., 864 F. Supp. 991, 3 AD Cases 1141 (D. Or. 1994) (employer who knew of its employee's alcohol problem has duty to accommodate such employee).

In this regard, the U.S. Court of Appeals for the Third Circuit has held that when a disabled employee identifies positions into which he or she might be transferred—even if he or she fails to formally apply for such slots—this communication is enough essentially to shift the burden to the employer to establish that reassignment would not constitute a reasonable accommodation within the meaning of the ADA.[61] Moreover, the U.S. Court of Appeals for the First Circuit has held that the failure of an employer to engage in an interactive process takes on significance only if the plaintiff can demonstrate that a reasonable accommodation existed at the time of the challenged action.[62] Where a plaintiff can successfully demonstrate that a reasonable accommodation existed, that it was not made available and the employer failed to engage in an interactive process around the question of accommodation, the employer may face the burden of demonstrating either that a reasonable accommodation was made available, or that the failure to engage in the interactive process was harmful because no true reasonable accommodation was possible.[63]

Where an employer fails to participate in the interactive process, it may be found to be prima facie evidence of bad faith, and render an award of summary judgment to the defendant inappropriate.[64] In some instances, an employer may be required to make multiple efforts to identify and implement a reasonable accommodation. For example, the U.S. Court of Appeals for the Seventh Circuit has noted that while an employer cannot be held liable because an attempted reasonable accommodation is not successful, experimentation might be required to find one that is appropriate.[65] Where an employer

---

[61] Shapiro v. Township of Lakewood, 292 F.3d 356, 13 AD Cases 106 (3d Cir. 2002).

[62] Kvorjak v. Maine, 259 F.3d 48, 12 AD Cases 160 (1st Cir. 2001). *See also* Donahue v. Consolidated Rail Corp., 224 F.3d 226, 10 AD Cases 1505 (3d Cir. 2000).

[63] Mays v. Principi, 301 F.3d 866, 13 AD Cases 985 (7th Cir. 2002).

[64] Cravens v. Blue Cross & Blue Shield of Kansas City, 214 F.3d 1011, 10 AD Cases 1057 (8th Cir. 2000).

[65] EEOC v. Humiston-Keeling, Inc., 227 F.3d 1024, 10 AD Cases 1665 (7th Cir. 2000).

initially provided accommodations, but there were factual issues regarding its failure to carry the interactive process further, the award of summary judgment to the defendant may be inappropriate.[66]

2. Form of the Request

To request an accommodation, the employee simply needs to put the employer on notice that he or she needs a job adjustment or modification because of a medical condition.[67] The request for reasonable accommodation does not have to be in writing. Rather, the employee need only notify the employer in "plain English" that he or she needs an accommodation.[68]

Additionally, an employer must consider requests for accommodation that are not made by the disabled employee, but are made by a person other than the employee on his or her behalf.[69] A letter to an employer from an employee's psychiatrist articulating that the employee/patient needed to be in a less stressful environment was sufficient to create a triable issue as to whether the employer failed to accommodate the employee's disability.[70] Similarly, a request for an "accommodation" made by the employee's son, after the employee was hospitalized for a psychotic episode at work, was sufficient

---

[66] Humphrey v. Memorial Hosps. Ass'n, 239 F.3d 1128, 11 AD Cases 765 (9th Cir. 2001). *See also* Zvkovic v. Southern Cal. Edison Co., 302 F.3d 1080 (9th Cir. 2002) (where factual issues exist as to employer's continued participation in interactive process, award of summary judgment in challenge to failure to reasonably accommodate employee not proper).

[67] *Cravens*, 214 F.3d 1011 (once employee sought employer's assistance in locating more suitable position because of her disability, it became employer's duty to initiate interactive process to find her appropriate reasonable accommodation).

[68] EEOC ENFORCEMENT GUIDE, *supra* note 40, at 5.

[69] Bultemeyer v. Ft. Wayne Cmty. Sch., 100 F.3d 1281, 6 AD Cases 67 (7th Cir. 1996) (mere fact that mentally ill employee's request for accommodation came in form of his doctor's note, did not relieve employer of its duty to reasonably accommodate him); Taylor v. Phoenixville Sch. Dist., 184 F.3d 296, 9 AD Cases 1187 (3d Cir. 1999) (disabled employee's son could make request for accommodation on behalf of his mother).

[70] *Bultemeyer*, 100 F.3d at 1286.

to trigger the employer's obligation to engage in the interactive process.[71]

3. Employer's Responsibility to Engage in the Interactive Process to Formulate an Effective Accommodation

Generally, an employer must not make disability-related inquiries as to whether an employee requires a reasonable accommodation; it is up to the disabled employee to inform the employer that one is needed. An exception to this general rule, according to the EEOC, occurs when the employer (1) knows that the employee is disabled; (2) knows or has reason to know that the employee is experiencing difficulties in the workplace because of such disability; or (3) knows or has reason to know that the employee is unable to ask for a reasonable accommodation, precisely because of the disability.[72]

Once an employee informs the employer of a need for an accommodation, or once the employer becomes apprised of such a need, the employer must participate in good faith in the interactive process in an attempt to decide on a reasonable accommodation.[73] In *Garcia-Ayala v. Lederle Parenterals, Inc.*,[74] the court held that an employer, by rejecting its employee's request for an extension of leave without discussion, failed to engage in the interactive process required by the ADA. Similarly, in *Taylor v. Phoenixville School District*,[75] the court held that an employer's failure to respond to the employee's request for an accommodation created a genuine issue of fact as to whether the employer participated in good faith in an interactive process with the employee.

One of the consequences for an employer who fails to engage in the interactive process is that the employer may fail

---

[71] *Taylor*, 184 F.3d at 313.
[72] EEOC. ENFORCEMENT GUIDE, *supra* note 40, at 23.
[73] 29 C.F.R. §1630.2(o)(3) (2003); *see* Schmidt v. Safeway, Inc., 864 F. Supp. 991, 3 AD Cases 1141 (D. Or. 1994) (employee does not need to mention statute or use words "reasonable accommodation" to trigger employer's obligation to consider appropriate accommodations).
[74] 212 F.3d 638, 648, 10 AD Cases 865 (1st Cir. 2000).
[75] 184 F.3d 296, 9 AD Cases 1187 (3d Cir. 1999).

to discover an appropriate accommodation for the employee's disability. If a reasonable accommodation is possible, and the employer fails to provide one, such failure is a violation of the ADA. However, where an employee cannot demonstrate that a reasonable accommodation would have been possible, the employer's lack of investigation into reasonable accommodation does not give rise to liability under the ADA.[76] An employer will not be held independently liable under the ADA for failing to engage in an interactive process to determine reasonable accommodations.[77] Rather, liability stems from the refusal to grant a reasonable accommodation occasioned by the refusal to engage in the process.

4. *The Responsibility of the Employee to Provide Requested Information*

The EEOC and the courts have described the interactive process that may be necessary to determine whether a reasonable accommodation can be made.[78] An employee's failure to fully engage in an interactive process by summarily rejecting an offered reasonable accommodation without explanation may result in the rejection of his or her claim.[79] In *Beck v.*

---

[76]Donahue v. Consolidated Rail Corp., 224 F.3d 226, 10 AD Cases 1505 (3d Cir. 2000) (employer did not violate Rehabilitation Act by refusing to transfer employee suffering from heart condition to train dispatcher position, because of possibility of harm such accommodation would pose to others).

[77]*See* Fjellestad v. Pizza Hut of Am., Inc., 188 F.3d 944, 952, 9 AD Cases 1153 (8th Cir. 1999); Willis v. Conopco, Inc., 108 F.3d 282, 285, 6 AD Cases 806 (11th Cir. 1997); White v. York Int'l Corp., 45 F.3d 357, 363, 3 AD Cases 1746 (10th Cir. 1995).

[78]29 C.F.R. §1630.2(o)(3) (2003); *see* Rehling v. City of Chi., 207 F.3d 1009, 10 AD Cases 589 (7th Cir. 2000) (employer's failure to engage in interactive process is not in of itself ADA violation because employee still must allege that failure to engage in interactive process resulted in failure to identify appropriate accommodation); Loulseged v. Akzo Nobel, Inc., 178 F.3d 731, 9 AD Cases 783 (5th Cir. 1999) (failure to participate in talks with employer about possible accommodation barred employee's lawsuit); Beck v. University of Wis. Bd. of Regents, 75 F.3d 1130, 5 AD Cases 304 (7th Cir. 1996) (employee's failure to provide employer with relevant medical information led to breakdown of interactive process, because employer did not know what action to take).

[79]EEOC v. Yellow Freight Sys., Inc., 253 F.3d 943, 11 AD Cases 1569 (7th Cir. 2001) (en banc).

University of Wisconsin Board of Regents,[80] the U.S. Court of Appeals for the Seventh Circuit found that a secretary disabled by osteoarthritis and major depression frustrated her university employer's efforts to determine how to reasonably accommodate her disabilities. She refused to sign a release that would have enabled her employer to obtain more information from her doctor and failed to respond to reasonable requests for additional information about how to accommodate her disability. Noting that there was no evidence that the employer had tried to "sweep the problem under the rug," the court concluded that the employer was unable to obtain a satisfactory understanding of what action it should take, and could not be found liable for failing to accommodate the employee's disability.

At times, the breakdown in the interactive process can be attributed to the actions (or inaction) of the employee. For example, in *Davis v. Guardian Life Ins. Co. of America,*[81] the court found that in telling her employer "I don't think we should talk anymore" after the employer had made attempts to initiate the interactive process, the employee had caused the breakdown of the interactive process and the employer could not be charged with the failure to accommodate the employee. In *Wells v. Shalala,*[82] a case arising under the Rehabilitation Act, the U.S. Court of Appeals for the Tenth Circuit upheld the award of summary judgment to an employer, where it found that the employee had failed consistently to engage meaningfully in an interactive process aimed at finding a reasonable accommodation. In *Wells,* a major point of contention was the employer's insistence that travel, an essential function of the position in question, remain an element of the position. It proposed various accommodations directed to the employee's limitations, but these were rejected. The employee's insistence on removal of this essential job function from any reasonable

---

[80] *Beck,* 75 F.3d at 1135–36.
[81] 11 AD Cases 550 (E.D. Pa. 2000).
[82] 228 F.3d 1137, 10 AD Cases 1795 (10th Cir. 2000).

accommodation, and subsequently, his rejection of a reassignment, led to the court's adverse conclusion.[83] Where a plaintiff is not able to demonstrate that a reasonable accommodation existed that would have permitted the employee to meet the job's essential functions without imposing an undue hardship, the employer's failure to engage in the interactive process does not appear to have independent significance.[84]

5. Interactive Process Examples

The law does not require the employer to adopt the accommodation requested by the employee.[85] While the employer must consider the employee's needs (as defined by the employee's medical provider), it may choose among reasonable accommodations as long as the chosen accommodation is effective (i.e., it enables the employee to perform the essential functions of the position). One court found that by simply acceding to the employee's requested accommodation, without analysis, an employer had failed to accommodate the employee's disability because the requested accommodation was not effective.[86] Although the desires of the disabled employee should be given consideration, the employer has the ultimate discretion and responsibility to select a reasonable accommodation.[87]

---

[83]*See also* Loulseged v. Akzo Nobel, Inc, 178 F.3d 731, 9 AD Cases 783 (5th Cir. 1999).

[84]Dropinski v. Douglas County, 298 F.3d 704, 13 AD Cases 676 (8th Cir. 2002). *See also* Kvorjak v. Maine, 259 F.3d 48, 12 AD Cases 160 (1st Cir. 2001).

[85]Jay v. Internet Wagner, Inc., 233 F.3d 1014, 11 AD Cases 471 (7th Cir. 2000) (where employee's requested accommodation infringes on rights of other employees, employer is not obligated to grant employee his choice of accommodation); Gaines v. Runyon, 107 F.3d 1171, 6 AD Cases 688 (6th Cir. 1997) (where employee's medical documentation simply showed that employee needed straight shift, employer did not have to assign employee to shift he requested).

[86]Feliberty v. Kemper Corp., 98 F.3d 274, 280, 5 AD Cases 1729 (7th Cir. 1996) (where employer provided requested modification to employee's workstation, but modifications did not relieve his problems relating to his carpal tunnel syndrome, employer failed to provide reasonable accommodation).

[87]*Id. See also* EEOC ENFORCEMENT GUIDE, *supra* note 40, at 8–9.

According to the EEOC, as part of the interactive process, the employer may, and should, also offer alternative suggestions for reasonable accommodations and discuss the effectiveness of all potential accommodations in removing the workplace barrier that is impeding the disabled employee. The employer may not rely solely on cost considerations in selecting or rejecting any particular proposed accommodation, according to the EEOC, unless such accommodation would pose an undue hardship. However, if there are two possible reasonable accommodations, and one costs more or is more burdensome than the other, the agency has recognized that the employer may choose the less expensive or burdensome accommodation as long as it is effective, without having to prove that the rejected accommodation would pose an undue hardship.[88]

The *Enforcement Guidance* provides several examples that illustrate the manner in which the EEOC believes employers comply with the interactive process. For example, an employer may not be required under the ADA to provide a computer with speech output to an employee with a learning disability, where providing tape-recorded memoranda will serve the same objective. Because both accommodations are effective, the employer may choose to provide the supervisor and employee with a tape recorder so that the supervisor can record her memoranda and the employee can listen to them. Thus, the U.S. Court of Appeals for the Seventh Circuit has held that where an employee's requested accommodation is unreasonable, and the employer counters with one that is reasonable that the employee summarily rejects, the employer has satisfied its obligation to participate in the interactive process.[89]

However, the opposite result is achieved where, instead of providing an assistant to read printed materials as requested by an employee with a severe vision disability, the employer provides her with a print magnification device. Although the employee can read using the device, she does so with such

---

[88]EEOC ENFORCEMENT GUIDE, *supra* note 40, at 9.
[89]EEOC v. Yellow Freight Sys., Inc., 253 F.3d 943, 11 AD Cases 1569 (7th Cir. 2001).

great difficulty that it significantly slows down her ability to review written materials. The magnifying device is ineffective as a reasonable accommodation because it does not provide the employee with an equal opportunity to attain the same level of performance as her colleagues. Thus, failure to provide the reader, absent undue hardship, would violate the ADA.[90] The determination of what accommodations are reasonable may involve communication and analysis of the best manner to ensure the appropriate opportunity to perform the essential functions of the position.

B. Documentation Requests by Employer

As part of the interactive process, the employer has the right to request further documentation from the employee's treating physician, if the employee's disability or need for accommodation is not obvious to the employer.[91] However, the employer is only entitled to documentation that would be necessary in determining whether the employee has a qualifying disability under the ADA. For this reason, the employer is not entitled to review the employee's entire medical file, the contents of which may not all be relevant in determining whether the employee is disabled and requires a reasonable accommodation.[92]

For example, in *Beck v. University of Wisconsin Board of Regents*,[93] the employee's failure to specify the job accommodations needed and failure to provide medical documentation excused the employer's failure to accommodate her alleged disability. Likewise, in *McAlpin v. National Semiconductor Corp.*,[94] the court found that the employer had not violated the ADA where a disabled employee who suffered from a lung condition

---

[90] EEOC ENFORCEMENT GUIDE, *supra* note 40, at 9. *But cf.* Coleman v. Darden, 595 F.2d 533, 1 AD Cases 49 (10th Cir. 1979) (employer not required to employ assistant for blind employee, where seeing is essential function of position).
[91] EEOC ENFORCEMENT GUIDE, *supra* note 40, at 6–7.
[92] 29 C.F.R. pt. 1630, app. §1630.9 (2003); EEOC ENFORCEMENT GUIDE, *supra* note 40, at 6.
[93] 75 F.3d 1130, 5 AD Cases 304 (7th Cir. 1996).
[94] 921 F. Supp. 1518, 1525, 5 AD Cases 1047 (N.D. Tex. 1996).

refused to provide it with a list of chemicals she was to avoid, thereby causing a breakdown in the interactive process. Finally, in *Templeton v. Neodata Services*,[95] the U.S. Court of Appeals for the Tenth Circuit found that the employer was justified in terminating an employee who could not perform the essential functions of her job, where the employee refused to authorize her doctor to release medical information that would have assisted the employer in framing an appropriate accommodation to enable her to perform those functions.

C. Requirement of Additional Certification by Physician Selected by Employer

A medical certification is an important step in determining a reasonable accommodation under the ADA.[96] The ADA permits employers to require that existing employees submit to medical examinations or medical inquiries that are "job-related and consistent with medical necessity."[97] Such examinations or questions are prohibited if used to determine whether an employee has a disability or to determine the nature or severity of a disability. According to the EEOC, an employer may ask an employee to undergo a medical examination only in limited circumstances:

1. "When an employee is having difficulty performing [the] job effectively";
2. "When an employee becomes disabled," either on or off the job;
3. When an examination is necessary to determine reasonable accommodation; or

---

[95] 162 F.3d 617, 8 AD Cases 1615 (10th Cir. 1998).
[96] *See* 29 C.F.R. pt. 1630, app. §1630.14(c) (2003).
[97] 42 U.S.C. §12112(d)(4)(A):
A covered entity shall not require a medical examination and shall not make medical inquiries of an employee as to whether such employee is an individual with a disability or as to the nature or severity of the disability, unless such examination or inquiry is shown to be job-related and consistent with business necessity.

4. When examinations or medical "screening and monitoring [are] required by other laws."[98]

In *Yin v. California*,[99] an employee used up to six times as much sick leave as other employees for a period of 4 straight years. The employee sued her employer when her manager asked her to submit to an independent medical examination after she missed almost 4 full months of work in 1 year. The court concluded that "when health problems have had a substantial and injurious impact on an employee's job performance, the employer can require the employee to undergo a physical examination designed to determine his or her ability to work, even if the examination might disclose whether the employee is disabled or the extent of any disability."[100]

In *EEOC v. Prevo's Family Market, Inc.*,[101] the U.S. Court of Appeals for the Sixth Circuit found that the employer did not violate the ADA when it discharged an employee allegedly infected with the human immunodeficiency virus (HIV) for refusing to submit to a medical examination. The employer insisted on the medical exam in order to ascertain whether the employee, who worked as a produce clerk and was prone to cuts and scrapes while preparing produce for show, needed to be reassigned to a different position. The court sided with the employer, holding that the employer's medical examination request was reasonable in order to determine whether the employee "could safely perform the function of his job involving cuts and scrapes without exposing others to HIV infection."[102]

The employer may rely on a doctor's certification only to the extent that it provides sufficient information on which to base a reasonable decision. In *Pesterfield v. Tennessee Valley*

---

[98] *See* A Technical Assistance Manual on the Employment Provisions (Title I) of the Americans with Disabilities Act §6.6.
[99] 95 F.3d 864, 5 AD Cases 1487 (9th Cir. 1996), *cert. denied*, 519 U.S. 1114, 117 S. Ct. 955 (1997).
[100] *Id.* at 868–69, 5 AD Cases at 1489.
[101] 135 F.3d 1089, 8 AD Cases 401 (6th Cir. 1998).
[102] *Id.* at 1095, 8 AD Cases at 407.

Authority,[103] the U.S. Court of Appeals for the Sixth Circuit found that an employer's discharge of a construction worker did not violate the Rehabilitation Act, where the employer relied on a psychiatrist's report stating that the employee was unable to return to work due to his psychological condition. However, in *Holiday v. City of Chattanooga*,[104] the Sixth Circuit found that it could not conclude as a matter of law that a city was entitled to rely on a doctor's report stating that an applicant for a police officer position could not perform the essential functions of his job safely. The court found that the doctor's report lacked detail and suggested that the physician had not made an individualized determination as required by the ADA, but had made a cursory determination after learning of the applicant's HIV-positive status.[105]

D. Employer Policies

Although an employer's policies may provide some insight into the types of accommodations an employer may find reasonable, they will not be dispositive of whether a denial of a particular accommodation is reasonable.[106] A California district court, in *Wood v. Alameda*,[107] also found that the duty to accommodate employees with disabilities reasonably "may require employers to alter existing policies or procedures that they would not change for non handicapped employees, [as] that is the essence of reasonable accommodation."[108] The U.S.

---

[103] 941 F.2d 437, 1 AD Cases 1858 (6th Cir. 1991).
[104] 206 F.3d 637, 10 AD Cases 501 (6th Cir. 2000).
[105] *Id.*
[106] *E.g.,* EEOC v. Sara Lee Corp., 237 F.3d 349, 11 AD Cases 595 (4th Cir. 2001) (even outside context of collective bargaining agreement, employers should not have to deviate from their seniority systems in order to accommodate disabled employee under ADA); Wood v. County of Alameda, 1995 U.S. Dist. LEXIS 17514, *33 (N.D. Cal. 1995) (duty to reasonably accommodate may require alteration of employer policies or procedures); *but see* Earl v. Mervyns, 207 F.3d 1361, 10 AD Cases 673 (11th Cir. 2000) (strong policies regarding tardiness evidence that punctuality was "essential function" of position).
[107] *Wood,* 1995 U.S. Dist. LEXIS 17514, *33.
[108] *Id.*

Court of Appeals for the Fourth Circuit reached the opposite conclusion in *EEOC v. Sara Lee Corp.*,[109] in holding that employers should not have to deviate from their seniority systems to accommodate a disabled employee under the ADA.

In 2002, the Supreme Court shed further light on these issues. In *U.S. Airways v. Barnett*,[110] the Court vacated and remanded the decision of the U.S. Court of Appeals for the Ninth Circuit, sitting en banc, in which it found that the presence of a seniority system is merely "a factor" in the undue hardship analysis.[111] That court held that a case-by-case, fact-intensive analysis would be required to determine if any particular reassignment constituted an undue hardship on the employer.

The Supreme Court held that when the interests of a disabled worker who seeks assignment to a particular job as a reasonable accommodation collide with those of other workers with superior bidding rights under the employer's seniority system, "the seniority system will prevail in the run of cases."[112] As Justice Breyer, writing for the Court, stated:

> As we interpret the statute, to show that a requested accommodation conflicts with the rules of a seniority system is ordinarily to show that the accommodation is not "reasonable." Hence such a showing will entitle an employer/defendant to summary judgment on the question—unless there is more. The plaintiff remains free to present evidence of special circumstances that make "reasonable" a seniority rule exception in the particular case. And such a showing will defeat the employer's demand for summary judgment.[113]

Thus, in the Court's view, ordinarily, the ADA does not require an employer to assign a disabled employee to a particular position where another employee is entitled to the slot under the employer's established seniority system. In such a case, it is reasonable nonetheless that the plaintiff must present evidence of special circumstances surrounding the assignment.

---

[109] 237 F.3d 349, 11 AD Cases 595 (4th Cir. 2001).
[110] 535 U.S. 391, 12 AD Cases 1729 (2002).
[111] Barnett v. U.S. Air, 228 F.3d 1105, 1120, 10 AD Cases 1761 (9th Cir. 2000).
[112] *U.S. Airways*, 535 U.S. at 394, 12 AD Cases at 1730.
[113] *Id.* at 394, 12 AD Cases at 1730–31 (citing F. R. Civ. P. 56(e)).

This might be accomplished by showing "that the employer, having retained the right to change the seniority system unilaterally, exercises that right fairly frequently, [thus] reducing employee expectations that the system will be followed—to the point where one more departure needed to accommodate an individual with a disability, will not likely make a difference. [Alternatively,] [t]he plaintiff might show that the [employer's] system already contains [sufficient] exceptions such that . . . one further exception" will have little significance. If a plaintiff can make this showing, the defendant/employer then must show special (typically case-specific) circumstances that demonstrate undue hardship in the particular circumstances.[114]

It should be noted that policies that impose restrictions on an employee's ability to transfer, take a leave, or engage in any conduct that may be deemed a reasonable accommodation, may impose liability on employers.[115] An employee need not request a reasonable accommodation where the employer's policies make it obvious that to do so would be futile. Thus, in *Davoll v. Webb*,[116] a police department had a strict policy against reassignment of any employees to vacant positions in other aspects of the city government. The U.S. Court of Appeals for the Tenth Circuit held that it was appropriate for the trial court to instruct the jury that it would have been a "futile gesture" for the plaintiff-employees to request reassignment.[117] It further held that the employer had failed to provide a reasonable accommodation by maintaining a policy that prohibited reassignment, even though the plaintiffs never made any request for an accommodation.

---

[114] *Id.* at 405, 12 AD Cases at 1735.

[115] *See* Davoll v. Webb, 194 F.3d 1116, 9 AD Cases 1533 (10th Cir. 1999) (employer failed to provide reasonable accommodation, where policy against reassignment created situation where it would have been futile for employee to request accommodation).

[116] 194 F.3d 1116, 9 AD Cases 1533 (10th Cir. 1999).

[117] *Id.* at 1132–33.

E. Effect of a Collective Bargaining Agreement

During the first years of litigation after the statute's effective dates, a conflict emerged between the EEOC's interpretation of the ADA and the federal circuit courts regarding an employer's duty to provide a disabled employee an accommodation that would violate the terms of a collective bargaining agreement. The EEOC's *Technical Assistance Manual* stated that the terms of a collective bargaining agreement may be relevant in determining whether an accommodation would impose an undue hardship.[118] However, the *Manual* was clear that the existence of a collective bargaining agreement would not be determinative.[119] This was consistent with several cases that held that, where a collective bargaining agreement is not in place, the duty to reasonably accommodate an employee may require employers to alter their existing policies.[120] Most courts that have considered the issue, however, found that an employer should not be required to disrupt a bona fide seniority system contained in a collective bargaining agreement to accommodate an individual with a disability.[121]

---

[118] A TECHNICAL ASSISTANCE MANUAL ON THE EMPLOYMENT PROVISIONS (TITLE I) OF THE AMERICANS WITH DISABILITIES ACT, III-16 (1992); *see* H.R. REP. No. 101-485, pt. 2, at 63 (1990), *reprinted in* 1990 U.S.C.C.A.N. 303, 345; S. REP. No. 101-116, at 32 (1989).

[119] *Id. See also* Buckingham v. United States, 998 F.2d 735, 740–41, 2 AD Cases 1009 (9th Cir. 1993) (rejecting argument that Rehabilitation Act of 1973, 29 U.S.C. §794, enacted a per se ban against transfers that impinged on collective bargaining agreements).

[120] *See, e.g.*, Garcia-Ayala v. Lederle Parenterals, Inc., 212 F.3d 638, 10 AD Cases 865 (1st Cir. 2000) (requiring leave in excess of that allowed under company's regular leave policy); Hendricks-Robinson v. Excel Corp., 154 F.3d 685, 8 AD Cases 875 (7th Cir. 1998) (exception required with respect to employer's neutral physical fitness standard).

[121] *See, e.g.*, Willis v. Pacific Maritime Ass'n, 236 F.3d 1160, 11 AD Cases 588 (9th Cir. 2001) (employer not required to violate terms of seniority system under collective bargaining agreement to accommodate disabled employee); Cravens v. Blue Cross & Blue Shield of Kansas City, 214 F.3d 1011, 1020, 10 AD Cases 1057 (8th Cir. 2000) (employer not required to transfer employee if that transfer interfered with other employees' rights via collective bargaining agreement); Davis v. Florida Power & Light Co., 205 F.3d 1301, 10 AD Cases 492 (11th Cir.), *cert. denied*, 531 U.S. 927 (2000) (employer not required to violate terms of seniority system under collective bargaining agreement to accommodate disabled employee); Kralik v. Durbin, 130 F.3d 76, 83, 7 AD Cases 1040 (3d Cir. 1997) (proposed accommoda-

For example, in *Eckles v. Consolidated Rail Corp.*,[122] the U.S. Court of Appeals for the Seventh Circuit held that a disabled employee could not displace a more senior employee as a form of reasonable accommodation if such accommodation would violate the terms of the collective bargaining agreement. Similarly, in *Boersig v. Union Electric Co.*,[123] the court held that the employer was not required to take an action that was inconsistent with the collectively bargained rights of other workers, where an employee with a lifting restriction claimed that he was passed over for a promotion.

In *Willis v. Pacific Maritime Ass'n*,[124] the U.S. Court of Appeals for the Ninth Circuit determined that it would not interfere with a Dock Preference Board, a placement system run by the International Longshore and Warehouse Union (ILWU) and contained in a collective bargaining agreement negotiated by the ILWU and the Pacific Maritime Association (PMA).[125] Two employees who suffered from disabilities covered under the ADA were denied their requests to be placed on the Dock Placement Board because they did not have the requisite seniority under the collective bargaining agreement and ILWU rules. The Ninth Circuit decided to follow the decisions of the U.S. Courts of Appeals for the Third, Fifth, Seventh, Eighth,

---

tion not reasonable, because it would infringe on collectively bargained seniority rights of others); Eckles v. Consolidated Rail Corp., 94 F.3d 1041, 5 AD Cases 1367 (7th Cir. 1996), *cert. denied*, 520 U.S. 1146 (1997) (disabled employee could not displace more senior employee in violation of collective bargaining agreement). *See also* Feliciano v. Rhode Island, 160 F.3d 780, 787, 8 AD Cases 1520 (1st Cir. 1998); Cassidy v. Detroit Edison Co., 138 F.3d 629, 634, 8 AD Cases 326 (6th Cir. 1998); Foreman v. Babcock & Wilcox Co., 117 F.3d 800, 810, 7 AD Cases 331 (5th Cir. 1997), *cert. denied*, 522 U.S. 1115 (1998); Benson v. Northwest Airlines, 62 F.3d 1108, 1114, 4 AD Cases 1234 (8th Cir. 1995); Milton v. Scrivner, Inc., 53 F.3d 1118, 1125, 4 AD Cases 432 (10th Cir. 1995).

[122]94 F.3d 1041, 5 AD Cases 1367 (7th Cir. 1996), *cert. denied*, 520 U.S. 1146 (1997).

[123]219 F.3d 816, 821, 10 AD Cases 1249 (8th Cir. 2000), *cert. denied*, 531 U.S. 1113 (2001); *see also* Spitzer v. Good Guys, Inc., 80 Cal. App. 4th 1376, 1389, 10 AD Cases 1638 (2000) (responsibility to reassign disabled employee who cannot be otherwise accommodated does not require creating new job, moving another employee, promoting disabled employee, or violating another employee's rights under collective bargaining agreement).

[124]236 F.3d 1160, 11 AD Cases 588 (9th Cir. 2001).

[125]*Id.* at 1168, 11 AD Cases at 594.

and Tenth Circuits in applying a per se rule that it would not interfere with a bona fide seniority system under a collective bargaining agreement. The court specifically rejected the argument of the plaintiffs that the prohibition of "'participating in a contractual or other arrangement or relationship that has the effect of subjecting a covered entity's qualified applicant or employee with a disability to the discrimination prohibited by this subchapter'" in the ADA operated to show that the PMA and ILWU discriminated against them.[126] According to the court, "the operation of a bona fide seniority system is not discriminatory simply because it does not allow for accommodations which would upset the operation of the seniority system itself."[127]

F. Confidentiality Issues

An employer is not allowed to disclose to others in the workplace that an individual employee is receiving a reasonable

---

[126] *Id.* at 1165, 11 AD Cases at 592 (quoting 42 U.S.C. §12112(b)(2)).

[127] *Id.* at 1165, 11 AD Cases at 592. The court also rejected the appellant's argument that Congress intended the provisions of a collective bargaining agreement to be only one factor in the reasonable accommodation analysis. The court, citing to the ADA's legislative history (H.R. REP. No. 101-485, pt. 2, at 63 (1990), *reprinted in* 1990 U.S.C.C.A.N. 303, 345), explained that "we, like our sister circuits which have confronted the issue, must also recognize that Congress enacted the ADA fully aware of the 'well established precedent' under the Rehabilitation Act which refused to require employers to violate a CBA's [collective bargaining agreement's] bona fide seniority system, and yet failed to include any provision to counter that precedent in the plain language of the ADA." *Id.* (citing Kralik v. Durbin, 130 F.3d 76, 82, 7 AD Cases 1040 (3d Cir. 1997), which quoted Eckles v. Consolidated Rail Corp., 94 F.3d 1041, 1048, 5 AD Cases 1367 (7th Cir. 1996)). The court also rejected one commentator's suggestion of a "multi-factored" test to determine when the proposed accommodation is reasonable, where there are conflicting seniority provisions in a collective bargaining agreement. The court noted that such a balancing approach "would leave employers too vulnerable to the possibility of guessing wrong when trying to weigh the relative benefits and burdens on disabled and nondisabled employees." *Id.* The U.S. Court of Appeals for the Ninth Circuit clarified that the "per se rule" applies only "where there is a *direct conflict* between the proposed accommodation and the collectively-bargained seniority rights of other employees." *Id.* at 1166, 11 AD Cases at 592 (emphasis in original). The court further noted that "our holding is limited to an accommodation request that conflicts with a CBA's bona fide seniority system, [i.e.,] 'one that was created for legitimate purposes, rather than for the purpose of discrimination.'" *Id.* at 1166, 11 AD Cases at 593 (quoting *Eckles*, 94 F.3d at 1046 n. 7).

accommodation. Such disclosure would violate the individual employee's right to keep private the fact that he or she suffers from a disability.[128] If and when an individual's coworkers ask their employer why an individual is receiving special or different treatment, the EEOC recommends that the employer respond by "emphasizing its policy of assisting any employee who encounters difficulties in the workplace."[129]

IV. WHAT TYPE OF ACCOMMODATION IS "REASONABLE"?

Every accommodation must be evaluated on a case-by-case basis, taking into consideration the employer's resources, the employee's abilities, the functional requirements of the job, and the employee's functional limitations. When identifying a reasonable accommodation, the EEOC regulations advance the requirement that an employer should observe the following steps:

1. Examine "the particular job involved and determine its purpose and essential functions";
2. "Consult with the individual . . . to ascertain" his or her specific physical or mental abilities and limitations as they relate to the essential job functions;
3. "In consultation with the individual . . . identify potential accommodations and assess" how effective each

---

[128] 42 U.S.C. §12112(d)(3)(B), (d)(4)(C); 29 C.F.R. §1630.14(b)(1) (2003). The limited exceptions to the ADA confidentiality requirements are: (1) "Supervisors and managers may be [told about] necessary restrictions on the work or duties of the employee and [about] necessary accommodations"; (2) "First aid and safety personnel may be [told] . . . if the disability might require emergency treatment"; and (3) "Government officials investigating compliance with [the ADA must be given] relevant information on request". *Id.* §1630.14(b)(1)(i–iii). In addition, the EEOC has interpreted the ADA to allow employers to disclose medical information in the following circumstances: (1) in accordance with state workers' compensation laws, employers may disclose information to state workers' compensation offices, state second injury funds, or workers' compensation insurance carriers; and (2) employers are permitted to use medical information for insurance purposes. *See* 29 C.F.R. pt. 1630, app. §1630.14(b) (2003).

[129] EEOC ENFORCEMENT GUIDE, *supra* note 40, at 24.

would be "in enabling the individual to perform the essential functions of the" job.[130]

If there are several effective accommodations, the employer should consider the preference of the individual and select the accommodation that best serves the needs of the individual and the employer. The employer is free, however, to choose among effective accommodations, and may choose one that is less expensive or easier to provide.[131]

An employer is not required to provide the employee with accommodations that are not directly related to performing the essential functions of a job, such as prosthetic limbs, eyeglasses, hearing aids, or similar devices. For example, it may be a reasonable accommodation to allow a vision-impaired employee to bring a service dog into the workplace, but it is not expected that the employer would provide the service dog to the employee.[132]

The ADA identifies as appropriate the following suggested accommodations:

1. "making existing facilities used by employees readily accessible to and usable by individuals with disabilities";
2. "job restructuring";
3. "part-time or modified work schedules";
4. reassigning a disabled individual to a vacant position;
5. acquiring or modifying equipment or devices;
6. appropriately adjusting or modifying "examinations, training materials or policies";
7. providing "qualified readers or interpreters"; and
8. "other similar accommodations for individuals with disabilities."[133]

Other solutions that have been identified as appropriate under the regulations and case law are providing the employee

---
[130] 29 C.F.R. pt. 1630, app. §1630.9 (2003).
[131] Id.
[132] Id. app. §1630.2(o) (2003).
[133] 42 U.S.C. §12111(9)(A), (B).

with additional leave time, providing transportation to the employee, providing a travel attendant to a blind employee, and permitting individuals to use equipment, aids, or services possessed by the employee, even if the employer is not required to provide them to the employee. The ADA regulations make clear that the lists provided by the statute and the regulations are not intended to be exhaustive.[134]

A. Making Existing Facilities Accessible to Disabled Employees

Under the ADA, one type of reasonable accommodation includes "making existing facilities . . . readily accessible" to the disabled employee.[135] This entails making accessible to the employee all areas that the employee needs to perform the essential functions of the job and nonwork areas such as break rooms, lunchrooms, training rooms, and restrooms.[136] An employer can offer such an accommodation by removing, among other things, architectural, communication and transportation barriers such as stairs, revolving doors, and rampless sidewalks.[137]

For example, an employer may accommodate an employee with a hearing disability—whose job requires him or her to contact the public via telephone—by providing the employee with a teletypewriter, a device that allows him or her to communicate by telephone. Providing such a device would constitute a reasonable accommodation, because it would be effective in that it would allow the disabled employee to communicate with the public via telephone.[138]

An employer can also reasonably (and effectively) accommodate a cashier/employee suffering from lupus by providing him or her with a stool to alleviate the fatigue he or she endures

---

[134] *Id.*
[135] 29 C.F.R. pt. 1630, app. §1630.2(o) (2003).
[136] *Id.*
[137] *See, e.g.*, EEOC Enforcement Guidance, "Reasonable Accommodation and Undue Harship Under the Americans with Disabilities Act" (Oct. 17, 2002).
[138] EEOC Enforcement Guide, General Principles.

from standing as a result of the disability. Such an accommodation removes the workplace barrier of having to stand and permits the employee to perform just as well and effectively as the other cashiers.[139]

Moreover, with regard to transportation barriers, some courts have held that an employer may be required to provide a disabled employee with a paid parking space near the workplace as a form of reasonable accommodation, although such a paid parking space is not offered to nondisabled employees.[140]

B. Job Restructuring

The ADA and its implementing regulations suggest that job restructuring can be an appropriate accommodation for an individual with a disability.[141] While the employer must consider whether nonessential functions can be reassigned or modified, the ADA does not require that an employer reallocate the essential functions of a position.[142] For example, in *Fjellestad v. Pizza Hut of America, Inc.*,[143] the court held that creating a comanager position for a disabled employee who was unable to work the required hours was unreasonable, because an essential function of her job as manager was to work 50 hours a week. According to the court, the employer was under no obligation to reallocate or eliminate the essential functions of the job in order to accommodate the disabled employee.[144]

---

[139] *Id.*

[140] *See* Lyons v. Legal Aid Soc'y, 68 F.3d 1512, 4 AD Cases 1694 (2d Cir. 1995); *see also* Smallwood v. Witco Corp., 1995 U.S. Dist. LEXIS (S.D.N.Y. 1995) (employer may have to offer commuting assistance to disabled employee as form of reasonable accommodation).

[141] 42 U.S.C. §12111(9)(B); 29 C.F.R. pt. 1630, app. §§1630.2(o), 1630.9 (2003).

[142] Benson v. Northwest Airlines, Inc., 62 F.3d 1108, 1112–13, 4 AD Cases 1234 (8th Cir. 1995) (ADA does not require employer to reallocate essential functions of job); *see also* 29 C.F.R. pt. 1630, app. §1630.2(o) (2003).

[143] 188 F.3d 944, 952, 9 AD Cases 1153 (8th Cir. 1999).

[144] *Id.*; *see also* Bratten v. SSI Servs., Inc., 185 F.3d 625, 9 AD Cases 1045 (6th Cir. 1999) (employer not required to eliminate overhead lifting as requirement of disabled auto mechanic's job as form of reasonable accommodation).

Similarly, in *Anderson v. Coors Brewing Co.*,[145] the court found that fundamentally altering the nature of the Temporary Production Operator position held by an employee suffering from multiple sclerosis was not a reasonable accommodation. Apparently, the employee had sought a transfer from a position where she had to perform multiple tasks in a wide range of environments to one where she only had to perform one sedentary task.[146] As these cases make clear, the definition of "essential functions" becomes critical in determining whether a particular reallocation is appropriate.

An important issue for many employers relates to the question of potential reassignment under the ADA and state disability statutes and the "light duty" programs they design for employees that are injured on-the-job and/or those injured away from work who need a period of transitional duty before returning to normal job activity. Similarly, systems in which employees rotate through a range of work tasks, in order to minimize ergonomic stressors, equalize exertion throughout the workforce, or accomplish other goals, often come into play when individuals focus on the potential to restructure jobs as a form of reasonable accommodation. In *Watson v. Lithonia Lighting & National Serv. Indus., Inc.*[147] a plaintiff sought exemption from the employer's task rotation system on its assembly line due to limitations on her ability to engage in repetitive motions. She failed in her efforts to establish that her desired position would constitute a reasonable accommodation, due to the business purpose of the rotation system and her inability to establish that exceptions had been made for other employees. Of significance was the court's holding that the statute does not require employers who set aside temporary light duty positions for recovering employees to make those slots available on an indefinite basis for those with long-term disabilities that are not expected to improve over time. By contrast, in circumstances in

---

[145] 181 F.3d 1171, 9 AD Cases 835 (10th Cir. 1999).
[146] *Id.*
[147] 304 F.3d 749 (7th Cir. 2002), *cert. denied*, 537 U.S. 1193 (2003).

which rotation was not clearly established as an essential function of a position, an employer's failure to reassign a disabled employee until the individual could perform all of the rotating tasks of the position's job assignments could leave a jury free to find in favor of the employee on a refusal to accommodate claim.[148]

Lifting and other specific exertions often are the subject of dispute in the accommodation context. In *Mays v. Principi*,[149] the U.S. Court of Appeals for the Seventh Circuit held that a hospital was not required to provide a nurse limited from lifting more than 10 pounds with the assistance of another staff member, because doing so would result essentially in two employees performing the same job. Similarly, in *Dropinski v. Douglas County*,[150] the employer was not required to restructure the job of an equipment operator who was limited in his ability to bend, squat, twist, or lift anything in excess of 50 pounds. However, the fact that an employer believes that restructuring a job in order to accommodate an individual with a disability would be "inconvenient" would not serve as an adequate defense to an allegation that it has failed to satisfy its reasonable accommodation obligation.

C. Job Reassignment

Employers must consider transfers and reassignments of disabled employees, even where a disability may preclude an employee from performing the essential functions of his or her position.[151] Employers must consider offering a disabled employee a transfer to a different position that the employee

---

[148] Kiphart v. Saturn Corp., 251 F.3d 573, 11 AD Cases 1473 (6th Cir. 2001).
[149] 301 F.3d 866, 13 AD Cases 985 (7th Cir. 2002).
[150] 298 F.3d 704, 13 AD Cases 676 (8th Cir. 2002). *See also* Phelps v. Optima Health, Inc., 251 F.3d 21, 11 AD Cases 1487 (1st Cir. 2001) (because lifting 50 pounds was essential function of nursing position, employer was not required to have other nurses assist nurse with back impairment in all patient lifts).
[151] *See* Cravens v. Blue Cross & Blue Shield of Kansas City, 214 F.3d 1011, 1018, 10 AD Cases 1057, 1061 (8th Cir. 2000) ("definition of 'qualified individual with a disability' includes a disabled employee who cannot do his or her current job, but who desires and can perform, with or without reasonable accommodation, the essential functions of a vacant job within the company").

might be able to perform as an accommodation for the employee's disability.[152] However, reassignment should be considered "only when accommodation within the individual's current position would pose an undue hardship ... [and] may not be used to limit, segregate, or otherwise discriminate against employees with disabilities by forcing reassignments to undesirable positions or to designated offices or facilities."[153] Thus, in *Skerski v. Time Warner Cable Co.*,[154] the company considered the circumstances of an employee with a panic disorder who had been excused from climbing duties. When the employee's new supervisor required him to resume those duties, it rejected his request for the use of a bucket truck, and he agreed to a reassignment under pressure. The court held that the reassignment may not have satisfied the employer's reasonable accommodation obligation, as reassignment should only be considered as a last resort, which was not the employer's approach.[155]

Viewing the limits on an employer's potential obligation to reassign an employee with a disability, the U.S. Court of Appeals for the Eleventh Circuit noted that the statute does not require employers to "bump" an employee to create a vacancy, promote an employee, change a temporary job into a permanent one, or eliminate essential functions of the job in question.[156] The U.S. Court of Appeals for the Seventh Circuit, similarly, has observed that the ADA does not require employers to promote an employee as a form of accommodation, nor

---

[152] *See* Aka v. Washington Hosp. Ctr., 156 F.3d 1284, 1305, 8 AD Cases 1093 (D.C. Cir. 1998) (refusal to reassign may be violation of ADA, where employee was unable to perform his job following bypass surgery); Gile v. United Airlines, Inc., 95 F.3d 492, 5 AD Cases 1466 (7th Cir. 1996) (by refusing to change employee's shift, employer failed to reasonably accommodate depressed and insomniac employee).

[153] 29 C.F.R. pt. 1630, app. §1630.2 (o) (2003).

[154] 257 F.3d 273, 11 AD Cases 1665 (3d Cir. 2001).

[155] *See also* Lovejoy-Wilson v. NOCO Motor Fuel, Inc., 263 F.3d 208, 12 AD Cases 340 (2d Cir. 2001) (employer's reasonable accommodation obligation could not be satisfied by promoting employee in another location, where problem task was not an issue, because it had to consider potential ability to reasonably accommodate her in her prior position or location of her choice).

[156] Lucas v. W.W. Grainger, Inc., 257 F.3d 1249, 11 AD Cases 1761 (11th Cir. 2001).

must it provide training so that the employee obtains qualifications that are required in order to perform a new job.[157]

In *Vollmert v. Wisconsin Department of Transportation*,[158] the court held that the employer had not provided a dyslexic employee a reasonable accommodation when it had transferred her to a position that did not provide the same opportunities for advancement within the company as her former position and did not "address the problems posed by her disability."[159] The employee was transferred from a position that entailed processing applications for special license plates for disabled persons using a new computer system to a position that did not require any computer use. The court held that such a transfer did not constitute a reasonable accommodation and that the employer could have reasonably accommodated her at her former position by training her on the new computer system.

1. Legitimate Policies Prohibiting a Transfer

There has been a substantial split in authority over the last several years as to whether an employer must reassign an employee in spite of a legitimate policy of the employer that would prohibit such a transfer. Many courts have held that where the transfer of a disabled employee would violate an employer's policies, the employer is typically justified in refusing the transfer.[160] However, other courts have held that an employer must place a disabled employee in a vacant position, even where the employer's seniority system or other policy

---

[157]Williams v. United Ins. Co. of Am., 253 F.3d 280, 11 AD Cases 1613 (7th Cir.), *cert. denied*, 534 U.S. 1025 (2001).

[158]197 F.3d 293, 9 AD Cases 1704 (7th Cir. 1999).

[159]*Id.* at 302, 9 AD Cases 1711.

[160]*See* Foreman v. Babcock & Wilcox Co., 117 F.3d 800, 810, 7 AD Cases 331 (5th Cir. 1997), *cert. denied*, 522 U.S. 1115 (1998) (with or without collective bargaining agreement employer not required to reassign employee in violation of bona fide seniority system); Daugherty v. City of El Paso, 56 F.3d 695, 700, 4 AD Cases 993 (5th Cir. 1995), *cert. denied*, 516 U.S. 1172 (1996) (city not required to alter its hiring and reassignment practices for part-time driver disqualified from driving by insulin-dependent diabetes).

would require placing another employee in that position.[161] Courts have been more willing to give deference to policies negotiated as part of a collective bargaining agreement. As to seniority systems outside the collective bargaining framework, the Supreme Court's decision in *U.S. Airways, Inc. v. Barnett*,[162] is most relevant. Applying *Barnett*, the U.S. Court of Appeals for the Third Circuit found that the identification by a disabled employee of positions for a potential reassignment was sufficient to shift the burden to the employer to establish that such a shift would not be a reasonable accommodation under the ADA.[163]

The responsibility to reassign disabled employee who cannot be otherwise accommodated does not require that the employer create a new job,[164] promote the disabled employee if such promotion is not warranted,[165] or violate another employee's rights under a collective bargaining agreement.[166] Similarly, an employer is not obligated to convert a temporary "light-duty" job into a permanent position in order to accommodate a disabled employee.[167]

---

[161] United States v. City & County of Denver, 943 F. Supp. 1304, 1312, 6 AD Cases 245 (D. Colo. 1996), *aff'd in part sub nom.* Davoll v. Webb, 194 F.3d 1116, 9 AD Cases 1533 (10th Cir. 1999) (policy of barring reassignment of disabled police officers to vacant positions for which they are qualified violates ADA despite employer policy to contrary).

[162] 535 U.S. 391, 12 AD Cases 1729 (2002).

[163] Shapiro v. Township of Lakewood, 292 F.3d 356, 13 AD Cases 106 (3d Cir. 2002).

[164] *See* Cravens v. Blue Cross & Blue Shield of Kansas City, 214 F.3d 1011, 1019, 10 AD Cases 1057 (8th Cir. 2000); *see also* Donahue v. Consolidated Rail Corp., 224 F.3d 226, 10 AD Cases 1505 (3d Cir. 2000) (employer's obligation to provide reasonable accommodation does not require employer to create new job).

[165] Malabarba v. Chicago Tribune Co., 149 F.3d 690, 697, 8 AD Cases 1505 (7th Cir. 1998); White v. York Int'l Corp., 45 F.3d 357, 362, 3 AD Cases 1746 (10th Cir. 1995).

[166] Spitzer v. Good Guys, Inc., 80 Cal. App. 4th 1376, 1389, 10 AD Cases 1638 (2000).

[167] *Id. See also* Watson v. Lithonia Lighting & Nat'l Serv. Indus., Inc., 304 F.3d 749 (7th Cir. 2002), *cert. denied*, 537 U.S. 1193 (2003); Dalton v. Subaru-Isuzu Auto., 141 F.3d 667, 680–81, 7 AD Cases 1872 (7th Cir. 1998) (employer with policy providing for reassignment of workers with temporary disabilities not required to reassign employee with permanent injury); Howell v. Michelin Tire Corp., 860 F. Supp. 1488, 1492, 3 AD Cases 929, 931 (M.D. Ala. 1994) ("Reasonable accommoda-

2. Vacant Positions

The ADA requires only that the employer consider "reassignment to a vacant position," indicating that the employer is not required to displace/reassign another employee to provide an accommodation to an employee with a disability.[168] Specifically, "vacant positions"[169] include those found within the entire company,[170] meaning that the employer must reassign the employee to any open position available in the employee's office, branch, agency, department, or geographic area, so long as it is still within the company. Moreover, some courts have placed the burden of identifying a vacant position to which the disabled employee can be transferred on the employer.[171]

The employer's duty to reassign a disabled employee to a vacant position ends, however, if the reassignment is deemed unreasonable or if it imposes an undue hardship on the employer.[172] For example, in *Gaul v. Lucent Technologies, Inc.*,[173] the court held that an employer had no duty to transfer an employee suffering from depression and anxiety when the employee complained that certain coworkers caused him too much stress. According to the court, such a request was unreasonable as a matter of law.[174]

---

tion . . . does not require that an employer create a light-duty position or a new permanent position.").

[168]42 U.S.C. §12111(9)(B); *see also* Gile v. United Airlines, 95 F.3d 492, 499, 5 AD Cases 1466 (7th Cir. 1996) (employer has no duty to "bump" incumbent from position in order to accommodate disabled employee).

[169]Cravens v. Blue Cross & Blue Shield of Kansas City, 214 F.3d 1011, 1019 n.5, 10 AD Cases 1057, 1062 n.5 (8th Cir. 2000) ("vacant position" includes those employer reasonably anticipates becoming vacant shortly) (citing Monette v. Electronic Data Sys. Corp., 90 F.3d 1173, 1187, 5 AD Cases 1326 (6th Cir. 1996)).

[170]Smith v. Midland Brake, 180 F.3d 1154, 9 AD Cases 738 (10th Cir. 1999).

[171]Hines v. Chrysler Corp., 2000 U.S. App. LEXIS 11338 (10th Cir. May 19, 2000) (unpublished opinion) (failure to identify any vacant positions to which disabled employee can be transferred can constitute discrimination).

[172]EEOC ENFORCEMENT GUIDE, *supra* note 40, at 19.

[173]134 F.3d 576, 7 AD Cases 1223 (3d Cir. 1998); *see also* Potter v. Xerox Corp., 88 F. Supp. 2d 109, 82 FEP Cases 1116 (W.D.N.Y. 2000), *aff'd*, 2001 U.S. App. LEXIS 329 (2d Cir. 2001) (unpublished opinion) (no employer is required to provide its employees with completely stress-free environment).

[174]*See Gaul*, 134 F.3d 576.

In *Gile v. United Airlines*,[175] the employer violated the ADA when it failed to transfer a night-shift employee to a vacant daytime position. The court found that the employer had not explored accommodation options adequately through the required interactive process, and if it had, it would have learned from the employee and his social worker that a transfer to the day shift was a desired accommodation.[176] Continuing obligations have been rejected by courts in certain circumstances. For example, in *Boykin v. ATC/Vancom of Colorado*,[177] the court held that the employer committed no violation when a driver was terminated after turning down an appropriate vacant position when it did not assign the individual to the dispatcher position he sought months after discharge. The U.S. Court of Appeals for the Seventh Circuit, in *EEOC v. Humiston-Keeling*,[178] found that the ADA does not require an employer to reassign a disabled employee to a job for which there is a better applicant, provided that the employer's consistent and honest policy was to hire the best applicant for the particular job rather than the first qualified applicant.

Under the interpretative guidelines provided by the EEOC, the employer may reassign the employee to a lower grade and paid position if the employee cannot be accommodated in his or her current position, and a comparable position is not available.[179] However, some courts have stated that employers should first consider lateral moves and assignments to positions that are equivalent to those previously occupied by the employee, as certain positions may be found deficient in meeting the employer's reasonable accommodation obligation.[180]

---

[175] 213 F.3d 365, 373–74, 10 AD Cases 968 (7th Cir. 2000).
[176] *Id.*
[177] 247 F.3d 1061, 11 AD Cases 1204 (10th Cir. 2001).
[178] EEOC v. Humiston-Keeling, Inc., 227 F.3d 1024, 10 AD Cases 1665 (7th Cir. 2000).
[179] 29 C.F.R. pt. 1630, app. §1630.2(o) (2003); *see also* Cravens v. Blue Cross & Blue Shield of Kansas City, 214 F.3d 1011, 1019, 10 AD Cases 1057 (8th Cir. 2000); Cassidy v. Detroit Edison Co., 138 F.3d 629, 624, 8 AD Cases 326 (6th Cir. 1998).
[180] *See, e.g.,* Dilley v. SuperValu, Inc., 296 F.3d 958, 13 AD Cases 486 (10th Cir. 2002).

D. Obligation to Provide a Leave of Absence as a Reasonable Accommodation

One form of reasonable accommodation is allowing a qualified individual with a disability to use accrued paid leave or to provide additional unpaid leave for necessary treatment.[181] Thus, in *Smith v. Diffee Ford-Lincoln-Mercury, Inc.*,[182] the U.S. Court of Appeals for the Tenth Circuit found that the award of summary judgment to the employer was inappropriate in a case where the evidence suggested that the company terminated an individual with a disability who required leave as a reasonable accommodation. According to the EEOC, the ADA does not require an employer to provide paid leave to disabled employees in excess of that provided to similarly situated employees, however, there may be obligations to provide additional unpaid leave for many purposes related to the disability.[183]

In *Garcia-Ayala v. Lederle Parenterals, Inc.*,[184] the court specified the factors to be considered in determining whether requests for a leave of absence are unreasonable:

1. Where "employee gives no indication as to when [he or she can] return to work," but demands that employer hold job open indefinitely;
2. Where the employee has "erratic" and "unexplained" absences;
3. Where the employer hired the "employee to complete a specific task"; or
4. Where employer had a policy to permit additional leave rather than "hire and train a new employee."[185]

---

[181] *See* 29 C.F.R. pt. 1630, app. §1630.2(o) (2003).

[182] 298 F.3d 955, 13 AD Cases 588 (10th Cir. 2002).

[183] EEOC ENFORCEMENT GUIDE, *supra* note 40, at 13. These might include (but not be limited to) obtaining medical treatment, recuperating from illness or an episodic manifestation of the disability, obtaining repairs on a wheelchair, accessible van or prosthetic device, avoiding temporary adverse conditions in the work environment, receiving training in the use of braille or sign language, or training a service animal. *Id.*

[184] 212 F.3d 638, 650, 10 AD Cases 865, 872–873 (1st Cir. 2000).

[185] *Id. See also* Taylor v. Pepsi-Cola, 196 F.3d 1106, 9 AD Cases 1731 (10th Cir. 1999) (indefinite leave is not reasonable accommodation). *But see* Parker v. Columbia Pictures Indus., 204 F.3d 326, 10 AD Cases 396 (2d Cir. 2000) (employer may

Applying these factors, the court held that the employer had failed to meet its burden of proof on the issue of undue hardship because it had failed to illustrate that the employee's requested accommodation of more than 1 year of unpaid leave to receive cancer treatment would cause it any undue hardship.[186]

In most cases, however, while courts recognize that additional leave may be a form of reasonable accommodation, most find that requests for indefinite sick leave, or excessive absenteeism are beyond the scope of a reasonable accommodation required by the statute. Thus, in *EEOC v. Yellow Freight System, Inc.*,[187] the court found that an individual's request for unlimited sick leave without penalty or discipline to be unreasonable when weighing an employer's accommodation obligation. Similarly, when it weighed the record and request of an employee that he be allowed to work when he wanted as a form of reasonable accommodation, the U.S. Court of Appeals for the Eighth Circuit concluded that the individual's failure to demonstrate regularity in attendance for most of the year prior to the request made his desired accommodation unreasonable as a matter of law.[188] The U.S. Court of Appeals for the Sixth Circuit, in reviewing a case in which the employer previously provided a very substantial amount of medical leave, found that mandating further leave when there were no clear prospects for recovery was not a reasonable accommodation that the ADA would mandate.[189]

---

violate ADA if it terminates employee who could perform essential job functions but could not return after medical leave because of employer's summary rejection of part-time schedule request); Nunes v. Wal-Mart Stores, Inc., 164 F.3d 1243, 8 AD Cases 1813 (1999) (employee cannot be found unqualified for sole reason that she cannot work during period of leave, because unpaid medical leave, extended medical leave, or extension of existing leave periods may be forms of reasonable accommodation); Criado v. I.B.M. Corp., 145 F.3d 437, 444–45, 8 AD Cases 336 (1st Cir. 1998) (employer's refusal to grant additional leave following employee's psychiatrist's request, unreasonable because extra leave was not going to be prolonged or perpetual).

[186] *Garcia-Ayala*, 212 F.3d at 650.
[187] 253 F.3d 943, 11 AD Cases 1569 (7th Cir. 2001) (en banc).
[188] Pickens v. Soo Line R.R., 264 F.3d 773, 12 AD Cases 333 (8th Cir. 2001), *cert. denied*, 535 U.S. 1057 (2002).
[189] Walsh v. United Parcel Serv., Inc., 201 F.3d 718, 10 AD Cases 161 (6th Cir. 2000) (employee had been out on medical leave for nearly 18 months when he sought additional 90 days for further medical evaluations of his condition).

1. Employer Policies Regarding Leaves of Absence and Attendance

Generally, a "no-fault" leave policy, in which the employee is automatically terminated after being on leave for a certain period of time, cannot be applied to an employee with a disability who requires leave beyond the period specified in the policy. Instead, the employer is required to modify its no-fault leave policy to permit employees to take additional leave as needed for a qualifying disability.[190] An employer cannot penalize an employee with a disability for missing work during a leave taken as a form of reasonable accommodation.[191] However, as least one circuit has held that an employer's leave policy that required termination after 1 year of leave did not violate the ADA because disabled and nondisabled employees were treated the same.[192] The employer also is not required to alter its no-fault leave policies if it can establish that: "(1) there is another effective accommodation that would enable the person to perform the essential functions of his or her position, or (2) granting additional leave would cause an undue hardship."[193]

2. Employee's Job Security While on Medical Leave

A disabled employee who is granted leave as a form of reasonable accommodation can expect to return to his or her same position unless the employer can show that holding the position open would impose an undue hardship. If keeping the position unoccupied does in fact pose an undue hardship to the employer, the employer may then have to transfer the employee to a vacant, equivalent position for which the employee is qualified so that once the employee returns from his or her leave, he or she can return to this new position.[194]

---

[190] EEOC ENFORCEMENT GUIDE, *supra* note 40, at 13.
[191] EEOC ENFORCEMENT GUIDE, *supra* note 40, at 14. *But see* Matthews v. Commonwealth Edison Co., 128 F.3d 1194, 7 AD Cases 1651 (7th Cir. 1997) (employee who had returned to work on part-time basis after taking leave for several months could be terminated during reduction in force based on his lower productivity).
[192] Gantt v. Wilson Sporting Goods Co., 143 F.3d 1042, 8 AD Cases 308 (6th Cir. 1998).
[193] EEOC ENFORCEMENT GUIDE, *supra* note 40, at 13.
[194] *Id.*

3. Requiring Employee to Stay on the Job Rather Than Take a Leave as a Form of Reasonable Accommodation

If an employer is able to reasonably accommodate a disabled employee without granting the employee's request for a leave, the employer can do so, as long as the employer provides the employee with an effective accommodation.[195] However, if an employee is covered under the Family and Medical Leave Act (FMLA),[196] the employer cannot refuse to provide an FMLA-required leave of absence.[197]

4. Providing a Modified or Part-Time Schedule

An employer must allow a disabled employee to work a modified or part-time schedule as a reasonable accommodation if doing so would not impose an undue hardship on the employer.[198] A modified schedule could entail adjusting the employee's arrival or departure times, providing the employee with periodic breaks, or allowing the employee to use accrued paid leave and/or vacation time, among other adjustments. An employer is required to modify its workplace policies to accommodate an employee with a disability as long as such modification does not impose an undue burden on the employer. The employer, however, only has to modify its policies as to the individual employee with a disability, not to all employees across the company.[199]

Having to adjust the time for which an essential function of the job is performed would be sufficient for an employer to show that a specified accommodation would pose an undue hardship. Similarly, a modification of one employee's work hours that would prevent other employees from performing their jobs and/or significantly disrupt the operations of the

---

[195] *Id., supra* note 40, at 14.
[196] 29 U.S.C. §2601 et al.
[197] *See* 29 C.F.R. §825.702 (2003).
[198] EEOC ENFORCEMENT GUIDE, *supra* note 40, at 15–16; *see also* Ralph v. Lucent Techs., 135 F.3d 166, 172, 7 AD Cases 1345 (1st Cir. 1998) (modified schedule is form of reasonable accommodation).
[199] EEOC ENFORCEMENT GUIDE, *supra* note 40, at 17.

employer would also be an undue hardship.[200] An employer is not required to create a position for a disabled employee that would be inconsistent with the overall structure of the company. For example, in *Terrell v. U.S. Air*,[201] the court held that the employer had no duty to create a part-time position for the employee requesting such a position as a reasonable accommodation, where the employer had eliminated all part-time positions from the company.

Courts have viewed requests for adoption of part-time or flexible work schedules as reasonable accommodations in different ways, rejecting such proposals in some instances,[202] while requiring employers to meet an "undue hardship" proof analysis in others.[203] At least some courts have concluded, however, that even though part-time work may be a form of reasonable accommodation, an employer is not required by the ADA to create a new part-time position where one had not existed previously.[204] Moreover, if the employer can demonstrate that full-time work is an essential function of the job, termination of an employee after rejecting a request for a part-time schedule may not violate the ADA.[205] Similarly, when an employee was regularly late for work because of her disability and punctuality was essential for the position she occupied (a retail store area coordinator), the court rejected the plaintiff's requested accommodation that she be allowed to arrive whenever she was

---

[200] *Id., supra* note 40, at 25–26.

[201] Terrell v. USAir, 132 F.3d 621, 626, 8 AD Cases 529 (11th Cir. 1998).

[202] *See, e.g.,* Hatchett v. Philander Smith Coll., 251 F.3d 826, 12 AD Cases 640 (8th Cir. 2001).

[203] Ward v. Massachusetts Health Research Inst., Inc., 209 F.3d 29, 10 AD Cases 776 (1st Cir. 2000). In at least some cases, courts have rejected certain attempts by employees to secure exemption from overtime on the basis of their conditions. *See, e.g.,* Boerst v. General Mills Operations, Inc., 25 Fed. Appx. 403, 2002 WL 59637, 2002 U.S. App. LEXIS 813 (6th Cir.), *cert. denied,* 535 U.S. 1097 (2002).

[204] Treanor v. MCI Telecomms. Corp., 200 F.3d 570, 10 AD Cases 80 (8th Cir. 2000).

[205] Lamb v. Qualex, Inc., 2002 U.S. App. LEXIS 5982 (4th Cir. 2002). In the case of a full-time job, employees must be capable of working full time; "[o]ddly, this is assumed rather than stated in most of the cases." DeVito v. Chicago Park Dist., 270 F.3d 532, 534, 12 AD Cases 705, 705–06 (7th Cir. 2001) (rejecting ADA claim of park laborer who had not worked full-time for 13 years).

able to make it to work, without discipline or reprimand, even though she was willing to make up time at the end of her shift.[206]

E. Work at Home

An employer may also modify its policies to allow an employee with a disability to work from home if such an arrangement would reasonably accommodate the employee, would effectively allow the employee to perform the essential functions of the job, and would not cause an undue hardship for the employer.[207] In a number of reported cases, however, employers have been found to have no obligation to allow employees to work at home. In most cases, these findings have been based on conclusions that the discretion sought by the individual was not reasonable,[208] or that the individual would not be able to perform all of the job's essential functions at home.[209] In *Smith v. Ameritech*,[210] the court held that the employer was not required to allow a disabled employee to work at home if the quality of his or her work performance would be reduced. Similarly, in *Vande Zande v. Wisconsin Department of Administration*,[211] the court held that the employer was not required to accommodate a paraplegic employee who requested that her employer provide her with a desktop computer so that she could work from home. According to the court, such a request was unreasonable because the employer demonstrated that it did not have enough work for her to perform individually at home, and the nature of her job required teamwork under supervision to maintain its optimal quality.[212]

---

[206]Earl v. Mervyn's, Inc., 207 F.3d 1361, 10 AD Cases 673 (11th Cir. 2000).
[207]EEOC ENFORCEMENT GUIDE, *supra* note 40, at 21.
[208]Rauen v. United States Tobacco Mfg., 319 F.3d 891, 13 AD Cases 1797 (7th Cir. 2003).
[209]Kvorjak v, Maine, 259 F.3d 48, 12 AD Cases 160 (1st Cir. 2001); Heaser v. Toro Co., 247 F.3d 826, 11 AD Cases 1320 (8th Cir. 2001).
[210]129 F.3d 857, 867, 7 AD Cases 917 (6th Cir. 1997).
[211]44 F.3d 538, 545, 3 AD Cases 1636 (7th Cir. 1995).
[212]*See also* Whillock v. Delta Air Lines, Inc., 926 F. Supp. 1555, 5 AD Cases 1027 (N.D. Ga. 1995) (plaintiff's request to work at home was unreasonable accommodation for her disability, because employer would sacrifice security, supervision, and availability of computer resources if it were to accommodate request).

Also, in *Tyndall v. National Education Centers of California, Inc.*,[213] the court held that an employee suffering from lupus was not a qualified person with a disability for purposes of his position as an instructor. The employee's request to work from home could not be granted, because attending the classes he taught was an essential function of the employee's job as an instructor.[214]

In *Carr v. Reno*,[215] however, the court held that "in appropriate cases, [the Rehabilitation Act] requires an agency to consider work at home, as well as reassignment in another position, as potential forms of accommodation."[216] Likewise, in *Humphrey v. Memorial Hospitals Ass'n*,[217] the court held that it would be reasonable for an employer to allow an employee who suffered from obsessive-compulsive disorder, which prevented her from arriving on time to work, to work from home. Specifically, the court found that the employee, a transcriptionist, could have performed the essential functions of her job—transcribing medical records—from her home without causing any hardship on the employer.[218]

F. Issues Relating to Medication of a Disabled Employee

According to the *Enforcement Guidance*, an employer is not obligated to monitor a disabled employee's medication as a form of reasonable accommodation.[219] Nor is an employer responsible for ensuring that the employee is receiving appropriate treatment. In *Robertson v. Neuromedical Center*,[220] the court rejected an employee's argument that his employer should have ensured that he take his medication. The court held that the decision to take medication was a personal one and rested

---

[213] 31 F.3d 209, 213, 3 AD Cases 868 (4th Cir. 1994).
[214] *Id.*
[215] 23 F.3d 525, 3 AD Cases 434 (D.C. Cir. 1994).
[216] *Id.* at 530, 3 AD Cases at 437.
[217] 239 F.3d 1128, 11 AD Cases 765 (9th Cir. 2001).
[218] *Id.* at 1136–37, 11 AD Cases at 772.
[219] EEOC ENFORCEMENT GUIDE, *supra* note 40, at 22.
[220] 161 F.3d 292, 296 (5th Cir. 1998), *cert. denied*, 526 U.S. 1098 (1999).

solely with the employee, not the employer.[221] However, an employer is required to reasonably accommodate an employee who suffers from side effects as a result of his or her disability-related medication or treatment or an employee who suffers from disability-related symptoms or medical conditions that cause limitations.[222]

G. Modification of the Employer's Work Site or Equipment

An employer may be required to modify an employee's desk, work station, or other equipment as a form of reasonable accommodation. However, a delay in making such modifications does not necessarily imply a failure to make an accommodation on the part of the employer. For example, in *Terrell v. USAir*,[223] the court held that an employer's delay in providing a "drop keyboard" to an employee suffering from carpal tunnel syndrome was reasonable where the employer had provided the employee with some access to the drop keyboard and had not required the employee to type when access was unavailable. In *Feliberty v. Kemper Corp.*,[224] however, the court held that a triable issue of fact existed as to whether retrieval of medical files by typing on a keyboard was an essential function of the employee's job, when the employee claimed that the employer's untimely response to a request for accommodation was a failure to make a reasonable accommodation.

H. Effect on Workplace Conduct Rules

An employer may terminate or discipline a disabled employee who violates a uniformly applied conduct rule so long

---

[221] *See also* Siefken v. Village of Arlington Heights, 65 F.3d 664, 4 AD Cases 1441 (7th Cir. 1995).
[222] *See* Vande Zande v. Wisconsin Dep't of Admin., 44 F.3d 538, 3 AD Cases 1636 (7th Cir. 1995).
[223] 132 F.3d 621, 628, 8 AD Cases 529 (11th Cir. 1998).
[224] 98 F.3d 274, 5 AD Cases 1729 (7th Cir. 1996).

as the rule is job-related and consistent with business necessity.[225] For example, in *Harris v. Polk County, Iowa*,[226] the court held that the employer could properly deny a stenographer a job because she had a criminal record despite her assertion that her shoplifting was caused by an ADA-protected mental disorder. Regarding threatening workplace conduct, an employee was found to have been lawfully terminated for egregious misconduct when he threatened his supervisor's life, despite the fact that he suffered from certain psychological disorders.[227] A load operator, whose duties includes welding and operating heavy machinery, and who often fell asleep on the job, was found to have been terminated lawfully despite his sleep apnea.[228]

V. Undue Hardship Issues

An employer is not required to provide an employee reasonable accommodations that would cause the employer to suffer "undue hardship." The ADA defines "undue hardship" as "an action requiring significant difficulty or expense . . . ."[229] In making a claim of undue hardship, the employer is required to provide sufficient evidence that the reasonable "accommodation will, in fact, cause it undue hardship"; it is not enough for the employer to simply assert that it will suffer undue hardship.[230]

A. Undue Hardship Defined

Although the determination of whether an employer will suffer undue hardship is made on a case-by-case basis, there

---

[225]EEOC Enforcement Guide, *supra* note 40, at 21–22; *see* Harris v. Polk County, Iowa, 103 F.3d 696, 6 AD Cases 545 (8th Cir. 1996).
[226]103 F.3d 696, 6 AD Cases 545 (8th Cir. 1996).
[227]Jones v. Postal Workers Local 4755, 192 F.3d 417, 9 AD Cases 1249 (4th Cir. 1999).
[228]Leonberger v. Martin Marietta Materials Inc., 231 F.3d 396, 11 AD Cases 103 (7th Cir. 2000) (employee indicated he chose to fall asleep and that his impairment did not cause him to do so).
[229]42 U.S.C. §12111(10)(A).
[230]*See* 29 C.F.R. pt. 1630, app. §1630.15(d) (2003).

are some factors to consider in establishing whether an undue hardship would be imposed on the employer. These factors include the following:

1. "the nature and cost of the accommodation needed";
2. "the overall financial resources of the facility" making the reasonable accommodation;
3. "the overall financial resources," size, number of employees, and the type and location of facilities of the employer (if the facility involved in the reasonable accommodation is part of a larger entity);
4. "the type of operation" of the employer, including the "structure [ ] and functions of the workforce; the geographic separateness," and the "administrative, or fiscal relationship of the facility" involved in making the accommodation to the employer; and
5. "the impact of" the accommodation "upon the operation of the facility."[231]

Although the language of the ADA and it legislative history do not allow for a consideration of the cost-benefit analysis of the requested accommodation, some courts have nonetheless applied such an analysis to determine whether an undue hardship exists. For example, in *Vande Zande v. Wisconsin Department of Administration*,[232] the court applied cost-benefit analysis in finding that a wheelchair-bound employee's request that she be accommodated with a desktop computer for her home and lowered sinks in kitchenettes near her office was unreasonable because the costs of such adjustments outweighed the benefits.[233] In applying the cost-benefit analysis to show undue hardship, however, the employer has to go beyond showing that providing an accommodation would require the employer to

---

[231] 42 U.S.C. §12111(10)(B). Still, even if a determination is made that the cost of the accommodation would unduly burden the employer, the employer may still have to provide the accommodation if the employee can cover the portion of the cost that exceeds the undue hardship level. *See* 29 C.F.R. pt. 1630, app. §1630.15(d) (2003).

[232] 44 F.3d 538, 545, 3 AD Cases 1636 (7th Cir. 1995).

[233] *Id.*

make changes to the property of another (e.g., changes to the structure in which the employer is a tenant).[234] Similarly, in *Kennedy v. Dresser Rand Co.*,[235] the court applied the cost-benefit analysis and determined that the disabled employee had not met her burden of identifying an accommodation the costs of which exceeded the benefits. In this case, the employee had requested an accommodation that necessitated reassigning her to an entirely new supervisor and ensuring that she never came into contact with her former supervisor.[236]

In *Buckles v. First Data Resources, Inc.*,[237] the U.S. Court of Appeals for the Eight Circuit granted judgment for the employer as a matter of law, reversing a jury verdict, in a case in which the plaintiff sought to require that the employer provide him a workplace wholly free of irritants and unlimited leave. The financial and administrative burdens of the measures sought by the employee were found to be unreasonable and amounted to an undue hardship.

B. Undue Hardship Applied to Leave Cases

Although providing a leave for an employee who is unable to ascertain a set date of return is a reasonable accommodation, if the abstractness of the employee's return date creates an undue hardship for the employer, then the employer can rightfully deny the leave.[238] For example, in *Myers v. Hose*,[239] the employee's request for leave was deemed unreasonable by the court because the employee failed to set a time limit and

---

[234]EEOC ENFORCEMENT GUIDE, *supra* note 40, at 26.
[235]193 F.3d 120, 9 AD Cases 1335 (2d Cir. 1999), *cert. denied*, 528 U.S. 1190 (2000).
[236]*Id.*
[237]176 F.3d 1098, 9 AD Cases 765 (8th Cir. 1999).
[238]EEOC ENFORCEMENT GUIDE, *supra* note 40, at 26.
[239]50 F.3d 278, 4 AD Cases 391 (4th Cir. 1995); *see also* Walsh v. United Parcel Serv., Inc., 201 F.3d 718, 10 AD Cases 161 (6th Cir. 2000) (employer not required to extend leave indefinitely, where employee already had 1½ years of disability leave and failed to provide adequate documentation regarding his condition and possible return to work); Evans v. Federal Express Corp., 133 F.3d 137, 140–41, 8 AD Cases 151 (1st Cir. 1998) (employer may deny request for additional leave due to employee's alcohol problem, where employer had previously granted leave for employee's cocaine addiction).

offered no evidence as to the certainty of his improvement. In *Garcia-Ayala v. Lederle Parenterals, Inc.*,[240] however, the court held that a leave period beyond the employer's 1-year leave policy was a reasonable accommodation, where the employer had temporary help available at no additional cost.[241]

VI. Direct-Threat Defense

The ADA provides employers with a "direct-threat" defense, by which employers can refuse to accommodate a disabled employee whose disability poses a direct threat to other employees.[242] The employer also is not required to provide an accommodation that would pose a direct threat ("significant risk of substantial harm") to the health and safety of other employees.[243] However, in determining whether an individual poses a significant risk of substantial harm to others, the employer should rely on an objective evaluation and "not on subjective perceptions, irrational fears, patronizing attitudes, or stereotypes."[244]

The EEOC and several courts of appeals have interpreted the statutory "direct-threat" defense to apply to situations where

---

[240] 212 F.3d 638, 649, 10 AD Cases 865 (1st Cir. 2000); *see also* Cehrs v. Northeast Ohio Alzheimer's Research Ctr., 155 F.3d 775, 783, 8 AD Cases 825 (6th Cir. 1998) (leave request by employee with psoriasis and arthritis would not create an undue hardship, because employer routinely granted leave to other employees); Haschmann v. Time Warner Entm't Co., 151 F.3d 591, 602, 8 AD Cases 692 (7th Cir. 1998) (2–4 weeks of leave did not constitute undue hardship, where requesting employee's position had been vacant for 6 months prior to his hiring).

[241] *See also* Ward v. Massachusetts Health Research Inst., Inc., 209 F.3d 29, 10 AD Cases 776 (1st Cir. 2000) (employer must produce evidence that requests for schedule or leave policy alteration would impose undue hardship); Nunes v. Wal-Mart Stores, Inc., 164 F.3d 1243, 8 AD Cases 1813 (9th Cir. 1999) (9-month leave sought by plaintiff presented fact question as to whether it would impose undue hardship in light of employer's policy of allowing extended leaves and hiring temporary help).

[242] 42 U.S.C. §12113(b); *see also* Robertson v. Neuromedical Ctr., 161 F.3d 292, 296 (5th Cir. 1998) (employers not required to accommodate employee pursuant to ADA if employee would pose direct threat to health and safety of others) (citing 42 U.S.C. §12113(b)).

[243] 29 C.F.R. §1630.15 (2003).

[244] 29 C.F.R. pt. 1630, app. §1630.2(r) (2003).

the work environment would pose a direct threat to the health of the disabled employee as well as to other employees. For example, in *LaChance v. Duffy's Draft House*,[245] the court held that, because an epileptic employee working as a line cook posed a direct threat to himself and others in the workplace, he was not a qualified individual under the ADA. In 2002, the Supreme Court—reversing the U.S. Court of Appeals for the Ninth Circuit—held, in *Echazabal v. Chevron USA, Inc.*,[246] that the "direct-threat" defense applies to instances where the individual's employment poses or would pose a direct threat to the health and safety of the workers' own health and safety, as well as to circumstances in which the individual poses a direct threat to others. In *Echazabal*, the disabled employee who suffered from chronic active hepatitis C was denied a position because his employer feared that working in an oil refinery might exacerbate his condition.

In a number of cases, employers have been able to establish the existence of a direct threat to others posed by employees' conditions in circumstances in which they had mental/psychological/suicidal conditions and issued threats of physical violence,[247] experienced panic attacks in a job in which the worker was responsible for handling life-threatening emergencies,[248] or had HIV conditions and were involved in invasive patient care procedures,[249] among other situations. In other circumstances, however, courts have not embraced such asserted defenses.[250]

---

[245] 146 F.3d 832, 8 AD Cases 652 (11th Cir. 1998).

[246] 536 U.S. 73, 13 AD Cases 97 (2002).

[247] Green v. Burton Rubber Processing, 2002 U.S. App. LEXIS 2959 (6th Cir. 2002); Borigialli v. Thunder Basin Coal Co., 235 F.3d 1284, 11 AD Cases 484 (10th Cir. 2000); Palesch v. Missouri Comm'n on Human Rights, 233 F.3d 560 (8th Cir. 2000).

[248] Emerson v. Northern States Power Co., 256 F.3d 506, 11 AD Cases 1683 (7th Cir. 2001).

[249] Waddell v. Valley Forge Dental Assocs., Inc., 276 F.3d 1275, 12 AD Cases 1029 (11th Cir. 2001), *cert. denied*, 535 U.S. 1096 (2002); Estate of Mauro v. Borgess Med. Ctr., 137 F.3d 398, 7 AD Cases 1571 (6th Cir. 1998), *cert. denied*, 525 U.S. 815 (1998).

[250] *See, e.g.*, Lovejoy-Wilson v. NOCO Motor Fuel, Inc. 263 F.3d 208, 12 AD Cases 340 (2d Cir. 2001); Lowe v. Alabama Power Co., 244 F.3d 1305 (11th Cir.

When considering an employer's policy to exclude from specified positions (safety-sensitive jobs, with no immediate supervision) individuals with a history of alcoholism or drug addiction, the U.S. Court of Appeals for the Fifth Circuit concluded that the employer's safety-based qualification standard was adopted as a matter of business necessity and that defense would be applied to the employer's actions, rather than the direct-threat defense, which the court held was applicable to individual safety risks that are not addressed by that overall standard.[251]

VII. REASONABLE ACCOMMODATION AND JOB APPLICANTS

A. Duty to Provide Reasonable Accommodation to New Hires

An employer is required to provide a reasonable accommodation to a qualified applicant with a disability so long as the accommodation provides the applicant with an equal opportunity to engage in the application process and to be considered for the job.[252] The employer does not need to provide the applicant with a reasonable accommodation, however, if doing so would amount to undue hardship for the employer.[253]

In *Hoffman v. Fidelity Brokerage Services, Inc.*,[254] the court held that reassignments are not available for job applicants. Specifically, the court found that where the particular function of the job is not essential to that job, the employer must either provide an accommodation that will assist the applicant in performing the job, transfer the function to another position,

---

2001); Rizzo v. Children's World Learning Ctrs., 213 F.3d 209, 10 AD Cases 976 (5th Cir.), *cert. denied*, 531 U.S. 958 (2000).
    [251]EEOC v. Exxon Corp., 203 F.3d 871, 10 AD Cases 225 (5th Cir. 2000).
    [252]EEOC ENFORCEMENT GUIDE, *supra* note 40, at 10–11.
    [253]*Id.*
    [254]959 F. Supp. 452, 6 AD Cases 651 (S.D. Ohio 1997).

or exchange the function to one that the applicant can perform. However, in *Spitzer v. Good Guys, Inc.*,[255] the court held that the employer had a duty to reassign a disabled employee if an already funded, vacant position at the same level existed. According to the court, "'the ADA may require an employer to reassign a disabled employee to a different position as reasonable accommodation where the employee can no longer perform the essential functions of [his or her] current position.'"[256]

B. Preemployment Inquiries by an Employer as to the Need for a Reasonable Accommodation

Once an employer has described to the applicant what the hiring process involves (e.g., an interview, timed written test, or job demonstration), the employer may ask the applicant if he or she requires a reasonable accommodation for the hiring process.[257] However, whether or not an employer can inquire from an applicant whether or not he or she requires a reasonable accommodation to perform the job depends on whether or not an offer of employment has been extended.

1. Preemployment Offer

Generally, the ADA prohibits an employer from conducting any preemployment offer inquiries or medical examinations of a job applicant as to whether the applicant is disabled.[258] This restriction, however, does not apply to former employees who have applied to be rehired.[259] Also, in *Harris v. Harris &*

---

[255]80 Cal. App. 4th 1376, 10 AD Cases 1638 (2000).
[256]*Id.* at 1389, 10 AD Cases 1645 (quoting Gile v. United Air Lines, 95 F.3d 492, 498, 5 AD Cases 1466 (7th Cir. 1996)).
[257]EEOC ENFORCEMENET GUIDE, *supra* note 40, at 10–11.
[258]42 U.S.C. §12112(d)(2)(A).
[259]Grenier v. Cyanamid Plastics, 70 F.3d 667, 5 AD Cases 75 (1st Cir. 1995) (employer's request that former employee provide certification from his doctor that (1) identified necessary reasonable accommodations, and (2) provided that employee could work without restrictions, did not violate ADA); Harris v. Harris & Hart, Inc., 206 F.3d 838, 845, 10 AD Cases 481 (9th Cir. 2000) (employer's request for medical release prior to rehiring former employee with known disability did not violate ADA).

Hart, Inc.,[260] the court outlined three other exceptions to the ADA's general rule barring pre-offer medical inquiries: (1) inquiries relating to the applicant's ability to perform job-related functions, (2) when employer reasonably believes that the "applicant's known disability will interfere with the performance of a job-related function," and (3) "when an applicant requests a reasonable accommodation" for the job or the application process itself.[261]

2. Post-Employment Offer

An employer that extends a conditional offer of employment to an applicant who has not yet begun working may inquire as to whether the applicant will need a reasonable accommodation and may seek a medical examination if such an inquiry or examination in shown to be related to the job.[262] For example, in *Barnes v. Cochran*,[263] the court found that an employer's requirement of a preemployment psychological exam violated the ADA.

VIII. OTHER REASONABLE ACCOMMODATION ISSUES

A. Interplay With Other Laws

In determining who is a "qualified individual with a disability," courts may consider admissions made by the disabled employee on, for example, applications for social security disability benefits. In *Cleveland v. Policy Management Systems Corp.*,[264] the Supreme Court held that an individual who claims to be totally disabled for the purposes of a Social Security Disability Insurance (SSDI) application, should not be barred from also bringing a claim under the ADA, so long as the individual proffers

---

[260] 206 F.3d 838, 10 AD Cases 481 (9th Cir. 2000).
[261] *Id.* at 841–42.
[262] 42 U.S.C. §12112(d)(3).
[263] 944 F. Supp. 897, 5 AD Cases 1685 (S.D. Fla. 1996), *aff'd*, 130 F.3d 443 (11th Cir. 1997) (employer's preemployment psychological exam violated ADA).
[264] 526 U.S. 795, 805, 9 AD Cases 491 (1999).

a sufficient explanation for the apparent contradiction between his or her two statements on the application and the desire to continue working. In *Cleveland,* the employee's job required her to perform background checks on prospective employees of Policy Management System's clients. The employee suffered a stroke that damaged her concentration, memory, and language skills. Three weeks later, she filed an SSDI application, in which she stated that she was "disabled" and "unable to work." After the employee returned to work the Social Security Administration (SSA) terminated her application for benefits. Shortly thereafter, her employer fired her. At a subsequent SSDI hearing for reconsideration, the employee reiterated that "I am unable to work due to my disability."[265] The employee alleged that Policy Management had failed to accommodate her disability by providing training or additional time to complete her work. One week later, she received an award of benefits from the SSA.

Prior to *Cleveland,* some courts viewed an SSDI application, or the receipt of benefits, as an absolute bar to pursuing an ADA claim,[266] while others only viewed the application as relevant evidence on the employee's ADA claim.[267] The Supreme Court resolved this division by holding that the employee's application and award of SSDI benefits did not automatically bar any claim under the ADA. In so holding, the Court explained that the "Social Security Act and the ADA both help individuals with disabilities, but in different ways."[268] Because the Social Security Act tries to provide critical financial support to disabled individuals, which requires the processing of more than 2.5 million claims per year, the Social Security Act defines disability in the simplest of terms and does not consider the highly fact-specific (and often highly disputed) question of

---

[265] *Id.* at 799, 9 AD Cases at 493.

[266] *See* McNemar v. Disney Store, Inc., 91 F.3d 610, 618–20, 5 AD Cases 1227 (3d Cir. 1996), *cert. denied,* 519 U.S. 1115 (1997).

[267] *See* Rascon v. U.S. W. Communications, Inc., 143 F.3d 1324, 1332, 8 AD Cases 541 (10th Cir. 1998); Griffith v. Wal-Mart Stores, Inc., 135 F.3d 376, 382, 7 AD Cases 1233 (6th Cir. 1998), *cert. denied,* 526 U.S. 1144 (1999); Swanks v. Washington Metro. Area Transit Auth., 116 F.3d 582, 586, 6 AD Cases 1544 (D.C. Cir. 1997).

[268] *Cleveland,* 526 U.S. at 801, 9 AD Cases at 494.

reasonable accommodation. Therefore, a person who is totally disabled under the SSA may still be a qualified individual under the ADA if that person can perform the job with reasonable accommodation.

However, the Court also held that "in some cases an earlier SSDI claim may turn out genuinely to conflict with an ADA claim,"[269] so an ADA plaintiff cannot simply ignore an apparent contradiction. Therefore, even though Cleveland's claim was not automatically barred, the Court still required her to "sufficiently explain" the discrepancy between her SSDI application, in which she claimed to be "totally disabled," and her ADA claim that she could "'perform the essential functions' of her job."[270]

As noted earlier,[271] an employee who is covered by the FMLA may not be denied benefits of the FMLA under the guise that an FMLA leave is not a reasonable accommodation. Similarly, the employer cannot use the 12-week FMLA leave to limit the amount of leave that may be reasonable to accommodate a disability under the ADA.[272]

B. Providing Additional Accommodations

The EEOC has stated that the employer has an ongoing duty to provide reasonable accommodations for a disabled employee, so long as the accommodations are necessitated by

---

[269] Id. at 805, 9 AD Cases at 496.

[270] Id. at 806, 9 AD Cases at 496 (quoting 42 U.S.C. §12111(8)); see also EEOC v. Stowe-Pharr Mills, Inc., 216 F.3d 373, 378, 10 AD Cases 1153, 1156 (4th Cir. 2000) (requiring employee to "proffer a sufficient explanation for any apparent contradiction between the [ADA and the SSDI] claims"). But see Disanto v. McGraw Hill, Inc., 220 F.3d 61, 10 AD Cases 1364 (2d Cir. 2000) (failure to reconcile inconsistent statement could not recover under ADA); Reed v. Petroleum Helicopters, Inc., 218 F.3d 477, 10 AD Cases 1426 (5th Cir. 2000) (same); Motley v. New Jersey State Police, 196 F.3d 160, 9 AD Cases 1505 (3d Cir. 1999) (same), cert. denied, 529 U.S. 1087 (2000).

[271] See section IV.D.3., "Rather Than Take a Leave as a Form of Reasonable Accommodation," above.

[272] 29 C.F.R. §825.702 (2003).

the employee's disability, are effective, and would not impose an undue hardship on the employer.[273]

Courts are in agreement with the EEOC that an employer does not have to change the employee's supervisor as a form of reasonable accommodation.[274] In *Palmer v. Circuit Court of Cook County Social Services Dep't*,[275] as well as in *Schneiker v. Fortis Insurance Co.*,[276] the U.S. Court of Appeals for the Seventh Circuit held that an employee who suffers from anxiety and/or depression as a result of working with his or her supervisor is not disabled. According to the court, because the employee is still able to work under a different supervisor, he or she is not limited in the major life activity of working.

IX. PUBLIC ACCOMMODATIONS

Title III of the ADA establishes access requirements for private entities defined as public accommodations. Under Title III, a public accommodation must make "reasonable accommodations" to provide for access to the accommodation's facility and/or its goods and services.[277]

The U.S. Court of Appeals for the Sixth Circuit, in *Parker v. Metropolitan Life Insurance Co.*,[278] denied an employee's Title III claim against her employer and found that the plain language of the ADA "expressly limits discrimination in employment practices to Title I of the ADA."[279] The employee sued the

---

[273] EEOC ENFORCEMENT GUIDE, *supra* note 40, at 20–21; *see also* Ralph v. Lucent Techs., Inc., 135 F.3d 166, 171, 172, 7 AD Cases 1345, 1349 (1st Cir. 1998) ("The duty to provide reasonable accommodation is a continuing one . . . and not exhausted by one effort.").

[274] EEOC ENFORCEMENT GUIDE, *supra* note 40, at 32. (employer may be required to change supervisory methods as form of reasonable accommodation).

[275] 117 F.3d 351, 6 AD Cases 1569 (7th Cir. 1997), *cert. denied*, 522 U.S. 1096 (1998).

[276] 200 F.3d 1055, 10 AD Cases 75 (7th Cir. 2000).

[277] 42 U.S.C. §12181(7).

[278] 121 F.3d 1006, 6 AD Cases 1865 (6th Cir. 1997) (en banc), *cert. denied*, 522 U.S. 1084 (1998).

[279] *Id.* at 1015, 6 AD Cases at 1872; *see also* Menkowitz v. Pottstown Mem'l Med. Ctr., 154 F.3d 113, 118, 8 AD Cases 725, 729 (3d Cir. 1998) ("[I]t is evident that Congress sought to regulate disability discrimination in the area of employment

employer and its insurance carrier for alleged discriminatory practices under their available insurance policies.[280] The *Parker* court affirmed the lower court's dismissal of the plaintiff's claim against the employer.[281] The lower court analyzed the legislative history of the ADA, which revealed that "Title III was not intended . . . to govern any terms or conditions of employment by providers of public accommodations . . . '[E]mployment practices are governed by title I of this legislation.'"[282] A Massachusetts district court reached a similar conclusion in a claim under Title III seeking redress for alleged employment disability discrimination under Title III.[283] The court found that "to [allow the plaintiff to sue his employer under Title III] might wreak havoc with the careful balance that Congress attempted to strike in Title I between the rights of employers and the rights of workers with disabilities."[284] These cases are clear that the public accommodations provisions of Title III of the ADA do not apply to the employees of a public accommodation.

---

exclusively through Title I . . . ."); Ford v. Schering-Plough Corp., 145 F.3d 601, 612, 8 AD Cases 190, 199 (3d Cir. 1998), *cert. denied,* 525 U.S. 1093 (1999) ("Terms and conditions of employment are covered under Title I, not Title III."); Motzkin v. Trustees of Boston Univ., 938 F. Supp. 983, 996, 7 AD Cases 101 (D. Mass. 1996) (Title III of ADA does not apply to employment discrimination).

[280] *Parker,* 121 F.3d at 1008.

[281] Parker v. Metropolitan Life Ins. Co., 875 F. Supp. 1321, 1328, 4 AD Cases 34 (W.D. Tenn. 1995).

[282] *Id.* (quoting S. REP. No. 101-116, at 56 (1989)).

[283] *Motzkin,* 938 F. Supp at 985.

[284] *Id.* at 996, 7 AD Cases at 111.

CHAPTER 9

INTERPLAY OF RELATED WORKPLACE STATUTES

I. The Family and Medical Leave Act 839
   A. Employer Coverage Under the ADA and the FMLA 841
   B. Employee Coverage Under the ADA and the FMLA 841
      1. Threshold Requirements as to Duration of Employment 841
      2. "Disability" Versus "Serious Health Condition" 842
         a. "Disability" 843
         b. "Serious Health Condition" 843
         c. Differing Requirements 845
   C. Terms and Conditions of Leave Under the ADA and the FMLA 847
      1. Limitations on the Availability of Leave Based on Hardship to the Employer Under the ADA and the FMLA 847
      2. Duration of Leave Under the ADA and the FMLA 850
      3. Availability of Reduced Schedule or Intermittent Leave 852
      4. Compensation While on Leave Under the ADA and the FMLA 854
      5. Continuation of Benefits While on Leave Under the ADA and the FMLA 855
      6. Treatment of Absenteeism under the ADA and the FMLA 856
   D. Availability of Light-Duty Work Under the ADA and the FMLA 857

	E.	Medical Examinations and Inquiries Under the ADA and the FMLA	858
	F.	Fitness-for-Duty Requirements Under the ADA and the FMLA	861
	G.	Reinstatement Rights Under the ADA and the FMLA	862
	H.	Antiretaliation Provisions Under the ADA and the FMLA	864
	I.	Remedies Under the ADA and the FMLA	865
II.	Workers' Compensation Laws	865
	A.	The ADA and the Exclusive Remedy Provisions of Workers' Compensation Laws	867
	B.	Pursuit of Discrimination Charges and Workers' Compensation Claims	869
		1. Judicial Estoppel	869
		2. EEOC Position	870
		3. Disability Benefits Versus ADA Claims	871
	C.	Medical Inquiries and Confidentiality of Medical Information	873
		1. Medical Records	873
		2. Medical Examinations	873
		3. Fitness to Return-to-Work Policies	874
		4. Physical Agility Tests	875
		5. Medical Inquiries	875
	D.	Accommodations, Light-Duty, and Leave Under the ADA and Workers' Compensation Laws	877
III.	Social Security and Other Disability Benefits Programs	879
	A.	"Disability" Under the Social Security Programs	881
		1. Duration of Social Security Benefits	883
	B.	"Disability" Under the ADA	885
	C.	Recognition of Conflict Between Social Security Disability and ADA Disability	887
		1. Administrative Recognition of Conflict	887
		2. Court Recognition of Conflict	887
	D.	Receipt of Disability Benefits and ADA Recovery	890

	1. Social Security and ADA Disability Claims Conflict	890
	2. Genuine Conflicts	892
	3. "Sufficient Explanation" Burden	893
IV.	Safety and Health Statutes and Regulations	895
	A. Balancing Individual Rights Against the Duty to Provide a Safe Workplace	897
	1. The Business Necessity Defense	898
	2. The Undue Hardship Defense	899
	3. The Direct-Threat Defense	900
	a. Opposing View	901
	4. The ADA's Conflict With Other Federal Laws as a Defense	904
	B. Specific Occupational Safety and Health Act and ADA Tensions	907
	1. Employee Records	907
	2. Medical Examinations	909
	3. Abatement Requirements	910
	C. State Medical and Safety Requirements	911
V.	The National Labor Relations Act	912
	A. How the ADA and tje NLRA Interrelate	913
	B. Conflicts Between the ADA and the NLRA	914
	1. The Implicit Duty to Meet Informally Versus the Prohibition Against Direct Dealing	914
	2. The Duty to Maintain Confidentiality Versus the Duty to Disclose	915
	3. The Duty to Reasonably Accommodate Versus the Duty to Bargain	917
	a. Collective Bargaining Agreement	917
	C. Arbitration Issues Under the ADA	921
	D. The Duty of Fair Representation	923
VI.	ERISA and the ADA's Application to Employee Benefits Plans	924
	A. ADA Section 501(c)	927
	1. Historical Background/Legislative History	928
	a. Effect on ERISA's Preemption Provision	930

	b. Effect on Insurance Industry		930
	2. No Subterfuge		931
	3. Permitted Limitations		932
B.	EEOC Guidance		934
	1. Level 1: Are Benefits "Unequal"?		937
	2. Level 2: Do the "Unequal" Benefits Arise from a "Disability-Based" Distinction?		937
	3. Level 3: Is the "Disability-Based" Distinction a "Subterfuge"?		939
		a. Circumstance 1	940
		b. Circumstance 2	941
		c. Circumstance 3	942
		d. Circumstance 4	943
		e. Circumstance 5	944
		f. Summary	944
C.	Recurring Questions		944
	1. Standing to Sue Under the ADA		945
		a. No Longer Covered Under the ADA	946
		b. Judicial Estoppel	947
		c. EEOC's Position	947
		d. Disability-Based Risk Classifications	949
	2. Mental Versus Physical Health Care Coverage		952
D.	Violations and Permitted Distinctions		954

The American with Disabilities Act (ADA)[1] protects important individual rights, but neither this landmark legislation—nor the Rehabilitation Act of 1973,[2] which preceded it at the federal level, nor the comparable state disability discrimination statutes—stands alone. There are other employment statutes, at both the federal and state levels, that also protect the rights of individuals and groups of individuals. At times, overlapping legislation complements the requirements of the ADA, but there also are instances in which there appear to be substantive

---

[1] 42 U.S.C. §12101 et seq.
[2] 29 U.S.C. §701 et seq.

conflicts. The ADA is a statute of relatively recent vintage, and courts—as well as administrative agencies—are continually struggling to define the interrelationship of the ADA and other statutes. This chapter describes such measures and explores their connections to the ADA.

I. THE FAMILY AND MEDICAL LEAVE ACT

In addition to providing rights to care for new children and close relatives with serious health conditions, the Family and Medical Leave Act (FMLA)[3] offers benefits and protection to employees with certain medical conditions. Where the employee's health condition also entitles the individual to protection under the ADA, employers are subject to concurrent and sometimes conflicting obligations under each statutory scheme. This section discusses the intersection between the ADA and FMLA.

The FMLA became effective for most employers on August 5, 1993.[4] It generally requires that employers provide employees up to 12 weeks of unpaid, job-protected leave for situations involving their own medical condition or those of a family member. Title I of the ADA first became effective more than 1 year earlier, on July 26, 1992. It prohibits discrimination against employees and applicants for employment based on a physical or mental disability. Coverage under the ADA and FMLA overlaps most often when an employee with a physical or mental condition that constitutes both a "disability" within the meaning of the ADA and a "serious health condition" under the FMLA desires to utilize continuous or intermittent leave.

---

[3] 29 U.S.C. §2601 et seq. and implementing regulations are at 29 C.F.R. §825.101 et seq. (2003).

[4] A number of states have enacted family and medical leave laws, including some of general application and others limited to public sector employees. In addition to broad family and medical leave laws, see, e.g., the District of Columbia Family and Medical Leave Act, D.C. CODE ANN., §36-1301 et seq., some states have enacted distinct leave protections for women who are pregnant, or which allow leave to deal with children's school needs or the health-care concerns of elderly relatives. See, e.g., The Massachusetts "Small Necessities Leave Act," MASS. GEN. LAWS ch. 149, §52D.

While the goals of Title I of the ADA are to eliminate employment discrimination against qualified individuals with disabilities and to expand employment opportunities for such persons, the specific purpose of the FMLA is to provide leave for employees to deal with medical situations and emergencies of their own or family members without fear of the termination of employment or loss of health benefits.[5] An employer's obligation to provide leave to a disabled employee as a reasonable accommodation under the ADA[6] often will involve the need to take into consideration an employee's rights and employer's obligations under the FMLA. Both the ADA and the FMLA recognize that their terms do not provide the sole sources of guidance regarding potentially affected individuals. Rather, each contemplates that other measures will merit consideration in certain circumstances. The ADA provides that "[n]othing in this chapter shall be construed to invalidate or limit the remedies, rights, and procedures of any Federal law ... that provides greater or equal protection for the rights of individuals with disabilities than are afforded by this chapter."[7] The FMLA similarly provides that its provisions should not be construed to modify or affect any federal or state law prohibiting discrimination on a variety of bases, including disability discrimination. Its implementing regulations provide further that the leave requirements of the FMLA are wholly distinct from the reasonable accommodation obligations of an employer under the ADA.[8] Clearly, there are overlapping areas of application of both the ADA and FMLA including (but not limited

---

[5] 29 U.S.C. §2601.

[6] *See Revised Enforcement Guidance: Reasonable Accommodation and Undue Hardship Under the Americans with Disabilities Act* (Oct. 2002) [hereinafter *Revised Enforcement Guidance*] (under section on Leave, providing that "[p]ermitting the use of accrued paid leave, or unpaid leave, is a form of reasonable accommodation when necessitated by an employee's disability," citing Cehrs v. Northeast Ohio Alzheimer's Research Ctr., 155 F.3d 775, 8 AD Cases 825 (6th Cir. 1998)); *see also* Schmidt v. Safeway Inc., 864 F. Supp. 991, 3 AD Cases 1141 (D. Or. 1994); Dutton v. Johnson County Bd. of County Comm'rs, 859 F. Supp. 498, 3 AD Cases 808 (D. Kan. 1994) (recognizing that temporary leave may be reasonable accommodation under ADA).

[7] 42 U.S.C. §12201(b).

[8] 29 C.F.R. §825.701(a) (2003).

to) circumstances in which employees enjoy leave and reinstatement rights under both statutes.

A. Employer Coverage Under the ADA and the FMLA

In determining whether there will be any interplay at all between the ADA and FMLA, a threshold question is the determination of employer coverage. Title I of the ADA is the broader classification, as its provisions apply to employers "engaged in an industry affecting commerce that has 15 or more employees for each working day in each of 20 or more calendar weeks in the current or preceding calendar year."[9] The FMLA covers employers engaged in similar activities, however, the number of employees necessary for an employer to be covered is 50 or more employees.[10] Thus, the potential for overlapping application of the ADA and FMLA exists only for employers that meet the 50-plus employee standard of the FMLA.

B. Employee Coverage Under the ADA and the FMLA

1. Threshold Requirements as to Duration of Employment

In addition to concurrent coverage for the employer, the employee must qualify for coverage under each statute. The ADA ultimately applies only to employees and applicants who are qualified individuals with a disability who can perform the essential functions of their current job or the one that they seek, "with or without reasonable accommodation."[11] "Qualified individuals" under the ADA are persons who have the requisite skill, experience, education, and other job-related requirements that would enable them to perform the essential functions of the job.[12] Under the regulations implementing

---

[9] 42 U.S.C. §12111(5)(A).
[10] 29 U.S.C. §2611(4)(A)(i); 29 C.F.R. §825.104(a) (2003). Employers covered by the FMLA also include persons "acting, directly or indirectly, in the interest of a covered employer [with respect] to any of the employees of [a covered] employer, any successor in interest to a covered employer, and any public agency." *Id.*
[11] 42 U.S.C. §§12111(8), 12112(a).
[12] *Id.* §12111(8).

the ADA, an "essential function" of a job includes the "fundamental job duties" of the position.[13] There is no requirement that an employee (or applicant) be employed for a particular duration to be entitled to coverage under the ADA.

By contrast, to be eligible for leave under the FMLA, an employee must have worked at least 12 months (not necessarily consecutively) for the employer and worked at least 1,250 hours in the 12 months preceding leave.[14] Whether an employee has worked 1,250 hours for purposes of the FMLA "is determined according to principles established under the Fair Labor Standards Act [29 U.S.C. §201 et seq.] for determining compensable hours of work."[15]

Although Title I of the ADA applies to applicants for employment, the FMLA, in general, does not apply to applicants or prospective employees. However, some courts have interpreted the FMLA's antiretaliation provision to provide a cognizable claim for violation of the FMLA where an employee is not hired or is not rehired based on that person's record of having utilized the FMLA's leave provisions.[16]

2. *"Disability" Versus "Serious Health Condition"*

The key definitional terms of the ADA and the FMLA that relate to covered conditions suggest that overlapping coverage may be a regular occurrence. Yet, the concepts that are key to coverage—"disability" under the ADA and "serious health condition" under the FMLA—are different concepts, and must be analyzed separately."[17]

---

[13]29 C.F.R. §1630.2(n) (2003).
[14]29 U.S.C. §2611(2)(A); 29 C.F.R. §825.110 (2003).
[15]29 C.F.R. §825.110(c) (2003).
[16]*Compare* Wenzlaff v. NationsBank, 940 F. Supp. 889, 9 AD Cases 582 (D. Md. 1996) (dismissing claim of post-termination violations of FMLA by former employee on basis of its finding that last possible day for cognizable claim of violation of FMLA is employee's last day of employment) *and* Duckworth v. Pratt & Whitney, Div. of United Techs. Corp., 152 F.3d 1, 4 WH Cases 2d 1281 (1st Cir. 1998) (overruled lower court finding that job applicant may not bring suit against potential employer alleging violation of FMLA, where applicant claimed that company interfered with his FMLA rights by refusing to rehire him based on his past use of FMLA leave).
[17]29 C.F.R. §825.702(a) (2003); *see also* Vincent v. Wells Fargo Guard Servs., Inc. of Fla., 3 F. Supp. 2d 1405 (S.D. Fla. 1998) (separate analysis for entitled to

a. "Disability"

The ADA defines a disability, in relevant part, as "[a] physical or mental impairment that substantially limits one or more of the major life activities of such individual."[18] Major life activities include, but are not limited to, things "such as caring for oneself, performing manual tasks, walking, seeing, hearing, speaking, breathing, learning, and working."[19] Factors to be considered in determining whether a major life activity is substantially impaired include the type of impairment, the severity of the impairment, the anticipated duration of the impairment, and the projected long-term impact of the impairment.[20] In many cases, physical limitations that amount to "disabilities" under the ADA also are quite likely to be classified as protected "serious health conditions," but that is not true in all cases. For example, severe hearing loss well might constitute an ADA-protected disability, but it may not constitute an FMLA-covered serious health condition.

Temporary, nonchronic conditions such as "broken limbs, sprained joints, concussions, appendicitis, and influenza" generally do not qualify as ADA-protected disabilities.[21] However, some, if not all of these conditions well may qualify as a "serious health condition" for purposes of the FMLA. The ADA also protects employees who have a record of such an impairment or are regarded as having such an impairment.

b. "Serious Health Condition"

Among other coverage triggers (such as the arrival of new children or illnesses of close relations), the FMLA provides leave for employees who suffer from a "serious health condition" that renders the employee incapable of performing an

---

leave under ADA and FMLA must be performed); Ellis v. Mohenis Servs., Inc., 8 AD Cases 939 (E.D. Pa. 1998) (employee who has serious health condition for purposes of FMLA not necessarily disabled under ADA).

[18] 42 U.S.C. §12102(2).

[19] 29 C.F.R. §1630.2(i) (2003).

[20] *Id.* §1630(j)(2) (2003); *see also* Oswalt v. Sara Lee Corp., 74 F.3d 91, 5 AD Cases 385 (5th Cir. 1996); Bolton v. Scrivner, Inc., 36 F.3d 939, 3 AD Cases 1089 (10th Cir. 1994), *cert. denied*, 513 U.S. 1152 (1995).

[21] 29 C.F.R. pt. 1630, app. §1630.2(j) (2003).

essential function of the individual's job.[22] The definition of "essential function" under the FMLA is given the same meaning as that phrase is under the ADA.[23]

Under the FMLA, a serious health condition is an illness, injury, impairment, or physical or mental condition that involves either inpatient care (including time for recovery and subsequent treatment in connection with the inpatient care) or continuing treatment by a health care provider.[24] Continuing treatment by a health care provider is defined under the regulations to exist in five circumstances: (1) during "[a] period of incapacity ... of more than three consecutive calendar days ... that also involves: ... [t]reatment two or more times by a health care provider [or a single] [t]reatment by a health care provider ... which results in a regimen of continuing treatment under the supervision of the health care provider.... (2) [a]ny period of incapacity due to pregnancy, or for prenatal care; (3) ... [a]ny period of incapacity or treatment ... due to a chronic serious health condition [requiring] periodic visits for treatment" such as diabetes or epilepsy; (4) "[a] period of incapacity which is permanent or long-term due to a condition for which treatment may not be effective" even though the individual remains "under the continuing supervision of ... a health care provider," such as Alzheimer's disease or a stroke; and (5) [a]ny period of absence to receive multiple treatments [from] a health care provider ... for restorative surgery ... or for a condition that would likely result in an absence "of more than three consecutive calendar days" without treatment such as cancer chemotherapy and radiation.[25] "Ordinarily, unless complications arise, the common cold, the flu, ear aches, [stomach aches], headaches," for example, are not considered

---

[22] 29 C.F.R. §825.114 (2003).

[23] *Id.* §825.115 (2003) ("An employee is 'unable to perform the functions of the position' where the health care provider finds that the employee is unable to work at all or is unable to perform any one of the essential functions of the employee's position within the meaning of the Americans with Disabilities Act....").

[24] 29 U.S.C. §2612(a)(1).

[25] 29 C.F.R. §825.114(a)(2) (2003).

to be "serious health conditions" for purposes of the FMLA under the regulations.[26]

c. Differing Requirements

It is clear that under these differing standards, a particular health condition may qualify as a "serious health condition" for purposes of the FMLA, but not a "disability" for purposes of the ADA. For example, a pregnancy or routine broken bone generally will qualify as a serious health condition, but not as a disability because they most likely do not substantially limit a major life activity. In addition, human immunodeficiency virus (HIV)–positive status has been accepted as a disability under the ADA, but it is not clear that HIV-positive status, alone, qualifies as a serious health condition.[27] Similarly, the permanent visual impairment of an individual who can perform the essential job functions of his or her position with or without reasonable accommodation may constitute a disability under the ADA, but not a serious health condition under the FMLA, unless it requires continuing treatment. The lack of overlapping coverage in these instances is largely due to the fact that the definition of disability under the ADA is tied to a substantial limitation of a major life activity, while the definition of serious health condition is not. Therefore, the expected duration of a mental or physical condition is an important factor in determining whether there is a substantial limitation under the ADA, but this same analysis is not relevant to the

---

[26] *Id.* §825.114(c) (2003); *see also* Seidle v. Provident Mut. Life Ins. Co., 871 F. Supp. 238, 246, 2 WH Cases 2d 913, 920 (E.D. Pa. 1994) ("To construe the FMLA to include conditions which, although minor in their initial stages, could evolve into serious illnesses would bring within the protections of the statute virtually every common malady, an out come which is in direct conflict with Congress' intention to exclude from the protections of the FMLA those minor illnesses with short recovery periods."); *but see* Serious Health Condition, FMLA Op. 87 (Dec. 12, 1996), BNA Wage & Hour Manual 99:3092 (illnesses such common cold, flu, and bronchitis, will be considered serious health conditions if they result in incapacity for more than 3 calendar days and employee received continuing treatment); Price v. City of Fort Wayne, 117 F.3d 1022, 3 WH Cases 2d 1729 (7th Cir. 1997) (ailments that would not in and of themselves qualify as a serious health condition under FMLA may combine to constitute serious health condition).

[27] *See* Mora v. Chem-Tronics, Inc., 16 F. Supp. 2d 1192, 5 WH Cases 2d 475 (S.D. Cal. 1998) (citing Bragdon v. Abbott, 524 U.S. 624 (1998)).

question of whether a serious health condition exists for purposes of the FMLA.[28]

In addition, the requirements for showing entitlement to leave under the ADA and FMLA differ in another important respect. To qualify as a serious health condition under the FMLA, an employee must only show that he or she cannot perform the essential functions of a particular position. Such a showing of limitations would not be adequate to establish the presence of a disability under the ADA, even if the focus is on the major life activity of "working." Rather, in order to qualify for protection under the ADA, the employee must establish that he or she cannot perform the essential functions of a broad range of jobs to show the existence of a disability under the ADA.[29]

Thus, the standards for determining whether leave is available to an employee under the ADA and FMLA are quite different. Under the ADA, an employee seeking leave as a reasonable accommodation must generally show that he or she is: (1) disabled as defined by the ADA; (2) qualified to perform the job either with or without reasonable accommodation.[30] Under the FMLA, an employee need only have a serious health condition and show that he or she has worked for the employer for 12 months and 1,250 hours.[31] Unlike the ADA, the FMLA does not require that the person seeking leave demonstrate that he or she is qualified for the position he or she holds. There is no single test to determine whether an employee's physical or mental condition qualifies as both a serious health condition under the FMLA and as a disability under the ADA. Rather, these are separate inquiries that must be undertaken, when appropriate, on a case-by-case basis.[32]

---

[28] 29 U.S.C. §2611(11); 29 U.S.C. §825.114.

[29] *See* Barfield v. Bell S. Telecomms. Inc., 886 F. Supp. 1321, 4 AD Cases 1159 (S.D. Miss. 1995) (employee must establish his or her inability to perform broad range of jobs to be "disabled" for purposes of ADA).

[30] *See* Jessie v. Carter Health Care Ctr., 926 F. Supp. 613, 616 n.2, 3 WH Cases 2d 549, 551 n.2 (E.D. Ky. 1996) (what employee must do to show entitlement to leave under ADA and FMLA).

[31] 29 U.S.C. §2611(2)(A).

[32] 29 C.F.R. §825.310 (2003).

There likely will be no overlapping application of the FMLA and ADA in situations in which an employee qualifies for ADA coverage by virtue of the fact that they are "regarded as" disabled or have a "record" of being disabled. This is so because there are no analogous provisions under the FMLA, and that statute's coverage trigger that deals with the employee's condition focuses on actual, current health limitations, not perceptions or past records of illness. Rather, an employee seeking FMLA leave based on his or her own health status always must establish the current existence of a serious health condition to be covered under the FMLA. Some courts have addressed and rejected the related contention that an employee's record of having a serious health condition under the FMLA establishes that an employee is "regarded as" disabled under the ADA.[33] Similarly, there will be no overlap between the ADA and FMLA in situations where an employee requests leave on the basis of a serious health condition of a family member. While the ADA bars "associational discrimination," it would only require accommodation in the form of leave in some circumstances, based on the employee's own disability, not the disability of a family member.[34]

C. Terms and Conditions of Leave Under the ADA and the FMLA

1. *Limitations on the Availability of Leave Based on Hardship to the Employer Under the ADA and the FMLA*

Under the ADA, employers are required to "reasonably accommodate" the "known physical or mental limitations of

---

[33] *See EEOC Fact Sheet on the Family and Medical Leave Act, the Americans with Disabilities Act, and Title VII of the Civil Rights Act of 1964*, available at www.eeoc.gov (just because someone has serious health condition does not mean that employer regards him or her as having ADA disability; rather, to satisfy this prong of ADA definition of "disability," employer must treat individual as having impairment that substantially limits one or more major life activities).

[34] *See* Tyndall v. National Educ. Ctrs., Inc. of Cal., 31 F.3d 209, 3 AD Cases 868 (4th Cir. 1994) (ADA does not require employer to reasonably accommodate employee's work schedule to enable employee to care for family member with disability).

[a] qualified individual with a disability who is an applicant or employee, unless [the employer] demonstrate[s] that the accommodations would impose an undue hardship on the operation of the business. . . . ."[35] As explored elsewhere,[36] the concept of reasonable accommodation encompasses a broad range of potential actions or modifications of standard requirements or policies. The principal ADA reasonable accommodation that might result in overlapping obligations with the FMLA involves leave, including reduced schedule or intermittent leave.

Though the ADA does not provide for leave, many courts have held that a reasonable accommodation may be a part-time schedule in a current position or intermittent leave.[37] Reassignment to a vacant position also may be a reasonable accommodation.[38] However, there appear to be conflicting authorities on whether excessive absenteeism related to a disability requires accommodation. A number of courts have held that an indefinite leave of absence may be unreasonable and may constitute an undue hardship for an employer under the ADA.[39] Some courts, however, have held that termination based on absenteeism resulting from disability may be tantamount

---

[35] 42 U.S.C. §12112(b)(5)(A).

[36] *See* Chapter 8, "Reasonable Accommodation."

[37] Weiler v. Household Fin. Corp., 101 F.3d 519, 526, 6 AD Cases 106 (7th Cir. 1996) (employer's decision to grant short-term and extended leave was reasonable accommodation); Hankins v. Gap, Inc., 84 F.3d 797, 5 AD Cases 924 (6th Cir. 1996) (affirming summary judgment decision that employee who was granted leave was reasonably accommodated); *see also* 29 C.F.R. §1630.2(o) (2003).

[38] 42 U.S.C. §12111(9)(B); 29 C.F.R. 1630.2(o)(2)(ii) (2003).

[39] *See, e.g.,* Cehrs v. Northeast Ohio Alzheimer's Research Ctr., 155 F.3d 775, 8 AD Cases 825 (6th Cir. 1998) (genuine issue of fact as to whether employee's requested temporary leave was reasonable accommodation); Haschmann v. Time Warner Entm't Co., 151 F.3d 591, 8 AD Cases 692 (7th Cir. 1998) (jury could reasonably determine that two 4-week leaves employee sought for treatment were reasonable accommodation); Criado v. IBM Corp., 145 F.3d 437, 8 AD Cases 336 (1st Cir. 1998) (1-month leave for medical treatment was reasonable accommodation, particularly given that employer gave all of its employees 52 weeks of paid disability leave); Hypes ex rel. Hypes v. First Commerce Corp., 134 F.3d 721, 726–27, 7 AD Cases 1546 (5th Cir. 1998); Kennedy v. Applause, Inc., 90 F.3d 1477, 1482, 5 AD Cases 1249, 1251–52 (9th Cir. 1996) (totally disabled individual could not have "performed her job with the proposed [leave], or any other, accommodation"); Monette v. Electronic Data Sys. Corp., 90 F.3d 1173, 1187, 5 AD Cases 1326, 1338 (6th Cir. 1996) ("employers are under no duty to keep employees on unpaid leaves indefinitely"); Rogers v. International Marine Terminals, Inc., 87 F.3d 755, 759, 5

to termination because of that disability.[40] The majority of courts now recognize that regular attendance is an essential job function and that accommodating a disabled employee's irregular attendance may impose an undue hardship. Stated another way, where the absenteeism is significant and sporadic or indefinite, any accommodation would be unreasonable and would impose an undue burden on the employer.[41]

An example of how this rule is applied is found in *Haschmann v. Time Warner Entertainment Co.*.[42] In *Haschmann*, the plaintiff, who suffered from lupus, took several weeks of medical leave. When she returned to work, her performance began to suffer and she requested another 2 to 4 weeks for leave.[43] The employer denied the request and terminated the plaintiff for poor attendance.[44] Although the court acknowledged that an employer is not obligated to tolerate erratic, unreliable attendance, the court also recognized that the employer must make a good-faith effort to reasonably accommodate the plaintiff's disability. In holding the employer liable, the court set forth its basic test for determining whether an individual may be discharged for excessive absences under the ADA: "[I]t is not the absence itself but rather the excessive frequency of an employee's absence in relation to that employee's job responsibilities that may lead to a finding that an employee is unable to perform the duties of his job."[45]

AD Cases 1115 (5th Cir. 1996) (inability to report to work rendered employee not "otherwise qualified").

[40]*See* Teahan v. Metro-North Commuter R.R., 951 F.2d 511, 517, 2 AD Cases 84 (2d Cir. 1991), *cert. denied*, 506 U.S. 815 (1992).

[41]*See, e.g.*, Watkins v. J&S Oil Co., 164 F.3d 55, 5 WH Cases 2d 1 (1st Cir. 1998); Nesser v. Trans World Airlines, Inc., 160 F.3d 442, 445–46, 8 AD Cases 1348 (8th Cir. 1998); Nowak v. St. Rita High Sch., 142 F.3d 999, 1002–04, 8 AD Cases 106 (7th Cir. 1998); Halperin v. Abacus Tech. Corp., 128 F.3d 191, 197, 7 AD Cases 406 (4th Cir. 1997) (inability to work on regular basis meant that plaintiff could not perform any functions of job); Bultemeyer v. Fort Wayne Cmty. Sch., 100 F.3d 1281, 1284, 6 AD Cases 67 (7th Cir. 1996) (ability to report to work is essential job function); Tyndall v. National Educ. Ctrs. of Cal., Inc., 31 F.3d 209, 213, 3 AD Cases 868 (4th Cir. 1994); Carr v. Reno, 23 F.3d 525, 530, 3 AD 434 (D.C. Cir. 1994).

[42]151 F.3d 591, 601, 8 AD Cases 692 (7th Cir. 1998).

[43]*Id.* at 591.

[44]*Id.* at 595.

[45]*Id.* at 602, 8 AD Cases at 701.

The determination of whether a reasonable accommodation under the ADA, in this case a leave, constitutes an "undue hardship" under the ADA is determined on a case-by-case basis, taking into account such factors as the nature and cost of the accommodation.[46] There is no analogous "undue hardship" defense under the FMLA. An employer must provide up to 12 weeks of leave in a 12-month period regardless of the hardship that will be imposed on the employer. Indeed, there is no limit under the FMLA on the number of employees that can take FMLA leave at the same time, regardless of the hardship on the employer. However, under the FMLA, an exception to an employee's right to reinstatement following leave exists for so-called "key employees." A key employee is a salaried FMLA-eligible employee who is among the highest paid 10 percent of all the employees employed by the employer within 75 miles of the employee's work site. A key employee can be denied reinstatement if such denial is "necessary to prevent substantial and grievous economic injury to the operations of the employer."[47] The FMLA's regulations specifically provide that the "substantial and grievous economic injury" standard is different from and more stringent than the "undue hardship" test under the ADA. Individuals so classified must be notified of their status as "key employees" prior to commencement of leave under the FMLA. The Labor Department's FMLA regulations provide that when an employee requires intermittent or reduced-schedule leave, the employee "must attempt to schedule their leave so as not to disrupt the employer's operations."[48] In addition, "an employer may assign an employee to an alternative position with equivalent pay and benefits that better accommodates the employee's intermittent or reduced leave schedule."[49]

2. *Duration of Leave Under the ADA and the FMLA*

A major distinction between the FMLA and the ADA—insofar as they both might require leave in a given

---

[46] 42 U.S.C. §12111(10)(A).
[47] 29 C.F.R. §825.216(c).
[48] 29 C.F.R. §825.117 (2003).
[49] *Id.*

circumstance—relates to the specific nature and duration of potentially mandated leave. The FMLA entitles eligible employees to a specific quantity of protected job absences, that is, a maximum of 12 weeks of leave in a 12-month period. Therefore, under the FMLA, an employee who exhausts his or her entitlement to leave, but cannot perform an essential function of the job at the end of that period, can be terminated (from an FMLA perspective). There is no such limitation on the amount of leave available to a disabled employee as a reasonable accommodation under the ADA in the absence of an "undue hardship." In fact, *EEOC Policy Guidance* on this subject provides that an employer may not apply a policy of automatically terminating employees "after they have been on leave . . . to an employee with a disability who needs leave beyond" a standardized period of time.[50] It further provides that the employer must modify any no-fault policy to provide a qualified employee with a disability with additional unpaid leave, unless it can show that: (1) there is another effective accommodation that would enable the person to perform the essential functions of his or her position, or (2) granting additional leave would constitute an undue hardship. In other words, an employee who exhausts his or her entitlement to 12 weeks of leave under the FMLA may still be entitled to some additional period of leave as a reasonable accommodation if that person also meets the ADA's definition of "disability."

An additional issue for consideration is whether an employee who requires leave or is not able to regularly attend work, can be judged to be a "qualified individual with a disability." Courts are grappling with questions presented by an employee request for leave for an indefinite period and whether indefinite leave can ever be a reasonable accommodation under the ADA.[51]

---

[50] *See Revised Enforcement Guidance, supra* note 6, at Question 17.

[51] Myers v. Hose, 50 F.3d 278, 283, 4 AD Cases 391, 395 (4th Cir. 1995) ("Nothing in the text of the reasonable accommodation provision requires an employer to wait an indefinite period for an accommodation to achieve its intended effect."). *See also* Johnson v. Foulds, 111 F.3d 133 (7th Cir. 1997); Hudson v. MCI Telecommunications Corp., 87 F.3d 1167, 5 AD Cases 1099 (10th Cir. 1996); Pegues v. Emerson Elec. Co., 913 F. Supp. 976, 5 AD Cases 376, (N.D. Miss. 1996); Howell v. Michelin Tire Corp., 860 F. Supp. 1488, 3 AD Cases 929, (M.D. Ala. 1994).

Under the ADA, the choice of accommodation is left to the employer as long as the accommodation chosen allows the employee to perform the essential functions of the job.[52] By contrast, an employee entitled to leave under the FMLA cannot be forced to accept an accommodation in place of taking leave. An employee is entitled to take FMLA leave despite the fact that he or she may currently be provided an alternative reasonable accommodation for a disability.

3. Availability of Reduced Schedule or Intermittent Leave

Reduced schedules, such as a part-time schedule, or a schedule permitting intermittent leave, have been described by the Equal Employment Opportunity Commission (EEOC) as forms of reasonable accommodation under the ADA in all regulatory, interpretive, and guidance pronouncements involving such issues. Although the ADA itself is silent on the subject of whether a leave of absence may be required as a reasonable accommodation, it provides that job restructuring or part-time or modified work are examples of possible accommodations. The appellate courts have considered many circumstances in

---

[52] *See* Weiler v. Household Fin. Corp., 101 F.3d 519, 6 AD Cases 106 (7th Cir. 1996); Feliberty v. Kemper Corp., 98 F.3d 274, 5 AD Cases 1729 (7th Cir. 1996); Schmidt v. Methodist Hosp. of Ind., Inc., 89 F.3d 342, 5 AD Cases 1340 (7th Cir. 1996); Whillock v. Delta Air Lines, Inc., 926 F. Supp. 1555, 5 AD Cases 1027 (N.D. Ga. 1995), *aff'd*, 86 F.3d 1171, 7 AD Cases 1267 (11th Cir. 1996); Kuehl v. Wal-Mart Stores, Inc., 909 F. Supp. 794, 5 AD Cases 91 (D. Colo. 1995); Kemer v. Johnson, 900 F. Supp. 677, 4 AD Cases 1823 (S.D.N.Y. 1995); Williams v. City of Charlotte, N.C., 899 F. Supp. 1484, 4 AD Cases 1675 (W.D.N.C. 1995); Eckles v. Consolidated Rail Corp., 890 F. Supp. 1391, 4 AD Cases 1134 (S.D. Ind. 1995), *aff'd*, 94 F.3d 1041, 5 AD Cases 1367 (7th Cir. 1996), *cert. denied*, 520 U.S. 1146 (1997); Robinson v. City of Friendswood, 890 F. Supp. 616, 5 AD Cases 105 (S.D. Tex. 1995); Marschand v. Norfolk & W. Ry., 876 F. Supp. 1528, 4 AD Cases 1099 (N.D. Ind. 1995), *aff'd*, 81 F.3d 714, 5 AD Cases 1184 (7th Cir. 1996); Valdez v. Albuquerque Pub. Sch., 875 F. Supp. 740, 4 AD Cases 70 (D.N.M. 1994); Vande Zande v. Wisconsin Dep't of Admin., 851 F. Supp. 353, 2 AD Cases 1846 (W.D. Wis. 1994), *aff'd*, 44 F.3d 538, 3 AD Cases 1636 (7th Cir. 1995) (employer reasonably accommodated its paraplegic employee who was unable to reach kitchen sink by allowing employee to use bathroom sink); Stolmeier v. Yellow Freight Sys., Inc., 3 AD Cases 65 (D. Or. 1994) (employer reasonably accommodated employee truck driver by providing back support pillow instead of special seat and power steering, where there was no evidence that additional accommodations were medically necessary).

which employees have sought flexible or part-time schedules as a form of reasonable accommodation under the ADA. Some have found part-time work to be a form of reasonable accommodation, while others have rejected its use in specific circumstances.[53] They also have considered whether a regular and predictable schedule is an "essential function" of a job, and—in some cases—concluded that it is not.[54]

Likewise, reduced schedule and intermittent leave are also available under the FMLA if medically necessary, and such medical needs can be best accommodated through an intermittent or reduced leave schedule.[55] Under the FMLA, reduced schedule or intermittent leave for an employee's serious health condition is available without regard to any hardship its use may impose on the employer, so long as that particular type of leave is medically necessary.[56] The use of intermittent leave triggers some of the loudest employer complaints about the administrative and productivity drains imposed by the FMLA, particularly when its use comes with little or no prior notice (based on recurrence of symptoms or complications). An employer only may limit leave increments under the FMLA to

---

[53] *Compare* Ralph v. Lucent Techs., 135 F.3d 166, 7 AD Cases 1345 (1st Cir. 1998) (plaintiff with depression entitled to period of part-time work after returning from leave) *with* Hypes v. First Commerce Corp., 134 F.3d 721, 7 AD Cases 1546 (5th Cir. 1998) (where no evidence that later starting time was required by individual's disabling lung disease or would enable him to perform his job's essential functions, flex-time required could be denied).

[54] *See, e.g.* Ward v. Massachusetts Health Research Inst., 209 F.3d 29, 10 AD Cases 776 (1st Cir. 2000).

[55] 29 C.F.R. §825.117 (2003) provides:

For intermittent leave or leave on a reduced leave schedule, there must be a medical need for leave (as distinguished from voluntary treatments and procedures) and it must be that such medical need can be best accommodated through an intermittent or reduced leave schedule. The treatment regimen and other information described in the certification of a serious health condition . . . meets the requirement for certification of the medical necessity of intermittent leave or leave on a reduced leave schedule. Employees needing intermittent FMLA leave or leave on a reduced leave schedule must attempt to schedule their leave so as not to disrupt the employer's operations. In addition, an employer may assign an employee to an alternative position with equivalent pay and benefits that better accommodates the employee's intermittent or reduced leave schedule.

[56] *Id.*

"the shortest period of time that the employer's payroll system uses to account for absences or use of leave, provided it is one hour or less."[57] Moreover, when a reduced schedule or intermittent leave is taken under the FMLA, only the actual period of absence from work is counted toward the 12-week maximum. In this manner, employees with covered serious health conditions may be able to extend certain variations of intermittent leave—for example, 1 day per week for necessary treatment—throughout the entire year.

In the absence of undue hardship, it does not appear that the ADA would permit an employer to transfer an employee needing a reduced schedule as a reasonable accommodation against his or her wishes to a different position based solely on the fact that the new position, utilizing a reduced schedule, works better for the employer.[58] Although there is no "undue hardship" defense under the FMLA, it provides that "[e]mployees needing intermittent or reduced schedule leave" attempt to schedule their leave so as not to disrupt the employer's operations.[59] In addition, the FMLA permits an employer to transfer an employee on reduced schedule or intermittent leave to an alternative position with equivalent pay and benefits if the other position better accommodates the employee's schedule.[60]

4. Compensation While on Leave Under the ADA and the FMLA

The ADA does not require that employees be paid while on leave, unless the employer's policies would require payment generally. This is so because an employer may not discriminate against individuals with disabilities on leave as a reasonable accommodation as opposed to its treatment of employees on leave for reasons other than a disability. Similarly, there is no broad requirement that FMLA leave be paid. An employer on

---

[57] *Id.* §825.203(d) (2003).

[58] *Id.* §§1630.2(o) (2003) and 1630.9 (2003).

[59] *Id.* §825.117 (2003).

[60] *Id.* In circumstances in which intermittent or reduced schedule FMLA leave is sought to provide care for a newborn or newly adopted child, the use of intermittent leave is at the employer's discretion. 29 C.F.R. §825.203(b).

giving proper notice under the FMLA can require an employee to use paid sick, vacation or disability leave to be substituted unless workers' compensation benefits are being received.[61] Likewise, an employee has the right to apply appropriate accrued paid leave to periods of FMLA leave that otherwise would be unpaid.[62]

5. Continuation of Benefits While on Leave Under the ADA and the FMLA

Under the FMLA, an employee is entitled to continue to participate in group health insurance plans on the same basis as active employees during the period of statutorily protected leave.[63] The assurance that group health insurance benefits will be maintained for employees using statutory leave for a serious health condition was one of the primary goals of the FMLA. Of course, an employee on leave still is required to make the same premium contributions that were required as an active employee.[64] There is no comparable provision of the ADA that explicitly requires employers to maintain health care benefits for employees who are on leave as a reasonable accommodation. However, an employer may not discriminate against individuals with disabilities on leave as a reasonable accommodation as opposed to its treatment of employees who are on leave for purposes other than a disability. Thus, according to the EEOC, an employer whose policies require continuation of group health care coverage for leaves other than those provided under the ADA may be required to continue coverage for employees on leave as a reasonable accommodation.[65]

---

[61] See Cline v. Wal-Mart Stores, Inc., 144 F.3d 294, 8 AD Cases 154 (4th Cir. 1998) (as result of employer's failure to give proper notice that employee had to use vacation days for FMLA leave meant that employee was entitled to 12 weeks of leave under FMLA in addition to any accrued paid vacation leave, employer had improperly terminated employee following 12 weeks of FMLA leave because employee was entitled to his accrued vacation leave).

[62] 29 C.F.R. §825.207 (2003).

[63] Id. §825.209 (2003).

[64] Id.

[65] EEOC Fact Sheet, "The Family and Medical Leave Act, the Americans with Disabilities Act and Title VII of the Civil Rights Act of 1964" (Nov. 1995) Q. 15.

For purposes of eligibility to participate in pension and other benefit plans, the FMLA provides that time off for leave taken under the FMLA must be treated by the employer as "continued service." The FMLA does not require that employers allow employees to continue to accrue any additional benefits or seniority during unpaid FMLA leave, although it permits employers to voluntarily choose to allow such accrual.[66] Again, there are no such specific requirements under the ADA. However, the ADA's provision prohibiting discrimination against individuals on leave well may have the effect of prohibiting any reduction or limitations on participation in a benefit plan.

The FMLA also permits employers to require an employee to use accrued vacation, personal, or sick leave for all or part of periods of absence that also meet the relevant definitional criteria for the form of FMLA leave that is applicable. The ADA contains no analogous provision.

6. Treatment of Absenteeism Under the ADA and the FMLA

The ADA and the FMLA also overlap in that both prohibit employers from adversely treating employee absences due to leave protected under either statute. Leave under the FMLA cannot be counted against an employee under an employer's absenteeism policy, even if it is a no-fault policy.[67] In other words, an employee absence due to leave taken under the FMLA cannot be taken into account when making decisions such as promotion, discipline, firing, or layoff.

According to the EEOC, the ADA similarly prohibits employers from treating absences from work due to a reasonable accommodation negatively.[68] However, under the ADA, additional issues often entail consideration of whether regular attendance is an essential function of the position and, if so, whether an employee who cannot regularly attend work is a

---

[66] 29 C.F.R. §825.209(h) (2003).

[67] *See* Viereck v. City of Gloucester City, 961 F. Supp. 703, 3 WH Cases 2d 1763 (D.N.J. 1997); George v. Associated Stationers, 932 F. Supp. 1012, 3 WH Cases 2d 1234 (N.D. Ohio 1996).

[68] *See Revised Enforcement Guidance, supra* note 6, at Question 19.

"qualified" individual under the ADA.[69] Some courts have held that termination based on absenteeism resulting from a disability constitutes a termination on the basis of a disability.[70]

D. Availability of Light-Duty Work Under the ADA and the FMLA

While light-duty work may be a reasonable accommodation under the ADA, the FMLA prohibits an employer from forcing an employee to take a light-duty assignment in lieu of leave under the FMLA.[71] An employee may insist on taking an FMLA leave if he or she is eligible for such treatment. There is no FMLA prohibition against *offering* a light-duty assignment. If an employee accepts an employer's offer of a light-duty assignment in lieu of leave, the employee's time spent performing the light-duty assignment is not counted as time spent on leave under the FMLA.

An employer may—but is not necessarily required, in all instances, to—offer a light-duty position as a reasonable accommodation under the ADA. An employer may be required to restructure a job to provide light-duty work only if the more demanding duties are not essential functions of the position. In addition, it generally has been held that there is no duty for an employer to create a light-duty position as a reasonable accommodation when one is not available. However, reassignment to a vacant light-duty position may be a reasonable accommodation in certain circumstances, and, in some cases, it may

---

[69]Rogers v. International Marine Terminals, Inc., 87 F.3d 755, 5 AD Cases 1115 (5th Cir. 1996); Tyndall v. National Educ. Ctrs. of Cal., Inc., 31 F.3d 209, 3 AD Cases 868 (4th Cir. 1994); Carr v. Reno, 23 F.3d 525, 3 AD Cases 434 (D.C. Cir. 1994); Jackson v. Department of Veterans Affairs, 22 F.3d 277, 3 AD Cases 483, *reh'g denied*, 30 F.3d 1500 (11th Cir. 1994); Kotlowski v. Eastman Kodak Co., 922 F. Supp. 790, 6 AD Cases 609 (W.D.N.Y. 1996); Gore v. GTE S., Inc., 917 F. Supp. 1564, (M.D. Ala. 1996); Hendry v. GTE N., Inc., 896 F. Supp. 816, 6 AD Cases 451 (N.D. Ind. 1995); Haysman v. Food Lion, Inc., 893 F. Supp. 1092, 4 AD Cases 1297 (S.D. Ga. 1995); Wilder v. Southeastern Pub. Serv. Auth., 869 F. Supp. 409, 4 AD Cases 838 (E.D. Va. 1994), *aff'd*, 69 F.3d 534, 5 AD Cases 256 (4th Cir. 1995).

[70]*See* Teahan v. Metro-North Commuter R.R., 951 F.2d 511, 2 AD Cases 84 (2d Cir. 1991), *cert. denied*, 506 U.S. 815 (1992).

[71]29 C.F.R. §825.220(d) (2003); *see also* Light Duty, FMLA Op. 17 (Nov. 15, 1993), BNA Wage & Hour Manual 99:3012.

be more preferable to the employer than other alternative accommodations that the disabled employee might seek.[72] In viewing these two statutory treatments in combination, where an employee's medical condition qualifies as a "serious health condition" under the FMLA in addition to a "disability" under the ADA, an employer may not have the option of refusing the employee's request for leave and opt for an alternative reasonable accommodation even if leave would constitute an undue hardship.[73]

E. Medical Examinations and Inquiries Under the ADA and the FMLA

Under the FMLA, employers are permitted to require submission of a medical certification providing certain (limited) information in order for an employee to establish entitlement to FMLA leave.[74] However, the certification generally must be limited to requiring a statement regarding (1) "which part of the definition of 'serious health condition,'" if any, applies to the patient's condition; (2) "the medical facts" supporting the certification; (3) "[t]he approximate date the serious health condition commenced, and [(4)] its probable duration," and whether intermittent or reduced schedule leave is necessary.[75] If clarification of a medical certification is needed, the Labor Department's FMLA regulations only permit the employer's doctor to contact the employee's doctor, if the

---

[72] *See* Mott v. Synthetic Indus., 4 AD Cases 1393 (N.D. Ga. 1995) (although reasonable accommodation may include reassignment to vacant light-duty position, it would not require employer to create light-duty position or convert temporary light-duty position into permanent position); Smith v. Midland Brake, Inc., 911 F. Supp. 1351, 5 AD Cases 386 (D. Kan. 1995), *aff'd*, 138 F.3d 1304, 7 AD 1560 (10th Cir. 1998) (although assigning employee to different position may be reasonable accommodation, this duty does not necessarily require providing disabled employee with different position, where he or she cannot perform essential functions of their present position).

[73] *See, e.g.*, EEOC Fact Sheet, "The Family and Medical Leave Act, the Americans with Disabilities Act and Title VII of the Civil Rights Act of 1964" (Nov. 1995), Q. 18.

[74] 29 C.F.R. §825.305 (2003).

[75] *Id.* §825.306(b)(1)–2(i)–(ii) (2003).

employee consents. The employer is not permitted direct contact with the employee's health care provider under those agency rules.[76]

An employer that questions a medical certification provided by an employee under the FMLA is permitted to request a second opinion.[77] The second opinion must be at the employer's expense, and be provided by a health care provider who is not regularly used by the employer. In the event that this opinion conflicts with the certification provided by the employer, the opinion of a third health care provider may be obtained.[78]

The ADA limits an employer's ability to make inquiry or request documentation regarding an employee's medical condition except to determine the ability of the employee to perform job functions and the need for an accommodation.[79] Employers are prohibited from making pre-job offer medical inquiries or examinations.[80]

The EEOC has taken the position that there is no conflict between the FMLA provision allowing employers to ask for certification that an employee has a serious health condition and the ADA's restrictions on disability-related inquiries of employees.[81] In this circumstance, the EEOC states that when an employer is seeking information limited to that allowed by the FMLA's certification forms, the employer only is inquiring into what it is entitled to know to determine eligibility for FMLA leave. In circumstances in which information sought is strictly limited in this fashion, the inquiry is job-related and consistent with business necessity as required by the ADA.[82] However, there clearly is the potential for conflict regarding medical examinations under the ADA and the FMLA with

---

[76] 29 C.F.R. §825.307(a) (2003).
[77] Id. §825.307(a)(2) (2003).
[78] Id. §825.307(a)(2)(c) (2003).
[79] 42 U.S.C. §12112(d)(4)(A).
[80] Id. §12112(d)(2)(A).
[81] See EEOC Fact Sheet on the Family and Medical Leave Act, the Americans with Disabilities Act, and Title VII of the Civil Rights Act of 1964, available at www.eeoc.gov.
[82] Id.

respect to whether the medical examination should be performed by a health care provider engaged by the employer or the employee. Under the ADA, the employer's physician may administer medical examinations.[83] The FMLA, however, envisions that medical certifications will be provided by the employee's health care provider, at least for a first opinion regarding the existence of a serious health condition or other condition qualifying for FMLA leave.[84]

The ADA and the FMLA also have overlapping requirements regarding the retention of employee medical records and documents reflecting employees' medical conditions. The FMLA provides that

> [r]ecords and documents relating to medical certifications, recertifications or medical histories of employees or employees' family members, created for purposes of FMLA, shall be maintained as confidential medical records in separate files/records from the usual personnel files, and if ADA is also applicable, such records shall be maintained in conformance with ADA confidentiality requirements....[85]

The following are the only exceptions to these rules:

> (1) Supervisors and managers may be informed regarding necessary restrictions on the work or duties of an employee and necessary accommodations;
> (2) First aid and safety personnel may be informed (when appropriate) if the employee's physical or medical condition might require emergency treatment; and
> (3) Government officials investigating compliance with FMLA (or other pertinent law) shall be provided relevant information upon request.[86]

Under the FMLA, employers are further obligated to maintain records reflecting "[b]asic payroll and identifying employee data, . . . daily and weekly hours worked per pay period, . . . [d]ates FMLA leave is taken," and copies of any notices

---

[83] 42 U.S.C. §12112(d)(3–4).
[84] 29 U.S.C. §2613(a); 29 C.F.R. §825.305(a) (2003).
[85] 29 C.F.R. §825.500(g) (2003); *see also* 29 C.F.R. §1630.14(c)(1) (2003).
[86] *Id.* §825.500(g) (2003).

provided pursuant to the FMLA.[87] Such records must be maintained for a period of 3 years.[88] In addition to requiring that employers maintain the confidentiality of information regarding an employee's medical condition, all medical-related information must be maintained in separate medical files.[89]

F. Fitness-for-Duty Requirements Under the ADA and the FMLA

The FMLA permits employers to require employees returning from FMLA leave "to obtain and present certification from the employee's health care provider that the employee is able to resume work" if pursuant to an established "policy or practice that requires all similarly-situated employees ... who take leave" to do so.[90] The return to work certification must be limited "to the particular health condition that caused the employee's need for FMLA leave."[91] Moreover, all that is required is certification by the employee's health care provider that the employee is fit to return to work.[92]

The ADA permits employers to require an examination or inquiry when an employee wishes to return to work after an injury or illness, provided it is "job-related and consistent with business necessity," to (1) determine if the employee is covered by the ADA if that person has requested an accommodation, (2) determine if the employee can perform the essential functions of the job, or (3) identify an effective accommodation.[93]

From the foregoing, it appears that under the ADA, an employer is permitted to require a prereinstatement medical examination. Such an examination is not permitted under the

---

[87] *Id.* §825.500(c)(1), (2), (4) (2003).
[88] *Id.* §825.500(b) (2003).
[89] 42 U.S.C. §12112(d)(4)(C); 29 C.F.R. §1630.14(c)(1) (2003).
[90] 29 C.F.R. §825.310(a) (2003).
[91] *Id.* §825.310(c) (2003).
[92] *Id.*
[93] *Id.* §1630.14(c) (2003); *see also* A TECHNICAL ASSISTANCE MANUAL ON THE EMPLOYMENT PROVISIONS (TITLE I) OF THE AMERICANS WITH DISABILITIES ACT §6.2 [hereinafter TITLE I TECHNICAL ASSISTANCE MANUAL].

FMLA. The FMLA limits employers to requiring a certification of fitness from the employee's health care provider. At least one court has specifically considered the distinction regarding the return to duty requirements permitted employers under the ADA and the FMLA. In *Albert v. Runyon*,[94] the employer was found to have violated the FMLA by requiring an employee returning from FMLA leave to submit to a fitness-for-duty medical examination when the employee's treating physician had already provided the employer with a statement that the employee was fit for reinstatement. The court held that an employer is not authorized to make its own determination of whether an employee is fit to return from FMLA leave. In reaching this conclusion, the court rejected the employer's argument that the medical examination should be permitted because it was allowed by the FMLA. The court found that the ADA's "business necessity" requirement for medical examinations is not triggered by an employee's having taken FMLA leave.[95]

G. Reinstatement Rights Under the ADA and the FMLA

The ADA and the FMLA contain competing and overlapping requirements with regard to the reinstatement rights of an employee returning from leave taken under both the ADA and FMLA. Under the FMLA, an employee returning from leave "is entitled to be returned to the same position the employee held when leave commenced, or to an equivalent position . . . ."[96] There is no obligation under the FMLA that an employee's position be held open while he or she is on FMLA-qualifying leave.[97] However, where the employee's position has been filled, that employee must be returned to an

---

[94] 6 F. Supp. 2d 57, 4 WH Cases 2d 1128 (D. Mass. 1998).
[95] But see, TITLE I TECHNICAL ASSISTANCE MANUAL, *supra* note 93, at §6.b, providing that an examination may be required to determine if an employee returning from incapacity can perform the essential functions of his or her job.
[96] 29 C.F.R. §825.214(a) (2003).
[97] *Id.*

equivalent position on his or her return from leave.[98] For purposes of the FMLA, "[a]n equivalent position is one that is virtually identical to the employee's former position in terms of pay, benefits" (including life insurance, health insurance, sick leave, educational benefits), privileges, status, duties, and responsibilities.[99]

In addition, employees returning from FMLA leave have no greater rights to their former positions than they would have had if leave had not been taken.[100] Thus, for example, if a reduction-in-force occurred that would have eliminated the employee's position while he or she was on FMLA leave, that employee would not be entitled to reinstatement. Similarly, if a shift were eliminated while an employee was on FMLA leave, that employee would not be entitled to reinstatement to the eliminated shift.[101]

Most importantly, under the FMLA, if an employee returning from leave is unable to perform one or more of the essential functions of the position because of a physical or mental condition, including the continuation of the serious health condition for which he or she took leave, the employee has no right to reinstatement to that position or any other position under the FMLA.[102] However, the FMLA regulations specifically state that, under this circumstance, the employer's obligations regarding reinstatement of the employee may be governed by the ADA.[103]

The ADA may provide even greater rights to reinstatement than the FMLA. If an employee returning from leave taken as a reasonable accommodation cannot perform an essential function of the previous job in the former manner, he or she will nonetheless be entitled to reinstatement to that position so long as the individual can perform the essential functions of the position with a "reasonable accommodation." In addition, where the employee *is* qualified for the previous position, he

---

[98] *Id.* §825.214(a) (2003).
[99] *Id.* §825.215(a), (d) (2003).
[100] *Id.* §825.216 (2003).
[101] *Id.* §825.216(a)(1), (2).
[102] *Id.* §825.114 (2003).
[103] *Id.* §825.216(d) (2003).

or she must be returned to that position. If a position was not held open based on undue hardship to the employer, the employer must determine whether it has other positions open to which the employee could be reassigned.[104]

As noted previously, the "undue hardship" defense is not available under the FMLA to deny reinstatement.[105] However, the FMLA limits the right to reinstatement of so-called "key employees" taking leave under the FMLA. A key employee can be denied reinstatement "if such denial is necessary to prevent substantial and grievous economic injury to the operations of the employer."[106] The FMLA's regulations specifically provide that the " 'substantial and grievous economic injury' standard is different from and more stringent than the 'undue hardship' test under the ADA."[107] So-called key employees must be notified of their status as "key employees" prior to commencement of leave under the FMLA.

H. Antiretaliation Provisions Under the ADA and the FMLA

Under the FMLA, it is "unlawful for any employer to interfere with, restrain, or deny the exercise of," or attempted exercise of, an employee's ability to take leave under the FMLA.[108] In addition, it is "unlawful for any employer to discharge or [otherwise] discriminate against any individual for opposing" an employer's attempt to interfere with an employee's rights under the FMLA.[109] The FMLA also has been interpreted to prohibit retaliation against an employee for exercising his or her rights under the FMLA.[110] The ADA contains similar antiretaliation provisions.

---

[104] 42 U.S.C. §12111(9); 29 C.F.R. §1630.2(o)(2)(ii) (2003).
[105] See 29 C.F.R. §§825.214, 825.216.
[106] 29 C.F.R. §825.216(c) (2003).
[107] Id. §825.218(d).
[108] 29 U.S.C. §2615(a)(1).
[109] Id. §2615(a)(2), (b).
[110] See Haschmann v. Time Warner Entm't Co., 151 F.3d 591, 8 AD Cases 692 (7th Cir. 1998); Cline v. Wal-Mart Stores, Inc., 144 F.3d 294, 8 AD Cases 154 (4th Cir. 1998); Hodgens v. General Dynamics Corp., 144 F.3d 151, 4 WH Cases 2d 993 (1st Cir. 1998).

I. Remedies Under the ADA and the FMLA

An employer that violates the provisions of the FMLA may be held liable for lost compensation (or, if no compensation was lost, any actual monetary losses incurred by the employee as a result of being denied leave) and an equal amount in liquidated damages unless the employer can establish it acted in good faith.[111] Equitable relief, such as reinstatement and promotion, and attorneys' fees and costs are also available under the FMLA. The FMLA has been interpreted to exclude punitive damages.[112]

Pursuant to the Civil Rights Act of 1991,[113] the remedy provisions of Title VII of the Civil Rights Act of 1964[114] have been adopted for violations of the ADA.[115] Thus, an employer that has failed to reasonably accommodate an individual or otherwise discriminated against a qualified individual with a disability may be held liable for compensatory and punitive damages.[116] Equitable relief, attorneys' fees, and costs may also be recovered. Thus, unlike under the ADA, recovery under the FMLA is limited to lost earnings and benefits plus an equivalent amount in liquidated damages, and does not provide for the recovery of damages such as emotional distress and punitive damages that are available under the ADA.

II. Workers' Compensation Laws

The ADA was enacted to prevent discrimination against disabled individuals and to integrate disabled citizens into the workplace.[117] The law prohibits discrimination against a qualified disabled individual in connection with a job application,

---

[111] 29 U.S.C. §2617(a)(1).
[112] McAnnally v. Wyn S. Molded Prods., Inc., 912 F. Supp. 512, 3 WH Cases 2d 433 (N.D. Ala. 1996).
[113] 42 U.S.C. §1981.
[114] Id. §2000e et seq.
[115] Id. §12117.
[116] Id. §1981(a).
[117] Id. §12101(b)(4).

"hiring, advancement, or discharge."[118] The law also prohibits discrimination against a qualified disabled individual with regard to "compensation, job training, and other terms, conditions, and privileges of employment."[119]

Workers' compensation laws, however, are designed as a "non-fault mechanism for providing cash and/or wage benefits and medical care to victims of work-connected injuries."[120] These measures also are designed to pass the cost of these injuries ultimately onto the consumer, through the medium of insurance. Workers' compensation statutes are found in the laws of the individual states because the federal government has not passed any statute of general application that governs such issues.

As a general matter, the ADA does not preempt existing state laws that are consistent with the ADA.[121] Thus, employers must comply with both the ADA and state workers' compensation laws, where the laws do not conflict. However, to the extent that there is such a conflict, the ADA may preempt those conflicting provisions. An employer, therefore, cannot "assert, as a valid defense to a charge of discrimination, that it failed to hire or [reinstate] an individual with a disability because doing so would violate a state workers' compensation law that required exclusion of this individual."[122]

The ADA (and to some extent, the various state disability discrimination statutes) and workers' compensation laws have different goals, and can lead to divergent duties and conflicting requirements. One area of arguable conflict is the "exclusive remedy" provision of most states' workers' compensation statutes and the remedial provisions of the ADA.[123] A second area of conflict involves circumstances in which an injured worker is found to be unable to work under state workers' compensation

---

[118] *Id.* §12112(a).
[119] *Id.*
[120] LARSON & LARSON, WORKERS' COMPENSATION LAW: CASES, MATERIALS AND TEXT §1, at 1 (3d ed. 2003).
[121] 42 U.S.C. §12201(b).
[122] TITLE I TECHNICAL ASSISTANCE MANUAL, *supra* note 93, §9.6.
[123] 42 U.S.C. §12117(a).

laws, but the employee claims that he or she is able to work with a reasonable accommodation under the ADA.[124] A third area of conflict occurs with regard to medical inquiries and the confidentiality of employees' medical records. (The ADA provides for strict need-to-know confidentiality of medical records,[125] while most workers' compensation laws allow broad access to the medical records of injured workers.) In addition, the ADA limits the type and scope of medical inquiries that can be posed to employees and potential employees,[126] while most workers' compensation statutes provide no such limits, and often encourage employers to gather medical information on employees.

A. The ADA and the Exclusive Remedy Provisions of Workers' Compensation Laws

Typically, the compensatory remedies provided by workers' compensation laws are deemed to be the exclusive remedy for any injury or accident that is covered by workers' compensation. The state statutes typically are construed to cover all injuries that arise "out of" and "in the course" of employment. As at least one commentator explains, once a workers' compensation act has become applicable, it affords the exclusive remedy for the injury of the employee or his dependents against the employer and insurance carrier.[127] The exclusive remedy concept typically is incorporated into the statutory provisions of each state's workers' compensation law. The workers' compensation system is a result of a legislated quid pro quo between employees and employers with respect to their legal rights. The employer assumes financial responsibility for such liabilities without proof of fault, while the employee gives up the right to pursue claims for damages in the court system, and in this

---

[124] 42 U.S.C. §12111(9)(a) & (b).
[125] 42 U.S.C. §12112(d).
[126] Id.
[127] LARSON & LARSON, WORKERS' COMPENSATION LAW: CASES, MATERIALS AND TEXT §69.10, at 557 (3d ed. 2003).

manner, workers' compensation benefits become the "exclusive remedy" of workers for such job-related occurrences.[128] However, when an injured employee receives workers' compensation benefits and also happens to be covered by the ADA, the traditional exclusive remedy doctrine may not apply.

A federal district court, in *Wood v. County of Alameda*,[129] considered this precise question. In *Wood*, an employer attempted to argue that the exclusive remedy provision of California's workers' compensation law prevented recovery under the ADA. In determining whether the ADA could preempt this provision of California's workers' compensation statute, the court relied on the two-part test employed by the Supreme Court in *Adam's Fruit Co. v. Barrett*.[130] Based on the *Adam's Fruit* formula, the court in *Wood* considered two questions. First, whether the ADA explicitly or implicitly indicates that Congress intended to yield to state law in similar situations.[131] The court found that Congress did not intend for the ADA to defer to state workers' compensation statutes.[132] In looking at Congress' intent, the court concluded that the ADA seeks to "ensure that plaintiffs are not denied the benefits of compatible state statutes on the ground that the ADA precludes any cause of action under the state law."[133] Thus, the court determined that there is no indication that Congress intended to defer to state workers' compensation laws.

The second question analyzed by *Wood* required the court to consider whether preemption principles mandated that all or part of the state law be denied effect in light of Congress' intent in enacting the federal law. The court found that the ADA preempts the exclusive remedy provision because the state

---

[128] *Id.*
[129] 875 F. Supp. 659, 4 AD Cases 43 (N.D. Cal. 1995).
[130] 494 U.S. 638, 648–49 (1990) (Court considered whether exclusive remedy provision in state workers' compensation case precluded action under federal Migrant and Seasonal Agricultural Worker Protection Act, 29 U.S.C. §1801 et seq., and held that federal law preempts state law to limited extent that it does not permit states to supplant, rather than to supplement, federal statute's remedial scheme).
[131] *Id.* at 662.
[132] *Id.* at 664.
[133] *Id.*

provision would be an obstacle to the congressional objective behind the ADA, primarily the elimination of discrimination against disabled persons. The court reasoned that the objectives of the ADA would be weakened if each state were allowed effectively to supersede the ADA by placing exclusivity provisions in its state workers' compensation statutes and thereby precluding remedial actions pursuant to the ADA.[134]

B. Pursuit of Discrimination Charges and Workers' Compensation Claims

1. Judicial Estoppel

In many cases, obvious contradictions may appear when a claimant makes concurrent claims under the ADA and under workers' compensation laws. Under workers' compensation and other disability programs, such as Social Security,[135] an injured employee represents that he or she is unable to work or is totally disabled.[136] In contrast, when an employee seeks a remedy under the ADA, he or she represents that he or she is an individual with a disability who *is* able to work, with or without reasonable accommodation.[137] Such an apparent contradiction has often led employers to argue that the doctrine of judicial estoppel is applicable.[138] Judicial estoppel may be applied where a party to litigation has taken "inconsistent" legal positions regarding the same or nearly identical legal issues involving the same parties and the same essential fact pattern.[139]

"Judicial estoppel, sometimes also known as the doctrine of preclusion of inconsistent positions, precludes a party from gaining an advantage by taking one position, and then seeking

---

[134] *Id.* at 665.
[135] *See* section II.B.3., "EEOC Position," below.
[136] *See, e.g.,* NEV. REV. STAT. ch. 616C.435 (2000); Haschmann v. Time Warner Entm't Co., 151 F.3d 591, 603, 8 AD Cases 692, 701 (7th Cir. 1998).
[137] *Haschman,* 151 F.3d 603.
[138] *Id.*
[139] Yanez v. United States, 989 F.2d 323 (9th Cir. 1993).

a second advantage by taking an incompatible position."[140] This doctrine has also been stated to be based on the equitable principle that " 'if a party wins a suit on one ground, it can't turn around and in further litigation with the same opponent repudiate the ground in order to win a further victory.' "[141]

2. EEOC Position

In an effort to shape the manner in which employers and courts addressed this issue, the EEOC issued an interpretive memorandum[142] that set forth the EEOC's position that representations made in applications for Social Security, workers' compensation, disability insurance, and other disability benefits should not be an automatic bar to ADA claims. The EEOC advanced several reasons for this guidance.

First, it is possible for an individual to meet the eligibility requirements for receipt of disability benefits and still be a "qualified individual with a disability" for ADA purposes. Specifically, in terms of workers' compensation, such statutes' typical definitions of "disability" are distinct from the ADA's definition of the same term. For example, most workers' compensation laws define disability more generally. They often permit generalized presumptions about an individual's ability to work and fail to distinguish between marginal and essential functions. Many of the statutes consider whether an individual's ability to do any kind of work for which there is a reasonably stable employment market rather focusing on whether he or she can perform the essential functions of a particular job. They also typically do not consider whether an individual can work with a reasonable accommodation.[143]

---

[140] Rissetto v. Plumbers & Steamfitters Local 343, 94 F.3d 597, 600, 71 FEP Cases 1057, 1059 (9th Cir. 1996) (citing 18 CHARLES ALAN WRIGHT, ARTHUR R. MILLER & EDWARD H. COOPER, FEDERAL PRACTICE AND PROCEDURE §4477 (1981 & Supp. 1995)); Yanez, 989 F.2d at 326; Russell v. Rolfs, 893 F.2d 1033, 1037 (9th Cir. 1990), cert. denied, 501 U.S. 1260 (1991).

[141] Haschmann v. Time Warner Entm't Co., 151 F.3d 591, 603, 8 AD Cases 692, 701 (7th Cir. 1998).

[142] EEOC, *Guidance on the Effect of Disability Representations in Benefits Applications on ADA Coverage* (Feb. 1997).

[143] *See* NEV. REV. STAT. ch. 616C et seq. (2000).

Second, the *EEOC Guidance* referenced the public policy favoring an individual's right to choose between applying for disability benefits and vindicating his or her rights under the ADA. Moreover, according to the EEOC, the ADA's purposes and standards are fundamentally different from the purposes and standards of other statutory schemes. Thus, the EEOC concluded in its *Guidance* that a determination of what, if any, weight to give to representations made in support of applications for disability benefits depends on the context and timing of the representations.

The lower federal courts' initial decisions were split on the issue of whether an ADA plaintiff is judicially estopped from proving his or her ADA claim simply because he or she has sought or received disability benefits. Some courts held that the positions are not necessarily inconsistent.[144] However, other courts found that the two positions are almost always inconsistent and apply the rule of judicial estoppel.[145]

3. Disability Benefits Versus ADA Claims

At first blush, the judicial estoppel concept logically would appear to apply in most cases where ADA and disability claims for benefits (including workers' compensation claims) are

---

[144] *See, e.g., Haschmann*, 151 F.3d at 605 (declining to adopt per se rule that plaintiff is judicially estopped from asserting ADA claim if plaintiff received disability payments); Rascon v. U.S. W. Communications, 143 F.2d 1324, 8 AD Cases 541 (10th Cir. 1998); Johnson v. Oregon Dep't of Human Res., Rehab. Div., 141 F.3d 1361, 1367, 8 AD Cases 283 (9th Cir. 1998); Griffith v. Wal-Mart Stores, Inc., 135 F.3d 376, 383, 7 AD Cases 1233 (6th Cir. 1998), *cert. denied*, 526 U.S. 1144 (1999); Talavera v. Palm Beach County Sch. Bd., 129 F.3d 1214, 1220, 7 AD Cases 1025 (11th Cir. 1997); Weigel v. Target Stores, 122 F.3d 461, 7 AD Cases 358 (7th Cir. 1997); Swanks v. Washington Metro. Area Transit Auth., 116 F.3d 582, 586–87, 6 AD Cases 1544 (D.C. Cir. 1997).

[145] Dush v. Appleton Elec. Co., 124 F.3d 957, 7 AD Cases 183 (8th Cir. 1997); McNemar v. Disney Store, Inc., 91 F.3d 610, 5 AD Cases 1227 (3d Cir. 1996), *cert. denied*, 519 U.S. 1115 (1997) (statement to Social Security Administration that plaintiff was disabled and unable to work, barred his subsequent ADA claim); August v. Offices Unlimited, Inc., 981 F.2d 576, 2 AD Cases 401 (1st Cir. 1992); Violette v. International Bus. Machs. Corp., 962 F. Supp. 446, 7 AD Cases 395 (D. Vt. 1996), *aff'd*, 116 F.3d 466, 7 AD Cases 544 (2d Cir. 1997); Thomas v. Fort Myers Hous. Auth., 955 F. Supp. 1463, 6 AD 735 (M.D. Fla. 1997); Bennett v. United Parcel Serv., 5 AD Cases 260 (S.D. Tex. 1995); Reigel v. Kaiser Found. Health Plan of N.C., 859 F. Supp. 963, 3 AD Cases 577 (E.D.N.C. 1994).

brought concurrently. On the one hand, workers' compensation laws tend to focus on the extent to which an injured worker *cannot* perform the job as a result of an on-the-job accident.[146] On the other hand, the ADA focuses on the extent to which an impaired employee *can* perform his or her job with or without reasonable accommodation.[147] Thus, "[t]he conflict in the system is obvious: an [injured worker] receives maximum workers' compensation benefits by proving that he or she is totally disabled, but receives maximum protection under the ADA by establishing that he or she can perform the essential functions of his or her job."[148]

The Supreme Court addressed the issue of whether the receipt of disability benefits precludes ADA relief, though not in the context of a workers' compensation claim.[149] As discussed more fully below,[150] in *Cleveland v. Policy Management System Corp.*,[151] the Court considered whether an application for, or receipt of, disability insurance benefits under the Social Security Act creates a rebuttable presumption that the applicant or recipient is judicially estopped from asserting that she is a "qualified individual with a disability" under the Americans with Disabilities Act.[152] The Supreme Court held that a claimant is *not* automatically estopped from making a claim under the ADA when the claimant applies for Social Security benefits. The Court also recognized, however, that there could be circumstances in which such claims would be irreconcilably inconsistent, and found that in order to survive a summary judgment motion on the judicial estoppel grounds, a claimant "cannot simply ignore the apparent contradiction that arises" and therefore must proffer a sufficient explanation. In other words, a

---

[146] *See, e.g.*, NEV. REV. STAT. ch. 616C.435 & .475 (2000); Gabel, Mansfield, & Klein, The New Relationship Between Injured Worker and Employer: An Opportunity for Restructuring the System, 35 AM. BUS. L.J. 403, 415 (1998).

[147] *Gabel*, at 415.

[148] *Id.*

[149] Cleveland v. Policy Mgmt. Sys. Corp., 526 U.S. 795, 9 AD Cases 491 (1999).

[150] See section III, "Social Security and Other Disability Benefits Programs, below.

[151] 526 U.S. 795, 9 AD Cases 491 (1999).

[152] *Id.* at 797.

claimant must come forward with a logical explanation as to how the two claims are not inconsistent.[153]

C. Medical Inquiries and Confidentiality of Medical Information

1. Medical Records

In the case of a disabled employee, an employer normally is precluded from obtaining medical records from the employee unless it is obvious that an accommodation will be necessary or the applicant voluntarily discloses the need for accommodation.[154] Postoffer inquiries must be limited to determining the ability to perform job functions.[155] In the postoffer stage, an employer can obtain information about prior occupational injuries, provided it requires all entering employees in the same job category to provide the same medical information.[156]

2. Medical Examinations

Employers are not permitted to require a job applicant to undergo a medical examination to determine if the individual has a disability or to assess the severity or nature of a disability.[157] The ADA prohibits an employer from asking any questions about disability or prior workers' compensation claims before an offer of employment.[158] An employer may, however, require an applicant to demonstrate or describe how he or she would perform the essential functions of the job, assuming that all applicants must make the same demonstration regardless of disability.[159] Moreover, after an employment offer has been made, but before the individual has started work, an employer may require a medical examination (an

---

[153] *Id.* at 806, 9 AD Cases at 492.
[154] 42 U.S.C. §12112(d)(2)(A); TITLE I TECHNICAL ASSISTANCE MANUAL *supra* note 93, §6.3.
[155] 42 U.S.C. §12112(d)(3).
[156] *Id.* §12112(d)(3)(A).
[157] 29 C.F.R. §1630.13(a) (2003).
[158] *Id.* §1630.12(a) (2003).
[159] *Id.* §1630.14(a) (2003).

"employment entrance examination") to identify the nature and severity of a disability.[160] However, once an employee begins work, any medical examination must be "job-related and consistent with business necessity."[161]

Under the ADA, medical certification relating to leaves of absence is potentially problematic. Employers cannot require employees requesting leave or returning from leave to subject themselves to full medical examinations. Medical examinations must be "job-related and consistent with business necessity."[162] However, an employer may request medical documentation directly related to a request for leave, because the employee is claiming inability to work, and the employer is permitted to ask current employees whether they are able to perform the functions of their jobs.[163]

Under most workers' compensation laws, an employer has the right to require one or more independent medical examinations of an employee.[164] Similar to second and third health provider examinations under the FMLA, workers' compensation exams are paid for by the employer. Typically, they can be used only to determine whether the employee (1) is entitled to benefits, (2) should continue receiving benefits, or (3) has reached maximum medical improvement.[165]

3. Fitness to Return-to-Work Policies

In workers' compensation cases, many employers traditionally have required employees to be "100 percent fit" before they return to work. This policy may be inconsistent with the right of an employee to secure a reasonable accommodation in some cases under the ADA. For example, the "100 percent fit" policy likely would violate the ADA where the employee is restricted but still may perform the essential functions of the

---

[160] Id. §1630.14(b) (2003).
[161] 42 U.S.C. §12112(d)(4).
[162] Id. §12112(d)(4)(A).
[163] 29 C.F.R. §825.305(a) (2003).
[164] See MINN. STAT. ANN. §176.155 (West 1993).
[165] See id.

job with accommodations.[166] Therefore, employers must consider whether the enforcement of a full and complete fitness policy violates the rights of an employee where there is a potential disability under the ADA.

4. Physical Agility Tests

The EEOC's regulations under the statute provide that physical agility tests are not medical examinations and thus may be given at any point in the application process so long as all similarly situated applicants are tested.[167] It is unclear whether the physical agility provision allows employers to administer strength tests or functional capacity assessments. If these are desired, it is advisable to perform them after a conditional offer of employment is made.

5. Medical Inquiries

Once an offer has been made, an employer is granted greater latitude in testing and in permissible questioning of employees. However, a potential conflict arises where an employer seeks a preemployment postoffer examination that is permitted under the ADA—and the employer attempts to ascertain information about an employee's workers' compensation history.[168] Such inquiries should be analyzed carefully under each applicable state workers' compensation law in order to determine if they are lawful. Further, even though the ADA allows an employer to inquire about workers' compensation history in a medical inquiry or examination after a conditional job offer has been made but before an employee starts work, the inquiry may be made only if all applicants in the same job category also are required to submit to such an examination

---

[166]Bolton v. Scrivner, Inc., 836 F. Supp. 783, 788–89 n.4, 3 AD Cases 86 (W.D. Okla. 1993) (discussing employer 100% fitness return to work policy), *aff'd*, 36 F.3d 939, 3 AD Cases 1089 (10th Cir. 1994), *cert. denied*, 513 U.S. 1152 (1995).

[167]29 C.F.R. pt. 1630, app. §1630.14(a) (2003).

[168]Downs v. Massachusetts Bay Transp. Auth., 13 F. Supp. 2d 130, 138, 8 AD Cases 447 (D. Mass. 1998).

or inquiry.[169] If the employer withdraws a job offer after engaging in the medical inquiry, it should be prepared to demonstrate that implementation of the reasonable accommodations necessary to enable the employee to perform the essential functions of the job would constitute an "undue hardship."[170]

In addition, even if the inquiry is permitted, under EEOC guidelines, medical information regarding workers' compensation claims must be kept confidential.[171] The ADA's confidentiality requirement requires that the medical information be maintained in a separate medical file and that access to the file may only be granted to (1) supervisory personnel who need to know the employee's work restrictions and necessary accommodations, (2) first aid or safety personnel, (3) and "[g]overnment officials investigating compliance" with the ADA.[172] The EEOC has taken the position that the ADA's confidentiality requirements extend to medical records maintained by an employer regarding an individual's workers' compensation claims, requiring that such records be kept in a separate medical file.[173]

General medical inquiries related to a pending workers' compensation claim resulting from an on-the-job injury are more liberal than those normally permitted are under the ADA. If an employee suffers a work-related injury, the ADA does not prohibit the employer from asking questions about the injury or from requiring the employee to submit to a medical examination so that the employer may assess the nature and extent of its workers' compensation liability.[174] Importantly, where discrimination and accommodation matters under the ADA are at issue, employers may have to disregard the

---

[169] 29 C.F.R. pt. 1630, app. §1630.14(a), (b) (2003).

[170] An "undue hardship" means "significant difficulty or expense." 42 U.S.C. §12111(10). The factors to be considered include: (1) "the nature and cost of the accommodation"; (2) "the overall financial resources of" and the number of employees at the facility; (3) the size and financial resources of the employer; and (4) "the type of operation involved." *Id.*

[171] *Revised Enforcement Guidance, supra* note 6, at Question 42.

[172] 29 C.F.R. §1630.14(b)(1)–(d)(1) (2003).

[173] *EEOC Enforcement Guidance: Workers' Compensation and the ADA*, EEOC Notice No. 915.002 (Sept. 3, 1996), at Question 10.

[174] *Id.* at Question 8.

information obtained through a workers' compensation claim that does not relate to the individual's ability to perform the essential functions of the job.[175]

D. Accommodations, Light-Duty, and Leave Under the ADA and Workers' Compensation Laws

As discussed above,[176] leave is not a specified requirement of the ADA, but it may be required as an accommodation. If leave was taken as an accommodation, reinstatement to the employee's former position is only required if the employee is qualified to perform the essential functions of the job with or without reasonable accommodations.[177] Further, the ADA does not require reinstatement if it would pose an undue hardship for the employer.[178] Employers also may wish to reassign a returning employee to a vacant position. The EEOC has declared that such reassignments may be considered a reasonable accommodation of the type required by the ADA if both the employer and employee agree that reassignment is more appropriate than accommodation in the present position.[179] Light-duty work may also be offered as a possible accommodation, but the creation of light-duty positions and permanent light-duty assignments are not required as a reasonable accommodation.[180] Nevertheless, if an employee requests light-duty work, at least one court has held that an employer's failure to determine whether any light-duty assignments were available can be an indication of bad faith.[181]

Under workers' compensation statutes, if an employee's injury is such that he or she cannot return to work at all,

---

[175] *See generally* EEOC Enforcement Guidance, "Workers' Compensation and the ADA" (Sept. 1996).

[176] *See* section I.G., "Reinstatement Rights Under the ADA and the FMLA," above.

[177] 29 C.F.R. §825.702(c)(1) (2003).

[178] *Id.* §825.702(c)(4) (2003) (by allowing the employee to work part-time or by reassigning the employee to a vacant position, barring undue hardship).

[179] 29 C.F.R. pt. 1630, app. §1630.2(o) (2003).

[180] Turco v. Hoechst Celanese Chem. Group, 101 F.3d 1090, 1094, 6 AD Cases 278 (5th Cir. 1996).

[181] Harrison v. Landis Plastics, Inc., 1998 U.S. Dist. LEXIS 11311 (N.D. Ill. 1998).

permanent total disability benefits will be paid until the employee reaches a certain designated age (e.g., 65 or 67) even if the employee is terminated because of habitual absences or inability to work.[182] When an employee is off from work due to a workers' compensation injury, some state laws expressly provide reinstatement rights to injured employees, while others have been construed to provide an implied right to reinstatement.[183] However, under most workers' compensation statutes, an employee is not entitled to reinstatement to his or her former position; rather, workers' compensation laws focus on his or her return to "suitable" work.[184] As with the ADA, this may include light-duty work. Under Nevada and Minnesota law, for example, light-duty work is not required, but an employee who unreasonably refuses an offer of suitable work, including light-duty assignments, risks losing workers' compensation benefits.[185]

When an employee is ready to return to work following a work-related injury, employers must consider the implications of the ADA. Some employers historically took the position that employees could not return to work until they had reached their full capacity and had no medically imposed physical restrictions; with the enactment of the ADA, this may no longer be a reasonable position.[186] If the ADA covers the employee's impairment, then the employer should examine if the employee can be reasonably accommodated, regardless of whether the employee has a medically imposed limitation. Reasonable accommodation may include modification of the employee's work structure, restructuring of the job, reassignment of the employee to a vacant position, or obtaining the necessary

---

[182] *See, e.g.*, MINN. STAT. ANN. §176.101(4) (Supp. 2000).

[183] Judson Steel Corp. v. Workers' Comp. Appeals Bd., 22 Cal. 3d 658, 586 P.2d 564, 150 Cal. Rptr. 250 (1978).

[184] *See* Karst v. F.C. Hayer Co., 447 N.W.2d 180, 186, 1 AD Cases 1530 (Minn. 1989) (unlike Wisconsin, Minnesota does not have statutory provision guaranteeing reinstatement to employee on workers' compensation–related leave).

[185] MINN. STAT. ANN. §176.101, subd. 3e(b).

[186] *See generally* EEOC Enforcement Guidance, "Workers' Compensation and the ADA" (Sept. 1996).

adaptive equipment.[187] Under the ADA, if the employee is unable to perform the essential functions of the job with or without accommodation, or if the employee's return to work constitutes an undue hardship on the employer, or is a direct threat to the health and safety of the workforce, the employer may prohibit the employee from returning to work after a workers' compensation injury.[188]

III. SOCIAL SECURITY AND OTHER DISABILITY BENEFITS PROGRAMS

In addition to state workers' compensation laws, individuals may secure disability benefits through other statutory mechanisms at the federal and/or state levels, as well as through private insurance programs. The federal government's Social Security system—administered by the Social Security Administration (SSA), an agency of the U.S. Department of Health and Human Services—includes a very substantial disability benefits program that pays cash and other benefits to individuals who meet the standards for such a determination.[189] Some (but by no means all) states have disability benefits programs that provide a form of disability insurance coverage to individuals, with premiums mandated for payment by employers, in some instances.[190] Finally, some employers voluntarily provide disability benefits to employees without regard to whether the limiting injury or illness arises at work.[191] Such benefits may be provided under a company's personnel policies, individual employment contracts, or collective bargaining agreements,

---

[187] 42 U.S.C. §12111(9).

[188] 42 U.S.C.§§12111(3), (9), (10).

[189] See http:/www.ssa.gov/dibplan/index.htm.

[190] Among the states with temporary disability programs are Hawaii, HAW. REV. STAT. §392-1 et seq.; New Jersey, N.J. STAT. ANN. §43:21-26 et seq.; Rhode Island, R.I. GEN. LAWS §28-38-1 et seq.; and California, CAL. UNEMP. INS. CODE §3301(d).

[191] See "An Employer's Guide to Disability Income Insurance," Health Insurance Association of America (2004).

and they may be insured programs or paid out of the employer's general assets. In addition, individual employees may themselves independently maintain disability insurance coverage to pay benefits in the event that they become disabled.[192] Each of these mechanisms—in addition to workers' compensation programs—may become relevant to cases litigated under the ADA, as often there may be evidence and representations potentially relevant to both that are generated in the course of the parallel proceedings.

When Congress passed Title I of the ADA in 1990,[193] one of the major effects envisioned for this legislation was approximately $222 million in revenue generated through a combination of decreased support payments made under the Social Security Disability Insurance (SSDI)[194] and Supplemental Security Income (SSI)[195] statutes[196] and increased taxes collected as a result of these disabled workers returning to the workforce.[197] Nearly 15 years after the ADA's enactment, any beneficial economic effects from the passage of the statute remain the subject of debate.[198] Nonetheless, an almost immediate effect of the ADA was to focus the attention of the courts on the effect of an apparently unforeseen conflict between the definition of disability under the Social Security disability statutes and the

---

[192] *See id.*

[193] The ADA incorporated amendments of the Civil Rights Act of 1991. Title I of the ADA applies to discrimination in employment, which is the focus of this section. Unless otherwise indicated, all further references to the ADA in this section will refer exclusively to Title I.

[194] 42 U.S.C. §§401–431. The Social Security Disability Insurance (SSDI) program under the Social Security Act, was added to the Social Security Act of 1934 by the Social Security Amendments of 1956, Pub. L. No. 84-880 §183(a), 70 Stat. 807, 815–824 (1956). Further references referring specifically to this statutory program will identify it as the SSDI.

[195] 42 U.S.C. §§1381–1383. The Supplemental Security Income program under the Social Security Act, was added to the Social Security Act of 1934 by the Social Security Amendments of 1972, Pub. L. No. 92-603, 86 Stat. 1329 (1972). Further references referring specifically to this statutory program will identify it as the SSI.

[196] When referred to collectively, the SSDI and SSI statutory programs will be identified as the "Social Security disability statutes."

[197] *See* Equal Opportunity for Individuals With Disabilities, 56 Fed. Reg. 8578, 8579 (Feb. 28, 1991).

[198] *See* Schwochau & Blanck, *The Economics of the Americans With Disabilities Act, Part III: Does the ADA Disable the Disabled?* 21 BERKELEY J. EMP. & LAB. L. 271 (2000).

definition of "qualified individual with a disability" under the ADA. This unforeseen conflict threatened the legal viability of ADA claims in situations where the plaintiff had first applied for and/or obtained Social Security disability benefits based on a claim that the employee was "totally disabled."

As ultimately recognized by the Supreme Court in *Cleveland v. Policy Management Systems Corp.*,[199] the conflict arose as a result of the differing purposes and approaches to disability in the ADA and the Social Security disability statutes.[200] While the legal battle over the apparently conflicting statutory approaches to defining disability has been effectively resolved as a result of Supreme Court's decision in *Cleveland*, it is necessary to review the differences between the approaches to disability in these statutes in order to understand the reasoning of the *Cleveland* Court and the factual analysis that must be conducted by the lower courts when applying that holding.

A. "Disability" Under the Social Security Programs

Under the Social Security disability statutes, a disability is defined as the "inability to engage in any substantial gainful activity by reason of any medically determinable physical or mental impairment which can be expected to result in death or which has lasted or can be expected to last for a continuous period of not less than 12 months."[201] A "physical or mental impairment" is defined by the statue as "an impairment that results from anatomical, physiological, or psychological abnormalities which are demonstrable by medically acceptable clinical and laboratory diagnostic techniques."[202] To further clarify the nature of the impairment required in order to obtain benefits, the Social Security disability statutes state that "[a]n individual shall be determined to be under a disability only if his physical or mental impairment or impairments are of such severity that he is not only unable to do his previous work but

---

[199] 526 U.S. 795, 9 AD Cases 491 (1999).
[200] *Id.* at 801.
[201] 42 U.S.C. §§423(d)(1)(a), 1382c(a)(3)(A).
[202] *Id.* §423(d)(3).

cannot, considering his age, education, and work experience, engage in any other kind of substantial gainful work which exists in the national economy . . . ."[203] Substantial gainful work is defined in the regulations as "work that (a) [i]nvolves doing significant and productive physical or mental duties; and (b) [i]s done (or intended) for pay or profit."[204]

To determine whether an applicant is eligible to receive disability benefits under the Social Security disability statutes, the SSA employs a five-step interview procedure,[205] which consists of asking the applicant certain questions that are intended to elicit responses that will allow the SSA to establish the existence of a disability as defined under those statutes. The process is as follows:

> *Step One*: Are you working? If you are and your earnings average more than $700 a month, you generally cannot be considered disabled. If you are not working, we go to the next step.[206]
>
> *Step Two*: Is your condition "severe"? Your condition must interfere with basic work-related activities for your claim to be considered. If it does not, we will find that you are not disabled. If it does, we will go to the next step.[207]

Thus, the first two steps of the SSA's inquiry concentrate solely on the ability of the person to work, and further consideration of the application is made only if the applicant states that he or she is not working and it is his or her medical condition that is interfering with his or her ability to work.

> *Step Three*: Is your condition found in the list of disabling impairments? We maintain a list of impairments for each of the major body systems that are so severe they automatically mean you are disabled. If your condition is not on the list, we have to decide if

---

[203] *Id.* §§423(d)(2)(a), 1382c(a)(3)(B).

[204] 20 C.F.R. §404.1510 (2003); *see also* 20 C.F.R. §404.1572 (2003) (adding that substantial gainful activity need not be full-time).

[205] The step-by-step format is outlined in Part 2 of *Social Security Disability Benefits*, 05-10029 (Sept. 29, 1999), *available at* www.ssa.gov.

[206] *Id.*; *see also* 20 C.F.R. §404.1520(b) (2003).

[207] *Social Security Disability Benefits*; *see also* 20 C.F.R. §404.1520(c) (2003).

it is of equal severity to an impairment on the list. If it is, we will find that you are disabled. If it is not, we go to the next step.[208]

If the answers to Step One and Step Two establish that the person's medical condition is currently preventing him or her from working, and if the condition is on the SSA's list as set forth in Step Three, the person is presumptively considered to be disabled and will be awarded Social Security disability benefits. If the applicant answers "yes" to Step One and Step Two, but the applicant's condition is not on the SSA's presumptive impairment list, the applicant must proceed to Step Four.

> *Step Four:* Can you do the work you did previously? If your condition is severe, but not at the same or equal severity as an impairment on the list, then we must determine if it interferes with your ability to do the work you did previously. If it does not, your claim will be denied. If it does, we go to the next step.[209]
>
> *Step Five:* Can you do any other type of work? If you cannot do the work you did in the past, we see if you are able to adjust to other work. We consider your medical conditions and your age, education, past work experience, and transferable skills you may have. If you cannot adjust to other kind of work, your claim will be approved. If you can, your claim will be denied.[210]

1. Duration of Social Security Benefits

Once the SSA makes a determination that an award of disability benefits is appropriate, Social Security disability benefits generally continue for as long as the individual remains disabled.[211] However, the SSA is required to review disability cases periodically, with the frequency of the review depending on the initial assessment by the SSA of the expectations of recovery or improvement.[212] For example, if medical improvement is "expected," the disability is normally scheduled to

---

[208] *Social Security Disability Benefits*; *see also* 20 C.F.R. §§404.1520(d) (2003), 404.1525 (2003), 1526 (2003). For the list of impairments, see 20 C.F.R. §404, app. 1, Subpart P—Listing of Impairments.
[209] *Social Security Disability Benefits*, 20 C.F.R. §404.1520(e) (2003).
[210] *Social Security Disability Benefits*, 20 C.F.R. §§404.1520(f) (2003), 404.1560(c) (2003).
[211] 42 U.S.C. §423.
[212] 20 C.F.R. §§404.1590(a) (2003), 404.1594(a) (2003).

be reviewed within 6 to 18 months.[213] If the disability is not considered permanent but medical improvement cannot be predicted accurately, the review of continuing eligibility for disability benefits will be scheduled at least once every 3 years. If the disability is considered permanent, the SSA will make its review of continuing eligibility for benefits no less frequently than once every 7 years but no more frequently than once every 5 years.

Notwithstanding these general review guidelines, the SSA may schedule a review of continuing eligibility for disability benefits immediately if, among other various factors: (1) the individual returns to work and successfully completes a period of trial work;[214] (2) if substantial earnings are reported on the individual's wage record;[215] (3) if the individual voluntarily informs the SSA that he or she has recovered from the disability or has returned to work;[216] (4) if the state vocational rehabilitation agency informs the SSA that rehabilitation services have been completed, or that the individual is now working, or that the individual is now able to work;[217] (5) if a person in a position to know the individual's physical or mental condition informs the SSA that the individual is either not disabled, is not following prescribed treatment, has returned to work, or is otherwise failing to follow the provisions of the Social Security Act or its regulations;[218] or (6) the SSA otherwise receives evidence that raises a question as to whether the individual's disability still exists.[219]

The discontinuation of SSDI benefits is authorized when the SSA is provided with evidence of medical improvement sufficient to allow the individual to resume substantial gainful

---

[213] 20 C.F.R. §404.1590(d) (2003).
[214] *Id.* §404.1590(b)(4) (2003).
[215] *Id.* §404.1590(b)(5) (2003).
[216] *Id.* §404.1590(b)(6) (2003).
[217] *Id.* §404.1590(b)(7) (2003).
[218] *Id.* §404.1590(b)(8) (2003). The regulation further requires that the SSA must be convinced that the report could be "substantially correct."
[219] *Id.* §404.1590(b)(9) (2003).

activity in the workforce.[220] The Social Security disability statutes provide for a brief continuation of full SSDI benefits during a 9-month period of time while the disabled worker reenters the workforce.[221] Congress passed additional legislation, known as the Ticket to Work and Work Incentive Improvement Act of 1999,[222] which was intended to create further incentives to encourage individuals receiving SSDI and SSI disability benefits to reenter the workforce.[223] As such, while the initial and immediate focus of the Social Security disability programs is to assess the existence of a disability and to provide replacement income to those who qualify as disabled under these programs, there appears to be a developing legislative movement to attempt to focus on rehabilitating disabled workers and returning them to the workforce.[224]

B. "Disability" Under the ADA

The focus of Title I of the ADA in the legislative scheme of things is to eliminate discrimination against individuals with disabilities "to assure equality of opportunity" in employment by providing individuals with disabilities a legal right to compete for employment on an equal basis with other citizens.[225] Thus, while the Social Security disability statutes are focused on providing financial relief for individuals who potentially are

---

[220] 42 U.S.C. §423(f); 20 C.F.R. §§404.1579(b) (2003), 404.1594(b) (2003).
[221] 20 C.F.R. §404.1592 (2003).
[222] Pub. L. 106-170, 113 Stat. 1860 (1999).
[223] As stated in the preface of the act, its purpose is "[t]o amend the Social Security Act to expand the availability of health care coverage for working individuals with disabilities, to establish a Ticket to Work and Self-Sufficiency Program in the Social Security Administration to provide such individuals with meaningful opportunities to work, and for other purposes."
[224] See, e.g., Exec. Order No. 13,078, Presidential Task Force on Employment of Adults With Disabilities (Mar. 13, 1998). This Task Force is comprised of representatives of the Secretary of Labor, Secretary of Education, Secretary of Veterans Affairs, Secretary of Health and Human Services, Commissioner of Social Security, Secretary of the Treasury, Secretary of Commerce, Secretary of Transportation, Director of the Office of Personnel Management, Administrator of the Small Business Administration, the Chair of the EEOC, the Chair of the National Council on Disability, and the Chair of the President's Committee on Employment of People With Disabilities.
[225] 42 U.S.C. §12101(a)(8)–(9).

unable to work for at least a year due to physical or mental impairments, the ADA is focused on finding and making available employment positions that exist within the economy that can be performed by persons with disabilities.

Under the ADA, a "disability" is defined as "a physical or mental impairment that substantially limits one or more of the major life activities of such individual."[226] Under the ADA regulations, "temporary, non-chronic impairments of short duration, with little or no long term or permanent impact, are usually not disabilities."[227] The ADA regulations also state that to be considered substantially limited means, among other things, that an individual is "[u]nable to perform a major life activity that the average person in the general population can perform";[228] or "[s]ignificantly restricted as to the condition, manner or duration under which an individual can perform a particular major life activity as compared to the condition, manner, or duration under which the average person in the general population can perform that same major life activity."[229] Major life activities as described by the ADA regulations include "functions such as caring for oneself, performing manual tasks, walking, seeing, hearing, speaking, breathing, learning, and working."[230]

Unlike the Social Security disability statutes, under the ADA, the determination of the existence of a covered disability is only the first step in the analysis of whether an individual is entitled to the protections of the ADA. Under the ADA, in addition to demonstrating that he or she has a disability as defined by the ADA, the employee is required to demonstrate that he or she is a "qualified individual with a disability."[231] To be a qualified individual with a disability, the employee seeking relief under the ADA bears the burden of demonstrating that he or she is capable of performing the essential functions of

---

[226] 42 U.S.C. §12102(2)(A); 29 C.F.R. §1630.2(g) (2003).
[227] 29 C.F.R. pt. 1630, app. §1630.2(j) (2003).
[228] 29 C.F.R. §1630.2(j)(i) (2003).
[229] Id. §1630.2(j)(ii) (2003).
[230] Id. §1630.2(i) (2003).
[231] 42 U.S.C. §12112(a).

the current or desired employment position either with or without reasonable accommodation.[232] If an employee fails to establish that he or she is capable of performing the essential functions of the position desired either with or without a reasonable accommodation, the employee is not a qualified individual with a disability and is not entitled to the protections of the ADA.[233]

C. Recognition of Conflict Between Social Security Disability and ADA Disability

1. Administrative Recognition of Conflict

In 1993, in response to the passage of the ADA, the SSA made an attempt to distinguish Social Security disability determinations and ADA disability determinations by promulgating a special memorandum to administrative law judges and staff addressing the effect of language in the ADA on determinations of eligibility for SSDI or SSI benefits.[234] In that memorandum, the SSA's Associate Commissioner for Hearings and Appeals instructed all SSA administrative law judges and staff that in assessing initial or continued disability "[t]he fact that an individual may be able to return to a past relevant job, provided that the employer makes accommodations, is not relevant to the issues to be resolved," and thus "hypothetical inquiries about whether an employer would or could make accommodations that would allow return to a prior job would not be appropriate."[235]

2. Court Recognition of Conflict

While the SSA moved to distinguish the effect of the ADA concept of reasonable accommodation on the administration

---

[232] *Id.* §12111(8).
[233] *Id.*
[234] Memorandum from Daniel Skoler, SSA Associate Commissioner for Hearings and Appeals, on the Americans with Disabilities Act, to Administrative Law Judges and Staff (June 2, 1993).
[235] *Id.*

and award of benefits under the Social Security disability statutes, the courts were faced with the task of interpreting claims of ADA qualified disability in light of, or in spite of, applications by ADA plaintiffs for and/or awards of Social Security disability benefits. The initial holdings of numerous courts was that the doctrine of judicial estoppel[236] barred applicants who had made sworn representations of "total disability" in Social Security disability benefit applications from claiming in later or concurrent ADA litigation that the applicant was capable of performing the essential functions of the job.[237]

---

[236]Judicial estoppel is a court-created equitable doctrine that is intended to prevent a litigant from attempting to assert a position inconsistent with one that he or she has asserted in a previous judicial proceeding. *See* Boyers, *Precluding Inconsistent Statements: The Doctrine of Judicial Estoppel*, 80 Nw. U. L. REV. 1244 (1986). For another treatment of the history and application of the doctrine of judicial estoppel, see Henkin, *Judicial Estoppel—Beating Shields Into Swords and Back Again*, 139 U. PA. L. REV. 1711, 1711 (1991). For more in-depth looks into the application of the doctrine of judicial estoppel in the context of the SSA and ADA, see Diller, *Dissonant Disability Policies: The Tension Between the Americans With Disabilities Act and Federal Disability Programs*, 76 TEX. L. REV. 1003 (1998); Sims, *Estop It! Judicial Estoppel and Its use in Americans with Disabilities Act Litigation*, 34 HOUS. L. REV. 843 (1997); Hamilton, *Judicial Estoppel, Social Security Disability Benefits and the ADA: The Circuits Diverge*, 9 DEPAUL BUS. L.J. 127 (1996).

[237]*See, e.g.*, Blanton v. Inco Alloys Int'l, Inc., 108 F.3d 104, 6 AD Cases 673, *aff'd in part and rev'd in part, remanded*, 123 F.3d 916, 7 AD Cases 1475 (6th Cir. 1997); Budd v. ADT Sec. Sys., Inc., 103 F.3d 699, 6 AD Cases 867 (8th Cir. 1996); Rissetto v. Plumbers & Steamfitters Local 343, 94 F.3d 597, 71 FEP Cases 1057 (9th Cir. 1996); McNemar v. Disney Store, Inc., 91 F.3d 610, 5 AD Cases 1227 (3d Cir. 1996), *cert. denied*, 519 U.S. 1115 (1997); Aucutt v. Six Flags Over Mid-America, Inc., 85 F.3d 1311, 5 AD Cases 902 (8th Cir. 1996); DeGiuseppe v. Village of Bellwood, 68 F.3d 187 (7th Cir. 1995); Lemons v. US Air Group, Inc., 43 F. Supp. 2d 571 (M.D.N.C.), *vacated and remanded*, 194 F.3d 1304 (4th Cir. 1999); Violette v. International Bus. Machs. Corp., 962 F. Supp. 446, 7 AD Cases 395 (D. Vt. 1996), *aff'd*, 116 F.3d 466, 7 AD Cases 544 (2d Cir. 1997); Erit v. Judge, Inc., 961 F. Supp. 774, 6 AD Cases 1353 (D.N.J. 1997); Thomas v. Fort Myers Hous. Auth., 955 F. Supp. 1463, 6 AD Cases 735 (M.D. Fla. 1997); Johnson v. Hines Nurseries, Inc., 950 F. Supp. 175, 7 AD Cases 867 (N.D. Tex. 1996); Terry v. Norfolk S. Ry., 948 F. Supp. 1058, 6 AD Cases 802 (N.D. Ga. 1996); Harris v. Marathon Oil Co., 948 F. Supp. 27, 7 AD Cases 873 (W.D. Tex. 1996), *aff'd*, 108 F.3d 332, 7 AD Cases 960 (5th Cir. 1997); Hindman v. Greenville Hosp. Sys., 947 F. Supp. 215, 7 AD Cases 963 (D.S.C. 1996), aff'd, 133 F.3d 915, 7 AD Cases 1267 (4th Cir. 1997); Wilmarth v. City of Santa Rosa, 945 F. Supp. 1271, 7 AD Cases 1131 (N.D. Cal. 1996); Johnson v. U.S. Steel Corp., 943 F. Supp. 1108, 7 AD Cases 999 (D. Minn. 1996); Miller v. U.S. Bancorp, 926 F. Supp. 994, 5 AD Cases 968 (D. Or. 1996), *aff'd*, 139 F.3d 906 (9th Cir. 1998); Cline v. Western Horseman, Inc., 922 F. Supp. 442, 5 AD Cases 714 (D. Colo. 1996); Hatfield v. Quantum Chem. Corp., 920 F. Supp. 108, 5 AD

Other courts rejected the use of judicial estoppel in this context, holding that statements made by individuals in Social Security disability applications that appeared to conflict with representations of one's ability to perform a particular position in an ADA claim should not automatically bar the ADA claim, but should be treated as evidence to be factored into the determination of whether the plaintiff could prove that he or she was a qualified individual with a disability.[238]

In response to the estoppel arguments being made by employers and recognized by some courts as a bar to ADA claims, the EEOC promulgated an *Enforcement Guidance* wherein it stated its official position that representations made by individuals in applications for disability benefits would not be viewed by the EEOC as an automatic bar to maintaining an ADA claim.[239] Following the issuance of the February 1997 EEOC Guidance, several courts definitively renounced the use

---

Cases 765 (S.D. Tex. 1996); Reiff v. Interim Pers., Inc., 906 F. Supp. 1280, 5 AD Cases 740 (D. Minn. 1995); Nguyen v. IBP, Inc., 905 F. Supp. 1471, 5 AD Cases 465 (D. Kan. 1995); Garcia-Paz v. Swift Textiles, Inc., 873 F. Supp. 547, 3 AD Cases 1844 (D. Kan. 1995); Reigel v. Kaiser Found. Health Plan of N.C., 859 F. Supp. 963, 3 AD Cases 577 (E.D.N.C. 1994) (all holding that claim for disability benefits precludes claim for ADA disability discrimination).

[238] *See, e.g.,* Weiler v. Household Fin. Corp., 101 F.3d 519, 6 AD Cases 106 (7th Cir. 1996); Robinson v. Neodata Servs., Inc., 94 F.3d 499, 5 AD Cases 1441 (8th Cir. 1996); D'Aprile v. Fleet Servs. Corp., 92 F.3d 1, 5 AD Cases 1343 (1st Cir. 1996); Kennedy v. Applause, Inc., 90 F.3d 1477, 5 AD Cases 1249 (9th Cir. 1996); Hughes v. Reinsurance Group of Am., 957 F. Supp. 1097, 6 AD Cases 888 (E.D. Mo. 1996); Morton v. GTE N., Inc., 922 F. Supp. 1169, 5 AD Cases 524 (N.D. Tex. 1996), *aff'd,* 114 F.3d 1182, 7 AD Cases 544 (5th Cir.), *cert. denied,* 522 U.S. 880 (1997); Pegues v. Emerson Elec. Co., 913 F. Supp. 976, 5 AD Cases 376 (N.D. Miss. 1996).

[239] *EEOC Enforcement Guidance on the Effect of Representations Made in Applications for Benefits on the Determination of Whether a Person Is a "Qualified Individual with a Disability" Under the Americans with Disabilities Act of 1990 (ADA),* EEOC Notice No. 915.002 (Feb. 12, 1997) [hereinafter 1997 EEOC Notice]. It should be recognized that the Supreme Court has stated that EEOC guidelines do not have the force and effect of law or regulations, but are merely entitled to some consideration by the courts. *See* General Elec. Co. v. Gilbert, 429 U.S. 125, 13 FEP Cases 1657, 1 EB Cases 1046 (1976). In fact, numerous courts have declined to follow guidelines set forth in EEOC Guidances, and the Supreme Court itself has rejected certain EEOC guidelines in the context of ADA enforcement. *See* Sutton v. United Air Lines, Inc., 527 U.S. 471, 9 AD Cases 673 (1999) (rejecting EEOC guidelines stating that ADA disability must be addressed without reference to mitigating measures).

of judicial estoppel to address conflicting statements of disability in SSDI and ADA claims.[240]

D. Receipt of Disability Benefits and ADA Recovery

1. Social Security and ADA Disability Claims Conflict

The decision of the U.S. Court of Appeals for the Fifth Circuit in *Cleveland v. Policy Management Systems, Inc.*[241] brought the conflict between Social Security and ADA disability claims to a head. While the Fifth Circuit in *Cleveland* refused to adopt a per se rule that would "automatically estop[] an applicant for or recipient of social security disability benefits from asserting a claim of discrimination under the ADA,"[242] it instead created a rebuttable legal presumption that an individual who pursues or receives Social Security disability benefits would be unable to demonstrate that he or she was also a qualified individual with a disability under the ADA.[243] In its analysis of the apparent

---

[240] *See* Griffith v. Wal-Mart Stores, 135 F.3d 376 (6th Cir. 1998) ("[J]udicial estoppel does not apply because the answers given in a Social Security disability benefit application are not necessarily inconsistent with a plaintiff's claim that he could have worked at his job, during the relevant period, with a reasonable accommodation."); Johnson v. Oregon Dep't of Human Res., Rehab. Div., 141 F.3d 1361, 1367, 8 AD Cases 283, 288 (9th Cir. 1998) (emphasis in original) ("[N]either application for nor receipt of disability benefits *automatically* bars a claimant from establishing that she is a qualified person with a disability under the ADA."); Griffith v. Wal-Mart Stores, Inc., 135 F.3d 376, 382, 7 AD Cases 1233, 1237 (6th Cir. 1998) ("[J]udicial estoppel does not apply because the answers given in a Social Security disability benefit application are not necessarily inconsistent with a plaintiff's claim that he could have worked at his job, during the relevant period, with a reasonable accommodation."); Talavera v. Palm Beach County Sch. Bd., 129 F.3d 1214, 1220, 7 AD Cases 1025, 1030 (11th Cir. 1997) ("We agree with the majority of our sister circuits that a certification of total disability on an SSD [social security disability] benefits application is not inherently inconsistent with being a 'qualified individual with a disability' under the ADA.'"); Blanton v. Inco Alloys Int'l, Inc., 123 F.3d 916, 6 AD Cases 1476, *modifying* 108 F.3d 104, 6 AD Cases 673 (6th Cir. 1997); Weigel v. Target Stores, 122 F.3d 461, 7 AD Cases 358 (7th Cir. 1997); Swanks v. Washington Metro. Area Transit Auth., 116 F.3d 582, 584, 6 AD Cases 1544, 1546 (D.C.Cir. 1997) ("[I]n assessing eligibility for disability benefits, the Social Security Administration gives no consideration to a claimant's ability to work with reasonable accommodation.").

[241] 120 F.3d 513, 7 AD Cases 1031 (5th Cir. 1997), *vacated and remanded*, 526 U.S. 795, 9 AD Cases 491 (1999).

[242] *Id.* at 517, 7 AD Cases at 1033.

[243] *Id.* at 518.

conflict, the Fifth Circuit recognized that different factors governed the disability determinations under the Social Security programs and the ADA,[244] and conceded that it was "at least theoretically conceivable" that the factual circumstances of Social Security disability would not necessarily be mutually exclusive with the factual circumstances of performing the essential functions of one's job with reasonable accommodation.[245] Nevertheless, because it determined that it would be only under "some limited and highly unusual set of circumstances" that a plaintiff could demonstrate that the two claims would not necessarily be mutually exclusive, the Fifth Circuit chose to impose a rebuttable presumption that a plaintiff who had applied for or received Social Security disability benefits was judicially estopped from asserting that she was a "qualified individual with a disability" under the ADA.[246] The Fifth Circuit's decision in *Cleveland*, combined with the *1997 EEOC Guidance*[247] and the numerous approaches to the conflict being utilized by the federal courts, set the stage for Supreme Court review.

The Supreme Court granted a limited review on writ of certiorari for the Fifth Circuit's holding in *Cleveland*.[248] The Court framed the specific issue addressed as follows: "whether the law erects a special presumption that would significantly inhibit an SSDI recipient from simultaneously pursuing an action for disability discrimination under the Americans with Disabilities Act of 1990 (ADA), claiming that 'with . . . reasonable accommodation' she could 'perform the essential functions' of her job."[249] In a unanimous decision, the Supreme Court reversed the holding of the Fifth Circuit in *Cleveland*, finding that it was unnecessary and improper to create a negative legal presumption that plaintiffs who had applied for and been granted SSDI benefits could not recover under the ADA, and that the pursuit of and receipt of SSDI benefits did not

---

[244] *Id.* at 517–18.
[245] *Id.* at 517, 7 AD Cases at 1033.
[246] *Id.*, 7 AD Cases at 1034.
[247] 1997 EEOC Notice, *supra* note 239.
[248] Cleveland v. Policy Mgmt. Sys. Corp., 526 U.S. 795, 9 AD Cases 491 (1999).
[249] *Id.* at 797, 9 AD Cases at 492.

automatically estop the recipient from pursuing an ADA claim.[250]

Finding that "there are too many situations in which an SSDI claim and an ADA claim can comfortably exist side by side,"[251] the Supreme Court rejected the premise that a claim by an individual of "total disability" in a Social Security disability application was necessarily in direct factual conflict with a claim of being a qualified individual with a disability for purposes of pursuing relief under the ADA. The Supreme Court found that due to the context and framework of the differing statutes, representations of disability made by applicants for Social Security disability benefits did not necessarily involve directly conflicting statements about the same purely factual matters.[252]

2. Genuine Conflicts

The Supreme Court in *Cleveland* did not, however, eliminate the possibility that a genuine factual conflict could exist between SSDI claims and ADA claims that would justify the summary dismissal of the plaintiff's ADA claim.[253] To the contrary, because the plaintiff bears the burden of proof in an ADA case to demonstrate that he or she is a qualified individual with a disability, the Supreme Court held that there could be situations where no reasonable juror could find that a plaintiff's prior sworn statement of "total disability" to the SSA could be consistent with a claim that the plaintiff is able to perform the essential functions of his or her employment position either with or without reasonable accommodation. Thus, although it refused to create a rebuttable presumption, the Supreme Court recognized that sworn statements made by persons in applications for Social Security disability benefits may negate their

---

[250] *Id.* at 797–98.

[251] *Id.* at 802–03, 9 AD Cases at 495.

[252] *Id.* at 804–05. The examples given by the Supreme Court of such directly conflicting statements would be "The light was red/green," or "I can/cannot raise my arm above my head." *Id.* at 802, 9 AD Cases at 494.

[253] *Id.* at 806.

ability to prove an essential element of their ADA case, that is, that they are qualified individuals with a disability.[254]

3. *"Sufficient Explanation" Burden*

In light of the ultimate burden of proof remaining with the ADA plaintiffs to demonstrate the essential elements of their case, and because of the potential direct factual conflict between sworn representations of "total disability" and "qualified individual" status, the Supreme Court imposed on the ADA plaintiff the burden to provide a "sufficient explanation" where the prior statements made to the SSA directly conflict with a later position taken in the ADA litigation.[255] The Supreme Court found that, in the face of prior statements of "total" disability or inability to perform any work, which statements must be assumed by the trier of fact to be true or made with a good-faith belief in their truth at the time they were made, the plaintiff must give an explanation sufficient to convince a reasonable juror that despite the earlier statement the plaintiff is able to perform the essential functions of the job in question, either with or without reasonable accommodation.[256]

Given the subjective "sufficient explanation" approach taken by the Supreme Court in *Cleveland*, it is not surprising that judicial interpretation of the Supreme Court's test has resulted in a "mixed-bag" of decisions, some finding sufficient facts to allow the cases to go forward[257] and others affirming

---

[254] *Id.* at 806–07.
[255] *Id.*
[256] *Id.* at 807.
[257] *See, e.g.,* Pals v. Schepel Buick & GMC Truck, Inc., 220 F.3d 495, 10 AD Cases 1345 (7th Cir. 2000) (plaintiff's explanation, while weak, was not so weak as to reverse jury finding); EEOC v. Stowe-Pharr Mills, Inc., 216 F.3d 373, 10 AD Cases 1153 (4th Cir. 2000) (plaintiff provided sufficient explanation through affidavit indicating that she discussed her belief that she could work with reasonable accommodation with Social Security); Parker v. Columbia Pictures Indus., 204 F.3d 326, 10 AD Cases 396 (2d Cir. 2000) (plaintiff explained that statement to Social Security reflected why his employer told him he could no longer work); Norris v. Sysco Corp., 191 F.3d 1043, 9 AD Cases 1262 (9th Cir. 1999) (court refused to reverse jury verdict, finding without analyzing explanation that it was not so deficient that jury verdict was erroneous); Dayoub v. Penn-Del Directory Co., 90 F. Supp. 2d. 636, 10 AD Cases 935 (E.D. Pa. 2000) (plaintiff's statement that he was totally disabled

summary judgment by finding the plaintiff unable to provide "sufficient" explanation for the conflicting statements.[258] As noted by the U.S. Court of Appeals for the Ninth Circuit in *Norris v. Sysco Corp.*,[259] the test adopted by the Supreme Court in *Cleveland* is essentially nothing more than the normal application of the summary judgment and judgment as a matter of law standards.[260]

Thus, from a legal standpoint, the issue of conflict between representations of total disability in Social Security applications and representations of ability to perform with reasonable accommodation in ADA litigation has been addressed and effectively resolved by the Supreme Court in *Cleveland*. It is now clear that representations of total disability or similar inability to work made in applications for Social Security disability benefits do not automatically estop or otherwise bar the applicant (or recipient of benefits) from seeking relief under the ADA, and that those same representations do not create a legal presumption that such person cannot seek relief under the

---

from performing his position for purposes of SSDI was not inherently inconsistent with his claim for relief under ADA).

[258] *See, e.g.*, DiSanto v. McGraw-Hill, Inc., 220 F.3d 61, 10 AD Cases 1364 (2d Cir. 2000) (plaintiff's explanation insufficient where statement of total disability preceded date of actual discharge); Reed v. Petroleum Helicopters, Inc., 218 F.3d 477, 10 AD Cases 1426 (5th Cir. 2000) (plaintiff's sworn statements that she could not sit for extended periods of time and that her back problems made her "totally unpredictable" precluded her from claiming she could fly helicopter or obtain valid airmen's certificate); Lloyd v. Hardin County, Iowa, 207 F.3d 1080, 10 AD Cases 703 (8th Cir. 2000) (plaintiff's explanation that he could have performed job that was not reasonable accommodation insufficient to avoid summary judgment); Motley v. New Jersey State Police, 196 F.3d 160, 9 AD Cases 1505 (3d Cir. 1999) (assertions of permanent and total disability, along with additional statements describing type and extent of injuries, and uncontroverted medical diagnoses patently inconsistent with plaintiff's present claims that he was "qualified individual" under ADA), *cert. denied*, 529 U.S. 1087 (2000); Feldman v. American Mem'l Life Ins. Co., 196 F.3d 783, 9 AD Cases 1717 (7th Cir. 1999); Mitchell v. Washingtonville Cent. Sch. Dist., 190 F.3d 1, 9 AD Cases 1123 (2d Cir. 1999) (summary judgment affirmed, where plaintiff stated to SSA that he was unable to stand or walk, but then claimed in his subsequent ADA action that he was capable of both standing and walking); Lincoln v. Momentum Sys. Ltd., 86 F. Supp. 2d 421, 10 AD Cases 946 (D.N.J. 2000) (sworn statements by plaintiff to SSA in direct conflict with claim under ADA warranted use of judicial estoppel of ADA claim).

[259] 191 F.3d 1043, 9 AD Cases 1262 (9th Cir. 1999).

[260] *Id.* at 1048.

ADA. However, the law now requires that the person who has applied for and/or received Social Security disability benefits, who then chooses to pursue an ADA claim, bears the burden of explaining the circumstances surrounding his or her prior representations of disability in a manner that could convince a reasonable juror that the two factual positions taken are not mutually exclusive. If the ADA plaintiff fails to provide a sufficient explanation, summary judgment or judgment as a matter of law still may be appropriate remedies.

At least some ADA plaintiffs have had favorable judgments upheld,[261] or been permitted to proceed with a disability discrimination claim,[262] despite seemingly contradictory statements made while seeking or receiving disability benefits. It appears, however, that the majority of plaintiffs experience serious difficulty in explaining conflicting statements and assertions made in the disability benefit context when they seek disability discrimination claims.[263]

IV. SAFETY AND HEALTH STATUTES AND REGULATIONS

The Occupational Safety and Health Act (OSH Act)[264] is the primary workplace safety and health law in the United States. Applicable to a very broad scope of employment settings, it requires employers to provide their employees with a safe workplace. In addition to the OSH Act, other federal statutes and regulations that are focused on safe operations of industrial and commercial functions also prescribe a range of requirements. Among these are the specific criteria established for

---

[261] Giles v. General Elec. Co., 245 F.3d 474, 11 AD Cases 1242 (5th Cir. 2001).

[262] Trowbridge v. Scranton Artificial Limb Co., 560 Pa. 640, 747 A.2d 862, 10 AD Cases 725 (2000).

[263] Sullivan v. Raytheon Co., 262 F.3d 41, 12 AD Cases 634 (1st Cir. 2001); Lee v. City of Salem, Ind., 259 F.3d 667, 12 AD Cases 10 (7th Cir. 2001); Lane v. BFI Waste Sys. of N. Am., 11 AD Cases 1795 (8th Cir. 2001); Reed v. Petroleum Helicopters, Inc., 218 F.3d 477, 10 AD Cases 1426 (5th Cir. 2000); Feldman v. American Mem'l Life Ins. Co., 196 F.3d 783, 9 AD Cases 1717 (7th Cir. 1999).

[264] 29 U.S.C. §651 et seq.

transportation operations by the various operating administrations of the Department of Transportation (DOT), as illustrated by the specific physical qualification standards for commercial truck drivers as regulated by the Federal Motor Carrier Safety Administration (FMCSA).[265] The intersection of such safety and health rules, or regulated physical qualification criteria, with the ADA are explored in the section that follows.

Obligations on employers under the OSH Act are derived from both general statutory obligations and more specific promulgated standards that relate to particular safety and health hazards. The basic—and most far-reaching—obligation placed on employers is expressed in the OSH Act's "General Duty Clause," which imposes on each employer a broad obligation to furnish to each of his employees employment and a place of employment which are free from recognized hazards that are causing or are likely to cause death or serious physical harm to his employees.[266] The Occupational Safety and Health Administration (OSHA) of the U.S. Department of Labor, the administrative agency that enforces the OSH Act, has promulgated a large number of regulations and standards to promote workplace safety and health. Employers who fail to comply with the statutory and regulatory mandates are subject to civil penalties, government-ordered abatement, and, in limited circumstances, criminal liability.[267] It is significant to note that while the OSH Act contains sweeping preemption provisions, certain states have regained authority to enforce safety and health laws in their jurisdictions under the statute's "state plan" process. Most requirements enforced by the state plans are equivalent to or more demanding than standards and rules promulgated by the federal agency.

The OSH Act has a very broad reach. In fact, unless subject to separate federal safety regulation or specifically excepted from the statute, the OSH Act has been interpreted to reach employers to the full extent permitted by the U.S. Constitution.

---

[265] 49 C.F.R. §391.41 (2003).
[266] 29 U.S.C. §654(a)(1).
[267] *Id.* §666.

The OSH Act defines a covered "employer" as: "a person engaged in a business affecting commerce who has employees, but does not include the United States (not including the United States Postal Service) or any State or political subdivision of a State."[268] Thus, few employers and workplaces escape coverage under the standards and regulations promulgated under the OSH Act, although OSHA's limited enforcement staffing has made routine agency visits somewhat unusual, particularly for the bulk of the nation's (small) employers.

The goals of the workplace safety and health statute are primarily preventive in nature. While the OSH Act imposes certain duties when an injury occurs, the clear emphasis of the OSH Act is to ensure that serious, preventable accidents never occur in the first place. Thus, employers bear the burden of continually evaluating the workplace for recognizable hazards, and of removing those hazards. The OSH Act and the ADA are somewhat similar in those respects. The ADA seeks to prevent discrimination against those individuals with disabilities who can work with reasonable accommodation and the OSH Act seeks to assure safe work environments. However, tension arises—in some instances—between the goals of these statutes where the rights of an individual impact safety in the workplace. Specifically, an employer may be caught in a situation of either complying with the OSH Act or the ADA, or, at a minimum, considering the safety and health implications of each statute. Such a dilemma may arise in the context of recordkeeping, medical examinations, or mandated abatement requirements.[269]

A. Balancing Individual Rights Against the Duty to Provide a Safe Workplace

The ADA requires an employer to reasonably accommodate a qualified individual with a disability.[270] There are three exceptions for a failure to accommodate: (1) that "an alleged

---

[268] *Id.* §652(5).
[269] 42 U.S.C. §12112.
[270] 42 U.S.C. §12112(a), (b)(5)(A).

application of qualification standards, tests, or selection criteria that screen out or tend to screen out" individuals with disabilities is "job-related and consistent with business necessity";[271] (2) that the disabled individual poses a "direct threat to the health or safety of other individuals in the workplace";[272] and (3) that reasonable accommodation "would impose an undue hardship on the operation of the business."[273] The EEOC has further stated in the regulations implementing the ADA that: "It may be a defense to a charge of discrimination ... that a challenged action is required or necessitated by another Federal law or regulation, or that another Federal law or regulation prohibits an action (including the provision of a particular reasonable accommodation) that would otherwise be required...."[274] All of these defenses may be raised in the context of a conflict between the OSH Act and the ADA.

1. The Business Necessity Defense

An action by an employer that is "job related and consistent with business necessity" is a complete defense to a claim of discrimination under the ADA, despite any incidental discriminatory effect. In order for a discriminatory criteria to be "job related and consistent with business necessity," it must be necessary to determine whether the individual can perform the essential functions of the job with reasonable accommodation.[275] Thus, the business necessity defense applies to the initial determination of whether an individual is a "qualified individual" under the ADA. For example, in *Fitzpatrick v. City of Atlanta*,[276] an employer argued that its compliance with OSHA regulations provided an affirmative defense to a claim of disability discrimination. Under the applicable OSHA regulation, firefighters were required to be clean-shaven, so that respirators could be properly worn and used. Several firefighters who

---

[271] *Id.* §12113(a).
[272] *Id.* §12113(b).
[273] *Id.* §12112(b)(5)(A).
[274] 29 C.F.R. §1630.15(e) (2003).
[275] 42 U.S.C. §12111(8).
[276] 2 F.3d 1112, 2 AD Cases 1270 (11th Cir. 1993).

suffered from a bacterial disorder, which precluded them from shaving, brought suit challenging the fire department's policy. The U.S. Court of Appeals for the Eleventh Circuit found that the fire department's policy was not violative of the Rehabilitation Act because the evidence demonstrated that the policy was motivated by safety concerns, and not discriminatory animus.[277] Thus, the policy was deemed to be job related and consistent with business necessity. The court further stated that, "Although public employers such as the City are not required by law to comply with OSHA standards . . . such standards certainly provide a trustworthy bench mark for assessing safety-based business necessity claims."[278] Thus, employers conflicted in their duties under the ADA and the OSH Act, may defend their failure to reasonably accommodate by arguing that an individual requesting accommodation must first meet the qualifications of the position, including any applicable OSHA standard or regulation.

2. The Undue Hardship Defense

The ADA defines "undue hardship" as "an action requiring significant difficulty or expense" in light of specific factors, including the size and resources of the employer.[279] An employer does not have to reasonably accommodate an individual with a disability if it "would impose an undue hardship on the operation of the" employer's business.[280] Thus, the undue hardship defense also is a complete defense to a claim of discrimination under the ADA. This defense often is raised in the context of the financial burden posed by the suggested

---

[277] Although *Fitzpatrick, see id.*, focused on the Rehabilitation Act of 1973, the ADA defines "disability" in substantially the same manner as the Rehabilitation Act then defined the term "handicap," and, thus, cases interpreting the Rehabilitation Act are instructive in interpreting the ADA. *See* Francis v. City of Meriden, 129 F.3d 281, 7 AD Cases 955 (2d Cir. 1997); Chandler v. City of Dallas, 2 F.3d 1385, 2 AD Cases 1326 (5th Cir. 1993), *cert. denied*, 511 U.S. 1011 (1994).
[278] *Fitzpatrick*, 2 F.3d at 1121.
[279] 42 U.S.C. §12111(10)(A), (B)(iii).
[280] 42 U.S.C. §12112(5)(A).

reasonable accommodation.[281] In this regard, something of an economic argument might be advanced in the context of a conflict between the OSH Act and the ADA by raising the financial burden imposed by an OSHA citation and any resulting enforcement litigation that might occur for an employer's failure to eliminate a known hazard in the workplace.[282]

3. The Direct-Threat Defense

Perhaps more significant—and more common—are concerns with whether the characteristics of an individual seeking placement or accommodation in a position may pose some type of threat in that job, based on its normal tasks and responsibilities. The language of the ADA provides, in the "defenses" section of Title I, that "[t]he term 'qualification standards' may include a requirement that an individual shall not pose a direct threat to the health or safety of other individuals in the workplace."[283] "Direct threat" is defined under the ADA as "a significant risk to the health or safety of others that cannot be eliminated by reasonable accommodation."[284] The EEOC has stated in its regulations that the "significant risk" must be a "significant risk of substantial harm."[285] The EEOC regulations further define "significant risk of substantial harm" to mean a "high probability" of its occurrence.[286] The direct-threat defense is another complete defense to a claim under the ADA, and often is raised in the context of workplace safety.[287]

---

[281] *See* Stone v. City of Mount Vernon, 118 F.3d 92, 6 AD Cases 1685 (2d Cir. 1997), *cert. denied*, 522 U.S. 1112 (1998) (concept of undue hardship looks at relation of costs to employer versus benefits to individual).

[282] *See* Campbell v. Federal Express Corp. 918 F. Supp. 912, 6 AD Cases 835 (D. Md. 1996) (requirement that driver obtain proper federal certification found to be job-related and consistent with necessity, and, thus, did not require reasonable accommodation).

[283] 42 U.S.C. §12113(b).
[284] *Id.* §12111(3).
[285] 29 C.F.R. §1630.2(r) (2003).
[286] 29 C.F.R. pt. 1630, app. §1630.2(r) (2003).
[287] *See* EEOC v. Exxon Corp., 203 F.3d 871, 10 AD Cases 225 (5th Cir. 2000); Moses v. American Nonwovens, Inc., 97 F.3d 446, 5 AD Cases 1651 (11th Cir. 1996), *cert. denied*, 519 U.S. 1118 (1997); Daugherty v. City of El Paso, 56 F.3d 695, 4 AD Cases 993 (5th Cir. 1995), *cert. denied*, 516 U.S. 1172 (1996).

The EEOC's regulations state that an assessment as to whether an individual poses a direct threat requires a case-by-case analysis "of the individual's present ability to safely perform the" job.[288] In making this assessment, employers should rely on "reasonable medical judgment" and "the best available objective evidence."[289] According to the EEOC, the following factors are used to determine the existence of a direct threat:

(1) The duration of the risk;
(2) The nature and severity of the potential harm;
(3) The likelihood that the potential harm will occur; and
(4) The imminence of the potential harm.[290]

Many courts have accepted this framework of analysis.[291]

a. Opposing View

A substantial debate has surrounded the question of whether the "direct-threat" defense provided by the ADA extends to circumstances in which it is alleged that the individual poses a direct threat to his or her own health. In its regulations, the EEOC stated that an employer may assert a direct-threat defense with respect to individuals who pose a threat to the health or safety of others or—more controversially—those whose conditions only pose a threat to their own health or safety.[292] A number of appellate courts have agreed with this proposition, either in holdings[293] or in dicta.[294] The U.S. Court of Appeals for the Ninth Circuit took the contrary view, finding that the statutory language and its legislative history pointed

---

[288]29 C.F.R. §1630.2(r) (2003).
[289]*Id.*
[290]*Id.*
[291]*See, e.g.,* Hamlin v. Charter Township of Flint, 165 F.3d 426, 8 AD Cases 1688 (6th Cir., 1999); Rizzo v. Children's World Learning Ctrs., Inc., 84 F.3d 758, 5 AD Cases 1155 (5th Cir. 1996).
[292]29 C.F.R. §§1630.15(b)(2), 1630.2(r) (2003).
[293]Moses v. American Nonwovens, Inc. 97 F.3d 446, 5 AD Cases 1651 (11th Cir. 1996), *cert. denied,* 519 U.S. 1118 (1997).
[294]La Chance v. Duffy's Draft House, Inc., 146 F.3d 832, 8 AD Cases 652 (11th Cir. 1998); EEOC v. Amego, Inc., 110 F.3d 135, 6 AD Cases 997 (1st Cir. 1997); Daugherty v. City of El Paso, 56 F.3d 695, 4 AD Cases 993 (5th Cir. 1995).

to the conclusion that such a defense is not envisioned by the ADA.[295]

The Supreme Court subsequently reversed the Ninth Circuit and upheld the validity of the EEOC's regulation.[296] In the case before the Court, Mario Echazabal worked for independent contractors performing services at a Chevron oil refinery. On two occasions, he applied directly to Chevron for a position; on both occasions, Echazabal was offered employment conditioned on his ability to pass the company's physical examination. Each time, the physical examination showed that Echazabal suffered from a liver abnormality or damage caused by hepatitis C. Chevron's doctors said that Echazabal's medical condition would be aggravated by continued exposure to toxins at the refinery.[297]

Following the first physical examination, Chevron withdrew its employment offer based on the threat of danger to Echazabal's own health from working in the refinery. Following the second physical examination, Chevron requested that the contractor employing Echazabal reassign him to a position where he would not be exposed to toxins. Instead, the contractor laid off Echazabal. Echazabal filed suit against Chevron alleging that Chevron's refusal to hire him because of the alleged threat to his health caused by his disability violated the ADA. The parties did not dispute and the issue was not litigated as to whether Echazabal's medical condition actually constituted a disability under the ADA.[298]

Chevron defended its actions as authorized by the EEOC's regulation, which provides that it is permissible for an employer to require "that an individual shall not pose a direct threat to the health or safety of the individual or others in the workplace."[299] This regulation was promulgated based on the text of the ADA that permits employers to implement "qualification

---

[295] Echazabal v. Chevron, U.S.A., Inc., 213 F.3d 1098, 10 AD Cases 961, *amended*, 226 F.3d 1063, 11 AD Cases 70 (9th Cir. 2000), *rev'd*, 536 U.S. 73, 13 AD Cases 97 (2002).

[296] Chevron, U.S.A., Inc. v. Echazabal, 536 U.S. 73 (2002).

[297] *Id.* at 76.

[298] *Id.*

[299] *Id.* at 77. *See also* 29 C.F.R. §1630.15(b)(2).

standards" (such as physical examinations) even if they might screen out persons with disabilities as long as the qualification standards are "job-related and consistent with business necessity."[300]

The Supreme Court rejected the Ninth Circuit's holding that the EEOC overstepped its bounds by implementing a regulation permitting employers to consider the danger to a disabled individual in the workplace posed by his own medical condition. It rejected the interpretation that because the ADA stated that permissible qualification standards "may include a requirement that an individual shall not pose a direct threat to the health or safety of other individuals in the workplace,"[301] Congress meant to exclude the danger posed to the disabled employee, himself, as a permissible consideration for employers. It found nothing in the text of the ADA or the legislative history to indicate that Congress intended to omit the safety of the disabled individual deliberately as a proper consideration for employers. Finally, the Court found that the Ninth Circuit's strict interpretation of the ADA, only permitting employers to consider the danger to "others in the workplace," led to the illogical conclusion that an employer would not be allowed to consider the safety of anyone other than potential coworkers. The Court, however, cautioned that an employer's ability to make employment decisions based on whether a disabled individual posed a threat to himself or others was not meant to insulate covert discrimination. Instead, an employer's decision based on a safety risk posed by a disabled individual must be based on a reasonable medical judgment that relies on the most current medical knowledge and/or the best available objective evidence and on an expressly "individualized assessment of the individual's present ability to safely perform the essential functions of the job reached after considering, among other things, the imminence of the risk and the severity of the harm portended."[302]

---

[300] 42 U.S.C. §12113(a).
[301] *Chevron*, 536 U.S. at 80.
[302] *Id.* at 86.

4. The ADA's Conflict With Other Federal Laws as a Defense

Under EEOC regulations, an employer may defend a charge of disability discrimination by demonstrating that a challenged action is either required or prohibited by the OSH Act. Although the EEOC regulations are not binding on the courts, the courts generally give them deference.[303] In such cases, it is important, of course, for the employer to have actually relied on the relevant regulation—which allegedly has an exclusionary effect—in order to avoid liability for discrimination. An employee who can demonstrate that the employer's use of the regulations is merely a pretext for unlawful discrimination could prevail on a claim of disability discrimination.

Many of the ADA cases that have involved the interpretation and application of qualification criteria that allegedly have produced a discriminatory exclusionary effect relate to the rules promulgated by the DOT and its various operating administrations. In a number of cases, those agencies—including the Federal Aviation Administration and the Federal Motor Carrier Safety Administration (FMCSA)—have adopted rules that mandate specific physical qualifications for an individual to perform certain commercial transportation functions. A number of the cases challenging the application of regulatory criteria to exclude individuals from jobs have involved these requirements; in most instances, an employer's application of regulatory criteria to candidates for appropriate jobs will be enforced. For example, in *Tate v. Farmland Industries, Inc.*,[304] a driver who was terminated after his employer—a commercial motor carrier—discovered that he was taking antiseizure medication for his history of "seizures, fits, convulsions or fainting" failed to establish that he was a "qualified" individual with a disability, and was found to have no claim under the ADA. The U.S. Court of Appeals for the Tenth Circuit, in *Tate*, made reference to authority provided by the Commercial Motor Vehicle Safety

---

[303]*See* McAlindin v. County of San Diego, 192 F.3d 1226, 9 AD Cases 1217 (9th Cir. 1999), *cert. denied*, 530 U.S. 1243 (2000).

[304]268 F.3d 989, 12 AD Cases 519 (10th Cir. 2001).

Act of 1986,[305] the DOT's regulations, and the FMCSA's Medical Advisory Criteria, in supporting the employer's application of criteria that excluded a driver who had worked for the company for 10 years (including 2 years while taking the medication in question).[306]

The most definitive analysis of the role of regulatory standards and exclusionary criteria appeared in the Supreme Court's 1999 decision[307] involving the federal vision standards for commercial truck drivers. In that case, the Court considered the role of the decades-old standards developed by the DOT or its predecessors for individuals who drive commercial vehicles in interstate commerce.[308] In that case, a grocery chain hired a commercial truck driver who suffered from amblyopia, a condition that left him with 20/200 vision in one eye which was uncorrectable, essentially leaving him with monocular vision. The company was unaware of the limitation until after a return-to-work physical following a workers' compensation leave uncovered the visual deficiency that had been erroneously certified as DOT-compliant in his prehire medical exam. When the limitation came to light, Albertsons fired the driver and refused to rehire him subsequently, after he received a waiver from the DOT from its usual vision standards.

In his lawsuit under the ADA, the employer was successful in moving for summary judgment in the district court, based on its judgment that Kirkingburg was not "otherwise qualified" to perform the truck driver job, as he could not meet the basic DOT vision standards. The U.S. Court of Appeals for the Ninth

---

[305] 49 U.S.C. §31100 et al.

[306] *See also* EEOC v. J.B. Hunt Transp., Inc., 321 F.3d 69, 13 AD Cases 1697 (2d Cir. 2003) (rejecting EEOC's argument that motor carrier's refusal to hire truck drivers who took prescriptions that could impair their driving abilities violated statute, as carrier did not view applicants as substantially limited in broad range of jobs); EEOC v. United Parcel Serv., Inc., 306 F.3d 794, 13 AD Cases 961 (9th Cir. 2002) (company ban on drivers with monocular vision not blanket violation of ADA, as condition did not substantially limit workers in their daily lives).

[307] Albertson's, Inc. v. Kinkingburg, 527 U.S. 555, 9 AD Cases 694 (1999).

[308] *See* Motor Carrier Act, §204(a), 49 Stat. 546; Department of Transportation Act, §6 (e)(6)(C), 80 Stat. 939–940; 49 C.F.R. §1.4(c)(9) (1968); Motor Carrier Safety Act of 1984, §206, 98 Stat. 2835, as amended, 49 U.S.C. §31136(a)(3); 49 C.F.R. §1.48(aa) (1998).

Circuit reversed,[309] concluding that the employer could use compliance with the government regulation as a justification for adhering to its vision requirement, because it viewed the agency's waiver program as "a lawful and legitimate part of the DOT regulatory scheme."[310] It concluded that the employer would be required to justify its standard, which it characterized as different from that overall DOT mandate, providing it could establish that it was necessary to prevent a "direct threat."[311]

In its review, the Supreme Court found that the appellate court had committed several missteps in its analysis.[312] As to the role of an employer's compliance with mandatory regulation, it found the Ninth Circuit's conclusions to be wholly off the mark. The Court concluded that it was an error to read the regulations that established the DOT vision waiver program as modifying the basic visual acuity requirements contained in the agency's physical qualification standards. Rather, its analysis of the regulatory record made it clear that the waiver rule did not rest on a factual conclusion that placed it on a par with the general visual acuity standards. Rather, it was an experiment with safety, which rested on a hypothesis that might be confirmed or refuted and provide a later basis for reconsidering the existing standards. Nothing in that waiver rule mandated that employers of commercial truck drivers accept this theory and participate in the government's experiment.[313]

---

[309] Kinkinburg v. Albertson's, Inc., 143 F.3d 1228, 8 AD Cases 180 (9th Cir.1998), *rev'd*, 527 U.S. 555, 9 AD Cases 694 (1999).

[310] *Id.* at 1236, 8 AD Cases at 187. For some of the prior and subsequent history of the Federal Highway Administration's vision waiver program, see *Albertson's Inc.,* 527 U.S. at 576 n.21. That program was the subject of multiple appellate court challenges—see, e.g., Rauenhorst v. U.S. Dep't of Transp., 95 F.3d 715, 5 AD Cases 1621 (8th Cir. 1996); Advocates for Highway & Auto Safety v. Federal Highway Admin., 28 F.3d 1288, 3 AD Cases 842 (D.C. Cir. 1994)—and further legislative and regulatory action. *See* Federal Motor Carrier Safety Regulations; Waivers, Exemptions, and Pilot Programs; Rules and Procedures, 63 Fed. Reg. 67,600 (Dec. 8, 1998) (discusses the Transportation Equity Act for the 21st Century, Pub. L. No. 105-178, 112 Stat. 107). Reg. 67,600 (Dec. 8, 1998).

[311] *Kinkinburg,* 143 F.3d at 1236.

[312] *Albertson's,* 527 U.S. at 562, 9 AD Cases at 698.

[313] *Id.* at 576, 9 AD Cases at 703.

According to the Court, this left the question as to whether the ADA required the employer to defend its decision to decline to participate in this experiment. Should Albertsons have to bear the burden of justifying a job qualification contained in a clearly applicable, unamended substantive regulatory standard, despite the government's willingness to waive it experimentally without its having reached a finding that such action is appropriate from a safety and policy standpoint?[314] If so, stated the Court, the employer

> would be required in effect to justify *de novo* an existing and otherwise applicable safety regulation issued by the Government itself. The employer would be required on a case-by-case basis to reinvent the Government's own wheel when the Government had merely begun an experiment to provide data to consider changing the underlying specifications.[315]

B. Specific Occupational Safety and Health Act and ADA Tensions

1. Employee Records

OSHA imposes requirements on employers to maintain records and reports regarding occupational safety and health. These requirements are set forth in Department of Labor regulations. For example, each employer is required to keep a log and summary of occupational injuries and illnesses and to provide an annual summary of injuries and illnesses.[316] The agency's regulations also have required employers to provide employees, employee representatives with signed authorizations, and OSHA personnel access to medical information in the interest of exposing potential hazards and their causes.[317]

The ADA does not require employers to keep any particular records or reports. However, EEOC regulations impose

---

[314]*Id.* at 577, 9 AD Cases at 704.
[315]*Id.*
[316]OSHA Form No. 200, 29 C.F.R. §1904.2, .5 (2001). On January 19, 2001, OSHA promulgated revised injury and illness recordkeeping regulations and forms that took effect on January 1, 2002. 66 Fed. Reg. 5916 (Jan. 19, 2001) (codified at a revised 29 C.F.R. pt. 1904 (2003)).
[317]29 C.F.R. §1910.1020 (2003).

requirements on those employers who make or keep records of personnel action to keep such records for a period of 1 year.[318] This includes records of any request for reasonable accommodations by an individual with a purported disability. Additionally, the ADA requires medical records to be kept confidential.[319] Specifically, medical information must be maintained in a separate file with limited access.[320]

Thus, there is an obvious tension between the ADA and the OSH Act in regard to the release of medical information. The tension is most evident where an OSHA compliance officer requests access to medical records. Because OSHA compliance officers do not investigate compliance with the ADA, they are not among the individuals identified in the ADA as being authorized to obtain information about an individual's possible disability.[321] OSHA compliance officers also do not typically obtain authorization forms from employees whose information will be reviewed. OSHA's regulation on access to employee exposure and medical records provides the following:

> "Each employer shall, upon request . . . assure the prompt access of [compliance officers] to employee exposure in medical records and to analyses using exposure [in] medical records."[322]

Thus, the employer may, potentially, be caught in a conflict between the confidentiality requirements of the ADA and the disclosure requirements of the OSH Act.

However, as set forth above, the EEOC states in its regulations that compliance with other federal laws is a complete defense to a claim of discrimination under the ADA.[323] It is unclear if this defense will be entirely successful if the release of medical information is challenged. Thus, some employers choose to release such data only after OSHA issues and serves an appropriate subpoena, in order to protect their position

---

[318] *Id.* §1602.14 (2003).
[319] 42 U.S.C. §12112(d)(3)(B), (4)(C).
[320] *Id.*
[321] *Id.* §12112(d)(3)(B).
[322] 29 C.F.R. §1910.1020(e)(3)(i) (2001).
[323] *Id.* §1630.15(e) (2003).

that they have been required to act under the OSH Act and its regulations.[324]

2. Medical Examinations

Although the OSH Act does not itself specifically address the question of medical examinations, various OSHA standards require employers to administer periodic examinations of employees. Examples of standards requiring medical examinations are those addressing noise, hazardous waste, asbestos, and lead.[325]

The ADA, however, limits medical inquiries,[326] and, as discussed above, imposes strict confidentiality requirements on medical information received by an employer.[327] Under the ADA, an employer may not require a medical examination or make a medical inquiry of a current employee regarding the existence of a disability, or the extent of the disability, unless the examination or inquiry is shown to be "job related and consistent with business necessity."[328] To be "job-related and consistent with business necessity" essentially means that the examination or inquiry must be necessary to determine whether the individual can perform, with reasonable accommodation, the essential functions of the job.[329]

The EEOC has made clear that medical examinations required by federal law, for example, the OSH Act, are considered job-related and consistent with business necessity.[330] Thus, compliance with the OSH Act requirements should not be violative of the ADA. However, if the scope of employee examinations goes beyond the areas required by OSHA and its regulations, broader constraints will apply, and employer actions may be subject to challenge.[331]

---

[324] 29 U.S.C. §657(b).
[325] *See* 29 C.F.R. Part 1910 (2003).
[326] 42 U.S.C. §12112(d)(4).
[327] *Id.* §§12112(d)(3)(B), (d)(4)(c).
[328] *Id.* §12112(d)(4).
[329] *Id.* §12111(8).
[330] 56 Fed. Reg. 35,751 (July 26, 1991).
[331] *See generally* EEOC Enforcement Guidance,"Pre-Employment Disability-Related Questions and Medical Examinations" (Oct. 10, 1995).

3. Abatement Requirements

Under the OSH Act, an employer may be cited for "failure to abate" or "failure to correct" a previously cited violation.[332] Additionally, an employer may be cited for failure to comply with any abatement requirements set forth in the regulations.[333] Various abatement requirements may raise issues of conflict with the requirements of the ADA.

By way of illustration, OSHA has taken the position in connection with citations for ergonomics hazards that an employer with such cited hazards may not simply permit employees with symptoms of allegedly related musculoskeletal disorder to continue performing the job that OSHA believes are contributors to those problems.[334] Among the abatement steps that OSHA has repeatedly advanced in individual enforcement cases is the removal of relevant employees from positions where exposure may occur.[335] Under the ADA, however, it is possible that such a condition could be considered a disability, raising discrimination and reasonable accommodation concerns.[336] Employers who fear being "whipsawed" between two competing schemes have been heartened by any number of rulings that have found certain conditions linked to OSHA's ergonomics focus, such as carpal tunnel syndrome, to be outside the category of disabilities protected under the ADA.[337] In this regard, the EEOC and private litigants have pursued discrimination allegations against companies that utilized or relied on nerve

---

[332] 29 U.S.C. §658(a).

[333] *Id.* §666.

[334] OSHA Corporate Wide Settlement Agreement with United Biscuits, Ltd., OSHR Docket No. 89-2807 (Apr. 26, 1990), *available at* www.osha-slc.gov.

[335] *Id.*

[336] *See, e.g.,* Cravens v. Blue Cross & Blue Shield of Kansas City, 214 F.3d 1011, 10 AD Cases 1057 (8th Cir. 2000) (claims adjuster, discharged after diagnosed with carpal tunnel syndrome kept her from working on keyboard job, permitted to proceed with disability discrimination lawsuit).

[337] *See, e.g.,* Gelabert-Ladenheim v. American Airlines, Inc., 252 F.3d 54, 11 AD Cases 1581 (1st Cir. 2001); Browning v. Liberty Mut. Ins. Co., 178 F.3d 1043, 9 AD Cases 730 (8th Cir.), *cert. denied,* 528 U.S. 1050 (1999); Gutridge v. Clure, 153 F.3d 898, 8 AD Cases 705 (8th Cir. 1998), *cert. denied sub nom.* Gutridge v. Midland Computer, Inc., 526 U.S. 1113 (1999). *See also* Dunn v. Lear Seating Corp., 12 AD Cases 990 (W.D. Ky. 2001).

testing to uncover susceptibility to carpal tunnel syndrome, but without notable success up to this point.[338]

Another example of current OSHA concerns that arguably could impact ADA considerations relates to workplace violence and its prevention, a subject that OSHA has approached under the OSH Act's General Duty Clause.[339] OSHA has issued citations (and targeted guidance documents focused on specific industry sectors) in some circumstances in which the employer allegedly had knowledge of an employee's exposure to persons with violent tendencies, yet failed to adequately protect its employees.[340] A Chicago psychiatric hospital settled such a citation because its employees were routinely exposed to patients with violent propensities. One of the abatement requirements was for the hospital to establish a "do not admit" list of violent offenders.[341] Logically, this could be extended to employers who continue to employ those individuals with a propensity for violence. However, a coworker with a propensity for violence could require accommodation under the ADA if the employee suffered from a mental disability.[342] Although all of the applicable defenses discussed above could be asserted by an employer in such a situation, the application of the direct-threat defense as well as safety requirements of other federal agencies may be more ambiguous in such settings.

C. State Medical and Safety Requirements

State medical and safety requirements are commonplace and constitute a significant body of the regulation in the form

---

[338] *See, e.g.*, EEOC v. Woodbridge Corp., 263 F.3d 812, 12 AD Cases 254 (8th Cir. 2001); EEOC v. Cambridge Indus., Inc., 10 AD Cases 1747 (N.D. Ill. 2000); EEOC v. Rockwell Int'l Corp., 60 F. Supp. 2d 791, 9 AD Cases 1092 (N.D. Ill. 1999).

[339] 29 U.S.C. §654(a)(1).

[340] 23 OSH Cases 646 (1993). *See also* Howard-Martin & Howard, *How OSHA's Response to Workplace Violence Will Affect Health Care Facilities*, 11 HEALTH SPAN 21 (1994) (discussing OSHA's handling of Charter Barclay Hospital).

[341] *Id.*

[342] *See* Palmer v. Circuit Court of Cook County, Ill., 117 F.3d 351, 6 AD Cases 1569 (7th Cir. 1997), *cert. denied*, 522 U.S. 1096 (1998) (employee who threatens coworkers with threats of violence and death is not "qualified" employee under ADA); Hardy v. Sears, Roebuck & Co., 1996 WL 735565 (N.D. Ga. Aug. 28, 1996)

of licensing, health-related laws, and other "state plan" requirements that exceed or differ from those promulgated by the federal agency. The EEOC regulations that provide a defense when the requirements of the ADA conflict with other federal laws do not explicitly apply to state laws.[343] However, the EEOC has issued a statement that employers may comply with state laws and requirements to the extent they are not inconsistent with the ADA.[344] Nevertheless, there are no definitive safe harbors where a conflict arises between the ADA and state laws that are designed to further safety or health interests in the workplace.

V. THE NATIONAL LABOR RELATIONS ACT

While the ADA is a significant piece of civil rights legislation that promotes employment opportunities for millions of individuals, it raises potential conflicts with the National Labor Relations Act (NLRA),[345] which promotes the rights of employees to deal collectively with their employer. The conflicts are greatest in a unionized setting and fall in roughly three areas: (1) the requirements of the ADA to meet informally with a potentially disabled employee in contrast to the restrictions against direct dealing under the NLRA, (2) the duty to make a reasonable accommodation to a disabled employee in contrast to an employer's collective bargaining agreement and other employer bargaining obligations, and (3) the duty to maintain confidentiality of the employee's medical condition under the ADA in contrast to the employer's duty to provide relevant information to the union. It also should be noted that the ADA requirements also may impact the union's duty of fair representation.

(bipolar disorder with manic episodes of hostile and threatening behavior regarded as mental impairment under ADA).

[343] 29 C.F.R. §1630.15(e) (2003).

[344] 29 C.F.R. pt. 1630, app. §1630.1(b) & (c).

[345] 29 U.S.C. §151 et seq.

A. How the ADA and the NLRA Interrelate

Title I of the ADA provides that "[n]o covered entity shall discriminate [in an employment setting] against a qualified individual with a disability because of the disability...."[346] It is important to note that both employers and unions are subject to the provisions of the ADA. Specifically, the ADA defines a "covered entity" as "an employer, employment agency, labor organization, or joint labor-management committee."[347]

The ADA lists seven actions that would constitute discrimination, two of which pose significant issues in a unionized setting: the failure to provide a reasonable accommodation, and contractual discrimination. A covered entity discriminates by not making a reasonable accommodation to "the known physical or mental limitations of an otherwise qualified individual with a disability ... unless such covered entity can demonstrate that the accommodation would impose an undue hardship on the operation of the business of such covered entity...."[348] A covered entity also discriminates by "participating in a contractual or other arrangement or relationship that has the effect of subjecting a covered entity's qualified applicant or employee with a disability to the discrimination prohibited ... [by the ADA] (such relationship includes a relationship with ... [a] labor union ...)."[349]

The ADA also provides that all "information obtained regarding the medical condition or history of the applicant is collected and maintained on separate forms and in separate medical files and is treated as a confidential medical record...."[350] The confidentiality requirements were adopted in recognition of the privacy rights of disabled employees and to further the goals of the ADA to encourage employees to come forward to seek accommodation and other protections of the ADA.

---

[346] 42 U.S.C. §12112(a).
[347] Id. §12111(2).
[348] Id. §12112(b)(5)(A).
[349] Id. §12112(b)(2).
[350] Id. §12112(d)(3)(B).

B. Conflicts Between the ADA and the NLRA

1. The Implicit Duty to Meet Informally Versus the Prohibition Against Direct Dealing

The duty to provide a reasonable accommodation normally does not arise until there is a request for an accommodation. Under the ADA, an employer faced with such a request has a right and a duty to discuss the disability and all proposed accommodations with the employee or applicant. The legislative history and EEOC regulations adopted shortly after the enactment of the ADA emphasize the need for informal discussions between the employee and the employer. The regulations instructed that the process should be flexible and interactive and involve both the employer and the employee or applicant. In such communications, potential accommodations would be discussed and evaluated based on the particular disability of the employee or applicant.[351]

This duty of an employer under the ADA arguably conflicts with the mandates imposed on an employer under the NLRA to bargain in good faith with a labor organization that represents a majority of its employees.[352] The National Labor Relations Board (NLRB) has held that the duty to bargain collectively with the employees' collective representative is inconsistent with direct dealing with individual employees over terms and conditions of employment.[353] Therefore, an employer that deals directly with an employee over terms and conditions of employment without affording the union an opportunity to be involved in the bargaining might be alleged to violate the NLRA. Accordingly, an employer could be faced with an unfair labor practice charge filed under the NLRA if it "bargains" directly with the disabled employee to explore potential reasonable accommodations for the employee's disability. Alternatively, if the employer invites and permits the union to be

---

[351] 29 C.F.R. §1630.2(o)(3) (2003); *see also* H.R. Rep. No. 101-485, pt. 2, at 66 (1990), *reprinted in* 1990 U.S.C.C.A.N. 303, 348.

[352] 29 U.S.C. §158(a)(5).

[353] General Elec. Co., 150 NLRB 192, 194, 57 LRRM 1491 (1964), *enforced*, 418 F.2d 736, 72 LRRM 2530 (2d Cir. 1969), *cert. denied*, 397 U.S. 965 (1970).

present, the employer could be faced with a complaint from the EEOC alleging a failure to meet informally in violation of the ADA.

2. The Duty to Maintain Confidentiality Versus the Duty to Disclose

Permitting a union to be present in accommodation discussions with individual employees also could conflict with the duty of an employer to maintain the confidentiality of information submitted to the employer pursuant to the ADA. Under the NLRA, an employer's obligation to bargain in good faith with the employees' representative has been held to include an employer's obligation to provide to the collective bargaining representative relevant information necessary for the union to bargain on behalf of the employees it represents.[354] This not only includes information at the bargaining table when the parties are bargaining for a new collective bargaining contract, it includes information necessary for the union to enforce a contract and to process grievances.[355]

In 1993, the EEOC and the general counsel of the NLRB entered into a memorandum of understanding to seek guidance from their counterpart agencies in cases they were investigating that posed issues with potential conflicts between the ADA and the NLRA.[356] In 1996, the EEOC issued an opinion letter to the NLRB General Counsel's office pursuant to its request for the position of the EEOC on whether an employer can refuse to supply a union with requested medical information needed to process a grievance by raising a defense that it is prohibited from doing so under the ADA.[357]

---

[354] NLRB v. Truitt Mfg. Co., 351 U.S. 149, 38 LRRM 2042 (1956).

[355] NLRB v. Acme Indus. Co., 385 U.S. 432, 64 LRRM 2069 (1967).

[356] Memorandum of Understanding Between the General Counsel of the National Labor Relations Board and the Equal Employment Opportunity Commission (Nov. 16, 1993), *available at* www.eeoc.gov.

[357] Equal Employment Opportunity Commission Opinion Letter on ADA Confidentiality Requirements and Union Rights (Nov. 1, 1996) (http://www.eeoc.gov/policy/docs/nlrblet.html).

The case arose where an employer gave a vacant position to a disabled employee as a reasonable accommodation under the ADA despite the fact that another employee would have been entitled to the position under the seniority provisions of the collective bargaining contract.[358] The union processed the grievance of the employee that had been denied the position and argued that the selection violated the seniority provisions of the contract. In response to the employer's position that the assignment was made as a reasonable accommodation under the ADA, the union demanded to see the medical information to determine if it was in fact a reasonable accommodation and to weigh the respective rights of the employees it represented. The employer refused, contending the ADA required that the information remain confidential, and the union filed a charge with the NLRB.[359]

The EEOC noted that a union was a covered entity under the ADA and had an obligation to provide a reasonable accommodation under the ADA. The EEOC took the position that, based on this dual obligation of an employer and a union, where an employer sought to provide a reasonable accommodation pursuant to the ADA that would conflict with a collective bargaining agreement, and where no other reasonable accommodation exists, the union and the employer would have a joint obligation to bargain to provide a variance, so long as it would not impose an undue hardship.[360]

Although this approach envisions a role of a union in the accommodation process, it should be noted that the EEOC envisioned that the duty to supply information to the union where a conflict with a collective bargaining agreement existed, only arises when no other reasonable accommodation exists, and also that the duty imposed on both the union and the employer is to bargain to find a variance so long as it does not result in an undue hardship. The approach does not envision a union's role in the initial process of communications between

---

[358] *Id.*
[359] *Id.*
[360] *Id.*

an employer and an employee to determine if there is a reasonable accommodation, and it does not focus on the union's obligation to protect the rights and interests of other employees.[361]

3. The Duty to Reasonably Accommodate Versus the Duty to Bargain

The position expressed by the EEOC—that is, that the union and the employer have an obligation to bargain to seek a variance to a collective bargaining agreement that conflicts with an otherwise reasonable accommodation—assumes that a reasonable accommodation inconsistent with a collective bargaining agreement is required by the ADA when there is no undue hardship to other employees. This position has not been adopted by the courts and highlights the most significant conflict between the ADA and the NLRA.[362]

a. Collective Bargaining Agreement

The duty to bargain in good faith imposed by section 8(a)(5) of the NLRA prohibits unilateral action by employers in changing terms and conditions of employment of those employees represented by a union. In the absence of a collective bargaining agreement, such employers are obligated to give a union an opportunity to bargain over terms and conditions of employment and, if the union engages in such bargaining, the employer can implement changes in such terms and

---

[361]The House of Representatives highlighted the potential conflict between the ADA and the NLRA when it stated: "Conflicts between provisions of a collective bargaining agreement and an employer's duty to provide reasonable accommodations may be avoided by ensuring that agreements negotiated after the effective date of this title contain a provision permitting the employer to take all actions necessary to comply with this legislation." H.R. Rep. No. 101-485, pt. 2, at 63 (1990), *reprinted in* 1990 U.S.C.C.A.N. 303, 346.

[362]*See, e.g.,* Davis v. Florida Power & Light Co., 205 F.3d 1301, 10 AD Cases 492 (11th Cir. 2000) (stating that an employer is not required to grant accommodation that would conflict with seniority under collective bargaining agreement); *see also* Kralik v. Durbin, 130 F.3d 76, 7 AD Cases 1040 (3d Cir. 1997) (stating that requested accommodation is unreasonable if it would require employer to violate collective bargaining agreement).

conditions without the union's acquiescence only after bargaining to impasse with the union.[363] If there is a collective bargaining agreement, the employer cannot make any unilateral changes in the terms of the agreement without violating the NLRA.[364] The employer could request a change in the terms of a collective bargaining agreement, but traditionally a union would have no obligation to discuss such changes.[365] Accordingly, under traditional labor law principles as developed under the NLRA, an employer that unilaterally deviates from the terms of a collective bargaining agreement by making a reasonable accommodation to a qualified employee under the ADA, might be seen as violating the NLRA. If the employer sought to bargain with the union over such an accommodation, the union traditionally would have no obligation to discuss the matter.

(i) Seniority Provisions. These issues have surfaced in litigation in which attempts to make a reasonable accommodation allegedly have violated the seniority provisions of collective bargaining agreements. Specifically, the terms of the ADA implicated in these disputes are those that provide that a reasonable accommodation may include reassignment to a vacant position, part-time or modified work schedules, and job restructuring.[366] Such conduct is often directly affected by seniority provisions in collective bargaining agreements. The ADA is silent on the affect that a collective bargaining agreement would have on such reasonable accommodations. However, as noted above, the ADA prohibits discrimination by agreement between a union and an employer where such discrimination would otherwise be unlawful.[367] Furthermore, the House of Representatives Report on the ADA stated that "a collective bargaining agreement could be relevant . . . in determining

---

[363] NLRB v. Katz, 369 U.S. 736, 50 LRRM 2177 (1962); Schmidt-Tiago Constr. Co., 286 NLRB 342, 127 LRRM 1246 (1987).

[364] *Katz,* 369 U.S. 736.

[365] Bricklayers Local 17 (Ruhm Tile & Marble), 278 NLRB 924, 121 LRRM 1347 (1986).

[366] 42 U.S.C. §12111(9)(B).

[367] 42 U.S.C. §12112(b)(2).

whether a given accommodation is reasonable," but that "the agreement would not be determinative on the issue."[368]

(ii) Rehabilitation Act of 1973. Courts have reviewed case law under the Rehabilitation Act of 1973 for guidance in interpreting the ADA on this issue, however. The Rehabilitation Act of 1973 was the only federal law protecting employees with disabilities from workplace discrimination prior to the ADA. It was limited to employees of agencies of the federal government, federal contractors, and organizations receiving federal funding.[369] Its principles had a substantial effect on the development of the ADA, and Congress incorporated many provisions of the Rehabilitation Act into the ADA. Numerous courts of appeals held that the Rehabilitation Act did not require an employer to violate the terms of a collective bargaining agreement. They held that the seniority provisions of a collective bargaining agreement override the obligation to provide a reasonable accommodation under the Rehabilitation Act.[370]

(iii) Court Rulings. Following enactment of the ADA, a number of federal appellate courts concluded that such provisions trump the obligation to provide a reasonable accommodation under the ADA. They have adopted a per se rule that such accommodations are not reasonable when they violate a bona fide seniority provision of a collective bargaining agreement. A seniority provision is bona fide if it is not adopted for the purpose of avoiding the provisions of the ADA.[371]

---

[368]H.R. Rep. No. 101-485, pt. 1, at 63 (1990), *reprinted in* 1990 U.S.C.C.A.N. 303, 345.

[369]29 U.S.C. §§791(b), 793(a), & 794(a).

[370]Shea v. Tisch, 870 F.2d 786, 1 AD Cases 1461 (1st Cir. 1989); Carter v. Tisch, 822 F.2d 465, 1 AD Cases 1114 (4th Cir. 1987); Daubert v. U.S. Postal Serv., 733 F.2d 1367, 1 AD Cases 597 (10th Cir. 1984).

[371]Eckles v Consolidated Rail Corp., 94 F.3d 1041, 5 AD Cases 1367 (7th Cir. 1996); Kralik v. Durbin, 130 F.3d 76, 7 AD Cases 1040 (3d Cir. 1997); Foreman v. Babcock & Wilcox Co., 117 F.3d 800, 7 AD Cases 331 (5th Cir. 1997), *cert. denied*, 522 U.S. 1115 (1998); Benson v. Northwest Airlines, Inc., 62 F.3d 1108, 4 AD Cases 1234 (8th Cir. 1995); Davis v. Florida Power & Light Co., 205 F.3d 1301, 1307, 10 AD Cases 492 (11th Cir.), *cert. denied*, 531 U.S. 927 (2000); Feliciano v. Rhode Island, 160 F.3d 780, 787, 8 AD Cases 1520 (1st Cir. 1998); Cassidy v. Detroit Edison Co., 138 F.3d 629, 634, 8 AD Cases 326 (6th Cir. 1998). The U.S. Court of Appeals for the Ninth Circuit reached the same result in *Willis v. Pacific Maritime Ass'n*, 162 F.3d 561, 8 AD Cases 1632 (9th Cir. 1998). With respect to the impact of seniority

Because of these views, courts do not proceed to "balance" any rights of employees to determine reasonableness and do not even reach the defense of undue hardship. It should be noted that even if a court finds that the seniority provision would not necessarily "trump" an accommodation, the seniority provision could possibly be relevant to determine the reasonableness of the accommodation based on the legislative history noted above. Furthermore, the EEOC suggests that a collective bargaining agreement may be relevant in determining whether an otherwise reasonable accommodation would create an "undue hardship."[372]

(iv) Arbitration. Arbitration decisions have not been uniform on the issue. In *In re City of Dearborn Heights, Michigan*,[373] the arbitrator upheld an employer's accommodation under the ADA of transferring an employee even though the transfer violated the terms of the seniority provision of the collective bargaining agreement. The arbitrator found that the accommodation was the only one possible and outweighed the inconvenience to the employees that were moved to other shifts to accommodate the transfer.

In *In re Clark County, Ohio, Sheriff's Dep't*,[374] the arbitrator found that the employer's attempted accommodation through a transfer of the disabled employee was inconsistent with the seniority provisions of the collective bargaining agreement, but held that the employer violated the agreement by ignoring the agreement without first bargaining over the issue with the union. The arbitrator indicated that it could have implemented the change, even in the face of the agreement, if it reached an impasse in negotiations with the union over the change.

In *In re Olin Corp.*,[375] the arbitrator found that employer violated the collective bargaining agreement by instituting an

---

systems on duties of reasonable accommodation, see Barnett v. U.S. Air, Inc., 535 U.S. 391, 12 AD Cases 1729 (2002) (did not involve collectively bargained seniority system).

[372] 29 C.F.R. pt. 1630, app. §1630.15(d) (2003).
[373] 101 LA 809 (Kanner, 1993).
[374] 102 LA 193 (Kindig, 1994).
[375] 103 LA 481 (Helburn, 1994).

ADA accommodation that was inconsistent with a seniority provision in the agreement. The arbitrator based the decision on the cases decided under the Rehabilitation Act of 1973.

C. Arbitration Issues Under the ADA

The arbitration decisions referenced above[376] involved grievances in which the union was advancing a position against the accommodation made by the employer under the ADA. Any final decision by an arbitrator in such circumstances may not resolve all issues between the participants, even if the collective bargaining agreements call for final and binding arbitration. The rights of employees under the ADA to proceed to redress rights under the provisions of the ADA are not precluded by the existence of a collective bargaining agreement covering such an employee, despite the provisions of the ADA that specifically encourage "alternative means of dispute resolution."[377] The conference report during final congressional consideration of the ADA indicates that an agreement to submit disputed issues to arbitration did "not preclude the affected person from seeking relief under the" provisions of the ADA.[378]

Courts have upheld enforceability of individual agreements to arbitrate statutory employment claims but have required a showing of specific indicia of a clear, knowing, and voluntary waiver of statutory rights on the part of the employee before they preclude redress to the courts. Courts have generally not found that union-negotiated agreements provide such a waiver. The U.S. Court of Appeals for the Eleventh Circuit, in *Brisentine v. Stone & Webster Engineering Corp.*,[379] recognized a substantial legal distinction between an individual's agreement to arbitrate statutory claims, with a waiver of statutory rights, from an arbitration clause in a collective bargaining agreement that attempts to waive statutory rights of employees.

---

[376] *See* section V.B.3.a.(4), "Arbitration," above.

[377] 42 U.S.C. §12212.

[378] H.R. Rep. No. 101-596 (1998), *reprinted in* 36 CONG. REC. H4582, 4606 (daily ed. July 12, 1990); H.R. Rep. No. 101-485, pt. 3, at 76–77 (1990), *reprinted in* 1990 U.S.C.C.A.N. 445, 449–50.

[379] 117 F.3d 519, 6 AD Cases 1878 (11th Cir. 1997).

The court ruled that a union cannot collectively waive the statutory rights of individual employees to bring most employment discrimination suits in federal court, including claims under the ADA.

The U.S. Court of Appeals for the Fourth Circuit reached a contrary result in *Austin v. Owens-Brockway Glass Container, Inc.*[380] This issue reached the Supreme Court in *Wright v. Universal Maritime Service*,[381] where the Court vacated a Fourth Circuit decision that held that an employee was required to arbitrate his ADA claim pursuant to an arbitration clause in a collective bargaining agreement. The Supreme Court held that the "very general" arbitration clause did not cover statutory claims. The Supreme Court, however, specifically declined to more broadly resolve the issue of whether a union specifically could waive an individual's right to address statutory discrimination claims through the courts.

The terms of the ADA also pose the potential that an arbitrator's award under a collective bargaining agreement could itself be a violation of the ADA. The ADA prohibits agreements between employers and unions that have the "effect of" subjecting disabled employees to discrimination that is otherwise unlawful under the ADA. In this regard, the general counsel of the NLRB issued an advice memo, in *Food & Commercial Workers Local 876 (The Kroger Co.)*,[382] on the issue of whether a union had violated its duty of fair representation by rejecting a proposed accommodation that would have violated the seniority provisions of the collective bargaining agreement. The general counsel determined that the union did not violate section 8(b)(1)(A) in this regard, noting that a union "may balance the rights of individual employees against the collective good."[383] However, the general counsel specifically left open the possibility that the union violated the ADA prohibition against contractual discrimination on the grounds that the

---

[380] 78 F.3d 875, 5 AD Cases 488 (4th Cir.), *cert. denied*, 519 U.S. 980 (1996).
[381] 525 U.S. 70, 8 AD Cases 1429 (1998).
[382] National Labor Relations Board Advice Memorandum, *Kroger Co.*, Case 7-CB-9518 (June 23, 1993) (available at www.nlrb.gov).
[383] *Id.*

seniority provision blocking the transfer had the effect of discriminating against the employee.

D. The Duty of Fair Representation

If the conduct of a union in refusing to process a grievance could constitute an "agreement" in violation of the ADA, the underlying collective bargaining agreement, or an arbitration award interpreting the collective bargaining agreement, could arguably be considered agreements in violation of the ADA.[384] However, it is unlikely that these issues will be addressed in those circuits that hold that collective bargaining agreements "trump" accommodations otherwise available under the ADA. There remains at least some possibility, however, that a member might seek to recover some form of judgment against the union in these or other ADA-related circumstances based on an allegation that its handling of his or her grievance or other element of the factual circumstances reflected a violation of the duty of fair representation.

As far back as the Supreme Court's landmark 1944 decision in *Steele v. Louisville & Nashville Railroad*,[385] it has been recognized that private-sector unions owe a duty of fair representation to individual members of the bargaining units they serve. This obligation is derived from both statutory provisions (under the NLRA and the Railway Labor Act)[386] as well as collective bargaining agreements that recognize the union's role as exclusive bargaining representative for employees in the unit. (Similar obligations have been found under state law and union contracts with respect to obligations to members owed by public-sector unions.)

The duty of fair representation requires labor organizations to process grievances in a fair manner, and to otherwise represent each unit employee without arbitrariness, discrimination, or hostility.[387] Although unions have a wide range of latitude in resolving disputes, including grievances, they face the

---

[384] 42 U.S.C. §12112(a), (b)(2).
[385] 323 U.S. 192, 15 LRRM 708 (1944).
[386] 45 U.S.C. §151 et seq.
[387] *See, e.g.*, Vaca v. Sipes, 386 U.S. 171, 64 LRRM 2369 (1967); Ford Motor Co. v. Huffman, 345 U.S. 330, 31 LRRM 2548 (1953).

possibility of liability to their members if they breach this responsibility. However, in many cases, this type of exposure can be avoided if the union provides a "legitimate and rational explanation" for its conduct.[388]

It is almost inherent in the union's role as representative of the bargaining unit as a whole and each employee that comprises that unit that differing perspectives regarding obligations and rights relating to accommodation may arise. They have the potential for placing the union in an uncomfortable position at best and in a defensive posture at worst if it is unable to reconcile fully all conflicting interests within its membership with respect to individual issues and cases. Nonetheless, certain labor organizations have concluded that embracing relevant responsibilities—for example, through the adoption of contract language recognizing and communicating all parties' obligations to refrain from unlawful discrimination (including that based on disability)—can be beneficial. Some unions have taken the further step of initiating awareness training for members and staff employees of the union with respect to disability discrimination issues.[389] As in other areas, avoiding actions in the role of representative that evidence or appear to reflect bad faith or hostility toward the member/grievant is frequently the critical factor in minimizing the union's exposure to liability in this area.

VI. ERISA AND THE ADA'S APPLICATION TO EMPLOYEE BENEFITS PLANS

Employee benefit plans, such as health insurance, prescription plans, and short- and long-term disability coverage, are main staples of most places of employment. In 1999, approximately 73.3 percent of working adults received some sort

---

[388] Air Line Pilots v. O'Neill, 499 U.S. 65, 136 LRRM 2721 (1991).
[389] See, e.g., Claude, Whitehead, *Enlisting Labor Union Participation to Ensure Expanded Employment Options—Vocational Rehabilitation and Competitive Employment*, American Rehabilitation, Spring 1991 (discussing American Federation of State,

of employment-related health benefit.[390] In fact, an employer's health care package is often promoted as a hiring incentive.[391] For individuals with disabilities, or those individuals who become disabled, an employer's health benefits take on added importance.

Most employees are unaware, however, of how tenuous the provision of health benefits can be. While the ADA prohibits discrimination "against a qualified individual with a disability because of the disability of such individual in regard to . . . employee compensation, . . . and other terms, conditions, and privileges of employment,"[392] the ADA does not necessarily prevent an employer from being discriminatory in the selection, reduction, or elimination of health benefits. The line between an employer's permissible selection/modification of health benefits and illegal disability-based discrimination is elusive at best. The purpose of this section is to better define that line by examining the laws governing employee health benefits, legislative intent, federal agency guidelines, and court opinions.

The federal law governing the provision of employer-provided health benefit plans is the Employee Retirement Income Security Act (ERISA).[393] ERISA was intended as a remedial statute to benefit both employers and employees. The statute's broad preemption provision permitting ERISA to "supersede any and all State laws insofar as they may now or hereafter relate to any employee benefit plan . . . ,"[394] was intended to protect employers from "conflicting and inconsistent state and

---

County, and Municipal Employees (AFSCME) resolution to establish disability advisory committees and to include disability training for union staff and officers).

[390] *Employment-Based Health Benefits: Trends and Outlook*, EBRI Issue Brief No. 233 (Employee Benfit Research Institute: Washington, D.C., May 2001).

[391] The Employee Benefit Research Institute found that in 2001, 77 percent of employees reported that the benefits package a prospective employer offers is very important in their decision to accept or reject the job offer. *Value of Benefits Constant in a Changing World: Findings From the 2001 EBRI/MGA Value of Benefits Survey*, (Employee Benefit Research Institute: Washington, D.C., Mar. 2002).

[392] 42 U.S.C. §12112(a).

[393] 29 U.S.C. §1001 et seq. For a further explanation of ERISA, see EMPLOYEE BENEFITS LAW (Sacher & Singer eds., BNA Books, 2d ed. 2000).

[394] 29 U.S.C. §1144.

local regulation" of employee benefit plans.[395] Employees benefit by having a statutory safeguard of their interests and promised benefits. For example, section 510 of ERISA provides that:

> It shall be unlawful for any person to discharge, fine, suspend, expel, discipline, or discriminate against a participant or beneficiary for exercising any right to which he is entitled under the provisions of an employee benefit plan, . . . or for the purpose of interfering with the attainment of any right to which such participant may become entitled under the plan. . . .[396]

This provision, however, protects only employer actions that specifically intend to deprive employees of their benefits.[397] Therefore, if an employer reduces coverage for cancer treatment, an employee afflicted with cancer may not necessarily be able to invoke the protections of section 510, because this benefit modification presumably affects *all* employees who have or one day may have this disease. The employee would have to prove that reducing these benefits was done with the *intention* of depriving the one individual of his or her rights. This is a difficult hurdle, as "employers rarely, if ever, memorialize their specific intent to act unlawfully."[398] Therefore, individuals with disabilities may find ERISA's health benefit protection lacking.

Moreover, employee health plans lack an important ERISA safeguard afforded to employee pension plans—vesting requirements. Welfare benefit plans—which include health plans—were specifically exempted from ERISA's vesting requirements.[399] Employers, therefore, have more liberty to modify or eliminate health benefits than is the case with pension benefits. Thus, the health benefits protections provided by ERISA often are limited in nature and scope.

---

[395] *See* Scott v. Gulf Oil Corp., 754 F.2d 1499, 1501 (9th Cir. 1985) (citing Shaw v. Delta Air Lines, Inc., 463 U.S. 85, 4 EB Cases 1593 (1983)).

[396] 29 U.S.C. §1140.

[397] *See* Conkwright v. Westinghouse Elec. Corp., 933 F.2d 231, 239, 13 EB Cases 2202 (4th Cir. 1991); Simmons v. Wilcox, 911 F.2d 1077, 1082 (5th Cir. 1990); Dister v. Continental Group, Inc., 859 F.2d 1108, 111–13, 10 EB Cases 1169 (2d Cir. 1988); Gavalik v. Continental Can Co., 812 F.2d 834, 851, 8 EB Cases 1047 (3d Cir.), *cert. denied*, 484 U.S. 979 (1987).

[398] *Conkwright*, 933 F.3d at 238.

[399] 29 U.S.C. §1051(1).

A. ADA Section 501(c)

The ADA fills in some of the benefit protection gaps ERISA leaves open. Although the regulation of an employer's benefit plan is ordinarily ERISA's domain, the ADA extended its reach to preclude some types of discrimination relating to the provision of these plans. However, what constitutes disability-based discrimination in the provision of employee benefit plans is not always clear and remains subject to intense debate.[400]

The ADA aims to prohibit discrimination against qualified disabled employees with regard to "employee compensation, ... and other terms, conditions, and privileges of employment."[401] With respect to employee benefits, section 501(c)[402] of the ADA contains "safe harbor" language that specifically addresses the ADA's impact on insurance.

Generally, under the ADA, a person with a disability cannot be denied insurance or be subject to different terms or conditions of insurance based on disability alone, if the disability does not impose increased actuarial risks. However, the ADA does not prevent an employer or insurance provider from classifying risks, or otherwise drafting benefit plans that may adversely affect individuals with disabilities.[403]

Section 501(c) specifically states that the ADA's general goal of eliminating discrimination against individuals with disabilities, reflected in Titles I through IV, should *not* be construed to prevent insurers and plan sponsors from underwriting, classifying, or administering risks, or prevent organizations from sponsoring or administering bona fide benefit plans, as long as the means used are in compliance with existing law.[404] Additionally, section 501(c) emphasizes that the ADA should not

---

[400] *See, e.g.,* "Sharing the Risk and Ensuring Independence: A Disability Perspective on Access to Health Insurance and Health-Related Services," National Council on Disability (Mar. 4, 2003).

[401] 42 U.S.C. §12112(a).

[402] 42 U.S.C. §12201(c).

[403] *Id.*

[404] Section 501(c) states that the ADA shall not be construed to prohibit or restrict—

(1) an insurer, hospital or medical service company, health maintenance

be construed to subject insurance plans to state law if they are currently exempt under ERISA.[405] In essence, section 501(c) sanctions certain types of insurance-related practices that ordinarily would be deemed discriminatory against individuals with disabilities. However, insurance providers and employers do not have free reign in modifying benefit plans. The subsection of section 501(c) clarifies that this safe harbor provision may "not be used as a subterfuge to evade the purposes of title I and III" of the ADA.[406] Of course, what constitutes "subterfuge" is another subject for debate, and will be discussed below.[407]

1. *Historical Background/Legislative History*[408]

The decision to include section 501(c) in the ADA was not made lightly. The House[409] and Senate[410] reports accompanying the ADA indicate that the ADA was not intended to affect the way the insurance industry operated, or impact the regulatory structure for self-insured employers by disrupting underwriting practices. Section 501(c) codifies this intent. Indeed, without this provision, Title I's broad nondiscrimination standards

---

organization, or any agent, or entity that administers benefits plans, or similar organizations from underwriting risks, classifying risks, or administering such risks that are based on or not inconsistent with State law; or

(2) a person or organization covered by this Act from establishing, sponsoring, observing or administering the terms of a bona fide benefits plan that are based on underwriting risks, classifying risks, or administering such risks that are based on or not inconsistent with State law; or

(3) a person or organization covered by this chapter from establishing, sponsoring, observing or administering the terms of a bona fide benefit plan that is not subject to State laws that regulate insurance.

[405] *Id.*

[406] Title I of the ADA prohibits discrimination against a qualified individual with a disability in the employment arena; title III of the ADA applies to public accommodations and commercial facilities.

[407] See section VI.A.2., "No Subterfuge," below.

[408] For a more complete discussion of the ADA's legislative history, see Chapter 3, "Legislative History of the Americans With Disabilities Act."

[409] *See* H.R. Rep. No. 101-485, pt. 1, at 45 (1990), *reprinted in* 1990 U.S.C.C.A.N. 267, 289; H.R. Rep. No. 101-485, pt. 2, at 59, 136–38 (1990), *reprinted in* 1990 U.S.C.C.A.N. 303, 341, 419–21; H.R. Rep. No. 101-485, pt. 3, at 37–38, 70–71 (1990), *reprinted in* 1990 U.S.C.C.A.N. 445, 459–61, 493–94; H.R. Rep. No. 101-485, pt. 4, at 70 (1990); H.R. Rep. No. 101-596, at 84, 85 (1990).

[410] S. Rep. No. 101-116, at 29, 84–86 (1989).

could be found to permit both disparate treatment and disparate impact challenges to health-related distinctions in employee health benefit plans that allegedly discriminate on the basis of disability. Recognizing the substantial impact that the ADA would have in the workplace and throughout society, Congress essentially chose to moderate its effects in the area of employee benefits by insulating longstanding accepted practices.

The congressional reports also note that employee benefit plans should not be deemed in violation of the ADA under disparate impact analysis merely because they do not address the unique needs of each disabled individual, for example, the need for additional sick leave or medical coverage. The FMLA[411] provided some degree of leave protection for the serious health conditions of eligible employees, among other circumstances, when it was enacted in 1993.

Specifically, section 501(c)(1) makes it clear that insurers may continue to sell to and underwrite individuals applying for life, health, or other insurance on an individually underwritten basis, or to service such insurance products, so long as the standards used are based on sound actuarial data and not on speculation.[412] This section also recognizes the need for employers, and their agents, to establish and observe the terms of employee benefits plans, so long as these plans are based on legitimate underwriting or classification of risks.[413]

Finally, section 501(c)(3) provides that persons or organizations covered by the ADA may continue to establish, sponsor, observe, or administer "the terms of a bona fide benefit plan that is not subject to State laws that regulate insurance." Section 501(c)(3) is designed to clarify that self-insurance plans, which are currently governed by the preemption provision of ERISA are still governed by that preemption provision and are not subject to state insurance laws.

---

[411] *See* section I., "The Family and Medical Leave Act," above.

[412] REAMS, JR., MCGOVERN & SCHULTZ, DISABILITY LAW IN THE UNITED STATES: A LEGISLATIVE HISTORY OF THE AMERICANS WITH DISABILITY ACT OF 1990 PUBLIC LAW 101-335, Vol. I, 70–71 (William S. Hein & Co., 1992).

[413] *Id.*

a. Effect on ERISA's Preemption Provision

Concerns had been raised that section 501(c)(1) and (2) could be interpreted as affecting the preemption provision of ERISA. Committee reports state that such an implication was not intended; that is, "[u]ntil the preemption provision of ERISA is modified, these self-insured plans are subject to state law only to the extent determined by the courts in their interpretation of ERISA's preemption provision."[414]

b. Effect on Insurance Industry

Section 501(c) was not originally included in the first draft of the ADA.[415] The bills that were adopted did not mention how insurance would be treated and the broadly drafted employment discrimination prohibition in the ADA appeared to prohibit discriminatory employee benefit practices. In fact, soon after the ADA's introduction in 1989, the insurance industry began to express concerns that the definition section[416] could be interpreted as requiring major changes in the manner in which the insurance industry operates. For example, some might suggest that any differential treatment based on disability can and should be called into question. However, insurance, by its very nature, requires insurers to distinguish among a variety of risks. This results in classifications that differentiate between experimental and nonexperimental treatments, physical and mental/nervous disorders, inpatient and outpatient care, preexisting and after-acquired conditions, and specific diseases, conditions, and treatments, each with varying degrees of coverage.[417] Longstanding insurance practices, such as limits based on preexisting conditions, annual and lifetime caps, and limits on reimbursement of medical treatments and procedures, tend to have a disparate impact on individuals with disabilities, and might therefore have violated the ADA. The

---

[414] *Id.*

[415] *See* 135 CONG. REC. 8509–8513 (1989).

[416] 42 U.S.C. §12112.

[417] Farber, *Note, Subterfuge: Do Coverage Limitations and Exclusions in Employer-Provided Health Care Plans Violate the Americans with Disabilities Act?*, 69 N.Y.U. L. REV. 850 (Oct–Nov. 1994).

industry therefore sought clarification.[418] Without such a clarification, the ADA could arguably find violative of its provisions any action taken by an insurer or employer that treated disabled persons differently under an insurance or benefit plan because they represented an increased hazard of death or illness.

During joint hearings before the Subcommittees on Select Education and Employment Opportunities of the House Committee on Education and Labor in July 1989, the need for clarification of the ADA's impact on insurance was addressed.[419] Congressional ADA sponsors brokered a compromise in consultation with representatives of the insurance industry and the disability community.[420] This compromise resulted in the first two provisions of what became section 501(c), the clauses stating that insurers and plan sponsors would not be proscribed from continuing accepted underwriting practices that were in compliance with existing law and based on legitimate actuarial data or real experience. These clauses were included in the substitute bill passed by the Senate Labor and Human Resources Committee in August 1989. A third clause, clarifying that the ADA does not interfere with ERISA exemption from state law, was negotiated and drafted the day prior to Senate consideration of the ADA; the language was adopted as a technical amendment by the Senate during passage.[421]

2. *No Subterfuge*

The language regarding continued use of bona fide actuarial data and practices and proscribing the use of underwriting

---

[418] Many of the insurance companies expressing concern were based in Iowa, the state of Sen. Tom Harkin, a chief ADA sponsor.

[419] *The Americans with Disabilities Act, 1989: Joint Hearing on H.R. 2273 Before the Subcomm. on Select Education and Employment Opportunities of the House Comm. on Education and Labor,* 101st Cong., 1st Sess. 110 (1989).

[420] Letter from Leadership Conference on Civil Rights, to The Honorable Major R. Owens, Chairperson, Subcommittee on Select Education, Committee on Education and Labor (Sept. 11, 1989) (on file with author); STAFF OF HOUSE COMM. ON EDUCATION AND LABOR, 101st CONG., 2D SESS., Letter from American Civil Liberties Union to The Honorable F. James Sensenbrenner (Comm. Print 1990). Although the insurance industry helped draft the actual language of §501(c), no hearings were held on the insurance issue, and the legislative history does not document the initial development of the language. *See Farber,* 69 N.Y.U. L. REV. at 863.

[421] 135 CONG. REC. 19,830 (1989).

as a subterfuge to evade the ADA was the focus of intense negotiations. The goal was a compromise that would allow the continued use of existing insurance practices but prohibit discrimination targeted at the disabled based on prejudice or animus. Section 501(c) seemed to accomplish this goal, as the insurance industry retained the ability to engage in differential treatment based on real data or experience, while disability advocates gained at least some assurance that the disabled could not be singled out for adverse insurance treatment. Incidentally, the House and Senate reports note that the term "subterfuge" is to be construed broadly and not as requiring malicious intent. The ADA drafters explicitly rejected the narrower use of the term articulated by the Supreme Court in *Public Employees Retirement System of Ohio v. Betts*.[422] In this case, the Supreme Court held that the term "subterfuge" means " 'a scheme, plan, stratagem, or artifice of evasion.' "[423] Stated differently, subterfuge implies a specific intent to evade. The significance of this term would make itself apparent in future discrimination lawsuits, in which an employer's motive in altering or discontinuing a benefit plan would become a decisive issue. At this point in the legislative process, however, the official interpretation of "subterfuge" was far from settled.

Another interesting feature of the ADA is that does not contain a blanket exception for insurance plans adopted prior to its enactment. Thus, an employer cannot deny a qualified applicant a job because the employer's current insurance plan does not cover the person's disability or because of an anticipated increase in the costs of the insurance.[424]

3. Permitted Limitations

The intent to require equal access to health coverage for the disabled is clarified in discussions of Title I of the ADA in the same congressional reports, which state that limitations

---

[422] 492 U.S. 158, 11 EB Cases 1049 (1989).
[423] *Id.* at 167 (quoting United Air Lines v. McMann, 434 U.S. 192, 203, 1 EB Cases 1556, 1561 (1977)).
[424] *See id.*

can be placed on benefits as long as the limitations are applied equally to persons with or without disabilities. To illustrate what is meant by this intent, the reports provide that a limitation can "be placed on reimbursements for a procedure [and on] the types of drugs or procedures covered, e.g., a limit on the number of x-rays or the non-coverage of experimental drugs or procedures" would be allowed, but that limitation had "to apply to persons with or without disabilities."[425]

Additionally, differential treatment of those with disabilities is permissible under the ADA as long as legitimate actuarial data and practices are used and they are not used simply to evade the purposes of the ADA. "For example, a blind person may not be denied coverage based on blindness independent of actuarial risk classification."[426]

The legislative history on this section also explains that the ADA is not intended to prohibit health insurance exclusions for preexisting conditions. Thus, employers can continue to offer policies that contain preexisting condition exclusions, even though such exclusions adversely affect persons with disabilities, so long as such clauses are not used as a subterfuge to evade the purposes of the Act.[427] However, such exclusions were subsequently addressed in the 1996 Health Insurance Portability and Accountability Act (HIPAA).[428] HIPAA placed certain limitations on an employer's or insurer's ability to use preexisting condition exclusions or limitations in their benefit plans.[429]

---

[425]S. Rep. No. 101-116, at 29 (1989); H.R. Rep. No. 101-485, pt. 2, at 59 (1990), *reprinted in* 1990 U.S.C.C.A.N., 303, 341.

[426]S. Rep. No. 101-116, at 84–86 (1989); H.R. Rep. No. 101-485, pt. 2, at 136–38 (1990), *reprinted in* 1990 U.S.C.C.A.N. 303, 419–21.

[427]H.R. Rep. No. 101-485, pt. 3, at 37–38 (1990), *reprinted in* 1990 U.S.C.C.A.N. 445, 460–461.

[428]Pub. L. No. 104-191, 110 Stat. 1936 (1996) (codified at 42 U.S.C. §300gg and 29 U.S.C. §1181 et seq.).

[429]Under HIPAA, a group health plan can apply a preexisting condition exclusion for no more than 12 months (18 months for a late enrollee) after an enrollment date. The preexisting condition exclusion period must be reduced by an individual's prior creditable coverage. Additionally, no preexisting condition limitation may be applied to an individual who was continuously covered for 12 months or more under the prior employer's health plan.

Another portion of the ADA's legislative history articulates that employers cannot "deny health insurance coverage completely to an individual based on the person's diagnosis or disability."[430] As an example, the reports hold that although it is permissible to offer insurance policies that limit coverage for certain procedures or treatments—for example, only a specified amount per year for mental health coverage—a person who has a mental health condition may not be denied coverage for other conditions, such as for a broken leg or for heart surgery, because of the existence of the mental health condition.[431] Likewise, while

> it is permissible for an employer to offer insurance policies that limit coverage for certain procedures or treatments (e.g., a limit on the extent of kidneys dialysis or whether dialysis will be covered at all, or a limit on the amount of blood transfusions or whether transfusions will be covered), [it is not permissible] to deny coverage to individuals, such as persons with kidney disease or hemophilia, who are affected by these limits on coverage for procedures or treatments, for other procedures or treatments connected with their disability.[432]

Despite this record of the ADA's legislative history with respect to the provision of health insurance, there remains confusion over what types of exclusions/limitations are deemed unlawful. The EEOC and various judicial circuits also have weighed in on this topic.

B. EEOC Guidance

In order to aid its investigators and attorneys in handling claims involving discrimination in employee benefits, the EEOC amended its *Compliance Manual*[433] to add a section that provided the commission's first comprehensive analysis of employee benefits issues under the myriad antidiscrimination

---

[430]S. Rep. No. 101-116, at 29 (1989); H.R. Rep. No. 101-485, pt. 2, at 59 (1990), *reprinted in* 1990 U.S.C.C.A.N. 303, 341.
[431]S. Rep. No. 101-116, at 29.
[432]H.R. Rep. No. 101-485, pt. 3, at 37–38 (1990), *reprinted in* 1990 U.S.C.C.A.N. 445, 460–461.
[433]EEOC Compliance Manual, §3, EEOC Notice No. 915.003 (Oct. 3, 2000) [hereinafter Compliance Manual].

laws, including the ADA. Despite the fact that they were drafted for internal use, these compliance guidelines are beneficial to anyone seeking guidance on the proper interpretation of an employer's obligations with respect to the provision of employee health and welfare benefit plans under the ADA, or the other antidiscrimination laws enforced by the EEOC. This section of the *Compliance Manual* is applicable to all employee benefit plans relating to "life and health insurance, long-term and short-term disability, severance, pension or other retirement benefits, and early retirement incentive plans" and separately covers these topics with respect to the ADA and other antidiscrimination laws.[434]

Notably, these guidelines superseded several previously issued EEOC policy documents relating to discrimination in the provision of employee benefits.[435] The guidelines did not, however, replace or supersede the *Interim Enforcement Guidance on the Application of the Americans with Disabilities Act of 1990 to Disability-Based Distinctions in Employer-Provided Health Insurance*.[436] Instead, the *Compliance Manual* section supplements the *Interim Enforcement Guidance*, providing more detailed information and analysis.[437]

---

[434]The other acts discussed in the COMPLIANCE MANUAL, *supra* note 433, are the Age Discrimination in Employment Act (ADEA), 29 U.S.C. §621 et seq.; Title VII of the Civil Rights Act of 1964, as amended, and the Equal Pay Act, 29 U.S.C. §206(d) (EPA). On August 20, 2001, the EEOC rescinded §IV(B) of the COMPLIANCE MANUAL chapter on Employee Benefits. This section dealt with the relationship between certain employer practices regarding the provision of retiree health benefits and the ADEA. In late 2003, the EEOC indicated that it was close to finalizing a final rule under the ADEA allowing employers to reduce or end benefits when a retiree becomes eligible for Medicare or comparable state benefits without violating the federal age discrimination statute. 68 Fed. Reg. 73,694 (Dec. 22, 2003). Portions of the COMPLIANCE MANUAL dealing with the relationship between employee benefits and the ADA remain in effect.

[435]Including, with respect to the ADA, the *Questions and Answers About Disability and Service Retirement Plans Under the ADA*, EEOC Notice No. 915.002 (May 11, 1995).

[436]EEOC Notice No. 915.002 (June 8, 1993) [hereinafter *Interim Enforcement Guidance*].

This COMPLIANCE MANUAL, *supra* note 433, section also does not replace or supersede any guidance with respect to the provision of employee benefits set forth in TITLE I TECHNICAL ASSISTANCE MANUAL, *supra* note 93. Instead, as with the *Interim Enforcement Guidance*, *supra* note 436, the COMPLIANCE MANUAL section merely supplements the guidance found in the TECHNICAL ASSISTANCE MANUAL.

[437]One point of distinction is that the *Interim Enforcement Guidance*, *supra* note 436, assesses an employer's obligations under the ADA with respect to health

With respect to the ADA, both the Compliance Manual and the *Interim Enforcement Guidance* were issued in furtherance of the commission's enforcement authority under 29 C.F.R. §1630.4 of the commission's regulations implementing the employment provisions of the ADA. In pertinent part, that provision makes it unlawful for an employer to discriminate on the basis of disability against a qualified individual with a disability in regard to "[f]ringe benefits available by virtue of employment, whether or not administered by the [employer]."[438] At the same time, however, both of these guidance tools also clarify the exceptions under the ADA permitting employers, in defined circumstances, to make certain disability-based distinctions in the provision of employee benefits. In particular, both the Compliance Manual section and the *Interim Enforcement Guidance* explain section 501(c) of the ADA, which, as discussed, permits employers to establish and/or observe the terms of a "bona fide" insured or self-insured health insurance plan that is based on "underwriting risks, classifying risks, or administering such risks that are—in the case of insured plans—based on or not inconsistent with State law," and that are not being used as a "subterfuge" to evade the purposes of the ADA.[439]

Under the framework established by the EEOC, there are essentially three levels of analysis in determining whether, under the ADA, an employer has unlawfully discriminated against

---

insurance plans only. In fact, the *Interim Enforcement Guidance* explicitly reserved the analysis of "other types of 'fringe benefits,' such as employer provided pension plans, life insurance, and disability insurance" to "future documents." *Id.* at §1. The COMPLIANCE MANUAL, *supra* note 433, represents the first of these future documents, by expanding its analysis to life and health insurance, long-term and short-term disability, severance, pension or other retirement benefits, and early retirement incentive plans.

[438] 29 C.F.R. §1630.4(f) (2003); *see also* 42 U.S.C. §12112(b)(2); 29 C.F.R. §1630.6(a) (2003) (prohibiting employers from indirectly discriminating on the basis of disability in the provision of health insurance by entering into or participating in a contractual or other arrangement or relationship that has the effect of discrimination against their own qualified applicants or employees with disabilities).

[439] 42 U.S.C. §12201(c); *see also* 29 C.F.R. §1630.16(f) (2003).

its employees in the provision of employee health and welfare benefits. Progression to each successive level of analysis is dependent on an affirmative response to the preceding analytical question.

1. Level 1: Are Benefits "Unequal"?

The first level of analysis seeks to determine whether, in fact, the employer has provided any benefits to a qualified employee with a disability that are *unequal* to the benefits provided to its employees generally. In order for benefits to be *equal*, the EEOC requires that "the same coverage . . . be provided, on the same terms, to all similarly situated employees."[440] The EEOC *Compliance Manual* further provides that benefits are *equal* when the coverage provided is the same with regard to "premiums, deductibles, caps on coverage, and waiting periods."[441] Conversely, the *Manual* provides as an example of *unequal* benefits a health insurance plan that has "a lifetime cap of $50,000 for the treatment of HIV/acquired immunodeficiency syndrome (AIDS), but a . . . lifetime cap of $2,000,000 for the treatment of all other medical conditions."[442] Under the multileveled analysis outlined by the EEOC, however, even assuming a plan does provide unequal benefits, the plan must be further scrutinized before determining that the plan is unlawfully discriminatory under the ADA.[443]

2. Level 2: Do the "Unequal" Benefits Arise from a "Disability-Based" Distinction?

After determining that an employer-sponsored health and welfare benefit plan *does* provide unequal benefits to disabled employees, the EEOC's second level of analysis asks whether the particular plan distinction resulting in unequal benefits is a "disability-based distinction" or if the distinction is merely

---

[440] COMPLIANCE MANUAL, *supra* note 433, at 627:0022.
[441] *Id.* at 627:0018.
[442] *Id.*
[443] *Id.* at 627:0018–627:0019.

"health-related" with an impact on persons with certain disabilities. The former leads to the final step of the analysis. The latter would result in an EEOC finding of no unlawful discrimination under the ADA.[444]

A "disability-based distinction" is a plan distinction that singles out either: (1) "a particular disability"; (2) "a discrete group of disabilities"; or (3) "disability in general," or singles out a procedure/treatment used exclusively or nearly exclusively for the treatment of a particular disability or a discrete group of disabilities.[445] Conversely, a "health-related distinction" is a "broad distinction which applies to a multitude of dissimilar conditions, *and* . . . constrains both individuals with and individuals without disabilities."[446] For instance, many health insurance plans distinguish between treatment for physical conditions, on the one hand, and mental/nervous conditions, on the other, by providing different levels of benefits for each.[447] Such a distinction is "health-related" but *not* "disability-based," because a distinction based on the broad category of mental/nervous conditions is applicable to a multitude of dissimilar conditions and would impact both individuals with disabilities (such as schizophrenia and major depression) and individuals without disabilities (such as individuals seeking grief or marital counseling).[448] Even though such a distinction may have a greater impact on certain individuals with disabilities (such as depression), it does not intentionally discriminate on the basis of disability and, therefore, is not "disability-based," but "health-related."[449] Health-related distinctions do not violate the ADA.

Using this same example, however, a plan that covers all physical and mental disorders except major depression is a

---

[444] *Id.*
[445] *Id.*
[446] *Id.*
[447] Usually a lower level of benefits for mental/nervous conditions. *See Interim Enforcement Guidance, supra* note 436, at 6.
[448] COMPLIANCE MANUAL, *supra* note 433, at 627:0023.
[449] Another common example of a "health-related" but *not* "disability-based" distinction is a long-term disability plan with "a 6-month waiting period for all pre-existing conditions." *Id.*

"disability-based" distinction, because it singles out a particular disability—major depression. Equally, a plan that requires employees who are no longer able to work because of a physical or mental disorder to retire on disability retirement, even if they are also eligible to retire under the employer's service retirement plan is also a disability-based distinction, because it singles out disability in general.[450] If a plan contains such a disability-based distinction, it violates the ADA *unless* the employer can show that the "disability-based" distinction is not a "subterfuge to evade the purposes of the ADA," in other words, that the distinction is justified.[451]

3. Level 3: Is the "Disability-Based" Distinction a "Subterfuge"?

This represents the final and most complex level of the EEOC analysis. In order to avoid liability under the ADA, under this step of the analysis, the employer would be required to demonstrate that: (1) "the benefit plan is *bona fide*"; *and* (2) "the plan is not a subterfuge to evade the purposes of the ADA," that is, is the distinction justified.[452] The easier element of this two-pronged burden of proof is demonstrating that the plan is bona fide. All that is necessary to demonstrate that an employee benefit plan is bona fide is to establish that the plan exists, the plan pays benefits, and that "the terms of the plan have been accurately communicated to eligible employees."[453] This can usually be accomplished simply by providing a copy of the plan documents and payment records.[454]

Establishing that a plan containing a disability-based distinction is not a subterfuge to evade the purposes of the ADA is a decidedly more difficult and complex matter. Nevertheless, the EEOC has defined several circumstances that, if proven,

---

[450] *Id.* at 627:0022. An example of a "disability-based" distinction that "singles out a discrete group of disabilities" is a health plan that "caps coverage for the treatment of cancers [i.e., a "discrete group of disabilities,"] at one million dollars, but caps coverage for the treatment of all other physical conditions at 20 million dollars." *Id.*

[451] *Id.*

[452] *Id.* at 627:0023.

[453] *Id.*; *see also Interim Enforcement Guidance, supra* note 436, at 11.

[454] COMPLIANCE MANUAL, *supra* note 433, at 627.0023.

will justify a disability-based distinction and relieve an employer of liability under the ADA. These circumstances include proof that:[455]

1. the employer is "not engaged in the disability-based disparate treatment alleged," because there is no "unequal treatment" of similar conditions; *or*
2. the disability-based distinction "is justified by legitimate actuarial data, or by actual or reasonably anticipated experience, and that conditions with comparable actuarial data and/or experience are treated" in the same fashion; *or*
3. the disability-based distinction "is necessary to maintain the solvency of the plan"; *or*
4. the disability-based distinction "is necessary to avoid unacceptable changes in the coverage of, or the premiums for, a benefit plan"; *or*
5. the particular treatment excluded from the "plan provides *no* medical benefit," based on "reliable scientific evidence" that the treatment does not cure, slow deterioration, alleviate symptoms, or maintain the current health status of those treated and the plan does not cover any other medical treatment which similarly provides no medical benefit.[456]

This list, however, is not exhaustive. Instead, each disability-based plan distinction must be assessed on a case-by-case basis, rendering this level of the analysis illustrative but, unlike the previous levels of analysis, not conclusive.[457]

a. Circumstance 1

While Circumstance 1 may seem to be an inquiry that was addressed at the first or second level of the analysis, there is a distinction being drawn here.[458] For example, under the first

---

[455] COMPLIANCE MANUAL, *supra* note 433, at 627:0023–0024; *see also Interim Enforcement Guidance, supra* note 426, at 12–15.

[456] COMPLIANCE MANUAL, *supra* note 433, at 627:0024; *see also Interim Enforcement Guidance, supra* note 426, at 14–15 n.17.

[457] COMPLIANCE MANUAL, *supra* note 433, at 627:0023; *see also Interim Enforcement Guidance, supra* note 426, at 12.

[458] COMPLIANCE MANUAL, *supra* note 433, at 627:0023.

two levels of the analysis, it may appear that an employee benefit plan provides benefits that are "unequal" with respect to persons with disabilities. It may further appear that this inequality is the result of a disability-based plan distinction. Nevertheless, at this level of the analysis, an employer may offer proof that these conclusions were improperly drawn based on the particular facts of a given case. For instance, a plan may be challenged for its failure to provide coverage for diabetes treatments while at the same time providing coverage for treatments relating to rheumatoid arthritis, a seemingly unequal benefit resulting from a disability-based distinction. However, the employer in such a circumstance could offer proof that the denial of coverage for the diabetes treatment was due to the fact that the diabetes was a preexisting condition under the terms of the policy, for which coverage is consistently denied for individuals both with and without disabilities. Such proof would relieve the employer of liability at this level of the analysis because, under the particular facts at issue, "there is no 'unequal treatment' of similar [pre-existing] conditions."[459]

b. Circumstance 2

In order to meet the necessary burden of proof for demonstrating that a disability-based plan distinction is "justified by legitimate actuarial data," Circumstance 2, an employer must show, by the use of specific and detailed factual data and actuarial assumptions, that the disability-based plan distinction resulting in unequal benefits is necessary "to account for an increased possibility that the benefit will be claimed or that the amounts required for coverage will be higher."[460] In other words, the employer must prove that the unequal benefits are the result of legitimate risk classifications and underwriting procedures associated with the disability, and not mere disparate treatment of the disability per se.[461] In particular, where the distinction is based on "actual or reasonably anticipated

---

[459] *Id.* at 627:0019–627:0020.
[460] *Id.* at 627:0024.
[461] "Legitimate risk classification and underwriting procedures" means that the assessment of the disability must be fact-based, including characteristics such as age, occupation, personal habits (i.e., smoking), and medical history, and not

experience," the employer must present proof of its insurance claims experience. In addition, the employer must demonstrate that there is consistency in its treatment of other conditions posing similar risks with similar associated costs.[462]

c. Circumstance 3

An employer also may avoid liability under the ADA for disability-based plan distinctions by proving that the distinction is "necessary to maintain the solvency of the plan."[463] In order to meet this burden of proof, an employer must demonstrate that providing equal coverage for the disability

- would require such substantial payments of benefits that it would threaten the fiscal soundness of the plan under commonly accepted or legally required standards, *and*
- that there is no non-disability-based plan change that could be made to the plan to limit those fiscal consequences.[464]

In demonstrating that there is no "non-disability-based change" that could achieve the desired result, the employer must offer proof of the nondisability-based options that were considered in reaching the conclusion that none were adequate to achieve fiscal soundness and the reasons for the inadequacy of each.[465]

Unfortunately, the terms "fiscal soundness" and "commonly accepted or legally required standards" have not been defined or delineated by example in either the *Compliance Manual* or the *Interim Enforcement Guidance*.[466] While it is reasonable to presume that, consistent with legal principles of construction, these terms will be given their ordinary meaning,

---

based on fears, stereotypes, or assumptions about the disability. *Id.; see also Interim Enforcement Guidance, supra* note 426, at 13 n.15.

[462] COMPLIANCE MANUAL, *supra* note 433, at 627:0024.
[463] *Id.*
[464] *Id.*
[465] *Id.*
[466] In fact, the COMPLIANCE MANUAL indicates that if an employer raises this defense, the investigator should contact the Office of the Legal Counsel. *Id.*

the uncertainty already inherent at this level of the analysis is amplified by this ambiguity and the predictability of results based on this standard is diminished.[467]

d. Circumstance 4

A disability-based plan distinction is equally justified and will not be deemed a subterfuge if the employer can demonstrate, as noted in Circumstance 4, that the distinction is "necessary to avoid unacceptable changes in the coverage of, or in the premiums for, a benefit plan."[468] Similar to Circumstance 3, "necessary" means that there is no "non-disability-based distinction" that could avoid the "unacceptable changes," and the same level of proof is required as outlined above.[469] By way of definition, the *EEOC Compliance Manual* instructs that an "unacceptable change" is a drastic increase in premium payments, copayments, or deductibles, or a drastic alteration to the scope of coverage or level of benefits provided that either:

1. "increase the cost to other employees so substantially that the benefit plan would be effectively unavailable to a significant number of them"; *or*
2. "make the benefit plan so unattractive as to result in significant adverse selection";[470] *or*

---

[467] *Compare* Section 501(c), 42 U.S.C. §12201 (providing that the ADA will not be construed to prohibit or restrict insurance companies or plan administrators from underwriting, classifying or administering benefit plans in a manner not barred by state law), *with* statements in the ADA's legislative history alluding to state law limitations on unfair discrimination among people of the same class and equal expectation of life. H.R. REP. 101-85, pt. 2 at 136, reprinted in 1990 U.S.C.C.A.N. at 419.

[468] COMPLIANCE MANUAL at 627:0020.

[469] *Id.; see also Interim Enforcement Guidance, supra* note 436, at 14.

[470] "Adverse selection" is defined as "the tendency of people who represent greater risks to apply for and/or retain a fringe benefit to a greater extent than people who represent average or below average risks. A benefit plan that is subjected to a significant rate of adverse selection may, as a result of the increase in the proportion of 'poor risk/high use' enrollees to 'good risk/low use' enrollees, become not viable or financially unsound." *Id.* at COMPLIANCE MANUAL, *supra* note 433 n.82; *see also Interim Enforcement Guidance, supra* note 436, at 14 n.16.

3. "make the plan so unattractive that the employer cannot compete in recruiting and maintaining qualified workers" in the community "due to the superiority of other" employers' plans.[471]

e. Circumstance 5

Finally, an employer may avoid liability by offering proof that the lack of coverage resulting in "unequal benefits" merely excludes a treatment that provides no medical benefit. This burden of proof is clear on its face. However, an employer should take note that it similarly must exclude coverage for any and all similar treatments equally lacking in medical benefits in order to successfully assert this defense.[472]

f. Summary

It is clear from both the *Compliance Manual* and the *Interim Enforcement Guidance* that if any of the foregoing circumstances are proven, an employer will be relieved of liability under the ADA for any "disability-based" distinction resulting in "unequal" plan benefits to disabled employees. Yet, it is equally clear that these are not the only circumstances that may relieve an employer of such liability, but it remains unclear what these other circumstances might be. Therefore, the EEOC's guidance, while instructive, does not offer the answer to all employee benefit questions with respect to disability law. Moreover, the EEOC's guidance does not necessarily represent the law in all jurisdictions.[473]

C. Recurring Questions

Despite the ADA's legislative history of section 501(c) and the EEOC's interpretive guidance, disability law with respect to employee benefits remains far from clear. Titles I, III, and section 501(c) of the ADA continue to raise legal questions.

---

[471] COMPLIANCE MANUAL, *supra* note 433; *see also Interim Enforcement Guidance, supra* note 436.

[472] *Id.*

[473] *See* O'Neal v. City of New Albany, 293 F.3d 998, 13 AD Cases 289 (7th Cir. 2002) (noting that EEOC guidance is not binding on the court).

1. Standing to Sue Under the ADA

Title I raises the question of whether, under certain circumstances, a disabled employee may bring a lawsuit under the ADA against an employer that unilaterally modifies/discontinues health or disability benefits. Title I specifically prohibits an employer from discriminating against an individual with disabilities through its relationship with "an organization providing fringe benefits to an employee."[474] However, in order to raise a claim under Title I, an individual must be a "qualified individual with a disability."[475] A disabled employee is "qualified" if he or she can perform the essential functions of the job with or without a reasonable accommodation.[476] Therefore, assuming an employee becomes permanently disabled to the extent he or she can no longer perform the major job functions with or without a reasonable accommodation, does the employee have the ability to sue over disability benefits under Title I? There is no firm answer to this question.

Employees who have filed for disability benefits claiming that they can no longer perform their everyday job functions have been precluded from bringing or prevailing in ADA lawsuits in one of two ways. First, some courts have found that disabled individuals who are no longer able to work are not protected under the ADA.[477] Second, the principle of judicial estoppel—or the preclusion of inconsistent positions—bars employees from claiming they are totally disabled and unable to work in one proceeding, then reversing course and claiming they are qualified individuals with disabilities for ADA purposes.[478]

---

[474] 42 U.S.C. §12112(b)(2).

[475] *Id.* §12111(5)(A).

[476] *Id.* §12111(8)–(9). For further information on what constitutes a qualified individual with a disability, see Chapter 5, §III.

[477] *See* Rogers v. International Marine Terminals, 87 F.3d 755, 5 AD Cases 1115 (5th Cir. 1996) (mechanic's absenteeism and inability to come to work for over 1 year resulted in his not being protected by the ADA); Waggoner v. Olin Corp, 169 F.3d 481, 9 AD Cases 88 (7th Cir. 1999) (in most cases, a disabled employee with erratic unexplained absences caused by the disability will not be protected under the ADA because attendance is a basic requirement of most jobs).

[478] *See* Reed v. Petroleum Helicopters, Inc., 218 F.3d 477, 10 AD Cases 1426 (5th Cir. 2000) (in an ADA action, summary judgment was proper because the

a. No Longer Covered Under the ADA

In order to prevail in an ADA lawsuit, the plaintiff must first establish a prima facie case of discrimination. The first element of a prima facie case in an ADA case is proving that the person raising the claim is, indeed, a qualified individual with a disability.[479] Under the ADA, a qualified individual with a disability is "an individual with a disability who satisfies the requisite skill, experience, education and other job-related requirements of the employment position such individual holds or desires, and who, with or without reasonable accommodation, can perform the essential functions of such position."[480] An employee who receives disability benefits because he or she has been rendered "totally disabled" may therefore be considered unqualified to perform the job's essential functions, and therefore unable to set forth a viable ADA claim.

The U.S. Courts of Appeals for the Seventh, Ninth, and Eleventh Circuits, as well as the U.S. District Court for the District of Columbia, have held that Title I of the ADA provides no protection to a totally disabled former employee because that person is no longer a qualified individual with a disability.[481] The U.S. Courts of Appeal for the Second and Third Circuits, however, have reached the opposite conclusion.[482]

---

employee was unable to reconcile statements made in the course of litigation of being able to work with reasonable accommodation and statements made to obtain total disability benefits); Pena v. Houston Lighting & Power Co., 154 F.3d 267, 8 AD Cases 961 (5th Cir. 1998) (claimant could not demonstrate that he was qualified individual with disability under ADA after having stated on disability benefits application that he could not perform his job with or without reasonable accommodations.)

[479] The ADA defines "disability" as: "(A) a physical or mental impairment that substantially limits one or more of the major life activities of [an] individual; (B) a record of such an impairment; or (C) being regarded as having such an impairment." 42 U.S.C. §12102(2); 29 C.F.R. §1630.2(g) (2003).

[480] 29 C.F.R. §1630.2(m) (2003).

[481] *See* Weyer v. Twentieth Century Fox Film Corp., 198 F.3d 1104, 10 AD Cases 65 (9th Cir. 2000); EEOC v. CNA Ins. Cos., 96 F.3d 1039, 1045, 5 AD Cases 1769 (7th Cir. 1996); Gonzales v. Garner Food Servs., Inc., 89 F.3d 1523, 1531, 5 AD Cases 1202 (11th Cir. 1996); Fennell v. Aetna Life Ins. Co., 37 F. Supp. 2d 40 (D.D.C. 1999).

[482] *See* Ford v. Schering-Plough Corp., 145 F.3d 601, 608, 8 AD Cases 190 (3d Cir. 1998), *cert. denied*, 525 U.S. 1093 (1999); Castellano v. City of New York, 142 F.3d 58, 68, 9 AD Cases 67 (2d Cir.), *cert. denied*, 525 U.S. 820 (1998).

These courts have held that that former employees who had earned fringe benfits while employed could bring a discrimination lawsuit under Title I of the ADA regarding post-employment benefits even if at the time of filing the suit the employees were completely disabled and no longer considered qualified individuals with disabilities. Therefore, where the ADA suit is brought could very well be dispositive of the issue.

b. Judicial Estoppel

The doctrine of judicial estoppel prevents an individual who successfully has asserted one position in a judicial proceeding from asserting an inconsistent position in another. In ADA cases, the doctrine of judicial estoppel has been invoked in situations where an employee represents that he or she is unable to work in order to receive disability benefits, then attempts to file a charge of disability discrimination if those benefits are perceived to violate the ADA. However, this principle usually applies only when the employee takes a position in an official judicial proceeding.[483] Claiming that one is disabled on an application for disability benefits, therefore, does not necessarily preclude the employee from filing a subsequent ADA claim.[484] It is unclear whether the same rule would apply if the employee first initiated an ADA claim in court, then reversed course and represented that he or she was "totally disabled" in order to receive disability benefits.

c. EEOC's Position

It is the EEOC's official position that "representations made in connection with an application for disability benefits should not be an automatic bar to an ADA claim."[485] One reason for asserting this position is that, according to the EEOC, there

---

[483] *See, e.g.,* Shell Oil Co. v. Trailer & Truck Repair Co., 828 F.2d 205, 209–10 (3d Cir. 1987); Smith v. Travelers Ins. Co., 438 F.2d 373, 377 (6th Cir.), *cert. denied,* 404 U.S. 832 (1971).

[484] *See, e.g.,* Marvello v. Chemical Bank, 923 F. Supp. 487, 491–92, 5 AD Cases 1400 (S.D.N.Y. 1996); Mohamed v. Marriott Int'l, 905 F. Supp. 141, 5 AD Cases 50 (S.D.N.Y. 1995).

[485] 1997 EEOC Notice, *supra* note 239, at 38.

are fundamental differences between the ADA and contractual disability benefits programs.

For example, the definition of disability under a disability benefit plan often deviates from that under the ADA. As discussed, the ADA's definition of "disability" requires a factfinder to focus on the employee's essential job tasks and whether the employee can complete these tasks with the aid of a reasonable accommodation. Such accommodations can include physical aids and flexible scheduling.[486]

In contrast, disability insurance plans may not always distinguish between the essential and marginal functions of the employee's position, and do not always consider whether an employee is able to perform the essential functions of the job with a reasonable accommodation. The eligibility requirements to receive disability benefits are usually spelled out in the insurance policy itself. Thus, the definition of disability for insurance purposes varies from policy to policy. Disability is often defined "as the incapacity to perform one or more duties of the insured's regular occupation."[487] Therefore, an individual may be "unable to work" under the terms of the insurance policy, but still could be able to perform the essential job tasks with reasonable accommodations, and thus be considered a qualified individual with a disability under the ADA.

Some courts have echoed the EEOC's position. In *D'Aprile v. Fleet Services Corp.*,[488] the U.S. Court of Appeals for the First Circuit reversed a lower court's grant of summary judgment for an employer where the plaintiff had applied for disability benefits after the employer denied her request to work part-time. The plaintiff's insurance policy defined a "totally disabled" individual as one "who is unable to perform the material duties of his/her job for the entire regularly scheduled work week as a result of illness or injury...."[489] The First Circuit found that the plaintiff's claim that she was unable to work

---

[486]42 U.S.C. §12111(9).
[487]1997 EEOC Notice, *supra* note 239.
[488]92 F.3d 1, 6 AD Cases 501 (1st Cir. 1996).
[489]*Id.* at 4–5, 6 AD Cases at 604.

without a flexible schedule was "entirely consistent with her claim to have been 'totally disabled' within the meaning of the policy."[490] Whether the plaintiff would have been physically able to work with an accommodation—which would render her a qualified individual with a disability under the ADA— was not relevant to her application for benefits.[491]

While some appellate courts disagreed with this approach, the Supreme Court enunciated a view in accord with this rationale in *Cleveland v. Policy Management Systems Corp.*[492] In that case, the Court held that the application for or receipt of Social Security disability benefits did not create a presumption that the employee was judicially estopped from later claiming that he or she is a qualified individual with a disability. While the plaintiff would have the burden of explaining any logical inconsistency between the two claims, he or she would not be barred from bringing both actions.

d. Disability-Based Risk Classifications

Title III of the ADA raises questions with respect to an employer or insurance provider's ability to make disability-based risk classifications in providing health or life insurance policies, or to discontinue such policies entirely. Title III— which prohibits public accommodations from discriminating on the basis of disability—is rife with textual ambiguity with respect to insurance.

Specifically, Title III prohibits discrimination on the "basis of disability in the full and equal enjoyment of the goods, services, facilities, privileges, advantages, or accommodations of any place of public accommodation . . . ."[493] Under the ADA,

---

[490] *Id.* at 5, 6 AD Cases at 604–05.

[491] *See also* Anzalone v. Allstate Ins. Co., 5 AD Cases 223 (E.D. La. 1995) (because definition of disability differs in insurance policy and ADA, plaintiff's receipt of disability benefits did not bar his ADA claim.); Ward v. Westvaco Corp., 859 F. Supp. 608, 615, 3 AD Cases 739 (D. Mass. 1994) (plaintiff allowed to demonstrate that he would have been able to perform job duties with reasonable accommodation for ADA purposes.).

[492] 526 U.S. 795, 9 AD Cases 491 (1999).

[493] 42 U.S.C. §12182(a).

a "public accommodation" is defined as a "private entity that owns, leases (or leases to), or operates a place of public accommodation."[494] Title III lists 12 categories of entities that constitute public accommodations, all of which describe physical locales.[495] One category of entities in this list includes: "a laundromat, dry-cleaner, bank, barber shop, beauty shop, travel service, shoe repair service, funeral parlor, gas station, office of an accountant or lawyer, pharmacy, *insurance office*, professional office of a health care provider, hospital, or other service establishment."[496]

Despite this comprehensive list of categories, what constitutes a "public accommodation" meriting ADA protection is still awaiting interpretation. Currently, there is a split among the judicial circuits on this very issue. The U.S. Courts of Appeal for the Third and Sixth Circuits have held that Title III mandates that individuals with disabilities be given access to physical structures only, such as insurance offices.[497] This interpretation sanctions disability-based risk classifications.

In contrast, the U.S. Courts of Appeal for the First and Second Circuits have interpreted the scope of Title III more broadly, holding that the ADA's prohibition on disability-based discrimination in the products and services of places of public accommodation may extend to insurance policies and underwriting practices, not just the insurance office itself.[498] In other words, these decisions hold that Title III requires that the disabled have access to the *substantive* terms of the policy. This interpretation could render certain disability-based risk classifications illegal.

---

[494] 28 C.F.R. §36.104 (2002).

[495] 42 U.S.C. §12181(7).

[496] *Id.* §12181(7)(F) (emphasis added).

[497] *See* Ford v. Schering-Plough Corp., 145 F.3d 601, 608, 8 AD Cases 190 (3d Cir. 1998), *cert. denied*, 525 U.S. 1093 (1999); Parker v. Metropolitan Life Ins. Co., 121 F.3d 1006, 1014, 6 AD Cases 1865 (6th Cir. 1997) (en banc), *cert. denied*, 522 U.S. 1084 (1998).

[498] *See* Pallozzi v. Allstate Life Ins. Co., 198 F.3d 28, 9 AD Cases 1697 (2d Cir. 1999), *amended on denial of reh'g*, 204 F.3d 392, 10 AD Cases 338 (2d Cir. 2000); Carparts Distribution Ctr., Inc. v. Automotive Wholesaler's Ass'n of New England, Inc., 37 F.3d 12, 19, 3 AD Cases 1237 (1st Cir. 1994).

Section 501(c) or the "safe harbor provision"—further complicates matters. As previously discussed, this section of the ADA addresses health benefit plans, and provides employers with some degree of flexibility in structuring health-benefits plans based on "underwriting risks, classifying risks, or administering . . . risks . . ." in accordance with state laws.[499] This section also reaffirms an employer's ability to provide health benefits under self-insured plans that do not implicate state insurance laws.[500] The caveat, of course, is that this safe harbor provision for employers may not be used as "subterfuge" to evade the antidiscrimination intent of the ADA.[501] Unfortunately, the term "subterfuge" is undefined. Therefore, while some have seized on the safe harbor provisions of the ADA to argue that Title III does not regulate the *terms* of the policies, as the provisions clearly sanction some types of risk-based classifications, others rely on the subterfuge qualification to argue the opposite.

The Supreme Court has defined "subterfuge" in the context of two Age Discrimination in Employment Act cases as having its "ordinary meaning as 'a scheme, plan, stratagem, or artifice of evasion.' "[502] This definition requires that the party specifically intends to evade the purpose of the statute in question. It is the EEOC's position, howver, that any benefit plan that includes disability-based distinctions is a subterfuge if those distinctions are not based on sound actuarial principles.[503] Thus, the EEOC takes the position that an intent to evade the ADA is not necessary.

In *EEOC v. Aramark Corp., Inc.*,[504] the U.S. Court of Appeals for the District of Columbia Circuit rejected the EEOC's interpretation of the term. In *Aramark*, a former employee filed

---

[499] 42 U.S.C. §12201(c)(2).

[500] *Id.* §12201(c)(3).

[501] *Id.*

[502] *See* Public Employees Ret. Sys. of Ohio v. Betts, 492 U.S. 158, 167, 11 EB Cases 1049 (1989); United Air Lines, Inc. v. McMann, 434 U.S. 192, 203, 1 EB Cases 1556 (1977).

[503] COMPLIANCE MANUAL, *supra* note 433.

[504] EEOC v. Aramark Corp., Inc., 208 F.3d 266, 10 AD Cases 798 (D.C. Cir. 2000).

suit against his employer under the ADA, claiming that his employee benefit plan unfairly provided a shorter period of long-term disability benefits for individuals suffering from mental or psychological disabilities than that provided for physical disabilities. The court denied this claim on the grounds that the insurance benefit plan was protected by the ADA's safe harbor provision, and that no subterfuge could exist because the benefit plan was instituted prior to the ADA's enactment. The court's rationale was that the employer could not have intended to evade the purpose of a statute not yet enacted.[505]

All other circuits that have addressed the issue have also rejected the EEOC's equating "subterfuge to evade" with a lack of actuarial justification.[506] Therefore, the judicial trend appears to favor the specific intent requirement, even though the legislative history of the ADA suggests otherwise.

2. Mental Versus Physical Health Care Coverage

Another big area of contention is whether and to what extent may a benefits plan provide different levels of coverage for mental health as opposed to physical health care. For example, many insurance plans cap benefits for mental health care at a lower level than that provided for physical health care,

---

[505] *Id.* at 270.

[506] *See* Leonard F. v. Israel Discount Bank of N.Y., 199 F.3d 99, 105, 10 AD Cases 13, 18 (2d Cir. 1999) ("In the context of the subterfuge clause of Section 501(c) of the ADA, neither the dictionary definition nor the Supreme Court's reasoning suggests that the absence of actuarial justification for different insurance benefits is sufficient to demonstrate a 'subterfuge' to evade the purposes of an Act, at least where the insurance policy was adopted prior to the Act's passage."); Rogers v. Department of Health & Envtl. Control, 174 F.3d 431, 437, 9 AD Cases 257, 261 (4th Cir. 1999) ("[W]e do not find anything in §501(c) of the ADA (or anywhere else in the Act) that requires a plan sponsor or administrator to justify a plan's separate classification of mental disability with actuarial data."); Ford v. Schering-Plough Corp., 145 F.3d 601, 611–12, 8 AD Cases 190, 198 (3d Cir. 1998), *cert. denied*, 525 U.S. 1093 (1999) ("[W]e will not construe section 501(c) to require a seismic shift in the insurance business, namely requiring insurers to justify their coverage plans in court after a mere allegation by a plaintiff."); Parker v. Metropolitan Life Ins. Co., 121 F.3d 1006, 1012, 6 AD Cases 1865, 1867 (6th Cir. 1997) (en banc), *cert. denied*, 525 U.S. 820 (1998) (rejecting argument that different insurance benefit or coverage levels based on disability are permitted only where "based on sound actuarial principles" or "related to actual or reasonably anticipated experience"); Krauel v. Iowa Methodist Med. Ctr., 95 F.3d 674, 678–79, 5 AD Cases 1503 (8th Cir. 1996) (rejecting EEOC's interim guidance and refusing to grant it

allow a smaller number of hospital visits for mental health care than for physical care, and/or increase a participant's copayment or coinsurance for mental health above that required for physical ailments. The most common reasons benefits providers cite for discriminating against mental health care are the high costs of mental health coverage and the perceived subjectivity of mental health treatment and diagnosis.[507]

Whether a disparity in mental health coverage is unlawful depends on what types of limitations are stipulated in the plan itself. Not only is the ADA implicated, but also the Mental Health Parity Act of 1996 (MHPA).[508] Despite its name, the MHPA does not require that employer health benefit plans place mental and physical health care coverage on equal footing. In fact, the MHPA does not require that mental health benefits be provided at all.[509] Rather, the MHPA is a somewhat effete piece of legislation that simply prohibits an employer from providing different annual and cumulative lifetime dollar limits for mental and physical health coverage in group health plans.[510] Any aggregate or lifetime dollar limits for medical/surgical coverage in a health plan that also contains mental health benefits must include those mental health benefits under the dollar limit umbrella, or create separate but equal limits for mental and health coverage.[511] However, the MHPA *does not* mandate that any other terms, quality of benefits, or contribution levels be made equal.[512]

---

deference, explaining actuarial justification defense as contrary to the plain language of the statute).

[507] *See* Gold, *Must Insurers Treat All Illnesses Equally?—Mental vs. Physical Illness: Congressional and Administrative Failure to End Limitations to and Exclusions From Coverage for Mental Illness in Employer-Provided Health Benefits Under the Mental Health Parity Act and the Americans with Disabilities Act*, 4 CONN. INS. L.J. 767, 770 (1997/1998).

[508] Pub. L. No. 104-204, 110 Stat. 2944 (1996) (codified at 29 U.S.C. §1185a).
[509] *See* 42 U.S.C. §300gg-5(b)(1).
[510] *Id.* §300gg-5.
[511] *Id.*
[512] *Id.* §300gg-5(b)(2). The vitality of the MHPA was extended by The Mental Health Parity Reauthorization Act of 2003, Pub. L. 108-197, amending ERISA, 29 U.S.C. §1185a(f) and Public Health Service Act, 42 U.S.C. §300gg-5(f). More expansive legislation to require group health plans to provide broader coverage for mental health conditions and treatment was advanced during the 108th Congress, with supporters led by Senators Pete Dominici (R-NM) and Edward Kennedy (D-MA).

For example, employers or insurance providers can evade the restrictions imposed by the MHPA by not creating an annual or lifetime cap on benefits. Instead, a benefit provider may still cap the number of a participant's mental health hospital visits, increase a participant's coshare or coinsurance for mental health benefits, or impose any other additional restrictions for mental health coverage without violating the MHPA. The next questions is whether doing so violates the ADA.

The majority of jurisdictions have held that it does not.[513] The main reason why offering different amounts for coverage for different types of disabilities does not violate the ADA is that there is no discrimination under the ADA where disabled individuals are given the same opportunity as everyone else. In essence, individuals with mental disabilities are presented with the same insurance coverage *options* as individuals with physical disabilities and individuals without any disabilities at all. Furthermore, because of the increased costs involved in covering mental health disabilities, there are actuarial justifications for such limitations. Thus, offering different coverage for mental and physical disabilities is most likely permissible as long as there is an economic rationale behind doing so.

Additionally, as discussed, the EEOC has made a distinction between disability-related and health-related benefits.[514] A prohibition or limitation on the provision of mental health–related benefits would likely fall into the latter category, and thus not be deemed discriminatory.

D. Violations and Permitted Distinctions

The ADA's safe harbor provision—which courts have broadly applied in a variety of circumstances—has given employers and insurance providers considerable leeway in crafting

---

[513] *See, e.g.*, Weyer v. Twentieth Century Fox Film Corp., 198 F.3d 1104, 10 AD Cases 65 (9th Cir. 2000); Rogers v. Department of Health & Envtl. Control, 174 F.3d 431, 435, 9 AD Cases 257 (4th Cir. 1999); Ford v. Schering-Plough Corp., 145 F.3d 601, 609, 8 AD Cases 190 (3d Cir. 1998); Parker v. Metropolitan Life Ins. Co., 121 F.3d 1006, 1015, 6 AD Cases 1865 (6th Cir. 1997), *cert. denied*, 522 U.S. 1084 (1998); EEOC v. CNA Ins. Cos., 96 F.3d 1039, 1044, 5 AD Cases 1769 (7th Cir. 1996); Krauel v. Iowa Methodist Med. Ctr., 95 F.3d 674, 678, 5 AD Cases 1503 (8th Cir. 1996).

[514] COMPLIANCE MANUAL, *supra* note 433, at 627:0022.

benefits coverage.[515] However, there are certain practices that would almost certainly constitute a violation of the ADA. Primarily, offering a disabled employee a different benefits package from that offered to a nondisabled employee is a violation of the ADA. In general, failing to treat employees equally raises a red flag for discrimination.

Second, creating a disability-based distinction, such as covering hospital stays for accidents and injuries but not for disability-related conditions, would be unlawful *unless* justified by one of the following reasons: (1) the distinction is based on sound actuarial data or on actual or reasonably anticipated experience; (2) failing to make the disability-based distinction would cause the benefit plan to go insolvent; (3) failing to make the disability-based distinction would cause significant adverse affects on the plan costs or on the availability of plan coverage for other employees; and/or (4) the disallowed benefit for the employee is not necessary to treat the disability.[516]

In essence, an employer or insurer may be able to provide a legitimate justification for making a disability-based distinction in a health benefit plan. As long as a nondiscriminatory rationale can be applied to the decision, it would not likely violate the ADA.

While no provision in particular is immune from challenge, employer and insurance providers should keep the following in mind to ensure that their policies comply with the ADA.

First, as long as the benefit does not make a disability-based distinction, it is permissible.[517] For example, placing a cap on all prescription costs does not specifically discriminate against individuals with disabilities, because presumably all employees are subject to this limitation. It is irrelevant that an employee with a disability would be more likely than a nondisabled employee to incur high medical costs.

---

[515] *See* EEOC v. Aramark Corp., 341 U.S. App. D.C. 38, 10 AD Cases 798 (D.C. Cir. 2000) (court affirmed summary judgment for employer in action challenging employee benefit plan under the ADA because plan was adopted prior to ADA's enactment and was protected by safe harbor provision).

[516] *Interim Enforcement Guidance, supra* note 436, at 5317–18.

[517] COMPLIANCE MANUAL, *supra*, note 433, at 627:0018.

Second, if a policy *does* make a disability-based distinction—placing a lower cap on the cost of cancer-fighting drugs than on medications used to treat other conditions, for example—then the employer or insurance provider should make sure that this decision is based on sound actuarial or viability principles, rather than on an intention to discriminate.[518] Thus, noncoverage for preexisting conditions, coverage for certain ailments and not others, and different coverage levels for different conditions are entirely permissible as long as the insurer's motivation is other than discriminatory.[519]

Third, employers and insurance providers may continue to make coverage distinctions as long as they are not based on a disability and are uniformly applied to all employees.[520] For example, employers may exclude certain ailments or procedures from coverage so long as nondisabled employees are subject to the same limitations.[521]

In addition to the permissible restrictions outlined above, employers should also be aware that there are other ways in which they may limit the benefits/coverage provided under an employee benefit plan without necessarily violating the ADA. The most important of these limitations, as noted in the EEOC's *Compliance Manual* and the *Interim Enforcement Guidance*, includes limitations in the provision of dependent coverage, disability retirement, and service retirement benefits.[522] Employers should note the following with respect to these limitations.

While employee benefit coverage provided to dependents is subject to the ADA, the ADA does not require that the coverage provided or the level of coverage accorded to dependents be the same as that accorded to an employee.[523] Moreover, because the law does not require that employers provide

---

[518] *Id.*

[519] *Id.* at 627:0019–627:0020.

[520] *Id.* at 627:0018.

[521] *Id.* at 627:0019.

[522] COMPLIANCE MANUAL, *supra* at note 433, INTERIM ENFORCEMENT GUIDANCE, *supra* at note 436.

[523] *Interim Enforcement Guidance, supra* note 436, at 15.

disability or service retirement plans, the failure to provide either, or both, does not violate the ADA.[524] Nor does it violate the ADA for an employer to preclude an employee who has voluntarily exercised his or her rights under one plan, that is. disability retirement plan, from simultaneously exercising her rights under the other alternative plan, that is, service retirement plan.[525] Nevertheless, if an employer does provide either or both types of plans, it may not discriminate against qualified employees with disabilities in the provision of such plan benefits or coverage. That is, while the provision of different levels of benefits and/or coverage under either of the plans vis-à-vis the other does not violate the ADA, because they serve different purposes and are not required to provide the same benefits, the employer may not provide different levels of benefits and/or coverage under the plans based on disability. For instance, no distinction is permitted in the provision of benefits and/or coverage under a service retirement plan based on disability. In other words, an employer may not require different lengths of employment for participation in a service retirement plan for employees with and without disabilities.[526] Likewise, as previously mentioned, an employer many not *require* an employee to exercise rights under a disability plan if the employee also is eligible to exercise rights under the service retirement plan and desires to do so.[527]

While the ADA affords certain protections against intentional discrimination in the provision and elimination of health benefits, it is not a panacea for employees who are adversely affected by benefit plan changes or limitations. The legislative history, EEOC guidance, and interpretive case law all indicate that providers of insurance—while not completely immune from ADA scrutiny—have been granted considerable leeway in crafting and implementing health benefit plans. Because

---

[524] COMPLIANCE MANUAL, *supra* note 433, at 627:0024, 25.
[525] *Id.* at 627:0025.
[526] *Id.*
[527] *Id.*

judicial circuits remain conflicted over various gray area issues, however, the parameters of this leeway are still being defined. In the interim, employers and other insurance providers should make certain that any benefit plan decisions are justified by legitimate, nondiscriminatory reasons.[528]

---

[528] *Id.* at 627:0019.

CHAPTER 10

REMEDIES, LITIGATION STRATEGIES, AND ALTERNATIVE DISPUTE RESOLUTION

I.	Introduction	961
II.	Administrative Procedures	962
	A. The Americans with Disabilities Act, Title I	962
	1. Filing a Discrimination Charge With the EEOC	962
	2. Exception to Time-Period Limitations: The *Edelman* Case	964
	3. EEOC Procedures: Probable Cause	965
	4. Civil Lawsuit	967
	B. The Americans with Disabilities Act, Title II	968
	C. The Americans with Disabilities Act, Title III ...	972
	D. The Rehabilitation Act of 1973	972
	1. Section 501	973
	2. Section 503	974
	3. Section 504	975
III.	Sovereign Immunity	977
	A. The Americans With Disabilities Act	980
	B. The Rehabilitation Act of 1973	984
IV.	Remedies	986
	A. Damages	986
	1. The Americans with Disabilities Act	986
	a. Title I	986
	b. Title II	989
	c. Title III	990
	2. The Rehabilitation Act of 1973	992
	B. Injunctions	994
V.	Litigation Strategies	995
	A. Plaintiff's Strategies	995

1. Filing the Charge of Discrimination at the Administrative Level 996
2. Filing the Lawsuit in Court 997
3. Establishing a *Prima Facie* Case 999
   a. Proving the Employee's Impairment Is a Disability 999
      i. Providing Proof 1000
   b. Proving the Employee Is a Qualified Individual With a Disability 1003
   c. Reasonable Accommodation 1005
   d. Making a Case for Punitive Damages 1009
B. Defendant's Strategies 1010
   1. Disproving Plaintiff's Prima Facie Case 1011
      a. Is the Employee Disabled? 1011
      b. Affirmative Defenses 1014
         i. Job-Related and Consistent With Business Necessity 1016
         ii. Leave Policies 1017
         iii. Safety-Based Qualification Standards 1017
         iv. Direct Threat 1018
         v. Undue Hardship 1021
         vi. Seniority Systems and Collective Bargaining Agreements 1024
         vii. Conflict with Federal Law 1024
         viii. Miscellaneous Defense 1025
VI. Arbitration 1026
   A. Americans With Disabilities Act 1026
      1. Unresolved Issues 1028
      2. Exceptions 1030
      3. Procedural Elements 1032
      4. Challenges to Arbitration Agreements 1033
      5. Unconscionable Arbitration Agreements 1035
      6. Collective Bargaining Agreements 1037
   B. The Rehabilitation Act of 1973 1039
VII. Attorneys' Fees, Costs, and Expenses 1041
   A. Americans With Disabilities Act 1041
      1. Legislative History 1042
      2. Obtaining an Award 1043

   a. Unsuccessful 1044
   b. Successful 1045
  3. Awards Against EEOC 1046
 B. The Rehabilitation Act of 1973 1047
 C. Claiming Attorneys' Fees Against
   State Governments 1047
 D. Recovery of Attorneys' Fees by the Prevailing
   Plaintiff for an Administrative Proceeding 1049

I. Introduction

This chapter provides an overview of the enforcement tools available to federal agencies, courts, and private plaintiffs in seeking to enforce or vindicate rights provided by the Americans with Disabilities Act of 1990 (ADA)[1] as well as the Rehabilitation Act of 1973.[2] The agencies charged with enforcement of the ADA include the Equal Employment Opportunity Commission (EEOC) and the Department of Justice (DOJ). Many states and some local governments also have enacted protective statutes that prohibit discrimination on the basis of disability, and those mechanisms may provide additional remedies, or extend to circumstances in which federal protections may not be applicable.

  The ADA's predecessor, in many respects, was the Rehabilitation Act of 1973, which prohibits discrimination on the basis of a disability in programs conducted by federal agencies, programs receiving federal financial assistance, federal employment, and in the employment practices of private parties that contract with the federal government. In addition to the two federal agencies noted above, the Department of Labor (DOL) is involved in the regulation of contactor activity under the Rehabilitation Act. The ADA provided more expansive remedies, including damages claims that could be sought through private litigation initiated by job applicants or employees.

---

[1] 42 U.S.C. §12101 et seq.
[2] 29 U.S.C. §701 et seq.

II. Administrative Procedures

A. The Americans with Disabilities Act, Title I

Title I of the ADA prohibits employers from discriminating against qualified individuals with disabilities.[3] The ADA expressly incorporates the enforcement procedures, powers, and remedies set forth in several sections of the Civil Rights Act of 1964,[4] which govern the employment provisions of the ADA.[5] With respect to these avenues for relief, the EEOC, U.S. Attorney General, and individuals alleging employment discrimination on a disability-related basis, possess the same authority and rights as provided under Title VII of the Civil Rights Act.[6] Therefore, individuals seeking redress for employment discrimination under Title I of the ADA follow the same procedures as those pursuing claims under Title VII of the Civil Rights Act of 1964.

1. Filing a Discrimination Charge With the EEOC

As the primary enforcement agency, the EEOC promulgated regulations interpeting the rights and requirements established by Title I of the ADA.[7] To commence the administrative process, the aggrieved individual typically files a charge of discrimination with the EEOC.[8] The charge must be in writing and under oath or affirmation, attesting that an unlawful employment practice occurred. The complaint must be filed with the EEOC within 180 days of the occurrence of the alleged wrongful act.[9]

There are limited circumstances in which new allegations contained in a plaintiff's complaint, amended or otherwise, may relate back to a charge filed with the EEOC. However,

---

[3] 42 U.S.C. §12112(a).
[4] Id. §2000e-4, 2000e-5, 2000e-6, 2000e-8, 2000e-9.
[5] Id. §12117(a).
[6] Id. §2000e.
[7] Id. §§12116, 2000e-5.
[8] Id. §2000e-5(a)–(b).
[9] Id. §2000e-5(e)(1).

such circumstances are fact-specific, and may require a determination from the court as to whether a claim properly relates back to an original EEOC charge in order not to be barred by the statute of limitations.[10]

States and local governments may enact their own antidiscrimination laws, and may create "deferral agencies" to enforce these state antidiscrimination laws. These state and local human rights commissions have concurrent jurisdiction with the EEOC over discrimination charges.[11] When such state and local agencies exist, no charge may be filed with the EEOC until the state or local human rights commission has had 60 days in which to address the matter.[12] The federal statute provides relevant state agencies with the first opportunity to act on the complaint if it so desires. The purpose of this requirement is to avoid premature federal intervention in suits that could be resolved at the local administrative level.[13] When a charge is

---

[10] Hornsby v. Conoco, Inc., 777 F.2d 243, 39 FEP Cases 766, *reh'g denied*, 780 F.2d 532 (5th Cir. 1985) (where discharged employee's original EEOC complaint alleged age and sex discrimination when construed liberally and not sexual harassment, amended complaint filed outside of 180-day limitation period that alleged sexual harassment, did not properly relate back to original complaint filed with EEOC, thus sexual harassment claim was time-barred); Ramirez v. National Distillers & Chem. Corp., 586 F.2d 1315, 18 FEP Cases 966 (9th Cir. 1978) (second employment charge virtually identical to earlier charge with only difference being that employer's address was listed differently in second charge, so that second charge related back to earlier charge and was timely).

[11] *See* 42 U.S.C. §12117(a)–(b). State courts have concurrent jurisdiction with federal courts over ADA claims. Yellow Freight Sys., Inc. v. Donnelly, 494 U.S. 820, 52 FEP Cases 875 (1990). The existence of concurrent jurisdiction does not alter the fact that ADA actions are federal question cases. Jones v. Illinois Cent. R.R., 859 F. Supp. 1144, 3 AD Cases 838 (N.D. Ill. 1994).

[12] 42 U.S.C. §2000e-5(c)–(e) (the 60-day deferral period extends to 120 days during the first year after the effective date of any such state or local statue prohibiting employment discrimination). In deferral states, which are states with fair employment agencies, claimants must file charges with the state agency before pursuing their claims with the EEOC. The EEOC will not formally file charges it receives until the state agency has terminated its proceedings or 60 days have elapsed, whichever occurs earlier. Rasimas v. Michigan Dep't of Mental Health, 714 F.2d 614, 32 FEP Cases 688 (6th Cir. 1983), *cert. denied*, 466 U.S. 950 (1984).

[13] 42 U.S.C. §2000e-5(c)–(e). Regardless of the fact that the state complaint may have technically been filed after the EEOC complaint, the purpose of the Civil Rights Act of 1964, requiring the state agency to be given the first opportunity to resolve the matter, is satisfied and the action may proceed as long as the state agency had the first opportunity to resolve the employment discrimination dispute.

filed with such a deferral agency, the time period for filing a charge with the EEOC is extended to the earlier of 300 days after the alleged unlawful employment practice occurred, or within 30 days after receiving notice that the state or local agency terminated the proceedings.[14]

2. Exception to Time-Period Limitations: The Edelman Case

There may be circumstances in which an exception is made to this statute of limitations. In *Edelman v. Lynchburg College*,[15] the Supreme Court held that a charge of discrimination filed with the EEOC 313 days after the alleged discrimination occurred could "relate back" to a letter that the charging party had faxed to the EEOC within the 300-day statute of limitations. In doing so, the Court determined that the EEOC's relation-back regulation was a correct interpretation of Title VII of the Civil Rights Act of 1964,[16] and that treatment almost certainly will extend to ADA filings.

In the *Edelman* case, Edelman had been denied tenure by Lynchburg College on June 6, 1997, and had faxed a letter to the EEOC on November 14, 1997, claiming discrimination based on sex, national origin, and religion. The letter lacked an oath or affirmation. The EEOC advised Edelman that he had to file a charge within the 300-day limitations period. Edelman finally returned a verified charge 13 days after the limitations period had expired. After completing an investigation into Edelman's allegations, the EEOC issued a right-to-sue letter.

When Edelman sued, the college moved to dismiss on the ground that he had failed to file a verified charge within the

---

Albano v. General Adjustment Bureau, Inc., 478 F. Supp. 1209, 21 FEP Cases 323 (S.D.N.Y. 1979), *aff'd*, 622 F.2d 572, 22 FEP Cases 840 (2d Cir. 1980).

[14]A Title VII complainant generally has 180 days from the time the alleged discrimination occurred in which to file a charge with the EEOC, but a 300-day filing period applies if the charging party institutes proceedings with a state or local human rights agency possessing the authority to grant relief from unlawful employment practices. 42 U.S.C. §2000e-5(e)(1); *see also* EEOC v. Commercial Office Prods. Co., 486 U.S. 107, 110, 46 FEP Cases 1265 (1988).

[15]535 U.S. 106, 88 FEP Cases 321 (2002).

[16]*Id.* at 118–19, 88 FEP Cases at 326.

300-day limitations period.[17] Edelman countered that the November letter faxed to the EEOC constituted a timely filed charge, pursuant to EEOC regulation 29 C.F.R. §1601.12(b), which permitted the verification to "relate back" to the letter.

The Supreme Court found that Title VII's filing and verification provisions do not require that a verified charge be filed with the EEOC within the limitations period. The Court determined that the EEOC's relation-back regulation is a reasonable interpretation of the statute's independent requirements that a charge be filed within the limitations period and that the charge be verified. The Court emphasized that Title VII does not specify a time frame within which the required verification must occur. However, the Court declined to decide whether Edelman's November letter actually qualified as a charge.[18] The case is significant because, in effect, it appears to permit charging parties to file a formal charge late at the EEOC so long as they file some document by the 300-day deadline.

3. EEOC Procedures: Probable Cause

Once a charge is filed with the EEOC, the commission notifies the respondent (the party charged with the alleged unlawful conduct) that a charge has been filed, and conducts an investigation of each allegation contained in the charge.[19] The investigatory period varies on a case-by-case basis, and the EEOC will pursue the investigation until it has sufficient evidence to make a finding on the merits.[20] To assess the merits of a charge, the EEOC can make specific requests for information from the respondent. For example, the EEOC can request copies of other employees' personnel files in order to compare them with the complainant's personnel file, and the EEOC can request policies or affidavits as historical evidence of past

---

[17] *Id.*
[18] The Court remanded the case for further proceedings on that issue. *Id.*
[19] *See* EEOC COMPLIANCE MANUAL (CCH) §22.3(a), *Scope of Investigation*; 42 U.S.C. §2000e-5(b).
[20] EEOC COMPLIANCE MANUAL §22.3(a).

employment practices.[21] In a bona fide occupational qualification case or reasonable accommodation case, such evidence of past practice may establish the lack of undue hardship on the employer or show that an employee is not qualified for a job, because the employee cannot perform the essential functions of a position.[22]

If an administrative investigation results in a determination by the EEOC that there is no probable cause to believe that discrimination occurred, the commission "will take no further action."[23] The EEOC will dismiss the charge when sufficient evidence to support a reasonable cause does not exist.[24] The letter of determination will contain a dismissal and right-to-sue notice and the charging party will have 90 days to file a civil lawsuit in federal district court.[25]

If, after concluding the investigation, however, the EEOC makes a finding that there exists probable cause to believe that a violation occurred, it may issue a determination letter to the parties.[26] The EEOC's determination of a probable cause finding indicates that the agency found that it is more likely than not that the charging party was discriminated against because of a prohibited basis.[27] The determination letter will also notify the charging party and the respondent of the commission's intent to eliminate any unlawful practices through

---

[21] *Id.* (stating that EEOC investigation procedure guidelines provide that the period of investigation should cover as much time as necessary to obtain sufficient comparative and/or historical evidence to make a finding on the merits. Data on wage histories and employment practices may be needed to demonstrate the extent of violations and fashion appropriate remedial relief). *Id.* §22.2(b), specifying that the EEOC's request for information should be tailored to the scope of the investigation.

[22] *Id.*

[23] A TECHNICAL ASSISTANCE MANUAL ON THE EMPLOYMENT PROVISIONS (TITLE I) OF THE AMERICANS WITH DISABILITIES ACT, at §10.3 [hereinafter TITLE I TECHNICAL ASSISTANCE MANUAL].

[24] *Id.*; *see also* 42 U.S.C. §2000e-5(b).

[25] *Id.*

[26] EEOC COMPLIANCE MANUAL, at §22.18.

[27] *Id.* §40.2.

voluntary conciliation.[28] Conciliation is a voluntary and informal procedure where both parties to a charge are invited to participate in a meeting where the EEOC acts as a facilitator. The goal is to reach a joint resolution to eliminate the problems underlying the charge. Although the EEOC cannot force conciliation on an unwilling employer, it is required by statute to conciliate the matter.[29]

Communications by the charging party and the respondent during the informal mediation may not be made public or used as evidence in subsequent proceedings. Violations are punishable by a fine up to $1,000 and imprisonment for up to 1 year.[30] If the EEOC finds "cause to believe that discrimination occurred, but cannot resolve the issue through conciliation, the case will be considered for litigation."[31] If the EEOC decides to litigate the matter, it will file suit in federal district court so long as the respondent is not a government, governmental agency, or political subdivision named in the charge.[32] If the EEOC decides not to litigate, it will send the charging party a "right-to-sue" letter and the charging party will have 90 days within which to file a civil suit. Regardless of when conciliation is concluded, the EEOC must issue the right-to-sue letter within 180 days after the charge was initially filed. The right-to-sue letter may also be issued earlier if the charging party so requests.

4. Civil Lawsuit

The individual complainant first must exhaust the administrative remedies prior to filing a civil lawsuit in the federal

---

[28] If after conducting an investigation the EEOC finds that there is reasonable cause to support an unlawful discriminatory act, it "shall endeavor to eliminate any such alleged unlawful employment practice by informal methods of conference, conciliation, and persuasion." 42 U.S.C. §2000e-5(b).

[29] EEOC v. Asplundh Tree Expert Co., 340 F.3d 1256, 92 FEP Cases 661 (11th Cir. 2003) (race discrimination suit filed by EEOC dismissed, because agency failed to pursue conciliation in appropriate manner before going to court, and EEOC ordered to pay costs, expenses, and attorneys' fees to employer).

[30] 42 U.S.C. §2000e-5(b).

[31] TITLE I TECHNICAL ASSISTANCE MANUAL, *supra* note 23, at 10.3.

[32] 42 U.S.C. §2000e-5(f)(1). If the respondent named in the charge is a government, governmental agency, or political subdivision, the EEOC will refer the case to the U.S. Attorney General, who may bring a civil action against the respondent

court system.[33] Generally, the charging party satisfies this by filing the required charge of discrimination with the EEOC, and obtaining a right-to-sue letter from the agency at the conclusion of its investigation or handling of the matter.[34] Circumstances may require the EEOC to issue a notice of right-to-sue to the charging party prior to completion of the administrative process. Such notices may be issued on request by the charging party so as not to impede an individual's ability to proceed with a lawsuit.[35] Also, there are limited circumstances in which a right-to-sue letter may not be necessary for exhaustion. However, such cases are fact-specific, and may require a determination from the court as to whether a plaintiff with an ADA claim actually exhausted the administrative remedies.[36]

B. The Americans with Disabilities Act, Title II

Title II of the ADA prohibits discrimination in public services by public entities, and the agencies with responsibilities

---

in the appropriate district court. The process for handling such complaints is described in the DOJ Title II regulations, 28 C.F.R. Part 35 (2004).

[33]42 U.S.C. §12117(a).

[34]Bishop v. Okidata, Inc., 864 F. Supp. 416, 3 AD Cases 1283 (D.N.J. 1994) (filing discrimination charge with EEOC and receiving right-to-sue letter before bringing private lawsuit against respondent is not jurisdictional issue, but charging party must exhaust administrative remedies before suing in federal court); Osborn v. E.J. Branch, Inc., 864 F. Supp. 56, 4 AD Cases 88 (N.D. Ill. 1994) (employee must timely file charge with EEOC and receive right-to-sue letter before filing civil suit against employer under ADA).

[35]EEOC Form 161-B, Notice of Right to Sue (Issued on Request) (Oct. 1996).

[36]EEOC v. Farmer Bros. Co., 31 F.3d 891, 899 n.5, 65 FEP Cases 857 (9th Cir. 1994) (trial court must examine both EEOC charge and EEOC investigation to determine if claims are exhausted, and exhausted claims include those actually investigated as well as those that "would have been within the scope of a 'reasonably thorough investigation'") (quoting Gibbs v. Pierce County Law Enforcement Support, 785 F.2d 1396, 1400, 40 FEP Cases 673 (9th Cir. 1986); Doe v. Kohn Nast & Graf, P.C., 866 F. Supp. 190, 3 AD Cases 1322 (E.D. Pa. 1994) (even though human immunodeficiency virus (HIV)–infected plaintiff did not file charge with EEOC for certain ADA claims, which were added in second-amended complaint, plaintiff had exhausted his administrative remedies given facts supporting claims appeared in administrative charge and it was reasonable to expect that ADA claims would have grown out of proper EEOC investigation).

for compliance with issues arising from Title II are the EEOC and the DOJ.[37]

The language of this section is ambiguous as to whether Title II prohibits discrimination in employment situations, and there exists a split among the circuits as to whether or not claims of employment discrimination can be brought against public entities under Title II.[38]

Courts that apply Title II to employment situations have been persuaded by the legislative history, applicable DOJ regulations, and past legal precedents, to support that Title II covers employment discrimination claims against public entities. The legislative history makes clear that the purpose of Title II was to extend the reach of Section 504 of the Rehabilitation Act to state and local governments as Section 504 only prohibited discrimination by recipients of federal financial assistance.[39]

---

[37]"Subject to the provisions of this subchapter, no qualified individual with a disability shall, by reason of such disability, be excluded from participation in or be denied the benefits of services, programs, or activities of a public entity, or be subjected to discrimination by any such entity." 42 U.S.C. §12132; 28 C.F.R. §§35.170–178 (2003).

[38]The earlier cases of employment discrimination brought against public entities under Title II of the ADA, uniformly applied Title II to employment discrimination claims. Ethridge v. Alabama, 847 F. Supp. 903, 906, 3 AD Cases 162, 165 (M.D. Ala. 1993) (analyzing legislative history, applicable regulations, and past legal precedents, Title II "clearly reaches employment discrimination by public entities"); Finley v. Giacobbe, 827 F. Supp. 215, 2 AD Cases 1117 (S.D.N.Y. 1993); Petersen v. University of Wis. Bd. of Regents, 818 F. Supp. 1276, 2 AD Cases 735 (W.D. Wis. 1993). However, more recently, judicial circuits have split on this point, and the matter has yet to be resolved. *Compare* Bledsoe v. Palm Beach County Soil & Water Conservation Dist., 133 F.3d 816, 820, 7 AD Cases 1433 (11th Cir.), *cert. denied*, 525 U.S. 826 (1998) (applying Title II in employment discrimination context), *with* Zimmerman v. Oregon Dep't of Justice, 170 F.3d 1169, 1173, 9 AD Cases 215, *reh'g en banc denied*, 183 F.3d 1161, 9 AD Cases 954 (9th Cir. 1999), *cert. denied*, 531 U.S. 1189 (2001) (Title II does not apply to employment discrimination claims). Within the Seventh Circuit the district courts have also held inapposite positions on this issue. *Compare* Dertz v. City of Chicago, 912 F. Supp. 319, 323–24, 7 AD Cases 1507 (N.D. Ill. 1995) (applying Title II to employment claim against public entity), *with* Patterson v. Illinois Dep't of Corr., 35 F. Supp. 2d 1103, 1109–10 (C.D. Ill. 1999), *aff'd*, 2002 U.S. App. LEXIS 12012 (7th Cir. 2002) (Title II does not cover employment disputes between public employers and their employees).

[39]Regulations promulgated under the Rehabilitation Act §504 provides, "No qualified handicapped person shall, on the basis of handicap, be subjected to discrimination in employment under any program or activity that receives or benefits from federal financial assistance." 28 C.F.R. §41.52(a) (2003). Section 504 applies

The House Report regarding discussions of Section 12132 of the ADA also expressly indicates that the discriminatory practices that are prohibited under Titles I and III of the ADA are to be identical to the forms of discrimination prohibited under Title II.[40]

This understanding is consistent with the explanation of the cross-reference to Title I in 28 C.F.R. §35.140 that was published in the *Federal Register*, which explained that it was to cover the employment practices of all public entities beginning January 26, 1992.[41] Also, the regulations implementing Title II of the ADA state that, "[n]o qualified individual with a disability shall, on the basis of disability, be subjected to discrimination in employment under any service, program, or activity conducted by a public entity."[42] Despite supporting authority for the application of Title II to employment discrimination, legal opinions vary on this point as the statute itself is silent as to its applicability in the employment context.

Jurisdictions applying Title II of the ADA to prohibit employment discrimination by public entities hold that the charging individuals have the option of pursuing their claims through the available administrative procedures or foregoing the administrative procedures altogether and filing a complaint in federal court. Title II adopts the remedies, rights, and procedures of Section 504 of the Rehabilitation Act of 1973.[43] The

---

to employment discrimination claims. Consolidated Rail Corp. v. Darrone, 465 U.S. 624, 626, 1 AD Cases 567 (1984). The legislative history of ADA Title II shows that the primary purpose of §12131 of the ADA was to extend the reach of §504 of the Rehabilitation Act, "to all programs, activities, and services provided or made available by state and local governments or instrumentalities or agencies thereto, regardless of whether or not such entities receive Federal financial assistance. Currently, section 504 prohibits discrimination only by recipients of Federal financial assistance." H. REP. No. 101-485, pt. 2, at 84 (1990), *reprinted in* 1990 U.S.C.C.A.N. 303, 366.

[40]"The Committee intends, however, that the forms of discrimination prohibited by [§12132] be identical to those set out in the applicable provisions of titles I and III of this legislation." H. REP. No. 101-485, at 84 (1990), *reprinted in* 1990 U.S.C.C.A.N. 303, 367.

[41]56 Fed. Reg. 35,707–08 (July 26, 1991).

[42]28 C.F.R. §35.140(a) (2002).

[43]The enforcement section of Title II provides that, "[t]he remedies, procedures, and rights set forth in section 794a of title 29 [the Rehabilitation Act of

Rehabilitation Act[44] adopts the remedies, procedures, and rights of Title VI of the Civil Rights Act of 1964,[45] and both the Rehabilitation Act and Title VI of the Civil Rights Act provide only for the termination of federal funding for violations of the statutory provisions and do not contain provisions for private lawsuits.[46]

Courts have reasoned that because "private plaintiffs may sue under these statutes only by virtue of private rights of action implied by the courts and because they receive no effective relief through administrative channels, these plaintiffs need not resort to administrative remedies before bringing an action in court."[47] Therefore, unlike Title I, Title II does not require the exhaustion of administrative procedures prior to the filing of a private lawsuit, and individuals pursuing legal claims against state and local governments under ADA Title II, have the option of filing their claims in federal court without having exhausted their administrative remedies.[48]

The unsettled state of this issue and resulting uncertainties in the lower courts are reflected in at least one 2002 trial court decision, holding that a plaintiff is able to pursue an employment discrimination claim under Title II.[49] The trial court noted that the U.S. Court of Appeals for the Seventh Circuit had not ruled on whether Title II applied to employment discrimination claims, and that other federal courts were split on this issue. Because of doubt on the proper application

---

1973] shall be the remedies, procedures, and rights this subchapter provides to any person alleging discrimination on the basis of disability in violation of section 12132 of this title." 42 U.S.C. §12133. The Rehabilitation Act does not require exhaustion of administrative remedies for nonfederal employees. 42 U.S.C. §§12117, 12133.

[44]29 U.S.C. §794a(a)(2).
[45]42 U.S.C. §2000d et seq.
[46]29 U.S.C. §794(a)(2); 42 U.S.C. §2000d, et seq. One complication is that a remedy under §504 of the Rehabilitation Act is the withdrawal of federal financial assistance. For an entity covered by Title II, but not by §504, the remedy obviously would be unavailable.
[47]Petersen v. University of Wis. Bd. of Regents, 818 F. Supp. 1276, 1278–79, 2 AD Cases 735, 737 (W.D. Wis. 1993) (citing Smith v. Barton, 914 F.2d 1330, 1338, 1 AD Cases 1689 (9th Cir. 1990), *cert. denied*, 501 U.S. 1217 (1991)).
[48]42 U.S.C. §12133.
[49]Jackson v. City of Chi., 24 NAT'L DISABILITY L. REP. 137 (N.D. Ill. 2002).

of the law and the likelihood that the Seventh Circuit or the Supreme Court would soon make a ruling on this matter, the court refrained from precluding the plaintiff's cause of action.[50]

C. The Americans With Disabilities Act, Title III

In contrast to certain state accessibility laws, relief under Title III of the ADA is limited. The statute's incorporation of 42 U.S.C. §2000a-3 makes it clear that the remedies available in private lawsuits under Title III are "limited to providing injunctive relief and *not* damages."[51] Attorneys' fees also may be recovered.[52] However, private plaintiffs may not recover compensatory or punitive damages.[53] In suits brought by the Department of Justice, monetary damages (*not* including punitive damages) can be awarded to individual victims of discrimination, and courts may assess civil penalties of up to $50,000 for first violations, and up to $100,000 for any subsequent violation.

D. The Rehabilitation Act of 1973

Certain claims brought under the Rehabilitation Act are like claims brought under Title VII in that they require the exhaustion of administrative remedies.[54] The procedures of Title VII also are incorporated into the statute for claims brought under the Rehabilitation Act,[55] and the federal implementation regulations for Title VII[56] also apply to claims under the Rehabilitation Act. The general purpose of the doctrine requiring the exhaustion of administrative remedies prior to commencing a lawsuit " 'is to permit an administrative agency to apply its special expertise in interpreting relevant statutes

---

[50]*Id.*

[51]A.R. v. Kogan, 964 F. Supp. 269, 271 (N.D. Ill. 1997) (dismissing claim for emotional distress under ADA Title III).

[52]"Subchapter III of the ADA does not provide for a private cause of action for damages." Howard v. Cherry Hills Cutters, Inc., 935 F. Supp. 1148, 1149, 5 AD Cases 1579, 1579 (D. Colo. 1996).

[53]*Id.*

[54]Hupka v. U.S. Dep't of Defense, 134 F. Supp. 2d 871 (E.D. Mich. 2001); Mickulicz v. Garthwaite, 2000 U.S. App. LEXIS 22248, at *1 (6th Cir. 2000) (citing Smith v. U.S. Postal Serv., 742 F.2d 257, 258–62, 1 AD Cases 620 (6th Cir. 1984).

[55]*Id.*

[56]29 C.F.R. §1614.105(a) (2003).

and in developing a factual record without premature judicial intervention.'"[57] The problem lies in determining which employees may proceed with their claims straight to court, and which employees first must exhaust the available administrative procedures.

Nonfederal employees are not required to exhaust their administrative remedies prior to bringing a private action in federal court under the Rehabilitation Act.[58] Both the Rehabilitation Act and Title VI of the Civil Rights Act provide only for the termination of federal funding for statutory violations and do not explicitly address private suits.[59] Because private plaintiffs may sue under these statutes only by virtue of private rights of action that are implied by the courts and because they do not receive effective relief through the administrative remedies available, these nonfederal employee plaintiffs are not required to exhaust their administrative remedies before bringing an action in court.[60]

1. Section 501

Federal courts require the exhaustion of administrative remedies prior to filing causes of action in federal court under Section 501.[61] The 1978 Amendments to the Rehabilitation Act made the Title VII remedies, procedures, and rights applicable

---

[57]*Hupka*, at 876 (quoting Southern Ohio Coal v. Donovan, 774 F.2d 693, 702 (6th Cir. 1985)).

[58]Petersen v. University of Wis. Bd. of Regents, 818 F. Supp. 1276, 1278–79, 2 AD Cases 735 (W.D. Wis. 1993).

[59]The Rehabilitation Act of 1973 adopts the remedies, procedures, and rights of Title VI of the Civil Rights Act of 1964, 42 U.S.C. §2000d et seq. *See* 29 U.S.C. §794a(a)(2).

[60]*Peterson*, 818 F. Supp. at 1279; Smith v. Barton, 914 F.2d 1330, 1338, 1 AD Cases 1689 (9th Cir. 1990), *cert. denied*, 501 U.S. 1217 (1990); Neighborhood Action Coalition v. Canton, 882 F.2d 1012, 1015 (6th Cir. 1989) ("litigants need not exhaust their administrative remedies prior to bringing a Title VI claim in federal court").

[61]Doe v. Garrett, 903 F.2d 1455, 1461, 1 AD Cases 1480 (11th Cir. 1990); Johnston v. Horne, 875 F.2d 1415, 49 FEP Cases 1806 (9th Cir. 1989); Morgan v. U.S. Postal Serv., 798 F.2d 1162, 1 AD Cases 963 (8th Cir. 1986), *cert. denied*, 480 U.S. 948 (1987); Prewitt v. U.S. Postal Serv., 662 F.2d 292, 1 AD Cases 273 (5th Cir. 1981); MacKay v. U.S. Postal Serv., 607 F. Supp. 271, 277–78, 42 FEP Cases 1197 (E.D. Pa. 1985).

to Section 501 complaints.[62] The court's holding in *Prewitt v. U.S. Postal Service*,[63] that Section 501 incorporates Title VII's requirement that administrative remedies must be exhausted prior to an individual's bringing a discrimination claim into federal court under Section 501, reflects the state of the laws on this issue.

2. Section 503

The majority of federal courts have concluded that a private right of action does not exist under Section 503.[64] The enforcement mechanism available under this section allows an individual to file a complaint with the DOL, which then permits the DOL to take enforcement action.[65] Those federal courts that recognize a private right of action have ruled that exhaustion of administrative remedies is not required prior to the individual pursuing a claim for disability discrimination under Section 503 in federal court.[66]

The Office of Federal Contract Compliance Programs (OFCCP), an agency within the DOL, is the governmental body that oversees the enforcement of Section 503.[67] The OFCCP

---

[62]Rehabilitation, Comprehensive Services, and Developmental Disabilities Amendments of 1978, Pub. L. No. 95-602, §120(a), 92 Stat. 2955, 2982 (codified at 29 U.S.C.A. §794a(a)(1)) (referring to the provisions of Title VII contained in 42 U.S.C. §2000e-16).

[63]662 F.2d 292, 1 AD Cases 273 (5th Cir. 1981).

[64]Clemmer v. Enron Corp., 882 F. Supp. 606, 611, 4 AD Cases 437 (S.D. Tex. 1995) (employee had no private right of action against employer that was federal contractor).

[65]The DOL is authorized to "take such action thereon as the facts and circumstances warrant. . . ." 29 U.S.C. §793(b).

[66]Chaplin v. Consolidated Edison Co. of N.Y., 482 F. Supp. 1165 (S.D.N.Y. 1980); Davis v. Modine Mfg. Co., 526 F. Supp 943, 28 FEP Cases 155 (D. Kan. 1981); California Paralyzed Veterans Ass'n v. Federal Communications Comm'n, 496 F. Supp. 125, 23 FEP Cases 1305 (C.D. Cal. 1980), *aff'd sub nom.* California Ass'n of the Physically Handicapped v. Federal Communications Comm'n, 721 F.2d 667, 1 AD Cases 538 (9th Cir. 1983), *cert. denied*, 469 U.S. 832 (1984). *Cf.* Thompson v. Spring Mills, Inc., 576 F. Supp. 651 (D.S.C. 1982) (claim dismissed for failure to exhaust administrative remedies).

[67]Under §503 of the Rehabilitation Act of 1973, 29 U.S.C.A. §793 (West Supp. 1998) and Exec. Order 11,246, 30 Fed. Reg. 12,319 (Sept. 24, 1965), the Secretary of Labor is authorized to enforce nondiscrimination and affirmative action obligations on parties to government contracts. The secretary has promulgated regulations to implement these laws, *see* 41 C.F.R. ch. 60 (2003), and has delegated certain enforcement duties to the Office of Federal Contract Compliance Programs

will investigate the complaint and may attempt informally to resolve the complaint prior to holding an administrative hearing.[68] If the complaint cannot be resolved at this stage, an administrative hearing on the merits of the complaint can be held.[69] If a violation is found, remedies may include withholding of payments due to the employer, cancellation of the federal contract or subcontract under which the violation occurred, and disqualification from obtaining future federal contracts.[70] The OFCCP may also award the individual financial relief in the form of back pay, job placement, and/or reinstatement. Administrative law judges conduct formal proceedings in these enforcement cases, and that adjudicator issues a recommended decision.[71] Following a period for both parties to file exceptions, the DOL's Administrative Review Board issues a final administrative order.[72]

3. Section 504

Section 504 established a private cause of action for disabled individuals who were discriminated against by entities receiving federal funds. In 1978, Congress amended the Rehabilitation Act so as to provide federal employees with a private right of action under Section 501.[73] Congress also extended the prohibition against disability discrimination in Section 504 to "any program or activity conducted by an Executive agency or by the United States Postal Service."[74] Thus, only since 1978 has the federal government been subject to suit under either Section 501 or 504.

(OFCCP) in the DOL. 41 C.F.R. §§60-1.2, 60-1.20 (2003). Pursuant to the Exec. Order and statutes, a covered contractor must "take affirmative action to ensure that applicants are employed, and that employees are treated during employment, without regard to their race, color, religion, sex or national origin," Exec. Order 11,246, and must "take affirmative action to employ and advance in employment" both "qualified individuals with disabilities," 29 U.S.C.A. §793; 41 C.F.R. §§60-741.1-.54 (2003).
[68] 41 C.F.R. §§60-741.26–28.
[69] *Id.* §§60-741.28(a)–29(a).
[70] *Id.* §§60-741.28(c)–(e).
[71] 41 C.F.R. §6-30.27 (2003).
[72] 41 C.F.R. §§60-30.29-30 (2003).
[73] 29 U.S.C.A. §794a(a)(1).
[74] *Id.*

A federal employee unquestionably can proceed under Section 501 so long as the administrative procedures have been exhausted. The body of law is not so clear as to whether a federal employee would be able to bring a private right of action under Section 504. Section 504 provides that disabled individuals may not "be excluded from participation in, be denied the benefits of, or be subjected to discrimination under any program or activity receiving Federal financial assistance or under any program or activity conducted by any Executive agency or by the United States Postal Service."[75] The definition of "program or activity"[76] suggests that Section 504 is not applicable to cases alleging disability discrimination against a federal agency.

There is a substantial split of authority among the circuits on this issue. The U.S. Courts of Appeals for the Second, Seventh, Ninth, and Tenth Circuits have held that Section 501 provides the exclusive remedy for federal employees.[77] However, the U.S. Courts of Appeals for the Third, Fifth, Sixth, Eighth, and Eleventh Circuits have held that federal agencies may be sued under either Section 501 or Section 504.[78]

For those categories of plaintiffs who are required to exhaust their administrative remedies prior to bringing a cause of action into court, case law interpreting Section 2000e-16 of Title VII is instructive in providing that the failure to comply with the procedural requirement of that section is grounds for dismissal of a Title VII action.[79] The failure to exhaust

---

[75] *Id.* §794a.

[76] 29 U.S.C.A. §794(b).

[77] Rivera v. Heyman, 157 F.3d 101, 104-05, 8 AD Cases 758 (2d Cir. 1998); Johnston v. Horne, 875 F.2d 1415, 1420–21, 49 FEP Cases 1806 (9th Cir. 1989), *overruled on other grounds by* Irwin v. Department of Veterans Affairs, 498 U.S. 89, 54 FEP Cases 577 (1990); Johnson v. U.S. Postal Serv., 861 F.2d 1475, 1477–78, 48 FEP Cases 686 (10th Cir. 1988); McGuinness v. U.S. Postal Serv., 744 F.2d 1318, 1321, 1 AD Cases 624 (7th Cir. 1984).

[78] *See* Spence v. Straw, 54 F.3d 196, 199 (3d Cir. 1995); de la Torres v. Bolger, 781 F.2d 1134, 1135–36 (5th Cir. 1986); Smith v. United States Postal Serv., 742 F.2d 257, 259–60 (6th Cir. 1984); Morgan v. United States Postal Serv., 798 F.2d 1162, 1164–65 (8th Cir. 1986), *cert. denied*, 480 U.S. 948, 94 L. Ed. 2d 794, 107 S. Ct. 1608 (1987); Treadwell v. Alexander, 707 F.2d 473 (11th Cir. 1983).

[79] *Irwin*, 498 U.S. at 96; Brown v. General Servs. Admin., 425 U.S. 820, 835, 12 FEP Cases 1361 (1976); Tolbert v. United States, 916 F.2d 245, 56 FEP Cases 152 (5th Cir. 1990); Hupka v. U.S. Dep't of Def., 134 F. Supp. 2d 871 (E.D. Mich. 2001).

administrative remedies prior to bringing a cause of action for discrimination in federal court is a condition precedent to filing a civil action in federal court.[80]

In situations where a public employee, whose employer is covered under the Rehabilitation Act, has entered into a contract (e.g., a collective bargaining agreement) that allows the allegations of employment discrimination to be raised in a negotiated grievance procedure, any complaint or grievance that the employee wishes to file regarding employment discrimination claims must be raised under the statutory scheme to the Merit Systems Protection Board (MSPB) or the negotiated grievance procedure.[81] However, the employee must choose one of the two resolution tracks, not both.[82]

If the employee elects to pursue the grievance under the collective bargaining agreement, the employee is required to process the grievance through the complete grievance procedure through arbitration.[83] The employee must then appeal any unfavorable arbitrator's decision to the MSPB.[84] Only then may the employee seek review of an unfavorable decision in federal court. Anything less would be a failure to exhaust the administrative procedures.

III. Sovereign Immunity

The Eleventh Amendment to the U.S. Constitution states, "The judicial power of the United States shall not be construed to extend to any suit in law or equity, commenced or prosecuted against one of the United States by citizens of another State, or by citizens or subjects of any foreign state." Although the amendment literally applies only to lawsuits against a state or by citizens of another state, the Supreme Court has extended the Amendment's applicability to lawsuits that citizens file

---

[80] Kubicki v. Brady, 829 F. Supp. 906, 910 (E.D. Mich. 1993), aff'd, 41 F.3d 1507 (6th Cir. 1994).

[81] 29 C.F.R. §1614.301(a).

[82] Id.

[83] Government Employees (AFGE), Local 2052 v. Reno, 992 F.2d 331, 336, 143 LRRM 2082 (D.C. Cir. 1993).

[84] Id.

against their own states.[85] The Supreme Court interprets the Eleventh Amendment as an "affirmation that the fundamental principle of sovereign immunity limits the grant of judicial authority in Article III of the Constitution."[86] As such, the Court has consistently held that an "unconsenting State is immune from suits brought in federal court by her own citizens as well as by citizens of another State."[87] It is also the well-established principle that a lawsuit may be barred by the Eleventh Amendment when a state is not a named party to the legal action if the action is in essence one for the recovery of money from the state.[88]

The doctrine of sovereign immunity is not absolute, however. A state may waive its immunity or Congress may abrogate the immunity through Section 5 of the Fourteenth Amendment.[89] In deciding whether a state has waived it constitutional protection under the Eleventh Amendment the waiver must be expressly stated.[90] Also, Congress may abrogate a state's Eleventh Amendment immunity "when it both unequivocally intends to do so," and " 'act[s] pursuant to a valid grant of

---

[85] Board of Trs. of the Univ. of Ala. v. Garrett, 531 U.S. 356, 11 AD Cases 737 (2001); Kimel v. Florida Bd. of Regents, 528 U.S. 62, 72–73, 81 FEP Cases 970 (2000) (ultimate guarantee of Eleventh Amendment is that nonconsenting states may not be sued by private individuals in federal court); Seminole Tribe of Fla. v. Florida, 517 U.S. 44, 54 (1996).

[86] Pennhurst State Sch. & Hosp. v. Halderman, 465 U.S. 89, 98 (1984).

[87] Edelman v. Jordan, 415 U.S. 651 (1974).

[88] Ford Motor Co. v. U.S. Dep't of Treasury, 323 U.S. 459, 464 (1945) ("[W]hen the action is in essence one for the recovery of money from the state, the state is the real, substantial party in interest and is entitled to invoke its sovereign immunity from suit even though individual officials are nominal defendants.").

[89] "No State shall make or enforce any law which shall abridge the privileges or immunities of citizens of the United States; nor shall any State deprive any person of life, liberty, or property, without due process of law; nor deny to any person within its jurisdiction the equal protection of the laws." U.S. CONST. amend. XIV, §1. The Congress shall have the power to enforce, by appropriate legislation, the provisions of this article." U.S. CONST. amend. XIV, §5.

[90] "In deciding whether a State has waived its constitutional protection under the Eleventh Amendment, we will find waiver only where stated 'by the most express language or by such overwhelming implications from the text as [will] leave no room for any other reasonable construction.'" *Edelman*, 415 U.S. at 673 (quoting Murray v. Wilson Distilling Co., 213 U.S. 151, 171 (1909)).

constitutional authority.' "[91] The Supreme Court, in *Seminole Tribe of Florida v. Florida*,[92] set forth a two-part test to determine whether Congress has abrogated a state's immunity when enacting legislation.

The initial inquiry is whether Congress unequivocally expressed its intent to abrogate the immunity. The second question is whether Congress acted pursuant to a valid exercise of its power in abrogating the immunity.[93]

In *Alden v. Maine*,[94] the Supreme Court held that "the powers delegated to Congress under Article I of the United States Constitution do not include the power to subject nonconsenting States to private suits for damages in state courts."[95] Since *Alden*, several state courts have addressed the issue of state immunity and held that a state has immunity from a lawsuit even when the action is brought in state court.[96]

---

[91] Board of Trs. of the Univ. of Ala. v. Garrett, 531 U.S. 356, 11 AD Cases 737 (2001) (citing Kimel v. Florida Bd. of Regents, 528 U.S. 62, 73, 81 FEP Cases 970 (2000)).

[92] 517 U.S. 44 (1996).

[93] *Id.* at 55.

[94] 527 U.S. 706, 5 WH Cases 2d 607 (1999).

[95] *Id.* at 712.

[96] *See* Erickson v. Board of Governors of State Colls. & Univs. for Northeastern Ill. Univ., 207 F.3d 945, 952, 10 AD Cases 577, 582 (7th Cir. 2000) (after *Alden*, states may "implement a blanket rule of sovereign immunity"), *cert. denied sub nom.* United States v. Board of Governors of State Colls. & Univs. for Northeastern Ill. Univ., 531 U.S. 1190 (2001); Whittington v. State, 129 N.M. 221, 4 P.3d 668, 6 WH Cases 2d 1023 (Ct. App. 2000), *aff'd*, 45 P.3d 889, 7 WH Cases 2d 1456 (2002) (vacating earlier *Whittington* decision in light of *Alden*, and that states enjoy immunity from FLSA lawsuits even when suit is brought in state court); Bachmeier v. Hoffman, 1 P.3d 1236, 6 WH Cases 2d 56 (Wyo. 2000) (*Alden* reaffirmed that states have sovereign immunity in action brought in state courts); Commonwealth v. Luzik, 259 Va. 198, 208, 524 S.E.2d 871, 5 WH Cases 2d 1735 (2000) (applying *Alden*, state has sovereign immunity from Fair Labor Standards Act (FLSA), 29 U.S.C. §201 et seq., claims even when claim is brought in state court); Lawson v. University of Tenn., 2000 Tenn. App. LEXIS 53 (Tenn. Ct. App. 2000) (state cannot be sued in action pursuant to FLSA even when suit is brought in state court following decision in *Alden*); Boise Cascade Corp. v. Board of Forestry, 164 Ore. App. 114, 118–19, 991 P.2d 563 (1999) (referring to *Alden* and considering defendant's immunity claims under Eleventh Amendment); Jacoby v. Arkansas Dep't of Educ., 338 Ark. 505, 506, 995 S.W.2d 353 (1999) (ordering rebriefing on issue of immunity following decision in *Alden*); Allen v. Fauver, 327 N.J. Super. 14, 18, 742 A.2d 594, 597 (1999) (quoting *Alden*, that state's immunity "flowed from the fundamental aspects of

Even though the *Alden* Court held that a state may assert its sovereign immunity when claims are brought against it in its own courts, it emphasized that the state's immunity may still be waived or be abrogated by Congress when legislation is passed pursuant to its power under Section 5 of the Fourteenth Amendment.[97]

A. The Americans With Disabilities Act

Congress sought to abrogate state sovereign immunity under the ADA by including express language in Section 12202 of Title V that meets the standard of an "unequivocal expression of congressional intent to overturn the constitutionally guaranteed immunity of the several states."[98] Title V of the ADA contains "Miscellaneous Provisions," and Section 12202, which is entitled "State Immunity," provides:

> A State shall not be immune under the eleventh amendment to the Constitution of the United States from an action in Federal or State court of competent jurisdiction for a violation of this chapter. In any action against a State for a violation of the requirements of this chapter, remedies (including remedies both at law and in equity) are available for such a violation to the same extent as such remedies are available for such a violation in an action against any public or private entity other than a State.

The ADA's statutory language leaves little doubt as to the congressional intent, and—prior to the Supreme Court's decision in *Board of Trustees of the University of Alabama v. Garrett*[99]—the majority of courts had allowed suits to be brought against states in federal courts under the ADA.[100] However, a

---

sovereignty enjoyed by the states before ratification of the United States Constitution"), *aff'd*, 167 N.J. 69, 768 A.2d 1055, 6 WH Cases 2d 1741 (2000).

[97] *Alden*, 527 U.S. at 713.

[98] Atascadero State Hosp. v. Scanlon, 473 U.S. 234, 240 (1985) (quoting Pennhurst State Sch. & Hosp. v. Halderman, 465 U.S. 89 (1984)).

[99] 531 U.S. 356, 11 AD Cases 737 (2001).

[100] Before *Garrett*, the majority of courts that addressed this issue held that Congress effectively abrogated the states' Eleventh Amendment rights when it enacted the ADA. *See* Garrett v. University of Ala. at Birmingham Bd. of Trs., 193 F.3d 1214, 1218, 9 AD Cases 1635 (11th Cir. 1999), *rev'd*, 531 U.S. 356, 11 AD Cases 737 (2001) (both ADA and Rehabilitation Act are within scope of congressional

CH. 10 III.A. REMEDIES AND STRATEGIES 981

contrary position was taken by a significant number of other courts, albeit a minority of panels, holding that Congress

power and states' Eleventh Amendment immunity was effectively abrogated by Congress); Dare v. California State Dep't of Motor Vehicles, 191 F.3d 1167, 1175, 9 AD Cases 1239 (9th Cir. 1999) (ADA is "congruent and proportional exercise" of Congress' enforcement powers under §5 of Fourteenth Amendment and Congress abrogated states' Eleventh Amendment immunity), *cert. denied,* 531 U.S. 1190 (2001); Martin v. Kansas, 190 F.3d 1120, 1129, 9 AD Cases 1075 (10th Cir. 1999) (affirming district court and joining majority of courts on this issue; Congress effectively abrogated state's immunity when it enacted ADA); Muller v. Costello, 187 F.3d 298, 311, 9 AD Cases 1064, 1072 (2d Cir. 1999) (distinguishing ADA from Religious Freedom Restoration Act, 42 U.S.C. §2000bb et seq.; ADA is narrowly tailored and is "reasonable response to the problem of discrimination against people with disabilities"); Amos v. Maryland Dep't of Pub. Safety & Corr. Servs., 178 F.3d 212, 222–23, 9 AD Cases 769 (4th Cir. 1999) (Congress properly enacted ADA within its constitutional powers pursuant to §5 of Fourteenth Amendment); Nelson v. Miller, 170 F.3d 641, 648, 9 AD Cases 234 (6th Cir.1999) ("it is clear from the language of the ADA" that Congress abrogated states' rights under Eleventh Amendment and that states cannot claim immunity in defending ADA claims from private citizens in federal court); Autio v. State, County & Mun. Employees (AFSCME), 140 F.3d 802, 806, 7 AD Cases 1706 (8th Cir. 1998) (enforcement of ADA is well within "spirit and letter of the Constitution" and ADA is proper exercise of Congress' enforcement power under §5 of Fourteenth Amendment, thereby abrogating states' immunity rights under Eleventh Amendment); Kimel v. Florida Bd. of Regents, 139 F.3d 1426, 1433, 8 AD Cases 1 (11th Cir. 1998), *aff'd,* 528 U.S. 62, 81 FEP Cases 970 (2000) (siding with majority of courts that have addressed this issue; ADA is valid abrogation of states' Eleventh Amendment immunity); Coolbaugh v. Louisiana, 136 F.3d 430, 438, 7 AD Cases 1730 (5th Cir.), *cert. denied,* 525 U.S. 819 (1998) (ADA is proper exercise of Congress' §5 enforcement power under Fourteenth Amendment, thereby depriving Louisiana of immunity defense pursuant to Eleventh Amendment); Clark v. California, 123 F.3d 1267, 1270, 7 AD Cases 292 (9th Cir. 1997), *cert. denied,* 524 U.S. 937 (1998) (affirming district court; both ADA and Rehabilitation Act were validly enacted under Fourteenth Amendment); Crawford v. Indiana Dep't of Corr., 115 F.3d 481, 487, 6 AD Cases 1416 (7th Cir. 1997) (ADA is similar to Age Discrimination in Employment Act, 29 U.S.C. §621 et seq., Congress was "well within its powers" under §5 of Fourteenth Amendment in addressing issue of disability discrimination, and states cannot use Eleventh Amendment to claim immunity from suits brought pursuant to ADA); Jones v. Pennsylvania, 2000 U.S. Dist. LEXIS 107 (E.D. Pa. 2000) (Eleventh Amendment offers no protection to states from ADA and "strong majority" has held likewise); Johnson v. State Tech. Ctr. at Memphis, 24 F. Supp. 2d 833, 842, 9 AD Cases 301 (W.D. Tenn. 1998) ("great weight of authority" has rejected states' claims of immunity under Eleventh Amendment when facing ADA claim brought by private citizen in federal court); Thrope v. Ohio, 19 F. Supp. 2d 816, 821–22, 8 AD Cases 1133 (S.D. Ohio 1998) ("clear majority" of courts have held that ADA is proper exercise of congressional power; Ohio could not claim immunity pursuant to Eleventh Amendment from claim brought in class action lawsuit); Lamb v. John Umstead Hosp., 19 F. Supp. 2d 498, 510, 9 AD Cases 401 (E.D.N.C. 1998) (ADA falls within Congress' power to adopt legislation pursuant to §5 of Fourteenth Amendment and ADA is an "effective abrogation" of states' immunity to suit under Eleventh Amendment);

failed to abrogate the states' immunity when it enacted the ADA.[101]

In 2001, the Supreme Court resolved the split among the courts of appeals in *Garrett* and decided that suits in federal court by state employees to recover money damages by reason of the State's failure to comply with Title I of the ADA are

---

Meekison v. Voinovich, 17 F. Supp. 2d 725, 730 (S.D. Ohio 1998) (Congress effectively abrogated states' immunity under Eleventh Amendment); Anderson v. Department of Pub. Welfare, 1 F. Supp. 2d 456, 468, 9 AD Cases 375 (E.D. Pa. 1998) (ADA is "congruent and proportional response to unconstitutional discrimination against disabled individuals," thereby preventing Pennsylvania from using Eleventh Amendment immunity as defense to ADA claims made by private citizens in federal court); Williams v. Ohio Dep't of Mental Health, 960 F. Supp. 1276, 1282-83, 7 AD Cases 1162 (S.D. Ohio 1997) ("number of other courts" have found that Congress abrogated states' Eleventh Amendment immunity when it enacted ADA and holding likewise); Mayer v. University of Minn., 940 F. Supp. 1474, 1480, 7 AD Cases 1551 (D. Minn. 1996) (Rehabilitation Act and ADA were valid exercises of congressional power and University could not assert Eleventh Amendment immunity); Martin v. Voinovich, 840 F. Supp. 1175, 1187 (S.D. Ohio 1993) (with very little analysis Congress unequivocally expressed its desire to abrogate states' Eleventh Amendment immunity; plaintiff could proceed with his ADA claim against state).

[101] *See* Erickson v. Board of Governors of State Colls. & Univs. for Northeastern Ill. Univ., 207 F.3d 945, 951, 10 AD Cases 577 (7th Cir. 2000), *cert. denied sub nom.* United States v. Board of Governors of State Colls. & Univ. for Northeastern Ill. Univ., 531 U.S. 1190 (2001) (ADA is not "prophylactic legislation" and Eleventh Amendment provides Illinois protection from suits brought in federal courts); DeBose v. Nebraska, 186 F.3d 1087, 1088, 9 AD Cases 832 (8th Cir.), *cert. denied*, 531 U.S. 1190 (1999) (Congress did not abrogate states' immunity when enacting ADA); Alsbrook v. City of Maumelle, Ark., 184 F.3d 999, 1009–10, 9 AD Cases 897 (8th Cir. 1999) (congressional record of ADA fails to support "proposition that most state programs and services discriminate arbitrarily against the disabled," therefore Congress did not validly abrogate Arkansas' Eleventh Amendment immunity from private suit in federal court); Brown v. North Carolina Div, of Motor Vehicles, 166 F.3d 698, 708, 11 AD Cases 831 (4th Cir. 1999), *cert. denied*, 531 U.S. 1190 (2001) (Congress went beyond mere remedy of violations of constitutional rights and attempted to define substance of those rights; Congress did not abrogate states' Eleventh Amendment immunity); Hedgepeth v. Tennessee, 33 F. Supp. 2d 668, 675, 9 AD Cases 163 (W.D. Tenn. 1998), *aff'd*, 215 F.3d 608 (6th Cir. 2000) (agreeing with minority of courts that ADA gives "the disabled a preferential right to treatment where no such right exists under the Equal Protection Clause," and Congress did not effectively abrogate states' immunity when it enacted ADA); Nihiser v. Ohio Envtl. Prot. Agency, 979 F. Supp. 1168, 1175, 7 AD Cases 751 (S.D. Ohio 1997), *aff'd in part, rev'd in part*, 269 F.3d 626, 12 AD Cases 530 (6th Cir. 2001), *cert. denied*, 536 U.S. 922 (2002) (ADA did not meet second prong of Katzenbach— Katzenbach v. Morgan, 384 U.S. 641 (1966)—test as there is no congruence and proportionality between injury to be prevented and remedies contained within ADA, thereby allowing Ohio Environmental Protection Agency to claim immunity under Eleventh Amendment).

barred by the Eleventh Amendment. The Court found that the two-part test to determine whether Congress has abrogated a state's immunity when enacting legislation under *Seminole Tribe of Florida v. Florida*,[102] had not been met. In order to "authorize private individuals to recover money damages against the States, there must be a pattern of discrimination by the States which violates the Fourteenth Amendment, and the remedy imposed by Congress must be congruent and proportional to the targeted violation."[103] As Congress was found to have lacked the requisite documentation of a marked pattern of unconstitutional action by the states against the disabled to justify such abrogation of state sovereign immunity under the ADA, the Court held that Congress did not validly abrogate the states' sovereign immunity from suit by private individuals for money damages under Title I.[104]

Apart from private actions, courts have noted that the Eleventh Amendment would not bar the federal government from instituting a lawsuit against a state employer on behalf of an individual employee. For example, in *United States v. Mississippi Department of Public Safety*,[105] the U.S. Court of Appeals for the Fifth Circuit noted that any bar on direct litigation by employees against the state would not limit the national government's ability to bring suit against the states for the benefit of the public.

---

[102] 517 U.S. 44, 55 (1996) (Congress must unequivocally express its intent to abrogate immunity, and then Congress must act pursuant to valid exercise of its power in abrogating immunity).

[103] *Garrett*, 531 U.S. at 374, 11 AD Cases at 744.

[104] *Id.* In a footnote, the Court noted that persons with disabilities still had available federal recourse against discrimination through enforcement by the United States in actions for money damages, private right of action for injunctive relief under *Ex parte Young*, 209 U.S. 123 (1908), and redress through state laws that protect the rights of the disabled in employment and other aspects of life. *Id.* at 374 n.9. Two years after *Garrett*, the Supreme Court agreed to hear *Medical Bd. of Cal. v. Hason*, 294 F.3d 1166, 13 AD Cases 477 (9th Cir. 2002), *cert. dismissed*, 538 U.S. 958 (2003), in which the court will determine if plaintiffs are permitted to sue state governments under the Title II of the ADA for failing to provide equal access to and treatment under services provided by public entities covered under this portion of the statute.

[105] 321 F.3d 495, 13 AD Cases 1706 (5th Cir. 2003).

B. The Rehabilitation Act of 1973

In 1985, the Supreme Court reviewed an employment discrimination case brought against a California State hospital under Section 504 of the Rehabilitation Act of 1973.[106] As Section 505(a) made available to any person aggrieved by any act of any recipient of federal assistance under the Rehabilitation Act the remedies for employment discrimination provided in Title VI of the Civil Rights Act of 1964, the U.S. Court of Appeals for the Ninth Circuit previously held that the Eleventh Amendment did not bar the action because by receiving the federal funds under the Rehabilitation Act, the state had implicitly consented to be sued as a recipient under Section 504. The Supreme Court reversed the appellate court's opinion on the grounds that as written, the Rehabilitation Act did not abrogate the Eleventh Amendment's bar of lawsuits against the states. To do so, Congress must express its intention in unmistakable language in the statute itself. The state's mere acceptance of federal funds and participation in programs funded under the Rehabilitation Act were insufficient to establish the state's consent to be sued in federal court.[107] The general authorization contained in the statute for suit in a federal court fell short of the "unequivocal statutory language sufficient to abrogate the Eleventh Amendment,"[108] and did not manifest the State's "clear intention" to consent to waive its constitutional immunity.[109]

In light of the Supreme Court's interpretation precluding the applicability of the Rehabilitation Act to states, Congress subsequently amended the Rehabilitation Act so that the statute expressly covered states under Section 504.[110] The Civil Rights Restoration Act of 1987[111] added this language under

---

[106] Atascadero State Hosp. v. Scanlon, 473 U.S. 234, 1 AD Cases 758 (1985).
[107] *Id.* at 246–47.
[108] *Id.* at 246, 1 AD Cases at 763.
[109] *Id.* at 246–47, 1 AD Cases at 763.
[110] Pub. L. No. 100-259, 102 Stat. 28 (1988) (codified at 20 U.S.C. §§1681, 1687, 1688; 29 U.S.C. §§706, 794; 42 U.S.C. §§6107, 2000d-4a).
[111] Pub. L. 100-259, 102 Stat. 28 (1988).

Section 794(b), which defined the programs and activities that are prohibited from discriminating on the basis of disability.[112]

Following the *Garrett*[113] ruling, several appellate courts considered whether states had waived their sovereign immunity through acceptance of federal funds under the Rehabilitation Act. In *Miller v. Texas Tech University Health Sciences Center*,[114] the U.S. Court of Appeals for the Fifth Circuit held that acceptance of funds prior to the *Garrett* decision could not be deemed a waiver of sovereign immunity by a defendant state, because it could not have known that it retained that capability in advance of the ruling. In *Koslow v. Commonwealth of Pennsylvania d/b/a Department of Corrections*,[115] the U.S. Court of Appeals for

---

[112]"Program or activity" is defined as follows:
For the purposes of this section, the term "program or activity" means all of the operations of—
(1)(A) a department, agency, special purpose district, or other instrumentality of a State or of a local government; or
(B) the entity of such State or local government that distributes such assistance and each such department or agency (and each other State or local government entity) to which the assistance is extended, in the case of assistance to a State or local government;
(2)(A) a college, university, or other postsecondary institution, or a public system of higher education; or
(B) a local educational agency (as defined in section 7801 of Title 20) system of vocational education, or other school system;
(3)(A) an entire corporation, partnership, or other private organization, or an entire sole proprietorship—
(i) if assistance is extended to such corporation, partnership, private organization, or sole proprietorship as a whole; or
(ii) which is principally engaged in the business of providing education, health care, housing, social services, or parks and recreation; or
(B) the entire plant or other comparable, geographically separate facility to which Federal financial assistance is extended, in the case of any other corporation, partnership, private organization, or sole proprietorship; or
(4) any other entity which is established by two or more of the entities described in paragraph (1), (2), or (3);
any part of which is extended Federal financial assistance.
29 U.S.C. §794(b).

[113]Board of Trs. of the Univ. of Ala. v. Garrett, 531 U.S. 356, 11 AD Cases 737 (2001).

[114]330 F.3d 691, 14 AD Cases 583, *rehearing, en banc, granted*, 342 F.3d 563, 14 AD Cases 1472 (5th Cir. 2003).

[115]302 F.3d 161, 13 AD Cases 769 (3d Cir. 2002), *cert. denied*, 537 U.S. 1232 (2003). *See also* Douglas v. California Dep't of Youth Auth., 271 F.3d 812, 12 AD Cases 826 (9th Cir. 2001), *cert. denied*, 536 U.S. 924 (2002).

the Third Circuit held that the state had waived its Eleventh Amendment immunity with respect to departments of government that received federal funds.

IV. REMEDIES

A. Damages

1. The Americans with Disabilities Act

a. Title I

Just as the enforcement procedures under the ADA Title I parallel those under Title VII of the Civil Rights Acts of 1964, as discussed above, the remedies available under the ADA Title I are the same as the remedies available under Title VII of the Civil Rights Acts of 1964.[116]

As initially enacted in 1990, Title I of the ADA provided only for equitable remedies.[117] Through the Civil Rights Act of 1991,[118] Congress provided for compensatory and punitive damages to be awarded under ADA Title I and Section 501 of the Rehabilitation Act against employers that engaged in

---

[116]42 U.S.C. §12117(a).

[117]Under §706(g) of the Civil Rights Act of 1964 as originally enacted, the court was authorized to award remedies such as injunctions, reinstatement, back pay, and lost benefits, on a finding that an employer intentionally engaged in an unlawful employment practice. Although reinstatement is the presumptive relief, front pay may be awarded when reinstatement is not practical. For example, plaintiffs may be reluctant to return to their former places of employment after winning their lawsuits, or there may have been so much disruption in the workplace over the plaintiff's case that it may be impractical to reinstate plaintiff in the same work environment.

Generally, front pay is the calculation of lost future compensation for the period between judgment and reinstatement that is provided in lieu of reinstatement. Pollard v. E.I. du Pont de Nemours & Co., 532 U.S. 843, 85 FEP Cases 1217 (2001). The scope of front pay is difficult to ascertain, and plaintiffs may have experts testify as to the proper scope of front pay to assist in determining how long one can reasonably expect it to take the plaintiff to find a job of comparable pay and stature. When there is a jury trial, judges may refer the question of the scope of front pay to the jury because it is a factual question.

[118]Pub. L. No. 102-166, 105 Stat. 1071.

unlawful intentional discrimination.[119] The amendments allowed a successful plaintiff to recover, in addition to the equitable remedies already allowed by statute, punitive damages and compensatory damages "for future pecuniary losses, emotional pain, suffering, inconvenience, mental anguish, loss of enjoyment of life, and other nonpecuniary losses."[120] The total damages amount for compensatory and punitive damages cannot exceed a combined total of: (1) $50,000 when the defendant employer has between 15 and 100 employees (including temporary and part-time employees according to the EEOC) in each of 20 or more calendar weeks in the current or preceding calendar year; (2) $100,000 when the defendant employer has between 101 and 200 employees during that period; (3) $200,000 when the defendant employer has between 201 and 500 employees during that period; or (4) $300,000 when the defendant employer has more than 500 employees during that period. When a claim is filed against an employer by more than one person, each individual may claim the maximum amount of damages.[121]

As written, the amendment appeared to limit an individual plaintiff's recovery to $300,000 against an employer that intentionally discriminates on the basis of a disability in violation of ADA Title I and Section 501. However, the Supreme Court clarified, in *Pollard v. E.I. du Pont de Nemours & Co.*,[122] that the newly authorized remedies of compensatory and punitive damages under Section 1981a, as amended by the Civil Rights Act of 1991, for violations of intentional discrimination were remedies available in addition to the equitable relief already authorized under the Civil Rights Act of 1964. Therefore, jury awards for back pay and front pay would not be included in

---

[119] *See* 137 CONG. REC. S15503–04 (Oct. 30, 1991).

[120] Pub. L. No. 166, 105 Stat. 1071, at Sec. 102(b)(3).

[121] *EEOC Enforcement Guidance: Compensatory and Punitive Damages Available Under §102 of the Civil Rights Act of 1991* (July 14, 1992).

[122] 532 U.S. 843, 85 FEP Cases 1217 (2001) (front pay is not element of compensatory damages under 42 U.S.C. §1981a, as amended by Civil Rights Act of 1991, as front pay was type of equitable relief already authorized under §706(g) of Civil Rights Act of 1964 (42 U.S.C. §2000e-5(g)) and thus not subject to damages cap imposed by §1981a(b)(3) as plain language of amendment makes clear that

calculating the statutory cap for compensatory and punitive damage awards.[123]

Further, the Civil Rights Act of 1991 expressly provides that where a discriminatory practice involves the provision of reasonable accommodations pursuant to the ADA, damages may not be awarded where the employer makes a good-faith effort to engage in consultation with the disabled employee who requested a reasonable accommodation, to make a reasonable accommodation that would not cause an undue hardship on the operation of the business.[124]

At least four appellate courts—the U.S. Courts of Appeals for the First, Fourth, Seventh, and Eleventh Circuits—permit an award of punitive damages in a claim under Title VII in the absence of compensatory damages so long as an award of back pay was present.[125] Because the back-pay award was likened to serve a similar purpose as compensatory damage awards, the doctrine that punitive damages may not be assessed in the absence of compensatory damages, was not applicable in the case.[126] As the remedies available under the ADA Title I are the same as the remedies available under Title VII of the Civil Rights Acts of 1964, the availability of punitive damages in this circumstance will also apply to Title I claims.[127]

---

newly authorized §1981a remedies were in addition to relief already authorized by §706(g)).

[123] *Id. See also* Burch v. Coca-Cola Co., 119 F.3d 305, 7 AD Cases 241 (5th Cir. 1997), *rev'd on other grounds*, (5th Cir. 1997).

[124] The statute provides that compensatory and punitive damages are not available in cases involving the provision of a reasonable accommodation when the covered entity "demonstrates good faith efforts, in consultation with the person with the disability who has informed the covered entity that accommodation is needed." 42 U.S.C. §1981a-(a)(3). This provision only insulates a defendant from compensatory and punitive damages, where the employer actively engaged in the interactive reasonable accommodation process that is recommended in the EEOC's Interpretive Guidance (*see* 29 C.F.R. pt. 1630, app. (Reasonable Accommodation Process Illustrated) (2003). This good-faith defense is not available in all ADA employment cases. The Civil Rights Act of 1991 refers only to cases brought under 42 U.S.C. §12112(b)(5). Thus, it is generally more advantageous to plaintiffs to bring their legal actions under theories of discrimination other than §12112(b)(5) to avoid the applicability of the good-faith defense.

[125] Conti v. Storage Tech. Corp., No. 01-1833 (4th Cir. Sept. 18, 2002).

[126] *Id.*

[127] *Id.*; *see also* §12117(a).

b. Title II

Title II appears to take a two-tier approach to available remedies. The statute provides that the remedies for violations of the ADA by state and local governments are the same as those available under Section 505 of the Rehabilitation Act.[128] Section 505 in turn provides that the remedies available under Section 504 are those available under Title VI of the Civil Rights Act of 1964.[129] Title II conjunctively states that state and local government employers having the requisite number of employees (i.e., 15) to otherwise fall within the coverage of Title I must comply with the provisions of Title I.[130] Therefore, where the entity at issue has fewer employees than the 15 employees specified for coverage by Title I, the Section 504 remedies will govern. It is interesting to note that such an application of remedies will result in the possibility that the smaller sized government entities would be subject to the larger damage awards available under Section 504 for intentional discrimination.

In a unanimous decision, the Supreme Court broadly held that punitive damages are unavailable in private suits brought under Title II of the ADA and Section 504 of the Rehabilitation Act,[131] because the remedies for violating Title II and Section 504 are coextensive with the remedies available under Title VI of the Civil Rights Act of 1964. Under Title VI, private individuals may pursue a cause of action, but they cannot recover punitive damages. The mere acceptance of federal funds also was found not to constitute an implicit consent to be liable for punitive damages. Because punitive damages cannot be awarded under Title VI, neither can they be awarded under Title II of the ADA or Section 504 of the Rehabilitation Act.[132]

---

[128] 29 U.S.C. §794a.
[129] 29 U.S.C. §794a(a)(1).
[130] 28 C.F.R. §35.140.
[131] Barnes v. Gorman, 536 U.S. 181 (2002).
[132] *Id.*

c. *Title III*

Title III prohibits public accommodations from discriminating on the basis of disability in their programs or activities.[133] It also applies to any commercial facility or entity that offers examinations or courses related to certain applications, licensing, certification, or credentiality.[134] Private suits may be brought by individuals who are being subjected to discrimination. Also, the DOJ will investigate complaints and conduct compliance reviews of covered entities. The DOJ will pursue lawsuits when it has reasonable cause to believe that there is a pattern or practice of discrimination or discrimination that raises an issue of general public importance.[135]

There is no statutory provision for state or local civil rights agencies to enforce directly Title III of the ADA. They can, however, enact and enforce state or local laws that incorporate the standards of the ADA.[136]

Within this specific realm of coverage, the relief available under Title III is limited. Remedies available in a private suit may include a permanent or temporary injunction, restraining order, or other order. The remedies may not include compensatory or punitive money damages or civil penalties. In cases where violations of the readily achievable barrier removal or accessible new construction and alterations are found, remedies may include an order to alter the facilities to make them readily accessible and usable by individuals with disabilities. Remedies may also include the provision of an auxiliary aid or service, the modification of a policy, or providing an alternative method of barrier removal.[137]

---

[133] 42 U.S.C. §12181 et seq.

[134] 42 U.S.C. §12189; 28 C.F.R. §36.102 (2003).

[135] AMERICANS WITH DISABILITIES ACT TITLE III TECHNICAL ASSISTANCE MANUAL (1993) §III-8.1000.

[136] There are vast numbers of code jurisdictions across the country that enforce various combinations of state and local building codes (which may, or may not, incorporate accessibility requirements). Compliance with local codes does not constitute compliance with ADA Title III requirements unless the Department of Justice certifies that those ordinances meet or exceed applicable ADA standards for alterations and new construction to public accommodations and commercial facilities. 42 U.S.C. §12188(b)(1)(A)(ii) of the ADA; 28 C.F.R. §36.604.

[137] Title III, TECHNICAL ASSISTANCE MANUAL §III-1.1000.

The U.S. Attorney General may bring a lawsuit against an entity covered under Title III where the entity is charged with engaging in a pattern or practice of discrimination or the discrimination raises an issue is of general public importance.[138] In addition to the remedies available to a private plaintiff bringing suit under this title, compensatory damages to individual victims are available when the Attorney General brings suit, but punitive damages are not. Additionally civil penalties of up to $50,000 for the first violation and $100,000 for each subsequent violation are available. In determining whether such penalties are warranted, the court must consider an entity's good-faith effort or attempt to comply with the ADA.

The requirements of Title III for new construction and alterations cover commercial facilities whose operations affect commerce, "such as office buildings, factories, and warehouses."[139] This category includes places of employment that may not constitute public accommodations or may place additional obligations on sites that fall under the description of both commercial facilities and public accommodations.[140] Commercial facilities do not include rail vehicles or facilities covered by the Fair Housing Act.[141]

Religious organizations are exempt from all requirements of Title III.[142] The exemption for religious entities is construed broadly and includes religious organizations as well as entities that are controlled by religious organizations.[143] This exemption covers all of the religious entity's activities, including activities that are secular or religious.[144] For example, a church operating a private elementary school that is open to members as well as nonmembers is exempt from Title III coverage. Furthermore, a nonreligious entity operating a place of public accommodation in space donated by a religious entity is not

---

[138] *Id.* §III-8.4000.
[139] *Id.* §III-1.3000.
[140] *Id.*
[141] *Id.* §III-1.3100; Fair Housing Act of 1968, 42 U.S.C. §3601 et seq.
[142] *Id.* at §III-1.5000.
[143] *Id.* §III.5100; *see also* 42 U.S.C. §12187.
[144] TITLE III TECHNICAL ASSISTANCE MANUAL, *supra* note 135, at §III-1.5200.

covered under Title III. The nonreligious entity would be subject to Title III "only if a lease exist[ed] under which rent or other consideration is paid."[145]

Private clubs are also wholly exempt from the obligations imposed by Title III.[146] The ADA uses the same definition of a private club that is found under Title II of the Civil Rights Act of 1964.[147] A private club will lose its exemption status to the extent the facilities "are made available for use by nonmembers as places of public accommodation."[148]

2. The Rehabilitation Act of 1973

Pursuant to the Rehabilitation Act amendments of 1992, the standards used to determine whether an employer has impermissibly discriminated against an individual on the basis of a disability are the same under Sections 501, 503, and 504 of the Rehabilitation Act and Title I of the ADA.[149] Thus, to the extent an employer is found to have intentionally discriminated against a disabled employee or job applicant under ADA Title I, an employer that is a covered entity under the Rehabilitation Act will also be found to have discriminated against the individual under the Rehabilitation Act.

Although Title I of the ADA and Sections 501 and 504 of the Rehabilitation Act are to be interpreted in the same manner with regard to employment discrimination, the remedies available for intentional discrimination under 504 may provide for

---

[145] *Id.*

[146] *Id.* §III-1.6000.

[147] *Id.*
Courts have been most inclined to find private club status in cases where—
  1) Members exercise a high degree of control over club operations.
  2) The membersip selection process is highly selective.
  3) Substantial membership fees are charged.
  4) The entity is operated on a nonprofit basis.
  5) The club was not founded specifically to avoid compliance with Federal civil rights laws.
Id.

[148] *Id.*

[149] Pub. L. No. 102-973. *See* 138 CONG. REC. H10714-77 (Oct. 2, 1992). The damage provisions of the Civil Rights Act of 1991 apply to Section 501 and ADA Title I.

a greater recovery for the plaintiff than under Title I or Section 501. The damage provisions of the Civil Rights Act of 1991, the purpose of which was to amend Title VII, do not apply to Section 504 because Section 504 was premised on Title VI of the Civil Rights Act of 1964 rather than Title VII.[150] Therefore, the compensatory damages available against employers who are found to have intentionally discriminated on the basis of a disability in violation of Section 504 are governed by applicable case law rather than the recovery limitations mandated by the ADA and the Civil Rights Act of 1991.[151] However, in *Barnes v. Gorman*,[152] the Supreme Court held that punitive damages are not a potential remedy for violations of Section 504.

Prior to the 1992 Supreme Court decision in *Franklin v. Gwinnett County Public Schools*,[153] there existed divergent opinions among various courts as to the availability of compensatory damages under Section 504.[154] Also, prior to *Franklin*, most courts held that punitive damages were not available under Section 504.[155]

In *Franklin*, the Supreme Court held that monetary damages are available in actions brought under Title IX of the 1972 Educational Amendments, which prohibits discrimination on

---

[150]The Rehabilitation Act provides that the "remedies, procedures, and rights" available in Title VI actions shall be available to plaintiffs proceeding under §504 against federal fund recipients. 29 U.S.C.A. §794a(a)(2).

[151]Title VI of the Civil Rights Act mentions no remedies and fails to specify a private right of action. Nonetheless, the Supreme Court has found an implied right of action (*Cannon v. University of Chicago*, 441 U.S. 677, 703 (1979)), and Congress' subsequent acknowledgment of this right in statutory amendments made clear that private individuals may sue to enforce that statutory provision. Alexander v. Sandoval, 532 U.S. 275 (2001).

[152]536 U.S. 181 (2002). The Court's conclusions also applied to actions brought against public entities under Section 202 of the ADA, 42 U.S.C. §12132.

[153]503 U.S. 60, 59 FEP Cases 213 (1992).

[154]*Compare, e.g.,* Miener v. Missouri, 673 F.2d 969 (8th Cir.), *cert. denied,* 459 U.S. 909 (1982) (compensatory damages available); Ruth Anne M. v. Alvin Indep. Sch. Dist., 532 F. Supp. 450 (S.D. Tex. 1982) (compensatory damages not available); Carter v. Orleans Parish Pub. Sch., 725 F.2d 261 (5th Cir. 1984) (compensatory damages available under Section 504 for intentional discrimination, but not for disparate impact causes of action).

[155]Shinault v. American Airlines, Inc., 738 F. Supp. 193 (S.D. Miss. 1990), *aff'd in part, rev'd in part,* 936 F.2d 796 (5th Cir. 1991); Gelman v. Department of Educ., 544 F. Supp. 651, 654, 1 AD Cases 359 (D. Colo. 1982).

the basis of sex in any educational program or activity receiving federal financial assistance.[156] Subsequent to this decision, courts have applied the reasoning underlying the *Franklin* decision to Section 504 because the issues in both Section 504 and Title IX were deemed identical.[157] The developed body of case law on this issue holds that compensatory damages are available when intentional discrimination is found.[158]

B. Injunctions

Many disability-related claims require emergency action by a court in order for effective relief to be granted to a plaintiff. Typically, plaintiff's lawyers may seek a temporary restraining order (TRO) from the court to enjoin a defendant from certain action.[159] The TRO can then be converted into a preliminary injunction and eventually into a permanent injunction.

One key to obtaining injunctive relief is demonstrating a threat of immediate and irreparable harm to the individual moving for a protective order before the adverse party can be heard in opposition. In situations involving an employment relationship, the plaintiff may emphasize the importance of continuing work in his or her chosen profession.

The dilemma faced by plaintiff's lawyers is how to stress strategically to the court the importance of continuing with employment due to the possible short life expectancy of the

---

[156] 20 U.S.C. §§1681–1688.

[157] Tanberg v. Weld County Sheriff, 787 F. Supp. 970, 2 AD Cases 148 (D. Colo. 1992) (following *Franklin*—compensatory damages available as implied remedy under §504 just as they are available as implied remedy under Title IX); Doe v. District of Columbia, 796 F. Supp. 559, 572, 2 AD Cases 197, 208 (D.D.C. 1992) (reasoning that "*Franklin* must authorize the award of damages for intentional discrimination under §504," because Congress intended same remedies to be available under Title IX, Title VI of the Civil Rights Act of 1964, and §504).

[158] The courts have yet to opine affirmatively that *compensatory* damages are available under §504 for unintentional discrimination. *See e.g.,* Wood v. President & Trs. of Spring Hill Coll., 978 F.2d 1214 (11th Cir. 1992). In *Franklin*, the court believed that "all" appropriate remedies were available; therefore, arguably punitive damages may be available under §504. As noted above, the Supreme Court's decision in *Barnes v. Gorman*, 536 U.S. 181 (2002), holds that *punitive* damages are not a potential remedy for violations of Section 504.

[159] FED. R. CIV. P. 65.

plaintiff (e.g., due to a human immunodeficiency virus (HIV) infection), while at the same time argue that the individual is otherwise qualified. Whether seeking injunctive relief will predispose the judge against the plaintiff on the merits is a legal strategy question the answer to which may turn on the facts of the case.

V. Litigation Strategies

The ADA is a complex piece of legislation with a host of procedural and administrative requirements. Prevailing in an ADA lawsuit, whether on the merits or at a pretrial stage, is a challenging task for both plaintiffs and defendants. The following highlights some tips and information litigants should keep in mind before filing/defending against an ADA claim.

A. Plaintiff's Strategies

As a number of academics and practitioners have observed after a decade of litigation under the ADA, those litigating discrimination claims under the statute on behalf of individuals alleging that their rights have been violated can face multiple hurdles and challenges. In a recent American Bar Association survey analyzing the outcomes of cases under the ADA, plaintiffs were victorious in only 4 percent of those cases decided in 2002.[160] Although a plaintiff's success at the administrative level was slightly higher,[161] employers still have a significant edge over employees. In fact, only 3.9 percent of the 310 cases

---

[160] Allbright, *2002 Employment Decisions Under the ADA Title I—Survey Update*, Law Rep., *available at* http://www.abanet.org/disability/reporter/employment.pdf. A plaintiff is considered the victor if he or she prevails on the merits.

[161] Employees prevailed in 21.9% of complaints filed with the EEOC. Under the EEOC's definitions, employees prevail in their administrative complaints if they are successful on the merits of their claims via negotiated settlement, employer capitulation, or conciliation, or if the EEOC determines that reasonable cause exists to believe that discrimination has occurred. Employers are deemed prevailing parties if the case is administratively closed because the plaintiff's claim is invalid, or because he or she failed to follow proper procedures. An employer is also deemed victorious if the agency issues a "no probably cause of discrimination" finding.

won by employers in 2002 actually were decided on the merits.[162] Thus, the majority of ADA cases are resolved at the summary judgment or other pretrial stage, and typically in the employer's favor.

These statistics indicate that the ADA imposes substantial technical and procedural hurdles for employees aggrieved by disability-based employment discrimination. Meeting the ADA's stringent definitions of "disability" and "qualified individual with a disability,"[163] in addition to overcoming an employer's defenses to an ADA claim, are considerable barriers to prevailing in an ADA suit. Despite the odds, there are a number of steps a plaintiff can take to increase the chances that his or her claim will survive summary judgment.

1. Filing the Charge of Discrimination at the Administrative Level

Because plaintiffs are required to exhaust their administrative remedies before filing a lawsuit in court,[164] it is crucial that they do so within the applicable statute of limitations period. Any allegations of disability discrimination must be filed with the EEOC within 180 days of the alleged discriminatory act. Alternatively, many states have enacted their own disability discrimination laws, and enforce these laws through appropriate state or local "deferral" agencies. Thus, if the employee first files the charge with an analogous state or local agency, the time period for filing the charge with the EEOC is extended to within 300 days after the alleged unlawful act occurred, or within 30 days after receiving notice that the state or local agency has terminated its processing of the charge, whichever is sooner.[165] In these deferral jurisdictions, the EEOC has no authority to process a charge of discrimination until the charge is timely filed with the state or local agency. Often, if the EEOC

---

[162] *Allbright*, at 2.

[163] 42 U.S.C. §§12103(2), 12111(8).

[164] A plaintiff must file a charge of discrimination with the EEOC within 180 days of the alleged discriminatory practice, or within 300 days if the plaintiff files the initial complaint with an analogous state agency. 42 U.S.C. §2000e-5(e)(1).

[165] 42 U.S.C. §2000e-5(e)(1).

receives the initial charge of discrimination, it will file that charge with the appropriate deferral agency simultaneously. However, an employee should not rely on the EEOC to do so, and should therefore inquire as to whether all appropriate agencies will be receiving the charge, and/or directly file the charge with the deferral agency in order to reserve the right to file a lawsuit later on.

2. Filing the Lawsuit in Court

After either the EEOC or the deferral state agency completes its processing of the charge, the employee is free to initiate a lawsuit. Once the employee receives a right-to-sue letter, he or she has 90 days in which to file a complaint in court.[166] In addition to articulating a cause(s) of action under the ADA, the complaint should include state or local disability law claims, if applicable. There are two main reasons for doing so. First, state or local laws may define "disability" more broadly than does the ADA. Thus, while an employee's impairment may not rise to the level of a protected disability under the ADA, it could constitute a disability under an analogous state or local law.

Second, unlike the ADA, many state or local laws do not provide a cap for punitive damages. Under the ADA, the maximum amount of punitive damages a plaintiff may be awarded ranges from $50,000 to $300,000, depending on the size of the employer.[167] If a plaintiff prevails on both his or her ADA and state/local disability law claims, however, a large punitive damages award may be apportioned to the state law claim in order to circumvent this monetary limit.

This tactic was sanctioned in *Gagliardo v. Connaught Laboratories*.[168] In that case, a plaintiff with multiple sclerosis, who

---

[166] 42 U.S.C. §2000e-5(f)(1).

[167] *Id.* §1981a. Employers with 15–100 employees are subject to a punitive damages cap of $50,000; employers with 101–200 employees are subject to a $100,000 cap; employers with 201–500 employees are subject to a $200,000 cap; and employers with more than 500 employees are subject to the maximum cap of $300,000. *Id.* §1981a(b)(3).

[168] 311 F.3d 565, 13 AD Cases 1345 (3d Cir. 2002).

believed she was terminated because of her medical condition, sued her employer under the ADA and the Pennsylvania Human Relations Act (PHRA).[169] A jury found in favor of the plaintiff, and awarded her $2.5 million in compensatory and punitive damages, which was later reduced to $2.3 million.[170] In response to the employer's motion to alter or amend the judgment, the district court limited the amount of punitive damages to $300,000—which is the statutory cap under the ADA for a large employer—and apportioned this amount to the ADA claim, since the PHRA does not provide for punitive damages. At the same time, the court allocated the remaining $2 million as compensatory damages under the state law claim, which does not limit such damages.

On appeal to the U.S. Court of Appeals for the Third Circuit, the employer contended, among other things, that the statutory cap on damages applied to all related disability claims.[171] The appellate court disagreed, holding that a cap on federal employment disability discrimination damages does not preclude the allocation of damages in excess of the statutory cap to analogous state law claims. In arriving at this decision, the Third Circuit relied on the ADA's guarantee that "[n]othing in this chapter shall be construed to invalidate or limit the remedies, rights, and procedures of any Federal law or law of any State . . . that provides greater or equal protection for the rights of individuals with disabilities than are afforded by this chapter."[172] According to the court's reasoning, applying the federal damages cap to state disability discrimination laws would limit the state law remedies in contravention of the ADA's clear language. Thus, it was permissible for the court to apportion a damage award between capped federal law claims and uncapped state law claims "so that the verdict winner

---

[169] 43 Pa. Stat. §951 et seq.
[170] *Gagliardo*, 311 F.3d at 568, 13 AD Cases at 1347.
[171] *Id.* at 570, 13 AD Cases at 1348.
[172] 42 U.S.C. §12201(b).

gets the maximum amount of the jury award that is legally available."[173]

The U.S. Courts of Appeals for the Ninth and District of Columbia Circuits also have held that the federal damages cap does not prevent a plaintiff from being awarded greater monetary damage amounts under state statutes virtually identical to federal nondiscrimination laws.[174] Therefore, including causes of action under state or local laws identical to the ADA could significantly benefit a plaintiff in the event of large damage awards.

3. Establishing a Prima Facie Case

In order to establish a viable claim under the ADA, a plaintiff must prove that he or she is disabled within the meaning of the ADA, qualified to perform the essential functions of the job with or without a reasonable accommodation, and was discriminated against because of this disability.[175]

a. Proving the Employee's Impairment Is a Disability

Only a qualified group of physical or mental conditions rise to the level of "disability" under the ADA.[176] Thus, one of the first hurdles a plaintiff faces in pursuing an ADA suit is proving that his or her impairment is a bona fide disability meriting statutory protection. According to the statute, a person is disabled if he or she has either a physical or mental impairment that substantially limits one or more major life

---

[173]Gagliardo v. Connaught Labs., 311 F.3d 565, 572, 13 AD Cases 1345, 1349 (3d Cir. 2002).

[174]Passantino v. Johnson & Johnson, 212 F.3d 493, 510, 84 FEP Cases 1123 (9th Cir. 2000) (discussing Title VII of the Civil Rights Act of 1991 and the Washington Law Against Discrimination, RCW 49.60); Martini v. Federal Nat'l Mortgage Ass'n, 178 F.3d 1336, 1349–50, 80 FEP Cases 1 (D.C. Cir. 1999) (discussing Title VII and the District of Columbia Human Rights Act, D.C. CODE. ANN. §§1-2501-1-2557); *C.f.* Oliver v. Cole Gift Ctrs., Inc., 85 F. Supp. 2d 109, 114 (D. Conn. 2000) (apportionment "would contravene the policies underlying both the Congressional limitation on recovery under Title VII and the limitation on punitive damages under Connecticut law").

[175]42 U.S.C. §12101–12213; Doren v. Battle Creek Health Sys., 187 F.3d 595, 597 (6th Cir. 1999).

[176]29 C.F.R. §1630.2(h).

activities, a record of such an impairment, or is regarded as having an impairment.[177]

One of the primary steps in proving disability is to illustrate how an impairment substantially limits a major life activity, "such as caring for oneself, performing manual tasks, walking, seeing, hearing, speaking, breathing, learning, and working."[178] An individual is substantially limited in performing these tasks if he or she is "[s]ignificantly restricted as to the condition, manner or duration under which [he or she] can perform [them] as compared to the condition, manner, or duration under which the average person in the general population can perform that same major life activity."[179]

i. Providing Proof. Therefore, in order to prove that an individual is substantially limited in a major life activity, a plaintiff should be prepared to provide evidence of the duration or long-term impact of the impairment, its severity, and how an average member of the general public does not suffer the same degree of limitation. For example, it may not be enough to show that a person's carpal tunnel syndrome restricts his or her ability to perform certain manual tasks, if those tasks are not central to an ordinary person's daily life.[180] Similarly, an inability to sleep is not an impairment if the degree of sleep deprivation is no greater than that suffered by the general population.[181] Evidence could include expert medical or vocational expert opinions or witness testimonials.

The determination of whether a person is disabled must take into consideration whether the person is substantially limited in a major life activity when using a mitigating measure,

---

[177] 42 U.S.C. §12102(2).
[178] 29 C.F.R. §1630.2(h)(2)(i) (2003).
[179] *Id.* §1630(j)(1)(ii) (2003).
[180] *See* Toyota Motor Mfg., Ky., Inc. v. Williams, 534 U.S. 184, 198, 12 AD Cases 993 (2002).
[181] *See* EEOC v. Sara Lee Corp., 237 F.3d 349, 11 AD Cases 595 (4th Cir. 2001) (seizure disorder reduced quality of sleep, but not beyond that suffered by general public).

such as medication or corrective lenses.[182] However, just because a person uses a mitigating measure to cope with an impairment does not mean that he or she would not be considered disabled under the ADA. The impact of the measure itself needs to be evaluated to determine whether the individual is disabled. For example, does the mitigation measure allow the individual to function at a level experienced by the general population? If so, the impairment does not rise to the level of disability. Common examples include the use of corrective lenses to offset myopia, insulin to counteract the effects of diabetes, and counseling to alleviate the symptoms of depression.[183] However, if the mitigating measure does not sufficiently offset the impact of the impairment, or if the measure itself substantially limits a major life activity, then the individual may still be considered disabled.[184] For example, the use of a prosthesis does not completely compensate an amputee for the loss of limb function. Similarly, certain medications may produce side effects, such as extreme fatigue or dizziness, that adversely impact an individual's ability to care for oneself.[185] Because the effects of any impairment must be evaluated on a case-by-case basis, plaintiffs should be prepared to show how any mitigation measure does not adequately compensate for the effects of the impairment, and/or how the corrective measures themselves substantially limit one or more major life activities.

In order to prove that one is substantially limited in the ability to work, an employee must show that a disability prevents

---

[182] Albertsons, Inc. v. Kirkingburg, 527 U.S. 555, 9 AD Cases 694 (1999); Murphy v. United Parcel Serv., Inc., 527 U.S. 516, 9 AD Cases 691 (1999); Sutton v. United Air Lines, Inc., 527 U.S. 471, 9 AD Cases 673 (1999).

[183] See note 182, supra.

[184] See, e.g., EEOC v. Sears, Roebuck & Co., 233 F.3d 432, 11 AD Cases 193 (7th Cir. 2000) (individual with neuropathy substantially limited in her ability to walk even though she uses cane for support).

[185] See, e.g., Sutton v. United Airlines, 527 U.S. 471, 9 AD Cases 673 (1999) (recognizing that the effects of mitigating measures—both positive and negative—need to be considered in assessing impairment and disability under the ADA).

him or her from working in a class or broad range of jobs.[186] This showing will necessarily require the provision of information about the relevant labor market, including job variety and availability and the skills/experience needed to obtain those jobs. A plaintiff also should provide information regarding the jobs he or she can no longer perform because of an impairment.[187]

Merely claiming that one cannot work at a particular job will not suffice as proof that an individual is substantially limited in the ability to work. Plaintiffs must show how their impairments limit their employment opportunities in the relevant

---

[186] *See, e.g., Murphy,* 527 U.S. 516 (mechanic with hypertension regarded as being unable to perform only small subset of mechanics jobs, not mechanic positions generally); *Sutton,* 527 U.S. 471 (pilot with substandard vision precluded from only narrow range of jobs, so was not regarded as disabled); EEOC v. J.B. Hunt Transp., Inc., 321 F.3d 69, 13 AD Cases 1697 (2d Cir. 2003) (over-the-road truck driver applicants rejected because of their use of prescription medications not regarded as substantially limited in their ability to work, as they did not prove that employer thought they were unqualified to be drivers at all); Sheehan v. City of Gloucester, 321 F.3d 21, 14 AD Cases 1 (1st Cir. 2003) (police officer involuntarily retired from service because of his hypertension could not prove that employer regarded him as unable to perform broad range of jobs); Blanks v. Southwestern Bell Communications, Inc., 310 F.3d 398, 13 AD Cases 1253 (5th Cir. 2002) (HIV positive employee could not prove that employer believed he was unable to perform broad range of jobs); Mack v. Great Dane Trailers, 308 F.3d 776, 13 AD Cases 1153 (7th Cir. 2002) (limitations on lifting and squatting were occupation-specific, and did not prevent employee from working entirely); EEOC v. Woodbridge Corp., 263 F.3d 812, 12 AD Cases 254 (8th Cir. 2001) (inability to perform single job does not constitute disability); EEOC v. Rockwell Int'l Corp., 243 F.3d 1012, 11 AD Cases 929 (7th Cir. 2001) (plaintiff must provide some demographic information from relevant labor market as evidence that employer regarded employee as precluded from broad range of jobs, and not merely discrete set of jobs requiring particular skill); Cash v. Smith, 231 F.3d 1301, 11 AD Cases 203 (11th Cir. 2000) (firefighter must show he was regarded as being unable to perform broad class of jobs); Shipley v. City of University City, 195 F.3d 1020, 9 AD Cases 1775 (8th Cir. 1999) (same), *reh'g denied* (2000).

[187] *See, e.g.,* Duncan v. Washington Metro. Area Transit Auth., 240 F.3d 1110, 11 AD Cases 833 (D.C. Cir.) (en banc), *cert. denied,* 534 U.S. 818 (2001) (employee with degenerative disc disease resulting in lifting restriction failed to present evidence of number and types of jobs available in local labor market, and thus could not establish that he could not perform class or broad range of jobs).

labor market as a whole.[188] Although not required, vocation expert testimony can be instructive in this area.[189]

In addition to proving that an individual is disabled under the ADA, it is important to prove that an individual's disability was known to the employer at the time of the adverse employment action. An employer cannot discriminate on the basis of an individual's disability if it had no knowledge of that disability.[190] Employer comments or memoranda regarding the disability—assuming the impairment is not obvious—in addition to medical documents in one's employee file may serve as evidence of employer knowledge.

b. Proving the Employee Is a Qualified Individual With a Disability

Once plaintiffs prove that they are legitimately disabled under the ADA, they must demonstrate that they are "qualified" individuals with disabilities. A "qualified" individual with a disability possess the requisite "skill, experience, education and other job-related requirements of the employment position such individual holds or desires," and is able to perform the

---

[188] *See* Mahon v. Crowell, 295 F.3d 585, 13 AD Cases 390 (6th Cir. 2002) (injured steamfitter who presented evidence he suffered 47% loss of access to job market not substantially limited in his ability to work, as he was still qualified to perform over half the jobs he was qualified for prior to being injured); Gelabert-Ladenheim v. American Airlines, Inc., 252 F.3d 54, 11 AD Cases 1581 (1st Cir. 2001) (multilevel analysis of whether impairment substantially limits working requires individual to present evidence of how impairment restricts one's ability to work in job market); *Rockwell Int'l*, 243 F.3d 1012 (plaintiff must provide some demographic information from relevant labor market as evidence that employer regarded employee as precluded from broad range of jobs, and not merely discrete set of jobs requiring particular skill); *Duncan*, 240 F.3d 1110 (employee with degenerative disc disease resulting in lifting restriction failed to present evidence of number and types of jobs available in local labor market, and thus could not establish that he could not perform class or broad range of jobs).

[189] *Id. See also* Mullins v. Crowell, 228 F.3d 1305, 11 AD Cases 38 (11th Cir. 2000) (vocational expert testimony may be persuasive, but is not necessary to satisfy evidentiary burden).

[190] *See, e.g.*, Amadio v. Ford Motor Co., 238 F.3d 919, 11 AD Cases 641 (7th Cir. 2001) (auto assembly worker with many medical conditions not regarded as disabled, as he never informed employer of these conditions).

essential functions of that position "with or without reasonable accommodation."[191] Thus, the first step in this process is to prove that the plaintiff has the necessary credentials for the job, including the education, training, licensing, or experience.[192] These criteria are usually listed in the job advertisement or position description.

A more difficult task is proving that the employee can perform the essential functions of the job with or without a reasonable accommodation. A job task is considered "essential" if "the reason the position exists is to perform that function,"[193] a limited number of employees are available to perform that function, or if the job task is so specialized that the employee was hired specifically to perform that function.[194] Although a great amount of deference is given to an employer's judgment as to which job functions are considered essential, a plaintiff may be able to show that a job task is or is not essential by providing a copy of the position's written job description, and/or indicating which job tasks past or current employees in the same or similar position(s) perform, and how much time is devoted to that particular activity.[195]

If the employee does not have a copy of the written job description, he or she should obtain one from the company's web site, employee handbook, collective bargaining agreement, or via discovery. The plaintiff's performance evaluations or the evaluations of past or present employees in the same position may also provide written confirmation of the most important job tasks. If an employer claims that an employee's disability precludes him or her from performing a particular activity, the employee may be able to show that the activity is nonessential by its omission from these documents.

Similarly, if other employees in the same position do not perform a particular function, it is harder to maintain that that task is essential. For example, if an employer argues that

---

[191] 29 C.F.R. §1630.2(m) (2003).
[192] TITLE I TECHNICAL ASSISTANCE MANUAL, *supra* note 23, at §2.3.
[193] 29 C.F.R. §1630(n)(2) (2003).
[194] *Id.*
[195] 29 C.F.R. §1630(n)(3) (2003).

a hearing impaired employee is not a qualified individual with a disability because he or she cannot answer the phone, a plaintiff must be able to demonstrate that answering the phone is a marginal job function. If other employees in the same position do not or rarely perform telephone work, then the employee has a better chance of proving that the function is not essential to the position.[196]

Moreover, if there are various methods of performing an essential job function, then any one particular method cannot be deemed essential. In *Skerski v. Time Warner Cable Co.*,[197] for example, the U.S. Court of Appeals for the Third Circuit determined that "climbing" was not an essential function for a cable installer even though this skill was listed as a job requirement in the position description, where climbing was just one method of performing the essential function of working at great heights. Because the employee was able to show that using a bucket truck would enable him to perform the necessary work, climbing was a marginal, not an essential, job function.[198]

In sum, a plaintiff must be able to demonstrate that he or she is a qualified individual with a disability at the outset of litigation in order to survive summary judgment. A plaintiff should be prepared to demonstrate the nature and severity of the impairment, how the impairment impacts his or her major life activities, and the plaintiff's ability to perform the essential functions of the job with or without a reasonable accommodation.[199]

c. Reasonable Accommodation

In order to defeat a defendant's motion for summary judgment on the issue of the reasonableness of an accommodation, a plaintiff need only demonstrate how a particular accommodation would enable him or her to perform the essential

---

[196] *See* 29 C.F.R. §1630.2(n)(3).
[197] 257 F.3d 273, 11 AD Cases 1665 (3d Cir. 2001).
[198] *Id.*
[199] *See supra* at n.175.

functions of the job[200] and how the accommodation seems reasonable on its face.[201] It is then up to the employer to prove that the accommodation would constitute an undue hardship.[202] While not an onerous burden, the plaintiff ultimately must show that the accommodation is at least feasible.[203] Thus, the request for an accommodation must take into consideration the difficulty or expense imposed on the employer in providing that accommodation.[204] For example, if a plaintiff with hearing impairments requests that an employer hire an interpreter, he or she must articulate how this accommodation would be reasonable in light of such factors as the size of the organization, its financial resources, and the impact the accommodation would have on other employees. While a plaintiff is not required to provide exact budgetary numbers or a detailed feasibility analysis, the plaintiff must at least address the reasonableness issue.

If the issue is not the reasonableness of a given accommodation, but rather the failure to accommodate in general, a

---

[200] *See* Cannice v. Norwest Bank Iowa N.A., 189 F.3d 723, 9 AD Cases 1103 (8th Cir. 1999), *cert. denied*, 529 U.S. 1019 (2000) (employee suffering from anxiety disorder failed to provide evidence that private phone line to call his doctor or family members would enable him to continue working); Buckles v. First Data Resources, Inc., 176 F.3d 1098, 9 AD Cases 765 (8th Cir. 1999) (jury verdict in favor of plaintiff reversed on grounds that he failed to identify reasonable accommodation that would enable him to work).

[201] U.S. Airways, Inc. v. Barnett, 535 U.S. 391, 12 AD Cases 1729 (2002).

[202] *Id.*

[203] *See, e.g.,* Reed v. LePage Bakeries, Inc., 244 F.3d 254, 11 AD Cases 1150 (1st Cir. 2001) (employee must demonstrate that requested accommodation is feasible as part of prima facie case if arguing that he or she is able to perform essential functions of job); Hoskins v. Oakland County Sheriff's Dep't, 227 F.3d 719, 728, 10 AD Cases 1417 (6th Cir. 2000); Willis v. Conopco, Inc., 108 F.3d 282, 285–86, 6 AD Cases 806 (11th Cir. 1997); Riel v. Electronic Data Sys. Corp., 99 F.3d 678, 682–83, 6 AD Cases 26 (5th Cir. 1996); Monette v. Electronic Data Sys. Corp., 90 F.3d 1173, 1183 & n.10, 1186 n.12, 5 AD Cases 1326 (6th Cir. 1996); Borkowski v. Valley Cent. Sch. Dist., 63 F.3d 131, 138, 4 AD Cases 1264, 1270 (2d Cir. 1995) (plaintiff satisfies "burden of production" by showing "plausible accommodation"); Vande Zande v. Wisconsin Dep't of Admin., 44 F.3d 538, 542–43, 3 AD Cases 1636 (7th Cir. 1995); Barth v. Gelb, 2 F.3d 1180, 1187, 2 AD Cases 1180, 1185 (D.C. Cir. 1993) (interpreting parallel language in Rehabilitation Act, stating that plaintiff need only show he seeks "*method of accommodation* that is reasonable in the run of cases" (emphasis in original)).

[204] *See, e.g., Vande Zande*, 44 F.3d at 542–43.

plaintiff needs to provide reliable evidence that an employer failed to provide a reasonable accommodation despite the knowledge that the employee needed such an accommodation, and was otherwise qualified to perform the job.[205] This step entails a showing that the employer was made aware of the need for an accommodation, assuming such a need is not obvious. The employer is then required to engage in an "informal, interactive process" with the employee to identify the employee's limitations and devise an appropriate reasonable accommodation.[206] If an employee alleges that an employer failed to participate in this interactive process, an employ must show that: (1) the employer knew about the employee's disability; (2) the employee requested accommodations or assistance for his or her disability; (3) the employer did not make a good-faith effort to assist the employee in seeking accommodations; and (4) the employee could have been reasonably accommodated but for the employer's lack of good faith.[207] Failure to engage in this interactive process can constitute prima facie evidence that the employer may be acting in bad faith.[208] The request for the accommodation must, however, be made prior to the challenged disciplinary action.[209] Moreover, the plaintiff must prove that a reasonable accommodation existed; if not, the interaction process would have been a futile exercise, and

---

[205] *See* Higgins v. New Balance Athletic Shoe, Inc., 194 F.3d 252, 9 AD Cases 1555 (1st Cir. 1999).

[206] 29 C.F.R. §1630.2(o)(3) (2003).

To determine the appropriate reasonable accommodation it may be necessary for the covered entity to initiate an informal, interactive process with the qualified individual with a disability in need of the accommodation. This process should identify the precise limitations resulting from the disability and potential reasonable accommodations that could overcome those limitations.

[207] *See, e.g.*, Ballard v. Rubin, 284 F.3d 957, 12 AD Cases 1646 (8th Cir. 2002); Taylor v. Phoenixville Sch. Dist., 174 F.3d 142, 165, 9 AD Cases 311 (3d Cir. 1999); Cravens v. Blue Cross & Blue Shield of Kansas City, 214 F.3d 1011, 10 AD Cases 1057 (8th Cir. 2000).

[208] *See, e.g., Ballard*, 284 F.3d 957 (citing Fjellestad v. Pizza Hut of Am., Inc., 188 F.3d 944, 9 AD Cases 1153 (8th Cir. 1999)).

[209] *See, e.g.*, Hill v. Kansas City Area Transp. Auth., 181 F.3d 891, 9 AD Cases 833 (8th Cir. 1999) (employee bus driver's request for reasonable accommodation only after he was terminated for falling asleep on job was made too late).

the employer would be excused from failing to participate in this exchange.[210]

Some courts have held that the absence of an express request for a reasonable accommodation is not always necessary when pursuing a failure-to-accommodate claim. For example, in *Taylor v. Phoenixville School District*,[211] the U.S. Court of Appeals for the Third Circuit stated,

> The EEOC's manual makes clear . . . that while the notice does not have to be in writing, be made by the employee, or formally invoke the magic words "reasonable accommodation," the notice nonetheless must make clear that the employee wants assistance for his or her disability. In other words, the employer must know of both the disability and the employee's desire for accommodations for that disability.[212]

According to the court in *Taylor*, "What matters . . . are not formalisms about the manner of the request, but whether the employee or a representative for the employee provides the employer with enough information that, under the circumstances, the employer can be fairly said to know of both the disability and desire for an accommodation."[213] This approach is especially applicable to situations in which the employee suffers from a mental disability, and would be less likely to articulate specifically the need for a reasonable accommodation.[214] Thus, if plaintiffs cannot prove that they specifically requested reasonable accommodations, they should provide evidence that the employer at least knew of their disabilities

---

[210] *See, e.g.*, Mays v. Principi, 301 F.3d 866, 13 AD Cases 985 (7th Cir. 2002); Dropinski v. Douglas County, Neb., 298 F.3d 704. 13 AD Cases 676 (8th Cir. 2002); Kvorjak v. Maine, 259 F.3d 48, 12 AD Cases 160 (1st Cir. 2001).

[211] 174 F.3d 142, 9 AD Cases 311 (3d Cir. 1999).

[212] *Id.* at 158–59, 9 AD Cases at 322.

[213] *Id.* at 159, 9 AD Cases at 322.

[214] *See, e.g.*, Bultemeyer v. Fort Wayne Cmty. Sch., 100 F.3d 1281, 1285, 6 AD Cases 67, 71 (7th Cir. 1996) ([P]roperly participating in the interactive process means that an employer cannot expect an employee to read its mind and know that he or she must specifically say 'I want a reasonable accommodation,' particularly when the employee has a mental illness. . . . [I]f it appears that the employee may need an accommodation but doesn't know how to ask for it, the employer should do what it can to help.").

and need for accommodations, yet did nothing to further this goal.[215]

d. Making a Case for Punitive Damages

As previously discussed, an award of punitive damages can be significant in an ADA case, especially if the plaintiff also prevails on a virtually identical state law claim that does not impose a damages cap. However, in order to merit punitive damages in the first place, a plaintiff must demonstrate his or her eligibility for such an award.

Under the ADA, punitive damages are limited to those intentional acts of discrimination that are done "with malice or with reckless indifference to the federally protected rights of an aggrieved individual."[216] An employer acts with "malice" and "reckless indifference" if it knows that its actions violate the law, not simply that it is aware that its actions are discriminatory.[217] An employer need not commit "egregious" or "outrageous" acts to be liable for punitive damages, although evidence of such behavior may support an inference of malice or reckless indifference to an individual's rights.[218] An employer simply must know that its actions violate the ADA.

Circumstances may arise where an employer intentionally discriminates against a disabled individual, but would not be subject to punitive damages liability. For example, an employer may believe that the disabled employee poses a direct threat to himself or herself or others, or that the person is not a "qualified" individual with a disability under the ADA.[219] Alternatively, the employer may prove that it was unaware of the ADA's protections, or that the underlying theory of discrimination has not been judicially sanctioned. In these instances, the intentional acts of discrimination would warrant an award of

---

[215] See id.

[216] 42 U.S.C. §1981a(b)(1).

[217] See, e.g., Kolstad v. American Dental Ass'n, 527 U.S. 526, 536, 79 FEP Cases 1697, 1701 (1999) ("[A]n employer must at least discriminate in the face of a perceived risk that its actions will violate federal law to be liable in punitive damages.").

[218] Id.

[219] Bragdon v. Abbott, 524 U.S. 624, 629 (1999).

compensatory damages only, as the employer did not purposely violate the ADA.

Given the procedural and administrative burdens a plaintiff must face in order to prevail in an ADA suit, and some of the difficulties in achieving ultimate success, it is crucial that employees clearly and decisively prove that they are qualified individuals with disabilities before even addressing the employer's alleged discriminatory actions. If the employer's failure to provide a reasonable accommodation becomes an issue, a plaintiff must demonstrate that a viable accommodation existed, the employer was aware of the plaintiff's disability, and that an accommodation was needed and/or requested.[220] Because a plaintiff's burden is so great, however, employees should consider alternative options to a trial on the merits—such as settlement or alternative dispute resolution—if their cases seem too vulnerable to withstand summary judgment.

B. Defendant's Strategies

Employers win a substantial percentage of employment-based disability discrimination suits on summary judgment.[221] One reason may be the plaintiff's inability to prove that he or she is a qualified individual with a disability under the ADA. Meeting the elements of a claim under the ADA is a difficult burden, as the ADA imposes high standards for its definitions of "disability" and "qualified individual with a disability." Thus, many employers are successful at the summary judgment stage by challenging each element of the plaintiff's prima facie case. Alternatively, the ADA lists a number of defenses an employer may take under Title I of the Act, including claims that the disabled individuals would pose a direct threat to themselves or others, and that reasonably accommodating their disabilities would pose an undue burden on the business. These employer defenses will be discussed in turn.

---

[220] Hoffman v. Caterpillar, Inc., 256 F.3d 568, 572 (7th Cir. 2001).

[221] Approximately 67% of ADA cases resolved in 2002 were dispensed with via summary judgment in favor of the employer. *See Allbright, 2002 Employment Decisions*

1. Disproving Plaintiff's Prima Facie Case

Before resorting to statutory defenses to a disability discrimination claim, an employer should examine whether the employee has a legitimate disability under the ADA, and, if so, whether he or she is a qualified individual with a disability.[222]

a. Is the Employee Disabled?

When faced with a disability discrimination lawsuit under the ADA, an employer needs to ask the following questions:

- Is the employee's condition a legitimate impairment?

Under the ADA, an impairment must be a physiological or mental disorder or condition that affects one or more body systems.[223] Cultural and economic characteristics are not impairments, nor are "physical characteristics such as eye color, hair color, left-handedness, or height, weight or muscle tone that are within 'normal' range and are not the result of a physiological disorder."[224] Thus, if an individual alleges that his or her quick temper or predisposition to illness, for example, constitutes an impairment, an employer should challenge the person's status as a disabled individual.

Additionally, an employer is entitled to obtain verification from the employee's doctor(s) regarding the impairment. Therefore, through discovery, an employer should seek all documents pertaining to the employee's condition. This documentation may show that the individual suffers from an impairment that is not considered a disability under the ADA, and/or provide information regarding the severity of the impairment.

If the individual does, indeed, have a legitimate impairment, the next question an employer should ask is:

- How does the impairment affect the individual's ability to perform major life activities?

Under the ADA Title I—Survey Update, LAW REP., *available at* http://www.abanet.org/disability/reporter/employment.pdf.

[222] 42 U.S.C. §12112(a).
[223] 29 C.F.R. §1630.2(h) (2003).
[224] 29 C.F.R. pt. 1630, app. §1630.2(h) (2003).

If the impairment does not *substantially limit* one or more major life activities, the individual is not disabled under the ADA.[225] An employer should determine whether the impairment is temporary or short-term in duration or impact, and/or whether the plaintiff is still able to perform major life activities at a level comparable to that of the general public. Impairments that are not severe or long term do not render an individual disabled under the ADA.

The plaintiff's medical documentation obtained through discovery may describe the characteristics and severity of the impairment. An employer's request for medical information is limited, however, to those records regarding the condition at issue; a defendant is not given carte blanche to seek irrelevant medical information.[226]

Another way to obtain this information is through the plaintiff's deposition testimony. First, an employer should ask the plaintiff a series of questions designed to pinpoint which life functions are allegedly affected by the disability. For example, a typical question would be: "Does your condition affect your ability to walk (breathe, eat, perform manual tasks, etc.)?" If no major life activities are affected by the individual's condition, then he or she is not disabled under the ADA.[227] If the response is "yes" to any of these questions, the next step is to determine the extent of this limitation. If, for instance, a plaintiff claims that an impairment affects his or her ability to sleep, the employer needs to obtain specific information, such as how many hours of sleep per night and days per week are affected. To what extent and how often a life activity is affected by the plaintiff's condition is a crucial determination. The degree of the plaintiff's limitation will resolve whether he or she is truly disabled under the ADA.[228]

- Are the life functions "major"?

---

[225] 29 C.F.R. §1630.2(j) (2003).
[226] EEOC Enforcement Guidance: Disability-Related Inquiries & Medical Examinations, Question 10.
[227] 42 U.S.C. §12102(2)(A).
[228] EEOC Technical Assistance Manual §2.2(a)(iii).

Not all life functions are considered "major" under the ADA. Major life activities include "caring for oneself, performing manual tasks, walking, seeing, hearing, speaking, breathing, learning, and working."[229] Although this list is not exhaustive, many ordinary activities of daily life do not qualify as major for purposes of the ADA. Driving[230] and concentrating,[231] for example, are not considered major life activities. In the plaintiff's deposition, an employer should make sure to elicit which life activities the plaintiff alleges are affected by his or her disability. If the major life activity at issue is the individual's ability to work, a defendant should determine the following:

- Is the individual precluded from working in one job, or all jobs at the work site? In the community?

An employee is substantially limited in the ability to work only if he or she is excluded from a class or broad range of jobs. Therefore, if the employer can prove that the employee could work in another position within the company, or could find work in the general labor market, then the employee is not considered disabled.[232] An employer should be prepared to challenge a plaintiff's labor market data or vocational expert, or present evidence of its own. If it can be shown that the plaintiff can find employment in the relevant labor market despite his or her impairment, he or she is not substantially limited in working, and thus not disabled for ADA purposes.

If the employee is, indeed, disabled, he or she must also prove that he or she is a qualified individual with a disability under the ADA. Thus, an employer should determine:

- Does the individual have the requisite credentials to perform the job?

---

[229] 29 C.F.R. §1630.2(i) (2003).
[230] Chenoweth v. Hillsborough County, 250 F.3d 1328, 11 AD Cases 1421 (11th Cir. 2001), *cert. denied*, 534 U.S. 1131 (2002).
[231] Boerst v. General Mills Operations, Inc., 25 Fed. Appx. 403, 2002 WL 59637, 2002 U.S. App. LEXIS 813 (6th Cir.), *cert. denied*, 535 U.S. 1097 (2002).
[232] 29 C.F.R. §1630.2(i) (2003).

If an individual does not meet the employer's standards for the job in terms of education, licenses, skills, and experience, it is irrelevant whether the employee could perform the essential functions of that position with or without a reasonable accommodation.[233] So long as those standards are relevant to the position in question and are uniformly applied to all potential job applicants regardless of disability, they are legitimate. Assuming the individual *does* possess the requisite credentials for the position, the next question is:

- Can he or she perform the essential functions of the position with or without a reasonable accommodation?

Determining the essential functions of a position is an important step in answering this question. A written job description for the position at issue may contain a list of the job's essential functions, if that description is current and was prepared prior to the filing of the discrimination charge.[234] A corrective discipline policy that addresses the failure to perform any one job function may also indicate that that job task is essential.[235] Demonstrating that other past or current employees in the plaintiff's position were or are required to perform the function at issue is another means of proving that that job function is essential. If an individual cannot perform these essential functions with or without a reasonable accommodation, he or she is not a qualified individual with a disability.

Deconstructing a plaintiff's prima facie case is one way of defeating a claim of disability discrimination under the ADA. Alternatively, an employer may rely on a number of affirmative defenses to challenge a plaintiff's case.

b. Affirmative Defenses

If an employee *is* a qualified individual with a disability under the ADA, an employer has a number of affirmative

---

[233] TITLE I TECHNICAL ASSISTANCE MANUAL, *supra* note 23, at §2.3.
[234] *Id.* §2.3(a).
[235] *See, e.g.,* Earl v. Mervyns, Inc., 207 F.3d 1361, 10 AD Cases 673 (11th Cir. 2000) (employer's priority on punctuality evident by its mention in employee hand-

defenses at its disposal. First, if an individual with a disability alleges that an employer took adverse action against him or her because of a disability, an employer may counter this claim by providing "a legitimate, nondiscriminatory reason" for the action.[236] This is a traditional disparate treatment defense articulated in *McDonnell Douglas Corp. v. Green*,[237] *Texas Department of Community Affairs v. Burdine*,[238] and other cases addressing the burden-shifting analysis to be used in discrimination cases under Title VII of the Civil Rights Act of 1991. Under this framework, after a plaintiff establishes a prima facie case of discrimination by showing that he or she is a disabled individual under the ADA who is qualified to perform the essential functions of the job with or without a reasonable accommodation, and that he or she suffered an adverse employment action because of his or her disability, the burden shifts to the employer to produce a legitimate, nondiscriminatory rationale for making the adverse decision. For example, an employer may allege that the employee's poor performance or excessive absenteeism—as opposed to his or her disability—was to blame for the termination, demotion, or other adverse action. That an individual's particular disability was not covered by the employer's insurance policy or would increase the employer's insurance premiums or workers' compensation costs, however, is not a legitimate defense to an adverse employment action.[239]

Under this burden-shifting framework, a plaintiff may rebut the proffered legitimate, nondiscriminatory reason by showing pretext. For example, if an individual with a disability was fired for excessive tardiness, yet other, nondisabled employees did not receive similar discipline for the same offense, the employer's rationale for the employment decision appears to be pretext for unlawful discrimination. Therefore, an employer

---

book, and by comprehensive system of warnings and reprimands in place for tardiness).

[236] 29 C.F.R. §1630.15 (2003).
[237] 411 U.S. 792, 5 FEP Cases 965 (1973).
[238] 450 U.S. 248, 25 FEP Cases 113 (1981).
[239] 29 C.F.R. pt. 1630, app. §1630.2(m) (2003).

should anticipate challenges to its nondiscriminatory reasons for its actions.

i. Job-Related and Consistent With Business Necessity. Ordinarily, an employer may not use a qualification standard in its application or hiring process that tends to screen out individuals with disabilities.[240] Such a facially neutral policy or practice may disparately impact individuals with disabilities. An employer can defend against such a disparate impact claim by proving that the policy or procedure in question is uniformly applied, job-related, and consistent with business necessity.[241] Additionally, it must be shown that the use of a reasonable accommodation would not overcome the need for the exclusionary qualification standard.[242]

For instance, a requirement that all employees posses valid driver's licenses would have a negative impact on individuals who have vision impairments or other medical conditions that preclude them from obtaining such a license. Thus, if challenged, an employer would need to show that this requirement is job-related and consistent with business necessity—that is, that driving is an essential function of the job. For example, driving is likely a job-related and necessary skill in a delivery service business. The ability to drive is less crucial in an office setting, even if it is convenient to have employees know how to drive in the event someone is needed to run errands.

Even if a policy is job-related and consistent with business necessity, an employer is required to provide, if possible, a reasonable accommodation to enable the job criterion or policy to be met or performed by an individual with a disability. If an employer requires all new hires to be interviewed, for example, an employer cannot justify the exclusion of an individual with hearing impairments from the applicant pool on the grounds that an interview is job-related and consistent with business necessity. In this instance, the use of an interpreter

---

[240] 42 U.S.C. §12112(b)(6).
[241] *Id.* §§12112(b)(6), 12113(a).
[242] *Id.*

would serve as a suitable reasonable accommodation to both comply with the employer's policy and the ADA.[243]

ii. Leave Policies. Some facially neutral and uniformly applied employment policies and practices are immune from adverse impact scrutiny. Thus, it is unnecessary to prove that these policies or practices are job-related and consistent with business necessity. Leave policies, for example, are not subject to such challenge.[244] For instance, although an employer's policy that provides only a set number of sick days may have a disproportionate impact on individuals with disabilities, the policy is not unlawful under a disparate impact theory of discrimination. Nonetheless, an employer may still be required to modify that policy as a reasonable accommodation unless doing so would constitute an undue hardship.

iii. Safety-Based Qualification Standards. The defense that a policy or practice is job-related and consistent with business necessity is often invoked when an employer institutes a safety-based qualification standard that excludes individuals with certain disabilities. For example, a trucking company may require that all new drivers meet the Department of Transportation's (DOT's) visual acuity standards, thereby weeding out individuals with visual impairments from its workforce.[245] Similarly, firefighters are often held to minimum weight requirements, as rescue operations often necessitate heavy lifting. This "business necessity" defense, however, is a stringent standard, requiring an employer to prove that the selection criteria are crucial to the operation of the business, and that no reasonable, nondiscriminatory alternative exists.

In deciding whether a safety-based qualification standard is job-related and consistent with business necessity, the court will likely examine the magnitude of potential harm that could

---

[243] 29 C.F.R. pt. 1630, app. §1630.15(b) & (c) (2003).
[244] *Id.*
[245] *See, e.g.,* Albertson's, Inc. v. Kirkingburg, 527 U.S. 555, 9 AD Cases 694 (1999) (employer could enforce DOT visual acuity standard as essential job function); *see also* Tate v. Farmland Indus., Inc., 268 F.3d 989, 12 AD Cases 519 (10th Cir. 2001) (employer may use DOT's advisory Medical Advisory Criteria as essential job functions for its truck drivers, where criteria are job-related and consistent with business necessity).

result, as well as the probability of that harm occurring.[246] Additionally, a court may examine whether the selection criteria at issue substantially promotes the employer's business needs[247] and is necessary and related to "the specific skills and physical requirements of the sought-after position."[248] Other considerations include the adequacy of the connection between the employer's qualification standard and alleviation of the feared safety risk and a showing of the necessity of across-the-board rather than individualized safety measures.[249] Finally, an employer should be prepared to demonstrate the difficulty or ineffectiveness of using less restrictive alternatives to the general safety standard.[250]

Providing evidence to demonstrate the above factors will increase an employer's chance of succeeding with the business necessity defense. In asserting this defense, it is not necessary for an employer to prove that an individual excluded by a safety-related qualification standard would pose a direct threat to others in the workplace.[251] The direct threat analysis is a separate defense to an individual's ADA suit.

iv. Direct Threat. An employer may exclude individuals from employment if the individual poses a direct threat to the

---

[246] EEOC v. Exxon Corp., 203 F.3d 871, 10 AD Cases 225 (5th Cir. 2000).

[247] *See, e.g.*, Cripe v. City of San Jose, 261 F.3d 877, 12 AD Cases 225 (9th Cir. 2001) (requirement that police officers serve as patrol officers prior to receiving specialized assignments, which screens out officers whose injuries preclude them from serving as patrol officers, must be examined under business necessity standard, not undue hardship defense).

[248] Belk v. Southwestern Bell Tel. Co., 194 F.3d 946, 951, 9 AD Cases 1621, 1624 (8th Cir. 1999).

[249] Morton v. United Parcel Serv., Inc., 272 F.3d 1249, 12 AD Cases 897 (9th Cir. 2001), *cert. denied*, 535 U.S. 1054 (2002).

[250] *Id.*

[251] *See, e.g.* EEOC v. Exxon Corp., 203 F.3d 871, 10 AD Cases 225 (5th Cir. 2000); *Morton*, 272 F.3d 1249. It is the EEOC's position, however, that with regard to safety requirements that screen out or tend to screen out an individual with a disability or a class of individuals with disabilities, an employer must demonstrate that the requirement, as applied to the individual, satisfies the "direct threat" standard in 29 C.F.R. §1630.2(r) (2003) in order to show that the requirement is job-related and consistent with business necessity. 29 C.F.R. pt. 1630, app. §1630.15(b) & (c) (2003). However, because this position was asserted in the 29 C.F.R. pt. 1630 (2003), and not in the regulations, it has not been given a great deal of deference.

health or safety of himself or herself[252] or other individuals in the workplace.[253] The EEOC regulations and interpretative guidance have construed this defense narrowly, requiring an employer to demonstrate that the individual poses "a significant risk of substantial and imminent harm" that cannot be diminished through the use of a reasonable accommodation.[254] The assessment of the direct threat an individual may pose must be conducted on a case-by-case basis, evaluating the person's "ability to safely perform the essential functions of the job."[255] An employer must base this assessment "on a reasonable medical judgment that relies on the most current medical knowledge and/or on the best available objective evidence."[256] The four factors to consider include "(1) [t]he duration of the risk; (2) [t]he nature and severity of the potential harm; (3) [t]he likelihood that the potential harm will occur; and (4) [t]he imminence of the potential harm."[257]

An employer need not prove that all of these factors apply when evaluating whether individuals pose a direct threat to themselves or others. For example, an employer does not need to prove that a potential hazard is imminent if it is impossible to predict. For instance, an employee with Type I diabetes who suffers from periodic diabetic episodes can pose a direct threat to others while working in a safety-sensitive position, even though the imminence of each episode is impossible to foretell.[258] Similarly, a train dispatcher whose heart condition causes him to occasionally lose consciousness poses a direct threat,

---

[252]Chevron U.S.A., Inc. v. Echazabal, 536 U.S. 73, 13 AD Cases 97 (2002).

[253]42 U.S.C. §12113(b). Under the ADA, "the term 'qualification standards' may include a requirement that an individual shall not pose a direct threat to the health or safety of other individuals in the workplace." *Id.*

[254]29 C.F.R. §1630.2(r) (2003).

[255]*Id.*

[256]*Id.*

[257]*Id.*

[258]*See* Hutton v. Elf Atochem N. Am., Inc., 273 F.3d 884, 12 AD Cases 909 (9th Cir. 2001) (diabetic chlorine finishing operator posed direct threat in his position because his mental and physical lapses caused by diabetic episodes, even though unpredictable, could cause substantial harm to others).

even though the imminence of these attacks cannot be anticipated.[259]

While there is no specific formula for weighing one of the four risk factors against another, the nature and severity of the potential harm often overshadows its probability. For example, in *Estate of William C. Mauro v. Borgess Medical Center*,[260] a surgical technician who was HIV-positive was found to pose a direct threat to patients, as the nature of his work required him to place his hands into body cavities during operations, risking the possibility of having his blood mix with that of the patient's in the event of a needle stick or minor laceration. Although the likelihood of this event was determined to be relatively small, the repercussions of such an accident would almost certainly be fatal for the patient. Thus, the magnitude of the potential harm outweighed its probability. Similarly, a dental hygienist who tested HIV-positive posed a direct threat to patients even though the risk of HIV transmission was small, as the potential harm would be certain death for the patient.[261]

An employer is not required to change a position's essential job functions as a reasonable accommodation to eliminate a direct threat. For example, in *Emerson v. Northern States Power Co.*,[262] a customer information associate who suffered from panic attacks was found to pose a direct threat to the public, as her condition prevented her from responding to emergency calls, an essential function of her job. The employer was not required to shift the employee's responsibility for handling emergency calls to a supervisor.

---

[259]Donahue v. Consolidated Rail Corp., 10 AD Cases 1505, 224 F.3d 226 (3d Cir. 2000).

[260]137 F.3d 398, 7 AD Cases 1571 (6th Cir.), *cert. denied*, 525 U.S. 815 (1998).

[261]Waddell v. Valley Forge Dental Assocs., Inc., 276 F.3d 1275, 12 AD Cases 1029 (11th Cir. 2001), *cert. denied*, 535 U.S. 1096 (2002). *See also* Doe v. University of Md. Med. Sys. Corp., 50 F.3d 1261, 4 AD Cases 379 (4th Cir. 1995); Bradley v. University of Tex. M.D. Anderson Cancer Ctr., 3 F.3d 922, 2 AD Cases 1297 (5th Cir. 1993) (per curiam), *cert. denied*, 510 U.S. 1119 (1994) (both cases determined that severity of risk posed by HIV-positive employees in medical positions outweighed its probability).

[262]256 F.3d 506, 11 AD Cases 1683 (7th Cir. 2001).

Verbal threats may serve as evidence that an individual poses a direct threat in the workplace. In *Williams v. Widnall*,[263] an employee who made threats against his supervisor and co-workers was justifiably terminated, even though the threats were the likely result of alcoholism. Similarly, in *Green v. Burton Rubber Processing, Inc.*,[264] an employer informed by mental hospital personnel of an employee's verbal threat to kill his supervisors was justified in terminating the employee. Even an offhand remark suggesting violence can be evidence that an individual poses a direct threat. In *Palesch v. Missouri Commission on Human Rights*,[265] an employer reasonably put an employee suffering from depression on leave after she made the comment: "If I had come in on Friday, I could have shot somebody."[266] Even though the employee alleged that she was making a joke, and her doctor informed the employer that the employee posed no threat, the employer was within its right to take precautionary measures.

The above cases indicate that while all four factors should be addressed in making the direct threat determination a strong showing in one or more of the four can outweigh a weaker showing in the remaining categories. If an employer can demonstrate that the potential harm is great, for example, it need not always prove that the probability of that harm is very likely or imminent.[267]

v. Undue Hardship. A defense to a failure to make a reasonable accommodation for an individual with a disability is that doing so would pose an undue hardship on the operation of the employer's business.[268] The ADA defines "undue hardship" as "an action requiring significant difficulty or expense"[269] when considered in light of the following factors:

---

[263] 79 F.3d 1003, 5 AD Cases 663 (10th Cir. 1996).
[264] 2002 U.S. App. LEXIS 2959 (6th Cir. 2002) (not recommended for full publication).
[265] 233 F.3d 560, 85 FEP Cases 75 (8th Cir. 2000).
[266] *Id.* at 564, 85 FEP at 77.
[267] 42 U.S.C. §12111(10).
[268] 42 U.S.C. §12112(b)(5); 29 C.F.R. §1630.15(d) (2003).
[269] 42 U.S.C. §12111(10); 29 C.F.R. §1630.2(p)(2) (2003).

- "the nature and cost of the accommodation," taking into consideration the availability of tax credits and deductions, and/or outside funding;
- "the overall financial resources of the [employer's] facility or facilities involved in the provision of the reasonable accommodation";
- "[t]he impact of the accommodation on the operation of the facility, including the impact on the ability of other employees to perform their duties and the impact on the facility's ability to conduct business";
- "the overall size of the business . . . with respect to the number of its employees"; and
- the financial and operational relationship of the facility or facilities providing the accommodaiton to the business as a whole.[270]

An employer that believes that a requested accommodation would pose an undue hardship is obligated to provide evidence of this hardship taking the above factors into consideration. The assessment of whether an accommodation poses an undue hardship must be made on a case-by-case basis.[271]

For many employers, a requested reasonable accommodation would pose an undue hardship because of the expense. However, an accommodation that results in a financial undue hardship for one employer may not do the same for another. The cost of a reasonable accommodation must be evaluated in light of the particular employer's budget, resources (such as a subsidiary's access to its parent company's funds), and overall operations. Thus, a small, family-owned business will have different economic obligations under the ADA than would a large corporation.[272]

Merely comparing the cost of the accommodation with the requesting employee's salary is not enough to prove undue

---

[270] *Id.*
[271] EEOC Enforcement Guidance: Reasonable Accommodation & Undue Hardship Under the Americans with Disabilities Act.
[272] 42 U.S.C. §12111(10)(iii); 29 C.F.R. §1630.2(g)(2)(11).

hardship. Also, if cost is the only factor rendering an accommodation an undue hardship, and the employee agrees to cover the expense, then the employer can no longer assert an undue hardship defense.

Although many of the undue hardship assessment factors address the financial difficulty an employer may face in providing an accommodation, an undue hardship refers to any accommodation that would be "unduly costly, extensive, substantial, or disruptive, or that would fundamentally alter the nature of the business."[273] Thus, it would be an undue hardship on a nightclub to increase the brightness of the lights to accommodate an employee with poor vision, as doing so would fundamentally change the nature of the establishment.[274] Similarly, an employer is not required to create an unlimited absentee policy for an employee whose condition results in poor job attendance, as doing so would create an undue administrative as well as financial burden on the employer.[275]

An employer's common policies and practices factor into whether a requested accommodation would be judged an undue hardship. For example, a request for a flexible start time as an accommodation will be deemed more reasonable for an employer who regularly permits employees to arrive to work within a particular timeframe, as opposed to a strict start time.[276] While arriving to work on time is an essential function of most jobs, it likely would not be an undue hardship to allow an employee a later arrival time if those employers already implement flexible work schedules.

In essence, once an employee requests a reasonable accommodation, it is incumbent on the employer to prove that

---

[273] 29 C.F.R. pt. 1630, app. §1630.2(p) (2003).
[274] Id.
[275] Buckles v. First Data Resources, Inc., 176 F.3d 1098, 9 AD Cases 765 (8th Cir. 1999) (employee suffering from acute recurrent rhino sinusitis not entitled to unlimited leave policy or irritant-free work space, as such accommodations would pose undue hardship on employer).
[276] See, e.g., Ward v. Massachusetts Health Research Inst., Inc., 209 F.3d 29, 10 AD Cases 776 (1st Cir. 2000) (employer that allows employees to start work between 7:00 am. and 9:00 a.m. would not suffer undue hardship by allowing employee suffering from arthritis to arrive to work at later time).

providing the accommodation would pose an undue hardship. Information about the employer's budget, profits, policies and practices, and financial resources may serve as evidence of the potential hardship.[277] Additionally, it may be an undue hardship for an employer to provide a reasonable accommodation that violates a collective bargaining agreement or established seniority system.

vi. Seniority Systems and Collective Bargaining Agreements. Job reassignment as a reasonable accommodation would constitute an undue hardship if it conflicts with an established seniority system.[278] Thus, an employer may lawfully deny an employee a reasonable accommodation if doing so would displace another employee entitled to that position via the seniority system.[279] However, an employee can counter this defense by indicating that the employer has the ability to make unilateral changes to the seniority system, and does, in fact, exercise this option. Also, an employee can counter this defense by demonstrating that the seniority system itself provides for changes to its policy. The reasoning behind these exceptions is that employees have diminished expectations that they will benefit by the seniority system if the employer deviates from it on a regular basis. This defense applies only when the proposed job reassignment directly violates an established seniority system. Speculation about whether the job reassignment may disrupt the seniority system at a future date will not suffice.[280]

vii. Conflict With Federal Law. If a federal law or regulation requires or prohibits an action, then an employer is not in violation of the ADA for complying with that law or regulation, even if doing so discriminates against individuals with disabilities.[281]

---

[277] 42 U.S.C.§12111(10)(B).

[278] U.S. Airways, Inc. v. Barnett, 535 U.S. 391, 12 AD Cases 1729 (2002).

[279] *Id. See also* Pond v. Michelin N. Am., Inc., 183 F.3d 592, 9 AD Cases 795 (7th Cir. 1999).

[280] *See, e.g.*, Dilley v. SuperValu, Inc., 296 F.3d 958, 13 AD Cases 486 (10th Cir. 2002) (argument that reassigning employee would prevent fellow employees from exercising seniority-based "bumping" rights in future cannot serve as defense for failing to reassign employee to accommodate his lifting restriction).

[281] 29 C.F.R. §1630.15(e) (2003):
   Conflict with other Federal laws. It may be a defense to a charge of discrimination under this part that a challenged action is required or necessitated

For example, the DOT has implemented a number of standards and regulations for employers engaged in the trucking industry. Subchapter III of the Commercial Motor Vehicle Safety Act,[282] for instance, authorizes the Secretary of Transportation to prescribe "minimum safety standards" to ensure "the physical condition of operators of commercial motor vehicles is adequate to enable them to operate the vehicles safely."[283] Among other minimum standards, the DOT's regulations explain that an individual is physically qualified to drive a commercial motor vehicle if that person "[h]as no established medical history or clinical diagnosis of . . . any . . . condition which is likely to cause loss of consciousness or any loss of ability to control a commercial motor vehicle."[284] Thus, individuals with—among other conditions—epilepsy, diabetes, or heart disease, would be precluded from becoming a commercial motor vehicle driver under these regulations. While complying with this federal requirement would necessarily require an employer to discriminate against individuals with certain disabilities in making hiring decisions, doing so would not violate the ADA. Thus, showing an obligation to adhere to federal standards that conflict with ADA's principles is a defense to a disability discrimination claim. However, an employee may rebut this defense by showing pretext or that an employer has an alternate, nondiscriminatory means of compliance with the federal law or regulation at issue.[285]

viii. Miscellaneous Defenses. A "religious corporation, association, educational institution, or society" is permitted to give hiring preferences to individuals belonging to the entity's particular faith.[286] Therefore, it is a defense to a charge of disability discrimination that the reason a religion-based entity did not hire an individual with a disability was because he or she did

---

by another Federal law or regulation, or that another Federal law or regulation prohibits an action (including the provision of a particular reasonable accommodation) that would otherwise be required by this part.
[282] 49 U.S.C. §§31131–31148.
[283] *Id.* §31136(a)(3).
[284] 49 C.F.R. §391.41(b)(8) (2003).
[285] 29 C.F.R. pt. 1630, app. §1630.15(e) (2003).
[286] 49 U.S.C. §12113(c)(1).

not practice the entity's religion. However, a religious entity still must adhere to the nondiscriminatory provisions of the ADA. Thus, an individual with a disability who satisfies the religious criteria of an entity must be given the same considerations as those given to nondisabled individuals with similar qualifications.[287]

VI. Arbitration

A. Americans With Disabilities Act

The question of whether nonunion arbitration mechanisms might be appropriate for the resolution of statutory claims of disability discrimination in employment appeared within the context of a legal debate that was reignited shortly after the ADA was signed into law. Litigation that developed years before the ADA was signed into law first explored the question of whether statutory discrimination claims might be foreclosed through private agreements that incorporate an arbitration mechanism. The question of nonunion employees waiving their right to pursue—through court litigation—claims of discrimination under federal law came to the forefront with the 1991 decision of the Supreme Court's in *Gilmer v. Interstate/Johnson Lane Corp.*[288] In *Gilmer*, the Supreme Court held for the first time that an agreement to arbitrate an employment discrimination claim—specifically, an age discrimination claim under the federal Age Discrimination in Employment Act (ADEA)[289]—was enforceable under the Federal Arbitration Act.[290] The Court also held that such an enforceable agreement effectively could bar a legal action based on a statutory claim of discrimination by the employee. Thus, it held that the right to a judicial forum for the trial of a federal age discrimination

---

[287]29 C.F.R. pt. 1630, app. §1630.16(a) (2003).
[288]500 U.S. 20, 55 FEP Cases 1116 (1991).
[289]29 U.S.C. §621 et seq.
[290]9 U.S.C. §1 et seq.

claim was subject to waiver by the employee. In the years following that ruling, most courts extended its holding to require arbitration of Title VII of the Civil Rights Act of 1964, ADA, Family and Medical Leave Act,[291] Employee Retirement Income Security Act,[292] and state law discrimination and tort claims. Adding to the debate was language incorporated into a number of antidiscrimination and employment-related statutes, in which Congress encouraged the use of alternative dispute resolution procedures, including arbitration.[293]

In *Gilmer*, the employee had been required as a condition of employment to register as a securities representative with the New York Stock Exchange (NYSE). That registration application provided that the employee agreed to arbitrate any dispute arising between him and his employer that was required to be arbitrated under NYSE rules. The NYSE rules, in turn, provided for arbitration of any dispute between a registered representative and any member of the NYSE that arose out of the individual's employment or the termination of that employment. The Court's emphasis in *Gilmer*, as reflected in its close review of the arbitration rules utilized by the stock exchange, was that the plaintiff did not give up a substantive right or lose his opportunity to fully and fairly present his claim by agreeing to arbitrate any dispute that arose between the two parties. It did not negate or alter his claim; rather, it only changed the forum in which such a claim would be heard. For that reason, the Court essentially concluded that the agreed-upon arbitration mechanism did not impede the antidiscrimination purpose of the ADEA. In this regard, the Court stated: "'[b]y agreeing to arbitrate a statutory claim, a party does not forgo the substantive rights afforded by the statute; it only submits to their resolution in an arbitral, rather than a judicial, forum.'"[294]

---

[291]29 U.S.C. §2601 et seq.
[292]29 U.S.C. §1001 et seq.
[293]*See* 42 U.S.C. §12212, 42 U.S.C. §118.
[294]Gilmer v. Interstate/Johnson Lane Corp., 500 U.S. 20, 26, 55 FEP Cases 1116 (1991) (quoting Mitsubishi Motors Corp. v. Soler Chrysler-Plymouth, Inc., 473 U.S. 614, 628 (1985)).

Moreover, even though the arbitration agreement was contained in a form application that Gilmer was required to sign as a condition of employment, the Court did not view that origin as an impediment to the arbitration agreement's enforcement. Under the FAA, arbitration agreements are enforceable except where grounds for revocation, such as coercion or fraud, are shown.[295] In *Gilmer*, the Court held that, "[m]ere inequality in bargaining power ... is not a sufficient reason to hold that arbitration agreements are never enforceable in the employment context."[296] (It noted, however, that claims of unequal bargaining power, like claims of procedural inadequacies in the arbitration agreement, should be left for review on a case-by-case basis.)

1. Unresolved Issues

While the *Gilmer* ruling enunciated the proposition that, under the FAA, a person can agree to arbitrate claims under those employment statutes in which the judicial forum is waivable, it left a number of important questions unresolved. Among these were whether the FAA even applies to contracts between employers and employees, under what circumstances will a contract to arbitrate employment disputes be enforceable, and did Congress intend to allow employees to waive their right to a judicial forum under statutes other than the ADEA? For a decade following the Court's decision in *Gilmer*, courts, employers, and individual workers struggled with these unresolved issues.[297]

---

[295] *See* 9 U.S.C. §2.

[296] *Gilmer*, 500 U.S. at 33.

[297] *See, e.g.*, Rosenberg v. Merrill Lynch, Pierce, Fenner & Smith, Inc., 170 F.3d 1 (1st Cir. 1999) (holding that waiver of court forum must be "knowing and voluntary"); Seus v. John Nuveen & Co., 146 F.3d 175 (3d Cir. 1998) (rejecting a "knowing and voluntary" standard for waiver of court forum); Cole v. Burns Int'l Sec. Servs., Inc., 105 F.3d 1465 (D.C. Cir. 1997) (arbitration procedure must provide the same substantive protections and access to a neutral forum); Shankle v. B-G Maint. Mgmt. of Colorado, Inc., 163 F.3d 1230 (10th Cir. 1999) (holding that substantive rights must be the same and there must be access to neutral forum, and that splitting arbitrator's fee with employee denies access); Paladino v. Avnet Computer Techs., Inc., 134 F.3d 1054 (11th Cir. 1998) (cannot limit remedies arbitrator may award).

In 2001, much of the cloud created by this uncertainty was lifted when a narrow 5-4 majority of the Supreme Court—in *Circuit City Stores, Inc. v. Adams*[298]—determined conclusively that the FAA applies to most employment-related contracts. In *Circuit City*, the Court considered whether the FAA excludes all arbitration agreements with employees, or whether the FAA's exclusion language applies only to a limited category of employment contracts. The Court held that the FAA applies to most employment contracts and only excludes those contracts involving transportation workers.[299] In reaching its decision, the Court noted that all of the federal circuits except the U.S. Court of Appeals for the Ninth Circuit found that the FAA applied to all employment contracts except those involving transportation workers.[300] To resolve the conflict between the Ninth Circuit and the other circuits, the Supreme Court looked at both the statute's construction and legislative history arguments made by Adams and the Ninth Circuit. The Court then agreed with the majority of the other appellate courts and concluded that, "Section 1 [the exclusion provision] exempts from the FAA only contracts of employment of transportation workers."[301] As a result, it is now clear that where the FAA applies and one party to the written arbitration agreement covered by the FAA fails or refuses to arbitrate, the other party may petition the court for an order compelling arbitration in lieu of court litigation with confidence that the FAA standards for enforcement will be applied.[302]

The Court rejected the position of the EEOC and others that argued that mandatory arbitration was somehow contrary to the remedial purposes of antidiscrimination statutes. It noted:

> The Court has been quite specific in holding that arbitration agreements can be enforced under the FAA without contravening the policies of congressional enactments giving employees specific

---

[298] 532 U.S. 105, 85 FEP Cases 266 (2001).
[299] *Id.* at 109.
[300] *Id.*
[301] *Id.* 532 U.S. at 119.
[302] 9 U.S.C. §4.

protection against discrimination prohibited by federal law; as we noted in *Gilmer*, "[b]y agreeing to arbitrate a statutory claim, a party does not forgo the substantive rights afforded by the statute; it only submits to their resolution in an arbitral, rather than a judicial, forum."[303]

2. Exceptions

The *Circuit City* holding did not mean, however, that arbitration agreements will always be enforced. In fact, some of the basic equity-based exceptions to contract enforcement first noted in *Gilmer* are still present and are the focus of many arbitration agreement challenges. In addition, arbitration agreements, like any other contracts, are subject to state law rules relating to the formation of contracts.[304] Therefore, in order to be enforceable, there must be consideration for entering into the contract. For example, some jurisdictions have held that continued at-will employment may be adequate consideration on the part of the employee in order to find a valid arbitration agreement.[305] Other courts have held that there must be a mutual agreement on the part of the employer and the employee to submit their respective claims in order to find sufficient consideration to enforce an arbitration agreement.[306]

---

[303] Circuit City Stores v. Adams, 532 U.S. 105, 123, 85 FEP Cases 266 (2001) (quoting Gilmer v. Interstate/Johnson Lane Corp., 500 U.S. 20, 26, 55 FEP Cases 1116 (1991)). The Ninth Circuit's decision in *Duffield v. Robertson Stephens & Co.*, 144 F.3d 1182, 76 FEP Cases 1450 (9th Cir.), *cert. denied*, 525 U.S. 982 (1998), which had held that for policy reasons Title VII claims could not be the subject of a predispute mandatory arbitration clause was not expressly addressed. However, it certainly appeared that the Supreme Court was sending a strong message that it did not agree with the reasoning used in *Duffield*. The Ninth Circuit understood the Court's message, and in 2003, it expressly overruled *Duffield* in *EEOC v. Luce, Forward, Hamilton, & Scripps*, 345 F.3d 742 (9th Cir. 2003).

[304] *See* First Options of Chi. v. Kaplan, 514 U.S. 938, 944 (1995).

[305] *See, e.g.* Tinder v. Pinkerton Sec., 305 F.3d 728, 736, 89 FEP Cases 1537 (7th Cir. 2002); Hightower v. GMRI, Inc., 272 F.3d 239, 243, 87 FEP Cases 461 (4th Cir. 2001); Gibson v. Neighborhood Health Clinics, Inc., 121 F.3d 1126, 1132, 8 AD Cases 483, 487 (7th Cir. 1997) ("An employer's specific promise to continue to employ an at-will employee may provide valid consideration for an employee's promise to forgo certain rights."); Scaglione v. Kraftmaid Cabinetry, Inc., 2002 Ohio 6917, 19 IER Cases 764 (2002); Quigley v. KPMG Peat Marwick LLP, 330 N.J. Super. 252, 749 A.2d 405, 413, 82 FEP Cases 988 (2000).

[306] *See* Michalski v. Circuit City Stores, Inc., 177 F.3d 634, 637, 79 FEP Cases 1160 (7th Cir. 1999); Hardwick v. Sherwin-Williams Co., 2002 Ohio App. LEXIS 7273, 91 FEP Cases 142 (2003).

Section 2 of the FAA states, "A written provision in . . . a contract evidencing a transaction involving commerce to settle by arbitration a controversy thereafter arising out of such contract . . . shall be valid, irrevocable, and enforceable, save upon such grounds as exist at law or in equity for the revocation of any contract."[307] Arbitration agreements are thus enforceable unless there are circumstances that render the agreement itself deficient. These circumstances generally are established by state contract law.

Following remand of the *Circuit City* case by the Supreme Court, the U.S. Court of Appeals for the Ninth Circuit used California state law to employ a slightly different test. The court divided the factors to be considered into two groups. The first group measures the comparative bargaining power of the parties to the arbitration agreement and whether the agreement is clear in its requirements. These factors require a court to consider the equilibrium of bargaining power between the parties, whether the stronger party drafted the agreement, whether the terms of the agreement are clearly disclosed, whether the arbitration agreement is a condition of employment, and whether the employee had the ability or opportunity to negotiate the agreement. (With the exception of the disclosure factor, these invariably weigh against the employer.) However, the court ruled that the arbitration agreement is unenforceable only if it fails to meet the requirements of both sets of factors. The second set of factors measures the degree to which the terms and obligations of the parties are similar and whether the agreement limits available relief or the time to bring a suit set by an applicable statue.[308] In this portion of the *Circuit City* saga, the court ruled that the arbitration agreement violated the first set of "procedural" factors because it was written by the employer, was a condition of the employee's hire, and was not negotiable by the employee. The Ninth Circuit held that the agreement also violated the second set of

---

[307] 9 U.S.C. §2.
[308] Circuit City Stores, Inc. v. Adams, 279 F.3d 889, 87 FEP Cases 1509 (9th Cir. 2002).

factors because the employer reserved a right to sue the employee in court that was not justified by business necessity, the employer limited the amounts of recoverable pay and damages as well as the statute of limitations, and the agreement raised the possibility that an employee would have to split the arbitration fees.[309]

3. Procedural Elements

The procedural elements needed for an enforceable program have been the subject of significant litigation. The U.S. Court of Appeals for the District of Columbia Circuit indicated some of the procedural elements it would require for an enforceable arbitration agreement in *Cole v. Burns International Security Services*.[310] Specifically, it referred to five factors that fulfilled *Gilmer's* requirement that the employee not be required to give up any substantive rights provided by the statute at issue: (1) a neutral arbitrator appointed through the American Arbitration Association (AAA), (2) adequate discovery, (3) a written award, (4) all relief otherwise available in court, and (5) no requirement to pay unreasonable costs or arbitrator's fees or expenses.[311] Courts applying an analysis similar to that in *Cole* are more likely to strike down arbitration agreements that are one-sided in favor of the employer.[312]

---

[309] *Id.*
[310] 105 F.3d 1465, 72 FEP Cases 1775 (D.C. Cir. 1997).
[311] *Id.* at 1482–84.
[312] *See, e.g.*, Hooters of Am., Inc. v. Phillips, 173 F.3d 933, 938–40, 79 FEP Cases 629, 633 (4th Cir. 1999). In the *Hooters* case, the court refused to enforce an arbitration agreement that contained the following provisions: (1) a requirement that the employee provide the company notice of a claim, but no similar requirement on the employer's part to file any responsive pleadings or put the plaintiff on notice of its defenses; (2) a provision that required the employee only to provide the company with a list of fact witnesses and a brief summary of their likely knowledge; (3) an arbitrator selection process that gave the company control over the panel by requiring the employee to select an arbitrator from a company provided list; (4) provisions allowing the company to move for summary judgment whereas the employee was not permitted to seek summary judgment; (5) a provision allowing the company, but not the employee, to record the arbitration hearing; (6) provisions permitting the company, but not the employee, to file suit in court to vacate or modify an arbitral award where the company could show the panel exceeded its authority; (7) a rule providing that, upon 30 days' notice, the company, but not

4. Challenges to Arbitration Agreements

Challenges to arbitration agreements based on state-law fraud in the inducement, equitable adhesion doctrine, or overwhelming economic power arguments have generally proven unsuccessful. The Supreme Court rejected the concept that mere inequality of bargaining power was enough to set aside the arbitration contract in *Gilmer*.[313] In addition, state laws that attempt to place stricter contract formation rules on arbitration agreements under the FAA than would normally apply to other contracts are preempted by the FAA and will not control.[314] Importantly, many courts have held that the issue of unconscionability in the formation or terms of the contract are for the arbitrator, not the court, to decide.[315] However, there is a split among the courts on this issue.[316] Moreover, courts have become increasingly willing to examine the provisions of an arbitration agreement and determine, prior to arbitration, that the nature of the provisions are themselves unconscionable and

---

the employee, could cancel the agreement to arbitrate; and (8) a provision reserving for the company the right to modify the rules in whole or in part, with or without notice to the employee. While no one of these provisions was singled out by the court, an overall procedural framework that is heavily tilted in favor of the employer will be reviewed with close scrutiny.

[313] Gilmer v. Interstate/Johnson Lane Corp., 500 U.S. 20, 33, 55 FEP Cases 1116 (1991).

[314] *See* Doctor's Assocs., Inc. v. Casarotto, 517 U.S. 681 (1996).

[315] Miller v. Public Storage Mgmt., Inc., 121 F.3d 215, 218, 7 AD Cases 416 (5th Cir. 1997) (claim of fraudulent inducement in contract as whole is properly left to arbitrator); Rojas v. TK Communications, 87 F.3d 745, 749, 71 FEP Cases 664 (5th Cir. 1996) (challenge to formation of contract as whole for arbitrator to decide); Freeman v. Minolta Bus. Sys., Inc., 699 So. 2d 1182 (La. Ct. App. 1997), *writ denied*, 706 So. 2d 1977 (La. 1998); Satarino v. A.G. Edwards & Sons, Inc., 941 F. Supp. 609, 613, 3 WH Cases 2d 934 (N.D. Tex. 1996); Johnson v. Hubbard Broad., Inc., 940 F. Supp. 1447, 1459–62, 73 FEP Cases 8 (D. Minn. 1996) (challenges to provisions of arbitration agreement regarding 180-day statute of limitations, limitation on damages, and costs of arbitration are for arbitrator to interpret in first instance, but indicating belief that provisions may be unconscionable).

[316] *See* Garten v. Kurth, 265 F.3d 136 (2d Cir. 2001) (question of fraud is judicial one, which must be determined by court); Kelly v. UHC Mgmt. Co., 967 F. Supp. 1240 (N.D. Ala. 1997) (fraud issue decided by court, because only arbitration agreement involved and arbitration clause not broad enough to cover contract claim); Cular v. Metropolitan Life Ins. Co., 961 F. Supp. 550, 555 (S.D.N.Y. 1997) (allegation of fraudulent inducement to enter arbitration agreement is for court to decide).

therefore preclude the court's ability to allow the arbitration to commence.[317]

Despite certain successes achieved by proponents of arbitration, courts have rejected their application to bar the litigation of discrimination claims in certain cases. For example, agreements that bind only the employee, and not the employer, are frequently found to be unenforceable. In *Gibson v. Neighborhood Health Clinics, Inc.*,[318] the U.S. Court of Appeals for the Seventh Circuit found an arbitration clause in an employee handbook unenforceable because the employer was not required to submit its claims to arbitration. Five years later, the same court struck down another arbitration agreement, finding that there was insufficient mutuality of obligation between the employer and the employee where the agreement did not clearly require the employer to arbitrate its claims.[319] The court rejected the idea that the employer's promise to consider the applicant for employment was adequate consideration for the agreement. (At the same time, other courts have held that continued employment or even possible employment is sufficient consideration to support an arbitration agreement.)[320]

---

[317]*See* Circuit City Stores, Inc. v. Adams, 279 F.3d 889, 87 FEP Cases 1509 (9th Cir.2002); Perez v. Globe Airport Sec. Servs., Inc., 253 F.3d 1280, 86 FEP Cases 613 (11th Cir. 2001).

[318]121 F.3d 1126, 1131–32, 8 AD Cases 483 (7th Cir. 1997).

[319]Penn v. Ryan's Family Steak Houses, Inc., 269 F.3d 753, 12 AD Cases 615 (7th Cir. 2001).

[320]Herko v. Metropolitan Life Ins. Co., 978 F. Supp. 141 (W.D.N.Y. 1997) (consideration of application for membership sufficient to support arbitration agreement); Sheller v. Frank's Nursery & Crafts, Inc., 957 F. Supp. 150, 73 FEP Cases 870 (N.D. Ill. 1997) (arbitration agreement in employment application enforceable, because supported by promise to consider application); Reese v. Commercial Credit Corp., 955 F. Supp. 567, 3 WH Cases 2d 1428 (D.S.C. 1997) (arbitration agreement accepted by continued employment after receiving notice of arbitration policy); Butcher v. Bally Total Fitness Corp., 2003 Ohio 1734 (2003) (employment offer sufficient consideration to support arbitration agreement, even though agreement not read by employee); Jenks v. Workman, 83 FEP Cases 761 (S.D. Ind. 2000) (arbitration agreement deemed as accepted and enforceable by first knowingly signing form and later by continued employment); Towles v. United Healthcare Corp., 524 S.E.2d 839 (S.C. Ct. App. 1999) (continued employment sufficient consideration to render arbitration agreement legally binding); Ball v. SFX Broad., 665 N.Y.S.2d 444 (N.Y. App. Div. 1997) (arbitration agreement accepted by continued employment after receiving notice of arbitration policy).

In *Johnson v. Circuit City Stores*,[321] the U.S. Court of Appeals for the Fourth Circuit held that even if the language of an arbitration agreement only requires employees to arbitrate their disputes, a court should infer that the employer's overall endorsement of the arbitration process means that it also is bound to arbitration. Accordingly, the court ordered enforcement of an arbitration provision in an employment application that was signed only by the employee and that, at least by its terms, purported to bind only the employee. Similarly, in *Michalski v. Circuit City Stores, Inc.*,[322] the U.S. Court of Appeals for the Seventh Circuit distinguished its earlier decision in *Gibson* and upheld an arbitration agreement even though the document the employee signed did not expressly state that the employer would be bound by arbitration. As in the *Johnson* case, the court found that the agreement as a whole bound the employer to arbitration.[323]

5. *Unconscionable Arbitration Agreements*

Arbitration agreements have also been found unconscionable where they compel arbitration of claims typically brought by employees and exempt claims typically brought by employers (such as claims for intellectual property violations, unfair competition, and misuse of trade secrets or other confidential information).[324] Arbitration agreements have also been subject to attack when they have sought to limit remedies available to employees.[325] It should be noted that most courts are willing

---

[321] 148 F.3d 373, 77 FEP Cases 139 (4th Cir. 1998).

[322] 177 F.3d 634, 636, 79 FEP Cases 1160 (7th Cir. 1999).

[323] *See also* Howard v. Oakwood Homes Corp., 134 N.C. App. 116, 516 S.E.2d 879, 15 IER Cases 678, 681 (1999).

[324] Mercuro v. Superior Court, 96 Cal. App. 4th 167, 175–76 (2002); *see also* O'Hare v. Municipal Resource Consultants, 107 Cal. App. 4th 267, 275–76, 19 IER Cases 1340 (2003).

[325] Johnson v. Circuit City Stores, Inc., 203 F.3d 821, 83 FEP Cases 320 (4th Cir. 2000); Paladino v. Avnet Computer Techs., 134 F.3d 1054, 76 FEP Cases 1315 (11th Cir. 1998); Rembert v. Ryan's Family Steak Houses, Inc., 596 N.W. 2d 208 (Mich. Ct. App. 1999) (mandatory predispute arbitration agreements enforceable even when statutory rights are at issue so long as no statutory rights or remedies are waived and procedure is fair).

to sever unenforceable limitations on remedies and will order arbitration subject to severance.[326]

In 2002, the Supreme Court provided further guidance regarding matters pertaining to arbitration of employment disputes in the context of the ADA, with particular focus on the role of the federal antidiscrimination agency. In *EEOC v. Waffle House, Inc.*,[327] the Court ruled that a private predispute arbitration agreement between an individual and that individual's employer does not prevent the EEOC from filing a court action in its own name and recovering monetary damages for the individual. In the *Waffle House* case, an individual signed an application containing an agreement to arbitrate all employment claims. After working for 16 days, he suffered a seizure at work and was discharged soon thereafter. The former grill operator did not seek to arbitrate any dispute, but he did file a complaint with the EEOC alleging that his termination violated the ADA. The EEOC filed an enforcement action in federal court requesting injunctive relief, monetary damages for the grill operator, and punitive damages against the restaurant. Waffle House insisted that the EEOC's claim should wait until the grill operator had pursued the claim on his own through arbitration, as agreed to in his application. The court of appeals rejected the restaurant's petition to stay the EEOC's lawsuit and allowed the EEOC to continue with the claim.[328] However, the court of appeals reasoned that the public policy favoring arbitration of the grill operator's dispute under the FAA should limit the EEOC to pursuing injunctive relief and not "victim specific" monetary damages.

---

[326]*See, e.g.,* Gannon v. Circuit City Stores, Inc., 262 F.3d 677, 86 FEP Cases 755 (8th Cir. 2001) (arbitration agreement provision limiting remedies can be severed, especially if agreement provides specifically for severance of provisions found to be in conflict with applicable law); Wright v. Circuit City Stores, Inc., 82 F. Supp. 2d 1279, 83 FEP Cases 877 (N.D. Ala. 2000); *but see* Perez v. Globe Airport Sec. Servs., Inc., 253 F.3d 1280, 86 FEP Cases 613 (11th Cir. 2001) (refusing to sever unenforceable fee-splitting provision, reasoning that such severance would provide incentive for employers to include unlawful provisions in arbitration agreements).

[327]534 U.S. 279, 12 AD Cases 1001 (2002).

[328]EEOC v. Waffle House, 193 F.3d 805, 9 AD Cases 1313 (4th Cir. 1999).

The Supreme Court rejected these contentions by ruling that the EEOC was not a party to the arbitration agreement made between the grill operator and the restaurant. For that reason, the arbitration agreement could not limit the EEOC in its ability to bring the claim or in the type and amount of relief sought by the EEOC.[329] Thus, after *Waffle House*, if the EEOC chooses to litigate a discrimination claim, it is permitted to do so notwithstanding an inability on the employee's part to pursue civil litigation as a result of a valid arbitration agreement. Although the EEOC has favored alternative dispute resolution generally, it has been opposed to predispute binding arbitration agreements.[330] The agency initiated litigation against certain employers who implemented mandatory arbitration programs, arguing that mandatory arbitration can take away substantive rights granted by Title VII. Arbitration agreements that do not permit employees to file charges with the EEOC have been another concern to the EEOC.

6. Collective Bargaining Agreements

The interplay between contractual arbitration mechanisms for dispute resolution and court procedures for the enforcement of statutory rights under federal discrimination laws first were considered under collective bargaining agreements. In those cases, the rights of union members covered by labor contracts with arbitration procedures to proceed with a Title VII claim of discrimination in court were examined. The Supreme Court, in *Alexander v. Gardner-Denver Co.*,[331] first held that a union member did not agree to submit Title VII claims to arbitration through an arbitration clause in the collective bargaining agreement. *Gilmer*[332] distinguished this case and its progeny on three separate grounds:

---

[329] *Waffle House*, 534 U.S. at 296–98, 12 AD Cases at 1009.

[330] *See EEOC Policy Statement on Mandatory Binding Arbitration of Employment Discrimination Disputes as a Condition of Employment* (July 10, 1997), EEOC COMPLIANCE MANUAL, N:3101-3106 (BNA 1997).

[331] 415 U.S. 36, 7 FEP Cases 81 (1974).

[332] Gilmer v. Interstate/Johnson Lane Corp., 500 U.S. 20, 55 FEP Cases 1116 (1991).

First, those cases [the *Gardner-Denver* line of cases] did not involve the issue of the enforceability of an agreement to arbitrate statutory claims. Rather, they involved the quite different issue whether arbitration of contract-based claims precluded subsequent judicial resolution of statutory claims.... Second, because the arbitration in those cases occurred in the context of a collective-bargaining agreement... [a]n important concern... was the tension between collective representation and individual statutory rights.... Finally, those cases were not decided under the FAA, which ... reflects a "liberal federal policy favoring arbitration agreements."[333]

The Court did not say, however, which ground was dispositive in distinguishing *Gardner-Denver*. As a result, some lower courts construing *Gardner-Denver* have cut away at the decision by holding, in effect, that all three grounds must be present in order for it to be controlling. For example, the U.S. Court of Appeals for the Seventh Circuit, in *Matthews v. Rollins Hudig Hall Co.*,[334] required arbitration of an employee's age discrimination claim when there was a question as to whether or not the employee was terminated "for cause" and the arbitration agreement applied to all claims "relating to a breach of this Agreement."[335]

In *Wright v. Universal Maritime Service Corp.*,[336] the Supreme Court addressed but did not resolve the issue. While confirming the continued vitality of *Gardner-Denver*, the Court left open the question as to whether a union in a collective bargaining agreement may prospectively waive a member's right to pursue federal statutory claims in court. The Court did hold that any such waiver must be "clear and unmistakable." Under the facts in *Wright*, the Court refused to require arbitration where the collective bargaining agreement provided that the agreement was "intended to cover all matters affecting wages, hours, and other terms and conditions of employment."[337] The Court held

---

[333] *Id.* at 35 (quoting Mitsubishi Motors Corp. v. Soler Chrysler-Plymouth, 473 U.S. 614, 625 (1985)).

[334] 72 F.3d 50, 69 FEP Cases 641 (7th Cir. 1995).

[335] *Id.* at 53, 69 FEP Cases at 643. *See also* Austin v. Owens-Brockway Glass Container, Inc., 78 F.3d 875, 5 AD Cases 488 (4th Cir.), *cert. denied*, 519 U.S. 980 (1996) (arbitration ordered where clause at issue contained express reference to statutory claims by employee).

[336] 525 U.S. 70, 8 AD Cases 1429 (1998).

[337] *Id.* at 81.

this to be a less than explicit union waiver and failed under the Court's "clear and unmistakable" standard.

The U.S. Court of Appeals for the Fourth Circuit, in *Carson v. Giant Food, Inc.*,[338] adopted a two-part test for applying *Wright*. The court held that the requirement of a "clear and unmistakable" waiver can be satisfied through the drafting of an "explicit arbitration clause" pursuant to which the union agrees to submit all statutory employment discrimination claims to arbitration. Alternatively, where the arbitration clause is "not so clear," employees might yet be bound to arbitrate their federal claims if "another provision, like a nondiscrimination clause, makes it unmistakably clear that the discrimination statutes at issue are part of the agreement...."[339]

Courts applying *Wright* have uniformly held that, at a minimum, a statute must be specifically referenced in a collective bargaining agreement for it to approach *Wright's* "clear and unmistakable" standard.[340]

B. The Rehabilitation Act of 1973

As discussed above,[341] the effect of arbitration agreements on an individual's ability to pursue disability discrimination claims arising out of the Rehabilitation Act tracked the legal

---

[338] 175 F.3d 325, 79 FEP Cases 976 (4th Cir. 1999).

[339] *Id.* at 331, 79 FEP Cases at 981.

[340] Fayer v. Town of Middlebury, 258 F.3d 117, 123 (2d Cir. 2001) (terminated employee free to bring lawsuit based on First Amendment where collective bargaining agreement covered only disputes arising under it); Safrit v. Cone Mills Corp., 248 F.3d 306, 85 FEP Cases 833 (4th Cir. 2001) (antidiscrimination provision that states that union will abide by Title VII and that unresolved grievances under provision are proper subjects of arbitration "indubitably provides" clear and unmistakable waiver); Bratten v. SSI Servs., Inc., 185 F.3d 625, 631, 9 AD Cases 1045 (6th Cir. 1999); Brown v. ABF Freight Sys., Inc., 183 F.3d 319, 161 LRRM 2769 (4th Cir. 1999); Quint v. A.E. Staley Mfg. Co., 172 F.3d 1, 9, 9 AD Cases 242 (1st Cir. 1999) (agreement did not explicitly mention ADA or other federal antidiscrimination statutes); Kelly v. Classic Rests. Corp., 92 FEP Cases 1222 (S.D.N.Y. 2003) (arbitration clause in collective bargaining agreement not preclude employee from raising ADEA claims in federal court); Giles v. City of New York, 41 F. Supp. 2d 308, 311–12, 160 LRRM 2879, 2882 (S.D.N.Y. 1999) ("list of covered grievances did not clearly include FLSA or other statutory claims"); Beason v. United Techs. Corp., 37 F. Supp. 2d 127, 130, 164 LRRM 2372 (D. Conn. 1999) (agreement did not specifically refer to federal or state antidisability discrimination statutes).

[341] *See* section VI.A.4., "Challenges to Arbitration Agreements," above.

history of the similar issue under the ADA. Also, despite otherwise valid and enforceable contract terms, plaintiffs were not required to exhaust the contractual administrative procedures before bringing forward their legal claims under the Rehabilitation Act.[342]

The current state of the law is simply the latest position on the legal continuum of this issue. The strong federal presumption in favor of enforcing arbitration agreements is clear, and this presumption extends to federal statutory employment discrimination claims such as claims arising out of the Rehabilitation Act.[343]

"A plaintiff can waive his right to bring an employment discrimination claim if he does so knowingly and voluntarily."[344] Therefore an individual can waive all claims arising out of a federal statute such as the Rehabilitation Act through a contract or by entering into a pre-arbitration settlement of the grievance.[345] Therefore an individual can waive all of the claims arising out of an adverse employment action by entering into a pre-arbitration settlement of the grievance.[346]

---

[342] Bowe v. Colgate Palmolive, 272 F. Supp. 332, 337, 1 FEP Cases 201 (S.D. Ind. 1967), aff'd in part, rev'd on other grounds, 416 F.2d 711, 2 FEP Cases 223 (7th Cir. 1969) (fundamental difference between claim for violation of collective bargaining agreement and violation of Civil Rights Act of 1964); Alexander v. Gardner-Denver Co., 415 U.S. 36, 51, 7 FEP Cases 81 (1974) (distinguishing civil rights claims for employment agreements, court reasoned that employees rights under Rehabilitation Act like those under Title VII, should not be affected by contracts such as arbitration agreements).

[343] Thoele v. Henderson, 2001 U.S. Dist. LEXIS 3522, at *1 (N.D. Ill. 2001).

[344] Id. at *1 ("A postal service employee who settles, with the help of a union representative, a union grievance brought contemporaneously with an EEO claim, does so knowingly and voluntarily.") (citing Lockhart v. United States, 961 F. Supp. 1260, 1267 (N.D. Ind. 1997); see also Wagner v. NutraSweet Co., 95 F.3d 527, 531, 72 FEP Cases 284 (7th Cir. 1996).

[345] Thoele, 2001 U.S. Dist. LEXIS 3522, at *8 (specifically included in release a phrase such as "any/all EEO complaints (formal or informal)....").

[346] Id.

VII. ATTORNEYS' FEES, COSTS, AND EXPENSES

A. Americans With Disabilities Act

Title I of the ADA incorporates the remedial provisions of Title VII of the Civil Rights Acts of 1964.[347] Therefore, the standards for recovering attorneys' fees in disability-based employment actions under the ADA follow those established under Title VII.[348] Additionally, the ADA expressly provides that,

> In any action or administrative proceeding commenced pursuant to this Act, the court or agency, in its discretion, may allow the prevailing party, other than the United States, a reasonable attorney's fee, including litigation expenses, and costs, and the United States shall be liable for the foregoing the same as a private individual.[349]

This provision was carefully worded in response to the Supreme Court decision mandating that statutes expressly include other costs within the provision for "attorney's' fees" rather than "costs" if congressional intent is to allow full recovery of such expenses to the successful party.[350] Otherwise, costs such as expert witness fees would be subject to the federal guidelines regulating the recoupement of costs under 28 U.S.C. §1821, which limits the federal court's discretion to award witness fee expenses to $30-per-day.[351] The House Judiciary Committee Report explained that expenses awarded under the statute are "included under the rubric of 'attorney's fees' rather than 'costs.'...."[352] As such, the attorneys' fees and other litigation expenses that appropriately fall under this category are

---

[347] 42 U.S.C. §12117(a).
[348] *Id.*
[349] 42 U.S.C. §12205.
[350] H.R. REP. No. 101-485, pt. 3, at 73 (1990), *reprinted in* 1990 U.S.C.C.A.N. 445, 496 (citing Crawford Fitting Co. v. J.T. Gibbons, Inc., 482 U.S. 437, 43 FEP Cases 1775 (1987)).
[351] *Crawford* held that absent express "statutory or contractual authorization" providing for the expenses of a litigant's witness as costs, FED. R. CIV. P. 54(d) was subject to the limitations set forth in 28 U.S.C. §1821(b) so that the district courts would have the discretion to allow that up to $30-per-day was reimbursable for witness fees or decline to do so. *Id.* at 445, 43 FEP Cases at 1778.
[352] H.R. REP. No. 101-485, pt. 3, at 73.

awarded at the discretion of the court,[353] in accordance with the legal standard set forth under *Christiansburg Garment Co. v. EEOC.*[354]

The general rule in the United States is that litigants must pay their own attorneys' fees in the absence of legislation providing otherwise.[355] Congress provides limited exceptions to this rule through "selected statutes granting or protecting various federal rights."[356] Some statutes make the award of attorneys' fees mandatory for prevailing plaintiffs.[357] Other statutes treat the award of attorneys' fees as permissive and limit the availability of the award to certain parties, usually the prevailing plaintiff.[358] Many statutes take another approach, which is more flexible and make the award of attorney's fees available to either the plaintiff or defendant.[359] The implementation of the effectuation of the statutory policy is left to the discretion of the trial court.[360] Title VII of the Civil Rights Act of 1964 falls into this last category as it provides that a district court may in its discretion allow an attorneys' fee to the prevailing party.[361]

1. Legislative History

The legislative history of the statutory provision in Title VII indicates that the fee provision was included to "make it

---

[353] *Id.* at 73 n.77.

[354] 434 U.S. 412, 420, 16 FEP Cases 502 (1978).

[355] Also referred to as the "American rule," the American common law rule as to the payment of attorneys' fees also provides that fees may be awarded against a party that proceeds in bad faith. Alyeska Pipeline Serv. Co. v. Wilderness Soc'y, 421 U.S. 240, 258–59, 10 FEP Cases 826 (1975); *Christiansburg,* 434 U.S. at 420.

[356] *Alyeska,* 421 U.S. at 260.

[357] *See, e.g.,* Clayton Antitrust Act, 15 U.S.C. §15; FLSA, 29 U.S.C. §216(b); Truth in Lending Act, 15 U.S.C. §1640(a).

[358] *See, e.g.,* Privacy Act of 1974, 5 U.S.C. §552a(g)(2)(B); Fair Housing Act of 1968, 42 U.S.C. §3612(p).

[359] *See, e.g.,* Securities Exchange Act of 1934, 15 U.S.C. §§78i(e) & 78r(a); Federal Water Pollution Control Act, 33 U.S.C. §1365(d); Clean Air Act, 42 U.S.C. §7604(d).

[360] *Id.*

[361] "In any action or proceeding under this title the court, in its discretion, may allow the prevailing party, other than the Commission or the United States, a reasonable attorney's fee as part of the costs, and the Commission and the United States shall be liable for costs the same as a private person." 42 U.S.C. §2000e-5(k).

easier for a plaintiff of limited means to bring a meritorious suit."[362] An additional purpose for the fee provision is indicated in the Senate floor discussions of the almost identical fee provision of Title II, where several Senators commented on the purposes of the fee provision to deter the bringing of lawsuits without merit or foundation.[363] The U.S. Court of Appeals for the District of Columbia Circuit concluded from these Senate debates that the two congressional purposes of the fee provisions in Title VII were to "make it easier for a plaintiff of limited means to bring a meritorious suit" and to "deter the bringing of lawsuits without foundation" by providing the "prevailing party," regardless of being a defendant or plaintiff, with the ability to obtain legal fees.[364]

2. Obtaining an Award

The conditions for obtaining such an award vary depending on whether or not the prevailing party is a defendant or a plaintiff.[365] In *Newman v. Piggy Park Enterprises*,[366] the Supreme Court considered the award of attorneys' fees under Title II of the Civil Rights Act of 1964. The statutory language permitting the award of attorneys' fees stated, "In any action commenced pursuant to this subchapter, the court, in its discretion, may allow the prevailing party, other than the United States, a reasonable attorney's fee as part of the costs, and the United States shall be liable for costs the same as a private person."[367] In *Piggy Park* the plaintiffs had prevailed, and the Supreme

---

[362] 110 Cong. Rec. 12,724 (1964) (remarks of Sen. Humphrey (D-Minn.) referring to §706(k) of Title VII).

[363] *Id.* at 13,668 (remarks of Sen. Lausche (D-Ohio) explaining that purpose of fee provision in Title II is to "deter the bringing of lawsuits without foundation"); *id.* at 14,214 (remarks of Sen. Pastore (D-R.I.) explaining that purpose of fee provision in Title II is to "discourage frivolous suits"); *id.* at 6534 (remarks of Sen. Humphrey explaining that purpose of fee provision in Title II is to "diminish the likelihood of unjustified suits being brought").

[364] Grubbs v. Butz, 548 F.2d 973, 975, 13 FEP Cases 245, 246–47 (D.C. Cir. 1976).

[365] Christiansburg Garment Co. v. EEOC, 434 U.S. 412, 16 FEP Cases 502 (1978).

[366] 390 U.S. 400 (1968).

[367] 42 U.S.C. §2000a-3(b).

Court held that a prevailing plaintiff under the statute "should ordinarily recover an attorney's fee unless special circumstances would render such an award unjust."[368] "Special circumstances" cited by the courts to deny an award of attorneys' fees have included poor performance of a plaintiff's attorneys, sponsorship of a plaintiff by a third party, and when a corporate defendant did not have unilateral power to avoid the violation and was supported by the EEOC.[369] In making this determination, the *Piggy Park* Court relied on the intent of Congress to cast the Title II plaintiff in the role of a private attorney general, vindicating a policy that Congress considered of the highest priority.[370]

In *Albemarle Paper Co. v. Moody*,[371] the Supreme Court made clear that the *Piggy Park* standard for awarding attorneys' fees to a successful plaintiff is applicable to legal actions commenced under Title VII of the Civil Rights Act. It has therefore, been established that under Title VII a prevailing plaintiff is ordinarily to be awarded attorneys' fees in all but special circumstances.[372]

a. Unsuccessful

At least one court has held that in certain circumstances an employee's misconduct may preclude an award of attorneys' fees.[373] In this case, the trial court exercised its discretion not to award the plaintiff with attorneys' fees on the basis that the

---

[368] *Piggy Park*, 390 U.S. at 402.
[369] Drake v. Southwestern Bell Tel. Co., 533 F.2d 1185, 1189, 15 FEP Cases 577 (8th Cir. 1977); Chastang v. Flynn & Emrich Co., 541 F.2d 1040, 12 FEP Cases 1533 (4th Cir. 1976); Sprogis v. United Air Lines, 517 F.2d 387, 10 FEP Cases 1249 (7th Cir. 1975).
[370] *Id.*
[371] 422 U.S. 405, 415, 10 FEP Cases 1181 (1975).
[372] *Chastang*, 541 F.2d at 1045, 12 FEP Cases at 1538 ("special circumstances" justified denial of an award of attorneys' fees to the prevailing plaintiff); Carrion v. Yeshiva Univ., 535 F.2d 722, 727, 13 FEP Cases 1521 (2d Cir. 1976); Johnson v. Georgia Highway Express, Inc. 488 F.2d 714, 716, 7 FEP Cases 1 (5th Cir. 1974); Parham v. Southwestern Bell Tel. Co., 433 F.2d 421, 429–30, 2 FEP Cases 1017 (8th Cir. 1970).
[373] Edwards v. Rosewood Health Ctr., 14 AD Cases 766 (N.D. Ill. 2002).

defendant would have discharged the employee for misconduct regardless of the finding of discrimination at the workplace. In this "mixed motive" case, the court considered " 'the relationship between the fees and the degree of plaintiff's success.' "[374] Factors considered included whether public purposes justified the attorneys' fees. The court noted that attorneys' fees are appropriate where an employer engages in widespread or intolerable animus to disabled employees. Under this reasoning, the court found that the public purpose was minor in that the act of discrimination was isolated and the plaintiff did not show that the improper conduct was widespread. Because the plaintiff's own misconduct was the impetus for her termination despite the employer's consideration of her disability when making the decision to terminate the plaintiff's employment, attorneys' fees were not warranted.

In 2001, the Supreme Court issued a significant attorneys' fees decision that narrowed the circumstances in which a plaintiff is viewed as a "prevailing party," triggering potential entitlement to attorneys' fees. It held in *Buckhannon Board & Care Home, Inc. v. West Virginia Department of Health & Human Services*,[375] that in circumstances in which the lawsuit initiated by the plaintiff may have served as the "catalyst" for a voluntary change in conduct on the defendant's part prior to judgment that brings about the desired result, attorneys' fees would not be available.

b. *Successful*

The standard for an award of attorney's fees is different, however, for successful defendants. In a unanimous opinion, the Supreme Court held that under the applicable provisions of Title VII a federal district court could in its discretion award attorneys' fees to a prevailing defendant only on a finding that the plaintiff's action was frivolous, unreasonable, or without

---

[374]*Id.* at 766 (quoting Akrabawi v. Carnes Co., 152 F.3d 688, 696 (3d Cir. 1988) (quoting in turn, Sheppard v. Riverview Nursing Ctr., 88 F.3d 1332, 1335, 71 FEP Cases 218 (4th Cir. 1996))).

[375]532 U.S. 598, 11 AD Cases 1300 (2001).

foundation, even though not brought in subjective bad faith.[376] The Court's rationale relied on distinguishing the differences between the equitable considerations inherent in a Title VII plaintiff's position.[377] Unlike the defendant in a Title VII action, the plaintiff is the chosen instrument of Congress to vindicate a "policy that Congress considered of the highest priority."[378] Also, when a trial court awards attorneys' fees to a prevailing plaintiff, it is awarding such fees against a violator of federal law.[379] Therefore, to the extent a district court may award a prevailing defendant in a Title VII case attorneys' fees, it may only do so on a finding that the plaintiff's action was frivolous, unreasonable, or without foundation, even though nor brought in subjective bad faith.[380]

3. Awards Against EEOC

Fee awards against the EEOC are explicitly provided in Title VII as it states that "the Commission and the United States shall be liable for costs the same as a private person."[381] No distinction is made between the EEOC and private plaintiffs in treatment when a prevailing defendant seeks to recover attorneys' fees.[382] The applicable standard used in the determination of whether attorneys' fees are warranted in such a situation is the same against an unsuccessful plaintiff and the EEOC.[383]

---

[376] Christiansburg Garment Co. v. EEOC, 434 U.S. 412, 421, 16 FEP Cases 502 (1978).

[377] *Id.* at 419–20.

[378] *Id.* at 419, 16 FEP Cases at 505 (quoting *Piggy Park Enters.*, 390 U.S. 400, 402 (1968)).

[379] *Id.*

[380] *Id.* Bolton v. Murray Envelope Corp., 553 F,2d 881, 884 n.2, 15 FEP Cases 478 (5th Cir. 1977); Grubbs v. Butz, 548 F.2d 973, 975–76, 13 FEP Cases 245 (D.C. Cir. 1976); Carrion v. Yeshiva Univ., 535 F.2d 722, 727, 13 FEP Cases 1521 (2d Cir. 1976); Wright v. Stone Container Corp., 524 F.2d 1058, 1063–64, 11 FEP Cases 1322 (8th Cir. 1975) (basing its holding United States Steel Corp. v. United States, 519 F.2d 359, 10 FEP Cases 1106 (3d Cir. 1975)).

[381] 42 U.S.C. §2000e-5(k).

[382] Christiansburg Garment Co. v. EEOC, 434 U.S. 412, 422, 16 FEP Cases 502 (1978).

[383] A district court may consider distinctions between the EEOC and private plaintiffs when determining the reasonableness of the EEOC's litigation efforts,

B. The Rehabilitation Act of 1973

Section 505(b) of the Rehabilitation Act states that "[i]n any action or proceeding to enforce or charge a violation of a provision of this subchapter, the court, in its discretion, may allow the prevailing party, other than the United States, a reasonable attorney's fee as part of the costs."[384] The 1978 Amendments to the Rehabilitation Act made the Title VII remedies, procedures, and rights applicable to Section 501 complaints.[385] Therefore, the award of attorneys' fees under Section 501 follows the standard established under Title VII as discussed earlier,[386] and the fee provision under Section 505(b) is not necessary to move the court for an award.[387]

Section 503 constitutes a "provision of this subchapter" as provided under Section 505(b), and a complaint initiated under Section 503 constitutes a process that is an "action or proceeding to enforce or charge a violation of" such a provision.[388] Section 505(b), however, authorizes "the court" to provide attorneys' fees using its discretion.[389] Given the difficulties an individual complainant faces in getting to court under a Section 503 complaint, the opportunity for an adjudication, let alone the issue of an award of attorneys' fees, would be very difficult for an aggrieved employee. Section 505(b) expressly permits the availability of attorneys' fees in Section 504 actions.

C. Claiming Attorneys' Fees Against State Governments

The question as to whether or not attorneys' fees were recoverable against state defendants in employment discrimination suits was affirmatively decided by the Supreme Court

---

however a different standard cannot be applied as to the determination of an attorneys' fee award. *Id.*

[384]29 U.S.C. §794a(b).

[385]29 U.S.C. §794a(a)(1) (referring to the provisions of Title VII contained in 42 U.S.C. §2000e-16).

[386]*See* section VII.A.2., "Obtaining an Award," above.

[387]42 U.S.C. §2000e-5(k).

[388]29 U.S.C. §794a(b).

[389]*Id.*

in *Fitzpatrick v. Bitzer*.[390] In this case, a class of retired, male, state employees successfully sued the state of Connecticut under their claim that the state's statutory retirement benefit plan discriminated against them because of their sex in violation of Title VII of the Civil Rights Act of 1964. As to damages, the trial court denied plaintiffs an award of retroactive retirement benefits and attorney fees on the basis that both constituted recovery of money damages from the state treasury and were thus precluded by the Eleventh Amendment.[391] The Court held that the Eleventh Amendment did not bar a back-pay award because that amendment and the principle of state sovereignty it embodies are limited by the enforcement provisions of Section 5 of the Fourteenth Amendment.[392]

Congress exercised its power under Section 5 of the Fourteenth Amendment when it enacted the 1972 Amendments to Title VII.[393] When Congress acts pursuant to Section 5 it exercises legislative authority that is "plenary within the terms of the constitutional grant."[394] As such, the Court determined that Congress may, in determining what is "appropriate legislation" for the purpose of enforcing the Fourteenth Amendment, allow for private suits against states or state officials, which may be constitutionally impermissible in other contexts.[395] Given the express congressional authority for an award of attorneys' fees under Title VII,[396] the Court reasoned that Congress' exercise of power in this respect was not barred by the Eleventh Amendment.[397] *Bitzer* established that prevailing plaintiffs in Title VII actions against state governments may recover reasonable attorneys' fees.

---

[390] 427 U.S. 445, 12 FEP Cases 1586 (1976).

[391] *Id.* at 450.

[392] The Fourteenth Amendment grants Congress the "authority to enforce, 'by appropriate legislation,' the substantive provisions of the Fourteenth Amendment, which [embody] significant limitations on state authority." *Id.* at 446, 12 FEP Cases at 1590.

[393] H.R. Rep. No. 92-238, at 19 (1971); S. Rep. No. 92-415, at 10–11 (1971); *cf.* National League of Cities v. Usery, 426 U.S. 833, 22 WH Cases 1064 (1976).

[394] *Bitzer*, 427 U.S. at 446, 12 FEP Cases at 1590.

[395] *Id.*

[396] 42 U.S.C. §2000e-5k.

[397] Fitzpatrick v. Bitzer, 427 U.S. 445, 457, 12 FEP Cases 1586 (1976).

D. Recovery of Attorneys' Fees by the Prevailing Plaintiff for an Administrative Proceeding

The broad statutory language of Title VII providing for the "prevailing party" of "any action or proceeding" to recover attorneys' fees has been determined in *New York Gaslight Club, Inc. v. Carey*,[398] to extend to successful complainants the ability to recover attorneys' fees for legal services conducted at the administrative level. A complainant exhaust the available administrative remedies prior to filing an action for discrimination in federal court and this state agency proceeding is mandatory as the enforcement system established under Title VII requires state and local deferral agencies initially to attempt to resolve the controversy prior to federal involvement at the district court level.[399] It is clear from this interrelated procedure for enforcement that Congress viewed the proceedings before the EEOC and the federal courts as part of a continuum running from the available state remedies for employment discrimination.[400] As a qualifying "proceeding" under the statute, attorneys' fees thus may be recovered for legal services provided at the federal stage.

The *Carey* analysis has also been applied in *Chrapliwy v. Uniroyal, Inc.*,[401] to justify an award of attorneys' fees to a successful plaintiff for time expended in debarment proceedings before the OFCCP. In that case, Title VII action was well underway

---

[398] 447 U.S. 54, 22 FEP Cases 1642 (1980).

[399] Accordingly,

Title VII establishes a comprehensive enforcement scheme in which state agencies are given "a limited opportunity to resolve problems of employment discrimination and thereby to make unnecessary, resort to federal relief by victims of the discrimination." . . . Congress envisioned that Title VII's procedures and remedies would "mes[h] nicely, logically, and coherently with the State and city legislation," and that remedying employment discrimination would be an area in which "[t]he Federal Government and the State governments could cooperate effectively."

Id. at 63–64, 22 FEP Cases at 1646 (quoting 110 CONG. REC. 7205 (1964) (remarks of Sen. Clark)).

[400] *Id.* at 65.

[401] 670 F.2d 760, 28 FEP Cases 19 (7th Cir. 1982) (on appeal of trial court's award of attorneys' fees to prevailing plaintiff pursuant to 42 U.S.C. §2000e-5(k), court held that plaintiffs' attorneys entitled to recover fees for time spent in attempt-

when the plaintiffs began their activities with regard to the debarment proceedings against the defendant, a federal contractor.[402] The issues and factual background forming the basis for debarment of the defendant from its federal contracts under Executive Order 11,246 were the same as the basis for the Title VII class action.[403] The plaintiff's effort at persuading the government to debar the defendant from its federal contracts was successful in that these efforts led to the settlement of the Title VII action. As both efforts by the plaintiffs were undertaken to move the Title VII case toward ultimate resolution, the reviewing court found that plaintiff's efforts to pursue debarment were within the Title VII action.[404]

Such an award of attorneys' fees is generally preconditioned on a filing of an actual Title VII complaint.[405] The *Mertz*[406] court distinguished the circumstances arising from the case at bar with *Carey*, in that the legal services provided at issue had been rendered in relation to pre-complaint processing. The court noted that,

> Attorney's fees shall be paid only for services performed after the filing of the complaint required in [29 C.F.R.] §1613.214 and

---

ing to have federal government debar employer as means of encouraging settlement after liability was determined).

[402]*Id.* at 766. The debarment proceeding commenced after the action had been filed due to, in part, the defendant's delay in responding to discovery requests and the delay caused by the unexpected death of the original trial judge. Therefore, the plaintiffs sought relief through the debarment process as an efficacious way to bring about the end of the Title VII action.

[403]*Id.*

[404]*Id.* at 767, 28 FEP Cases at 25.
We therefore conclude that neither Section 706(k) nor the *Carey* interpretation thereof precludes an award of attorneys' fees to the prevailing plaintiffs for their efforts in persuading the federal government to enforce Executive Order 11246. Rather, Section 706(k) should be interpreted as allowing attorneys' fees to the prevailing plaintiffs for services which contribute to the ultimate termination of the Title VII action.

Id.

[405]Mertz v. Marsh, 786 F.2d 1578, 40 FEP Cases 1110 (11th Cir. 1986).

[406]Mertz v. Marsh, 786 F.2d 1578, 1580, 40 FEP Cases 1110 (11th Cir. 1986) (civilian employee working as EEOC manager at Army base was denied claim for attorneys' fees, as legal services rendered with regard to settlement obtained for alleged employment discrimination occurred within context of Army base's internal efforts to address employee's grievance and formal complaint did not exist).

after the complainant has notified the agency that he or she is represented by an attorney, except that the fees are allowable for a reasonable period of time prior to the notification of representation for any services performed in reaching a determination to represent the complainant.[407]

This language does not treat the precomplaint processing as part of the "proceeding" for which attorneys' fees may be granted, but rather an informal, ameliorative procedure.[408] Title VII does not support an award of attorneys' fees for an optional internal grievance procedure, which is not a prerequisite to filing a Title VII action.[409]

---

[407] *Id.* at 1580, 40 FEP Cases at 1111 (quoting 29 C.F.R. §1613.271(c)(iv)).
[408] *Id.* at 1581.
[409] *Id.*

Appendix

LIST OF DOCUMENTS INCLUDED ON CD-ROM

Statutory and regulatory documents included on the CD-ROM accompanying this volume are separated by agency responsible for administering them—i.e., either

- Equal Employment Opportunity Commission (EEOC) or
- U.S. Department of Justice (DOJ), or
- U.S. Access Board

Thus,

- Title I and Title V of the ADA, for example, appear in the "EEOC" section, not including Sec. 102 of the Civil Rights Recovery Act concerning compensatory and punitive damages, which is not specific to the ADA, whereas
- Title III of the ADA appears in the "DOJ" section.

The various documents in each collection are listed below. These documents are also available on the agency websites at the web addresses shown, and can be accessed on those sites from the web addresses provided on the accompanying CD.

EEOC

Statute

Title I and Title V of the ADA, not including Sec. 102 of the Civil Rights Recovery Act concerning compensatory and punitive damages, which is not specific to the ADA.
http://www.eeoc.gov/policy/ada.html

Regulations

Regulations to Implement the Equal Employment Provisions of the Americans With Disabilities Act (29 C.F.R. §§ 1630.1–16) http://www.access.gpo.gov/nara/cfr/waisidx_03/29cfr1630_03.html

Procedures for Coordinating the Investigation of Complaints or Charges of Employment Discrimination Based on Disability Subject to the Americans with Disabilities Act and Section 504 of the Rehabilitation Act of 1973 (29 C.F.R § 1640)
http://www.access.gpo.gov/nara/cfr/waisidx_03/29cfr1640_03.html

Procedures for Complaints/Charges of Employment Discrimination Based on Disability Filed Against Employers Holding Government Contracts or Subcontracts (29 C.F.R. § 1641)
http://www.access.gpo.gov/nara/cfr/waisidx_03/29cfr1641_03.html

Other Documents

Enforcement Guidance

- Americans with Disabilities Act and Psychiatric Disabilities March, 1997
  http://www.eeoc.gov/policy/docs/psych.html *(last modified, February 1, 2000)*

- Application Of The ADA To Contingent Workers Placed By Temporary Agencies And Other Staffing Firms
  http://www.eeoc.gov/policy/docs/guidance-contingent.html *(last modified January 23, 2001)*
  - —*See also* Questions and Answers: Enforcement Guidance: Application of the ADA to Contingent Workers Placed by Temporary Agencies and Other Staffing Firms
    - http://www.eeoc.gov/policy/docs/qanda-contingent.html *(last modified December 27, 2000)*

- Application of the Americans with Disabilities Act of 1990 to Disability-Based Distinctions in Employer Provided Health Insurance *(Interim Enforcement Guidance)*
  http://www.eeoc.gov/policy/docs/health.html *(last modified July 6, 2000)*

- Disability-Related Inquiries and Medical Examinations of Employees Under the Americans with Disabilities Act (ADA) (July 27, 2000)
  http://www.eeoc.gov/policy/docs/guidance-inquiries.html (last modified March 24, 2005)
  - —*See also* Questions and Answers: Enforcement Guidance on Disability-Related Inquiries and Medical Examinations of Employees Under the Americans with Disabilities Act (ADA)
    http://www.eeoc.gov/policy/docs/qanda-inquiries.html

- Effect of Representations Made in Applications for Benefits on the Determination of Whether a Person Is a "Qualified Individual with a Disability" Under the Americans with Disabilities Act of 1990 (ADA) (February 12, 1997)
  http://www.eeoc.gov/policy/docs/qidreps.html (last modified July 6, 2000)

- Preemployment Disability-Related Questions and Medical Examinations (October 10, 1995)
  http://www.eeoc.gov/policy/docs/preemp.html (last modified July 6, 2000)

- Reasonable Accommodation and Undue Hardship Under the Americans With Disabilities Act (October 17, 2002)
  http://www.eeoc.gov/policy/docs/accommodation.html (last modified October 22, 2002)
  - —*See also* ADA Technical Assistance Manual: Addendum (October 17, 2002)
  - *http://www.eeoc.gov/policy/docs/adamanual_add.html (last modified October 29, 2002)*
  - —*See also* Small Employers and Reasonable Accommodation (March 1,1999)
  - *http://www.eeoc.gov/facts/accommodation.html (last modified March 1, 1999)*
    —*See also* The Family and Medical Leave Act, the Americans with Disabilities Act, and Title VII of the Civil Rights Act of 1964 Fact Sheet (March 1,1999)

- *http://www.eeoc.gov/facts/accommodation.html (last modified March 1, 1999)*

- Workers' Compensation and the ADA (September 1996) *http://www.eeoc.gov/policy/docs/workcomp.html (last modified July 6, 2000)*

Policy Guidance

- Executive Order 13145: To Prohibit Discrimination in Federal Employment Based on Genetic Information (July 26, 2000) *http://www.eeoc.gov/policy/docs/guidance-genetic.html (last modified July 27, 2000)*
    - —*See also*: Questions and Answers: EEOC Policy Guidance on Executive Order 13145 Prohibiting Discrimination in Federal Employment Based on Genetic Information
    - *http://www.eeoc.gov/policy/docs/qanda-genetic.html (last modified July 27, 2000)*

- Executive Order 13164: Establishing Procedures to Facilitate the Provision of Reasonable Accommodation (October 20, 2000)
    - *http://www.eeoc.gov/policy/docs/accommodation_procedures.html (last modified October 20, 2000)*
    - —*See also* Questions And Answers: Policy Guidance On Executive Order 13164: Establishing Procedures To Facilitate The Provision Of Reasonable Accommodation
    - *http://www.eeoc.gov/policy/docs/qanda-accommodation_procedures.html (last modified October 19, 2000)*

Additional Documents

- Compliance Manual Section 902: Definition of the Term Disability—Addendum *(March 1995, last modified February 1, 2000)* *http://www.eeoc.gov/policy/docs/902cm.html (last modified February 1, 2000)*

—*See also* Executive Summary: Compliance Manual Section 902: Definition of the Term "Disability"—Addendum *(last modified February 1, 2000)*
http://www.eeoc.gov/policy/docs/902cm.html *(last modified February 1, 2000)*

- Instructions for Field Offices Analyzing ADA Charges After Supreme Court Decisions Addressing "Disability" and "Qualified" (December 13, 1999)
http://www.eeoc.gov/policy/docs/field-ada.html *(last modified December 13, 1999)*

DOJ

Statute

Title III of the Americans with Disabilities Act, 42 U.S.C. §§ 12181, et seq. (Link includes entire law)
http://www.usdoj.gov/crt/ada/pubs/ada.txt

Regulations

Title II & III Regulation Amendment Regarding Detectable Warnings
http://www.usdoj.gov/crt/ada/detwarn.htm *(last revised January 22, 1999)*

U.S. Department of Justice Regulations under Title III of the ADA (28 C.F.R. Part 36)
http://www.usdoj.gov/crt/ada/reg3a.html *(last revised January 22, 2000)*
—*See also* Advance Notice of Proposed Rulemaking to amend 28 CFR Part 35: Nondiscrimination on the Basis of Disability in State and Local Government Services and 28 CFR Part 36: Nondiscrimination on the Basis of Disability by Public Accommodations and in Commercial Facilities
http://www.usdoj.gov/crt/ada/anprm04.htm *(last updated January 19, 2005)*
—*See also* Appendix A— Proposed Framework for the Regulatory Analysis

http://www.usdoj.gov/crt/ada/anprm04appa.htm (last updated September 30, 2004)
—*See also* Advance notice of proposed rulemaking; extension of comment period until May 31, 2005
http://www.usdoj.gov/crt/ada/anprm04ext.htm (last updated January 19, 2005)

Other Documents

Technical Assistance Manual for ADA Title III Compliance
http://www.usdoj.gov/crt/ada/taman3.html
—*See also* 1994 Supplement
http://www.usdoj.gov/crt/ada/taman3up.html

Access Board

ADA Accessibility Guidelines for Buildings and Facilities (ADAAG), as amended through September 2002
http://www.access-board.gov/adaag/html/adaag.htm

Proposed Revisions to ADA Accessibility Guidelines for Buildings and Facilities, as approved by ACTCB (published in the Federal Register on July 23, 2004), forming the basis for the Advance Notice of Proposed Rulemaking published by the Department of Justice to implement the Guidelines, on September 30, 2004
http://www.access-board.gov/ada-aba/final.htm

Uniform Federal Accessibility Standards (UFAS)
http://www.access-board.gov/ufas/ufas-html/ufas.htm

—*See also* Figures in Uniform Federal Accessibility Standards
http://www.access-board.gov/ufas/ufas-html/figures.htm

TABLE OF CASES

References are to chapters and footnote numbers (e.g., 3: 374; 10: 331 refers to footnote 374 in Chapter 3 and footnote 331 in Chapter 10). Alphabetization is letter-by-letter (e.g., "DeGiuseppe" precedes "de la Torres").

A

Access Now, Inc.
—v. Claire's Stores, Inc., No. 00-14017-CIV-MOORE, 2002 WL 1162422 (S.D. Fla. May 7, 2002) **6:** 97
—v. Holland Am. Line-Westours, Inc., 147 F. Supp. 2d 1311 (S.D. Fla. 2001) **6:** 187
—v. South Fla. Stadium Corp., 161 F. Supp. 2d 1357, 12 AD Cases 1384 (S.D. Fla. 2001) **6:** 208
—v. Southwest Airlines Co., 227 F. Supp. 2d 1312, 13 AD Cases 1186 (S.D. Fla. 2002) **6:** 87, 88, 94–96
Acme Indus. Co.; NLRB v., 385 U.S. 432, 64 LRRM 2069 (1967) **9:** 355
Adams
—v. Master Carvers of Jamestown Ltd., 2004 U.S. App. LEXIS 3381 (2d Cir. 2004) **5:** 161
—v. Rite Aid of Me., Inc., 6 WH Cases 2d 1481 (D. Me. 2001) **5:** 253
Adam's Fruit Co. v. Barrett, 494 U.S. 638 (1990) **9:** 130–34
Advocates for Highway & Auto Safety v. Federal Highway Admin., 28 F.3d 1288, 3 AD Cases 842 (D.C. Cir. 1994) **9:** 310
AIC Sec. Investigations, Ltd.; EEOC v., 820 F. Supp. 1060, 2 AD Cases 561 (N.D. Ill. 1993) **5:** 492
Air Line Pilots v. O'Neill, 499 U.S. 65, 136 LRRM 2721 (1991) **9:** 388
Aka v. Washington Hosp. Ctr., 156 F.3d 1284, 8 AD Cases 1093 (D.C. Cir. 1998) **7:** 41–47; **8:** 152
Akrabawi v. Carrier Co., 152 F.3d 688 (3d Cir. 1988) **10:** 374
Albano v. General Adjustment Bureau, Inc., 478 F. Supp. 1209, 21 FEP Cases 323 (S.D.N.Y. 1979), *aff'd*, 622 F.2d 572, 22 FEP Cases 840 (2d Cir. 1980) **10:** 13
Albemarle Paper Co. v. Moody, 422 U.S. 405, 10 FEP Cases 1181 (1975) **10:** 371
Albert v. Runyon, 6 F. Supp. 2d 57, 4 WH Cases 2d 1128 (D. Mass. 1998) **9:** 94
Alden v. Maine, 527 U.S. 706, 5 WH Cases 2d 607 (1999) **10:** 94, 95, 97
Aldrich v. Boeing Co., 146 F.3d 1265, 8 AD Cases 424 (10th Cir. 1998), *cert. denied*, 526 U.S. 1144 (1999) **5:** 121
Aldrup v. Caldera, 274 F.3d 282, 12 AD Cases 1044 (5th Cir. 2001) **5:** 104, 424
Alexander
—v. Choate, 469 U.S. 287 (1985) **1:** 5; **2:** 7, 8, 12; **5:** 10
—v. Gardner-Denver Co., 415 U.S. 36, 7 FEP Cases 81 (1974) **3:** 374; **10:** 331, 342
—v. Sandoval, 532 U.S. 275 (2001) **10:** 151
Allen
—v. A.G. Thomas, 161 F.3d 667 (11th Cir. 1998) **6:** 94
—v. Fauver, 327 N.J. Super. 14, 742 A.2d

Allen—*Cont'd*
594 (1999), *aff'd,* 167 N.J. 69, 768 A.2d 1055, 6 WH Cases 2d 1741 (2000) **10:** 96

Alsbrook v. City of Maumelle, Ark., 184 F.3d 999, 9 AD Cases 897 (8th Cir. 1999) **10:** 101

Altman v. New York City Health & Hosps. Corp., 100 F.3d 1054, 6 AD Cases 73 (2d Cir. 1996) **5:** 314

Alyeska Pipeline Serv. Co. v. Wilderness Soc'y, 421 U.S. 240, 10 FEP Cases 826 (1975) **10:** 355, 356

Amadio v. Ford Motor Co., 238 F.3d 919, 11 AD Cases 641 (7th Cir. 2001) **5:** 169; **10:** 190

Amego, Inc.; EEOC v., 110 F.3d 135, 6 AD Cases 997 (1st Cir. 1997) **9:** 294

American Disability Ass'n Inc. v. Chmielarz, No. 01-15366 (11th Cir. 2002) **6:** 412

Amir v. St. Louis Univ., 184 F.3d 1017, 9 AD Cases 999 (8th Cir. 1999) **5:** 410

Amos v. Maryland Dep't of Pub. Safety & Corr. Servs., 178 F.3d 212, 9 AD Cases 769 (4th Cir. 1999) **10:** 100

Anchor Hocking Corp.; EEOC v., 666 F.2d 1037, 27 FEP Cases 809 (6th Cir. 1981) **2:** 227

Anderson
—v. Coors Brewing Co., 181 F.3d 1171, 9 AD Cases 835 (10th Cir. 1999) **5:** 208, 216; **8:** 145, 146
—v. Department of Pub. Welfare, 1 F. Supp. 2d 456, 9 AD Cases 375 (E.D. Pa. 1998) **10:** 100
—v. Live Plants, Inc., 187 W. Va. 365, 419 S.E. 2d 305, 6 AD Cases 1045 (1992) **4:** 1081
—v. Pass Christian Isles Golf Club, Inc., 488 F.2d 855 (5th Cir. 1974) **6:** 126

Andrews
—v. Consolidated Rail Corp., 831 F.2d 678, 1 AD Cases 1122 (7th Cir. 1987) **2:** 250
—v. Ohio, 104 F.3d 803, 6 AD Cases 322 (6th Cir. 1997) **7:** 274, 275

Anzalone v. Allstate Ins. Co., 5 AD Cases 223 (E.D. La. 1995) **9:** 491

A.R. v. Kogan, 964 F. Supp. 269 (N.D. Ill. 1997) **10:** 51

Aramark Corp., Inc.; EEOC v., 208 F.3d 266, 341 U.S. App. D.C. 38, 10 AD Cases 798 (D.C. Cir. 2000) **9:** 504, 505, 515

Armstrong
—v. Lockheed Martin Beryllium Co., 990 F. Supp. 1395 (M.D. Fla. 1997) **4:** 161
—v. Turner Indus., 141 F.3d 554, 8 AD Cases 118 (5th Cir. 1998) **7:** 77

Arnold
—v. Appleton, Wis., City of, 97 F. Supp. 2d 937, 10 AD Cases 1474 (D. Wis. 2000) **5:** 502
—v. United Parcel Serv., 136 F.3d 854, 7 AD Cases 1489 (1st Cir. 1998) **5:** 130

Asplundh Tree Expert Co.; EEOC v., 340 F.3d 1256, 92 FEP Cases 661 (11th Cir. 2003) **10:** 29

Association for Disabled Americans Inc.
—v. Concorde Gaming Corp., 158 F. Supp. 2d 1353, 12 AD Cases 453 (S.D. Fla. 2001) **6:** 237
—v. 7-Eleven, Inc., No. 3:01-CV-0230-H (N.D. Tex. 2002) **6:** 405, 406

Association of Relatives & Friends of AIDS Patients v. Regulations & Permits Admin., 740 F. Supp. 95 (D.P.R. 1990) **5:** 337

AT&T Techs. v. Royston, 772 P.2d 1182, 2 AD Cases 1564 (Colo. Ct. App. 1989) **4:** 80

Atascadero State Hosp. v. Scanlon, 473 U.S. 234, 1 AD Cases 758 (1985) **10:** 98, 106–09

Aucutt v. Six Flags Over Mid-America, Inc., 85 F.3d 1311, 5 AD Cases 902 (8th Cir. 1996) **9:** 237

August v. Offices Unlimited, Inc., 981 F.2d 576, 2 AD Cases 401 (1st Cir. 1992) **9:** 145

Austin v. Owens-Brockway Glass Container, Inc., 78 F.3d 875, 5 AD Cases 488 (4th Cir.), *cert. denied,* 519 U.S. 980 (1996) **9:** 380; **10:** 335

Autio v. State, County & Mun. Employees (AFSCME), 140 F.3d 802, 7 AD Cases 1706 (8th Cir. 1998) **10:** 100

B

Bachman v. American Soc'y of Clinical Pathologists, 577 F. Supp. 1257 (D.N.J. 1983) *2:* 98
Bachmeier v. Hoffman, 1 P.3d 1236, 6 WH Cases 2d 56 (Wyo. 2000) *10:* 96
Baert v. Euclid Beverage, Ltd., 149 F.3d 626, 8 AD Cases 973 (7th Cir. 1998) *5:* 130
Bailey v. Georgia-Pacific Corp., 306 F.3d 1162, 13 AD Cases 1066 (1st Cir. 2002) *5:* 182, 269
Baker v. Board of Regents of State of Kan., 991 F.2d 628 (10th Cir. 1993) *2:* 302
Ball v. SFX Broad., 665 N.Y.S.2d 444 (N.Y. App. Div. 1997) *10:* 320
Ballard
—v. Healthsouth Corp., 147 F. Supp. 2d 529, 11 AD Cases 1717 (N.D. Tex. 2001) *5:* 392
—v. Rubin, 284 F.3d 957, 12 AD Cases 1646 (8th Cir. 2002) *2:* 302; *8:* 52; *10:* 207, 208
Barbera v. Di Martino, 305 N.J. Super. 617, 702 A.2d 1370, 7 AD Cases 1178 (1997), *cert. denied,* 708 A.2d 64 (1998) *5:* 431
Barfield v. Bell S. Telecommunications, Inc., 886 F. Supp. 1321, 4 AD Cases 1159 (S.D. Miss. 1995) *9:* 29
Barnes
—v. Cochran, 944 F. Supp. 897, 5 AD Cases 1685 (S.D. Fla. 1996), *aff'd,* 130 F.3d 443 (11th Cir. 1997) *7:* 95, 98, 115, 142–46, 203; *8:* 263
—v. Gorman, 536 U.S. 181 (2002) *10:* 131, 152, 158
Barnett v. U.S. Air, 228 F.3d 1105, 10 AD Cases 1761 (9th Cir. 2000), *vacated & remanded,* 535 U.S. 391, 12 AD Cases 1729 (2002) *4:* 691, 692; *8:* 110–14; *9:* 371
Barrios v. California Interscholastic Fed'n, 277 F.3d 1128, 12 AD Cases 1145 (9th Cir.), *cert. denied,* 537 U.S. 820 (2002) *6:* 411
Barth v. Gelb, 2 F.3d 1180, 2 AD Cases 1180 (D.C. Cir. 1993), *cert. denied,* 511 U.S. 1030 (1994) *2:* 305; *10:* 203
Bartlett v. New York State Bd. of Law Exam'rs, 156 F.3d 321, 8 AD Cases 1004 (2d Cir. 1998), *vacated,* 527 U.S. 1031, 9 AD Cases 768 (1999) *5:* 130
Bates v. Long Island R.R., 997 F.2d 1028, 2 AD Cases 1038 (2d Cir.), *cert. denied,* 510 U.S. 992 (1993) *2:* 302
Baxter v. City of Belleville, 720 F. Supp. 720 (S.D. Ill. 1989) *5:* 336
Beason v. United Techs. Corp.
—337 F.3d 271, 14 AD Cases 1121 (2d Cir. 2003) *4:* 107, 109
—37 F. Supp. 2d 127, 164 LRRM 2372 (D. Conn. 1999) *10:* 340
Beck v. University of Wis. Bd. of Regents, 75 F.3d 1130, 5 AD Cases 304 (7th Cir. 1996) *1:* 76; *8:* 78, 80, 93
Beele v. Donohue & Donohue, P.C., 20 MDLR 5 (1998) *4:* 519, 532
Bekker v. Humana Health Plan, Inc., 229 F.3d 662, 10 AD Cases 1776 (7th Cir. 2000), *cert. denied,* 532 U.S. 972 (2001) *1:* 96; *5:* 170, 318, 327
Belk v. Southwestern Bell Tel. Co., 194 F.3d 946, 9 AD Cases 1621 (8th Cir. 1999) *10:* 248
Bell
—v. Hood, 327 U.S. 678 (1946) *2:* 294
—v. Wells Fargo Bank, N.A., 62 Cal. App. 4th 1382, 73 Cal. Rptr. 2d 354, 8 AD Cases 95 (1998) *4:* 66
Benajmin R. v. Orkin Exterminating Co., 182 W.Va. 615, 390 S.E. 2d 814, 2 AD Cases 389 (1990) *4:* 1081
Bennett v. United Parcel Serv., 5 AD Cases 260 (S.D. Tex. 1995) *9:* 145
Benson v. Northwest Airlines, Inc., 62 F.3d 1108, 4 AD Cases 1234 (8th Cir. 1995) *7:* 228; *8:* 121, 142; *9:* 371
Bento v. I.T.O. Corp. of R.I., 599 F. Supp. 731, 1 AD Cases 653 (D.R.I. 1984) *5:* 26
Bercovitch v. Baldwin Sch., 964 F. Supp. 597, 7 AD Cases 1378 (D.P.R. 1997), *rev'd,* 133 F.3d 141, 8 AD Cases 259 (1st Cir. 1998) *6:* 395
Berg v. Norand Corp., 169 F.3d 1140, 9

Berg—*Cont'd*
AD Cases 207 (8th Cir.), *cert. denied*, 528 U.S. 872 (1999)   **5:** 100, 103, 458
Bishop v. Okidata, Inc., 864 F. Supp. 416, 3 AD Cases 1283 (D.N.J. 1994)   **10:** 34
Black v. Roadway Express, Inc., 297 F.3d 445, 13 AD Cases 581 (6th Cir. 2002)   **5:** 111
Blanks v. Southwestern Bell Commc'ns, Inc., 310 F.3d 398, 13 AD Cases 1253 (5th Cir. 2002)   **5:** 61, 155, 351; **10:** 186
Blanton v. Inco Alloys Int'l, Inc., 108 F.3d 104, 6 AD Cases 673, *aff'd in part & rev'd in part, remanded*, 123 F.3d 916, 7 AD Cases 1475 (6th Cir. 1997)   **9:** 237, 240
Bledsoe v. Palm Beach County Soil & Water Conservation Dist., 133 F.3d 816, 7 AD Cases 1433 (11th Cir.), *cert. denied*, 525 U.S. 826 (1998)   **10:** 38
Blue Cross Blue Shield of Conn.; EEOC v., 30 F. Supp. 2d 296 (D. Conn. 1998)   **7:** 118, 131, 133
Board of Governors of State Colls. & Univs. for N.E. Ill. Univ.; United States v. *See* Erickson v. Board of Governors of State Colls. & Univs. for N.E. Ill. Univ.
Boeing Co.; Doe v., 121 Wash. 2d 8, 846 P.2d 531, 2 AD Cases 548 (1993)   **4:** 1070
Boemio v. Loves Rest., 954 F. Supp. 204 (S.D. Cal. 1997)   **6:** 2
Boersig v. Union Elec. Co., 219 F.3d 816, 10 AD Cases 1249 (8th Cir. 2000), *cert. denied*, 531 U.S. 1113 (2001)   **8:** 123
Boerst v. General Mills Operations, Inc., 25 Fed. Appx. 403, 2002 WL 59637, 2002 U.S. App. LEXIS 813 (6th Cir. 2002), *cert. denied*, 535 U.S. 1097 (2002)   **5:** 64–66, 103; **8:** 203; **10:** 231
Boise Cascade Corp. v. Board of Forestry, 164 Ore. App. 114, 991 P.2d 563 (1999)   **10:** 96
Bolton
—v. Murray Envelope Corp., 553 F.2d 881, 15 FEP Cases 478 (5th Cir. 1977)   **10:** 380
—v. Scrivner, Inc., 836 F. Supp. 783, 3 AD Cases 86 (W.D. Okla. 1993), *aff'd*, 36 F.3d 939, 3 AD Cases 1089 (10th Cir. 1994), *cert. denied*, 513 U.S. 1152 (1995)   **9:** 20, 166
Boone v. Kent Feeds, Inc., 2001 U.S. Dist. LEXIS 9616, 2001 WL 1775375 (W.D. Ky. July 10, 2001)   **4:** 417
Boos v. Runyon, 201 F.3d 178, 10 AD Cases 198 (2d Cir. 2000)   **2:** 205
Borigialli v. Thunder Basin Coal Co., 235 F.3d 1284, 11 AD Cases 484 (10th Cir. 2000)   **8:** 247
Borkowski v. Valley Cent. Sch. Dist., 63 F.3d 131, 4 AD Cases 1264 (2d Cir. 1995)   **10:** 203
Botosan v. Paul McNally Realty, 216 F.3d 827, 10 AD Cases 1185 (9th Cir. 2000)   **6:** 269, 270, 395
Bowe v. Colgate Palmolive, 272 F. Supp. 332, 1 FEP Cases 201 (S.D. Ind. 1967), *aff'd in part, rev'd in part*, 416 F.2d 711, 2 FEP Cases 223 (7th Cir. 1969)   **10:** 342
Bowerman v. Malloy Lithographing, Inc., 171 Mich. App. 110, 430 N.W.2d 742, 48 FEP Cases 635 (1988)   **4:** 555
Bowers
—v. Estep, 204 Ga. App. 615, 420 S.E. 2d 336 (1992)   **4:** 209
—v. Multimedia Cablevision, Inc., 10 AD Cases 671 (D. Kan. 1999)   **5:** 428
—v. National Collegiate Athletic Ass'n, 118 F. Supp. 2d 494, 11 AD Cases 415 (D.N.J. 2000)   **6:** 72
Boyd v. U.S. Postal Serv., 752 F.2d 410, 1 AD Cases 686 (9th Cir. 1985)   **2:** 305
Boykin v. ATC/Vancom of Colo., 247 F.3d 1061, 11 AD Cases 1204 (10th Cir. 2001)   **8:** 177
Brace v. International Bus. Machs. Corp., 953 F. Supp. 561 (D. Vt. 1997)   **4:** 1041
Bradley
—v. Pizzaco of Neb., Inc., 939 F.2d 610 (8th Cir. 1991)   **4:** 665
—v. University of Tex. M.D. Anderson Cancer Ctr., 3 F.3d 922, 2 AD Cases 1297 (5th Cir. 1993), *cert. denied*, 510 U.S. 1119 (1994)   **10:** 261
Bragdon v. Abbott, 912 F. Supp. 580, 5 AD Cases 1673 (D. Me. 1995), *aff'd*,

107 F.3d 934, 6 AD Cases 780 (1st Cir. 1997), *vacated*, 524 U.S. 624, 8 AD Cases 239 (1998)   *1:* 53; *5:* 13, 51, 52, 60, 333, 340–45, 349, 421; *6:* 7, 151, 152; *9:* 27; *10:* 219
Branham v. Snow, 392 F.3d 896, 16 AD Cases 454 (7th Cir. 2004)   *5:* 453
Bratten v. SSI Servs., Inc., 185 F.3d 625, 9 AD Cases 1045 (6th Cir. 1999)   *8:* 144; *10:* 340
Breen v. Dep't of Transp., 282 F.3d 839, 12 AD Cases 1652 (D.C. Cir. 2002)   *2:* 188
Brennan
—v. King, 139 F.3d 258 (1st Cir. 1998)   *2:* 286
—v. Mercedes Benz USA, 388 F.3d 133, 16 AD Cases 15 (5th Cir. 2004)   *7:* 13, 24, 75
Brenneman v. MedCentral Health Sys., 366 F.3d 412, 15 AD Cases 769, *reh'g denied*, 2004 U.S. App. LEXIS 16569 (2004), *cert. denied*, 125 S. Ct. 1300 (2005)   *5:* 460
Bricklayers Local 17 (Ruhm Tile & Marble), 278 NLRB 924, 121 LRRM 1347 (1986)   *9:* 365
Brisentine v. Stone & Webster Eng'g Corp., 117 F.3d 519, 6 AD Cases 1878 (11th Cir. 1997)   *9:* 379
Brohm v. JH Props., Inc., 947 F. Supp. 299, 6 AD Cases 1489 (W.D. Ky. 1996)   *4:* 410
Brooklyn Union Gas Co. v. New York State Human Rights Appeal Bd., 41 N.Y.2d 84, 390 N.Y.S.2d 884, 359 N.E.2d 393, 14 FEP Cases 42 (1976)   *4:* 773
Brookman v. Wyoming Dep't of Family Servs., 342 F.3d 1159, 14 AD Cases 1423 (10th Cir. 2003), *cert. denied*, 124 S. Ct. 1509 (2004)   *2:* 101
Brown
—v. ABF Freight Sys., Inc., 183 F.3d 319, 161 LRRM 2769 (4th Cir. 1999)   *10:* 340
—v. General Servs. Admin., 425 U.S. 820, 12 FEP Cases 1361 (1976)   *10:* 79
—v. Loudoun Golf & Country Club, Inc.,

573 F. Supp. 399 (E.D. Va. 1983)   *6:* 126
—v. Lucky Stores Inc., 246 F.3d 1182, 11 AD Cases 1195 (9th Cir. 2001)   *5:* 287
—v. 1995 Tenet ParaAmerica Bicycle Challenge, 959 F. Supp. 496, 6 AD Cases 1137 (N.D. Ill. 1997)   *6:* 74
—v. North Carolina Div. of Motor Vehicles, 166 F.3d 698, 11 AD Cases 831 (4th Cir. 1999), *cert. denied*, 531 U.S. 1190 (2001)   *10:* 101
—v. Scott Paper Worldwide Co., 98 Wash. App. 349, 989 P.2d 1187, 81 FEP Cases 1267 (1999)   *4:* 1073
—v. Sibley, 650 F.2d 760, 1 AD Cases 254 (5th Cir. 1981)   *2:* 80
Browning v. Liberty Mut. Ins. Co., 178 F.3d 1043, 9 AD Cases 730 (8th Cir.), *cert. denied*, 528 U.S. 1050 (1999)   *9:* 337
Brunko v. Mercy Hosp., 260 F.3d 939, 12 AD Cases 256 (8th Cir. 2001)   *5:* 98, 100
Bryan v. United Parcel Serv. Inc., 2004 U.S. Dist. LEXIS 3382 (N.D. Cal. Mar. 2, 2004)   *4:* 44
Bryant v. Madigan, 84 F.3d 246, 5 AD Cases 833 (7th Cir. 1996)   *5:* 268
Buckhannon Bd. & Care Home, Inc. v. West Va. Dep't of Health & Human Serv., 532 U.S. 598, 11 AD Cases 1300 (2001)   *6:* 409, 410; *10:* 375
Buckingham v. United States, 998 F.2d 735, 2 AD Cases 1009 (9th Cir. 1993)   *8:* 119
Buckles v. First Data Res., Inc., 176 F.3d 1098, 9 AD Cases 765 (8th Cir. 1999)   *5:* 195; *8:* 237; *10:* 200, 275
Budd v. ADT Sec. Sys., Inc., 103 F.3d 699, 6 AD Cases 867 (8th Cir. 1996)   *9:* 237
Buie v. Quad/Graphics Inc., 366 F.3d 496, 15 AD Cases 790 (7th Cir. 2004)   *5:* 370
Bultemeyer v. Fort Wayne Cmty. Sch., 100 F.3d 1281, 6 AD Cases 67 (7th Cir. 1996)   *8:* 69, 70; *9:* 41; *10:* 214, 215
Burch v. Coca-Cola Co., 119 F.3d 305, 7 AD Cases 241 (5th Cir. 1997), *cert.*

Burch—*Cont'd*
denied, 522 U.S. 1084 (1998) **5:** 183, 270, 278, 281; **10:** 123
Burchett v. Target Corp., 340 F.3d 510, 14 AD Cases 1296 (8th Cir. 2003) **8:** 47
Burgess
—v. Joseph Schlitz Brewing Co., 298 N.C. 520, 259 S.E.2d 248, 1 AD Cases 121 (1979) **4:** 791
—v. Your House of Raleigh, Inc., 326 N.C. 205, 388 S.E.2d 134, 2 AD Cases 672 (1990) **4:** 779
Burke; United States v., 504 U.S. 229, 58 FEP Cases 1323 (1992) **2:** 230, 231
Burkhart v. Widener Univ., Inc., 2003 U.S. App. LEXIS 9004 (3d Cir. 2003) **6:** 395
Burnett
—v. Brock, 806 F.2d 265 (11th Cir. 1986) **2:** 68, 308, 310, 354
—v. Tyco Corp., 932 F. Supp. 1039 (W.D. Tenn. 1996) **4:** 972
Burns v. Coca-Cola Enters., Inc., 222 F.3d 247, 10 AD Cases 1409 (6th Cir. 2000) **5:** 99; **8:** 45, 46
Burriola v. Greater Toledo YMCA, 133 F. Supp. 2d 1034, 12 AD Cases 1710 (N.D. Ohio 2001) **6:** 153
Bush v. Commonwealth Edison Co., 990 F.2d 928, 2 AD Cases 679 (7th Cir. 1993) **2:** 302
Buskirk v. Apollo Metals, 307 F.3d 160 (3d Cir. 2002) **5:** 161
Butcher v. Bally Total Fitness Corp., 2003 Ohio 1734 (2003) **10:** 320

C

Calef v. Gillette Co., 322 F.3d 75, 14 AD Cases 110 (1st Cir. 2003) **5:** 414
California Paralyzed Veterans Ass'n v. Federal Commc'ns Comm'n, 496 F. Supp. 125, 23 FEP Cases 1305 (C.D. Cal. 1980), *aff'd sub nom.* California Ass'n of the Physically Handicapped v. Federal Commc'ns Comm'n, 721 F.2d 667, 1 AD Cases 538 (9th Cir. 1983), *cert. denied*, 469 U.S. 832 (1984) **10:** 66
Cambridge Indus., Inc.; EEOC v., 10 AD Cases 1747 (N.D. Ill. 2000) **9:** 338
Campbell
—v. Arco Marine, Inc., 42 Cal. App. 4th 1850, 50 Cal. Rptr. 2d 626, 70 FEP Cases 262 (1996) **4:** 59
—v. Federal Express Corp. 918 F. Supp. 912, 6 AD Cases 835 (D. Md. 1996) **9:** 282
Cannice v. Norwest Bank Iowa, N.A., 189 F.3d 723, 9 AD Cases 1103 (8th Cir. 1999), *cert. denied*, 529 U.S. 1019 (2000) **5:** 445; **10:** 200
Cannon v. University of Chicago, 441 U.S. 677 (1979) **10:** 151
Carparts Distrib. Ctr., Inc. v. Automotive Wholesaler's Ass'n of New England, Inc., 37 F.3d 12, 3 AD Cases 1237 (1st Cir. 1994), *on remand*, 987 F. Supp. 77, 7 AD Cases 759 (D.N.H. 1997) **4:** 698; **5:** 385; **6:** 67, 68, 70, 71; **7:** 93; **9:** 498
Carr
—v. Reno, 23 F.3d 525, 3 AD Cases 434 (D.C. Cir. 1994) **7:** 254, 255; **8:** 215, 216; **9:** 41, 69
—v. United Parcel Serv., 955 S.W.2d 832, 83 FEP Cases 341 (Tenn. 1997) **4:** 972
Carrion v. Yeshiva Univ., 535 F.2d 722, 13 FEP Cases 1521 (2d Cir. 1976) **10:** 372, 380
Carroll v. Xerox Corp., 294 F.3d 231, 13 AD Cases 396 (1st Cir. 2002) **5:** 92
Carson v. Giant Foods, Inc., 175 F.3d 325, 79 FEP Cases 976 (4th Cir. 1999) **10:** 338, 339
Carter
—v. Orleans Parish Pub. Sch., 725 F.2d 261 (5th Cir. 1984) **2:** 147, 148; **10:** 154
—v. Tisch, 822 F.2d 465, 1 AD Cases 1114 (4th Cir. 1987) **9:** 370
Caruso v. Blockbuster-Sony Music En-tm't Ctr. at the Waterfront, 193 F.3d 730, 9 AD Cases 1601 (3d Cir. 1999) **6:** 298

Cash v. Smith, 231 F.3d 1301, 11 AD Cases 203 (11th Cir. 2000) *5:* 155, 471; *10:* 186

Cassidy v. Detroit Edison Co., 138 F.3d 629, 8 AD Cases 326 (6th Cir. 1998) *8:* 121, 179; *9:* 371

Castellano v. City of New York, 142 F.3d 58, 9 AD Cases 67 (2d Cir.), *cert. denied,* 525 U.S. 820 (1998) *9:* 482

Cehrs v. Northeast Ohio Alzheimer's Research Ctr., 155 F.3d 775, 8 AD Cases 825 (6th Cir. 1998) *5:* 122; *8:* 240; *9:* 6, 39

Chabner v. United of Omaha Life Ins. Co., 225 F.3d 1042, 10 AD Cases 1705 (9th Cir. 2000) *5:* 383; *6:* 64

Chalk v. U.S. Dist. Ct. Cent. Dist. of Cal., 840 F.2d 701, 1 AD Cases 1210 (9th Cir. 1988) *2:* 299; *5:* 337

Chandler v. City of Dallas, 2 F.3d 1385, 2 AD Cases 1326 (5th Cir. 1993), *cert. denied,* 511 U.S. 1011 (1994) *7:* 283; *9:* 277

Chaplin v. Consolidated Edison Co. of N.Y., 482 F. Supp. 1165 (S.D.N.Y. 1980) *10:* 66

Charbonneau v. United Grinding, Inc., 1995 Conn. Super. LEXIS 3305 (Nov. 20, 1995) *4:* 105

Chastang v. Flynn & Emrich Co., 541 F.2d 1040, 12 FEP Cases 1533 (4th Cir. 1976) *10:* 369, 372

Chaveriat v. Williams Pipe Line Co., 11 F.3d 1420 (7th Cir. 1993) *5:* 233

Chenoweth v. Hillsborough County, 250 F.3d 1328, 11 AD Cases 1421 (11th Cir. 2001), *cert. denied,* 534 U.S. 1131 (2002) *2:* 136; *5:* 68, 498, 499; *10:* 230

Cherosky v. Henderson, 330 F.3d 1243, 14 AD Cases 673 (9th Cir. 2003) *2:* 206

Chevron U.S.A., Inc. v. Echazabal, 536 U.S. 73, 13 AD Cases 97 (2002) *10:* 252

Cheyenne Mountain Conference Resort, Inc.; Roe v., 124 F.3d 1221, 7 AD Cases 779 (10th Cir. 1997) *5:* 179, 312; *7:* 73, 124

Chiari v. City of League City, 920 F.2d 311, 1 AD Cases 1721 (5th Cir. 1991) *7:* 261

Chmielewski v. Xermac, Inc., 457 Mich. 593, 580 N.W. 2d 817 (Mich. 1998) *4:* 552

Chrapliwy v. Uniroyal, Inc., 670 F.2d 760, 28 FEP Cases 19 (7th Cir. 1982) *10:* 401–4

Christiansburg Garment Co. v. EEOC, 434 U.S. 412, 16 FEP Cases 502 (1978) *10:* 354, 355, 365, 376–80, 382, 383

Cinemark USA Inc.; United States v., 348 F.3d 569, 14 AD Cases 1788 (6th Cir. 2003), *cert. denied,* 124 S. Ct. 2905, 15 AD Cases 1216 (2004) *6:* 392

Circuit City Stores, Inc. v. Adams, 532 U.S. 105, 85 FEP Cases 266 (2001), *on remand,* 279 F.3d 889, 87 FEP Cases 1509 (9th Cir. 2002) *10:* 298–301, 303, 308, 309, 317

City of. *See name of city*

Clark v. California, 123 F.3d 1267, 7 AD Cases 292 (9th Cir. 1997), *cert. denied,* 524 U.S. 937 (1998) *10:* 100

Clark County, Ohio, Sheriff's Dep't, In re, 102 LA 193 (Kindig, 1994) *9:* 374

Clemente v. Executive Airlines, Inc., 213 F.3d 25, 10 AD Cases 996 (1st Cir. 2000) *5:* 80

Clemmer v. Enron Corp., 882 F. Supp. 606, 4 AD Cases 437 (S.D. Tex. 1995) *10:* 64

Cleveland v. Policy Mgt. Sys. Corp., 120 F.3d 513, 7 AD Cases 1031 (5th Cir. 1997), *vacated & remanded,* 526 U.S. 795, 9 AD Cases 491 (1999) *2:* 156; *4:* 521; *5:* 234–41, 354–56; *8:* 264, 265, 268–70; *9:* 149, 151–53, 199, 200, 241–46, 248–56, 492

Cline

—v. Wal-Mart Stores, Inc., 144 F.3d 294, 8 AD Cases 154 (4th Cir. 1998) *9:* 61, 110

—v. Western Horseman, Inc., 922 F. Supp. 442, 5 AD Cases 714 (D. Colo. 1996) *9:* 237

Clopton v. Global Computer Assocs., 4 AD Cases 360 (C.D. Cal. 1995) *4:* 58

CNA Ins. Cos.; EEOC v., 96 F.3d 1039, 5 AD Cases 1769 (7th Cir. 1996) **5:** 443; **9:** 482, 513

Cody v. CIGNA Healthcare of St. Louis, 139 F.3d 595, 7 AD Cases 1716 (8th Cir. 1998) **5:** 407, 436

Cole
—v. Burns Int'l Sec. Servs., Inc., 105 F.3d 1465, 72 FEP Cases 1775 (D.C. Cir. 1997) **10:** 297, 310, 311
—v. Staff Temps, 554 N.W.2d 699 (Iowa 1996) **7:** 11, 65, 96, 97

Coleman v. Darden
—595 F.2d 533, 1 AD Cases 49 (10th Cir. 1979) **2:** 313, 314; **8:** 90
—15 FEP Cases 272 (D. Colo. 1977), *cert. denied*, 444 U.S. 927 (1979) **2:** 203

Collings v. Longview Fibre Co., 63 F.3d 828, 4 AD Cases 1278 (9th Cir. 1995), *cert. denied*, 516 U.S. 1048 (1996) **5:** 171, 259, 283

Collins v. Blue Cross/Blue Shield of Mich., 228 Mich. App. 560, 579 N.W.2d 435 (1998) **5:** 433

Colorado Civil Rights Comm'n
—v. ConAgra Flour Milling Co., 736 P.2d 842, 2 AD Cases 1554 (Colo. Ct. App. 1987) **4:** 85
—v. North Wash. Fire Prot. Dist., 772 P.2d 70, 2 AD Cases 1545 (Colo. 1989) **4:** 86, 87

Colorado Cross Disability Coalition v. Hermanson Family Ltd. P'ship I, 264 F.3d 999, 12 AD Cases 351 (10th Cir. 2001) **6:** 165, 200

Columbus, City of v. Liebhart, 86 Ohio App. 3d 469, 621 N.E.2d 554, 2 AD Cases 1508 (1993) **4:** 829

Colwell v. Suffolk County Police Dep't, 158 F.3d 635, 8 AD Cases 1232 (2d Cir. 1998), *cert. denied*, 526 U.S. 1018 (1999) **5:** 69, 116, 504

Commercial Office Prods. Co.; EEOC v., 486 U.S. 107, 46 FEP Cases 1265 (1988) **10:** 14

Commonwealth v. *See name of commonwealth*

Conkwright v. Westinghouse Elec. Corp., 933 F.2d 231, 13 EB Cases 2202 (4th Cir. 1991) **9:** 397, 398

Connecticut Comm'n on Human Rights & Opportunities
—v. General Dynamics Corp., 1995 Conn. Super. LEXIS 1318 (Conn. Super. Ct. May 1, 1995) **4:** 114
—ex rel. Kowalczyk v. City of New Britain, CHRO No. 9810482 (Mar. 15, 2002) **4:** 108
—ex rel. Saksena v. State, CHRO No. 9940089 (Aug. 9, 2001) **4:** 108
—ex rel. Secondo v. Housing Auth., CHRO No. 9710713 (June 9, 2000) **4:** 108
—ex rel. Tucker v. General Dynamics Corp., No. 517054, 1991 Conn. Super. LEXIS 2704 (Conn. Super. Ct. Nov. 22, 1991) **4:** 91

Consolidated Rail Corp. v. Darrone, 465 U.S. 624, 1 AD Cases 567 (1984) **2:** 83, 92, 93, 285, 291; **5:** 8, 10; **10:** 39

Conti v. Storage Tech. Corp., No. 01-1833 (4th Cir. Sept. 18, 2002) **10:** 125–27

Conway v. City of Hartford, Civ. 950553003, 1997 Conn. Super. LEXIS 282 (Feb. 4, 1997) **4:** 98, 106

Cook v. Rhode Island Dep't of Mental Health, Retardation, & Hosps., 783 F. Supp. 1569, 2 AD Cases 143 (D.R.I. 1992), *aff'd*, 10 F.3d 17, 2 AD Cases 1476 (1st Cir. 1993) **2:** 120, 121

Coolbaugh v. Louisiana, 136 F.3d 430, 7 AD Cases 1730 (5th Cir.), *cert. denied*, 525 U.S. 819 (1998) **10:** 100

Cornelius v. Benevolent Protective Order of Elks, 382 F. Supp. 1182 (D. Conn. 1974) **6:** 126

Corr v. MTA Long Island Bus, 27 F. Supp. 2d 359 (E.D.N.Y. 1998) **5:** 444

Cort v. Ash, 422 U.S. 66 (1975) **2:** 282, 283

Cortes v. Board of Governors, 766 F. Supp. 623, 3 AD Cases 271 (N.D. Ill. 1991) **2:** 296

Coski v. City & County of Denver, 795 P.2d 1364, 2 AD Cases 1525 (Colo. App. 1990) **4:** 84

Counts v. U.S. Postal Serv., 17 FEP Cases 1161 (N.D. Fla. 1978), *rev'd,* 631 F.2d 46, 24 FEP Cases 677 (5th Cir. 1980) *2:* 203

Cousins v. Secretary, Department of Transp., 880 F.2d 603, 1 AD Cases 1502 (1st Cir. 1989) *2:* 305

Cravens v. Blue Cross & Blue Shield of Kansas City, 214 F.3d 1011, 10 AD Cases 1057 (8th Cir. 2000) *8:* 48, 49, 59, 60, 64, 67, 121, 151, 164, 169, 179; *9:* 336; *10:* 207

Crawford v. Indiana Dep't of Corr., 115 F.3d 481, 6 AD Cases 1416 (7th Cir. 1997) *10:* 100

Crawford Fitting Co. v. J.T. Gibbons, Inc., 482 U.S. 437, 43 FEP Cases 1775 (1987) *10:* 350, 351

Crewe v. Office of Pers. Mgmt., 834 F.2d 140, 1 AD Cases 1167 (8th Cir. 1987) *2:* 126, 127

Criado v. IBM Corp., 145 F.3d 437, 8 AD Cases 336 (1st Cir. 1998) *5:* 448; *8:* 16, 17, 185; *9:* 39

Cripe v. City of San Jose, 261 F.3d 877, 12 AD Cases 225 (9th Cir. 2001) *5:* 211, 219; *10:* 247

Cromer v. Greenwood Comm'n of Pub. Works, 2 AD Cases 683 (S.C. Ct. Com. Pl. 1993) *7:* 254

Cular v. Metropolitan Life Ins. Co., 961 F. Supp. 550 (S.D.N.Y. 1997) *10:* 316

Curtis v. Security Bank of Wash., 69 Wash. App. 12, 847 P.2d 507, 2 AD Cases 573 (1993) *4:* 1076

D

Dahill v. Police Dep't of Boston, 434 Mass. 233, 748 N.E. 3d 956, 11 AD Cases 1377 (2001) *4:* 518

Daigle v. Friendly Ice Cream Corp., 957 F. Supp. 8, 6 AD Cases 554 (D.N.H. 1997) *6:* 397

Daley v. Koch, 892 F.2d 212, 1 AD Cases 1549 (2d Cir. 1989) *7:* 245

Dalton v. Subaru-Isuzu Auto., Inc., 141 F.3d 667, 7 AD Cases 1872 (7th Cir. 1998) *7:* 218; *8:* 167

Dana Tank Container, Inc. v. Human Rights Comm'n, 687 N.E.2d 102 (Ill. Ct. App. 1997) *4:* 268

Daniel v. Paul, 395 U.S. 298 (1969) *6:* 126

D'Antonio v. Runyon, 3 AD Cases 1658 (E.D. Pa. 1994) *7:* 254

D'Aprile v. Fleet Servs. Corp., 92 F.3d 1, 5 AD Cases 1343 (1st Cir. 1996) *9:* 238, 488–90

Dare v. California State Dep't of Motor Vehicles, 191 F.3d 1167, 9 AD Cases 1239 (9th Cir. 1999), *cert. denied,* 531 U.S. 1190 (2001) *10:* 100

Daubert v. U.S. Postal Serv., 733 F.2d 1367, 1 AD Cases 597 (10th Cir. 1984) *9:* 370

Daugherty
—v. El Paso, City of, 56 F.3d 695, 4 AD Cases 993 (5th Cir. 1995), *cert. denied,* 516 U.S. 1172 (1996) *7:* 283; *8:* 160; *9:* 287, 294
—v. Metropolitan Atlanta Rapid Transit Auth., 187 Ga. App. 864, 371 S.E.2d 677, 4 AD Cases 1315 (1988) *4:* 204

Davidson
—v. America Online, Inc., 337 F.3d 1179, 14 AD Cases 1185 (10th Cir. 2003) *7:* 60, 185
—v. Iona-McGregor Fire Prot. & Rescue Dist., 674 So. 2d 858 (Fla. Dist. Ct. App. 1996) *4:* 186
—v. Midelfort Clinic Ltd., 133 F.3d 499, 8 AD Cases 77 (7th Cir. 1998) *5:* 158

Davis
—v. Florida Power & Light Co., 205 F.3d 1301, 10 AD Cases 492 (11th Cir.), *cert. denied,* 531 U.S. 927 (2000) *8:* 121; *9:* 362, 371
—v. Guardian Life Ins. Co. of Am., 11 AD Cases 550 (E.D. Pa. 2000) *8:* 81
—v. Modine Mfg. Co., 526 F. Supp. 943, 28 FEP Cases 155 (D. Kan. 1981) *10:* 66
—v. Sea Island Co., 43 FEP Cases 997 (Ga. Super. Ct. 1987) *4:* 217
—v. Southeastern Cmty. Coll., 574 F.2d

Davis—*Cont'd*
1158 (4th Cir. 1978), *rev'd*, 442 U.S. 397, 2 AD Cases 1 (1979) **2:** 163
—v. University of N.C. at Wilmington, 263 F.3d 95, 12 AD Cases 243 (4th Cir. 2001) **2:** 139
Davoll v. Webb. *See* Denver, City & County of; United States v.
Dayoub v. Penn-Del Directory Co., 90 F. Supp. 2d. 636, 10 AD Cases 935 (E.D. Pa. 2000) **9:** 257
Dean v. American Sec. Ins. Co., 559 F.2d 1036 (5th Cir. 1977), *cert. denied*, 434 U.S. 1066 (1978) **3:** 503
Deane v. Pocono Med. Ctr., 142 F.3d 138, 7 AD Cases 1809 (3d Cir. 1998) **5:** 163; **7:** 56; **8:** 18
Dearborn Heights, Mich., In re, 101 LA 809 (Kanner, 1993) **9:** 373
Deas v. River W., L.P., 152 F.3d 471, 8 AD Cases 989 (5th Cir. 1998), *cert. denied*, 527 U.S. 1035 (1999) **5:** 67, 507, 508
DeBose v. Nebraska, 186 F.3d 1087, 9 AD Cases 832 (8th Cir.), *cert. denied*, 531 U.S. 1190 (1999) **10:** 101
Decker v. Vermont Educ. Television, 13 F. Supp. 2d 569 (D. Vt. 1998) **4:** 1039
DeGiuseppe v. Village of Bellwood, 68 F.3d 187 (7th Cir. 1995) **9:** 237
de la Torres v. Bolger, 781 F.2d 1134, 1 AD Cases 852 (5th Cir. 1986) **2:** 305; **10:** 78
DeLeo v. City of Stamford, 919 F. Supp. 70, 4 AD Cases 427 (D. Conn. 1995) **2:** 296
Delta Air Lines v. New York State Div. of Human Rights, 91 N.Y.2d 65, 666 N.Y.S.2d 1004, 689 N.E.2d 898 (1997) **4:** 769
Den Hartog v. Wasatch Acad., 129 F.3d 1076, 7 AD Cases 764 (10th Cir. 1997) **5:** 372
Denver, City & County of; United States v., 943 F. Supp. 1304, 6 AD Cases 245 (D. Colo. 1996), *aff'd in part sub nom.* Davoll v. Webb 194 F.3d 1116, 9 AD Cases 1533 (10th Cir. 1999) **8:** 115–17, 161

DePaoli v. Abbott Labs., 140 F.3d 668, 7 AD Cases 1828 (7th Cir. 1998) **7:** 219
Department of Corr. v. Illinois Human Rights Comm'n, 298 Ill. App. 3d 536, 699 N.E.2d 143 (1998) **4:** 271, 278
Department of Transp. v. Paralyzed Veterans of Am., 477 U.S. 597 (1986) **2:** 96, 97, 332, 333
Dertz v. City of Chicago, 912 F. Supp. 319, 7 AD Cases 1507 (N.D. Ill. 1995) **10:** 38
DeSpears v. Milwaukee County, 63 F.3d 635, 4 AD Cases 1313 (7th Cir. 1995) **5:** 268, 292
DeVito v. Chicago Park Dist., 270 F.3d 532, 12 AD Cases 705 (7th Cir. 2001) **8:** 205
Dilley v. SuperValu, Inc., 296 F.3d 958, 13 AD Cases 486 (10th Cir. 2002) **8:** 180; **10:** 280
DiPompo v. West Point Military Acad., 708 F. Supp. 540, 1 AD Cases 1432 (S.D.N.Y. 1989), *aff'd*, 960 F.2d 326, 2 AD Cases 1514 (2d Cir. 1992) **2:** 305
Disabled Rights Action Comm. v. Santa Fe Gaming Corp., 2002 U.S. App. LEXIS 4803 (9th Cir. 2002) **6:** 373
DiSanto v. McGraw-Hill, Inc., 220 F.3d 61, 10 AD Cases 1364 (2d Cir. 2000) **5:** 353; **8:** 270; **9:** 258
Dister v. Continental Group, Inc., 859 F.2d 1108, 10 EB Cases 1169 (2d Cir. 1988) **9:** 397
District of Columbia; Doe v., 796 F. Supp. 559, 2 AD Cases 197 (D.D.C. 1992) **1:** 47; **7:** 136; **10:** 157
District 27 Cmty. Sch. Bd. v. Board of Educ. of New York, 130 Misc. 2d 398, 502 N.Y.S.2d 325 (Sup. Ct. Queens County 1986) **5:** 336
Doane v. City of Omaha, 115 F.3d 624, 6 AD Cases 1553 (8th Cir. 1997) **5:** 130
Doctor's Assocs., Inc. v. Casarotto, 517 U.S. 681 (1996) **10:** 314
Doebele v. Sprint/United Mgmt. Co., 342 F.3d 1117, 14 AD Cases 1281 (10th Cir. 2003) **5:** 412
Doe v. *See name of opposing party*
Dolphin Cruise Line, Inc.; EEOC v., 945

F. Supp. 1550, 6 AD Cases 187 (S.D. Fla. 1996)   *7:* 136, 280
Dolton Elementary Sch. Dist. No. 148; Doe v., 694 F. Supp. 440 (N.D. Ill. 1988)   *5:* 337
Doman v. City of Grosse Pointe Farms, 170 Mich. App. 536, 428 N.W.2d 708, 50 FEP Cases 982 (1988)   *4:* 549
Donahue v. Consolidated Rail Corp., 224 F.3d 226, 10 AD Cases 1505 (3d Cir. 2000)   *8:* 45, 62, 76, 164; *10:* 259
Doren v. Battle Creek Health Sys., 187 F.3d 595 (6th Cir. 1999)   *10:* 175
Dorsey v. Department of Labor, 41 F.3d 1551, 3 AD Cases 1651 (D.C. Cir. 1994)   *2:* 306
Dotson v. Pike County Bd. of Educ., 2001 WL 1216998 (6th Cir. 2001)   *2:* 157
Douglas v. California Dep't of Youth Auth., 271 F.3d 812, 12 AD Cases 826 (9th Cir. 2001), *cert. denied,* 536 U.S. 924 (2002)   *2:* 101; *10:* 115
Dowden v. Tisch, 729 F. Supp. 1137, 52 FEP Cases 93 (E.D. Tex. 1989), *aff'd,* 902 F.2d 957, 53 FEP Cases 912 (5th Cir. 1990)   *7:* 292
Downs v. Massachusetts Bay Transp. Auth., 13 F. Supp. 2d 130, 8 AD Cases 447 (D. Mass. 1998)   *7:* 35, 76, 91, 93; *9:* 168
Drake v. Southwestern Bell Tel. Co., 533 F.2d 1185, 15 FEP Cases 577 (8th Cir. 1977)   *10:* 369
Dropinski v. Douglas County, Neb., 298 F.3d 704, 13 AD Cases 676 (8th Cir. 2002)   *5:* 215; *8:* 28, 84, 150; *10:* 210
Duckworth v. Pratt & Whitney, Div. of United Techs. Corp., 152 F.3d 1, 4 WH Cases 2d 1281 (1st Cir. 1998)   *9:* 16
Duda v. Board of Educ. of Franklin Park Pub. Sch. Dist. No. 84, 133 F.3d 1054, 8 AD Cases 99 (7th Cir. 1998)   *5:* 45, 268
Dudley v. Hannaford Bros. Co., 333 F.3d 299, 14 AD Cases 901 (1st Cir. 2003)   *6:* 404
Duffield v. Robertson Stephens & Co., 144 F.3d 1182, 76 FEP Cases 1450 (9th Cir.), *cert. denied,* 525 U.S. 982 (1998)   *10:* 303
Dugger v. Delta Airlines, 325 S.E.2d 394 (Ga. Ct. App. 1984)   *4:* 218
Duncan v. Washington Metro. Area Transit Auth., 240 F.3d 1110, 11 AD Cases 833 (D.C. Cir.), *cert. denied,* 534 U.S. 818 (2001)   *5:* 106, 107; *10:* 187, 188
Dunn v. Lear Seating Corp., 12 AD Cases 990 (W.D. Ky. 2001)   *9:* 337
Duren v. Johnson, Dkt. No. 01934068, 1995 WL 114286 (EEOC)   *7:* 246
Durham v. Red Lake Fishing & Hunting Club, Inc., 666 F. Supp. 954 (W.D. Tex. 1987)   *6:* 126
Durning v. Duffens Optical, Inc., 1996 U.S. Dist. LEXIS 1685, 1996 WL 67640 (E.D. La. 1996)   *1:* 69; *8:* 33–35
Dush v. Appleton Elec. Co., 124 F.3d 957, 7 AD Cases 183 (8th Cir. 1997)   *9:* 145
Dutcher v. Ingalls Shipbuilding, 53 F.3d 723, 4 AD Cases 802 (5th Cir. 1995)   *7:* 245
Dutton v. Johnson County Bd. of County Comm'rs, 859 F. Supp. 498, 3 AD Cases 808 (D. Kan. 1994)   *7:* 254; *9:* 6
Dyke v. O'Neal Steel, Inc., 2003 WL 21000819, 14 AD Cases 481 (7th Cir. 2003)   *5:* 79, 153

E

Earl v. Mervyns, Inc., 207 F.3d 1361, 10 AD Cases 673 (11th Cir. 2000)   *5:* 195, 202; *8:* 30–32, 106, 206; *10:* 235
Echazabal v. Chevron U.S.A., Inc., 213 F.3d 1098, 10 AD Cases 961, *amended,* 226 F.3d 1063, 11 AD Cases 70 (9th Cir. 2000), *rev'd,* 536 U.S. 73, 13 AD Cases 97 (2002), *on remand,* 336 F.3d 1023, 14 AD Cases 1089 (9th Cir. 2003)   *1:* 97; *7:* 161, 162, 273; *8:* 246; *9:* 295, 296–99, 301, 302
Eckles v. Consolidated Rail Corp., 890 F. Supp. 1391, 4 AD Cases 1134 (S.D. Ind. 1995), *aff'd,* 94 F.3d 1041, 5 AD

Eckles—*Cont'd*
   Cases 1367 (7th Cir. 1996), *cert. denied*, 520 U.S. 1146 (1997)   **8:** 121, 122, 127; **9:** 52, 371
Edelman
—v. Jordan, 415 U.S. 651 (1974)   **10:** 87, 90
—v. Lynchburg Coll., 535 U.S. 106, 88 FEP Cases 321 (2002)   **10:** 15–17
Edwards v. Rosewood Health Ctr., 14 AD Cases 766 (N.D. Ill. 2002)   **10:** 373, 374
E.E. Black, Ltd. v. Marshall, 497 F. Supp. 1088, 1 AD Cases 220 (D. Haw. 1980), *vacated*, 1981 WL 265, 1 AD Cases 266 (D. Haw. 1981)   **1:** 108
EEOC v. *See name of opposing party*
Effinger v. Philip Morris, Inc., 984 F. Supp. 1043 (W.D. Ky. 1997)   **4:** 416
Electro-Craft Corp.; Doe v., No. 87-E-132 (Rockingham Super. Ct. 1988)   **4:** 709
Elitt v. USA Hockey, 922 F. Supp. 217, 5 AD Cases 648 (E.D. Mo. 1996)   **6:** 75
Ellis v. Mohenis Servs., Inc., 8 AD Cases 939 (E.D. Pa. 1998)   **9:** 17
Emerson
—v. Northern States Power Co., 256 F.3d 506, 11 AD Cases 1683 (7th Cir. 2001)   **5:** 220; **8:** 248; **10:** 262
—v. Thiel Coll., 296 F.3d 184, 13 AD Cases 493 (3d Cir. 2002)   **6:** 376
Erickson v. Board of Governors of State Colls. & Univs. for N.E. Ill. Univ., 207 F.3d 945, 10 AD Cases 577 (7th Cir. 2000), *cert. denied sub nom.* United States v. Board of Governors of State Colls. & Univs. for N.E. Ill. Univ., 531 U.S. 1190 (2001)   **10:** 96, 101
Erit v. Judge, Inc., 961 F. Supp. 774, 6 AD Cases 1353 (D.N.J. 1997)   **9:** 237
Estate of. *See name of estate*
Ethridge v. Alabama
—847 F. Supp. 903, 3 AD Cases 162 (M.D. Ala. 1993)   **10:** 38
—860 F. Supp. 808, 3 AD Cases 1013 (M.D. Ala. 1994)   **7:** 164–68, 256, 260, 266, 267, 298
Evans v. Federal Express Corp., 133 F.3d 137, 8 AD Cases 151 (1st Cir. 1998)   **8:** 239
Everett v. Cobb County Sch. Dist., 138 F.3d 1407, 8 AD Cases 65 (11th Cir. 1998)   **2:** 302
Ex parte. *See name of party*
Exxon Corp.
—EEOC v., 203 F.3d 871, 10 AD Cases 225 (5th Cir. 2000)   **2:** 350; **5:** 175, 176, 307–9; **8:** 251; **9:** 287; **10:** 246, 251
—v. U.S. Dep't of Labor, 2002 U.S. Dist. LEXIS 3540, 12 AD Cases 1665 (N.D. Tex. 2002)   **2:** 349

F

Failla v. City of Passaic, 146 F.3d 149, 8 AD Cases 275 (3d Cir. 1998)   **4:** 731
Farmer Bros. Co.; EEOC v., 31 F.3d 891, 65 FEP Cases 857 (9th Cir. 1994)   **10:** 36
Father Flannagan's Boy's Home v. Goerke, 401 N.W.2d 461 (Neb. 1987)   **4:** 665
Fayer v. Town of Middlebury, 258 F.3d 117 (2d Cir. 2001)   **10:** 340
Feldman v. American Mem'l Life Ins. Co., 196 F.3d 783, 9 AD Cases 1717 (7th Cir. 1999)   **9:** 258, 263
Feliberty v. Kemper Corp., 98 F.3d 274, 5 AD Cases 1729 (7th Cir. 1996)   **8:** 86, 224; **9:** 52
Feliciano v. Rhode Island, 160 F.3d 780, 8 AD Cases 1520 (1st Cir. 1998)   **8:** 121; **9:** 371
Felix v. New York City Transit Auth., 324 F.3d 102, 14 AD Cases 193 (2d Cir. 2003)   **8:** 19
Fennell v. Aetna Life Ins. Co., 37 F. Supp. 2d 40 (D.D.C. 1999)   **9:** 481
Fenney v. Dakota, Minnesota & R.R. Co., 327 F.3d 707, 14 AD Cases 385 (8th Cir.), *reh'g denied*, 2003 U.S. App. LEXIS 10769 (8th Cir. 2003)   **5:** 89
Fernot v. Crafts Inn, Inc., 895 F. Supp. 668 (D. Vt. 1995)   **4:** 1040
Fiedler v. American Multi-Cinema, Inc.,

871 F. Supp. 35, 3 AD Cases 1610 (D.D.C. 1994) *6:* 150
Figueroa v. Fajardo, 1 F. Supp. 2d 117 (D.P.R. 1998) *5:* 283
Finley v. Giacobbe, 827 F. Supp. 215, 2 AD Cases 1117 (S.D.N.Y. 1993) *10:* 38
First Options of Chi. v. Kaplan, 514 U.S. 938 (1995) *10:* 304
Fiscus v. Wal-Mart Stores Inc., 385 F.3d 378, 16 AD Cases 10 (3d Cir. 2004) *5:* 62
Fitzgerald
—v. Caldera, 216 F.3d 1087 (10th Cir. 2000) *5:* 283
—v. Green Area Educ. Agency, 589 F. Supp. 1130, 1 AD Cases 601 (S.D. Iowa 1984) *5:* 30
Fitzpatrick
—v. Atlanta, City of, 2 F.3d 1112, 2 AD Cases 1270 (11th Cir. 1993) *7:* 298; *9:* 276–78
—v. Bitzer, 427 U.S. 445, 12 FEP Cases 1586 (1976) *10:* 390–92, 394, 395, 397
Fjellestad v. Pizza Hut of Am., Inc., 188 F.3d 944, 9 AD Cases 1153 (8th Cir. 1999) *8:* 77, 143, 144; *10:* 208
Flowers v. Southern Reg'l Physician Serv., Inc., 247 F.3d 229, 11 AD Cases 1129 (5th Cir. 2001) *5:* 395, 396
Flynn v. Raytheon Co., 868 F. Supp. 383, 3 AD Cases 1495 (D. Mass. 1994) *5:* 265, 296
Forbes v. Wilson County Emergency, 966 S.W.2d 421 (Tenn. 1998) *4:* 971
Ford v. Schering-Plough Corp., 145 F.3d 601, 8 AD Cases 190 (3d Cir. 1998), *cert. denied,* 525 U.S. 1093 (1999) *5:* 383, 439; *6:* 64; *8:* 279; *9:* 482, 497, 506, 513
Ford Motor Co.
—v. Huffman, 345 U.S. 330, 31 LRRM 2548 (1953) *9:* 387
—v. U.S. Dep't of Treasury, 323 U.S. 459 (1945) *10:* 88
Foreman v. Babcock & Wilcox Co., 117 F.3d 800, 7 AD Cases 331 (5th Cir. 1997), *cert. denied,* 522 U.S. 1115 (1998) *8:* 121, 160; *9:* 371
Forest City Daly Hous., Inc. v. Town of N. Hempstead, 175 F.3d 144 (2d Cir. 1999) *5:* 58
Forrisi v. Bowen, 794 F.2d 931, 1 AD Cases 921 (4th Cir. 1986) *5:* 33
Foster v. Shore Club Lodge, Inc., 127 Idaho 921, 908 P.2d 1228 (1995) *4:* 250
Fox v. General Motors Corp., 247 F.3d 169, 11 AD Cases 1121 (4th Cir. 2001) *5:* 395
Francis v. City of Meriden, 129 F.3d 281, 7 AD Cases 955 (2d Cir. 1997) *7:* 10; *9:* 277
Franklin v. Gwinnett County Pub. Sch., 503 U.S. 60, 59 FEP Cases 213 (1992) *2:* 292–94, 345; *10:* 153, 158
Fraser v. Goodale, 342 F.3d 1032, 10 AD Cases 1377 (9th Cir. 2003), *cert. denied,* 541 U.S. 937, 15 AD Cases 608 (2004) *5:* 58
Fredenburg v. Contra Costa County Dep't of Health Servs., 172 F.3d 1176, 9 AD Cases 385 (9th Cir. 1999) *7:* 124, 127–29
Freed v. Consolidated Rail Corp., 201 F.3d 188, 10 AD Cases 169 (3d Cir. 2000) *2:* 286
Freeman v. Minolta Bus. Sys., Inc., 699 So. 2d 1182 (La. Ct. App. 1997), *writ denied,* 706 So. 2d 1977 (La. 1998) *10:* 315
Fuentes v. Perskie, 32 F.3d 759, 63 FEP Cases 890 (3d Cir. 1994) *7:* 19
Fuzy v. S&B Eng'rs & Constrs., Ltd., 332 F.3d 301, 14 AD Cases 676 (5th Cir. 2003), *cert. denied,* 540 U.S. 1108, 15 AD Cases 128 (2004) *7:* 152, 238

G

Gabriel v. City of Chicago, 9 F. Supp. 2d 974, 9 AD Cases 483 (N.D. Ill. 1998) *1:* 52

Gagliardo v. Connaught Labs., 311 F.3d 565, 13 AD Cases 1345 (3d Cir. 2002) *10:* 168, 170, 171, 173
Gaines v. Runyon, 107 F.3d 1171, 6 AD Cases 688 (6th Cir. 1997) *8:* 85
Gamble v. Levitz Furniture Co. of Midwest, 759 P.2d 761, 2 AD Cases 1539 (Colo. Ct. App. 1988) *4:* 78
Gannon v. Circuit City Stores, Inc., 262 F.3d 677, 86 FEP Cases 755 (8th Cir. 2001) *10:* 326
Gantt v. Wilson Sporting Goods Co., 143 F.3d 1042, 8 AD Cases 308 (6th Cir. 1998) *8:* 51, 192
Garcia-Ayala v. Lederle Parenterals, Inc., 212 F.3d 638, 10 AD Cases 865 (1st Cir. 2000) *8:* 74, 120, 184–86, 240
Garcia-Paz v. Swift Textiles, Inc., 873 F. Supp. 547, 3 AD Cases 1844 (D. Kan. 1995) *9:* 237
Gardner v. Morris, 752 F.2d 1271, 1 AD Cases 673 (8th Cir. 1985) *5:* 24
Garraway v. Diversified Material Handling, Inc., 975 F. Supp. 1026, 74 FEP Cases 1593 (N.D. Ohio 1997) *4:* 841
Garrett
—Doe v., 903 F.2d 1455, 1 AD Cases 1606 (11th Cir. 1990), *cert. denied,* 499 U.S. 904 (1991) *2:* 203, 287; *5:* 336; *10:* 61
—v. University of Ala. at Birmingham Bd. of Trs.
——193 F.3d 1214, 9 AD Cases 1635 (11th Cir. 1999), *rev'd,* 531 U.S. 356, 11 AD Cases 737 (2001) *6:* 25; *10:* 85, 91, 99, 100, 103, 104, 113
——344 F.3d 1288, 14 AD Cases 1386 (11th Cir. 2003) *2:* 101
Garrison v. Baker Hughes Oilfield Operations, Inc., 287 F.3d 955 (10th Cir. 2002) *7:* 139
Garrity v. Gallen, 522 F. Supp. 171 (D.N.H. 1981) *2:* 81
Garten v. Kurth, 265 F.3d 136 (2d Cir. 2001) *10:* 316
GASP v. Mecklenburg County, 42 N.C. App. 225, 256 S.E.2d 477 (1979) *4:* 791
Gaston v. Bellingrath Gardens & Home, Inc., 167 F.3d 1361, 8 AD Cases 1862 (11th Cir. 1999) *8:* 51
Gaul v. AT&T, Inc., 955 F. Supp. 346, 6 AD Cases 705 (D.N.J. 1997), *aff'd,* 134 F.3d 576, 7 AD Cases 1223 (3d Cir. 1998) *5:* 424, 447; *8:* 173, 174
Gauthier v. Natick, 20 MDLR 41 (M.C.A.D. 1998) *4:* 519
Gavalik v. Continental Can Co., 812 F.2d 834, 8 EB Cases 1047 (3d Cir.), *cert. denied,* 484 U.S. 979 (1987) *9:* 397
Gelabert-Ladenheim v. American Airlines, Inc., 252 F.3d 54, 11 AD Cases 1581 (1st Cir. 2001) *5:* 108; *9:* 337; *10:* 188
Gelman v. Department of Educ., 544 F. Supp. 651, 1 AD Cases 359 (D. Colo. 1982) *10:* 155
General Elec. Co.
—150 NLRB 192, 57 LRRM 1491 (1964), *enforced,* 418 F.2d 736, 72 LRRM 2530 (2d Cir. 1969), *cert. denied,* 397 U.S. 965 (1970) *9:* 353
—v. Gilbert, 429 U.S. 125, 13 FEP Cases 1657, 1 EB Cases 1046 (1976) *9:* 239
Genthe v. Quebecor World Lincoln, 383 F.3d 713, 15 AD Cases 1697, *reh'g denied,* 2004 U.S. App. LEXIS 21634 (8th Cir. 2004), *cert. denied,* 2005 U.S. LEXIS 2805 (2005) *5:* 162
George v. Associated Stationers, 932 F. Supp. 1012, 3 WH Cases 2d 1234 (N.D. Ohio 1996) *9:* 67
Giacobbi v. Biermann, 780 F. Supp. 33, 2 AD Cases 104 (D.D.C. 1992) *2:* 250
Gibbs v. Pierce County Law Enforcement Support, 785 F.2d 1396, 40 FEP Cases 673 (9th Cir. 1986) *10:* 36
Gibson v. Neighborhood Health Clinics, Inc., 121 F.3d 1126, 8 AD Cases 483 (7th Cir. 1997) *10:* 305, 318
Gile v. United Air Lines, Inc.
—95 F.3d 492, 5 AD Cases 1466 (7th Cir. 1996) *8:* 152, 168, 256
—213 F.3d 365, 10 AD Cases 968 (7th Cir. 2000) *8:* 175, 176
Giles
—v. General Elec. Co., 245 F.3d 474, 11 AD Cases 1242 (5th Cir. 2001) *9:* 261

—v. New York City, 41 F. Supp. 2d 308, 160 LRRM 2879 (S.D.N.Y. 1999) *10:* 340
Gillen v. Fallon Ambulance Serv., Inc., 283 F.3d 11, 12 AD Cases 1633 (1st Cir. 2002) *7:* 238, 265
Gilman Bros. Co. v. Connecticut Comm'n on Human Rights & Opportunities, No. CV 950536075, 1997 Conn. Super. LEXIS 1311 (Conn. Super. Ct. May 14, 1997) *4:* 104, 107
Gilmer v. Interstate/Johnson Lane Corp., 500 U.S. 20, 55 FEP Cases 1116 (1991) *10:* 288, 294, 296, 303, 313, 332, 333
Giordano v. City of New York, 274 F.3d 740, 12 AD Cases 1053 (2d Cir. 2001) *5:* 156
Gonzales v. Garner Food Servs., Inc., 89 F.3d 1523, 5 AD Cases 1202 (11th Cir. 1996) *9:* 481
Gonzalez v. El Dia, Inc., 304 F.3d 63, 13 AD Cases 889 (1st Cir. 2002) *5:* 100, 457, 459
Goodman v. Lukens Steel Co., 482 U.S. 656, 44 FEP Cases 1 (1987) *2:* 301
Gordon v. Runyon, 1994 U.S. Dist. LEXIS 4959, 3 AD Cases 784 (E.D. Pa. 1994) *7:* 288, 289
Gore v. GTE S., Inc., 917 F. Supp. 1564 (M.D. Ala. 1996) *9:* 69
Government Employees (AFGE)
—Local 1812 v. U.S. Dep't of State, 662 F. Supp. 50, 1 AD Cases 1060 (D.D.C. 1987) *5:* 337
—Local 2052 v. Reno, 992 F.2d 331, 143 LRRM 2082 (D.C. Cir. 1993) *10:* 83, 84
Grant v. May Dep't Store Co., 786 A.2d 580, 12 AD Cases 1308 (D.C. 2001) *4:* 147
Gravitte v. Mitsubishi Semiconductor Am., Inc., 109 N.C. App. 466, 428 S.E.2d 254, 2 AD Cases 669 (1993) *4:* 796
Greater Cleveland Reg'l Transit Auth. v. Ohio Civil Rights Comm'n, 58 Ohio App. 3d 20, 567 N.E.2d 1325, 55 FEP Cases 826 (1989) *4:* 844

Green
—v. Burton Rubber Processing, Inc., 2002 U.S. App. LEXIS 2959 (6th Cir. 2002) *8:* 247; *10:* 264
—v. Joy Cone Co., 2004 U.S. App. LEXIS 16612 (3d Cir. 2004) *7:* 24, 75
—v. Rosemont Indus., 5 F. Supp. 2d 568, 9 AD Cases 121 (S.D. Ohio 1998) *5:* 118
Greenberg v. New York State Dep't of Corr. Servs., 919 F. Supp. 637, 5 AD Cases 1851 (E.D.N.Y. 1996) *5:* 47
Greene v. Seminole Elec. Coop., 701 So. 2d 646 (Fla. Dist Ct. App. 1997) *4:* 175
Greer v. Emerson Elec. Co., 185 F.3d 917, 9 AD 1100 (8th Cir. 1999) *5:* 429
Grenier v. Cyanamid Plastics, Inc., 70 F.3d 667, 5 AD Cases 75 (1st Cir. 1995) *7:* 64, 66, 93–96, 98, 102, 105, 108–10, 142, 203, 253, 286; *8:* 41, 259
Greser v. Department of Corr., 145 F.3d 979 (8th Cir. 1998) *4:* 582
Griel v. Franklin Med. Ctr., 234 F.3d 731, 11 AD Cases 469 (1st Cir. 2000) *5:* 319
Griffin v. Steeltek, Inc., 261 F.3d 1026, 12 AD Cases 248 (10th Cir. 2001) *7:* 74, 75, 111
Griffith v. Wal-Mart Stores, Inc., 135 F.3d 376, 7 AD Cases 1233 (6th Cir. 1998), *cert. denied,* 526 U.S. 1144 (1999) *5:* 231; *8:* 267; *9:* 144, 240
Grimes v. Canadian Am. Transp. Inc., 72 F. Supp. 2d 629, 81 FEP Cases 428 (W.D. Va. 1999) *4:* 1049
Grove City Coll. v. Bell, 465 U.S. 555 (1984) *2:* 82, 95, 330, 331
Grozdanich v. Leisure Hills Health Ctr., Inc., 25 F. Supp. 2d 953 (D. Minn. 1998) *4:* 582
Grubbs v. Butz, 548 F.2d 973, 13 FEP Cases 245 (D.C. Cir. 1976) *10:* 364, 380
Guardians Ass'n v. City Civil Serv. Comm'n, 463 U.S. 582, 32 FEP Cases 250 (1983) *2:* 289, 290

Gudenkauf v. Stauffer Communications, 922 F. Supp. 465, 5 AD Cases 1739, 77 FEP Cases 1723 (D. Kan. 1996), *aff'd*, 158 F.3d 1074, 77 FEP Cases 1742 (10th Cir. 1998)   *1:* 54
Guinn v. Bolger, 598 F. Supp. 196, 36 FEP Cases 506 (D.D.C. 1984)   *5:* 29
Gutridge v. Clure, 153 F.3d 898, 8 AD Cases 705 (8th Cir. 1998), *cert. denied sub nom.* Gutridge v. Midland Computer, Inc., 526 U.S. 1113 (1999)   *7:* 245; *9:* 337
Gutwaks v. American Airlines, Inc., No. 3:98-CV-2120-BF, 1999 WL 1611328 (N.D. Tex. Sept. 2, 1999)   *5:* 352

H

Hall
—v. Hackley Hosp., 210 Mich. App. 48 532 N.W.2d 893, 4 AD Cases 961 (1995)   *4:* 558
—v. Knott County Bd. of Educ., 941 F.2d 402 (6th Cir. 1991), *cert. denied*, 502 U.S. 1077 (1992)   *2:* 302
—v. U.S. Postal Serv., 857 F.2d 1073, 1 AD Cases 1368 (6th Cir. 1988)   *7:* 31, 32, 182, 229
Halperin v. Abacus Tech. Corp., 128 F.3d 191, 7 AD Cases 406 (4th Cir. 1997)   *8:* 29; *9:* 41
Hamilton v. Southwestern Bell Tel. Co., 136 F.3d 1047, 8 AD Cases 1219 (5th Cir. 1998)   *5:* 92, 431
Hamlin v. Charter Township of Flint, 165 F.3d 426, 8 AD Cases 1688 (6th Cir. 1999)   *5:* 191; *9:* 291
Hammon v. DHL Airways, Inc., 165 F.3d 441, 8 AD Cases 1707 (6th Cir. 1999)   *8:* 51
Hankins v. Gap, Inc., 84 F.3d 797, 5 AD Cases 924 (6th Cir. 1996)   *9:* 37
Hardwick v. Sherwin-Williams Co., 2002 Ohio App. LEXIS 7273, 91 FEP Cases 142 (2003)   *10:* 306
Hardy v. Sears, Roebuck & Co., 1996 WL 735565 (N.D. Ga. Aug. 28, 1996)   *9:* 342

Harris
—v. H&W Contracting Co., 102 F.3d 516, 6 AD Cases 460 (11th Cir. 1996)   *5:* 130
—v. Harris & Hart, Inc., 206 F.3d 838, 10 AD Cases 481 (9th Cir. 2000)   *7:* 67, 78, 81–84, 96, 98, 203; *8:* 259–61
—v. Marathon Oil Co., 948 F. Supp. 27, 7 AD Cases 873 (W.D. Tex. 1996), *aff'd*, 108 F.3d 332, 7 AD Cases 960 (5th Cir. 1997)   *9:* 237
—v. Polk County, Iowa, 103 F.3d 696, 6 AD Cases 545 (8th Cir. 1996)   *8:* 225, 226
Harrison v. Landis Plastics, Inc., 1998 U.S. Dist. LEXIS 11311 (N.D. Ill. 1998)   *9:* 181
Hart v. Alameda County Prob. Dep't, 485 F. Supp. 66, 21 FEP Cases 233 (N.D. Cal. 1979)   *2:* 25
Haschmann v. Time Warner Entm't Co., 151 F.3d 591, 8 AD Cases 692 (7th Cir. 1998)   *8:* 240; *9:* 39, 42–45, 110, 136–38, 141, 144
Hatchett v. Philander Smith Coll., 251 F.3d 826, 12 AD Cases 640 (8th Cir. 2001)   *8:* 202
Hatfield v. Quantum Chem. Corp., 920 F. Supp. 108, 5 AD Cases 765 (S.D. Tex. 1996)   *9:* 237
Haulbrook v. Michelin N. Am., Inc., 252 F.3d 696, 11 AD Cases 1407 (4th Cir. 2001)   *5:* 167
Hayes v. Cleveland Pneumatic Co., 92 Ohio App. 3d 36, 634 N.E.2d 228, 3 AD Cases 646 (1993)   *4:* 835
Haysman v. Food Lion, Inc., 893 F. Supp. 1092, 4 AD Cases 1297 (S.D. Ga. 1995)   *9:* 69
Hazeldine v. Beverage Media, 954 F. Supp. 697, 6 AD Cases 1821 (S.D.N.Y. 1997)   *4:* 776
Healion v. Great-West Life Assurance Co., 830 F. Supp. 1372 (D. Colo. 1993)   *4:* 82, 83
Heaser v. Toro Co., 247 F.3d 826, 11 AD Cases 1320 (8th Cir. 2001)   *8:* 209
Hedberg v. Indiana Bell Tel. Co., 47 F.3d

928, 4 AD Cases 65 (7th Cir. 1995) *1:* 70; *5:* 444; *7:* 20; *8:* 51
Hedgepeth v. Tennessee, 33 F. Supp. 2d 668, 9 AD Cases 163 (W.D. Tenn. 1998), *aff'd,* 215 F.3d 608 (6th Cir. 2000)   *10:* 101
Hein v. All Am. Plywood Co., 232 F.3d 482, 11 AD Cases 308 (6th Cir. 2000) *5:* 135, 480
Hendricks-Robinson v. Excel Corp., 154 F.3d 685, 8 AD Cases 875 (7th Cir. 1998)   *8:* 120
Hendry v. GTE N., Inc., 896 F. Supp. 816, 6 AD Cases 451 (N.D. Ind. 1995) *9:* 69
Henrickson
—v. Potter, 327 F.3d 444 (5th Cir.), *cert. denied,* 124 S. Ct. 579 (2003)   *2:* 206
—v. Sammons, 263 Ga. 331, 434 S.E.2d 51, 2 AD Cases 1358 (1993)   *2:* 302
Herko v. Metropolitan Life Ins. Co., 978 F. Supp. 141 (W.D.N.Y. 1997)   *10:* 320
Hernandez
—v. Hartford, City of, 30 F. Supp. 2d 268 (D. Conn. 1998)   *2:* 296
—v. Hughes Missile Sys. Co., 292 F.3d 1038, *as amended,* 298 F.3d 1030, 13 AD Cases 198 (9th Cir. 2002), *vacated sub nom.* Raytheon Co. v. Hernandez, 540 U.S. 44, 14 AD Cases 1825 (2003) *5:* 148, 172, 311, 340
—v. Prudential Ins. Co., 977 F. Supp. 1160 (M.D. Fla. 1997)   *4:* 181
Heyman v. Queens Vill. Comm. for Mental Health for Jamaica Cmty. Adolescent Program, Inc., 198 F.3d 68, 10 AD Cases 27 (2d Cir. 1999)   *5:* 161
Hickey v. Irving Indep. Sch. Dist., 976 F.2d 980 (5th Cir. 1992)   *2:* 302
Higgins v. New Balance Athletic Shoe, Inc., 194 F.3d 252, 9 AD Cases 1555 (1st Cir. 1999)   *10:* 205
Hightower v. GMRI, Inc., 272 F.3d 239, 87 FEP Cases 461 (4th Cir. 2001) *10:* 305
Hilburn v. Murata Elec. N. Am., Inc., 181 F.3d 1220, 9 AD Cases 908 (11th Cir. 1999)   *5:* 147, 485, 486

Hill v. Kansas City Area Transp. Auth., 181 F.3d 891, 9 AD Cases 833 (8th Cir. 1999)   *8:* 51; *10:* 209
Hindman
—v. Greenville Hosp. Sys., 947 F. Supp. 215, 7 AD Cases 963 (D.S.C. 1996), *aff'd,* 133 F.3d 915, 7 AD Cases 1267 (4th Cir. 1997)   *9:* 237
—v. GTE Data Servs., 3 AD Cases 641 (M.D. Fla. 1994)   *7:* 293
Hines v. Chrysler Corp., 2000 U.S. App. LEXIS 11338 (10th Cir. May 19, 2000) *8:* 50, 171
Hodgdon v. Mt. Mansfield Co., 160 Vt. 150, 624 A.2d 1122, 2 AD Cases 499 (1992)   *4:* 1036
Hodgens v. General Dynamics Corp., 144 F.3d 151, 4 WH Cases 2d 993 (1st Cir. 1998)   *9:* 110
Hoeller v. Eaton Corp., 149 F.3d 621, 8 AD Cases 537 (7th Cir. 1998)   *5:* 91
Hoffman
—v. Caterpillar, Inc., 256 F.3d 568, 11 AD Cases 1674 (7th Cir. 2001)   *5:* 228; *10:* 220
—v. Fidelity Brokerage Servs., Inc., 959 F. Supp. 452, 6 AD Cases 651 (S.D. Ohio 1997)   *7:* 28, 51–53, 95, 99–101, 103, 104, 106, 107, 163, 167–70, 196, 259, 262–64; *8:* 254
Holiday v. City of Chattanooga, 206 F.3d 637, 10 AD Cases 501 (6th Cir. 2000) *7:* 4, 15, 136; *8:* 36, 37, 104, 105
Holihan v. Lucky Stores, Inc., 87 F.3d 362, 5 AD Cases 1068 (9th Cir. 1996), *cert. denied,* 520 U.S. 1162 (1997)   *5:* 130
Holly v. City of Naperville, Ill., 603 F. Supp. 220, 37 FEP Cases 1615 (N.D. Ill. 1985), *aff'd,* 861 F.2d 723, 48 FEP Cases 235 (7th Cir. 1988)   *5:* 23
Holstein v. Norandex, Inc., 194 W. Va. 727, 461 S.E. 2d 473 (1995)   *4:* 1084
Holt v. Continental Group, Inc., 708 F.2d 87, 31 FEP Cases 1468 (2d Cir. 1983), *cert. denied,* 465 U.S. 1030 (1984)   *2:* 227
Hooks v. Okbridge, Inc., 232 F.3d 208 (5th Cir. 2000)   *6:* 103, 105

Hooters of Am., Inc. v. Phillips, 173 F.3d 933, 79 FEP Cases 629 (4th Cir. 1999) *10:* 312

Hoover v. Norwest Private Mortgage Banking, 632 N.W.2d 534, 12 AD Cases 360 (Minn. 2001) *4:* 585

Hornsby v. Conoco, Inc., 777 F.2d 243, 39 FEP Cases 766, *reh'g denied,* 780 F.2d 532 (5th Cir. 1985) *10:* 10

Hoskins v. Oakland County Sheriff's Dep't, 227 F.3d 719, 10 AD Cases 1417 (6th Cir. 2000) *10:* 203

Howard
—v. Cherry Hills Cutters, Inc., 935 F. Supp. 1148, 5 AD Cases 1579 (D. Colo. 1996) *6:* 397; *10:* 52, 53
—v. North Miss. Med. Ctr., 939 F. Supp. 505, 5 AD Cases 1723 (N.D. Miss. 1996) *7:* 255
—v. Oakwood Homes Corp., 134 N.C. App. 116, 516 S.E.2d 879, 15 IER Cases 678 (1999) *10:* 323

Howard Baer Inc. v. Schave, 127 S.W.3d 589 (Ky. 2003) *4:* 409

Howell v. Michelin Tire Corp., 860 F. Supp. 1488, 3 AD Cases 929 (M.D. Ala. 1994) *8:* 167; *9:* 51

Hoyts Cinemas Corp.; United States v., 380 F.3d 558, 15 AD Cases 1774 (1st Cir. 2004) *6:* 392

Huckans v. U.S. Postal Serv., 1999 U.S. App. LEXIS 30755 (10th Cir. 1999) *5:* 70

Hudson v. MCI Telecommunications Corp., 87 F.3d 1167, 5 AD Cases 1099 (10th Cir. 1996) *9:* 51

Huels v. Exxon Coal USA, Inc., 121 F.3d 1047, 7 AD Cases 10 (7th Cir. 1997) *5:* 268

Hughes v. Reinsurance Group of Am., 957 F. Supp. 1097, 6 AD Cases 888 (E.D. Mo. 1996) *9:* 238

Hume v. American Disposal Co., 124 Wash. 2d 656, 880 P.2d 988, 3 AD Cases 1208 (1994) *4:* 1070

Humiston-Keeling, Inc.; EEOC v., 227 F.3d 1024, 10 AD Cases 1665 (7th Cir. 2000) *8:* 65, 178

Humphrey v. Memorial Hosps. Ass'n, 239 F.3d 1128, 11 AD Cases 765 (9th Cir. 2001), *cert. denied,* 535 U.S. 1011 (2002) *5:* 82; *8:* 66, 217, 218

Hunt-Golliday v. Metropolitan Water Reclamation Dist. of Greater Ohio, 104 F.3d 1004, 6 AD Cases 725 (7th Cir. 1997) *8:* 51

Hupka v. U.S. Dep't of Defense, 134 F. Supp. 2d 871 (E.D. Mich. 2001) *10:* 54, 55, 57, 79

Hurst v. St. Mary's Hosp., 867 F. Supp. 435 (S.D. W. Va. 1994) *4:* 1085

Hutton v. Elf Atochem N. Am., Inc., 273 F.3d 884, 12 AD Cases 909 (9th Cir. 2001) *5:* 464; *10:* 258

Hypes ex rel. Hypes v. First Commerce Corp., 134 F.3d 721, 7 AD Cases 1546 (5th Cir. 1998) *9:* 39, 53

I

Independent Living Res. v. Oregon Arena Corp., 982 F. Supp. 698 (D. Or. 1997), *supplemented,* 1 F. Supp. 2d 1159 (D. Or. 1998) *6:* 208, 264, 274

Indiana Civil Rights Comm'n v. Southern Ind. Gas & Elec. Co., 553 N.E.2d 840 (Ind. 1990) *4:* 289, 323

In re. *See name of party*

Irwin v. Department of Veterans Affairs, 498 U.S. 89, 54 FEP Cases 577 (1990) *10:* 77, 79

J

Jackson
—v. Chicago, City of, 24 Nat'l Disability L. Rep. 137 (N.D. Ill. 2002) *10:* 49, 50
—v. Department of Veterans Affairs, 22 F.3d 277, 3 AD Cases 483, *reh'g denied,* 30 F.3d 1500 (11th Cir. 1994) *7:* 254; *8:* 30; *9:* 69

Jacoby v. Arkansas Dep't of Educ., 338 Ark. 505, 995 S.W.2d 353 (1999) *10:* 96

Jacques
—v. Clean-Up Group, Inc., 96 F.3d 506, 5 AD Cases 1594 (1st Cir. 1996)   **5:** 510
—v. DiMarzio, Inc., 200 F. Supp. 2d 151, 13 AD Cases 1014 (E.D.N.Y. 2002), *aff'd*, 386 F.3d 192, 16 AD Cases 1 (2d Cir. 2004)   **5:** 59; **8:** 18
James v. U.S. Dep't of Health & Human Servs., 824 F.2d 1132 (D.C. Cir. 1987)   **2:** 205
Jankey v. Twentieth Century Fox Film Corp., 14 F. Supp. 2d 1174 (C.D. Cal. 1998), *aff'd*, 212 F.3d 1159, 10 AD Cases 1002 (9th Cir. 2000)   **6:** 38, 40
Jasany v. U.S. Postal Serv., 755 F.2d 1244, 1 AD Cases 706 (6th Cir. 1985)   **8:** 39
Jay v. Internet Wagner, Inc., 233 F.3d 1014, 11 AD Cases 471 (7th Cir. 2000)   **8:** 85
J.B. Hunt Transp., Inc.; EEOC v., 128 F. Supp. 2d 117, 12 AD Cases 1805 (N.D.N.Y. 2001), *aff'd*, 321 F.3d 69, 13 AD Cases 1697 (2d Cir. 2003)   **5:** 155, 300, 479; **7:** 89, 90; **9:** 306; **10:** 186
Jenks v. Workman, 83 FEP Cases 761 (S.D. Ind. 2000)   **10:** 320
Jessie v. Carter Health Care Ctr., 926 F. Supp. 613, 3 WH Cases 2d 549 (E.D. Ky. 1996)   **9:** 30
Johnson
—v. Al Tech Specialties Steel Corp., 34 FEP Cases 861 (1984)   **3:** 503
—v. Boardman Petroleum, Inc., 923 F. Supp. 1563, 5 AD Cases 983 (S.D. Ga. 1996)   **5:** 46
—v. Brown, 26 F. Supp. 2d 147 (D.D.C. 1998)   **7:** 244
—v. Circuit City Stores, Inc.
——148 F.3d 373, 77 FEP Cases 139 (4th Cir. 1998)   **10:** 321
——203 F.3d 821, 83 FEP Cases 320 (4th Cir. 2000)   **10:** 325
—v. Foulds, 111 F.3d 133 (7th Cir. 1997)   **9:** 51
—v. Gambrinus Co./Spoetzl Brewery, 116 F.3d 1052, 7 AD Cases 837 (5th Cir. 1997)   **6:** 165, 200
—v. Georgia Highway Express, Inc. 488 F.2d 714, 7 FEP Cases 1 (5th Cir. 1974)   **10:** 372
—v. Hines Nurseries, Inc., 950 F. Supp. 175, 7 AD Cases 867 (N.D. Tex. 1996)   **9:** 237
—v. Hubbard Broad., Inc., 940 F. Supp. 1447, 73 FEP Cases 8 (D. Minn. 1996)   **10:** 315
—v. New York Hosp., 96 F.3d 33, 5 AD Cases 1537 (2d Cir. 1996)   **5:** 181, 290, 291
—v. Oregon Dep't of Human Resources, Rehab. Div., 141 F.3d 1361, 8 AD Cases 283 (9th Cir. 1998)   **9:** 144, 240
—v. Saline, City of, 151 F.3d 564, 8 AD Cases 629 (6th Cir. 1998)   **2:** 295
—v. State Tech. Ctr. at Memphis, 24 F. Supp. 2d 833, 9 AD Cases 301 (W.D. Tenn. 1998)   **10:** 100
—v. U.S. Postal Serv., 861 F.2d 1475, 48 FEP Cases 686 (10th Cir. 1988), *cert. denied*, 493 U.S. 811 (1989)   **2:** 305; **10:** 77
—v. U.S. Steel Corp., 943 F. Supp. 1108, 7 AD Cases 999 (D. Minn. 1996)   **9:** 237
Johnston v. Horne, 875 F.2d 1415, 49 FEP Cases 1806 (9th Cir. 1989), *overruled by* Irwin v. Department of Veterans Affairs, 498 U.S. 89, 54 FEP Cases 577 (1990)   **2:** 305; **10:** 61, 77
Jones
—v. Corrections Corp. of Am., 993 F. Supp. 1384, 8 AD Cases 1561 (D. Kan. 1998)   **5:** 275
—v. Illinois Cent. R.R., 859 F. Supp. 1144, 3 AD Cases 838 (N.D. Ill. 1994)   **10:** 11
—v. Pennsylvania, 2000 U.S. Dist. LEXIS 107 (E.D. Pa. 2000)   **10:** 100
—v. Postal Workers Local 4755, 192 F.3d 417, 9 AD Cases 1249 (4th Cir. 1999)   **8:** 227
—v. United Parcel Serv., 214 F.3d 402, 10 AD Cases 1064 (3d Cir. 2000)   **8:** 44, 56
Jovanovic v. In-Sink-Erator Div., Emerson Elec. Co., 201 F.3d 894, 10 AD Cases 193 (7th Cir. 2000)   **8:** 51

Judson Steel Corp. v. Workers' Comp. Appeals Bd., 22 Cal. 3d 658, 586 P.2d 564, 150 Cal. Rptr. 250 (1978) **9:** 183
Justice v. Pike County Bd. of Educ., 348 F.3d 554, 14 AD Cases 1761 (6th Cir. 2003) **2:** 157

K

Kalekiristos v. CTF Hotel Mgmt. Corp., 958 F. Supp. 641, 6 AD Cases 1725 (D.D.C.), *aff'd*, 132 F.3d 1481 (D.C. Cir. 1997) **7:** 230
Kansas Gas & Elec. Co. v. Kansas Comm'n on Civil Rights, 750 P.2d 1055 (Kan. 1988) **4:** 372
Kapche v. City of San Antonio
—176 F.3d 840, 9 AD Cases 623 (5th Cir. 1999) **7:** 282–85
—304 F.3d 493, 13 AD Cases 907 (5th Cir. 2002) **5:** 133, 463; **7:** 160
Kaplan v. City of North Las Vegas, 323 F.3d 1226, 14 AD Cases 295 (9th Cir.), *cert. denied*, 14 AD Cases 1920 (2003) **8:** 18
Karbusicky v. City of Park Ridge, 950 F. Supp. 878, 6 AD Cases 661 (N.D. Ill. 1997) **7:** 257
Karst v. F.C. Hayer Co., 447 N.W.2d 180, 1 AD Cases 1530 (Minn. 1989) **9:** 184
Katz
—v. City Metal Co., 87 F.3d 26, 5 AD Cases 1120 (1st Cir. 1996) **8:** 18
—NLRB v., 369 U.S. 736, 50 LRRM 2177 (1962) **9:** 363, 364
Katzenbach v. Morgan, 384 U.S. 641 (1966) **10:** 101
Kedra v. Nazareth Hosp., 868 F. Supp. 733, 3 AD Cases 1550 (E.D. Pa. 1994) **2:** 296
Keever v. City of Middletown, 145 F.3d 809, 8 AD Cases 388 (6th Cir.), *cert. denied*, 525 U.S. 963 (1998) **5:** 446
Kellogg v. Union Pac. R.R., 233 F.3d 1083, 11 AD Cases 385 (8th Cir. 2000) **5:** 103, 426

Kelly
—v. Classic Rests. Corp., 92 FEP Cases 1222 (S.D.N.Y. 2003) **10:** 340
—v. UHC Mgmt. Co., 967 F. Supp. 1240 (N.D. Ala. 1997) **10:** 316
Kelsey v. University Club of Orlando, 845 F. Supp. 1526, 3 AD Cases 459 (M.D. Fla. 1994) **6:** 125
Kemer v. Johnson, 900 F. Supp. 677, 4 AD Cases 1823 (S.D.N.Y. 1995) **9:** 52
Kennedy
—v. Applause, Inc.
——90 F.3d 1477, 5 AD Cases 1249 (9th Cir. 1996) **5:** 231; **9:** 39, 238
——3 AD Cases 1734 (C.D. Cal. 1994) **7:** 255
—v. Chemical Waste Mgmt., Inc., 79 F.3d 49, 5 AD Cases 565 (7th Cir. 1996) **8:** 55, 56
—v. Dresser Rand Co., 193 F.3d 120, 9 AD Cases 1335 (2d Cir. 1999), *cert. denied*, 528 U.S. 1190 (2000) **5:** 447; **8:** 235, 236
Kent State Univ. v. Ohio Civil Rights Comm'n, 64 Ohio App. 3d 427, 581 N.E.2d 1135, 2 AD Cases 1496 (1989) **4:** 835
Kilmer v. U.S. Dep't of Labor, 1 AD Cases 1535 (S.D.N.Y. 1989) **2:** 250
Kilroy v. Husson Coll., 959 F. Supp. 22, 6 AD Cases 1033 (D. Me. 1997) **2:** 296
Kimbro v. Atlantic Richfield Co., 889 F.2d 869, 1 AD Cases 1537 (9th Cir. 1989) **4:** 1070
Kimel v. Florida Bd. of Regents, 139 F.3d 1426, 8 AD Cases 1 (11th Cir. 1998), *aff'd*, 528 U.S. 62, 81 FEP Cases 970 (2000) **10:** 85, 91, 100
Kiphart v. Saturn Corp., 251 F.3d 573, 11 AD Cases 1473 (6th Cir. 2001) **5:** 191; **8:** 148
Kirkingburg v. Albertson's, Inc., 143 F.3d 1228, 8 AD Cases 180 (9th Cir. 1998), *rev'd*, 527 U.S. 555, 9 AD Cases 694 (1999) **1:** 86; **5:** 138, 139, 209, 350, 417, 501; **9:** 307, 309–15; **10:** 182, 245
Kitchell v. Public Serv. Co., 126 N.M. 525, 972 P.2d 344 (1998) **4:** 745

Kohn Nast & Graf, P.C.; Doe v., 866 F. Supp. 190, 3 AD Cases 1322 (E.D. Pa. 1994)   *10:* 36
Kolling v. Blue Cross Blue Shield of Mich., 318 F.3d 715, 14 AD Cases 384, 29 EB Cases 2597 (6th Cir. 2003)   *5:* 383; *6:* 64
Kolpas v. G.D. Searle & Co., 959 F. Supp. 525, 8 AD Cases 1285 (N.D. Ill. 1997)   *5:* 44
Kolstad v. American Dental Ass'n, 527 U.S. 526, 79 FEP Cases 1697 (1999)   *1:* 112, 113; *10:* 217, 218
Kolton v. Anoka County, 645 N.W.2d 403, 13 AD Cases 337 (Minn. 2002)   *4:* 581
Korzeniowski v. ABF Freight Sys., Inc., 38 F. Supp. 2d 688, 9 AD Cases 393 (N.D. Ill. 1999)   *5:* 119
Koshinski v. Decatur Foundry, Inc., 177 F.3d 599, 9 AD Cases 353 (7th Cir. 1999)   *7:* 274
Koslow v. Pennsylvania, 302 F.3d 161, 13 AD Cases 769 (3d Cir. 2002), *cert. denied,* 537 U.S. 1232 (2003)   *2:* 101; *10:* 115
Kotlowski v. Eastman Kodak Co., 922 F. Supp. 790, 6 AD Cases 609 (W.D.N.Y. 1996)   *9:* 69
Kralik v. Durbin, 130 F.3d 76, 7 AD Cases 1040 (3d Cir. 1997)   *8:* 121, 127; *9:* 362, 371
Krauel v. Iowa Methodist Med. Ctr., 95 F.3d 674, 5 AD Cases 1503 (8th Cir. 1996)   *9:* 506, 513
Krein v. Martin Manor Nursing Home, 415 N.W.2d 793 (N.D. 1987)   *4:* 811
Krocka v. City of Chi., 203 F.3d 507, 10 AD Cases 289 (7th Cir. 2000)   *5:* 436, 438
Kubicki v. Brady, 829 F. Supp. 906 (E.D. Mich. 1993), *aff'd,* 41 F.3d 1507 (6th Cir. 1994)   *10:* 80
Kuehl v. Wal-Mart Stores, Inc., 909 F. Supp. 794, 5 AD Cases 91 (D. Colo. 1995)   *9:* 52
Kvorjak v. Maine, 259 F.3d 48, 12 AD Cases 160 (1st Cir. 2001)   *2:* 190; *8:* 62, 84, 209; *10:* 210

L

LaChance v. Duffy's Draft House, Inc., 146 F.3d 832, 8 AD Cases 652 (11th Cir. 1998)   *4:* 184, 190; *5:* 493, 517; *8:* 245; *9:* 294
Lakota v. Sonoco Prod. Co., 2002 U.S. Dist. LEXIS 6422 (D. Mass. 2002)   *4:* 519
Lamb
—v. John Umstead Hosp., 19 F. Supp. 2d 498, 9 AD Cases 401 (E.D.N.C. 1998)   *10:* 100
—v. Qualex, Inc., 2002 U.S. App. LEXIS 5982 (4th Cir. 2002)   *8:* 205
Land v. Baptist Med. Ctr., 164 F.3d 423 (8th Cir. 1999)   *5:* 58
Lane
—v. BFI Waste Sys. of N. Am., 11 AD Cases 1795 (8th Cir. 2001)   *9:* 263
—v. Pena, 518 U.S. 187, 5 AD Cases 973 (1996)   *2:* 306, 307
Lansdowne Swim Club; United States v., 713 F. Supp. 785 (E.D. Pa. 1989)   *6:* 126
Lara v. Cinemark USA, Inc., 207 F.3d 783, 10 AD Cases 683 (5th Cir.), *cert. denied,* 531 U.S. 944 (2000)   *6:* 296, 392
Larimer v. International Bus. Machs. Corp., 370 F.3d 698, 15 AD Cases 1070 (7th Cir.), *cert. denied,* 125 S. Ct. 477, 33 EB Cases 3015 (2004)   *5:* 376
Laurin v. Providence Hosp. & Mass. Nurses Ass'n, 150 F.3d 52, 8 AD Cases 768 (1st Cir. 1998)   *8:* 39
Lawson
—v. CSX Transp., Inc., 245 F.3d 916, 11 AD Cases 1025 (7th Cir. 2001)   *5:* 58, 133, 150, 453
—v. University of Tenn., 2000 Tenn. App. LEXIS 53 (Tenn. Ct. App. 2000)   *10:* 96
Leatherwood v. Houston Post Co., 59 F.3d 533, 4 AD Cases 1091 (5th Cir. 1995)   *7:* 254
LeBourgeois v. Fireplace Mfrs., Inc., 68 Cal. App. 4th 1049 (1998)   *4:* 68, 72

Lebron-Torres v. Whitehall Robins Labs., 251 F.3d 236, 11 AD Cases 1491 (1st Cir. 2001) **5:** 110
Lee v. City of Salem, Ind., 259 F.3d 667, 12 AD Cases 10 (7th Cir. 2001) **9:** 263
Legal Aid Soc'y v. Brennan, 608 F.2d 1319, 21 FEP Cases 605 (9th Cir. 1979), *cert. denied,* 447 U.S. 921 (1980) **2:** 261, 262, 264
Leisen v. City of Shelbyville, 135 F.3d 805, 8 AD Cases 892 (7th Cir. 1998) **5:** 404, 425, 430
Lemons v. US Air Group, Inc., 43 F. Supp. 2d 571 (M.D.N.C.), *vacated & remanded,* 194 F.3d 1304 (4th Cir. 1999) **9:** 237
Lenker v. Methodist Hosp., 210 F.3d 792, 10 AD Cases 782 (7th Cir. 2000) **5:** 194
Lenox v. Healthwise of Ky., 149 F.3d 453, 8 AD Cases 521 (6th Cir. 1998) **5:** 439
Leonard F. v. Israel Discount Bank of N.Y., 199 F.3d 99, 10 AD Cases 13 (2d Cir. 1999) **9:** 506
Leonberger v. Martin Marietta Materials Inc., 231 F.3d 396, 11 AD Cases 103 (7th Cir. 2000) **8:** 228
Lesane v. Hawaiian Airlines, 75 F. Supp. 2d 1113 (D. Haw. 1999) **4:** 224
Leverett v. City of Indianapolis, 51 F. Supp. 2d 949, 9 AD Cases 1812 (S.D. Ind. 1999) **7:** 51, 257, 258
Library of Congress v. Shaw, 478 U.S. 310, 41 FEP Cases 85 (1986) **2:** 235
Lieber v. Macy's W., Inc., 80 F. Supp. 2d 1065 (N.D. Cal. 1999) **6:** 186
Liljedahl v. Ryder Student Transp. Serv., Inc., 341 F.3d 836, 14 AD Cases 1390 (8th Cir. 2003) **4:** 584
Lincoln v. Momentum Syst. Ltd., 86 F. Supp. 2d 421, 10 AD Cases 946 (D.N.J. 2000) **9:** 258
Lloyd
—v. Hardin County, Iowa, 207 F.3d 1080, 10 AD Cases 703 (8th Cir. 2000) **9:** 258
—v. Regional Transp. Auth., 548 F.2d 1277 (7th Cir. 1977) **2:** 281, 284, 286

Local unions. *See name of national or international organization*
Lockhart v. United States, 961 F. Supp. 1260 (N.D. Ind. 1997) **10:** 344
Longoria v. Harris, 554 F. Supp. 102, 38 FEP Cases 738 (S.D. Tex. 1982) **5:** 31
Lopez v. Johnson, 333 F.3d 459, 14 AD Cases 893 (9th Cir. 2003) **2:** 50
Louie
—v. Ideal Cleaners, 1999 WL 1269191 (N.D. Cal. 1999) **6:** 41
—v. National Football League, 185 F. Supp. 2d 1306, 12 AD Cases 1394 (S.D. Fla. 2002) **6:** 209
Loulseged v. Akzo Nobel, Inc., 178 F.3d 731, 9 AD Cases 783 (5th Cir. 1999) **8:** 78, 83
Lovejoy-Wilson v. NOCO Motor Fuel, Inc., 263 F.3d 208, 12 AD Cases 340 (2d Cir. 2001) **5:** 499, 518, 532, 533; **8:** 155, 250
Lowe v. Alabama Power Co., 244 F.3d 1305 (11th Cir. 2001) **8:** 250
Lowell v. International Bus. Machs. Corp., 955 F. Supp. 300, 6 AD Cases 1269 (D. Vt. 1997) **4:** 1035
Lucas v. W.W. Grainger, Inc., 257 F.3d 1249, 11 AD Cases 1761 (11th Cir. 2001) **8:** 156
Luce, Forward, Hamilton, & Scripps; EEOC v., 345 F.3d 742 (9th Cir. 2003) **10:** 303
Lusk v. Christ Hosp., 10 AD Cases 534 (N.D. Ill. 2000) **5:** 425
Luzik; Commonwealth v., 259 Va. 198, 524 S.E.2d 871, 5 WH Cases 2d 1735 (2000) **10:** 96
Lyons v. Legal Aid Soc'y, 68 F.3d 1512, 4 AD Cases 1694 (2d Cir. 1995) **8:** 140

M

Mack v. Great Dane Trailers, 308 F.3d 776, 13 AD Cases 1153 (7th Cir. 2002) **5:** 89, 155; **10:** 186
Mackay v. U.S. Postal Serv., 607 F. Supp. 271, 42 FEP Cases 1197 (E.D. Pa. 1985) **10:** 61

Mackie v. Runyon, 804 F. Supp. 1508, 2 AD Cases 260 (M.D. Fla. 1992) *8:* 39
Maddox v. University of Tenn., 62 F.3d 843, 4 AD Cases 1253 (6th Cir. 1995) *5:* 181, 293
Maes v. Henderson, 33 F. Supp. 2d 1281 (D. Nev. 1999) *4:* 690
Magruder v. Runyon, 844 F. Supp. 696, 3 AD Cases 120 (D. Kan. 1994), *aff'd,* 54 F.3d 787, 6 AD Cases 1440 (10th Cir. 1995) *7:* 291
Mahon v. Crowell, 295 F.3d 585, 13 AD Cases 390 (6th Cir. 2002) *2:* 138; *5:* 109; *10:* 188, 189
Malabarba v. Chicago Tribune Co., 149 F.3d 690, 8 AD Cases 1505 (7th Cir. 1998) *8:* 165
Mancini v. General Elec. Co., 820 F. Supp. 141, 2 AD Cases 764 (D. Vt. 1993) *7:* 287, 292
Mantolete v. Bolger, 767 F.2d 1416, 1 AD Cases 811 (9th Cir. 1985) *8:* 44
Mararri v. WCI Steel, Inc., 130 F.3d 1180, 7 AD Cases 978 (6th Cir. 1997) *5:* 265, 289
Marinelli v. City of Erie, Pa., 216 F.3d 354, 10 AD Cases 1157 (3d Cir. 2000) *5:* 101
Marschand v. Norfolk & W. Ry., 876 F. Supp. 1528, 4 AD Cases 1099 (N.D. Ind. 1995), *aff'd,* 81 F.3d 714, 5 AD Cases 1184 (7th Cir. 1996) *9:* 52
Martin
—In re, No. 01954089, 1997 WL 151524 (EEOC, Mar. 27, 1997) *5:* 335
—v. Allegheny Airlines, Inc., 126 F. Supp. 2d 809 (E.D. Pa. 2000) *7:* 12
—v. Barnesville Exempted Vill. Sch. Dist. Bd. of Educ., 209 F.3d 931, 10 AD Cases 787 (6th Cir.), *cert. denied,* 531 U.S. 992 (2000) *5:* 177, 178, 277, 286
—v. Kansas, 190 F.3d 1120, 9 AD Cases 1075 (10th Cir. 1999) *10:* 100
—v. Voinovich, 840 F. Supp. 1175 (S.D. Ohio 1993) *10:* 100
Martinez v. Ohio Dep't of Admin. Servs., 118 Ohio App. 3d 687, 693 N.E.2d 1152 (1997) *4:* 844
Martinez ex. rel. Martinez v. School Bd. of Hillsborough County, 861 F.2d 1502 (11th Cir. 1988) *5:* 337
Martini v. Federal Nat'l Mortgage Ass'n, 178 F.3d 1336, 80 FEP Cases 1 (D.C. Cir. 1999) *10:* 174
Martinson v. Kinney Shoe Corp., 104 F.3d 683, 6 AD Cases 434 (4th Cir. 1997) *5:* 493, 511; *8:* 39
Marvello v. Chemical Bank, 923 F. Supp. 487, 5 AD Cases 1400 (S.D.N.Y. 1996) *9:* 484
Mason v. South Bend Cmty. Sch. Corp., 9 AD Cases 979 (N.D. Ind. 1998) *7:* 219
Matczak v. Frankford Candy & Chocolate Co., 136 F.3d 933, 7 AD Cases 1050 (3d Cir. 1997), *aff'd,* 261 F.3d 492 (3d Cir. 2001) *5:* 130, 496; *7:* 12, 58
Mathews v. Denver Post, 263 F.3d 1164, 12 AD Cases 250 (10th Cir. 2001) *5:* 513
Mathieson v. American Elec. Power, 2002 U.S. Dist. LEXIS 6560 (W.D. Mich. 2002) *5:* 325
Matthews
—v. Commonwealth Edison Co., 128 F.3d 1194, 7 AD Cases 1651 (7th Cir. 1997) *8:* 191
—v. National Collegiate Athletic Ass'n, 179 F. Supp. 2d 1209 (E.D. Wash. 2001) *6:* 72
—v. Rollins Hudig Hall Co., 72 F.3d 50, 69 FEP Cases 641 (7th Cir. 1995) *10:* 334, 335
Mattice v. Memorial Hosp. of South Bend, Inc., 249 F.3d 682, 11 AD Cases 1339 (7th Cir. 2001) *5:* 435
Mauro, Estate of v. Borgess Med. Ctr., 137 F.3d 398, 7 AD Cases 1571 (6th Cir.), *cert. denied,* 525 U.S. 815 (1998) *5:* 362; *8:* 249; *10:* 260
Maxwell v. State, 91 Wash. App. 171, 956 P.2d 1110 (1998) *4:* 1076
Mayer v. University of Minn., 940 F. Supp. 1474, 7 AD Cases 1551 (D. Minn. 1996) *10:* 100
Mayes v. Allison, 983 F. Supp. 923, 7 AD Cases 1063 (D. Nev. 1997) *6:* 398, 400

Mays v. Principi, 301 F.3d 866, 13 AD Cases 985 (7th Cir. 2002) *5:* 536; *8:* 63, 149; *10:* 210

Maziarka v. Mills Fleet Farm, Inc., 245 F.3d 675, 11 AD Cases 1140 (8th Cir. 2001) *5:* 195

Mazzarella v. U.S. Postal Serv., 849 F. Supp. 89, 3 AD Cases 232 (D. Mass. 1994) *7:* 289, 290

McAlindin v. County of San Diego
—192 F.3d 1226, 9 AD Cases 1217 (9th Cir. 1999), *cert. denied*, 530 U.S. 1243 (2000) *9:* 303
—201 F.3d 1211, 10 AD Cases 252 (9th Cir. 1999), *cert. denied*, 530 U.S. 1243 (2000) *5:* 420

McAlpin v. National Semiconductor Corp., 921 F. Supp. 1518, 5 AD Cases 1047 (N.D. Tex. 1996) *8:* 51, 94

McAnnally v. Wyn S. Molded Prods., Inc., 912 F. Supp. 512, 3 WH Cases 2d 433 (N.D. Ala. 1996) *9:* 112

McBrearity v. Connecticut Comm'n on Human Rights & Opportunities, 1995 Conn. Super. LEXIS 2669 (Conn. Super. Ct. Sept. 19, 1995) *4:* 113

McConnell v. Pioneer Hi-Bred Int'l, 10 AD Cases 578 (D.S.D. 2000) *5:* 419

McDaniel v. Mississippi Baptist Med. Ctr., 877 F. Supp. 321, 4 AD Cases 241 (S.D. Miss.), *aff'd*, 74 F.3d 1238, 6 AD Cases 800 (5th Cir. 1995) *5:* 261

McDonnell Douglas Corp. v. Green, 411 U.S. 792, 5 FEP Cases 965 (1973) *7:* 12; *10:* 237

McGuiness v. University of N.M. Sch. of Med., 170 F.3d 974, 9 AD Cases 297 (10th Cir. 1998), *cert. denied*, 526 U.S. 1051 (1999) *5:* 91

McGuinness v. U.S. Postal Serv., 744 F.2d 1318, 5 FEP Cases 1762, 1 AD Cases 624 (7th Cir. 1984) *2:* 287, 305; *10:* 77

McKay v. Toyota Motor Mfg. U.S.A., Inc., 110 F.3d 369, 6 AD Cases 933 (6th Cir. 1997) *7:* 245

McKiver v. General Elec. Co., 11 F. Supp. 2d 755, 9 AD Cases 30 (M.D.N.C. 1997) *5:* 118

McNeil v. Times Ins. Co., 2000 U.S. App. LEXIS 2710 (5th Cir. 2000) *5:* 383; *6:* 64

McNemar v. Disney Store, Inc., 91 F.3d 610, 5 AD Cases 1227 (3d Cir. 1996), *cert. denied*, 519 U.S. 1115 (1997) *5:* 231, 357; *8:* 266; *9:* 145, 237

Means v. Iowa Sec. Servs., 440 N.W.2d 23 (Mich. Ct. App. 1989) *4:* 549

Mears v. Gulfstream Aerospace Corp., 905 F. Supp. 1075, 5 AD Cases 1295 (S.D. Ga. 1995), *aff'd*, 87 F.3d 1331, 6 AD Cases 1152 (11th Cir. 1996) *8:* 51

Medical Bd. of Cal. v. Hason, 294 F.3d 1166, 13 AD Cases 477 (9th Cir. 2002), *cert. dismissed*, 538 U.S. 958 (2003) *10:* 104

Meekison v. Voinovich, 17 F. Supp. 2d 725 (S.D. Ohio 1998) *10:* 100

Menkowitz v. Pottstown Mem'l Med. Ctr., 154 F.3d 113, 8 AD Cases 725 (3d Cir. 1998) *8:* 279

Mercuro v. Superior Court, 96 Cal. App. 4th 167 (2002) *10:* 324

Meritor Sav. Bank v. Vinson, 477 U.S. 57, 40 FEP Cases 1822 (1986) *7:* 94; *8:* 41

Mertz v. Marsh, 786 F.2d 1578, 40 FEP Cases 1110 (11th Cir. 1986) *10:* 405–9

Michalski v. Circuit City Stores, Inc., 177 F.3d 634, 79 FEP Cases 1160 (7th Cir. 1999) *10:* 306, 322

Mickulicz v. Garthwaite, 2000 U.S. App. LEXIS 22248 (6th Cir. 2000) *10:* 54

Miener v. Missouri, 673 F.2d 969 (8th Cir.), *cert. denied*, 459 U.S. 909 (1982) *2:* 286, 288; *10:* 154

Milbert v. Koop, 830 F.2d 354, 1 AD Cases 1148 (D.C. Cir. 1987) *2:* 205, 304

Miller
—v. American Coalition of Citizens with Disabilities, Inc., 485 A.2d 186, 1 AD Cases 649 (D.C. 1984) *4:* 153
—v. National Cas. Co., 61 F.3d 627, 4 AD Cases 1089 (8th Cir. 1995) *8:* 51
—v. Public Storage Mgmt., Inc., 121 F.3d 215, 7 AD Cases 416 (5th Cir. 1997) *10:* 315

—v. Springfield, City of, 146 F.3d 612, 8 AD Cases 321 (8th Cir. 1998) **5:** 436

—v. Texas Tech Univ. Health Sci. Ctr., 330 F.3d 691, 14 AD Cases 583, *rehearing en banc granted,* 342 F.3d 563, 14 AD Cases 1472 (5th Cir. 2003) **10:** 114

—v. U.S. Bancorp, 926 F. Supp. 994, 5 AD Cases 968 (D. Or. 1996), *aff'd,* 139 F.3d 906 (9th Cir. 1998) **9:** 237

Milton v. Scrivner, Inc., 53 F.3d 1118, 4 AD Cases 432 (10th Cir. 1995) **8:** 121

Miners v. Cargill Communications, Inc., 113 F.3d 820, 6 AD Cases 1229 (8th Cir.), *cert. denied,* 522 U.S. 981 (1997) **5:** 184, 274

Misek-Falkoff v. International Bus. Machs. Corp., 854 F. Supp. 215, 3 AD Cases 449 (S.D.N.Y. 1994), *aff'd,* 60 F.3d 811, 6 AD Cases 576 (2d Cir.), *cert. denied,* 516 U.S. 991 (1995) **7:** 293

Mississippi Dep't of Pub. Safety; United States v., 321 F.3d 495, 13 AD Cases 1706 (5th Cir. 2003) **10:** 105

Mitchell v. Washingtonville Cent. Sch. Dist., 190 F.3d 1, 9 AD Cases 1123 (2d Cir. 1999) **9:** 258

Mitsubishi Motors Corp. v. Soler Chrysler-Plymouth, Inc., 473 U.S. 614 (1985) **10:** 294, 333

Mohamed v. Marriott Int'l, 905 F. Supp. 141, 5 AD Cases 50 (S.D.N.Y. 1995) **9:** 484

Mohr v. Hoover Co., 2004 U.S. App. LEXIS 9689 (6th Cir. 2004) **5:** 459

Mole v. Buckhorn Rubber Prods., Inc., 185 F.3d 1212, 8 AD Cases 1873 (8th Cir.), *cert. denied,* 528 U.S. 821 (1999) **8:** 51

Monette v. Electronic Data Sys. Corp., 90 F.3d 1173, 5 AD Cases 1326 (6th Cir. 1996) **8:** 169; **9:** 39; **10:** 203

Montalvo v. Radcliffe, 167 F.3d 873, 9 AD Cases 15 (4th Cir.), *cert. denied,* 528 U.S. 813 (1999) **5:** 381; **6:** 154

Montegue v. City of New Orleans, No. Civ. A. 95-2420, 1997 WL 327113 (E.D. La. 1997) **5:** 247

Moody-Herrara v. State, 967 P.2d 79 (Alaska 1998) **4:** 12

Moon v. Secretary, U.S. Dep't of Labor, 747 F.2d 599, 1 AD Cases 642 (11th Cir. 1984), *cert. denied,* 471 U.S. 1055 (1985) **2:** 251

Mora v. Chem-Tronics, Inc., 16 F. Supp. 2d 1192, 5 WH Cases 2d 475 (S.D. Cal. 1998) **9:** 27

Moran v. State Comm'n for Human Rights, 121 R.I. 978, 404 A.2d 857 (1979) **4:** 932

Moreno

—v. American Ingredients Co., 10 AD Cases 1483, 2000 WL 527808 (D. Kan. Apr. 7, 2000) **5:** 506

—v. Consolidated Rail Corp., 63 F.3d 1404, 4 AD Cases 1364 (6th Cir. 1995), *aff'd en banc,* 99 F.3d 782, 6 AD Cases 86 (6th Cir. 1996) **2:** 296

Morgan

—v. N.W. Permanente, P.C., 989 F. Supp. 1330 (D. Or. 1997) **5:** 330

—v. U.S. Postal Serv., 798 F.2d 1162, 1 AD Cases 963 (8th Cir. 1986), *cert. denied,* 480 U.S. 948, 94 L. Ed. 2d 794, 107 S. Ct. 1608 (1987) **2:** 305; **10:** 61, 78

Morisky v. Broward County, 80 F.3d 445, 5 AD Cases 737 (11th Cir. 1996) **4:** 182; **7:** 20; **8:** 53, 54

Morse v. University of Vt., 973 F.2d 122 (2d Cir. 1992) **2:** 302

Morton

—v. GTE N., Inc., 922 F. Supp. 1169, 5 AD Cases 524 (N.D. Tex. 1996), *aff'd,* 114 F.3d 1182, 7 AD Cases 544 (5th Cir.), *cert. denied,* 522 U.S. 880 (1997) **9:** 238

—v. United Parcel Serv., Inc., 272 F.3d 1249, 12 AD Cases 897 (9th Cir. 2001), *cert. denied,* 535 U.S. 1054, 13 AD Cases 96 (2002) **1:** 90, 91; **5:** 212–14, 307, 523; **10:** 249–51

Moses v. American Nonwovens, Inc., 97 F.3d 446, 5 AD Cases 1651 (11th Cir. 1996), *cert. denied,* 519 U.S. 1118 (1997) **5:** 517; **9:** 287, 293

Motley v. New Jersey State Police, 196 F.3d 160, 9 AD Cases 1505 (3d Cir. 1999), *cert. denied,* 529 U.S. 1087 (2000) **8:** 270; **9:** 258

Mott v. Synthetic Indus., 4 AD Cases 1393 (N.D. Ga. 1995) *9:* 72

Motzkin v. Trustees of Boston Univ., 938 F. Supp. 983, 7 AD Cases 101 (D. Mass. 1996) *8:* 279, 283, 284

Muellner v. Mars, Inc., 714 F. Supp. 351 (N.D. Ill. 1989) *5:* 233

Mulholland v. Pharmacia & Upjohn, Inc., 2002 U.S. App. LEXIS 24200, 13 AD Cases 1632 (6th Cir. 2002) *5:* 89

Muller v. Costello, 187 F.3d 298, 9 AD Cases 1064 (2d Cir. 1999) *10:* 100

Mullins v. Crowell, 228 F.3d 1305, 11 AD Cases 38 (11th Cir. 2000) *5:* 107; *10:* 189

Mundo v. Sanus Health Plan of Greater N.Y., 966 F. Supp. 171, 8 AD Cases 937 (E.D.N.Y. 1997) *5:* 44

Murphy
—v. Cartex Corp., 377 Pa. Super. 181, 546 A.2d 1217, 52 FEP Cases 1267 (1988) *4:* 906
—v. United Parcel Serv., Inc., 527 U.S. 516, 9 AD Cases 691 (1999) *1:* 86; *2:* 319; *5:* 124, 126, 155, 350, 417, 423, 476, 477, 501; *10:* 182, 186

Murray
—v. John D. Archbold Mem'l Hosp., Inc., 50 F. Supp. 2d 1368 (M.D. Ga. 1999) *7:* 14, 85, 86
—v. Wilson Distilling Co., 213 U.S. 151 (1909) *10:* 90

Mustafa v. Clark County Sch. Dist., 157 F.3d 1169, 8 AD Cases 1119 (9th Cir. 1998) *5:* 93

Mutual of Omaha Ins. Co.; Doe v., 179 F.3d 557, 9 AD Cases 657 (7th Cir. 1999), *cert. denied*, 528 U.S. 1106 (2000) *5:* 385, 387; *6:* 67, 101, 102

Myers v. Hose, 50 F.3d 278, 4 AD Cases 391 (4th Cir. 1995) *8:* 239; *9:* 51

N

National Fed'n of the Blind (NFB) v. America Online, Inc., No. 99CV12303 EFH (D. Mass 1999) *6:* 85

National League of Cities v. Usery, 426 U.S. 833, 22 WH Cases 1064 (1976) *10:* 393

Nawrot v. CPC Int'l, 277 F.3d 896, 12 AD Cases 1138 (7th Cir. 2002) *5:* 132, 454–56

Nedder v. Rivier Coll., 944 F. Supp. 111, 5 AD Cases 1691 (D.N.H. 1996) *4:* 698

Neff v. American Dairy Queen Corp., 58 F.3d 1063, 4 AD Cases 1170 (5th Cir. 1995), *cert. denied*, 516 U.S. 1045 (1996) *6:* 264, 265

Neighborhood Action Coalition v. Canton, 882 F.2d 1012 (6th Cir. 1989) *10:* 60

Nelson
—v. Miller, 170 F.3d 641, 9 AD Cases 234 (6th Cir. 1999) *10:* 100
—v. Thornburgh, 567 F. Supp. 369, 1 AD Cases 463 (E.D. Pa. 1983), *aff'd*, 732 F.2d 146, 1 AD Cases 573 (3d Cir. 1984), *cert. denied*, 469 U.S. 118 (1985) *3:* 380, 381; *7:* 213, 229
—v. Williams Field Serv. Co., Nos. 99-8041, 98-CV-242-D, 2000 WL 743684 (10th Cir. 2000) *5:* 271, 289

Nesmith v. YMCA, 397 F.2d 96 (4th Cir. 1968) *6:* 126

Nesser v. Trans World Airlines, Inc., 160 F.3d 442, 8 AD Cases 1348 (8th Cir. 1998) *8:* 29; *9:* 41

Newberry v. East Tex. State Univ., 161 F.3d 276, 8 AD Cases 1595 (5th Cir. 1998) *8:* 18

Newland v. Dalton, 81 F.3d 904, 5 AD Cases 735 (9th Cir. 1996) *5:* 294, 295

Newman v. Piggy Park Enters., 390 U.S. 400 (1968) *10:* 366, 368, 370, 378

New York Gaslight Club, Inc. v. Carey, 447 U.S. 54, 22 FEP Cases 1642 (1980) *10:* 398–400

New York v. Ocean Club, Inc., 602 F. Supp. 489 (E.D.N.Y. 1984) *6:* 126

New York Univ.; Doe v., 666 F.2d 761 (2d Cir. 1981) *7:* 54

Nguyen v. IBP, Inc., 905 F. Supp. 1471, 5 AD Cases 465 (D. Kan. 1995) *9:* 237

Nihiser v. Ohio Envtl. Prot. Agency, 979 F. Supp. 1168, 7 AD Cases 751 (S.D. Ohio 1997), *aff'd in part, rev'd in part*, 269 F.3d 626, 12 AD Cases 530 (6th

Cir. 2001), *cert. denied*, 536 U.S. 922 (2002)   **10:** 101
NLRB v. *See name of opposing party*
Norcross v. Sneed, 755 F.2d 113, 1 AD Cases 689 (8th Cir. 1985)   **5:** 22
Norman-Bloodsaw v. Lawrence Berkeley Lab., 135 F.3d 1260, 7 AD Cases 1395 (9th Cir. 1998)   **7:** 118, 131
Norris v. Sysco Corp., 191 F.3d 1043, 9 AD Cases 1262 (9th Cir. 1999)   **9:** 257, 259, 260
Nowak v. St. Rita High Sch., 142 F.3d 999, 8 AD Cases 106 (7th Cir. 1998)   **9:** 41
Nunes v. Wal-Mart Stores, Inc., 164 F.3d 1243, 8 AD Cases 1813 (9th Cir. 1999)   **8:** 185, 241

O

Oesterling v. Walters, 760 F.2d 859, 1 AD Cases 722 (8th Cir. 1985)   **1:** 47; **2:** 133
Office of Senate Sergeant-at-Arms v. Office of Senate Fair Employment Practices, 95 F.3d 1102, 6 AD Cases 1237 (Fed. Cir. 1996)   **8:** 51
Ogburn v. United Food & Commercial Workers Local 881, 305 F.3d 763, 13 AD Cases 1071 (7th Cir.), *reh'g denied*, 2002 U.S. App. LEXIS 7394 (7th Cir. 2002)   **5:** 117, 427
O'Hare v. Municipal Resource Consultants, 107 Cal. App. 4th 267, 19 IER Cases 1340 (2003)   **10:** 324
Ohio Envtl. Prot. Agency v. Nihiser, 269 F.3d 626, 12 AD Cases 530 (6th Cir. 2001), *cert. denied*, 536 U.S. 922 (2002)   **2:** 101
Olin Corp., In re, 103 LA 481 (Helburn, 1994)   **9:** 375
Oliver v. Cole Gift Ctrs., Inc., 85 F. Supp. 2d 109 (D. Conn. 2000)   **10:** 174
Oliveras-Sifre v. Puerto Rico Dep't of Health, 214 F.3d 23, 10 AD Cases 1083 (1st Cir. 2000)   **5:** 375
Ollie v. Titan Tire Corp., 336 F.3d 680, 14 AD Cases 993 (8th Cir. 2003)   **7:** 119, 156–58

O'Loughlin v. Pinchback, 579 So. 2d 788 (Fla. Dist. Ct. App. 1991)   **4:** 187
Olson v. v. Dubuque Cmty. Sch. Dist., 137 F.3d 609, 7 AD Cases 1598 (8th Cir. 1998)   **5:** 405
Olzman v. Lake Hills Swim Club, Inc., 495 F.2d 1333 (2d Cir. 1974)   **6:** 126
O'Neal v. City of New Albany, 293 F.3d 998, 13 AD Cases 289 (7th Cir. 2002)   **7:** 138; **9:** 474
Oregon Paralyzed Veterans of Am. v. Regal Cinemas, Inc., 339 F.3d 1126, 14 AD Cases 1779 (9th Cir. 2003), *cert. denied*, 124 S. Ct. 2903 (2004)   **6:** 297, 392
Oregon Resort; Doe v., 11 AD Cases 1824 (D. Or. 2001)   **5:** 369
Orr v. Wal-Mart Stores, Inc., 297 F.3d 720, 13 AD Cases 577 (8th Cir. 2002), *cert. denied*, 541 U.S. 1070, 15 AD Cases 960 (2004)   **5:** 131, 452
Osborn v. E.J. Branch, Inc., 864 F. Supp. 56, 4 AD Cases 88 (N.D. Ill. 1994)   **10:** 34
Ostrander v. Farm Bureau Mut. Ins. Co., 123 Idaho 650, 851 P.2d 946, 8 IER Cases 1063 (1993)   **4:** 249
Oswalt v. Sara Lee Corp., 74 F.3d 91, 5 AD Cases 385 (5th Cir. 1996)   **9:** 20
Otting v. J.C. Penney Co., 223 F.3d 704, 10 AD Cases 1549 (8th Cir. 2000)   **5:** 123, 509
Owens v. Parker Drilling Co., 207 Mont. 446, 676 P.2d 162, 2 AD Cases 312 (1984)   **4:** 630
Ozlowski v. Henderson, 237 F.3d 837, 11 AD Cases 671 (7th Cir. 2001)   **1:** 81; **2:** 189

P

Pace v. Paris Maint. Co., 107 F. Supp. 2d 251, 11 AD Cases 990 (S.D.N.Y. 2000), *aff'd*, 14 AD Cases 672 (2d Cir. 2001)   **5:** 280
Pack v. Kmart Corp., 166 F.3d 1300, 8 AD Cases 1880 (10th Cir.), *cert. denied*, 528 U.S. 811 (1999)   **5:** 64, 411, 421, 504

Padilla v. City of Topeka, 238 Kan. 218, 708 P.2d 543, 2 AD Cases 1605 (1985) **4:** 375

Paladino v. Avnet Computer Techs., Inc., 134 F.3d 1054, 76 FEP Cases 1315 (11th Cir. 1998) **10:** 297, 325

Palesch v. Missouri Comm'n on Human Rights, 233 F.3d 560, 85 FEP Cases 75 (8th Cir. 2000) **5:** 433; **8:** 247; **10:** 265, 266

Pallozzi v. Allstate Life Ins. Co., 198 F.3d 28, 9 AD Cases 1697 (2d Cir. 1999), *amended on denial of reh'g,* 204 F.3d 392, 10 AD Cases 338 (2d Cir. 2000) **9:** 498

Palmer v. Circuit Court of Cook County Soc. Serv. Dep't, 117 F.3d 351, 6 AD Cases 1569 (7th Cir. 1997), *cert. denied,* 522 U.S. 1096 (1998) **8:** 275; **9:** 342

Palotai v. University of Md. at Coll. Park, 2002 U.S. App. LEXIS 12757 (4th Cir. 2002), *cert. denied,* 537 U.S. 1107 (2003) **5:** 415

Pals v. Schepel Buick & GMC Truck, Inc., 220 F.3d 495, 10 AD Cases 1345 (7th Cir. 2000) **9:** 257

Pandazides v. Virginia Bd. of Educ., 13 F.3d 823, 2 AD Cases 1711 (4th Cir. 1994) **2:** 295, 297

Paralyzed Veterans of Am. v. Ellerbe Becket Architects & Eng'rs, P.C., 945 F. Supp. 1, 5 AD Cases 1494 (D.D.C. 1996), *aff'd sub nom.* Paralyzed Veterans of Am. v. D.C. Arena L.P., 117 F.3d 579, 6 AD Cases 1614 (D.C. Cir. 1997), *cert. denied sub nom.* Pollin v. Paralyzed Veterans of Am., 523 U.S. 1003 (1998) **6:** 297, 300

Parham v. Southwestern Bell Tel. Co., 433 F.2d 421, 2 FEP Cases 1017 (8th Cir. 1970) **10:** 372

Parker
—v. Columbia Pictures Indus., 204 F.3d 326, 10 AD Cases 396 (2d Cir. 2000) **8:** 185; **9:** 257
—v. Metropolitan Life Ins. Co., 875 F. Supp. 1321, 4 AD Cases 34 (W.D. Tenn. 1995), *aff'd,* 121 F.3d 1006, 6 AD Cases 1865 (6th Cir. 1997), *cert. denied,* 522 U.S. 1084 (1998) **5:** 383; **6:** 64, 65; **8:** 278–82; **9:** 497, 506, 513

Parry v. Mohawk Motors of Mich., Inc., 236 F.3d 299, 11 AD Cases 538 (6th Cir. 2000), *cert. denied,* 533 U.S. 951 (2001) **5:** 174, 279

Passantino v. Johnson & Johnson, 212 F.3d 493, 84 FEP Cases 1123 (9th Cir. 2000) **10:** 174

Paterson v. State, 128 Idaho 494, 915 P.2d 724 (1996) **4:** 250

Patterson v. Illinois Dep't of Corr., 35 F. Supp. 2d 1103 (C.D. Ill. 1999), *aff'd,* 2002 U.S. App. LEXIS 12012 (7th Cir. 2002) **10:** 38

Peden v. City of Detroit, Detroit Police Dep't, 470 Mich. 195, 680 N.W. 2d 857 (2004) **4:** 552

Pegues v. Emerson Elec. Co., 913 F. Supp. 976, 5 AD Cases 376 (N.D. Miss. 1996) **9:** 51, 238

Pena v. Houston Lighting & Power Co., 154 F.3d 267, 8 AD Cases 961 (5th Cir. 1998) **9:** 478

Penn v. Ryan's Family Steak Houses, Inc., 269 F.3d 753, 12 AD Cases 615 (7th Cir. 2001) **10:** 319

Pennhurst State Sch. & Hosp. v. Halderman, 465 U.S. 89 (1984) **10:** 86, 98

Pennsylvania State Police v. Pennsylvania Human Relations Comm'n, 72 Pa. Commw. 520, 457 A.2d 584, 36 FEP Cases 602 (1983) **4:** 899

Perez v. Globe Airport Sec. Servs., Inc., 253 F.3d 1280, 86 FEP Cases 613 (11th Cir. 2001) **10:** 317, 326

Perfetti v. First Nat'l Bank of Chi., 950 F.2d 449, 57 FEP Cases 720 (7th Cir. 1991), *cert. denied,* 505 U.S. 1205 (1992) **7:** 44

Pernice v. City of Chi., 237 F.3d 783, 11 AD Cases 608 (7th Cir. 2001) **5:** 283

Pesterfield v. Tennessee Valley Auth., 941 F.2d 437, 1 AD Cases 1858 (6th Cir. 1991) **1:** 68; **7:** 287; **8:** 103

Peters
—v. Baldwin Union Free Sch. Dist., 320 F.3d 164, 13 AD Cases 1793 (2d Cir. 2003) **2:** 151; **5:** 434

—v. Mauston, City of, 311 F.3d 835, 13 AD Cases 1351 (7th Cir. 2002)   *2:* 191; *5:* 201
Petersen v. University of Wis. Bd. of Regents, 818 F. Supp. 1276, 2 AD Cases 735 (W.D. Wis. 1993)   *10:* 38, 47, 58, 60
Peyton v. Otis Elevator Co., 72 F. Supp. 2d 915, 10 AD Cases 1148 (N.D. Ill. 1999)   *5:* 331
PGA Tour, Inc. v. Martin, 532 U.S. 661, 11 AD Cases 1281 (2001)   *6:* 35, 45, 156, 401
Phelps v. Optima Health, Inc., 251 F.3d 21, 11 AD Cases 1487 (1st Cir. 2001)   *5:* 217; *8:* 150
Philadelphia Elec. Co. v. Pennsylvania Human Relations Comm'n, 68 Pa. Commw. 212, 448 A.2d 701, 36 FEP Cases 593 (1982)   *4:* 906
Pickens v. Soo Line R.R., 264 F.3d 773, 12 AD Cases 333 (8th Cir. 2001), *cert. denied*, 535 U.S. 1057 (2002)   *8:* 188
Pickern v. Holiday Quality Foods Inc., 293 F.3d 1133, 13 AD Cases 409 (9th Cir. 2002)   *6:* 380
Pollard
—v. E.I. du Pont de Nemours & Co., 532 U.S. 843, 85 FEP Cases 1217 (2001)   *10:* 117, 122, 123
—v. High's of Balt., Inc., 281 F.3d 462, 12 AD Cases 1409 (4th Cir.), *cert. denied*, 517 U.S. 827 (2002)   *5:* 115
Pollin v. Paralyzed Veterans of Am. *See* Paralyzed Veterans of Am. v. Ellerbe Becket Architects & Eng'rs, P.C.
Pona v. Whittaker's, Inc., 155 F.3d 1034, 8 AD Cases 968 (8th Cir. 1998), *cert. denied*, 526 U.S. 1131 (1999)   *6:* 263
Pond v. Michelin N. Am., Inc., 183 F.3d 592, 9 AD Cases 795 (7th Cir. 1999)   *10:* 279
Popko v. Pennsylvania State Univ., 994 F. Supp. 293, 9 AD Cases 131 (M.D. Pa. 1998), *on remand*, 84 F. Supp. 2d 589, 10 AD Cases 1404 (M.D. Pa. 2000), *aff'd*, 254 F.3d 1078 (3d Cir. 2001)   *5:* 58, 502

Porter v. Adams, 639 F.2d 273, 25 FEP Cases 1107 (5th Cir. 1981)   *2:* 227
Potter v. Xerox Corp., 88 F. Supp. 2d 109, 82 FEP Cases 1116 (W.D.N.Y. 2000), *aff'd*, 2001 U.S. App. LEXIS 329 (2d Cir. 2001)   *8:* 173
Potvin v. Champlain Cable Corp., 165 Vt. 504, 687 A.2d 95, 6 AD Cases 1493 (1996)   *4:* 1036
Prado v. Continental Air Transp. Co., 982 F. Supp. 1304 (N.D. Ill. 1997)   *7:* 121, 122
Presinzano v. Hoffman-LaRoche, Inc., 726 F.2d 105, 1 AD Cases 552 (3d Cir. 1984)   *2:* 251
Pressman v. UNC Charlotte, 78 N.C. App. 296, 337 S.E.2d 644 (1985)   *4:* 791
Prevo's Family Mkt., Inc.; EEOC v., 135 F.3d 1089, 8 AD Cases 401 (6th Cir. 1998)   *5:* 365; *8:* 101, 102
Prewitt v. U.S. Postal Serv., 662 F.2d 292, 1 AD Cases 273 (5th Cir. 1981)   *2:* 24, 155, 203, 287, 304; *8:* 44; *10:* 61, 63
Price v. City of Fort Wayne, 117 F.3d 1022, 3 WH Cases 2d 1729 (7th Cir. 1997)   *9:* 26
Prillman v. United Air Lines, Inc., 53 Cal. App. 4th 935 (1997)   *4:* 67, 73
Pryor v. Trane Co., 138 F.3d 1024, 8 AD Cases 271 (5th Cir. 1998)   *5:* 118
Public Employees Ret. Sys. of Ohio v. Betts, 492 U.S. 158, 11 EB Cases 1049 (1989)   *9:* 422–24, 502
Publix Supermarkets, Inc. v. Commission on Human Relations, 470 So. 2d 754 (Fla. Dist. Ct. App. 1985)   *4:* 160
Pushkin v. Regents of the Univ. of Colo., 658 F.2d 1372, 2 AD Cases 11 (10th Cir. 1981)   *2:* 286, 298; *5:* 28

Q

Quigley
—v. Austeel Lemont Co., 79 F. Supp. 2d 941, 10 AD Cases 351 (N.D. Ill. 2000)   *5:* 260
—v. KPMG Peat Marwick LLP, 330 N.J.

Quigley—*Cont'd*
Super. 252, 749 A.2d 405, 82 FEP Cases 988 (2000) *10:* 305
Quinn v. City of Los Angeles, 84 Cal. App. 4th 472, 11 AD Cases 207 (2000) *4:* 64
Quint v. A.E. Staley Mfg. Co., 172 F.3d 1, 9 AD Cases 242 (1st Cir.), *cert. denied*, 535 U.S. 1023 (1999) *5:* 120; *10:* 340

R

Rakity v. Dillon Cos., 302 F.3d 1152, 13 AD Cases 896 (10th Cir. 2002) *5:* 89, 146, 164
Ralph v. Lucent Techs., Inc., 135 F.3d 166, 7 AD Cases 1345 (1st Cir. 1998) *8:* 198, 273; *9:* 53
Ramirez v. National Distillers & Chem. Corp., 586 F.2d 1315, 18 FEP Cases 966 (9th Cir. 1978) *10:* 10
Randolph-Sheppard Vendors of Am. v. Weinberger, 795 F.2d 90 (D.C. Cir. 1986) *2:* 205
Rascon v. U.S. W. Communications, Inc., 143 F.3d 1324, 8 AD Cases 541 (10th Cir. 1998) *5:* 231; *8:* 267; *9:* 144
Rasimas v. Michigan Dep't of Mental Health, 714 F.2d 614, 32 FEP Cases 688 (6th Cir. 1983), *cert. denied*, 466 U.S. 950 (1984) *10:* 12
Rauen v. United States Tobacco Mfg., 319 F.3d 891, 13 AD Cases 1797 (7th Cir. 2003) *8:* 208
Rauenhorst v. U.S. Dep't of Transp., 95 F.3d 715, 5 AD Cases 1621 (8th Cir. 1996) *9:* 310
Ray
—v. Glidden Co., 85 F.3d 227, 5 AD Cases 991 (5th Cir. 1996) *5:* 70
—v. School Dist. of DeSoto County, 666 F. Supp. 1524 (M.D. Fla. 1987) *5:* 336
Raytheon Co. v. Hernandez. *See* Hernandez v. Hughes Missile Sys. Co.
Redd
—v. Rubin, 34 F. Supp. 2d 1, 8 AD Cases 1787 (D.D.C. 1998) *2:* 306

—v. Summers, 232 F.3d 933, 11 AD Cases 410 (D.C. Cir. 2000) *2:* 50
Redding v. Chicago Transit Auth., 11 AD Cases 157 (N.D. Ill. 2000) *5:* 327
Reed
—v. LePage Bakeries, Inc., 244 F.3d 254, 11 AD Cases 1150 (1st Cir. 2001) *5:* 444; *8:* 51; *10:* 203
—v. Petroleum Helicopters, Inc., 218 F.3d 477, 10 AD Cases 1426 (5th Cir. 2000) *8:* 270; *9:* 258, 263, 478
Reese
—v. Commercial Credit Corp., 955 F. Supp. 567, 3 WH Cases 870 (D.S.C. 1997) *10:* 320
—v. Sears, Roebuck & Co., 107 Wash. 2d 563, 731 P.2d 497, 1 AD Cases 1012 (1987) *4:* 1070
Reeves v. Johnson Controls World Servs., 140 F.3d 144, 7 AD Cases 1675 (2d Cir. 1998) *5:* 416
Rehling v. City of Chi., 207 F.3d 1009, 10 AD Cases 589 (7th Cir. 2000) *8:* 78
Reiff v. Interim Pers., Inc., 906 F. Supp. 1280, 5 AD Cases 740 (D. Minn. 1995) *9:* 237
Reigel v. Kaiser Found. Health Plan of N.C., 859 F. Supp. 963, 3 AD Cases 577 (E.D.N.C. 1994) *9:* 145, 237
Rembert v. Ryan's Family Steak Houses, Inc., 596 N.W. 2d 208 (Mich. Ct. App. 1999) *10:* 325
Renaud v. Wyoming Dep't of Family Servs., 203 F.3d 723, 5 WH Cases 2d 1505 (10th Cir. 2000) *5:* 287
Rendon v. Valleycrest Prods., 294 F.3d 1279, 13 AD Cases 404 (11th Cir. 2002) *6:* 98–100
Rhoads v. Federal Deposit Ins. Corp., 257 F.3d 373 (4th Cir. 2001), *cert. denied*, 535 U.S. 933 (2002) *5:* 157
Richards
—v. CH2M Hill, Inc., 26 Cal. 4th 798, 12 AD Cases 129 (2001) *4:* 62
—v. Topeka, City of, 173 F.3d 1247, 9 AD Cases 333 (10th Cir. 1999) *5:* 160
Richberg; United States v., 398 F.2d 523 (5th Cir. 1968) *6:* 126

Riel v. Electronic Data Sys. Corp., 99 F.3d 678 (5th Cir. 1996) *10:* 203
Rinehimer v. Cemcolift, Inc., 292 F.3d 375, 13 AD Cases 110 (3d Cir. 2002) *5:* 162, 163
Rissetto v. Plumbers & Steamfitters Local 343, 94 F.3d 597, 71 FEP Cases 1057 (9th Cir. 1996) *5:* 231; *9:* 140, 237
Ristrom v. Asbestos Workers Local 34 Joint Apprentice Comm., 370 F.3d 763, 15 AD Cases 1057 (8th Cir.), *reh'g denied*, 2004 U.S. App. LEXIS 15037 (2004) *5:* 413; *7:* 171
Rivera v. Heyman, 157 F.3d 101, 8 AD Cases 758 (2d Cir. 1998) *10:* 77
Rizzo v. Children's World Learning Ctrs., Inc.
—84 F.3d 758, 5 AD Cases 1155 (5th Cir. 1996), *cert. denied*, 531 U.S. 958 (2000) *7:* 280; *9:* 291
—213 F.3d 209, 10 AD Cases 976 (5th Cir.), *cert. denied*, 531 U.S. 958 (2000) *8:* 250
R.J. Gallagher Co.; EEOC v., 181 F.3d 645, 9 AD Cases 917 (5th Cir. 1999) *5:* 147, 490
Robb v. Horizon Credit Union, 66 F. Supp. 2d 913, 9 AD Cases 1365 (C.D. Ill. 1999) *5:* 418, 419
Robertson
—v. Granite City Cmty. Unit Sch. Dist. No. 9, 684 F. Supp. 1002 (S.D. Ill. 1988) *5:* 337
—v. Neuromedical Ctr., 161 F.3d 292 (5th Cir. 1998), *cert. denied*, 526 U.S. 1098 (1999) *8:* 220, 242
Robinson
—v. Dana Corp., 656 N.E.2d 540 (Ind. Ct. App. 1995) *4:* 321, 322
—v. Fair Employment & Hous. Comm'n, 2 Cal. 4th 226, 825 P.2d 781, 58 FEP Cases 887 (1992) *4:* 56
—v. Friendswood, City of, 890 F. Supp. 616, 5 AD Cases 105 (S.D. Tex. 1995) *9:* 52
—v. Neodata Servs., Inc., 94 F.3d 499, 5 AD Cases 1441 (8th Cir. 1996) *9:* 238
Rockwell Int'l Corp.; EEOC v., 60 F. Supp. 2d 791, 9 AD Cases 1092 (N.D. Ill. 1999), *aff'd*, 243 F.3d 1012, 11 AD Cases 929 (7th Cir. 2001) *5:* 155; *7:* 130; *9:* 338; *10:* 186, 188
Rodgers v. Magnet Cove Pub. Sch., 34 F.3d 642, 3 AD Cases 971 (8th Cir. 1994) *2:* 295
Roe v. *See name of opposing party*
Rogers
—v. Department of Health & Envtl. Control, 174 F.3d 431, 9 AD Cases 257 (4th Cir. 1999) *9:* 506, 513
—v. Exxon Research & Eng'g Co., 550 F.2d 834 (3d Cir. 1977) *3:* 503
—v. Frito Lay, Inc., 611 F.2d 1074, 1 AD Cases 131 (5th Cir.), *cert. denied*, 449 U.S. 889 (1980) *2:* 6, 7
—v. International Marine Terminals, Inc., 87 F.3d 755, 5 AD Cases 1115 (5th Cir. 1996) *9:* 39, 69, 477
Rohan v. Networks Presentations LLC, 375 F.3d 266, 15 AD Cases 1313 (4th Cir. 2004) *5:* 406
Rojas v. TK Communications, 87 F.3d 745, 71 FEP Cases 664 (5th Cir. 1996) *10:* 315
Rosebud Sioux Tribe, In re, No. 93-504-1, 1994 WL 603015 (Dep't of Health & Human Servs., Dep'tl App. Bd., Sept. 25, 1992) *5:* 335
Rosenberg v. Merrill Lynch, Pierce, Fenner & Smith, Inc., 170 F.3d 1 (1st Cir. 1999) *10:* 297
Ross v. Campbell Soup Co., 237 F.3d 701, 11 AD Cases 577 (6th Cir. 2001) *5:* 161
Rouke v. Oakwood Hosp. Corp., 580 N.W.2d 397 (Mich. App. 1998) *4:* 555
Rowles v. Automated Prod. Sys., Inc., 92 F. Supp. 2d 424, 10 AD Cases 1542 (M.D. Pa. 2000) *5:* 502, 506
Russell
—v. Clark County Sch. Dist., 2000 U.S. App. LEXIS 17460 (9th Cir. 2000) *5:* 84
—v. Cooley Dickinson Hosp., Inc., 437 Mass. 433, 772 N.E.2d 1054, 13 AD Cases 709 (2002) *4:* 522
—v. Frank, 2 AD Cases 243 (D. Mass.

Russell—*Cont'd*
1991), *aff'd*, 971 F.2d 744, 2 AD Cases 1872 (1st Cir. 1992), *cert. denied*, 507 U.S. 925 (1993)   **7:** 287
—v. Rolfs, 893 F.2d 1033 (9th Cir. 1990), *cert. denied*, 501 U.S. 1260 (1991)   **9:** 140
Ruth Anne M. v. Alvin Indep. Sch. Dist., 532 F. Supp. 450 (S.D. Tex. 1982) **10:** 154

S

Safrit v. Cone Mills Corp., 248 F.3d 306, 85 FEP Cases 833 (4th Cir. 2001) **10:** 340
St. Mary's Honor Ctr. v. Hicks, 509 U.S. 502, 62 FEP Cases 96 (1993)   **7:** 13, 16–18, 21, 22
St. Peter v. AMPAK-Div. of Gatewood Prods., Inc., 199 W. Va. 365, 484 S.E.2d 481, 7 AD Cases 1709 (1997)   **4:** 1084
Salisbury v. Art Van Furniture, 938 F. Supp. 435 (W.D. Mich. 1996)   **5:** 284
Salley v. Circuit City Stores, Inc., 7 AD Cases 852 (E.D. Pa. 1997), *aff'd*, 160 F.3d 977, 8 AD Cases 1407 (3d Cir. 1998)   **5:** 256
Salmon v. Dade County Sch. Bd., 4 F. Supp. 2d 1157 (S.D. Fla. 1998)   **4:** 183, 191, 192; **8:** 39
Sam Teague, Ltd. v. Hawaii Civil Rights Comm'n, 89 Haw. 269, 971 P.2d 1104 (1999)   **4:** 235
Sanchez v. Henderson, 188 F.3d 740, 9 AD Cases 1006 (7th Cir. 1999), *cert. denied*, 528 U.S. 1173 (2000)   **5:** 166
Sanders v. Arneson Prods., 91 F.3d 1351, 5 AD Cases 1292 (9th Cir. 1996), *cert. denied*, 520 U.S. 1116 (1997)   **7:** 15
Sant v. Mack Trucks, Inc., 424 F. Supp. 621 (N.D. Cal. 1976)   **3:** 503
Sapp v. MHI P'ship, 199 F. Supp. 2d 578 (N.D. Tex. 2002)   **6:** 49
Sara Lee Corp.; EEOC v., 237 F.3d 349, 11 AD Cases 595 (4th Cir. 2001)   **5:** 81, 123, 403, 503, 505, 535; **8:** 106, 109; **10:** 181

Satarino v. A.G. Edwards & Sons, Inc., 941 F. Supp. 609, 3 WH Cases 2d 934 (N.D. Tex. 1996)   **10:** 315
Savage v. Glendale Union High School Dist. No. 205, 343 F.3d 1036, 14 AD Cases 1412 (9th Cir. 2003), *cert. denied*, 124 S. Ct. 2067 (2004)   **2:** 101
Scaglione v. Kraftmaid Cabinetry, Inc., 2002 Ohio 6917, 19 IER Cases 764 (2002)   **10:** 305
Schaaf v. Association of Educ. Therapists, 1995 WL 381979 (N.D.Cal. 1995)   **6:** 76
Schmidt
—v. Methodist Hosp. of Ind., Inc., 89 F.3d 342, 5 AD Cases 1340 (7th Cir. 1996)   **9:** 52
—v. Safeway, Inc., 864 F. Supp. 991, 3 AD Cases 1141 (D. Or. 1994)   **8:** 60, 73; **9:** 6
Schmidt-Tiago Constr. Co., 286 NLRB 342, 127 LRRM 1246 (1987)   **9:** 363
Schneiker v. Fortis Ins. Co., 200 F.3d 1055, 10 AD Cases 75 (7th Cir. 2000) **5:** 105, 424; **8:** 276
School Bd. of Nassau County v. Arline, 480 U.S. 273, 1 AD Cases 1026 (1987) **1:** 63, 64; **2:** 145, 149, 152–54, 167, 168; **3:** 74, 75, 388; **5:** 18, 21, 74; **6:** 147; **7:** 243
Schrader v. Fred A. Ray M.D., P.C., 296 F.3d 968, 13 AD Cases 481 (10th Cir. 2002)   **2:** 81
Schuler v. SuperValu, Inc., 336 F.3d 702, 14 AD Cases 1115 (8th Cir. 2003)   **5:** 530; **7:** 137, 159
Scott
—v. Beverly Enter.-Kansas, Inc., 968 F. Supp. 1430 (D. Kan. 1997)   **5:** 260
—v. Gulf Oil Corp., 754 F.2d 1499 (9th Cir. 1985)   **9:** 395
Seaman v. CSPH, Inc., 179 F.3d 297, 5 WH Cases 2d 673 (5th Cir. 1999) **5:** 445
Sears, Roebuck & Co.; EEOC v., 233 F.3d 432, 11 AD Cases 193 (7th Cir. 2000) **5:** 136; **10:** 184
Seidle v. Provident Mut. Life Ins. Co.,

871 F. Supp. 238, 2 WH Cases 2d 913 (E.D. Pa. 1994) **9:** 26
Selenke v. Medical Imaging of Colo., 248 F.3d 1249, 11 AD Cases 1395 (10th Cir. 2001) **1:** 77
Seminole Tribe of Fla. v. Florida, 517 U.S. 44 (1996) **2:** 99; **10:** 85, 92, 93, 102
Seus v. John Nuveen & Co., 146 F.3d 175 (3d Cir. 1998) **10:** 297
Shafer v. Preston Mem'l Hosp. Corp., 107 F.3d 274, 6 AD Cases 682 (4th Cir. 1997) **5:** 171, 257, 258
Shankle v. B-G Maint. Mgmt. of Colorado, Inc., 163 F.3d 1230 (10th Cir. 1999) **10:** 297
Shapiro v. Township of Lakewood, 292 F.3d 356, 13 AD Cases 106 (3d Cir. 2002) **8:** 61, 163
Shaw
—v. Delta Air Lines, Inc., 463 U.S. 85, 4 EB Cases 1593 (1983) **9:** 395
—v. Greenwich Anesthesiology Assocs., P.C., 137 F. Supp. 2d 48, 11 AD Cases 1354 (D. Conn. 2001) **4:** 107
Shea v. Tisch, 870 F.2d 786, 1 AD Cases 1461 (1st Cir. 1989) **9:** 370
Sheehan v. City of Gloucester, 321 F.3d 21, 14 AD Cases 1 (1st Cir. 2003) **5:** 100, 155, 481; **10:** 186
Sheller v. Frank's Nursery & Crafts, Inc., 957 F. Supp. 150, 73 FEP Cases 870 (N.D. Ill. 1997) **10:** 320
Shell Oil Co. v. Trailer & Truck Repair Co., 828 F.2d 205 (3d Cir. 1987) **9:** 483
Sheppard v. Riverview Nursing Ctr., 88 F.3d 1332, 71 FEP Cases 218 (4th Cir. 1996) **10:** 374
Sherer v. GE Capital Corp., 59 F. Supp. 2d 1132, 9 AD Cases 1820 (D. Kan. 1999) **5:** 419
Shinault v. American Airlines, Inc., 738 F. Supp. 193 (S.D. Miss. 1990), *aff'd in part, rev'd in part*, 936 F.2d 796 (5th Cir. 1991) **10:** 155
Shiplett v. National R.R. Passenger Corp., 182 F.3d 918 (6th Cir. 1999), *cert. denied*, 528 U.S. 1078 (2000) **5:** 276
Shipley v. City of University City, Mo., 195 F.3d 1020, 9 AD Cases 1775 (8th Cir. 1999) **5:** 155; **10:** 186
Siefken v. Village of Arlington Heights, 65 F.3d 664, 4 AD Cases 1441 (7th Cir. 1995) **8:** 221
Simmons v. Wilcox, 911 F.2d 1077 (5th Cir. 1990) **9:** 397
Simo v. Home Health & Hospice Care, 906 F. Supp. 714, 5 AD Cases 1461 (D.N.H. 1995) **5:** 233
Simon v. St. Louis County, 656 F.2d 316, 1 AD Cases 268 (8th Cir. 1981) **7:** 54
Simpson v. Reynolds Metals Co., 629 F.2d 1226, 1 AD Cases 206 (7th Cir. 1980) **2:** 80
Sisson v. Helms, 751 F.2d 991, 1 AD Cases 670 (9th Cir.), *cert. denied*, 474 U.S. 846, 1 AD Cases 830 (1985) **5:** 25
Skaggs v. Elk Run Coal Co., 198 W. Va. 51, 479 S.E. 2d 561, 6 AD Cases 965 (1996) **4:** 1085
Skerski v. Time Warner Cable Co., 257 F.3d 273, 11 AD Cases 1665 (3d Cir. 2001) **5:** 205, 206; **8:** 154; **10:** 197, 198
Smallwood v. Witco Corp., 1995 U.S. Dist. LEXIS (S.D.N.Y. 1995) **8:** 140
Smith
—v. Ameritech, 129 F.3d 857, 7 AD Cases 917 (6th Cir. 1997) **8:** 38, 210
—v. Barton, 914 F.2d 1330, 1 AD Cases 1689 (9th Cir. 1990), *cert. denied*, 501 U.S. 1217 (1991) **2:** 286, 297; **10:** 47, 60
—v. Chrysler Corp., 155 F.3d 799, 8 AD Cases 1084 (6th Cir. 1988) **7:** 7
—v. City of Des Moines, Iowa, 99 F.3d 1466, 6 AD Cases 14 (8th Cir. 1996) **7:** 276
—v. Diffee Ford-Lincoln-Mercury, Inc., 298 F.3d 955, 13 AD Cases 588 (10th Cir. 2002) **8:** 182
—v. Midland Brake, Inc.
——180 F.3d 1154, 9 AD Cases 738 (10th Cir. 1999) **8:** 50, 170

Smith—*Cont'd*
——911 F. Supp. 1351, 5 AD Cases 386 (D. Kan. 1995), *aff'd*, 138 F.3d 1304, 7 AD 1560 (10th Cir. 1998)   **9:** 72
—v. Montgomery Ward & Co., 388 F.2d 291 (6th Cir. 1968)   **5:** 233
—v. Travelers Ins. Co., 438 F.2d 373 (6th Cir.), *cert. denied*, 404 U.S. 832 (1971)   **9:** 483
—v. U.S. Postal Serv., 742 F.2d 257, 1 AD Cases 620 (6th Cir. 1984)   **2:** 305; **10:** 54, 78
—v. Young Men's Christian Ass'n of Montgomery, 462 F.2d 634 (5th Cir. 1972)   **6:** 126

Snyder
—v. Medical Serv. Corp., 98 Wash. App. 315, 988 P.2d 1023, 16 IER Cases 1337 (1999)   **4:** 1076
—v. San Diego Flowers, 21 F. Supp. 2d 1207, 8 AD Cases 1050 (S.D. Cal. 1998)   **6:** 398

Soentgen v. Quain & Ramstad Clinic, 467 N.W.2d 73 (N.D. 1991)   **4:** 810

Sorensen v. University of Utah Hosp., 194 F.3d 1084, 9 AD Cases 1490 (10th Cir. 1999)   **5:** 147

Southeastern Cmty. Coll. v. Davis, 442 U.S. 397, 2 AD Cases 1 (1979)   **2:** 166; **5:** 7; **7:** 188, 229, 242

Southern Ohio Coal v. Donovan, 774 F.2d 693 (6th Cir. 1985)   **10:** 57

Spades v. City of Walnut Ridge, Ark., 186 F.3d 897, 9 AD Cases 1015 (8th Cir. 1999)   **5:** 134, 418

Spence v. Straw, 54 F.3d 196, 4 AD Cases 528 (3d Cir. 1995)   **2:** 287; **10:** 78

Spicer v. Martin-Brower Co., 177 Ga. App. 197, 338 S.E.2d 773, 58 FEP Cases 1372 (1985)   **4:** 204

Spitzer v. Good Guys, Inc., 80 Cal. App. 4th 1376, 96 Cal. Rptr. 2d 236, 10 AD Cases 1638 (2000)   **4:** 63; **7:** 201, 204; **8:** 123, 166, 167, 255, 256

Sprogis v. United Air Lines, 517 F.2d 387, 10 FEP Cases 1249 (7th Cir. 1975)   **10:** 369

State Div. of Human Rights v. Xerox Corp., 102 A.D. 2d 543, 478 N.Y.S.2d 982, 35 FEP Cases 819 (1984)   **4:** 769

Staub v. Boeing Co., 919 F. Supp. 366, 8 AD Cases 323 (W.D. Wash. 1996)   **4:** 1076

Steele
—v. Louisville & Nashville R.R., 323 U.S. 192, 15 LRRM 708 (1944)   **9:** 385
—v. Thiokol Corp., 241 F.3d 1248, 11 AD Cases 859 (10th Cir. 2001)   **5:** 83

Steger v. Franco, Inc., 228 F.3d 889, 11 AD Cases 51 (8th Cir. 2000)   **6:** 402, 403

Stein v. Ashcroft, 284 F.3d 721 (7th Cir. 2002)   **2:** 137

Stevanovic v. Modern Tool & Die Co., No. 67225, 1995 Ohio App. LEXIS 1628 (8th App. Dist. Apr. 20, 1995)   **4:** 835

Stevens
—v. Inland Waters, Inc., 220 Mich. App. 212, 559 N.W.2d 61, 6 AD Cases 490 (1996)   **5:** 49
—v. Stubbs, 576 F. Supp. 1409, 1 AD Cases 546 (N.D. Ga. 1983)   **1:** 50

Stinson v. West Suburban Hosp. Med. Ctr., 1998 WL 188938 (N.D. Ill. 1998)   **7:** 51, 134

Stock v. Grantham, 125 N.M. 564, 964 P.2d 125 (1998)   **4:** 744

Stolmeier v. Yellow Freight Sys., Inc., 3 AD Cases 65 (D. Or. 1994)   **9:** 52

Stone v. City of Mount Vernon, 118 F.3d 92, 6 AD Cases 1685 (2d Cir. 1997), *cert. denied*, 522 U.S. 1112 (1998)   **9:** 281

Stout v. Young Men's Christian Ass'n of Bessemer, Ala., 404 F.2d 687 (5th Cir. 1968)   **6:** 126

Stoutenborough v. National Football League, 59 F.3d 580, 4 AD Cases 1035 (6th Cir.) *cert. denied*, 516 U.S. 1028 (1995)   **6:** 75

Stowe-Pharr Mills, Inc.; EEOC v., 216 F.3d 373, 10 AD Cases 1153 (4th Cir. 2000)   **8:** 270; **9:** 257

Strathie v. Department of Transp., 716 F.2d 227, 1 AD Cases 486 (3d Cir. 1983)   **7:** 184

Sullivan
—v. Ratheon Corp., 262 F.3d 41, 12 AD Cases 634 (1st Cir. 2001), *cert. denied*, 534 U.S. 1118 (2002)   *4:* 520; *9:* 263
—v. River Valley Sch. Dist., 197 F.3d 804, 9 AD Cases 1711 (6th Cir. 1999), *cert. denied*, 530 U.S. 1262 (2000)   *5:* 436
Sutton v. United Air Lines, Inc., 527 U.S. 471, 9 AD Cases 673 (1999)   *1:* 59, 60, 86; *2:* 134, 149, 150, 319; *5:* 73, 74, 124, 125, 137, 155, 350, 417, 423, 450, 451, 493, 501, 528; *8:* 41; *9:* 239; *10:* 182, 185, 186
Swain v. Hillsborough County Sch. Bd., 146 F.3d 855, 8 AD Cases 488 (11th Cir. 1998)   *7:* 245
Swanks v. Washington Metro. Area Transit Auth., 116 F.3d 582, 6 AD Cases 1544 (D.C. Cir. 1997)   *5:* 231; *8:* 267; *9:* 144, 240
Swanson v. University of Cincinnati, 268 F.3d 307, 12 AD Cases 417 (6th Cir. 2001)   *2:* 140; *5:* 134, 157, 418

T

Tadie v. Rehabilitation Hosp., 6 F. Supp. 2d 125 (D.R.I. 1998)   *4:* 928
Talavera v. Palm Beach County Sch. Bd., 129 F.3d 1214, 7 AD Cases 1025 (11th Cir. 1997)   *9:* 144, 240
Talk v. Delta Airlines, Inc., 165 F.3d 1021, 9 AD Cases 5 (5th Cir. 1999)   *5:* 159
Tanberg v. Weld County Sheriff, 787 F. Supp. 970, 2 AD Cases 148 (D. Colo. 1992)   *10:* 157
Tate v. Farmland Indus., Inc., 268 F.3d 989, 12 AD Cases 519 (10th Cir. 2001)   *5:* 209; *9:* 304; *10:* 245
Taylor
—v. Nimock's Oil Co., 214 F.3d 957, 10 AD Cases 1069 (8th Cir. 2000)   *5:* 168, 486
—v. Pathmark Stores, 177 F.3d 180, 9 AD Cases 497 (3d Cir. 1999)   *5:* 165
—v. Pepsi-Cola 196 F.3d 1106, 9 AD Cases 1731 (10th Cir. 1999)   *8:* 185

—v. Phoenixville Sch. Dist.
——174 F.3d 142, 9 AD Cases 311 (3d Cir. 1999)   *5:* 422; *10:* 207, 211–13
——184 F.3d 296, 9 AD Cases 1187 (3d Cir. 1999)   *5:* 90, 123; *8:* 44, 69, 71, 75
Teahan v. Metro-North Commuter R.R. Co.
—951 F.2d 511, 2 AD Cases 84 (2d Cir. 1991), *cert. denied*, 506 U.S. 815 (1992)   *9:* 40, 70
—80 F.3d 50, 5 AD Cases 603 (2d Cir. 1996)   *5:* 263
Templeton v. Neodata Servs., 162 F.3d 617, 8 AD Cases 1615 (10th Cir. 1998)   *8:* 95
Tennessee v. Lane, 541 U.S. 509, 15 AD Cases 865 (2004)   *6:* 25
Terrell v. USAir, 132 F.3d 621, 8 AD Cases 529 (11th Cir. 1998)   *8:* 201, 223
Terry v. Norfolk S. Ry., 948 F. Supp. 1058, 6 AD Cases 802 (N.D. Ga. 1996)   *9:* 237
Texas Bus Lines; EEOC v., 923 F. Supp. 965, 5 AD Cases 878 (S.D. Tex. 1996)   *7:* 36–38, 121, 123, 154, 155
Texas Dep't of Cmty. Affairs v. Burdine, 450 U.S. 248, 25 FEP Cases 113 (1981)   *10:* 238
Thoele v. Henderson, 2001 U.S. Dist. LEXIS 3522 (N.D. Ill. 2001)   *10:* 343–46
Thomas
—v. Atascadero Unified Sch. Dist., 662 F. Supp. 376 (C.D. Cal. 1987)   *5:* 336
—v. Fort Myers Hous. Auth., 955 F. Supp. 1463, 6 AD Cases 735 (M.D. Fla. 1997)   *9:* 145, 237
—v. General Servs. Admin., No. 49 FEP Cases 1602 (D.D.C. 1989)   *7:* 292
Thompson
—v. Berta Enters., Inc., 72 Wash. App. 531, 864 P.2d 983, 68 FEP Cases 1643 (1994)   *4:* 1073
—v. Borg-Warner Protective Servs. Corp., 1996 U.S. Dist. LEXIS 4781 (N.D. Cal. Mar. 11, 1996)   *7:* 140

Thompson—*Cont'd*
—v. Holy Family Hosp., 121 F.3d 537, 7 AD Cases 308 (9th Cir. 1997)   **7:** 245
—v. Spring Mills, Inc., 576 F. Supp. 651 (D.S.C. 1982)   **10:** 66
Thornton v. McClatchy Newspapers, Inc.
—261 F.3d 789, 12 AD Cases 211 (9th Cir. 2001)   **1:** 58
—292 F.3d 1045, 13 AD Cases 203 (9th Cir. 2002)   **5:** 71
Thrope v. Ohio, 19 F. Supp. 2d 816, 8 AD Cases 1133 (S.D. Ohio 1998)   **10:** 100
Tice v. Centre Area Transp. Auth., 247 F.3d 506, 11 AD Cases (3d Cir. 2001)   **5:** 166
Tillman v. Wheaton-Haven Recreation Ass'n, 410 U.S. 431 (1973)   **6:** 126
Tinder v. Pinkerton Sec., 305 F.3d 728, 89 FEP Cases 1537 (7th Cir. 2002)   **10:** 305
Tockes v. Air-Land Transp. Serv., Inc., 343 F.3d 895, 14 AD Cases 1389 (7th Cir. 2003), *cert. denied*, 124 S. Ct. 1414, 15 AD Cases 416 (2004)   **5:** 161
Todd v. Academy Corp., 57 F. Supp. 2d 448, 9 AD Cases 1306 (S.D. Tex. 1999)   **5:** 502
Tolbert v. United States, 916 F.2d 245, 56 FEP Cases 152 (5th Cir. 1990)   **10:** 79
Tompkins v. United Healthcare of New England, Inc., 203 F.3d 90, 23 EB Cases 2967 (1st Cir. 2000)   **5:** 385; **6:** 67
Tordonato v. Colt's Mfg. Co., No. CV 9704816l0S, 2000 Conn. Super. LEXIS 3615 (Conn. Super. Ct. Dec. 26, 2000)   **4:** 107
Torres v. AT&T Broadband, LLC, 158 F. Supp. 2d 1035 (N.D. Cal. 2001)   **6:** 97
Toscano v. National Broad. Co., 12 AD Cases 768 (S.D.N.Y. 2000)   **5:** 251
Toussaint v. Sheriff of Cook County, No. 97 C 7866, 2000 WL 656642 (N.D. Ill. 2000)   **5:** 284
Towles v. United Healthcare Corp., 524 S.E.2d 839 (S.C. Ct. App. 1999)   **10:** 320
Toyota Motor Mfg., Ky. Inc. v. Williams, 534 U.S. 184, 12 AD Cases 993 (2002)   **1:** 43, 56, 57, 86; **5:** 77, 86–88; **10:** 180
Treadwell v. Alexander, 707 F.2d 473, 1 AD Cases 459 (11th Cir. 1983)   **1:** 93; **5:** 27; **7:** 260; **8:** 24, 44; **10:** 78
Treanor v. MCI Telecommunications Corp., 200 F.3d 570, 10 AD Cases 80 (8th Cir. 2000)   **8:** 204
Treglia v. Town of Manlius, 68 F. Supp. 2d 153, 10 AD Cases 1486 (N.D.N.Y. 1999), *vacated in part*, 313 F.3d 713, 13 AD Cases 1537 (2d Cir. 2002)   **5:** 502
Trowbridge v. Scranton Artificial Limb Co., 560 Pa. 640, 747 A.2d 862, 10 AD Cases 725 (2000)   **9:** 262
Truitt Mfg. Co.; NLRB v., 351 U.S. 149, 38 LRRM 2042 (1956)   **9:** 354
Trustees of Fraternal Order of Eagles, Milwaukee; United States v., 472 F. Supp. 1174 (E.D. Wis. 1979)   **6:** 126
Tsetseranos v. Tech Prototype, Inc., 893 F. Supp. 109, 4 AD Cases 1635 (D.N.H. 1995)   **4:** 698
Tuck v. HCA Health Servs. of Tenn., Inc., 7 F.3d 465, 2 AD Cases 1349 (6th Cir. 1993)   **2:** 286
Turco v. Hoechst Celanese Chem. Group, Inc., 101 F.3d 1090, 6 AD Cases 278 (5th Cir. 1996)   **5:** 460, 465; **9:** 180
Turkette; United States v., 425 U.S. 576 (1981)   **6:** 94
Tyndall v. National Educ. Ctrs. of Cal., Inc., 31 F.3d 209, 3 AD Cases 868 (4th Cir. 1994)   **8:** 213, 214; **9:** 34, 41, 69

U

United Air Lines, Inc. v. McMann, 434 U.S. 192, 1 EB Cases 1556 (1977)   **9:** 423, 502
United Parcel Serv., Inc.; EEOC v., 306 F.3d 794, 13 AD Cases 961 (9th Cir. 2002)   **5:** 79, 89; **9:** 306
United States v. *See name of opposing party*
United States Steel Corp. v. United States, 519 F.2d 359, 10 FEP Cases 1106 (3d Cir. 1975)   **10:** 380

University of Ala. v. Garrett, 531 U.S. 356, 11 AD Cases 737 (2001) *2:* 100
University of Md. Med. Sys. Corp.; Doe v., 50 F.3d 1261, 4 AD Cases 379 (4th Cir. 1995) *5:* 361; *10:* 261
UNUM Corp. v. United States, 886 F. Supp. 150 (D. Me. 1995) *5:* 233
U.S. Airways, Inc. v. Barnett, 535 U.S. 391, 12 AD Cases 1729 (2002) *5:* 535; *8:* 162; *10:* 201, 202, 278, 279
U.S. Postal Serv.; Doe v., 317 F.3d 339, 13 AD Cases 1801 (D.C. Cir. 2003) *5:* 393, 394

Voytek v. University of Cal., 5 AD Cases 1255 (N.D. Cal. 1994) *7:* 253, 286

W

Waddell v. Valley Forge Dental Assocs., Inc., 276 F.3d 1275, 12 AD Cases 1029 (11th Cir. 2001), *cert. denied*, 535 U.S. 1096, 13 AD Cases 192 (2002) *5:* 363; *8:* 249; *10:* 261
Waffle House, Inc.; EEOC v., 193 F.3d 805, 9 AD Cases 1313 (4th Cir. 1999), *rev'd and remanded*, 534 U.S. 279, 12 AD Cases 1001 (2002) *10:* 327–29
Waggoner v. Olin Corp, 169 F.3d 481, 9 AD Cases 88 (7th Cir. 1999) *9:* 477
Wagner v. NutraSweet Co., 95 F.3d 527, 72 FEP Cases 284 (7th Cir. 1996) *10:* 344
Wai v. Allstate Ins. Co., 75 F. Supp. 2d 1, 9 AD Cases 1588 (D.D.C. 1999) *5:* 385; *6:* 67
Waldrip v. General Elec. Co., 325 F.3d 652, 14 AD Cases 301 (5th Cir. 2003) *5:* 63, 89
Waldron v. SL Indus., 56 F.3d 491, 67 FEP Cases 1577 (3d Cir. 1995) *7:* 58
Waldrop v. Southern Co. Servs., 24 F.3d 152, 3 AD Cases 595 (11th Cir. 1994) *2:* 295, 297
Walker v. Ford Motor Co., 684 F.2d 1355, 29 FEP Cases 1259 (11th Cir. 1982) *2:* 230
Wallace v. Skadden, Arps, Slate, Meagher & Flom, 715 A.2d 873, 14 IER Cases 851 (D.C. 1998) *4:* 149
Walsh v. United Parcel Serv., Inc., 201 F.3d 718, 10 AD Cases 161 (6th Cir. 2000) *8:* 189, 239
Walton v. Mental Health Ass'n of S.E. Pa., 168 F.3d 661, 9 AD Cases 34 (3d Cir. 1999) *5:* 449
Wander v. Kaus, 304 F.3d 856, 13 AD Cases 1619 (9th Cir. 2002) *6:* 373
Ward
—v. Massachusetts Health Research Inst., Inc., 209 F.3d 29, 10 AD Cases

V

Vaca v. Sipes, 386 U.S. 171, 64 LRRM 2369 (1967) *9:* 387
Valdez v. Albuquerque Pub. Sch., 875 F. Supp. 740, 4 AD Cases 70 (D.N.M. 1994) *9:* 52
Vande Zande v. Wisconsin Dep't of Admin., 851 F. Supp. 353, 2 AD Cases 1846 (W.D. Wis. 1994), *aff'd*, 44 F.3d 538, 3 AD Cases 1636 (7th Cir. 1995) *8:* 211, 222, 232, 233; *9:* 52; *10:* 203, 204
Venclauskas v. State, No. CV 960471879, 1997 Conn. Super. LEXIS 1643 (Conn. Super. Ct. May 14, 1997) *4:* 107
Vickers v. Veterans Admin., 549 F. Supp. 85, 1 AD Cases 366 (W.D. Wash. 1982) *5:* 32
Viereck v. City of Gloucester City, 961 F. Supp. 703, 3 WH Cases 2d 1763 (D.N.J. 1997) *9:* 67
Vincent v. Wells Fargo Guard Servs., Inc. of Fla., 3 F. Supp. 2d 1405 (S.D. Fla. 1998) *4:* 178; *9:* 17
Violette v. International Bus. Machs. Corp., 962 F. Supp. 446, 7 AD Cases 395 (D. Vt. 1996), *aff'd*, 116 F.3d 466, 7 AD Cases 544 (2d Cir. 1997) *9:* 145, 237
Vollmert v. Wisconsin Dep't of Transp., 197 F.3d 293, 9 AD Cases 1704 (7th Cir. 1999) *8:* 158, 159

Ward—*Cont'd*
776 (1st Cir. 2000)   **5:** 188, 189, 222; **8:** 203, 241; **9:** 54; **10:** 276
—v. Westvaco Corp., 859 F. Supp. 608, 3 AD Cases 739 (D. Mass. 1994)   **9:** 491
Washington v. HCA Health Servs. of Tex., Inc., 152 F.3d 464, 8 AD Cases 1044 (5th Cir. 1998), *vacated,* 527 U.S. 1032, 9 AD Cases 768 (1999)   **5:** 130
Washington Metro. Area Transit Auth. v. DeArment, 1991 U.S. Dist. LEXIS 10391 (D.D.C. 1991)   **2:** 75, 76
Watkins v. J&S Oil Co., 164 F.3d 55, 5 WH Cases 2d 1 (1st Cir. 1998)   **9:** 41
Watson
—v. Lithonia Lighting & Nat'l Serv. Indus., Inc., 304 F.3d 749 (7th Cir. 2002), *cert. denied,* 537 U.S. 1193 (2003)   **8:** 147, 167
—v. Miami Beach, City of, 177 F.3d 932, 9 AD Cases 760 (11th Cir. 1999)   **5:** 48, 436
W.B. v. Matula, 67 F.3d 484 (3d Cir. 1995)   **2:** 295
Webb v. Clyde Choate Mental Heath Ctr., 230 F.3d 991, 11 AD Cases 97 (7th Cir. 2000)   **5:** 198, 199
Weber v. Strippit, Inc., 186 F.3d 907, 9 AD Cases 961 (8th Cir. 1999), *cert. denied,* 528 U.S. 1078 (2000)   **5:** 69, 482, 484; **8:** 18
Webner v. Titan Distribution, Inc., 267 F.3d 828, 12 AD Cases 513 (8th Cir. 2001)   **5:** 99
Webster
—v. Henderson, 2002 U.S. App. LEXIS 2877 (4th Cir. 2002)   **2:** 192
—v. Methodist Occupational Health Ctrs., Inc., 141 F.3d 1236, 8 AD Cases 33 (7th Cir. 1998)   **7:** 218
Weigel v. Target Stores, 122 F.3d 461, 7 AD Cases 358 (7th Cir. 1997)   **9:** 144, 240
Weiler v. Household Fin. Corp., 101 F.3d 519, 6 AD Cases 106 (7th Cir. 1996)   **9:** 37, 52, 238
Wellington v. Lyon County Sch. Dist., 187 F.3d 1150, 9 AD Cases 1177 (9th Cir. 1999)   **5:** 99

Wells v. Shalala, 228 F.3d 1137, 10 AD Cases 1795 (10th Cir. 2000)   **8:** 82
Wenzlaff v. NationsBank, 940 F. Supp. 889, 9 AD Cases 582 (D. Md. 1996)   **9:** 16
Weyer v. Twentieth Century Fox Film Corp., 198 F.3d 1104, 10 AD Cases 65 (9th Cir. 2000)   **5:** 383, 439; **6:** 64; **9:** 481, 513
Whillock v. Delta Air Lines, Inc., 926 F. Supp. 1555, 5 AD Cases 1027 (N.D. Ga. 1995), *aff'd,* 86 F.3d 1171, 7 AD Cases 1267 (11th Cir. 1996)   **8:** 51, 212; **9:** 52
Whitbeck v. Vital Signs, Inc., 116 F.3d 588, 6 AD Cases 1540 (D.C. Cir. 1997)   **4:** 154
White v. York Int'l Corp., 45 F.3d 357, 3 AD Cases 1746 (10th Cir. 1995)   **8:** 77, 165
Whitlock v. Donovan, 598 F. Supp. 126, 1 AD Cases 630 (D.D.C. 1984), *aff'd,* 790 F.2d 964, 2 AD Cases 624 (D.C. Cir. 1986)   **2:** 126
Whitlow v. Kentucky Mfg. Co., 762 S.W.2d 808 (Ky. Ct. App. 1988)   **4:** 401
Whittington v. State, 129 N.M. 221, 4 P.3d 668, 6 WH Cases 2d 1023 (Ct. App. 2000), *aff'd,* 45 P.3d 889, 7 WH Cases 2d 1456 (2002)   **10:** 96
Wilder v. Southeastern Pub. Serv. Auth., 869 F. Supp. 409, 4 AD Cases 838 (E.D. Va. 1994), *aff'd,* 69 F.3d 534, 5 AD Cases 256 (4th Cir. 1995)   **9:** 69
Williams
—v. Channel Master Satellite Sys., 101 F.3d 346, 6 AD Case 131 (4th Cir. 1996)   **4:** 779
—v. Charlotte, N.C., City of, 899 F. Supp. 1484, 4 AD Cases 1675 (W.D.N.C. 1995)   **9:** 52
—v. Ohio Dep't of Mental Health, 960 F. Supp. 1276, 7 AD Cases 1162 (S.D. Ohio 1997)   **10:** 100
—v. United Ins. Co. of Am., 253 F.3d 280, 11 AD Cases 1613 (7th Cir.), *cert. denied,* 534 U.S. 1025 (2001)   **1:** 83, 84; **8:** 157

—v. Widnall, 79 F.3d 1003, 5 AD Cases 663 (10th Cir. 1996) *5:* 180, 288, 320; *10:* 263
Willis
—v. Conopco, Inc., 108 F.3d 282, 6 AD Cases 806 (11th Cir. 1997) *8:* 77; *10:* 203
—v. Pacific Maritime Ass'n
——162 F.3d 561, 8 AD Cases 1632 (9th Cir. 1998) *9:* 371
——236 F.3d 1160, 11 AD Cases 588 (9th Cir. 2001) *8:* 121, 124–27
Wilmarth v. City of Santa Rosa, 945 F. Supp. 1271, 7 AD Cases 1131 (N.D. Cal. 1996) *9:* 237
Wilson
—v. Acacia Park Cemetery Ass'n, 162 Mich. App. 638, 413 N.W.2d 79, 47 FEP Cases 1309 (1987) *4:* 549
—v. Garcia, 471 U.S. 261 (1985) *2:* 300
—v. Teamsters, 47 F. Supp. 2d 8 (D.D.C. 1999) *5:* 272
Winfrey v. City of Chi.
—259 F.3d 610, 12 AD Cases 21 (7th Cir. 2001) *5:* 216
—957 F. Supp. 1014, 7 AD Cases 1525 (N.D. Ill. 1997) *2:* 296
Witter v. Delta Air Lines, Inc., 138 F.3d 1366, 8 AD Cases 747 (11th Cir. 1998) *5:* 437
Wobser v. PPG Indus., Inc., 208 F.3d 224 (9th Cir. 2000) *5:* 289
Women's Equity Action League v. Cavazos, 906 F.2d 742 (D.C. Cir. 1990) *2:* 263
Wood
—v. Alameda, County of
——875 F. Supp. 659, 4 AD Cases 43 (N.D. Cal. 1995) *9:* 129
——1995 U.S. Dist. LEXIS 17514 (N.D. Cal. 1995) *8:* 106–8
—v. Crown Redi-Mix, 339 F.3d 682, 14 AD Cases 1204 (8th Cir. 2003) *8:* 19
—v. Indianapolis Power & Light Co., 210 F.3d 377 (7th Cir. 2000) *5:* 329
—v. President & Trs. of Spring Hill Coll., 978 F.2d 1214 (11th Cir. 1992) *10:* 158
Woodbridge Corp.; EEOC v., 263 F.3d 812, 12 AD Cases 254 (8th Cir. 2001) *5:* 155; *7:* 130; *9:* 338; *10:* 186
Woodland v. State, County & Mun. Employees Dist. Council 20, 777 A.2d 795, 7 WH Cases 2d 312 (D.C. 2001) *4:* 147
Woodman v. Runyon, 132 F.3d 1330, 7 AD Cases 1189 (10th Cir. 1997) *2:* 324
Woodyard v. Hoover Group, Inc., 985 F.2d 421, 2 AD Cases 467 (8th Cir. 1993) *4:* 667
Wooten v. City of Columbus, 91 Ohio App. 3d 326, 632 N.E.2d 605, 3 AD Cases 631 (1993) *4:* 844
Workman v. Frito-Lay, Inc., 165 F.3d 460, 8 AD Cases 1761 (6th Cir. 1999) *8:* 18
Wright
—v. Circuit City Stores, Inc., 82 F. Supp. 2d 1279, 83 FEP Cases 877 (N.D. Ala. 2000) *10:* 326
—v. Columbia Univ., 520 F. Supp. 789 (E.D. Pa. 1981) *2:* 81
—v. Stone Container Corp., 524 F.2d 1058, 11 FEP Cases 1322 (8th Cir. 1975) *10:* 380
—v. Universal Maritime Serv. Corp., 525 U.S. 70, 8 AD Cases 1429 (1998) *9:* 381; *10:* 336, 337
Wyss v. General Dynamics Corp., 24 F. Supp. 2d 202 (D.R.I. 1998) *4:* 920

Y

Yanez v. United States, 989 F.2d 323 (9th Cir. 1993) *9:* 139, 140
Yates v. Volunteer Health Care Sys., 783 F. Supp. 1002 (W.D. Va. 1992) *4:* 1047
Yellow Freight Sys., Inc.
—v. Donnelly, 494 U.S. 820, 52 FEP Cases 875 (1990) *10:* 11
—EEOC v., 253 F.3d 943, 11 AD Cases 1569 (7th Cir. 2001) *5:* 195; *8:* 79, 89, 187
Yin v. California, 95 F.3d 864, 5 AD Cases 1487 (9th Cir. 1996), *cert. denied,* 519

Yin—*Cont'd*
  U.S. 1114, 117 S. Ct. 955 (1997)   **8:** 99, 100
Young, Ex parte, 209 U.S. 123 (1908)   ***10:*** 104
Yount v. Hesston Corp., 124 Ill. App. 3d 943, 464 N.E.2d 1214, 45 FEP Cases 371 (Ill. Ct. App. 1984)   **4:** 258

Z

Zapata Gulf Marine Corp. v. Puerto Rico Mar. Shipping Auth., 731 F. Supp. 747 (E.D. La. 1990)   **5:** 233

Zenor v. El Paso Healthcare Sys., Ltd., 176 F.3d 847, 9 AD Cases 609 (5th Cir. 1999)   **5:** 262, 278
Zimmerman v. Oregon Dep't of Justice, 170 F.3d 1169, 9 AD Cases 215, *reh'g en banc denied,* 183 F.3d 1161, 9 AD Cases 954 (9th Cir. 1999), *cert. denied,* 531 U.S. 1189 (2001)   ***10:*** 38
Zvkovic v. Southern Cal. Edison Co., 302 F.3d 1080 (9th Cir. 2002)   **8:** 66

INDEX

*References are to chapter and section numbers (e.g., "**6:** II.E.1, II.E.2" refers to sections II.E.1 and II.E.2 in Chapter 6). Alphabetization is word-by-word (e.g., "Work sites" precedes "Workers' compensation").*

A

Abatement requirements
  OSH Act and, **9:** IV.B.3
Absence, leaves of. See Leaves of absence
Absenteeism
  treatment under FMLA and ADA, **9:** I.C.6
Access Board (Architectural Barriers Compliance Board)
  Title III compliance and, **6:** I
Accessibility issues
  ADA and, **3:** II.B
  covered entities, **6:** II
    commercial facilities, **6:** II.F
    Internet-only businesses, **6:** II.E.3, II.E.4
    mixed-use facilities, **6:** II.B
    nontangible public accommodations, **6:** II.D
    physical vs. nonphysical, **6:** II.C
    private companies, **6:** II.E
    public accommodations, defined, **6:** II.A
    Web sites, **6:** II.E.1, II.E.2
  enforcement, **6:** V
    administrative remedies,
    exhaustion requirement, **6:** V.C
    attorney general's role, **6:** V.B
    attorneys' fees, **6:** V.E
    Justice Department and, **6:** V.F
    remedies, **6:** V.A
    standing issues, **6:** V.D
  exemptions, **6:** III
    government entities, **6:** III.C
    private clubs, **6:** III.B
    religious organizations, **6:** III.A
  hiring process and, **7:** IV
    hearing-impaired applicants, **7:** IV.C.1
    interviews, **7:** IV.B
    mobility-impaired applicants, **7:** IV.C.3
    physical access, **7:** IV.A
    speech-impaired applicants, **7:** IV.C.4
    visually-impaired applicants, **7:** IV.C.2
  historic landmarks, **6:** IV.E.4.b
  requirements, **6:** IV
    alterations, **6:** IV.I
    alternatives, **6:** IV.G
    architect liability, **6:** IV.O
    auxiliary aids, provision of, **6:** IV.H
    barrier removal, **6:** IV.E
    direct threat defense, **6:** IV.B
    equal participation, **6:** IV.A
    franchise liability, **6:** IV.L
    guidelines, **6:** IV.F
    integrated settings, **6:** IV.D
    landlord/tenant liability, **6:** IV.M
    new construction, **6:** IV.N
    primary function areas, **6:** IV.J
    reasonable modifications, **6:** IV.C
    tax credits, **6:** IV.K
    transportation services, **6:** IV.P
  Title III compliance, **6:** I
  wilderness areas, **3:** III.E.4

1099

Accommodation
  public. See Public accommodation, places of
  reasonable, obligation under ADA. See Reasonable accommodation obligation
  as remedy for ADA violation, **1:** I.G.3
Actual disability
  defined, **2:** IV.B
  impairment, generally, **2:** IV.B.1.a
ADA. See Americans with Disabilities Act
Addictions. See Drug or alcohol addiction
Administrative relief
  ADA remedies and, **1:** I.G.1
  attorneys' fee awards and, **10:** VII.D
  exhaustion requirement, **6:** V.C
  filing ADA charges, **10:** V.A.1
  Title I, ADA, **10:** II.A
    discrimination charge, filing with EEOC, **10:** II.A.1
    exhaustion of administrative remedies requirement, **10:** II.A.4
    probable cause investigation, **10:** II.A.3
    state agencies, concurrent jurisdiction, **10:** II.A.1
    time period limitations and exceptions, **10:** II.A.2
  Title II, **10:** II.B
  Title III, **10:** II.C
Affirmative action plans
  government contractors and, **2:** VI.C.4
  government employees and, **1:** I.A.1; **2:** III.B, VI.B.4
  state antidiscrimination laws and, **4:** IA.I.E.2.a, KS.I.E.2.a, LA.I.E.2.a, MO.I.E.2.a
Affirmative defenses in ADA cases, 10: V.B.1.b
  collective bargaining act requirements, **10:** V.B.1.b.vi
  direct threat, **10:** V.B.1.b.iv
  federal law, conflicts with, **10:** V.B.1.b.vii

  job-related qualifications and business necessity, **10:** V.B.1.b.i
  liberal leave policies, **10:** V.B.1.b.ii
  religious entity defense, **10:** V.B.1.b.viii
  safety-based qualifications, **10:** V.B.1.b.iii
  seniority requirements, **10:** V.B.1.b.vi
  undue hardship, **10:** V.B.1.b.v
Agencies, federal
  Rehabilitation Act
    application, **2:** III.B
    defenses, **2:** VII.D
    enforcement of, **2:** VI.B
Agility tests
  workers' compensation laws and, **9:** II.C.4
AIDS
  Americans with Disabilities Act and, **3:** I.B; **5:** V.B
    association provision, **5:** V.B.1.c
    inquiries and tests, **5:** V.B.1.b
    insurance benefits, employer's obligation regarding, **5:** V.B.1.e
    privacy, duty to maintain, **5:** V.B.1.f
    qualified individual with disability, **5:** V.B.1
    reasonable accommodation, **5:** V.B.1.d
    unqualified due to risk, **5:** V.B.1.a
  discrimination laws and, **1:** I.B
  food industry issues and, **1:** I.B.3; **3:** III.E.5
  impairment, defined as, **5:** II.A
  state antidiscrimination laws and, **4:** CA.I.B, FL.I.B.3, NY.I.C.1, PA.I.B.1
Air Carrier Access Act, 1: II.D
Alabama
  disability discrimination laws, **4:** AL.I
Alaska, disability discrimination laws, 4: AK.I
  covered employees, **4:** AK.I.D
  defenses, **4:** AK.I.E
  definitions, **4:** AK.I.C
    disability, **4:** AK.I.C.1
    impairment, **4:** AK.I.C.1
  overview, **4:** AK.I.A

prohibited discriminations, **4:** AK.I.B
reasonable accommodation
  obligations, **4:** AK.I.E
Alcohol addiction. See Drug or alcohol
  addiction
Alterations
  ADA Title III requirements and, **6:**
    IV.I
Amendments to ADA, 3: III.E
  commuter trains, **3:** III.E.6
  food-handling jobs, **3:** III.E.5
  miscellaneous amendments, **3:**
    III.E.6
  public transportation, **3:** III.E.6
  remedies, **3:** III.E.6
  small business grace period, **3:**
    III.E.1
  small community amendments, **3:**
    III.E.6
  undue hardship, quantifying, **3:**
    III.E.3
  wilderness area accessibility issues, **3:**
    III.E.4
  written job descriptions, assessment
    of job function and, **3:** III.E.2
Americans with Disabilities Act (ADA)
  accessibility standards, **3:** II.B
    See also Accessibility issues
  administration approval, **3:** II.F, IV
  administration deliberations, **3:** II.E
  AIDS/HIV and. See AIDS
  amendments. See Amendments to
    ADA
  arbitration and, **10:** VI.A
  arbitration issues and, **9:** V.C
  attorneys' fees and related matters,
    10: VII.A
  business necessity defense, **1:** I.F
  common illnesses and conditions,
    5: V
  conflict with other laws defense, **9:**
    IV.A.4
  damages. See Damages
  defenses. See Defenses to ADA
  direct threat defense, **1:** I.F
  disability, defined, **5:** II
  drafts, first, **3:** I.A
  enforcement, **1:** I.G
  entities, covered, **1:** I.C
  essential job function, defined. See
    Essential job function
  exempted conditions, **1:** I.B.1
  final law, scope of coverage, **1:** I.B.4
  FMLA, comparisons with. See Family
    and Medical Leave Act
  food industry issues, **1:** I.B.3
  generally, **1:** I.B
  hiring provisions. See Hiring
  House consideration. See House of
    Representatives
  illnesses and conditions. See
    Illnesses and conditions under
    ADA
  impairment, defined, **1:** I.D.1; **5:**
    II.A
  legislative history
    House, progress in, **1:** I.B.2; **3:** III
    revised bill, **3:** II.C
    Senate, introduction in, **1:** I.B.1;
      3: I, II
  limitation on major life activity,
    defined, **1:** I.D.2
  litigation strategies. See Litigation
    strategies, ADA
  mental disorders. See Mental
    impairment
  National Council on Disability
    reports, **3:** I
  obligations, employer, **1:** I.E, I.F
    defenses and limitations, **1:** I.F
  preemployment discrimination,
    prima facie case, **7:** II
  preliminary analysis, **3:** I
  previous or misconceived
    impairments, defined, **1:** I.D.3
  protected disability, defined, **1:** I.D
  qualified individuals, defined, **5:** III
    otherwise qualified, **5:** III.A
  reasonable accommodation. See
    Reasonable accommodation
    obligation
  record of impairment, **5:** II.D
  regarded as disabled definition, **5:**
    II.E
  Rehabilitation Act, overlapping
    coverage, **2:** I
  remedies, **1:** I.G
  revisions, **3:** II.A

Americans with Disabilities Act (ADA)—*Cont'd*
safety and health laws, interplay with. See Safety and health statutes
Senate. See Senate proceedings on ADA
signing, **3:** IV
sovereign immunity and, **10:** III.A
Title III. See Title III, ADA
undue hardship, factors, **1:** I.F
workers' compensation laws. See Workers' compensation laws

Antiretaliation provisions. See Retaliation

Applicants
ADA coverage and, **1:** I.C
disparate treatment,
 nondiscriminatory reasons for, **7:** X.C
 direct threat defense, **7:** X.C.1, X.C.2
 mitigation of threat through reasonable accommodation, **7:** X.C.3
 threat assessment, **7:** X.C.4
executive branch, discrimination protection, **1:** I.A.1; **2:** III.A
hearing-impaired, **7:** IV.C.1
mobility-impaired, **7:** IV.C.3
reasonable accommodation obligation
 ADA, **7:** VIII.B
 employer's duties, **7:** VIII.B.2; **8:** VII
 employment agencies, use of, **7:** VIII.B.4
 equal employment opportunity requirements, **7:** VIII.B.1
 essential function analysis, **7:** VIII.B.8
 generally, **7:** VIII
 job information, access to, **7:** VIII.B.3
 recruitment, **7:** VIII.B.5
 Rehabilitation Act, **7:** VIII.A
 requests for, **7:** VIII.B.6
 undue hardship analysis, **7:** VIII.B.7

speech-impaired, **7:** IV.C.4
visually-impaired, **7:** IV.C.2

Applications
forms as evidence, **7:** V.A.1
hiring process and, **7:** V.A
qualifications comparisons, **7:** V.A.2

Arbitration
ADA issues, **9:** V.C; **10:** VI.A
challenging arbitration agreements, **10:** VI.A.4
collective bargaining agreements and, **9:** V.B.3.a.iv; **10:** VI.A.6
enforcement exceptions, **10:** VI.A.2
FAA applicability to employment contracts, **10:** VI.A.1
procedural elements, **10:** VI.A.3
Rehabilitation Act and, **10:** VI.B
unconscionability defense, **10:** VI.A.5

Architects
ADA Title III requirements, liability for, **6:** IV.O

Architectural Barriers Act, 1: II.A
ADA Title III and, **6:** I

Architectural Barriers Compliance Board (Access Board)
Title III compliance and, **6:** I

Arizona, disability discrimination laws
covered employers, **4:** AZ.I.D
defenses, **4:** AZ.I.E.2
 direct threat defense, **4:** AZ.I.E.2.a
 undue hardship defense, **4:** AZ.I.E.2.b
definitions, **4:** AZ.I.C
 disability, **4:** AZ.I.C.1
 essential job function, **4:** AZ.I.C.2
overview, **4:** AZ.I.A
preemployment issues, **4:** AZ.I.B.1
 medical examinations, **4:** AZ.I.B.1.a
prohibited discrimination, **4:** AZ.I.B
reasonable accommodation obligation, **4:** AZ.I.E.1

Arkansas, disability discrimination laws
covered employers, **4:** AR.I.D
defenses, **4:** AR.I.E
definition of disability, **4:** AR.I.C.1
overview, **4:** AR.I.A
prohibited discrimination, **4:** AR.I.B
 genetic testing, **4:** AR.I.B.1

reasonable accommodation
obligations, **4:** AR.I.E
Assembly seating
barrier removal and, **6:** IV.E.2
Attendance policies
absenteeism, treatment under FMLA
and ADA, **9:** I.C.6
leaves of absence and, **8:** IV.D.1
Attorney general
role in enforcing Title III, **6:** V.B
Attorneys' fees
ADA
Title I enforcement and, **10:** VII.A
EEOC, awards against, **10:**
VII.A.3
employee's misconduct as
discharging, **10:** VII.A.2.a
legislative history, **10:** VII.A.1
obtaining, **10:** VII.A.2
successful defendants, **10:**
VII.A.2.b
Title III enforcement and, **6:** V.E;
10: II.C
administrative proceedings, **10:**
VII.D
Rehabilitation Act, **10:** VII.B
state government defendants, **10:**
VII.C
Auxiliary aids
ADA Title III requirements and, **6:**
IV.H

B

Back pay
as remedy for ADA violation, **1:**
I.G.3
as remedy for Rehabilitation Act
violation, **2:** VI.B.3, VI.D.3
Bargaining
NLRA duty and, **9:** V.B.3
Barrier removal
additional measures, **6:** IV.E.4
historic landmarks, **6:** IV.E.4.b
public areas, **6:** IV.E.4.a
alternatives, **6:** IV.G
assembly seating, **6:** IV.E.2
guidelines, **6:** IV.F
priorities, **6:** IV.E.3

readily available standard and
factors, **6:** IV.E.1
Title III requirements, **6:** IV.E; **10:**
IV.A.1.c
types of barriers, **6:** IV.E
Barriers
types, **6:** IV.E
Benefits and privileges of employment
accommodation required to provide,
8: II.C
circumstances justifying disability-
based distinction
legitimate actuarial data justifies,
9: VI.B.3.b
necessary to avoid changes in
coverage or premium, **9:**
VI.B.3.d
necessary to maintain solvency of
benefit plan, **9:** VI.B.3.c
no medical benefit, **9:** VI.B.3.e
no unequal treatment, **9:** VI.B.3.a
continuation of, **9:** I.C.5
discrimination in, EEOC guidance
and, **9:** VI.B
disability-based distinction,
inequality based on, **9:** VI.B.2
inequality of benefits, **9:** VI.B.1
outstanding questions, **9:** VI.C
particular circumstances, **9:** VI.B.3
subterfuge, determining, **9:** VI.B.3
distinguishing between mental and
physical disabilities, **5:** V.C.6
ERISA, ADA interplay with, **9:** VI
Mental Health Parity Act and, **9:**
VI.C.2
mental vs. physical health care
coverage, **9:** VI.C.2
violations and permitted
distinctions, **9:** VI.D
BFOQ. *See* Bona fide occupational
qualification
Bisexuality
as exempt from Rehabilitation Act,
2: II.E, IV.B.1.a
Blind job applicants
hiring procedures and, **7:** IV.C.2
**Bona fide occupational qualification
(BFOQ)**
state antidiscrimination laws and, **4:**

Bona fide occupational qualification (BFOQ)—*Cont'd*
  CO.I.E.1.a, CT.I.E.1.a, FL.I.E.2.a, HI.I.E.2.a, IA.I.E.2.b, IL.I.E.2.a, MA.I.E.2.a, MD.I.E.2.a, MT.I.E.2.a, NV.I.E.2.a
Buses, over-the-road
  ADA Title III requirements and, **6:** IV.P.4
Business necessity defense, 1: I.F; **5:** V.A.6.a; **10:** V.B.1.b.i
  OSH Act and, **9:** IV.A.1
  state laws and, **4:** CO.I.E.1.b, LA.I.E.2.b, TX.I.E.2.a
Businesses
  ADA accommodation issues and, **6:** II.E
    Internet-only businesses, **6:** II.E.3, II.E.4
    Web sites, **6:** II.E.1, II.E.2

C

California, disability discrimination laws
  AIDS issues, **4:** CA.I.B
  covered employers, **4:** CA.I.D
  defenses, **4:** CA.I.E.2
    undue hardship, **4:** CA.I.E.2.a
  definitions
    disability, **4:** CA.I.C.1
    essential job functions, **4:** CA.I.C.2
    major life activities, **4:** CA.I.C.3
    medical conditions, **4:** CA.I.C.4
  local laws, **4:** CA.II
  overview, **4:** CA.I.A
  prohibited discrimination, **4:** CA.I.B
  reasonable accommodation obligation, **4:** CA.I.E.1
Cancer
  ADA treatment of, **5:** V.G
Caps on damages, 10: V.A.2
Categories of reasonable accommodation, 8: II.A
Certification of disability by employer-selected doctor
  reasonable accommodation and, **8:** III.C

Civil remedies for ADA violations. See Remedies for ADA violations
Civil Rights Act of 1964. See Title VII
Civil Rights Act of 1991
  damages provisions, **10:** IV.A.1.a
Civil Rights Restoration Act, 2: III.D.1
Clubs, private
  ADA exemptions and, **6:** III.B; **10:** IV.A.1.c
Collective bargaining agreements
  arbitration, **9:** V.B.3.a.iv; **10:** VI.A.6
  conflicts between ADA and NLRA, **9:** V.B.3.a
  seniority provisions, **9:** V.B.3.a.i
  court rulings, **9:** V.B.3.a.iii
  defenses to ADA claims and, **10:** V.B.1.b.vi
  Rehabilitation Act provisions, **9:** V.B.3.a.ii
  requests for reasonable accommodation, effect on, **8:** III.E
Colorado, disability discrimination laws
  covered employers, **4:** CO.I.D
  defenses, **4:** CO.I.E.1
    bona fide occupational qualification (BFOQ), **4:** CO.I.E.1.a
    business necessity, **4:** CO.I.E.1.b
    undue hardship, **4:** CO.I.E.1.c
  definition of disability, **4:** CO.I.C.1
  overview, **4:** CO.I.A
  prohibited discrimination, **4:** CO.I.B
  reasonable accommodation obligation, **4:** CO.I.E
Commercial facilities
  See also Businesses
  defined, **6:** II.F
  public accommodation, as places of, **6:** II.F
Commercial Motor Vehicle Safety Act
  ADA interplay with, **9:** IV.A.4
Communicable diseases
  AIDS and HIV. See AIDS
  state antidiscrimination laws and. See Infectious or communicable diseases

INDEX

Commuter trains
  ADA and, **3:** III.E.6
Compensation issues
  leaves and, **9:** I.C.4
Compensatory damages
  as remedy for ADA violation, **1:** I.G.3; **10:** IV.A.1.a
  as remedy for Rehabilitation Act violation, **2:** VI.B.3, VI.D.3
Compliance reviews
  Rehabilitation Act and, **2:** VI.C.5
Concurrent jurisdiction of states
  ADA claims and, **10:** II.A.1
Conditions and illnesses, common. See Illnesses and conditions under ADA
Conduct rules in workplace
  reasonable accommodations and, **8:** IV.H
Confidentiality issues
  AIDS/HIV, employer's duty, **5:** V.B.1.f
  NLRA conflicts and, **9:** V.B.2
  requests for reasonable accommodation and, **8:** III.F
  workers' compensation claims, **9:** II.C
Conflict of ADA with other laws defense, 9: IV.A.4; **10:** V.B.1.b.vii
Conflicts between NLRA and ADA, 9: V.B
  bargaining and reasonable accommodation, **9:** V.B.3
  confidentiality and disclosures duties, **9:** V.B.2
  direct dealing prohibition and duty to meet informally, **9:** V.B.1
Congress, U.S. See House of Representatives; Senate
Connecticut, disability discrimination laws
  covered employers, **4:** CT.I.D
  defenses, bona fide occupational qualification (BFOQ), **4:** CT.I.E.1.a
  definition of disability, **4:** CT.I.C.1
  overview, **4:** CT.I.A
  prohibited discrimination, **4:** CT.I.B

  genetic testing, **4:** CT.I.B.1
  reasonable accommodation obligation, **4:** CT.I.E
Constitution, U.S.
  Eleventh Amendment, **10:** III
  Seventh Amendment jury trial right, **2:** VI.D.3
  Spending Clause, **2:** III.D.3
Construction, new
  ADA Title III requirements, **6:** IV.N
  scoping requirements, **6:** IV.N.1
  unclear accessibility guidelines, **6:** IV.N.2
Contractors, government. See Government contractors
Corrective measures. See Mitigating or corrective measures
Courses and examinations for transportation services
  ADA Title III requirements and, **6:** IV.Q
Covered entities, 1: I.C
  defenses and, **2:** VII.A.1
  state laws. See *specific state*
Credits, tax
  ADA Title III requirements, compliance with, **6:** IV.K
Criteria for establishing job requirements
  preemployment practices, **7:** VIX.C

D

Damages
  ADA
    Title I, parallel to Title VII, **10:** IV.A.1.a
    Title II, two-tier approach, **10:** IV.A.1.b
  caps, **10:** V.A.2
  compensatory, **1:** I.G.3; **2:** VI.B.3, VI.D.3; **10:** IV.A.1.a
  limitations on, **1:** I.G.3
  punitive. See Punitive damages
Deaf job applicants
  hiring procedures and, **7:** IV.C.1
Defendant's litigation strategies, 10: V.B
  affirmative defenses, **10:** V.B.1.b

Defendant's litigation strategies—
Cont'd
    collective bargaining act requirements, **10:** V.B.1.b.vi
    direct threat, **10:** V.B.1.b.iv
    federal law, conflicts with, **10:** V.B.1.b.vii
    job-related or business necessity, **10:** V.B.1.b.i
    liberal leave policies, **10:** V.B.1.b.ii
    religious entity defense, **10:** V.B.1.b.viii
    safety-based qualifications, **10:** V.B.1.b.iii
    seniority requirements, **10:** V.B.1.b.vi
    undue hardship, **10:** V.B.1.b.v
    plaintiff's case, disproving, **10:** V.B.1
    disability, disproving, **10:** V.B.1.a
    summary judgment, motion for, **10:** V.B

Defenses to ADA liability
    See also Affirmative defenses in ADA cases
    business necessity defense, **1:** I.F; **5:** V.A.6.a
    direct threat, **1:** I.F; **5:** V.A.6.a
    job standards and qualifications, **1:** I.F
    preemployment practices. See Discrimination in hiring procedures
    undue hardship, factors, **1:** I.F

Defenses to Rehabilitation Act liability
    employee not covered by act, **2:** VII.A.2
    employee not disabled, **2:** VII.A.2.b
    employee not qualified for job, **2:** VII.A.2.a
    employer not covered entity, **2:** VII.A.1
    government contractors, **2:** VII.C
    government employees, **2:** VII.D
    job qualifications, education and experience requirements, **2:** VII.A.2.a
    knowledge of employee's disability, **2:** VII.A.4
    procedural defenses, **2:** VII.A.5
    programs receiving financial assistance, **2:** VII.B
    indirect recipient of financial aid, **2:** VII.B.1
    partial or sector coverage, **2:** VII.B.2
    reasonable accommodation impossible, **2:** VII.A.3
    types, **2:** VII.A

Defenses to state disability discrimination laws. See *specific state*

Definitions
    actual disability, **2:** IV.B
    commercial facilities, **6:** II.F
    disability, **3:** II.A; **9:** I.B.2.a, III.A, III.B
    state antidiscrimination laws. See *specific state*
    disability, protected, **1:** I.D
    disability-based distinction, **9:** VI.B.2
    employee, **4:** IN.I.C.2
    employment, **4:** HI.I.C.2
    essential job function, **4:** AZ.I.C.2, CA.I.C.2, FL.I.C.2, KS.I.C.2; **5:** III.B
    government contracts, **2:** III.C
    impairment, **1:** I.D.1; **4:** AK.I.C.1
    major life activity
    limitation on, **1:** I.D.2; **2:** IV.B.2.a
    state antidiscrimination laws. See *specific state*
    medical conditions, **4:** CA.I.C.4
    medical examination, **7:** VI.B.3
    mental impairment, **2:** IV.B.1.a
    person, **4:** IN.I.C.3
    physical impairment, **2:** IV.B.1.a
    previous or misconceived impairment, **1:** I.D.3
    program or activity subject to Rehabilitation Act, **2:** III.D.1
    protected individual, **2:** IV.A
    public accommodations, **6:** II.A
    qualified handicap, **4:** DE.I.C.1
    qualified individual with disability, **2:** IV.E
    reasonable accommodation, **2:** V.B
    receipt of federal financial assistance, **2:** III.D.2

INDEX 1107

serious medical conditions, **9:** I.B.2.b
substantially limits, **2:** IV.B.2.b
undue hardship, **8:** V.A
Delaware, disability discrimination laws
covered employers, **4:** DE.I.D
defenses, **4:** DE.I.E.2
  risk to others, **4:** DE.I.E.2.a
  undue hardship, **4:** DE.I.E.2.a
definitions
  disability, **4:** DE.I.C.1
  qualified handicap, **4:** DE.I.C.1
overview, **4:** DE.I.A
prohibited discrimination, **4:** DE.I.B
  genetic testing, **4:** DE.I.B.2
  medical examinations, **4:** DE.I.B.1.a
  preemployment inquiries, **4:** DE.I.B.1
reasonable accommodation obligation, **4:** DE.I.E.1
Demand-responsive transportation systems
ADA Title III requirements, **6:** IV.P.2
Developmental Disabilities Assistance and Bill of Rights Act, 1: II.C
Diabetes
ADA treatment of, **5:** V.D
Direct dealing prohibition
NLRA and, **9:** V.B.1
Direct threat defense, 1: I.F; **5:** V.A.6.a; **6:** IV.B; **7:** X.C.1, X.C.2; **10:** V.B.1.b.iv
  assessment of threat, **7:** X.C.4
  mitigation of threat, **7:** X.C.3
  OSH Act and, **9:** IV.A.3
  reasonable accommodations and, **8:** VI
  state law and, **4:** AZ.I.E.2.a, FL.I.E.2.b, ID.I.E.2.a, KS.I.E.2.b, MN.I.E.2.a, OR.I.E.2.a, VA.I.E.2.a
Disability
actual disability, defined, **2:** IV.B
ADA definitions, **5:** II
conflicts, **2:** IV.B.1.b
defined, **3:** II.A; **9:** I.B.2.a, III.A, III.B

state antidiscrimination laws. See *specific state*
disproving, **10:** V.B.1.a
duration or long-time impact, proof of, **10:** V.A.3.a.1
impairment, generally, **2:** IV.B.1.a
knowledge of, defense to liability, **2:** VII.A.4
mental impairment, defined, **2:** IV.B.1.a
physical impairment, defined, **2:** IV.B.1.a
protected, defined, **1:** I.D
proving, **10:** V.A.3.a
record of, **2:** IV.C
"regarded as" disabled, **2:** IV.C
Rehabilitation Act definition, **5:** I
Disability discrimination and related laws
ADA. See Americans with Disabilities Act
Air Carrier Access Act, **1:** II.D
Architectural Barriers Act, **1:** II.A
Developmental Disabilities Assistance and Bill of Rights Act, **1:** II.C
Fair Housing Act, **1:** II.F
federal, **1:** I
Individuals with Disabilities Education Act (IDEA), **1:** II.B
Rehabilitation Act, **1:** I.A
Social Security Act, **1:** II.G
state laws, **Ch. 4**
Telecommunications Act, **1:** II.E
Disability-related preemployment inquiries
permissible inquiries, **7:** VI.A.3
  job-related function inquiries, **7:** VI.A.3.b
  known disabilities, **7:** VI.A.3.c
  nondisabling impairments, **7:** VI.A.3.a
prima facie case, **7:** VI.A.1
prohibition, reasons for, **7:** VI.A.2
Disclosure
NLRA duties and, **9:** V.B.2
Discrimination in hiring procedures
accessibility and accommodation issues, **7:** IV

Discrimination in hiring procedures—
Cont'd
    hearing-impaired applicants, **7:** IV.C.1
    interviews, **7:** IV.B
    mobility-impaired applicants, **7:** IV.C.3
    physical accessibility, **7:** IV.A
    speech-impaired applicants, **7:** IV.C.4
    visually-impaired applicants, **7:** IV.C.2
  applications, **7:** V.A
    as evidence, **7:** V.A.1
    qualifications comparisons, **7:** V.A.2
  defenses, **7:** X
    employee insubordination, **7:** X.C.5
    inability to perform essential job function, **7:** X.B
    legitimate nondiscriminatory reason, **7:** X.C
    nonstatutory defenses, **7:** X.D
    reasonable accommodation impossible, **7:** X.A
    threat-related issues, **7:** X.C.1, X.C.2, X.C.3, X.C.4
  equal employment opportunity requirements, **7:** VIII.B.1
  job descriptions, **7:** V.B
  job-related requirements
    establishing, criteria, **7:** VIX.C
    justified, **7:** VIX.A
    not justified, **7:** VIX.B
  medical examinations, **7:** VI, VI.B
    defined, **7:** VI.B.3
    disputed results, **7:** VI.B.4
    postoffer exams, **7:** VI.B.2
    pre-offer exams, **7:** VI.B.1
  preemployment discrimination, prima facie case, **7:** II
  preemployment inquiries, **7:** VI
    disability-related inquiries, **7:** VI.A
  preemployment training programs, **7:** VII
  proving, **7:** III
  reasonable accommodation obligation
    ADA, **7:** VIII.B
    employer's duties, **7:** VIII.B.2
    employment agencies, use of, **7:** VIII.B.4
    equal employment opportunity requirements, **7:** VIII.B.1
    essential function analysis, **7:** VIII.B.8
    generally, **7:** VIII
    job information, access to, **7:** VIII.B.3
    recruitment, **7:** VIII.B.5
    Rehabilitation Act, **7:** VIII.A
    requests for, **7:** VIII.B.6
    undue hardship analysis, **7:** VIII.B.7

Diseases
  ADA treatment of
    cancer, **5:** V.G
    diabetes, **5:** V.D
    epilepsy, **5:** V.H
    heart disease, **5:** V.F
    hypertension, **5:** V.E
  AIDS and HIV. See AIDS
  common illnesses. See Illnesses and conditions under ADA
  state antidiscrimination laws and. See Infectious or communicable diseases

Disparate treatment of applicants
  nondiscriminatory reasons, **7:** X.C
    direct threat defense, **7:** X.C.1, X.C.2
    mitigation of threat through reasonable accommodation, **7:** X.C.3
    threat assessment, **7:** X.C.4

District of Columbia, disability discrimination laws
  covered employers, **4:** DC.I.D
  defenses, **4:** DC.I.E.2
  definition of disability, **4:** DC.I.C.1
  overview, **4:** DC.I.A
  prohibited discrimination, **4:** DC.I.B
    preemployment inquiries, **4:** DC.I.B.1
  reasonable accommodation obligation, **4:** DC.I.E.1

Doctrine of sovereign immunity. See Sovereign immunity
Documentation requests
  reasonable accommodation and, **8:** III.B
Drug-Free Workplace Act
  compliance with, **5:** V.A.7
Drug or alcohol addiction
  ADA and, **5:** II.D, II.F, V.A
  alcohol only, **5:** V.A.2
  compliance with other laws and regulations, **5:** V.A.7
  current use, **5:** V.A.1
  drug testing, **5:** V.A.5.a
  employer defenses, **5:** V.A.6
  employer rights, **5:** V.A.4
  inquiries and examinations regarding, **5:** V.A.5
  reasonable accommodation, **5:** V.A.8
  "regarded as," **5:** V.A.3
  Rehabilitation Act and, **2:** II.D, IV.B.1.b.ii
Drug testing, 5: V.A.5.a
Duration of employment
  threshold requirements for FMLA and ADA coverage, **9:** I.B.1
Duration of leave
  ADA and FMLA compared, **9:** I.C.2
Duration of Social Security benefits, 9: III.A.1

E

Electronic and information technology
  Rehabilitation Act, application to, **1:** I.A.4
Eleventh Amendment and sovereign immunity, 10: III
Employee benefits. See Benefits and privileges of employment
Employee Retirement Income Security Act (ERISA)
  ADA interplay with, **9:** VI
  coverage gaps filled by ADA, **9:** VI.A
  EEOC guidance on benefits, **9:** VI.B
  disability-based distinction, **9:** VI.B.2
  outstanding questions, **9:** VI.C
  subterfuge, determining, **9:** VI.B.3
  unequal benefits, **9:** VI.B.1
  insurance-related practices, ADA's safe harbor provisions, **9:** VI.A
  disability-based risk classifications, **9:** VI.A.1.d
  HIPAA, effect of, **9:** VI.A.3
  insurance industry, effect on, **9:** VI.A.1.b
  legislative history, **9:** VI.A.1
  limitations on coverage, permitted, **9:** VI.A.3
  no subterfuge provision, **9:** VI.A.2
  preemption provisions, effect on, **9:** VI.A.1.a
  judicial estoppel, **9:** VI.C.1.b
  mental vs. physical health care coverage, **9:** VI.C.2
  MHPA and, **9:** VI.C.2
  representations regarding disability as bar, **9:** VI.C.1.c
  standing to sue, **9:** VI.C.1
  totally disabled former employees, **9:** VI.C.1.a
  violations and permitted distinctions, **9:** VI.D
Employees
  defined, **4:** IN.I.C.2
  government. See Government employees
  records, ADA and OSH Act treatment compared, **9:** IV.B.1
Employer defenses to ADA liability. See Defenses to ADA liability
Employer policies
  absenteeism, treatment under FMLA and ADA, **9:** I.C.6
  fitness to return to work, **9:** II.C.3
  leaves of absences, **8:** IV.D.1
  reasonable accommodation requests, **8:** III.D
Employer rights
  reasonable accommodation and, **8:** II.B.2
  substance abuse and, **5:** V.A.4
  defenses, **5:** V.A.6
  discrimination or pretext, **5:** V.A.4.c
  drug testing, **5:** V.A.5.a

Employer rights—*Cont'd*
  last-chance agreements, **5:** V.A.4.a
  off-duty conduct, **5:** V.A.4.b
Employment
  ADA coverage and, **1:** I.B.4
  defined, **4:** HI.I.C.2
Employment agencies
  ADA compliance and, **7:** VIII.B.4
Employment contracts
  FAA applicability to, **10:** VI.A.1
Enforcement of ADA, 1: I.G
  overview, **10:** I
  Title I, administrative procedures, **10:** II.A
    discrimination charge, filing with EEOC, **10:** II.A.1
    exhaustion of administrative remedies, **10:** II.A.4
    probable cause investigation, **10:** II.A.3
    state agencies, concurrent jurisdiction, **10:** II.A.1
    time period limitations and exceptions, **10:** II.A.2
  Title II, administrative procedures, **10:** II.B
  Title III provisions, **6:** V; **10:** II.C
    attorney general's role, **6:** V.B
    attorneys' fees, **6:** V.E; **10:** II.C
    exhaustion of administrative remedies, **6:** V.C
    Justice Department and, **6:** V.F
    limitations on, **10:** II.C
    remedies, **6:** V.A; **10:** IV.A.1.c
    standing, **6:** V.D
Enforcement of Rehabilitation Act, 2: II.C
  executive agencies and, **2:** VI.B
  generally, **2:** VI.A
  procedures, **2:** VI.B.2
  remedies, **2:** VI.B.3
  scope, **2:** VI.B.1
  exhaustion of administrative remedies, **2:** II.D
  federal employees, **10:** II.D.1
  government contractors
    affirmative action plan requirements, **2:** VI.C.4
    compliance reviews, **2:** VI.C.5
    procedures, **2:** VI.C.2

  remedies, **2:** VI.C.3
  scope, **2:** VI.C.1
  private rights of action under, federal contractors, **10:** II.D.2
  programs receiving financial assistance
    private rights of action, **10:** II.D.3
    procedures, **2:** VI.D.2
    remedies, **2:** VI.D.3
    scope, **2:** VI.D.1
  statute of limitations, **2:** VI.D.3
  Title VII, incorporation in, **10:** II.D
Entities covered. See Covered entities
Epilepsy
  ADA treatment of, **5:** V.H
Equal Employment Opportunity Commission (EEOC)
  discrimination and workers' compensation claims, pursuing, **9:** II.B.2
Equal employment opportunity requirements, 7: VIII.B.1
Equal participation
  Title III requirements, **6:** IV.A
Equipment
  reasonable accommodation and modification of, **8:** IV.G
Equitable remedies
  ADA violations and, **1:** I.G.3
  front pay, **1:** I.G.3
  injunctions, **1:** I.G.3
  job accommodation, **1:** I.G.3
  Rehabilitation Act violations and, **2:** VI.B.3, VI.C.3, VI.D.3
ERISA. See Employee Retirement Income Security Act
Essential job function
  ADA/Rehabilitation Act guidelines, **7:** VIII.B.8.b
  consequences of nonperformance, **5:** III.B.4
  defined, **5:** III.B
    state laws, **4:** AZ.I.C.2, CA.I.C.2, FL.I.C.2, KS.I.C.2
  EEO guidelines, **7:** VIII.B.8.a
  essentially, determining, **8:** II.B.1
  factors, additional, **5:** III.B.5
  government safety standards, **5:** III.B.2
  inability to perform, **7:** X.B

preemployment practices and, **7:** VIII.B.8
private employer requirements, **7:** VIII.B.8.c
reasonable accommodation
   identification of, **8:** II.B.1
   performance with or without, **5:** III.C
   time devoted to task, **5:** III.B.3
   written job descriptions, **3:** III.E.2; **5:** III.B.1
Estoppel. See Judicial estoppel
Evidence
   application forms, **7:** V.A.1
   discrimination in hiring procedure, proving, **7:** III
Examinations and courses for transportation services
   ADA Title III requirements and, **6:** IV.Q
Exclusive remedy provisions of workers' compensation laws
   ADA and, **9:** II.A
Executive branch employees
   discrimination protection. See Government employees
Exempted conditions
   See also *specific exempted conditions*
   Rehabilitation Act and, **2:** II.E, IV.B.1.a, IV.B.1.b
Exemptions to ADA Title III, 6: III
   government entities, **6:** III.C
   private clubs, **6:** III.B; **10:** IV.A.1.c
   religious organizations, **6:** III.A; **10:** IV.A.1.c
Exhaustion of administrative remedies
   as prerequisite to civil suit, **10:** II.A.4
   Rehabilitation Act enforcement, **10:** II.D
   Title III enforcement, **6:** V.C
Exhibitionism
   as exempt from Rehabilitation Act, **2:** II.E

F

FAA. See Federal Arbitration Act
Failure to provide reasonable accommodation, 8: II.D
Fair Housing Act, 1: II.F; **10:** IV.A.1.c

Fair representation, duty of, 9: V.D
Family and Medical Leave Act (FMLA)
   ADA interplay with, **8:** VIII.A; **9:** I
   antiretaliation provisions, **9:** I.H
   employee coverage, **9:** I.B
      ADA requirements distinguished, **9:** I.B.2.c
      disability and serious health conditions, distinguishing, **9:** I.B.2
      duration of employment, threshold requirements, **9:** I.B.1
   employer coverage, **9:** I.A
   fitness-for-duty requirements, **9:** I.F
   leave, terms and conditions of, **9:** I.C
      absenteeism, treatment of, **9:** I.C.6
      benefits, continuation of, **9:** I.C.5
      compensation issues, **9:** I.C.4
      duration of, **9:** I.C.2
      hardship limitations, **9:** I.C.1
      reduced schedule or intermittent leave, **9:** I.C.3
   light-duty work, availability of, **9:** I.D
   medical examinations, **9:** I.E
   preemployment inquiries, **9:** I.E
   reinstatement rights, **9:** I.G
   remedies, **9:** I.I
Federal Arbitration Act (FAA)
   ADA issues and, **10:** VI.A
   employment contracts, applicability to, **10:** VI.A.1
   enforcement exceptions, **10:** VI.A.2
Federal financial assistance. See Financial assistance, programs receiving
Fees. See Attorneys' fees
Financial assistance, programs receiving
   defenses to liability, **2:** VII.B
      indirect recipient of financial aid, **2:** VII.B.1
      partial or sector coverage, **2:** VII.B.2
   discrimination protection, **1:** I.A.3; **2:** III.A, III.D
   enforcement
      procedures, **2:** VI.D.2
      remedies, **2:** VI.D.3
      scope, **2:** VI.D.1

Financial assistance, programs receiving—*Cont'd*
  indirect benefits, **2:** III.D.2
  program or activity, defined, **2:** III.D.1
  receipt of, defined, **2:** III.D.2
  states, application to, **2:** III.D.3
Fitness-for-duty requirements
  FMLA and ADA compared, **9:** I.F
Fitness to return to work policies
  workers' compensation claims and, **9:** II.C.3
Fixed-route transportation systems
  ADA Title III requirements, **6:** IV.P.1
Florida, disability discrimination laws
  covered employers, **4:** FL.I.D
  defenses, **4:** FL.I.E.2
    bona fide occupational qualification (BFOQ), **4:** FL.I.E.2.a
    direct threat defense, **4:** FL.I.E.2.b
    undue hardship, **4:** FL.I.E.2.c
  definitions, **4:** FL.I.C
    disability, **4:** FL.I.C.1
    essential job function, **4:** FL.I.C.2
  local laws, **4:** FL.II
  overview, **4:** FL.I.A
  prohibited discrimination, **4:** FL.I.B
    AIDS, **4:** FL.I.B.3
    genetic testing, **4:** FL.I.B.1
    harassment, **4:** FL.I.B.2
    medical conditions, **4:** FL.I.B.3
  reasonable accommodation obligation, **4:** FL.I.E.1
FMLA. *See* Family and Medical Leave Act
Food industry
  ADA issues, **1:** I.B.3; **3:** III.E.5
Franchises
  ADA Title III requirements and, **6:** IV.L
Front pay
  as remedy for ADA violation, **1:** I.G.3
Future hazard
  state antidiscrimination laws and, **4:** MD.I.E.2.c

G

Gambling, compulsive
  as exempt from Rehabilitation Act, **2:** II.E
Gender identity disorders
  as exempt from Rehabilitation Act, **2:** II.E, IV.B.1.a
Genetic testing
  state antidiscrimination laws and, **4:** AR.I.B.1, CT.I.B.1, DE.I.B.2, FL.I.B.1, HI.I.B.1, IA.I.B.2, KS.I.B.2, LA.I.B.1, MA.I.B.2, MD.I.B.1, ME.I.B.2, MI.I.B.1, MN.I.B.3, NC.I.B.1, NE.I.B.2, NH.I.B.2, NV.I.B.1, NY.I.B.1, OK.I.B.1, OR.I.B.1, RI.I.B.1, SD.I.B.1, TX.I.B.1, UT.I.B.2, VA.I.B.1, VT.I.B.1, WI.I.B.1
Georgia, disability discrimination laws
  covered employers, **4:** GA.I.D
  defenses, **4:** GA.I.E.2
    infectious or communicable diseases, **4:** GA.I.E.2.a
  definition of disability, **4:** GA.I.C.1
  overview, **4:** GA.I.A
  prohibited discrimination, **4:** GA.I.B
    preemployment inquiries, **4:** GA.I.B.1
    retaliation, **4:** GA.I.B.2
  reasonable accommodation obligation, **4:** GA.I.E.1
Government contractors
  administrative relief, **1:** I.G.1
  defenses to liability, **2:** VII.C
  discrimination protection, **1:** I.A.2; **2:** III.A, III.C
  enforcement, **2:** VI.C
    affirmative action plan requirements, **2:** VI.C.4
    compliance reviews, **2:** VI.C.5
    procedures, **2:** VI.C.2
    remedies, **2:** VI.C.3
    scope, **2:** VI.C.1
  government contract defined, **2:** III.C
  private right of action and, **1:** I.G.2; **10:** II.D.2
  sanctions, **2:** VI.C.3
  waivers, **1:** I.A.2; **2:** III.C

Government employees
ADA coverage and, **1:** I.C
administrative relief, **1:** I.G.1
defenses to liability, **2:** VII.D
enforcement
affirmative action plan
requirements, **2:** VI.B.4
procedures, **2:** VI.B.2
remedies, **2:** VI.B.3
scope, **2:** VI.B.1
executive branch agencies, **1:** I.A.1; **2:** III.A, III.B
private right of action and, **1:** I.G.2
Government entities
ADA Title III exemptions and, **6:** III.C
Government safety standards
essential job function, element of, **5:** III.B.2
Grace periods
small businesses, **3:** III.E.1

H

Harassment
state antidiscrimination laws and, **4:** FL.I.B.2
Hardship. See Undue hardship
Hawaii, disability discrimination laws
covered employers, **4:** HI.I.D
defenses, bona fide occupational qualification (BFOQ), **4:** HI.I.E.2.a
definitions, **4:** HI.I.C
disability, **4:** HI.I.C.1
employment, **4:** HI.I.C.2
overview, **4:** HI.I.A
prohibited discrimination, **4:** HI.I.B
genetic testing, **4:** HI.I.B.1
reasonable accommodation obligation, **4:** HI.I.E.1
Hazard, future
state antidiscrimination laws and, **4:** MD.I.E.2.c
Health, Education, and Welfare Department regulations, 5: I
Health and safety statutes. See Safety and health statutes

Health care coverage
See also Benefits and privileges of employment
mental vs. physical, **9:** VI.C.2
Health Insurance Portability and Accounting Act (HIPAA)
insurance-related practices, ADA's safe harbor provisions and, **9:** VI.A.3
Hearing-impaired applicants
hiring procedures and, **7:** IV.C.1
Hearings on ADA
House Committee on Education and Labor, **3:** III.A.1
House Committee on Energy and Commerce, **3:** III.B.1
House Committee on Judiciary, **3:** III.D.1
House Committee on Public Works and Transportation, **3:** III.C.1
Senate, **3:** II.D
Heart disease
ADA treatment of, **5:** V.F
High blood pressure
ADA treatment of, **5:** V.E
HIPAA (Health Insurance Portability and Accounting Act)
insurance-related practices, ADA's safe harbor provisions and, **9:** VI.A.3
Hiring
accessibility and accommodation issues, **7:** IV
hearing-impaired applicants, **7:** IV.C.1
interviews, **7:** IV.B
mobility-impaired applicants, **7:** IV.C.3
physical accessibility, **7:** IV.A
speech-impaired applicants, **7:** IV.C.4
visually-impaired applicants, **7:** IV.C.2
ADA provisions applicable to, **7:** I
applications, **7:** V.A
as evidence, **7:** V.A.1
qualifications comparisons, **7:** V.A.2
defenses, **7:** X

Hiring—*Cont'd*
  employee insubordination, **7:** X.C.5
  inability to perform essential job function, **7:** X.B
  legitimate nondiscriminatory reason, **7:** X.C
  nonstatutory defenses, **7:** X.D
  reasonable accommodation impossible, **7:** X.A
  threat-related issues, **7:** X.C.1, X.C.2, X.C.3, X.C.4
  discrimination in, proving, **7:** III
  job descriptions, **7:** V.B
  job-related requirements
    establishing, criteria, **7:** VIX.C
    justified, **7:** VIX.A
    not justified, **7:** VIX.B
  medical examinations, **7:** VI, VI.B
    defined, **7:** VI.B.3
    disputed results, **7:** VI.B.4
    postoffer exams, **7:** VI.B.2
    pre-offer exams, **7:** VI.B.1
  preemployment discrimination, prima facie case, **7:** II
  preemployment inquiries, **7:** VI
    disability-related inquiries, **7:** VI.A
  preemployment training programs, **7:** VII
  reasonable accommodation obligation
    ADA, **7:** VIII.B
    employer's duties, **7:** VIII.B.2
    employment agencies, use of, **7:** VIII.B.4
    equal employment opportunity requirements, **7:** VIII.B.1
    essential function analysis, **7:** VIII.B.8
    generally, **7:** VIII
    job information, access to, **7:** VIII.B.3
    recruitment, **7:** VIII.B.5
    Rehabilitation Act, **7:** VIII.A
    requests for, **7:** VIII.B.6
    undue hardship analysis, **7:** VIII.B.7
  as remedy for ADA violation, **1:** I.G.3
  as remedy for Rehabilitation Act violation, **2:** VI.B.3
Historic landmarks
  barrier removal and, **6:** IV.E.4.b
HIV. See **AIDS**
Home-based employment
  reasonable accommodation and, **8:** IV.E
Homosexuality
  as exempt from Rehabilitation Act, **2:** II.E, IV.B.1.a
House of Representatives
  Committee on Education and Labor, **3:** III.A
    hearings, **3:** III.A.1
    report, **3:** III.A.2
  Committee on Energy and Commerce
    hearings, **3:** III.B.1
    reports, **3:** III.B.2
  Committee on Judiciary
    hearings, **3:** III.D.1
    reports, **3:** III.D.2
  Committee on Public Works and Transportation
    hearings, **3:** III.C.1
    reports, **3:** III.C.2
  consideration of, **3:** III
  floor action, **3:** III.E
  House/Senate conference, **3:** IV
  progress in, **1:** I.B.2
Hypertension
  ADA treatment of, **5:** V.E

I

Idaho, disability discrimination laws
  covered employers, **4:** ID.I.D
  defenses, direct threat, **4:** ID.I.E.2.a
  definition of disability, **4:** ID.I.C.1
  overview, **4:** ID.I.A
  prohibited discrimination, **4:** ID.I.B
  reasonable accommodation obligation, **4:** ID.I.E.1
Illinois, disability discrimination laws
  covered employers, **4:** IL.I.D
  defenses, **4:** IL.I.E.2
    bona fide occupational

qualification (BFOQ), **4:** IL.I.E.2.a
undue hardship, **4:** IL.I.E.2.b
definition of disability, **4:** IL.I.C.1
local laws, **4:** IL.II
overview, **4:** IL.I.A
prohibited discrimination, **4:** IL.I.B
pregnancy-related disability, **4:** IL.I.B.1
reasonable accommodation obligation, **4:** IL.I.E.1
Illnesses and conditions under ADA, 5: V
AIDS/HIV. See AIDS
cancer, **5:** V.G
diabetes, **5:** V.D
epilepsy, **5:** V.H
heart disease, **5:** V.F
hypertension, **5:** V.E
mental disorders. See Mental impairment
substance abuse. See Substance abuse
Impairment
ADA definitions, **5:** II.A
AIDS, **5:** II.A
conflicts, **2:** IV.B.1.b
defined, **1:** I.D.1; **4:** AK.I.C.1
disproving, **10:** V.B.1.a
exempted conditions, **2:** IV.B.1.a
generally, **2:** IV.B.1.a
mental impairment, defined, **2:** IV.B.1.a
physical impairment, defined, **2:** IV.B.1.a
previous or misconceived, defined, **1:** I.D.3
record of, **2:** IV.C; **5:** II.D
Rehabilitation Act definitions, **5:** I
Impossibility defense
reasonable accommodation and, **2:** VII.A.3; **7:** X.A
Indiana, disability discrimination laws
covered employer, **4:** IN.I.D
defenses, **4:** IN.I.E.2
infectious or communicable diseases, **4:** IN.I.E.2.a
qualification standards, **4:** IN.I.E.2.b

undue hardship, **4:** IN.I.E.2.c
definitions, **4:** IN.I.C
disability, **4:** IN.I.C.1
employee, **4:** IN.I.C.2
person, **4:** IN.I.C.3
overview, **4:** IN.I.A
prohibited discrimination, **4:** IN.I.B
preemployment inquiries, medical examinations, **4:** IN.I.B.1.a
reasonable accommodation obligation, **4:** IN.I.E.1
Indirect benefits, programs receiving
Rehabilitation Act and, **2:** III.D.2, VII.B.1
Individuals with Disabilities Education Act (IDEA), 1: II.B
Infectious or communicable diseases
AIDS/HIV. See AIDS
state antidiscrimination laws and, **4:** GA.I.E.2.a, IN.I.E.2.a, KS.I.E.2.c
Information, employee's duty to provide, 8: III.A.4
Information and electronic technology
Rehabilitation Act, application to, **1:** I.A.4
Injunctions
as remedy for ADA violation, **1:** I.G.3; **10:** IV.B
as remedy for Rehabilitation Act violation, **2:** VI.C.3, VI.D.3; **10:** IV.B
Insubordination
as justifying non-hire, **7:** X.C.5
Insurance benefits
AIDS/HIV, employer's obligation to provide, **5:** V.B.1.e
distinguishing between mental and physical disabilities, **5:** V.C.6
nonphysical public accommodation lawsuits, **6:** II.C.1
viability of claim, **6:** II.C.2
safe harbor provisions, ADA, **9:** VI.A
ERISA preemption provisions and, **9:** VI.A.1.a
insurance industry, effect on, **9:** VI.A.1.b
Integrated settings requirement, 6: IV.D

Interactive process for requesting reasonable accommodation, 8: III.A
  employee's responsibility, **8:** III.A.1
  employer's duty, **8:** III.A.1.a
  examples, **8:** III.A.5
  form of, **8:** III.A.2
  formulating effective accommodation, employer's duty, **8:** III.A.3
  information, employee's duty to provide, **8:** III.A.4
Intermittent leave
  FMLA and ADA compared, **9:** I.C.3
Internet
  Internet-only businesses, **6:** II.E.3, II.E.4
  Web sites, as places of public accommodation, **6:** II.E.1, II.E.2
Interviews
  accessibility and accommodation issues, **7:** IV.B
Iowa, disability discrimination laws
  covered employers, **4:** IA.I.D
  defenses
    affirmative action, **4:** IA.I.E.2.a
    bona fide occupational qualification (BFOQ), **4:** IA.I.E.2.b
    undue hardship, **4:** IA.I.E.2.c
  definitions, **4:** IA.I.C
    disability, **4:** IA.I.C.1
    major life activities, **4:** IA.I.C.2
  overview, **4:** IA.I.A
  prohibited discrimination, **4:** IA.I.B
    genetic testing, **4:** IA.I.B.2
    preemployment inquiries, medical examinations, **4:** IA.I.B.1.a
    pregnancy-related disabilities, **4:** IA.I.B.3
  reasonable accommodation obligation, **4:** IA.I.E.1

J

Job applicants. See Applicants
Job applications. See Applications
Job descriptions. See Written job descriptions

Job function, essential. See Essential job function
Job information, access to
  ADA requirements and, **7:** VIII.B.3
Job security issues
  reasonable accommodation leave of absence and, **8:** IV.D.2
Job standards and qualifications
  establishing, criteria, **7:** VIX.C
  justified, **7:** VIX.A
  as limiting employer ADA obligations, **1:** I.F
  as limiting employer Rehabilitation Act obligations, **2:** VII.A.2.a
  not justified, **7:** VIX.B
Judicial estoppel
  benefits, discrimination claims and, **9:** VI.C.1.b
  discrimination charges and compensation claims, pursuing, **9:** II.B.1
Jury trial, right to
  Rehabilitation Act and, **2:** VI.D.3
Justice Department (DOJ)
  ADA Title III enforcement, role in, **6:** V.F

K

Kansas, disability discrimination laws
  covered employers, **4:** KS.I.D
  defenses, **4:** KS.I.E.2
    affirmative action, **4:** KS.I.E.2.a
    direct threat, **4:** KS.I.E.2.b
    infectious or communicable diseases, **4:** KS.I.E.2.c
    undue hardship, **4:** KS.I.E.2.d
  definitions, **4:** KS.I.C
    disability, **4:** KS.I.C.1
    essential job function, **4:** KS.I.C.2
    major life activities, **4:** KS.I.C.3
  overview, **4:** KS.I.A
  prohibited discrimination, **4:** KS.I.B
    genetic testing, **4:** KS.I.B.2
    preemployment inquiries, medical examinations, **4:** KS.I.B.1.a
    pregnancy-related disabilities, **4:** KS.I.B.3

reasonable accommodation
obligation, **4:** KS.I.E.1
Kentucky, disability discrimination laws
covered employers, **4:** KY.I.D
defenses, **4:** KY.I.E.2
undue hardship, **4:** KY.I.E.2.a
definition of disability, **4:** KY.I.C.1
overview, **4:** KY.I.A
prohibited discrimination, **4:** KY.I.B
reasonable accommodation
obligation, **4:** KY.I.E.1
Kleptomania
as exempt from Rehabilitation Act,
2: II.E

L

Landlord/tenant liability
ADA Title III requirements and, **6:** IV.M
Landmarks, historical
barrier removal and, **6:** IV.E.4.b
Last-chance agreements
substance abuse and, **5:** V.A.4.a
Leases and rentals
ADA Title III requirements and, **6:** IV.M
Leaves of absence
benefits, continuation of, **9:** I.C.5
compensation issues, **9:** I.C.4
denial and accommodation, **8:** IV.D.3
duration of, FMLA and ADA compared, **9:** I.C.2
employer policies regarding, **8:** IV.D.1
intermittent leave, **9:** I.C.3
job security issues, **8:** IV.D.2
medical leave, **8:** IV.D.2
modified or part-time schedule, **8:** IV.D.4
policy as defense to ADA claim, **10:** V.B.1.b.ii
reasonable accommodations and, **8:** IV.D
terms and conditions, FMLA and ADA compared, **9:** I.C
undue hardship and, **8:** V.B

workers' compensation laws and, **9:** II.D
Legislative history of ADA
See also Amendments to ADA;
Hearings on ADA; Reports on
ADA
House, progress in, **1:** I.B.2
Senate, introduction in, **1:** I.B.1; **3:** I, II
Life functions or activities. See Major life activities
Light-duty work
available under FMLA and ADA, **9:** I.D
workers' compensation laws and, **9:** II.D
Limitation on major life activity
conflicting areas, **2:** IV.B.2.b
defined, **1:** I.D.2; **2:** IV.B.2.a
substantially limits, defined, **2:** IV.B.2.b
Limitations, statutes of. See Statutes of limitations
Litigation strategies, ADA, 10: V
defendants, **10:** V.B
affirmative defenses, **10:** V.B.1.b
disproving plaintiff's case, **10:** V.B.1
plaintiffs, **10:** V.A
administrative charges, filing, **10:** V.A.1
lawsuits, filing, **10:** V.A.2
prima facie case, establishing, **10:** V.A.3
success rates, **10:** V.A
Local antidiscrimination laws
California, **4:** CA.II
Florida, **4:** FL.II
Illinois, **4:** IL.II
New York, **4:** NY.II
Louisiana, disability discrimination laws
covered employers, **4:** LA.I.D
defenses, **4:** LA.I.E.2
affirmative action, **4:** LA.I.E.2.a
business necessity, **4:** LA.I.E.2.b
qualification standards, **4:** LA.I.E.2.c
undue hardship, **4:** LA.I.E.2.d

Louisiana, disability discrimination laws—*Cont'd*
definitions, **4:** LA.I.C
  disability, **4:** LA.I.C.1
  major life activities, **4:** LA.I.C.2
overview, **4:** LA.I.A
prohibited discrimination, **4:** LA.I.B
  genetic testing, **4:** LA.I.B.1
  pregnancy-related disabilities, **4:** LA.I.B.2
reasonable accommodation obligation, **4:** LA.I.E.1

M

Maine, disability discrimination laws
covered employers, **4:** ME.I.D
defenses, **4:** ME.I.E.2
  undue hardship, **4:** ME.I.E.2.a
definition of disability, **4:** ME.I.C.1
overview, **4:** ME.I.A
prohibited discrimination, **4:** ME.I.B
  genetic testing, **4:** ME.I.B.2
  preemployment inquiries, medical examinations, **4:** ME.I.B.1.a
reasonable accommodation obligation, **4:** ME.I.E.1

Major life activities
ADA definitions, **5:** II.B
  working, **5:** II.B.1
conflicting areas, **2:** IV.B.2.b
defined, **1:** I.D.2
state antidiscrimination laws. See *specific state*
disproving plaintiff's ADA case and, **10:** V.B.1.a
mental impairments, **5:** V.C.1
substantial limitation, defined, **2:** IV.B.2.b; **5:** II.C
  mitigating measures, effect of, **5:** II.C.4
  nature and severity of impairment, **5:** II.C.1
  temporary vs. permanent, **5:** II.C.3
  working, substantially limited, **5:** II.C.2

Maryland, disability discrimination laws
covered employers, **4:** MD.I.D

defenses, **4:** MD.I.E.2
  bona fide occupational qualification (BFOQ), **4:** MD.I.E.2.a
  future hazard, **4:** MD.I.E.2.b
  preferential treatment, **4:** MD.I.E.2.c
definitions
  disability, **4:** MD.I.C.1
  major life activity, **4:** MD.I.C.2
overview, **4:** MD.I.A
prohibited discrimination, **4:** MD.I.B
  genetic testing, **4:** MD.I.B.1
  pregnancy-related disabilities, **4:** MD.I.B.2
reasonable accommodation obligation, **4:** MD.I.E.1

Massachusetts, disability discrimination laws
covered employers, **4:** MA.I.D
defenses, **4:** MA.I.E.2
  bona fide occupational qualification (BFOQ), **4:** MA.I.E.2.a
  undue hardship, **4:** MA.I.E.2.b
definitions
  disability, **4:** MA.I.C.1
  major life activity, **4:** MA.I.C.2
overview, **4:** MA.I.A
prohibited discrimination, **4:** MA.I.B
  genetic testing, **4:** MA.I.B.2
  preemployment inquiries, **4:** MA.I.B.1
  retaliation, **4:** MA.I.B.3
reasonable accommodation obligation, **4:** MA.I.E.1

Medical conditions
defined, **4:** CA.I.C.4
distinguishing from disabilities, **9:** I.B.2
state antidiscrimination laws and, **4:** FL.I.B.3, NM.I.C.2, PA.I.B.1

Medical examinations
ADA and OSH Act treatment compared, **9:** IV.B.2
FMLA treatment compared, **9:** I.E
hiring process and ADA, **7:** VI, VI.B
defined, **7:** VI.B.3
disputed results, **7:** VI.B.4

postoffer exams, **7:** VI.B.2
pre-offer exams, **7:** VI.B.1
requests for reasonable accommodation and, **8:** III.C
state antidiscrimination laws, **4:** AZ.I.B.1.a, DE.I.B.1.a, IA.I.B.1.a, IN.I.B.1.a, KS.I.B.1.a, ME.I.B.1.a, MN.I.B.1.a, MO.I.B.1.a, MT.I.B.1.a, NE.I.B.1.a, SC.I.B.1.a, WA.I.B.1.a
workers' compensation claims and, **9:** II.C.2

Medical leave
job security issues and, **8:** IV.D.2

Medical records
workers' compensation claims and, **9:** II.C.1

Medication issues
reasonable accommodation and, **8:** IV.F

Mental Health Parity Act (MHPA), 9: VI.C.2

Mental impairment
defined, **2:** IV.B.1.a; **5:** V.C
employee benefits and, **5:** V.C.6
major life activity, substantial limit on, **5:** V.C.1
mitigating or corrective measures, **5:** V.C.1, V.C.2
perceived as disabled, **5:** V.C.5
qualified individuals, **5:** V.C.4
reasonable accommodation obligation, **5:** V.C.7
working, substantial limitation on, **5:** V.C.3

Michigan, disability discrimination laws
covered employers, **4:** MI.I.D
defenses, undue hardship, **4:** MI.I.E.2.a
definitions
  disability, **4:** MI.I.C.1
  major life activity, **4:** MI.I.C.2
overview, **4:** MI.I.A
prohibited discrimination, **4:** MI.I.B
  genetic testing, **4:** MI.I.B.1
reasonable accommodation obligation, **4:** MI.I.E.1

Minnesota, disability discrimination laws
covered employers, **4:** MN.I.D
defenses, **4:** MN.I.E.2
  direct threat, **4:** MN.I.E.2.a
  undue hardship, **4:** MN.I.E.2.b
definition of disability, **4:** MN.I.C.1
overview, **4:** MN.I.A
prohibited discrimination, **4:** MN.I.B
  genetic testing, **4:** MN.I.B.3
  preemployment inquiries, medical examinations, **4:** MN.I.B.1.a
  pregnancy-related disabilities, **4:** MN.I.B.2
  retaliation, **4:** MN.I.B.4
reasonable accommodation obligation, **4:** MN.I.E.1

Misconceived impairment
defined, **1:** I.D.3

Mississippi, disability discrimination laws
covered employers, **4:** MS.I.D
defenses, **4:** MS.I.E
definition of disability, **4:** MS.I.C.1
overview, **4:** MS.I.A
prohibited discrimination, **4:** MS.I.B
reasonable accommodation obligation, **4:** MS.I.E

Missouri, disability discrimination laws
covered employers, **4:** MO.I.D
defenses, **4:** MO.I.E.2
  affirmative action, **4:** MO.I.E.2.a
  preferential treatment, **4:** MO.I.E.2.b
definitions, **4:** MO.I.C
  disability, **4:** MO.I.C.1
  major life activity, **4:** MO.I.C.2
overview, **4:** MO.I.A
prohibited discrimination, **4:** MO.I.B
  medical examinations, **4:** MO.I.B.1.a
  preemployment inquiries, **4:** MO.I.B.1
reasonable accommodation obligation, **4:** MO.I.E.1

Mitigating or corrective measures
effect on substantial limitation, **5:** II.C.4
mental impairments and, **5:** V.C.2

Mixed-use facilities
  ADA accommodation obligations
    and, **6:** II.B
Mobility-impaired applicants
  hiring process and, **7:** IV.C.3
"Model" employer provisions
  Rehabilitation Act and, **2:** III.B
Modifications, reasonable
  barrier removal. See Barrier removal
  Title III requirements, **6:** IV.C
  work site or equipment, **8:** IV.G
Modified or part-time schedule
  reasonable accommodation and, **8:** IV.D.4
Montana, disability discrimination laws
  covered employers, **4:** MT.I.D
  defenses, **4:** MT.I.E.2
    BFOQ, **4:** MT.I.E.2.a
    undue hardship, **4:** MT.I.E.2.b
  definition of disability, **4:** MT.I.C.1
  overview, **4:** MT.I.A
  prohibited discrimination, **4:** MT.I.B
    medical examinations, **4:** MT.I.B.1.a
    preemployment inquiries, **4:** MT.I.B.1
  reasonable accommodation
    obligation, **4:** MT.I.E.1
Motion for summary judgment
  defendant's litigation strategies and, **10:** V.B

N

National Council on Disability, 1: I.B
  reports, **3:** I
National Labor Relations Act (NLRA)
  ADA interplay with, **9:** V
    collective bargaining agreements.
      See Collective bargaining
      agreements
    conflicts between NLRA and ADA, **9:** V.B
    bargaining and reasonable
      accommodation, **9:** V.B.3
    confidentiality and disclosures
      duties, **9:** V.B.2
    direct dealing prohibition and
      duty to meet informally, **9:** V.B.1
    fair representation, duty of, **9:** V.D
    interrelation with ADA, **9:** V.A
Nebraska, disability discrimination laws
  covered employers, **4:** NE.I.D
  defenses, undue hardship, **4:** NE.I.E.2.a
  definition of disability, **4:** NE.I.C.1
  overview, **4:** NE.I.A
  prohibited discrimination, **4:** NE.I.B
    genetic testing, **4:** NE.I.B.2
    medical examinations, **4:** NE.I.B.1.a
    preemployment inquiries, **4:** NE.I.B.1
  reasonable accommodation
    obligation, **4:** NE.I.E.1
Nevada, disability discrimination laws
  covered employers, **4:** NV.I.D
  defenses
    bona fide occupational
      qualification (BFOQ), **4:** NV.I.E.2.a
    preferential treatment, **4:** NV.I.E.2.b
  definition of disability, **4:** NV.I.C.1
  overview, **4:** NV.I.A
  prohibited discrimination, **4:** NV.I.B
    genetic testing, **4:** NV.I.B.1
    pregnancy-related disabilities, **4:** NV.I.B.2
  reasonable accommodation
    obligation, **4:** NV.I.E.1
New construction
  ADA Title III requirements, **6:** IV.N
  scoping requirements, **6:** IV.N.1
  unclear accessibility guidelines, **6:** IV.N.2
New Hampshire, disability discrimination laws
  covered employers, **4:** NH.I.D
  defenses, **4:** NH.I.E
  definition of disability, **4:** NH.I.C.1
  overview, **4:** NH.I.A
  prohibited discrimination, **4:** NH.I.B
    genetic testing, **4:** NH.I.B.2
    preemployment issues, **4:** NH.I.B.1

reasonable accommodation
obligation, **4:** NH.I.E
New hires
reasonable accommodation
obligations, **8:** VII.A
**New Jersey, disability discrimination
laws**
covered employers, **4:** NJ.I.D
defenses, **4:** NJ.I.E.2
undue hardship, **4:** NJ.I.E.2.a
definition of disability, **4:** NJ.I.C.1
overview, **4:** NJ.I.A
prohibited discrimination, **4:**
NJ.I.B
reasonable accommodation
obligation, **4:** NJ.I.E.1
**New Mexico, disability discrimination
laws**
covered employers, **4:** NM.I.D
definitions
disability, **4:** NM.I.C.1
medical condition, **4:** NM.I.C.2
overview, **4:** NM.I.A
prohibited discrimination, **4:**
NM.I.B
reasonable accommodation
obligation, **4:** NM.I.E.1
**New York, disability discrimination
laws**
AIDS, **4:** NY.I.C.1
covered employers, **4:** NY.I.D
definition of disability, **4:** NY.I.C.1
local laws, **4:** NY.II
overview, **4:** NY.I.A
prohibited discrimination, **4:** NY.I.B
genetic testing, **4:** NY.I.B.1
reasonable accommodation
obligation, **4:** NY.I.E.1
NLRA. See National Labor Relations
Act
**Nonphysical places of public
accommodation**
lawsuits, **6:** II.C.1
viability of claim, **6:** II.C.2
**Nonstatutory defenses to
discrimination charges, 7:** X.D
Normal physical characteristics
as exempt from Rehabilitation Act,
2: IV.B.1.a

**North Carolina, disability
discrimination laws**
covered employers, **4:** NC.I.D
defenses, **4:** NC.I.E.2
undue hardship, **4:** NC.I.E.2.a
definition of disability, **4:** NC.I.C.1
overview, **4:** NC.I.A
prohibited discrimination, **4:** NC.I.B
genetic testing, **4:** NC.I.B.1
retaliation, **4:** NC.I.B.2
reasonable accommodation
obligation, **4:** NC.I.E.1
**North Dakota, disability discrimination
laws**
covered employers, **4:** ND.I.D
defenses, undue hardship, **4:**
ND.I.E.2.a
definition of disability, **4:** ND.I.C.1
overview, **4:** ND.I.A
prohibited discrimination, **4:** ND.I.B
reasonable accommodation
obligation, **4:** ND.I.E.1

O

Obesity
Rehabilitation Act coverage and, **2:**
IV.B.1.b.i
**Occupational Safety and Health Act
(OSH Act)**
ADA compared, **9:** IV
conflict defense, **9:** IV.A.4
direct threat defense, **9:** IV.A.3
application debate, **9:** IV.A.3.a
duty to provide safe workplace, **9:**
IV.A
business necessity defense, **9:**
IV.A.1
employer defined, **9:** IV
tensions with ADA, **9:** IV.B
abatement requirements, **9:**
IV.B.3
employee records, **9:** IV.B.1
medical examinations, **9:** IV.B.2
undue hardship defense, **9:** IV.A.2
Off-duty conduct
substance abuse and, **5:** V.A.4.b

Offers
  post-employment, reasonable
    accommodation need and, **8:**
    VII.B.2
  preemployment, reasonable
    accommodation need and, **8:**
    VII.B.1

Ohio, disability discrimination laws
  covered employers, **4:** OH.I.D
  defenses, undue hardship, **4:**
    OH.I.E.2.a
  definitions
    disability, **4:** OH.I.C.1
    major life activity, **4:** OH.I.C.2
  overview, **4:** OH.I.A
  prohibited discrimination, **4:** OH.I.B
    preemployment inquiries, **4:**
    OH.I.B.1
  reasonable accommodation
    obligation, **4:** OH.I.E.1

Oklahoma, disability discrimination laws
  covered employers, **4:** OK.I.D
  defenses, undue hardship, **4:**
    OK.I.E.2.a
  definition of disability, **4:** OK.I.C.1
  overview, **4:** OK.I.A
  prohibited discrimination, **4:** OK.I.B
    genetic testing, **4:** OK.I.B.1
  reasonable accommodation
    obligation, **4:** OK.I.E.1

Ordinances, antidiscrimination
  California, **4:** CA.II
  Florida, **4:** FL.II
  Illinois, **4:** IL.II
  New York, **4:** NY.II

Oregon, disability discrimination laws
  covered employers, **4:** OR.I.D
  defenses, direct threat, **4:** OR.I.E.2.a
  definitions
    disability, **4:** OR.I.C.1
    major life activities, **4:** OR.I.C.2
  overview, **4:** OR.I.A
  prohibited discrimination, **4:** OR.I.B
    genetic testing, **4:** OR.I.B.1
  reasonable accommodation
    obligation, **4:** OR.I.E.1

OSH Act. See Occupational Safety and Health Act

Over-the-road buses
  ADA Title III requirements and, **6:**
    IV.P.4

P

Part-time or modified schedule
  reasonable accommodation and, **8:**
    IV.D.4

Pedophilia
  as exempt from Rehabilitation Act,
    2: II.E

Pennsylvania, disability discrimination laws
  covered employers, **4:** PA.I.D
  defenses, undue hardship, **4:**
    PA.I.E.2.a
  definitions
    disability, **4:** PA.I.C.1
    major life activities, **4:** PA.I.C.2
  overview, **4:** PA.I.A
  prohibited discrimination, **4:** PA.I.B
    AIDS, **4:** PA.I.B.1
    medical condition, **4:** PA.I.B.1
  reasonable accommodation
    obligation, **4:** PA.I.E.1

Person
  defined, **4:** IN.I.C.3

Personnel offices
  accessibility to, **7:** IV.A

Physical impairment
  defined, **2:** IV.B.1.a

Plaintiff's litigation strategies, 10: V.A
  administrative charges, filing, **10:**
    V.A.1
  lawsuits, filing, **10:** V.A.2
  prima facie case, establishing, **10:**
    V.A.3
    disability, proving, **10:** V.A.3.a
    duration or long-time impact,
      proof of, **10:** V.A.3.a.1
    punitive damages, making case
      for, **10:** V.A.3.d
    qualified individual, proving status
      as, **10:** V.A.3.b
    reasonable accommodation and,
      10: V.A.3.c
  success rates, **10:** V.A

Policies, employer
  fitness to return to work, **9:** II.C.3

reasonable accommodation requests and, **8:** III.D
absenteeism, treatment under FMLA and ADA, **9:** I.C.6
leaves of absences and, **8:** IV.D.1
Post-employment offers
reasonable accommodation need and, **8:** VII.B.2
Preemployment discrimination
prima facie case under ADA, **7:** II
Preemployment inquiries
ADA, hiring process and, **7:** VI
disability-related inquiries, **7:** VI.A
job-related function inquiries, **7:** VI.A.3.b
known disabilities, **7:** VI.A.3.c
nondisabling impairments, **7:** VI.A.3.a
permissible inquiries, **7:** VI.A.3
prima facie case, **7:** VI.A.1
prohibition, reasons for, **7:** VI.A.2
FMLA treatment compared, **9:** I.E
reasonable accommodation, need for, **8:** VII.B
post-employment offers, **8:** VII.B.2
preemployment offers, **8:** VII.B.1
state antidiscrimination laws
generally, **4:** GA.I.B.1, MA.I.B.1, NH.I.B.1, OH.I.B.1, UT.I.B.1
medical examinations. See Medical examinations
physical condition or medical history, **4:** DC.I.B.1
workers' compensation laws and, **9:** II.C.5
Preemployment offers
reasonable accommodation need and, **8:** VII.B.1
Preemployment training programs, 7: VII
Preemption issues
ERISA and ADA safe harbor provisions, **9:** VI.A.1.a
workers' compensation laws and ADA, **9:** II
Preferential treatment
state antidiscrimination laws and, **4:** MD.I.E.2.c, MO.I.E.2.b, NV.I.E.2.b

Pregnancy-related disabilities
state antidiscrimination laws, **4:** IA.I.B.3, IL.I.B.1, KS.I.B.3, LA.I.B.2, MD.I.B.2, MN.I.B.2, NV.I.B.2
Pretext
substance abuse and, **5:** V.A.4.c
Previous impairment
defined, **1:** I.D.3
Prima facie case, ADA
establishing, **10:** V.A.3
disability, proving, **10:** V.A.3.a
duration or long-time impact, proof of, **10:** V.A.3.a.1
punitive damages, making case for, **10:** V.A.3.d
qualified individual, proving status as, **10:** V.A.3.b
reasonable accommodation and, **10:** V.A.3.c
Primary function areas
ADA Title III requirements and, **6:** IV.J
Privacy
AIDS/HIV, employer's duty, **5:** V.B.1.f
requests for reasonable accommodation and, **8:** III.F
workers' compensation claims, **9:** II.C
Private clubs
ADA exemptions and, **6:** III.B; **10:** IV.A.1.c
Private companies
ADA accommodation issues and, **6:** II.E
Internet-only businesses, **6:** II.E.3, II.E.4
Web sites, **6:** II.E.1, II.E.2
Private right of action
Rehabilitation Act
federal contractor provisions, **10:** II.D.2
programs receiving federal funds, **10:** II.D.3
Probable cause for discrimination claim
EEOC investigation and, **10:** II.A.3
Procedural defenses, 2: VII.A.5

Protected individual
defined, **2:** IV.A
Public accommodation, places of,
8: IX
ADA coverage and, **1:** I.B.4
alterations, **6:** IV.I
alternatives, **6:** IV.G
architect liability, **6:** IV.O
auxiliary aids, provision of, **6:** IV.H
barrier removal, **6:** IV.E
commercial facilities, **6:** II.F
defined, **6:** II.A
direct threat defense, **6:** IV.B
enforcement, **6:** V
  administrative remedies,
    exhaustion requirement, **6:** V.C
  attorney general's role, **6:** V.B
  attorneys' fees, **6:** V.E
  Justice Department and, **6:** V.F
  remedies, **6:** V.A
  standing issues, **6:** V.D
equal participation, **6:** IV.A
exemptions, **6:** III
  government entities, **6:** III.C
  private clubs, **6:** III.B
  religious organizations, **6:** III.A
franchise liability, **6:** IV.L
guidelines, **6:** IV.F
historic landmarks, **6:** IV.E.4.b
intangible public accommodations, **6:** II.D
integrated settings, **6:** IV.D
Internet-only businesses, **6:** II.E.3, II.E.4
landlord/tenant liability, **6:** IV.M
mixed-use facilities, **6:** II.B
new construction, **6:** IV.N
physical vs. nonphysical, **6:** II.C
primary function areas, **6:** IV.J
private companies, **6:** II.E
reasonable modifications, **6:** IV.C
requirements, **6:** IV
tax credits, **6:** IV.K
transportation services, **6:** IV.P
Web sites, **6:** II.E.1, II.E.2
Public entity activities
ADA coverage and, **1:** I.B.4
Public transportation
ADA, proposed amendments, **3:** III.E.6

Punitive damages
as remedy for ADA violation, **1:** I.G.3; **10:** IV.A.1.a, IV.A.1.b, V.A.2, V.A.3.d
as remedy for Rehabilitation Act violation, **2:** VI.D.3; **10:** IV.A.1.b
Pyromania
as exempt from Rehabilitation Act, **2:** II.E

Q

Qualifications and standards
comparison of applicants, **7:** V.A.2
as limiting employer ADA obligations, **1:** I.F
as limiting employer Rehabilitation Act obligations, **2:** VII.A.2.a
preemployment practices
  establishing, criteria, **7:** VIX.C
  justified, **7:** VIX.A
  not justified, **7:** VIX.B
state antidiscrimination laws, **4:** IN.I.E.2.b, LA.I.E.2.c
Qualified handicap
defined, **4:** DE.I.C.1
Qualified individual with disability
AIDS/HIV, **5:** V.B.1
  association provision, **5:** V.B.1.c
  inquiries and tests, **5:** V.B.1.b
  insurance benefits, employer's obligation regarding, **5:** V.B.1.e
  privacy, duty to maintain, **5:** V.B.1.f
  reasonable accommodation, **5:** V.B.1.d
  unqualified due to risk, **5:** V.B.1.a
defined, **2:** IV.E; **5:** III
disproving plaintiff's status as, **10:** V.B.1.a
essential job functions, defined, **5:** III.B
mental impairments, **5:** V.C.4
otherwise qualified, **5:** III.A
proving status as, **10:** V.A.3.b
reasonable accommodation and, **8:** II.B
  essential job function, **8:** II.B.1
tests, **2:** IV.E

R

Reasonable accommodation obligation, 1: I.E
  accommodations, types required, **8:** II.C
  ADA, **8:** I.B
    interplay with other laws, **8:** VIII.A
    additional accommodations, **8:** VIII.B
  AIDS/HIV, **5:** V.B.1.d
  applicants, **8:** VII
    ADA, **7:** VIII.B
    employer's duties, **7:** VIII.B.2
    employment agencies, use of, **7:** VIII.B.4
    equal employment opportunity requirements, **7:** VIII.B.1
    essential function analysis, **7:** VIII.B.8
    generally, **7:** VIII
    job information, access to, **7:** VIII.B.3
    recruitment, **7:** VIII.B.5
    Rehabilitation Act, **7:** VIII.A; **8:** I.A
    requests for, **7:** VIII.B.6
    undue hardship analysis, **7:** VIII.B.7
  aspects of employment, **1:** I.E
  benefits and privileges of employment, **8:** II.C
  business necessity defense, **1:** I.F
  categories, **8:** II.A
  defenses and limitations, **1:** I.F; **2:** VII.A.3
  direct threat defense, **1:** I.F; **8:** VI
  disproving plaintiff's ADA case, **10:** V.B.1.a
  employer's duties, **1:** I.E
  employer's rights, **8:** II.B.2
  essential job function and, **5:** III.C
  failure to provide, **8:** II.D
  impossibility defense, **2:** VII.A.3; **7:** X.A
  mental impairments, **5:** V.C.7
  mitigation of threat posed by applicant, **7:** X.C.3
  new hires, **8:** VII.A
  NLRA conflicts and, **9:** V.B.3
  other laws, interplay with, **8:** VIII.A
  preemployment inquiries, **8:** VII.B
  post-employment offers, **8:** VII.B.2
  preemployment offers, **8:** VII.B.1
  proving availability of, **10:** V.A.3.c
  public accommodations, **8:** IX
  qualified individuals with disabilities, **8:** II.B
    essential job functions, **8:** II.B.1
  reasonableness of accommodation, factors for determining, **8:** IV
  Rehabilitation Act
    defined, **2:** V.B
    origin of, **2:** V.A
    undue hardship and, **2:** V.B
  requests for, **8:** III
    certification by employer-selected doctor, **8:** III.C
    collective bargaining agreements, effect of, **8:** III.E
    confidentiality issues, **8:** III.F
    documentation requests, **8:** III.B
    employee's responsibility, **8:** III.A.1
    employer's duty, **8:** III.A.1.a
    employer's policies, **8:** III.D
    examples, **8:** III.A.5
    form of, **8:** III.A.2
    formulating effective accommodation, employer's duty, **8:** III.A.3
    information, employee's duty to provide, **8:** III.A.4
    interactive process, **8:** III.A
  state disability discrimination laws. See *specific state*
  substance abuse, **5:** V.A.8
  suggested accommodations, **8:** IV
    existing facilities, accessibility, **8:** IV.A
    home-based employment, **8:** IV.E
    job reassignment, **8:** IV.C
    job restructuring, **8:** IV.B
    leaves of absence, **8:** IV.D
    medication issues, **8:** IV.F
    modification of work site or equipment, **8:** IV.G
    workplace conduct rules and, **8:** IV.H

Reasonable accommodation obligation—*Cont'd*
  undue hardship issues. See Undue hardship
  violation by employer, factors, **1:** I.E
  workers' compensation laws and, **9:** II.D
Reasonableness of accommodation
  factors for determining, **8:** IV
  suggested accommodations, **8:** IV
    existing facilities, accessibility, **8:** IV.A
    job reassignment, **8:** IV.C
    job restructuring, **8:** IV.B
    leaves of absence, **8:** IV.D
Record of disability
  Rehabilitation Act and, **2:** IV.C
Record of impairment
  ADA and, **5:** II.D
Records, employee
  ADA and OSH Act treatment compared, **9:** IV.B.1
Records, medical
  workers' compensation claims and, **9:** II.C.1
Recruitment
  ADA preemployment practices requirements and, **7:** VIII.B.5
Reduced schedules
  FMLA and ADA compared, **9:** I.C.3
"Regarded as" disabled, 2: IV.C; **5:** II.E
  ability to work substantially limited, **5:** II.E.1
  mental impairments, **5:** V.C.5
Rehabilitation Act, 1: I.A
  actual disability, defined, **2:** IV.B
  ADA and
    overlapping coverage, **2:** I
    standards, incorporation in, **2:** II.E
  administrative relief, **1:** I.G.1
  affirmative action plans, **1:** I.A.1; **2:** III.B, VI.B.4
  alcohol or drug addiction and, **2:** II.D
  arbitration and, **10:** VI.B
  attorneys' fee awards and, **10:** VII.B
  conflicts, **2:** IV.B.1.b

  defenses. See Defenses to Rehabilitation Act liability
  disability, defined, **5:** I
  electronic and information technology, **1:** I.A.4
  enactment, **2:** II.A
  enforcement of. See Enforcement of Rehabilitation Act
  entities, covered, **1:** I.C
  executive branch employees, **1:** I.A.1; **2:** II.C, III.A, III.B
  exempted conditions, **2:** II.E, IV.B.1.a
  government contractors. See Government contractors
  government employees. See Government employees
  HEW regulations, **5:** I
  impairment. See Impairment
  indirect benefits, programs receiving, **2:** III.D.2
  "model" employer provisions, **2:** III.B
  1974 amendments, **2:** II.B
  1978 amendments, **2:** II.C
  1990 amendments, **2:** II.D
  1992 amendments, **2:** II.E
  overview, **2:** I
  private right of action and, **1:** I.G.2; **10:** II.D.2
  programs receiving federal financial assistance, **1:** I.A.3; **2:** III.A, III.D
  protected individual, defined, **2:** IV.A
  qualified individual with disability, defined, **2:** IV.E
  reasonable accommodation obligation. See Reasonable accommodation obligation
  record of disability, **2:** IV.C
  "regarded as" disabled, **2:** IV.C
  remedies for violations. See Remedies for Rehabilitation Act violations
  sovereign immunity and, **10:** III.B
  states, application to, **2:** III.D.3
  tests, **2:** IV.E

Vietnam Era Veterans' Readjustment
Assistance Act and, **2:** II.E
waivers, **1:** I.A.2; **2:** II.E, III.C
Reinstatement
as remedy for ADA violation, **1:** I.G.3
as remedy for Rehabilitation Act violation, **2:** VI.B.3
right to, FMLA and ADA compared, **9:** I.G
Religious organizations
ADA exemptions and, **6:** III.A; **10:** IV.A.1.c, V.B.1.b.viii
Remedies for ADA violations, 1: I.G, I.G.3
administrative relief, **1:** I.G.1
amendments, proposed, **3:** III.E.6
back pay, **1:** I.G.3
compensatory damages, **1:** I.G.3; **10:** IV.A.1.a
damages
limitations on, **1:** I.G.3
Title I, parallel to Title VII, **10:** IV.A.1.a
Title II, two-tier approach, **10:** IV.A.1.b
Title III, limited relief available, **10:** IV.A.1.c
equitable remedies, **1:** I.G.3
exhaustion of administrative remedies requirement, **10:** II.A.4
FMLA remedies compared, **9:** I.I
hiring, **1:** I.G.3
injunctions, **10:** IV.B
private right of action, **1:** I.G.2
punitive damages, **1:** I.G.3; **10:** IV.A.1.a, IV.A.1.b
reinstatement, **1:** I.G.3
Title III violations, **6:** V.A
types, **1:** I.G.3
Remedies for Rehabilitation Act violations, 2: VI.B.3; **10:** IV.A.2
back pay, **2:** VI.B.3, VI.D.3
compensatory damages, limits on, **2:** VI.B.3, VI.D.3
equitable relief, **2:** VI.B.3
injunctions, **2:** VI.C.3, VI.D.3; **10:** IV.B

punitive damages, **2:** VI.D.3
sanctions, **2:** VI.C.3
types, **2:** VI.B.3
Rental units
ADA Title III requirements and, **6:** IV.M
Reports on ADA
House Committee on Education and Labor, **3:** III.A.2
House Committee on Energy and Commerce, **3:** III.B.2
House Committee on Judiciary, **3:** III.D.2
House Committee on Public Works and Transportation, **3:** III.C.2
Requests for reasonable accommodation, 8: III
certification by employer-selected doctor, **8:** III.C
collective bargaining agreements, effect of, **8:** III.E
confidentiality issues, **8:** III.F
documentation requests, **8:** III.B
employer policies, **8:** III.D
interactive process, **8:** III.A
employee's responsibility, **8:** III.A.1
employer's duty, **8:** III.A.1.a
examples, **8:** III.A.5
form of, **8:** III.A.2
formulating effective accommodation, employer's duty, **8:** III.A.3
information, employee's duty to provide, **8:** III.A.4
Restaurants
ADA issues, **1:** I.B.3; **3:** III.E.5
Retaliation
antiretaliation provisions of FMLA and ADA compared, **9:** I.H
state antidiscrimination laws and, **4:** GA.I.B.2, MA.I.B.3, MN.I.B.4, NC.I.B.2, TN.I.B.1
Rhode Island, disability discrimination laws
covered employers, **4:** RI.I.D
definition of disability, **4:** RI.I.C.1
overview, **4:** RI.I.A
prohibited discrimination, **4:** RI.I.B
genetic testing, **4:** RI.I.B.1

Rhode Island, disability discrimination laws—*Cont'd*
  reasonable accommodation obligation, **4:** RI.I.E
Risk
  as disqualifying individual under ADA, **5:** V.B.1.a

S

Safe harbor provisions
  insurance-related practices, **9:** VI.A
Safety and health statutes
  Commercial Motor Vehicle Safety Act, **9:** IV.A.4
  Occupational Safety and Health Act, **9:** IV
    duty to provide safe workplace, **9:** IV.A
    employer defined, **9:** IV
  state laws, **9:** IV.C
Safety standards
  defenses to ADA claims, as, **10:** V.B.1.b.iii
  essential job function, element of, **5:** III.B.2
Sanctions
  government contractors and, **2:** VI.C.3
Scoping requirements for new construction
  ADA Title III requirements, **6:** IV.N.1
Seating, assembly
  barrier removal and, **6:** IV.E.2
Senate proceedings on ADA
  approval, **3:** II.G
  hearings, **3:** II.D
  House/Senate conference, **3:** IV
  introduction, **1:** I.B.1; **3:** I.B
Seniority provisions
  collective bargaining agreements and, **9:** V.B.3.a.i
  defenses to ADA claims, as, **10:** V.B.1.b.vi
Serious medical conditions
  defined, **9:** I.B.2.b
  distinguishing from disabilities, **9:** I.B.2

Seventh Amendment jury trial right
  Rehabilitation Act and, **2:** VI.D.3
Sexual behavior disorders
  as exempt from Rehabilitation Act, **2:** II.E
Small businesses
  grace period, **3:** III.E.1
Small communities
  ADA, proposed amendments, **3:** III.E.6
Social Security Act programs, 1: II.G; **9:** III
  disability
    ADA definition compared, **9:** III.B
    conflict between definitions, recognition by administration and courts, **9:** III.C.1, III.C.2
    defined, **9:** III.A
    duration of benefits, **9:** III.A.1
  receipt of benefits and ADA recovery, **9:** III.D
    conflicts, **9:** III.D.1
    genuine conflicts, **9:** III.D.2
    sufficient explanation burden, **9:** III.D.3
  SSDI benefits, interaction with ADA, **5:** IV; **8:** VIII.A
South Carolina, disability discrimination laws
  covered employers, **4:** SC.I.D
  definition of disability, **4:** SC.I.C.1
  overview, **4:** SC.I.A
  prohibited discrimination, **4:** SC.I.B
    medical examinations, **4:** SC.I.B.1.a
    preemployment inquiries, **4:** SC.I.B.1
  reasonable accommodation obligation, **4:** SC.I.E.1
South Dakota, disability discrimination laws
  covered employers, **4:** SD.I.D
  definition of disability, **4:** SD.I.C.1
  overview, **4:** SD.I.A
  prohibited discrimination, **4:** SD.I.B
    genetic testing, **4:** SD.I.B.1
  reasonable accommodation obligation, **4:** SD.I.E.1

Sovereign immunity, 10: III
  ADA and, **10:** III.A
  Eleventh Amendment and, **10:** III
  Rehabilitation Act, **10:** III.B
  waiver provisions, **10:** III
Speech-impaired applicants
  hiring process and, **7:** IV.C.4
Spending Clause, 2: III.D.3
SSDI benefits. See Social Security Act programs
Standing
  ADA Title III enforcement and, **6:** V.D
  benefits, discrimination in, **9:** VI.C.1
States
  attorneys' fee awards and, **10:** VII.C
  disability discrimination laws, **Ch. 4**
    See also *specific states*
  Rehabilitation Act, application to, **2:** III.D.3
  safety and health laws, ADA interplay with, **9:** IV.C
Statutes of limitations
  ADA and, **10:** II.A.2
  Rehabilitation Act violations and, **2:** VI.D.3
Substance abuse
  ADA treatment of, **5:** V.A
    alcohol only, **5:** V.A.2
    compliance with other laws and regulations, **5:** V.A.7
    current use, **5:** V.A.1
    drug testing, **5:** V.A.5.a
    employer defenses, **5:** V.A.6
    employer rights, **5:** V.A.4
    inquiries and examinations regarding, **5:** V.A.5
    reasonable accommodation, **5:** V.A.8
    "regarded as," **5:** V.A.3
Substantial limitation on major life activity
  defined, **2:** IV.B.2.b; **5:** II.C
  mitigating measures, effect of, **5:** II.C.4
  nature and severity of impairment, **5:** II.C.1
  temporary vs. permanent, **5:** II.C.3
  working, substantially limited, **5:** II.C.2
Sufficient explanation burden
  Social Security Act and ADA conflict, **9:** III.D.3
Suggested reasonable accommodations, 8: IV
  existing facilities, accessibility, **8:** IV.A
  job reassignment, **8:** IV.C
    transfer, restrictions on, **8:** IV.C.1
    vacant positions, **8:** IV.C.2
  job restructuring, **8:** IV.B
  leaves of absence, **8:** IV.D
    denial and accommodation, **8:** IV.D.3
    employer attendance policies and, **8:** IV.D.1
    job security issues, **8:** IV.D.2
    modified or part-time schedule, **8:** IV.D.4
  medication issues, **8:** IV.F
  modification of work site or equipment, **8:** IV.G
  work at home, **8:** IV.E
  workplace conduct rules and, **8:** IV.H
Summary judgment, motion for
  defendant's litigation strategies and, **10:** V.B

T

Tax credits
  ADA Title III requirements, compliance with, **6:** IV.K
Technology, electronic and information
  Rehabilitation Act, application to, **1:** I.A.4
Telecommunications Act, 1: II.E
Telecommunications services
  ADA coverage and, **1:** I.B.4
Telecommuting options
  reasonable accommodation and, **8:** IV.E
Tenant/landlord issues
  ADA Title III requirements and, **6:** IV.M

Tennessee, disability discrimination laws
  covered employers, **4:** TN.I.D
  defenses, **4:** TN.I.E
  definition of disability, **4:** TN.I.C.1
  overview, **4:** TN.I.A
  prohibited discrimination, **4:** TN.I.B
    retaliation, **4:** TN.I.B.1
  reasonable accommodation obligation, **4:** TN.I.E
Tests
  qualified individual with disability, determining, **2:** IV.E
Texas, disability discrimination laws
  covered employers, **4:** TX.I.D
  defenses, business necessity, **4:** TX.I.E.2.a
  definition of disability, **4:** TX.I.C.1
  overview, **4:** TX.I.A
  prohibited discrimination, **4:** TX.I.B
    genetic testing, **4:** TX.I.B.1
  reasonable accommodation obligation, **4:** TX.I.E.1
Threat. See Direct threat defense
Time limits
  See also Statutes of limitations
  discrimination claims, filing, **10:** II.A.2
Title III, ADA
  compliance issues, **6:** I
  covered entities, **6:** II
    commercial facilities, **6:** II.F
    Internet-only businesses, **6:** II.E.3, II.E.4
    mixed-use facilities, **6:** II.B
    nontangible public accommodations, **6:** II.D
    physical vs. nonphysical, **6:** II.C
    private companies, **6:** II.E
    public accommodations, defined, **6:** II.A
    Web sites, **6:** II.E.1, II.E.2
  enforcement, **6:** V
    administrative remedies, exhaustion requirement, **6:** V.C
    attorney general's role, **6:** V.B
    attorneys' fees, **6:** V.E
    Justice Department and, **6:** V.F
    remedies, **6:** V.A; **10:** IV.A.1.c
    standing issues, **6:** V.D
  exemptions, **6:** III
    government entities, **6:** III.C
    private clubs, **6:** III.B; **10:** IV.A.1.c
    religious organizations, **6:** III.A; **10:** IV.A.1.c
  generally, **Ch. 6**
  historic landmarks, **6:** IV.E.4.b
  requirements, **6:** IV
    alterations, **6:** IV.I
    alternatives, **6:** IV.G
    architect liability, **6:** IV.O
    auxiliary aids, provision of, **6:** IV.H
    barrier removal, **6:** IV.E; **10:** IV.A.1.c
    direct threat defense, **6:** IV.B
    equal participation, **6:** IV.A
    franchise liability, **6:** IV.L
    guidelines, **6:** IV.F
    integrated settings, **6:** IV.D
    landlord/tenant liability, **6:** IV.M
    new construction, **6:** IV.N
    primary function areas, **6:** IV.J
    reasonable modifications, **6:** IV.C
    tax credits, **6:** IV.K
    transportation services, **6:** IV.P
Title VII
  damages, ADA parallels, **10:** IV.A.1.a
  incorporation in ADA, **10:** II.D
  attorneys' fee provisions, **10:** VII.A
Training programs, preemployment, 7: VII
Trains, commuter
  ADA and, **3:** III.E.6
Transfers, restrictions on
  reasonable accommodations and, **8:** IV.C.1
Transportation services
  ADA Title III requirements and, **6:** IV.P
    companies primarily engaged in business of providing, **6:** IV.P.3
    demand-responsive transportation systems, **6:** IV.P.2
    examinations and courses, **6:** IV.Q
    fixed-route systems, **6:** IV.P.1
    over-the-road buses, **6:** IV.P.4

public, ADA proposed amendments, **3:** III.E.6
Transsexualism
as exempt from Rehabilitation Act, **2:** II.E, IV.B.1.a
Transvestitism
as exempt from Rehabilitation Act, **2:** II.E, IV.B.1.a

U

Unconscionability
arbitration agreements, as reason for voiding, **10:** VI.A.5
Undue hardship defense, 10: V.B.1.b.v
defined, **8:** V.A
factors for determining, **1:** I.F; **8:** V.A
leave cases, application to, **8:** V.B; **9:** I.C.1
OSH Act and, **9:** IV.A.2
preemployment practices and, **7:** VIII.B.7
quantifying, **3:** III.E.3
reasonable accommodation obligation and, **2:** V.B
reasonable accommodations and, **8:** V
Rehabilitation Act and, **2:** VII.A.3
state law and. See *specific state*
Utah, disability discrimination laws
covered employers, **4:** UT.I.D
definitions
disability, **4:** UT.I.C.1
major life activities, **4:** UT.I.C.2
overview, **4:** UT.I.A
prohibited discrimination, **4:** UT.I.B
genetic testing, **4:** UT.I.B.2
preemployment inquiries, **4:** UT.I.B.1
reasonable accommodation obligation, **4:** UT.I.E.1

V

Vacant positions
reasonable accommodation, transfer to as providing, **8:** IV.C.2

Vermont, disability discrimination laws
covered employers, **4:** VT.I.D
defenses, undue burden, **4:** VT.I.E.2.a
definition of disability, **4:** VT.I.C.1
overview, **4:** VT.I.A
prohibited discrimination, **4:** VT.I.B
genetic testing, **4:** VT.I.B.1
reasonable accommodation obligation, **4:** VT.I.E.1
Vietnam Era Veterans' Readjustment Assistance Act
Rehabilitation Act and, **2:** II.E
Virginia, disability discrimination laws
covered employers, **4:** VA.I.D
defenses
direct threat, **4:** VA.I.E.2.a
undue hardship, **4:** VA.I.E.2.b
definition of disability, **4:** VA.I.C.1
overview, **4:** VA.I.A
prohibited discrimination, **4:** VA.I.B
genetic testing, **4:** VA.I.B.1
reasonable accommodation obligation, **4:** VA.I.E.1
Visually-impaired job applicants
hiring procedures and, **7:** IV.C.2
Voyeurism
as exempt from Rehabilitation Act, **2:** II.E

W

Waivers
government contractors and, **1:** I.A.2; **2:** III.C
Rehabilitation Act, **2:** II.E
sovereign immunity, **10:** III
Washington, disability discrimination laws
covered employers, **4:** WA.I.D
definition of disability, **4:** WA.I.C.1
overview, **4:** WA.I.A
preemployment inquiries and medical exams, **4:** WA.I.B.1.a
prohibited discrimination, **4:** WA.I.B
reasonable accommodation obligation, **4:** WA.I.E.1

Web sites
 public accommodation, as places of, **6:** II.E.1, II.E.2
 Internet-only businesses, **6:** II.E.3, II.E.4
West Virginia, disability discrimination laws
 covered employers, **4:** WV.I.D
 definition of disability, **4:** WV.I.C.1
 overview, **4:** WV.I.A
 prohibited discrimination, **4:** WV.I.B
 reasonable accommodation obligation, **4:** WV.I.E.1
Wheelchair-bound applicants
 hiring process and, **7:** IV.C.3
Wilderness areas
 accessibility issues and, **3:** III.E.4
Wisconsin, disability discrimination laws
 covered employers, **4:** WI.I.D
 defenses, undue hardship, **4:** WI.I.E.1.a
 definition of disability, **4:** WI.I.C.1
 overview, **4:** WI.I.A
 prohibited discrimination, **4:** WI.I.B
 genetic testing, **4:** WI.I.B.1
Work sites
 reasonable accommodation and modification of, **8:** IV.G
Workers' compensation laws
 accommodations, **9:** II.D
 discrimination charges and compensation claims, pursuing, **9:** II.B
 disability benefits, distinguished, **9:** II.B.3

 EEOC position, **9:** II.B.2
 judicial estoppel, **9:** II.B.1
 exclusive remedy provisions, **9:** II.A
 interplay with ADA, **9:** II
 medical information and confidentiality issues, **9:** II.C
 agility tests, **9:** II.C.4
 fitness to return to work policies, **9:** II.C.3
 medical examinations, **9:** II.C.2
 medical records, **9:** II.C.1
 preemployment, post-offer inquiries, **9:** II.C.5
 preemption issues, **9:** II
Working
 as major life activity under ADA, **5:** II.B.1
 mental impairments and, **5:** V.C.3
 regarded as disabled provision, **5:** II.E.1
 substantial limitation, factors, **5:** II.C.2
Workplace conduct rules
 reasonable accommodations and, **8:** IV.H
Written job descriptions
 hiring process and, **7:** V.B
 job function assessment and, **3:** III.E.2; **5:** III.B.1
Wyoming, disability discrimination laws
 covered employers, **4:** WY.I.D
 defenses, **4:** WY.I.E.1
 definition of disability, **4:** WY.I.C.1
 overview, **4:** WY.I.A
 prohibited discrimination, **4:** WY.I.B

ABOUT THE AUTHOR

Peter A. Susser is a shareholder in the Washington, D.C., office of Littler Mendelson, P.C., the nation's largest employment and labor law firm. He has practiced employment and labor law for 25 years, and represents employers and national trade associations in these areas. He has participated in rulemaking proceedings under the Americans with Disabilities Act before several federal agencies and has authored articles on the statute that have appeared in law journals as well as human resources and trade publications. A graduate of Cornell University's School of Industrial and Labor Relations, and of the law school of the College of William and Mary, he also holds an LL.M. degree in Labor Law Studies from the Georgetown University Law Center.

PLEASE READ BEFORE USING THIS CD-ROM

This is a legal agreement between you, the individual or entity using this software (the "User"), and BNA Books ("BNA"). Use of these software files ("Software") is governed by the terms of the following license agreement ("Agreement"). By proceeding to use this CD-ROM you agree to accept each of the terms, conditions, and covenants set forth herein. If you do not agree to each of the terms of this Agreement, promptly return the CD-ROM package and the accompanying items (including associated book and packaging) to BNA Books for a full refund or cancellation of all charges.

BNA BOOKS LICENSE AGREEMENT

1. *Grant of License.* BNA grants to User a nonexclusive limited license to use the Software on a single-user computer.

2. *Transfer of License.* You may not rent, loan, or lease the Software, but you may transfer the Software and the accompanying written materials on a permanent basis provided you transfer this Agreement to the recipient, retain no copies, and the recipient agrees in writing to comply with each of the terms set forth in this Agreement. If the Software is an update, any transfer must include the update and all prior versions.

3. *Other Restrictions.* You may not: reproduce, publish, distribute, sell, or otherwise use any material retrieved from or contained in the CD-ROM in any manner whatsoever that may infringe any copyright or proprietary interest of BNA; distribute, rent, sublicense, lease, transfer, or assign the product or the License Agreement; decompile, disassemble, or otherwise reverse-engineer the CD-ROM. Nothing herein, however, shall prevent you from using the material (electronic or written) in the normal course of business for which the material is intended.

4. *Copyright.* The Software is owned by BNA or its successors, assigns, or suppliers (as determined solely by BNA) and is protected by United States copyright laws and international treaty provisions.

Therefore, you must treat the Software like any other copyrighted material (e.g., a book or musical recording) except that you may either (a) make one copy of the Software solely for backup or archival purposes, or (b) transfer the Software to a single hard disk provided you keep the original solely for backup or archival purposes.

DISCLAIMER

This publication is designed to provide accurate and authoritative information in regard to the subject matter covered. In publishing this book, neither the author nor the publisher is engaged in rendering legal, accounting, or other professional service. If legal advice or other expert assistance is required, the services of a competent professional should be sought.

LIMITED WARRANTY

BNA warrants the physical media (i.e., CD-ROM) on which the Software is furnished to be free from defects in materials and workmanship under normal use for a period of one year from the date of delivery to you. This limited warranty gives you specific legal rights. You may have others, which vary from state to state. Some states do not allow the limitation or exclusion of some warranties, so the above limitation may not apply to you.

BNA does not warrant that the functions contained in the program will meet your requirements. You assume responsibility for the installation, use, and results obtained from the program.

THE ENCLOSED SOFTWARE IS PROVIDED "AS IS" WITHOUT WARRANTY OF ANY KIND, EITHER EXPRESS OR IMPLIED, INCLUDING BUT NOT LIMITED TO IMPLIED WARRANTIES OF MERCHANTABILITY AND FITNESS FOR A PARTICULAR PURPOSE, WITH RESPECT TO THE SOFTWARE AND ANY OTHER ACCOMPANYING MATERIALS.

LIMITATION OF REMEDIES

If for any reason the limited warranty provided by this agreement should be determined to be invalid or inapplicable to any claim that is based upon the quality or performance of the licensed Software, the aggregate liability of BNA and anyone else who has been involved in the creation, production, or delivery of the licensed Software nevertheless shall be limited to the amount paid by you to BNA for the original version of the Software.

IN NO EVENT WILL BNA BE LIABLE TO YOU FOR ANY DAMAGES, INCLUDING ANY LOST PROFITS, BUSINESS INTERRUPTION, LOST SAVINGS, LOSS OF BUSINESS INFORMATION, OR OTHER INCIDENTAL OR CONSEQUENTIAL DAMAGES ARISING OUT OF THE USE OR INABILITY TO USE SUCH SOFTWARE EVEN IF BNA OR AN AUTHORIZED BNA DEALER HAS BEEN ADVISED OF THE POSSIBILITY OF SUCH DAMAGES. NOR SHALL BNA BE RESPONSIBLE FOR ANY CLAIM BY ANY OTHER PARTY ARISING FROM OR RELATED TO THE SOFTWARE.

SOME STATES DO NOT ALLOW THE LIMITATION OR EXCLUSION OF LIABILITY FOR INCIDENTAL OR CONSEQUENTIAL DAMAGES, SO THE ABOVE LIMITATION OR EXCLUSION MAY NOT APPLY TO YOU.

This Agreement is governed by the laws of the District of Columbia. If any provision of this Agreement shall be determined to be invalid or otherwise unenforceable, the enforceability of the remaining provisions shall not be impaired thereby. The failure of BNA to exercise any right provided for herein shall not be deemed a waiver of any right hereunder. This Agreement sets forth the entire understanding of BNA and the User with respect to the issues addressed herein and may not be modified except by a writing executed by both parties.

The CD-ROM contains files in html and Adobe® PDF* formats. The material will print on most printers; charts may not print without reformatting on some printers.

*Adobe® and Acrobat Reader® are registered trademarks or trademarks of Adobe Systems Incorporated.

Copyright © 2005 The Bureau of National Affairs, Inc. No copyright claimed as to U.S. government materials.